THE FIRST AMENDMENT
CASES—COMMENTS—QUESTIONS

Fifth Edition

■ ■ ■

By

Steven H. Shiffrin
Charles Frank Reavis, Sr., Professor of Law,
Cornell University

Jesse H. Choper
Earl Warren Professor of Public Law,
University of California, Berkeley

AMERICAN CASEBOOK SERIES®

WEST®

A Thomson Reuters business

Mat #40864707

American Casebook Series and West Group are trademarks registered in the U.S.Patent and Trademark Office.

COPYRIGHT © 1991, 1996 WEST PUBLISHING CO.
© West, a Thomson business, 2001
© 2006 Thomson/West
© 2011 Thomson Reuters
> 610 Opperman Drive
> P.O. Box 64526
> St. Paul, MN 55164–0526
> 1–800–328–9352

Printed in the United States of America

ISBN 978–0–314–90456–0

PREFACE

The First Amendment is an important cultural symbol in American society, but it is also an important part of American constitutional law. Unfortunately, first amendment law is a growth industry. It has outstripped the capacity of constitutional law books to provide materials that are sufficiently comprehensive for a separate first amendment course.

This book is designed for a two or three unit course in the First Amendment. It proceeds on three assumptions:

(1) The body of First Amendment law is sufficiently complicated and interconnected that a variety of organizational patterns can usefully be employed in teaching the course. For that reason we present the materials in a way that will permit instructors to depart from the organization of the casebook with relative ease.

(2) Students benefit from notes and questions that force them to come to grips with the diversity of perspectives arrayed in the rich literature of the First Amendment. In particular we try to expose students to original perspectives or perspectives they might otherwise tend to slide past.

(3) The First Amendment can be characterized as embodying a variety of competing values. In our view, those values are best studied in notes and questions as they emerge from concrete cases rather than from an abstract characterization and classification imposed on the student at the outset of study.

No Supreme Court term passes without further opinions addressing the First Amendment. Hence, we will continue to provide annual supplements for recent developments, including one for the 2010–11 term.

Case and statute citations, as well as footnotes, of the Court and commentators have been omitted without so specifying; other omissions are indicated by asterisks or by brackets. Numbered footnotes are from the original materials; lettered footnotes are ours.

In preparing this casebook we have drawn freely from the first amendment materials in the casebooks we have co-authored and continue to co-author with our friends Yale Kamisar and Richard Fallon. We owe them many thanks. We are grateful for insightful feedback from faculty and students, particularly Robert Cole, Owen Fiss and Abner Greene. Finally, thanks to Jan Rose and Catharine M. Schultz for secretarial and administrative assistance far beyond the call of duty.

TABLE OF CONTENTS

TABLE OF CASES

The principal cases are in bold type. Cases cited or discussed in the text are in roman type. References are to pages.

TABLE OF AUTHORITIES

If extracts have been taken, the page numbers
appear in bold; all others are roman.

Farber, Daniel A. & Nowak, John E., *Justice Harlan and the First Amendment*, 2 Const. Comm. 425 (1985), p. 137.

Farber, Daniel A. & Nowak, John E., *The Misleading Nature of Public Forum Analysis: Content and Context in First Amendment Adjudication*, 70 Va.L.Rev. 1219 (1984), p. 368.

Fargo, Anthony L., *Testing the Boundaries of the First Amendment Press Clause*, 32 Harv. J.L. & Pub. Pol'y 1093 (2009), p. 334.

Favata, Richard, *Filling the Void in First Amendment Jurisprudence: Is There a Solution for Replacing the Impotent System of Prior Restraints?*, 72 Fordham L.Rev. 169 (2003), p. 293.

Felcher, Peter & Rubin, Edward L., *Privacy, Publicity, and the Portrayal of Real People by the Media*, 88 Yale L.J. 1577 (1979), p. 238.

Feldblum, Chai R., *Moral Conflict and Liberty: Gay Rights and Religion*, 72 Brook. L.Rev. 61 (2006), p. 474.

Feldman, Noah, *From Liberty to Equality: The Transformation of the Establishment Clause*, 90 Calif.L.Rev. 673 (2002), p. 574.

Feldman, Noah, *The Framers' Church-State Problem—and Ours*, in The Constitution 2020, p. 221 (Jack Balkin & Reva Siegel, eds. 2009), p. 530.

Feldman, Noah, *The Intellectual Origins of the Establishment Clause*, 77 N.Y.U.L.Rev. 346 (2002), p. 529.

Feldman, Stephen M., *Free Expression and Education: Between Two Democracies*, 16 Wm. & Mary Bill Rts.J. 999 (2008), p. 408.

Fenner, G. Michael & Koley, James, *Access to Judicial Proceedings: To Richmond Newspapers and Beyond*, 16 Harv.Civ.Rts.–Civ. Lib.L.Rev. 415 (1981), p. 348.

Fialkow, David E., *The Media's First Amendment Rights and the Rape Victim's Right to Privacy*, 39 Suffolk L.Rev. 745 (2006), p. 85.

Figinski, M. Albert, *Military Chaplains—A Constitutionally Permissible Accommodation Between Church and State*, 24 Md. L.Rev. 377 (1964), p. 571.

Finnerty, Kevin and Redish, Martin H., *What Did You Learn in School Today? Free Speech, Values Inculcation, and the Democratic-Educational Paradox*, 88 Cornell L. Rev. 62 (2002), p. 400.

Finnis, John, *"Reason and Passion": The Constitutional Dialectic of Free Speech and Obscenity*, 116 U.Pa.L.Rev. 222 (1967), p. 106.

Fischette, Charles, *A New Architecture of Commercial Speech Law*, 31 Harv. J.L. & Pub. Pol'y 663 (2008), p. 250.

Fish, Stanley, *There's No Such Thing as Free Speech: And It's a Good Thing Too*, (1994), p. 195.

Fiss, Owen, *Free Speech and Social Structure*, 71 Iowa L.Rev. 1405 (1986), pp. 26, 61.

Fiss, Owen, *Money and Politics*, 97 Colum. L.Rev. 2470 (1997), p. 508.

Fiss, Owen, *The Censorship of Television*, 93 Nw.U.L.Rev. 1215 (1999), pp. 441, 446.

Fiss, Owen, *The Civil Rights Injunction* (1978), p. 294.

Fiss, Owen, *Why the State*, 100 Harv.L.Rev. 781 (1987), pp. 26, 61.

Fiss, Owen J., *State Activism and State Censorship*, 100 Yale L.J. 2087 (1991), pp. 26, 61, 397.

Fiss, Owen M., *The Censorship of Television*, in Eternally Vigilant: Free Speech in the Modern Era (Lee C. Bollinger & Geoffrey R. Stone eds., 2002), p. 446.

Fitts, Michael, *Look Before You Leap*, 97 Yale L.J. 1651 (1988), p. 508

Fitts, Michael, *The Vices of Virtue*, 136 U.Pa. L.Rev. 1567 (1988), p. 508.

Fletcher, George, *Loyalty* (1993), p. 196.

Foley, Edward B., *Equal–Dollars–Per Voter: A Constitutional Principle of Campaign Finance*, 94 Colum.L.Rev. 1204 (1994), p. 508.

Francione, Gary, *Experimentation and the Marketplace Theory of the First Amendment*, 136 U.Pa.L.Rev. 417 (1987), p. 200.

Frazer, Elizabeth & Cameron, Deborah, *On the Question of Pornography and Sexual Violence: Moving Beyond Cause and Effect*, in Feminism & Pornography 240 (Drucilla Cornell ed., 2000), p. 155.

Freed, Mayer G. & Polsby, Daniel D., *Race, Religion, and Public Policy: Bob Jones University v. United States*, 1983 Sup.Ct.Rev. 1, p. 614.

Freedman, Monroe H. & Starwood, Janet, *Prior Restraints on Freedom of Expression by Defendants and Defense Attorneys: Ratio Decidendi v. Obiter Dictum*, 29 Stan.L.Rev. 607 (1977), p. 323.

Freeman, III, George C., *The Misguided Search for the Constitutional Definition of "Religion,"* 71 Geo.L.J. 1519 (1983), p. 638.

Freund, Paul A., *On Understanding the Supreme Court* (1949), p. 34.

Freund, Paul A., *Public Aid to Parochial Schools*, 82 Harv.L.Rev. 1680 (1969), p. 536.

Freund, Paul A., *The Supreme Court and Civil Liberties*, 4 Vand.L.Rev. 533, p. 296.

Frickey, Phillip P. & Farber, Daniel A., *Practical Reason and the First Amendment*, 34 UCLA L.Rev. 1615 (1987), p. 3.

Fried, Charles, *Perfect Freedom, Perfect Justice*, 78 B.U.L.Rev. 717 (1998), pp. 9, 164.

Fried, Charles, *The New First Amendment Jurisprudence: A Threat to Liberty*, 59 U.Chi. L.Rev. 225 (1992), p. 26.

Friendly, Fred, *Minnesota Rag* (1981), p. 292.

Friendly, Fred, *The Good Guys, The Bad Guys and the First Amendment* (1975), p. 427.

Friendly, Fred & Elliot, Martha, *The Constitution: That Delicate Balance* (1984), pp. 165, 322, 507.

Furth, Alexandra D., *Secular Idolatry and Sacred Traditions: A Critique of the Supreme Court' Secularization Analysis*, 146 U.Pa. L.Rev. 579 (1998), p. 575.

The First Amendment

CASES—COMMENTS—QUESTIONS

Fifth Edition

PART 1

FREEDOM OF EXPRESSION AND ASSOCIATION

■ ■ ■

CHAPTER 1

WHAT SPEECH IS NOT PROTECTED?

■ ■ ■

The First Amendment provides that "Congress shall make no law * * * abridging the freedom of speech, or of the press." Some have stressed that no law means NO LAW. For example, Black, J., dissenting in *Konigsberg v. State Bar*, 366 U.S. 36 (1961) argued that the "First Amendment's unequivocal command [shows] that the men who drafted our Bill of Rights did all the 'balancing' that was to be done in this field."

Laws forbidding speech, however, are commonplace. Laws against perjury, blackmail, and fraud prohibit speech. So does much of the law of contracts. Black, J., himself conceded that speech pursued as an integral part of criminal conduct was beyond First Amendment protection. Indeed no one contends that citizens are free to say anything, anywhere, at any time. As Holmes, J., observed, citizens are not free to yell "fire" falsely in a theater.

The spectre of a man crying fire falsely in the theater, however, has plagued First Amendment theory. The task is to formulate principles that separate the protected from the unprotected. But speech interacts with too many other values in too many complicated ways to expect that a single formula will prove productive.

Are advocates of illegal action, pornographers selling magazines, or publishers of defamation like that person in the theater or are they engaged in freedom of speech? Do citizens have a right to speak on government property? Which property? Is there a right of access to the print or broadcast media? Can government force private owners to grant access for speakers? Does the First Amendment offer protection for the wealthy, powerful corporations, and media conglomerates against government attempts to assure greater equality in the intellectual marketplace? Can government demand information about private political associations or reporters' confidential sources without First Amendment limits? Does the First Amendment require government to produce information it might otherwise withhold?

The Court has approached questions such as these without much attention to the language[a] or history[b] of the First Amendment and without a commitment to any general theory.[c] Rather it has sought to develop principles on a case-by-case basis and has produced a complex and conflicting body of constitutional precedent. Many of the basic principles were developed in a line of cases involving the advocacy of illegal action.

I. ADVOCACY OF ILLEGAL ACTION

A. EMERGING PRINCIPLES

SCHENCK v. UNITED STATES, 249 U.S. 47 (1919): Defendants were convicted of a conspiracy to violate the 1917 Espionage Act by conspiring to cause and attempting to cause insubordination in the armed forces of the United States, and obstruction of the recruiting and enlistment service of the United States, when at war with Germany, by printing and circulating to men accepted for military service approximately fifteen thousand copies of the document described in the opinion. In affirming, HOLMES, J., said for a unanimous Court: "The document in question upon its first printed side recited the first section of the Thirteenth Amendment, said that the idea embodied in it was violated by the conscription act and that a conscript is little better than a convict. In impassioned language it intimated that conscription was despotism in its worst form

---

a. For the contention that comparing the speech clause with other clauses of the Constitution yields insight, see Akhil Reed Amar, *Intratextualism*, 112 Harv. L.Rev. 747, 810–17 (1999).

b. But see, *McIntyre v. Ohio Elections Comm'n*, Sec. 9, I (Thomas, J., concurring) (Scalia, J., dissenting). See, e.g., Michael Perry, *The Constitution, The Courts, and Human Rights*, 63–64 (1982). For a variety of views about the history surrounding the adoption of the first amendment, compare Leonard Levy, *Legacy of Suppression* (1960) with Leonard Levy, *Emergence of a Free Press* (1985); Leonard Levy, *The Legacy Reexamined*, 37 Stan.L.Rev. 767 (1985); Leonard Levy, *On the Origins of the Free Press Clause*, 32 U.C.L.A.L.Rev. 177 (1984) and George Anastaplo, *Book Review*, 39 N.Y.U.L.Rev. 735 (1964); David Anderson, *The Origins of the Press Clause*, 30 U.C.L.A.L.Rev. 455 (1983); Phillip Hamburger, *The Development of the Law of Seditious Libel and the Control of the Press*, 37 Stan.L.Rev. 661 (1985); William Mayton, *Seditious Libel and the Lost Guarantee of a Freedom of Expression*, 84 Colum.L.Rev. 91 (1984); William Mayton, *From a Legacy of Suppression to the 'Metaphor of the Fourth Estate,'* 39 Stan.L.Rev. 139 (1986); Lucas Powe, *The Fourth Estate and the Constitution* 22–50 (1991). David Rabban, *The Ahistorical Historian: Leonard Levy on Freedom of Expression in Early American History*, 37 Stan.L.Rev. 795 (1985).

For the contention that post-adoption history should play a larger role than philosophy in first amendment analysis, see L.A. Powe, *Situating Schauer,* 72 Notre D. L.Rev. 1519 (1997). For work focusing on post-adoption periods, see Michael Kent Curtis, *Free Speech, "The People's Darling Privilege"* (2000); David Rabban, *Free Speech in its Forgotten Years* (1997); Stewart Jay, *The Creation of the First Amendment Right to Free Expression: From the Eighteenth Century to the Mid-Twentieth Century*, 34 Wm. Mitch. L. Rev. 773 (2008); Michael Gibson, *The Supreme Court and Freedom of Expression from 1791 to 1917*, 55 Fordham L.Rev. 263 (1986). See also Zechariah Chafee, *Free Speech in the United States* (1941); Leon Whipple, *The Story of Civil Liberty in the United States* (1927); David Kairys, *Freedom of Speech* in The Politics of Law 160 (Kairys ed. 1982). For an ambitious attempt to marry history, philosophy, and the first amendment, see David Richards, *A Theory of Free Speech*, 34 UCLA L.Rev. 1837 (1987).

c. On the difficulties involved in developing general theory, see Larry Alexander, *Is There a Right of Freedom of Expression* (2005); Larry Alexander & Paul Horton, *The Impossibility of a Free Speech Principle,* 78 Nw.U.L.Rev. 1319 (1983); Daniel Farber & Phillip Frickey, *Practical Reason and the First Amendment,* 34 UCLA L.Rev. 1615 (1987); Steven Shiffrin, *The First Amendment and Economic Regulation: Away From a General Theory of the First Amendment,* 78 Nw.U.L.Rev. 1212 (1983); Laurence Tribe, *Toward A Metatheory of Free Speech,* 10 Sw.U.L.Rev. 237 (1978). For a survey of such attempts, see Matthew D. Bunker, *Critiquing Free Speech* (2001).

and a monstrous wrong against humanity in the interest of Wall Street's chosen few. It said, 'Do not submit to intimidation,' but in form at least confined itself to peaceful measures such as a petition for the repeal of the act. The other and later printed side of the sheet was headed 'Assert Your Rights.' It stated reasons for alleging that any one violated the Constitution when he refused to recognize 'your right to assert your opposition to the draft,' and went on, 'If you do not assert and support your rights, you are helping to deny or disparage rights which it is the solemn duty of all citizens and residents of the United States to retain.' It described the arguments on the other side as coming from cunning politicians and a mercenary capitalist press, and even silent consent to the conscription law as helping to support an infamous conspiracy. It denied the power to send our citizens away to foreign shores to shoot up the people of other lands, and added that words could not express the condemnation such cold-blooded ruthlessness deserves, & c., & c., winding up, 'You must do your share to maintain, support and uphold the rights of the people of this country.' Of course the document would not have been sent unless it had been intended to have some effect, and we do not see what effect it could be expected to have upon persons subject to the draft except to influence them to obstruct the carrying of it out. The defendants do not deny that the jury might find against them on this point.

"But it is said, suppose that that was the tendency of this circular, it is protected by the First Amendment to the Constitution. [We] admit that in many places and in ordinary times the defendants in saying all that was said in the circular would have been within their constitutional rights. But the character of every act depends upon the circumstances in which it is done. The most stringent protection of free speech would not protect a man in falsely shouting fire in a theatre and causing a panic. [The] question in every case is whether the words used are used in such circumstances and are of such a nature as to create a clear and present danger that they will bring about the substantive evils that Congress has a right to prevent. It is a question of proximity and degree.[a] When a nation is at war many things that might be said in time of peace are such a hindrance to its effort that their utterance will not be endured so long as men fight and that no Court could regard them as protected by any constitutional right. It seems to be admitted that if an actual obstruction of the recruiting service were proved, liability for words that produced that effect might be enforced. The statute of 1917 punishes conspiracies to obstruct as well as actual obstruction. If the act, (speaking, or circulating

---

a. Although Schenck was convicted for violating a conspiracy statute, Holmes appears to have used the occasion to import the law of criminal attempts into the freedom of expression area. "In *Schenck,* 'clear and present danger,' 'a question of proximity and degree' bridged the gap between the defendant's acts of publication and the [prohibited interferences with the war.] This connection was strikingly similar to the Holmesian analysis of the requirement of 'dangerous proximity to success' [quoting from an earlier Holmes opinion] that, in the law of attempts, bridges the gap between the defendant's acts and the completed crime. In either context, innocuous efforts are to be ignored." Yogal Rogat, *Mr. Justice Holmes: Some Modern Views—The Judge as Spectator,* 31 U.Chi.L.Rev. 213, 215 (1964). But see Holmes, J., dissenting in *Abrams* infra, and fn. b below.

a paper), its tendency and the intent with which it is done are the same, we perceive no ground for saying that success alone warrants making the act a crime."[b]

DEBS v. UNITED STATES, 249 U.S. 211 (1919): Defendant was convicted of violating the Espionage Act for obstructing and attempting to obstruct the recruiting service and for causing and attempting to cause insubordination and disloyalty in the armed services. He was given a ten-year prison sentence on each count, to run concurrently. His criminal conduct consisted of giving the anti-war speech described in the opinion at the state convention of the Socialist Party of Ohio, held at a park in Canton, Ohio, on a June 16, 1918 Sunday afternoon before a general audience of 1,200 persons. At the time of the speech, defendant was a national political figure.[a] In affirming, HOLMES, J., observed for a unanimous Court:

"The main theme of the speech was socialism, its growth, and a prophecy of its ultimate success. With that we have nothing to do, but if a part or the manifest intent of the more general utterances was to encourage those present to obstruct the recruiting service and if in passages such encouragement was directly given, the immunity of the general theme may not be enough to protect the speech. [Defendant had come to the park directly from a nearby jail, where he had visited three socialists imprisoned for obstructing the recruiting service. He expressed sympathy and admiration for these persons and others convicted of similar offenses, and then] said that the master class has always declared the war and the subject class has always fought the battles—that the subject class has had nothing to gain and all to lose, including their lives; [and that] 'You have your lives to lose; you certainly ought to have the right to declare war if you consider a war necessary.' [He next said of a woman serving a ten-year sentence for obstructing the recruiting service] that she had said no more than the speaker had said that afternoon; that if she was guilty so was [he].

---

b. See also *Frohwerk v. United States,* 249 U.S. 204 (1919), where a unanimous Court, per Holmes, J., sustained a conviction for conspiracy to obstruct recruiting in violation of the Espionage Act, by means of a dozen newspaper articles praising the spirit and strength of the German nation, criticizing the decision to send American troops to France, maintaining that the government was giving false and hypocritical reasons for its course of action and implying that "the guilt of those who voted the unnatural sacrifice" is greater than the wrong of those who seek to escape by resistance: "[*Schenck* decided] that a person may be convicted of a conspiracy to obstruct recruiting by words of persuasion. [S]o far as the language of the articles goes there is not much to choose between expressions to be found in them and those before us in *Schenck.*" Consider Powe, supra, at 71: "The case against Frohwerk was [weaker] than that against Schenck on both contested points; the recipients of the writing and the intensity of the writing. [Even] the government attorney who prevailed in *Frohwerk* [concluded that Frowerk was] 'one of the clearest examples of the political prisoner.'"

a. Debs had run for the Presidency on the Socialist ticket for the fourth time in 1912. At the 1920 election, while in prison, Debs ran again and received over 900,000 votes as the Socialist candidate.

"There followed personal experiences and illustrations of the growth of socialism, a glorification of minorities, and a prophecy of the success of [socialism], with the interjection that 'you need to know that you are fit for something better than slavery and cannon fodder.' [Defendant's] final exhortation [was] 'Don't worry about the charge of treason to your masters; but be concerned about the treason that involves yourselves.' The defendant addressed the jury himself, and while contending that his speech did not warrant the charges said 'I have been accused of obstructing the war. I admit it. Gentlemen, I abhor war. I would oppose the war if I stood alone.' The statement was not necessary to warrant the jury in finding that one purpose of the speech, whether incidental or not does not matter, was to oppose not only war in general but this war, and that the opposition was so expressed that its natural and intended effect would be to obstruct recruiting. If that was intended and if, in all the circumstances, that would be its probable effect, it would not be protected by reason of its being part of a general program and expressions of a general and conscientious belief.

"[Defendant's constitutional objections] based upon the First Amendment [were] disposed of in *Schenck*. [T]he admission in evidence of the record of the conviction [of various persons he mentioned in his speech was proper] to show what he was talking about, to explain the true import of his expression of sympathy and to throw light on the intent of the address. [Properly admitted, too, was an 'Anti-war Proclamation and Program' adopted the previous year, coupled with testimony that shortly before his speech defendant had stated that he approved it]. Its first recommendation was, 'continuous, active, and public opposition to the war, through demonstrations, mass petitions, and all other means within our power.' Evidence that the defendant accepted this view and this declaration of his duties at the time that he made his speech is evidence that if in that speech he used words tending to obstruct the recruiting service he meant that they should have that effect. [T]he jury were most carefully instructed that they could not find the defendant guilty for advocacy of any of his opinions unless the words used had as their natural tendency and reasonably probable effect to obstruct the recruiting service [and] unless the defendant had the specific intent to do so in his mind."

NOTES AND QUESTIONS

1. ***War criticism.*** Geoffrey R. Stone, *Perilous Times* xxii-xxiii (2004): "It is often said that dissent in wartime is disloyal. This claim puzzles civil libertarians, who see a clear distinction. In their view, dissent in wartime can be the highest form of patriotism. Whether, when, for how long, and on what terms to fight a war are among the most profound decisions a nation encounters. A democratic society must debate these issues throughout the conflict. Dissent that questions the conduct and morality of a war is, on this view, the very essence of responsible and courageous citizenship.

"At the same time, however, dissent can readily be cast as disloyal. A critic who argues that troops are poorly trained or the war is unjust may make a significant contribution to public discourse. But he also gives 'aid and comfort' to the enemy. The enemy is more likely to fight fiercely if it is confident and believes its adversary to be divided and uncertain. Public disagreement during a war can strengthen the enemy's resolve. [T]he United States has had a long and unfortunate history of overreacting to the perceived dangers of wartime. Time and again, Americans have allowed fear and fury to get the better of them. Time and again, Americans have suppressed dissent, imprisoned and deported dissenters, and then—later—regretted their actions."

2. ***The man in the theater.*** Consider Harry Kalven, *A Worthy Tradition* 133–34 (1988): "*Schenck*—and perhaps even Holmes himself—are best remembered for the example of the man 'falsely shouting fire' in a crowded theater. Judge Hand said in *Masses* that 'words are not only the keys of persuasion, but the triggers of action.' Justice Holmes makes the same point by means of the 'fire' example, an image which was to catch the fancy of the culture. But the example has long seemed to me trivial and misleading. It is as if the only conceivable controversy over speech policy were with an adversary who asserts that *all* use of words is absolutely immunized under the First Amendment. The 'fire' example then triumphantly impeaches this massive major premise. Beyond that, it adds nothing to our understanding. If the point were that *only* speech which is a comparable 'trigger of action' could be regulated, the example might prove a stirring way of drawing the line at incitement, but it is abundantly clear that Justice Holmes is not comparing Schenck's leaflet to the shouting of 'fire.' Moreover, because the example is so wholly apolitical, it lacks the requisite complexity for dealing with any serious speech problem likely to confront the legal system. The man shouting 'fire' does not offer premises resembling those underlying radical political rhetoric—premises that constitute criticism of government."

3. ***Schenck and Debs.*** Consider Harry Kalven, *Ernst Freund and the First Amendment Tradition,* 40 U.Chi.L.Rev. 235, 236–38 (1973): "It has been customary to lavish care and attention on the *Schenck* case, [but *Debs*, argued well before *Schenck* was handed down and decided just one week later,] represented the first effort by Justice Holmes to apply what he had worked out about freedom of speech in *Schenck*. The start of the law of the First Amendment is not *Schenck;* it is *Schenck* and *Debs* read together. [Debs' speech] fell into the genre of bitter criticism of government and government policy, sometimes called seditious libel; freedom of such criticism from government marks, we have come to understand, 'the central meaning of the First Amendment' [*New York Times v. Sullivan,* Ch.. 1, II, B infra] *Debs* raises serious questions as to what the First Amendment, and more especially, what the clear and present danger formula can possibly have meant at the time. [Holmes] does not comment on the fact difference between [*Schenck* and *Debs*]: the defendant in *Schenck* had sent his leaflets directly to men who awaited draft call whereas [*Debs*] was addressing a general audience at a public meeting. Holmes offers no discussion of the sense in which Debs's speech presented a clear and present danger. [In fact, *Debs*] did not move [Holmes] to discuss free speech at all; his brief opinion is occupied with two points about admissibility of [evidence]. It was for Holmes a routine criminal appeal."

4. *Governmental legitimacy.* Consider Lawrence B. Solum, *Freedom of Communicative Action*, 83 Nw.U.L.Rev. 54, 122–23 (1989): "Government claims a legitimate monopoly on the use of force. Any fundamental challenge to the legitimacy of this monopoly must include implicit justification or explicit advocacy of illegal action, either of nonviolent civil disobedience or of violent revolution. [S]uch fundamental challenges must be allowed if the government claims that the rightfulness of its monopoly on the use of force would be accepted in rational discourse. [I]f a violent revolutionary movement were actually likely to succeed in overthrowing the present government and if we had good reason to believe that the new regime would be worse than the present government, then we would have good reasons to temporarily suspend the right to question fundamental legitimacy in order to avoid this immediate and serious danger. The 'clear and present danger' test operationalizes a qualification of the right to advocate illegal conduct." But see Seana Valentine Shiffrin, *Speech, Death, and Double Effect*, 78 N.Y.U. L. Rev. 1135, 1159–1160 (2003): "The state is a poor and deeply biased judge about what visions for stability and change are defective. [O]ur vitality as a democratic collectivity depends on our joint engagement with and evaluation of competing visions * * *. We want speakers to have full freedom in the construction and dissemination of their intent. Our legitimacy depends on it. Protection of the bitter alongside the sweet, then, may be a necessary condition of protecting those valuable processes and outcomes provoked by insightful speech."

5. MASSES PUBLISHING CO. v. PATTEN, 244 Fed. 535 (S.D.N.Y. 1917): The Postmaster of New York advised plaintiff that an issue of his monthly revolutionary journal, *The Masses,* would be denied the mails under the Espionage Act since it tended to encourage the enemies of the United States and to hamper the government in its conduct of the war. The Postmaster subsequently specified as objectionable several cartoons entitled, e.g., "Conscription," "Making the World Safe for Capitalism"; several articles admiring the "sacrifice" of conscientious objectors and a poem praising two persons imprisoned for conspiracy to resist the draft. Plaintiff sought a preliminary injunction against the postmaster from excluding its magazine from the mails. LEARNED HAND, D.J., granted relief:

"[The postmaster maintains] that to arouse discontent and disaffection among the people with the prosecution of the war and with the draft tends to promote a mutinous and insubordinate temper among the troops. This [is] true; men who become satisfied that they are engaged in an enterprise dictated by the unconscionable selfishness of the rich, and effectuated by a tyrannous disregard for the will of those who must suffer and die, will be more prone to insubordination than those who have faith in the cause and acquiesce in the means. Yet to interpret the word 'cause' [in the statutory language forbidding one to 'willfully cause' insubordination in the armed forces] so broadly would [necessarily involve] the suppression of all hostile criticism, and of all opinion except what encouraged and supported the existing policies, or which fell within the range of temperate argument. * * * Assuming that the power to repress such opinion may rest in Congress in the throes of a struggle for the very existence of the state, its exercise is so contrary to the use and wont of our people that only the clearest expression of such a power justifies the conclusion that it was intended.

"The defendant's position, therefore, in so far as it involves the suppression of the free utterance of abuse and criticism of the existing law, or of the policies of the war, is not, in my judgment, supported by the language of the statute. Yet there has always been a recognized limit to such expressions, incident indeed to the existence of any compulsive power of the state itself. One may not counsel or advise others to violate the law as it stands. Words are not only the keys of persuasion, but the triggers of action, and those which have no purport but to counsel the violation of law cannot by any latitude of interpretation be a part of that public opinion which is the final source of government in a democratic state. [If] one stops short of urging upon others that it is their duty or their interest to resist the law, it seems to me one should not be held to have attempted to cause its violation.[b] If that be not the test, I can see no escape from the conclusion that under this section every political agitation which can be shown to be apt to create a seditious temper is illegal. I am confident that by such language Congress had no such revolutionary purpose in view.

"It seems to me, however, quite plain that none of the language and none of the cartoons in this paper can be thought directly to counsel or advise insubordination or mutiny, without a violation of their meaning quite beyond any tolerable understanding. I come, therefore to the [provision of the Act forbidding] any one from willfully obstructing [recruiting or enlistment]. I am not prepared to assent to the plaintiff's position that this only refers to acts other than words, nor that the act thus defined must be shown to have been successful. One may obstruct without preventing, and the mere obstruction is an injury to the service; for it throws impediments in its way. Here again, however, since the question is of the expression of opinion, I construe the sentence, so far as it restrains public utterance, [as] limited to the direct advocacy of resistance to the recruiting and enlistment service. If so, the inquiry is narrowed to the question whether any of the challenged matter may be said to advocate resistance to the draft, taking the meaning of the words with the utmost latitude which they can bear.

"[It] is plain enough that the [magazine] has the fullest sympathy for [those who resist the draft or obstruct recruiting], that it admires their courage, and that it presumptively approves their conduct. [Moreover,] these passages, it must be remembered, occur in a magazine which attacks with the utmost violence the draft and the war. That such comments have a tendency to arouse emulation in others is clear enough, but that they counsel others to follow these examples is not so plain. Literally at least they do not, and while, as I have said, the words are to be taken, not literally, but according to their full import,[c] the literal meaning is the starting point for interpretation. One may admire and approve the course of a hero without feeling any duty to follow him. There is not the least implied intimation in these words that

_____

b.   Charles Fried, *Perfect Freedom, Perfect Justice*, 78 B.U.L.Rev. 717, 725 (1998): "Hand's test both excludes and includes too much. It denies First Amendment protection to pacifist teaching that it is a person's duty peaceably to disobey certain laws, while granting it—to use Mill's example—to the inflammatory denunciation of food speculation to a hungry mob assembled at a corn dealer's house."

c.   On the extent to which it is feasible and desirable to require clarity of expression before the imposition of sanctions in this and other doctrinal parts of free speech law, see Charlotte Taylor, *Free Expression and Expressness*, 33 N.Y.U. Rev. L. & Soc. Change 375 (2009).

others are under a duty to follow. The most that can be said is that, if others do follow, they will get the same admiration and the same approval. * * *

"When the question is of a statute constituting a crime, it seems to me that there should be more definite evidence of the act. The question before me is quite the same as what would arise upon a motion to dismiss an indictment at the close of the proof: Could any reasonable man say, not that the indirect result of the language might be to arouse a seditious disposition, for that would not be enough, but that the language directly advocated resistance to the draft? I cannot think that upon such language any verdict would stand."[d]

JUSTICE HOLMES—DISSENTING IN
ABRAMS v. UNITED STATES

250 U.S. 616, 624, 40 S.Ct. 17, 20, 63 L.Ed. 1173, 1178 (1919).

[In the summer of 1918, the United States sent a small body of marines to Siberia. Although the defendants maintained a strong socialist opposition to "German militarism," they opposed the "capitalist" invasion of Russia, and characterized it as an attempt to crush the Russian Revolution. Shortly thereafter, they printed two leaflets and distributed several thousand copies in New York City. Many of the copies were thrown from a window where one defendant was employed; others were passed around at radical meetings. Both leaflets supported Russia against the United States; one called upon workers to unite in a general strike. There was no evidence that workers responded to the call.

[The Court upheld the defendants' convictions for conspiring to violate two provisions of the 1918 amendments to the Espionage Act. One count prohibited language intended to "incite, provoke and encourage resistance to the United States"; the other punished those who urged curtailment of war production. As the Court interpreted the statute, an intent to interfere with efforts against a *declared* war was a necessary element of both offenses. Since the United States had not declared war upon Russia, "the main task of the government was to establish an [*intention*] *to interfere with the war with Germany.*" Chafee, supra, at 115. The Court found intent on the principle that "Men must be held to have

---

d. In reversing, 246 Fed. 24 (1917), the Second Circuit observed: "If the natural and probable effect of what is said is to encourage resistance to a law, and the words are used in an endeavor to persuade to resistance, it is immaterial that the duty to resist is not mentioned, or the interest of the person addressed in resistance is not suggested. That one may willfully obstruct the enlistment service, without advising in direct language against enlistments, and without stating that to refrain from enlistment is a duty or in one's interest, seems to us too plain for controversy." Geoffrey R. Stone, *Perilous Times* 159–160 (2004): "Attorney General Gregory charged that Hand had gutted the Espionage Act, and Hand's opinion in *Masses* was promptly and emphatically reversed by the court of appeals. Referring to his opinion in *Masses*, Hand wistfully 'bid a long farewell to my little toy ship which set out quite bravely on the shortest voyage ever made.' He was passed over for the court of appeals appointment, which went to a less distinguished jurist. Hand reflected later, 'The case cost me something, at least at the time,' but added, 'I have been very happy to do what I believe was some service to temperateness and sanity.'" For diverse views concerning Judge Hand's opinion and its importance, see Gerald Gunther, *Learned Hand* 151–70, 603 (1994); Bernard Schwartz, *Holmes v. Hand,* 1994 S.Ct.Rev. 209; Vincent Blasi, *Learned Hand and the Self-Government Theory of the First Amendment,* 61 U.Col.L.Rev. 1 (1990).

intended, and to be accountable for, the effects which their acts were likely to produce. Even if their primary purpose and intent was to aid the cause of the Russian Revolution, the plan of action which they adopted necessarily involved, before it could be realized, defeat of the war program of the United States * * *."

[HOLMES, J., dissented in an opinion with which Brandeis, J., concurred:][a]

[I] am aware of course that the word "intent" as vaguely used in ordinary legal discussion means no more than knowledge at the time of the act that the consequences said to be intended will ensue. [But,] when words are used exactly, a deed is not done with intent to produce a consequence unless that consequence is the aim of the deed. It may be obvious, and obvious to the actor, that the consequence will follow, and he may be liable for it even if he regrets it, but he does not do the act with intent to produce it unless the aim to produce it is the proximate motive of the specific act although there may be some deeper motive behind.

It seems to me that this statute must be taken to use its words in a strict and accurate sense. They would be absurd in any other. A patriot might think that we were wasting money on aeroplanes, or making more cannon of a certain kind than we needed, and might advocate curtailment with success, yet even if it turned out that the curtailment hindered and was thought by other minds to have been obviously likely to hinder the United States in the prosecution of the war, no one would hold such conduct a crime. * * *

I never have seen any reason to doubt that the questions of law that alone were before this Court in the cases of *Schenck, Frohwerk* and *Debs* were rightly decided. I do not doubt for a moment that by the same reasoning that would justify punishing persuasion to murder, the United States constitutionally may punish speech that produces or is intended to produce a clear and imminent danger that it will bring about forthwith certain substantive evils that the United States constitutionally may seek to prevent. The power undoubtedly is greater in time of war than in time of peace because war opens dangers that do not exist at other times.

But as against dangers peculiar to war, as against others, the principle of the right to free speech is always the same. It is only the present danger of immediate evil or an intent to bring it about that warrants Congress in setting a limit to the expression of opinion where private rights are not concerned. Congress certainly cannot forbid all effort to change the mind of the country. Now nobody can suppose that the surreptitious publishing of a silly leaflet by an unknown man, without more, would present any immediate danger that its opinions would hinder the success of the government arms or have any appreciable tendency to

---

a. Consider Sheldon Novick, *Honorable Justice, The Life of Oliver Wendell Holmes* 331 (1989): "The majority did very highly disapprove of Holmes's dissent, and White tried to persuade him to be silent. When Holmes clung to what he thought his duty, three of the justices came to call on him in his library, and [his wife] Fanny joined them in trying to dissuade him from publishing his dissent."

do so.[b] Publishing those opinions for the very purpose of obstructing, however, might indicate a greater danger and at any rate would have the quality of an attempt.[c] * * *

I do not see how anyone can find the intent required by the statute in any of the defendants' words. The leaflet advocating a general strike is the only one that affords even a foundation for the charge, and [its only object] is to help Russia and stop American intervention there against the popular government—not to impede the United States in the war that it was carrying on. * * *

In this case sentences of twenty years imprisonment have been imposed for the publishing of two leaflets that I believe the defendants had as much right to publish as the Government has to publish the Constitution of the United States now vainly invoked by them. [E]ven if what I think the necessary intent were shown; the most nominal punishment seems to me all that possibly could be inflicted, unless the defendants are to be made to suffer not for what the indictment alleges but for the creed that they avow—[which,] although made the subject of examination at the trial, no one has a right even to consider in dealing with the charges before the Court.

Persecution for the expression of opinions seems to me perfectly logical. If you have no doubt of your premises or your power and want a certain result with all your heart you naturally express your wishes in law and sweep away all opposition. To allow opposition by speech seems to indicate that you think the speech impotent, as when a man says that he has squared the circle, or that you do not care whole-heartedly for the result, or that you doubt either your power or your premises. But when men have realized that time has upset many fighting faiths,[d] they may

---

b. But cf. John Wigmore, *Abrams v. U.S.: Freedom of Speech and Freedom of Thuggery in War–Time and Peace–Time,* 14 Ill.L.Rev. 539, 549–50 (1920): "[The *Abrams* dissent] is dallying with the facts and the law. None know better than judges that what is lawful for one is lawful for a thousand others. If these five men could, without the law's restraint, urge munition workers to a general strike and armed violences then others could lawfully do so; and a thousand disaffected undesirables, aliens and natives alike, were ready and waiting to do so. Though this circular was 'surreptitious,' the next ones need not be so. If such urgings were lawful, every munitions factory in the country could be stopped by them. The relative amount of harm that one criminal act can effect is no measure of its criminality, and no measure of the danger of its criminality. [At a time] when the fate of the civilized world hung in the balance, how could the Minority Opinion interpret law and conduct in such a way as to let loose men who were doing their hardest to paralyze the supreme war efforts of our country?"

c. Would it, if, under the circumstances, the defendant had no reasonable prospect of success? If his efforts were utterly ineffectual? Cf. Oliver Wendall Holmes, *The Common Law* 65–66, 68–69 (1881): "Intent to commit a crime is not itself criminal. [Moreover], the law does not punish every act which is done with the intent to bring about a crime. [We] have seen what amounts to an attempt to burn a haystack [lighting a match with intent to start fire to a haystack]; but it was said in the same case, that, if the defendant had gone no further than to buy a box of matches for the purpose, he would not have been liable. [Relevant considerations are] the nearness of the danger, the greatness of the harm and the degree of apprehension felt."

d. "In referring to 'fighting faiths,' Holmes may well have been thinking in part of the abolitionism to which he had been committed in his youth, and which he believed had led to the devastation of the Civil War. In this way, he laid the foundations of modern free speech jurisprudence on the ruins of the natural rights theory which originally supported the First

come to believe even more than they believe the very foundations of their own conduct that the ultimate good desired is better reached by free trade in ideas—that the best test of truth is the power of the thought to get itself accepted in the competition of the market, and that truth is the only ground upon which their wishes safely can be carried out. That at any rate is the theory of our Constitution. It is an experiment, as all life is an experiment. Every year if not every day we have to wager our salvation upon some prophecy based upon imperfect knowledge. While that experiment is part of our system I think that we should be eternally vigilant against attempts to check the expression of opinions that we loathe and believe to be fraught with death, unless they so imminently threaten immediate interference with the lawful and pressing purposes of the law that an immediate check is required to save the country. [Only] the emergency that makes it immediately dangerous to leave the correction of evil counsels to time warrants making any exception to the sweeping command, "Congress shall make no law * * * abridging the freedom of speech." Of course I am speaking only of expressions of opinion and exhortations, which were all that were uttered [here].[e]

NOTES AND QUESTIONS

1. ***"Marketplace of ideas."*** (a) Consider Frederick Schauer, *Facts and the First Amendment,* 57 UCLA L.Rev. 897, 909 (2010): "Once we fathom the full scope of factors other than the truth of a proposition that might determine which propositions individuals or groups will accept and which they will reject-the charisma, authority, or persuasiveness of the speaker; the consistency between the proposition and the prior beliefs of the hearer; the consistency between the proposition and what the hearer believes that other hearers believe; the frequency with which the proposition is uttered; the extent to which the proposition is communicated with photographs and other visual or aural embellishments; the extent to which the proposition will make the reader or listener feel good or happy for content-independent reasons; and almost countless others-we can see that placing faith in the superiority of truth over all of these other attributes of a proposition in explaining acceptance and rejection requires a substantial degree of faith in pervasive human rationality and an almost willful disregard of the masses of scientific and marketing research to the contrary."[f]

Amendment." Steven J. Heyman, *Righting the Balance: An Inquiry into the Foundations and Limits of Freedom of Expression,* 78 B.U.L.Rev. 1275, 1303 (1998).

e. Consider Vincent Blasi, *Reading Holmes through the Lens of Schauer: The Abrams Dissent,* 72 Notre Dame L. Rev. 1343, 1354–55 (1997): "Nothing [Holmes] says in *Abrams* by his own injunction, applies to regulations of speech predicated on misstatements of verifiable fact, such as the standard action for defamation. Likewise, disclosures of sensitive information remain outside the ambit of Holmes's argument for free speech, however much such disclosures might contribute to public debate or the checking of government power. The graphic depictions of pornographers, even the soft-core variety, also appear not to be the type of speech that Holmes insists must be tested in the competition of the market."

f. Despite the weaknesses of the rationality assumption, is it wiser to presume it as a matter of First Amendment policy? See Lyrissa Barnett Lidsky, *Nobody's Fools: The Rational Audience as First Amendment Ideal,* 2010 U.Ill. L.Rev. 799.

(b) Contrast Holmes, J.'s statement of the "marketplace of ideas" argument with John Milton's statement in *Areopagitica:* "And though all the winds of doctrine were let loose to play upon the earth, so Truth be in the field, we do injuriously by licensing and prohibiting to misdoubt her strength. Let her and Falsehood grapple; who ever knew Truth put to the worse, in a free and open encounter?" Holmes, J., claims that the competition of the market is the best test of truth; Milton maintains that truth will emerge in a free and open encounter. How would one verify either hypothesis?

Is the "marketplace of ideas" a "free and open encounter"? Consider Charles Lindblom, *Politics and Markets* 207 (1977): "Early, persuasive, unconscious conditioning—[to] believe in the fundamental politico-economic institutions of one's society is ubiquitous in every society. These institutions come to be taken for granted. Many people grow up to regard them not as institutions to be tested but as standards against which the correctness of new policies and institutions can be tested. When that happens, as is common, processes of critical judgment are short-circuited." Consider also Tribe 2d ed., at 786: "Especially when the wealthy have more access to the most potent media of communication than the poor, how sure can we be that 'free trade in ideas' is likely to generate truth?"

For a specific example, see Steven Shiffrin, *The First Amendment and Economic Regulation: Away From A General Theory of the First Amendment,* 78 Nw.U.L.Rev. 1212, 1281 (1983): "Living in a society in which children and adults are daily confronted with multiple communications that ask them to purchase products inevitably places emphasis on materialistic values. The authors of the individual messages may not intend that general emphasis, but the whole is greater than the sum of the parts. [Advertisers] spend some sixty billion dollars per year. [Those] who would oppose the materialist message must combat forces that have a massive economic advantage. Any confidence that we will know what is truth by seeing what emerges from such combat is ill placed."

Do the different market failure considerations offered by Lindblom, Tribe, and Shiffrin add up to a rebuttal of the marketplace argument? Consider Melvin Nimmer, *Nimmer on Freedom of Speech* 1–12 (1984): "If acceptance of an idea in the competition of the market is not the 'best test' [what] is the alternative? It can only be acceptance of an idea by some individual or group narrower than that of the public at large. Thus, the alternative to competition in the market must be some form of elitism. It seems hardly necessary to enlarge on the dangers of that path." Is elitism the only alternative to the marketplace perspective? Is elitism always wrong?

(c) Evaluate the following hypothetical commentary: "Liberals have favored government intervention in the economic marketplace but pressed for laissez-faire in the intellectual marketplace. Conservatives have done the reverse. Liberals and conservatives have one thing in common: inconsistent positions."

(d) Does the marketplace argument overvalue truth? Consider Frederick Schauer, *Free Speech: A Philosophical Enquiry* 23 (1982). Government may seek to suppress opinions "because their expression is thought to impair the authority of a lawful and effective government, interfere with the administration of justice (such as publication of a defendant's criminal record in advance of a jury trial), cause offence, invade someone's privacy, or cause a decrease in public order. When these are the motives for suppression, the possibility of losing some truth is relevant but hardly dispositive. [In such circumstances] the argument from truth [is] not wholly to the point." See also Robert Wolff, *The Poverty of Liberalism* 18 (1968) "[I]t is not to assist the advance of knowledge that free debate is needed. Rather, it is in order to guarantee that every legitimate interest shall make itself known and felt in the political [process]. Justice, not truth, is the ideal served by liberty of speech." Compare Paul Chevigny, *Philosophy of Language and Free Expression*, 55 N.Y.U.L.Rev. 157 (1980); Mark Leitner, *Liberalism, Separation and Speech*, 1985 Wis. L.Rev. 79, 89–90 & 103–04. The standard discussion of free speech values continues to be Thomas Emerson, *The System of Freedom of Expression* 6–9 (1970).

(e) Would an emphasis on dissent be preferable to an emphasis on the marketplace metaphor? Consider Steven Shiffrin, *The First Amendment, Democracy, and Romance* (1990): "[A] commitment to sponsoring dissent does not require a belief that what emerges in the 'market' is usually right or that the 'market' is the best test of truth. Quite the contrary, the commitment to sponsor dissent assumes that societal pressures to conform are strong and that incentives to keep quiet are often great. If the marketplace metaphor encourages the view that an invisible hand or voluntaristic arrangements have guided us patiently, but slowly, to Burkean harmony, the commitment to sponsoring dissent encourages us to believe that the cozy arrangements of the status quo have settled on something less than the true or the just. If the marketplace metaphor encourages the view that conventions, habits, and traditions have emerged as our best sense of the truth from the rigorous testing ground of the marketplace of ideas, the commitment to sponsoring dissent encourages the view that conventions, habits, and traditions are compromises open to challenge. If the marketplace metaphor counsels us that the market's version of truth is more worthy of trust than any that the government might dictate, a commitment to sponsoring dissent counsels us to be suspicious of both. If the marketplace metaphor encourages a sloppy form of relativism (whatever has emerged in the marketplace is right for now), the commitment to sponsoring dissent emphasizes that truth is not decided in public opinion polls."

2. ***Pragmatism and scientific method.*** Consider Vincent Blasi, *Reading Holmes through the Lens of Schauer: The Abrams Dissent*, 72 Notre D. L. Rev. 1343, 1344–45 (1997): "Once the eloquence has been savored (and the false modesty noted), the reader wonders whether Holmes can possibly mean what he seems to be saying about 'the best test of truth.' Is he really so cynical, or fatalistic? Is he asserting a Chicago-school level of faith in markets combined with a willingness both to commodify truth and to ignore the various sources of market failure that operate in the flesh-and-blood society he is supposedly discussing? And even if Holmes wishes to embrace such a mundane conception of truth, how then does truth become 'the only ground' of social organization and aspiration? [H]ow does the author of the quip 'the Fourteenth Amendment does not enact Mr. Herbert Spencer's Social Statics'

justify the position that the First Amendment enacts an extreme version of epistemological skepticism and/or moral relativism?

"One possible response is to read Holmes as neither a borderline cynic nor a model-building neoclassical economist but rather a pragmatist impressed by how free speech can foster a culture of productive adaptation. In this view, the reference to 'the market'—observe that Holmes never employs the phrase 'marketplace of ideas'—is not meant to evoke anything so elegant and implausible as a fair procedure for determining society's finely calibrated, self-correcting cognitive equilibrium. Rather the claim is simply that the human understanding is eternally fluctuating and incomplete, and constantly in need of inquisitive energy much the way commercial prosperity depends on entrepreneurial energy. In addition, Holmes's allusion to Darwinian forces and his assertion that life is an experiment suggests his embrace of the scientific method, with the implication that the First Amendment represents a commitment by this society to test its truths continually and revise them regularly."[g]

B. STATE SEDITION LAWS

The second main group of cases in the initial development of First Amendment doctrine involved state "sedition laws" of two basic types: criminal anarchy laws, typified by the New York statute in *Gitlow*, infra, and criminal syndicalism laws similar to the California statute in *Whitney*, infra. Most states enacted anarchy and syndicalism statutes between 1917 and 1921, in response to World War I and the fear of Bolshevism that developed in its wake, but the first modern sedition law was passed by New York in 1902, soon after the assassination of President McKinley. The law, which prohibited not only actual or attempted assassinations or conspiracies to assassinate, but advocacy of anarchy as well, lay idle for nearly twenty years, until the *Gitlow* prosecution.

GITLOW v. NEW YORK, 268 U.S. 652 (1925): Defendant was a member of the Left Wing Section of the Socialist Party and a member of its National Council, which adopted a "Left Wing Manifesto," condemning the dominant "moderate Socialism" for its recognition of the necessity of the democratic parliamentary state; advocating the necessity of accomplishing the "Communist Revolution" by a militant and "revolutionary Socialism" based on "the class struggle"; and urging the development of mass political strikes for the destruction of the parliamentary state. Defendant arranged for printing and distributing, through the mails and

---

g. The literature on Holmes, J.'s first amendment views and their connection to his larger world view is substantial. See, e.g., Albert W. Alschuler, *Law Without Values: The Life, Work, and Legacy of Justice Holmes* (2000); Ronald K.L. Collins, *The Fundamental Holmes* (2010); Vincent Blasi, *Holmes and the Marketplace of Ideas*, 2004 Sup. Ct. Rev. 1 (2004); G. Edward White, *Justice Oliver Wendell Holmes* 412–54 (1993); Yogal Rogat & James O'Fallon, *Mr. Justice Holmes: A Dissenting Opinion—The Speech Cases*, 36 Stan.L.Rev. 1349 (1984); David Rabban, *The Emergence of Modern First Amendment Doctrine*, 50 U.Chi.L.Rev. 1205 (1983); David M. Rabban, *Free Speech in Progressive Social Thought*, 74 Texas L.Rev. 951 (1996). For further analysis of the Holmes–Hand correspondence, see Gerald Gunther, *Learned Hand and the Origins of Modern First Amendment Doctrine: Some Fragments of History*, 27 Stan.L.Rev. 719 (1975). For illuminating discussion of *Abrams* and the period of which it is a part, see Richard Polenberg, *Fighting Faiths* (1987).

otherwise, 16,000 copies of the Manifesto in the Left Wing's official organ, The Revolutionary Age. There was no evidence of any effect from the publication and circulation of the Manifesto.

In sustaining a conviction under the New York "criminal anarchy" statutes, prohibiting the "advocacy, advising or teaching the duty, necessity or propriety of overthrowing or overturning organized government by force or violence" and the publication or distribution of such matter, the majority, per Sanford, J., stated that for present purposes we may and do assume[a] that First Amendment freedoms of expression "are among the fundamental personal rights and 'liberties' protected by the due process clause of the Fourteenth Amendment from impairment by the States," but ruled:

"By enacting the present statute the State has determined, through its legislative body, that utterances advocating the overthrow of organized government by force, violence and unlawful means, are so inimical to the general welfare and involve such danger of substantive evil that they may be penalized in the exercise of its police power. That determination must be given great weight. Every presumption is to be indulged in favor of the validity of the statute. And the case is to be considered 'in the light of the principle that the State is primarily the judge of regulations required in the interest of public safety and welfare'; and that its police 'statutes may only be declared unconstitutional where they are arbitrary or unreasonable attempts to exercise authority vested in the State in the public interest.' That utterances inciting to the overthrow of organized government by unlawful means, present a sufficient danger of substantive evil to bring their punishment within the range of legislative discretion, is clear. Such utterances, by their very nature, involve danger to the public peace and to the security of the State. They threaten breaches of the peace and ultimate revolution. And the immediate danger is none the less real and substantial, because the effect of a given utterance cannot be accurately foreseen. The State cannot reasonably be required to measure the danger from every such utterance in the nice balance of a jeweler's scale. A single revolutionary spark may kindle a fire that, smoldering for a time, may burst into a sweeping and destructive conflagration. It cannot be said that the State is acting arbitrarily or unreasonably when in the exercise of its judgment as to the measures necessary to protect the public peace and safety, it seeks to extinguish the spark without waiting until it has enkindled the flame or blazed into the conflagration. It cannot reasonably be required to defer the adoption of measures for its own peace and safety until the revolutionary utterances lead to actual disturbances of the public

---

a. Although *Gitlow* is often cited for the proposition that First Amendment freedoms apply to restrict state conduct, its language is dictum. Some would say the first case so holding is *Fiske v. Kansas*, 274 U.S. 380 (1927) (no evidence to support criminal syndicalism conviction) even though no reference to the First Amendment appears in the opinion. Perhaps the honor belongs to *Near v. Minnesota* (1931), Ch. 4, I, B infra. Although the doctrine is that the First Amendment applies equally to states, localities, and the federal government, the Court may generally have given more leeway to the federal government. See Adam Winkler, *Free Speech Federalism*, 108 Mich. L.Rev. 153 (2009).

peace or imminent and immediate danger of its own destruction; but it may, in the exercise of its judgment, suppress the threatened danger in its incipiency.

"[It] is clear that the question in [this case] is entirely different from that involved in those cases where the statute merely prohibits certain acts involving the danger of substantive evil, without any reference to language itself, and it is sought to apply its provisions to language used by the defendant for the purpose of bringing about the prohibited results. There, if it be contended that the statute cannot be applied to the language used by the defendant because of its protection by the freedom of speech or press, it must necessarily be found, as an original question, without any previous determination by the legislative body, whether the specific language used involved such likelihood of bringing about the substantive evil as to deprive it of the constitutional protection. In such cases it has been held that the general provisions of the statute may be constitutionally applied to the specific utterance of the defendant if its natural tendency and probable effect was to bring about the substantive evil which the legislative body might prevent. *Schenck; Debs.* And the general statement in the *Schenck* case that the 'question in every case is whether the words are used in such circumstances and are of such a nature as to create a clear and present danger that they will bring about the substantive evils,' [was] manifestly intended, as shown by the context, to apply only in cases of this class, and has no application to those like the present, where the legislative body itself has previously determined the danger of substantive evil arising from utterances of a specified character."

HOLMES, J., joined by Brandeis, J., dissented: "The general principle of free speech, it seems to me, must be taken to be included in the Fourteenth Amendment, in view of the scope that has been given to the word 'liberty' as there used, although perhaps it may be accepted with a somewhat larger latitude of interpretation than is allowed to Congress by the sweeping language that governs or ought to govern the laws of the United States. If I am right then I think that the criterion sanctioned by the full Court in *Schenck* applies. [It] is true that in my opinion this criterion was departed from in *Abrams,* but the convictions that I expressed in that case are too deep for it to be possible for me as yet to believe that it [has] settled the law. If what I think the correct test is applied it is manifest that there was no present danger of an attempt to overthrow the government by force on the part of the admittedly small minority who shared the defendant's views. It is said that this manifesto was more than a theory, that it was an incitement. Every idea is an incitement. It offers itself for belief and if believed it is acted on unless some other belief outweighs it or some failure of energy stifles the movement at its birth. The only difference between the expression of an opinion and an incitement in the narrower sense is the speaker's enthusiasm for the result. Eloquence may set fire to reason. But whatever may be thought of the redundant discourse before us it had no chance of starting a present conflagration.[b] If in the long run the beliefs expressed in proletarian dictatorship are destined to be accepted by the dominant forces of the community, the only meaning of free speech is that they should be given their chance and have their way.[c]

"If the publication of this document had been laid as an attempt to induce an uprising against government at once and not at some indefinite time in the future it would have presented a different question. The object would have been one with which the law might deal, subject to the doubt whether there was any danger that the publication could produce any result, or in other words, whether it was not futile and too remote from possible consequences. But the indictment alleges the publication and nothing more."

NOTES AND QUESTIONS

1. The statute in *Schenck* was not aimed directly at expression, but at conduct, i.e., certain actual or attempted interferences with the war effort. Thus, an analysis in terms of proximity between the words and the conduct prohibited (by a concededly valid law) seemed useful. But in *Gitlow* (and *Dennis*, Ch. 1, I, C infra) the statute was directed expressly against *advocacy* of a certain doctrine. Once the legislature *designates the point at which words became unlawful,* how helpful is the clear and present danger test? Is the question still how close words come to achieving certain consequences? In *Gitlow*, did Holmes "evade" the difficulty of applying an unmodified *Schenck* test to a different kind of problem? See Yogal Rogat, *Mr. Justice Holmes: Some Modern Views—The Judge as Spectator,* 31 U.Chi.L.Rev. 213, 217 (1964).

2. Consider Hans Linde, *"Clear and Present Danger" Reexamined,* 22 Stan.L.Rev. 1163, 1171 (1970): "Since New York's law itself defined the prohibited speech, the [*Gitlow*] Court could choose among three positions. It could (1) accept this legislative judgment of the harmful potential of the proscribed words, subject to conventional judicial review; (2) independently

---

b. Consider Harry Kalven, *A Worthy Tradition* 156 (1988): "This famous passage points up the ironies in tradition building. The basic problem of finding an accommodation between speech too close to action and censorship too close to criticism might, we have argued, have been tolerably solved by settling on 'incitement' as the key term. It is a term which came easily to the mind of Learned Hand. But for Holmes it does not resonate as it did for Hand. It strikes his ear as a loose, expansible term. At an inopportune moment in the history of free speech the great master of the common law turns poet: 'Every idea is an incitement.' There is of course a sense in which this is true and in which it is a 'scholastic subterfuge' to pretend that speech can be arrayed in firm categories. But the defendants' proposed instruction had offered a sense in which it was not true, in which incitement required advocacy of some definite and immediate acts of force. The weakness of the prosecution's case was not that the defendants' radicalism was not dangerous; it was that their manifesto was not concrete enough to be an incitement."

"Justice Holmes's dissent in *Gitlow,* like his *Abrams* peroration, is extraordinary prose to find in a judicial opinion, and I suspect it has contributed beyond measure to the charisma of the First Amendment. But it also carries the disturbing suggestion that the defendants' speech is to be protected precisely because it is harmless and unimportant. It smacks, as will the later protections of Jehovah's Witnesses, of a luxury civil liberty."

c. But see Richard Posner, *Free Speech in an Economic Perspective,* 20 Suff.L.Rev. 1, 7 (1986): "If those beliefs are destined to prevail, free speech is irrelevant. Holmes is not describing a competitive market in ideas but a natural monopoly."

scrutinize the facts to see whether a 'danger,' as stated in *Schenck,* justified suppression of the particular expression; or (3) hold that by legislating directly against the words rather than the effects, the lawmaker had gone beyond the leeway left to trial and proof by the holding in *Schenck* and had made a law forbidden by the First Amendment." Which course did the *Gitlow* majority choose? The dissenters? Which position should the Court have chosen?

———

Cases such as *Whitney,* infra, raise questions not only about freedom of speech, but also about the right of assembly. In turn, *Whitney* raises the issue of the existence and scope of a right not mentioned in the First Amendment: freedom of association, explored in Ch. 9 infra. Several of the cases which follow are primarily characterized as speech cases because the assemblies or associations at issue were designed for the purpose of organizing future speech activity.

WHITNEY v. CALIFORNIA

274 U.S. 357, 47 S.Ct. 641, 71 L.Ed. 1095 (1927).

JUSTICE SANFORD delivered the opinion of the Court.

[Charlotte Anita Whitney was convicted of violating the 1919 Criminal Syndicalism Act of California whose pertinent provisions were]:

"Section 1. The term 'criminal syndicalism' as used in this act is hereby defined as any doctrine or precept advocating, teaching or aiding and abetting the commission of crime, sabotage (which word is hereby defined as meaning willful and malicious physical damage or injury to physical property), or unlawful acts of force and violence or unlawful methods of terrorism as a means of accomplishing a change in industrial ownership or control, or effecting any political change.

"Sec. 2. Any person who: * * * 4. Organizes or assists in organizing, or is or knowingly becomes a member of, any organization, society, group or assemblage of persons organized or assembled to advocate, teach or aid and abet criminal syndicalism; * * *

"Is guilty of a felony and punishable by imprisonment."

The first count of the information, on which the conviction was had, charged that on or about November 28, 1919, in Alameda County, the defendant, in violation of the Criminal Syndicalism Act, "did then and there unlawfully, willfully, wrongfully, deliberately and feloniously organize and assist in organizing, and was, is, and knowingly became a member of [a group] organized and assembled to advocate, teach, aid and abet criminal syndicalism." * * *

1. While it is not denied that the evidence warranted the jury in finding that the defendant became a member of and assisted in organizing the Communist Labor Party of California, and that this was organized to

advocate, teach, aid or abet criminal syndicalism as defined by the Act, it is urged that the Act, as here construed and applied, deprived the defendant of her liberty without due process of law. [Defendant's] argument is, in effect, that the character of the state organization could not be forecast when she attended the convention; that she had no purpose of helping to create an instrument of terrorism and violence; that she "took part in formulating and presenting to the convention a resolution which, if adopted, would have committed the new organization to a legitimate policy of political reform by the use of the ballot"; that it was not until after the majority of the convention turned out to be "contrary minded, and other less temperate policies prevailed" that the convention could have taken on the character of criminal syndicalism; and that as this was done over her protest, her mere presence in the convention, however violent the opinions expressed therein, could not thereby become a crime. This contention [is in effect] an effort to review the weight of the evidence for the purpose of showing that the defendant did not join and assist in organizing the Communist Labor Party of California with a knowledge of its unlawful character and purpose. This question, which is foreclosed by the verdict of the jury, [is] one of fact merely which is not open to review in this Court, involving as it does no constitutional question whatever. * * *

[That a state] may punish those who abuse [freedom of speech] by utterances inimical to the public welfare, tending to incite to crime, disturb the public peace, or endanger the foundations of organized government and threaten its overthrow by unlawful means, is not open to question. [*Gitlow*].

The essence of the offense denounced by the Act is the combining with others in an association for the accomplishment of the desired ends through the advocacy and use of criminal and unlawful methods. It partakes of the nature of a criminal conspiracy. That such united and joint action involves even greater danger to the public peace and security than the isolated utterances and acts of individuals is clear. We cannot hold that, as here applied, the Act is an unreasonable or arbitrary exercise of the police power of the State, unwarrantably infringing any right of free speech, assembly or association, or that those persons are protected from punishment by the due process clause who abuse such rights by joining and furthering an organization thus menacing the peace and welfare of the State. * * *

Affirmed.

Justice Brandeis (concurring.) * * *

The felony which the statute created is a crime very unlike the old felony of conspiracy or the old misdemeanor of unlawful assembly. The mere act of assisting in forming a society for teaching syndicalism, of becoming a member of it, or assembling with others for that purpose is given the dynamic quality of crime. There is guilt although the society may not contemplate immediate promulgation of the doctrine. Thus the accused is to be punished, not for attempt, incitement or conspiracy, but for a step in preparation, which, if it threatens the public order at all, does so only remotely. The novelty in the prohibition introduced is that the statute aims, not at the practice of criminal syndicalism, nor even directly at the preaching of it, but at association with those who propose to preach it.

Despite arguments to the contrary which had seemed to me persuasive, it is settled that the due process clause of the Fourteenth Amendment applies to matters of substantive law as well as to matters of procedure. Thus all fundamental rights comprised within the term liberty are protected by the federal Constitution from invasion by the states. The right of free speech, the right to teach and the right of assembly are, of course, fundamental rights. These may not be denied or abridged. But, although the rights of free speech and assembly are fundamental, they are not in their nature absolute. Their exercise is subject to restriction, if the particular restriction proposed is required in order to protect the state from destruction or from serious injury, political, economic or moral. That the necessity which is essential to a valid restriction does not exist unless speech would produce, or is intended to produce, a clear and imminent danger of some substantive evil which the state constitutionally may seek to prevent has been settled. See *Schenck.*

[The] Legislature must obviously decide, in the first instance, whether a danger exists which calls for a particular protective measure. But where a statute is valid only in case certain conditions exist, the enactment of the statute cannot alone establish the facts which are essential to its validity. Prohibitory legislation has repeatedly been held invalid, because unnecessary, where the denial of liberty involved was that of engaging in a particular business. The powers of the courts to strike down an offending law are no less when the interests involved are not property rights, but the fundamental personal rights of free speech and assembly.

This Court has not yet fixed the standard by which to determine when a danger shall be deemed clear; how remote the danger may be and yet be deemed present; and what degree of evil shall be deemed sufficiently substantial to justify resort to abridgment of free speech and assembly as the means of protection. To reach sound conclusions on these matters, we must bear in mind why a state is, ordinarily, denied the power to prohibit dissemination of social, economic and political doctrine which a vast majority of its citizens believes to be false and fraught with evil consequence.

Those who won our independence believed that the final end of the state was to make men free to develop their faculties, and that in its government the deliberative forces should prevail over the arbitrary.[a]

---

a. For commentary on Brandeis, J.'s use of history, see Bradley C. Bobertz, *The Brandeis Gambit: The Making of America's "First Freedom," 1909–1931,* 40 Wm. & Mary L.Rev. 557 (1999). See also Stewart Jay, *The Creation of the First Amendment Right to Free Expression: From the Eighteenth Century to the Mid-Twentieth Century,* 34 Wm. Mitch. L. Rev. 773, 872

They valued liberty both as an end and as a means. They believed liberty to be the secret of happiness and courage to be the secret of liberty. They believed that freedom to think as you will and to speak as you think are means indispensable to the discovery and spread of political truth;[b] that without free speech and assembly discussion would be futile; that with them, discussion affords ordinarily adequate protection against the dissemination of noxious doctrine;[c] that the greatest menace to freedom is an inert people; that public discussion is a political duty; and that this should be a fundamental principle of the American government. They recognized the risks to which all human institutions are subject. But they knew that order cannot be secured merely through fear of punishment for its infraction; that it is hazardous to discourage thought, hope and imagination; that fear breeds repression; that repression breeds hate; that hate menaces stable government; that the path of safety lies in the opportunity to discuss freely supposed grievances and proposed remedies; and that the fitting remedy for evil counsels is good ones. Believing in the power of reason as applied through public discussion, they eschewed silence coerced by law—the argument of force in its worst form. Recognizing the occasional tyrannies of governing majorities, they amended the Constitution so that free speech and assembly should be guaranteed.

Fear of serious injury cannot alone justify suppression of free speech and assembly. Men feared witches and burnt women. It is the function of speech to free men from the bondage of irrational fears. To justify suppression of free speech there must be reasonable ground to fear that serious evil will result if free speech is practiced. There must be reasonable ground to believe that the danger apprehended is imminent. There must be reasonable ground to believe that the evil to be prevented is a serious one. Every denunciation of existing law tends in some measure to increase the probability that there will be violation of it. Condonation of a breach enhances the probability. Expressions of approval add to the probability. Propagation of the criminal state of mind by teaching syndicalism increases it. Advocacy of lawbreaking heightens it still further. But even advocacy of violation, however reprehensible morally, is not a

---

(2008). On the development of the free speech thought of Brandeis, J., see Phillipa Strum, *Brandeis: The Public Activist and Freedom of Speech,* 45 Brand. L.J. 659 (2007).

b. Consider Vincent Blasi, *The First Amendment and the Ideal of Civic Courage,* 29 Wm. & Mary L.Rev. 653, 673–74 (1988): "This is as close as Brandeis gets to the claim that unregulated discussion yields truth. Notice that, in contrast to Holmes, Brandeis never tells us what is 'the best test of truth.' He never employs the metaphor of the marketplace. He speaks only of 'political truth,' and he uses the phrase 'means indispensable' to link activities described in highly personal terms—'think as you will,' 'speak as you think'—with the collective social goal of 'political truth.' I think his emphasis in this passage is on the attitudes and atmosphere that must prevail if the ideals of self-government and happiness through courage are to be realized. Brandeis is sketching a good society here, but not, I think, an all-conquering dialectic."

c. Consider Blasi, supra, at 674–75: "It is noteworthy that Brandeis never speaks of noxious doctrine being refuted or eliminated or defeated. He talks of societal self-protection and the fitting remedy. He warns us not to underestimate the value of discussion, education, good counsels. To me, his point is that noxious doctrine is most likely to flourish when its opponents lack the personal qualities of wisdom, creativity, and confidence. And those qualities, he suggests, are best developed by discussion and education, not by lazy and impatient reliance on the coercive authority of the state."

justification for denying free speech where the advocacy falls short of incitement and there is nothing to indicate that the advocacy would be immediately acted on. The wide difference between advocacy and incitement, between preparation and attempt, between assembling and conspiracy, must be borne in mind. In order to support a finding of clear and present danger it must be shown either that immediate serious violence was to be expected or was advocated, or that the past conduct furnished reason to believe that such advocacy was then contemplated.

Those who won our independence by revolution were not cowards. They did not fear political change. They did not exalt order at the cost of liberty. To courageous, self-reliant men, with confidence in the power of free and fearless reasoning applied through the processes of popular government, no danger flowing from speech can be deemed clear and present, unless the incidence of the evil apprehended is so imminent that it may befall before there is opportunity for full discussion. If there be time to expose through discussion the falsehood and fallacies, to avert the evil by the processes of education, the remedy to be applied is more speech, not enforced silence.[d] Only an emergency can justify repression. Such must be the rule if authority is to be reconciled with freedom. Such, in my opinion, is the command of the Constitution. It is therefore always open to Americans to challenge a law abridging free speech and assembly by showing that there was no emergency justifying it.

Moreover, even imminent danger cannot justify resort to prohibition of these functions essential to effective democracy, unless the evil apprehended is relatively serious. Prohibition of free speech and assembly is a measure so stringent that it would be inappropriate as the means for averting a relatively trivial harm to society. A police measure may be unconstitutional merely because the remedy, although effective as means of protection, is unduly harsh or oppressive. Thus, a state might, in the exercise of its police power, make any trespass upon the land of another a crime, regardless of the results or of the intent or purpose of the trespasser. It might, also, punish an attempt, a conspiracy, or an incitement to commit the trespass. But it is hardly conceivable that this court would hold constitutional a statute which punished as a felony the mere voluntary assembly with a society formed to teach that pedestrians had the moral right to cross uninclosed, unposted, waste lands and to advocate their doing so, even if there was imminent danger that advocacy would lead to a trespass. The fact that speech is likely to result in some violence or in destruction of property is not enough to justify its suppression. There must be the probability of serious injury to the State.[e] Among free

---

d. But see Richard Delgado & Jean Stefanic, *Images of the Outsider in American Law and Culture: Can Free Expression Remedy Systematic Social Ills?*, 77 Corn.L.Rev. 1258 (1992); Lawrence Lessig, *The Regulation of Social Meaning*, 62 U.Chi.L.Rev. 943, 1036–39 (1995).

e. But see Robert Bork, *Neutral Principles and Some First Amendment Problems*, 47 Ind.L.J. 1, 34 (1971): "It is difficult to see how a constitutional court could properly draw the distinction proposed. Brandeis offered no analysis to show that advocacy of law violation merited protection by the Court. Worse, the criterion he advanced is the importance, in the judge's eye, of the law whose violation is urged."

men, the deterrents ordinarily to be applied to prevent crime are education and punishment for violations of the law, not abridgement of the rights of free speech and assembly.

* * * Whenever the fundamental rights of free speech and assembly are alleged to have been invaded, it must remain open to a defendant to present the issue whether there actually did exist at the time a clear danger, whether the danger, if any, was imminent, and whether the evil apprehended was one so substantial as to justify the stringent restriction interposed by the Legislature. The legislative declaration, like the fact that the statute was passed and was sustained by the highest court of the State, creates merely a rebuttable presumption that these conditions have been satisfied.

Whether in 1919, when Miss Whitney did the things complained of, there was in California such clear and present danger of serious evil, might have been made the important issue in the case. She might have required that the issue be determined either by the court or the jury. She claimed below that the statute as applied to her violated the federal Constitution; but she did not claim that it was void because there was no clear and present danger of serious evil, nor did she request that the existence of these conditions of a valid measure thus restricting the rights of free speech and assembly be passed upon by the court or a jury. On the other hand, there was evidence on which the court or jury might have found that such danger existed. I am unable to assent to the suggestion in the opinion of the court that assembling with a political party, formed to advocate the desirability of a proletarian revolution by mass action at some date necessarily far in the future, is not a right within the protection of the Fourteenth Amendment. In the present case, however, there was other testimony which tended to establish the existence of a conspiracy, on the part of members of the International Workers of the World, to commit present serious crimes, and likewise to show that such a conspiracy would be furthered by the activity of the society of which Miss Whitney was a member. Under these circumstances the judgment of the State court cannot be disturbed. * * *

JUSTICE HOLMES joins in this opinion.

NOTES AND QUESTIONS

1. *"They valued liberty both as an end and as a means."* Should recognition of the value of liberty as an end augment the marketplace perspective? Replace it?[f] Is autonomy preferable to liberty (or self-realization)

---

f. Compare C. Edwin Baker, *Harm, Liberty, and Free Speech,* 70 So.Cal.L.Rev. 979 (1997)(harm does not justify invasion of liberty); Steven J. Heyman, *Righting the Balance: An Inquiry into the Foundations and Limits of Freedom of Expression,* 78 B.U.L.Rev. 1275 (1998)(endorsing natural rights theory of liberty as basis for free speech); and Martin Redish, *The Value of Free Speech,* 130 U.Pa.L.Rev. 591 (1982) (self-realization should be regarded as the first amendment's exclusive value) and Rodney Smolla, *Free Speech in an Open Society* 5 (1992) ("There is no logical reason, however, why the preferred position of freedom of speech might not be buttressed by multiple rationales. Acceptance of one rationale need not bump another from the

as an organizing principle for First Amendment theory? Does a focus on autonomy help determine the appropriate scope of liberty? C. Edwin Baker, *Human Liberty and Freedom of Speech* 47–51 (1989).**g** Even if we engage the philosophical assumption that human beings are capable of making autonomous choices, are empirical claims of human autonomy somewhat dubious? Richard Fallon, *Two Senses of Autonomy,* 46 Stan.L.Rev. 875 (1994). C. Edwin Baker, *Autonomy and Informational Privacy, or Gossip: The Central Meaning of the First Amendment,* 21 Social Phil. & Pol'y 215, 223 (2004): "The law affirms the formal conception of autonomy to the extent that the law recognizes an agent's legal right to choose what to do with herself (and her property * * *). The law recognizes her dominion over her own mind and body, given the inherent constraints of the environment and given her lack of any right to interfere directly with another's decisions about himself (and his property). This formal autonomy implies nothing about actual capacity, opportunity, or the availability of needed resources."

2. ***Brandeis and Republicanism.*** Consider Pnina Lahav, *Holmes and Brandeis: Libertarian and Republican Justifications for Free Speech,* 4 J.L. & Pol. 451, 460–461 (1987): "[I]n his *Whitney* concurrence, Brandeis tells us, that in the American polity, 'the deliberative forces should prevail over the arbitrary,' that 'public discussion is a political duty,' and that 'the occasional tyranny of governing majorities' should be thwarted. This is radically different from the notion that individuals are free to remain aloof from politics if they so choose (a notion espoused by Holmes), and from the principle of the separation of the state from society. Implied here is the notion of civic virtue—the duty to participate in politics, the importance of deliberation, and the notion that the end of the state is not neutrality but active assistance in providing conditions of freedom which in turn are the 'secret of happiness.'

list, as if this were First Amendment musical chairs"); Steven Shiffrin, *The First Amendment and Economic Regulation: Away From a General Theory of the First Amendment,* 78 Nw.U.L.Rev. 1212 (1983) (many values including liberty and self-realization underpin the first amendment; single valued orientations are reductionist); Brian C. Murchison, *Speech and the Self–Realization Value,* 33 Harv.C.R.-C.L. L.Rev. 443 (1998)(emphasizing and illuminating the self-realization value while recognizing other values); But see Frederick Schauer, *Must Speech Be Special,* 78 Nw.U.L.Rev. 1284 (1983) (neither liberty nor self-realization should play *any* role in first amendment theory). See also Joshua Cohen, *Freedom of Expression,* 22 Phil. & Pub.Aff. 207 (1993); Joseph Raz, *Free Expression and Personal Identification,* 11 Oxford J.Legal St. 311 (1991).

g. See also David Richards, Toleration and the Constitution 165–77 (1986); Robert Post, *Constitutional Domains* 268–331 (1995); Charles Fried, *The New First Amendment Jurisprudence: A Threat to Liberty,* 59 U.Chi.L.Rev. 225, 233–37 (1992); Robert Post, *Managing Deliberation: The Quandary of Democratic Dialogue,* 103 Ethics 654, 664–66 (1993); Robert Post, *Racist Speech, Democracy, and the First Amendment,* 32 Wm. & Mary L.Rev. 267, 279–85 (1991); Thomas Scanlon, *A Theory of Freedom of Expression,* 1 Phil. & Pub.Aff. 204, 215–22 (1972); David Strauss, *Persuasion, Autonomy, and Freedom of Expression,* 91 Colum.L.Rev. 334, 353–71 (1991); Christina Wells, *Reinvigorating Autonomy,* 32 Harv. C.R.-C.L. L. Rev. 159 (1997). Cf. D.F.B. Tucker, *Law, Liberalism, and Free Speech* (1985)(qualified endorsement of autonomy from a Rawlsian perspective).

For commentary on the differences between speaker and listener autonomy, see Cass Sunstein, *Democracy and the Problem of Free Speech* 139–44 (1993); C. Edwin Baker, *Turner Broadcasting: Content–Based Regulation of Persons and Presses,* 1994 Sup.Ct.Rev. 57, 72–80. For the suggestion that the value of autonomy depends upon open and rich public discussion, see Sunstein, supra. For the contention that the value of autonomy should be subservient to open and rich discussion, see Owen Fiss, *State Activism and State Censorship,* 100 Yale L.J. 2087 (1991). Owen Fiss, *Why the State,* 100 Harv.L.Rev. 781 (1987); Owen Fiss, *Free Speech and Social Structure,* 71 Iowa L.Rev. 1405 (1986); but see Robert Post, *Equality and Autonomy in First Amendment Discourse,* 95 Mich. L.Rev. 1517 (1997).

One may even speculate that Brandeis, the progressive leader, believed that the final end of the state was the happiness of mankind.

"These ingredients of the Brandeis position in *Whitney* resonate with republican theory. The theory rests on two central themes: the idea of civic virtue and the idea that the end of politics (or the state) is the common good, which in turn is more than the sum of individual wills. Thus, the state is not separated from society, but rather is committed to the public good, and to a substantive notion of public morality. The members of society are not individuals encased in their autonomous zones, but rather social beings who recognize that they are an integral part of the society. This organic sense of belonging implicitly rejects the notion of combat zones. The republic and its citizens care for the welfare of all. Correctly understood, Brandeis' concurrence in *Whitney* is more than a justification from self-fulfillment or from self-rule. It is a justification from civic virtue."

3. ***Character.*** In keeping with the positions of Holmes and Brandeis, is the First Amendment best defended as proceeding from a "special kind of argument from character that builds from the claim that a culture that prizes and protects expressive liberty nurtures in its members certain character traits such as inquisitiveness, independence of judgment, distrust of authority, willingness to take initiative, perseverance, and the courage to confront evil"? Vincent Blasi, *Free Speech and Good Character*, 46 UCLA L.Rev. 1567 (1999). See also Vincent Blasi, *Free Speech and Good Character: From Milton to Brandeis to the Present*, in Eternally Vigilant: Free Speech in the Modern Era 77 (Lee C. Bollinger & Geoffrey R. Stone eds., 2002): "I do not think Brandeis wanted hopeful, vital, imaginative dissidents because he thought they could be mollified by civil liberties. Rather, he believed that in a political community personal qualities such as hope and imagination tend to be contagious and reciprocal. If the marginal, powerless members of the community retain some semblance of spirit, the mainstream is more likely to sustain its own vitality. And when dissidents become gripped by fear and hate, so too does the majority. The phrase 'repression breeds hate' can be read as a double entendre: it is not just the hate experienced by the dissidents that concerns Brandeis, but also the hate that is felt by those who possess the power to punish dissent. The passage is not primarily about consequences or tactics; it is about character."

4. Ten years after *Whitney*, *DeJonge v. Oregon*, 299 U.S. 353 (1937) held that mere participation in a meeting called by the Communist party could not be made a crime. The right of peaceable assembly was declared to be "cognate to those of free speech and free press and is equally fundamental."

C. COMMUNISM AND ILLEGAL ADVOCACY

Kent Greenawalt has well described the pattern of decisions for much of the period between *Whitney* and *Dennis* infra: "[T]he clear and present danger formula emerged as the applicable standard not only for the kinds of issues with respect to which it originated but also for a wide variety of other First Amendment problems. If the Court was not always very clear about the relevance of that formula to those different problems, its use of the test, and its employment of ancillary doctrines, did evince a growing disposition to protect expression." *Speech and Crime,* 1980 Am.B.Found. Res.J. 645, 706. By 1951, however, anti-communist sentiment was a powerful theme in American politics. The Soviet Union had detonated a nuclear weapon; communists had firm control of the Chinese mainland; the Korean War had reached a stalemate; Alger Hiss had been convicted of perjury in congressional testimony concerning alleged spying activities for the Soviet Union while he was a State Department official; and Senator Joseph McCarthy of Wisconsin had created a national sensation by accusations that many "card carrying Communists" held important State Department jobs. In this context, the top leaders of the American Communist Party asked the Court to reverse their criminal conspiracy convictions.

DENNIS v. UNITED STATES

341 U.S. 494, 71 S.Ct. 857, 95 L.Ed. 1137 (1951).

CHIEF JUSTICE VINSON announced the judgment of the Court and an opinion in which JUSTICE REED, JUSTICE BURTON and JUSTICE MINTON join.

Petitioners were indicted in July, 1948, for violation of the conspiracy provisions of the Smith Act during the period of April, 1945, to July, 1948. * * * A verdict of guilty as to all the petitioners was [affirmed by the Second Circuit]. We granted certiorari, limited to the following two questions: (1) Whether either § 2 or § 3 of the Smith Act, inherently or as construed and applied in the instant case, violates the First Amendment and other provisions of the Bill of Rights; (2) whether either § 2 or § 3 of the Act, inherently or as construed and applied in the instant case, violates the First and Fifth Amendments, because of indefiniteness.

Sections 2 and 3 of the Smith Act provide as follows:

"Sec. 2.

"(a) It shall be unlawful for any person—

"(1) to knowingly or willfully advocate, abet, advise, or teach the duty, necessity, desirability, or propriety of overthrowing or destroying any government in the United States by force or violence, or by the assassination of any officer of any such government; * * *

"Sec. 3. It shall be unlawful for any person to attempt to commit, or to conspire to commit, any of the acts prohibited by the provisions [of] this title."

The indictment charged the petitioners with wilfully and knowingly conspiring (1) to organize as the Communist Party of the United States of America a society, group and assembly of persons who teach and advocate the overthrow and destruction of the Government of the United States by force and violence, and (2) knowingly and wilfully to advocate and teach the duty and necessity of overthrowing and destroying the Government of the United States by force and violence. The indictment further alleged that § 2 of the Smith Act proscribes these acts and that any conspiracy to take such action is a violation of § 3 of the Act.

The trial of the case extended over nine months, six of which were devoted to the taking of evidence, resulting in a record of 16,000 pages. Our limited grant of the writ of certiorari has removed from our consideration any question as to the sufficiency of the evidence to support the jury's determination that petitioners are guilty of the offense charged. Whether on this record petitioners did in fact advocate the overthrow of the Government by force and violence is not before us, and we must base any discussion of this point upon the conclusions stated in the opinion of the Court of Appeals, which treated the issue in great detail [and] held that the record supports the following broad conclusions: [that] the Communist Party is a highly disciplined organization, adept at infiltration into strategic positions, use of aliases, and double-meaning language; that the Party is rigidly controlled; that Communists, unlike other political parties, tolerate no dissension from the policy laid down by the guiding [forces]; that the literature of the Party and the statements and activities of its leaders, petitioners here, advocate, and the general goal of the Party was, during the period in question, to achieve a successful overthrow of the existing order by force and violence. * * *

The obvious purpose of the statute is to protect existing Government, not from change by peaceable, lawful and constitutional means, but from change by violence, revolution and terrorism. That it is within the *power* of the Congress to protect the Government of the United States from armed rebellion is a proposition which requires little discussion. Whatever theoretical merit there may be to the argument that there is a "right" to rebellion against dictatorial governments is without force where the existing structure of the government provides for peaceful and orderly change. We reject any principle of governmental helplessness in the face of preparation for revolution, which principle, carried to its logical conclusion, must lead to anarchy. No one could conceive that it is not within the power of Congress to prohibit acts intended to overthrow the Government by force and violence. The question with which we are concerned here is not whether Congress has such *power,* but whether the *means* which it has employed conflict with the First and Fifth Amendments to the Constitution.

One of the bases for the contention that the means which Congress has employed are invalid takes the form of an attack on the face of the statute on the grounds that by its terms it prohibits academic discussion of the merits of Marxism–Leninism, that it stifles ideas and is contrary to all concepts of a free speech and a free press. [This] is a federal statute which we must interpret as well as judge. Herein lies the fallacy of reliance upon the manner in which this Court has treated judgments of state courts. Where the statute as construed by the state court transgressed the First Amendment, we could not but invalidate the judgments of conviction.

The very language of the Smith Act negates the interpretation which petitioners would have us impose on that Act. It is directed at advocacy, not discussion. Thus, the trial judge properly charged the jury that they could not convict if they found that petitioners did "no more than pursue peaceful studies and discussions or teaching and advocacy in the realm of ideas." * * * Congress did not intend to eradicate the free discussion of political theories, to destroy the traditional rights of Americans to discuss and evaluate ideas without fear of governmental sanction. * * *

But although the statute is not directed at the hypothetical cases which petitioners have conjured, its application in this case has resulted in convictions for the teaching and advocacy of the overthrow of the Government by force and violence, which, even though coupled with the intent to accomplish that overthrow, contains an element of speech. For this reason, we must pay special heed to the demands of the First Amendment marking out the boundaries of speech.

[T]he basis of the First Amendment is the hypothesis that speech can rebut speech, propaganda will answer propaganda, free debate of ideas will result in the wisest governmental policies. [An] analysis of the leading cases in this Court which have involved direct limitations on speech, however, will demonstrate that both the majority of the Court and the dissenters in particular cases have recognized that this is not an unlimited, unqualified right, but that the societal value of speech must, on occasion, be subordinated to other values and considerations. * * *

Although no case subsequent to *Whitney* and *Gitlow* has expressly overruled the majority opinions in those cases, there is little doubt that subsequent opinions have inclined toward the Holmes–Brandeis rationale. * * *

In this case we are squarely presented with the application of the "clear and present danger" test, and must decide what that phrase imports.[a] We first note that many of the cases in which this Court has reversed convictions by use of this or similar tests have been based on the fact that the interest which the State was attempting to protect was itself too insubstantial to warrant restriction of speech. * * * Overthrow of the Government by force and violence is certainly a substantial enough interest for the Government to limit speech. Indeed, this is the ultimate value of any society, for if a society cannot protect its very structure from armed internal attack, it must follow that no subordinate value can be protected. If, then, this interest may be protected, the literal problem which is presented is what has been meant by the use of the phrase "clear and present danger" of the utterances bringing about the evil within the power of Congress to punish.

Obviously, the words cannot mean that before the Government may act, it must wait until the putsch is about to be executed, the plans have been laid and the signal is awaited. If Government is aware that a group aiming at its overthrow is attempting to indoctrinate its members and to

---

a. Consider Harry Kalven, *A Worthy Tradition* 190–91 (1988): "The [Vinson opinion] acknowledges clear and present danger as the constitutional measure of free speech, but in the process, to meet the political exigencies of the case, it officially adjusts the test, giving it the kiss of death."

commit them to a course whereby they will strike when the leaders feel the circumstances permit, action by the Government is required. The argument that there is no need for Government to concern itself, for Government is strong, it possesses ample powers to put down a rebellion, it may defeat the revolution with ease needs no answer. For that is not the question. Certainly an attempt to overthrow the Government by force, even though doomed from the outset because of inadequate numbers or power of the revolutionists, is a sufficient evil for Congress to prevent. The damage which such attempts create both physically and politically to a nation makes it impossible to measure the validity in terms of the probability of success, or the immediacy of a successful attempt. In the instant case the trial judge charged the jury that they could not convict unless they found that petitioners intended to overthrow the Government "as speedily as circumstances would permit." This does not mean, and could not properly mean, that they would not strike until there was certainty of success. What was meant was that the revolutionists would strike when they thought the time was ripe. We must therefore reject the contention that success or probability of success is the criterion.

The situation with which Justices Holmes and Brandeis were concerned in *Gitlow* was a comparatively isolated event, bearing little relation in their minds to any substantial threat to the safety of the community. [They] were not confronted with any situation comparable to the instant one—the development of an apparatus designed and dedicated to the overthrow of the Government, in the context of world crisis after crisis.

Chief Judge Learned Hand, writing for the majority below, interpreted the phrase as follows: "In each case [courts] must ask whether the gravity of the 'evil,' discounted by its improbability, justifies such invasion of free speech as is necessary to avoid the danger." We adopt this statement of the rule. As articulated by Chief Judge Hand, it is as succinct and inclusive as any other we might devise at this time. * * *

Likewise, we are in accord with the court below, which affirmed the trial court's finding that the requisite danger existed. The mere fact that from the period 1945 to 1948 petitioners' activities did not result in an attempt to overthrow the Government by force and violence is of course no answer to the fact that there was a group that was ready to make the attempt. The formation by petitioners of such a highly organized conspiracy, with rigidly disciplined members subject to call when the leaders, these petitioners, felt that the time had come for action, coupled with the inflammable nature of world conditions, similar uprisings in other countries, and the touch-and-go nature of our relations with countries with whom petitioners were in the very least ideologically attuned, convince us that their convictions were justified on this score. And this analysis disposes of the contention that a conspiracy to advocate, as distinguished from the advocacy itself, cannot be constitutionally restrained, because it comprises only the preparation. It is the existence of the conspiracy which creates the danger. * * *

Although we have concluded that the finding that there was a sufficient danger to warrant the application of the statute was justified on the merits, there remains the problem of whether the trial judge's treatment of the issue was correct. He charged the jury, in relevant part, as follows:

"In further construction and interpretation of the statute I charge you that it is not the abstract doctrine of overthrowing or destroying organized government by unlawful means which is denounced by this law, but the teaching and advocacy of action for the accomplishment of that purpose, by language reasonably and ordinarily calculated to incite persons to such action. Accordingly, you cannot find the defendants or any of them guilty of the crime charged unless you are satisfied beyond a reasonable doubt that they conspired to organize a society, group and assembly of persons who teach and advocate the overthrow or destruction of the Government of the United States by force and violence and to advocate and teach the duty and necessity of overthrowing or destroying the Government of the United States by force and violence, with the intent that such teaching and advocacy be of a rule or principle of action and by language reasonably and ordinarily calculated to incite persons to such action, all with the intent to cause the overthrow or destruction of the Government of the United States by force and violence as speedily as circumstances would permit. * * *

"If you are satisfied that the evidence establishes beyond a reasonable doubt that the defendants, or any of them, are guilty of a violation of the statute, as I have interpreted it to you, I find as matter of law that there is sufficient danger of a substantive evil that the Congress has a right to prevent to justify the application of the statute under the First Amendment of the Constitution. This is matter of law about which you have no concern. * * * "

It is thus clear that he reserved the question of the existence of the danger for his own determination, and the question becomes whether the issue is of such a nature that it should have been submitted to the jury.

[When] facts are found that establish the violation of a statute, the protection against conviction afforded by the First Amendment is a matter of law. The doctrine that there must be a clear and present danger of a substantive evil that Congress has a right to prevent is a judicial rule to be applied as a matter of law by the courts. The guilt is established by proof of facts. Whether the First Amendment protects the activity which constitutes the violation of the statute must depend upon a judicial determination of the scope of the First Amendment applied to the circumstances of the case.

[In] *Schenck* this Court itself examined the record to find whether the requisite danger appeared, and the issue was not submitted to a jury. And in every later case in which the Court has measured the validity of a statute by the "clear and present danger" test, that determination has been by the court, the question of the danger not being submitted to the jury. * * * Petitioners intended to overthrow the Government of the United States as speedily as the circumstances would permit. Their conspiracy to organize the Communist Party and to teach and advocate the overthrow of the Government of the United States by force and violence created a "clear and present danger" of an attempt to overthrow the Government by force and violence. They were properly and constitutionally convicted * * *.

Affirmed.

JUSTICE CLARK took no part in the consideration or decision of this case.

JUSTICE FRANKFURTER, concurring in affirmance of the judgment.

[The] demands of free speech in a democratic society as well as the interest in national security are better served by candid and informed weighing of the competing interests, within the confines of the judicial process, than by announcing dogmas too inflexible for the non-Euclidian problems to be solved.

But how are competing interests to be assessed? Since they are not subject to quantitative ascertainment, the issue necessarily resolves itself into asking, who is to make the adjustment?—who is to balance the relevant factors and ascertain which interest is in the circumstances to prevail? Full responsibility for the choice cannot be given to the courts. Courts are not representative bodies. They are not designed to be a good reflex of a democratic society. Their judgment is best informed, and therefore most dependable, within narrow limits. Their essential quality is detachment, founded on independence. History teaches that the independence of the judiciary is jeopardized when courts become embroiled in the passions of the day and assume primary responsibility in choosing between competing political, economic and social pressures.

Primary responsibility for adjusting the interests which compete in the situation before us of necessity belongs to the Congress. [We] are to set aside the judgment of those whose duty it is to legislate only if there is no reasonable basis for [it]. Free-speech cases are not an exception to the principle that we are not legislators, that direct policy-making is not our province. How best to reconcile competing interests is the business of legislatures, and the balance they strike is a judgment not to be displaced by ours, but to be respected unless outside the pale of fair judgment. [A] survey of the relevant decisions indicates that the results which we have reached are on the whole those that would ensue from careful weighing of conflicting interests. The complex issues presented by regulation of speech in public places by picketing, and by legislation prohibiting advocacy of crime have been resolved by scrutiny of many factors besides the imminence and gravity of the evil threatened. The matter has been well summarized by a reflective student of the Court's work. "The truth is that the clear-and-present-danger test is an oversimplified judgment unless it takes account also of a number of other factors: the relative seriousness of the danger in comparison with the value of the occasion for speech or political activity; the availability of more moderate controls than those which the state has imposed; and perhaps the specific intent with which the speech or activity is launched. No matter how rapidly we utter the phrase 'clear and present danger,' or how closely we hyphenate the words, they are not a substitute for the weighing of values. They tend to convey a delusion of certitude when what is most certain is the complexity of the strands in the web of freedoms which the judge must disentangle." Paul Freund, *On Understanding the Supreme Court* 27–28 [1949]. * * *

To make validity of legislation depend on judicial reading of events still in the womb of time—a forecast, that is, of the outcome of forces at best appreciated only with knowledge of the topmost secrets of nations—is to charge the judiciary with duties beyond its equipment. * * *

Even when moving strictly within the limits of constitutional adjudication, judges are concerned with issues that may be said to involve vital finalities. The too easy transition from disapproval of what is undesirable to condemnation as unconstitutional, has led some of the wisest judges to question the wisdom of our scheme in lodging such authority in courts. But it is relevant to remind that in sustaining the power of Congress in a case like this nothing irrevocable is done. The democratic process at all events is not impaired or restricted. Power and responsibility remain with the people and immediately with their representation. All the Court says is that Congress was not forbidden by the Constitution to pass this enactment and that a prosecution under it may be brought against a conspiracy such as the one before us. * * *

JUSTICE JACKSON, concurring.

[E]ither by accident or design, the Communist stratagem outwits the antianarchist pattern of statute aimed against "overthrow by force and violence" if qualified by the doctrine that only "clear and present danger" of accomplishing that result will sustain the prosecution.

The "clear and present danger" test was an innovation by Mr. Justice Holmes in the *Schenck* case, reiterated and refined by him and Mr. Justice Brandeis in later cases, all arising before the era of World War II revealed the subtlety and efficacy of modernized revolutionary techniques used by totalitarian parties. In those cases, they were faced with convictions under so-called criminal syndicalism statutes aimed at anarchists but which, loosely construed, had been applied to punish socialism, pacifism, and left-wing ideologies, the charges often resting on farfetched inferences which, if true, would establish only technical or trivial violations. They proposed "clear and present danger" as a test for the sufficiency of evidence in particular cases.

I would save it, unmodified, for application as a "rule of reason" in the kind of case for which it was devised. When the issue is criminality of a hotheaded speech on a street corner, or circulation of a few incendiary pamphlets, or parading by some zealots behind a red flag, or refusal of a handful of school children to salute our flag, it is not beyond the capacity of the judicial process to gather, comprehend, and weigh the necessary materials for decision whether it is a clear and present danger of substantive evil or a harmless letting off of steam. It is not a prophecy, for the danger in such cases has matured by the time of trial or it was never present. The test applies and has meaning where a conviction is sought to be based on a speech or writing which does not directly or explicitly advocate a crime but to which such tendency is sought to be attributed by construction or by implication from external circumstances. The formula in such cases favors freedoms that are vital to our society, and, even if sometimes applied too generously, the consequences cannot be grave. But its recent expansion has extended, in particular to Communists, unprecedented immunities. Unless we are to hold our Government captive in a judge-made verbal trap, we must approach the problem of a well-organized, nation-wide conspiracy, such as I have described, as realistically as our predecessors faced the trivialities that were being prosecuted until they were checked with a rule of reason.

I think reason is lacking for applying that test to this case. *clear & present danger*

If we must decide that this Act and its application are constitutional only if we are convinced that petitioner's conduct creates a "clear and present danger" of violent overthrow, we must appraise imponderables, including international and national phenomena which baffle the best informed foreign offices and our most experienced politicians. We would have to foresee and predict the effectiveness of Communist propaganda, opportunities for infiltration, whether, and when, a time will come that they consider propitious for action, and whether and how fast our existing government will deteriorate. And we would have to speculate as to whether an approaching Communist coup would not be anticipated by a nationalistic fascist movement. No doctrine can be sound whose application requires us to make a prophecy of that sort in the guise of a legal decision. The judicial process simply is not adequate to a trial of such far-flung issues. The answers given would reflect our own political predilections and nothing more.

The authors of the clear and present danger test never applied it to a case like this, nor would I. If applied as it is proposed here, it means that the Communist plotting is protected during its period of incubation; its preliminary stages of organization and preparation are immune from the law; the Government can move only after imminent action is manifest, when it would, of course, be too late.

The highest degree of constitutional protection is due to the individual acting without conspiracy. But even an individual cannot claim that the Constitution protects him in advocating or teaching overthrow of government by force or violence. I should suppose no one would doubt that Congress has power to make such attempted overthrow a crime. But the contention is that one has the constitutional right to work up a public desire and will to do what it is a crime to attempt. I think direct incitement by speech or writing can be made a crime, and I think there can be a conviction without also proving that the odds favored its success by 99 to 1, or some other extremely high ratio. * * *

What really is under review here is a conviction of conspiracy, after a trial for conspiracy, on an indictment charging conspiracy, brought under a statute outlawing conspiracy. With due respect to my colleagues, they seem to me to discuss anything under the sun except the law of conspiracy. * * *

The Constitution does not make conspiracy a civil right. [Although] I consider criminal conspiracy a dragnet device capable of perversion into an instrument of injustice in the hands of a partisan or complacent judiciary, it has an established place in our system of law, and no reason appears for applying it only to concerted action claimed to disturb interstate commerce and withholding it from those claimed to undermine our whole Government. * * *

I do not suggest that Congress could punish conspiracy to advocate something, the doing of which it may not punish. Advocacy or exposition of the doctrine of communal property ownership, or any political philosophy unassociated with advocacy of its imposition by force or seizure of government by unlawful means could not be reached through conspiracy prosecution. But it is not forbidden to put down force or violence, it is not forbidden to punish its teaching or advocacy, and the end being punishable, there is no doubt of the power to punish conspiracy for the purpose. * * *

JUSTICE BLACK, dissenting. * * *

So long as this Court exercises the power of judicial review of legislation, I cannot agree that the First Amendment permits us to sustain laws suppressing freedom of speech and press on the basis of Congress' or our own notions of mere "reasonableness." Such a doctrine waters down the First Amendment so that it amounts to little more than an admonition to Congress. The Amendment as so construed is not likely to protect any but those "safe" or orthodox views which rarely need its protection. I must also express my objection to the holding because, as Mr. Justice Douglas' dissent shows, it sanctions the determination of a crucial issue of fact by the judge rather than by the jury. * * *

Public opinion being what it now is, few will protest the conviction of these Communist petitioners. There is hope, however, that in calmer times, when present pressures, passions and fears subside, this or some later Court will restore the First Amendment liberties to the high preferred place where they belong in a free society.

JUSTICE DOUGLAS, dissenting.

If this were a case where those who claimed protection under the First Amendment were teaching the techniques of sabotage, the assassination of the President, the filching of documents from public files, the planting of bombs, the art of street warfare, and the like, I would have no doubts. The freedom to speak is not absolute; the teaching of methods of terror and other seditious conduct should be beyond the pale along with obscenity and immorality. This case was argued as if those were the facts. The argument imported much seditious conduct into the record. That is easy and it has popular appeal, for the activities of Communists in plotting and scheming against the free world are common knowledge. But the fact is that no such evidence was introduced at the trial. There is a statute which makes a seditious conspiracy unlawful. Petitioners, however, were not charged with a "conspiracy to overthrow" the Government. They were charged with a conspiracy to form a party and groups and assemblies of people who teach and advocate the overthrow of our Government by force or violence and with a conspiracy to advocate and teach its overthrow by force and violence. It may well be that indoctrination in the techniques of terror to destroy the Government would be indictable under either statute. But the teaching which is condemned here is of a different character.

So far as the present record is concerned, what petitioners did was to organize people to teach and themselves teach the Marxist–Leninist doctrine contained chiefly in four books: *Foundations of Leninism* by Stalin (1924); *The Communist Manifesto* by Marx and Engels (1848); *State and Revolution* by Lenin (1917); *History of the Communist Party of the Soviet Union* (B.) (1939).

Those books are to Soviet Communism what *Mein Kampf* was to Nazism. If they are understood, the ugliness of Communism is revealed, its deceit and cunning are exposed, the nature of its activities becomes apparent, and the chances of its success less likely. That is not, of course, the reason why petitioners chose these books for their classrooms. They are fervent Communists to whom these volumes are gospel. They preached the creed with the hope that some day it would be acted upon.

The opinion of the Court does not outlaw these texts nor condemn them to the fire, as the Communists do literature offensive to their creed. But if the books themselves are not outlawed, if they can lawfully remain on library shelves, by what reasoning does their use in a classroom become a crime? It would not be a crime under the Act to introduce these books to a class, though that would be teaching what the creed of violent overthrow of the Government is. The Act, as construed, requires the element of intent—that those who teach the creed believe in it. The crime then depends not on what is taught but on who the teacher is. That is to make freedom of speech turn not on *what is said,* but on the *intent* with which it is said. Once we start down that road we enter territory dangerous to the liberties of every citizen. * * *

The vice of treating speech as the equivalent of overt acts of a treasonable or seditious character is emphasized by a concurring opinion, which by invoking the law of conspiracy makes speech do service for deeds which are dangerous to society. [N]ever until today has anyone seriously thought that the ancient law of conspiracy could constitutionally be used to turn speech into seditious conduct. Yet that is precisely what is suggested. I repeat that we deal here with speech alone, not with speech *plus* acts of sabotage or unlawful conduct. Not a single seditious act is charged in the indictment. To make a lawful speech unlawful because two men conceive it is to raise the law of conspiracy to appalling proportions. * * *

There comes a time when even speech loses its constitutional immunity. Speech innocuous one year may at another time fan such destructive flames that it must be halted in the interests of the safety of the Republic. That is the meaning of the clear and present danger test. When conditions are so critical that there will be no time to avoid the evil that the speech threatens, it is time to call a halt. Otherwise, free speech which is the strength of the Nation will be the cause of its destruction.

Yet free speech is the rule, not the exception. The restraint to be constitutional must be based on more than fear, on more than passionate opposition against the speech, on more than a revolted dislike for its contents. There must be some immediate injury to society that is likely if speech is allowed. * * *

I had assumed that the question of the clear and present danger, being so critical an issue in the case, would be a matter for submission to the jury. [The] Court, I think, errs when it treats the question as one of law.

Yet, whether the question is one for the Court or the jury, there should be evidence of record on the issue. This record, however, contains no evidence whatsoever showing that the acts charged viz., the teaching of the Soviet theory of revolution with the hope that it will be realized, have created any clear and present danger to the Nation. The Court, however, rules to the contrary. [The majority] might as well say that the speech of petitioners is outlawed because Soviet Russia and her Red Army are a threat to world peace.

The nature of Communism as a force on the world scene would, of course, be relevant to the issue of clear and present danger of petitioners' advocacy within the United States. But the primary consideration is the strength and tactical position of petitioners and their converts in this country. On that there is no evidence in the record. If we are to take judicial notice of the threat of Communists within the nation, it should not be difficult to conclude that *as a political party* they are of little consequence. Communists in this country have never made a respectable or serious showing in any election. I would doubt that there is a village, let alone a city or county or state, which the Communists could carry. Communism in the world scene is no bogeyman; but Communism as a political faction or party in this country plainly is. Communism has been so thoroughly exposed in this country that it has been crippled as a political force. Free speech has destroyed it as an effective political party. It is inconceivable that those who went up and down this country preaching the doctrine of revolution which petitioners espouse would have any success. In days of trouble and confusion, when bread lines were long, when the unemployed walked the streets, when people were starving, the advocates of a short-cut by revolution might have a chance to gain adherents. But today there are no such conditions. The country is not in despair; the people know Soviet Communism; the doctrine of Soviet revolution is exposed in all of its ugliness and the American people want none of it.

[Unless] and until extreme and necessitous circumstances are shown our aim should be to keep speech unfettered and to allow the processes of law to be invoked only when the provocateurs among us move from speech to action. * * *[b]

Notes and Questions

1. *The test.* Is the *Dennis* test problematic on its face, as applied, or both? Consider Wilson Huhn, *Scienter, Causation, and Harm in Freedom of Expression Analysis: The Right Hand Side of the Constitutional Calculus*, 13 Wm. & Mary Bill Rts. J. 125, 166 (2004): "The central problem [with] *Dennis* was not that it utilized Judge Hand's balancing approach, but rather that it failed to estimate properly the remoteness of the threatened harm, and accordingly, it failed to evaluate properly the relative weight of the freedom to advocate for unpopular political positions."

2. **Suppression of "totalitarian movements."** Consider Carl Auerbach, *The Communist Control Act of 1954*, 23 U.Chi.L.Rev. 173, 188–89 (1956): "[I]n suppressing totalitarian movements a democratic society is not acting to protect the status quo, but the very same interests which freedom of speech itself seeks to secure—the possibility of peaceful progress under freedom. That suppression may sometimes have to be the means of securing and enlarging freedom is a paradox which is not unknown in other areas of the law of modern democratic states. The basic 'postulate,' therefore, which should 'limit and control' the First Amendment is that it is part of the framework for a constitutional democracy and should, therefore, not be used to curb the power of Congress to exclude from the political struggle those groups which, if victorious, would crush democracy and impose totalitarianism."[c]

Was the *Dennis* prosecution a net positive because of the moral culpability of the Communist leaders and because they themselves did not believe in free speech? See David E. Bernstein, *The Red Menace, Revisited*, 100 Nw. U.L. Rev. 1295 (2006).

---

b. Eighteen years later, concurring in *Brandenburg*, Ch. 1, I, D infra, Douglas, J., declared: "I see no place in the regime of the First Amendment for any 'clear and present danger' test whether strict and tight as some would make it or free-wheeling as the Court in *Dennis* rephrased it. When one reads the opinions closely and sees when and how the 'clear and present danger' test has been applied, great misgivings are aroused. First, the threats were often loud but always puny and made serious only by judges so wedded to the status quo that critical analysis made them nervous. Second, the test was so twisted and perverted in *Dennis* as to make the trial of those teachers of Marxism an all-out political trial which was part and parcel of the cold war that has eroded substantial parts of the First Amendment."

c. For different perspectives, see John Rawls, *A Theory of Justice* 216–21 (1971); Steven Shiffrin, *Racist Speech Outsider Jurisprudence, and the Meaning of America*, 80 Cornell L.Rev. 43, 88 n. 220, 90 n. 232 (1994); Stephen Smith, *Radically Subversive Speech and the Authority of Law*, 94 Mich.L.Rev. 348 (1995).

3. *The Second Amendment.* Does the second amendment guarantee individuals (or groups) the right to bear arms for protection including protection against government tyranny?[d] If the second amendment is so construed, does the second amendment shed light on the first?

4. *Dennis distinguished.* In 1954, Senator McCarthy was censured by the United States Senate for acting contrary to its ethics and impairing its dignity. In 1957, when the convictions of 14 "second string" communist leaders reached the Supreme Court in YATES v. UNITED STATES, 354 U.S. 298 (1957), McCarthy had died, and so had McCarthyism. Although strong anti-communist sentiment persisted, the political atmosphere in *Yates'* 1957 was profoundly different from that of *Dennis'* 1951. HARLAN, J., distinguishing *Dennis,* construed the Smith Act narrowly: "[The] essence of the *Dennis* holding was that indoctrination of a group in preparation for future violent action, as well as exhortation to immediate action, by advocacy found to be directed to 'action for the accomplishment' of forcible overthrow, to violence as 'a rule or principle of action,' and employing 'language of incitement,' is not constitutionally protected when the group is of sufficient size and cohesiveness, is sufficiently oriented towards action, and other circumstances are such as reasonably to justify apprehension that action will occur. This is quite a different thing from the view of the District Court here that mere doctrinal justification of forcible overthrow, if engaged in with the intent to accomplish overthrow, is punishable per se under the Smith Act. [T]he trial court's statement that the proscribed advocacy must include the 'urging,' 'necessity,' and 'duty' of forcible overthrow, and not merely its 'desirability' and 'propriety,' may not be regarded as a sufficient substitute for charging that the Smith Act reaches only advocacy of action for the overthrow of government by force and violence. The essential distinction is that those to whom the advocacy is addressed must be urged to *do* something, now or in the future, rather than merely to *believe* in something." Applying this standard, Harlan J., acquitted 5 defendants and remanded to the lower court for proceedings against the remaining defendants.[e]

5. *The membership clause of the Smith Act.* After *Yates,* the government sought to prosecute communists for being members of an organization advocating the overthrow of the government by force and violence. The Court in *Scales v. United States,* 367 U.S. 203 (1961) and *Noto v. United States,* 367 U.S. 290 (1961) interpreted the membership clause to require that the organization engage in advocacy of the sort described in *Yates* and that the members be active with knowledge of the organization's advocacy and the group's specific intent to bring about violent overthrow as speedily as circumstances permit.

6. *Spock.* Dr. Spock, Rev. Coffin and others were convicted of conspiring to counsel and abet Selective Service registrants to refuse to have their

---

d. Is the second amendment an embarrassment to liberals? See Sanford Levinson, *The Embarrassing Second Amendment,* 99 Yale L.J. 637 (1989). For comparative analysis of the methodology employed in First and Second Amendment cases, see Joseph Blocher, *Categoricalism and Balancing in First and Second Amendment Cases,* 84 N.Y.U. L.Rev. 375 (2009).

e. Burton, J., concurred. Black, joined by Douglas, JJ., dissenting, would have acquitted all defendants. Clark, J., dissenting, would have affirmed the convictions of all defendants. Brennan and Whittaker, JJ., took no part. On remand, the government requested dismissal of the indictments, explaining that it could not meet *Yates'* evidentiary requirements.

draft cards in their possession and to disobey other duties imposed by the Selective Service Act of 1967. Spock signed a document entitled "A Call to Resist Illegitimate Authority," which "had 'a double aspect: in part it was a denunciation of governmental policy [in Vietnam] and, in part, it involved a public call to resist the duties imposed by the [Selective Service] Act.' " Several weeks later, Spock attended a demonstration in Washington, D.C., where an unsuccessful attempt was made to present collected draft cards to the Attorney General. UNITED STATES v. SPOCK, 416 F.2d 165 (1st Cir.1969), per ALDRICH, J., ruled that Spock should have been acquitted: "[Spock] was one of the drafters of the Call, but this does not evidence the necessary intent to adhere to its illegal aspects. [H]is speech was limited to condemnation of the war and the draft, and lacked any words or content of counselling. The jury could not find proscribed advocacy from the mere fact [that] he hoped the frequent stating of his views might give young men 'courage to take active steps in draft resistance.' This is a natural consequence of vigorous speech. Similarly, Spock's actions lacked the clear character necessary to imply specific intent under the First Amendment standard. [H]e was at the Washington demonstration, [but took] no part in its planning. [His statements at this demonstration did not extend] beyond the general anti-war, anti-draft remarks he had made before. His attendance is as consistent with a desire to repeat this speech as it is to aid a violation of the law. The dissent would fault us for drawing such distinctions, but it forgets the teaching of [*Bond v. Floyd*[f]] that expressing one's views in broad areas is not foreclosed by knowledge of the consequences, and the important lesson of *Noto, Scales* and *Yates* that one may belong to a group, knowing of its illegal aspects, and still not be found to adhere thereto."

D. A MODERN "RESTATEMENT"

BRANDENBURG v. OHIO

395 U.S. 444, 89 S.Ct. 1827, 23 L.Ed.2d 430 (1969).

PER CURIAM.[a]

The appellant, a leader of a Ku Klux Klan group, was convicted under [a 1919] Ohio Criminal Syndicalism statute of "advocat[ing] the duty, necessity, or propriety of crime, sabotage, violence, or unlawful methods of terrorism as a means of accomplishing industrial or political reform" and

---

f. *Bond,* 385 U.S. 116 (1966) found ambiguity in expressions of support for those unwilling to respond to the draft that earlier opinions would have characterized as clear advocacy of illegal action. As Thomas Emerson puts it "the distance traversed [from *Schenck* and *Debs* to *Bond*] is quite apparent." *Freedom of Expression in Wartime,* 116 U.Pa.L.Rev. 975, 988 (1968).

a. See Bernard Schwartz, *Holmes Versus Hand: Clear and Present Danger or Advocacy of Unlawful Action?* 1995 S.Ct.Rev. 237: "*Brandenburg* was assigned to Justice Fortas. The draft opinion that he circulated stated a modified version of the Clear and Present test. [As] it turned out, *Brandenburg* did not come down as a Fortas opinion. Though the Justice had circulated his draft opinion in April 1969 and quickly secured the necessary votes, he followed Justice Harlan's suggestion to delay its announcement. Before then, the events occurred that led to Justice Fortas's forced resignation from the Court. The *Brandenburg* opinion was then redrafted by Justice Brennan, who eliminated all references to the Clear and Present Danger test and substituted the present *Brandenburg* language: 'where such advocacy is directed to inciting or producing imminent lawless action and is likely to incite or produce such action.' The Brennan redraft was issued as a per curiam opinion."

of "voluntarily assembl[ing] with any society, group or assemblage of persons formed to teach or advocate the doctrines of criminal syndicalism." He was fined $1,000 and sentenced to one to 10 years' imprisonment. * * *

The record shows that a man, identified at trial as the appellant, telephoned an announcer-reporter on the staff of a Cincinnati television station and invited him to come to a Ku Klux Klan "rally" to be held at a farm in Hamilton County. With the cooperation of the organizers, the reporter and a cameraman attended the meeting and filmed the events. Portions of the films were later broadcast on the local station and on a national network.

The prosecution's case rested on the films and on testimony identifying the appellant as the person who communicated with the reporter and who spoke at the rally. The State also introduced into evidence several articles appearing in the film, including a pistol, a rifle, a shotgun, ammunition, a Bible, and a red hood worn by the speaker in the films.

One film showed 12 hooded figures, some of whom carried firearms. They were gathered around a large wooden cross, which they burned. No one was present other than the participants and the newsmen who made the film. Most of the words uttered during the scene were incomprehensible when the film was projected, but scattered phrases could be understood that were derogatory of Negroes and, in one instance, of Jews. Another scene on the same film showed the appellant, in Klan regalia, making a speech. The speech, in full, was as follows:

"This is an organizers' meeting. We have had quite a few members here today which are—we have hundreds, hundreds of members throughout the State of Ohio. I can quote from a newspaper clipping from the Columbus Ohio Dispatch, five weeks ago Sunday morning. The Klan has more members in the State of Ohio than does any other organization. We're not a revengent organization, but if our President, our Congress, our Supreme Court, continues to suppress the white, Caucasian race, it's possible that there might have to be some revengence taken.

"We are marching on Congress July the Fourth, four hundred thousand strong. From there we are dividing into two groups, one group to march on St. Augustine, Florida, the other group to march into Mississippi. Thank you."

The second film showed six hooded figures one of whom, later identified as the appellant, repeated a speech very similar to that recorded on the first film. The reference to the possibility of "revengence" was omitted, and one sentence was added: "Personally, I believe the nigger should be returned to Africa, the Jew returned to Israel." Though some of the figures in the films carried weapons, the speaker did not.

[*Whitney*] sustained the constitutionality of California's Criminal Syndicalism Act, the text of which is quite similar to that of the laws of Ohio. The Court upheld the statute on the ground that, without more, "advocating" violent means to effect political and economic change involves such danger to the security of the State that the State may outlaw it. But *Whitney* has been thoroughly discredited by later decisions [such as *Dennis* which] have fashioned the principle that the constitutional guarantees of free speech and free press do not permit a State to forbid or proscribe advocacy of the use of force or of law violation except where such advocacy is directed[b] to inciting or producing imminent lawless action[c] and is likely to incite or produce such action.[2] As we said in *Noto*, "the mere abstract teaching [of] the moral propriety or even moral necessity for a resort to force and violence, is not the same as preparing a group for violent action and steeling it to such action." See also *Bond v. Floyd*. A statute which fails to draw this distinction impermissibly intrudes upon the freedoms guaranteed by the First and Fourteenth Amendments. It sweeps within its condemnation speech which our Constitution has immunized from governmental control. Cf. *Yates* * * *.

Measured by this test, Ohio's Criminal Syndicalism Act cannot be sustained. The Act punishes persons who "advocate or teach the duty, necessity, or propriety" of violence "as a means of accomplishing industrial or political reform"; or who publish or circulate or display any book or paper containing such advocacy; or who "justify" the commission of violent acts "with intent to exemplify, spread or advocate the propriety of the doctrines of criminal syndicalism"; or [who] "voluntarily assemble" with a group formed "to teach or advocate the doctrines of criminal syndicalism." Neither the indictment nor the trial judge's instructions to the jury in any way refined the statute's bald definition of the crime in terms of mere advocacy not distinguished from incitement to imminent lawless action.[3]

---

b. Consider Eugene Volokh, *Crime-Facilitating Speech*, 57 STAN. L. REV. 1095, 1193 (2005):"The incitement cases [have] never fully explained why an intent-imminence-likelihood test is the proper approach (as opposed to, say, a knowledge-imminence-likelihood test)."

c. Consider Christina Wells, *Reinvigorating Autonomy*, 32 Harv. C.R.-C.L. L. Rev. 159, 179 (1997), "The Court's requirement of imminent lawless action is easily justified as based upon concern for autonomy. Speech designed to incite immediate violence or lawless action does not appeal to our thought processes. Rather, it disrespects our rationality and is designed to elicit an unthinking, animalistic response. * * * Speech designed to persuade people to violate the law is not coercive in the same sense as speech designed to incite imminent lawlessness; the former contributes to rather than detracts from our deliberative processes." Compare David R. Dow & R. Scott Shieldes, *Rethinking the Clear and Present Danger Test*, 73 Indiana L.J. 1217 (1998); David R. Dow, 6 Wm. & Mary Bill of Rts. J. 733 (1998)(clear and present danger test inconsistent with appropriate notions of moral responsibility).

2. It was on the theory that the Smith Act embodied such a principle and that it had been applied only in conformity with it that this Court sustained the Act's constitutionality. That this was the basis for *Dennis* was emphasized in *Yates*, in which the Court overturned convictions for advocacy of the forcible overthrow of the Government under the Smith Act, because the trial judge's instructions had allowed conviction for mere advocacy, unrelated to its tendency to produce forcible action.

3. The first count of the indictment charged that appellant "did unlawfully by word of mouth advocate the necessity, or propriety of crime, violence, or unlawful methods of terrorism as a means of accomplishing political reform * * *." The second count charged that appellant "did unlawfully voluntarily assemble with a group or assemblage of persons formed to advocate the doctrines of criminal syndicalism * * *." The trial judge's charge merely followed the language of the indictment. * * *

Accordingly, we are here confronted with a statute which, by its own words and as applied, purports to punish mere advocacy and to forbid, on pain of criminal punishment, assembly with others merely to advocate the described type of action.[4] Such a statute falls within the condemnation of the First and Fourteenth Amendments. The contrary teaching of *Whitney* cannot be supported, and that decision is therefore overruled.

Reversed.

JUSTICE BLACK, concurring.

I agree with the views expressed by Mr. Justice Douglas in his concurring opinion in this case that the "clear and present danger" doctrine should have no place in the interpretation of the First Amendment. I join the Court's opinion, which, as I understand it, simply cites *Dennis*, but does not indicate any agreement on the Court's part with the "clear and present danger" doctrine on which *Dennis* purported to rely.

JUSTICE DOUGLAS, concurring.

While I join the opinion of the Court, I desire to enter a caveat.

[Whether] the war power—the greatest leveler of them all—is adequate to sustain [the "clear and present danger"] doctrine is debatable. The dissents in *Abrams* [and other cases] show how easily "clear and present danger" is manipulated to crush what Brandeis called "the fundamental right of free men to strive for better conditions through new legislation and new institutions" by argument and discourse even in time of war. Though I doubt if the "clear and present danger" test is congenial to the First Amendment in time of a declared war, I am certain it is not reconcilable with the First Amendment in days of peace. * * *

Mr. Justice Holmes, though never formally abandoning the "clear and present danger" test, moved closer to the First Amendment ideal when he said in dissent in *Gitlow* [quoting the passage beginning, "Every idea is an incitement."] We have never been faithful to the philosophy of that dissent.

"[In *Dennis,* we distorted] the 'clear and present danger' test beyond recognition. [I] see no place in the regime of the First Amendment for any 'clear and present danger' test whether strict and tight as some would make it or free-wheeling as the Court in *Dennis* rephrased it.

NOTES AND QUESTIONS

1.   What pre-*Brandenburg* decisions, if any, "have fashioned the principle" that advocacy may not be prohibited "except [where] directed to inciting or producing *imminent* lawless action *and* * * * *likely* to incite or produce such action"? (Emphasis added.) Did *Dennis, Yates* and *Scales* take pains to *deny* that the unlawful action advocated need be "imminent" or that the

---

4.   Statutes affecting the right of assembly, like those touching on freedom of speech, must observe the established distinctions between mere advocacy and incitement to lawless action * * *.

advocacy must be "likely" to produce the forbidden action? See Hans Linde, *"Clear and Present Danger" Reexamined,* 22 Stan.L.Rev. 1163, 1166–67, 1183–86 (1970).

2. Does *Brandenburg* adopt the *Masses* incitement test as a major part of the required showing? Consider Gerald Gunther, *Learned Hand and the Origins of Modern First Amendment Doctrine: Some Fragments of History,* 27 Stan.L.Rev. 719, 754–55 (1975): "An incitement-nonincitement distinction had only fragmentary and ambiguous antecedents in the pre-*Brandenburg* era; it was *Brandenburg* that really 'established' it; and, it was essentially an establishment of the legacy of Learned Hand. [Under] *Brandenburg,* probability of harm is no longer the central criterion for speech limitations. The inciting language of the speaker—the Hand focus on 'objective' words—is the major consideration. And punishment of the harmless inciter is prevented by the *Schenck*–derived requirement of a likelihood of dangerous consequences." (citing *Brandenburg*'s note 4.) But see Steven Shiffrin, *Defamatory Non-Media Speech and First Amendment Methodology,* 25 UCLA L.Rev. 915, 947 n. 206 (1978): "Several leading commentators assume that *Brandenburg* adopts an incitement requirement. [The] conclusion is apparently based on this line from *Brandenburg:* 'Neither the indictment nor the trial judge's instructions to the jury in any way refined the statute's bald definition of the crime in terms of mere advocacy, not distinguished from incitement to imminent lawless action' [also citing note 4]. The difficulty with attaching significance to this ambiguous statement is that the term 'incitement' is used in the alternative in the Court's statement of its test. Thus, advocacy of imminent lawless action is protected unless it is directed to inciting *or* producing imminent lawless action and is likely to incite *or* produce imminent lawless action. Thus, even assuming that the use of the word incitement refers to express use of language, as opposed to the nature of results (an interpretation which is strained in light of the Court's wording of the test), incitement is not necessary to divorce the speech from First Amendment protection. It is enough that the speech is directed to producing imminent lawless action and is likely to produce such action."

If one wants to argue that *Brandenburg* adopted *Masses,* is there anything to be made of the phrase "directed to" in the *Brandenburg* test? Alternatively, did *Yates* adopt the *Masses* test? If so, does its favorable citation in *Brandenburg* constitute an adoption of the *Masses* test?

3. The *Brandenburg* "inciting or producing imminent lawless action" standard was the basis for reversal of a disorderly conduct conviction in HESS v. INDIANA, 414 U.S. 105 (1973) (per curiam). After antiwar demonstrators on the Indiana University campus had blocked a public street, police moved them to the curbs on either side. As an officer passed him, appellant stated loudly, "We'll take the fucking street later [or again]," which led to his disorderly conduct conviction. His statement, observed the Court, "was not addressed to any person or group in particular" and "his tone, although loud, was no louder than that of the other people in the area. [At] best, [the] statement could be taken as counsel for present moderation; at worst, it amounted to nothing more than advocacy of illegal action at some indefinite future time." This was insufficient, under *Brandenburg,* to punish appellant's words, as the State had, on the ground that they had a "tendency to produce

violence." It could not be said that appellant "was advocating, in the normal sense, any action" and there was "no evidence" that "his words were intended to produce, and likely to produce, *imminent* disorder."

REHNQUIST, J., joined by Burger, C.J., and Blackmun, J., dissented: "The simple explanation for the result in this case is that the majority has interpreted the evidence differently from the courts below." The dissenters quarreled with the Court's conclusion that appellant's advocacy "was not directed towards inciting imminent action. [T]here are surely possible constructions of the statement which would encompass more or less immediate and continuing action against the police. They should not be rejected out of hand because of an unexplained preference for other acceptable alternatives."

4. Does *Yates* survive *Brandenburg*'s emphasis on *imminent* lawless action? Consider Harry Kalven, *A Worthy Tradition* 234 (1988): "It is [possible] that [*Brandenburg*] has preserved the group/individual distinction. Under such an approach the *Yates* incitement-to-future-action standard would apply to group speech and the *Brandenburg* incitement-to-immediate-action standard would apply to the individual speaker." Is light shed on the question by *Communist Party of Indiana v. Whitcomb*, 414 U.S. 441 (1974), invalidating an Indiana statute denying a political party or its candidates access to the ballot unless the party files an affidavit that it "does not advocate the overthrow of local, state or national government by force or violence"? The Court, per Brennan J., maintained that the required oath (which had been interpreted to include advocacy of abstract doctrine) violated the principle of *Brandenburg* and stated that the principle applied not only to attempted denials of public employment, bar licensing, and tax exemption, but also to ballot access denials. The flaw with the state's position was that it furnished access to the ballot "not because the Party urges others 'to *do* something now *or in the future* [but] merely to believe in something,' [*Yates*]" (second emphasis added).

What happened to the "imminent lawless action" requirement? Does the *Whitcomb* language clarify *Brandenburg*? Modify it?

5. Does *Brandenburg* apply to the advocacy of trivial crimes whether politically motivated or not? Suppose the advocacy of trespass across a lawn? What result under *Brandenburg*? What result under *Dennis*? Is *Dennis* potentially more speech protective than *Brandenburg*? Is Vinson, C.J.'s approach in *Dennis* superior to *Brandenburg* because it takes into account the magnitude of the harm (whether trivial or grave) or is it inferior because it is likely to be administered in a manner that would overestimate the costs of free speech? See Jonathan S. Masur, *Probability Threshholds*, 92 Iowa L.Rev. 1293 (2007).

6. Does *Brandenburg* apply to solicitation of crime in private or non-ideological contexts? Consider Shiffrin, note 2 supra, at 950: "How different it might be if the factual context were to involve advocacy of murder in a non-socio-political context. One suspects that little rhetoric about the marketplace of ideas or other First Amendment values would be employed and that the serious and explicit advocacy of murder in a concrete way would suffice to divorce the speech from First Amendment protection even in the absence of a specific showing of likelihood." Would it matter if it were not explicit or not

concrete? For trenchant analysis of the issues raised by the shift in context from public to private or in subject matter from ideological to non-ideological, see Kent Greenawalt, *Speech and Crime,* 1980 Am.B.Found.Res.J. 645.

7. Should *Brandenburg* be construed to protect threats?[d] Nuremberg Files, an anti-abortion Web site included the names, addresses, photographs, and license plate numbers of those who provided abortions or were prominent pro-choice advocates together with their family members. Protected? *Planned Parenthood of Columbia/Willamette Inc. v. American Coalition of Life Activists,* 290 F.3d 1058 (9th Cir. 2002). Consider Steven G. Gey, *The Nuremberg Files and the First Amendment Value of Threats,* 78 Tex. L. Rev. 541, 592 (2000): "It seems clear that the *Brandenburg* standard should apply unmodified in public situations. The situation is more complicated in cases where the speech does not occur in public, but is communicated surreptitiously to the target of the threat. Should *Brandenburg* also apply to these cases? What makes threats communicated privately more disturbing than publicly threatening speech is the intuitive judgment that the private communication of a threat is more likely to indicate a seriousness of purpose than the attention-grabbing public bluster that characterizes cases such as [the] Nuremberg Files litigation."

Is it clear that *Brandenburg* should apply unmodified in public situations? Consider Rodney A. Smolla, *Should the Brandenburg v. Ohio incitement Test Apply in Media Violence Tort Cases?* 27 N. Ky. L. Rev. 1, 45 (2000): "What makes the abortion web page case difficult [is] the injection of an element not present in *Brandenburg,* the detailed provision of material on the doctors' names, business locations, residential addresses, social security numbers, vehicle license plates, phone numbers, and other identifying information. This evidence adds some highly perplexing aspects to the case. First, it may well take it beyond the realm of abstract advocacy, and into the realm of detailed information provided to assist in violent crime. Second, it is highly probative of an intent by the defendants either to assist in crime or to threaten abortion providers, itself a crime. In this fact pattern, the details of the record are likely to be critical. You are likely to find yourself closely examining the facts to determine whether or not a case can be made that these defendants subjectively intended this material as a threat or as a vehicle for aiding and abetting crime,[e] and whether, objectively, the material was so understood or used."

---

d. See also *NAACP v. Claiborne Hardware Co.,* 458 U.S. 886 (1982). The Court stated that remarks of Charles Evers "might have been understood" as inviting violence, but stated that when "such appeals do not incite lawless action, they must be regarded as protected speech." If violent action had followed his remarks, a "substantial question" of liability would have been raised. The Court also observed, however, that the defendant might be held criminally liable for the acts of others if the speeches could be taken as evidence that the defendant gave "other specific instructions to carry out violent acts or threats." Compare *Watts v. United States,* 394 U.S. 705 (1969) (statute prohibiting knowing and wilful threat of bodily harm upon the President is constitutional on its face) (dictum); *Rankin v. McPherson,* Ch. 7, III infra (clerical employee's private expression of desire that Presidential assassination attempt be successful is insufficient justification for dismissal even in a law enforcement agency).

e. Should Brandenburg be construed to protect the provision of information when it is overwhelmingly likely to facilitate crime? Paladin Press published *Hit Man: A Technical Manual for Independent Contractors.* James Perry relied on the book's instructions to kill three people. Protected? *Rice v. Paladin Enterprises,* 128 F.3d 233 (4th Cir. 1997). David A. Anderson, *Incitement and Tort Law,* 37 Wake Forest L. Rev. 957, 986–987 (2002): "I have found no case in

If threats should be unprotected without regard to the *Brandenburg* standard, is it enough that a "reasonable person" would foresee that the recipients of the speaker's statement would see it a serious expression of intent to physically harm or is a "mere negligence standard [simply] not compatible with a constitutional guarantee as fundamental as free speech"? G. Robert Blakey and Brian J. Murray, *Threats, Free Speech, and the Jurisprudence of the Federal Criminal Law*, 2002 B.Y.U.L. Rev. 829, 880 (2002). Should subjective intent to threaten be necessary? Does it matter if the threat reaches its target? If the speaker has no intention of carrying out the threat? If the speaker maintains that the threat will be carried out by unrelated third parties rather the speaker or co-conspirators? See Jennifer E. Rothman, *Freedom of Speech and True Threats*, 25 Harv. J.L. & Pub. Pol'y 283 (2001). For additional commentary on threats, see Justice Linde's opinion in *State v. Robertson*, 293 Or. 402, 649 P.2d 569 (1982); C. Edwin Baker, *Human Liberty and Freedom of Speech* 5469 (1989); Kent Greenawalt, *Criminal Coercion and Freedom of Speech*, 78 Nw.U.L.Rev. 1081 (1984); Andrew P. Stanner, *Toward an Improved True Threat Doctrine for Student Speakers*, 81 N.Y.U. L.Rev. 385 (2006); Note, *United States v. Jake Baker: Revisiting Threats and the First Amendment*, 84 Va. L.Rev. 287 (1998).

8. Congress prohibits the providing of material support or resources to any organization designated by the Secretary of State to be a foreign terrorist organization. Plaintiffs sought to provide support to either of two such organizations: the Kurdistan Workers Party ("PKK") and the Liberation Tigers of Tamil Eelam ("LTTE"). Specifically, they wished to provide support in order to train members of the PKK to use law to peacefully resolve disputes; to teach PKK how to petition representative bodies such as the United Nations for relief; and/or to engage in political advocacy on behalf of Kurds who live in Turkey or on behalf of the LTTE. HOLDER v. HUMANITARIAN LAW PROJECT, 130 S.Ct. 2705 (2010), per ROBERTS, C.J., held that the congressional prohibition could constitutionally be applied to training and expert advice for peaceful speech activities even if the provision of such support was not intended to assist in the unlawful activities of the organization. Roberts, C.J., emphasized that the statute does not cover independent advocacy on behalf of such organizations or even membership in such organizations.[f] Rather it covers support including training, expert advice, or speech under the direction of or in coordination with an organization designated as terrorist in character.

Roberts, C.J., did not deny that the support offered in the case was a form of presumptively protected speech, but he deferred to the findings of the Congressional and Executive Branches that the organizations were "so tainted by their criminal conduct that any contribution to such an organization

---

which a media defendant has been held liable on the ground that it incited physical harm, and only one case [*Rice*] in which liability has been approved on the ground of aiding and abetting. Media are simply not in the business of 'inciting . . . imminent lawless action' as that phrase is understood in *Brandenburg*. [This] is why media lawyers are so insistent that incitement, or something close to it, is the only permissible basis for liability—it effectively forecloses liability." See generally Rodney Smolla, *Deliberate Intent* (1999); Cass Sunstein, *One Case at a Time* 191–96 (1999).

f. Roberts, C.J., stated that the record did not disclose whether the plaintiffs sought to engage in independent or coordinated advocacy.

facilitates that conduct." He argued that support frees up other resources, helps to legitimize such organizations, and strains U.S. relationships with its allies. The skills taught could be used in manipulative ways and might gain further monetary gains for such organizations. Roberts, C.J., concluded that the prohibitions were necessary to further an urgent objective of the highest order.

BREYER, J., joined by Ginsburg and Sotomayor, JJ., dissenting, argued that the decision interfered with centrally important peaceful speech activities. He argued that peaceful advocacy should ordinarily be protected whether or not it was coordinated with a designated terrorist organization. Nor did he find a sufficient governmental showing to justify limiting this speech: "I believe the Court has failed to examine the Government's justification with sufficient care. It has failed to insist upon specific evidence, rather than general assertion. It has failed to require tailoring of means to fit compelling ends. And ultimately it deprives the individuals before us of the protection that the First Amendment demands."

Even assuming that *Brandenburg* applies in all cases involving advocacy of illegal action, it has little explanatory power across the broad range of First Amendment cases. Consider Rodney A. Smolla, *Should the Brandenburg v. Ohio Incitement Test Apply in Media Violence Tort Cases?* 27 N. Ky. L. Rev. 1, 12 (2000): "The *Brandenburg* case is an important First Amendment landmark, but it is not the only First Amendment landmark and does not restate the legal doctrine applied in all First Amendment contexts. To the contrary, modern First Amendment law is a complex maze of doctrinal formulas employing specific standards that have been tailored to particular topics of speech, modes of legal liability, and social contexts. There are innumerable other First Amendment contexts in which the *Brandenburg* standard just does not apply, contexts in which the Supreme Court has fashioned special standards suited for the balance of interests at hand. Because free speech issues arise in an extraordinarily wide range of circumstances and settings, the Supreme Court has not attempted to jam all free speech analysis into the "incitement" standard of *Brandenburg*, but rather has employed *Brandenburg*-style analysis only in cases dealing with *Brandenburg*-like settings."[g]

9. Should the line of cases from *Schenck* to *Humanitarian Law Project* fuel cynicism about the binding force of legal doctrine and about the willingness or capacity of the judiciary to protect dissent?[h] To what extent does the focus on Supreme Court cases exaggerate the frailty of legal doctrine?[i]

---

g. For the claim that *Brandenburg* should be applied across a broader range of factual contexts, see Stephen G. Gey, *The Brandenburg Paradigm and Other First Amendments*, 12 U.Pa.J. Const.L. 971 (2010).

h. In fashioning First Amendment doctrine, should the overriding objective be at "all times [to] equip the First Amendment to do maximum service in those historical periods when intolerance of unorthodox ideas is most prevalent and when governments are most able and most likely to stifle dissent systematically"? Should the First Amendment "be targeted for the worst of times"? What impact would such a perspective have on the general development of First Amendment doctrine? See Vincent Blasi, *The Pathological Perspective and the First Amendment*, 85 Colum.L.Rev. 449 (1985).

i. Are other countries likely to provide less protection than the United States for advocacy of illegal action? See Zana v. Turkey, 1997–VII Eur. Ct. H.R. 2533; Ruth Gavison, *Incitement and the Limits of Law* in *Censorship and Silencing* 43 (Post ed. 1998) (discussing Israeli law and the speech surrounding the assassination of Prime Minister Rabin). If so, why?

II. REPUTATION AND PRIVACY

In an important article, Harry Kalven coined the phrase "two level theory," *The Metaphysics of the Law of Obscenity,* 1960 Sup.Ct.Rev. 1, 11. As he described it, *Beauharnais,* infra, and other cases employed a First Amendment methodology that classified speech at two levels. Some speech—libel, obscenity, "fighting words"—was thought to be so bereft of social utility as to be beneath First Amendment protection. At the second level, speech of constitutional value was thought to be protected unless it presented a clear and present danger of a substantive evil.

In considering libel and privacy, we will witness the collapse of "two level theory." The purpose is not a detailed examination of libel and privacy law. Our interests include the initial exclusion of defamation from First Amendment protection, the themes and methods contributing to the erosion of that exclusion, and the articulation of basic First Amendment values having implications and applications beyond defamation and the right to privacy.

A. GROUP LIBEL

BEAUHARNAIS v. ILLINOIS, 343 U.S. 250 (1952), per FRANKFURTER, J., sustained a statute prohibiting exhibition in any public place of any publication portraying "depravity, criminality, unchastity, or lack of virtue of a class of citizens, of any race, color, creed or religion [which exposes such citizens] to contempt, derision or obloquy or which is productive of breach of the peace or riots." The Court affirmed a conviction for organizing the distribution of a leaflet which petitioned the Mayor and City Council of Chicago "to halt the further encroachment, harassment and invasion of white people, their property, neighborhoods and persons by the Negro"; called for "one million self respecting white people in Chicago to unite"; and warned that if "the need to prevent the white race from becoming mongrelized by the Negro will not unite us, then the [aggressions], rapes, robberies, knives, guns, and marijuana of the Negro, surely will.":

"Today every American jurisdiction [punishes] libels directed at individuals. '[There] are certain well-defined and narrowly limited classes of speech, the prevention and punishment of which have never been thought to raise any constitutional problem. These include the lewd and obscene, the profane, the libelous, and the insulting or "fighting" words—those which by their very utterance inflict injury or tend to incite to an immediate breach of the peace. It has been well observed that such utterances are no essential part of any exposition of ideas, and are of such slight social value as a step to truth that any benefit that may be derived from them is clearly outweighed by the social interest in order and morality. "Resort to epithets or personal abuse is not in any proper sense communication of information or opinion safeguarded by the Constitution, and its punishment as a criminal act would raise no question under that instrument." *Cantwell v. Connecticut,* [Ch. 12, I].' Such were the views of a unanimous Court in *Chaplinsky v. New Hampshire,* Ch. 1, IV, A infra.[6]

"No one will gainsay that it is libelous falsely to charge another with being a rapist, robber, carrier of knives and guns, and user of marijuana. The [question is whether the fourteenth amendment] prevents a State from punishing such libels—as criminal libel has been defined, limited and constitutionally recognized time out of mind—directed at designated collectivities and flagrantly disseminated. [I]f an utterance directed at an individual may be the object of criminal sanctions, we cannot deny to a State power to punish the same utterance directed at a defined group, unless we can say that this is a wilful and purposeless restriction unrelated to the peace and well-being of the State.

"Illinois did not have to look beyond her own borders to await the tragic experience of the last three decades to conclude that wilful purveyors of falsehood concerning racial and religious groups promote strife and tend powerfully to obstruct the manifold adjustments required for free, orderly life in a metropolitan, polyglot community. From the murder of the abolitionist Lovejoy in 1837 to the Cicero riots of 1951, Illinois has been the scene of exacerbated tension between races, often flaring into violence and destruction. In many of these outbreaks, utterances of the character here in question, so the Illinois legislature could conclude, played a significant [part].

"In the face of this history and its frequent obligato of extreme racial and religious propaganda, we would deny experience to say that the Illinois legislature was without reason in seeking ways to curb false or malicious defamation of racial and religious groups, made in public places and by means calculated to have a powerful emotional impact on those to whom it was presented.

"[It would] be arrant dogmatism, quite outside the scope of our authority [, for] us to deny that the Illinois Legislature may warrantably believe that a man's job and his educational opportunities and the dignity accorded him may depend as much on the reputation of the racial and religious group to which he willynilly belongs, as on his own merits. This being so, we are precluded from saying that speech concededly punishable when immediately directed at individuals cannot be outlawed if directed at groups with whose position and esteem in society the affiliated individual may be inextricably involved. * * *[18]

"As to the defense of truth, Illinois in common with many States requires a showing not only that the utterance state the facts, but also that the publication be made 'with good motives and for justifiable ends'.

---

6. In all but five States, the constitutional guarantee of free speech to every person is explicitly qualified by holding him "responsible for the abuse of that right." * * *

18. [If] a statute sought to outlaw libels of political parties, quite different problems not now before us would be raised. For one thing, the whole doctrine of fair comment as indispensable to the democratic political process would come into play. Political parties, like public men, are, as it were, public property.

Both elements are necessary if the defense is to prevail. [The] teaching of a century and a half of criminal libel prosecutions in this country would go by the board if we were to hold that Illinois was not within her rights in making this combined requirement. Assuming that defendant's offer of proof directed to a part of the defense was adequate, it did not satisfy the entire requirement which Illinois could exact."

The Court ruled that the trial court properly declined to require the jury to find a "clear and present danger": "Libelous utterances not being within the area of constitutionally protected speech, it is unnecessary, either for us or for the State courts, to consider the issues behind the phrase 'clear and present danger.' Certainly no one would contend that obscene speech, for example, may be punished only upon a showing of such circumstances. Libel, as we have seen, is in the same class."

BLACK, J., joined by Douglas, J., dissented: "[The Court] acts on the bland assumption that the First Amendment is wholly irrelevant. [Today's] case degrades First Amendment freedoms to the 'rational basis' level. [We] are cautioned that state legislatures must be left free to 'experiment' and to make legislative judgments. [State] experimentation in curbing freedom of expression is startling and frightening doctrine in a country dedicated to self-government by its people.

"[As] 'constitutionally recognized,' [criminal libel] has provided for punishment of false, malicious, scurrilous charges against individuals, not against huge groups. This limited scope of the law of criminal libel is of no small importance. It has confined state punishment of speech and expression to the narrowest of areas involving nothing more than private feuds. Every expansion of the law of criminal libel so as to punish discussion of matters of public concern means a corresponding invasion of the area dedicated to free expression by the First Amendment.

"[If] there be minority groups who hail this holding as their victory, they might consider the possible relevancy of this ancient remark: 'Another such victory and I am undone.' "

REED, J., joined by Douglas, J., dissenting, argued that the statute was unconstitutionally vague: "These words—'virtue,' 'derision,' and 'obloquy'—have neither general nor special meanings well enough known to apprise those within their reach as to limitations on speech. Philosophers and poets, thinkers of high and low degree from every age and race have sought to expound the meaning of virtue. [Are] the tests of the Puritan or the Cavalier to be applied, those of the city or the farm, the Christian or non-Christian, the old or the young?"

DOUGLAS, J., dissented: "Hitler and his Nazis showed how evil a conspiracy could be which was aimed at destroying a race by exposing it to contempt, derision, and obloquy. I would be willing to concede that such conduct directed at a race or group in this country could be made an indictable offense. For such a project would be more than the exercise of free speech. [It] would be free speech plus.

"I would also be willing to concede that even without the element of conspiracy there might be times and occasions when the legislative or executive branch might call a halt to inflammatory talk, such as the shouting of 'fire' in a school or a theatre.

"My view is that if in any case other public interests are to override the plain command of the First Amendment, the peril of speech must be clear and present, leaving no room for argument, raising no doubts as to the necessity of curbing speech in order to prevent disaster."

JACKSON, J., dissenting, argued that the fourteenth amendment does not incorporate the first, as such, but permits the states more latitude than the Congress. He concluded, however, that due process required the trier of fact to evaluate the evidence as to the truth and good faith of the speaker and the clarity and presence of the danger. He was unwilling to assume danger from the tendency of the words and felt that the trial court had precluded the defendant's efforts to show truth and good motives.

NOTES AND QUESTIONS

1. ***The right to petition.*** Should it make a difference that the leaflet was in the form of a petition to the mayor and city council? Does the right of the people "to petition the Government for a redress of grievances" add anything of substance to Beauharnais' other First Amendment arguments? Consider Harry Kalven, *The Negro and the First Amendment* 40 (1965): "If it would make a difference whether the petition was genuine and not just a trick of form, can the Court penetrate the form and appraise the true motivation or must it, as it does with congressional committees accept the official motivation?"[a]

2. ***Equality and freedom of speech.*** Consider the following hypothetical commentary: "Group libel statutes pose uniquely difficult issues for they involve a clash between two constitutional commitments: the principle of equality and the principle of free speech. They force us to decide what we want to express as a nation: Do we want a powerful symbol of our belief in uninhibited debate or do we want to be the kind of nation that will not tolerate the public calumny of religious, ethnic, and racial groups?"[b]

3. ***Tolerance and freedom of speech.*** Should the First Amendment be a means of institutionalizing a national commitment to the value of tolerance? By tolerating the intolerable, would we carve out one area of social interaction for extraordinary self-restraint and thereby develop[c] and demonstrate a vital

---

a. See *McDonald v. Smith*, 472 U.S. 479 (1985) (denying any special First Amendment status for the Petition Clause).

b. See, e.g., *The Price We Pay: The Case Against Racist Speech* (Laura J. Lederer & Richard Delgado eds. 1995); Robin West, *Progressive Constitutionalism: Reconstructing the Fourteenth Amendment* (1994); Mari J. Matsuda et al., *Words that Wound* (Itzin ed. 1993); Gary Goodpaster, *Equality and Free Speech: The Case Against Substantive Equality,* 82 Ia. L.Rev. 645 (1997); Loren Beth, *Group Libel and Free Speech,* 39 Minn.L.Rev. 167, 180–81 (1955) and sources cited in Ch. 1, V, C.

c. For skepticism about the capacity of courts to achieve any substantial impact in promoting tolerance, see Robert Nagel, *Constitutional Cultures* 27–59 (1989); Stephen E. Gottlieb & David Schultz, *The Empirical Basis for First Amendment Principles,* 19 J. of L. & Politics 145 (2003).

social capacity? See generally Lee Bollinger, *The Tolerant Society: Freedom of Speech and Extremist Speech in America* (1986); Lee Bollinger, *Free Speech and Intellectual Values,* 92 Yale L.J. 438 (1983); Lee Bollinger, *Book Review,* 80 Mich.L.Rev. 617 (1982).

4. **Dignity and Group Libel.** Wholly apart from any message that group libel statutes signal about our polity, do group libel statutes safeguard individual rights to dignity that outweigh any expressive interests in this context? See Jeremy Waldron, *Dignity and Defamation: The Visibility of Hate,* 123 Harv. L.Rev. 1596 (2010). For the argument that many free speech issues involve dignity interests expressed by opposing claimants, see Steven J. Heyman, *Free Speech and Human Dignity* (2008).

5. ***Libel, group libel, and seditious libel.*** Consider Kalven, supra, at 15, 16 and 50–51: Seditious libel "is the doctrine that criticism of government officials and policy may be viewed as defamation of government and may be punished as a serious crime. [On] my view, the absence of seditious libel as a crime is the true pragmatic test of freedom of speech. This I would argue is what freedom of speech is about. [The] most revealing aspect of the opinions, and particularly that of Justice Frankfurter, is the absence of any sense of the proximity of the case before them to seditious libel. The case presents almost a perfect instance of that competition among analogies which Edward Levi has emphasized as the essential circumstance of legal reasoning. In the middle we have group libel and Justice Frankfurter's urging its many resemblances to individual libel. [If] the Court's speech theory had been more grounded, as it seems to me it should be, on the relevance of the concept of seditious libel and less on the analogy to the law of attempts found in the slogan 'clear and present danger,' it is difficult to believe that either the debate or the result in *Beauharnais* would have been the same."

B. PUBLIC OFFICIALS AND SEDITIOUS LIBEL

NEW YORK TIMES CO. v. SULLIVAN
376 U.S. 254, 84 S.Ct. 710, 11 L.Ed.2d 686 (1964).

JUSTICE BRENNAN delivered the opinion of the Court.

[Sullivan, the Montgomery, Ala. police commissioner, sued the New York Times and four black Alabama clergymen for alleged libelous statements in a paid, full-page fund-raising advertisement signed by a "Committee to defend Martin Luther King and the struggle for freedom in the South." The advertisement stated that "truckloads of police armed with shotguns and tear-gas ringed Alabama State College Campus" in Montgomery, and that "the Southern violators [have] bombed [Dr. King's] home, assaulted his person [and] arrested him seven times." In several respects the statements were untrue. Several witnesses testified that they understood the statements to refer to Sullivan because he supervised Montgomery police. Sullivan proved he did not participate in the events described. He offered no proof of pecuniary loss.[3] Pursuant to Alabama

---

3. Approximately 394 copies of the edition of the Times containing the advertisement were circulated in Alabama. Of these, about 35 copies were distributed in Montgomery County. The total circulation of the Times for that day was approximately 650,000 copies.

law, the trial court submitted the libel issue to the jury, giving general and punitive damages instructions. It returned a $500,000 verdict for Sullivan against all of the defendants.[a] We hold that the rule of law applied by the Alabama courts is constitutionally deficient for failure to provide the safeguards for freedom of speech and of the press that are required by the First and Fourteenth Amendments in a libel action brought by a public official against critics of his official conduct.[4] We further hold that under the proper safeguards the evidence presented in this case is constitutionally insufficient to support the judgment for respondent.

I. [The] publication here [communicated] information, expressed opinion, recited grievances, protested claimed abuses, and sought financial support on behalf of a movement whose existence and objectives are matters of the highest public interest and concern. That the Times was paid for publishing the advertisement is as immaterial in this connection as is the fact that newspapers and books are sold. *Smith v. California*, Ch. 1, III, B infra. Any other conclusion would discourage newspapers from carrying "editorial advertisements" of this type, and so might shut off an important outlet for the promulgation of information and ideas by persons who do not themselves have access to publishing facilities.

II. Under Alabama law [once] "libel per se" has been established, the defendant has no defense as to stated facts unless he can persuade the jury that they were true in all their particulars. [His] privilege of "fair comment" for expressions of opinion depends on the truth of the facts upon which the comment is based. [Unless] he can discharge the burden of proving truth, general damages are presumed, and may be awarded without proof of pecuniary injury.

[Respondent] relies heavily, as did the Alabama courts, on statements of this Court to the effect that the Constitution does not protect libelous publications. Those statements do not foreclose our inquiry here. None of the cases sustained the use of libel laws to impose sanctions upon expression critical of the official conduct of public officials. [L]ibel can claim no talismanic immunity from constitutional limitations. It must be measured by standards that satisfy the First Amendment.

The First Amendment, said Judge Learned Hand, "presupposes that right conclusions are more likely to be gathered out of a multitude of tongues, than through any kind of authoritative selection. To many this is,

---

a. This was the highest award in the history of the state. David A. Logan, *Libel Law in the Trenches: Reflections on Current Data on Libel Litigation*, 87 Va.L.Rev. 503, 504 (2001).

4. [The] Times contends that the assumption of jurisdiction over its corporate person by the Alabama courts overreaches the territorial limits of the Due Process Clause. The latter claim is foreclosed from our review by the ruling of the Alabama courts that the Times entered a general appearance in the action and thus waived its jurisdictional objection. * * *

[Since *New York Times* the Court has upheld expansive personal jurisdiction against media defendants. *Calder v. Jones*, 465 U.S. 783 (1984); *Keeton v. Hustler*, 465 U.S. 770 (1984). *Calder* rejected the suggestion that First Amendment concerns enter into jurisdictional analysis. It feared complicating the inquiry and argued that because First Amendment concerns are taken into account in limiting the substantive law of defamation, "to reintroduce those concerns at the jurisdictional stage would be a form of double counting."]

and always will be, folly; but we have staked upon it our all." [Thus] we consider this case against the background of a profound national commitment to the principle that debate on public issues should be uninhibited, robust, and wide-open, and that it may well include vehement, caustic, and sometimes unpleasantly sharp attacks on government and public officials.[b] The present advertisement, as an expression of grievance and protest on one of the major public issues of our time, would seem clearly to qualify for the constitutional protection. The question is whether it forfeits that protection by the falsity of some of its factual statements and by its alleged defamation of respondent.

Authoritative interpretations of the First Amendment guarantees have consistently refused to recognize an exception for any test of truth— whether administered by judges, juries, or administrative officials—and especially not one that puts the burden of proving truth on the speaker. [E]rroneous statement is inevitable in free debate, and [it] must be protected if the freedoms of expression are to have the "breathing space" that they "need [to] survive."

[Injury] to official reputation affords no more warrant for repressing speech that would otherwise be free than does factual error. Where judicial officers are involved, this Court has held that concern for the dignity and reputation of the courts does not justify the punishment as criminal contempt of criticism of the judge or his decision. This is true even though the utterance contains "half-truths" and "misinformation." Such repression can be justified, if at all, only by a clear and present danger of the obstruction of justice. If judges are to be treated as "men of fortitude, able to thrive in a hardy climate,"[c] surely the same must be true of other government officials, such as elected city commissioners. Criticism of their official conduct does not lose its constitutional protection merely because it is effective criticism and hence diminishes their official reputations.

If neither factual error nor defamatory content suffices to remove the constitutional shield from criticism of official conduct, the combination of the two elements is no less inadequate. This is the lesson to be drawn from the great controversy over the Sedition Act of 1798, 1 Stat. 596, which first crystallized a national awareness of the central meaning of the First Amendment. [Although] the Sedition Act was never tested in this Court, the attack upon its validity has carried the day in the court of history. Fines levied in its prosecution were repaid by Act of Congress on the ground that it was unconstitutional. * * * Jefferson, as President,

---

b. Consider Brian C. Murchison, *Speech and the Self-Governance Value*, 14 Wm. & Mary Bill Rts. J. 1251, 1293 (2006): "[Brennan, J.'s] adjectives suggest the risk of people speaking past each other. In this way, democratic consciousness can suffer slippage: from dialogue based on equal respect to potentially uncompromising debate among subjects who view each other warily from havens of walled off 'dignity.'"

c. Ironically, in the post-*Sullivan* era, critical speech regarding judges is now punished by judges on standards far less stringent than those that apply to other public officials. Margaret Tarkington, *The Truth Be Damned: The First Amendment, Attorney Speech, and Judicial Reputation*, 97 Geo. L.J. 1567 (2009).

pardoned those who had been convicted and sentenced under the Act and remitted their fines. [Its] invalidity [has] also been assumed by Justices of this Court. [These] views reflect a broad consensus that the Act, because of the restraint it imposed upon criticism of government and public officials, was inconsistent with the First Amendment. * * *

What a State may not constitutionally bring about by means of a criminal statute is likewise beyond the reach of its civil law of libel. The fear of damage awards under a rule such as that invoked by the Alabama courts here may be markedly more inhibiting than the fear of prosecution under a criminal statute. [The] judgment awarded in this case—without the need for any proof of actual pecuniary loss—was one thousand times greater than the maximum fine provided by the Alabama criminal [libel law], and one hundred times greater than that provided by the Sedition Act. And since there is no double-jeopardy limitation applicable to civil lawsuits, this is not the only judgment that may be awarded against petitioners for the same publication.[18] Whether or not a newspaper can survive a succession of such judgments, the pall of fear and timidity imposed upon those who would give voice to public criticism is an atmosphere in which the First Amendment freedoms cannot [survive].

The state rule of law is not saved by its allowance of the defense of truth. A defense for erroneous statements honestly made is no less essential here than was the requirement of proof of guilty knowledge which, in *Smith v. California*, we held indispensable to a valid conviction of a bookseller for possessing obscene writings for [sale].

A rule compelling the critic of official conduct to guarantee the truth of all his factual assertions—and to do so on pain of libel judgments virtually unlimited in amount—leads to a comparable "self-censorship." Allowance of the defense of truth, with the burden of proving it on the defendant, does not mean that only false speech will be deterred.[19] [Under] such a rule, would-be critics of official conduct may be deterred from voicing their criticism, even though it is believed to be true and even though it is in fact true, because of doubt whether it can be proved in court or fear of the expense of having to do so. They tend to make only statements which "steer far wider of the unlawful zone." The rule thus dampens the vigor and limits the variety of public [debate].

The constitutional guarantees require, we think, a federal rule that prohibits a public official from recovering damages for a defamatory falsehood relating to his official conduct unless he proves that the statement was made with "actual malice"—that is, with knowledge that it was false or with reckless disregard of whether it was false or [not].[d]

---

18. The Times states that four other libel suits based on the advertisement have been filed against it by [others]; that another $500,000 verdict has been awarded in [one]; and that the damages sought in the other three total $2,000,000.

19. Even a false statement may be deemed to make a valuable contribution to the public debate, since it brings about "the clearer perception and livelier impression of truth, produced by its collision with error." Mill, *On Liberty* 15 (1955).

d. Compare *St. Amant v. Thompson*, 390 U.S. 727 (1968) (publishing while "in fact entertain[ing] serious doubts about the truth of the publication" satisfies standard) with *Garrison v.*

Such a privilege for criticism of official conduct is appropriately analogous to the protection accorded a public official when he is sued for libel by a private citizen. In *Barr v. Matteo,* 360 U.S. 564, 575 (1959), this Court held the utterance of a federal official to be absolutely privileged if made "within the outer perimeter" of his duties. The States accord the same immunity to statements of their highest officers, although some differentiate their lesser officials and qualify the privilege they enjoy. But all hold that all officials are protected unless actual malice can be proved. The reason for the official privilege is said to be that the threat of damage suits would otherwise "inhibit the fearless, vigorous, and effective administration of policies of government" and "dampen the ardor of all but the most resolute, or the most irresponsible, in the unflinching discharge of their duties." *Barr.* Analogous considerations support the privilege for the citizen-critic of government. It is as much his duty to criticize as it is the official's duty to administer. [It] would give public servants an unjustified preference over the public they serve, if critics of official conduct did not have a fair equivalent of the immunity granted to the officials themselves. We conclude that such a privilege is required by the First and Fourteenth Amendments.[23]

III. [W]e consider that the proof presented to show actual malice lacks the convincing clarity[e] which the constitutional standard demands, and hence that it would not constitutionally sustain the judgment for respondent under the proper rule of law. [T]here is evidence that the Times published the advertisement without checking its accuracy against the news stories in the Times' own files. The mere presence of the stories in the files does [not] establish that the Times "knew" the advertisement was false, since the state of mind required for actual malice would have to be brought home to the persons in the Times' organization having responsibility for the publication of the advertisement. With respect to the failure of those persons to make the check, the record shows that they relied upon their knowledge of the good reputation of many [whose] names were listed as sponsors of the advertisement, and upon the letter from A. Philip Randolph, known to them as a responsible individual, certifying that the use of the names was authorized. There was testimony that the persons handling the advertisement saw nothing in it that would

---

Louisiana, 379 U.S. 64 (1964) (standard requires "high degree of awareness of probable falsity"). See also *Masson v. New Yorker Magazine, Inc.,* 501 U.S. 496 (1991) ("a deliberate alteration of the words uttered by a plaintiff does not equate with knowledge of falsity [unless] the alteration results in a material change of meaning conveyed by the statement").

23. We have no occasion here to determine how far down into the lower ranks of government employees the "public official" designation would extend for purposes of this rule, or otherwise to specify categories of persons who would or would not be included. [Nor] need we here determine the boundaries of the "official conduct" concept. * * *

e. Compare *Bose Corp. v. Consumers Union,* 466 U.S. 485 (1984) (appellate courts "must exercise independent judgment and determine whether the record establishes actual malice with convincing clarity."). Accord *Harte–Hanks Communications, Inc. v. Connaughton,* 491 U.S. 657 (1989). See also *Anderson v. Liberty Lobby, Inc.,* 477 U.S. 242 (1986) (same standard at summary judgment). Should *Bose* apply when the lower court finds a First Amendment violation or only when it does not? See Stuart Minor Benjamin, *Proactive Legislation and the First Amendment,* 99 Mich. L. Rev. 281, 346–47 (2000). Should independent appellate judgment be required in all First Amendment cases? All constitutional cases?

render it unacceptable under the Times' policy of rejecting advertisements containing "attacks of a personal character"; their failure to reject it on this ground was not unreasonable. We think the evidence against the Times supports at most a finding of negligence in failing to discover the misstatements, and is constitutionally insufficient to show the recklessness that is required for a finding of actual malice.

[T]he evidence was constitutionally defective in another respect: it was incapable of supporting the jury's finding that the allegedly libelous statements were made "of and concerning" respondent. [On this point, the Supreme Court of Alabama] based its ruling on the proposition that: "[The] average person knows that municipal agents, such as police and firemen, and others, are under the control and direction of the city governing body, and more particularly under the direction and control of a single commissioner. In measuring the performance or deficiencies of such groups, praise or criticism is usually attached to the official in complete control of the body."

This proposition has disquieting implications for criticism of governmental conduct. [It would transmute] criticism of government, however impersonal it may seem on its face, into personal criticism, and hence potential libel, of the officials of whom the government is composed. [Raising] as it does the possibility that a good-faith critic of government will be penalized for his criticism, the proposition relied on by the Alabama courts strikes at the very center of the constitutionally protected area of free expression. We hold that such a proposition may not constitutionally be utilized to establish that an otherwise impersonal attack on governmental operations was a libel of an official responsible for those operations. Since it was relied on exclusively here, and there was no other evidence to connect the statements with respondent, the evidence was constitutionally insufficient to support a finding that the statements referred to respondent. * * *f

JUSTICE BLACK, with whom JUSTICE DOUGLAS joins (concurring).

* * * "Malice," even as defined by the Court, is an elusive, abstract concept, hard to prove and hard to disprove. The requirement that malice be proved provides at best an evanescent protection for the right critically to discuss public affairs and certainly does not measure up to the sturdy safeguard embodied in the First Amendment. Unlike the Court, therefore, I vote to reverse exclusively on the ground that the Times and the individual defendants had an absolute, unconditional constitutional right to publish in the Times advertisement their criticisms of the Montgomery agencies and [officials].

The half-million-dollar verdict [gives] dramatic proof [that] state libel laws threaten the very existence of an American press virile enough to publish unpopular views on public affairs and bold enough to criticize the

f. For a similar ruling that impersonal criticism of a government operation cannot be the basis for defamation "of and concerning" the supervisor of the operation, see *Rosenblatt v. Baer*, 383 U.S. 75 (1966): "[T]antamount to a demand for recovery based on libel of government."

conduct of public officials. [B]riefs before us show that in Alabama there are now pending eleven libel suits by local and state officials against the Times seeking $5,600,000, and five such suits against the Columbia Broadcasting System seeking $1,700,000. Moreover, this technique for harassing and punishing a free press—now that it has been shown to be possible—is by no means limited to cases with racial overtones; it can be used in other fields where public feelings may make local as well as out-of-state newspapers easy prey for libel verdict seekers.

In my opinion the Federal Constitution has dealt with this deadly danger to the press in the only way possible without leaving the press open to destruction—by granting the press an absolute immunity for criticism of the way public officials do their public duty.

[This] Nation, I suspect, can live in peace without libel suits based on public discussions of public affairs and public officials. But I doubt that a country can live in freedom where its people can be made to suffer physically or financially for criticizing their government, its actions, or its officials. * * *g

---

NOTES AND QUESTIONS

1. ***The First Amendment and democracy.*** Professor Harry Kalven observed that the Court in *New York Times* was moving toward "the theory of free speech that Alexander Meiklejohn has been offering us for some fifteen years now." Harry Kalven, *The New York Times Case: A Note On "The Central Meaning of the First Amendment,"* 1964 Sup.Ct.Rev. 191, 221. Indeed Kalven reported Alexander Meiklejohn's view that the case was " 'an occasion for dancing in the streets.' " Id. at 221 n. 125. Meiklejohn argued that "[The] principle of the freedom of speech springs from the necessities of the program of self-government. [It] is a deduction from the basic American agreement that public issues shall be decided by universal suffrage. [When] a question of policy is 'before the house,' free men choose to meet it not with their eyes shut, but with their eyes open. To be afraid of ideas, any idea, is to be unfit for self-government. [The] guarantee given by the First Amendment is not, then, assured to all speaking. It is assured only to speech which bears, directly or indirectly, upon issues with which voters have to deal—only, therefore, to the consideration of matters of public interest. Private speech, or private interest in speech, on the other hand, has no claim whatever to the protection of the First Amendment." Alexander Meiklejohn, *Free Speech And Its Relation To Self-Government* (1948).

To what extent does *New York Times* incorporate Meiklejohn's perspec-

---

g. Goldberg, J., joined by Douglas, J., concurring, also asserted for "the citizen and [the] press an absolute unconditional privilege to criticize official conduct," but maintained that the imposition of liability for "[p]urely private defamation" did not abridge the First Amendment because it had "little to do with the political ends of a self-governing society." For the Canadian approach, see *Hill v. Church of Scientology of Ontario* [1995], 126 D.L.R. 4th 129.

tive?[h] What is the "central meaning" of the First Amendment? Consider Burt Neuborne, *Toward a Democracy–Centered Reading of the First Amendment,* 93 Nw.U.L.Rev. 1055, 1069 (1999): "It is no coincidence that the textual rhythm of the First Amendment moves from protection of internal conscience in the religion clauses, to protection of individual expression in the speech clause, to broad community-wide discussion in the press clause, to concerted action in the assembly (and implied association) clause, and, finally, to formal political activity in the petition clause. Indeed, no rights-bearing document in the Western tradition approximates the precise organizational clarity of the First Amendment as a road map of democracy." Consider Susan H. Williams, *Truth, Autonomy, and Speech: Feminist Theory and the First Amendment* 2 (2004): "The democracy theory is really a conjoining of two different arguments about the connection between speech and democracy. The first is a programmatic argument about the practical effects of speech on democratic decision making: when we hear all the speech available, we have more of the information we need to make good decisions in the democratic process. The second argument is about the relationship between speech and full participation as a democratic citizen: speech is a primary mechanism through which we participate fully in creating and shaping the public opinion that guides a democracy."[i]

If the First Amendment is rooted in a conception of democracy, is it obvious that the idea of democracy is politically centered?[j] Consider Jack M. Balkin, *Digital Speech and Democratic Culture: A Theory of Freedom of Expression for the Information Society,* 79 N.Y.U. L. Rev. 1, 3–5 (2004): "The purpose of freedom of speech [is] to promote a democratic culture. A democratic culture is more than representative institutions of democracy, and it is more than deliberation about public issues. Rather, a democratic culture is a

---

h. For elaboration and modification of Meiklejohn's views, see Alexander Meiklejohn, *The First Amendment Is an Absolute,* 1961 Sup.Ct.Rev. 245. For commentary, see Zechariah Chafee,Jr., *Book Review,* 62 Harv. L.Rev. 891 (1949); Lee Bollinger, *Free Speech and Intellectual Values,* 92 Yale L.J. 438 (1983); Kalven, supra.

i. For emphasis on the participatory aspects of democracy, see Robert Post, *Constitutional Domains* (1995); James Weinstein, *Hate Speech, Pornography, and the Radical Attack on Free Speech Doctrine* (1999). For criticism of Post's position, see Martin H. Redish & Abby Marie Molen, *Understanding Post's and Meiklejohn's Mistakes,* 103 Nw. U.L. L.Rev. 1303 (2009).

j. For work proceeding from a politically based interpretation of the First Amendment, see Robert Post, fn. i; James Weinstein, fn. i; Cass R. Sunstein, *Democracy and the Problem of Free Speech* (1993). For criticism of Sunstein's position, see J.M. Balkin, *Populism and Progressivism as Constitutional Categories,* 104 Yale L.J. (1995); Robert Lipkin, *The Quest for the Common Good: Neutrality and Deliberative Democracy in Sunstein's Conception of American Constitutionalism,* 26 Conn.L.Rev. 1039 (1994); William Marshall, *Free Speech and the "Problem" of Democracy,* 89 Nw.U.L.Rev. 191 (1994).

For additional commentary proceeding from a politically based interpretation, see Akhil Reed Amar, *The Bill of Rights* 20–32 (1998); George Anastaplo, *The Constitutionalist* (1971); Cass Sunstein, *Democracy and the Problem of Free Speech* (1993); Lillian BeVier, *The First Amendment and Political Speech: An Inquiry Into the Substance and Limits of Principle,* 30 Stan.L.Rev. 299 (1978); Edward Bloustein, *The First Amendment and Privacy: The Supreme Court Justice and the Philosopher,* 28 Rutg.L.Rev. 41 (1974); Robert Bork, *Neutral Principles and Some First Amendment Problems,* 47 Ind.L.J. 1 (1971); Owen Fiss, *State Activism and State Censorship,* 100 Yale L.J. 2087 (1991). Owen Fiss, *Why the State,* 100 Harv.L.Rev. 781 (1987); Owen Fiss, *Free Speech and Social Structure,* 71 Iowa L.Rev. 1405 (1986). See also William Brennan, *The Supreme Court and the Meiklejohn Interpretation of the First Amendment,* 79 Harv.L.Rev. 1 (1965); Daniel Farber, *Free Speech Without Romance,* 105 Harv.L.Rev. 554 (1991) (arriving at a politically centered perspective after applying economic analysis).

culture in which individuals have a fair opportunity to participate in the forms of meaning-making that constitute them as individuals. Democratic culture is about individual liberty as well as collective self-governance; it is about each individual's ability to participate in the production and distribution of culture. [As] people express themselves, make music, create works of art, sing, gossip, converse, accuse, deny, complain, celebrate, enthuse, boast, and parody, they continually add something to the cultural mixture in which they live. They reshape, however imperceptibly, cultural conventions about what things mean, what is proper and improper, what is important and less important, how things are done and how they are not done. Through communicative interaction, through expression, through exchange, individual people become the architects of their culture, building on what others did before them and shaping the world that will shape them and those who follow them." See also Kenneth L. Karst, *Local Discourse and the Social Issues*, 12 Cardozo Stud. L. & Literature 1, 26–27 (2000).

Is the concept of cultural democracy itself too narrow? Consider Seana Valentine Shiffrin, *Speech, Death, and Double Effect*, 78 N.Y.U. L. Rev. 1135, 1159 (2003): "Although there is quite substantial value associated with the pure act of self-articulation and self-expression associated with speech, a predominant value of speech lies in its nature as a communicative enterprise. We prize speech, in large part, because it communicates content to others and stimulates thought, understanding, critical reflection, emotional reactions, subtle and radical changes in self-conception and behavior, and other responses in audiences about that content. Speakers offer visions of what our lives represent and what they should become; that is, how we, as citizens and moral agents, should act."

Assuming the idea of democracy is central to the First Amendment, and assuming the idea of democracy is politically centered, what is the theory of political democracy lying at the heart of the First Amendment? What is the appropriate role for citizens, political leaders, and the press in democratic theory? For the suggestion that the particular theory of democracy entertained has implications for a range of First Amendment questions, see, C. Edwin Baker, *The Media That Citizens Need,* 147 U.Pa.L.Rev. 317 (1998).

2. **Providing leadership in a globalized setting.** In a globalized setting with an increased need for an international free press, should the Court try to provide leadership and broaden its rationale in a way that might be appealing to countries that do not accept Madisonian self-government? Might an "emphasis on how a system of openness helps to moderate authoritarian tendencies and helps to generate capacities to deal with social conflict meet with a better reception in many societies." See Lee C. Bollinger, *Uninhibited, Robust, and Wide-Open* 118 (2010).

3. Consider Richard A. Epstein, *Privacy, Publication, and the First Amendment: The Dangers of First Amendment Exceptionalism*, 52 Stan. L. Rev. 1003, 1010–1011 (2000): "[T]he press in the United States and other common law countries had flourished under the general rules in force prior to the advent of *New York Times.* While the reversal of the Alabama court could easily be justified on the ground that Alabama played fast and loose with two elements of the common law account of the wrong—what it means for

statements to be "of and concerning the plaintiff," and what is needed to prove hefty awards of general damages—the Supreme Court had little reason to fashion a broad 'actual malice' privilege out of whole cloth that would become applicable to all sorts of defamation cases that had none of the tragic overtones of the civil rights struggle in the South." But cf. Rodney A. Smolla, *Information as Contraband: The First Amendment and Liability for Trafficking in Speech*, 96 Nw. U. L. Rev. 1099, 1138–1139 (2002): "[I]f the Supreme Court ever required genuine hard evidence that the 'chilling effect' of the negligence standard repudiated in *New York Times* actually exists, the media might well be fearful that the evidence could not be garnered. The point here is not that the *New York Times* rule is indefensible—it is better described as indispensable—but rather that its defense is more comfortably made by arguing principle than sociology." What is the principle? See Richard H. Fallon, Jr., *Implementing the Constitution* 29–30 (2001)(arguing that the defamation rules depend upon empirical judgments).

4. ***New York Times, definitional balancing, and the two-level theory of the First Amendment.*** By holding that some libel was within the protection of the First Amendment, did the Court dismantle its two-level theory? See Kalven, supra, at 217–218. Or did the Court merely rearrange its conception of what was protected and what was not?

Does *Garrison v. Louisiana,* 379 U.S. 64 (1964) shed light on the question? The Court stated: "Calculated falsehood falls into that class of utterances '[of] such slight social value as a step to truth that any benefit that may be derived from them is clearly outweighed by the social interest in order and morality.' *Chaplinsky.*"

Could the judicial process here fairly be called *definitional* classification—defining which categories of libel are to be viewed as "speech" within the First Amendment, and which are not? Consider Melville Nimmer, *The Right to Speak from Times to Time: First Amendment Theory Applied to Libel and Misapplied to Privacy*, 56 Calif.L.Rev. 935, 942–43 (1968): "[*New York Times*] points the way to the employment of the balancing process on the definitional rather than the litigation or ad hoc level, [that is,] balancing not for the purpose of determining which litigant deserves to prevail in the particular case, but only for the purpose of defining which forms of speech are to be regarded as 'speech' within the meaning of the First Amendment. [By] in effect holding that knowingly and recklessly false speech was not 'speech' within the meaning of the First Amendment, the Court must have implicitly (since no explicit explanation was offered) referred to certain competing policy considerations. This is surely a kind of balancing, but it is just as surely not ad hoc balancing."

5. ***Scope of New York Times.*** Professor Kalven argued that given the Court's conception of freedom of speech, its holding could not be confined: "the invitation to follow a dialectic progression from public official to government policy to public policy to matters in the public domain, like art, seems * * * overwhelming." Kalven, supra, at 221.

(a) ***Public officials.*** *New York Times,* fn. 23 left open "how far down into the lower ranks of governmental employees" the rule would extend, and *Rosenblatt v. Baer*, 383 U.S. 75 (1966) suggested the rule might apply to the supervisor of a publicly owned ski resort, saying it applies among other things to those who "appear to the public to [have] substantial responsibility for or control over the conduct of government affairs." Should criticism of the official conduct of *very* high ranking government officials (e.g., the President, the Secretary of State, a general commanding troops in war) be given greater protection than that afforded in *New York Times*?

(b) *Private conduct of public officials and candidates. Garrison,* extended *New York Times* to "anything which might touch on an official's fitness for office," even if the defamation did not concern official conduct in office. Invoking that standard, *Monitor Patriot Co. v. Roy,* 401 U.S. 265 (1971) applied *New York Times* to a news column describing a candidate for public office as a "former small-time bootlegger."

(c) *Public figures.* In CURTIS PUB. CO. v. BUTTS and ASSOCIATED PRESS v. WALKER, 388 U.S. 130 (1967), HARLAN, J., contended that because public figures were not subject to the restraints of the political process, any criticism of them was not akin to seditious libel and was, therefore, a step removed from the central meaning of the First Amendment. Nonetheless, he argued that public figure actions should not be left entirely to the vagaries of state defamation law and would have required that public figures show "highly unreasonable conduct constituting an extreme departure from the standards of investigation and reporting ordinarily adhered to by responsible publishers" as a prerequisite to recovery. In response, WARREN, C.J., argued that the inapplicability of the restraints of the political process to public figures underscored the importance for uninhibited debate about their activities since "public opinion may be the only instrument by which society can attempt to influence their conduct." He observed that increasingly "the distinctions between governmental and private sectors are blurred," that public figures, like public officials, "often play an influential role in ordering society," and as a class have a ready access to the mass media "both to influence policy and to counter criticism of their views and activities." He accordingly concluded that the *New York Times* rule should be extended to public figures. Four other justices in *Butts* and *Walker* were willing to go at least as far as Warren, C.J., and subsequent cases have settled on the position that public figures must meet the *New York Times* requirements in order to recover in a defamation action. The critical issues are how to define the concept of public figure and how to apply it in practice.[k] See *Gertz,* infra. Does this encourage media overreaching and irresponsibility? Would a negligence regime be better? See Gerald Ashdown, *Journalism Police,* 89 Marq. L.Rev. 739 (2006).

(d) *Private plaintiffs and public issues.* Without deciding whether any First Amendment protection should extend to matters not of general or public interest, a plurality led by BRENNAN, J., joined by Burger, C.J., and Blackmun, J., argued in ROSENBLOOM v. METROMEDIA, INC., 403 U.S. 29 (1971), that the *New York Times* rule should be extended to defamatory statements involving matters of public or general interest "without regard to whether the persons involved are famous or anonymous." Black, J., would

---

k. For close analysis of the genesis of public figure doctrine, see Catherine Hancock, *Origins of the Public Figure Doctrine in First Amendment Defamation Law,* 50 N.Y.L.Sch.L.Rev. 81 (2005–06).

have gone further, opining that the First Amendment "does not permit the recovery of libel judgments against the news media even when statements are broadcast with knowledge they are false," and Douglas, J., shared Black, J.'s approach (at least with respect to matters of public interest, although he did not participate in *Rosenbloom*.) WHITE, J., felt that the *New York Times* rule should apply to reporting on the official actions of public servants and to reporting on those involved in or affected by their official action. That principle was broad enough to cover Rosenbloom, a distributor of nudist magazines who had been arrested by the Philadelphia police for distributing obscene materials. The defamatory broadcast wrongly assumed his guilt. Dissenting, Harlan, Stewart and Marshall, JJ., counseled an approach similar to that taken in *Gertz*, infra.

After *Rosenbloom* the lower courts rather uniformly followed the approach taken by the plurality. By 1974, however, the composition of the Court had changed and so had the minds of some of the justices.

C. PRIVATE INDIVIDUALS AND PUBLIC FIGURES

GERTZ v. ROBERT WELCH, INC.
418 U.S. 323, 94 S.Ct. 2997, 41 L.Ed.2d 789 (1974).

JUSTICE POWELL delivered the opinion of the Court.

[Respondent published *American Opinion*, a monthly outlet for the John Birch Society. It published an article falsely stating that Gertz, a lawyer, was the "architect" in a "communist frameup" of a policeman convicted of murdering a youth whose family Gertz represented in resultant civil proceedings, and that Gertz had a "criminal record" and had been an officer in a named "Communist-fronter" organization that advocated violent seizure of our government. In Gertz' libel action there was evidence that *Opinion*'s managing editor did not know the statements were false and had relied on the reputation of the article's author and prior experience with the accuracy of his articles. After a $50,000 verdict for Gertz, the trial court entered judgment n.o.v., concluding that the *New York Times* rule applied to any discussion of a "public issue." The court of appeals affirmed, ruling that the publisher did not have the requisite "awareness of probable falsity." The Court held that *New York Times* did not apply to defamation of private individuals, but remanded for a new trial "because the jury was allowed to impose liability without fault [and] to presume damages without proof of injury."]

II. The principal issue in this case is whether a newspaper or broadcaster that publishes defamatory falsehoods about an individual who is neither a public official nor a public figure may claim a constitutional privilege against liability for the injury inflicted by those statements.
* * *

In his opinion for the plurality in *Rosenbloom,* Mr. Justice Brennan took the *Times* privilege one step further [than *Butts* and *Walker*]. He concluded that its protection should extend to defamatory falsehoods relating to private persons if the statements concerned matters of general or public interest. He abjured the suggested distinction between public officials and public figures on the one hand and private individuals on the other. He focused instead on society's interest in learning about certain issues: "If a matter is a subject of public or general interest, it cannot suddenly become less so merely because a private individual is involved or because in some sense the individual did not choose to become involved." Thus, under the plurality opinion, a private citizen involuntarily associated with a matter of general interest has no recourse for injury to his reputation unless he can satisfy the demanding requirements of the *Times* [test].

III.   [Under] the First Amendment there is no such thing as a false idea.[a] However pernicious an opinion may seem, we depend for its correction not on the conscience of the judges and juries but on the competition of other ideas.[b] But there is no constitutional value in false statements of fact. Neither the intentional lie nor the careless error materially advances society's interest in "uninhibited, robust, and wide-open" debate on public issues. * * *

Although the erroneous statement of fact is not worthy of constitutional protection, it is nevertheless inevitable in free debate. [P]unishment of error runs the risk of inducing a cautious and restrictive exercise of the constitutionally guaranteed freedoms of speech and press. [The] First Amendment requires that we protect some falsehood in order to protect speech that matters.

The need to avoid self-censorship by the news media is, however, not the only societal value at issue. [The] legitimate state interest underlying the law of libel is the compensation of individuals for the harm inflicted on them by defamatory falsehoods. We would not lightly require the State to abandon this purpose, for, as Mr. Justice Stewart has reminded us, the individual's right to the protection of his own good name "reflects no more than our basic concept of the essential dignity and worth of every human being—a concept at the root of any decent system of ordered liberty. * * * " *Rosenblatt*.[c]

---

a.   But see Shannon Gilreath, *"Tell Your Faggot Friend He Owes Me $500 for my Broken Hand": Thoughts on a Substantive Equality Theory of Free Speech*, 44 Wake For. L.Rev. 557, 570 (2009): "There are false ideas. In the American democratic order, we have determined that the equality of every person is a paramount principle—perhaps the ultimate principle of ordered liberty. [E]xpression that is targeted to undermine equality, to subjugate an individual or group purely because of group identity, and to exclude the victim from meaningful, equal citizenship is—constitutionally speaking—false."

b.   For many years the lower courts took this language seriously and deemed opinion to be absolutely protected (see, e.g., *Ollman v. Evans*, 750 F.2d 970 (D.C.Cir.1984)), but *Milkovich v. Lorain Journal Co.*, 497 U.S. 1 (1990), per Rehnquist, C.J., ultimately denied that there is any "wholesale defamation exception for anything that might be labeled 'opinion.' " Should opinions about non-public matters be subject to different standards than opinions about public matters? Robert D. Sack, *Protection of Opinion Under the First Amendment: Reflections on Alfred Hill, "Defamation and Privacy Under the First Amendment,"* 100 Colum.L.Rev. 294, 326–327 (2000).

c.   Stewart J., continued: "The protection of private personality, like the protection of life itself, is left primarily to the individual States under the Ninth and Tenth Amendments. But this does not mean that the right is entitled to any less recognition by this Court as a basic of our

Some tension necessarily exists between the need for a vigorous and uninhibited press and the legitimate interest in redressing wrongful injury. [In] our continuing effort to define the proper accommodation between these competing concerns, we have been especially anxious to assure to the freedoms of speech and press that "breathing space" essential to their fruitful exercise. To that end this Court has extended a measure of strategic protection to defamatory falsehood.

The *New York Times* standard defines the level of constitutional protection appropriate to the context of defamation of [public figures and those who hold governmental office]. Plainly many deserving plaintiffs, including some intentionally subjected to injury, will be unable to surmount the barrier of the *New York Times* test. [For] the reasons stated below, we conclude that the state interest in compensating injury to the reputation of private individuals requires that a different rule should obtain with respect to them.

[W]e have no difficulty in distinguishing among defamation plaintiffs. The first remedy of any victim of defamation is self-help—using available opportunities to contradict the lie or correct the error and thereby to minimize its adverse impact on reputation. Public officials and public figures usually enjoy significantly greater access to the channels of effective communication and hence have a more realistic opportunity to counteract false statements than private individuals normally enjoy.[9] Private individuals are therefore more vulnerable to injury, and the state interest in protecting them is correspondingly greater.

More important than the likelihood that private individuals will lack effective opportunities for rebuttal, there is a compelling normative consideration underlying the distinction between public and private defamation plaintiffs. An individual who decides to seek governmental office must accept certain necessary consequences of that involvement in public affairs. He runs the risk of closer public scrutiny than might otherwise be the case. [Those] classed as public figures stand in a similar [position.][d]

---

constitutional system." Consider Robert Post, *The Social Foundations of Defamation Law*, 74 Calif.L.Rev. 691, 708 (1986): "[I]t is not immediately clear how reputation, which is social and public, and which resides in the 'common or general estimate of person,' can possibly affect the 'essential dignity' of a person's 'private personality.' The gulf that appears to separate reputation from dignity can be spanned only if defamation law contains an implicit theory of the relationship between the private and public aspects of the self."

9. Of course, an opportunity for rebuttal seldom suffices to undo harm of defamatory falsehood. Indeed, the law of defamation is rooted in our experience that the truth rarely catches up with a lie. But the fact that the self-help remedy of rebuttal, standing alone, is inadequate to its task does not mean that it is irrelevant to our inquiry. [Consider Steven Shiffrin, *Defamatory Non-Media Speech and First Amendment Methodology*, 25 UCLA L.Rev. 915, 952–53 (1978): "[F]ootnote nine, has seemingly left the First Amendment in a peculiar spot. *Gertz* holds that the First Amendment offers some protection for defamatory utterances presumably so that our Constitution can continue 'to preserve an uninhibited marketplace of ideas in which truth will ultimately prevail. * * *' And yet the Court recognizes that 'an opportunity for rebuttal seldom suffices to undo [the] harm of defamatory falsehood,' i.e., truth does not emerge in the marketplace of ideas. Is the Court trapped in an obvious contradiction?"]

d. Consider Lee Bollinger, *Images of a Free Press* 25–26 (1994): "Essentially, the Court has said that, since these individuals have freely chosen a public life, what happens to them is their own doing, just as it is for a man who breaks his leg while hiking in the wilderness. Putting aside

Even if the foregoing generalities do not obtain in every instance, the communications media are entitled to act on the assumption that public officials and public figures have voluntarily exposed themselves to increased risk of injury from defamatory falsehoods concerning them. No such assumption is justified with respect to a private individual. He has not accepted public office nor assumed an "influential role in ordering society." *Butts.* He has relinquished no part of his interest in the protection of his own good name, and consequently he has a more compelling call on the courts for redress of injury inflicted by defamatory falsehood. Thus, private individuals are not only more vulnerable to injury than public officials and public figures; they are also more deserving of recovery.

For these reasons we conclude that the States should retain substantial latitude in their efforts to enforce a legal remedy for defamatory falsehood injurious to the reputation of a private individual. The extension of the *Times* test proposed by the *Rosenbloom* plurality would abridge this legitimate state interest to a degree that we find unacceptable. And it would occasion the additional difficulty of forcing state and federal judges to decide on an ad hoc basis which publications address issues of "general or public interest" and which do not—to determine, in the words of Mr. Justice Marshall, "what information is relevant to self-government." *Rosenbloom.* We doubt the wisdom of committing this task to the conscience of judges. [The] "public or general interest" test for determining the applicability of the *Times* standard to private defamation actions inadequately serves both of the competing values at stake. On the one hand, a private individual whose reputation is injured by defamatory falsehood that does concern an issue of public or general interest has no recourse unless he can meet the rigorous requirements of *Times*. This is true despite the factors that distinguish the state interest in compensating private individuals from the analogous interest involved in the context of public persons. On the other hand, a publisher or broadcaster of a defamatory error which a court deems unrelated to an issue of public or general interest may be held liable in damages even if it took every reasonable precaution to ensure the accuracy of its assertions. And liability may far exceed compensation for any actual injury to the plaintiff, for the jury may be permitted to presume damages without proof of loss and even to award punitive damages.

We hold that, so long as they do not impose liability without fault, the States may define for themselves the appropriate standard of liability for a publisher or broadcaster of defamatory falsehood injurious to a private individual. This approach provides a more equitable boundary between the competing concerns involved here. It recognizes the strength of the

---

for the moment the fact that we also have an interest in encouraging people to enter public affairs, it simply is wrong to suppose that the pain inflicted by defamatory statements about public officials and figures is not our responsibility or concern. It should always be open to people to object to the way the world works under the rules we create, and not be dismissed by the claim that they have chosen to continue living in that world and, therefore, can be taken as having assented to it."

legitimate state interest in compensating private individuals for wrongful injury to reputation, yet shields the press and broadcast media from the rigors of strict liability for defamation. At least this conclusion obtains where, as here, the substance of the defamatory statement "makes substantial danger to reputation apparent." *Butts.* This phrase places in perspective the conclusion we announce today. Our inquiry would involve considerations somewhat different from those discussed above if a State purported to condition civil liability on a factual misstatement whose content did not warn a reasonably prudent editor or broadcaster of its defamatory potential. Cf. *Time, Inc. v. Hill* [Part D infra]. Such a case is not now before us, and we intimate no view as to its proper resolution.

IV. [T]he strong and legitimate state interest in compensating private individuals for injury to reputation [extends] no further than compensation for actual injury. For the reasons stated below, we hold that the States may not permit recovery of presumed or punitive damages, at least when liability is not based on a showing of knowledge of falsity or reckless disregard for the truth.

The common law of defamation is an oddity of tort [law]. Juries may award substantial sums as compensation for supposed damage to reputation without any proof that such harm actually occurred. [This] unnecessarily compounds the potential of any system of liability for defamatory falsehood to inhibit the vigorous exercise of First Amendment freedoms [and] invites juries to punish unpopular opinion rather than to compensate individuals for injury sustained by the publication of a false fact. More to the point, the States have no substantial interest in securing for plaintiffs such as this petitioner gratuitous awards of money damages far in excess of any actual injury.

We would not, of course, invalidate state law simply because we doubt its wisdom, but here we are attempting to reconcile state law with a competing interest grounded in the constitutional command of the First Amendment. It is therefore appropriate to require that state remedies for defamatory falsehood reach no farther than is necessary to protect the legitimate interest involved. It is necessary to restrict defamation plaintiffs who do not prove knowledge of falsity or reckless disregard for the truth to compensation for actual injury. We need not define "actual injury," as trial courts have wide experience in framing appropriate jury instructions in tort action. Suffice it to say that actual injury is not limited to out-of-pocket loss. Indeed, the more customary types of actual harm inflicted by defamatory falsehood include impairment of reputation and standing in the community, personal humiliation, and mental anguish and suffering. Of course, juries must be limited by appropriate instructions, and all awards must be supported by competent evidence concerning the injury, although there need be no evidence which assigns an actual dollar value to the injury.

We also find no justification for allowing awards of punitive damages against publishers and broadcasters held liable under state-defined standards of liability for defamation. In most jurisdictions jury discretion over the amounts awarded is limited only by the gentle rule that they not be excessive. Consequently, juries assess punitive damages in wholly unpredictable amounts bearing no necessary relation to the actual harm caused. And they remain free to use their discretion selectively to punish expressions of unpopular views. [J]ury discretion to award punitive damages unnecessarily exacerbates the danger of media self-censorship; [punitive] damages are wholly irrelevant to the state interest that justifies a negligence standard for private defamation actions. They are not compensation for injury. Instead, they are private fines levied by civil juries to punish reprehensible conduct and to deter its future occurrence. In short, the private defamation plaintiff who establishes liability under a less demanding standard than that stated by *Times* may recover only such damages as are sufficient to compensate him for actual injury.[e]

V. Notwithstanding our refusal to extend the *New York Times* privilege to defamation of private individuals, respondent contends that we should affirm the judgment below on the ground that petitioner is [a] public figure. [That] designation may rest on either of two alternative bases. In some instances an individual may achieve such pervasive fame or notoriety that he becomes a public figure for all purposes and in all contexts. More commonly, an individual voluntarily injects himself or is drawn into a particular public controversy and thereby becomes a public figure for a limited range of issues. In either case such persons assume special prominence in the resolution of public questions.

Petitioner has long been active in community and professional affairs. He has served as an officer of local civic groups and of various professional organizations, and he has published several books and articles on legal subjects. Although petitioner was consequently well known in some circles, he had achieved no general fame or notoriety in the community. None of the prospective jurors called at the trial had ever heard of petitioner prior to this litigation, and respondent offered no proof that this response was atypical of the local population. We would not lightly assume that a citizen's participation in community and professional affairs rendered him a public figure for all purposes. Absent clear evidence of general fame or notoriety in the community, and pervasive involvement in the affairs of society, an individual should not be deemed a public personality for all aspects of his life. It is preferable to reduce the public-figure question to a more meaningful context by looking to the nature and extent of an individual's participation in the particular controversy giving rise to the defamation.

In this context it is plain that petitioner was not a public figure. He played a minimal role at the coroner's inquest, and his participation related solely to his representation of a private client. He took no part in the criminal prosecution of Officer Nuccio. Moreover, he never discussed

---

e. On remand, Gertz was awarded $100,000 in compensatory damages and $300,000 in punitive damages. In the prior trial, he had been awarded only $50,000 in damages.

either the criminal or civil litigation with the press and was never quoted as having done so. He plainly did not thrust himself into the vortex of this public issue, nor did he engage the public's attention in an attempt to influence its outcome. We are persuaded that the trial court did not err in refusing to characterize petitioner as a public figure for the purpose of this litigation.

We therefore conclude that the *New York Times* standard is inapplicable to this case and that the trial court erred in entering judgment for respondent. Because the jury was allowed to impose liability without fault and was permitted to presume damages without proof of injury, a new trial is necessary.[f]

Justice Brennan, dissenting.

[While the Court's] arguments are forcefully and eloquently presented, I cannot accept them for the reasons I stated in *Rosenbloom:* "The *New York Times* standard was applied to libel of a public official or public figure to give effect to the Amendment's function to encourage ventilation of public issues, not because the public official has any less interest in protecting his reputation than an individual in private life. [In] the vast majority of libels involving public officials or public figures, the ability to respond through the media will depend on the same complex factor on which the ability of a private individual depends: the unpredictable event of the media's continuing interest in the story. Thus the unproved, and highly improbable, generalization that an as yet [not fully defined] class of 'public figures' involved in matters of public concern will be better able to respond through the media than private individuals also involved in such matters seems too insubstantial a reed on which to rest a constitutional distinction."

[Adoption], by many States, of a reasonable care standard in cases where private individuals are involved in matters of public interest—the probable result of today's decision—[will] lead to self-censorship since publishers will be required carefully to weigh a myriad of uncertain factors before publication. The reasonable care standard is "elusive," *Time, Inc. v. Hill;* it saddles the press with "the intolerable burden of guessing how a jury might assess the reasonableness of steps taken by it to verify the accuracy of every reference to a name, picture or portrait." Ibid. Under a reasonable care regime, publishers and broadcasters will

---

f. Blackmun, J., concurred: "[Although I joined Brennan, J.'s plurality opinion in *Rosenbloom,* from which the Court's opinion in the present case departs, I join] the Court's opinion and its judgment for two reasons:

"1. By removing the spectres of presumed and punitive damages in the absence of *Times* malice, the Court eliminates significant and powerful motives for self-censorship that otherwise are present in the traditional libel action. By so doing, the Court leaves what should prove to be sufficient and adequate breathing space for a vigorous press. What the Court has done, I believe, will have little, if any, practical effect on the functioning of responsible journalism.

"2. The Court was sadly fractionated in *Rosenbloom.* A result of that kind inevitably leads to uncertainty. I feel that it is of profound importance for the Court to come to rest in the defamation area and to have a clearly defined majority position that eliminates the unsureness engendered by *Rosenbloom's* diversity. If my vote were not needed to create a majority, I would adhere to my prior view. A definitive ruling, however, is paramount."

have to make pre-publication judgments about juror assessment of such diverse considerations as the size, operating procedures, and financial condition of the news gathering system, as well as the relative costs and benefits of instituting less frequent and more costly reporting at a higher level of accuracy. [And] most hazardous, the flexibility which inheres in the reasonable care standard will create the danger that a jury will convert it into "an instrument for the suppression of those 'vehement, caustic, and sometimes unpleasantly sharp attacks,' [which] must be protected if the guarantees of the First and Fourteenth Amendments are to prevail." *Monitor Patriot Co.*

[A] jury's latitude to impose liability for want of due care poses a far greater threat of suppressing unpopular views than does a possible recovery of presumed or punitive damages. Moreover, the Court's broad-ranging examples of "actual injury" [allow] a jury bent on punishing expression of unpopular views a formidable weapon for doing so. [E]ven a limitation of recovery to "actual injury"—however much it reduces the size or frequency of recoveries—will not provide the necessary elbow room for First Amendment expression. "[The] very possibility of having to engage in litigation, an expensive and protracted process, is threat enough to cause discussion and debate to 'steer far wider of the unlawful zone' thereby keeping protected discussion from public cognizance. * * * " *Rosenbloom.*

[I] reject the argument that my *Rosenbloom* view improperly commits to judges the task of determining what is and what is not an issue of "general or public interest."[3] I noted in *Rosenbloom* that performance of this task would not always be easy. But surely the courts, the ultimate arbiters of all disputes concerning clashes of constitutional values, would only be performing one of their traditional functions in undertaking this duty. [The] public interest is necessarily broad; any residual self-censorship that may result from the uncertain contours of the "general or public interest" concept should be of far less concern to publishers and broadcasters than that occasioned by state laws imposing liability for negligent falsehood. * * *[g]

---

3. The Court, taking a novel step, would not limit application of First Amendment protection to private libels involving issues of general or public interest, but would forbid the States from imposing liability without fault in any case where the substance of the defamatory statement made substantial danger to reputation apparent. As in *Rosenbloom,* I would leave open the question of what constitutional standard, if any, applies when defamatory falsehoods are published or broadcast concerning either a private or public person's activities not within the scope of the general or public interest.

Parenthetically, my Brother White argues that the Court's view and mine will prevent a plaintiff—unable to demonstrate some degree of fault—from vindicating his reputation by securing a judgment that the publication was false. This argument overlooks the possible enactment of statutes, not requiring proof of fault, which provide for an action for retraction or for publication of a court's determination of falsity if the plaintiff is able to demonstrate that false statements have been published concerning his activities. Although it may be that questions could be raised concerning the constitutionality of such statutes, certainly nothing I have said today (and, as I read the Court's opinion, nothing said there) should be read to imply that a private plaintiff, unable to prove fault, must inevitably be denied the opportunity to secure a judgment upon the truth or falsity of statements published about him.

g. Douglas, J., dissented, objecting to "continued recognition of the possibility of state libel suits for public discussion of public issues" as diluting First Amendment protection. He added:

JUSTICE WHITE, dissenting.

[T]he Court, in a few printed pages, has federalized major aspects of libel law by declaring unconstitutional in important respects the prevailing defamation law in all or most of the 50 States. * * *

I.   [These] radical changes in the law and severe invasions of the prerogatives of the States [should] at least be shown to be required by the First Amendment or necessitated by our present circumstances. Neither has been [demonstrated.]

The central meaning of *New York Times,* and for me the First Amendment as it relates to libel laws, is that seditious libel—criticism of government and public officials—falls beyond the police power of the State. In a democratic society such as ours, the citizen has the privilege of criticizing his government and its officials. But neither *New York Times* nor its progeny suggest that the First Amendment intended in all circumstances to deprive the private citizen of his historic recourse to redress published falsehoods damaging to reputation or that, contrary to history and precedent, the amendment should now be so interpreted. Simply put, the First Amendment did not confer a "license to defame the citizen." Douglas, *The Right of the People* 38 (1958).

[T]he law has heretofore put the risk of falsehood on the publisher where the victim is a private citizen and no grounds of special privilege are invoked. The Court would now shift this risk to the victim, even though he has done nothing to invite the calumny, is wholly innocent of fault, and is helpless to avoid his injury. I doubt that jurisprudential resistance to liability without fault is sufficient ground for employing the First Amendment to revolutionize the law of libel, and in my view, that body of legal rules poses no realistic threat to the press and its service to the public. The press today is vigorous and robust. To me, it is quite incredible to suggest that threats of libel suits from private citizens are causing the press to refrain from publishing the truth. I know of no hard facts to support that proposition, and the Court furnishes none.

[I]f the Court's principal concern is to protect the communications industry from large libel judgments, it would appear that its new requirements with respect to general and punitive damages would be ample protection. Why it also feels compelled to escalate the threshold standard of liability I cannot fathom, particularly when this will eliminate in many instances the plaintiff's possibility of securing a judicial determination that the damaging publication was indeed false, whether or not he is entitled to recover money damages. [I] find it unacceptable to distribute the risk in this manner and force the wholly innocent victim to bear the

---

"Since this case involves a discussion of public affairs, I need not decide at this point whether the First Amendment prohibits all libel actions. 'An unconditional right to say what one pleases about public affairs is what I consider to be *the minimum guarantee* of the First Amendment.' *New York Times* (Black, J., concurring) (emphasis added). But 'public affairs' includes a great deal more than merely political affairs. Matters of science, economics, business, art, literature, etc., are all matters of interest to the general public. Indeed, any matter of sufficient general interest to prompt media coverage may be said to be a public affair. Certainly police killings, 'Communist conspiracies,' and the like qualify."

injury; for, as between the two, the defamer is the only culpable party. It is he who circulated a falsehood that he was not required to publish. * * *h

V. [I] fail to see how the quality or quantity of public debate will be promoted by further emasculation of state libel laws for the benefit of the news media.[41] If anything, this trend may provoke a new and radical imbalance in the communications process. Cf. Jerome Barron, *Access to the Press—A New First Amendment Right,* 80 Harv.L.Rev. 1641, 1657 (1967). It is not at all inconceivable that virtually unrestrained defamatory remarks about private citizens will discourage them from speaking out and concerning themselves with social problems. This would turn the First Amendment on its head. * * *i

NOTES AND QUESTIONS

1. ***Gertz and Meiklejohn.*** By affording some constitutional protection to all media defamatory speech whether or not it relates to public issues, does the Court squarely reject the Meiklejohn theory of the First Amendment? Consider Steven Shiffrin, *Defamatory Non–Media Speech and First Amendment Methodology,* 25 UCLA L.Rev. 915, 929 (1978): "It may be that the Court has refused to adopt the Meiklejohn 'public issues' test not because it believes that private speech (i.e., speech unrelated to public issues) is as important as public speech but rather because it doubts its ability to distinguish unerringly between the two. [B]y placing all defamatory media speech within the scope of the First Amendment, the Court may believe it has protected relatively little non-public speech. On the other hand, [putting aside comments about public officials and public figures], the Court may fear that if *Gertz* were extended to non-media speech, the result would be to protect much speech having nothing to do with public issues, while safeguarding relatively little that does." For consideration of the distinction between public and private speech and of the media/non-media distinction, see *Greenmoss*, Ch. 3, III, infra. See also *Philadelphia Newspapers, Inc. v. Hepps,* 475 U.S. 767 (1986) (private figure plaintiff has burden of showing falsity at least when issue is of "public concern" and leaving open the question of what standards apply to non-media defendants).

---

h. White, J., also argued strongly against the Court's rulings on presumed and punitive damages.

41. Cf. Willard Pedrick, *Freedom of the Press and the Law of Libel: The Modern Revised Translation,* 49 Cornell L.Q. 581, 601–02 (1964): "A great many forces in our society operate to determine the extent to which men are free in fact to express their ideas. Whether there is a privilege for good faith defamatory misstatements on matters of public concern or whether there is strict liability for such statements may not greatly affect the course of public discussion. How different has life been in those states which heretofore followed the majority rule imposing strict liability for misstatements of fact defaming public figures from life in the minority states where the good faith privilege held sway?"

i. Burger, C.J., also dissented: "I am frank to say I do not know the parameters of a 'negligence' doctrine as applied to the news media. [I] would prefer to allow this area of law to continue to evolve as it has up to now with respect to private citizens rather then embark on a new doctrinal theory which has no jurisprudential ancestry. [I would remand] for reinstatement of the verdict of the jury and the entry of an appropriate judgment on that verdict."

2. **Public figures.** TIME, INC. v. FIRESTONE, 424 U.S. 448 (1976), per REHNQUIST, J., declared that persons who have not assumed a role of especial prominence in the affairs of society are not public figures unless they have " 'thrust themselves to the forefront of particular public controversies in order to influence the resolution of the issues involved.' " It held that a divorce proceeding involving one of America's wealthiest industrial families and containing testimony concerning the extramarital sexual activities of the parties did not involve a "public controversy," "even though the marital difficulties of extremely wealthy individuals may be of interest to some portion of the reading public." Nor was the filing of a divorce suit, or the holding of press conferences ("to satisfy inquiring reporters") thought to be freely publicizing the issues in order to influence their outcome. Recall *Gertz* doubted the wisdom of forcing judges to determine on an ad hoc basis what is and is not of "general or public interest." Is there a basis for distinguishing a public figure test requiring judges to determine on an ad hoc basis what is or is not a "public controversy"?

What does it mean to assume a role of especial prominence in the affairs of society? If Elmer Gertz, a prominent Illinois attorney, does not qualify, does Wolfgang Puck? Naomi Campbell? If so, is the slide from public officials to chefs and models too precipitous because the latter "have little, if any, effect, on questions of politics, public policy, or the organization and determination of societal affairs"? See Frederick Schauer, *Public Figures,* 25 Wm. & Mary L.Rev. 905 (1984): Consider Marie A. Failinger, *Five Modern Notions in Search of an Author: The Ideology of the Intimate Society in Constitutional Speech Law,* 30 U.Tol. L.Rev. 251, 299 (1999): "[T]he Court merely adds fuel to the cultural fire created by [the] 'star' system—people who want to know intimate details that confirm their trust in those selected by the public to be 'stars,' and yet, they have a secret desire to know 'dirt' on those same persons to justify their beliefs that people just like themselves have been randomly enriched with fame, power, and wealth. [T]his politics of resentment, parlay[s] the shame and envy of those who find themselves in a lower-than-deserved status into a rising backlash against those who have unfairly taken 'their' place. Thus, protection of the cult of personality in the Court's speech doctrine only serves to fuel the fires of self-interested, mean-spirited public life." Does a narrow definition of public figures discriminate in favor of orthodox media and discourage attempts "to illuminate previously unexposed aspects of society"? Does the negligence concept itself threaten to discriminate "against media or outlets whose philosophies and methods deviate from those of the mainstream"? See generally David Anderson, *Libel and Press Self–Censorship,* 53 Tex.L.Rev. 422, 453, 455 (1975).

3. **Taking reputation too seriously?** Consider Rodney Smolla, *Suing the Press* 257 (1986): "[I]f we take the libel suit too seriously, we are in danger of raising our collective cultural sensitivity to reputation to unhealthy levels. We are in danger of surrendering a wonderful part of our national identity—our strapping, scrambling, free-wheeling individualism, in danger of becoming less American, less robust, wild-eyed, pluralistic and free, and more decorous, image-conscious, and narcissistic. The media is itself partly to blame for this direction, and it would be dangerous to release it totally from the important check and balance that the libel laws provide. But in the United

States, the balance that must be struck between reputation and expression should never be tilted too far against expression, for the right to defiantly, robustly, and irreverently speak one's mind just because it is one's mind is quintessentially what it means to be an American."[j]

D. EMOTIONAL DISTRESS

HUSTLER MAGAZINE v. FALWELL, 485 U.S. 46 (1988), per REHN-QUIST, C.J., held that public figures and public officials offended by a mass media parody could not recover for the tort of intentional infliction of emotional distress without a showing of *New York Times* malice. Parodying a series of liquor advertisements in which celebrities speak about their "first time," the editors of *Hustler* chose plaintiff Jerry Falwell (a nationally famous minister, host of a nationally syndicated television show, and founder of the Moral Majority political organization) "as the featured celebrity and drafted an alleged 'interview' with him in which he states that his 'first time' was during a drunken incestuous rendezvous with his mother in an outhouse. The *Hustler* parody portrays [Falwell] and his mother[a] 'as drunk and immoral,' and suggests that [Falwell] is a hypocrite who preaches only when he is drunk. In small print at the bottom of the page, the ad contains the disclaimer, 'ad parody—not to be taken seriously.' The magazine's table of contents also lists the ad as 'Fiction; Ad and Personality Parody.' * * *

"We must decide whether a public figure may recover damages for emotional harm caused by the publication of an ad parody offensive to him, and doubtless gross and repugnant in the eyes of most.[3] [Falwell] would have us find that a State's interest in protecting public figures from emotional distress is sufficient to deny First Amendment protection to speech that is patently offensive and is intended to inflict emotional injury, even when that speech could not reasonably have been interpreted as stating actual facts about the public figure involved. * * *

"Generally speaking the law does not regard the intent to inflict emotional distress as one which should receive much solicitude, and it is quite understandable that most if not all jurisdictions have chosen to make it civilly culpable where the conduct in question is sufficiently 'outrageous.' But in the world of debate about public affairs, many things done with motives that are less than admirable are protected by the First Amendment. '[Debate] on public issues will not be uninhibited if the speaker must run the risk that it will be proved in court that he spoke out of hatred; even if he did speak out of hatred, utterances honestly believed

---

j. For historical perspective on the social messages communicated by defamation law, see Norman Rosenberg, *Protecting the Best Men* (1986). For discussion of factors causing few cases to go to trial against media defendants, see David A. Anderson, *Rethinking Defamation*, 48 Ariz. L.Rev. 1047 (2006).

a. Falwell's mother was not a plaintiff. What result if she were?

3. Under Virginia law, in an action for intentional infliction of emotional distress a plaintiff must show that the defendant's conduct (1) is intentional or reckless; (2) offends generally accepted standards of decency or morality; (3) is causally connected with the plaintiff's emotional distress; and (4) caused emotional distress that was severe.

contribute to the free interchange of ideas and the ascertainment of truth.' *Garrison.* Thus while such a bad motive may be deemed controlling for purposes of tort liability in other areas of the law, we think the First Amendment prohibits such a result in the area of public debate about public figures.

"Were we to hold otherwise, there can be little doubt that political cartoonists and satirists would be subjected to damage awards without any showing that their work falsely defamed its subject. * * *

"There is no doubt that the caricature of [Falwell] and his mother published in Hustler is at best a distant cousin of [traditional] political cartoons [and] a rather poor relation at that. If it were possible by laying down a principled standard to separate the one from the other, public discourse would probably suffer little or no harm. But we doubt that there is any such standard, and we are quite sure that the pejorative description 'outrageous' does not supply one. 'Outrageousness' in the area of political and social discourse has an inherent subjectiveness about it which would allow a jury to impose liability on the basis of the jurors' tastes or views, or perhaps on the basis of their dislike of a particular expression.

"We conclude that public figures and public officials may not recover for the tort of intentional infliction of emotional distress by reason of publications such as the one here at issue without showing in addition that the publication contains a false statement of fact which was made with 'actual malice,' i.e., with knowledge that the statement was false or with reckless disregard as to whether or not it was true."[b]

NOTES AND QUESTIONS

1. Does the rationale sweep beyond the holding? If debate on public issues should be uninhibited and if speakers filled with hatred have a place in that debate, why is the holding confined to suits brought by public officials and public figures? Is the holding likely to follow a "dialectic progression" from public official and public figure to all matters in the public domain? Should it? Is that far enough? Should the holding encompass all media speech? All non-media speech? Consider Rodney Smolla, *Emotional Distress and the First Amendment,* 20 Ariz.St.L.J. 423, 427 (1988): "The intellectual challenge posed by Falwell's suit is not how to construct a convincing rationale for rejecting his claim, but rather how to articulate limits on that rationale that will permit suits for emotional distress inflicted through speech in other contexts to survive." To what extent should the tort of intentional infliction of emotional distress raise constitutional problems?

2. Is the problem with the outrageousness standard less its subjectivity than its enabling "a single community to use the authority of the state to confine speech within its own notions of propriety." Does *Falwell* exhibit a need to respect a "marketplace of communities?" Can we respect that marketplace without "blunt[ing the] rules of civility that define the essence of

---

b. White, J., concurred, but stated that *New York Times* was irrelevant because of the jury's finding that the parody contained no assertion of fact. Kennedy, J., took no part.

reason and dignity within community life?" Compare Robert Post, *The Constitutional Concept of Public Discourse,* 103 Harv.L.Rev. 601, 632, 643 (1990) with Joshua Cohen, *Freedom of Expression*, 22 Phil. & Pub. Aff. 207, 227 n. 62 (1993).

3. ***False light privacy.*** TIME, INC. v. HILL, 385 U.S. 374 (1967) applied the *New York Times* knowing and reckless falsity standard to a right of privacy action for publishing an erroneous but not defamatory report about private individuals involved in an incident of public interest. The Court maintained that "[N]egligence would be a most elusive standard, especially when the content of the speech itself affords no warning of prospective harm to another through falsity. A negligence test would place on the press the intolerable burden of guessing how a jury might assess the reasonableness of steps taken by it to verify the accuracy of every reference to a name, picture or [portrait]." Does *Hill* survive *Gertz*? Would it make a difference if the law suit were for intentional infliction of emotional distress?

Compare *Hill* with ZACCHINI v. SCRIPPS–HOWARD BROADCASTING CO., 433 U.S. 562 (1977): Zacchini performed as a "human cannonball," being shot from a cannon into a net some 200 feet away. Without Zacchini's permission to film or broadcast his act, Scripps–Howard obtained and broadcast the tape of his "shot" on the news. The Ohio Supreme Court held the telecast was protected under *Time, Inc. v. Hill* as a newsworthy event. The Court, per WHITE, J., reversed. *Hill* was distinguishable because Zacchini's claim was based not on privacy or reputation but "in protecting the proprietary interest," an interest "closely analogous to the goals of patent and copyright law." Unlike *Hill,* the issue was not whether Zacchini's act would be available to the public: "[T]he only question is who gets to do the publishing."[c]

4. ***False news.*** Should injury to any particular person be a prerequisite to state regulation of false publications? Consider *Keeton v. Hustler Magazine, Inc.,* 465 U.S. 770 (1984): "False statements of fact harm both the subject of the falsehood *and* the readers of the statement. New Hampshire may rightly employ its libel laws to discourage the deception of its citizens." Could New Hampshire make it a criminal offense to publish false statements with knowledge of their falsity without any requirement of injury to any particular person?[d]

E. DISCLOSURE OF PRIVATE FACTS

FLORIDA STAR v. B.J.F.
491 U.S. 524, 109 S.Ct. 2603, 105 L.Ed.2d 443 (1989).

JUSTICE MARSHALL delivered the opinion of the Court.

---

c. Powell, J., joined by Brennan and Marshall, JJ., dissented, observing that there was no showing that the broadcast was a "subterfuge or cover for private or commercial exploitation." Stevens, J., dissented on procedural grounds. For commentary on the right to publicity, see J. Thomas McCarthy, The Rights of Publicity and Privacy (2d ed. 2000); Russell S. Jones, Jr., *The Flip Side of Privacy*, 39 Creigh. L.Rev. 939 (2006).

d. See Jonathan Varat, *Deception and the First Amendment: A Central, Complex, and Somewhat Curious Relationship*, 53 UCLA L.Rev. 1107, 1119–22 (2007).

Florida Stat. § 794.03 (1987) makes it unlawful to "print, publish, or broadcast [in] any instrument of mass communication" the name of the victim of a sexual offense. Pursuant to this statute, appellant The Florida Star was found civilly liable for publishing the name of a rape victim which it had obtained from a publicly released police report. [B.J.F.] testified that she had suffered emotional distress from the publication of her name. She stated that she had heard about the article from fellow workers and acquaintances; that her mother had received several threatening phone calls from a man who stated that he would rape B.J.F. again; and that these events had forced B.J.F. to change her phone number and residence, to seek police protection, and to obtain mental health counseling. [The jury] awarded B.J.F. $75,000 in compensatory damages and $25,000 in punitive damages. * * *

[We do not] accept appellant's invitation to hold broadly that truthful publication may never be punished consistent with the First Amendment. Our cases have carefully eschewed reaching this ultimate question, mindful that the future may bring scenarios which prudence counsels our not resolving anticipatorily. See, e.g., *Near v. Minnesota*, [Section 4, I, B] (hypothesizing "publication of the sailing dates of transports or the number and location of troops"); see also *Garrison v. Louisiana* (endorsing absolute defense of truth "where discussion of public affairs is concerned," but leaving unsettled the constitutional implications of truthfulness "in the discrete area of purely private libels"). Indeed, in [*Cox Broadcasting v. Cohn*, 420 U.S. 469 (1975)], we pointedly refused to answer even the less sweeping question "whether truthful publications may ever be subjected to civil or criminal liability" for invading "an area of privacy" defined by the State. [We] continue to believe that the sensitivity and significance of the interests presented in clashes between First Amendment and privacy rights counsel relying on limited principles that sweep no more broadly than the appropriate context of the instant case.

In our view, this case is appropriately analyzed with reference to such a limited First Amendment principle. It is the one, in fact, which we articulated in *Smith v. Daily Mail Pub. Co.*, [Ch. 5, I] in our synthesis of prior cases involving attempts to punish truthful publication: "[I]f a newspaper lawfully obtains truthful information about a matter of public significance then state officials may not constitutionally punish publication of the information, absent a need to further a state interest of the highest order."[a] * * *

Applied to the instant case, the *Daily Mail* principle clearly commands reversal. The first inquiry is whether the newspaper "lawfully obtain[ed] truthful information about a matter of public significance." It is undisputed that the news article describing the assault on B.J.F. was accurate. In

---

a. Suppose a newspaper publishes the name of a confidential source who it believes has misled it for political reasons and suppose the source sues the newspaper for breach of contract? Should the *Daily Mail* principle apply? See *Cohen v. Cowles Media Co.*, 501 U.S. 663 (1991). Should the *Daily Mail* principle apply in copyright cases?

addition, appellant lawfully obtained B.J.F.'s name. Appellee's argument to the contrary is based on the fact that under Florida law, police reports which reveal the identity of the victim of a sexual offense are not among the matters of "public record" which the public, by law, is entitled to inspect. But the fact that state officials are not required to disclose such reports does not make it unlawful for a newspaper to receive them when furnished by the government. Nor does the fact that the Department apparently failed to fulfill its obligation under § 794.03 not to "cause or allow to [be] published" the name of a sexual offense victim make the newspaper's ensuing receipt of this information unlawful. Even assuming the Constitution permitted a State to proscribe *receipt* of information, Florida has not taken this step. It is, clear, furthermore, that the news article concerned "a matter of public significance[.]" That is, the article generally, as opposed to the specific identity contained within it, involved a matter of paramount public import: the commission, and investigation, of a violent crime which had been reported to authorities.

The second inquiry is whether imposing liability on appellant pursuant to § 794.03 serves "a need to further a state interest of the highest order." Appellee argues that a rule punishing publication furthers three closely related interests: the privacy of victims of sexual offenses; the physical safety of such victims, who may be targeted for retaliation if their names become known to their assailants; and the goal of encouraging victims of such crimes to report these offenses without fear of exposure.

At a time in which we are daily reminded of the tragic reality of rape, it is undeniable that these are highly significant interests. [We] accordingly do not rule out the possibility that, in a proper case, imposing civil sanctions for publication of the name of a rape victim might be so overwhelmingly necessary to advance these interests as to satisfy the *Daily Mail* standard. For three independent reasons, however, imposing liability for publication under the circumstances of this case is too precipitous a means of advancing these interests to convince us that there is a "need" within the meaning of the *Daily Mail* formulation for Florida to take this extreme step.

First is the manner in which appellant obtained the identifying information in question. [B.J.F.'s] identity would never have come to light were it not for the erroneous, if inadvertent, inclusion by the Department of her full name in an incident report made available in a press room open to the public. [Where] as here, the government has failed to police itself in disseminating information, it is clear [that] the imposition of damages against the press for its subsequent publication can hardly be said to be a narrowly tailored means of safeguarding anonymity.

That appellant gained access to the information in question through a government news release makes it especially likely that, if liability were to be imposed, self-censorship would result. Reliance on a news release is a paradigmatically "routine newspaper reporting techniqu[e]." The government's issuance of such a release, without qualification, can only convey to recipients that the government considered dissemination lawful, and indeed expected the recipients to disseminate the information further. Had appellant merely reproduced the news release prepared and released by the Department, imposing civil damages would surely violate the First Amendment. The fact that appellant converted the police report into a news story by adding the linguistic connecting tissue necessary to transform the report's facts into full sentences cannot change this result.

A second problem with Florida's imposition of liability for publication is the broad sweep of the negligence per se standard applied under the civil cause of action implied from § 794.03. Unlike claims based on the common law tort of invasion of privacy, civil actions based on § 794.03 require no case-by-case findings that the disclosure of a fact about a person's private life was one that a reasonable person would find highly offensive. On the contrary, under the per se theory of negligence adopted by the courts below, liability follows automatically from publication. This is so regardless of whether the identity of the victim is already known throughout the community; whether the victim has voluntarily called public attention to the offense; or whether the identity of the victim has otherwise become a reasonable subject of public concern—because, perhaps, questions have arisen whether the victim fabricated an assault by a particular person. Nor is there a scienter requirement of any kind under § 794.03, engendering the perverse result that truthful publications challenged pursuant to this cause of action are less protected by the First Amendment than even the least protected defamatory falsehoods: those involving purely private figures, where liability is evaluated under a standard, usually applied by a jury, of ordinary negligence. See *Gertz.*
* * *

Third, and finally, the facial underinclusiveness of § 794.03 raises serious doubts about whether Florida is, in fact, serving, with this statute, the significant interests which appellee invokes in support of affirmance. Section 794.03 prohibits the publication of identifying information only if this information appears in an "instrument of mass communication," a term the statute does not define. Section 794.03 does not prohibit the spread by other means of the identities of victims of sexual offenses. An individual who maliciously spreads word of the identity of a rape victim is thus not covered, despite the fact that the communication of such information to persons who live near, or work with, the victim may have consequences equally devastating as the exposure of her name to large numbers of strangers.

When a State attempts the extraordinary measure of punishing truthful publication in the name of privacy, it must demonstrate its commitment to advancing this interest by applying its prohibition evenhandedly, to the small-time disseminator as well as the media giant. Where important First Amendment interests are at stake, the mass scope of disclosure is not an acceptable surrogate for injury. Without more careful and inclusive precautions against alternative forms of dissemination, we cannot conclude that Florida's selective ban on publication by the mass media satisfactorily accomplishes its stated purpose.

Our holding today is limited. We do not hold that truthful publication is automatically constitutionally protected, or that there is no zone of personal privacy within which the State may protect the individual from intrusion by the press, or even that a State may never punish publication of the name of a victim of a sexual offense. We hold only that where a newspaper publishes truthful information which it has lawfully obtained, punishment may lawfully be imposed, if at all, only when narrowly tailored to a state interest of the highest order, and that no such interest is satisfactorily served by imposing liability under § 794.03 to appellant under the facts of this case. * * *

JUSTICE SCALIA, concurring in part and concurring in the judgment.

I think it sufficient to decide this case to rely upon the third ground set forth in the Court's opinion: that a law cannot be regarded as protecting an interest "of the highest order" and thus as justifying a restriction upon truthful speech, when it leaves appreciable damage to that supposedly vital interest unprohibited. In the present case, I would anticipate that the rape victim's discomfort at the dissemination of news of her misfortune among friends and acquaintances would be at least as great as her discomfort at its publication by the media to people to whom she is only a name. Yet the law in question does not prohibit the former in either oral or written form. Nor is it at all clear, as I think it must be to validate this statute, that Florida's general privacy law would prohibit such gossip. Nor, finally, is it credible that the interest meant to be served by the statute is the protection of the victim against a rapist still at large—an interest that arguably would extend only to mass publication. There would be little reason to limit a statute with that objective to rape alone; or to extend it to all rapes, whether or not the felon has been apprehended and confined. In any case, the instructions here did not require the jury to find that the rapist was at large.

This law has every appearance of a prohibition that society is prepared to impose upon the press but not upon itself. Such a prohibition does not protect an interest "of the highest order." For that reason, I agree that the judgment of the court below must be reversed.

JUSTICE WHITE, with whom THE CHIEF JUSTICE and JUSTICE O'CONNOR join, dissenting.

"Short of homicide, [rape] is the 'ultimate violation of self.'" *Coker v. Georgia,* [433 U.S. 584 (1977)] (opinion of White, J.). For B.J.F., however, the violation she suffered at a rapist's knife-point marked only the beginning of her ordeal. [Yet] today, the Court holds that a jury award of $75,000 to compensate B.J.F. for the harm she suffered due to the Star's negligence is at odds with the First Amendment. I do not accept this result.

[T]he three "independent reasons" the Court cites for reversing the judgment for B.J.F. [do not] support its result.

The first of these reasons [is] the fact "appellant gained access to [B.J.F.'s name] through a government news release." [But the] "release" of information provided by the government was not, as the Court says, "without qualification." As the Star's own reporter conceded at trial, the crime incident report that inadvertently included B.J.F.'s name was posted in a room that contained signs making it clear that the names of rape victims were not matters of public record, and were not to be published. The Star's reporter indicated that she understood that she "[was not] allowed to take down that information" (i.e., B.J.F.'s name) and that she "[was] not supposed to take the information from the police department." Thus, by her own admission the posting of the incident report did not convey to the Star's reporter the idea that "the government considered dissemination lawful"; the Court's suggestion to the contrary is inapt. * * *

Unfortunately, as this case illustrates, mistakes happen: even when States take measures to "avoid" disclosure, sometimes rape victim's names are found out. As I see it, it is not too much to ask the press, in instances such as this, to respect simple standards of decency and refrain from publishing a victim's name, address, and/or phone number.

Second, the Court complains [that] a newspaper might be found liable under the Florida courts' negligence per se theory without regard to a newspaper's scienter or degree of fault. The short answer to this complaint is that whatever merit the Court's argument might have, it is wholly inapposite here, where the jury found that appellant acted with "reckless indifference towards the rights of others," a standard far higher than the *Gertz* standard the Court urges as a constitutional minimum today.

But even taking the Court's concerns in the abstract, they miss the mark. [The] Court says that negligence per se permits a plaintiff to hold a defendant liable without a showing that the disclosure was "of a fact about a person's private life [that] a reasonable person would find highly offensive." But the point here is that the legislature—reflecting popular sentiment—has determined that disclosure of the fact that a person was raped is categorically a revelation that reasonable people find offensive. And as for the Court's suggestion that the Florida courts' theory permits liability without regard for whether the victim's identity is already known, or whether she herself has made it known—these are facts that would surely enter into the calculation of damages in such a case. In any event, none of these mitigating factors was present [here].

Third, the Court faults the Florida criminal statute for being underinclusive. [But] our cases which have struck down laws that limit or burden the press due to their underinclusiveness have involved situations where a legislature has singled out one segment of the news media or press for adverse treatment. Here, the Florida law evenhandedly covers all "instrument[s] of mass communication" no matter their form, media, content, nature or purpose. It excludes neighborhood gossips because presumably the Florida Legislature has determined that neighborhood gossips do not pose the danger and intrusion to rape victims that "instrument[s] of mass communication" do. Simply put: Florida wanted to prevent the widespread distribution of rape victim's names, and therefore enacted a statute tailored almost as precisely as possible to achieving that end. * * *

At issue in this case is whether there is any information about people, which—though true—may not be published in the press. [The] Court accepts appellant's invitation to obliterate one of the most note-worthy legal inventions of the 20th–Century: the tort of the publication of private facts. William Prosser, John Wade, & Victor Schwartz, *Torts* 951–952 (8th ed. 1988). Even if the Court's opinion does not say as much today, such obliteration will follow inevitably from the Court's conclusion here. [The] Court's ruling has been foreshadowed. In *Time, Inc. v. Hill,* we observed that—after a brief period early in this century where Brandeis' view was ascendant—the trend in "modern" jurisprudence has been to eclipse an individual's right to maintain private any truthful information that the press wished to publish. More recently, in *Cox Broadcasting,* we acknowledged the possibility that the First Amendment may prevent a State from ever subjecting the publication of truthful but private information to civil liability. Today, we hit the bottom of the slippery slope.

I would find a place to draw the line higher on the hillside: a spot high enough to protect B.J.F.'s desire for privacy and peace-of-mind in the wake of a horrible personal tragedy. There is no public interest in publishing the names, addresses, and phone numbers of persons who are the victims of crime—and no public interest in immunizing the press from liability in the rare cases where a State's efforts to protect a victim's privacy have failed. Consequently, I respectfully dissent.[5]

NOTES AND QUESTIONS

1. **First Amendment value?** Consider Gavin Phillipson, *Trial By Media: The Betrayal of the First Amendment's Purpose,* 71 Law & Contemp. Probs. 15, 21 (2008): "The glaring omission in this case was the complete absence of any attempt to ask just how and why public understanding of the criminal justice system was served by its being informed of the name and address of a particular rape victim—in other words, by the particular news report in question."

2. *Privacy: interest or right?* Consider Steven J. Heyman, *Spheres of Autonomy: Reforming the Content Neutrality Doctrine in First Amendment Jurisprudence,* 10 Wm. & Mary Bill Rts. J. 647, 684–685 (2002): "The Court's refusal to protect informational privacy may be attributed to several factors:

---

5. The Court does not address the distinct constitutional questions raised by the award of punitive damages in this case. Consequently, I do not do so either. That award is more troublesome than the compensatory award discussed above. Cf. Note, *Punitive Damages and Libel Law,* 98 Harv.L.Rev. 847 (1985).

...tegories of regulable speech; the
...mendment, the state may rarely
...modern tendency to frame First
...he right to free speech and 'state
...he issue is viewed from a rights-
...t privacy is no less deserving of
...sential aspects of the right to an
...erally should be entitled to decide
...ighly personal information to oth-
...d without consent, the subject in

...accidentally sends the press a rape
...ior sexual history of an alleged rape
...publication of the transcript or the
...vid E. Fialkow, *The Media's First
...s Right to Privacy,* 39 Suf. L.Rev. 745

...ndment preclude a privacy cause of
...e that a private person is gay? What if
...member of a board of education?[b]

...'Jack posts private details about Jill's
...a small readership. Marty, a blogger
...thousands of readers, thinks that the
...pts of Jack's post." Who should be
...niel J. Solove, *The Future of Reputation*

...ernment prohibits or provides tort relief
...information about the buying habits of
...in similar data. Constitutional? Consider
...*and Information Privacy: The Troubling
...le from Speaking About You,* 52 Stan. L.
...difficulty is that the right to information
...communication of personally identifiable
...to have the government stop you from

...ion of television programming less about
...and more about encouraging a nation of
..., but do not engage with them, people who
...ers? Do voyeuristic desires deserve substan-
...? See Clay Calvert, *The Voyeurism Value in
...17 Cardoza Arts & Ent.L.J. 273 (1999). Do

...lney Smolla, *Free Speech in an Open Society,* 137–39
...of Publicly Outing Private People,* 73 Ore.L.Rev. 159
...iable or Unwarranted Invasion of Privacy? The Private
...of Sexual Orientation,* 11 Cardozo Arts & Ent.L.J. 857
...set,* 46 U.Miami L.Rev. 413 (1992); Note, *Outing, Privacy,*
...J. 747 (1992); Note, *"Outing" and Freedom of the Press:*
...upreme Court's Categorical Jurisprudence,* 77 Corn.L.Rev.

they exploit a "weakness that drives out (or at least diminishes) public attention to official actions and policies when offered more prurient alternatives." Paul Gewirtz, *Privacy and Speech*, 2001 Sup.Ct.Rev. 139, 175.[c]

———

During the course of a cell phone conversation, the president of a local teacher's union, Kane, told his chief labor negotiator, Bartnicki: "If they're not gonna move for three percent, we're gonna have to go to their, their homes * * * To blow off their front porches, we'll have to do some work on some of those guys. (PAUSES). Really, uh, really and truthfully because this is, you know, this is bad news." The conversation was illegally intercepted by an unknown person and was sent to the head of a local taxpayer's organization, Yocum, who in turn, shared it with school board members and a local broadcaster, Vopper. Vopper played the tape on his radio show. Bartnicki and Kane brought an action against Yocum and Vopper invoking state and federal laws prohibiting the disclosure of material known to be unlawfully intercepted.

BARTNICKI v. VOPPER, 532 U.S. 514 (2001), per STEVENS, J., held the statutes unconstitutional as applied to circumstances in which the defendants played no role in the illegal acquisition of the material, their access to the conversation was obtained lawfully, and the conversation was about a public issue: "We agree with petitioners that 18 U.S.C. § 2511(1)(c), as well as its Pennsylvania analog, is in fact a content-neutral law of general applicability. [In] this case, the basic purpose of the statute at issue is to 'protec[t] the privacy of wire[, electronic,] and oral communications.' S.Rep. No. 1097, 90th Cong., 2d Sess., 66 (1968). The statute does not distinguish based on the content of the intercepted conversations, nor is it justified by reference to the content of those conversations. Rather, the communications at issue are singled out by virtue of the fact that they were illegally intercepted—by virtue of the source, rather than the subject matter.

"On the other hand, the naked prohibition against disclosures is fairly characterized as a regulation of pure speech. Unlike the prohibition against the 'use' of the contents of an illegal interception in § 2511(1)(d), subsection (c) is not a regulation of conduct. It is true that the delivery of a tape recording might be regarded as conduct, but given that the purpose of such a delivery is to provide the recipient with the text of recorded statements, it is like the delivery of a handbill or a pamphlet, and as such, it is the kind of 'speech' that the First Amendment protects.

---

c. On the relationship between privacy and public discourse, see J.M. Balkin, *How Mass Media Simulate Political Transparency*, 3 Cultural Values 393 (1999); Lee Bollinger, *Images of a Free Press* 34–35 (1991); Lili Levi, *Challenging the Autonomous Press*, 78 Cornell L.Rev. 665, 669–700 (1993); Robert. F. Nagel, *Privacy and Celebrity: An Essay on the Nationalization of Intimacy*, 33 U.Rich.L.Rev. 1121 (2000); Sean M. Scott, *The Hidden First Amendment Values of Privacy*, 71 Wash.L.Rev. 683 (1996); Neil M. Richards, *The Puzzle of Brandeis, Privacy, and Speech*, 63 Vand. L.Rev. 1295 (2010).

"[As] a general matter, 'state action to punish the publication of truthful information seldom can satisfy constitutional standards.' *Daily Mail*. [The] Government identifies two interests served by the statute— first, the interest in removing an incentive for parties to intercept private conversations, and second, the interest in minimizing the harm to persons whose conversations have been illegally intercepted. We assume that those interests adequately justify the prohibition in § 2511(1)(d) against the interceptor's own use of information that he or she acquired by violating § 2511(1)(a), but it by no means follows that punishing disclosures of lawfully obtained information of public interest by one not involved in the initial illegality is an acceptable means of serving those ends.

"The normal method of deterring unlawful conduct is to impose an appropriate punishment on the person who engages in it. If the sanctions that presently attach to a violation of § 2511(1)(a) do not provide sufficient deterrence, perhaps those sanctions should be made more severe. But it would be quite remarkable to hold that speech by a law-abiding possessor of information can be suppressed in order to deter conduct by a non-law-abiding third party.[a]

"[With] only a handful of exceptions, the violations of § 2511(1)(a) that have been described in litigated cases have been motivated by either financial gain or domestic disputes. In virtually all of those cases, the identity of the person or persons intercepting the communication has been known. Moreover, petitioners cite no evidence that Congress viewed the prohibition against disclosures as a response to the difficulty of identifying persons making improper use of scanners and other surveillance devices and accordingly of deterring such conduct, and there is no empirical evidence to support the assumption that the prohibition against disclosures reduces the number of illegal interceptions.

"Although this case demonstrates that there may be an occasional situation in which an anonymous scanner will risk criminal prosecution by passing on information without any expectation of financial reward or public praise, surely this is the exceptional case. Moreover, there is no basis for assuming that imposing sanctions upon respondents will deter the unidentified scanner from continuing to engage in surreptitious interceptions. Unusual cases fall far short of a showing that there is a 'need of the highest order' for a rule supplementing the traditional means of deterring antisocial conduct. The justification for any such novel burden on expression must be 'far stronger than mere speculation about serious harms.' Accordingly, the Government's first suggested justification for applying § 2511(1)(c) to an otherwise innocent disclosure of public information is plainly insufficient.[19]

---

a. The Court recognized some exceptional cases, but stated the speech implicated was of minimal value, *New York v. Ferber*, Ch. 1, VI, A, infra (child pornography), or did not involve a prohibition of speech (possession or receipt of stolen mail or other property).

19. Our holding, of course, does not apply to punishing parties for obtaining the relevant information unlawfully. "It would be frivolous to assert—and no one does in these cases—that the First Amendment, in the interest of securing news or otherwise, confers a license on either the

"The Government's second argument, however, is considerably stronger. Privacy of communication is an important interest, [and] the fear of public disclosure of private conversations might well have a chilling effect on private speech. [Accordingly], it seems to us that there are important interests to be considered on both sides of the constitutional calculus. In considering that balance, we acknowledge that some intrusions on privacy are more offensive than others, and that the disclosure of the contents of a private conversation can be an even greater intrusion on privacy than the interception itself. As a result, there is a valid independent justification for prohibiting such disclosures by persons who lawfully obtained access to the contents of an illegally intercepted message, even if that prohibition does not play a significant role in preventing such interceptions from occurring in the first place.

"We need not decide whether that interest is strong enough to justify the application of § 2511(c) to disclosures of trade secrets or domestic gossip or other information of purely private concern. In other words, the outcome of the case does not turn on whether § 2511(1)(c) may be enforced with respect to most violations of the statute without offending the First Amendment. The enforcement of that provision in this case, however, implicates the core purposes of the First Amendment because it imposes sanctions on the publication of truthful information of public concern.

"In this case, privacy concerns give way when balanced against the interest in publishing matters of public importance. [The] months of negotiations over the proper level of compensation for teachers at the Wyoming Valley West High School were unquestionably a matter of public concern, and respondents were clearly engaged in debate about that concern. That debate may be more mundane than the Communist rhetoric that inspired Justice Brandeis' classic opinion in *Whitney v. California*, but it is no less worthy of constitutional protection."

BREYER, J., joined by O'Connor, J., concurred: "I write separately to explain why, in my view, the Court's holding does not imply a significantly broader constitutional immunity for the media.

"[As] a general matter, despite the statutes' direct restrictions on speech, the Federal Constitution must tolerate laws of this kind because of the importance of these privacy and speech-related objectives. [Nonetheless], looked at more specifically, the statutes, as applied in these circumstances, do not reasonably reconcile the competing constitutional objectives. Rather, they disproportionately interfere with media freedom. For one thing, the broadcasters here engaged in no unlawful activity other than the ultimate publication of the information another had previously obtained. [For] another thing, the speakers had little or no legitimate interest in maintaining the privacy of the particular conversation. That

---

reporter or his news sources to violate valid criminal laws. Although stealing documents or private wiretapping could provide newsworthy information, neither reporter nor source is immune from conviction for such conduct, whatever the impact on the flow of news." *Branzburg.*

conversation involved a suggestion about 'blow[ing] off ... front porches' and 'do[ing] some work on some of these guys,' thereby raising a significant concern for the safety of others. Where publication of private information constitutes a wrongful act, the law recognizes a privilege allowing the reporting of threats to public safety. [Even] where the danger may have passed by the time of publication, that fact cannot legitimize the speaker's earlier privacy expectation. Nor should editors, who must make a publication decision quickly, have to determine present or continued danger before publishing this kind of threat.

"Further, the speakers themselves, the president of a teacher's union and the union's chief negotiator, were 'limited public figures,' for they voluntarily engaged in a public controversy. They thereby subjected themselves to somewhat greater public scrutiny and had a lesser interest in privacy than an individual engaged in purely private affairs. [This] is not to say that the Constitution requires anyone, including public figures, to give up entirely the right to private communication, i.e., communication free from telephone taps or interceptions. But the subject matter of the conversation at issue here is far removed from that in situations where the media publicizes truly private matters.

"Thus, in finding a constitutional privilege to publish unlawfully intercepted conversations of the kind here at issue, the Court does not create a 'public interest' exception that swallows up the statutes' privacy-protecting general rule. Rather, it finds constitutional protection for publication of intercepted information of a special kind. Here, the speakers' legitimate privacy expectations are unusually low, and the public interest in defeating those expectations is unusually high."

Rehnquist, C.J., joined by Scalia and Thomas, JJ., dissented: "Technology now permits millions of important and confidential conversations to occur through a vast system of electronic networks. These advances, however, raise significant privacy concerns. We are placed in the uncomfortable position of not knowing who might have access to our personal and business e-mails, our medical and financial records, or our cordless and cellular telephone conversations. In an attempt to prevent some of the most egregious violations of privacy, the United States, the District of Columbia, and 40 States have enacted laws prohibiting the intentional interception and knowing disclosure of electronic communications. The Court holds that all of these statutes violate the First Amendment insofar as the illegally intercepted conversation touches upon a matter of 'public concern,' an amorphous concept that the Court does not even attempt to define. But the Court's decision diminishes, rather than enhances, the purposes of the First Amendment: chilling the speech of the millions of Americans who rely upon electronic technology to communicate each day.
* * *

"The Court correctly observes that these are 'content-neutral law[s] of general applicability' which serve recognized interests of the 'highest order': 'the interest in individual privacy [and] in fostering private speech.' It nonetheless subjects these laws to the strict scrutiny normally reserved for governmental attempts to censor different viewpoints or ideas. There is scant support, either in precedent or in reason, for the Court's tacit application of strict scrutiny.

"[Here], Congress and the Pennsylvania Legislature have acted 'without reference to the content of the regulated speech.' There is no intimation that these laws seek 'to suppress unpopular ideas or information or manipulate the public debate' or that they 'distinguish favored speech from disfavored speech on the basis of the ideas or views expressed.' [As] the concerns motivating strict scrutiny are absent, these content-neutral restrictions upon speech need pass only intermediate scrutiny.

"[I]t is obvious that the *Daily Mail* cases upon which the Court relies do not address the question presented here. Our decisions themselves made this clear: 'The *Daily Mail* principle does not settle the issue whether, in cases where information has been acquired unlawfully by a newspaper or by a source, the government may ever punish not only the unlawful acquisition, but the ensuing publication as well.' *Florida Star.* [Undaunted], the Court places an inordinate amount of weight upon the fact that the receipt of an illegally intercepted communication has not been criminalized. But this hardly renders those who knowingly receive and disclose such communications 'law-abiding,' and it certainly does not bring them under the *Daily Mail* principle. The transmission of the intercepted communication from the eavesdropper to the third party is itself illegal; and where, as here, the third party then knowingly discloses that communication, another illegal act has been committed. The third party in this situation cannot be likened to the reporters in the *Daily Mail* cases, who lawfully obtained their information through consensual interviews or public documents. * * *

"The 'dry up the market' theory, which posits that it is possible to deter an illegal act that is difficult to police by preventing the wrongdoer from enjoying the fruits of the crime, is neither novel nor implausible. It is a time-tested theory that undergirds numerous laws, such as the prohibition of the knowing possession of stolen goods. See 2 W. LaFave & A. Scott, *Substantive Criminal Law* § 8.10(a), p. 422 (1986) ("Without such receivers, theft ceases to be profitable. It is obvious that the receiver must be a principal target of any society anxious to stamp out theft in its various forms"). We ourselves adopted the exclusionary rule based upon similar reasoning, believing that it would 'deter unreasonable searches,' *Oregon v. Elstad*, 470 U.S. 298, 306 (1985), by removing an officer's 'incentive to disregard [the Fourth Amendment],' *Elkins v. United States*, 364 U.S. 206, 217 (1960). * * * Reliance upon the 'dry up the market' theory is both logical and eminently reasonable, and our precedents make plain that it is 'far stronger than mere speculation.'

"These statutes also protect the important interests of deterring clandestine invasions of privacy and preventing the involuntary broadcast of private communications. [These] statutes undeniably protect this venerable right of privacy. [The] Court concludes that the private conversation between Gloria Bartnicki and Anthony Kane is somehow a 'debate * * * worthy of constitutional protection.' Perhaps the Court is correct that '[i]f the statements about the labor negotiations had been made in a public arena—during a bargaining session, for example—they would have been newsworthy.' The point, however, is that Bartnicki and Kane had no intention of contributing to a public 'debate' at all, and it is perverse to hold that another's unlawful interception and knowing disclosure of their conversation is speech 'worthy of constitutional protection.' * * *

"The Constitution should not protect the involuntary broadcast of personal conversations. Even where the communications involve public figures or concern public matters, the conversations are nonetheless private and worthy of protection. Although public persons may have forgone the right to live their lives screened from public scrutiny in some areas, it does not and should not follow that they also have abandoned their right to have a private conversation without fear of it being intentionally intercepted and knowingly disclosed."

NOTES AND QUESTIONS

1. **The free speech value of privacy**. Consider Daniel J. Solove, *Understanding Privacy*, 143 (2008): "Although protecting against disclosure can limit free speech, disclosure protections can promote the same interests free speech furthers. * * * Privacy encourages uninhibited speech by enabling individuals to direct frank communications to those people they trust and who will not cause them harm because of what they [say]. Without protections against disclosure, people might be more reluctant to criticize aspects of their public lives, such as their employers." Solove also argues that disclosure inhibits autonomy, self-development, freedom of association, and the reading and consumption of ideas.

2. **The value of a narrow audience**. Consider Paul Gewirtz, *Privacy and Speech*, 2001 Supreme Court Review 139, 167 (2001): " 'Private speech' might be related to public issues or might be preparation for an ultimately more 'public' formulation, but its value does not depend only on that, and that is not the primary reason we protect it from disclosure. We protect its privateness. We protect the right to choose a narrow audience, or no audience except oneself—to be what William Carlos Williams called 'lonely, lonely,' and as such to be 'the happy genius of my household.' "

3. **The right to tell the truth**. Consider Rodney A. Smolla, *Information as Contraband: The First Amendment and Liability for Trafficking in Speech*, 96 Nw. U.L. Rev. 1099, 1126 (2002): "The truism that truth is presumptively protected under the First Amendment is, like most truisms, true only as far as it goes. The 'right to print the truth' cases presented a formidable analytic problem for those seeking to justify Title III, but they were by no means self-evidently invincible. First, the *Daily Mail* principle clearly did not apply all the time. [If] the First Amendment were understood to create a presumptive right to publish anything that might be deemed 'true,' legal recourse for a vast array of injuries effectuated through the revelation of truthful material

would be eviscerated, from the revelation of trade secrets to disclosure of information that one is contractually bound to keep confidential."[b]

4. **Public/private.** If the Court doubted the wisdom of distinguishing between matters of public and private concern in *Gertz*, is it wiser here? Can the Court adequately distinguish between the two? If it can, "should we be happy about placing final editorial review in the hands of judges who, after all, are agents of the government." Randall Bezanson, *How Free Can the Press Be?* 208 (2003).

5. **The right to joke in private.** Jeffrey Rosen, *The Purposes of Privacy: A Response*, 89 Geo. L.J. 2136–2137 (2001): "Of course Kane was not serious when he talked about blowing off the front porches of his opponents; he was engaging in the kind of hyperbole that many of us use in private to shock or amuse friends with our heretical thoughts, and so forth. Instead of putting the conversation in context, however, Vopper, the host of the radio station, exacerbated the danger of misunderstanding by airing the tape repeatedly on his show for three days, spicing up the broadcast with harsh criticism of the union leaders."

III. OWNERSHIP OF SPEECH

Former President Ford had contracted with Harper & Row and Readers Digest to publish his memoirs and granted them the right to license prepublication excerpts concentrating on his pardon of former President Nixon. Some weeks before a licensed article in Time was to appear, an unknown person presented the editor of The Nation with an unauthorized copy of the 200,000 word Ford manuscript from which the editor wrote a 2,250 word article entitled, "The Ford Memoirs—Behind the Nixon Pardon." The article included 26 verbatim quotations totaling 300 words of Ford's copyrighted expression and was timed to scoop Time. Accordingly, Time cancelled its article and refused to pay the publishers the remaining half of its $25,000 contract price.

In defense against the publishers' copyright claim, The Nation maintained that its publication was protected by the fair use provision of the Copyright Revision Act of 1976, 17 U.S.C. § 107 and by the First Amendment. HARPER & ROW v. NATION ENTERPRISES, 471 U.S. 539 (1985), per O'CONNOR, J., concluded that neither defense was viable and that the fair use provision properly accommodated the relevant First Amendment interests: "Article I, § 8, of the Constitution provides that: 'The Congress shall have Power * * * to Promote the Progress of Science and useful Arts, by securing for limited Times to Authors and Inventors the exclusive Right to their respective Writings and Discoveries.' '[This] limited grant is a means by which an important public purpose may be achieved. It is intended to motivate the creative activity of authors and inventors by the provision of a special reward, and to allow the public access to the products of their genius after the limited period of exclusive control has expired.' The monopoly created by copyright thus rewards the

---

b.   See also Howard M. Wasserman, *Bartnicki as Lockner,* 33 N.Ky.L. Rev. 421 (2006).

individual author in order to benefit the public. This principle applies equally to works of fiction and nonfiction. The book at issue here, for example, was two years in the making, and began with a contract giving the author's copyright to the publishers in exchange for their services in producing and marketing the work. In preparing the book, Mr. Ford drafted essays and word portraits of public figures and participated in hundreds of taped interviews that were later distilled to chronicle his personal viewpoint. It is evident that the monopoly granted by copyright actively served its intended purpose of inducing the creation of new material of potential historical value.

"Section 106 of the Copyright Act confers a bundle of exclusive rights to the owner of the copyright. [T]hese rights—to publish, copy, and distribute the author's work—vest in the author of an original work from the time of its creation. In practice, the author commonly sells his rights to publishers who offer royalties in exchange for their services in producing and marketing the author's work. The copyright owner's rights, however, are subject to certain statutory exceptions. Among these is § 107 which codifies the traditional privilege of other authors to make 'fair use' of an earlier writer's work.[1] In addition, no author may copyright facts or ideas. § 102. The copyright is limited to those aspects of the work— termed 'expression'—that display the stamp of the author's originality.

"[T]here is no dispute that the unpublished manuscript of 'A Time to Heal,' as a whole, was protected by § 106 from unauthorized reproduction. Nor do respondents dispute that verbatim copying of excerpts of the manuscript's original form of expression would constitute infringement unless excused as fair use. Yet copyright does not prevent subsequent users from copying from a prior author's work those constituent elements that are not original—for example, quotations borrowed under the rubric of fair use from other copyrighted works, facts, or materials in the public domain—as long as such use does not unfairly appropriate the author's original contributions. Perhaps the controversy between the lower courts in this case over copyrightability is more aptly styled a dispute over whether The Nation's appropriation of unoriginal and uncopyrightable elements encroached on the originality embodied in the work as a whole. Especially in the realm of factual narrative, the law is currently unsettled

---

1. Section 107 states: "Notwithstanding the provisions of section 106, the fair use of a copyrighted work [for] purposes such as criticism, comment, news reporting, teaching (including multiple copies for classroom use), scholarship, or research, is not an infringement of copyright. In determining whether the use made of a work in any particular case is a fair use the factors to be considered shall include—

"(1) the purpose and character of the use, including whether such use is of a commercial nature or is for nonprofit educational purposes;

"(2) the nature of the copyrighted work;

"(3) the amount and substantiality of the portion used in relation to the copyrighted work as a whole; and

"(4) the effect of the use upon the potential market for or value of the copyrighted work."

[For discussion of fair use in the trademark context, see William McGeveran, *Rethinking Trademark Fair Use,* 94 Iowa L.Rev. 49 (2008)].

regarding the ways in which uncopyrightable elements combine with the author's original contributions to form protected expression.

"We need not reach these issues, however, as The Nation has admitted to lifting verbatim quotes of the author's original language [constituting] some 13% of The Nation article. [To thereby] lend authenticity to its account of the forthcoming memoirs, The Nation effectively arrogated to itself the right of first publication, an important marketable subsidiary right. For the reasons set forth below, we find that this use of the copyrighted manuscript, even stripped to the verbatim quotes conceded by The Nation to be copyrightable expression, was not a fair use within the meaning of the Copyright Act.

"[The] nature of the interest at stake is highly relevant to whether a given use is fair. [The] right of first publication implicates a threshold decision by the author whether and in what form to release his work. First publication is inherently different from other § 106 rights in that only one person can be the first publisher; as the contract with Time illustrates, the commercial value of the right lies primarily in exclusivity. [Under] ordinary circumstances, the author's right to control the first public appearance of his undisseminated expression will outweigh a claim of fair use.

"Respondents, however, contend that First Amendment values require a different rule under the circumstances of this case. [Respondents] advance the substantial public import of the subject matter of the Ford memoirs as grounds for excusing a use that would ordinarily not pass muster as a fair use—the piracy of verbatim quotations for the purpose of 'scooping' the authorized first serialization. Respondents explain their copying of Mr. Ford's expression as essential to reporting the news story it claims the book itself represents. In respondents' view, not only the facts contained in Mr. Ford's memoirs, but 'the precise manner in which [he] expressed himself was as newsworthy as what he had to say.' Respondents argue that the public's interest in learning this news as fast as possible outweighs the right of the author to control its first publication.

"The Second Circuit noted, correctly, that copyright's idea/expression dichotomy 'strike[s] a definitional balance between the First Amendment and the Copyright Act by permitting free communication of facts while still protecting an author's expression.' No author may copyright his ideas or the facts he narrates.

"Respondents' theory, however, would expand fair use to effectively destroy any expectation of copyright protection in the work of a public figure. Absent such protection, there would be little incentive to create or profit in financing such memoirs and the public would be denied an important source of significant historical information. The promise of copyright would be an empty one if it could be avoided merely by dubbing the infringement a fair use 'news report' of the book. * * *

"In our haste to disseminate news, it should not be forgotten that the Framers intended copyright itself to be the engine of free expression. By establishing a marketable right to the use of one's expression, copyright supplies the economic incentive to create and disseminate ideas. * * *

"Moreover, freedom of thought and expression 'includes both the right to speak freely and the right to refrain from speaking at all.' We do not suggest this right not to speak would sanction abuse of the copyright owner's monopoly as an instrument to suppress facts. [But] 'the essential thrust of the First Amendment is to prohibit improper restraints on the *voluntary* public expression of ideas; it shields the man who wants to speak or publish when others wish him to be quiet. There is necessarily, and within suitably defined areas, a concomitant freedom *not* to speak publicly, one which serves the same ultimate end as freedom of speech in its affirmative aspect.' *Estate of Hemingway v. Random House, Inc.*, 23 N.Y.2d 341, 348, 296 N.Y.S.2d 771, 776, 244 N.E.2d 250, 255 (1968). * * *

"In view of the First Amendment protections already embodied in the Copyright Act's distinction between copyrightable expression and uncopyrightable facts and ideas, and the latitude for scholarship and comment traditionally afforded by fair use, we see no warrant for expanding the doctrine of fair use to create what amounts to a public figure exception to copyright. Whether verbatim copying from a public figure's manuscript in a given case is or is not fair must be judged according to the traditional equities of fair use."

In assessing the equities, the Court found the purpose of the article to count against fair use, noting that the publication "went beyond simply reporting uncopyrightable information" and made "a 'news event' out of its unauthorized first publication," that the publication was "commercial as opposed to non-profit," that The Nation intended to supplant the "right of first publication," and that it acted in bad faith, for it "knowingly exploited a purloined manuscript." In considering the nature of the copyrighted work, the Court found it significant not only that Ford's work was yet unpublished, but also that The Nation had focused "on the most expressive elements of the work" in a way that exceeded "that necessary to disseminate the facts" and in a "clandestine" fashion that afforded no "opportunity for creative or quality control" by the copyright holder. In evaluating the amount and substantiality of the portion used, the Court cited the district court finding that "The Nation took what was essentially the heart of the book" and pointed to the "expressive value of the excerpts and their key role in the infringing work." Finally, the Court observed that the effect of the use on the market for the copyrighted work was the most important element. It found the Time contract cancellation to be "clear cut evidence of actual damage."

BRENNAN, J., joined by White and Marshall, JJ., dissented: "When The Nation was not quoting Mr. Ford, [its] efforts to convey the historical information in the Ford manuscript did not so closely and substantially track Mr. Ford's language and structure as to constitute an appropriation of literary form.

"[The] Nation is thus liable in copyright only if the quotation of 300 words infringed any of Harper & Row's exclusive rights under § 106 of the Act. [Limiting] the inquiry to the propriety of a subsequent author's use of the copyright owner's literary form is not easy in the case of a work of history. Protection against only substantial appropriation of literary form does not ensure historians a return commensurate with the full value of their labors. The literary form contained in works like 'A Time to Heal' reflects only a part of the labor that goes into the book. It is the labor of collecting, sifting, organizing and reflecting that predominates in the creation of works of history such as this one. The value this labor produces lies primarily in the information and ideas revealed, and not in the particular collocation of words through which the information and ideas are expressed. Copyright thus does not protect that which is often of most value in a work of history and courts must resist the tendency to reject the fair use defense on the basis of their feeling that an author of history has been deprived of the full value of his or her labor. A subsequent author's taking of information and ideas is in no sense piratical because copyright law simply does not create any property interest in information and ideas.

"The urge to compensate for subsequent use of information and ideas is perhaps understandable. An inequity seems to lurk in the idea that much of the fruit of the historian's labor may be used without compensation. This, however, is not some unforeseen by-product of a statutory scheme intended primarily to ensure a return for works of the imagination. Congress made the affirmative choice that the copyright laws should apply in this way: 'Copyright does not preclude others from using the ideas or information revealed by the author's work. It pertains to the literary [form] in which the author expressed intellectual concepts.' This distinction is at the essence of copyright. The copyright laws serve as the 'engine of free expression,' only when the statutory monopoly does not choke off multifarious indirect uses and consequent broad dissemination of information and ideas. To ensure the progress of arts and sciences and the integrity of First Amendment values, ideas and information must not be freighted with claims of proprietary right.[13]

"In my judgment, the Court's fair use analysis has fallen to the temptation to find copyright violation based on a minimal use of literary form in order to provide compensation for the appropriation of information from a work of history."

Since news reporting is ordinarily conducted for profit and marked by attempts to "scoop" the opposition and by attempts to create "news events," Brennan, J., found the drawing of any negative implications from these factors to be inconsistent with congressional recognition in § 107

---

13. This congressional limitation on the scope of copyright does not threaten the production of history. That this limitation results in significant diminution of economic incentives is far from apparent. In any event noneconomic incentives motivate much historical research and writing. For example, former public officials often have great incentive to "tell their side of the story." And much history is the product of academic scholarship. Perhaps most importantly, the urge to preserve the past is as old as human kind.

that news reporting is a prime example of fair use. He found reliance on bad faith to be equally unwarranted: "No court has found that The Nation possessed the Ford manuscript illegally or in violation of any common law interest of Harper & Row; all common law causes of action have been abandoned or dismissed in this case. Even if the manuscript had been 'purloined' by someone, nothing in this record imputes culpability to The Nation. On the basis of the record in this case, the most that can be said is that The Nation made use of the contents of the manuscript knowing the copyright owner would not sanction the use.

"[T]he Court purports to rely on [the] factual findings that The Nation had taken 'the heart of the book.' This reliance is misplaced, and would appear to be another result of the Court's failure to distinguish between information and literary form. When the District Court made this finding, it was evaluating not the quoted words at issue here but the 'totality' of the information and reflective commentary in the Ford work. The vast majority of what the District Court considered the heart of the Ford work, therefore, consisted of ideas and information The Nation was free to use. It may well be that, as a qualitative matter, most of the value of the manuscript did lie in the information and ideas the Nation used. But appropriation of the 'heart' of the manuscript in this sense is irrelevant to copyright analysis because copyright does not preclude a second author's use of information and ideas.

"At least with respect to the six particular quotes of Mr. Ford's observations and reflections about President Nixon, I agree with the Court's conclusion that The Nation appropriated some literary form of substantial quality. I do not agree, however, that the substantiality of the expression taken was clearly excessive or inappropriate to The Nation's news reporting purpose.

"Had these quotations been used in the context of a critical book review of the Ford work, there is little question that such a use would be fair use within the meaning of § 107 of the Act. The amount and substantiality of the use—in both quantitative and qualitative terms— would have certainly been appropriate to the purpose of such a use. It is difficult to see how the use of these quoted words in a news report is less appropriate.

"The Nation's publication indisputably precipitated Time's eventual cancellation. But that does not mean that The Nation's use of the 300 quoted words caused this injury to Harper & Row. Wholly apart from these quoted words, The Nation published significant information and ideas from the Ford manuscript. [If] The Nation competed with Time, the competition was not for a share of the market in excerpts of literary form but for a share of the market in the new information in the Ford work.
* * *

"Because The Nation was the first to convey the information in this case, it did perhaps take from Harper & Row some of the value that publisher sought to garner for itself through the contractual arrangement with Ford and the license to Time. Harper & Row had every right to seek to monopolize revenue from that potential market through contractual arrangements but it has no right to set up copyright [as] a shield from competition in that market because copyright does not protect information. The Nation had every right to seek to be the first to publish that information. * * *

"The Court's exceedingly narrow approach to fair use permits Harper & Row to monopolize information. This holding 'effect[s] an important extension of property rights and a corresponding curtailment in the free use of knowledge and of ideas.' The Court has perhaps advanced the ability of the historian—or at least the public official who has recently left office—to capture the full economic value of information in his or her possession. But the Court does so only by risking the robust debate of public issues that is the 'essence of self-government.' *Garrison.* The Nation was providing the grist for that robust debate. The Court imposes liability upon The Nation for no other reason than that The Nation succeeded in being the first to provide certain information to the public."

NOTES AND QUESTIONS

1. ***Copyright and content discrimination.*** Consider C. Edwin Baker, *First Amendment Limits on Copyright*, 55 Vand. L. Rev. 891, 927, 931 (2002): "Copyright's policy concern arises only because the audience of purported infringers see or hear—mentally assimilate—the infringing content. If they did not—if they used the infringing material to wrap fish—the receipt of the infringing content would not (negatively) affect the market for the original content. [Nevertheless], copyright differs from typical cases of content suppression. It is designed to promote the very content—but not the same speaker—that it also suppresses. It suppresses content as a means of promoting the original creation, and presumably the subsequent commercial distribution, of the *same* content. Its aim is to have *more* of the content that, in relation to some speakers, it also suppresses." Is that aim consistently realized? Consider Rebecca Tushnet, *Copy This Essay: How Fair Use Doctrine Harms Free Speech and How Copying Serves It*, 114 Yale L.J. 535, 540–41 (2004): "Copyright is undoubtedly an engine of free expression, as it supports both large corporations and individual artists so that they can afford to be in the business of speaking. Unfortunately, however, there is not much evidence about the ideal scope of copyright or its ideal term." For a Lockean perspective on copyright, see Seana Shiffrin, Lockean Arguments for Private Intellectual Property, in *New Essays in the Legal and Political Theory of Property* 138 (Stephen Munzer, ed. 2001).

2. ***Copyright and fair use.*** Consider Jed Rubenfeld, *The Freedom of Imagination: Copyright's Constitutionality*, 112 Yale L.J. 1, 17 (2002): "Under the first factor of fair use doctrine (nature or purpose of the use), 'parodic' and 'critical' treatments of copyrighted material are highly favored. In other words, if you and I borrow exactly the same amount of material from a copyrighted work, I may escape liability because my speech criticized the copyrighted work, while you may be forced to pay damages because yours did

not. Commentators typically present the 'parody' and 'criticism' features of fair use doctrine as a First Amendment plus or even a First Amendment 'surrogate.' They do not seem to notice that it renders copyright law viewpoint-discriminatory, which, as noted earlier, amount almost everywhere else in free speech law to virtually a per se constitutional violation." Cf. Rebecca Tushnet, *Copyright as a Model for Free Speech Law: What Copyright Has in Common with Anti–Pornography Laws, Campaign Finance Reform, and Telecommunications Regulation*, 42 B.C. L. Rev. 1, 25–26 (2000): "Even without the public interest subfactor, one might wonder whether fair use is unconstitutional because it discriminates on the basis of content. Fair use favors copying, even pure copying, for educational and news reporting purposes. The Supreme Court, evaluating an anticounterfeiting law that prohibited certain reproductions of images of currency but made exceptions for newsworthiness or educational value, found that these exceptions were impermissibly content-based. There seems to be no reason that the exceptions would lose their content-based nature when applied to copyright." See also Eugene Volokh, *Freedom of Speech and Intellectual Property: Some Thoughts After Eldred, 44 Liquormart, and Bartnicki*, 40 Hous. L. Rev. 706–707 (2003). But consider Christopher L. Eisgruber, *Censorship, Copyright, and Free Speech: Some Tentative Skepticism About the Campaign to Impose First Amendment Restrictions on Copyright Law*, 2 J. Telecomm. & High Tech. L. 17, 23–24 (2003): "There is something odd about this argument. It asks us to believe that copyright law becomes worse from a First Amendment perspective because of a restriction that not only makes it less restrictive, but does so with regard to core First Amendment subjects. Indeed, First Amendment doctrine itself contains a discrimination like the one in the "fair use" provisions. Under *Times v. Sullivan* and its progeny, defendants in libel suits acquire special First Amendment protection if their speech deals with matters of public concern. It would be strange if copyright law became subject to heightened First Amendment scrutiny only because it afforded speakers protections comparable to those recommended by the First Amendment itself."

Gertz was reluctant to make ad hoc judgments as to whether statements are or are not of general or public interest. Should the Court be similarly reluctant to make ad hoc judgments as to the bona fide news purpose of an article,[a] as to whether expression goes to the "heart of the book," or whether quoted words are "necessary" to communicate the "facts"? Is there an alternative to the making of such judgments?[b]

---

a. Compare *Regan v. Time, Inc.*, 468 U.S. 641 (1984): 18 U.S.C. § 474 makes it a crime to photograph United States currency, but exceptions for articles and books for newsworthy purposes are permitted so long as certain size and color requirements are satisfied. 18 U.S.C. § 504. The Court, per White, J., invalidated the purpose requirement: "A determination concerning the newsworthiness [of] a photograph cannot help but be based on the content of the photograph and the message it delivers. [Regulations] which permit the Government to discriminate on the basis of the content of the message cannot be tolerated under the First Amendment. The purpose requirement of § 504 is therefore constitutionally infirm." Stevens, J., dissenting on this point, observed that if the Court's language were applied literally, the constitutionality of the fair use provision of the Copyright Act would be "highly suspect." See Eugene Volokh, *Freedom of Speech and Intellectual Property: Some Thoughts After Eldred, 44 Liquormart, and Bartnicki*, 40 Hous. L. Rev. 697, 706–707 (2003).

b. For additional criticism of the Court's copyright jurisprudence, see Matthew D. Bunker, *Adventures in Copyright Zone,* 14 Comm. L.& Pol'y 273 (2009); Jed Rubenfeld, *The Freedom of*

3. Melville Nimmer had argued that in most cases the idea/expression dichotomy is central to resolving the clash between copyright and the First Amendment. *Does Copyright Abridge the First Amendment Guarantees of Free Speech and Press?* 17 U.C.L.A.L.Rev. 1180 (1970). Is the distinction satisfactory? Consider *Cohen v. California,* protecting Cohen's use of the phrase "Fuck the Draft": "[W]e cannot indulge the facile assumption that one can forbid particular words without running a substantial risk of suppressing ideas in the process." Cohen's counsel was—Professor Nimmer. Does *Nimmer On Copyright* collide with *Nimmer on Freedom of Speech?* For Nimmer's answer, see id. § 2.05(c), at 72–77; § 3.04, at 28 n. 11.

———

The 1976 Copyright Act generally provided copyright protection until 50 years after an author's death. The Copyright Term Extension Act of 1998 ("CTEA") extended the term to 70 years for new and existing copyrights. ELDRED v. ASHCROFT, 537 U.S. 186 (2003), per GINSBURG, J., upheld the Act against a claim that the extended copyright protection to already existing intellectual property was unconstitutional: "Petitioners [argue] that the CTEA is a content-neutral regulation of speech that fails heightened judicial review under the First Amendment. We reject petitioners' plea for imposition of uncommonly strict scrutiny on a copyright scheme that incorporates its own speech-protective purposes and safeguards. The Copyright Clause and First Amendment were adopted close in time. This proximity indicates that, in the Framers' view, copyright's limited monopolies are compatible with free speech principles. Indeed, copyright's purpose is to *promote* the creation and publication of free expression. * * *

"In addition to spurring the creation and publication of new expression, copyright law contains built-in First Amendment accommodations. First, it distinguishes between ideas and expression and makes only the latter eligible for copyright protection. [Due] to this distinction, every idea, theory, and fact in a copyrighted work becomes instantly available for public exploitation at the moment of publication. * * *

"Second, the 'fair use' defense allows the public to use not only facts and ideas contained in a copyrighted work, but also expression itself in certain circumstances. [The] fair use defense affords considerable 'latitude for scholarship and comment,' and even for parody. The CTEA itself supplements these traditional First Amendment safeguards. First, it allows libraries, archives, and similar institutions to 'reproduce' and 'distribute, display, or perform in facsimile or digital form' copies of certain published works 'during the last 20 years of any term of copyright [for] purposes of preservation, scholarship, or research' if the work is not already being exploited commercially and further copies are unavailable at a reasonable price. Second, Title II of the CTEA, known as the Fairness in

Imagination, 112 Yale L.J. 1 (2002); Lawrence Lessig, *Copyright's First Amendment,* 48 UCLA L.Rev. 1057 (2001).

Music Licensing Act of 1998, exempts small businesses, restaurants, and like entities from having to pay performance royalties on music played from licensed radio, television, and similar facilities. * * *

"The First Amendment securely protects the freedom to make—or decline to make—one's own speech; it bears less heavily when speakers assert the right to make other people's speeches. To the extent such assertions raise First Amendment concerns, copyright's built-in free speech safeguards are generally adequate to address them. [W]hen, as in this case, Congress has not altered the traditional contours of copyright protection, further First Amendment scrutiny is unnecessary."[a]

Breyer, J., dissented: "The Copyright Clause and the First Amendment seek related objectives—the creation and dissemination of information. When working in tandem, these provisions mutually reinforce each other, the first serving as an 'engine of free expression,' the second assuring that government throws up no obstacle to its dissemination. At the same time, a particular statute that exceeds proper Copyright Clause bounds may set Clause and Amendment at cross-purposes, thereby depriving the public of the speech-related benefits that the Founders, through both, have promised. [The] majority [invokes] the 'fair use' exception, and it notes that copyright law itself is restricted to protection of a work's expression, not its substantive content. Neither the exception nor the restriction, however, would necessarily help those who wish to obtain from electronic databases material that is not there—say, teachers wishing their students to see albums of Depression Era photographs, to read the recorded words of those who actually lived under slavery, or to contrast, say, Gary Cooper's heroic portrayal of Sergeant York with filmed reality from the battlefield of Verdun. Such harm, and more, will occur despite the 1998 Act's exemptions and despite the other 'First Amendment safeguards' in which the majority places its trust. The statute falls outside the scope of legislative power that the Copyright Clause, read in light of the First Amendment, grants to Congress."[b]

Notes and Questions

1. Consider David McGowan, *Why the First Amendment Cannot Dictate*

---

a. For discussion of issues regarding the "traditional contours" of copyright law, see *Golan v. Gonzales*, 501 F.3d 1179 (10th Cir. 2007).

b. Although the majority argued that the act created incentives for the copyright holders to further invest in and disseminate their property, Breyer, J., rejoined: "This claim cannot justify this statute, however, because the rationale is inconsistent with the basic purpose of the Copyright Clause—as understood by the Framers and by this Court. The Clause assumes an initial grant of monopoly, designed primarily to encourage creation, followed by termination of the monopoly grant in order to promote dissemination of already-created works. It assumes that it is the *disappearance* of the monopoly grant, not its *perpetuation,* that will, on balance, promote the dissemination of works already in existence. This view of the Clause does not deny the empirical possibility that grant of a copyright monopoly to the heirs or successors of a long-dead author could *on occasion* help publishers resurrect the work, say, of a long-lost Shakespeare. But it does deny Congress the Copyright Clause power to base its actions primarily upon that empirical possibility—lest copyright grants become perpetual, lest on balance they restrict dissemination, lest too often they seek to bestow benefits that are solely retroactive." Stevens, J., also dissented.

Copyright Policy, 65 U. Pitt. L. Rev. 281, 286 (2004): "The Supreme Court in *Eldred* was right to imply that authors who do their own work advance some free speech values that copiers do not. Autonomy of speakers and diversity of expression are two such values. They are not the only First Amendment values, of course, but they are important. Giving upstream authors strong rights, which is what we do now, gives downstream users an incentive to do more of their own work than they would have to do if they could copy at will. Congress is not required to adopt laws that give people incentives to do their own work rather than copying others, but the First Amendment certainly does not prohibit it from doing so." See also Daniel A. Farber, *Conflicting Visions and Contested Baselines: Intellectual Property and Free Speech in the "Digital Millennium"*, 89 Minn. L. Rev. 1318, 1349 2005); But compare Rebecca Tushnet, note 1 after *Harper & Row*, at 564, 567: "First Amendment doctrine should recognize the value of copying, which can be an important part of self-definition and of participation in culture, from singing the national anthem to discussing The West Wing online in exact detail."

2.   Consider Neil Weinstock Netanel, *Copyright and a Democratic Civil Society*, 106 Yale L.J. 283, 285 (1996): "Copyright law strikes a precarious balance. To encourage authors to create and disseminate original expression, it accords them a bundle of proprietary rights in their works. But to promote public education and creative exchange, it invites audiences and subsequent authors to use existing works in every conceivable manner that falls outside the province of the copyright owner's exclusive rights." Does *Eldred* strike an appropriate balance?

3.   Consider William W. Van Alstyne, *Reconciling What the First Amendment Forbids With What the Copyright Clause Permits: A Summary Explanation and Review*, 66–SPG Law & Contemp. Probs. 238 (2003): "The clause, again, is meant to put an end to one more kind of federalism question, and on that front, it deserves to be generously interpreted and applied in what it may confide to the discretion of Congress to legislate as it thinks best to do, in preemption of various regimes that might otherwise riddle the field. It 'preempts' nothing within the protection of the First Amendment, however, and any feature of any portion of any act Congress has, or may in the future, provide under sanction of this clause, may always be brought into question respecting whether, on its face or as applied, it offends against the larger freedom of speech and of the press provided constitutional sanctuary in the First Amendment still unfolding in the United States."

IV.   OBSCENITY

A.   THE SEARCH FOR A RATIONALE

Roth v. United States, 354 U.S. 476 (1957) held that obscenity was "not within the area of constitutionally protected speech or press" because, drawing from *Chaplinsky*, such utterances were *"no essential part of any exposition of ideas, and are of such slight social value as a step to truth that any benefit that may be derived from them is clearly outweighed by the social interest in order and morality."* [Emphasis in original]. The Court determined that sexually explicit material was not necessarily obscene. Instead the question was "whether to the average person, applying contemporary community standards, the dominant theme of the material taken as a whole appeals to prurient interest." Such material, according to the Court, was "utterly without redeeming social importance."

Despite *Roth*'s view that obscene speech had no First Amendment value, *Stanley v. Georgia,* 394 U.S. 557 (1969) concluded that the First Amendment protected the possession of obscene material in the home. The Court argued that the constitutional right "to receive information and ideas, regardless of their social worth, is fundamental to our free society." The Court distinguished the public distribution of obscene materials on the ground that there was a greater danger that such material might fall into the hands of children or "intrude on the sensibilities or privacy of the general public."

Many commentators believed that *Roth* and *Stanley* left the law in an unstable position. *Roth* had insufficiently supported the view that obscenity was without constitutional value and, as interpreted, had offered an approach to defining obscenity that was difficult for prosecutors; *Stanley's* logic went further and seemed to suggest that public showings of obscene material might be constitutional if children were excluded and if individuals were not exposed to the material without informed consent. *Paris Adult Theatre,* infra, attempted to provide a rationale for the regulation of obscenity that would prevent the showing of obscene material in public theaters; *Miller,* infra, sought to loosen the definition of obscenity.

PARIS ADULT THEATRE I v. SLATON

413 U.S. 49, 93 S.Ct. 2628, 37 L.Ed.2d 446 (1973).

Chief Justice Burger delivered the opinion of the Court.

[The entrance to Paris Adult Theatres I & II was conventional and inoffensive without any pictures. Signs read: "Adult Theatre—You must be 21 and able to prove it. If viewing the nude body offends you, Please Do Not Enter." The District Attorney, nonetheless, had brought an action to enjoin the showing of two films that the Georgia Supreme Court described as "hard core pornography" leaving "little to the imagination." The Georgia Supreme Court assumed that the adult theaters in question barred minors and gave a full warning to the general public of the nature of the films involved, but held that the showing of the films was not constitutionally protected.]

[We] categorically disapprove the theory [that] obscene, pornographic films acquire constitutional immunity from state regulation simply because they are exhibited for consenting adults only. [Although we have] recognized the high importance of the state interest in regulating the exposure of obscene materials to juveniles and unconsenting adults, this Court has never declared these to be the only legitimate state interests permitting regulation of obscene material.

[W]e hold that there are legitimate state interests at stake in stemming the tide of commercialized obscenity, even assuming it is feasible to enforce effective safeguards against exposure to juveniles and to the passerby.[7] [These] include the interest of the public in the quality of life and the total community environment, the tone of commerce in the great city centers, and, possibly, the public safety itself. The Hill–Link Minority Report of the Commission on Obscenity and Pornography indicates that there is at least an arguable correlation between obscene material and crime. Quite apart from sex crimes, however, there remains one problem of large proportions aptly described by Professor Bickel: "It concerns the tone of the society, the mode, or to use terms that have perhaps greater currency, the style and quality of life, now and in the future. A man may be entitled to read an obscene book in his room, or expose himself indecently there. [We] should protect his privacy. But if he demands a right to obtain the books and pictures he wants in the market, and to foregather in public places—discreet, if you will, but accessible to all— with others who share his tastes, *then to grant him his right is to affect the world about the rest of us, and to impinge on other privacies.* Even supposing that each of us can, if he wishes, effectively avert the eye and stop the ear (which, in truth, we cannot), what is commonly read and seen and heard and done intrudes upon us all, want it or not." 22 *The Public Interest* 25, 25–26 (Winter, 1971). (Emphasis supplied.) [T]here is a "right of the Nation and of the States to maintain a decent [society]," *Jacobellis* (Warren, C.J., dissenting).

But, it is argued, there is no scientific data which conclusively demonstrates that exposure to obscene materials adversely affects men and women or their society. It is urged [that], absent such a demonstration, any kind of state regulation is "impermissible." We reject this argument. It is not for us to resolve empirical uncertainties underlying state legislation, save in the exceptional case where that legislation plainly impinges upon rights protected by the Constitution itself. [Although] there is no conclusive proof of a connection between antisocial behavior and obscene material, the legislature of Georgia could quite reasonably determine that such a connection does or might exist. In deciding *Roth,* this Court implicitly accepted that a legislature could legitimately act on such a conclusion to protect *"the social interest in order and morality."*

From the beginning of civilized societies, legislators and judges have acted on various unprovable assumptions. Such assumptions underlie much lawful state regulation of commercial and business affairs. The same

---

7. It is conceivable that an "adult" theatre can—if it really insists—prevent the exposure of its obscene wares to juveniles. An "adult" bookstore, dealing in obscene books, magazines, and pictures, cannot realistically make this claim. The Hill–Link Minority Report of the Commission on Obscenity and Pornography emphasizes evidence (the Abelson National Survey of Youth and Adults) that, although most pornography may be bought by elders, "the heavy users and most highly exposed people to pornography are adolescent females (among women) and adolescent and young males (among men)." *The Report of the Commission on Obscenity* 401 (1970). The legitimate interest in preventing exposure of juveniles to obscene materials cannot be fully served by simply barring juveniles from the immediate physical premises of "adult" bookstores, when there is a flourishing "outside business" in these materials.

is true of the federal securities, antitrust laws and a host of other federal regulations. [Likewise], when legislatures and administrators act to protect the physical environment from pollution and to preserve our resources of forests, streams and parks, they must act on such imponderables as the impact of a new highway near or through an existing park or wilderness area. [The] fact that a congressional directive reflects unprovable assumptions about what is good for the people, including imponderable aesthetic assumptions, is not a sufficient reason to find that statute unconstitutional.

If we accept the unprovable assumption that a complete education requires certain books, and the well nigh universal belief that good books, plays, and art lift the spirit, improve the mind, enrich the human personality and develop character, can we then say that a state legislature may not act on the corollary assumption that commerce in obscene books,[a] or public exhibitions focused on obscene conduct, have a tendency to exert a corrupting and debasing impact leading to antisocial behavior? [The] sum of experience, including that of the past two decades, affords an ample basis for legislatures to conclude that a sensitive, key relationship of human existence, central to family life, community welfare, and the development of human personality, can be debased and distorted by crass commercial exploitation of sex. Nothing in the Constitution prohibits a State from reaching such a conclusion and acting on it legislatively simply because there is no conclusive evidence or empirical data.

[Nothing] in this Court's decisions intimates that there is any "fundamental" privacy right "implicit in the concept of ordered liberty" to watch obscene movies in places of public accommodation. [W]e have declined to equate the privacy of the home relied on in *Stanley* with a "zone" of "privacy" that follows a distributor or a consumer of obscene materials wherever he goes.[b]

---

a. The only case after *Roth* in which the Court upheld a conviction based upon books was in *Mishkin* [Ch. 1, III, B infra] and most, if not all, of those books were illustrated. *Kaplan v. California,* 413 U.S. 115 (1973) held that books without pictures can be legally obscene "in the sense of being unprotected by the First Amendment." It observed that books are "passed hand to hand, and we can take note of the tendency of widely circulated books of this category to reach the impressionable young and have a continuing impact. A State could reasonably regard the 'hard core' conduct described by *Suite 69* as capable of encouraging or causing antisocial behavior, especially in its impact on young people." Is *Kaplan's* explanation in tension with *Butler v. Michigan* [Ch. 1, III, B infra]? Why should the obscenity standard focus on the average adult if the underlying worry is that books will fall in the hands of children?

b. In a series of cases, the Court limited *Stanley* strictly to its facts. It held that Stanley did not apply to the possession of child pornography even in the home. *Osborne v. Ohio,* 495 U.S. 103 (1990). It held that *Stanley* did not protect the mailing of obscene material to consenting adults, *United States v. Reidel,* 402 U.S. 351, 91 S.Ct. 1410, 28 L.Ed.2d 813 (1971) or the transporting or importing of obscene materials for private use, *United States v. Orito,* 413 U.S. 139 (1973) (transporting); *United States v. 12 200–Ft. Reels,* 413 U.S. 123 (1973) (importing). Dissenting in *Reels,* Douglas, J., argued that *Stanley* rights could legally be realized "only if one wrote or designed a tract in his attic and printed or processed it in his basement, so as to be able to read it in his study." Do these decisions take the First Amendment out of *Stanley*? Are they justified by the rationale in *Paris Adult Theatre*? For example, does importation for personal use intrude "upon us all"? Affect the total community environment?

For the declaration that *Stanley's* "privacy of the home" principle is "firmly grounded" in the First Amendment while resisting the principle's expansion to protect consensual adult homosexu-

[W]e reject the claim that Georgia is here attempting to control the minds or thoughts of those who patronize theatres. Preventing unlimited display or distribution of obscene material, which by definition lacks any serious literary, artistic, political, or scientific value as communication, is distinct from a control of reason and the intellect. Cf. John Finnis, *"Reason and Passion": The Constitutional Dialectic of Free Speech and Obscenity,* 116 U.Pa.L.Rev. 222, 229–230, 241–243 (1967).

[Finally], petitioners argue that conduct which directly involves "consenting adults" only has, for that sole reason, a special claim to constitutional protection. Our Constitution establishes a broad range of conditions on the exercise of power by the States, but for us to say that our Constitution incorporates the proposition that conduct involving consenting adults only is always beyond state regulation,[14] is a step we are unable to take.[15] [The] issue in this context goes beyond whether someone, or even the majority, considers the conduct depicted as "wrong" or "sinful." The States have the power to make a morally neutral judgment that public exhibition of obscene material, or commerce in such material, has a tendency to injure the community as a whole, to endanger the public safety, or to jeopardize, in Mr. Chief Justice Warren's words, the States' "right [to] maintain a decent society." *Jacobellis* (dissenting). * * *

JUSTICE BRENNAN, with whom JUSTICE STEWART and JUSTICE MARSHALL join, dissenting.

[I] am convinced that the approach initiated 15 years ago in *Roth* and culminating in the Court's decision today, cannot bring stability to this area of the law without jeopardizing fundamental First Amendment values, and I have concluded that the time has come to make a significant departure from that [approach.]

[The] decision of the Georgia Supreme Court rested squarely on its conclusion that the State could constitutionally suppress these films even if they were displayed only to persons over the age of 21 who were aware of the nature of their contents and who had consented to viewing them. [I] am convinced of the invalidity of that conclusion [and] would therefore vacate the [judgment]. I have no occasion to consider the extent of State power to regulate the distribution of sexually oriented materials to juveniles or to unconsenting [adults.] [*Stanley*] reflected our emerging view that the state interests in protecting children and in protecting unconsenting adults may stand on a different footing from the other asserted state interests. It may well be, as one commentator has argued, that "exposure to [erotic material] is for some persons an intense emotional experience. A

---

al sodomy in the home, see *Bowers v. Hardwick,* 478 U.S. 186 (1986). But see Blackmun, J., joined by Brennan, Marshall, and Stevens, JJ., dissenting in *Bowers* ("*Stanley* rested as much on the Court's understanding of the Fourth Amendment as it did on the First").

14. Cf. John Stuart Mill, *On Liberty* 13 (1955).

15. The state statute books are replete with constitutionally unchallenged laws against prostitution, suicide, voluntary self-mutilation, brutalizing "bare fist" prize fights, and duels, although these crimes may only directly involve "consenting adults." Statutes making bigamy a crime surely cut into an individual's freedom to associate, but few today seriously claim such statutes violate the First Amendment or any other constitutional provision.

communication of this nature, imposed upon a person contrary to his wishes, has all the characteristics of a physical assault. [And it] constitutes an invasion of his [privacy]." [But] whatever the strength of the state interests in protecting juveniles and unconsenting adults from exposure to sexually oriented materials, those interests cannot be asserted in defense of the holding of the Georgia Supreme Court, [which] assumed for the purposes of its decision that the films in issue were exhibited only to persons over the age of 21 who viewed them willingly and with prior knowledge of the nature of their contents. [The] justification for the suppression must be found, therefore, in some independent interest in regulating the reading and viewing habits of consenting [adults].

In *Stanley* we pointed out that "[t]here appears to be little empirical basis for" the assertion that "exposure to obscene materials may lead to deviant sexual behavior or crimes of sexual violence." In any event, we added that "if the State is only concerned about printed or filmed materials inducing antisocial conduct, we believe that in the context of private consumption of ideas and information we should adhere to the view that '[a]mong free men, the deterrents ordinarily to be applied to prevent crime are education and punishment for violations of the [law].'"

Moreover, in *Stanley* we rejected as "wholly inconsistent with the philosophy of the First Amendment," the notion that there is a legitimate state concern in the "control [of] the moral content of a person's thoughts." [The] traditional description of state police power does embrace the regulation of morals as well as the health, safety, and general welfare of the citizenry. [But] the State's interest in regulating morality by suppressing obscenity, while often asserted, remains essentially unfocused and ill-defined. And, since the attempt to curtail unprotected speech necessarily spills over into the area of protected speech, the effort to serve this speculative interest through the suppression of obscene material must tread heavily on rights protected by the First Amendment. * * *

In short, while I cannot say that the interests of the State—apart from the question of juveniles and unconsenting adults—are trivial or nonexistent, I am compelled to conclude that these interests cannot justify the substantial damage to constitutional rights and to this Nation's judicial machinery that inevitably results from state efforts to bar the distribution even of unprotected material to consenting adults.[c]

JUSTICE DOUGLAS, dissenting. * * *

"Obscenity" at most is the expression of offensive ideas. There are regimes in the world where ideas "offensive" to the majority (or at least to those who control the majority) are suppressed. There life proceeds at a monotonous pace. Most of us would find that world offensive. One of the most offensive experiences in my life was a visit to a nation where bookstalls were filled only with books on mathematics and books on religion.

---

c. For the portion of Brennan, J.'s dissent addressing the difficulties of formulating an acceptable constitutional standard, see *Miller v. California, infra.*

I am sure I would find offensive most of the books and movies charged with being obscene. But in a life that has not been short, I have yet to be trapped into seeing or reading something that would offend me. I never read or see the materials coming to the Court under charges of "obscenity," because I have thought the First Amendment made it unconstitutional for me to act as a censor. * * *

NOTES AND QUESTIONS

1. **Speech v. conduct.** Is pornography predominantly a form of sexual conduct rather than a communicative process? Frederick Schauer, *Speech and "Speech"—Obscenity and "Obscenity": An Exercise in the Interpretation of Constitutional Language,* 67 Geo. L.J. 899, 922 (1979). Is this reflected in the Court's definition? Consider James Weinstein, *Democracy, Sex, and the First Amendment,* 31 N.Y.U. Rev. L. & Soc. Change 865, 892 (2007): "[I]n accordance with the basic rule that any use of a medium essential to public discourse is presumptively protected, graphic depictions of sexual conduct in these media are, despite the physical effect they produce for many viewers, deemed public discourse rather than sexual conduct; this material loses protection only if a court determines that, taken as a whole, it is merely an appeal 'to the prurient interest in sex' rather than a 'serious' attempt to engage in informal politics or some other activity having First Amendment value."[d]

2. **Ideas and the First Amendment.** KINGSLEY INT'L PICTURES CORP. v. REGENTS, 360 U.S. 684 (1959), per STEWART, J., underlined the distinction between obscenity and non-obscene "portrayal of sex" in art and literature. *Kingsley* held invalid New York's denial of a license to exhibit the film *Lady Chatterley's Lover* pursuant to a statute requiring such denial when a film "portrays acts of sexual immorality [as] desirable, acceptable or proper patterns of behavior": "[What] New York has done, [is] to prevent the exhibition of a motion picture because that picture advocates an idea—that adultery under certain circumstances may be proper behavior. Yet the First Amendment's basic guarantee is of freedom to advocate ideas. The State, quite simply, has thus struck at the very heart of constitutionally protected liberty."

3. **Beauty and imagination.** Does the protection of art depend upon the advocacy of ideas? Consider Harry Kalven, *The Metaphysics of the Law of Obscenity,* 1960 Sup.Ct.Rev. 1, 15–16: "The classic defense of John Stuart Mill and the modern defense of Alexander Meiklejohn do not help much when the question is why the novel, the poem, the painting, the drama, or the piece of sculpture falls within the protection of the First Amendment. Nor do the famous opinions of Hand, Holmes, and Brandeis. [The] people do not need novels or dramas or paintings or poems because they will be called upon to vote. Art and belles-lettres do not deal in such ideas—at least not good art or belles-lettres—and it makes little sense here to talk [of] whether there is still time for counter-speech.

---

d. For commentary, see Andrew Koppelman, *Free Speech and Pornography,* 31 N.Y.U. Rev. L. & Soc. Change 899 (2007).

"[B]eauty has constitutional status too, [and] the life of the imagination is as important to the human adult as the life of the intellect. I do not think that the Court would find it difficult to protect Shakespeare, even though it is hard to enumerate the important ideas in the plays and poems. I am only suggesting that Mr. Justice Brennan [in *Roth*] might not have found it so easy to dismiss obscenity because it lacked socially useful ideas if he had recognized that as to this point, at least, obscenity is in the same position as all art and literature."

See also Jed Rubenfeld, *The Freedom of Imagination: Copyright's Constitutionality*, 112 Yale L.J. 1, 59–60 (2002): "The freedom of imagination extends far beyond art and entertainment. Philosophy is an exercise of the imagination too. So is prayer. So is a call for political change. The freedom of imagination, in other words, protects 'core' First Amendment speech just as it protects novels or pictures. It does so not because imagination informs voting, nor because imagination is central to individual autonomy. It does so because the freedom of imagination articulates the First Amendment's core commitment: that no one may be legally punished for thinking an unauthorized thought or for expressing an unauthorized idea."

4. ***Politics v. art.*** Consider Steven D. Smith, *Believing Persons, Personal Believings: The Neglected Center of the First Amendment*, 2002 U. ILL. L. REV. 1233, 1310 (2002): "Whether or not it is rational or explicitly political, music, painting, and poetry is typically as self-consciously a manifestation of central beliefs and attitudes (in all of their subjective richness) as almost any kind of expression can be. Indeed, from this perspective, art would seem to be even more central to the First Amendment's purpose than political speech."[e]

5. ***The moral rationale for prohibition.*** Is the value of obscenity "outweighed by the social interest in order and morality?" Consider Andrew Koppelman, *Does Obscenity Cause Moral Harm?*, 105 Colum. L. Rev. 1635, 1651 (2005): "[P]eople are animals. Sexual need is part of what makes us human. Lust depersonalizes, but it also personalizes. When I am the object of lust, this sometimes means that I am appreciated in the full embodied particularity of my self, as I am not if you only love me for my mind. A person is dehumanized in a distinctive way if she is never the object of anyone's lust. The precise letting go, in sex, of one's sober self-control that Kant feared is what D.H. Lawrence thought particularly valuable about sex." David Richards, *Free Speech and Obscenity Law: Toward A Moral Theory of the First Amendment*, 123 U.Pa.L.Rev. 45, 81 (1974): "[P]ornography can be seen as the unique medium of a vision of sexuality [, a] view of sensual delight in the erotic celebration of the body, a concept of easy freedom without consequences, a fantasy of timelessly repetitive indulgence. In opposition to the Victorian view that narrowly defines proper sexual function in a rigid way that is analogous to ideas of excremental regularity and moderation, pornography builds a model of plastic variety and joyful excess in sexuality. In opposition to the sorrowing Catholic dismissal of sexuality as an unfortunate

---

e. On the relationship between art and the first amendment, see Marci A. Hamilton, *Art Speech*, 49 Vand.L.Rev. 73 (1996); Sheldon Nahmod, *Artistic Expression and Aesthetic Theory: The Beautiful, The Sublime and The First Amendment*, 1987 Wisc.L.Rev. 221.

and spiritually superficial concomitant of propagation, pornography affords the alternative idea of the independent status of sexuality as a profound and shattering ecstasy."[f]

Even if this perspective were rejected on moral grounds, consider John Stuart Mill's statement of the harm principle in *On Liberty:* "[T]he only purpose for which power can be rightfully exercised over any member of a civilized community, against his will is to prevent harm to others."

Does the liberal view overestimate human rational capacity and underestimate the importance of the state in promoting a virtuous citizenry? See generally Harry Clor, *Obscenity and Public Morality* (1969). Do liberals fail to appreciate the morally corrosive effects of obscenity? Consider the following observation: "Obscenity emphasizes the base animality of our nature, reduces the spirituality of humanity to mere bodily functions, and debases civilization by transforming the private into the public." Consider Irving Kristol, *Reflections of a Neoconservative* 45, 47 (1983): "Bearbaiting and cockfighting are prohibited only in part out of compassion for the suffering animals; the main reason they were abolished was because it was felt that they debased and brutalized the citizenry who flocked to witness such spectacles. And the question we face with regard to pornography and obscenity is whether [they] can or will brutalize and debase our citizenry. We are, after all, not dealing with one passing incident—one book, or one play, or one movie. We are dealing with a general tendency that is suffusing our entire culture. [W]hen men and women make love, as we say, they prefer to be alone—because it is only when you are alone that you can make love, as distinct from merely copulating in an animal and casual way. And that, too, is why those who are voyeurs, if they are not irredeemably sick, also feel ashamed at what they are witnessing. When sex is a public spectacle, a human relationship has been debased into a mere animal connection."

6. ***Low First Amendment value.*** Consider Geoffrey R. Stone, *Sex, Violence, and the First Amendment,* 74 U.Chi. L.Rev. 1857, 1863–64 (2007): "[W]hy is obscenity of only low First Amendment value? [C]ase law [suggests] that several factors are relevant to the analysis. First, categories of low-value speech [do] not primarily advance political discourse. Second, categories of low-value speech are not defined in terms of disfavored ideas or political viewpoints. Third low-value speech usually has a strong noncognitive effect on its audience. Fourth, categories of low-value speech have long been regulated without undue harm to the overall system of free expression." How many of these categories apply to literature in general?

---

f. For the view that pornography can best be defended as a form of anti-social dissent, consider Steven Gey, *The Apologetics of Suppression,* 86 Mich.L.Rev. 1564, 1630 (1988): "Porn exposes a rot in the framework of society, and the great popularity of porn makes the burghers uneasily suspicious that the surface rot may evidence a more deeply rooted degeneration of their moral and political primacy. Thus, the imperative to suppress pornography reveals a much deeper and more insidious insecurity than the moralists will ever acknowledge." Cf. Robin West, *The Feminist–Conservative Anti–Pornography Alliance and the 1986 Attorney General's Commission on Pornography Report,* 1987 Am.B.Found.Res.J. 681, 686–99 (discussing victimizing and liberating aspects of pornography from the perspectives of women while contending that women's experience of pornography, albeit diverse, is different from that of men).

B. A REVISED STANDARD

MILLER v. CALIFORNIA

413 U.S. 15, 93 S.Ct. 2607, 37 L.Ed.2d 419 (1973).

CHIEF JUSTICE BURGER delivered the opinion of the Court. [The Court remanded, "for proceedings not inconsistent" with the opinion's obscenity standard, Miller's conviction under California's obscenity law for mass mailing of unsolicited pictorial advertising brochures depicting men and women in a variety of group sexual activities.]

This is one of a group of "obscenity-pornography" cases being reviewed by the Court in a re-examination of standards enunciated in earlier cases involving what Mr. Justice Harlan called "the intractable obscenity problem." [I]n this context[a] [we] are called on to define the standards which must be used to identify obscene material that a State may [regulate].

[Nine years after *Roth*], in *Memoirs v. Massachusetts*, 383 U.S. 413 (1966), the Court veered sharply away from the Roth concept and, with only three Justices in the plurality opinion, articulated a new test of obscenity. The plurality held that under the Roth definition "as elaborated in subsequent cases, three elements must coalesce: it must be established that (a) the dominant theme of the material taken as a whole appeals to a prurient interest in sex; (b) the material is patently offensive because it affronts contemporary community standards relating to the description or representation of sexual matters; and (c) the material is utterly without redeeming social value." * * * → *change over Roth*
tough for prosecution to improve / impossible

While *Roth* presumed "obscenity" to be "utterly without redeeming social importance," *Memoirs* required that to prove obscenity it must be affirmatively established that the material is "*utterly* without redeeming social value."

Thus, even as they repeated the words of *Roth*, the *Memoirs* plurality produced a drastically altered test that called on the prosecution to prove a negative, i.e., that the material was "*utterly* without redeeming social value"—a burden virtually impossible to discharge under our criminal standards of proof. [Apart] from the initial formulation in *Roth,* no majority of the Court has at any given time been able to agree on a standard to determine what constitutes obscene, pornographic material subject to regulation under the States' police power. See, e.g., *Redrup v. New York*, 386 U.S. 767 (1967).[3] This is not remarkable, for in the area

a. The "context" was that in *Miller* "sexually explicit materials have been thrust by aggressive sales action upon unwilling recipients." But nothing in *Miller* limited the revised standard to that context, and the companion case, *Paris Adult Theatre,* applied the same standard to dissemination limited to consenting adults.

3. In the absence of a majority view, this Court was compelled to embark on the practice of summarily reversing convictions for the dissemination of materials that at least five members of the Court, applying their separate tests, found to be protected by the First Amendment. *Redrup.* [Beyond] the necessity of circumstances, however, no justification has ever been offered in support of the *Redrup* "policy." The *Redrup* procedure has cast us in the role of an unreviewable

of freedom of speech and press the courts must always remain sensitive to any infringement on genuinely serious literary, artistic, political, or scientific expression. * * *

II. This much has been categorically settled by the Court, that obscene material is unprotected by the First Amendment. [We] acknowledge, however, the inherent dangers of undertaking to regulate any form of expression. State statutes designed to regulate obscene materials must be carefully limited. As a result, we now confine the permissible scope of such regulation to works which depict or describe sexual conduct. That conduct must be specifically defined by the applicable state law, as written or authoritatively construed.[6] A state offense must also be limited to works which, taken as a whole, appeal to the prurient interest in sex, which portray sexual conduct in a patently offensive way, and which, taken as a whole, do not have serious literary, artistic, political, or scientific value.

The basic guidelines for the trier of fact must be: (a) whether "the average person, applying contemporary community standards" would find that the work, taken as a whole, appeals to the prurient interest, (b) whether the work depicts or describes, in a patently offensive way, sexual conduct specifically defined by the applicable state law,[b] and (c) whether the work, taken as a whole, lacks serious literary, artistic, political, or scientific value. We do not adopt as a constitutional standard the *utterly without redeeming social value* test of *Memoirs;* that concept has never commanded the adherence of more than three Justices at one time.[7] If a state law that regulates obscene material is thus limited, as written or construed, the First Amendment values applicable to the States [are] adequately protected by the ultimate power of appellate courts to conduct an independent review of constitutional claims when necessary.

We emphasize that it is not our function to propose regulatory schemes for the States. [It] is possible, however, to give a few plain

---

board of censorship for the 50 States, subjectively judging each piece of material brought before us.

6. See, e.g., Oregon Laws 1971, c. 743, Art. 29, §§ 255–262, and Hawaii Penal Code, Tit. 37, §§ 1210–1216, 1972 Hawaii Session Laws, pp. 126–129, Act 9, Pt. II, as examples of state laws directed at depiction of defined physical conduct, as opposed to expression. [We] do not hold, as Mr. Justice Brennan intimates, that all States other than Oregon must now enact new obscenity statutes. Other existing state statutes, as construed heretofore or hereafter, may well be adequate.

b. On the use of guidelines (a) and (b) against sexual minorities, see Comment, *Behind the Curtain of Privacy: How Obscenity Laws Inhibit the Expression of Ideas About Sex and Gender,* 1998 Wis. L. Rev. 625 (1998).

7. "[We] also reject, as a constitutional standard, the ambiguous concept of 'social importance'." [*Hamling v. United States,* 418 U.S. 87 (1974) upheld a conviction in which the jury had been instructed to find that the material was "utterly without redeeming social value." Defendant argued that the latter phrase was unconstitutionally vague and cited *Miller.* The Court rejected the vagueness challenge: "[O]ur opinion in *Miller* plainly indicates that we rejected the '[social] value' formulation, not because it was so vague as to deprive criminal defendants of adequate notice, but instead because it represented a departure from [*Roth*], and because in calling on the prosecution to 'prove a negative,' it imposed a '[prosecutorial] burden virtually impossible to discharge' and which was not constitutionally required."]

examples of what a state statute could define for regulation under the second part (b) of the standard announced in this opinion, supra:

(a) Patently offensive representations or descriptions of ultimate sexual acts, normal or perverted, actual or simulated.

(b) Patently offensive representations or descriptions of masturbation, excretory functions, and lewd exhibition of the genitals.[c]

Sex and nudity may not be exploited without limit by films or pictures exhibited or sold in places of public accommodation any more than live sex and nudity can be exhibited or sold without limit in such public places.[8] At a minimum, prurient,[d] patently offensive depiction or description of sexual conduct must have serious literary, artistic, political, or scientific value to merit First Amendment protection. For example, medical books for the education of physicians and related personnel necessarily use graphic illustrations and descriptions of human anatomy. In resolving the inevitably sensitive questions of fact and law, we must continue to rely on the jury system, accompanied by the safeguards that judges, rules of evidence, presumption of innocence and other protective features [provide].

Mr. Justice Brennan [has] abandoned his former positions and now maintains that no formulation of this Court, the Congress, or the States can adequately distinguish obscene material unprotected by the First Amendment from protected expression, *Paris Adult Theatre I v. Slaton* (Brennan, J., dissenting). Paradoxically, Mr. Justice Brennan indicates that suppression of unprotected obscene material is permissible to avoid exposure to unconsenting adults, as in this case, and to juveniles, although he gives no indication of how the division between protected and nonprotected materials may be drawn with greater precision for these purposes than for regulation of commercial exposure to consenting adults only. Nor does he indicate where in the Constitution he finds the authority to

---

c. *Jenkins v. Georgia,* 418 U.S. 153 (1974) held the film *Carnal Knowledge* not obscene because it did not "'depict or describe patently offensive 'hard core' sexual conduct'" as required by *Miller:* "[While there] are scenes in which sexual conduct including 'ultimate sexual acts' is to be understood to be taking place, the camera does not focus on the bodies of the actors at such times. There is no exhibition whatever of the actors' genitals, lewd or otherwise, during these scenes. There are occasional scenes of nudity, but nudity alone is not enough to make material legally obscene under the *Miller* standards." *Ward v. Illinois,* 431 U.S. 767 (1977) held that it was not necessary for the legislature or the courts to provide an "exhaustive list of the sexual conduct [the] description of which may be held obscene." It is enough that a state adopt *Miller*'s explanatory examples. Stevens, J., joined by Brennan, Stewart and Marshall, JJ., dissented: "[I]f the statute need only describe the 'kinds' of proscribed sexual conduct, it adds no protection to what the Constitution itself creates. [The] specificity requirement as described in *Miller* held out the promise of a principled effort to respond to [the vagueness] argument. By abandoning that effort today, the Court withdraws the cornerstone of the *Miller* [structure]."

8. Although we are not presented here with the problem of regulating lewd public conduct itself, the States have greater power to regulate nonverbal, physical conduct than to suppress depictions or descriptions of the same behavior. * * *

d. *Brockett v. Spokane Arcades, Inc.,* 472 U.S. 491 (1985) held that appeals to prurient interest could not be taken to include appeals to "normal" interests in sex. Only appeals to a "shameful or morbid interest in sex" are prurient. Although the Court was resolute in its position that appeals to "good, old fashioned, healthy" interests in sex were constitutionally protected, it did not further specify how "normal" sex was to be distinguished from the "shameful" or "morbid."

distinguish between a willing "adult" one month past the state law age of majority and a willing "juvenile" one month younger.[e]

Under the holdings announced today, no one will be subject to prosecution for the sale or exposure of obscene materials unless these materials depict or describe patently offensive "hard core" sexual conduct specifically defined by the regulating state law, as written or construed. We are satisfied that these specific prerequisites will provide fair notice to a dealer in such materials that his public and commercial activities may bring prosecution. If the inability to define regulated materials with ultimate, god-like precision altogether removes the power of the States or the Congress to regulate, then "hard core" pornography may be exposed without limit to the juvenile, the passerby, and the consenting adult alike, as indeed, Mr. Justice Douglas contends.

[N]o amount of "fatigue" should lead us to adopt a convenient "institutional" rationale—an absolutist, "anything goes" view of the First Amendment—because it will lighten our burdens. [Nor] should we remedy "tension between state and federal courts" by arbitrarily depriving the States of a power reserved to them under the Constitution, a power which they have enjoyed and exercised continuously from before the adoption of the First Amendment to this day. See *Roth.* "Our duty admits of no 'substitute for facing up to the tough individual problems of constitutional judgment involved in every obscenity case.'" *Jacobellis* (opinion of Brennan, J.).

III.   Under a national Constitution, fundamental First Amendment limitations on the powers of the States do not vary from community to community, but this does not mean that there are, or should or can be, fixed, uniform national standards of precisely what appeals to the "prurient interest" or is "patently offensive." These are essentially questions of fact, and our nation is simply too big and too diverse for this Court to reasonably expect that such standards could be articulated for all 50 States in a single formulation, even assuming the prerequisite consensus exists. When triers of fact are asked to decide whether "the average

---

e.   The suggestion that the same book may be obscene in some contexts but not in others has been endorsed in several different contexts. *Butler v. Michigan,* 352 U.S. 380 (1957) held that the state could not ban sales to the general public of material unsuitable for children: "The State insists that [by] quarantining the general reading public against books not too rugged for grown men and women in order to shield juvenile innocence, it is exercising its power to promote the general welfare. Surely, this is to burn the house to roast the pig. [The] incidence of this enactment is to reduce the adult population of Michigan to reading only what is fit for children." *Ginsberg v. New York,* 390 U.S. 629 (1968), however, held that the state could bar the distribution to children of books that were suitable for adults, the Court recognizing it was adopting a "variable" concept of obscenity. See also *Ginzburg v. United States,* 383 U.S. 463 (1966) ("pandering" method of marketing supports obscenity conviction even though the materials might not otherwise have been considered obscene); *Mishkin v. New York,* 383 U.S. 502 (1966) (material designed for and primarily disseminated to deviant sexual group can meet prurient appeal requirement even if the material lacks appeal to an average member of the general public; appeal is to be tested with reference to the sexual interests of the intended and probable recipient group).

The variable obscenity approach had previously been advocated and elaborated by William Lockhart & Robert McClure, *Censorship of Obscenity: The Developing Constitutional Standards,* 45 Minn.L.Rev. 5, 77 (1960).

person, applying contemporary community standards" would consider certain materials "prurient," it would be unrealistic to require that the answer be based on some abstract formulation. The adversary system, with lay jurors as the usual ultimate fact finders in criminal prosecutions, has historically permitted triers-of-fact to draw on the standards of their community, guided always by limiting instructions on the law. To require a State to structure obscenity proceedings around evidence of a *national* "community standard" would be an exercise in [futility].

We conclude that neither the State's alleged failure to offer evidence of "national standards," nor the trial court's charge that the jury consider state community standards, were constitutional errors. Nothing in the First Amendment requires that a jury must consider hypothetical and unascertainable "national standards" when attempting to determine whether certain materials are obscene as a matter of [fact].

It is neither realistic nor constitutionally sound to read the First Amendment as requiring that the people of Maine or Mississippi accept public depiction of conduct found tolerable in Las Vegas, or New York City. People in different States vary in their tastes and attitudes, and this diversity is not to be strangled by the absolutism of imposed uniformity. As the Court made clear in *Mishkin,* the primary concern with requiring a jury to apply the standard of "the average person, applying contemporary community standards" is to be certain that, so far as material is not aimed at a deviant group, it will be judged by its impact on an average person, rather than a particularly susceptible or sensitive person—or indeed a totally insensitive one.[f] [We] hold the requirement that the jury evaluate the materials with reference to "contemporary standards of the State of California" serves this protective purpose and is constitutionally adequate.[g] * * *

In sum we (a) reaffirm the *Roth* holding that obscene material is not protected by the First Amendment, (b) hold that such material can be regulated by the States, subject to the specific safeguards enunciated

---

f. *Pinkus v. United States,* 436 U.S. 293 (1978) upheld a jury instruction stating "you are to judge these materials by the standard of the hypothetical average person in the community, but in determining this average standard you must include the *sensitive and the insensitive,* in other words, [everyone] in the community." On the other hand, in the absence of evidence that "children were the intended recipients" or that defendant "had reason to know children were likely to receive the materials," it was considered erroneous to instruct the jury that children were part of the relevant community. *Butler.* When the evidence would support such a charge, the Court stated that prurient appeal to deviant sexual groups could be substituted for appeal to the average person; moreover, the jury was entitled to take pandering into account. *Ginzburg.*

g. *Jenkins,* fn. c supra, stated that a judge may instruct a jury to apply "contemporary community standards" without any further specification. Alternatively, the state may choose "to define the standards in more precise geographic terms, as was done by California in *Miller.*" *Hamling,* fn. 7 supra, interpreted a federal obscenity statute to make the relevant community the one from which the jury was drawn. The judge's instruction to consider the "community standards of the 'nation as a whole' delineated a wider geographical area than would be warranted by [*Miller*]" or the Court's construction of the statute, but the error was regarded as harmless under the circumstances. See also *Sable Communications v. FCC,* Ch. 8, II, infra ("dial-a-porn" company bears burden of complying with congressional obscenity ban despite diverse local community standards). After these decisions, what advice should lawyers give to publishers who distribute in national markets?

above, without a showing that the material is "*utterly* without redeeming social value," and (c) hold that obscenity is to be determined by applying "contemporary community standards," not "national standards." * * *

JUSTICE DOUGLAS, dissenting. * * *

My contention is that until a civil proceeding has placed a tract beyond the pale, no criminal prosecution should be sustained. For no more vivid illustration of vague and uncertain laws could be designed than those we have fashioned. [If] a specific book [or] motion picture has in a civil proceeding been condemned as obscene and review of that finding has been completed, and thereafter a person publishes [or] displays that particular book or film, then a vague law has been made specific. There would remain the underlying question whether the First Amendment allows an implied exception in the case of obscenity. I do not think it does and my views on the issue have been stated over and again. But at least a criminal prosecution brought at that juncture would not violate the time-honored void-for-vagueness test.[8]

No such protective procedure has been designed by California in this case. Obscenity—which even we cannot define with precision—is a hodge-podge. To send men to jail for violating standards they cannot understand, construe, and apply is a monstrous thing to do in a Nation dedicated to fair trials and due process. * * *

JUSTICE BRENNAN, with whom JUSTICE STEWART and JUSTICE MARSHALL join, dissenting.

In my dissent in *Paris Adult Theatre,* decided this date, I noted that I had no occasion to consider the extent of state power to regulate the distribution of sexually oriented material to juveniles or the offensive exposure of such material to unconsenting adults. [I] need not now decide whether a statute might be drawn to impose, within the requirements of the First Amendment, criminal penalties for the precise conduct at issue here. For it is clear that under my dissent in *Paris Adult Theatre,* the statute under which the prosecution was brought is unconstitutionally overbroad, and therefore invalid on its face. * * *

[In his *Paris Adult Theatre* dissent, Brennan, J., joined by Stewart and Marshall, JJ., argued that the state interests in regulating obscenity were not strong enough to justify the degree of vagueness. He criticized not only the Court's standard in *Miller,* but also a range of alternatives:]

II. [The] essence of our problem [is] that we have been unable to provide "sensitive tools" to separate obscenity from other sexually orient-ed but constitutionally protected speech, so that efforts to suppress the former do not spill over into the suppression of the latter. [The dissent traced the Court's experience with *Roth* and its progeny.]

III. Our experience with the *Roth* approach has certainly taught us that the outright suppression of obscenity cannot be reconciled with the

---

8. The Commission on Obscenity and Pornography has advocated such a procedure. [See] *Report of the Commission on Obscenity and Pornography* 70–71 (1970).

fundamental principles of the First and Fourteenth Amendments. For we have failed to formulate a standard that sharply distinguishes protected from unprotected speech, and out of necessity, we have resorted to the *Redrup* approach, which resolves cases as between the parties, but offers only the most obscure guidance to legislation, adjudication by other courts, and primary conduct. [T]he vagueness problem would be largely of our own creation if it stemmed primarily from our failure to reach a consensus on any one standard. But after 15 years of experimentation and debate I am reluctantly forced to the conclusion that none of the available formulas, including the one announced today, can reduce the vagueness to a tolerable level while at the same time striking an acceptable balance between the protections of the First and Fourteenth Amendments, on the one hand, and on the other the asserted state interest in regulating the dissemination of certain sexually oriented materials. Any effort to draw a constitutionally acceptable boundary on state power must resort to such indefinite concepts as "prurient interest," "patent offensiveness," "serious literary value," and the like. The meaning of these concepts necessarily varies with the experience, outlook, and even idiosyncrasies of the person defining them. Although we have assumed that obscenity does exist and that we "know it when [we] see it," *Jacobellis* (Stewart, J., concurring), we are manifestly unable to describe it in advance except by reference to concepts so elusive that they fail to distinguish clearly between protected and unprotected speech.

[Added to the inherent vagueness of standards] is the further complication that the obscenity of any particular item may depend upon nuances of presentation and the context of its dissemination. See *Ginzburg*. [N]o one definition, no matter how precisely or narrowly drawn, can possibly suffice for all situations, or carve out fully suppressible expression from all media without also creating a substantial risk of encroachment upon the guarantees of the Due Process Clause and the First Amendment.

[The] resulting level of uncertainty is utterly intolerable, not alone because it makes "[b]ookselling [a] hazardous profession," *Ginsberg* (Fortas, J., dissenting), but as well because it invites arbitrary and erratic enforcement of the law. [We] have indicated that "stricter standards of permissible statutory vagueness may be applied to a statute having a potentially inhibiting effect on speech; a man may the less be required to act at his peril here, because the free dissemination of ideas may be the loser." * * *

The problems of fair notice and chilling protected speech are very grave standing alone. But [a] vague statute in this area creates a third [set] of problems. These [concern] the institutional stress that inevitably results where the line separating protected from unprotected speech is excessively vague. [Almost] every obscenity case presents a constitutional question of exceptional difficulty. [As] a result of our failure to define standards with predictable application to any given piece of material, there is no probability of regularity in obscenity decisions by state and lower federal courts. [O]ne cannot say with certainty that material is obscene until at least five members of this Court, applying inevitably obscure standards, have pronounced it [so].

We have managed the burden of deciding scores of obscenity cases by relying on per curiam reversals or denials of certiorari—a practice which conceals the rationale of decision and gives at least the appearance of arbitrary action by this Court. More important, [the] practice effectively censors protected expression by leaving lower court determinations of obscenity intact even though the status of the allegedly obscene material is entirely unsettled until final review here. In addition, the uncertainty of the standards creates a continuing source of tension between state and federal [courts].

The severe problems arising from the lack of fair notice, from the chill on protected expression, and from the stress imposed on the state and federal judicial machinery persuade me that a significant change in direction is urgently required. I turn, therefore, to the alternatives that are now open.

IV.   1.   The approach requiring the smallest deviation from our present course would be to draw a new line between protected and unprotected speech, still permitting the States to suppress all material on the unprotected side of the line. In my view, clarity cannot be obtained pursuant to this approach except by drawing a line that resolves all doubts in favor of state power and against the guarantees of the First Amendment. We could hold, for example, that any depiction or description of human sexual organs, irrespective of the manner or purpose of the portrayal, is outside the protection of the First Amendment and therefore open to suppression by the States. That formula would, no doubt, offer much fairer notice [and] give rise to a substantial probability of regularity in most judicial determinations under the standard. But such a standard would be appallingly overbroad, permitting the suppression of a vast range of literary, scientific, and artistic masterpieces. Neither the First Amendment nor any free community could possibly tolerate such a standard.

2.   [T]he Court today recognizes that a prohibition against any depiction or description of human sexual organs could not be reconciled with the guarantees of the First Amendment. But the Court [adopts] a restatement of the *Roth-Memoirs* definition of obscenity [that] permits suppression if the government can prove that the materials lack "*serious* literary, artistic, political or scientific value." [In] *Roth* we held that certain expression is obscene, and thus outside the protection of the First Amendment, precisely *because* it lacks even the slightest redeeming social value. [The] Court's approach necessarily assumes that some works will be deemed obscene—even though they clearly have *some* social value— because the State was able to prove that the value, measured by some unspecified standard, was not sufficiently "serious" to warrant constitutional protection. That result [is] nothing less than a rejection of the fundamental First Amendment premises and rationale of the *Roth* opinion and an invitation to widespread suppression of sexually oriented speech.

Before today, the protections of the First Amendment have never been thought limited to expressions of *serious* literary or political value. *Gooding v. Wilson; Cohen v. California; Terminiello v. Chicago* [Ch. 1, V, B infra].

[T]he Court's approach [can] have no ameliorative impact on the cluster of problems that grow out of the vagueness of our current standards. Indeed, even the Court makes no argument that the reformulation will provide fairer notice to booksellers, theatre owners, and the reading and viewing public. Nor does the Court contend that the approach will provide clearer guidance to law enforcement officials or reduce the chill on protected expression [or] mitigate [the] institutional [problems].

Of course, the Court's restated *Roth* test does limit the definition of obscenity to depictions of physical conduct and explicit sexual acts. And that limitation may seem, at first glance, a welcome and clarifying addition to the *Roth-Memoirs* formula. But just as the agreement in *Roth* on an abstract definition of obscenity gave little hint of the extreme difficulty that was to follow in attempting to apply that definition to specific material, the mere formulation of a "physical conduct" test is no assurance that it can be applied with any greater facility. [The] Court surely demonstrates little sensitivity to our own institutional problems, much less the other vagueness-related difficulties, in establishing a system that requires us to consider whether a description of human genitals is sufficiently "lewd" to deprive it of constitutional protection; whether a sexual act is "ultimate"; whether the conduct depicted in materials before us fits within one of the categories of conduct whose depiction the state or federal governments have attempted to suppress; and a host of equally pointless inquiries. * * *

If the application of the "physical conduct" test to pictorial material is fraught with difficulty, its application to textual material carries the potential for extraordinary abuse. Surely we have passed the point where the mere written description of sexual conduct is deprived of First Amendment protection. Yet the test offers no guidance to us, or anyone else, in determining which written descriptions of sexual conduct are protected, and which are not.

Ultimately, the reformulation must fail because it still leaves in this Court the responsibility of determining in each case whether the materials are protected by the First Amendment. * * *

3. I have also considered the possibility of reducing our own role, and the role of appellate courts generally, in determining whether particular matter is obscene. Thus, [we] might adopt the position that where a lower federal or state court has conscientiously applied the constitutional standard, its finding of obscenity will be no more vulnerable to reversal by this Court than any finding of fact. [E]ven if the Constitution would permit us to refrain from judging for ourselves the alleged obscenity of particular materials, that approach would solve at best only a small part of our problem. For while it would mitigate the institutional stress, [it] would neither offer nor produce any cure for the other vices of vagueness.

Far from providing a clearer guide to permissible primary conduct, the approach would inevitably lead to even greater uncertainty and the consequent due process problems of fair notice. And the approach would expose much protected, sexually oriented expression to the vagaries of jury determinations. Plainly, the institutional gain would be more than offset by the unprecedented infringement of First Amendment rights.

4.   Finally, I have considered the view, urged so forcefully since 1957 by our Brothers Black and Douglas, that the First Amendment bars the suppression of any sexually oriented expression. That position would effect a sharp reduction, although perhaps not a total elimination, of the uncertainty that surrounds our current approach. Nevertheless, I am convinced that it would achieve that desirable goal only by stripping the States of power to an extent that cannot be justified by the commands of the Constitution, at least so long as there is available an alternative approach that strikes a better balance between the guarantee of free expression and the States' legitimate interests.

* * * I would hold, therefore, that at least in the absence of distribution to juveniles or obtrusive exposure to unconsenting adults, the First and Fourteenth Amendments prohibit the state and federal governments from attempting wholly to suppress sexually oriented materials on the basis of their allegedly "obscene" contents.[h] Nothing in this approach precludes those governments from taking action to serve what may be strong and legitimate interests through regulation of the manner of distribution of sexually oriented material.

VI.   * * * I do not pretend to have found a complete and infallible [answer]. Difficult questions must still be faced, notably in the areas of distribution to juveniles and offensive exposure to unconsenting adults. Whatever the extent of state power to regulate in those areas,[29] it should be clear that the view I espouse today would introduce a large measure of clarity to this troubled area, would reduce the institutional pressure on this Court and the rest of the State and Federal judiciary, and would guarantee fuller freedom of expression while leaving room for the protection of legitimate governmental interests. * * *

NOTES AND QUESTIONS

1.   *Serious value.* Consider Harry Clor, *Obscenity and the First Amendment: Round Three*, 7 Loy.L.A.L.Rev. 207, 210, 218 (1974): "The *Miller* decision abandons the requirement that a censorable work must be '*utterly* without redeeming social value' and substitutes the rule of 'serious value'— literary, artistic, political, or scientific. This is the most important innovation

---

h.   For the portion of Brennan, J.'s dissent addressing the strength and legitimacy of the state interests, see *Paris Adult Theatre,* supra.

29.   The Court erroneously states, *Miller,* that the author of this opinion "indicates that suppression of unprotected obscene material is permissible to avoid exposure to unconsenting adults [and] to juveniles * * *." I defer expression of my views as to the scope of state power in these areas until cases squarely presenting these questions are before the Court.

in the law of obscenity introduced by these decisions. [Serious] literature is to be protected regardless of majority opinions about prurience and offensiveness. *This* is the national principle which is not subject to variation from community to community. If it is to perform this function, the rule will have to be elaborated and the meaning of 'serious value' articulated in some measure. This is the most important item on the legal agenda."

(a) *An independent factor?* Under *Miller* would material found to have "serious artistic value" be entitled to First Amendment protection regardless of how offensive or prurient? Must each factor in the *Miller* guidelines be independently satisfied? *Should* that be so? Would or should that preclude the degree of offensiveness or prurient appeal from affecting the conclusion on the value factor?

(b) *"Serious."* Do you find any guidance for determining when a First Amendment value in material depicting sexual conduct is sufficiently "serious" to preclude finding it obscene? Does *Pope v. Illinois,* 481 U.S. 497 (1987) assist?: "The proper inquiry is not whether an ordinary member of any given community would find serious literary, artistic, political, or scientific value[,] but whether a reasonable person would find such value in the material taken as a whole." Consider Amy Adler, *Post–Modern Art and the Death of Obscenity Law,* 99 Yale L.J. 1359, 1365 (1990): "What did the Miller Court mean by 'serious artistic value'? There are at least three plausible interpretations: (1) the artwork makes an important and original rather than a marginal and derivative contribution to art; (2) the artwork is 'serious' in that it reflects the sanctity and solemnity of high art; (3) the artist was serious and sincere in his attempt to make art (rather than obscenity), no matter how successful his ultimate achievement."

(c) *Scope of protected values.* Could the Court consistent with the First Amendment exclude serious educational value from those that preclude a finding of obscenity? Serious entertainment value? Could the guidelines be interpreted to include such values? What might explain their omission?

2. *Relationship of definition to harm.* Consider Arnold H. Loewy, *Obscenity: An Outdated Concept for the Twenty–First Century,* 10 NEXUS 21, 25 (2005): "It is extremely doubtful that the actual obscenity of a particular book or movie makes any difference at all in regard to our concern for community environment, protecting children, or protecting unwilling adults. If a particular movie theater is showing a sexually-explicit film that a jury has just declared to be non-obscene, it is likely to have very nearly the same deleterious effects as last week's sexually-explicit film which had been declared obscene."

3. *Vagueness and scienter.* Is the *Miller* test intolerably vague? Are there any alternatives that could mitigate the problem? Consider William B. Lockhart, *Escape from the Chill of Uncertainty: Explicit Sex and the First Amendment,* 9 Ga.L.Rev. 533, 563 (1975): "[E]ither legislative action, or constitutional adjudication, could establish as a defense to a criminal obscenity prosecution that the defendant *reasonably believed* that the material involved was not obscene, that is, was constitutionally protected. [Material] that would support such a court or jury finding is not the kind that requires or justifies quick action by the police and prosecutor. The public interest in

preventing distribution of borderline material that can reasonably be believed not obscene is not so pressing as to require immediate criminal sanctions and can adequately be protected by a declaratory judgment or injunction action to establish the obscenity of the material."

Smith v. California, 361 U.S. 147 (1959) invalidated an ordinance that dispensed with any requirement that a seller of an obscene book have knowledge of its contents, but did not decide what sort of mental element was needed to prosecute. *Hamling v. United States,* supra, stated that it was constitutionally sufficient to show that a distributor of an advertising collage of pictures of sexual acts "had knowledge of the contents of the materials [and] that he knew the character and nature of the materials." Would it be consistent with *Hamling* to afford constitutional protection to a distributor who reasonably believed the material disseminated was not obscene? See Lockhart, supra, at 568.

4. ***The practical impact of Miller.*** Consider Edward de Grazia, *Girls Lean Back Everywhere: The Law of Obscenity and the Assault on Genius* 561–62, 571 (1992): Until Powell, J., switched his vote, Brennan, J., and "a Court majority were preparing to reverse [Miller's] obscenity conviction. [T]he Burger revision of the Brennan doctrine was soon revealed to be a sort of paper tiger[, however]; by and large, there in fact occurred no observable retardation of the country's move during the decade that followed toward nearly absolute freedom for sexual expression in literary and artistic modes, including graphic or pictorial pornography; no increase in lower court convictions for obscenity; and no increase in prosecutorial [activity]." Cf. Daniel Mark Cohen, *Unhappy Anniversary: Thirty Years Since Miller v. California: The Legacy of the Supreme Court's Misjudgment on Obscenity*, 15 St. Thomas L. Rev. 545, 711 (2003). See also David Cole, *Playing by Pornography's Rules: The Regulation of Sexual Expression,* 143 U.Pa.L.Rev. 111, 170, 173 (1994): "Because this prohibition is so narrow, it serves in practice not so much to purge the community of explicit sexually arousing speech as to validate everything that remains as nonoffensive, 'normal,' or socially valuable. In this way, obscenity doctrine collectively assures the community that the pornography it consumes at such a high rate is acceptable. [There] are the few who are actually prosecuted; given the remarkable amount and variety of sexual expression that goes without prosecution, to be prosecuted for obscenity these days is akin to being struck by lightning."

C. VAGUENESS AND OVERBREADTH: AN OVERVIEW

In *Paris Adult Theatre,* Brennan, J., dissents on the ground that the obscenity statute is unconstitutionally vague. He envisions the possibility that an obscenity statute might overcome his vagueness objection if it were tailored to combat distribution to unconsenting adults or to children. In *Miller,* the materials were in fact distributed to unconsenting adults. There Brennan, J., does not reach the vagueness question but objects on the ground that the statute is overbroad,—i.e., it is not confined to the protection of unconsenting adults and children, but also prohibits distribution of obscene materials to consenting adults. In Brennan, J.'s view, even if the particular conduct at issue in *Miller* might be constitutionally prohibited by a narrower statute, it cannot be reached under a statute that sweeps so much protected speech within its terms.

The doctrines of "vagueness" and "overbreadth" referred to in Brennan, J.'s dissents are deeply embedded in First Amendment jurisprudence. At first glance, the doctrines appear discrete. A statute that prohibits the use of the words "kill" and "President" in the same sentence may not be vague, but it is certainly overbroad even though some sentences using those words may be unprotected. Conversely, a vague statute may not be overbroad; it may not pertain to First Amendment freedoms at all, or it may clearly be intended to exclude all protected speech from its prohibition but use vague language to accomplish that purpose.

Ordinarily, however, the problems of "vagueness" and "overbreadth" are closely related. An Airport Commissioners resolution banning all "First Amendment activities" in the Los Angeles International Airport was declared overbroad in *Board of Airport Commissioners v. Jews for Jesus,* 482 U.S. 569 (1987). Literally read the statute would have prevented anyone from talking or reading in the airport. But if the language literally covers a variety of constitutionally protected activities, it *cannot be read literally.* If the statute cannot be read according to its terms, however, problems of vagueness will often emerge. To be sure, statutes may be interpreted in ways that will avoid vagueness or overbreadth difficulties. See, e.g., *Scales v. United States,* Ch. 1, I, D supra. It is established doctrine, for example, that an attack based either upon vagueness or overbreadth will be unsuccessful in federal court if the statute in question is "readily subject to a narrowing construction by the state courts." *Young v. American Mini Theatres, Inc.; Erznoznik v. Jacksonville,* Ch. 3, I infra. Moreover, "[f]or the purpose of determining whether a state statute is too vague and indefinite to constitute valid legislation [the Court takes] 'the statute as though it read precisely as the highest court of the State has interpreted it.' " *Wainwright v. Stone,* 414 U.S. 21 (1973). Under this policy, a litigant can be prosecuted successfully for violating a statute that by its terms appears vague or overbroad but is interpreted by the state court in the same prosecution to mean something clearer or narrower than its literal language would dictate. *Cox v. New Hampshire,* Ch. 6, I, A infra. The harshness of this doctrine is mitigated somewhat by the fact that "unexpected" or "unforeseeable" judicial constructions in such contexts violate due process. See *Marks v. United States,* 430 U.S. 188 (1977).[a]

Somewhat more complicated is the issue of when general attacks on a statute are permitted. Plainly litigants may argue that statutes are vague as to their own conduct or that their own speech is protected. In other words, litigants are always free to argue that a statute is invalid "as applied" to their own conduct. The dispute concerns when litigants can

---

a. For commentary on overbreadth with special focus on the implications of the doctrine mentioned in this paragraph, see Richard Fallon, *Making Sense of Overbreadth,* 100 Yale L.J. 853 (1991).

attack a statute without reference to their own conduct, an attack sometimes called "on its face."

A separate question is: when should such attacks result in partial or total invalidation of a statute? The terminology here has become as confused as the issues. The Court has frequently referred to facial attacks on statutes in a way that embraces attempts at either partial or total invalidation. In some opinions, however, including those quoted below, it uses the term "facial attack" or "on its face" to refer only to arguments seeking total invalidation of a statute.

Terminology aside, one of the recurrent questions has been the extent to which litigants may argue that a statute is unconstitutionally overbroad even though their own conduct would not otherwise be constitutionally protected. This is often characterized as a standing issue. Ordinarily litigants do not have standing to raise the rights of others. But it has been argued that litigants should have standing to challenge overbroad statutes even if their own conduct would be otherwise unprotected in order to prevent a chilling effect on freedom of speech. Alternatively, it has been argued that no standing problem is genuinely presented because "[u]nder 'conventional' standing principles, a litigant has always had the right to be judged in accordance with a constitutionally valid rule of law." Henry Monaghan, *Overbreadth,* 1981 S.Ct.Rev. 1, 3. On this view, if a statute is unconstitutionally overbroad, it is not a valid rule of law, and any defendant prosecuted under the statute has standing to make that claim.[b] However the issue may be characterized, White, J., contended for many years that a litigant whose own conduct is unprotected should not prevail on an overbreadth challenge without a showing that the statute's overbreadth is "real and substantial." After much litigation, White, J., finally prevailed. The "substantial" overbreadth doctrine now burdens all litigants who argue that a statute should be declared overbroad when their own conduct would otherwise be unprotected.[c] *Brockett v. Spokane Arcades, Inc.; New York v. Ferber,* Ch. 1, V, A infra.

Less clear are the circumstances in which a litigant whose conduct *is* protected can go beyond a claim that the statute is unconstitutional "as applied" because litigants are always free to argue that their own conduct is protected. Moreover, the Court has stated that "[t]here is no reason to

---

b. See also Henry Monaghan, *Third Party Standing,* 84 Colum.L.Rev. 277 (1984). See also Robert Sedler, *The Assertion of Constitutional Jus Tertii: A Substantive Approach,* 70 Calif.L.Rev. 1308, 1327 (1982) ("It may be the potential chilling effect upon others' expression that makes the statute invalid, but the litigant has his own right not to be subject to the operation of an invalid statute."). For criticism of the Monaghan position, see Richard Fallon, supra note a, at 871–75; Alfred Hill, *The Puzzling Overbreadth Doctrine,* 25 Hofstra L.Rev. 1063 (1997); Lawrence Gene Sager, *Foreword: State Courts and the Strategic Space Between the Norms and Rules of Constitutional Law,* 63 Tex. L.Rev. 959, 967 & n. 22 (1985).

For the claim that a focus on audience rights best explains the overbreadth doctrine, see Note, *Overbreadth and Listeners' Rights,* 123 Harv. L.Rev. 1749 (2010).

c. For commentary on the concept of "substantial" overbreadth, see Fallon, supra; Lawrence A. Alexander, *Is There an Overbreadth Doctrine,* 22 San Diego L.Rev. 541, 553–54 (1985); Martin Redish, *The Warren Court, The Burger Court and the First Amendment Overbreadth Doctrine,* 78 Nw.U.L.Rev. 1031, 1056–69 (1983).

limit challenges to case-by-case 'as applied' challenges when the statute [in] all its applications falls short of constitutional demands."[d] *Secretary of State of Maryland v. Joseph H. Munson Co.*, 467 U.S. 947 (1984). How far beyond this the Court will go is unclear. In *Brockett v. Spokane Arcades, Inc.*, Ch. 1, III, B supra, it referred to the "normal rule that partial, rather than facial invalidation" of statutes is to be preferred and observed that: "[A]n individual whose own speech or expressive conduct may validly be prohibited or sanctioned is permitted to challenge a statute on its face because it also threatens others not before the court—those who desire to engage in legally protected expression but who may refrain from doing so rather than risk prosecution or undertake to have the law declared partially invalid. If the overbreadth is 'substantial,' the law may not be enforced against anyone, including the party before the court, until it is narrowed to reach only unprotected activity, whether by legislative action or by judicial construction or partial invalidation.

"It is otherwise where the parties challenging the statute are those who desire to engage in protected speech that the overbroad statute purports to punish, or who seek to publish both protected and unprotected material. There is then no want of a proper party to challenge the statute, no concern that an attack on the statute will be unduly delayed or protected speech discouraged. The statute may forthwith be declared invalid to the extent that it reaches too far, but otherwise left intact."[e]

Brockett takes the view that it must give standing to the otherwise unprotected to raise an overbreadth challenge, in order to secure the rights of those whose speech should be protected. But it sees no purpose in giving standing to the protected in order to secure rights for those whose speech should not be protected. This position is not without its ironies. In some circumstances, a litigant whose speech is unprotected will be in a better position than one whose speech is protected, at least if the litigant's goal is completely to stop enforcement of a statute.

Finally, what of the cases when it is uncertain whether the litigant's speech is protected? Should courts consider as applied attacks before proceeding to overbreadth attacks? *Board of Trustees v. Fox*, Ch. 3, III infra, declared it "not the usual judicial practice" and "generally undesirable" to proceed to an overbreadth challenge without first determining whether the statute would be valid as applied.[f] Yet the Court has fre-

---

d. There is a terminological dispute here. Compare *Los Angeles City Council v. Taxpayers For Vincent*, Ch. 6, II infra (such challenges are not overbreadth challenges) with *Munson*, supra (such challenges are properly called overbreadth challenges).

e. After the Court has declared that the statute is invalid to the extent it reaches too far, the remaining portion of the statute will be examined to determine whether that portion is severable. That is, it could well be the intent of the legislature that the statute stands or falls as a single package. To invalidate a part, then, could be to invalidate the whole. Alternatively, the legislature may have intended to salvage whatever it might. The question of severability is regarded as one of legislative intent, but, at least with respect to federal legislation, courts will presume that severability was intended. See, e.g., *Regan v. Time, Inc.*, 468 U.S. 641 (1984). The question of whether a provision of a state statute is severable is one of state law.

f. The case arose in the federal courts, and the Court might be less likely to remand to a state court for an as applied determination, but the Court did not address that distinction.

quently (see, e.g., Ch. 1, IV, C infra (fighting words cases; *Jews For Jesus*)) declared statutes overbroad without an as applied determination. The Court has yet systematically to detail the considerations relevant to separating the "usual" judicial practice from the unusual.

The issues with respect to vagueness challenges are similar. White, J., maintained that vagueness challenges should be confined to "as applied" attacks unless a statute were vague in all of its applications. Accordingly, if a statute clearly proscribed the conduct of a particular defendant, to allow that defendant to challenge a statute for vagueness would in his view have been "to confound vagueness and overbreadth." *Kolender v. Lawson,* 461 U.S. 352 (1983) (White, J., dissenting). In response, the Court stated that a facial attack upon a statute need not depend upon a showing of vagueness in all of a statute's applications: "[W]e permit a facial challenge if a law reaches 'a substantial amount of constitutionally protected conduct,' " *Kolender.* Moreover, the Court has previously allowed litigants to raise the vagueness issue "even though there is no uncertainty about the impact of the ordinances on their own rights." *Young.* But see, e.g., *Broadrick v. Oklahoma,* Ch. 1, VI, A infra, in which White, J., writing for the Court suggested that standing to raise the vagueness argument should not be permitted in this situation.

Much less clear are the circumstances in which litigants whose conduct is *not* clearly covered by a statute can go beyond an "as applied" attack.[g] One approach would be to apply the same rule to all litigants, e.g., allowing total invalidation of statutes upon a showing of a "substantial" vagueness. In *Kolender,* the Court made no determination whether the statute involved was vague as to the defendant's own conduct; arguably, the opinion implied that it made no difference. Another approach would analogize to the approach suggested in *Brockett* for overbreadth challenges. Thus, a court might refrain from total invalidation of a statute and confine itself to striking the vague part insofar as the vague part seems to cover protected speech, leaving the balance of the statute intact. *Kolender* itself recites that the Court has "traditionally regarded vagueness and overbreadth as logically related and similar doctrines," but the Court's attitudes toward vagueness remain unclear. The questions of what standards should govern challenges to statutes that go beyond the facts before the Court, who should be able to raise the challenges, and under what circumstances have not been systematically and consistently addressed.[h]

---

g. Conceivably, it could make a difference whether the litigants in this class of those "not clearly covered" have engaged in protected or unprotected conduct.

h. For commentary on vagueness and overbreadth, see, e.g., Melville Nimmer, *Nimmer on Freedom of Speech,* 4–147—4–162 (1984); Larry Alexander, *Is There an Overbreadth Doctrine?,* 22 San Diego L.Rev. 541 (1985); Anthony Amsterdam, *The Void–For–Vagueness Doctrine in the Supreme Court,* 109 U.Pa.L.Rev. 67 (1960); David Bogen, *First Amendment Ancillary Doctrines,* 37 Md.L.Rev. 679, 705–26 (1978); Monaghan, supra; Redish, supra; Note, *The First Amendment Overbreadth Doctrine,* 83 Harv.L.Rev. 844 (1970).

V. "FIGHTING WORDS," OFFENSIVE WORDS AND HOSTILE AUDIENCES

A. FIGHTING WORDS

CHAPLINSKY v. NEW HAMPSHIRE, 315 U.S. 568 (1942): In the course of proselytizing on the streets, appellant, a Jehovah's Witness, denounced organized religion. Despite the city marshal's warning to "go slow" because his listeners were upset with his attacks on religion, appellant continued and a disturbance occurred. At this point, a police officer led appellant toward the police station, without arresting him. While en route, appellant again encountered the city marshal who had previously admonished him. Appellant then said to the marshal (he claimed, but the marshal denied, in response to the marshal's cursing him): "You are a God damned racketeer" and "a damned Fascist and the whole government of Rochester are Fascists or agents of Fascists."[a] He was convicted of violating a state statute forbidding anyone to address "any offensive, derisive or annoying word to any other person who is lawfully in any [public place] [or] call[ing] him by any offensive or derisive name." The Court, per MURPHY, J., upheld the conviction:

"There are certain well-defined and narrowly limited classes of speech, the prevention and punishment of which have never been thought to raise any Constitutional problem.[b] These include the lewd and obscene, the profane, the libelous, and the insulting or 'fighting' words—those which by their very utterance inflict injury or tend to incite an immediate breach of the peace. [S]uch utterances are no essential part of any exposition of ideas, and are of such slight social value as a step to truth that any benefit that may be derived from them is clearly outweighed by the social interest in order and morality. * * *[c]

   a. The Supreme Court's version of the facts is sanitized. Bowering, the city marshall, stood by as a companion named Bowman punched Chaplinsky and later used a flagstaff as a spear in an effort to impale him. Without intervention from Bowering, the crowd demanded that Chaplinsky salute the flag and assaulted him when he refused. When Chaplinsky asked Bowering to arrest those who had committed violence against him, Bowering called him a damned bastard and demanded that he come along. Then Chaplinsky responded with epithets. Burton Caine, *The Trouble With "Fighting Words": Chaplinsky v. New Hampshire Is a Threat to First Amendment Values and Should Be Overruled*, 88 MARQ. L. REV. 441, 446–447 (2004); Vincent Blasi & Seana V. Shiffrin, The Story of West Virginia State Board of Education v. Barnette, in *Constitutional Law Stories* 432, 444 (Michael C. Dorf ed. 2004).

   b. See Franklyn Haiman, *How Much of Our Speech is Free?*, The Civ.Lib.Rev., Winter, 1975, pp. 111, 123: "[T]his discrimination between two classes of speech made its first U.S. Supreme Court appearance in *Cantwell v. Connecticut* (1940) [Part 1, Ch. 12, I infra]." Jehovah's Witnesses had been convicted of religious solicitation without a permit and of breach of the peace. The Court set aside both convictions. It invalidated the permit system for "religious" solicitation, because it permitted the licensing official to determine what causes were "religious," thus allowing a "censorship of religion." In setting aside the breach of peace conviction, because the offense covered much protected conduct and left "too wide a discretion in its application," the Court, per Roberts, J., noted: "One may, however, be guilty of [breach of the peace] if he commits acts or makes statements likely to provoke violence and disturbance of good order. [I]n practically all [such decisions to this effect], the provocative language [held to constitute] a breach of the peace consisted of profane, indecent or abusive remarks directed to the person of the hearer. *Resort to epithets or personal abuse is not in any proper sense communication of information or opinion safeguarded by the Constitution,* and its punishment as a criminal act [under a narrowly drawn statute] would raise no question under that instrument." (Emphasis added).

   c. For commentary on this paragraph, see Rodney A. Smolla, *Words "Which By Their Very Utterance Inflict Injury": The Evolving Treatment of Inherently Dangerous Speech in Free Speech Law and Theory*, 36 Pepp. L.Rev. 317 (2009).

"On the authority of its earlier decisions, the state court declared that the statute's purpose was to preserve the public peace, no words being 'forbidden except such as have a direct tendency to cause acts of violence by the person to whom, individually, the remark is addressed'. It was further said: 'The word "offensive" is not to be defined in terms of what a particular addressee thinks. [The] test is what men of common intelligence would understand would be words likely to cause an average addressee to fight. [The] English language has a number of words and expressions which by general consent are "fighting words" when said without a disarming smile. [Such] words, as ordinary men know, are likely to cause a fight. So are threatening, profane or obscene revilings. Derisive and annoying words can be taken as coming within the purview of the statute as heretofore interpreted only when they have this characteristic of plainly tending to excite the addressee to a breach of the peace. [The] statute, as construed, does no more than prohibit the face-to-face words plainly likely to cause a breach of the peace by the addressee, words whose speaking constitute a breach of the peace by the speaker—including "classical fighting words", words in current use less "classical" but equally likely to cause violence, and other disorderly words, including profanity, obscenity and threats.'

"[A] statute punishing verbal acts, carefully drawn so as not unduly to impair liberty of expression, is not too vague for a criminal law. * * *[8]

"Nor can we say that the application of the statute to the facts disclosed by the record substantially or unreasonably impinges upon the privilege of free speech. Argument is unnecessary to demonstrate that the appellations 'damn racketeer' and 'damn Fascist' are epithets likely to provoke the average person to retaliation, and thereby cause a breach of the peace.

"The refusal of the state court to admit evidence of provocation and evidence bearing on the truth or falsity of the utterances is open to no Constitutional objection. Whether the facts sought to be proved by such evidence constitute a defense to the charge or may be shown in mitigation are questions for the state court to determine. Our function is fulfilled by a determination that the challenged statute, on its face and as applied, does not contravene the Fourteenth Amendment."

NOTES AND QUESTIONS

1. *Fighting words and free speech values.* (a) *Self realization.* Does speech have to step toward truth to be of First Amendment value? Consider Martin Redish, *The Value of Free Speech*, 130 U.Pa.L.Rev. 591, 626 (1982): "Why not view Chaplinsky's comments as a personal catharsis, as a

---

8. [Even] if the interpretative gloss placed on the statute by the court below be disregarded, the statute had been previously construed as intended to preserve the public peace by punishing conduct, the direct tendency of which was to provoke the person against whom it was directed to acts of violence.

Appellant need not therefore have been a prophet to understand what the statute condemned.

means to vent his frustration at a system he deemed—whether rightly or wrongly—to be oppressive? Is it not a mark of individuality to be able to cry out at a society viewed as crushing the individual? Under this analysis, so-called 'fighting words' represent a significant means of self-realization, whether or not they can be considered a means of attaining some elusive 'truth.' "

(b) *Fighting words and truth.* Are fighting words always false? Should truth be a defense? Always?

(c) *Fighting words and self-government.* Was Chaplinsky's statement *something other than* the expression of an idea? Did he wish to inform the marshal of his opinion of him and did he do so "in a way which was not only unquestionably clear, [but] all too clear"? Arnold Loewy, *Punishing Flag Desecrators,* 49 N.C.L.Rev. 48, 82 (1970). How significant is it that Chaplinsky's remarks were not made in the context of a public debate or discussion of political or social issues? Or were they? Taking into account the events preceding Chaplinsky's remarks, and that the addressee was complicit in the physical and verbal abuse against Chaplinsky, that the addressee was an important public official in dereliction of his duties, was Chaplinsky's remark simply sharp criticism of government. In any event, should provocation be a defence? Burton Caine, *The Trouble With "Fighting Words": Chaplinsky v. New Hampshire Is a Threat to First Amendment Values and Should Be Overruled,* 88 Marq. L. Rev. 441, 446–447 (2004).

2. *The social interest in order and morality.* What was the social interest in this case? (a) *The likelihood and immediacy of violent retaliation?* Should the Court have considered whether a *law enforcement officer* so reviled would have been provoked to retaliate? Whatever is assumed about the reaction of an average citizen to offensive words, may it be assumed that police are "trained to remain calm in the face of citizen anger such as that expressed by Chaplinsky"? Mark Rutzick, *Offensive Language and the Evolution of First Amendment Protection,* 9 Harv.Civ.Rts.—Civ.Lib.L.Rev. 1, 10 (1974). See also Powell, J., concurring in *Lewis v. New Orleans,* Ch. 1, IV, C supra; Note, 53 B.U.L.Rev. 834, 847 (1973). Does the breach of the peace interest invite discriminatory enforcement? Consider Wendy B. Reilly, *Fighting the Fighting Words Standard: A Call For It's Destruction,* 52 Rutgers L. Rev. 947, 948 (2000): "[I]t is possible that almost nothing one could say to a woman would be proscribed by the fighting words doctrine because women are presumed to be unlikely to respond to any words with physical violence. On the other hand, words said to Black or Latino men may be considered fighting words based on a perception that those men of color are particularly prone to violence."

(b) *Psychic harm?* May the *Chaplinsky* statute be viewed as "a special type of assault statute"? See Loewy, supra, at 83–84. Would this be superior to a statute based on breach of the peace?

B. HOSTILE AUDIENCES

TERMINIELLO v. CHICAGO, 337 U.S. 1 (1949): Petitioner "vigorously, if not viciously" criticized various political and racial groups and condemned "a surging, howling mob" gathered in protest outside the auditorium in which he spoke. He called his adversaries "slimy scum," "snakes," "bedbugs," and the like. Those inside the hall could hear those on the outside yell, "Fascists, Hitlers!" The crowd outside tried to tear the clothes off those who entered. About 28 windows were broken; stink bombs were thrown. But in charging the jury, the trial court defined "breach of the peace" to include speech which "stirs the public to anger, *invites dispute,* [or] brings about a condition of unrest (emphasis added)." A 5–4 majority, per DOUGLAS, J., struck down the breach of peace ordinance as thus construed: "[A] function of free speech under our system of government is to invite dispute. It may indeed best serve its high purpose when it induces a condition of unrest, creates dissatisfaction with conditions as they are, or even stirs people to anger. [That] is why freedom of speech, though not absolute, *Chaplinsky,* is nevertheless protected against censorship or punishment, unless shown likely to produce a clear and present danger of a serious substantive evil that rises far above public inconvenience, annoyance, or unrest."

––––––

FEINER v. NEW YORK, 340 U.S. 315 (1951): Petitioner made a speech on a street corner in a predominantly black residential section of Syracuse, N.Y. A crowd of 75 to 80 persons, black and white, gathered around him, and several pedestrians had to go into the highway in order to pass by. A few minutes after he started, two police officers arrived and observed the rest of the meeting. In the course of his speech, publicizing a meeting of the Young Progressives of America to be held that evening in a local hotel and protesting the revocation of a permit to hold the meeting in a public school auditorium, petitioner referred to the President as a "bum," to the American Legion as "a Nazi Gestapo," and to the Mayor of Syracuse as a "champagne-sipping bum" who "does not speak for the Negro people." He also indicated in an excited manner: "The Negroes don't have equal rights; they should rise up in arms and fight for them."

These statements "stirred up a little excitement." One man indicated that if the police did not get that "S * * * O * * * B* * * "off the stand, he would do so himself. There was not yet a disturbance, but according to police testimony "angry muttering and pushing." In the words of the arresting officer whose testimony was accepted by the trial judge, he "stepped in to prevent it from resulting in a fight." After disregarding two requests to stop speaking, petitioner was arrested and convicted for disorderly conduct. The Court, per VINSON, C.J., affirmed: "The language of *Cantwell* is appropriate here. '[Nobody would] suggest that the principle of freedom of speech sanctions incitement to riot or that religious liberty connotes the privilege to exhort others to physical attack upon those belonging to another sect. When clear and present danger of riot, disorder, interference with traffic upon the public street or other immediate threat to public safety, peace, or order, appears, the power of the State to prevent or punish is obvious.'

"[It] is one thing to say that the police cannot be used as an instrument for the suppression of unpopular views, and another to say that, when as here the speaker passes the bounds of argument or persuasion and undertakes incitement to riot, they are powerless to prevent a breach of the peace. Nor in this case can we condemn the considered judgment of three New York courts approving the means which the police, faced with a crisis, used in the exercise of their power and duty to preserve peace and order."

BLACK, J., dissented: "The Court's opinion apparently rests on this reasoning: The policeman, under the circumstances detailed, could reasonably conclude that serious fighting or even riot was imminent; therefore he could stop petitioner's speech to prevent a breach of peace; accordingly, it was 'disorderly conduct' for petitioner to continue speaking in disobedience of the officer's request. As to the existence of a dangerous situation on the street corner, it seems far-fetched to suggest that the 'facts' show any imminent threat of riot or uncontrollable disorder. It is neither unusual nor unexpected that some people at public street meetings mutter, mill about, push, shove, or disagree, even violently, with the speaker. Indeed, it is rare where controversial topics are discussed that an outdoor crowd does not do some or all of these things. Nor does one isolated threat to assault the speaker forebode disorder. Especially should the danger be discounted where, as here, the person threatening was a man whose wife and two small children accompanied him and who, so far as the record shows, was never close enough to petitioner to carry out the threat.

"Moreover, assuming that the 'facts' did indicate a critical situation, I reject the implication of the Court's opinion that the police had no obligation to protect petitioner's constitutional right to talk. The police of course have power to prevent breaches of the peace. But if, in the name of preserving order, they ever can interfere with a lawful public speaker, they first must make all reasonable efforts to protect him. Here the policemen did not even pretend to try to protect petitioner. According to the officers' testimony, the crowd was restless but there is no showing of any attempt to quiet it; pedestrians were forced to walk into the street, but there was no effort to clear a path on the sidewalk; one person threatened to assault petitioner but the officers did nothing to discourage this when even a word might have sufficed. Their duty was to protect petitioner's right to talk, even to the extent of arresting the man who threatened to interfere. Instead, they shirked that duty and acted only to suppress the right to speak.

"Finally, I cannot agree with the Court's statement that petitioner's disregard of the policeman's unexplained request amounted to such 'deliberate defiance' as would justify an arrest or conviction for disorderly conduct. On the contrary, I think that the policeman's action was a 'deliberate defiance' of ordinary official duty as well as of the constitutional right of free speech. For at least where time allows, courtesy and explanation of commands are basic elements of good official conduct in a democratic society. Here petitioner was 'asked' then 'told' then 'commanded' to stop speaking, but a man making a lawful address is certainly not required to be silent merely because an officer directs it. Petitioner was entitled to know why he should cease doing a lawful act. Not once was he told.''

DOUGLAS, J., joined by Minton, J., dissented: "A speaker may not, of course, incite a riot any more than he may incite a breach of the peace by the use of 'fighting words'. But this record shows no such extremes. It shows an unsympathetic audience and the threat of one man to haul the speaker from the stage. It is against that kind of threat that speakers need police protection. If they do not receive it and instead the police throw their weight on the side of those who would break up the meetings, the police become the new censors of speech. Police censorship has all the vices of the censorship from city halls which we have repeatedly struck down.''

NOTES AND QUESTIONS

1. What was the subject of disagreement in *Feiner*? (1) The standard for police interruption of a speech when danger of violence exists and the speaker intends to create disorder rather than to communicate ideas? (2) The standard when such danger exists, but the speaker only desires to communicate ideas? (3) Whether the danger of disorder and violence *was* plain and imminent? (4) Whether the speaker *did* intend to create disorder and violence?

May *Feiner* be limited to the proposition that when a speaker "incites to riot"—but only then—police may stop him without bothering to keep his audience in check? Cf. *Sellers v. Johnson,* 163 F.2d 877 (8th Cir.1947), cert. denied, 332 U.S. 851 (1948). See Richard Stewart, *Public Speech and Public Order in Britain and the United States,* 13 Vand.L.Rev. 625, 632–33 (1960).

2. *Edwards v. South Carolina,* 372 U.S. 229 (1963) reversed a breach of the peace conviction of civil rights demonstrators who refused to disperse within 15 minutes of a police command. The Court maintained that the 200 to 300 onlookers did not threaten violence and that the police protection was ample. It described the situation as a "far cry from [*Feiner*]." Clark, J., dissenting, pointed to the racially charged atmosphere ("200 youthful Negro demonstrators were being aroused to a 'fever pitch' before a crowd of some 300 people who undoubtedly were hostile.") and concluded that city officials in good faith believed that disorder and violence were imminent. Did *Edwards* miss a golden opportunity to clarify *Feiner*? What if the crowd had been pushing, shoving and pressing more closely around the demonstrators in *Edwards* ? Would the case still be a "far cry" from *Feiner* because the demonstrators had not "passed the bounds of argument or persuasion and undertaken incitement to riot"?

3. In the advocacy of illegal action context, the fear of violence arises from audience cooperation with the speaker. In the hostile audience context, the fear of violence arises from audience conflict with the speaker. How do the elements set out in *Brandenburg* relate to those implied in *Feiner*? How

should they relate? Should the standard for "fighting words" cases be different from the "hostile audience" cases?

4.   Should police be able to prosecute or silence disruptive audiences? Heckling audiences? In what contexts? See generally *In re Kay,* 1 Cal.3d 930, 83 Cal.Rptr. 686, 464 P.2d 142 (1970).

C.   OFFENSIVE WORDS

COHEN v. CALIFORNIA

403 U.S. 15, 91 S.Ct. 1780, 29 L.Ed.2d 284 (1971).

JUSTICE HARLAN delivered the opinion of the Court.

[Defendant was convicted of violating that part of a general California disturbing-the-peace statute which prohibits "maliciously and willfully disturb[ing] the peace or quiet of any neighborhood or person" by "offensive conduct." He had worn a jacket bearing the plainly visible words "Fuck the Draft" in a Los Angeles courthouse corridor, where women and children were present. He testified that he did so as a means of informing the public of the depth of his feelings against the Vietnam War and the draft. He did not engage in, nor threaten, any violence, nor was anyone who saw him violently aroused. Nor was there any evidence that he uttered any sound prior to his arrest. In affirming, the California Court of Appeal construed "offensive conduct" to mean "behavior which has a tendency to provoke *others* to acts of violence or to in turn disturb the peace" and held that the state had proved this element because it was "reasonably foreseeable" that defendant's conduct "might cause others to rise up to commit a violent act against [him] or attempt to forceably remove his jacket."]

In order to lay hands on the precise issue which this case involves, it is useful first to canvass various matters which this record does *not* present.

The conviction quite clearly rests upon the asserted offensiveness of the *words* Cohen used to convey his message to the public. The only "conduct" which the State sought to punish is the fact of communication. Thus, we deal here with a conviction resting solely upon "speech," not upon any separately identifiable conduct which allegedly was intended by Cohen to be perceived by others as expressive of particular views but which, on its face, does not necessarily convey any message and hence arguably could be regulated without effectively repressing Cohen's ability to express himself. Cf. *United States v. O'Brien* [Ch. 2 infra]. Further, the State certainly lacks power to punish Cohen for the underlying content of the message the inscription conveyed. At least so long as there is no showing of an intent to incite disobedience to or disruption of the draft, Cohen could not, consistently with the First and Fourteenth Amendments, be punished for asserting the evident position on the inutility or immorality of the draft his jacket reflected. *Yates.*

Appellant's conviction, then, rests squarely upon his exercise [of] "freedom of speech" [and] can be justified, if at all, only as a valid regulation of the manner in which he exercised that freedom, not as a permissible prohibition on the substantive message it conveys. This does not end the inquiry, of course, for the First and Fourteenth Amendments have never been thought to give absolute protection to every individual to speak whenever or wherever he pleases, or to use any form of address in any circumstances that he chooses. In this vein, too, however, we think it important to note that several issues typically associated with such problems are not presented here.

In the first place, Cohen was tried under a statute applicable throughout the entire State. Any attempt to support this conviction on the ground that the statute seeks to preserve an appropriately decorous atmosphere in the courthouse where Cohen was arrested must fail in the absence of any language in the statute that would have put appellant on notice that certain kinds of otherwise permissible speech or conduct would nevertheless, under California law, not be tolerated in certain places. No fair reading of the phrase "offensive conduct" can be said sufficiently to inform the ordinary person that distinctions between certain locations are thereby created.[3]

In the second place, as it comes to us, this case cannot be said to fall within those relatively few categories of instances where prior decisions have established the power of government to deal more comprehensively with certain forms of individual expression simply upon a showing that such a form was employed. This is not, for example, an obscenity case. Whatever else may be necessary to give rise to the States' broader power to prohibit obscene expression, such expression must be, in some significant way, erotic. *Roth.* It cannot plausibly be maintained that this vulgar allusion to the Selective Service System would conjure up such psychic stimulation in anyone likely to be confronted with Cohen's crudely defaced jacket.

This Court has also held that the States are free to ban the simple use, without a demonstration of additional justifying circumstances, of so-called "fighting words," those personally abusive epithets which, when addressed to the ordinary citizen, are, as a matter of common knowledge, inherently likely to provoke violent reaction. *Chaplinsky.* While the four-letter word displayed by Cohen in relation to the draft is not uncommonly employed in a personally provocative fashion, in this instance it was clearly not "directed to the person of the hearer." No individual actually or likely to be present could reasonably have regarded the words on appellant's jacket as a direct personal insult. Nor do we have here an instance of the exercise of the State's police power to prevent a speaker from intentionally provoking a given group to hostile reaction. Cf. *Feiner;*

---

3. It is illuminating to note what transpired when Cohen entered a courtroom in the building. He removed his jacket and stood with it folded over his arm. Meanwhile, a policeman sent the presiding judge a note suggesting that Cohen be held in contempt of court. The judge declined to do so and Cohen was arrested by the officer only after he emerged from the courtroom.

Terminiello. There is, as noted above, no showing that anyone who saw Cohen was in fact violently aroused or that appellant intended such a result.

[T]he mere presumed presence of unwitting listeners or viewers does not serve automatically to justify curtailing all speech capable of giving offense. While this Court has recognized that government may properly act in many situations to prohibit intrusion into the privacy of the home of unwelcome views and ideas which cannot be totally banned from the public dialogue, we have at the same time consistently stressed that "we are often 'captives' outside the sanctuary of the home and subject to objectionable speech."[a] The ability of government, consonant with the Constitution, to shut off discourse solely to protect others from hearing it is, in other words, dependent upon a showing that substantial privacy interests are being invaded in an essentially intolerable manner. Any broader view of this authority would effectively empower a majority to silence dissidents simply as a matter of personal predilections.

[Given] the subtlety and complexity of the factors involved if Cohen's "speech" was otherwise entitled to constitutional protection, we do not think the fact that some unwilling "listeners" in a public building may have been briefly exposed to it can serve to justify this breach of the peace conviction where, as here, there was no evidence that persons powerless to avoid appellant's conduct did in fact object to it, and where [unlike another portion of the same statute barring the use of "vulgar, profane or indecent language within [the] hearing of women or children, in a loud and boisterous manner"], the [challenged statutory provision] evinces no concern [with] the special plight of the captive auditor, but, instead, indiscriminately sweeps within its prohibitions all "offensive conduct" that disturbs "any neighborhood or person."

Against this background, the issue flushed by this case stands out in bold relief. It is whether California can excise, as "offensive conduct," one particular scurrilous epithet from the public discourse, either upon the theory of the court below that its use is inherently likely to cause violent reaction or upon a more general assertion that the States, acting as guardians of public morality, may properly remove this offensive word from the public vocabulary.

The rationale of the California court is plainly untenable. At most it reflects an "undifferentiated fear or apprehension of disturbance [which] is not enough to overcome the right to freedom of expression." *Tinker* [Ch. 7, II infra]. We have been shown no evidence that substantial numbers of citizens are standing ready to strike out physically at whoever may assault their sensibilities with execrations like that uttered by Cohen. There may be some persons about with such lawless and violent proclivities, but that is an insufficient base upon which to erect, consistently with constitutional values, a governmental power to force persons who wish to ventilate

---

a. For commentary on the captive audience concept, see J.M. Balkin, *Free Speech and Hostile Environments,* 99 Colum. L.Rev. 2295, 2306–18 (1999).

their dissident views into avoiding particular forms of expression. The argument amounts to little more than the self-defeating proposition that to avoid physical censorship of one who has not sought to provoke such a response by a hypothetical coterie of the violent and lawless, the States may more appropriately effectuate that censorship themselves.

Admittedly, it is not so obvious that the First and Fourteenth Amendments must be taken to disable the States from punishing public utterance of this unseemly expletive in order to maintain what they regard as a suitable level of discourse within the body politic. We think, however, that examination and reflection will reveal the shortcomings of a contrary viewpoint.

[The] constitutional right of free expression is powerful medicine in a society as diverse and populous as ours. It is designed and intended to remove governmental restraints from the arena of public discussion, putting the decision as to what views shall be voiced largely into the hands of each of us, in the hope that use of such freedom will ultimately produce a more capable citizenry and more perfect polity and in the belief that no other approach would comport with the premise of individual dignity and choice upon which our political system rests.[b]

To many, the immediate consequence of this freedom may often appear to be only verbal tumult, discord, and even offensive utterance. These are, however, within established limits, in truth necessary side effects of the broader enduring values which the process of open debate permits us to achieve. That the air may at times seem filled with verbal cacophony is, in this sense not a sign of weakness but of strength. We cannot lose sight of the fact that, in what otherwise might seem a trifling and annoying instance of individual distasteful abuse of a privilege, these fundamental societal values are truly implicated. * * *

Against this perception of the constitutional policies involved, we discern certain more particularized considerations that peculiarly call for reversal of this conviction. First, the principle contended for by the State seems inherently boundless. How is one to distinguish this from any other offensive word? Surely the State has no right to cleanse public debate to the point where it is grammatically palatable to the most squeamish among us. Yet no readily ascertainable general principle exists for stopping short of that result were we to affirm the judgment below. For, while the particular four-letter word being litigated here is perhaps more distasteful than most others of its genre, it is nevertheless often true that one man's vulgarity is another's lyric. Indeed, we think it is largely because governmental officials cannot make principled distinctions in this area that the Constitution leaves matters of taste and style so largely to the individual.

---

b. For theoretical and practical elaboration of this perspective, see Steven J. Heyman, *Free Speech and Human Dignity* (2008).

Additionally, we cannot overlook the fact, because it is well illustrated by the episode involved here, that much linguistic expression serves a dual communicative function: it conveys not only ideas capable of relatively precise, detached explication, but otherwise inexpressible emotions as well. In fact, words are often chosen as much for their emotive as their cognitive force. We cannot sanction the view that the Constitution, while solicitous of the cognitive content of individual speech, has little or no regard for that emotive function which, practically speaking, may often be the more important element of the overall message sought to be communicated. * * *

Finally, and in the same vein, we cannot indulge the facile assumption that one can forbid particular words without also running a substantial risk of suppressing ideas in the process. Indeed, governments might soon seize upon the censorship of particular words as a convenient guise for banning the expression of unpopular views. We have been able [to] discern little social benefit that might result from running the risk of opening the door to such grave results.

It is, in sum, our judgment that, absent a more particularized and compelling reason for its actions, the State may not, consistently with the First and Fourteenth Amendments, make the simple public display here involved of this single four-letter expletive a criminal offense. * * *

[Blackmun, J., joined by Burger, C.J., and Black, J., dissented for two reasons: (1) "Cohen's absurd and immature antic [was] mainly conduct and little speech" and the case falls "well within the sphere of *Chaplinsky*"; (2) although it declined to review the state court of appeals' decision in *Cohen,* the California Supreme Court subsequently narrowly construed the breach-of-the-peace statute in another case and *Cohen* should be remanded to the California Court of Appeal in the light of this subsequent construction. White, J., concurred with the dissent on the latter ground.]

Notes and Questions

1. For criticism of *Cohen,* see Alexander Bickel, *The Morality of Consent* 72 (1975) (Cohen's speech "constitutes an assault" and this sort of speech "may create [an] environment [in which] actions that were not possible before become possible"); Archibald Cox, *The Role of the Supreme Court in American Government* 47–48 (1976) (state has interest in "level at which public discourse is conducted"; state should not have to "allow exhibitionists and [others] trading upon our lower prurient interests to inflict themselves upon the public consciousness and dull its sensibilities"). For a defense (but what not a few would consider a narrow reading) of *Cohen,* see Daniel Farber, *Civilizing Public Discourse: An Essay on Professor Bickel, Justice Harlan, and the Enduring Significance of Cohen v. California,* 1980 Duke L.J. 283. See also John Hart Ely, *Democracy and Distrust* 114 (1980); Tribe, 2d ed., at 787–88, 851–52, 916–17, 953–54. For an overview of Harlan, J.'s approach to the First Amendment, see Daniel Farber & John Nowak, *Justice Harlan and the First Amendment,* 2 Const.Comm. 425 (1985).

2.   To what extent, if at all, and in what ways, if any, does *Cohen* restrict the "fighting words" doctrine? Consider Hadley Arkes, *Civility and the Restriction of Speech: Rediscovering the Defamation of Groups*, 1974 Sup.Ct. Rev. 281, 316: *Cohen* turned "the presumptions in *Chaplinsky* around: instead of presuming that profane or defamatory speech was beneath constitutional protection, he presumed that the speech was protected and that the burden of proof lay with those who would restrict it." If "one man's vulgarity is another's lyric," how are discriminations to be made in the "fighting words" area?

3.   What does *Cohen* decide? Consider William Cohen, *A Look Back at Cohen v. California*, 34 UCLA L.Rev. 1595, 1602–03 (1987): "Unless it is overruled or dishonestly distinguished, [*Cohen*] has settled [that] a criminal statute is unconstitutional if it punishes all public use of profanity without reference to details such as the nature of the location and the audience. The opinion, however, left much to be decided about government controls on the use of profanity based on considerations of time, place, and manner. To what extent can profanity be punished because of the nature of the audience, the nature of the occasion on which it is uttered or displayed, or the manner of its utterance or display." What if the word "draft" did not appear on Cohen's jacket? Protected? What if the word "you" were substituted for "draft"? Protected? See Robert M. O'Neil, *Rights in Conflict: The First Amendment's Third Century*, 65–SPG Law & Contemp. Probs. 7, 20–22 (2002). Do spectators have any free speech rights in the courtroom? See *Carey v. Musladin*, 549 U.S. 70 (2006) (Souter, J., concurring).

4.   A series of cases in the early 1970s reversed convictions involving abusive language. *Gooding v. Wilson*, 405 U.S. 518 (1972), invalidated a Georgia ordinance primarily because it had been previously applied to "utterances where there was no likelihood that the person addressed would make an immediate violent response." *Lewis v. New Orleans*, 415 U.S. 130 (1974), ruled that vulgar or offensive speech was protected under the First Amendment. Because the statute punished "opprobrious language," it was deemed by the Court to embrace words that do not " 'by their very utterance inflict injury or tend to invite an immediate breach of the peace.' "

Although *Gooding* seemed to require a danger of immediate violence, *Lewis* recited that infliction of injury was sufficient. Dissenting in both cases, BURGER, C.J., and Blackmun and Rehnquist, JJ., complained that the majority invoked vagueness and overbreadth analysis "indiscriminately without regard to the nature of the speech in question, the possible effect the statute or ordinance has upon such speech, the importance of the speech in relation to the exposition of ideas, or the purported or asserted community interest in preventing that speech." The dissenters focused upon the facts of the cases (e.g., Gooding to a police officer: "White son of a bitch, I'll kill you," "You son of a bitch, I'll choke you to death," and "You son of a bitch, if you ever put your hands on me again, I'll cut you to pieces."). They complained that the majority had relegated the facts to "footnote status, conveniently distant and in less disturbing focus." In *Gooding, Lewis,* and the other cases, POWELL, J., insisted upon the importance of context in decision making. Dissenting in *Rosenfeld v. New Jersey*, 408 U.S. 901 (1972), he suggested that *Chaplinsky* be extended to the "wilful use of scurrilous language calculated to offend the sensibilities of an unwilling audience"; concurring in *Lewis,* he maintained that allowing prosecutions for offensive language directed at police officers invited law enforcement abuse. Finally, he suggested in *Rosenfeld* that whatever the scope of the "fighting words" doctrine, overbreadth analysis was inappropriate in such cases. He doubted that such statutes deter others from exercising First Amendment rights.[c]

VI. SHOULD NEW CATEGORIES BE CREATED?

Steven J. Heyman argues in *Free Speech & Human Dignity* 96 (2008): "The courts should be extremely careful not to unduly expand the bounds of regulable expression. New categories should be recognized only when they are clearly justified. But there is no reason to assume that the categories established in previous cases are the only valid ones. As one would expect from a process of case-by case adjudication, the categories of unprotected speech have been determined in piecemeal fashion and have never been worked out in a logical or systematic way. Thus, the Court should not refuse to recognize a category simply because it has not done so in the past." Suppose a legislature were to outlaw speech whose dominant theme appeals to a morbid interest in violence, that is patently offensive to contemporary community standards, and that lacks serious literary, artistic, political or scientific value. Constitutional?[a] One approach would be to contend that speech is protected unless it falls into already established categorical exceptions to First Amendment protection. Another would be to argue by analogy, e.g., if obscenity is beneath First Amendment protection, this speech should (or should not) be beneath such protection. Similarly, one could argue that exceptions to First Amendment protection has been fashioned by resort to a balancing methodology and that balancing the relevant interests is the right approach. Alternatively, one could proceed from a particular substantive vision of the First Amendment, such as the Meiklejohn view. Which approach has been applied by the Court?[b]

---

c. For commentary on Powell, J.'s approach, see Gerald Gunther, *In Search of Judicial Quality on a Changing Court: The Case of Justice Powell,* 24 Stan.L.Rev. 1001, 1029–35 (1972).

a. See Kevin W. Saunders, *Media Violence and the Obscenity Exception to the First Amendment,* 3 Wm. & Mary Bill Rts. J. 107 (1994); Lucas Powe & Thomas Krattenmaker, *Televised Violence: First Amendment Principles and Social Science Theory,* 64 Va. L.Rev. 1123 (1978). See also Lorraine M. Buerger *The Safe Games Illinois Act,* 37 Loy. U.Chi. L.J. 617 (2006); Laura Tate Kagel, *Balancing the First Amendment and Child Protection Goals in Legal Approaches to Restricting Access to Violent Video Games,* 34 Ga. J.Int'l & Comp.L. 743 (2006); Barry Smith, *The Fight Over Video Game Violence,* 30 Law & Psychol. Rev. 185 (2006). Cf. Geoffrey R. Stone, *Sex, Violence, and the First Amendment,* 74 U.Chi. L.Rev. 1857 (2007).

b. For commentary on the Court's methodology, see Rodney A. Smolla, *Smolla and Nimmer on Freedom of Speech* (3d ed. 1996); Daniel A. Farber, *The First Amendment* (2d ed. 2003); Martin Redish, *Freedom of Expression: A Critical Analysis* (1984); Steven Shiffrin, *The First Amendment, Democracy, and Romance* (1990); Rodney A. Smolla, *Smolla and Nimmer on Freedom of Speech* (1996); William Van Alstyne, *Interpretations of the First Amendment* (1984); William Van Alstyne, *A Graphic Review of the Free Speech Clause,* 70 Calif.L.Rev. 107 (1982); James Weinstein, *Hate Speech, Pornography and the Radical Attack on Free Speech Doctrine* (1999); T. Alexander Aleinikoff, *Constitutional Law in the Age of Balancing,* 96 Yale L.J. 943 (1987); Randall P. Bezanson, *The Quality of First Amendment Speech,* 20 Hastings Comm/Ent L.J. 275 (1998); Joshua P. Davis & Joshua D. Rosenberg, *The Inherent Structure of First Amendment Law,* 19

New York v. Ferber, infra, is interesting because it involves the question of whether to create a new category.

A. HARM TO CHILDREN AND THE OVERBREADTH DOCTRINE

NEW YORK v. FERBER, 458 U.S. 747 (1982), per WHITE, J., upheld conviction of a seller of films depicting young boys masturbating, under N.Y.Penal Law § 263.15, for "promoting[a] a sexual performance," defined as "any performance [which] includes sexual conduct[b] by a child" under 16. The Court addressed the "single question": " 'To prevent the abuse of children who are made to engage in sexual conduct for commercial purposes, could the New York State Legislature, consistent with the First Amendment, prohibit the dissemination of material which shows children engaged in sexual conduct, regardless of whether such material is obscene?'[c] * * *

"The *Miller* standard, like its predecessors, was an accommodation between the state's interests in protecting the 'sensibilities of unwilling recipients' from exposure to pornographic material and the dangers of censorship inherent in unabashedly content-based laws. Like obscenity statutes, laws directed at the dissemination of child pornography run the risk of suppressing protected expression by allowing the hand of the censor to become unduly heavy. For the following reasons, however, we are persuaded that the States are entitled to greater leeway in the regulation of pornographic depictions of children.

"First. [The] prevention of sexual exploitation and abuse of children constitutes a government objective of surpassing importance. The legisla-

---

Wm. & Mary Bill Rts.J. 131 (2010); Richard Fallon, *A Constructivist Coherence Theory of Constitutional Interpretation*, 100 Harv.L.Rev. 1189, 1228 n.191 (1987); Elena Kagan, *Private Speech, Public Purpose: The Role of Governmental Motive in First Amendment Doctrine*, 63 U. Chi.L.Rev. 413 (1996); Robert Post, *Recuperating First Amendment Doctrine*, 47 Stan.L.Rev. 1249(1995); Frederick Schauer, *The Speech of Law and the Law of Speech*, Ark. L.Rev. 687 (1997); Frederick Schauer, *Mrs. Palsgraf and the First Amendment*, 47 Wash. & Lee L.Rev. 161 (1990); Frederick Schauer, *The Second–Best First Amendment*, 31 Wm. & M.L.Rev. 1 (1989); Frederick Schauer, *Categories and the First Amendment: A Play in Three Acts,* 34 Vand.L.Rev. 265 (1981); Pierre Schlag, *Rules and Standards,* 33 U.C.L.A.L.Rev. 379 (1985); Geoffrey Stone, *Content Regulation and the First Amendment*, 25 Wm. & Mary L.Rev. 189 (1983); Geoffrey Stone, *Content–Neutral Restrictions*, 54 U.Chi.L.Rev. 46 (1987); Cass R. Sunstein, *Trimming*, 122 Harv. L.Rev. 1049 (2009).

a. "Promote" was defined to include all aspects of production, distribution, exhibition and sale.

b. Sec. 263.3 defined "sexual conduct" as "actual or simulated sexual intercourse, deviate sexual intercourse, sexual bestiality, masturbation, sado-masochistic abuse, or lewd exhibition of the genitals."

c. The opinion gave the background for such legislation: "In recent years, the exploitive use of children in the production of pornography has become a serious national problem. The federal government and forty-seven States have sought to combat the problem with statutes specifically directed at the production of child pornography. At least half of such statutes do not require that the materials produced be legally obscene. Thirty-five States and the United States Congress have also passed legislation prohibiting the distribution of such materials; twenty States prohibit the distribution of material depicting children engaged in sexual conduct without requiring that the material be legally obscene. New York is one of the twenty."

tive findings accompanying passage of the New York laws reflect this concern. * * *

"We shall not second-guess this legislative judgment. Respondent has not intimated that we do so. Suffice it to say that virtually all of the States and the United States have passed legislation proscribing the production of or otherwise combating 'child pornography.' The legislative judgment, as well as the judgment found in the relevant literature, is that the use of children as subjects of pornographic materials is harmful to the physiological, emotional, and mental health of the child. That judgment, we think, easily passes muster under the First Amendment.

"Second. The distribution of photographs and films depicting sexual activity by juveniles is intrinsically related to the sexual abuse of children in at least two ways. First, the materials produced are a permanent record of the children's participation and the harm to the child is exacerbated by their circulation. Second, the distribution network for child pornography must be closed if the production of material which requires the sexual exploitation of children is to be effectively controlled. Indeed, there is no serious contention that the legislature was unjustified in believing that it is difficult, if not impossible, to halt the exploitation of children by pursuing only those who produce the photographs and movies. While the production of pornographic materials is a low-profile, clandestine industry, the need to market the resulting products requires a visible apparatus of distribution. The most expeditious if not the only practical method of law enforcement may be to dry up the market for this material by imposing severe criminal penalties on persons selling, advertising, or otherwise promoting the product. Thirty-five States and Congress have concluded that restraints on the distribution of pornographic materials are required in order to effectively combat the problem, and there is a body of literature and testimony to support these legislative conclusions.

"[The] *Miller* standard, like all general definitions of what may be banned as obscene, does not reflect the State's particular and more compelling interest in prosecuting those who promote the sexual exploitation of children. Thus, the question under the *Miller* test of whether a work, taken as a whole, appeals to the prurient interest of the average person bears no connection to the issue of whether a child has been physically or psychologically harmed in the production of the work. Similarly, a sexual explicit depiction need not be 'patently offensive' in order to have required the sexual exploitation of a child for its production. In addition, a work which, taken on the whole, contains serious literary, artistic, political, or scientific value may nevertheless embody the hardest core of child pornography. 'It is irrelevant to the child [who has been abused] whether or not the material [has] a literary, artistic, political, or social value.' We therefore cannot conclude that the *Miller* standard is a satisfactory solution to the child pornography problem.

"Third. The advertising and selling of child pornography provides an economic motive for and is thus an integral part of the production of such materials, an activity illegal throughout the nation. 'It rarely has been suggested that the constitutional freedom for speech and press extends its immunity to speech or writing used as an integral part of conduct in violation of a valid criminal statute.' * * *

"Fourth. The value of permitting live performances and photographic reproductions of children engaged in lewd sexual conduct is exceedingly modest, if not de minimis. We consider it unlikely that visual depictions of children performing sexual acts or lewdly exhibiting their genitals would often constitute an important and necessary part of a literary performance or scientific or educational work. As the trial court in this case observed, if it were necessary for literary or artistic value, a person over the statutory age who perhaps looked younger could be utilized. * * *

"Fifth. Recognizing and classifying child pornography as a category of material outside the protection of the First Amendment is not incompatible with our earlier decisions. 'The question whether speech is, or is not protected by the First Amendment often depends on the content of the speech.' *Young v. American Mini Theatres, Inc.* [Ch. 3, I infra]. '[I]t is the content of an utterance that determines whether it is a protected epithet or [an] unprotected "fighting comment" '. Leaving aside the special considerations when public officials are the target, *New York Times Co. v. Sullivan,* a libelous publication is not protected by the Constitution. *Beauharnais.* [It] is not rare that a content-based classification of speech has been accepted because it may be appropriately generalized that within the confines of the given classification, the evil to be restricted so overwhelmingly outweighs the expressive interests, if any, at stake, that no process of case-by-case adjudication is required. When a definable class of material, such as that covered by § 263.15, bears so heavily and pervasively on the welfare of children engaged in its production, we think the balance of competing interests is clearly struck and that it is permissible to consider these materials as without the protection of the First Amendment.

"There are, of course, limits on the category of child pornography which, like obscenity, is unprotected by the First Amendment. As with all legislation in this sensitive area, the conduct to be prohibited must be adequately defined by the applicable state law, as written or authoritatively construed. Here the nature of the harm to be combated requires that the state offense be limited to works that *visually* depict sexual conduct by children below a specified age. The category of 'sexual conduct' proscribed must also be suitably limited and described.

"The test for child pornography is separate from the obscenity standard enunciated in *Miller,* but may be compared to it for purpose of clarity. The *Miller* formulation is adjusted in the following respects: A trier of fact need not find that the material appeals to the prurient interest of the average person; it is not required that sexual conduct portrayed be done so in a patently offensive manner; and the material at issue need not be considered as a whole. We note that the distribution of descriptions or other depictions of sexual conduct, not otherwise obscene, which do not involve live performance or photographic or other visual reproduction of live performances, retains First Amendment protection. As with obscenity laws, criminal responsibility may not be imposed without some element of scienter on the part of the defendant. * * *

"It remains to address the claim that the New York statute is unconstitutionally overbroad because it would forbid the distribution of material with serious literary, scientific, or educational value or material which does not threaten the harms sought to be combated by the State. * * *

"The traditional rule is that a person to whom a statute may constitutionally be applied may not challenge that statute on the ground that it may conceivably be applied unconstitutionally to others in situations not before the Court. *Broadrick v. Oklahoma,* 413 U.S. 601 (1973). In *Broadrick,* we recognized that this rule reflects two cardinal principles of our constitutional order: the personal nature of constitutional rights and prudential limitations on constitutional adjudication.[20] [By] focusing on the factual situation before us, and similar cases necessary for development of a constitutional rule,[21] we face 'flesh-and-blood' legal problems with data 'relevant and adequate to an informed judgment.' This practice also fulfills a valuable institutional purpose: it allows state courts the opportunity to construe a law to avoid constitutional infirmities.

"What has come to be known as the First Amendment overbreadth doctrine is one of the few exceptions to this principle and must be justified by weighty countervailing policies. The doctrine is predicated on the sensitive nature of protected expression: persons whose expression is constitutionally protected may well refrain from exercising their rights for fear of criminal sanctions by a statute susceptible of application to protected expression. * * *

"In *Broadrick,* we explained [that]: '[T]he plain import of our cases is, at the very least, that facial overbreadth adjudication is an exception to our traditional rules of practice and that its function, a limited one at the outset, attenuates as the otherwise unprotected behavior that it forbids the State to sanction moves from "pure speech" toward conduct and that conduct—even if expressive—falls within the scope of otherwise valid criminal laws that reflect legitimate state interests in maintaining comprehensive controls over harmful, constitutionally unprotected conduct. * * *'

"[*Broadrick*] examined a regulation involving restrictions on political campaign activity, an area not considered 'pure speech,' and thus it was unnecessary to consider the proper overbreadth test when a law arguably

20. In addition to prudential restraints, the traditional rule is grounded in Art. III limits on the jurisdiction of federal courts to actual cases and controversies. * * *

21. Overbreadth challenges are only one type of facial attack. A person whose activity may be constitutionally regulated nevertheless may argue that the statute under which he is convicted or regulated is invalid on its face. See, e.g., *Terminiello.* See generally Henry Monaghan, *Overbreadth,* 1981 S.Ct.Rev. 1, 10–14.

reaches traditional forms of expression such as books and films. As we intimated in *Broadrick,* the requirement of substantial overbreadth extended 'at the very least' to cases involving conduct plus speech. This case, which poses the question squarely, convinces us that the rationale of *Broadrick* is sound and should be applied in the present context involving the harmful employment of children to make sexually explicit materials for distribution.

"The premise that a law should not be invalidated for overbreadth unless it reaches a substantial number of impermissible applications is hardly novel.[d] On most occasions involving facial invalidation, the Court has stressed the embracing sweep of the statute over protected expression.[26] Indeed, Justice Brennan observed in his dissenting opinion in *Broadrick*: 'We have never held that a statute should be held invalid on its face merely because it is possible to conceive of a single impermissible application, and in that sense a requirement of substantial overbreadth is already implicit in the doctrine.'

"The requirement of substantial overbreadth is directly derived from the purpose and nature of the doctrine. While a sweeping statute, or one incapable of limitation, has the potential to repeatedly chill the exercise of expressive activity by many individuals, the extent of deterrence of protected speech can be expected to decrease with the declining reach of the regulation. This observation appears equally applicable to the publication of books and films as it is to activities, such as picketing or participation in election campaigns, which have previously been categorized as involving conduct plus speech. We see no appreciable difference between the position of a publisher or bookseller in doubt as to the reach of New York's child pornography law and the situation faced by the Oklahoma state employees with respect to the State's restriction on partisan political activity.[e] * * *

"Applying these principles, we hold that § 263.15 is not substantially overbroad. We consider this the paradigmatic case of a state statute whose legitimate reach dwarfs its arguably impermissible applications. [While] the reach of the statute is directed at the hard core of child pornography, the Court of Appeals was understandably concerned that some protected expression, ranging from medical textbooks to pictorials in the National

---

d. Scalia, J., dissenting in *Chicago v. Morales*, 527 U.S. 41 (1999), argues that in order to avoid advisory opinions, federal courts should limit themselves to as applied attacks, but that if they insist on considering facial attacks, they should insist that a statute be unconstitutional in all its applications before declaring it unconstitutional. Are either of these positions acceptable?

26. In *Gooding v. Wilson,* the Court's invalidation of a Georgia statute making it a misdemeanor to use " 'opprobrious words or abusive language, tending to cause a breach of the peace' " followed from state judicial decisions indicating that "merely to speak words offensive to some who hear them" could constitute a "breach of the peace." * * *

e. *Brockett v. Spokane Arcades, Inc.,* Ch. 1, III, B supra, stated: "The Court of Appeals erred in holding that the *Broadrick* substantial overbreadth requirement is inapplicable where pure speech rather than conduct is at issue. *Ferber* specifically held to the contrary." For commentary on the overbreadth discussion in *Broadrick* and *Ferber,* see Martin Redish, *The Warren Court, The Burger Court and the First Amendment Overbreadth Doctrine,* 78 Nw.U.L.Rev. 1031, 1056–69 (1983).

Geographic would fall prey to the statute. How often, if ever, it may be necessary to employ children to engage in conduct clearly within the reach of § 263.15 in order to produce educational, medical, or artistic works cannot be known with certainty. Yet we seriously doubt, and it has not been suggested, that these arguably impermissible applications of the statute amount to more than a tiny fraction of the materials within the statute's reach."[f]

NOTES AND QUESTIONS

1. Consider Frederick Schauer, *Codifying the First Amendment: New York v. Ferber,* 1982 Sup.Ct.Rev. 285, 295: The new category created in *Ferber* "bears little resemblance to the category of obscenity delineated by *Miller.* The Court in *Ferber* explicitly held that child pornography need not appeal to the prurient interest, need not be patently offensive, and need not be based on a consideration of the material as a whole. This last aspect is most important, because it means that the presence of some serious literary, artistic, political, or scientific matter will not constitutionally redeem material containing depictions of sexual conduct by children. The Court referred to the foregoing factors in terms of having 'adjusted' the *Miller* test, but that is like saying a butterfly is an adjusted camel." What precisely is the new category created in *Ferber*?

2. What test or standard of review did the Court use to determine whether the speech should be protected? For general discussion, see Schauer, *supra.* Did it apply a different test or a standard of review when it formulated its rules in *Gertz*? Are tests or standards of review needed in these contexts? Desirable? Consider Steven Shiffrin, *The First Amendment and Economic Regulation: Away From a General Theory of the First Amendment,* 78 Nw.

---

f. Brennan, J., joined by Marshall, J., agreed "with much of what is said in the Court's opinion. [This] special and compelling interest (in protecting the well-being of the State's youth), and the particular vulnerability of children, afford the State the leeway to regulate pornographic material, the promotion of which is harmful to children, even though the State does not have such leeway when it seeks only to protect consenting adults from exposure to such materials. * * * I also agree with the Court that the 'tiny fraction' of material of serious artistic, scientific or educational value that could conceivably fall within the reach of the statute is insufficient to justify striking the statute on grounds of overbreadth." But the concurrence stated that application of the statute to such materials as "do have serious artistic, scientific or medical value would violate the First Amendment."

On that issue O'Connor, J., wrote a short concurrence: "Although I join the Court's opinion, I write separately to stress that the Court does not hold that New York must except 'material with serious literary, scientific or educational value' from its statute. The Court merely holds that, even if the First Amendment shelters such material, New York's current statute is not sufficiently overbroad to support respondent's facial attack. The compelling interests identified in today's opinion suggest that the Constitution might in fact permit New York to ban knowing distribution of works depicting minors engaged in explicit sexual conduct, regardless of the social value of the depictions. For example, a 12-year-old child photographed while masturbating surely suffers the same psychological harm whether the community labels the photograph 'edifying' or 'tasteless.' The audience's appreciation of the depiction is simply irrelevant to New York's asserted interest in protecting children from psychological, emotional, and mental harm."

Stevens, J., also concurred in the judgment in a short opinion that noted his conclusion that the films in the case were not entitled to First Amendment protection, and his view that overbreadth analysis should be avoided by waiting until the hypothetical case actually arises.

Blackmun, J., concurred in the result without opinion.

U.L.Rev. 1212, 1268 (1983): "The complex set of rules produced in *Gertz,* right or wrong, resulted from an appreciation that the protection of truth was important but that the protection of reputation also was important. The Court wisely avoided discussion of levels of scrutiny because any resort to such abstractions would have constitutionalized reductionism." Is "constitutionalized reductionism" desirable because it protects speech and provides guidance to the lower courts?

3. *Absence of children.* SIMON & SCHUSTER, INC. v. MEMBERS OF NEW YORK STATE CRIME VICTIMS BD., 502 U.S. 105 (1991), per O'CONNOR, J., struck down a law requiring that income derived from works in which individuals admit to crime involving victims be used to compensate the victims: "[T]he State has a compelling interest in compensating victims from the fruits of the crime, but little if any interest in limiting such compensation to the proceeds of the wrongdoer's speech about the crime."[g]

4. *Overbreadth without a chilling effect?* Massachusetts prohibited adults from posing or exhibiting nude children for purposes of photographs, publications, or pictures, moving or otherwise. Bona fide scientific or medical purposes were excepted as were educational or cultural purposes for a bona fide school, museum, or library. Douglas Oakes was prosecuted for taking 10 color photographs of his 14–year–old stepdaughter in a state of nudity covered by the statute. The Massachusetts Supreme Judicial Court declared the statute overbroad. After certiorari was granted in MASSACHUSETTS v. OAKES, 491 U.S. 576 (1989), Massachusetts added a "lascivious intent" requirement to the statute and eliminated the exemptions. O'CONNOR, J., joined by Rehnquist, C.J., and White and Kennedy, JJ., accordingly refused to entertain the overbreadth challenge and voted to remand the case for determination of the statute's constitutionality as applied: "Because it has been repealed, the former version of [the Massachusetts law] cannot chill protected speech."

SCALIA, J., joined by Blackmun, Brennan, Marshall, and Stevens, JJ., disagreed:[h] "It seems to me strange judicial theory that a conviction initially invalid can be resuscitated by postconviction alteration of the statute under which it was obtained. [Even as a policy matter, the] overbreadth doctrine serves to protect constitutionally legitimate speech not merely *ex post,* that is, after the offending statute is enacted, but also *ex ante,* that is, when the legislature is contemplating what sort of statute to enact. If the promulgation of overbroad laws affecting speech was cost free[,] if *no* conviction of constitutionally proscribable conduct would be lost, so long as the offending statute

---

g. Kennedy, J., concurring, would have stricken the statute without reference to the compelling state interest test which he condemned as ad hoc balancing. Blackmun, J., also concurred. Thomas, J., did not participate. For extensive criticism of the strict scrutiny test, see Eugene Volokh, *Freedom of Speech, Permissible Tailoring, and Transcending Strict Scrutiny,* 144 U.Pa. L.Rev. 2417, 2446 (1996).

h. Although these five justices agreed that the overbreadth challenge should be entertained, they divided on the merits of the challenge. Scalia, J., joined by Blackmun, J., found no merit in the overbreadth claim (see note 5 infra) and voted to reverse and to remand for determination of the statute's constitutionality as applied. The three remaining justices (see note 5 infra) agreed with the overbreadth challenge and voted to affirm the judgment below. O'Connor, J.'s opinion, therefore, became the plurality opinion, and the Court's judgment was to vacate the judgment below and to remand. In the end, six justices voted against the overbreadth challenge: four because it was moot; two because it did not meet the requirement of substantial overbreadth.

was narrowed before the final appeal—then legislatures would have significantly reduced incentive to stay within constitutional bounds in the first place.[i] [More] fundamentally, however, [it] seems to me that we are only free to pursue policy objectives through the modes of action traditionally followed by the courts and by the law. [I] have heard of a voidable contract, but never of a voidable law. The notion is bizarre."

5. *How substantial is substantial overbreadth?* Five justices addressed the overbreadth question in *Oakes,* but the substantive issue was not resolved. BRENNAN, J., joined by Marshall and Stevens, JJ., objected that the statute would make it criminal for parents "to photograph their infant children or toddlers in the bath or romping naked on the beach." More generally, he argued that the First Amendment "blocks the prohibition of nude posing by minors in connection with the production of works of art not depicting lewd behavior. [Many] of the world's great artists—Degas, Renoir, Donatello, to name but a few—have worked from models under 18 years of age, and many acclaimed photographs have included nude or partially clad minors."

SCALIA, J., joined by Blackmun, J., disagreed: "[G]iven the known extent of the kiddie-porn industry[,] I would estimate that the legitimate scope [of the statute] vastly exceeds the illegitimate. [Even] assuming that proscribing artistic depictions of preadolescent genitals and postadolescent breasts is impermissible,[2] the body of material that would be covered is, as far as I am aware, insignificant compared with the lawful scope of the statute. That leaves the family photos. [Assuming] that it is unconstitutional (as opposed to merely foolish) to prohibit such photography, I do not think it so common as to make the statute *substantially* overbroad. [My] perception differs, for example, from Justice Brennan's belief that there is an 'abundance of baby and child photographs taken every day' depicting genitals."[j]

Consider Amy Adler, *Inverting the First Amendment*, 149 U. Pa. L. Rev. 921, 947 (2001): "The Supreme Court and lower federal courts since *Ferber* have tolerated statutes that define this margin of child "sexual conduct" in increasingly broad and subjective terms. Each subtle reiteration of the definition of "lewd" or "lascivious exhibition of the genitals" since *Ferber* has expanded it. If we pushed the case law to the extreme, it seems to threaten all pictures of unclothed children, whether "lewd" or not, and even pictures of clothed children, if they meet the increasingly hazy definition of 'lascivious' or 'lewd.' " Does the increasing breadth make the failure to countenance a "serious value" exception more problematic? See id. at 967–69.

---

i. For criticism of this point, see Alfred Hill, *The Puzzling First Amendment Overbreadth Doctrine,* 25 Hof.L.Rev. 1063, 1071 (1997).

2. [Most] adults, I expect, would not hire themselves out as nude models, whatever the intention of the photographer or artist, and however unerotic the pose. There is no cause to think children are less sensitive. It is not unreasonable, therefore, for a State to regard parents' using (or permitting the use) of their children as nude models, or other adults' use of consenting minors, as a form of child exploitation.

j. For the argument that the Court should balance a number of factors including the "state's substantive interest in being able to impose sanctions for a particular kind of conduct under a particular legal standard, as opposed to being forced to rely on other, less restrictive substitutes" instead of trying to determine the number of constitutional and unconstitutional applications, see Richard Fallon, *Making Sense of Overbreadth,* 100 Yale L.J. 853, 894 (1991).

6. *Digital child pornography.* The Child Pornography Act of 1996 (the "CPPA") in addition to outlawing child pornography involving minors, extends its coverage to prohibit images that "appear to be, of a minor engaging in sexually explicit conduct" or marketed in a way that "conveys the impression" that it depicts a "minor engaging in sexually explicit conduct." ASHCROFT v. FREE SPEECH COALITION, 535 U.S. 234 (2002), per KENNE-DY, J., declared these provisions to be unconstitutional: "The CPPA [extends] to images that appear to depict a minor engaging in sexually explicit activity without regard to the *Miller* requirements. The materials need not appeal to the prurient interest. Any depiction of sexually explicit activity, no matter how it is presented, is proscribed. The CPPA applies to a picture in a psychology manual, as well as a movie depicting the horrors of sexual abuse. It is not necessary, moreover, that the image be patently offensive. Pictures of what appear to be 17-year-olds engaging in sexually explicit activity do not in every case contravene community standards.

"The CPPA prohibits speech despite its serious literary, artistic, political, or scientific value. The statute proscribes the visual depiction of [the idea] of teenagers engaging in sexual activity that is a fact of modern society and has been a theme in art and literature throughout the ages." Kennedy, J., argued that the Act could potentially apply to versions of Romeo and Juliet and films like Traffic and American Beauty.

"[The government] argues that the CPPA is necessary because pedophiles may use virtual child pornography to seduce children. There are many things innocent in themselves, however, such as cartoons, video games, and candy, that might be used for immoral purposes, yet we would not expect those to be prohibited because they can be misused. The Government, of course, may punish adults who provide unsuitable materials to children, and it may enforce criminal penalties for unlawful solicitation. The precedents establish, however, that speech within the rights of adults to hear may not be silenced completely in an attempt to shield children from it. [The Government] submits further that virtual child pornography whets the appetites of pedo-philes and encourages them to engage in illegal conduct. This rationale cannot sustain the provision in question. The mere tendency of speech to encourage unlawful acts is not a sufficient reason for banning it. * * *

"Finally, the Government says that the possibility of producing images by using computer imaging makes it very difficult for it to prosecute those who produce pornography by using real children. Experts, we are told, may have difficulty in saying whether the pictures were made by using real children or by using computer imaging. The necessary solution, the argument runs, is to prohibit both kinds of images. The argument, in essence, is that protected speech may be banned as a means to ban unprotected speech. This analysis turns the First Amendment upside down. The Government may not suppress lawful speech as the means to suppress unlawful speech."[k]

---

k. In overthrowing the "conveys the impression provision," Kennedy, J., argued that it applied to a substantial amount of material that could not be reached by anti-pandering obscenity law and wrongfully proscribed possession of material that was distributed in a manner conveying a false impression even when the possessor knew the material was mislabeled.

THOMAS, J., concurred: "In my view, the Government's most persuasive asserted interest [is] the prosecution rationale that persons who possess and disseminate pornographic images of real children may escape conviction by claiming that the images are computer-generated, thereby raising a reasonable doubt as to their guilt. At this time, however, the Government asserts only that defendants raise such defenses, not that they have done so successfully. In fact, the Government points to no case in which a defendant has been acquitted based on a computer-generated images defense. While this speculative interest cannot support the broad reach of the CPPA, technology may evolve to the point where it becomes impossible to enforce actual child pornography laws because the Government cannot prove that certain pornographic images are of real children. * * *

"The Court suggests that the Government's interest in enforcing prohibitions against real child pornography cannot justify prohibitions on virtual child pornography, because 'this analysis turns the First Amendment upside down.' [But] if technological advances thwart prosecution of unlawful speech, the Government may well have a compelling interest in barring or otherwise regulating some narrow category of lawful speech in order to enforce effectively laws against pornography made through the abuse of real children."

O'CONNOR, J., concurring in part and dissenting in part, agreed that the act's attempt to ban sexually explicit images of adults that appear to be children was overbroad, but, in a portion of her opinion joined by Rehnquist, C.J., and Scalia, J., she argued that the prohibitions of computer generated sexually explicit images appearing to be children or conveying that impression were constitutional: "[D]efendants indicted for the production, distribution, or possession of actual-child pornography may evade liability by claiming that the images attributed to them are in fact computer-generated. Respondents may be correct that no defendant has successfully employed this tactic. But, given the rapid pace of advances in computer-graphics technology, the Governments concern is reasonable. Computer-generated images lodged with the Court bear a remarkable likeness to actual human beings. [T]his Court's cases do not require Congress to wait for harm to occur before it can legislate against it.

"The Court concludes that the CPPAs ban on virtual-child pornography is overbroad. The basis for this holding is unclear. [Respondents] provide no examples of films or other materials that are wholly computer-generated and contain images that 'appea[r] to be' of minors engaging in indecent conduct, but that have serious value or do not facilitate child abuse."

REHNQUIST, C.J., joined in part by Scalia, J.,[1] dissenting, would have construed the statute to apply to "visual depictions of youthful looking adult actors engaged in actual sexual activity; mere suggestions of sexual activity, such as youthful looking adult actors squirming under a blanket, are more akin to written descriptions than visual depictions, and thus fall outside the purview of the statute. The reference to simulated has been part of the definition of sexually explicit conduct since the statute was first passed. But the inclusion of simulated conduct, alongside actual conduct, does not change

---

1. Scalia, J., did not join a portion of Rehnquist, C.J.'s opinion discussing the statute's legislative history.

the hard core nature of the image banned. The reference to simulated conduct simply brings within the statute's reach depictions of hard core pornography that are made to look genuine including the main target of the CPPA, computer generated images virtually indistinguishable from real children engaged in sexually explicit conduct. Neither actual conduct nor simulated conduct, however, is properly construed to reach depictions such as those in a film portrayal of Romeo and Juliet which are far removed from the hard core pornographic depictions that Congress intended to reach.

"To the extent the CPPA prohibits possession or distribution of materials that convey the impression of a child engaged in sexually explicit conduct, that prohibition can and should be limited to reach the sordid business of pandering which lies outside the bounds of First Amendment protection. [The] First Amendment may protect the video shopowner or film distributor who promotes material as 'entertaining' or 'acclaimed' regardless of whether the material contains depictions of youthful looking adult actors engaged in nonobscene but sexually suggestive conduct. The First Amendment does not, however, protect the panderer. Thus, materials promoted as conveying the impression that they depict actual minors engaged in sexually explicit conduct do not escape regulation merely because they might warrant First Amendment protection if promoted in a different manner. * * *

"In sum, while potentially impermissible applications of the CPPA may exist, I doubt that they would be substantial in relation to the statute's plainly legitimate sweep."

After *Free Speech Coalition*, UNITED STATES v. WILLIAMS, 553 U.S. 285 (2008), per SCALIA, J., held that "offers to provide or requests to obtain child pornography are categorically excluded from the First Amendment" even if the material offered is not actually child pornography. *Free Speech Coalition* was distinguished on the ground that it "went beyond pandering to prohibit possession of material that could not otherwise be proscribed."[m]

7. **"Autopornography."** Approximately 11% of girls ages thirteen to sixteen admit to producing and distributing nude or semi-nude pictures of themselves. Prosecutors have charged such girls under child pornography statutes. Do the materials constitute child pornography under *Ferber*? Does *Free Speech Coalition* shed light on this? Would prosecutions of those who possess such photographs be appropriate? Does it matter that some 40% of teenagers (including distributors and possessors) would be sex offenders if *Ferber* applies? See John A. Humbach, *'Sexting' and the First Amendment*, 37 Hastings Con. L.Q. 433 (2010). See also Sarah Wastler, *The Harm in "Sexting"?*, 33 Harv. J.L. & Gender 687 (2010).

B. HARM TO WOMEN: FEMINISM AND PORNOGRAPHY

Catharine MacKinnon and Andrea Dworkin drafted an anti-pornography ordinance that was considered in a number of jurisdictions.[a]

---

m. Stevens, J., joined by Breyer, J., concurred. Souter, J., joined by Ginsburg, J., dissented.

a. The ordinance was first considered in Minneapolis. For political, rhetorical, and sociological discussion, see Paul Brest & Ann Vandenberg, *Politics, Feminism, and the Constitution: The Anti–Pornography Movement in Minneapolis*, 39 Stan.L.Rev. 607 (1987). Different versions of the ordinance were passed in Indianapolis, Indiana and Bellingham, Washington (see Margaret

PROPOSED LOS ANGELES COUNTY ANTI–PORNOGRAPHY CIVIL RIGHTS LAW

Section 1. Statement of Policy

Pornography is sex discrimination. It exists in the County of Los Angeles, posing a substantial threat to the health, safety, welfare and equality of citizens in the community. Existing state and federal laws are inadequate to solve these problems in the County of Los Angeles.

Section 2. Findings

Pornography is a systematic practice of exploitation and subordination based on sex which differentially harms women. The harm of pornography includes dehumanization, sexual exploitation, forced sex, forced prostitution, physical injury, and social and sexual terrorism and inferiority presented as entertainment. The bigotry and contempt pornography promotes, with the acts of aggression it fosters, diminish opportunities for equality of rights in employment, education, property, public accommodations and public services; create public and private harassment, persecution and denigration; promote injury and degradation such as rape, battery, child sexual abuse, and prostitution and inhibit just enforcement of laws against these acts; contribute significantly to restricting women in particular from full exercise of citizenship and participation in public life, including in neighborhoods; damage relations between the sexes; and undermine women's equal exercise of rights to speech and action guaranteed to all citizens under the Constitutions and laws of the United States, the State of California and the County of Los Angeles.

Section 3. Definitions

1. *Pornography* is the graphic sexually explicit subordination of women through pictures and/or words that also includes one or more of the following: (i) women are presented dehumanized as sexual objects, things or commodities; or (ii) women are presented as sexual objects who enjoy pain or humiliation; or (iii) women are presented as sexual objects who experience sexual pleasure in being raped; or (iv) women are presented as sexual objects tied up or cut up or mutilated or bruised or physically hurt; or (v) women are presented in postures of sexual submission, servility, or display; or (vi) women's body parts—including but not limited to vaginas, breasts, or buttocks—are exhibited such that women are reduced to those parts; or (vii) women are presented as whores by nature; or (viii) women are presented as being penetrated by objects or animals; or (ix) women are presented in scenarios of degradation, injury, torture, shown as filthy or inferior, bleeding, bruised or hurt in a context that makes these conditions sexual.

Baldwin, *Pornography and the Traffic in Women*, 1 Yale J.L. & Fem. 111 (1989)). Both versions were declared unconstitutional.

2.   The use of men,[b] children, or transsexuals in the place of women in (1) above is also pornography for purposes of this law.

Section 4.   Unlawful Practices

1.   *Coercion into pornography*: It shall be sex discrimination to coerce, intimidate, or fraudulently induce (hereafter, "coerce") any person, including transsexual, into performing for pornography, which injury may date from any appearance or sale of any product(s) of such performance(s). The maker(s), seller(s), exhibitor(s) and/or distributor(s) of said pornography may be sued, including for an injunction to eliminate the product(s) of the performance(s) from the public view.

Proof of one or more of the following facts or conditions shall not, without more, negate a finding of coercion:

(i)   that the person is a woman; or

(ii)   that the person is or has been a prostitute; or

(iii)   that the person has attained the age of majority; or

(iv)   that the person is connected by blood or marriage to anyone involved in or related to the making of the pornography; or

(v)   that the person has previously had, or been thought to have had, sexual relations with anyone, including anyone involved in or related to the making of the pornography; or

(vi)   that the person has previously posed for sexually explicit pictures with or for anyone, including anyone involved in or related to the making of the pornography at issue; or

(vii)   that anyone else, including a spouse or other relative, has given permission on the person's behalf; or

(viii)   that the person actually consented to a use of the performance that is changed into pornography; or

(ix)   that the person knew that the purpose of the acts or events in question was to make pornography; or

(x)   that the person showed no resistance or appeared to cooperate actively in the photographic sessions or in the events that produced the pornography; or

(xi)   that the person signed a contract, or made statements affirming a willingness to cooperate in the production of pornography; or

(xii)   that no physical force, threats, or weapons were used in the making of the pornography; or

(xiii)   that the person was paid or otherwise compensated.

---

b.   Does this provision wrongly conflate gay pornography with stereotypical heterosexual pornography? See Leslie Green, *Pornographies,* 8 J. of Pol. Phil. 27 (2000). For criticism of the ordinance from a lesbian perspective, see Becki L. Ross, *'It's Merely Designed for Sexual Arousal,' Feminism & Pornography* 264–317 (Cornell ed. 1999).

2. *Trafficking in pornography:* It shall be sex discrimination to produce, sell, exhibit, or distribute pornography, including through private clubs.

(i) City, state, and federally funded public libraries or private and public university and college libraries in which pornography is available for study, including on open shelves but excluding special display presentations, shall not be construed to be trafficking in pornography.

(ii) Isolated passages or isolated parts shall not be actionable under this section.

(iii) Any woman has a claim hereunder as a woman acting against the subordination of women. Any man, child, or transsexual who alleges injury by pornography in the way women are injured by it also has a claim.

3. *Forcing pornography on a person:* It shall be sex discrimination to force pornography on a person, including child or transsexual, in any place of employment, education, home, or public place. Only the perpetrator of the force and/or institution responsible for the force may be sued.

4. *Assault or physical attack due to pornography:* It shall be sex discrimination to assault, physically attack or injure any person, including child or transsexual, in a way that is directly caused by specific pornography. The perpetrator of the assault or attack may be sued. The maker(s), distributor(s), seller(s), and/or exhibitor(s) may also be sued, including for an injunction against the specific pornography's further exhibition, distribution or sale.

Section 5. Defenses

1. It shall not be a defense that the defendant in an action under this law did not know or intend that the materials were pornography or sex discrimination.

2. No damages or compensation for losses shall be recoverable under Sec. 4(2) or other than against the perpetrator of the assault or attack in Sec. 4(4) unless the defendant knew or had reason to know that the materials were pornography.

3. In actions under Sec. 4(2) or other than against the perpetrator of the assault or attack in Sec. 4(4), no damages or compensation for losses shall be recoverable against maker(s) for pornography made, against distributor(s) for pornography distributed, against seller(s) for pornography sold, or against exhibitor(s) for pornography exhibited, prior to the effective date of this law.

Section 6. Enforcement

a. Civil Action: Any person, or their estate, aggrieved by violations of this law may enforce its provisions by means of a civil action. No criminal penalties shall attach for any violation of the provisions of this law. Relief for violations of this law, except as expressly restricted or precluded herein, may include compensatory and punitive damages and reasonable attorney's fees, costs and disbursements.

b. Injunction: Any person who violates this law may be enjoined except that:

(i) In actions under Sec. 4(2), and other than against the perpetrator of the assault or attack under Sec. 4(4), no temporary or permanent injunction shall issue prior to a final judicial determination that the challenged activities constitute a violation of this law.

(ii) No temporary or permanent injunction shall extend beyond such material(s) that, having been described with reasonable specificity by the injunction, have been determined to be validly proscribed under this law.

Section 7. Severability

Should any part(s) of this law be found legally invalid, the remaining part(s) remain valid. A judicial declaration that any part(s) of this law cannot be applied validly in a particular manner or to a particular case or category of cases shall not affect the validity of that part(s) as otherwise applied, unless such other application would clearly frustrate the intent of the Board of Supervisors in adopting this law.

Section 8. Limitation of Action

Actions under this law must be filed within one year of the alleged discriminatory acts.

NOTES AND QUESTIONS

1. ***The Ferber analogy.*** Consider Cass Sunstein, *Neutrality in Constitutional Law (With Special Reference to Pornography, Abortion, and Surrogacy)*, 92 Colum.L.Rev. 1, 24 (1992): "A successful action for rape and sexual assault is difficult enough. The difficulty becomes all the greater when the victims are young women coerced into, and abused during, the production of pornography. Often those victims will be reluctant to put themselves through the experience and possible humiliation and expense of initiating a proceeding. Often prosecutors will be reluctant to act on their behalf. Often they will have extremely little credibility even if they are willing to come forward. In this light, the only realistically effective way to eliminate the practice is to eliminate or reduce the financial benefits." If all women in pornographic films were coerced, would the analogy to *Ferber* be airtight? If not, how much coercion is acceptable? What is the relationship between prostitution and pornography? Consider Tonya R. Noldon, *Challenging First Amendment Protection of Adult Films with the Use of Prostitution Statutes*, 3 Va. Sports & Ent. L.J. 310, 311 (2004): "The stated purposes behind criminalizing prostitution—preventing the spread of communicable diseases, precluding the denigration and sexual exploitation of women, reducing the collateral criminal misconduct that tends to cluster with prostitution (such as drug, alcohol, and physical abuse)—are uncharacteristic of the mainstream movie industry, but

prevalent throughout the adult film industry. Not only is the adult film industry not illegal, however, it can barely be regulated at all because it has been labeled 'free speech' or 'free expression,' which is protected by the First Amendment of the United States Constitution. The purposes behind making prostitution illegal, however, are completely unrelated to suppressing free expression.''

2. ***Relationship between obscenity and pornography.*** Consider Catharine MacKinnon, *Pornography, Civil Rights, and Speech,* 20 Harv.Civ. Rts.—Civ.Lib.L.Rev. 1, 50–52 & 16–17 (1985): ''Under the obscenity rubric, much legal and psychological scholarship has centered on a search for the elusive link between pornography defined as obscenity and harm. They have looked high and low—in the mind of the male consumer, in society or in its 'moral fabric,' in correlations between variations in levels of anti-social acts and liberalization of obscenity laws. The only harm they have found has been one they have attributed to 'the social interests in order and morality.' Until recently, no one looked very persistently for harm to women, particularly harm to women through men. The rather obvious fact that the sexes *relate* has been overlooked in the inquiry into the male consumer and his mind. The pornography doesn't just drop out of the sky, go into his head and stop there. Specifically, men rape, batter, prostitute, molest, and sexually harass women. Under conditions of inequality, they also hire, fire, promote, and grade women, decide how much or whether or not we are worth paying and for what, define and approve and disapprove of women in ways that count, that determine our lives.

''In pornography, there it is, in one place, all of the abuses that women had to struggle so long even to begin to articulate, all the *unspeakable* abuse: the rape, the battery, the sexual harassment, the prostitution, and the sexual abuse of children. Only in the pornography it is called something else: sex, sex, sex, sex, and sex, respectively. Pornography sexualizes rape, battery, sexual harassment, prostitution, and child sexual abuse; it thereby celebrates, promotes, authorizes, and legitimizes them. More generally, it eroticizes the dominance and submission that is the dynamic common to them all. It makes hierarchy sexy and calls that 'the truth about sex' or just a mirror of reality.'' See also Deborah Cameron & Elizabeth Frazer, *On the Question of Pornography and Sexual Violence: Moving Beyond Cause and Effect,* in FEMINISM & PORNOGRAPHY 240, 241 (Drucilla Cornell ed., 2000): ''Whereas conservatives criticize almost all expressions of sexuality as immoral and recommend a return to traditional religious and family values, feminist analysis criticizes instead the oppressive and misogynistic forms such expressions typically take in male-dominated culture. Stressing the pervasiveness of misogyny through time–that is, denying that we are witnessing a moral decline–feminists identify religion and the family as part of the problem.''

3. ***The trafficking section.*** Is the trafficking section constitutional under *Miller?* Consider the following hypothetical commentary: ''The Dworkin–MacKinnon proposal focuses on a narrower class of material than *Miller* because it excludes erotic materials that do not involve subordination. That class of material upon which it does focus appeals to prurient interest because it is graphic and sexually explicit. Moreover, the eroticization of dominance in the ways specified in the ordinance is so patently offensive to community

standards that it can be said as a matter of law that this class of materials lacks *serious* literary, artistic, political, or scientific value as a matter of law." Do you agree?

Is there a good analogy to *Beauharnais?* To *Ferber?* Did more or less harm exist in *Gertz? Miller? Ferber?* Was there more or less of a threat to First Amendment values in *Gertz? Miller? Ferber?* Should this be accepted as a new category?

Consider Wendy Kaminer, *Pornography and the First Amendment: Prior Restraints and Private Action*, 239, 245 in *Take Back the Night: Women on Pornography* (Laura Lederer ed. 1980): "The Women's Movement is a Civil Rights Movement, and we should appreciate the importance and the danger of turning popular sentiment into law in areas affecting individual privacy.

"Legislative or judicial control of pornography is simply not possible without breaking down the legal principles and procedures that are essential to our own right to speak and, ultimately, our freedom to control our own lives. We must continue to organize against pornography and the degradation and abuse of women, but we must not ask the government to take up our struggle for us. The power it will assume to do so will be far more dangerous to us all than the 'power' of pornography."[c]

4. ***Pornography and harm.*** Consider Andrew Koppelman, *Does Obscenity Cause Moral Harm?*, 105 Colum. L. Rev. 1635, 1665 (2005): "[L]aboratory studies cannot establish what happens outside the lab. Short-term attitudinal and behavioral changes are all that laboratory studies, by their

---

c. Compare Nan Hunter & Sylvia Law, *Brief Amici Curiae of Feminist Anti–Censorship Taskforce* (on appeal in *Hudnut,* below), 21 U.Mich.J.L.Ref. 69, 109 & 129–30 (1987–88). The ordinance conceivably "would require the judiciary to impose its views of correct sexuality on a diverse community. The inevitable result would be to disapprove those images that are least conventional and privilege those that are closest to majoritarian beliefs about proper sexuality. [Moreover] [b]y defining sexually explicit images of women as subordinating and degrading to them, the ordinance reinforces the stereotypical view that 'good' women do not seek and enjoy sex. [Finally], the ordinance perpetuates a stereotype of women as helpless victims, incapable of consent, and in need of protection." See generally Nadine Strossen, *Defending Pornography* (1995).

For collections of feminist perspectives, see Drucilla Cornell, ed., *Feminism and* Pornography (2000); Take *Back the Night,* supra; Varda Burstyn, ed., *Women Against Censorship* (1985); Ann Snitow, Christine Stansell & Sharon Thompson, etc., *Powers of Desire* 419–67 (1983). For a variety of views (including feminist views), see James Weinstein, *Hate Speech, Pornography, and the Radical Attack on Free Speech Doctrine* (1999); Richard Delgado & Jean Stefanic, *Must We Defend Nazis* (1997); Nicholas Wolfson, *Hate Speech, Sex Speech, Free Speech* (1997); Michelle Chernikoff Anderson, *Speaking Freely About Reducing Violence Against Women*, 10 U.Fla. J.L. & Pub.Pol. 173 (1998); Joshua Cohen, *Freedom of Expression*, 21 Phil. & Pub.Aff. 207 (1993); Deborah Rhode, *Justice and Gender*, 263–73 (1989); Mark Tushnet, *Red, White, and Blue* 293–312 (1988); Donald Downs, *The Attorney General's Commission and the New Politics of Pornography*, 1987 Am.B.Found.Res.J. 641; Steven Gey, *The Apologetics of Suppression*, 86 Mich.L.Rev. 1564 (1988); Eric Hoffman, *Feminism, Pornography, and the Law*, 133 U.Pa.L.Rev. 497 (1985); Robert Post, *Cultural Heterogeneity and the Law*, 76 Calif.L.Rev. 297 (1988); David Richards, *Pornography Commissions and the First Amendment*, 39 Me.L.Rev. 275 (1987); Frederick Schauer, *Causation Theory and the Causes of Sexual Violence*, 1987 Am.B.Found.Res.J. 737; Suzanna Sherry, *An Essay Concerning Toleration*, 71 Minn.L.Rev. 963 (1987); Geoffrey Stone, *Anti–Pornography Legislation as Viewpoint–Discrimination*, 9 Harv.J.Pub.Pol'y 461 (1986); Nadine Strossen, *The Convergence of Feminist and Civil Liberties Principles in the Pornography Debate*, 62 N.Y.U.L.Rev. 201 (1987); Cass Sunstein, *Pornography and the First Amendment*, 1986 Duke L.J. 589; Robin West, *The Feminist–Conservative Anti–Pornography Alliance and the 1986 Attorney General's Commission on Pornography Report*, 1987 Am.B.Found.Res.J. 681. For the Canadian approach, see *Regina v. Butler*, [1992] 1 S.C.R. 452. For comparative commentary, see Kent Greenawalt, *Fighting Words* 99–123 (1995).

nature, could possibly show. Moreover, the laboratory studies also found that the effect of even this kind of pornography was not inevitably malign. When men who had been exposed to these misogynistic materials were later given debriefing sessions that included materials dispelling rape myths and detailing the harms women suffer as a consequence of rape, the net effect was striking. After these men were exposed both to violent pornography and to pro-feminist material, they had more positive, less discriminatory, and less stereotyped attitudes toward women than they did before the experiment." But see Rae Langton, *Speech Acts and Unspeakable Acts,* 22 Phil. & Pub.Aff. 293, 311–312 (1993): "What is important here is not whether the speech of pornographers is universally held in high esteem: it is not—hence the common assumption among liberals that in defending pornographers they are defending the underdog. What is important is whether it is authoritative in the domain that counts—the domain of speech about sex—and whether it is authoritative for the hearers that count: people, men, boys, who in addition to wanting 'entertainment,' want to discover the right way to do things, want to know which moves in the sexual game are legitimate. What is important is whether it is authoritative for those hearers who—one way or another—do seem to learn that violence is sexy and coercion legitimate: the fifty percent of boys who 'think it is okay for a man to rape a woman if he is sexually aroused by her,' the fifteen percent of male college undergraduates who say they have raped a woman on a date, the eighty-six percent who say that they enjoy the conquest part of sex, the thirty percent who rank faces of women displaying pain and fear to be more sexually attractive than faces showing pleasure."

5. **Pornography and the internet.** Does the prevalence of pornography on the internet make the case for regulation all the more pressing? Or does it afford increased opportunities for feminist inspired sexually oriented speech that could challenge the eroticization of patriarchy? See Courtenay W. Daum, *Feminism and Pornography in the Twenty-First Century,* 30 Women's Rts.L.Rep. 543 (2009) (arguing for the latter).

6. *Subordination.* Is the absence of subordination an appropriate ideal? Consider Carlin Meyer, *Sex, Sin, and Women's Liberation: Against Porn–Suppression,* 72 Tex.L.Rev. 1097, 1133 n. 156, 1154–55 (1994): "I am not suggesting that sex accompanied by intimacy, respect, and caring is not an appropriate ideal. Rather, I mean to argue that the sort of equality in which no one is ever the aggressor in fantasy or in reality is, at best, a 'utopian vision of sexual relations: sex without power, sex without persuasion, sex without pursuit.' [S]exual discourse needs to be free-wheeling and uncontrolled because of the hotly contested nature of issues concerning sexuality. Such issues as what constitutes pleasure for women and its connection to danger, to power, to men, and to aggression and inequality; of what sex is 'good' and 'bad'; and of whether women can escape inequality and coercion within Western sexual culture are debated and dissected with little agreement across boundaries of class, race, and nationality. Allies on other issues disagree about whether all violence is bad, over what constitutes violence or pleasure, and over the meaning of such terms as 'objectified,' 'degraded,' or 'demeaned.' " See also Susan Keller, *Viewing and Doing: Complicating Pornography's Meaning,* 81 Geo.L.J. 2195, 2231 (1993): "[R]obin West critiques MacKinnon and Dworkin for their failure to acknowledge the 'meaning and the value, to women, of the pleasure we take in our fantasies of eroticized

submission.' Some like Jessica Benjamin and Kate Ellis have attempted to explain psychologically why pleasure can be found by women, as well as men, in submission and power. Of the various meanings pornography could have for a variety of audience members, one meaning for women could be pleasure in depictions of power." Can domination be eliminated?

7. ***The pornography definition.*** Is the proposed definition too vague? Is it more or less vague than the terminology employed in *Miller?* Is there a core of clear meaning? How would you clarify its meaning? Is the definition overbroad? What revisions, if any, would you suggest to narrow its scope? Consider Thomas Emerson, *Pornography and the First Amendment: A Reply to Professor MacKinnon,* 3 Yale L. & Pol. Rev. 130, 131–32 (1985): "The sweep of the Indianapolis Ordinance is breathtaking. It would subject to governmental ban virtually all depictions of rape, verbal or pictorial, and a substantial proportion of other presentations of sexual encounters. More specifically, it would outlaw such works of literature as the *Arabian Nights,* John Cleland's *Fanny Hill,* Henry Miller's *Tropic of Cancer,* William Faulkner's *Sanctuary,* and Norman Mailer's *Ancient Evenings,* to name but a few. The ban would extend from Greek mythology and Shakespeare to the millions of copies of 'romance novels' now being sold in the supermarkets. It would embrace much of the world's art, from ancient carvings to Picasso, well-known films too numerous to mention, and a large amount of commercial advertising.

"The scope of the Indianapolis Ordinance is not accidental. [As] Mac-Kinnon emphasizes, male domination has deep, pervasive and ancient roots in our society, so it is not surprising that our literature, art, entertainment and commercial practices are permeated by attitudes and behavior that create and reflect the inferior status of women. If the answer to the problem, as Professor MacKinnon describes it, is government suppression of sexual expression that contributes to female subordination, then the net of restraint has to be cast on a nearly limitless scale." Would the ordinance inadvertently cover activist anti-pornographic art that uses violent sexual images to make its point. If not, does the intent of the artist excuse any unintended effects? See Amy Adler, *What's Left?: Hate Speech, Pornography, and the Problem of Artistic Expression,* 84 Calif.L.Rev. 1499 (1996).

8. ***The assault provision.*** Should the maker of a pornographic work be responsible for assaults prompted by the work? Should the maker of non-pornographic works be responsible for imitative assaults. In *Olivia N. v. NBC,* 126 Cal.App.3d 488, 178 Cal.Rptr. 888 (1981), the victim of a sexual assault allegedly imitating a sexual assault in NBC's "Born Innocent" sued the network. Olivia N. claimed that NBC negligently exposed her to serious risk because it knew or should have known that someone would imitate the act portrayed in the movie. Suppose Olivia N. could show that NBC had been advised that such an assault was likely if the movie were shown? Should a court analogize to cases like *Gertz?* The California court ruled that Olivia N. could not prevail unless she met the *Brandenburg* standard.[d]

---

d. For relevant commentary, see J.M. Balkin, *The Rhetoric of Responsibility,* 76 Va.L.Rev. 197 (1990); Frederick Schauer, *Uncoupling Free Speech,* 92 Colum.L.Rev. 1321 (1992); Frederick Schauer, *Mrs. Palsgraf and the First Amendment,* 47 Wash. & Lee L.Rev. 161 (1990).

The Indianapolis version of the anti-pornography civil rights ordinance was struck down in AMERICAN BOOKSELLERS ASS'N v. HUDNUT, 771 F.2d 323 (7th Cir.1985), affirmed, 475 U.S. 1001 (1986). The Seventh Circuit, per EASTERBROOK, J., ruled that the definition of pornography infected the entire ordinance (including provisions against trafficking, coercion into pornography, forcing pornography on a person, and assault or physical attack due to pornography) because it impermissibly discriminated on the basis of point of view: "Indianapolis enacted an ordinance defining 'pornography' as a practice that discriminates against women. * * *

"The Indianapolis ordinance does not refer to the prurient interest, to offensiveness, or to the standards of the community. It demands attention to particular depictions, not to the work judged as a whole. It is irrelevant under the ordinance whether the work has literary, artistic, political, or scientific value. The City and many amici point to these omissions as virtues. They maintain that pornography influences attitudes, and the statute is a way to alter the socialization of men and women rather than to vindicate community standards of offensiveness. And as one of the principal drafters of the ordinance has asserted, 'if a woman is subjected, why should it matter that the work has other value?' Catharine MacKinnon, *Pornography, Civil Rights, and Speech,* 20 Harv.Civ.Rts.—Civ. Lib.L.Rev. 1, 21 (1985).

"Civil rights groups and feminists have entered this case as amici on both sides. Those supporting the ordinance say that it will play an important role in reducing the tendency of men to view women as sexual objects, a tendency that leads to both unacceptable attitudes and discrimination in the workplace and violence away from it. Those opposing the ordinance point out that much radical feminist literature is explicit and depicts women in ways forbidden by the ordinance and that the ordinance would reopen old battles. It is unclear how Indianapolis would treat works from James Joyce's *Ulysses* to Homer's *Iliad;* both depict women as submissive objects for conquest and domination.

"We do not try to balance the arguments for and against an ordinance such as this. The ordinance discriminates on the ground of the content of the speech. Speech treating women in the approved way—in sexual encounters 'premised on equality' (MacKinnon, supra, at 22)—is lawful no matter how sexually explicit. Speech treating women in the disapproved way—as submissive in matters sexual or as enjoying humiliation—is unlawful no matter how significant the literary, artistic, or political qualities of the work taken as a whole. The state may not ordain preferred viewpoints in this way. The Constitution forbids the state to declare one perspective right and silence opponents.[a] [Under] the First Amendment

---

a. But consider Alon Harel, *Bigotry, Pornography, and The First Amendment: A Theory of Unprotected Speech,* 65 S.Cal.L.Rev. 1887, 1889 (1992): "Some ideas and values cannot aid in the process of shaping our political obligations. This is not because these 'values' do not, as a matter of fact, influence the output of the political process but because any influence they do exert does not generate legitimate political obligations. Racist and sexist values cannot participate in the

the government must leave to the people the evaluation of ideas. Bald or subtle, an idea is as powerful as the audience allows it to be. A belief may be pernicious—the beliefs of Nazis led to the death of millions, those of the Klan to the repression of millions. A pernicious belief may prevail. Totalitarian governments today rule much of the planet, practicing suppression of billions and spreading dogma that may enslave others. One of the things that separates our society from theirs is our absolute right to propagate opinions that the government finds wrong or even hateful. * * *

"Under the ordinance graphic sexually explicit speech is 'pornography' or not depending on the perspective the author adopts. Speech that 'subordinates' women and also, for example, presents women as enjoying pain, humiliation, or rape, or even simply presents women in 'positions of servility or submission or display' is forbidden, no matter how great the literary or political value of the work taken as a whole. Speech that portrays women in positions of equality is lawful, no matter how graphic the sexual content. This is thought control. It establishes an 'approved' view of women, of how they may react to sexual encounters, of how the sexes may relate to each other. Those who espouse the approved view may use sexual images; those who do not, may not.

"Indianapolis justifies the ordinance on the ground that pornography affects thoughts. Men who see women depicted as subordinate are more likely to treat them so. Pornography is an aspect of dominance.[1] It does not persuade people so much as change them. It works by socializing, by establishing the expected and the permissible. In this view pornography is not an idea; pornography is the injury.

"There is much to this perspective. Beliefs are also facts. People often act in accordance with the images and patterns they find around them. People raised in a religion tend to accept the tenets of that religion, often without independent examination. People taught from birth that black people are fit only for slavery rarely rebelled against that creed; beliefs coupled with the self-interest of the masters established a social structure that inflicted great harm while enduring for centuries. Words and images

---

shaping of political obligations because the legal obligations they generate do not have morally binding force."

1. "Pornography constructs what a woman is in terms of its view of what men want sexually. * * * Pornography's world of equality is a harmonious and balanced place. Men and women are perfectly complementary and perfectly bipolar. [All] the ways men love to take and violate women, women love to be taken and violated. [What] pornography *does* goes beyond its content: It eroticizes hierarchy, it sexualizes inequality. It makes dominance and submission sex. Inequality is its central dynamic; the illusion of freedom coming together with the reality of force is central to its working. [P]ornography is neither harmless fantasy nor a corrupt and confused misrepresentation of an otherwise neutral and healthy sexual situation. It institutionalizes the sexuality of male supremacy, fusing the erotization of dominance and submission with the social construction of male and female. * * * Men treat women as who they see women as being. Pornography constructs who that is. Men's power over women means that the way men see women defines who women can be. Pornography [is] a sexual reality." MacKinnon, supra, at 17–18 (emphasis in original). See also Andrea Dworkin, *Pornography: Men Possessing Women* (1981). A national commission in Canada recently adopted a similar rationale for controlling pornography. Special Commission on Pornography and Prostitution, 1 *Pornography and Prostitution in Canada* 49–59 (1985).

act at the level of the subconscious before they persuade at the level of the conscious. Even the truth has little chance unless a statement fits within the framework of beliefs that may never have been subjected to rational study.

"Therefore we accept the premises of this legislation. Depictions of subordination tend to perpetuate subordination. The subordinate status of women in turn leads to affront and lower pay at work, insult and injury at home, battery and rape on the streets.[2] * * *

"Yet this simply demonstrates the power of pornography as speech. All of these unhappy effects depend on mental intermediation. Pornography affects how people see the world, their fellows, and social relations. If pornography is what pornography does, so is other speech. Hitler's orations affected how some Germans saw Jews. Communism is a world view, not simply a *Manifesto* by Marx and Engels or a set of speeches. Efforts to suppress communist speech in the United States were based on the belief that the public acceptability of such ideas would increase the likelihood of totalitarian government. [Many] people believe that the existence of television, apart from the content of specific programs, leads to intellectual laziness, to a penchant for violence, to many other ills. The Alien and Sedition Acts passed during the administration of John Adams rested on a sincerely held belief that disrespect for the government leads to social collapse and revolution—a belief with support in the history of many nations. Most governments of the world act on this empirical regularity, suppressing critical speech. In the United States, however, the strength of the support for this belief is irrelevant. Seditious libel is protected speech unless the danger is not only grave but also imminent. See *New York Times*; cf. *Brandenburg*.

"Racial bigotry, anti-semitism, violence on television, reporters' biases—these and many more influence the culture and shape our socialization. None is directly answerable by more speech, unless that speech too finds its place in the popular culture. Yet all is protected as speech, however insidious. Any other answer leaves the government in control of all of the institutions of culture, the great censor and director of which thoughts are good for us.

"Sexual responses often are unthinking responses, and the association of sexual arousal with the subordination of women therefore may have a

---

2. MacKinnon's article collects empirical work that supports this proposition. The social science studies are very difficult to interpret, however, and they conflict. Because much of the effect of speech comes through a process of socialization, it is difficult to measure incremental benefits and injuries caused by particular speech. Several psychologists have found, for example, that those who see violent, sexually explicit films tend to have more violent thoughts. But how often does this lead to actual violence? National commissions on obscenity here, in the United Kingdom, and in Canada have found that it is not possible to demonstrate a direct link between obscenity and rape or exhibitionism. The opinions in *Miller* discuss the U.S. commission. See also *Report of the Committee on Obscenity and Film Censorship* 61–95 (Home Office, Her Majesty's Stationery Office, 1979); 1 *Pornography and Prostitution in Canada* 71–73, 95–103. In saying that we accept the finding that pornography as the ordinance defines it leads to unhappy consequences, we mean only that there is evidence to this effect, that this evidence is consistent with much human experience, and that as judges we must accept the legislative resolution of such disputed empirical questions.

substantial effect. But almost all cultural stimuli provoke unconscious responses. Religious ceremonies condition their participants. Teachers convey messages by selecting what not to cover; the implicit message about what is off limits or unthinkable may be more powerful than the messages for which they present rational argument. Television scripts contain unarticulated assumptions. People may be conditioned in subtle ways. If the fact that speech plays a role in a process of conditioning were enough to permit governmental regulation, that would be the end of freedom of speech. * * *

"Much of Indianapolis's argument rests on the belief that when speech is 'unanswerable,' and the metaphor that there is a 'marketplace of ideas' does not apply, the First Amendment does not apply either. The metaphor is honored; Milton's *Aeropagitica* and John Stuart Mill's *On Liberty* defend freedom of speech on the ground that the truth will prevail, and many of the most important cases under the First Amendment recite this position. The Framers undoubtedly believed it. As a general matter it is true. But the Constitution does not make the dominance of truth a necessary condition of freedom of speech. To say that it does would be to confuse an outcome of free speech with a necessary condition for the application of the amendment.

"A power to limit speech on the ground that truth has not yet prevailed and is not likely to prevail implies the power to declare truth. At some point the government must be able to say (as Indianapolis has said): 'We know what the truth is, yet a free exchange of speech has not driven out falsity, so that we must now prohibit falsity.' If the government may declare the truth, why wait for the failure of speech? Under the First Amendment, however, there is no such thing as a false idea, *Gertz,* so the government may not restrict speech on the ground that in a free exchange truth is not yet dominant. * * *

"We come, finally, to the argument that pornography is 'low value' speech, that it is enough like obscenity that Indianapolis may prohibit it. Some cases hold that speech far removed from politics and other subjects at the core of the Framers' concerns may be subjected to special regulation. E.g., *FCC v. Pacifica Foundation* [Ch. 8, II infra]; *Young v. American Mini Theatres*; *Chaplinsky*. These cases do not sustain statutes that select among viewpoints, however. In *Pacifica* the FCC sought to keep vile language off the air during certain times. The Court held that it may; but the Court would not have sustained a regulation prohibiting scatological descriptions of Republicans but not scatological descriptions of Democrats, or any other form of selection among viewpoints.

"At all events, pornography is not low value speech within the meaning of these cases. Indianapolis seeks to prohibit certain speech because it believes this speech influences social relations and politics on a grand scale, that it controls attitudes at home and in the legislature. This precludes a characterization of the speech as low value. True, pornography and obscenity have sex in common. But Indianapolis left out of its definition any reference to literary, artistic, political, or scientific value. The ordinance applies to graphic sexually explicit subordination in works great and small.[3] The Court sometimes balances the value of speech against the costs of its restriction, but it does this by category of speech and not by the content of particular works. See John Hart Ely, *Flag Desecration: A Case Study in the Roles of Categorization and Balancing in First Amendment Analysis,* 88 Harv.L.Rev. 1482 (1975); Geoffrey Stone, *Restrictions of Speech Because of its Content: The Strange Case of Subject–Matter Restrictions,* 46 U.Chi.L.Rev. 81 (1978). Indianapolis has created an approved point of view and so loses the support of these cases.

"Any rationale we could imagine in support of this ordinance could not be limited to sex discrimination. Free speech has been on balance an ally of those seeking change. Governments that want stasis start by restricting speech. Culture is a powerful force of continuity; Indianapolis paints pornography as a part of the culture of power. Change in any complex system ultimately depends on the ability of outsiders to challenge accepted views and the reigning institutions. Without a strong guarantee of freedom of speech, there is no effective right to challenge what is."[b]

NOTES AND QUESTIONS

1. In response to the last paragraph, supra, Professor Frank Michelman observes: "[I]t is a fair and obvious question why preservation of 'effective right[s] to challenge what is' does not require protection of a 'freedom of speech' more broadly conceived to protect social critics—'outsiders,' in Judge Easterbrook's phrase—against suppression by nongovernmental as well as by governmental power. It is a fair and obvious question why the assertion that '[g]overnments that want stasis start by restricting speech' does not apply equally to the nongovernmental agencies of power in society. It is a fair and obvious question why our society's openness to challenge does not need protection against repressive private as well as public action." *Conceptions of Democracy in American Constitutional Argument: The Case of Pornography Regulation,* 56 Tenn.L.Rev. 291 (1989), citing Catharine MacKinnon, *Feminism Unmodified* 155–58 (1987).

---

3. Indianapolis briefly argues that *Beauharnais,* which allowed a state to penalize "group libel," supports the ordinance. In *Collin v. Smith,* [Ch. 1, V, C infra], we concluded that cases such as *New York Times v. Sullivan* had so washed away the foundations of *Beauharnais* that it could not be considered authoritative. If we are wrong in this, however, the case still does not support the ordinance. It is not clear that depicting women as subordinate in sexually explicit ways, even combined with a depiction of pleasure in rape, would fit within the definition of a group libel. The well received film *Swept Away* used explicit sex, plus taking pleasure in rape, to make a political statement, not to defame. Work must be an insult or slur for its own sake to come within the ambit of *Beauharnais,* and a work need not be scurrilous at all to be pornography under the ordinance.

b. The balance of the opinion suggested ways that parts of the ordinance might be salvaged, if redrafted. It suggested, for example, that the city might forbid coerced participation in any film or in "any film containing explicit sex." If the latter were adopted, would it make a difference if the section applied to persons coerced into participation in such films without regard to whether they were forced into explicit sex scenes? Swygert, J., concurring, joined part of Easterbrook, J.'s opinion for the court, but objected both to the "questionable and broad assertions regarding how human behavior can be conditioned" and to the "advisory" opinion on how parts of the ordinance might be redrafted.

2. ***Free speech and silence.*** Consider Catharine MacKinnon, *Toward a Feminist Theory of the State* 206 (1989): "That pornography chills women's expression is difficult to demonstrate empirically because silence is not eloquent. Yet on no more of the same kind of evidence, the argument that suppressing pornography might chill legitimate speech has supported its protection. [T]he law of the First Amendment comprehends that freedom of expression, in the abstract, is a system but fails to comprehend that sexism (and racism), in the concrete, are also systems."[c] But see Charles Fried, *Perfect Freedom, Perfect Justice,* 78 B.U. L.Rev. 717, 737 (1998): "[R]acist or sexist speech, if it has the effect attributed to it, produces it through the mind: Potential speakers are persuaded that they are less worthy individuals and so they are less inclined to contribute their voices in debate; and potential listeners are persuaded that these speakers are not worth attending to. But as the argument must concede that the mechanism of the silencing is through persuasion, it must also concede that the government's countermeasures must be directed at silencing the attempt to persuade: The government stops the message because of what it says and the evil the government fears works through the channels of the mind. I do not see how we can escape the conclusion that the government is stopping the message because it is afraid that people might believe it. But that is precisely what the First Amendment has consistently identified as what government may not do * * *."

3. ***"We do not try to balance."*** Does the existence of point of view discrimination preclude balancing under existing law? Consider Marjorie Heins, *Viewpoint Discrimination,* 24 Hastings L.Q. 99, 136 (1996) "Judge Easterbrook's point is well-taken, but it reaches beyond the MacKinnon/Dworkin type of ordinance. The First Amendment does not allow the government to dictate 'which thoughts are good for us,' whether it be in the guise of 'feminist' antipornography laws, indecency laws that turn on notions of 'patent offensiveness,' or obscenity laws of the type upheld in *Miller* and *Slaton* because of the lascivious, family-undermining, personality-distorting, and generally immoral thoughts that the Court felt pornography inspires."

4. Does pornography as defined by Indianapolis (or some part of that category) implicate such little First Amendment value as to foreclose constitutional protection? How should such value be assessed? Consider Cass Sunstein, *Pornography and the First Amendment,* 1986 Duke Law Journal 603–04: "First, the speech must be far afield from the central concern of the First Amendment, which, broadly speaking, is effective popular control of public affairs. Speech that concerns governmental processes is entitled to the highest level of protection; speech that has little or nothing to do with public affairs may be accorded less protection. Second, a distinction is drawn between cognitive and noncognitive aspects of speech. Speech that has purely noncognitive appeal will be entitled to less constitutional protection.[d] Third, the

---

c. To what extent is discourse inherently empowering and silencing in its effects? To what extent is pornography unique? For rich commentary, see the essays collected in *Censorship and Silencing* (Post ed. 1998); Langton, note 4 supra; Jennifer Hornsby, *Disempowered Speech,* 23 Philos. Topics 127 (1997); Daniel Jacobson, *Freedom of Speech Acts?,* 24 Phil. & Pub. Aff. 64 (1995); Wojciech Sadurski, *On Seeing Speech Through An Equality Lens,* 16 Oxford J. of Leg. Stud. 713 (1996).

d. For debate about this factor compare Paul Chevigny, *Pornography and Cognition,* 1989 Duke L.J. 420 with Cass Sunstein, *The First Amendment and Cognition,* 1989 Duke L.J. 433. See

purpose of the speaker is relevant: if the speaker is seeking to communicate a message, he will be treated more favorably than if he is not. Fourth, the various classes of low-value speech reflect judgments that in certain areas, government is unlikely to be acting for constitutionally impermissible reasons or producing constitutionally troublesome harms."

How do Sunstein's factors apply to the Indianapolis ordinance? To what extent is it desirable to consider the value of speech in forging a balance?[e]

C. RACIST SPEECH REVISITED: THE NAZIS

"*What do you want to sell in the marketplace? What idea? The idea of murder?*"

Erna Gans, a concentration camp survivor and active leader in the Skokie B'nai B'rith.[a]

COLLIN v. SMITH, 578 F.2d 1197 (7th Cir.), cert. denied, 439 U.S. 916 (1978), per Pell, J., struck down a Village of Skokie "Racial Slur" Ordinance, making it a misdemeanor to disseminate any material (defined to include "public display of markings and clothing of symbolic significance") promoting and inciting racial or religious hatred. The Village would apparently apply this ordinance to the display of swastikas and military uniforms by the NSPA, a "Nazi organization" which planned to peacefully demonstrate for some 20–30 minutes in front of the Skokie Village Hall.

Although there was some evidence that some individuals "might have difficulty restraining their reactions to the Nazi demonstration," the Village "does not rely on a fear of responsive violence to justify the ordinance, and does not even suggest that there will be any physical violence if the march is held. This confession takes the case out of the scope of *Brandenburg* and *Feiner*. [It] also eliminates any argument based on the fighting words doctrine of *Chaplinsky*, [which] applied only to words with a direct tendency to cause violence by the persons to whom, individually, the words were addressed."

The court rejected, inter alia, the argument that the Nazi march, with its display of swastikas and uniforms, "will create a substantive evil that it has a right to prohibit: the infliction of psychic trauma on resident holocaust survivors [some 5,000] and other Jewish residents. [The] problem with engrafting an exception on the First Amendment for such situations is that they are indistinguishable in principle from speech that 'invite[s] dispute [or] induces a condition of unrest [or] even stirs people to anger,' *Terminiello*. Yet these are among the 'high purposes' of the

also Kenneth Karst, *Boundaries and Reasons: Freedom of Expression and the Subordination of Groups*, 1990 U.Ill.L.Rev. 95.

e. Compare, e.g., Martin Redish, *The Value of Free Speech*, 130 U.Pa.L.Rev. 591, 596–611 (1982) and Larry Alexander, *Low Value Speech*, 83 Nw.U.L.Rev. 547 (1989) with Cass Sunstein, *Low Value Speech Revisited*, 83 Nw.U.L.Rev. 555 (1989). Reconsider the question after completing Ch. 3.

a. Quoted in Fred Friendly & Martha Elliot, *The Constitution: That Delicate Balance* 83 (1984).

First Amendment. [Where,] as here, a crime is made of a silent march, attended only by symbols and not by extrinsic conduct offensive in itself, we think the words of *Street v. New York* [Ch. 2 infra] are very much on point: '[A]ny shock effect [must] be attributed to the content of the ideas expressed. [P]ublic expression of ideas may not be prohibited merely because the ideas are themselves offensive to some of their hearers.' "

Nor was the court impressed with the argument that the proposed march was "not speech, [but] rather an invasion, intensely menacing no matter how peacefully conducted" (most of Skokie's residents are Jewish): "There *need be* no captive audience, as Village residents may, if they wish, simply avoid the Village Hall for thirty minutes on a Sunday afternoon, which no doubt would be their normal course of conduct on a day when the Village Hall was not open in the regular course of business. Absent such intrusion or captivity, there is no justifiable substantial privacy interest to save [the ordinance], when it attempts, by fiat, to declare the entire Village, at all times, a privacy zone that may be sanitized from the offensiveness of Nazi ideology and symbols."[b]

NOTES AND QUESTIONS

1. Is *Beauharnais*, Ch. 1, II, A supra, still "good law"? Should it be?

2. ***Abstraction and the First Amendment.*** Consider Frederick Schauer, *Harry Kalven and the Perils of Particularism*, 56 U.Chi.L.Rev. 397, 408 (1989): "[O]ne sees in the *Skokie* litigation an available distinction between Nazis and others, an equally available distinction between speech designed to persuade and speech designed to assault, and a decision made by the people rather than a decision designed to interfere with the people's wishes. If doctrinal development under the free speech clause were merely an instance of common law decision making, one might expect to see some or all of these factors treated as relevant, and new distinctions developed in order to make relevant those factors, such as the ones just enumerated, that had been suppressed by previous formulations. Yet we know that this is not what happened. The particular events were abstracted in numerous ways. Nazis became political speakers, a suburban community populated by Holocaust survivors became a public forum, and popularly inspired restrictions became governmental censorship. The resolution of the controversy, therefore, stands not as a monument to the ever-more-sensitive development of common law doctrine, but instead as an embodiment of the way in which the First Amendment operates precisely by the entrenchment of categories whose breadth prevents the consideration of some number of relevant factors, and prevents the free speech decision maker from 'thinking small.' "

---

b. See also *Skokie v. National Socialist Party,* 69 Ill.2d 605, 373 N.E.2d 21 (1978). For commentary relating the Skokie issue to regulation of pornography, and of commercial speech, for the purpose of asking whether there are general principles of freedom of expression and whether freedom of expression should be category-dependent, see Thomas Scanlon, *Freedom of Expression and Categories of Expression,* 40 U.Pitt.L.Rev. 519 (1979). For assessment of the complicated connection between Skokie and equality values especially in light of the rest of First Amendment law, see Laurence Tribe, *Constitutional Choices* 219–20 (1985). Compare Donald Downs, *Skokie Revisited: Hate Group Speech and the First Amendment,* 60 Not.D.Law. 629 (1985). More generally, see David Kretzmer, *Freedom of Speech and Racism,* 8 Cardozo L.Rev. 445 (1987).

3. *Is racist speech high value?* Consider David O. Brink, *Millian Principles, Freedom of Expression, and Hate Speech*, 7 Legal Theory 119, 143 (2001): "On [one] view, if hate speech is not high-value, it must be low-value. But bivalence is not a necessary feature of First Amendment jurisprudence. An alternative approach is *scalar*; one assesses liberties of expression in terms of their *centrality* to First Amendment values and holds regulation of expression to a standard of review whose stringency is commensurate with the importance of the liberties at stake. Indeed, First Amendment doctrine is not consistently bivalent; under existing law, commercial speech such as advertising is treated as neither high-value nor low-value; it is accorded a kind of intermediate value, with the result that restrictions on commercial speech must satisfy an intermediate standard of review. Even on this scalar view, a good case can be made that hate speech is low-value speech. But perhaps this claim is more controversial on the scalar than on the bivalent view. However, even if we do not agree to treat hate speech as low-value speech, the case for doing so makes it very implausible to treat it as high-value speech. At most, it could be accorded a sort of intermediate value; if so, the regulation of hate speech should be subject, at most, to a standard of review intermediate between rational basis review and strict scrutiny—perhaps one that requires that the state have a significant or substantial interest that it pursues in a comparatively restrictive manner."

Is speech denying the holocaust clearly of low value? Or in the tradition of Holmes, J., is governmental agnosticism about truth and falsity a central First Amendment value that can be dispensed with only upon the demonstration of harm to reputation and the like. See Steven G. Gey, *The First Amendment and the Dissemination of Socially Worthless Untruths*, 36 Fla. St. U.L. Rev. 1 (2008).

4. *The Klan and the Communists.* Are the arguments of those who would prohibit racist speech (or pornography), the same as those who would have restricted the speech of the communists (or anarchists). See Steven G. Gey, *The Case Against Postmodern Censorship Theory*, 145 U.Pa. L.Rev. 193 (1996). But consider Steven H. Shiffrin, *Dissent, Injustice, and the Meanings of America* 78,79 n. 184 (1999): "Racist speakers seek to persuade people that government (and others) should not treat all persons with equal concern and respect. If our legal system has even a prayer of claiming to be legitimate, however, it must start from the premise that all citizens are worthy of equal concern and respect. [In] this limited context, the best test of truth is the system's foundational premise of equality,[c] not whether racist speech can emerge in the marketplace of ideas. [To] the extent the communists argue against free speech, [they] are in the same position as the Ku Klux Klan, but the harm of that speech is not in the same league as racist speech."

5. *European comparison.* Consider Sionaidh Douglas–Scott, *The Hatefulness of Protected Speech: A Comparison of the American and European Approaches,* 7 Wm. & Mary Bill Rts.J. 305, 343–44 (1999): "There clearly is a radical difference between the German or, more generally, the European and American approach to the regulation of speech. [First], European and, espe-

---

c. Are there many conceptions of equality in the American system which those who would regulate racist speech need to take account? See Gary Goodpaster, *Equality and Free Speech: The Case Against Substantive Equality,* 82 Iowa L. Rev 645 (1997).

cially, German jurisprudence emphasize particular values—dignity, protection of personal identity, and equality. German judgments stress the potential of racist insults and denials of Nazi atrocities to affect the very core of the identities of members of certain groups, even if those individuals have not been specifically targeted for abuse. [European] case law rejects a conception of individuals as beings who merely should be left to their own devices to make up their own minds about the value of expression in the public domain, to be free to ignore it, or to counter it with more speech. Such an approach isolates human beings by forcing them to take the consequences of painful conduct and ignores the particular susceptibility of certain groups to injury, especially when the offense of the speech seems to be targeted at such groups because of their identity. Under the American model, the individual will be left to his or her less communal and somewhat atomistic existence.[d]

"Second, the European approach is fundamentally more sympathetic to a conception in which the state plays a role in facilitating the realization of freedom, democracy, and equality. Under the European approach, it becomes natural for the state to assume a more affirmative role in actualizing specific constitutional rights. Within the area of freedom of speech this would require the state not only to refrain from violating certain constitutional norms, but also to participate in their realization—an approach which usually is assumed only to be required of socio-economic rights, such as the right to work. Surely it is not enough for societies that claim to be committed to the ideals of social and political equality and respect for individual dignity to remain neutral and passive when threats to these values exist. Sometimes the State must take steps to protect democracy itself, which may involve repressing speech."

Consider Michel Rosenfeld, *Hate Speech in Constitutional Jurisprudence: A Comparative Analysis*, 24 Cardozo L. Rev. 1523, 1559–60 (2003): "In terms of assumptions, the American approach either underestimates the potential for harm of hate speech that is short of incitement to violence, or it overestimates the potential of rational deliberation as a means to neutralize calls to hate. In terms of impact, given its long history of racial tensions, it is surprising that the United States does not exhibit greater concern for the injuries to security, dignity, autonomy and well being which officially tolerated hate speech causes to its black minority. Likewise, America's hate speech approach seems to unduly discount the pernicious impact that racist hate speech may have on lingering or dormant racist sentiments still harbored by a non-negligible segment of the white population."

6. *Face-to-face insults.* Should the First Amendment bar an action for intentional infliction of emotional distress for face-to-face racial insults?[e] Is it enough that the words in question inflict injury or must the victim show that the words were likely to promote a fight? Suppose a crowd of whites gathers to taunt a young black child on the way to a previously all white school? Suppose short of using violence, they do everything they can to harm the child? Is it the case that "no government that would call itself a decent government would fail to intervene [and] disperse the crowd" and that "the

---

d. See also Guy E. Carmi, *Dignity—The Enemy From Within*, 9 U.Pa.J. Const.L. 957 (2007).

e. On the relationship between discriminatory speech and the tort of intentional infliction of emotional distress, see Jean Love, *Discriminatory Speech and the Tort of Intentional Infliction of Emotional Distress*, 47 Wash. & Lee L.Rev. 123 (1990).

rights of the crowd [cannot] really stand on the same plane" as the child on the way to school? See Hadley Arkes, *Civility and the Restriction of Speech: Rediscovering the Defamation of Groups,* 1974 Sup.Ct.Rev. 281, 310–11. Should the First Amendment bar state criminal or civil actions precisely tailored to punish racial insults? Insults directed against the handicapped? For the case in favor of a tort action against racial insults, see Richard Delgado, *Words That Wound: A Tort Action for Racial Insults, Epithets, and Name–Calling,* 17 Harv.Civ.Rts.—Civ.Lib.L.Rev. 133 (1982). For a spirited exchange, see Marjorie Heins, *Banning Words: A Comment on "Words that Wound,"* 18 Harv.Civ.Rts.—Civ.Lib.L.Rev. 585 (1983) and *Professor Richard Delgado Replies,* Id. at 593.

7. ***Is one person's "racialist's plea" another person's act of intimidation?*** Are these responses patterned? Consider Mari Matsuda, *Public Response to Racist Speech: Considering the Victim's Story,* 87 Mich.L.Rev. 2320, 2326–27 (1989): "The typical reaction of target-group members to an incident of racist propaganda is alarm and immediate calls for redress. The typical reaction of non-target-group members is to consider the incidents isolated pranks, the product of sick-but-harmless minds. This is in part a defensive reaction: a refusal to believe that real people, people just like us, are racists. This disassociation leads logically to the claim that there is no institutional or state responsibility to respond to the incident.[f] It is not the kind of real and pervasive threat that requires the state's power to quell."[g]

See also Charles Lawrence, *If He Hollers Let Him Go: Regulating Racist Speech on Campus,* 1990 Duke L.J. 431, 474–75: "If one asks why we always begin by asking whether we can afford to fight racism rather than asking whether we can afford not to, or if one asks why my colleagues who oppose all regulation of racist speech do not feel the burden is theirs (to justify a reading of the First Amendment that requires sacrificing rights guaranteed under the equal protection clause), then one sees an example of how unconscious racism operates in the marketplace of ideas. [O]ur unconscious racism causes us (even those of us who are the direct victims of racism) to view the First Amendment as the 'regular' amendment—an amendment that works for all people—and the equal protection clause and racial equality as a special interest-amendment important to groups that are less valued."[h]

8. ***Effects of regulation.*** Consider Steven Shiffrin, *Racist Speech, Outsider Jurisprudence, and the Meaning of America,* 80 Corn.L.Rev. 43, 96–97, 103 (1994): "From the perspective of many millions of Americans, to enact racist speech regulations would be to pass yet another law exhibiting special favoritism for people of color. What makes this kind of law so potentially

---

f. For the argument that the best interpretation of *Brown v. Board of Education* requires government to respond, see Lawrence, infra. For response, see Strossen, infra.

g. Are victims in a better position to evaluate the truth? Compare Richard Delgado & Jean Stefanic, *Must We Defend Nazis* 86–87 (1997) with Gey, note 3 supra.

h. For discussion of the extent and character of the harm, see Delgado & Stefanic, fn. g supra, at 4–10; Matsuda, supra; Lawrence, infra; Richard Delgado, *Campus Antiracism Rules Constitutional Narratives in Collision,* 85 Nw.U.L.Rev. 343, 384 (1991) ("The ubiquity and incessancy of harmful racial depiction are [the] source of its virulence. Like water dripping on sandstone, it is a pervasive harm which only the most hardy can resist. Yet the prevailing First Amendment paradigm predisposes us to treat racist speech as individual harm, as though we only had to evaluate the effect of a single drop of water.").

counterproductive is that its transformation of public racists into public martyrs would tap into widespread political traditions and understanding in our culture. In short, the case of the martyr would be appealingly wrapped in the banner of the American flag. Millions of white Americans already resent people of color to some degree. To fuse that resentment with Americans' love for the First Amendment is risky business. [America] would still have a FIRST AMENDMENT and a strong First Amendment tradition even if it enacted general racist speech regulations. The problem is not the First Amendment; the problem is that racism is now and always has been a central part of the meaning of America." Would hate speech legislation have the "unfortunate effect of focusing on the individual perpetrator rather than on the victims or on social forces that assist and inform the perpetrator"? Would attention "more fruitfully turn to both the lives and the circumstances of the victims as well as the surrounding social traditions and practices that have made and continue to make that group subject to dehumanization"? Martha Minow, *Regulating Hatred*, 47 UCLA L.Rev. 1253, 1274 (2000).

9. ***Proposals to restrict hate speech.*** Consider Stanford University's definition of harassment by personal vilification: "Speech or other expression constitutes harassment by personal vilification if it a) is intended to insult or stigmatize an individual or a small number of individuals on the basis of their sex, race, color, handicap, religion, sexual orientation, or national and ethnic origin; and b) is addressed directly to the individual or individuals whom it insults or stigmatizes; and c) makes use of insulting or 'fighting words' or non-verbal symbols." Is this appropriate? See Thomas Grey, *Civil Rights v. Civil Liberties*, Soc. Phil. & Pol'y 81 (Spring 1991). Does this go too far? See Nadine Strossen, *Regulating Racist Speech on Campus: A Modest Proposal?* 1990 Duke L.J. 484. Does it not go far enough? See Lawrence, supra at 450 n. 82: "I supported a proposal which would have been broader in scope by prohibiting speech of this nature in all common areas, excepting organized rallies and speeches. It would have been narrower in its protection in that it would not have protected persons who were vilified on the basis of their membership in dominant majority groups." Compare Matsuda, supra at 2357, arguing that speech with a message of racial inferiority, that is directed against a historically oppressed group, and that is persecutorial, hateful, and degrading should be outlawed.[i]

---

i. For other relevant literature, see, e.g., Ch. 3, IV supra; James Weinstein, *Hate Speech, Pornography, and the Radical Attack on Free Speech Doctrine* (1999); Nicholas Wolfson, *Hate Speech, Sex Speech, Free Speech* (1997); Kent Greenawalt, *Fighting Words* (1995); Mari Matsuda, Charles Lawrence, Richard Delgado, & Kimberle Crenshaw, eds., *Words that Wound* (1993); Laura Lederer & Richard Delgado, eds., *The Price We Pay: The Case Against Racist Speech, Hate Propaganda and Pornography* (1995); Samuel Walker, *Hate Speech: The History of an American Controversy* (1994); Symposium, *Campus Hate Speech and the Constitution in the Aftermath of Doe v. University of Michigan,* 37 Wayne L.Rev. 1309 (1991); Symposium, *Free Speech & Religious, Racial & Sexual Harassment,* 32 Wm. & Mary L.Rev. 207 (1991); Symposium, *Frontiers of Legal Thought: The New First Amendment,* 1990 Duke L.J. 375; Symposium, *Hate Speech and the First Amendment: On A Collision Course?,* 37 Vill.L.Rev. 723 (1992); Symposium, *Hate Speech After R.A.V.: More Conflict Between Free Speech and Equality,* 18 Wm. Mitchell L.Rev. 889 (1992); See also sources cited in connection with *R.A.V. v. City of St. Paul,* Ch. 3, IV infra and sources cited in Steven Shiffrin, *Racist Speech, Outsider Jurisprudence, and the Meaning of America,* 80 Corn.L.Rev. 43, 44 n. 6 (1994). For the Canadian perspective, see *Regina v. Keegstra,* [1990] 3 S.C.R. 697. For relevant commentary, see Greenawalt, supra; Lawrence Douglas, *Policing the Past* in *Censorship and Silencing* 67 (Robert C. Post ed. 1998); Lorraine Weinrib, *Hate Promotion in a Democratic Society,* 36 McGill L.Rev. 1416 (1991).

D. ANIMAL CRUELTY AND THE FLIGHT FROM NEW CATEGORIES

18 U.S.C. § 48 criminalizes knowing creation, sale, or possession of a depiction of animal cruelty, if done for commercial gain in interstate or foreign commerce. A depiction of animal cruelty is defined as one "in which a living animal is intentionally maimed, mutilated, tortured, wounded, or killed," if that conduct violates federal or state law where "the creation, sale, or possession takes place." The law exempts any depiction "that has serious religious, political, scientific, educational, journalistic, historical, or artistic value." Respondent was convicted under the statute for selling videos of dog fighting, but argued that the statute violated the First Amendment on its face. UNITED STATES v. STEVENS, per ROBERTS, C.J., rejected this contention and held that the statute was substantially overbroad, but it left room for Congress to pass a more narrowly drawn statute: "The Government's primary submission is that [the] banned depictions of animal cruelty, as a class, are categorically unprotected by the First Amendment. We disagree.

"* * * 'From 1791 to the present,' [the] First Amendment has 'permitted restrictions upon the content of speech in a few limited areas,' and has never 'include[d] a freedom to disregard these traditional limitations.' These 'historic and traditional categories long familiar to the bar,'—including obscenity, *Roth*, defamation, *Beauharnais*, fraud, *Virginia Bd.*, incitement, *Brandenburg*, and speech integral to criminal conduct, *Giboney v. Empire Storage & Ice Co.*, 336 U.S. 490 (1949)—are 'well-defined and narrowly limited classes of speech, the prevention and punishment of which have never been thought to raise any Constitutional problem.' *Chaplinsky*.

"The Government argues that 'depictions of animal cruelty' should be added to the list. It contends that depictions of 'illegal acts of animal cruelty' that are 'made, sold, or possessed for commercial gain' necessarily 'lack expressive value,' and may accordingly 'be regulated as *unprotected* speech.' * * *

"The Government contends that 'historical evidence' about the reach of the First Amendment is not 'a necessary prerequisite for regulation today,' and that categories of speech may be exempted from the First Amendment's protection without any long-settled tradition of subjecting that speech to regulation. Instead, the Government points to Congress's 'legislative judgment that ... depictions of animals being intentionally tortured and killed [are] of such minimal redeeming value as to render [them] unworthy of First Amendment protection,' and asks the Court to uphold the ban on the same basis. The Government thus proposes that a claim of categorical exclusion should be considered under a simple balancing test: 'Whether a given category of speech enjoys First Amendment protection depends upon a categorical balancing of the value of the speech against its societal costs.'

"As a free-floating test for First Amendment coverage, that sentence is startling and dangerous. The First Amendment's guarantee of free speech does not extend only to categories of speech that survive an ad hoc balancing of relative social costs and benefits. The First Amendment itself reflects a judgment by the American people that the benefits of its restrictions on the Government outweigh the costs. * * *

"To be fair to the Government, its view did not emerge from a vacuum. As the Government correctly notes, this Court has often *described* historically unprotected categories of speech as being 'of such slight social value as a step to truth that any benefit that may be derived from them is clearly outweighed by the social interest in order and morality.' In *Ferber*, we noted that within these categories of unprotected speech, 'the evil to be restricted so overwhelmingly outweighs the expressive interests, if any, at stake, that no process of case-by-case adjudication is required,' because 'the balance of competing interests is clearly struck,' The Government derives its proposed test from these descriptions in our precedents.

"But such descriptions are just that-descriptive. They do not set forth a test that may be applied as a general matter to permit the Government to imprison any speaker so long as his speech is deemed valueless or unnecessary, or so long as an ad hoc calculus of costs and benefits tilts in a statute's favor. When we have identified categories of speech as fully outside the protection of the First Amendment, it has not been on the basis of a simple cost-benefit analysis. In *Ferber*, for example, we classified child pornography as such a category. We noted that the State of New York had a compelling interest in protecting children from abuse, and that the value of using children in these works (as opposed to simulated conduct or adult actors) was de minimis. But our decision did not rest on this 'balance of competing interests' alone. We made clear that *Ferber* presented a special case: The market for child pornography was 'intrinsically related' to the underlying abuse, and was therefore 'an integral part of the production of such materials, an activity illegal throughout the Nation.' As we noted, '[i]t rarely has been suggested that the constitutional freedom for speech and press extends its immunity to speech or writing used as an integral part of conduct in violation of a valid criminal statute.' (quoting *Giboney*). *Ferber* thus grounded its analysis in a previously recognized, long-established category of unprotected speech * * *.

"Our decisions in *Ferber* and other cases cannot be taken as establishing a freewheeling authority to declare new categories of speech outside the scope of the First Amendment. Maybe there are some categories of speech that have been historically unprotected, but have not yet been specifically identified or discussed as such in our case law. But if so, there is no evidence that 'depictions of animal cruelty' is among them. We need not foreclose the future recognition of such additional categories to reject the Government's highly manipulable balancing test as a means of identifying them.''

Roberts, C.J., thereafter argued that the statute was substantially overbroad. Depictions of maiming, mutilating, and torture convey cruelty, he said, but not depictions of wounding or killing, and he did not interpret the statute to apply exclusively to instances of animal cruelty. Nor was the illegality of the underlying activity a proxy for cruelty, he suggested, because many laws involving the proper treatment of animals are not related to cruelty. And the serious value section of the statute did not resolve the overbreadth issue because depictions of hunting might be protected even if they did not have *serious* value.

"Our construction of § 48 decides the constitutional question; the Government makes no effort to defend [its constitutionality] as applied beyond crush videos and depictions of animal fighting. It argues that those particular depictions are intrinsically related to criminal conduct or are analogous to obscenity (if not themselves obscene), and that the ban on such speech is narrowly tailored to reinforce restrictions on the underlying conduct, prevent additional crime arising from the depictions, or safeguard public mores. But the Government nowhere attempts to extend these arguments to depictions of any other activities—depictions that are presumptively protected by the First Amendment but that remain subject to the criminal sanctions of § 48.

"However 'growing' and 'lucrative' the markets for crush videos and dogfighting depictions might be, they are dwarfed by the market for other depictions, such as hunting magazines and videos. We therefore need not and do not decide whether a statute limited to crush videos or other depictions of extreme animal cruelty would be constitutional. We hold only that § 48 is not so limited but is instead substantially overbroad, and therefore invalid under the First Amendment."

Alito, J., dissented: "The Court strikes down in its entirety a valuable statute that was enacted not to suppress speech, but to prevent horrific acts of animal cruelty-in particular, the creation and commercial exploitation of 'crush videos,' a form of depraved entertainment that has no social value. [A] sample crush video, which has been lodged with the Clerk, records the following event: '[A] kitten, secured to the ground, watches and shrieks in pain as a woman thrusts her high-heeled shoe into its body, slams her heel into the kitten's eye socket and mouth loudly fracturing its skull, and stomps repeatedly on the animal's head. The kitten hemorrhages blood, screams blindly in pain, and is ultimately left dead in a moist pile of blood-soaked hair and bone.'

"It is undisputed that the *conduct* depicted in crush videos may constitutionally be prohibited. All 50 States and the District of Columbia have enacted statutes prohibiting animal cruelty. But before the enactment of § 48 the underlying conduct depicted in crush videos was nearly impossible to prosecute. These videos, which 'often appeal to persons with a very specific sexual fetish,' were made in secret, generally without a live audience, and 'the faces of the women inflicting the torture in the material often were not shown, nor could the location of the place where the cruelty was being inflicted or the date of the activity be ascertained from the depiction.' Thus, law enforcement authorities often were not able to identify the parties responsible for the torture. * * *

"In light of the practical problems thwarting the prosecution of the creators of crush videos under state animal cruelty laws, Congress concluded that the only effective way of stopping the underlying criminal conduct was to prohibit the commercial exploitation of the videos of that conduct. And Congress' strategy appears to have been vindicated. We are told that '[b]y 2007, sponsors of § 48 declared the crush video industry dead. Even overseas Websites shut down in the wake of § 48. Now, after the Third Circuit's decision [facially invalidating the statute], crush videos are already back online.'"

Alito, J., argued that the principles of *Ferber* lead easily to the conclusion that crush and dog fight videos were constitutionally unprotected though he conceded that the government interest was more significant in *Ferber*. He dissented from the Court's conclusion that the statute was overbroad: "I would hold that § 48 does not apply to depictions of hunting. First, because § 48 targets depictions of 'animal cruelty,' I would interpret that term to apply only to depictions involving acts of animal cruelty as defined by applicable state or federal law, not to depictions of acts that happen to be illegal for reasons having nothing to do with the prevention of animal cruelty. Virtually all state laws prohibiting animal cruelty either expressly define the term 'animal' to exclude wildlife or else specifically exempt lawful hunting activities, so the statutory prohibition [may] reasonably be interpreted not to reach most if not all hunting depictions. * * *

"Second, even if the hunting of wild animals were otherwise covered[,] I would hold that hunting depictions fall within the exception [for] depictions that have 'serious' (i.e., not "trifling") 'scientific,' 'educational,' or 'historical' value. [Thus,] it is widely thought that hunting has 'scientific' value in that it promotes conservation, 'historical' value in that it provides a link to past times when hunting played a critical role in daily life, and 'educational' value in that it furthers the understanding and appreciation of nature and our country's past and instills valuable character traits. And if hunting itself is widely thought to serve these values, then it takes but a small additional step to conclude that depictions of hunting make a non-trivial contribution to the exchange of ideas. Accordingly, I would hold that hunting depictions fall comfortably within the exception * * *.

"I do not have the slightest doubt that Congress, in enacting § 48, had no intention of restricting the creation, sale, or possession of depictions of hunting. Proponents of the law made this point clearly. [But] even if § 48 did impermissibly reach the sale or possession of depictions of hunting in a few unusual situations (for example, the sale in Oregon of a depiction of hunting with a crossbow in Virginia or the sale in Washington State of the hunting of a sharp-tailed grouse in Idaho, those isolated applications would hardly show that § 48 bans a substantial amount of protected speech."

After making similar arguments with other examples put forth by Roberts, C.J., Alito, J., concluded that the statute "has a substantial core of constitutionally permissible applications" and that the respondent had not met his burden of demonstrating that any impermissible applications of the statute were substantial.

CHAPTER 2

DISTINGUISHING BETWEEN CONTEN REGULATION AND MANNER REGULATION: UNCONVENTIONAL FORMS OF COMMUNICATION

■ ■ ■

Special First Amendment questions are often said to arise by regulation of the time, place, and manner of speech as opposed to regulation of its content. But the two types of regulation are not mutually exclusive. It is possible to regulate time, place, manner, and content in the same regulation. For example, in *Linmark,* Ch. 3, II infra, the township outlawed signs (but not leaflets) advertising a house for sale (but not other advertisements or other messages) on front lawns (but not other places).

Further, the terms, manner and content are strongly contested concepts. Indeed, an issue recurring in this section is whether the regulations in question are of manner or content. To the extent this section is about manner regulation, it is not exhaustive—much comes later. Most of the cases in this section involve unconventional forms of expression. Speakers claim protection for burning draft cards, wearing armbands, mutilating flags, nude dancing, wearing long hair. Fact patterns such as these fix renewed attention on the question of how "speech" should be defined. It may be a nice question as to whether obscenity is not speech within the First Amendment lexicon, whether it is such speech but has been balanced into an unprotected state, or whether it is not *freedom* of speech or *the* freedom of speech. But assassinating a public figure, even to send a message, raises no First Amendment problem. Robbing a bank does not raise a free speech issue. What does? How do we decide?

The fact patterns in this section also invite scrutiny of other issues that appear in succeeding sections. Should it make a difference if the state's interest in regulating speech is unrelated to what is being said? Suppose the state's concern arises from the non-communicative impact of the speech act—from its manner. Should that distinction make a constitutional difference, and, if so, how much? These questions become more complicated because in context it is often difficult to determine what the

176

state interest is and sometimes difficult to determine whether there is a meaningful distinction between what is said and how it is said.

Even when the distinction between the manner of the speech and the content of the speech is clear, further doctrinal complications abound. Sometimes the regulation considered by the Court is described as one regulating the "time, place, or manner" of speech, and the Court employs the "time, place, or manner test" which is itself differently phrased in different cases. On other occasions the regulation is described as having an "incidental" impact on freedom of speech, and the Court turns to a different test. These different tests are sometimes described by the Court as functional equivalents. Should there be different tests? In what circumstances? See generally Susan Williams, *Content Discrimination and the First Amendment,* 139 U.Pa.L.Rev. 201 (1991).

Finally, in this and succeeding sections the question arises of the extent to which freedom of speech should require special sensitivity to the methods and communications needs of the less powerful.

UNITED STATES v. O'BRIEN

391 U.S. 367, 88 S.Ct. 1673, 20 L.Ed.2d 672 (1968).

CHIEF JUSTICE WARREN delivered the opinion of the Court.

On the morning of March 31, 1966, David Paul O'Brien and three companions burned their Selective Service registration certificates on the steps of the South Boston Courthouse. A sizable crowd, including several [FBI agents] witnessed the event. Immediately after the burning, members of the crowd began attacking O'Brien [and he was ushered to safety by an FBI agent.] O'Brien stated to FBI agents that he had burned his registration certificate because of his beliefs, knowing that he was violating federal law.

[For this act, O'Brien was convicted in federal court.] He [told] the jury that he burned the certificate publicly to influence others to adopt his antiwar beliefs, as he put it, "so that other people would reevaluate their positions with Selective Service, with the armed forces, and reevaluate their place in the culture of today, to hopefully consider my position."

The indictment upon which he was tried charged that he "wilfully and knowingly did mutilate, destroy, and change by burning [his] Registration Certificate; in violation of [§ 462(b)(3) of the Universal Military Training and Service Act of 1948], amended by Congress in 1965 (adding the words italicized below), so that at the time O'Brien burned his certificate an offense was committed by any person, "who forges, alters, *knowingly destroys, knowingly mutilates,* or in any manner changes any such certificate * * *." (Italics supplied.)

[On appeal, the] First Circuit held the 1965 Amendment unconstitutional as a law abridging freedom of speech. At the time the Amendment was enacted, a regulation of the Selective Service System required registrants to keep their registration certificates in their "personal possession at all times." Wilful violations of regulations promulgated pursuant to the Universal Military Training and Service Act were made criminal by statute. The Court of Appeals, therefore, was of the opinion that conduct punishable under the 1965 Amendment was already punishable under the nonpossession regulation, and consequently that the Amendment served no valid purpose; further, that in light of the prior regulation, the Amendment must have been "directed at public as distinguished from private destruction." On this basis, the Court concluded that the 1965 Amendment ran afoul of the First Amendment by singling out persons engaged in protests for special treatment. * * *

When a male reaches the age of 18, he is required by the Universal Military Training and Service Act to register with a local draft board. He is assigned a Selective Service number, and within five days he is issued a registration certificate. Subsequently, and based on a questionnaire completed by the registrant, he is assigned a classification denoting his eligibility for induction, and "[a]s soon as practicable" thereafter he is issued a Notice of Classification. * * *

Both the registration and classification certificates bear notices that the registrant must notify his local board in writing of every change in address, physical condition, and occupational, marital, family, dependency, and military status, and of any other fact which might change his classification. Both also contain a notice that the registrant's Selective Service number should appear on all communications to his local board.

[The 1965] Amendment does not distinguish between public and private destruction, and it does not punish only destruction engaged in for the purpose of expressing views.[a] A law prohibiting destruction of Selective Service certificates no more abridges free speech on its face than a motor vehicle law prohibiting the destruction of drivers' licenses, or a tax law prohibiting the destruction of books and records.

O'Brien nonetheless argues [first] that the 1965 Amendment is unconstitutional [as] applied to him because his act of burning his registration certificate was protected "symbolic speech" within the First Amendment. [He claims that] the First Amendment guarantees include all modes of "communication of ideas by conduct," and that his conduct is within this definition because he did it in "demonstration against the war and against the draft."

We cannot accept the view that an apparently limitless variety of conduct can be labeled "speech" whenever the person engaging in the conduct intends thereby to express an idea. However, even on the assumption that the alleged communicative element in O'Brien's conduct is sufficient to bring into play the First Amendment, it does not necessarily follow that the destruction of a registration certificate is constitutionally

---

a. But compare Chief Judge Aldrich below, 376 F.2d at 541: "We would be closing our eyes in the light of the prior law if we did not see on the face of the amendment that it was precisely directed at public as distinguished from private destruction. [In] singling out persons engaging in protest for special treatment the amendment strikes at the very core of what the First Amendment protects."

protected activity. This Court has held that when "speech" and "non-speech" elements are combined in the same course of conduct, a sufficiently important governmental interest in regulating the nonspeech element can justify incidental limitations on First Amendment freedoms. To characterize the quality of the governmental interest which must appear, the Court has employed a variety of descriptive terms: compelling; substantial; subordinating; paramount; cogent; strong. [W]e think it clear that a government regulation is sufficiently justified if it is within the constitutional power of the government; if it furthers an important or substantial governmental interest; if the governmental interest is unrelated to the suppression of free expression; and if the incidental restriction on alleged First Amendment freedom is no greater than is essential to the furtherance of that interest.[b] We find that the 1965 Amendment meets all of these requirements, and consequently that O'Brien can be constitutionally convicted for violating it. [Pursuant to its power to classify and conscript manpower for military service], Congress may establish a system of registration for individuals liable for training and service, and may require such individuals within reason to cooperate in the registration system. The issuance of certificates indicating the registration and eligibility classification of individuals is a legitimate and substantial administrative aid in the functioning of this system. And legislation to insure the continuing availability of issued certificates serves a legitimate and substantial purpose in the system's administration.

[O'Brien] essentially adopts the position that [Selective Service] certificates are so many pieces of paper designed to notify registrants of their registration or classification, to be retained or tossed in the wastebasket according to the convenience or taste of the registrant. Once the registrant has received notification, according to this view, there is no reason for him to retain the certificates. [However, the registration and classification certificates serve] purposes in addition to initial notification. Many of these purposes would be defeated by the certificates' destruction or mutilation. Among these are [simplifying verification of the registration and classification of suspected delinquents, evidence of availability for induction in the event of emergency, ease of communication between registrants and local boards, continually reminding registrants of the need to notify local boards of changes in status].

The many functions performed by Selective Service certificates establish beyond doubt that Congress has a legitimate and substantial interest in preventing their wanton and unrestrained destruction and assuring their continuing availability by punishing people who knowingly and

---

b. Michael C. Dorf, *Incidental Burdens on Fundamental Rights*, 109 Harv. L. Rev. 1175, 1202 (1996): "Prong one is not properly part of First Amendment law, because *all* regulation must be within the government's constitutional power. Prong three merely restates the proposition that the challenged regulation must be content-neutral—which is a precondition for the application of the test in the first instance. The *O'Brien* test thus can be distilled into a two-part requirement that formally resembles conventional intermediate scrutiny: a regulation must serve a substantial government interest and must be narrowly tailored to that end in order to pass constitutional muster."

wilfully destroy or mutilate them. And we are unpersuaded that the pre-existence of the nonpossession regulations in any way negates this interest.

In the absence of a question as to multiple punishment, it has never been suggested that there is anything improper in Congress providing alternative statutory avenues of prosecution to assure the effective protection of one and the same interest. Here, the pre-existing avenue of prosecution was not even statutory. Regulations may be modified or revoked from time to time by administrative discretion. Certainly, the Congress may change or supplement a regulation.

[The] gravamen of the offense defined by the statute is the deliberate rendering of certificates unavailable for the various purposes which they may serve. Whether registrants keep their certificates in their personal possession at all times, as required by the regulations, is of no particular concern under the 1965 Amendment, as long as they do not mutilate or destroy the certificates so as to render them unavailable. [The 1965 amendment] is concerned with abuses involving *any* issued Selective Service certificates, not only with the registrant's own certificates. The knowing destruction or mutilation of someone else's certificates would therefore violate the statute but not the nonpossession regulations.

We think it apparent that the continuing availability to each registrant of his Selective Service certificates substantially furthers the smooth and proper functioning of the system that Congress has established to raise armies. * * *

It is equally clear that the 1965 Amendment specifically protects this substantial governmental interest. We perceive no alternative means that would more precisely and narrowly assure the continuing availability of issued Selective Service certificates than a law which prohibits their wilful mutilation or destruction. The 1965 Amendment prohibits such conduct and does nothing more. [The] governmental interest and the scope of the 1965 Amendment are limited to preventing a harm to the smooth and efficient functioning of the Selective Service System. When O'Brien deliberately rendered unavailable his registration certificate, he wilfully frustrated this governmental interest. For this noncommunicative impact of his conduct, and for nothing else, he was convicted.* * *

O'Brien finally argues that the 1965 Amendment is unconstitutional as enacted because what he calls the "purpose" of Congress was "to suppress freedom of speech." We reject this argument because under settled principles the purpose of Congress, as O'Brien uses that term, is not a basis for declaring this legislation unconstitutional.

It is a familiar principle of constitutional law that this Court will not strike down an otherwise constitutional statute on the basis of an alleged illicit legislative motive.

[I]f we were to examine legislative purpose in the instant case, we would be obliged to consider not only [the statements of the three members of Congress who addressed themselves to the amendment, all viewing draft-card burning as a brazen display of unpatriotism] but also the more authoritative reports of the Senate and House Armed Services Committees. [B]oth reports make clear a concern with the "defiant" destruction of so-called "draft cards" and with "open" encouragement to others to destroy their cards, [but they] also indicate that this concern stemmed from an apprehension that unrestrained destruction of cards would disrupt the smooth functioning of the Selective Service System. * * *

Reversed.[c]

JUSTICE HARLAN concurring. * * *

I wish to make explicit my understanding that [the Court's analysis] does not foreclose consideration of First Amendment claims in those rare instances when an "incidental" restriction upon expression, imposed by a regulation which furthers an "important or substantial" governmental interest and satisfies the Court's other criteria, in practice has the effect of entirely preventing a "speaker" from reaching a significant audience with whom he could not otherwise lawfully communicate. This is not such a case, since O'Brien manifestly could have conveyed his message in many ways other than by burning his draft card.

JUSTICE DOUGLAS, dissenting.

[Douglas, J., thought that "the underlying and basic problem in this case" was the constitutionality of a draft "in the absence of a declaration of war" and that the case should be put down for reargument on this question. The following Term, concurring in *Brandenburg*, he criticized *O'Brien* on the merits. After recalling that the Court had rejected O'Brien's First Amendment argument on the ground that "legislation to insure the continuing availability of issued certificates serves a legitimate and substantial purpose in the [selective service] system's administration," he commented: "But O'Brien was not prosecuted for not having his draft card available when asked for by a federal agent. He was indicted, tried, and convicted for burning the card. And this Court's affirmance [was not] consistent with the First Amendment." He observed, more generally in *Brandenburg*:

["Action is often a method of expression and within the protection of the First Amendment. Suppose one tears up his own copy of the Constitution in eloquent protest to a decision of this Court. May he be indicted? Suppose one rips his own Bible to shreds to celebrate his departure from one 'faith' and his embrace of atheism. May he be indicted? * * *

["The act of praying often involves body posture and movement as well as utterances. It is nonetheless protected by the Free Exercise Clause. Picketing [is] 'free speech plus.' [Therefore], it can be regulated when it comes to the 'plus' or 'action' side of the protest. It can be regulated as to the number of pickets and the place and hours, because traffic and other

---

c. Marshall, J., took no part.

community problems would otherwise suffer. But none of these considerations are implicated in the symbolic protest of the Vietnam war in the burning of a draft card.''']

NOTES AND QUESTIONS

1. ***Expression vs. action.*** What of the Court's rejection of the idea that conduct is speech "whenever the person engaging in the conduct intends thereby to express an idea." Was it right to question whether O'Brien's conduct was speech? What was it about O'Brien's conduct that made the Court doubt that it was speech? What if O'Brien had burned a copy of the Constitution? Consider Thomas Emerson, *The System of Freedom of Expression* 80 & 84 (1970): "To some extent expression and action are always mingled; most conduct includes elements of both. Even the clearest manifestations of expression involve some action, as in the case of holding a meeting, publishing a newspaper, or merely talking. At the other extreme, a political assassination includes a substantial mixture of expression. The guiding principle must be to determine which element is predominant in the conduct under consideration. Is expression the major element and the action only secondary? Or is the action the essence and the expression incidental? The answer, to a great extent, must be based on a common-sense reaction, made in light of the functions and operations of a system of freedom of expression. * * *

"The burning of a draft card is, of course, conduct that involves both communication and physical acts. Yet it seems quite clear that the predominant element in such conduct is expression (opposition to the draft) rather than action (destruction of a piece of cardboard). The registrant is not concerned with secret or inadvertent burning of his draft card, involving no communication with other persons. The main feature, for him, is the public nature of the burning, through which he expresses to the community his ideas and feelings about the war and the draft."

Compare John Hart Ely, *Flag Desecration: A Case Study in the Roles of Categorization and Balancing in First Amendment Analysis*, 88 Harv.L.Rev. 1482, 1495 (1975): "[B]urning a draft card to express opposition to the draft is an undifferentiated whole, 100% action and 100% expression. It involves no conduct that is not at the same time communication, and no communication that does not result from conduct. Attempts to determine which element 'predominates' will therefore inevitably degenerate into question-begging judgments about whether the activity should be protected. The *O'Brien* Court thus quite wisely dropped the 'speech-conduct' distinction as quickly as it had picked it up."[d]

2. ***Nature of the state interest and First Amendment methodology.*** Melville Nimmer, *The Meaning of Symbolic Speech under the First Amendment*, 21 UCLA L.Rev. 29 (1973), followed by Ely, note 1 supra, and

---

d. But, as Ely recognizes, the Court picked it up again in *Cohen*, Ch. 1, IV, C supra: "[W]e deal here with a conviction resting solely upon 'speech', cf. *Stromberg*, not upon any separately identifiable conduct which allegedly was intended by Cohen to be perceived by others as expressive of particular views but which, on its face, does not necessarily convey any message and hence arguably could be regulated without effectively repressing Cohen's ability to express himself. Cf. *O'Brien*."

Tribe 2d ed., at 791–92, proposed that the crucial starting point for First Amendment methodology is and should be the nature of the state interest.[e] As Ely put it, at 1497: "The critical question would therefore seem to be whether the harm that the state is seeking to avert is one that grows out of the fact that the defendant is communicating, and more particularly out of the way people can be expected to react to his message [Tribe calls this "track one"], or rather would arise even if the defendant's conduct had no communicative significance whatever [Tribe calls this "track two"]." In order to appreciate the difference this distinction makes, it is necessary to determine the standard or standards used on track one. The standard or standards used on track one are not obvious because some speech on track one can be prohibited or sanctioned (e.g., some forms of advocacy of illegal action and obscenity); some speech on track one is subject to a test whose stringency varies with the context and the membership of the Court (e.g., *Central Hudson*); some speech on track one is subject to little or no scrutiny (consider the application of the securities laws to corporate speech); and other speech on track one can be prohibited only if it is necessary to achieve a compelling state interest (e.g., speech on public issues that does not fall within recognized exceptions such as advocacy of illegal action under *Brandenburg*). Geoffrey Stone has argued for some years that the exceptions to stringent protection on what is ordinarily the functional equivalent to track one are based either on extraordinary circumstances or on the determination that the speech is of low or lesser value (e.g., obscenity, false statements of fact). See also Lee C. Bollinger & Geoffrey R. Stone, *Dialogue*, in Eternally Vigilant: Free Speech in the Modern Era 8 (Lee C. Bollinger & Geoffrey R. Stone eds., 2002). Steven Shiffrin, by contrast, has argued that different tests have been applied in different contexts on track one and that determinations of the degree of stringency are more complicated than Stone suggests. The weight placed upon the speech interest, he argues, depends upon the nature of the state interest, the extent to which the state regulation furthers the interest, the possibility of less restrictive alternatives together with an assessment of the extent to which the restriction has an impact on First Amendment values and an assessment of the importance of the values impacted. Steven H. Shiffrin, *The First Amendment, Democracy, and Romance* ch. 1 (1990). Commenting on the terms in which the Court has explained its behavior on track one, consider Steven J. Heyman, *Spheres of Autonomy: Reforming the Content Neutrality Doctrine in First Amendment Jurisprudence*, 10 Wm. & Mary Bill Rts. J. 647, 651–652 (2002): "[T]the Court has carved out two exceptions to the [protection of speech under track one]. First, the justices have adhered to the traditional view that some categories of speech are entitled to little or no protection under the First Amendment. Second, the Court has held in principle—though very rarely in practice—that even fully protected speech may be regulated based on content where necessary to achieve a compelling government interest. Unfortunately, however, the Court has never succeeded in explaining the rationale for these exceptions, or in squaring them with the general principle of content neutrality. If the First Amendment allows harm-based regulation in some cases, why not in others?"

---

    e. The distinction is a major organizing principle in Rodney Smolla, *Smolla and Nimmer on Freedom of Speech* (1984).

(a) *Normative value of the distinction between track one and track two.* How much weight should be put on the distinction between track one and track two? Consider a regulation governing express warranties in commercial advertising. Is much of contract law on track one?[f] Consider "a nationwide ban on *all* posters (intended to conserve paper)." Isn't that on track two? Do these examples suggest that too much emphasis is being placed on a single factor? See Daniel Farber, *Content Regulation and the First Amendment: A Revisionist View,* 68 Geo.U.L.Rev. 727, 746–47 (1980).[g] Does the distinction between track one and track two rest on an assumption that the First Amendment is primarily concerned with protecting against improper government motivation? For the suggestion that a concern with purpose or motive is at the heart of the First Amendment, see Larry Alexander, *Is There a Right of Freedom of Expression?* 38–81 (2005); Jed Rubenfeld, *The First Amendment's Purpose,* 53 Stan. L. Rev. 767, 768 (2001); Elena Kagan, *Private Speech, Public Purpose: The Role of Governmental Motive in First Amendment Doctrine,* 63 U.Chi. L.Rev. 413 (1996); David Bogen, *Bulwark of Liberty: The Court and the First Amendment* (1984); David Bogen, *Balancing Freedom of Speech,* 38 Md.L.Rev. 387 (1979); David Bogen, *The Supreme Court's Interpretation of the Guarantee of Freedom of Speech,* 35 Md.L.Rev. 555 (1976). See note 3 after *Arcara* infra. If so, does this perspective neglect the positive values of the First Amendment? Was there an impermissible legislative purpose in *Schenck v. U.S.? Falwell? Cohen v. California?* See Eugene Volokh, *Speech As Conduct: Generally Applicable Laws, Illegal Courses of Conduct, "Situation–Altering Utterances," and the Uncharted Zones,* 90 Cornell L.Rev. 1277, 1287–92 (2005). In *Minneapolis Star?* See Stuart Minor Benjamin, *Proactive Legislation and the First Amendment,* 99 Mich. L. Rev. 281, 287 (2000). Consider Volokh, supra, at 1285: "When a law generally applies to a wide range of conduct, and sweeps in speech together with such conduct, there is little reason to think that lawmakers had any motivation with regard to speech, much less an impermissible one. Nonetheless, such a law should still be unconstitutional when applied to speech based on its content—even though the legislature's motivations may have been quite benign." For further criticism, see Richard Posner, *Law, Pragmatism, and Democracy* 368–83 (2003).

(b) *Application to O'Brien.* Consider Ely, note 1 supra, at 1498–99: "The interests upon which the government relied were interests, having mainly to do with the preservation of selective service records, that would have been equally threatened had O'Brien's destruction of his draft card totally lacked communicative significance—had he, for example, used it to start a campfire for a solitary cookout or dropped it in his garbage disposal for a lark. (The law prohibited all knowing destructions, public or private)."

Compare Melville Nimmer, note 2 supra, at 41, contending that the *O'Brien* statute was "overnarrow": "[An overnarrow statute] may be said to

---

f. For the suggestion that virtually all laws have information effects and that track two embraces virtually all laws not covered by track one, see Larry Alexander, *Trouble on Track Two: Incidental Regulations of Speech and Free Speech,* 44 Hastings L.J. 921 (1993) (arguing that track two countenances an unconstitutional evaluation of the value of speech).

g. See generally Martin Redish, *The Content Distinction in First Amendment Analysis,* 34 Stan.L.Rev. 113 (1981). See notes after *Chicago Police Dept. v. Mosley,* Ch. 6, I, B infra.

create a conclusive presumption that in fact the state interest which the statute serves is an anti-rather than a non-speech interest. If the state interest asserted in *O'Brien* were truly the non-speech interest of assuring availability of draft cards, why did Congress choose not to prohibit any knowing conduct which leads to unavailability, rather than limiting the scope of the statute to those instances in which the proscribed conduct carries with it a speech component hostile to governmental policy? The obvious inference to be drawn is that in fact the Congress was completely indifferent to the 'availability' objective, and was concerned only with an interest which the *O'Brien* opinion states is impermissible—an interest in the suppression of free expression."[h]

3. *Dissent.* Does *O'Brien* shortchange the value of dissent? Consider Steven Shiffrin, *The First Amendment, Democracy, and Romance* 5–6, 81 (1990): "If an organizing symbol makes sense in First Amendment jurisprudence, it is not the image of a content-neutral government; it is not a town hall meeting or even a robust marketplace of ideas; still less is it liberty, equality, self-realization, respect, dignity, autonomy, or even tolerance. If the First Amendment is to have an organizing symbol, let it be an Emersonian[i] symbol, let it be the image of the dissenter. A major purpose of the First Amendment [is] to protect the romantics—those who would break out of classical forms: the dissenters, the unorthodox, the outcasts. [That] Emersonian ideal of freedom of speech has deep roots in the nation's culture, but it has been subtly denigrated in recent First Amendment theory and seriously abused in practice.

"[N]either the town hall metaphor nor the marketplace of ideas metaphor[, for example,] is quite apt as a symbol for why *O'Brien* is a First Amendment horror story. Town hall meetings can function without the burning of draft cards. And it is hard to claim that truth was kept from the marketplace of ideas. *O'Brien* is one of those not infrequent cases where government prosecutions assist the dissemination of the dissenter's message. Yet, *O'Brien* is perhaps the ultimate First Amendment insult. O'Brien is jailed because the authorities find his manner of expression unpatriotic, threatening, and offensive. When he complains that his freedom of speech has been abridged, the authorities deny that he has spoken."

4. *Scope of O'Brien.* Should the *O'Brien* test be confined to unconventional forms of communication? Would a distinction of this type be defensible? See Ely, note 1 supra, at 1489: "The distinction is its own objection."[j] Consider Richard H. Fallon, Jr., *The Dynamic Constitution* 43–44 (2004): "Over time, *O'Brien* has proved to be among the Court's most influential free-speech decisions of the modern era. Its significance reaches beyond the special

---

h. On the inadequacy of the *O'Brien* methodology to serve as a proxy for problematic motivation, see Lee Bollinger, *The Tolerant Society* 206–12 (1986). On its inadequacy as an organizing principle for First Amendment doctrine, see Shiffrin, note 3 infra, ch. 1.

i. See generally Joel Porte ed. (1983), *Ralph Waldo Emerson: Essays and Lectures.*

j. See also Dean Alfange, *Free Speech and Symbolic Conduct: The Draft–Card Burning Case,* 1968 Sup.Ct.Rev. 1, 23–24; Lawrence Velvel, *Freedom of Speech and the Draft Card Burning Cases,* 16 U.Kan.L.Rev. 149, 153 (1968); Louis Henkin, *On Drawing Lines,* 82 Harv.L.Rev. 63, 79 (1968). For evidence that the distinction would violate the original meaning of the First Amendment, see Eugene Volokh, *Symbolic Expression and the Original Meaning of the First Amendment,* 97 Geo. L.J. 1057 (2009).

problems posed by expressive conduct. As commentators quickly noticed, even when the government regulates 'pure' speech, it may sometimes act for reasons unrelated to the suppression of speech."

TEXAS v. JOHNSON

491 U.S. 397, 109 S.Ct. 2533, 105 L.Ed.2d 342 (1989).

JUSTICE BRENNAN delivered the opinion of the Court.

[Gregory] Lee Johnson was convicted of desecrating a flag in violation of Texas law.[1]

I. While the Republican National Convention was taking place in Dallas in 1984, respondent Johnson participated in a political demonstration dubbed the "Republican War Chest Tour." [The] demonstration ended in front of Dallas City Hall, where Johnson unfurled the American flag, doused it with kerosene, and set it on fire. While the flag burned, the protestors chanted, "America, the red, white, and blue, we spit on you." [No] one was physically injured or threatened with injury, though several witnesses testified that they had been seriously offended by the flag-burning. * * *

II. Johnson was convicted of flag desecration for burning the flag rather than for uttering insulting words.[2] [We] must first determine whether Johnson's burning of the flag constituted expressive conduct, permitting him to invoke the First Amendment in challenging his conviction. If his conduct was expressive, we next decide whether the State's regulation is related to the suppression of free expression. *O'Brien.* If the State's regulation is not related to expression, then the less stringent standard we announced in *O'Brien* for regulations of noncommunicative conduct controls. If it is, then we are outside of *O'Brien*'s test, and we must ask whether this interest justifies Johnson's conviction under a more

---

1. Tex.Penal Code Ann. § 42.09 (1989) provides in full: "§ 42.09. Desecration of Venerated Object

"(a) A person commits an offense if he intentionally or knowingly desecrates:

"(1) a public monument;

"(2) a place of worship or burial; or

"(3) a state or national flag.

"(b) For purposes of this section, 'desecrate' means deface, damage, or otherwise physically mistreat in a way that the actor knows will seriously offend one or more persons likely to observe or discover his action.

"(c) An offense under this section is a Class A misdemeanor."

2. Because the prosecutor's closing argument observed that Johnson had led the protestors in chants denouncing the flag while it burned, Johnson suggests that he may have been convicted for uttering critical words rather than for burning the flag. He relies on *Street v. New York*, 394 U.S. 576 (1969), in which we reversed a conviction obtained under a New York statute that prohibited publicly defying or casting contempt on the flag "either by words or act" because we were persuaded that the defendant may have been convicted for his words alone. Unlike the law we faced in *Street*, however, the Texas flag-desecration statute does not on its face permit conviction for remarks critical of the flag, as Johnson himself admits. Nor was the jury in this case told that it could convict Johnson of flag desecration if it found only that he had uttered words critical of the flag and its referents. * * *

demanding standard.[3] A third possibility is that the State's asserted interest is simply not implicated on these facts, and in that event the interest drops out of the picture. * * *

In deciding whether particular conduct possesses sufficient communicative elements to bring the First Amendment into play, we have asked whether "[a]n intent to convey a particularized message was present, and [whether] the likelihood was great that the message would be understood by those who viewed it." [In] *Spence v. Washington*, 418 U.S. 405 (1974), for example, we emphasized that Spence's taping of a peace sign to his flag was "roughly simultaneous with and concededly triggered by the Cambodian incursion and the Kent State tragedy." The State of Washington had conceded, in fact, that Spence's conduct was a form of communication, and we stated that "the State's concession is inevitable on this record."

III. In order to decide whether *O'Brien*'s test [applies] we must decide whether Texas has asserted an interest in support of Johnson's conviction that is unrelated to the suppression of expression.

A. Texas claims that its interest in preventing breaches of the peace justifies Johnson's conviction for flag desecration.[4] However, no disturbance of the peace actually occurred or threatened to occur because of Johnson's burning of the flag. [The] only evidence offered by the State at trial to show the reaction to Johnson's actions was the testimony of several persons who had been seriously offended by the flag-burning.

The State's position, therefore, amounts to a claim that an audience that takes serious offense at particular expression is necessarily likely to disturb the peace and that the expression may be prohibited on this basis. [W]e have not permitted the Government to assume that every expression of a provocative idea will incite a riot, but have instead required careful consideration of the actual circumstances surrounding such expression, asking whether the expression "is directed to inciting or producing imminent lawless action and is likely to incite or produce such action." *Brandenburg*. To accept Texas' arguments that it need only demonstrate

---

3. [Johnson] has raised a facial challenge to Texas' flag-desecration [statute]. Section 42.09 regulates only physical conduct with respect to the flag, not the written or spoken word, and although one violates the statute only if one "knows" that one's physical treatment of the flag "will seriously offend one or more persons likely to observe or discover his action," this fact does not necessarily mean that the statute applies only to *expressive* conduct protected by the First Amendment. A tired person might, for example, drag a flag through the mud, knowing that this conduct is likely to offend others, and yet have no thought of expressing any idea; neither the language nor the Texas courts' interpretations of the statute precludes the possibility that such a person would be prosecuted for flag desecration. Because the prosecution of a person who had not engaged in expressive conduct would pose a different case, and because we are capable of disposing of this case on narrower grounds, we address only Johnson's claim that § 42.09 as applied to political expression like his violates the First Amendment.

4. Relying on our decision in *Boos v. Barry*, Johnson argues [that] the violent reaction to flag-burning feared by Texas would be the result of the message conveyed by them, and that this fact connects the State's interest to the suppression of expression. This view has found some favor in the lower courts. Johnson's theory may overread *Boos* insofar as it suggests that a desire to prevent a violent audience reaction is "related to expression" in the same way that a desire to prevent an audience from being offended is "related to expression." Because we find that the State's interest in preventing breaches of the peace is not implicated on these facts, however, we need not venture further into this area.

"the potential for a breach of the peace," and that every flag-burning necessarily possesses that potential, would be to eviscerate our holding in *Brandenburg.* This we decline to do.

Nor does Johnson's expressive conduct fall within that small class of "fighting words" that are "likely to provoke the average person to retaliation, and thereby cause a breach of the peace." *Chaplinsky.* No reasonable onlooker would have regarded Johnson's generalized expression of dissatisfaction with the policies of the Federal Government as a direct personal insult or an invitation to exchange fisticuffs.

We thus conclude that the State's interest in maintaining order is not implicated on these facts. * * *

B.   The State also asserts an interest in preserving the flag as a symbol of nationhood and national unity. [The] State, apparently, is concerned that such conduct will lead people to believe either that the flag does not stand for nationhood and national unity, but instead reflects other, less positive concepts, or that the concepts reflected in the flag do not in fact exist, that is, we do not enjoy unity as a Nation. These concerns blossom only when a person's treatment of the flag communicates some message, and thus are related "to the suppression of free expression" within the meaning of *O'Brien.* We are thus outside of *O'Brien*'s test altogether.

IV.   It remains to consider whether the State's interest in preserving the flag as a symbol of nationhood and national unity justifies Johnson's conviction. [If Johnson] had burned the flag as a means of disposing of it because it was dirty or torn, he would not have been convicted of flag desecration under this Texas law: federal law designates burning as the preferred means of disposing of a flag "when it is in such condition that it is no longer a fitting emblem for display," 36 U.S.C. § 176(k), and Texas has no quarrel with this means of disposal. The Texas law is thus not aimed at protecting the physical integrity of the flag in all circumstances, but is designed instead to protect it only against impairments that would cause serious offense to others.[6]

Whether Johnson's treatment of the flag violated Texas law thus depended on the likely communicative impact of his expressive conduct. Our decision in *Boos v. Barry,* 485 U.S. 312 (1988), tells us that this restriction on Johnson's expression is content-based. In *Boos,* we considered the constitutionality of a law prohibiting "the display of any sign within 50 feet of a foreign embassy if that sign tends to bring that foreign government into 'public odium' or 'public disrepute.'" Rejecting the argument that the law was content-neutral because it was justified by "our international law obligation to shield diplomats from speech that

---

6.   *Cf. Smith v. Goguen,* 415 U.S. 566 (1974) (Blackmun, J., dissenting) (emphasizing that lower court appeared to have construed state statute so as to protect physical integrity of the flag in all circumstances); id. (Rehnquist, J., dissenting) (same). [In *Goguen,* Blackmun, J., argued that "Goguen's punishment was constitutionally permissible for harming the physical integrity of the flag by wearing it affixed to the seat of his pants" and emphasized that such punishment would not be for "speech—a communicative element."].

offends their dignity," we held that "[t]he emotive impact of speech on its audience is not a 'secondary effect'" unrelated to the content of the expression itself.

According to the principles announced in *Boos,* Johnson's political expression was restricted because of the content of the message he conveyed. We must therefore subject the State's asserted interest in preserving the special symbolic character of the flag to "the most exacting scrutiny." *Boos.*[8] * * *

If there is a bedrock principle underlying the First Amendment, it is that the Government may not prohibit the expression of an idea simply because society finds the idea itself offensive or disagreeable. [We] have not recognized an exception to this principle even where our flag has been involved. [We] never before have held that the Government may ensure that a symbol be used to express only one view of that symbol or its referents. Indeed, in *Schacht v. United States,* 398 U.S. 58 (1970), we invalidated a federal statute permitting an actor portraying a member of one of our armed forces to " 'wear the uniform of that armed force if the portrayal does not tend to discredit that armed force.' " This proviso, we held, "which leaves Americans free to praise the war in Vietnam but can send persons like Schacht to prison for opposing it, cannot survive in a country which has the First Amendment."

We perceive no basis on which to hold that the principle underlying our decision in *Schacht* does not apply to this case. To conclude that the Government may permit designated symbols to be used to communicate only a limited set of messages would be to enter territory having no discernible or defensible boundaries. Could the Government, on this theory, prohibit the burning of state flags? Of copies of the Presidential seal? Of the Constitution? In evaluating these choices under the First Amendment, how would we decide which symbols were sufficiently special to warrant this unique status? To do so, we would be forced to consult our own political preferences, and impose them on the citizenry, in the very way that the First Amendment forbids us to do.

There is, moreover, no indication—either in the text of the Constitution or in our cases interpreting it—that a separate judicial category exists for the American flag alone. Indeed, we would not be surprised to learn that the persons who framed our Constitution and wrote the Amendment that we now construe were not known for their reverence for the Union Jack. The First Amendment does not guarantee that other concepts virtually sacred to our Nation as a whole—such as the principle that discrimination on the basis of race is odious and destructive—will go unquestioned in the marketplace of ideas. See *Brandenburg.* We decline,

---

8. Our inquiry is, of course, bounded by the particular facts of this case and by the statute under which Johnson was convicted. There was no evidence that Johnson himself stole the flag he burned, nor did the prosecution or the arguments urged in support of it depend on the theory that the flag was stolen. [Thus] nothing in our opinion should be taken to suggest that one is free to steal a flag so long as one later uses it to communicate an idea. We also emphasize that Johnson was prosecuted *only* for flag desecration—not for trespass, disorderly conduct, or arson.

therefore, to create for the flag an exception to the joust of principles protected by the First Amendment.

It is not the State's ends, but its means, to which we object. It cannot be gainsaid that there is a special place reserved for the flag in this Nation, and thus we do not doubt that the Government has a legitimate interest in making efforts to "preserv[e] the national flag as an unalloyed symbol of our country." We reject the suggestion, urged at oral argument by counsel for Johnson, that the Government lacks "any state interest whatsoever" in regulating the manner in which the flag may be displayed. Congress has, for example, enacted precatory regulations describing the proper treatment of the flag, see 36 U.S.C. §§ 173–177, and we cast no doubt on the legitimacy of its interest in making such recommendations. To say that the Government has an interest in encouraging proper treatment of the flag, however, is not to say that it may criminally punish a person for burning a flag as a means of political protest. "National unity as an end which officials may foster by persuasion and example is not in question. The problem is whether under our Constitution compulsion as here employed is a permissible means for its achievement."

[W]e submit that nobody can suppose that this one gesture of an unknown man will change our Nation's attitude towards its flag. See *Abrams* (Holmes, J., dissenting). Indeed, Texas' argument that the burning of an American flag " 'is an act having a high likelihood to cause a breach of the peace,' " and its statute's implicit assumption that physical mistreatment of the flag will lead to "serious offense," tend to confirm that the flag's special role is not in danger; if it were, no one would riot or take offense because a flag had been burned.

We are tempted to say, in fact, that the flag's deservedly cherished place in our community will be strengthened, not weakened, by our holding today. Our decision is a reaffirmation of the principles of freedom and inclusiveness that the flag best reflects, and of the conviction that our toleration of criticism such as Johnson's is a sign and source of our strength. Indeed, one of the proudest images of our flag, the one immortalized in our own national anthem, is of the bombardment it survived at Fort McHenry. It is the Nation's resilience, not its rigidity, that Texas sees reflected in the flag—and it is that resilience that we reassert today.

The way to preserve the flag's special role is not to punish those who feel differently about these matters. It is to persuade them that they are wrong. [We] can imagine no more appropriate response to burning a flag than waving one's own, no better way to counter a flag-burner's message than by saluting the flag that burns, no surer means of preserving the dignity even of the flag that burned than by—as one witness here did— according its remains a respectful burial. * * *

JUSTICE KENNEDY, concurring. * * *

Our colleagues in dissent advance powerful arguments why respondent may be convicted for his expression, reminding us that among those who will be dismayed by our holding will be some who have had the singular honor of carrying the flag in battle. And I agree that the flag holds a lonely place of honor in an age when absolutes are distrusted and simple truths are burdened by unneeded apologetics.

With all respect to those views, I do not believe the Constitution gives us the right to rule as the dissenting members of the Court urge, however painful this judgment is to announce. Though symbols often are what we ourselves make of them, the flag is constant in expressing beliefs Americans share, beliefs in law and peace and that freedom which sustains the human spirit. The case here today forces recognition of the costs to which those beliefs commit us. It is poignant but fundamental that the flag protects those who hold it in contempt.

For all the record shows, this respondent was not a philosopher and perhaps did not even possess the ability to comprehend how repellent his statements must be to the Republic itself. But whether or not he could appreciate the enormity of the offense he gave, the fact remains that his acts were speech, in both the technical and the fundamental meaning of the Constitution. So I agree with the Court that he must go free.

CHIEF JUSTICE REHNQUIST, with whom JUSTICE WHITE and JUSTICE O'CONNOR join, dissenting.

In holding this Texas statute unconstitutional, the Court ignores Justice Holmes' familiar aphorism that "a page of history is worth a volume of logic." *New York Trust Co. v. Eisner,* 256 U.S. 345 (1921). * * *

The American flag [throughout] more than 200 years of our history, has come to be the visible symbol embodying our Nation.[a] It does not represent the views of any particular political party, and it does not represent any particular political philosophy. The flag is not simply another "idea" or "point of view" competing for recognition in the marketplace of ideas. Millions and millions of Americans regard it with an almost mystical reverence regardless of what sort of social, political, or philosophical beliefs they may have. I cannot agree that the First Amendment invalidates the Act of Congress, and the laws of 48 of the 50 States, which make criminal the public burning of the flag.

More than 80 years ago in *Halter v. Nebraska* [205 U.S. 34 (1907)], this Court upheld the constitutionality of a Nebraska statute that forbade the use of representations of the American flag for advertising purposes upon articles of merchandise. The Court there said: "For that flag every true American has not simply an appreciation but a deep affection. * * * Hence, it has often occurred that insults to a flag have been the cause of war, and indignities put upon it, in the presence of those who revere it, have often been resented and sometimes punished on the spot."

---

a. Rehnquist, C.J., invoked a legacy of prose, poetry, and law in honor of flags in general and the American flag in particular both in peace and in war, quoting from, among others, Ralph Waldo Emerson and John Greenleaf Whittier. Emerson's poem referred to the Union Jack, but he did not always speak warmly of the American flag. After passage of the Fugitive Slave Law Emerson wrote, "We sneak about with the infamy of crime in the streets, & cowardice in ourselves and frankly once for all the Union is sunk, the flag is hateful, and shall be hissed." *Emerson in His Journals* 421 (Joel Porte ed. 1982).

Only two Terms ago, in *San Francisco Arts & Athletics, Inc. v. United States Olympic Committee,* [483 U.S. 522 (1987)], the Court held that Congress could grant exclusive use of the word "Olympic" to the United States Olympic Committee. The Court thought that this "restrictio[n] on expressive speech properly [was] characterized as incidental to the primary congressional purpose of encouraging and rewarding the USOC's activities." As the Court stated, "when a word [or symbol] acquires value 'as the result of organization and the expenditure of labor, skill, and money' by an entity, that entity constitutionally may obtain a limited property right in the word [or symbol]."[b] Surely Congress or the States may recognize a similar interest in the flag.[c]

[T]he public burning of the American flag by Johnson was no essential part of any exposition of ideas, and at the same time it had a tendency to incite a breach of the peace. Johnson was free to make any verbal denunciation of the flag that he wished; indeed, he was free to burn the flag in private. He could publicly burn other symbols of the Government or effigies of political leaders. He did lead a march through the streets of Dallas, and conducted a rally in front of the Dallas City Hall. He engaged in a "die-in" to protest nuclear weapons. He shouted out various slogans during the march, including: "Reagan, Mondale which will it be? Either one means World War III"; "Ronald Reagan, killer of the hour, Perfect example of U.S. power"; and "red, white and blue, we spit on you, you stand for plunder, you will go under." For none of these acts was he arrested or prosecuted. [As] with "fighting words," so with flag burning, for purposes of the First Amendment: It is "no essential part of any exposition of ideas, and [is] of such slight social value as a step to truth that any benefit that may be derived from [it] is clearly outweighed" by the public interest in avoiding a probable breach of the peace. * * *

The result of the Texas statute is obviously to deny one in Johnson's frame of mind one of many means of "symbolic speech." Far from being a case of "one picture being worth a thousand words," flag burning is the equivalent of an inarticulate grunt or roar that, it seems fair to say, is most likely to be indulged in not to express any particular idea, but to antagonize others. [The] Texas statute [left Johnson] with a full panoply of other symbols and every conceivable form of verbal expression to express his deep disapproval of national policy. Thus, in no way can it be said that Texas is punishing him because his hearers—or any other group of people—were profoundly opposed to the message that he sought to convey. Such opposition is no proper basis for restricting speech or expression under the First Amendment. It was Johnson's use of this

---

b. For criticism, see James Boyle, *Shamans, Software, and Spleens* 145–48 (1996); Yochai Benkler, *Constitutional Bounds of Database Protection,* 15 Berkeley L.J. 535 (2000); Robert Kravitz, *Trademarks, Speech, and the Gay Olympics Case,* 69 B.U.L.Rev. 131 (1989).

c. In response, Brennan, J., observed that *Halter* was decided "nearly twenty years" before the First Amendment was applied to the states and "[m]ore important" that *Halter* involved "purely commercial rather than political speech." Similarly, he stated that the authorization "to prohibit certain commercial and promotional uses of the word 'Olympic' [does not] even begin to tell us whether the Government may criminally punish physical conduct towards the flag engaged in as a means of political protest."

particular symbol, and not the idea that he sought to convey by it or by his many other expressions, for which he was punished. * * *

The Court concludes its opinion with a regrettably patronizing civics lecture, presumably addressed to the Members of both Houses of Congress, the members of the 48 state legislatures that enacted prohibitions against flag burning, and the troops fighting under that flag in Vietnam who objected to its being burned: "The way to preserve the flag's special role is not to punish those who feel differently about these matters. It is to persuade them that they are wrong." The Court's role as the final expositor of the Constitution is well established, but its role as a platonic guardian admonishing those responsible to public opinion as if they were truant school children has no similar place in our system of government. * * *

Uncritical extension of constitutional protection to the burning of the flag risks the frustration of the very purpose for which organized governments are instituted. The Court decides that the American flag is just another symbol, about which not only must opinions pro and con be tolerated, but for which the most minimal public respect may not be enjoined. The government may conscript men into the Armed Forces where they must fight and perhaps die for the flag, but the government may not prohibit the public burning of the banner under which they fight. I would uphold the Texas statute as applied in this case.[2]

JUSTICE STEVENS, dissenting. * * *

Even if flag burning could be considered just another species of symbolic speech under the logical application of the rules that the Court has developed in its interpretation of the First Amendment in other contexts, this case has an intangible dimension that makes those rules inapplicable.

A country's flag is a symbol of more than "nationhood and national unity." [T]he American flag [is] more than a proud symbol of the courage, the determination, and the gifts of nature that transformed 13 fledgling Colonies into a world power. It is a symbol of freedom, of equal opportunity, of religious tolerance, and of goodwill for other peoples who share our aspirations. The symbol carries its message to dissidents both at home and abroad who may have no interest at all in our national unity or survival.

The value of the flag as a symbol cannot be measured. Even so, I have no doubt that the interest in preserving that value for the future is both significant and legitimate. Conceivably that value will be enhanced by the Court's conclusion that our national commitment to free expression is so strong that even the United States as ultimate guarantor of that freedom

---

2. In holding that the Texas statute as applied to Johnson violates the First Amendment, the Court does not consider Johnson's claims that the statute is unconstitutionally vague or overbroad. I think those claims are without merit. [By] defining "desecrate" as "deface," "damage" or otherwise "physically mistreat" in a manner that the actor knows will "seriously offend" others, § 42.09 only prohibits flagrant acts of physical abuse and destruction of the flag of the sort at issue here—soaking a flag with lighter fluid and igniting it in public—and not any of the examples of improper flag etiquette cited in Respondent's brief.

is without power to prohibit the desecration of its unique symbol. But I am unpersuaded. The creation of a federal right to post bulletin boards and graffiti on the Washington Monument might enlarge the market for free expression, but at a cost I would not pay. Similarly, in my considered judgment, sanctioning the public desecration of the flag will tarnish its value—both for those who cherish the ideas for which it waves and for those who desire to don the robes of martyrdom by burning it. That tarnish is not justified by the trivial burden on free expression occasioned by requiring that an available, alternative mode of expression—including uttering words critical of the flag be employed.

It is appropriate to emphasize certain propositions that are not implicated by this case. [The] statute does not compel any conduct or any profession of respect for any idea or any symbol. [Nor] does the statute violate "the government's paramount obligation of neutrality in its regulation of protected communication." The content of respondent's message has no relevance whatsoever to the case. The concept of "desecration" does not turn on the substance of the message the actor intends to convey, but rather on whether those who view the act will take serious offense. Accordingly, one intending to convey a message of respect for the flag by burning it in a public square might nonetheless be guilty of desecration if he knows that others—perhaps simply because they misperceive the intended message—will be seriously offended. Indeed, even if the actor knows that all possible witnesses will understand that he intends to send a message of respect, he might still be guilty of desecration if he also knows that this understanding does not lessen the offense taken by some of those witnesses. The case has nothing to do with "disagreeable ideas." It involves disagreeable conduct that, in my opinion, diminishes the value of an important national asset.

[Had respondent] chosen to spray paint—or perhaps convey with a motion picture projector—his message of dissatisfaction on the facade of the Lincoln Memorial, there would be no question about the power of the Government to prohibit his means of expression. The prohibition would be supported by the legitimate interest in preserving the quality of an important national asset. Though the asset at stake in this case is intangible, given its unique value, the same interest supports a prohibition on the desecration of the American flag.*

---

* The Court suggested that a prohibition against flag desecration is not content-neutral because this form of symbolic speech is only used by persons who are critical of the flag or the ideas it represents. In making this suggestion the Court does not pause to consider the far-reaching consequences of its introduction of disparate impact analysis into our First Amendment jurisprudence. It seems obvious that a prohibition against the desecration of a gravesite is content-neutral even if it denies some protesters the right to make a symbolic statement by extinguishing the flame in Arlington Cemetery where John F. Kennedy is buried while permitting others to salute the flame by bowing their heads. Few would doubt that a protester who extinguishes the flame has desecrated the gravesite, regardless of whether he prefaces that act with a speech explaining that his purpose is to express deep admiration or unmitigated scorn for the late President. Likewise, few would claim that the protester who bows his head has desecrated the gravesite, even if he makes clear that his purpose is to show disrespect. In such a case, as in a flag burning case, the prohibition against desecration has absolutely nothing to do with the content of the message that the symbolic speech is intended to convey.

The ideas of liberty and equality have been an irresistible force in motivating leaders like Patrick Henry, Susan B. Anthony, and Abraham Lincoln, schoolteachers like Nathan Hale and Booker T. Washington, the Philippine Scouts who fought at Bataan, and the soldiers who scaled the bluff at Omaha Beach. If those ideas are worth fighting for—and our history demonstrates that they are—it cannot be true that the flag that uniquely symbolizes their power is not itself worthy of protection from unnecessary desecration.

NOTES AND QUESTIONS

1. **The meaning of "speech."** If the *O'Brien* Court had inquired whether a particularized message was present, and whether likelihood was great that the message would be understood by those who viewed it, would it have had any difficulty in classifying draft card burning as speech? Must a particularized message be present for the First Amendment to be relevant? Would such a requirement wrongly fail to protect "a great deal of painting, music, dance, and sculpture"? Jed Rubenfeld, *The Freedom of Imagination: Copyright's Constitutionality*, 112 Yale L.J. 1, 32 (2002). Is the presence of a particularized message sufficient to implicate the First Amendment? Is the First Amendment generally implicated in contract negotiations? Navigation maps? Instructions for handling machinery? See Robert Post, *Recuperating First Amendment Doctrine,* 47 Stan.L.Rev. 1249 (1995). Cf. Frederick Schauer, *Free Speech and the Demise of the Soapbox* Book Review, 84 Colum.L.Rev. 558, 565 (1984) ("[T]he First Amendment importance of the messages from an automatic teller to the bank's central computer completely escapes me, as does the First Amendment importance of the mutual exchange of electronic and visual symbols between me and the Pac–Man machine."). Does the process of defining speech for First Amendment purposes require an understanding of the purposes of the First Amendment rather than a focus on the communicative character of the phenomena examined? See Post, supra (speech in its ordinary language sense has no inherent constitutional value and should be defined to include only those social practices which implicate free speech values).[d] Cf. Stanley Fish, *There's No Such Thing as Free Speech: And It's a Good Thing Too* 102 (1994) ("'Free speech' is just the name we give to verbal behavior that serves the substantive agendas we wish to advance"). What are the relevant purposes and values? For example, is begging speech for First Amendment purposes? Daniel Mark Cohen, *Begging the Court's Pardon: Justice Denied for the Poorest of the Poor,* 14 ST. THOMAS L. REV. 825, 828 (2002)(yes); Randall P. Bezanson, *Speaking Through Others' Voices: Authorship, Originality, and Free Speech,* 38 Wake Forest L. Rev. 983, 1034 (2003)(no). For an argument that all communicative utterances be considered speech regardless of purpose, Consider Eugene Volokh, *Speech As Conduct: Generally Applicable Laws, Illegal Courses of Conduct, "Situation-Altering Utterances," and the Uncharted Zones*, 90 Cornell L. Rev. 1277, 1336

---

d. For other important commentary, see Kent Greenawalt, *Speech, Crime and the Uses of Language* (1989); Frederick Schauer, *Free Speech: A Philosophical Enquiry* 181–84 (1982); Frederick Schauer, *Speech and "Speech"—Obscenity and "Obscenity": An Exercise in the Interpretation of Constitutional Language,* 67 Geo.L.J. 899 (1979); Larry Alexander & Paul Horton, *The Impossibility of a Free Speech Principle,* 78 Nw.U.L.Rev. 1319, 1331–34 (1984).

(2005): "Lying on the witness stand is not less speech than lying about the weather, [although] it may also be perjury. The shout of 'Fire!' is not less speech in the Holmes instance than the shout of 'Fire!' from the mouth of an actor on the state of the same theater, spoken as but a word in a play. It is futile to argue that an appropriately tailored law that punishes any or all of these utterances does not abridge speech. It does, it is meant to, and one should not take recourse to verbal subterfuge, e.g., that it is "speech-brigaded-with-action" or "conduct" alone that is curtailed. [They] are separately crafted rules that let the government punish speech in particular circumstances, based on arguments about the harm and value of speech that are specific to each exception."

2. ***Patriotism.*** Consider Amy Adler, *The Art of Censorship*, 103 W. Va. L. Rev. 205, 216–217 (2000): "Do people really die for the flag? Don't people actually die for what it represents? There is a confusion here between the image and reality. [H]ere and at another point where Rehnquist says the flag 'embodies' our nation, I think his slippage between the image and what it stands for reveals something deeper about images. They are so strong, such a plain 'short cut' to our minds, that they tempt us to conflate representation with reality. [For] a brief moment Justice Rehnquist has given way to idolatry." But see George Fletcher, *Loyalty* 141 (1993): "The [question] is whether the Congress has a sufficiently clear interest in promoting national loyalty to interpret the crime of flag burning as a sanction aimed not at the message of protest, but at the act, regardless of its political slant. Whether Congress and the country possess this interest depends, of course, on what one thinks of loyalty and devotion to country as a value. A high regard for patriotism, for sharing a common purpose in cherishing our people and seeking to solve our problems, leads one easily to perceive the expression of our unity as a value important in itself. The flag is at least as important—to go from the sublime to the ridiculous—as protecting draft cards so that the Selective Service System can function efficiently."

3. ***Dissent.*** Consider Steven Shiffrin, *The First Amendment and the Meaning of America,* in *Identities, Politics, and Rights* 318 (Sarat & Kearnes eds. 1996): "The flag-burning prohibition is uniquely troubling not because it interferes with the metaphorical marketplace of ideas, not because it topples our image of a content neutral government (*that* has fallen many times), and not merely because it suppresses political speech. The flag-burning prohibition is a naked attempt to smother dissent. If we must have a 'central meaning' of the First Amendment, we should recognize that the dissenters—those who attack existing customs, habits, traditions and authorities—stand at the center of the First Amendment and not at its periphery. Gregory Johnson was attacking a symbol which the vast majority of Americans regard with reverence. But that is *exactly* why he deserved First Amendment protection. The First Amendment has a special regard for those who swim against the current, for those who would shake us to our foundations, for those who reject prevailing authority. In burning the flag, Gregory Johnson rejected, opposed, even blasphemed the Nation's most important political, social, and cultural icon. Clearly Gregory Johnson's alleged act of burning the flag was a quintessential act of dissent. A dissent centered conception of the First Amendment would make it clear that *Johnson* was an easy case—rightly decided."

4. *The meaning of the flag.* Consider Kenneth Karst, *Law's Promise, Law's Expression: Visions of Power in the Politics of Race, Gender, and Religion* 165 (1993): "According to those opinions the flag stands for our nationhood or national unity (Brennan, paraphrasing the state's lawyers); for principles of freedom or inclusiveness (Brennan); for the nation's resiliency (Brennan); for the nation itself (Rehnquist); for something men will die for in war (Rehnquist); for 'America's imagined past and present' (Rehnquist, in Sheldon Nahmod's apt paraphrase); for courage, freedom, equal opportunity, religious tolerance, and 'goodwill for other peoples who share our aspirations' (Stevens); and for shared beliefs in law and peace and 'the freedom that sustains the human spirit' (Kennedy). So, even within the Supreme Court, the flag stands at once for freedom and for obedience to law, for war and for peace, for unity and for tolerance of difference." For perspectives on the relationship of the First Amendment to nationalism and national identity, Paul A. Passavant, *No Escape: Freedom of Speech and the Paradox of Rights* (2002); Steven H. Shiffrin, *The First Amendment, Democracy, and Romance* (1991).

5. *The flag's "physical integrity."* Brennan, J., observes that the Texas law is "not aimed at protecting the physical integrity of the flag in all circumstances." What if it were?[e]

In response to *Johnson*, Congress passed the Flag Protection Act of 1989, which attached criminal penalties to the knowing mutilation, defacement, burning, maintaining on the floor or ground, or trampling upon any flag of the United States. UNITED STATES v. EICHMAN, 496 U.S. 310 (1990), per BRENNAN, J., invalidated the statute: "Although the Flag Protection Act contains no explicit content-based limitation on the scope of prohibited conduct, it is nevertheless clear that the Government's asserted *interest* is 'related "to the suppression of free expression"' and concerned with the content of such expression. The Government's interest in protecting the 'physical integrity' of a privately owned flag rests upon a perceived need to preserve the flag's status as a symbol of our Nation and certain national ideals. But the mere destruction or disfigurement of a particular physical manifestation of the symbol, without more, does not diminish or otherwise affect the symbol itself in any way. For example, the secret destruction of a flag in one's own basement would not threaten the flag's recognized meaning. Rather, the Government's desire to preserve the flag as a symbol for certain national ideals is implicated 'only when a person's treatment of the flag communicates [a] message' to others that is inconsistent with those ideals."

STEVENS, J., joined by Rehnquist, C.J., White and O'Connor, JJ., dissenting, argued that the government's "legitimate interest in protecting the symbolic value of the American flag" outweighed the free speech interest. In describing the flag's symbolic value he stated that the flag "inspires and motivates the average citizen to make personal sacrifices in order to achieve

---

e. For commentary concerning the extent to which a focus on physical integrity can be separated from a concern with content, see Kent Greenawalt, *O'er the Land of the Free: Flag Burning as Speech*, 37 UCLA L.Rev. 925 (1990); Frank Michelman, *Saving Old Glory: On Constitutional Iconography*, 42 Stan.L.Rev. 1337 (1990); Geoffrey Stone, *Flag Burning and the Constitution*, 75 Ia.L.Rev. 111 (1989); Mark Tushnet, *The Flag–Burning Episode: An Essay on the Constitution*, 61 U.Col.L.Rev. 39 (1990).

societal goals of overriding importance; at all times, it serves as a reminder of the paramount importance of pursuing the ideals that characterize our society. * * * [T]he communicative value of a well-placed bomb in the Capital does not entitle it to the protection of the First Amendment. Burning a flag is not, of course, equivalent to burning a public building. Assuming that the protester is burning his own flag, it causes no physical harm to other persons or to their property. The impact is purely symbolic, and it is apparent that some thoughtful persons believe that impact far from depreciating the value of the symbol, will actually enhance its meaning. I most respectfully disagree."[f]

6. *Compromise?* Prior to adopting the Flag Protection Act, the Senate by a vote of 97–3 had passed a resolution expressing "profound disappointment with the [*Johnson*] decision." The House had approved a similar resolution by a vote of 411–5, and President Bush had proposed a constitutional amendment to overrule *Johnson.* Opponents of the amendment argued that a carefully drawn statute might (or would) be upheld by the Court. Suppose you were a member of the House or Senate at that time. Suppose you supported *Johnson* but believed that the statute might be held constitutional, even though you did not think it should be. Suppose you also believed that if a statute were not passed an amendment would.[g]

Consider this exchange during hearings of the House Subcommittee on Civil and Constitutional Rights in *Statutory and Constitutional Responses to the Supreme Court Decision in Texas v. Johnson* (1989): Former Solicitor General Charles Fried: "My good friends and colleagues, Rex Lee and Laurence Tribe, have testified that a statute might be drawn that would pass constitutional muster. [I] hope and urge and pray that we will not act—that no statute be passed and of course that the Constitution not be amended. In short, I believe that *Johnson* is right [in] principle." * * *

Representative Schroeder: "I thought your testimony was eloquent. I think in a purist world, that is where we should go. But [we] are not talking about a purist world. We are talking about a very political world." * * *

Mr. Fried: "There are times when you earn your rather inadequate salary by just doing the right thing, and where you seem to agree with me is that the right thing to do is to do neither one of these. [It] is called leadership."

Representative Schroeder: "It is called leadership. [But] I guess what I am saying is if we can't stop a stampede on an amendment without something, isn't it better to try to save the Bill of Rights and the Constitution?"

––––––––

f. But see Arnold Loewy, *The Flag–Burning Case: Freedom of Speech When We Need It Most,* 68 N.C.L.Rev. 165, 174 (1989): "Perhaps the ultimate irony is that *Johnson* has done more to preserve the flag as a symbol of liberty than any prior decision, while the decision's detractors would allow real desecration of the flag by making it a symbol of political oppression." Compare Robin West, *Taking Freedom Seriously,* 104 Harv.L.Rev. 43, 97–98 (1990) (the militaristic patriotism associated with the flag menaces dissent); see also Greenawalt, fn. e supra.

g. For commentary, compare Michelman, fn. e supra with Steven H. Shiffrin, *Dissent, Injustice, and the Meanings of America* ch. 1 (1990).

Community for Creative Non–Violence (CCNV) sought to conduct a wintertime demonstration near the White House in Lafayette Park and the Mall to dramatize the plight of the homeless. The National Park Service authorized the erection of two symbolic tent cities for purposes of the demonstration, but denied CCNV's request that demonstrators be permitted to sleep in the tents. National Park Service regulations permit camping (the "use of park land for living accommodation purposes such as sleeping activities") in National Parks only in campgrounds designated for that purpose.

CLARK v. COMMUNITY FOR CREATIVE NON–VIOLENCE, 468 U.S. 288 (1984), per WHITE, J., rejected CCNV's claim that the regulations could not be constitutionally applied against its demonstration: "We need not differ with the view of the Court of Appeals that overnight sleeping in connection with the demonstration is expressive conduct protected to some extent by the First Amendment.[5] We assume for present purposes, but do not decide, that such is the case, cf. *O'Brien*, but this assumption only begins the inquiry. Expression, whether oral or written or symbolized by conduct, is subject to reasonable time, place, or manner restrictions. We have often noted that restrictions of this kind are valid provided that they are justified without reference to the content of the regulated speech, that they are narrowly tailored to serve a significant governmental interest, and that they leave open ample alternative channels for communication of the information.

"It is also true that a message may be delivered by conduct that is intended to be communicative and that, in context, would reasonably be understood by the viewer to be communicative. Symbolic expression of this kind may be forbidden or regulated if the conduct itself may constitutionally be regulated, if the regulation is narrowly drawn to further a substantial governmental interest, and if the interest is unrelated to the suppression of free speech. *O'Brien*.

"[That] sleeping, like the symbolic tents themselves, may be expressive and part of the message delivered by the demonstration does not make the ban any less a limitation on the manner of demonstrating, for reasonable time, place, or manner regulations normally have the purpose and direct effect of limiting expression but are nevertheless valid. Neither does the fact that sleeping, arguendo, may be expressive conduct, rather than oral or written expression, render the sleeping prohibition any less a time, place, or manner regulation. To the contrary, the Park Service neither attempts to ban sleeping generally nor to ban it everywhere in the parks. It has established areas for camping and forbids it elsewhere, including Lafayette Park and the Mall. Considered as such, we have very

---

5. We reject the suggestion of the plurality below, however, that the burden on the demonstrators is limited to "the advancement of a plausible contention" that their conduct is expressive. Although it is common to place the burden upon the Government to justify impingements on First Amendment interests, it is the obligation of the person desiring to engage in assertedly expressive conduct to demonstrate that the First Amendment even applies. To hold otherwise would be to create a rule that all conduct is presumptively expressive.

little trouble concluding that the Park Service may prohibit overnight sleeping in the parks involved here.

"The requirement that the regulation be content-neutral is clearly satisfied. The courts below accepted that view, and it is not disputed here that the prohibition on camping, and on sleeping specifically, is content-neutral and is not being applied because of disagreement with the message presented.[a] Neither was the regulation faulted, nor could it be, on the ground that without overnight sleeping the plight of the homeless could not be communicated in other ways. The regulation otherwise left the demonstration intact, with its symbolic city, signs, and the presence of those who were willing to take their turns in a day-and-night vigil. Respondents do not suggest that there was, or is, any barrier to delivering to the media, or to the public by other means, the intended message concerning the plight of the homeless.

"It is also apparent to us that the regulation narrowly focuses on the Government's substantial interest in maintaining the parks in the heart of our Capital in an attractive and intact condition, readily available to the millions of people who wish to see and enjoy them by their presence. To permit camping—using these areas as living accommodations—would be totally inimical to these purposes, as would be readily understood by those who have frequented the National Parks across the country and observed the unfortunate consequences of the activities of those who refuse to confine their camping to designated areas.

"It is urged by [CCNV] that if the symbolic city of tents was to be permitted and if the demonstrators did not intend to cook, dig, or engage in aspects of camping other than sleeping, the incremental benefit to the parks could not justify the ban on sleeping, which was here an expressive activity said to enhance the message concerning the plight of the poor and homeless. We cannot agree. In the first place, we seriously doubt that the First Amendment requires the Park Service to permit a demonstration in Lafayette Park and the Mall involving a 24–hour vigil and the erection of tents to accommodate 150 people. Furthermore, although we have assumed for present purposes that the sleeping banned in this case would have an expressive element, it is evident that its major value to this demonstration would be facilitative. Without a permit to sleep, it would be difficult to get the poor and homeless to participate or to be present at all.[b]

"Beyond this, however, it is evident from our cases that the validity of this regulation need not be judged solely by reference to the demonstration at hand.[c] Absent the prohibition on sleeping, there would be other

---

a. Marshall, J., dissenting, observed that CCNV had held a demonstration the previous winter in which it set up nine tents and slept in Lafayette Park. The D.C. Circuit held that the regulations did not preclude such a demonstration. According to Marshall, J., "The regulations at issue in this case were passed in direct response" to that holding.

b. What if it were the exclusive value? For discussion, see Gary Francione, *Experimentation and the Marketplace Theory of the First Amendment,* 136 U.Pa.L.Rev. 417 (1987).

c. For debate about this point and its implications, compare Frank Easterbrook, *Foreword: The Court and the Economic System,* 98 Harv.L.Rev. 4, 19–21 (1984) with Laurence Tribe,

groups who would demand permission to deliver an asserted message by camping in Lafayette Park. Some of them would surely have as credible a claim in this regard as does CCNV, and the denial of permits to still others would present difficult problems for the Park Service. With the prohibition, however, as is evident in the case before us, at least some around-the-clock demonstrations lasting for days on end will not materialize, others will be limited in size and duration, and the purposes of the regulation will thus be materially served. Perhaps these purposes would be more effectively and not so clumsily achieved by preventing tents and 24–hour vigils entirely in the core areas. But the Park Service's decision to permit nonsleeping demonstrations does not, in our view, impugn the camping prohibition as a valuable, but perhaps imperfect, protection to the parks. If the Government has a legitimate interest in ensuring that the National Parks are adequately protected, which we think it has, and if the parks would be more exposed to harm without the sleeping prohibition than with it, the ban is safe from invalidation under the First Amendment as a reasonable regulation of the manner in which a demonstration may be carried out.[d] * * *

"[The] foregoing analysis demonstrates that the Park Service regulation is sustainable under the four-factor standard of O'Brien, for validating a regulation of expressive conduct, which, in the last analysis is little, if any, different[e] from the standard applied to time, place, or manner restrictions.[8] No one contends that aside from its impact on speech a rule against camping or overnight sleeping in public parks is beyond the constitutional power of the Government to enforce. And for the reasons we have discussed above, there is a substantial Government interest in

---

Constitutional Calculus: Equal Justice or Economic Efficiency? 98 Harv.L.Rev. 592, 599–603 (1985) and Frank Easterbrook, *Method, Result, and Authority: A Reply,* 98 Harv.L.Rev. 622, 626 (1985).

d. Alan E. Brownstein, *Alternative Maps for Navigating the First Amendment Maze,* 16 Const. Comm. 101, 117 (1999): "It seems clear that a similar argument could be applied to prohibit leafleting (or all demonstrations for that matter) in Lafayette Park. * * * I do not believe that a ban on leafleting in Lafayette Park would be as cavalierly upheld by the Court as the ban on camping, however."

e. Christopher Thomas Leahy, *The First Amendment Gone Awry: City of Erie v. Pap's A.M., Ailing Analytical Structures, and the Suppression of Protected Expression,* 150 U. Pa. L. Rev. 1021, 1034–1035 (2002): "While the tests may appear similar at first glance, they are distinct in several ways. First, the Court created the *O'Brien* test in the face of the preexisting TPM test—signaling an intention to create a distinct standard. Second, the TPM test's tailoring requirement is substantially weaker than the parallel requirement in the *O'Brien* test—it does not require that the restriction be 'no greater than is essential to the furtherance of [the governmental] interest.' Third, the TPM test requires consideration of 'alternative avenues of speech,' a prong completely absent from the *O'Brien* analysis."

8. Reasonable time, place, or manner restrictions are valid even though they directly limit oral or written expression. It would be odd to insist on a higher standard for limitations aimed at regulable conduct and having only an incidental impact on speech. Thus, if the time, place, or manner restriction on expressive sleeping, if that is what is involved in this case, sufficiently and narrowly serves a substantial enough governmental interest to escape First Amendment condemnation, it is untenable to invalidate it under *O'Brien* on the ground that the governmental interest is insufficient to warrant the intrusion on First Amendment concerns or that there is an inadequate nexus between the regulation and the interest sought to be served. We note that only recently, in a case dealing with the regulation of signs, the Court framed the issue under *O'Brien* and then based a crucial part of its analysis on the time, place, or manner cases.

conserving park property, an interest that is plainly served by, and requires for its implementation, measures such as the proscription of sleeping that are designed to limit the wear and tear on park properties. That interest is unrelated to suppression of expression.

"We are unmoved by the Court of Appeals' view that the challenged regulation is unnecessary, and hence invalid, because there are less speech-restrictive alternatives that could have satisfied the Government interest in preserving park lands. [The] Court of Appeals' suggestions that the Park Service minimize the possible injury by reducing the size, duration, or frequency of demonstrations would still curtail the total allowable expression in which demonstrators could engage, whether by sleeping or otherwise, and these suggestions represent no more than a disagreement with the Park Service over how much protection the core parks require or how an acceptable level of preservation is to be attained. We do not believe, however, that either *United States v. O'Brien* or the time, place, or manner decisions assign to the judiciary the authority to replace the Park Service as the manager of the Nation's parks or endow the judiciary with the competence to judge how much protection of park lands is wise and how that level of conservation is to be [attained.]"

BURGER, C.J., joined in the Court's opinion, adding: "[CCNV's] attempt at camping in the park is a form of 'picketing'; it is conduct, not speech. [It] trivializes the First Amendment to seek to use it as a shield in the manner asserted here."

MARSHALL, J., joined by Brennan, J., dissented: "The majority assumes, without deciding, that the respondents' conduct is entitled to constitutional protection. The problem with this assumption is that the Court thereby avoids examining closely the reality of respondents' planned expression. The majority's approach denatures respondents' asserted right and thus makes all too easy identification of a Government interest sufficient to warrant its abridgment.

"[Missing] from the majority's description is any inkling that Lafayette Park and the Mall have served as the sites for some of the most rousing political demonstrations in the Nation's history.[2] [The] primary purpose for making *sleep* an integral part of the demonstration was 'to reenact the central reality of homelessness' and to impress upon public consciousness, in as dramatic a way as possible, that homelessness is a widespread problem, often ignored, that confronts its victims with life-threatening deprivations. As one of the homeless men seeking to demonstrate explained: 'Sleeping in Lafayette Park or on the Mall, for me, is to

---

2. At oral argument, the Government informed the Court "that on any given day there will be an average of three or so demonstrations going on" in the Mall–Lafayette Park area. Respondents accurately describe Lafayette Park "as the American analogue to 'Speaker's Corner' in Hyde Park."

[For commentary on the inadequate conception of place in First Amendment law, see Timothy Zick, *Speech and Spatial* Tactics, 84 Tex. L.Rev. 581 (2006); Timothy Zick, *Space, Place, and Speech*, 74 Geo. Wash. L.Rev. 439 (2006); Timothy Zick, *Property, Place and Public Discourse*, 21 Wash U.J.L. & Pol'y 173 (2006). See also Elizabeth Craig, *Protecting the President from Protest*, 9 J.Gender Race & Just. 665 (2006).].

show people that conditions are so poor for the homeless and poor in this city that we would actually sleep *outside* in the winter to get the point across.' * * * Here respondents clearly intended to protest the reality of homelessness by sleeping outdoors in the winter in the near vicinity of the magisterial residence of the President of the United States. In addition to accentuating the political character of their protest by their choice of location and mode of communication, respondents also intended to underline the meaning of their protest by giving their demonstration satirical names. Respondents planned to name the demonstration on the Mall 'Congressional Village,' and the demonstration in Lafayette Park, 'Reaganville II.' * * *

"Although sleep in the context of this case is symbolic speech protected by the First Amendment, it is nonetheless subject to reasonable time, place, and manner restrictions. I agree with the standard enunciated by the majority.[6] I conclude, however, that the regulations at issue in this case, as applied to respondents, fail to satisfy this [standard].

"[T]here are no substantial Government interests advanced by the Government's regulations as applied to respondents. All that the Court's decision advances are the prerogatives of a bureaucracy that over the years has shown an implacable hostility toward citizens' exercise of First Amendment [rights].

"The disposition of this case impels me to make two additional observations. First, in this case, as in some others involving time, place, and manner restrictions, the Court has dramatically lowered its scrutiny of governmental regulations once it has determined that such regulations are content-neutral.[f] The result has been the creation of a two-tiered approach to First Amendment cases: while regulations that turn on the content of the expression are subjected to a strict form of judicial review, regulations that are aimed at matters other than expression receive only a minimal level of scrutiny. [The] Court has seemingly overlooked the fact that content-neutral restrictions are also capable of unnecessarily restricting protected expressive activity.[13] [The] Court [has] transformed the ban against content distinctions from a floor that offers all persons at least equal liberty under the First Amendment into a ceiling that restricts persons to the protection of First Amendment equality—but nothing more.[14] The consistent imposition of silence upon all may fulfill the

---

6. I also agree with the majority that no substantial difference distinguishes the test applicable to time, place, and manner restrictions and the test articulated in *O'Brien*.

f. In support of Marshall, J.'s contention, see generally William Lee, *Lonely Pamphleteers, Little People, and the Supreme Court,* 54 G.W.U.L.Rev. 757 (1986).

13. See Martin Redish, *The Content Distinction in First Amendment Analysis,* 34 Stan.L.Rev. 113 (1981).

14. Furthermore, [a] content-neutral regulation that restricts an inexpensive mode of communication will fall most heavily upon relatively poor speakers and to points of view that such speakers typically espouse. [See Lee, fn. f supra.] This sort of latent inequality is very much in evidence in this case, for respondents lack the financial means necessary to buy access to more conventional modes of persuasion.

dictates of an evenhanded content-neutrality. But it offends our 'profound national commitment to the principle that debate on public issues should be uninhibited, robust, and wide-open'. *New York Times v. Sullivan.*

"Second, the disposition of this case reveals a mistaken assumption regarding the motives and behavior of Government officials who create and administer content-neutral regulations. The Court's salutary skepticism of governmental decisionmaking in First Amendment matters suddenly dissipates once it determines that a restriction is not content-based. The Court evidently assumes that the balance struck by officials is deserving of deference so long as it does not appear to be tainted by content discrimination. What the Court fails to recognize is that public officials have strong incentives to overregulate even in the absence of an intent to censor particular views. This incentive stems from the fact that of the two groups whose interests officials must accommodate—on the one hand, the interests of the general public and, on the other, the interests of those who seek to use a particular forum for First Amendment activity— the political power of the former is likely to be far greater than that of the latter.[16]"

Notes and Questions

1. Consider Mark Tushnet, *Character as Argument,* 14 Law and Social Inquiry 539, 549 (1989) (reviewing Harry Kalven, *A Worthy Tradition*): "To capture the attention of a public accustomed to dignified protest, and able to screen it from consciousness, dissidents may have to adopt novel forms of protest, such as sleeping in a national park overnight to draw attention to the disgrace of a national policy that deprives many people of decent shelter. Yet, precisely because their protests take a novel form, they may not be covered by the worthy tradition that Kalven honors. In this sense the dynamics of protest may make the protection of free speech what Kalven tellingly calls a 'luxury civil liberty,' a civil liberty to be enjoyed when nothing of consequence turns on protecting speech and to be abandoned when it really matters."

2. Should the Court have decided whether sleeping in the park in these circumstances was a form of expression entitled to some degree of First Amendment protection? See *Schad v. Mount Ephraim,* Ch. 3, I infra: "[N]ude dancing is not without its First Amendment protections from official regulation." Should hair styles be afforded First Amendment protection? Are hair styles distinguishable from nude dancing on the ground that the latter is a form of expressive entertainment?

3. The "time, place, or manner" test set out in *Clark* is differently stated in different cases. For example, *U.S. Postal Service v. Council of Greenburgh,* 453 U.S. 114 (1981), speaks of "adequate" as opposed to "am-

---

A disquieting feature about the disposition of this case is that it lends credence to the charge that judicial administration of the First Amendment, in conjunction with a social order marked by large disparities of wealth and other sources of power, tends systematically to discriminate against efforts by the relatively disadvantaged to convey their political ideas. * * *

16. See David Goldberger, *Judicial Scrutiny in Public Forum Cases: Misplaced Trust in the Judgment of Public Officials,* 32 Buffalo L.Rev. 175, 208 (1983).

ple" alternative channels of communication, and *Renton v. Playtime Theatres, Inc.,* Ch. 3, I infra, transcends the difference by requiring that the restriction not "unreasonably limit" alternative channels of communication. Beyond these differences, a number of cases state that the regulation must serve a significant government interest without stating that it must be "narrowly tailored" to serve a significant government interest. See e.g., *Heffron v. International Soc. For Krishna Consciousness,* Ch. 6, I, A infra. But see *Ward v. Rock Against Racism,* Ch. 6, I, A infra (reaffirming and defining narrowly tailored requirement). Assuming sleeping in the *Clark* context implicates First Amendment values, what test should apply? For development of an argument that a form of intermediate scrutiny "has attained central importance in the overall structure of free speech law," see Ashutosh Bhagwat, *The Test that Ate Everything: Intermediate Scrutiny in First Amendment Jurisprudence,* 2007 U.Ill. L.Rev. 783.

New York Public Health law authorizes the forced closure of a building for one year if it has been used for the purpose of "lewdness, assignation or prostitution." A civil complaint alleged that prostitution solicitation and sexual activities by patrons were occurring at an adult bookstore within observation of the proprietor. Accordingly, the complaint called for the closure of the building for one year. There was no claim that any books in the store were obscene. The New York Court of Appeals held that the closure remedy violated the First Amendment because it was broader than necessary to achieve the restriction against illicit sexual activities. It reasoned that an injunction against the alleged sexual conduct could further the state interest without infringing on First Amendment values. ARCARA v. CLOUD BOOKS, INC., 478 U.S. 697 (1986), per Burger, C.J., reversed, holding that the closure remedy did not require any First Amendment scrutiny: "This Court has applied First Amendment scrutiny to a statute regulating conduct which has the incidental effect of burdening the expression of a particular political opinion. *O'Brien.* * * *

"We have also applied First Amendment scrutiny to some statutes which, although directed at activity with no expressive component, impose a disproportionate burden upon those engaged in protected First Amendment activities. In *Minneapolis Star & Tribune v. Minnesota Commissioner of Revenue,* 460 U.S. 575 (1983), we struck down a tax imposed on the sale of large quantities of newsprint and ink because the tax had the effect of singling out newspapers to shoulder its burden. [Even] while striking down the tax in *Minneapolis Star,* we emphasized: 'Clearly, the First Amendment does not prohibit all regulation of the press. It is beyond dispute that the States and the Federal Government can subject newspapers to generally applicable economic regulations without creating constitutional problems.'

"The New York Court of Appeals held that the *O'Brien* test for permissible governmental regulation was applicable to this case because the closure order sought by petitioner would also impose an incidental burden upon respondents' bookselling activities. [But] unlike the symbolic draft card burning in *O'Brien,* the sexual activity carried on in this case manifests absolutely no element of protected expression.[a] In *Paris Adult Theatre,* we underscored the fallacy of seeking to use the First Amendment as a cloak for obviously unlawful public sexual conduct by the diaphanous device of attributing protected expressive attributes to that conduct. First Amendment values may not be invoked by merely linking the words 'sex' and 'books.'

"Nor does the distinction drawn by the New York Public Health Law inevitably single out bookstores or others engaged in First Amendment protected activities for the imposition of its burden, as did the tax struck down in *Minneapolis Star.* [If] the city imposed closure penalties for demonstrated Fire Code violations or health hazards from inadequate sewage treatment, the First Amendment would not aid the owner of premises who had knowingly allowed such violations to persist. * * *

"It is true that the closure order in this case would require respondents to move their bookselling business to another location. Yet we have not traditionally subjected every criminal and civil sanction imposed through legal process to 'least restrictive means' scrutiny simply because each particular remedy will have some effect on the First Amendment activities of those subject to sanction.[4]"[b]

O'CONNOR, J., joined by Stevens, J., concurred: "I agree that the Court of Appeals erred in applying a First Amendment standard of review where, as here, the government is regulating neither speech nor an incidental, non-expressive effect of speech. Any other conclusion would lead to the absurd result that any government action that had some conceivable speech-inhibiting consequences, such as the arrest of a newscaster for a traffic violation, would require analysis under the First Amendment."

BLACKMUN, J., joined by Brennan and Marshall, JJ., dissented: "Until today, this Court has never suggested that a State may suppress speech as

---

a. In an earlier section of the opinion, Burger, C.J., stated that, "petitioners in *O'Brien* had, as respondents here do not, at least the semblance of expressive activity in their claim that the otherwise unlawful burning of a draft card was to 'carry a message' of the actor's opposition to the draft."

4. [T]here is no suggestion on the record before us that the closure of respondents' bookstore was sought under the public health nuisance statute as a pretext for the suppression of First Amendment protected material. Were respondents able to establish the existence of such a speech suppressive motivation or policy on the part of the District Attorney, they might have a claim of selective prosecution. Respondents in this case made no such assertion before the trial court.

b. On remand, the New York Court of Appeals held that, in the absence of a showing that the state had chosen a course no broader than necessary to accomplish its purpose, any forced closure of the bookstore would unduly impair the bookseller's rights of free expression under the New York State constitution. From New York's perspective, the question is not "who is aimed at but who is hit." *People ex rel. Arcara v. Cloud Books, Inc.,* 68 N.Y.2d 553, 510 N.Y.S.2d 844, 503 N.E.2d 492 (1986). New York has since retreated. Jeremy J. Bethel, *Freedom of Expression in New York State: What Remains of People Ex Rel. Arcara v. Cloud Books, Inc.?,* 28 FORDHAM URB. L.J. 1797, 1797 (2001). See also *Alexander v. United States,* 509 U.S. 544 (1993)(confiscation and destruction of protected materials for distribution of obscene materials does not violate First Amendment).

much as it likes, without justification, so long as it does so through generally applicable regulations that have 'nothing to do with any expressive conduct.' * * *

"At some point, of course, the impact of state regulation on First Amendment rights become so attenuated that it is easily outweighed by the state interest. But when a State directly and substantially impairs First Amendment activities, such as by shutting down a bookstore, I believe that the State must show, at a minimum, that it has chosen the least restrictive means of pursuing its legitimate objectives. The closure of a bookstore can no more be compared to a traffic arrest of a reporter than the closure of a church could be compared to the traffic arrest of its clergyman.

"A State has a legitimate interest in forbidding sexual acts committed in public, including a bookstore. An obvious method of eliminating such acts is to arrest the patron committing them. But the statute in issue does not provide for that. Instead, it imposes absolute liability on the bookstore simply because the activity occurs on the premises. And the penalty—a mandatory 1–year closure—imposes an unnecessary burden on speech. Of course 'linking the words "sex" and "books" is not enough to extend First Amendment protection to illegal sexual activity, but neither should it suffice to remove First Amendment protection from books situated near the site of such activity. The State's purpose in stopping public lewdness cannot justify such a substantial infringement of First Amendment rights. * * *

"Petitioner has not demonstrated that a less restrictive remedy would be inadequate to abate the nuisance. The Court improperly attempts to shift to the bookseller the responsibility for finding an alternative site. But surely the Court would not uphold a city ordinance banning all public debate on the theory that the residents could move somewhere else.

Notes and Questions

1. *A need for scrutiny?* Should the state's closing of a bookstore *always* trigger heightened judicial scrutiny? Should fire code regulations trigger First Amendment scrutiny? Consider Comment, *Padlock Orders and Nuisance Laws,* 51 Albany L.Rev. 1007, 1026–27 (1987): "Closure penalties for fire code violations or health hazards from inadequate sewage treatment were offered as examples of generally applicable regulations which could constitutionally be applied to bookstores where the owner 'had knowingly allowed such violations to persist.' Few would argue with this conclusion. These generally applicable regulations would be within the state's constitutional power, would further a substantial governmental interest unrelated to the suppression of free expression, and the incidental restriction on First Amendment freedoms, where the owner knowingly allowed the violations to persist, would be no greater than is essential to further the state's interest. Concluding that the *O'Brien* test is satisfied, however, does not support the conclusion that the test does not apply."

2. ***Generally applicable laws.*** A newspaper published the name of a confidential source who it believed had misled it for political reasons. The source sued for breach of contract and prevailed in the Minnesota Supreme Court. COHEN v. COWLES MEDIA CO., 501 U.S. 663 (1991), per White, J., affirmed, dismissing the First Amendment claim with the observation that "generally applicable laws do not offend the First Amendment simply because their enforcement against the press has incidental effects on its ability to gather and report the news."[c] Consistent with *O'Brien*? *Daily Mail*? Consider Eugene Volokh, *Speech As Conduct: Generally Applicable Laws, Illegal Courses of Conduct, "Situation–Altering Utterances," and the Uncharted Zones*, 90 Cornell L. Rev. 1277, 1297 (2005): " 'Minnesota law simply requires those making promises to keep them. The parties themselves, as in this case, determine the scope of their legal obligations, and any restrictions which may be placed on the publication of truthful information are self-imposed.' So the Court rejected the free speech argument based on the principle that free speech rights, like most other rights, are waivable, rather than on an assertion that speech-neutral laws are per se constitutional."

3. ***Negative theory.*** Should the scope of the First Amendment be confined to instances in which government may have acted in a biased way? Consider Ronald Cass, *Commercial Speech, Constitutionalism, Collective Choice*, 56 U.Cin.L.Rev. 1317, 1352 (1988): "There is widespread agreement that limitation of official bias is the principal aim of the First Amendment, historically and as amplified over the past half-century by the courts." See generally Ronald Cass, *The Perils of Positive Thinking: Constitutional Interpretation and Negative First Amendment Theory*, 34 UCLA L.Rev. 1405 (1987) (emphasizing official self interest and, to a lesser extent, intolerance as the principal motives of concern).

Professor Schauer has also attempted a justification for freedom of speech not based on any positive aspects of speech, but based on the premise that governments are "less capable of regulating speech than they are of regulating other forms of conduct."[d] He suggests that bias, self-interest, and a general urge to suppress that with which one disagrees are significant reasons for this incapability. Frederick Schauer, *Free Speech: A Philosophical Enquiry* 80–86 (1982). See also Frederick Schauer, *Must Speech Be Special?*, 78 Nw.U.L.Rev. 1284 (1983). As he interprets the First Amendment, therefore, its "focus [is] on the motivations of the government." Frederick Schauer, *Cuban Cigars, Cuban Books, and the Problem of Incidental Restrictions on Communications*, 26 Wm. & Mary L.Rev. 779, 780 (1985).[e]

Is negative theory consistent with what the Court has *said* about free speech? With the doctrine it has produced? Consider, e.g., *Arcara*. *O'Brien*. The defamation line of cases. Compare Frederick Schauer, *Cuban Cigars*, supra with Steven Shiffrin, *The First Amendment, Democracy, and Romance*

---

c. Blackmun, J., joined by Marshall & Souter, JJ., dissented; Souter, J., joined by Marshall, Blackmun, & O'Connor, JJ., and dissented.

d. But see Larry Alexander, *Is There a Right of Freedom of Expression?* 145 (2005).

e. See also Frederick Schauer, *The Phenomenology of Speech and Harm*, 103 Ethics 635 (1993) (disputing the hypothesis that the harmful consequences of speech are less than those associated with other forms of conduct); Frederick Schauer, *The Sociology of the Hate Speech Debate*, 37 Vill.L.Rev. 805 (1992).

(1990). Is the content-based/content-neutral distinction founded exclusively on a concern with government motive? See generally Geoffrey Stone, *Content Regulation and the First Amendment,* 25 Wm. & Mary L.Rev. 189 (1983) (arguing that the basis for the distinction is more complicated). Does an emphasis on motive or content unreasonably downplay the notion that the *effect* of government conduct on the quantity or quality of speech is of independent First Amendment value? See generally R. George Wright, *Content-Based and Content-Neutral Regulation of Speech: The Limitations of a Common Distinction,* 60 U.Miami L.Rev. 333, 354–55 (2006); Martin Redish, *The Content Distinction in First Amendment Analysis,* 34 Stan.L.Rev. 113 (1981); Susan Williams, *Content Discrimination and the First Amendment,* 139 U.Pa.L.Rev. 201 (1991).

4. ***Reading Arcara narrowly.*** Could *Arcara's* failure to find the First Amendment implicated be justified without resort to negative theory or motive theory? Consider Tribe 2d ed., at 978–79 n. 2: "[W]hen *neither* the law, *nor* the act triggering its enforcement has any significant First Amendment dimension,[f] the fact that the law *incidentally* operates to restrict First Amendment activity, and that some alternative state measure might offer a less restrictive means of pursuing the state's legitimate objectives, should not serve to condemn what the state has done as unconstitutional." Why not? For discussion of the foundations of *Arcara,* see Seana Valentine Shiffrin, *Speech, Death, and Double Effect,* 78 N.Y.U. L. Rev. 1135, 1150, 1152, 1163–64, 1165–71 (2003).

5. ***Arcara extended?*** The Richmond Redevelopment and Housing Authority barred Hicks from trespassing on property where public low income housing existed in the absence of permission from the manager of the housing project. VIRGINIA v. HICKS, 539 U.S. 113 (2003), per Scalia, J., held that the bar was not substantially overbroad since it prevented a wide range of conduct, and that even if Hicks wanted to enter the property to speak or leaflet, the bar would properly be applied: "Neither the basis for the barment sanction (the prior trespass) nor its purpose (preventing prior trespasses) has anything to do with the First Amendment."[g]

---

f. For relevant commentary, see Michael C. Dorf, *Incidental Burdens on Fundamental Rights,* 109 Harv. L. Rev. 1175 (1996).

g. Souter, J., joined by Breyer, J., concurred.

CHAPTER 3

IS SOME PROTECTED SPEECH LESS EQUAL THAN OTHER PROTECTED SPEECH?

■ ■ ■

I. NEAR OBSCENE SPEECH

RENTON v. PLAYTIME THEATRES, INC., 475 U.S. 41 (1986), per REHNQUIST, J., upheld a zoning ordinance that prohibited adult motion picture theaters from locating within 1,000 feet of any residential zone, church, park, or school. The effect was to exclude such theaters from approximately 94% of the land in the city. Of the remaining 520 acres, a substantial part was occupied by a sewage disposal and treatment plant, a horse racing track and environs, a warehouse and manufacturing facilities, a Mobil Oil tank farm, and a fully-developed shopping center: "[T]he resolution of this case is largely dictated by our decision in *Young v. American Mini Theatres, Inc.*, 427 U.S. 50 (1976). There, although five Members of the Court did not agree on a single rationale for the decision, we held that the city of Detroit's zoning ordinance, which prohibited locating an adult theater within 1,000 feet of any two other 'regulated uses' or within 500 feet of any residential zone, did not violate the First and Fourteenth amendments. The Renton ordinance, like the one in *Young*, does not ban adult theaters altogether, but merely provides that such theaters may not be located within 1,000 feet of any residential zone, single-or multiple-family dwelling, church, park, or school. The ordinance is therefore properly analyzed as a form of time, place, and manner regulation.

"This Court has long held that regulations enacted for the purpose of restraining speech on the basis of its content presumptively violate the First Amendment. See *Chicago Police Dept. v. Mosley*, Ch. 6, I, B infra.[a] On the other hand, so-called 'content-neutral' time, place, and manner regulations are acceptable so long as they are designed to serve a substantial governmental interest and do not unreasonably limit alternative avenues of communication.[b]

---

a. *Mosley* involved an ordinance that banned picketing near a school building except the "peaceful picketing of any school involved in a labor dispute." The Court stated: "The regulation '[slips] from the neutrality of time, place, and circumstance into a concern about content.' This is never permitted."

210

"At first glance, the Renton ordinance, like the ordinance in *Young,* does not appear to fit neatly into either the 'content-based' or the 'content-neutral' category. To be sure, the ordinance treats theaters that specialize in adult films differently from other kinds of theaters. Nevertheless, [the] City Council's *'predominate* concerns' were with the secondary effects of adult theaters, and not with the content of adult films themselves. * * *

"[This] finding as to 'predominate' intent is more than adequate to establish that the city's pursuit of its zoning interests here was unrelated to the suppression of free expression.[c] The ordinance by its terms is designed to prevent crime, protect the city's retail trade, maintain property values,[d] and generally 'protec[t] and preserv[e] the quality of [the city's] neighborhoods, commercial districts, and the quality of urban life,' not to suppress the expression of unpopular views. As Justice Powell observed in *Young,* '[i]f [the city] had been concerned with restricting the message purveyed by adult theaters, it would have tried to close them or restrict their number rather than circumscribe their choice as to location.'

"In short, the [ordinance] does not contravene the fundamental principle that underlies our concern about 'content-based' speech regulations: that 'government may not grant the use of a forum to people whose views it finds acceptable, but deny use to those wishing to express less favored or more controversial views.' *Mosley.*

"It was with this understanding in mind that, in *Young,* a majority of this Court decided that at least with respect to businesses that purvey sexually explicit materials,[e] zoning ordinances designed to combat the undesirable secondary effects of such businesses are to be reviewed under the standards applicable to 'content-neutral' time, place, and manner regulations.[2]

---

b. Compare the statement of the time, place, and manner test in *Clark,* Ch. 2 supra. For commentary, see David Day, *The Hybridization of the Content–Neutral Standards for the Free Speech Clause,* 19 Ariz.St.L.J. 195 (1987).

c. The Court interpreted the court of appeals opinion to require the invalidation of the ordinance if a "motivating factor" to restrict the exercise of First Amendment rights was present "apparently no matter how small a part this motivating factor may have played in the City Council's decision." This view of the law, the Court continued, "was rejected in *O'Brien:* 'It is a familiar principle of constitutional law that this Court will not strike down an otherwise constitutional statute on the basis of an alleged illicit legislative motive. [What] motivates one legislator to make a speech about a statute is not necessarily what motivates scores of others to enact it, and the stakes are sufficiently high for us to eschew guesswork.' "

d. For support, see Charles Clarke, *Freedom of Speech and the Problem of the Lawful Harmful Public Reaction,* 20 Akron L.Rev. 187 (1986).

e. The secondary effects justification was deemed to distinguish *Erznoznik v. City of Jacksonville,* 422 U.S. 205 (1975) (invalidating ordinance prohibiting drive-in theaters from showing films containing nudity) and *Schad v. Mount Ephraim,* 452 U.S. 61 (1981) (invalidating ordinance prohibiting live entertainment, as applied to nude dancing, in commercial zone).

2. See *Young* (plurality opinion) ("[I]t is manifest that society's interest in protecting this type of expression is of a wholly different, and lesser, magnitude than the interest in untrammeled political debate * * *."). [The plurality opinion in *Young* stated that "[f]ew of us would march our sons and daughters off to war to see 'Specified Sexual Activities' exhibited in the theaters of our choice."].

"The appropriate inquiry in this case, then, is whether the Renton ordinance is designed to serve a substantial governmental interest and allows for reasonable alternative avenues of communication."

After concluding that the ordinance was designed to serve substantial government interests, the Court ruled that the Renton ordinance allowed "for reasonable alternative avenues of communication": "[W]e note that the ordinance leaves some 520 acres, or more than five percent of the entire land area of Renton, open to use as adult theater sites. [Respondents] argue, however, that some of the land in question is already occupied by existing businesses, that 'practically none' of the undeveloped land is currently for sale or lease, and that in general there are no 'commercially viable' adult theater sites within the 520 acres left open by the Renton ordinance. The Court of Appeals accepted these arguments. * * *

"We disagree. [That] respondents must fend for themselves in the real estate market, on an equal footing with other prospective purchasers and lessees, does not give rise to a First Amendment violation. And although we have cautioned against the enactment of zoning regulations that have 'the effect of suppressing, or greatly restricting access to, lawful speech,' *Young* (plurality opinion), we have never suggested that the First Amendment compels the Government to ensure that adult theaters, or any other kinds of speech-related businesses for that matter, will be able to obtain sites at bargain prices. [T]he First Amendment requires only that Renton refrain from effectively denying respondents a reasonable opportunity to open and operate an adult theater within the city, and the ordinance before us easily meets this requirement. * * *[4]"[f]

BRENNAN, J., joined by Marshall, J., dissented: "The fact that adult movie theaters may cause harmful 'secondary' land use effects may arguably give Renton a compelling reason to regulate such establishments; it does not mean, however, that such regulations are content-neutral. * * *

"The ordinance discriminates on its face against certain forms of speech based on content. Movie theaters specializing in 'adult motion pictures' may not be located within 1,000 feet of any residential zone, single-or multiple-family dwelling, church, park, or school. Other motion picture theaters, and other forms of 'adult entertainment,' such as bars, massage parlors, and adult bookstores, are not subject to the same restrictions. This selective treatment strongly suggests that Renton was interested not in controlling the 'secondary effects' associated with adult businesses, but in discriminating against adult theaters based on the

---

4. [We] reject respondents' "vagueness" argument for the same reasons that led us to reject a similar challenge in *Young*. There, the Detroit ordinance applied to theaters "used to present material distinguished or characterized by an emphasis on [sexually explicit matter]." We held that "even if there may be some uncertainty about the effect of the ordinances on other litigants, they are unquestionably applicable to these respondents." We also held that the Detroit ordinance created no "significant deterrent effect" that might justify invocation of the First Amendment "overbreadth" doctrine.

f. Blackmun, J., concurred in the result without opinion.

content of the films they exhibit. [Moreover,] [a]s the Court of Appeals observed, '[b]oth the magistrate and the district court recognized that many of the stated reasons for the ordinance were no more than expressions of dislike for the subject matter.'[3] That some residents may be offended by the *content* of the films shown at adult movie theaters cannot form the basis for state regulation of speech. See *Terminiello*.

"Some of the 'findings' [do] relate to supposed 'secondary effects' associated with adult movie theaters[4] [but they were added by the City Council only after this law suit was filed and the Court should not] accept these post-hoc statements at face value. [As] the Court of Appeals concluded, '[t]he record presented by Renton to support its asserted interest in enacting the zoning ordinance is very thin.' [5] * * *[7]

"Even assuming that the ordinance should be treated like a content-neutral time, place, and manner restriction, I would still find it unconstitutional. [T]he ordinance is invalid because it does not provide for reasonable alternative avenues of communication.[g] [R]espondents do not ask Renton to guarantee low-price sites for their businesses, but seek, only a reasonable opportunity to operate adult theaters in the city. By denying them this opportunity, Renton can effectively ban a form of protected speech from its borders. The ordinance 'greatly restrict[s] access to, lawful speech,' *Young*, and is plainly unconstitutional."

---

3. For example, "finding" number 2 states that "[l]ocation of adult entertainment land uses on the main commercial thoroughfares of the City gives an impression of legitimacy to, and causes a loss of sensitivity to the adverse effect of pornography upon children, established family relations, respect for marital relationship and for the sanctity of marriage relations of others, and the concept of nonaggressive, consensual sexual relations."

"Finding" number 6 states that "[l]ocation of adult land uses in close proximity to residential uses, churches, parks, and other public facilities, and schools, will cause a degradation of the community standard of morality. Pornographic material has a degrading effect upon the relationship between spouses."

4. For example, "finding" number 12 states that "[l]ocation of adult entertainment land uses in proximity to residential uses, churches, parks and other public facilities, and schools, may lead to increased levels of criminal activities, including prostitution, rape, incest and assaults in the vicinity of such adult entertainment land uses."

5. As part of the amendment passed after this lawsuit commenced, the City Council added a statement that it had intended to rely on the Washington Supreme Court's opinion in *Northend Cinema, Inc. v. Seattle*, 90 Wash.2d 709, 585 P.2d 1153 (1978), cert. denied, 441 U.S. 946 (1979), which upheld Seattle's zoning regulations against constitutional attack. Again, despite the suspicious coincidental timing of the amendment, the Court holds that "Renton was entitled to rely [on] the 'detailed findings' summarized in [the] *Northend Cinema* opinion." In *Northend Cinema*, the court noted that "[t]he record is replete with testimony regarding the effects of adult movie theater locations on residential neighborhoods." The opinion however, does not explain the evidence it purports to summarize, and provided no basis for determining whether Seattle's experience is relevant to Renton's.

7. As one commentator has noted: "[A]nyone with any knowledge of human nature should naturally assume that the decision to adopt almost any content-based restriction might have been affected by an antipathy on the part of at least some legislators to the ideas or information being suppressed. The logical assumption, in other words, is not that there is not improper motivation but, rather, because legislators are only human, that there is a substantial risk that an impermissible consideration has in fact colored the deliberative process." Geoffrey Stone, *Restrictions on Speech Because of its Content: The Peculiar Case of Subject–Matter Restrictions*, 46 U.Chi.L.Rev. 81, 106 (1978).

g. Brennan, J., argued that the ordinance also failed as an acceptable time, place, and manner restriction because it was not narrowly tailored to serve a significant governmental interest.

NOTES AND QUESTIONS

1. ***Content neutral?*** Was the ordinance fairly characterized as content-neutral? Erwin Chemerinsky, *Content Neutrality as a Central Problem of Freedom of Speech: Problems in the Supreme Court's Application*, 74 S. Cal. L. Rev. 49, 60 (2000): "The *Renton* approach confuses whether a law is content based or content neutral with the question of whether a law is justified by a sufficient purpose. The law in Renton may have been properly upheld as needed to combat crime and the secondary effects of adult theaters, but it nonetheless was clearly content based. The law applied only to theaters showing films with sexually explicit content." See also Heidi Kitrosser, *From Marshall McLuhan to Anthropomorphic Cows: Communicative Manner and the First Amendment*, 96 Nw. U. L. REV. 1339, 1397–98 (2002). Is the focus on "secondary effects" convincing? Consider Geoffrey Stone, *Content–Neutral Restrictions*, 54 U.Chi.L.Rev. 46, 115–117 (1987): "[T]he Court had never before *Renton* suggested that the absence of a constitutionally disfavored justification is in itself a justification for treating an expressly content-based restriction as if it were content-neutral. To the contrary, with the single exception of *Renton,* the Court in such circumstances has always invoked the stringent standards of content-based review. [For example, *Ferber*] treated as content-based a law prohibiting 'child pornography,' even though the government defended the law not in terms of communicative impact, but on the ground that the law was necessary to protect children who participate in 'sexual performances.' [I]f taken seriously, and extended to other contexts, the Court's transmogrification in *Renton* of an expressly content-based restriction into one that is content-neutral threatens to undermine the very foundation of the content-based/content-neutral distinction. This would in turn erode the coherence and predictability of First Amendment doctrine. One can only hope that this aspect of *Renton* is soon forgotten." See also Kathleen M. Sullivan, *Sex, Money, and Groups: Free Speech and Association Decisions in the October 1999 Term*, 28 Pepp. L. Rev. 723, 730 (2001): "The Court uses the rationale of content-neutral 'secondary effects' to uphold otherwise content-based statutes whose political counterparts would readily be struck down; no one, for example, would sustain a ban on political rallies because they tend to be associated with litter and fistfights."

Are subject matter restrictions as a class less problematic than other forms of content discrimination in that they often do not discriminate on the basis of point of view? Should *Renton's* secondary effects emphasis be limited to subject-matter-based restrictions? See Note, *The Content Distinction in Free Speech Analysis After Renton*, 102 Harv.L.Rev. 1904 (1989). Even if some subject matter restrictions are less problematic, is the Renton ordinance neutral as to point of view? Consider Geoffrey Stone, *Restrictions of Speech Because of its Content: The Peculiar Case of Subject–Matter Restrictions*, 46 U.Chi.L.Rev. 81, 111–12 (1978): "[T]he speech suppressed by restrictions such as those involved in [cases like *Erznoznik* and *Young*] will almost invariably carry an implicit, if not explicit, message in favor of more relaxed sexual mores. Such restrictions, in other words, have a potent viewpoint-differential impact. [I]n our society, the very presence of sexual explicitness in speech seems ideologically significant, without regard to whatever other messages might be intended. To treat such restrictions as viewpoint-neutral seems simply to ignore reality. Finally, [a] large percentage of citizens apparently feel threatened by nonobscene, sexually-explicit speech and believe it to be morally reprehensible. If it were not for the Court's relatively narrow construction of the obscenity concept, much of this speech would undoubtedly be banned outright. Thus, any restriction along these lines will carry an extraordinarily high risk that its enactment was tainted by this fundamentally illegitimate consideration. Such restrictions, although superficially viewpoint-neutral, pose a uniquely compelling case for content-based scrutiny." Are feminist or neo-conservative objections to near obscene speech both "fundamentally illegitimate." Should all content-based scrutiny be the same? Does *Renton* reconstruct the Court's "narrow construction of the obscenity concept"?

Is the concept of viewpoint neutrality itself problematic? Consider Cass Sunstein, *Pornography and the First Amendment,* 1986 Duke L.J. 589, 615: "One does not 'see' a viewpoint-based restriction when the harms invoked in defense of a regulation are obvious and so widely supported by social consensus that they allay any concern about impermissible government motivation. Whether a classification is viewpoint-based thus ultimately turns on the viewpoint of the decisionmaker." See generally Catharine MacKinnon, *Feminism, Marxism, Method, and the State,* 7 Signs 515, 535–36 (1981).

2. Can *Renton* be squared with *Brandenburg*? Consider Seana Valentine Shiffrin, *Speech, Death, and Double Effect,* 78 N.Y.U. L. Rev. 1135, 1152 (2003): "If one puts the *Brandenburg* line of cases side by side with [the] *Young–Renton–Barnes–Erie* line of cases, it looks as though a speaker may be held responsible for incidental effects of her speech but not (except under special circumstances) for direct, intended effects. The negative or positive effects on an audience from its understanding and directly reacting to the contents of one's speech may not be the grounds for restriction, but the side effects of one's speech may be so used." Is this explainable because a "central reason for protecting speech is to permit a variety of ideas to be promulgated to, and evaluated and tested by, independent agents." Id. at 1163. Is interference with advocacy of illegal action, therefore, more problematic than interference on "secondary effects" grounds? Does it matter whether the speech in cases like *Renton* predisposes audience members to solicit prostitutes or seek drugs?

Can a distinction be drawn because advocacy of illegal action is political? Does *Renton*—see fn. 2—endorse a hierarchy of categories among types of protected speech? Consider Tribe 2d ed., at 939 n. 66: "[I]t is doubtful that *Renton* can fairly be read as endorsing the concept of a hierarchy of intermediate categories, because the case turned on the majority's characterization of the restriction as content-neutral, and the issue of the relative importance of the speech involved, was, strictly speaking, irrelevant." But cf. Philip Prygoski, *Low Value Speech: From Young to Fraser,* 32 St. L.U.L.J. 317, 345 (1987) (despite the content-neutral language, "antipathy toward the kind of expression involved" swayed the case).

3. *Renton's* "secondary effects" notion was revisited by several justices in BOOS v. BARRY, Ch. 2, supra: A District of Columbia ordinance banned the display of any sign within 500 feet of a foreign embassy that would tend to bring the embassy into "public odium" or "public disrepute." O'CONNOR, J., joined by Stevens and Scalia, JJ., distinguished *Renton:* "Respondents and the United States do not point to the 'secondary effects' of picket signs in front of embassies. They do not point to congestion, to interference with ingress or egress, to visual clutter, or to the need to protect the security of embassies. Rather, they rely on the need to protect the dignity of foreign diplomatic personnel by shielding them from speech that is critical of their governments. This justification focuses *only* on the content of the speech and the direct impact that speech has on its listeners. The emotive impact of speech on its audience is not a 'secondary effect.'[h] Because the display clause regulates speech due to its potential primary impact, we conclude it must be considered content-based."[i]

BRENNAN, J., joined by Marshall, J., agreed with the conclusion that the ordinance was content-based, but objected to O'Connor, J.'s "assumption that the *Renton* analysis applies not only outside the context of businesses purveying sexually explicit materials but even to political speech."[j]

4. ***The nature of content regulation reconsidered.*** LOS ANGELES v. ALAMEDA BOOKS, 535 U.S. 425 (2002), per O'CONNOR, J., reaffirmed *Renton* and found a sufficient showing of secondary effects to permit Los Angeles not only to disperse adult businesses, but also to prohibit more than one adult entertainment business within the same building, i.e., a company could not have an adult bookstore and an adult video arcade in the same building.

SCALIA, J., concurring, would have gone further: "[I]n a case such as this our First Amendment traditions make secondary effects analysis quite unnecessary. The Constitution does not prevent those communities that wish to do so from regulating, or indeed entirely suppressing, the business of pandering sex."

Four justices expressed doubts about the conception of "content" employed in *Renton*. KENNEDY, J., concurring, criticized *Renton's* conception of

---

h. See *Forsyth County v. The Nationalist Movement*, 505 U.S. 123 (1992)("Listener's reaction to speech is not a content-neutral basis for regulation,"—not secondary effects).

i. In an earlier passage O'Connor, J., responded to the argument that the ordinance was not content-based on the theory that the government was not selecting between viewpoints. The argument was instead that "the permissible message on a picket sign is determined solely by the policies of a foreign government. We reject this contention, although we agree the provision is not viewpoint-based. The display clause determines which viewpoint is acceptable in a neutral fashion by looking to the policies of foreign governments. While this prevents the display clause from being directly viewpoint-based, a label with potential First Amendment ramifications of its own, it does not render the statute content-neutral. Rather, we have held that a regulation that 'does not favor either side of a political controversy' is nonetheless impermissible because the 'First Amendment's hostility to content-based regulation extends [to] prohibition of public discussion of an entire topic.' Here the government has determined that an entire category of speech—signs or displays critical of foreign governments—is not to be permitted."

j. Rehnquist, J., joined by White and Blackmun, JJ., voted to uphold the ordinance on the basis of Bork, J.'s opinion below in *Finzer v. Barry*, 798 F.2d 1450 (D.C.Cir.1986). Bork, J., stated that the need to adhere to principles of international law might constitute a secondary effect under *Renton* but was not "entirely sure" whether *Renton* alone could dictate that result and did not resolve the issue. Id. at 1469–70 n. 15.

"content": "*Renton* described a similar ordinance as "content neutral," and I agree with the dissent that the designation is imprecise. [T]he ordinance in *Renton* 'treat[ed] theaters that specialize in adult films differently from other kinds of theaters.' The fiction that this sort of ordinance is content neutral— or 'content neutral'—is perhaps more confusing than helpful, as Justice Souter demonstrates. [These] ordinances are content based, and we should call them so."

Nonetheless, Kennedy, J., adhered to the "intermediate scrutiny" of *Renton* and required a city to "advance some basis to show that its regulation has the purpose and effect of suppressing secondary effects, while leaving the quantity and accessibility of speech substantially intact. The ordinance may identify the speech based on content, but only as a shorthand for identifying the secondary effects outside. A city may not assert that it will reduce secondary effects by reducing speech in the same proportion. [The] rationale of the ordinance must be that it will suppress secondary effects and not by suppressing speech." Kennedy, J., found that Los Angeles ordinance met this burden.

Souter, J., joined by Stevens and Ginsburg, and in part by Breyer, JJ., dissented:[a] "[W]hile it may be true that an adult business is burdened only because of its secondary effects, it is clearly burdened only if its expressive products have adult content. Thus, the Court has recognized that this kind of regulation, though called content neutral, occupies a kind of limbo between full-blown, content-based restrictions and regulations that apply without any reference to the substance of what is said.

"It would in fact make sense to give this kind of zoning regulation a First Amendment label of its own, and if we called it content correlated, we would not only describe it for what it is, but keep alert to a risk of content-based regulation that it poses. The risk lies in the fact that when a law applies selectively only to speech of particular content, the more precisely the content is identified, the greater is the opportunity for government censorship. Adult speech refers not merely to sexually explicit content, but to speech reflecting a favorable view of being explicit about sex and a favorable view of the practices it depicts; a restriction on adult content is thus also a restriction turning on a particular viewpoint, of which the government may disapprove.

"This risk of viewpoint discrimination is subject to a relatively simple safeguard, however. If combating secondary effects of property devaluation and crime is truly the reason for the regulation, it is possible to show by empirical evidence that the effects exist, that they are caused by the expressive activity subject to the zoning, and that the zoning can be expected either to ameliorate them or to enhance the capacity of the government to combat them (say, by concentrating them in one area), without suppressing the expressive activity itself. This capacity of zoning regulation to address the practical problems without eliminating the speech is, after all, the only possible excuse for speaking of secondary-effects zoning as akin to time, place, or manner regulations." Souter, J., argued that Los Angeles had not met this burden.

---

a. Breyer, J., joined this section of the opinion, but not the portion quoted here.

5. **Beyond secondary effects.** Consider Barry P. McDonald, *Speech and Distrust: Rethinking the Content Approach to Protecting the Freedom of Expression*, 81 Notre D. L.Rev. 1347 (2006): "[A] review of the Court's post-*Renton* cases indicates that the decision was anything but an aberration in calling a facially content discriminatory regulation content-neutral. [T]he vast majority of speech regulations reviewed by the Court make content distinctions on their face, and [the] Court has taken quite often to designating them as content-neutral without resort to any sort of secondary effects rationale."

———

Five years after *Renton*, the Court held that an Indiana statute prohibiting the knowing or intentional appearing in a public place in a state of nudity could constitutionally be applied to require that any female dancer at a minimum wear "pasties" and a "G-string" when she dances. BARNES v. GLEN THEATRE, INC., 501 U.S. 560 (1991). The Justices upholding the ordinance were divided upon the rationale for doing so. Rehnquist, C.J., joined by O'Connor and Kennedy, JJ., applied the *O'Brien* test, characterized the statute as a "public indecency" statute, and concluded that the interests in order and morality justified the statute. Souter, J., concurring, also applied the *O'Brien* test, but concluded that the statute was justified by the "secondary effects" of prostitution, sexual assaults, and other criminal activity even though this justification had not been articulated by the Indiana legislature or its courts. Scalia, J., argued that the case law did not support the plurality's contention that the interest in morality was substantial enough to pass muster under *O'Brien*; nonetheless, he voted to uphold the statute by repudiating the *O'Brien* test. White, J. joined by Marshall, Blackmun and Stevens, JJ., dissented.

———

The fragmented character of the *Barnes* majority created interpretive difficulties for the Pennsylvania Supreme Court in considering an Erie, Pennsylvania ordinance. Like Indiana, Erie's ordinance forbade knowingly or intentionally appearing in a public "state of nudity." Unlike Indiana, however, the preamble to the ordinance stated that the "Council specifically wishes to adopt the concept of Public Indecency prohibited by the laws of the State of Indiana, which was approved by the U.S. Supreme Court in *Barnes*, (for) the purpose of limiting a recent increase in nude live entertainment within the City," which led to prostitution and other crime.

Pap's A.M., operated "Kandyland," featuring nude erotic dancing by women. To comply with the ordinance, these dancers had to minimally wear "pasties" and a "G-string." Pap's sought an injunction against the ordinance's enforcement. The Pennsylvania Supreme Court, unable to find a lowest common denominator uniting the *Barnes* majority, felt free to reach an independent judgment, and found that the ordinance, although also directed at secondary effects, was primarily directed at expression and did not survive close scrutiny.

In ERIE v. PAP'S A.M., 529 U.S. 277 (2000), the plurality, per O'CONNOR, J., joined by Rehnquist, C.J., and Kennedy and Breyer, JJ., upheld application of the ordinance to prevent nude dancing:[a] "Being 'in a state of nudity' is not an inherently expressive condition. [N]ude dancing of the type at issue here is expressive conduct, although we think that it falls only within the outer ambit of the First Amendment's protection. [G]overnment restrictions on public nudity such as the ordinance at issue here should be evaluated under the framework set forth in *O'Brien* for content-neutral restrictions on symbolic speech. * * *

"The ordinance [bans] all public nudity, regardless of whether that nudity is accompanied by expressive activity [and] updates provisions of an 'Indecency and Immorality' ordinance that has been on the books since 1866, predating the prevalence of nude dancing establishments such as Kandyland. [T]he Pennsylvania Supreme Court [concluded] that the ordinance was nevertheless content based, relying on Justice White's position in dissent in *Barnes* for the proposition that a ban of this type *necessarily* has the purpose of suppressing the erotic message [, and] that '[s]ince the State permits the dancers to perform if they wear pasties and G-strings but forbids nude dancing, it is precisely because of the distinctive, expressive content of the nude dancing performances at issue in this case that the State seeks to apply the statutory prohibition.' A majority of the Court rejected that view in *Barnes*, and we do so again here.

"Respondent's argument that the ordinance is 'aimed' at suppressing expression through a ban on nude dancing—an argument that respondent supports by pointing to statements by the city attorney that the public nudity ban was not intended to apply to 'legitimate' theater productions—is really an argument that the city council also had an illicit motive in enacting the ordinance. As we have said before, however, this Court will not strike down an otherwise constitutional statute on the basis of an alleged illicit motive. In light of the Pennsylvania court's determination that one purpose of the ordinance is to combat harmful secondary effects, the ban on public nudity here is no different from the ban on burning draft registration cards in *O'Brien*, where the Government sought to prevent the means of the expression and not the expression of antiwar sentiment itself.

"Justice Stevens argues that the ordinance enacts a complete ban on expression. [But] simply to define what is being banned as the 'message' is to assume the conclusion. [Although] there may be cases in which banning the means of expression so interferes with the message that it essentially bans the message, that is not the case here. * * *

---

a. O'Connor, J., rebuffed a contention that the case was moot. Scalia, J., joined by Thomas, J., would have sustained the mootness claim. Stevens, J., joined by Ginsburg, J., did not address the issue.

"Similarly, even if Erie's public nudity ban has some minimal effect on the erotic message by muting that portion of the expression that occurs when the last stitch is dropped, [a]ny effect on the overall expression is de minimis. And as Justice Stevens eloquently stated for the plurality in *Young*, 'even though we recognize that the First Amendment will not tolerate the total suppression of erotic materials that have some arguably artistic value, it is manifest that society's interest in protecting this type of expression is of a wholly different, and lesser, magnitude than the interest in untrammeled political debate.' [If] States are to be able to regulate secondary effects, then de minimis intrusions on expression such as those at issue here cannot be sufficient to render the ordinance content based.

"This case is, in fact, similar to *O'Brien*, *Clark*, and *Ward*. The justification for the government regulation in each case prevents harmful 'secondary' effects that are unrelated to the suppression of expression. See, e.g., *Ward* (noting that '[t]he principal justification for the sound-amplification guideline is the city's desire to control noise levels at bandshell events, in order to retain the character of [the adjacent] Sheep Meadow and its more sedate activities,' and citing *Renton* for the proposition that '[a] regulation that serves purposes unrelated to the content of expression is deemed neutral, even if it has an incidental effect on some speakers or messages but not others'). While the doctrinal theories behind 'incidental burdens' and 'secondary effects' are, of course, not identical, there is nothing objectionable about a city passing a general ordinance to ban public nudity (even though such a ban may place incidental burdens on some protected speech) and at the same time recognizing that one specific occurrence of public nudity—nude erotic dancing—is particularly problematic because it produces harmful secondary effects.

"[E]rie's efforts to protect public health and safety are clearly within the city's police powers [and] are undeniably important. And [the] city need not 'conduct new studies or produce evidence independent of that already generated by other cities' to demonstrate the problem of secondary effects [*Renton*.] In fact, Erie expressly relied on *Barnes* and its discussion of secondary effects, including its reference to *Renton* and *American Mini Theatres*. * * *

"In any event, Erie also relied on its own findings. The preamble to the ordinance states that 'the Council of the City of Erie *has, at various times over more than a century, expressed its findings* that certain lewd, immoral activities carried on in public places for profit are highly detrimental to the public health, safety and welfare, and lead to the debasement of both women and men, promote violence, public intoxication, prostitution and other serious criminal activity.' The city council members, familiar with commercial downtown Erie, are the individuals who would likely have had first-hand knowledge of what took place at and around nude dancing establishments in Erie, and can make particularized, expert judgments about the resulting harmful secondary effects. * * *

"Justice Souter, however, would require Erie to develop a specific evidentiary record supporting its ordinance * * *. *O'Brien*, of course, required no evidentiary showing at all that the threatened harm was real. But that case is different, Justice Souter contends, because in *O'Brien* 'there could be no doubt' that a regulation prohibiting the destruction of draft cards would alleviate the harmful secondary effects flowing from the destruction of those cards.

"But whether the harm is evident to our 'intuition,' is not the proper inquiry. If it were, we would simply say there is no doubt that a regulation prohibiting public nudity would alleviate the harmful secondary effects associated with nude dancing. * * * Justice Souter [argues] that we cannot accept Erie's findings because the subject of nude dancing is 'fraught with some emotionalism.' Yet surely the subject of drafting our citizens into the military is 'fraught' with more emotionalism than the subject of regulating nude dancing.

"As to [whether] the regulation furthers the government interest—it is evident that, since crime and other public health and safety problems are caused by the presence of nude dancing establishments like Kandy-land, a ban on such nude dancing would further Erie's interest in preventing such secondary effects. To be sure, requiring dancers to wear pasties and G-strings may not greatly reduce these secondary effects, but *O'Brien* requires only that the regulation further the interest in combating such effects. [It may] be true that a pasties and G-string requirement would not be as effective as, for example, a requirement that the dancers be fully clothed, but the city must balance its efforts to address the problem with the requirement that the restriction be no greater than necessary to further the city's interest. [The] requirement that dancers wear pasties and G-strings is a minimal restriction in furtherance of the asserted government interests, and the restriction leaves ample capacity to convey the dancer's erotic message. Justice Souter points out that zoning is an alternative means of addressing this problem. It is far from clear, however, that zoning imposes less of a burden on expression than the minimal requirement implemented here. In any event, since this is a content-neutral restriction, least restrictive means analysis is not required."

SCALIA, J., joined by Thomas., J., concurred: "In *Barnes*, I voted to uphold the challenged Indiana statute 'not because it survives some lower level of First Amendment scrutiny, but because, as a general law regulating conduct and not specifically directed at expression, it is not subject to First Amendment scrutiny at all.' Erie's ordinance, too, by its terms prohibits not merely nude dancing, but the act—irrespective of whether it is engaged in for expressive purposes—of going nude in public. The facts that a preamble to the ordinance explains that its purpose, in part, is to 'limi[t] a recent increase in nude live entertainment,' that city council-members in supporting the ordinance commented to that effect, and that the ordinance includes in the definition of nudity the exposure of devices simulating that condition, neither make the law any less general in its reach nor demonstrate that what the municipal authorities *really* find objectionable is expression rather than public nakedness. As far as appears (and as seems overwhelmingly likely), [these] simply reflect the fact that Erie had recently been having a public nudity problem not with streakers, sunbathers or hot-dog vendors, but with lap dancers.

"There is no basis for the contention that the ordinance does not apply to nudity in theatrical productions such as Equus or Hair. Its text contains no such limitation. It was stipulated in the trial court that no effort was made to enforce the ordinance against a production of Equus involving nudity that was being staged in Erie at the time the ordinance became effective. [But], neither in the stipulation, nor elsewhere in the record, does it appear that the city was aware of the nudity—and before this Court counsel for the city attributed nonenforcement not to a general exception for theatrical productions, but to the fact that no one had complained. * * *

"Moreover, even were I to conclude that the city of Erie had specifically singled out the activity of nude dancing, I still would not find that this regulation violated the First Amendment unless I could be persuaded (as on this record I cannot) that it was the communicative character of nude dancing that prompted the ban. When conduct other than speech itself is regulated, it is my view that the First Amendment is violated only '[w]here the government prohibits conduct precisely because of its communicative attributes.' I do not feel the need, as the Court does, to identify some 'secondary effects.' [The] traditional power of government to foster good morals (bonos mores), and the acceptability of the traditional judgment (if Erie wishes to endorse it) that nude public dancing *itself* is immoral, have not been repealed by the First Amendment."

SOUTER, J., concurred in part and dissented in part: "I [agree] with the analytical approach that the plurality employs in deciding this case. [But] intermediate scrutiny requires a regulating government to make some demonstration of an evidentiary basis for the harm it claims to flow from the expressive activity, and for the alleviation expected from the restriction imposed. [What] is clear is that the evidence of reliance must be a matter of demonstrated fact, not speculative supposition.[b]

"By these standards, the record before us today is deficient. [The] plurality does the best it can with the materials to hand, but the pickings are slim. [T]he ordinance's preamble assert[s] that over the course of more than a century the city council had expressed 'findings' of detrimental

---

b. For evidence suggesting that adult nightclubs are less likely to be the sites for crime, see Daniel Linz, Kenneth C. Land, Jay R. Williams, Bryant Paul, and Michael E. Ezell, *An Examination of the Assumption that Adult Businesses are Associated with Crime in Surrounding Areas: A Secondary Effects Study in Charlotte, North Carolina*, 38 Law & Soc'y Rev. 99 (2004): "The establishments themselves have evolved more closely into legitimate businesses–establishments with management attention to profitability and continuity of existence. To meet these objectives, it is essential that the management and/or owners of the clubs provide their customers with some assurance of safety. Accordingly, adult nightclubs [often] appear to have better lighting in their parking lots and better security surveillance than is standard for non-nightclub business establishments. These may be factors producing fewer crime opportunities and lower numbers of reported crime incidents in the surrounding areas of the clubs."

secondary effects flowing from lewd and immoral profitmaking activity in public places. But however accurate the recital may be and however honestly the councilors may have held those conclusions to be true over the years, the recitation does not get beyond conclusions on a subject usually fraught with some emotionalism. * * *

"There is one point, however, on which an evidentiary record is not quite so hard to find, but it hurts, not helps, the city. The final *O'Brien* requirement is that the incidental speech restriction be shown to be no greater than essential to achieve the government's legitimate purpose. To deal with this issue, we have to ask what basis there is to think that the city would be unsuccessful in countering any secondary effects by the significantly lesser restriction of zoning to control the location of nude dancing, thus allowing for efficient law enforcement, restricting effects on property values, and limiting exposure of the public. The record shows that for 23 years there has been a zoning ordinance on the books to regulate the location of establishments like Kandyland, but the city has not enforced it. [T]his hurdle to the application of *O'Brien* requires an evidentiary response. * * *

"Careful readers, and not just those on the Erie City Council, will of course realize that my partial dissent rests on a demand for an evidentiary basis that I failed to make when I concurred in *Barnes*. [A]fter many subsequent occasions to think further about the needs of the First Amendment, I have come to believe that a government must toe the mark more carefully than I first insisted."

STEVENS, J., joined by Ginsburg, J., dissented: "Far more important than the question whether nude dancing is entitled to the protection of the First Amendment are the dramatic changes in legal doctrine that the Court endorses today. Until now, the 'secondary effects' of commercial enterprises featuring indecent entertainment have justified only the regulation of their location. For the first time, the Court has now held that such effects may justify the total suppression of protected speech. * * *

"As the preamble to Ordinance No. 75–1994 candidly acknowledges, the council of the city of Erie enacted the restriction at issue 'for the purpose of limiting a recent increase in nude live entertainment within the City.' Prior to the enactment of the ordinance, the dancers at Kandyland performed in the nude. As the Court recognizes, after its enactment they can perform precisely the same dances if they wear 'pasties and G-strings.' [The] plurality assumes, however, that the difference in the content of the message resulting from the mandated costume change is 'de minimis.' [The] crucial point to remember, however, is that whether one views the difference as large or small, nude dancing still receives First Amendment protection, even if that protection lies only in the 'outer ambit' of that Amendment. Erie's ordinance, therefore, burdens a message protected by the First Amendment. If one assumes that the same erotic message is conveyed by nude dancers as by those wearing miniscule costumes, one means of expressing that message is banned;[2] if one assumes that the messages are different, one of those messages is banned. In either event, the ordinance is a total ban.

"[Never] before have we approved the use of ['the so-called "secondary effects" test'] to justify a total ban on protected First Amendment expression. On the contrary, we have been quite clear that the doctrine would not support that end.[3] [4]

"The reason we have limited our secondary effects cases to zoning and declined to extend their reasoning to total bans is clear and straightforward: A dispersal that simply limits the places where speech may occur is a minimal imposition whereas a total ban is the most exacting of restrictions. [T]he Court's holding rejects the explicit reasoning in *American Mini Theatres* and *Renton* and the express holding in *Schad* [and] compounds that error by dramatically reducing the degree to which the State's interest must be furthered by the restriction imposed on speech, and by ignoring the critical difference between secondary effects caused by speech and the incidental effects on speech that may be caused by a regulation of conduct.

"[T]he plurality concedes that 'requiring dancers to wear pasties and G-strings may not greatly reduce these secondary effects.' To believe that the mandatory addition of pasties and a G-string will have *any* kind of noticeable impact on secondary effects requires nothing short of a titanic surrender to the implausible. * * *

"The Court is also mistaken in equating our secondary effects cases with the 'incidental burdens' doctrine applied in cases such as *O'Brien*; and it aggravates the error by invoking the latter line of cases to support its assertion that Erie's ordinance is unrelated to speech. The incidental

---

2. Although nude dancing might be described as one protected "means" of conveying an erotic message, it does not follow that a protected message has not been totally banned simply because there are other, similar ways to convey erotic messages. A State's prohibition of a particular book, for example, does not fail to be a total ban simply because other books conveying a similar message are available.

3. The Court contends *Ward* shows that we have used the secondary effects rationale to justify more burdensome restrictions than those approved in *Renton* and *American Mini Theatres*. That argument is unpersuasive for two reasons. First, as in the two cases just mentioned, the regulation in *Ward* was as a time, place, and manner restriction. Second, [*Ward*] is not a secondary effects case.

4. We [held] in *Renton* [that] the city [was] permitted to rely on a detailed study conducted by the city of Seattle that examined the relationship between zoning controls and the secondary effects of adult theaters. (It was permitted to rely as well on "the 'detailed findings' summarized" in an opinion of the Washington Supreme Court to the same effect.) Renton, having identified the same problem in its own city as that experienced in Seattle, quite logically drew on Seattle's experience and adopted a similar solution. But if Erie is relying on the Seattle study as well, its use of that study is most peculiar. After identifying a problem in its own city similar to that in Seattle, Erie has implemented a solution (pasties and G-strings) bearing no relationship to the efficacious remedy identified by the Seattle study (dispersal through zoning).

But the city of Erie, of course, has not in fact pointed to any study by anyone suggesting that the adverse secondary effects of commercial enterprises featuring erotic dancing depends in the slightest on the precise costume worn by the performers—it merely assumes it to be so. If the city is permitted simply to assume that a slight addition to the dancers' costumes will sufficiently decrease secondary effects, then presumably the city can require more and more clothing as long as any danger of adverse effects remains.

burdens doctrine applies when 'speech' and 'nonspeech' elements are combined in the same 'course of conduct,' and the government's interest in regulating the latter justifies incidental burdens on the former. *O'Brien.* Secondary effects, on the other hand, are indirect consequences of protected speech and may justify regulation of the places where that speech may occur. See *American Mini Theatres.* When a State enacts a regulation, it might focus on the secondary effects of speech as its aim, or it might concentrate on nonspeech related concerns, having no thoughts at all with respect to how its regulation will affect speech—and only later, when the regulation is found to burden speech, justify the imposition as an unintended incidental consequence. But those interests are not the same, and the Court cannot ignore their differences and insist that both aims are equally unrelated to speech simply because Erie might have 'recogniz[ed]' that it could possibly have had either aim in mind. One can think of an apple and an orange at the same time; that does not turn them into the same fruit.

"[Erie] has expressly justified its ordinance with reference to secondary effects. [Thus,] the Court's argument that 'this case is similar to *O'Brien*,' is quite wrong, as are its citations to *Clark* and *Ward*, neither of which involved secondary effects. [E]ither Erie's ordinance was not aimed at speech and the Court may attempt to justify the regulation under the incidental burdens test, or Erie has aimed its law at the secondary effects of speech, and the Court can try to justify the law under that doctrine. But it cannot conflate the two with the expectation that Erie's interests aimed at secondary effects will be rendered unrelated to speech by virtue of this doctrinal polyglot. * * *

"Erie's ordinance differs from the statute in *Barnes* [because] the city permitted a production of Equus to proceed without prosecution, even after the ordinance was in effect, and despite its awareness of the nudity involved in the production. [As] presented to us, the ordinance is deliberately targeted at Kandyland's type of nude dancing (to the exclusion of plays like Equus), in terms of both its applicable scope and the city's enforcement.[14]

"This narrow aim is confirmed by the expressed views of the Erie City Councilmembers who voted for the ordinance. [E]ach stated his or her view that the ordinance was aimed specifically at nude adult entertainment, and not at more mainstream forms of entertainment that include total nudity, nor even at nudity in general. One lawmaker observed: 'We're not talking about nudity. We're not talking about the theater or art * * * * We're talking about what is indecent and immoral* * * * We're not prohibiting nudity, we're prohibiting nudity when it's used in a lewd and immoral fashion.' * * *[16]"

---

14. Justice Scalia [opines] that here, the basis for singling out Kandyland is morality. But since the "morality" of the public nudity in Hair is left untouched by the ordinance, while the "immorality" of the public nudity in Kandyland is singled out, the distinction cannot be that 'nude public dancing *itself* is immoral.' Rather, the only arguable difference between the two is that one's message is more immoral than the other's.

NOTES AND QUESTIONS

1. *Is nude dancing speech?* Consider Robert Post, *Recuperating First Amendment Doctrine,* 47 Stan.L.Rev. 1249, 1259 (1995): "[T]he outcome in *Barnes* would have been different if Indiana were to have applied its statute to accepted media for the communication of ideas, as for example by attempting to prohibit nudity in movies or in the theater. Any such prohibition would serve interests deemed highly problematic by fully elaborated principles of First Amendment jurisprudence. Crucial to the result in *Barnes,* then, is the distinction between what the Court is prepared to accept as a medium for the communication of ideas, and its implicit understanding of nude dancing in nightclubs, which at least three of the majority Justices explicitly characterized as merely 'expressive conduct.'" For defense of the view that nude dancing should be protected speech, see Kevin Case, *"Lewd and Immoral": Nude Dancing, Sexual Expression, and the First Amendment,* 81 Chi.-Kent L. Rev. 1185 (2006).

2. *A First Amendment test?* Assuming nude dancing is speech, is Scalia, J., correct in arguing that no First Amendment test should apply? Is his analysis consistent with the language of *O'Brien?* The holding in *Falwell?* The approach taken in *Schenck?* Is *Arcara,* Ch. 2 supra, (no First Amendment scrutiny; statute directed at prostitution and premises used regardless of other uses) consistent with *Barnes* and *Pap's?*

3. **Law and morals.** Consider Christopher Thomas Leahy, *The First Amendment Gone Awry: City of Erie v. Pap's A.M., Ailing Analytical Structures, and the Suppression of Protected Expression,* 150 U. Pa. L. Rev. 1021, 1024 (2002): "'As of February 1997, Americans spend more money at strip clubs than at Broadway, off-Broadway, regional, and non-profit theaters; than at the opera, the ballet, and jazz and classical music performances–combined.' As such, the use of zoning and general laws to limit or eliminate adult entertainment establishments is a particularly thorny issue because it inextricably involves conflicts between passionate defenders and equally fervent detractors, as well as difficult questions of morality, government censorship, and legislative motive." Does this show the popularity of immorality or differences about the substance of morality? What accounts for political differences about the relationship between law and morals in the First Amendment context? Consider Vincent Blasi, *Six Conservatives in Search of the First Amendment: The Revealing Case of Nude Dancing,* 33 Wm. and Mary L.Rev. 611, 621–22 (1992): "Can a principled conservative approve the enforcement of morals in the context of group vilification? Can a principled

---

16. The Court dismisses this evidence, declaring that it "will not strike down an otherwise constitutional statute on the basis of an alleged illicit motive." *O'Brien* [said] only that we would not strike down a law "on the *assumption* that a wrongful purpose or motive has caused the power to be exerted," (emphasis added), and that statement was due to our recognition that it is a "hazardous matter" to determine the actual intent of a body as large as Congress "on the basis of what fewer than a handful of Congressmen said about [a law]." [We] need not base our inquiry on an "assumption," nor must we infer the collective intent of a large body based on the statements of a few, for we have in the record the actual statements of all the city councilmembers who voted in favor of the ordinance.

liberal argue that topless dancing is protected by the First Amendment but not the shouting of racial epithets? Important differences between the two categories of speech regulation may exist—hate speech ordinarily is not confined to settings in which every member of the audience has made a choice to receive the message, but hate speech also seems more political in character—but the response of many conservatives to the hate speech issue at least suggests that they do not invariably prefer a narrow interpretation of the First Amendment and do not always take a broad view of the state's power to enforce morality."

4. *Law and Psychology.* Consider Amy Adler, *Girls! Girls! Girls!: The Supreme Court Confronts the G–String,* 80 N.Y.U. L. Rev. 1108, 1129–1131, 1136–37 (2005): "The G-string conceals a very small part of the body, the sight of which is a very big deal. It covers [the evidence] that the woman does not have a penis. [T]he sight of the woman's 'lack' ushers in the panic of castration anxiety for the male viewer. [Freud] emphasizes the universality of castration anxiety: 'Probably no male human being is spared the fright of castration at the sight of a female genital.' [The] G-string as solution is hard to make sense of in the world of First Amendment or conscious logic. But in the drama of castration anxiety and fetishism, the function performed by the G-string could not be more urgent or necessary. By warding off the threat of castration, it restores order and function."

II. COMMERCIAL SPEECH

VIRGINIA STATE BOARD OF PHARMACY v. VIRGINIA CITIZENS CONSUMER COUNCIL

425 U.S. 748, 96 S.Ct. 1817, 48 L.Ed.2d 346 (1976).

JUSTICE BLACKMUN delivered the opinion of the Court.

[The Court held invalid a Virginia statute that made advertising the prices of prescription drugs "unprofessional conduct," subjecting pharmacists to license suspension or revocation. Prescription drug prices strikingly varied within the same locality, in Virginia and nationally, sometimes by several hundred percent. Such drugs were dispensed exclusively by licensed pharmacists but 95% were prepared by manufacturers, not compounded by the pharmacists.]

[Appellants] contend that the advertisement of prescription drug prices is outside the protection of the First Amendment because it is "commercial speech." There can be no question that in past decisions the Court has given some indication that commercial speech is unprotected.[a]

Last Term, in *Bigelow v. Virginia,* 421 U.S. 809 (1975), the notion of unprotected "commercial speech" all but passed from the scene. We reversed a conviction for violation of a Virginia statute that made the

---

a. Starting with *Valentine v. Chrestensen,* 316 U.S. 52 (1942), the opinion summarized the decisions and dicta that gave such "indication." Long after *Chrestensen,* strong arguments against a First Amendment exception for commercial speech had appeared. See Martin Redish, *The First Amendment in the Market Place,* 39 Geo.Wash.L.Rev. 420 (1971); Note, 50 Ore.L.Rev. 177 (1971); cf. Note, 78 Harv.L.Rev. 1191 (1965).

circulation of any publication to encourage or promote the processing of an abortion in Virginia a misdemeanor. The defendant had published in his newspaper the availability of abortions in New York. The advertisement in question, in addition to announcing that abortions were legal in New York, offered the services of a referral agency in that State. [We] concluded that "the Virginia courts erred in their assumptions that advertising, as such, was entitled to no First Amendment protection," and we observed that the "relationship of speech to the marketplace of products or of services does not make it valueless in the marketplace of ideas."

Some fragment of hope for the continuing validity of a "commercial speech" exception arguably might have persisted because of the subject matter of the advertisement in *Bigelow*. We noted that in announcing the availability of legal abortions in New York, the advertisement "did more than simply propose a commercial transaction. It contained factual material of clear 'public interest.' " And, of course, the advertisement related to activity with which, at least in some respects, the State could not interfere. See *Roe v. Wade*, 410 U.S. 113 (1973). Indeed, we observed: "We need not decide in this case the precise extent to which the First Amendment permits regulation of advertising that is related to activities the State may legitimately regulate or even prohibit."

Here, [the] question whether there is a First Amendment exception for "commercial speech" is squarely before us. Our pharmacist does not wish to editorialize on any subject, cultural, philosophical, or political. He does not wish to report any particularly newsworthy fact, or to make generalized observations even about commercial matters. The "idea" he wishes to communicate is simply this: "I will sell you the X prescription drug at the Y price." Our question, then, is whether this communication is wholly outside the protection of the First Amendment.

V.   [Speech] does not lose its First Amendment protection because money is spent to project it, as in a paid advertisement of one form or another. *New York Times Co. v. Sullivan.* Speech likewise is protected even though it is carried in a form that is "sold" for profit. *Smith v. California.* [Our] question is whether speech which does "no more than propose a commercial transaction," is so removed from any "exposition of ideas," and from "truth, science, morality, and arts in general, in its diffusion of liberal sentiments on the administration of Government", *Roth,* that it lacks all protection. Our answer is that it is not.

Focusing first on the individual parties to the transaction that is proposed in the commercial advertisement, we may assume that the advertiser's interest is a purely economic one. That hardly disqualifies him for protection under the First Amendment. The interests of the contestants in a labor dispute are primarily economic, but it has long been settled that both the employee and the employer are protected by the First

Amendment when they express themselves on the merits of the dispute in order to influence its outcome. * * *[17]

As to the particular consumer's interest in the free flow of commercial information, that interest may be as keen, if not keener by far, than his interest in the day's most urgent political debate.[b] Appellees' case in this respect is a convincing one. Those whom the suppression of prescription drug price information hits the hardest are the poor, the sick, and particularly the aged. A disproportionate amount of their income tends to be spent on prescription drugs; yet they are the least able to learn, by shopping from pharmacist to pharmacist, where their scarce dollars are best spent. When drug prices vary as strikingly as they do, information as to who is charging what becomes more than a convenience. It could mean the alleviation of physical pain or the enjoyment of basic necessities.

Generalizing, society also may have a strong interest in the free flow of commercial information. Even an individual advertisement, though entirely "commercial," may be of general public interest. The facts of decided cases furnish illustrations: advertisements stating that referral services for legal abortions are available, *Bigelow;* that a manufacturer of artificial furs promotes his product as an alternative to the extinction by his competitors of fur-bearing mammals, see *Fur Information & Fashion Council, Inc. v. E.F. Timme & Son,* 364 F.Supp. 16 (S.D.N.Y.1973); and that a domestic producer advertises his product as an alternative to imports that tend to deprive American residents of their jobs, cf. *Chicago Joint Board v. Chicago Tribune Co.,* 435 F.2d 470 (C.A.7 1970), cert. denied, 402 U.S. 973 (1971). Obviously, not all commercial messages contain the same or even a very great public interest element. There are few to which such an element, however, could not be added. Our pharmacist, for example, could cast himself as a commentator on store-to-store disparities in drug prices, giving his own and those of a competitor as proof. We see little point in requiring him to do so, and little difference if he does not.

---

17. The speech of labor disputants, of course, is subject to a number of restrictions. The Court stated in *NLRB v. Gissel Packing Co.,* 395 U.S., at 618 (1969), for example, that an employer's threats of retaliation for the labor actions of his employees are "without the protection of the First Amendment." The constitutionality of restrictions upon speech in the special context of labor disputes is not before us here. We express no views on that complex subject, and advert to cases in the labor field only to note that in some circumstances speech of an entirely private and economic character enjoys the protection of the First Amendment.

[For the contention that labor speech receives less protection than commercial speech, see James Pope, *The Three–Systems Ladder of First Amendment Values: Two Rungs and a Black Hole,* 11 Hast.Con.L.Q. 189 (1984)].

b. "After all. As the National Enquirer likes to observe, 'Inquiring Minds Want to Know.' They 'want to know' about the kind of creme rinse Cindi Lauper uses as much as, perhaps even more than, they want to know whether the CIA may have helped bring down the government in South Vietnam." William Van Alstyne, *Remembering Melville Nimmer: Some Cautionary Notes on Commercial Speech,* 43 UCLA L.Rev. 1635 (1996); Consider Mark Tushnet, *Red, White, and Blue* 290 (1988): "The listener's interest in receiving information, a private interest, thus prevails over a more republican vision of politics, in which political discussion is, at least on the level of public norms, 'keener by far' than private interest."

Moreover, there is another consideration that suggests that no line between publicly "interesting" or "important" commercial advertising and the opposite kind could ever be drawn. Advertising, however tasteless and excessive it sometimes may seem, is nonetheless dissemination of information as to who is producing and selling what product, for what reason, and at what price. So long as we preserve a predominantly free enterprise economy, the allocation of our resources in large measure will be made through numerous private economic decisions. It is a matter of public interest that those decisions, in the aggregate, be intelligent and well informed. To this end, the free flow of commercial information is indispensable. And if it is indispensable to the proper allocation of resources in a free enterprise system, it is also indispensable to the formation of intelligent opinions as to how that system ought to be regulated or altered. Therefore, even if the First Amendment were thought to be primarily an instrument to enlighten public decision making in a democracy, we could not say that the free flow of information does not serve that goal.[c]

Arrayed against these substantial individual and societal interests are a number of justifications for the advertising ban. These have to do principally with maintaining a high degree of professionalism on the part of licensed pharmacists. [Price] advertising, it is argued, will place in jeopardy the pharmacist's expertise and, with it, the customer's health. It is claimed that the aggressive price competition that will result from unlimited advertising will make it impossible for the pharmacist to supply professional services in the compounding, handling, and dispensing of prescription drugs. Such services are time-consuming and expensive; if competitors who economize by eliminating them are permitted to advertise their resulting lower prices, the more painstaking and conscientious pharmacist will be forced either to follow suit or to go out of business. [It] is further claimed that advertising will lead people to shop for their prescription drugs among the various pharmacists who offer the lowest prices, and the loss of stable pharmacist-customer relationships will make individual [attention] impossible. Finally, it is argued that damage will be done to the professional image of the pharmacist. This image, that of a skilled and specialized craftsman, attracts talent to the profession and reinforces the better habits of those who are in [it].

---

c. Consider Steven H. Shiffrin, *Dissent, Injustice, and the Meaning of America* 40 (1999): "Suppose that the private allocation of resources is a part of public decision making in a democracy. [Government allocation of resources[, however,] is also part of public decision making in a democracy. That one predominates over the other (for many wealthy corporations, of course, free enterprise is the exception, not the rule) seems quite beside the point. Even if we suppose that commercial advertising is political, protection of 'political speech' in this context seems dramatically less important than in others if all that is at stake is the efficient allocation of resources. Moreover, since government frequently departs from the enterprise with constitutional blessing, perhaps the proper allocation of resources as seen by the market should not be privileged at all. [Why] should allocation of resources be a First Amendment worry?" Compare James Weinstein, *Fools, Knaves, and the Protection of Commercial Speech*, 41 Loy. U.L. L.Rev. 133 (2007) (core value of First Amendment is democratic self governance and this suggests that commercial speech is of lesser value); Robert Post, *The Constitutional Status of Commercial Speech*, 48 UCLA L.Rev. 1 (2000)(commercial speech provides information necessary for public decision making though it is not as important as "public discourse").

The strength of these proffered justifications is greatly undermined by the fact that high professional standards, to a substantial extent, are guaranteed by the close regulation to which pharmacists in Virginia are subject. [At] the same time, we cannot discount the Board's justifications entirely. [The Court regarded justifications of this type sufficient to sustain the advertising bans challenged on due process and equal protection grounds].[d]

The challenge now made, however, is based on the First Amendment. This casts the Board's justifications in a different light, for on close inspection it is seen that the State's protectiveness of its citizens rests in large measure on the advantages of their being kept in ignorance. The advertising ban does not directly affect professional standards one way or the other. It affects them only through the reactions it is assumed people will have to the free flow of drug price information. There is no claim that the advertising ban in any way prevents the cutting of corners by the pharmacist who is so inclined. That pharmacist is likely to cut corners in any event. The only effect the advertising ban has on him is to insulate him from price competition and to open the way for him to make a substantial, and perhaps even excessive, profit in addition to providing an inferior service. The more painstaking pharmacist is also protected but, again, it is a protection based in large part on public ignorance.

It appears to be feared that if the pharmacist who wishes to provide low cost, and assertedly low quality, services is permitted to advertise, he will be taken up on his offer by too many unwitting customers. They will choose the low-cost, low-quality service and drive the "professional" pharmacist out of business. [They] will go from one pharmacist to another, following the discount, and destroy the pharmacist-customer relationship. They will lose respect for the profession because it advertises. All this is not in their best interests, and all this can be avoided if they are not permitted to know who is charging what.

[A]n alternative to this highly paternalistic[e] approach [is] to assume that this information is not in itself harmful, that people will perceive their own best interests if only they are well enough informed, and that the best means to that end is to open the channels of communication rather than to close them. If they are truly open, nothing prevents the "professional" pharmacist from marketing his own assertedly superior product, and contrasting it with that of the low-cost, high-volume prescription drug retailer. But the choice among these alternative approaches is not ours to make or the Virginia General Assembly's. It is precisely this

---

d. The Court referred here to cases upholding bans on advertising prices for eyeglass frames and optometrist and dental services.

e. Consider Frederick Schauer, *The Role of the People in First Amendment Theory,* 74 Calif.L.Rev. 761, 788 (1986): "We ought to recognize that popular control over nonpolitical speech may in some circumstances be a bad idea and address directly just why this is so. Perhaps it is time to face up to the paternalism of the First Amendment, and maybe much of the rest of the Constitution as well." Is the Court's anti-paternalism paternalistic? For the contention that the Virginia price advertising ban was not paternalistic, see Daniel Lowenstein, *"Too Much Puff": Persuasion, Paternalism, and Commercial Speech,* 56 U.Cin.L.Rev. 1205, 1238 (1988).

kind of choice, between the dangers of suppressing information, and the dangers of its misuse if it is freely available, that the First Amendment makes for [us].

VI. In concluding that commercial speech, like other varieties, is protected, we of course do not hold that it can never be regulated in any way. Some forms of commercial speech regulation are surely permissible. We mention a few. [There] is no claim, for example, that the prohibition on prescription drug price advertising is a mere time, place, and manner restriction. We have often approved restrictions of that kind provided that they are justified without reference to the content of the regulated speech, that they serve a significant governmental interest, and that in so doing they leave open ample alternative channels for communication of the information. Whatever may be the proper bounds of time, place, and manner restrictions on commercial speech, they are plainly exceeded by this Virginia statute, which singles out speech of a particular content and seeks to prevent its dissemination completely.

Nor is there any claim that prescription drug price advertisements are forbidden because they are false or misleading in any way.[f] Untruthful speech, commercial or otherwise, has never been protected for its own sake. *Gertz.* Obviously much commercial speech is not provably false, or even wholly false, but only deceptive or misleading. We foresee no obstacle to a State's dealing effectively with this problem.[24] The First Amendment, as we construe it today, does not prohibit the State from insuring that the stream of commercial information flows cleanly as well as freely.

Also, there is no claim that the transactions proposed in the forbidden advertisements are themselves illegal in any way. Finally, the special problems of the electronic broadcast media are likewise not in this case.

What is at issue is whether a State may completely suppress the dissemination of concededly truthful information about entirely lawful activity, fearful of that information's effect upon its disseminators and its recipients. Reserving other questions,[25] we conclude that the answer to this one is in the [negative].

---

f. On the difficulties of determining whether commercial speech is false and misleading, see Rebecca Tushnet, *It Depends on What the Meaning of "False" Is,* 41 Loy. L.A.L. Rev. 227 (2007).

24. [C]ommon sense differences between speech that does "no more than propose a commercial transaction," *Pittsburgh Press* and other varieties [suggest] that a different degree of protection is necessary to insure that the flow of truthful and legitimate commercial information is unimpaired. The truth of commercial speech, for example, may be more easily verifiable by its disseminator than, let us say, news reporting or political commentary, in that ordinarily the advertiser seeks to disseminate information about a specific product or service that he himself provides and presumably knows more about than anyone else. Also, commercial speech may be more durable than other kinds. Since advertising is the sine qua non of commercial profits, there is little likelihood of its being chilled by proper regulation and foregone entirely.

Attributes such as these, the greater objectivity and hardiness of commercial speech, may make it less necessary to tolerate inaccurate statements for fear of silencing the speaker. They may also make it appropriate to require that a commercial message appear in such a form, or include such additional information, warnings and disclaimers, as are necessary to prevent its being deceptive. They may also make inapplicable the prohibition on prior restraints. Compare *New York Times v. United States* [Ch. 4, III infra] with *Donaldson v. Read Magazine,* 333 U.S. 178 (1948).

25. We stress that we have considered in this case the regulation of commercial advertising by pharmacists. Although we express no opinion as to other professions, the distinctions, historical

JUSTICE STEWART, concurring.[g]

[I] write separately to explain why I think today's decision does not preclude [governmental regulation of false or deceptive advertising]. The Court has on several occasions addressed the problems posed by false statements of fact in libel cases. [Factual] errors are inevitable in free debate, and the imposition of liability for [such errors] can "dampe[n] the vigor and limi[t] the variety of public debate" by inducing "self-censorship." [In] contrast to the press, which must often attempt to assemble the true facts from sketchy and sometimes conflicting sources under the pressure of publication deadlines, the commercial advertiser generally knows the product or service he seeks to sell and is in a position to verify the accuracy of his factual representations before he disseminates them. The advertiser's access to the truth about his product and its price substantially eliminates any danger that governmental regulation of false or misleading price or product advertising will chill accurate and nondeceptive commercial [expression].

Since the factual claims contained in commercial price or product advertisements relate to tangible goods or services, they may be tested empirically and corrected to reflect the truth without in any manner jeopardizing the free dissemination of thought. Indeed, the elimination of false and deceptive claims serves to promote the one facet of commercial price and product advertising that warrants First Amendment protection—its contribution to the flow of accurate and reliable information relevant to public and private decision making.

JUSTICE REHNQUIST, dissenting.

[Under] the Court's opinion the way will be open not only for dissemination of price information but for active promotion of prescription drugs, liquor, cigarettes and other products the use of which it has previously been thought desirable to discourage. Now, however, such promotion is protected by the First Amendment so long as it is not misleading or does not promote an illegal product or [enterprise].

The Court speaks of the consumer's interest in the free flow of commercial information. [This] should presumptively be the concern of the Virginia Legislature, which sits to balance [this] and other claims in the process of making laws such as the one here under attack. The Court speaks of the importance in a "predominantly free enterprise economy" of intelligent and well-informed decisions as to allocation of resources. While there is again much to be said for the Court's observation as a matter of desirable public policy, there is certainly nothing in the United States

---

and functional, between professions, may require consideration of quite different factors. Physicians and lawyers, for example, do not dispense standardized products; they render professional *services* of almost infinite variety and nature, with the consequent enhanced possibility for confusion and deception if they were to undertake certain kinds of advertising. [Should there be limits placed on the advertising of specific drugs to consumers? See David C. Vladek, *The Difficult Case of Direct-To-Consumer Drug Advertising*, 41 Loy. L.A.L. 259 (2007).]

g. Burger, C.J., separately concurring, stressed the reservation in fn. 25 of the opinion with respect to advertising by attorneys and physicians. Stevens, J., took no part.

Constitution which requires the Virginia Legislature to hew to the teachings of Adam Smith in its legislative decisions regulating the pharmacy profession. E.g., *Nebbia v. New York*, 291 U.S. 502 (1934); *Olsen v. Nebraska*, 313 U.S. 236 (1941).

[There] are undoubted difficulties with an effort to draw a bright line between "commercial speech" on the one hand and "protected speech" on the other, and the Court does better to face up to these difficulties than to attempt to hide them under labels. In this case, however, the Court has unfortunately substituted for the wavering line previously thought to exist between commercial speech and protected speech a no more satisfactory line of its own—that between "truthful" commercial speech, on the one hand, and that which is "false and misleading" on the other. The difficulty with this line is not that it wavers, but on the contrary that it is simply too Procrustean to take into account the congeries of factors which I believe could, quite consistently with the First and Fourteenth Amendments, properly influence a legislative decision with respect to commercial advertising.

[S]uch a line simply makes no allowance whatever for what appears to have been a considered legislative judgment in most States that while prescription drugs are a necessary and vital part of medical care and treatment, there are sufficient dangers attending their widespread use that they simply may not be promoted in the same manner as hair creams, deodorants, and toothpaste. The very real dangers that general advertising for such drugs might create in terms of encouraging, even though not sanctioning, illicit use of them by individuals for whom they have not been prescribed, or by generating patient pressure upon physicians to prescribe them are simply not dealt with in the Court's [opinion].

NOTES AND QUESTIONS

1. ***Economic due process.*** As compared to political decision making, is commercial advertising "neither more nor less significant than a host of other market activities that legislatures concededly may regulate"? Is there an "absence of any principled distinction between commercial soliciting and other aspects of economic activity"? Has economic due process been "resurrected, clothed in the ill-fitting garb of the First Amendment"? See Thomas Jackson & John Jeffries, *Commercial Speech: Economic Due Process and the First Amendment*, 65 Va.L.Rev. 1, 18 and 30 (1979). See also Frederick Schauer, *First Amendment Opportunism*, in Eternally Vigilant: Free Speech in the Modern Era 175, 180 (Lee C. Bollinger & Geoffrey R. Stone eds., 2002).

2. ***Paternalism.*** Why may government "be paternalistic regarding the purchase of goods but may not be paternalistic regarding information about those goods"? Larry Alexander, *Speech in the Local Marketplace: Implications of Virginia State Board of Pharmacy v. Virginia Citizens Consumer Council, Inc. for Local Regulatory Power,* 14 San Diego L.Rev. 357, 376 (1977). Should the "strong anti-paternalism feature of free speech doctrine [apply] only when the government regulation addresses us qua citizen, not in various other capacities, such as consumer." With respect to ordinary commercial speech,

should people be considered "dependent and vulnerable rather than independent and rational." Does this follow from democratic theory? See James Weinstein, *Speech Categorization and the Limits of First Amendment Formalism: Lessons From Nike v. Kasky*, 54 Case W. Res. L. Rev. 1091, 1105–1106 (2004). Or is it a part of democratic theory that "individual citizens can be trusted to make legally valid life-affecting choices on the basis of an open marketplace of ideas of information and opinion ." Martin H. Redish, *Tobacco Advertising and the First Amendment*, 81 Ia. L.Rev. 589, 604–05 (1996). Consider Steven H. Shiffrin, *Dissent, Injustice, and the Meanings of America* 143–44 n. 41 (1999): "This argument would seem to prove too much. If democratic theory assumes citizens can be trusted to make such choices in an open marketplace, one would imagine government would be foreclosed not only from fixing prices to discourage consumption, but also from regulating false and misleading advertising. In addition, it would be unclear why government should be permitted to make products illegal for paternalistic reasons— if citizens can truly be trusted. Assuming it were consistent with this version of democratic theory for government to ban products, it would be unclear why its paternalism could not extend to product advertising of legal products. It would not do, for example, to claim that products not made illegal have been certified as safe. To outlaw cigarettes, for example, might create black markets and enormous attendant enforcement problems. The failure to outlaw cigarettes need not suggest that government thinks of them as any less a public health problem than numerous other drugs that are currently outlawed. Whether individual citizens can be 'trusted,' seems to bear no relationship to the legal status of the product. In addition, one could argue that the notion of democracy makes no claims about the quality of *individual* decision making, but makes some relative claims about the quality of *public* decision making."

3. ***Image advertising.*** Does the rationale of *Virginia Pharmacy* extend to image or non-informational advertising? Should such advertising be protected? For relevant discussion, see Daniel Lowenstein, *"Too Much Puff": Persuasion, Paternalism, and Commercial Speech*, 56 U.Cin.L.Rev. 1205 (1988). For the cultural implications of image advertising, see Ronald Collins & David Skover, *Commerce and Communication*, 71 Tex.L.Rev. 697 (1993).[h] But see Sylvia Law, *Addiction, Autonomy, and Advertising*, 77 Iowa L.Rev. 909, 932 (1992): "A broad-sweeping principle denying constitutional protection to noninformational commercial speech reinforces a narrow vision of First Amendment values focusing on political participation and rationality. * * * Film, music, and novels are protected, not because they necessarily provide 'information' or facilitate participation in formal political processes, but because the First Amendment protects 'not only ideas capable of relatively precise, detached explication, but otherwise inexpressible emotions as well.' "

4. ***Deception.*** Footnote 24 suggests that *deceptive* commercial speech may be regulated in ways that would be barred if the speech were political. Sound distinction?[i]

---

h. For the negative implications of advertising (informational or non-informational) for democratic politics and culture, see C. Edwin Baker, *Advertising and a Democratic Press* (1994). See also Ronald Collins, *Dictating Content: How Advertising Pressure Can Corrupt A Free Press* (1992).

(a) *"Commonsense" differences between commercial speech and other speech.* (1) *Verifiability.* Consider Daniel Farber, *Commercial Speech and First Amendment Theory,* 74 Nw.U.L.Rev. 372, 385–86 (1979): "[C]ommercial speech is not necessarily more verifiable than other speech. There may well be uncertainty about some quality of a product, such as the health effect of eggs. On the other hand, political speech is often quite verifiable by the speaker. A political candidate knows the truth about his own past and his present intentions, yet misrepresentations on these subjects are immune from state regulation." (2) *Durability.* Consider Martin Redish, *The Value of Free Speech,* 130 U.Pa.L.Rev. 591, 633 (1982): "[I]t is also incorrect to distinguish commercial from political expression on the ground that the former is somehow hardier because of the inherent profit motive. It could just as easily be said that we need not fear that commercial magazines and newspapers will cease publication for fear of governmental regulation, because they are in business for profit. Of course, the proper response to this contention is that our concern is not *whether* they will publish, but *what* they will publish: fear of regulation might deter them from dealing with controversial subjects."[j] Does the case for treating commercial speech as a stepchild ultimately rest upon subjective disagreement with the message expressed, i.e., viewpoint discrimination? See Martin H. Redish, *Commercial Speech, First Amendment Intuitionism, and the Twilight Zone of Viewpoint Discrimination,* 41 Loy. L.A.L. Rev. 67 (2007).

(b) *Commercial speech and self-expression.* Is commercial speech distinguishable from political speech because it is unrelated to self-expression? Consider C. Edwin Baker, *Commercial Speech: A Problem in the Theory of Freedom,* 62 Iowa L.Rev. 1, 17 (1976): In commercial speech, the dissemination of the profit motive "breaks the connection between speech and any vision, or attitude, or value of the individual or group engaged in advocacy. Thus the content and form of commercial speech cannot be attributed to individual value allegiances." See generally C. Edwin Baker, *Human Liberty and Freedom of Speech* chs. 3, 9, 10 (1989). For criticism, see, e.g., Pierre Schlag, *An Attack on Categorical Approaches to Freedom of Speech,* 30 UCLA L.Rev. 671, 710–21 (1983); Steven Shiffrin, *The First Amendment and Economic Regulation: Away From A General Theory of the First Amendment,* 78 Nw.U.L.Rev. 1212 (1983). Even if commercial speech is divorced from self expression (or dignity), should it merit substantial protection, nonetheless. See Aleita Estreicher, *Securities Regulation and the First Amendment,* 24 Ga.L.Rev. 223 (1990); Burt Neuborne, *The First Amendment and Government Regulation of Capital Markets,* 55 Brook.L.Rev. 5 (1989).

(c) *Contract approach to commercial speech.* Is commercial advertising distinguishable from other forms of speech because of the state interest in regulating contracts? Consider Farber, supra, at 389: "The unique aspect of commercial speech is that it is a prelude to, and therefore becomes integrated

---

i. On the market failures associated with commercial speech, see Tamara R. Piety, *Market Failure in the Market Place of Ideas,* 41 Loy. L.A.L. Rev. 181 (2007).

j. Ronald Cass, *Commercial Speech, Constitutionalism, Collective Choice,* 56 U.Cin.L.Rev. 1317, 1368–73 (1988); Bruce Johnson, *First Amendment Commercial Speech Protections: A Practitioner's Guide,* 41 Loy. L.A.L. Rev. 297, 302 (2007).

into, a contract, the essence of which is the presence of a promise. Because a promise is an undertaking to ensure that a certain state of affairs takes place, promises obviously have a closer connection with conduct than with self-expression. Second, [in] a fundamentally market economy, the government understandably is given particular deference in its enforcement of contractual expectations. Indeed, the Constitution itself gives special protection to contractual expectations in the contract clause. Finally, [the] technicalities of contract law, with its doctrines of privity, consideration, and the like, should not be blindly translated into First Amendment jurisprudence. The basic doctrines of contract law, however, provide a helpful guide in considering commercial speech problems." For discussion, see Larry Alexander & Daniel Farber, *Commercial Speech and First Amendment Theory: A Critical Exchange,* 75 Nw.U.L.Rev. 307 (1980).

(d) ***Error costs.*** Is commercial speech distinguishable because the risks of error are less? Consider Cass, supra at 1360: "[T]he inquiry can be framed as asking four questions: (1) will officials err less systematically or less often in regulation of commercial speech than in regulation of other speech?; (2) will officials err less systematically or less often in regulation of commerce than in regulation of speech?; (3) will the consequences of errors in regulation of one sort of activity generally be less significant than the consequences of errors in the other?; and (4) will the process costs associated with error correction be lower in respect of one activity than the other?" On the risks of error, see generally Cass, supra; Fred McChesney, *A Positive Regulatory Theory of the First Amendment,* 20 Conn.L.Rev. 335 (1988). See also Ronald Coase, *Advertising and Free Speech,* 6 J.Legal Stud. 1 (1977); Richard Posner, *Free Speech in an Economic Perspective,* 20 Suffolk U.L.Rev. 1 (1986); Thomas Scanlon, *Freedom of Expression and Categories of Expression,* 40 U.Pitt.L.Rev. 519 (1979).

(e) ***Limits on regulation of deceptive advertising.*** Bates v. State Bar, 433 U.S. 350 (1977), struck down an Arizona Supreme Court rule against a lawyer "publicizing himself" through advertising. It rejected the claim that attorney price advertising was inherently misleading, but left open the "peculiar problems" associated with advertising claims regarding the quality of legal services.[k] Has the Court made it difficult for states and communities to deal with a "considerable range of highly debatable conduct by which some individuals seek to profit from the inattentiveness or lack of sophistication of consumers of goods and services"? Paul D. Carrington, *Our Imperial First Amendment,* 34 U. Rich. L. Rev. 1167, 1188 (2001). Should the Court have deferred to the judgment of the State Bar of Arizona? If not, should it defer to the SEC when it regulates the advertising of securities? The FTC when it

---

k. *Zauderer v. Office of Disciplinary Counsel,* Ch. 9, I infra, held that a state may not discipline attorneys who solicit legal business through newspaper advertisements containing "truthful and nondeceptive information and advice regarding the legal rights of potential clients" or for the advertising use of "accurate and nondeceptive" illustrations. Zauderer had placed illustrated ads in 36 Ohio newspapers publicizing his availability to represent women who had suffered injuries from use of a contraceptive device known as the Dalkon Shield Intrauterine Device. In the ad Zauderer stated that he had represented other women in Dalkon Shield litigation. The Court observed that accurate statements of fact cannot be proscribed "merely because it is possible that some readers will infer that he has some expertise in those areas." But it continued to "leave open the possibility that States may prevent attorneys from making non-verifiable claims regarding the quality of their services. *Bates.*"

regulates automobile advertising? The Virginia Board of Pharmacy when it regulates quality advertising by pharmacists? For deferential treatment of a state ban on the use of trade names by optometrists, see *Friedman v. Rogers,* 440 U.S. 1 (1979).

5. ***Truth and commercial advertising.*** Should Mercedes Benz be able to truthfully advertise that Elton John drives its car without getting John's permission? Should the state be able to prevent homeowners from posting "for sale" signs in order to prevent panic selling in order to maintain an integrated neighborhood? See *Linmark Associates v. Willingboro,* 431 U.S. 85 (1977). May a state regulate the content of contraceptive advertising in order to minimize its offensive character? Cf. *Carey v. Population Services Int'l.,* 431 U.S. 678 (1977) (total ban on contraceptive advertising unconstitutional).[1]

———

OHRALIK v. OHIO STATE BAR ASS'N, 436 U.S. 447 (1978), upheld the indefinite suspension of an attorney for violating the anti-solicitation provisions of the Ohio Code of Professional Responsibility. Those provisions generally do not allow lawyers to recommend themselves to anyone who has not sought "their advice regarding employment of a lawyer." Albert Ohralik had approached two young accident victims to solicit employment—Carol McClintock in a hospital room where she lay in traction and Wanda Lou Holbert on the day she came home from the hospital. He employed a concealed tape recorder with Holbert, apparently to insure he would have evidence of her assent to his representation. The next day, when Holbert's mother informed Ohralik that she and her daughter did not want to have appellant represent them, he insisted that the daughter had entered into a binding agreement. McClintock also discharged Ohralik, and Ohralik sued her for breach of contract. The Court ruled, per POWELL, J., that a state may forbid in-person solicitation of clients by lawyers for pecuniary gain:

"Expression concerning purely commercial transactions has come within the ambit of the Amendment's protection only recently. In rejecting the notion that such speech is wholly outside the protection of the First Amendment, *Virginia Pharmacy,* we were careful not to hold that it is wholly undifferentiable from other forms of speech.

"We have not discarded the common sense distinction between speech proposing a commercial transaction, which occurs in an area traditionally

---

1. See Eugene Volokh, *Freedom of Speech and the Right of Publicity,* 40 Houston L.Rev. 903 (2003); Melissa B. Jacoby & Diane Leenheer Zimmerman, *Foreclosing On Fame: Exploring The Uncharted Boundaries Of The Right Of Publicity,* 77 N.Y.U. L. Rev. 1322 (2002); Michael Madow, *Private Ownership of Public Image: Popular Culture and Publicity Rights,* 81 Cal. L. Rev. 201–202 (1993). See also Alice Haemmerli, *Whose Who? The Case for a Kantian Right of Publicity,* 49 Duke L.J. 383 (1999); Diane Leenheer Zimmerman, *Who Put the Right in the Right of Publicity?,* 9 DePaul–LCA J. Art & Ent. L. 35, 43 (1998); Wesley Liebeler, *A Property Rights Approach to Judicial Decision Making,* 4 Cato J. 783, 802–03 (1985); Shiffrin, supra note 3, at 1257–58 n. 275; Peter Felcher & Edward Rubin, *Privacy, Publicity, and the Portrayal of Real People by the Media,* 88 Yale L.J. 1577 (1979); James Treece, *Commercial Exploitation of Names, Likenesses, and Personal Histories,* 51 Tex.L.Rev. 637 (1973).

subject to government regulation, and other varieties of speech. To require a parity of constitutional protection for commercial and noncommercial speech alike could invite dilution, simply by a leveling process, of the force of the Amendment's guarantee with respect to the latter kind of speech. Rather than subject the First Amendment to such a devitalization, we instead have afforded commercial speech a limited measure of protection, commensurate with its subordinate position in the scale of First Amendment values, while allowing modes of regulation that might be impermissible in the realm of noncommercial expression.

"Moreover, 'it has never been deemed an abridgment of freedom of speech or press to make a course of conduct illegal merely because the conduct was in part initiated, evidenced, or carried out by means of language, either spoken, written, or printed.' *Giboney v. Empire Storage & Ice Co.,* 336 U.S. 490, 502 (1949). Numerous examples could be cited of communications that are regulated without offending the First Amendment, such as the exchange of information about securities, *SEC v. Texas Gulf Sulphur Co.,* 401 F.2d 833 (C.A.2 1968), cert. denied, 394 U.S. 976 (1969), corporate proxy statements, *Mills v. Electric Auto–Lite Co.,* 396 U.S. 375 (1970), the exchange of price and production information among competitors, *American Column & Lumber Co. v. United States,* 257 U.S. 377 (1921), and employers' threats of retaliation for the labor activities of employees, *NLRB v. Gissel Packing Co.,* 395 U.S. 575, 618 (1969). [These examples [illustrate] that the State does not lose its power to regulate commercial activity deemed harmful to the public whenever speech is a component of that activity. Neither *Virginia Pharmacy* nor *Bates* purported to cast doubt on the permissibility of these kinds of commercial regulation.

"In-person solicitation by a lawyer of remunerative employment is a business transaction in which speech is an essential but subordinate component. While this does not remove the speech from the protection of the First Amendment, as was held in *Bates* and *Virginia Pharmacy,* it lowers the level of appropriate judicial scrutiny. [A] lawyer's procurement of remunerative employment is a subject only marginally affected with First Amendment concerns. It falls within the State's proper sphere of economic and professional regulation. While entitled to some constitutional protection, appellant's conduct is subject to regulation in furtherance of important state [interests].

" 'The interest of the States in regulating lawyers is especially great since lawyers are essential to the primary function of administering justice and have historically been officers of the courts' [and] act 'as trusted agents of their clients and as assistants to the court in search of a just solution to disputes.'

"[The] substantive evils of solicitation have been stated over the years in sweeping terms: stirring up litigation, assertion of fraudulent claims, debasing the legal profession,[a] and potential harm to the solicited client in

---

a. Is regulation of speech debasing the legal profession legitimate? Consider Rodney Smolla, *Lawyer Advertising and the Dignity of the Profession,* 59 Ark. L.Rev. 437, 455 (2006): "The

the form of overreaching, overcharging, underrepresentation, and misrepresentation." In providing information about the availability and terms of proposed legal services "in-person solicitation serves much the same function as the advertisement at issue in *Bates*. But there are significant differences as well. Unlike a public advertisement, which simply provides information and leaves the recipient free to act upon it or not, in-person solicitation may exert pressure and often demands an immediate response, without providing an opportunity for comparison or reflection. The aim and effect of in-person solicitation may be to provide a one-sided presentation and to encourage speedy and perhaps uninformed decision making; there is no opportunity for intervention or counter-education by agencies of the Bar, supervisory authorities, or persons close to the solicited individual. The admonition that 'the fitting remedy for evil counsels is good ones' is of little value when the circumstances provide no opportunity for any remedy at all. In-person solicitation is as likely as not to discourage persons needing counsel from engaging in a critical comparison of the 'availability, nature, and prices' of legal services; it actually may disserve the individual and societal interest, identified in *Bates,* in facilitating 'informed and reliable decision making.'

"[Appellant's argument that none of the evils of solicitation was found in his case] misconceives the nature of the State's interest. The rules prohibiting solicitation are prophylactic measures whose objective is the prevention of harm before it occurs.[b] The rules were applied in this case to discipline a lawyer for soliciting employment for pecuniary gain under circumstances likely to result in the adverse consequences the State seeks to avert. In such a situation, which is inherently conducive to overreaching and other forms of misconduct, the State has a strong interest in adopting and enforcing rules of conduct designed to protect the public from harmful solicitation by lawyers whom it has [licensed].

"The efficacy of the State's effort to prevent such harm to prospective clients would be substantially diminished if, having proved a solicitation in circumstances like those of this case, the State were required in addition to prove actual injury. Unlike the advertising in *Bates,* in-person solicitation is not visible or otherwise open to public scrutiny. Often there is no witness other than the lawyer and the lay person whom he has solicited, rendering it difficult or impossible to obtain reliable proof of what actually took place. This would be especially true if the lay person were so distressed at the time of the solicitation that he or she could not recall specific details at a later date. If appellant's view were sustained, in-person solicitation would be virtually immune to effective oversight and regulation by the State or by the legal profession, in contravention of the State's strong interest in regulating members of the Bar in an effective,

---

regulation of lawyer advertising on [the] ground that it is demeaning to the profession raises profound First Amendment questions. The central core of modern First Amendment jurisprudence is that the government may never stifle a message merely because it finds the content of the message disagreeable or offensive."

b. But see Fred McChesney, *Commercial Speech in the Professions,* 134 U.Pa.L.Rev. 45 (1985) (anti-solicitation provisions may be motivated by anti-competitive considerations).

objective, and self-enforcing manner. It therefore is not unreasonable, or violative of the Constitution, for a State to respond with what in effect is a prophylactic rule.''[c]

NOTES AND QUESTIONS

1. *Companion case.* IN RE PRIMUS, 436 U.S. 412 (1978), per POWELL, J., held that a state could not constitutionally discipline an ACLU "cooperating lawyer" who, after advising a gathering of allegedly illegally sterilized women of their rights, initiated further contact with one of the women by writing her a letter informing her of the ACLU's willingness to provide free legal representation for women in her situation and of the organization's desire to file a lawsuit on her behalf. "South Carolina's action in punishing appellant for soliciting a prospective litigant by mail, on behalf of ACLU, must withstand the 'exacting scrutiny applicable to limitations on core First Amendment rights.' [Where] political expression or association is at issue, this Court has not tolerated the degree of imprecision that often characterizes government regulation of the conduct of commercial affairs. The approach we adopt today in *Ohralik* that the State may proscribe in-person solicitation for pecuniary gain under circumstances likely to result in adverse consequences, cannot be applied to appellant's activity on behalf of the ACLU. Although a showing of potential danger may suffice in the former context, appellant may not be disciplined unless her activity in fact involved the type of misconduct at which South Carolina's broad prohibition is said to be directed. The record does not support appellee's contention that undue influence, overreaching, misrepresentation, or invasion of privacy actually occurred in this case."

2. *Related cases.* Edenfield v. Fane, 507 U.S. 761 (1993) held that direct personal solicitation of prospective business clients by Certified Public Accountants is protected under the First Amendment,[d] but *Florida Bar v. Went For It, Inc.,* 515 U.S. 618 (1995) held that targeted direct-mail solicitations by personal injury attorneys to victims and their relatives for thirty days following an accident were not protected under the First Amendment. See also *Brentwood Academy v. Tennessee Secondary School Athletic Ass'n,* 531 U.S. 288 (2001) (five justices maintain that *Ohralik* does not apply to rules designed to protect children from recruitment solicitations by high school coaches).

3. *A hierarchy of protected speech.* Consider Steven Shiffrin, note 3 supra, at 1218–21 (1983): In *Virginia Pharmacy,* "the Court never admitted that commercial speech was less valuable than political speech. The 'commonsense differences' had nothing to do with value. [Although] Justice Blackmun labored to defend the asserted equal relationship between commercial speech and political speech for the *Virginia Pharmacy* majority, Justice Powell in *Ohralik* was content to lead the Court to an opposite position without

---

    c. Marshall and Rehnquist, JJ., each separately concurred in the judgment. Brennan, J., did not participate.

    d. Blackmun, J., concurred; O'Connor, J., dissented. Compare Ibanez v. Florida Dep't of Business and Professional Regulation, 512 U.S. 136 (1994) (attorney's references in advertising, business cards and stationery to her credentials as a CPA and a Certified Financial Planner are not deceptive or misleading and are protected commercial speech); Accord, Peel v. Attorney Registration and Disciplinary Comm'n, 496 U.S. 91 (1990) (reference on letterhead to prestigious certification is protected speech).

explanation. In so doing, Justice Powell steered the Court to accept a hierarchy of protected speech for the first time, despite his own stated opposition [in *Young*] to creating any such hierarchy." Does the concern that the protection of non-commercial speech would be subject to dilution if it were placed on a par with commercial speech presuppose an unexplained difference between the two types of speech? See id. at 1221 n. 59. For discussion of the dilution argument, see William Marshall, *The Dilution of the First Amendment and the Equality of Ideas*, 38 Case W.Res.L.Rev. 566 (1988).

4. ***Muddying the hierarchy.*** Cincinnati permitted 1,500–2,000 news racks throughout the city for publications not classified as commercial speech, but refused to allow an additional 62 news racks that contained two publications classified as commercial speech. CINCINNATI v. DISCOVERY NETWORK, 507 U.S. 410 (1993), per STEVENS, J., held that this discrimination violated the First Amendment: "The major premise supporting the city's argument is the proposition that commercial speech has only a low value. Based on that premise, the city contends that the fact that assertedly more valuable publications are allowed to use news racks does not undermine its judgment that its esthetic and safety interests are stronger than the interest in allowing commercial speakers to have similar access to the reading public. [In] our view, the city's argument attaches more importance to the distinction between commercial and non-commercial speech than our cases warrant and seriously underestimates the value of commercial speech.[20]"e

5. ***The reach of Discovery Network.*** (a) In MARTIN v. STRUTHERS, 319 U.S. 141 (1943), a city forbade knocking on the door or ringing the doorbell of a resident in order to deliver handbills (in an industrial community where many worked night shifts and slept during the day). In striking down the ordinance, the Court, per BLACK, J., pointed out that the city's objectives could be achieved by means of a law making it an offense for any person to ring the doorbell of a householder who has "appropriately indicated that he is unwilling to be disturbed. This or any similar regulation leaves the decision as to whether distributors of literature may lawfully call at a home where it belongs—with the homeowner himself." By contrast, *Breard v. Alexandria*, 341 U.S. 622 (1951) upheld an ordinance forbidding the practice of going door

---

20. Metromedia, Inc. v. San Diego, 453 U.S. 490 (1981), upon which the city heavily relies, is not to the contrary. In that case, a plurality of the Court found as a permissible restriction on commercial speech a city ordinance that, for the most part, banned outdoor "offsite" advertising billboards, but permitted "onsite" advertising signs identifying the owner of the premises and the goods sold or manufactured on the site. Unlike this case, which involves discrimination between commercial and noncommercial speech, the "offsite-onsite" distinction involved disparate treatment of two types of commercial speech. Only the onsite signs served both the commercial and public interest in guiding potential visitors to their intended destinations; moreover, the plurality concluded that a "city may believe that offsite advertising, with its periodically changing content, presents a more acute problem than does onsite advertising." Neither of these bases has any application to the disparate treatment of news racks in this case.

The Chief Justice is correct that seven Justices in the Metromedia case were of the view that San Diego could completely ban offsite commercial billboards for reasons unrelated to the content of those billboards. Those seven Justices did not say, however, that San Diego could distinguish between commercial and noncommercial offsite billboards that cause the same esthetic and safety concerns. That question was not presented in Metromedia, for the regulation at issue in that case did not draw a distinction between commercial and noncommercial offsite billboards; with a few exceptions, it essentially banned all offsite billboards.

e. Rehnquist, C.J., joined by White & Thomas, JJ., dissented.

to door to solicit orders for the sale of goods. The commercial element was said to distinguish *Martin.* Does *Breard* survive *Virginia Pharmacy?* Does (should) *Discovery Network* settle the issue? What if, as in *Breard,* the solicitor is selling subscriptions for magazines?

(b) Compare *Schneider,* Ch. 6, I, A infra (prohibition against leaflet distribution on streets unconstitutional) with *Valentine,* Ch. 3, II supra (prohibition against distribution of commercial leaflets upheld). Does (should) the *holding* of *Valentine* survive *Virginia Pharmacy?* Does *Discovery Network* settle the issue?

(c) *Linmark* held it unconstitutional for a locality to prohibit "For Sale" signs on residential property. Similarly, the Court has held it unconstitutional to permit property owners to display "For Sale" signs while prohibiting most other signs including those with political, religious or personal messages. *Ladue v. Gilleo,* 512 U.S. 43 (1994). After *Linmark, Ladue,* and *Discovery Network,* would it be unconstitutional to prohibit signs on residential property that advertise goods and services sold elsewhere?

———

In CENTRAL HUDSON GAS & ELEC. CORP. v. PUBLIC SERV. COMM'N, 447 U.S. 557 (1980), the Court, per POWELL, J., characterized the prior commercial speech cases as embracing a special test: "In commercial speech cases, then, a four-part analysis has developed. At the outset, we must determine whether the expression is protected by the First Amendment. For commercial speech to come within that provision, it at least must concern lawful activity and not be misleading. Next, we ask whether the asserted governmental interest is substantial. If both inquiries yield positive answers, we must determine whether the regulation directly advances the governmental interest asserted, and whether it is not more extensive than is necessary to serve that interest."

LORILLARD TOBACCO CO. v. REILLY

533 U.S. 525, 121 S.Ct. 2404, 150 L.Ed.2d 532 (2001).

JUSTICE O'CONNOR delivered the opinion of the Court.

In January 1999, the Attorney General of Massachusetts promulgated comprehensive regulations governing the advertising and sale of cigarettes, smokeless tobacco, and cigars. Petitioners, a group of cigarette, smokeless tobacco, and cigar manufacturers and retailers, filed suit in Federal District Court claiming that the regulations violate federal law and the United States Constitution.

I. [The Court observed that the purpose of the restrictions was "to eliminate deception and unfairness in the way cigarettes and smokeless tobacco products are marketed, sold and distributed in Massachusetts in order to address the incidence of cigarette smoking and smokeless tobacco use by children under legal age [and] to prevent access to such products by underage consumers. The similar purpose of the cigar regulations is 'to eliminate [the] false perception that cigars are a safe alternative to cigarettes [and] to prevent access to such products by underage consumers.'" Among other things the restrictions prohibited outdoor advertising, "including advertising in enclosed stadiums and advertising from within a retail establishment that is directed toward or visible from the outside of the establishment, in any location that is within a 1,000 foot radius of any public playground, playground area in a public park, elementary school or secondary school."].[a]

II. [The Court concluded that the Federal Cigarette Labeling and Advertising Act of 1965 as amended, prevented states and localities from regulating the location of cigarette advertising.]

III. By its terms, the FCLAA's pre-emption provision only applies to cigarettes. Accordingly, we must evaluate the smokeless tobacco and cigar petitioners' First Amendment challenges to the State's outdoor and point-of-sale advertising regulations. The cigarette petitioners did not raise a pre-emption challenge to the sales practices regulations. Thus, we must analyze the cigarette as well as the smokeless tobacco and cigar petitioners' claim that certain sales practices regulations for tobacco products violate the First Amendment.

A. [Petitioners] urge us to reject the *Central Hudson* analysis and apply strict scrutiny. [S]everal Members of the Court have expressed doubts about the *Central Hudson* analysis and whether it should apply in particular cases. See, e.g., *44 Liquormart, Inc. v. Rhode Island*, 517 U.S. 484, 501 (1996) (joint opinion of Stevens, Kennedy, and Ginsburg, JJ.)(Scalia, J. concurring in part and concurring in judgment)(Thomas, J., concurring in part and concurring in judgment). [But] we see "no need to break new ground. *Central Hudson*, as applied in our more recent commercial speech cases, provides an adequate basis for decision."

Only the last two steps of *Central Hudson*'s four-part analysis are at issue here. The Attorney General has assumed for purposes of summary judgment that petitioners' speech is entitled to First Amendment protection. With respect to the second step, none of the petitioners contests the importance of the State's interest in preventing the use of tobacco products by minors.

The third step of *Central Hudson* [requires] that "the speech restriction directly and materially advanc[e] the asserted governmental interest. 'This burden is not satisfied by mere speculation or conjecture; rather, a governmental body seeking to sustain a restriction on commercial speech must demonstrate that the harms it recites are real and that its restriction will in fact alleviate them to a material degree.'" We do not, however,

---

a. The regulations also banned such advertising at the point of sale if they were within five feet of the floor of the retail establishment and within a 1000 feet radius of the places identified in the outdoor advertising restrictions. O'Connor, J., found that these regulations violated the third and fourth prongs of *Central Hudson*. Stevens, J., joined by Ginsburg and Breyer, JJ., dissenting, found these restrictions to be "little more than an adjunct" to rules prohibiting the placement of the products within the reach of customers and of only slight impact on the ability of adults to purchase "a poisonous product and may save some children from taking the first step on the road to addiction."

require that "empirical data [come] accompanied by a surfeit of background information. [W]e have permitted litigants to justify speech restrictions by reference to studies and anecdotes pertaining to different locales altogether, or even, in a case applying strict scrutiny, to justify restrictions based solely on history, consensus, and 'simple common sense.'"

The last step of the *Central Hudson* analysis "complements" the third step, "asking whether the speech restriction is not more extensive than necessary to serve the interests that support it." We have made it clear that "the least restrictive means" is not the standard; instead, the case law requires a reasonable "'fit between the legislature's ends and the means chosen to accomplish those ends, [a] means narrowly tailored to achieve the desired objective.'" * * *

B. [1.] The smokeless tobacco and cigar petitioners [maintain] that although the Attorney General may have identified a problem with underage cigarette smoking, he has not identified an equally severe problem with respect to underage use of smokeless tobacco or cigars. The smokeless tobacco petitioner emphasizes the "lack of parity" between cigarettes and smokeless tobacco. The cigar petitioners catalogue a list of differences between cigars and other tobacco products, including the characteristics of the products and marketing strategies. The petitioners finally contend that the Attorney General cannot prove that advertising has a causal link to tobacco use such that limiting advertising will materially alleviate any problem of underage use of their products.

In previous cases, we have acknowledged the theory that product advertising stimulates demand for products, while suppressed advertising may have the opposite effect. *United States v. Edge Broadcasting Co.*, 509 U.S. 418, 434 (1993). The Attorney General cites numerous studies to support this theory in the case of tobacco products [, providing] ample documentation of the problem with underage use of smokeless tobacco and cigars. In addition, we disagree with petitioners' claim that there is no evidence that preventing targeted campaigns and limiting youth exposure to advertising will decrease underage use of smokeless tobacco and cigars. On this record and in the posture of summary judgment, we are unable to conclude that the Attorney General's decision to regulate advertising of smokeless tobacco and cigars in an effort to combat the use of tobacco products by minors was based on mere "speculation [and] conjecture."

2. Whatever the strength of the Attorney General's evidence to justify the outdoor advertising regulations, however, we conclude that the regulations do not satisfy the fourth step of the *Central Hudson* analysis. * * *

The outdoor advertising regulations prohibit any smokeless tobacco or cigar advertising within 1,000 feet of schools or playgrounds. In the District Court, petitioners maintained that this prohibition would prevent advertising in 87% to 91% of Boston, Worcester, and Springfield. The 87% to 91% figure appears to include not only the effect of the regulations, but also the limitations imposed by other generally applicable zoning restrictions. The Attorney General disputed petitioners' figures but "concede[d] that the reach of the regulations is substantial." * * *

In some geographical areas, these regulations would constitute nearly a complete ban on the communication of truthful information about smokeless tobacco and cigars to adult consumers. The breadth and scope of the regulations, and the process by which the Attorney General adopted the regulations, do not demonstrate a careful calculation of the speech interests involved. * * *

The Attorney General apparently selected the 1,000–foot distance based on the FDA's decision to impose an identical 1,000–foot restriction when it attempted to regulate cigarette and smokeless tobacco advertising. But [the] degree to which speech is suppressed—or alternative avenues for speech remain available—under a particular regulatory scheme tends to be case specific [for] although a State or locality may have common interests and concerns about underage smoking and the effects of tobacco advertisements, the impact of a restriction on speech will undoubtedly vary from place to place. The FDA's regulations would have had widely disparate effects nationwide. Even in Massachusetts, the effect of the Attorney General's speech regulations will vary based on whether a locale is rural, suburban, or urban. The uniformly broad sweep of the geographical limitation demonstrates a lack of tailoring. * * *

The State's interest in preventing underage tobacco use is substantial, and even compelling, but it is no less true that the sale and use of tobacco products by adults is a legal activity. We must consider that tobacco retailers and manufacturers have an interest in conveying truthful information about their products to adults, and adults have a corresponding interest in receiving truthful information about tobacco products. [In] some instances, Massachusetts' outdoor advertising regulations would impose particularly onerous burdens on speech. For example, we disagree with the Court of Appeals' conclusion that because cigar manufacturers and retailers conduct a limited amount of advertising in comparison to other tobacco products, "the relative lack of cigar advertising also means that the burden imposed on cigar advertisers is correspondingly small." If some retailers have relatively small advertising budgets, and use few avenues of communication, then the Attorney General's outdoor advertising regulations potentially place a greater, not lesser, burden on those retailers' speech. * * *

JUSTICE KENNEDY, with whom JUSTICE SCALIA joins, concurring in part and concurring in the judgment.

The obvious overbreadth of the outdoor advertising restrictions suffices to invalidate them under the fourth part of the test in *Central Hudson*. [My] continuing concerns that the test gives insufficient protection to truthful, nonmisleading commercial speech require me to refrain from expressing agreement with the Court's application of the third part of *Central Hudson*. With the exception of Part III–B–1, then, I join the opinion of the Court.

JUSTICE THOMAS, concurring in part and concurring in the judgment

I join the opinion of the Court (with the exception of Part III–B–1). * * *

I have observed previously that there is no "philosophical or historical basis for asserting that 'commercial' speech is of 'lower value' than 'noncommercial' speech." Indeed, I doubt whether it is even possible to draw a coherent distinction between commercial and noncommercial speech.[2]

It should be clear that if these regulations targeted anything other than advertising for commercial products—if, for example, they were directed at billboards promoting political candidates—all would agree that the restrictions should be subjected to strict scrutiny. In my view, an asserted government interest in keeping people ignorant by suppressing expression "is per se illegitimate and can no more justify regulation of 'commercial' speech than it can justify regulation of 'noncommercial' speech." That is essentially the interest asserted here. * * *

[R]espondents [argue] that the regulations target deceptive and misleading speech. Second, they argue that the regulations restrict speech that promotes an illegal transaction—i.e., the sale of tobacco to minors. Neither theory is properly before the Court. For purposes of summary judgment, respondents were willing to assume "that the tobacco advertisements at issue here are truthful, nonmisleading speech about a lawful activity." [E]ven if we were to entertain these arguments, neither is persuasive. Respondents suggest that tobacco advertising is misleading because "its youthful imagery [and] sheer ubiquity" leads children to believe "that tobacco use is desirable and pervasive." This justification is belied, however, by the sweeping overinclusivity of the regulations. Massachusetts has done nothing to target its prohibition to advertisements appealing to "excitement, glamour, and independence"; the ban applies with equal force to appeals to torpor, homeliness, and servility. It has not focused on "youthful imagery"; smokers depicted on the sides of buildings may no more play shuffleboard than they may ride skateboards. * * *

[Viewed] as an effort to proscribe solicitation to unlawful conduct, these regulations clearly fail the *Brandenburg* test. [Even] if Massachusetts could prohibit advertisements reading, "Hey kids, buy cigarettes here," these regulations sweep much more broadly than that. They cover "[any] statement or representation [the] purpose or effect of which is to promote the use or sale" of tobacco products, whether or not the statement is directly or indirectly addressed to minors. [It] is difficult to see

---

2. Tobacco advertising provides a good illustration. The sale of tobacco products is the subject of considerable political controversy, and not surprisingly, some tobacco advertisements both promote a product and take a stand in this political debate. A recent cigarette advertisement, for example, displayed a brand logo next to text reading, "Why do politicians smoke cigars while taxing cigarettes?"

any stopping point to a rule that would allow a State to prohibit all speech in favor of an activity in which it is illegal for minors to engage. Presumably, the State could ban car advertisements in an effort to enforce its restrictions on underage driving. It could regulate advertisements urging people to vote, because children are not permitted to vote. * * *[b]

Underlying many of the arguments of respondents and their amici is the idea that tobacco is in some sense sui generis [so] that application of normal First Amendment principles should be suspended. [Nevertheless], it seems appropriate to point out that to uphold the Massachusetts tobacco regulations would be to accept a line of reasoning that would permit restrictions on advertising for a host of other products.

Tobacco use is, we are told, "the single leading cause of preventable death in the United States." The second largest contributor to mortality rates in the United States is obesity. [A] significant factor has been the increased availability of large quantities of high-calorie, high-fat foods. Such foods, of course, have been aggressively marketed and promoted by fast food companies. Respondents say that tobacco companies are covertly targeting children in their advertising. Fast food companies do so openly. Moreover, there is considerable evidence that they have been successful in changing children's eating behavior. * * *

To take another example, the third largest cause of preventable deaths in the United States is alcohol. [Although] every State prohibits the sale of alcohol to those under age 21, much alcohol advertising is viewed by children. Not surprisingly, there is considerable evidence that exposure to alcohol advertising is associated with underage drinking. * * *

Respondents have identified no principle of law or logic that would preclude the imposition of restrictions on fast food and alcohol advertising similar to those they seek to impose on tobacco advertising. In effect, they seek a "vice" exception to the First Amendment. No such exception exists. If it did, it would have almost no limit, for "any product that poses some threat to public health or public morals might reasonably be characterized by a state legislature as relating to 'vice activity.'"

No legislature has ever sought to restrict speech about an activity it regarded as harmless and inoffensive. [It] is therefore no answer for the State to say that the makers of cigarettes are doing harm: perhaps they are. But in that respect they are no different from the purveyors of other harmful products, or the advocates of harmful ideas. When the State seeks to silence them, they are all entitled to the protection of the First Amendment. * * *

JUSTICE SOUTER, concurring in part and dissenting in part.

---

b. For the contention that junk food advertising to children should not be protected, see David G. Yosifon, *Resisting Deep Capture: The Commercial Speech Doctrine and Junk-Food Advertising to Children*, 39 Loy. L.A.L. Rev. 507 (2006).

I join Parts I, II–C, II–D, III–A, III–B–1, III–C, and III–D of the Court's opinion. I join Part I of the opinion of Justice Stevens concurring in the judgment in part and dissenting in part. I respectfully dissent from Part III–B–2 of the opinion of the Court, and like Justice Stevens would remand for trial on the constitutionality of the 1,000–foot limit.

JUSTICE STEVENS, with whom JUSTICE GINSBURG and JUSTICE BREYER join, and with whom JUSTICE SOUTER joins as to Part I, concurring in part, concurring in the judgment in part, and dissenting in part. * * *

I. [Stevens, J., argued that the Federal Cigarette Labeling and Advertising Act of 1965 did not preclude state and local regulation of the location of cigarette advertising.]

II. *The 1,000–Foot Rule.* I am in complete accord with the Court's analysis of the importance of the interests served by the advertising restrictions. As the Court lucidly explains, few interests are more "compelling," than ensuring that minors do not become addicted to a dangerous drug before they are able to make a mature and informed decision as to the health risks associated with that substance. [Nevertheless,] noble ends do not save a speech-restricting statute whose means are poorly tailored. Such statutes may be invalid for two different reasons. First, the means chosen may be insufficiently related to the ends they purportedly serve. Alternatively, the statute may be so broadly drawn that, while effectively achieving its ends, it unduly restricts communications that are unrelated to its policy aims.

To my mind, the 1,000–foot rule does not present a tailoring problem of the first type. For reasons cogently explained in our prior opinions and in the opinion of the Court, we may fairly assume that advertising stimulates consumption and, therefore, that regulations limiting advertising will facilitate efforts to stem consumption. Furthermore, if the government's intention is to limit consumption by a particular segment of the community—in this case, minors—it is appropriate, indeed necessary, to tailor advertising restrictions to the areas where that segment of the community congregates—in this case, the area surrounding schools and playgrounds.

However, I share the majority's concern as to whether the 1,000–foot rule unduly restricts the ability of cigarette manufacturers to convey lawful information to adult consumers. This, of course, is a question of line-drawing. [E]fforts to protect children from exposure to harmful material will undoubtedly have some spillover effect on the free speech rights of adults. [Though] many factors plausibly enter the equation when calculating whether a child-directed location restriction goes too far in regulating adult speech, one crucial question is whether the regulatory scheme leaves available sufficient "alternative avenues of communication." Because I do not think the record contains sufficient information to enable us to answer that question, I would vacate the award of summary judgment upholding the 1,000–foot rule and remand for trial on that issue.

[For example,] depending on the answers to empirical questions on which we lack data, the ubiquity of print advertisements hawking particular brands of cigarettes might suffice to inform adult consumers of the special advantages of the respective brands. Similarly, print advertisements, circulars mailed to people's homes, word of mouth, and general information may or may not be sufficient to imbue the adult population with the knowledge that particular stores, chains of stores, or types of stores sell tobacco products.

I note, moreover, that the alleged "overinclusivity" of the advertising regulations while relevant to whether the regulations are narrowly tailored, does not "beli[e]" the claim that tobacco advertising imagery misleads children into believing that smoking is healthy, glamorous, or sophisticated. For purposes of summary judgment, the State conceded that the tobacco companies' advertising concerns lawful activity and is not misleading. Under the Court's disposition of the case today, the State remains free to proffer evidence that the advertising is in fact misleading. * * *

III. Because I strongly disagree with the Court's conclusion on the preemption issue, I dissent from Parts II–A and II–B of its opinion. Though I agree with much of what the Court has to say about the First Amendment, I ultimately disagree with its disposition or its reasoning on each of the regulations before us.[12]

NOTES AND QUESTIONS

1. Consider Richard H. Fallon, Jr., *The Dynamic Constitution* 50–51 (2004): "The decision in *Lorillard* * * * demonstrates the tendency of legal doctrine to deal in abstraction. In the eyes of the law, companies engaged in the business of selling cigarettes become 'speakers' protected under the First Amendment even though the sole aim of their 'speech'—consisting mostly of misleading images of healthy and sexy-looking people on billboards—was to promote the sale of a deadly product. [T]he same Justices who joined the *Lorillard* majority continue to hold that the states can regulate obscenity, simply to preserve state interests in morality."[c] Should corporations be denied First Amendment protection on the ground that they are not First Amendment speakers?

2. Consider Kathleen M. Sullivan, *Cheap Spirits, Cigarettes, and Free Speech: The Implications of 44 Liquormart,* 1996 Sup.Ct. Rev. 123, 160 (1996): "A plurality [is] willing to move commercial speech somewhat closer to the

---

12. Reflecting my partial agreement with the Court, I join Parts I, II–C, II–D, and III–B–1 and concur in the judgment reflected in Part III–D.

c. For material relevant to the prohibition of tobacco advertising, see Steven H. Shiffrin, *Dissent, Injustice, and the Meanings of America* ch. 2 (1999); Kathleen M. Sullivan, *Cheap Spirits, Cigarettes, and Free Speech: The Implications of 44 Liquormart,* 1996 Sup.Ct. Rev. 123 (1996); Martin H. Redish, *Tobacco Advertising and the First Amendment,* 81 Ia. L.Rev. 589 (1996); Sylvia Law, *Addiction, Autonomy, and Advertising,* 77 Iowa L.Rev. 909, 932 (1992); Daniel Lowenstein, *"Too Much Puff": Persuasion, Paternalism, and Commercial Speech,* 56 U.Cin.L.Rev. 1205, 1238 (1988); Charles Fischette, *A New Architecture of Commercial Speech Law,* 31 Harv. J.L. & Pub. Pol'y 663 (2008).

core of the First Amendment applying strict scrutiny to paternalistic interventions between speaker and listener for the listener's own good. It remains to be seen whether this group of Justices would extend that approach to all content-based commercial speech regulations, whether a fifth or more will join them, and whether such a move would prompt any change in the Court's currently exceptional treatment of false and misleading commercial speech." Will the category "commercial speech" be abandoned altogether?

3. Consider Akhil Reed Amar, *Intratextualism,* 112 Harv. L.Rev. 747, 810 (1999): "The Justices are beginning to detach the First Amendment from democracy and graft it onto property, moving from free speech to free markets."

4. Federal law permits compounding of drugs for the needs of specific patients without resort to FDA approval, so long as advertising of such drugs is not involved. The government rationale is that advertising would be indicative of mass manufacture rather than tailoring to the specific needs of individual patients. THOMPSON v. WESTERN STATES MEDICAL CENTER, 535 U.S. 357 (2002), per O'CONNOR, J., invalidated these restrictions in part by concluding that the government did not meet its burden to show that less restrictive alternatives were unavailable.[d]

BREYER, J., joined by Rehnquist, C.J., and Stevens and Ginsburg, JJ., dissenting, argued that the Court's approach to such issues should be flexible. He contended that the Court rightly applied the less demanding *Central Hudson* test because "it has concluded that, from a constitutional perspective, commercial speech does not warrant application of the Court's strictest speech-protective tests. And it has reached this conclusion in part because restrictions on commercial speech do not often repress individual self-expression; they rarely interfere with the functioning of democratic political processes; and they often reflect a democratically determined governmental decision to regulate a commercial venture in order to protect, for example, the consumer, the public health, individual safety, or the environment. [The] Court, in my view, gives insufficient weight to the Government's regulatory rationale, and too readily assumes the existence of practical alternatives. It thereby applies the commercial speech doctrine too strictly. [A]n overly rigid commercial speech doctrine will transform what ought to be a legislative or regulatory decision about the best way to protect the health and safety of the American public into a constitutional decision prohibiting the legislature from enacting necessary protections. As history in respect to the Due Process Clause shows, any such transformation would involve a tragic constitutional misunderstanding."

5. *Defining commercial speech.* In 1996 Nike, Inc. was confronted with allegations that it underpaid and otherwise mistreated workers at foreign facilities. Nike attempted to answer these charges with press releases, letters to editors, university presidents and athletic directors, and with a commissioned report by Andrew Young about working conditions in its

---

d. Elizabeth Spring, *Sales Versus Safety: The Loss of Balance in the Commercial Speech Standard in Thompson v. Western States Medical Center*, 37 U.C. Davis L. Rev. 1389, 1404 (2004): "The evolution of the commercial speech standard shows that the Court is now applying the *Central Hudson* test in a manner approaching strict scrutiny review."

factories. Kasky, a California resident, sued as a private attorney general under a California statute prohibiting unfair and deceptive practices.[e] Kasky alleged that in order to boost sales, Nike made a number of false statements and/or material omissions of fact. Assume that some of Nike's communications went to customers and that some did not. Are any of the communications "commercial speech"? All of them? Compare *Kasky v. Nike, Inc.*, 27 Cal.4th 939, 119 Cal.Rptr.2d 296, 45 P.3d 243 (2002) with *Nike, Inc. v. Kasky*, 539 U.S. 654 (2003)(Breyer, J., joined by O'Connor, J., dissenting from dismissal of the writ as improvidently granted).[f] Consider Robert M. O'Neil, *Nike v. Kasky—What Might Have Been* ..., 54 Case W. Res. L. Rev. 1259, 1273–1274 (2004): "Might there be some merit in recognizing a third category of expression—one that is neither classically commercial speech, nor fully protected speech? Consider the possibility of treating messages such as the overseas labor bulletins in the *Nike* case (or the utility promotions in *Central Hudson*, the off-label drug reprints in *WLF*, and the contraceptive pamphlets in *Bolger*) as less than fully protected speech on one hand, yet on the other hand as more protected than pure advertising. One of the limitations of the current analysis is the absence of any middle ground or intermediate option between the two poles—a disjunction which artificially compels courts to choose one extreme or the other, with drastic consequences, when in fact the real-world spectrum of corporate communications is far more varied and complex."[g]

In order to create a level playing field, should Nike's speech be entitled to the same protection afforded to those who might attack it? Rodney A. Smolla, *Afterword: Free the Fortune 500! The Debate over Corporate Speech and the First Amendment*, 54 Case W. Res. L. Rev. 1277, 1288 (2004). Would such treatment interfere with the enforcement of the Securities laws? Do corporate representations about manufacturing processes "provide consumers with an opportunity to engage in purposeful, expressive activity through the medium of conscientious consumption." Would "government's monitoring of the accuracy of process representations * * * impinge only on the commercial speech of product manufacturers, and * * * do so only in order to enable and support fundamental First Amendment activity by consumers." Douglas A. Kysar, *Preferences for Processes: The Process/Product Distinction and the Regulation of Consumer Choice*, 118 Harv. L. Rev. 525, 610, 612–13 (2004). Would it be wise to rule that "[t]ies go to the protection of the non-commercial elements of hybrid speech"? Jonathan Varat, *Deception and the First Amendment: A Central, Complex, and Somewhat Curious Relationship,* 53 UCLA L.Rev. 1107, 1129 (2007).

---

e. The Solicitor General argued that the private attorneys general provision should have doomed the statute on First Amendment grounds because of the potential chilling effect wholly apart from the status of the speech as commercial or political. For resistance to this contention in support of a general defense of private attorneys general, see Trevor W. Morrison, *Private Attorneys General and the First Amendment,* 103 Mich. L.Rev. 589 (2004).

f. For discussion, see Ronald K.L. Collins & David M. Skover, *The Landmark Case that Wasn't,* 54 Case W. Res. L. Rev. 965 (2004); Tom Bennigson, *Nike Revisited: Can Commercial Corporations Engage in Non-Commercial Speech?*, 39 Conn. L.Rev. 379 (2006).

g. Should there be a middle ground? Is it enough to qualify as commercial speech that Nike is involved in marketing its image and nothing more? See Tamara R. Piety, *Free Advertising*, 10 Lewis & Clark L.Rev. 367 (2006).

III. PRIVATE SPEECH

Before studying *Dun & Bradstreet,* below, review *Gertz,* Ch. 1, II, C supra.

Dun & Bradstreet, Inc., a credit reporting agency, falsely and negligently reported to five of its subscribers that Greenmoss Builders, Inc. had filed a petition for bankruptcy and also negligently misrepresented Greenmoss' assets and liabilities. In the ensuing defamation action, Greenmoss recovered $50,000 in compensatory damages and $300,000 in punitive damages. Dun & Bradstreet argued that, under *Gertz,* its First Amendment rights had been violated because presumed and punitive damages had been imposed without instructions requiring a showing of *New York Times* malice. Greenmoss argued that the *Gertz* protections did not extend to non-media defendants and, in any event, did not extend to commercial speech. DUN & BRADSTREET, INC. v. GREENMOSS BUILDERS, INC., 472 U.S. 749 (1985), rejected Dun & Bradstreet's contention, but there was no opinion of the Court. The common theme of the five justices siding with Greenmoss was that the First Amendment places less value on "private" speech than upon "public" speech.

POWELL, J., joined by Rehnquist and O'Connor, JJ., noted that the Vermont Supreme Court below had held "as a matter of federal constitutional law" that "the media protections outlined in *Gertz* are inapplicable to nonmedia defamation actions." In affirming, Powell, J., stated that his reasons were "different from those relied upon by the Vermont Supreme Court": "Like every other case in which this Court has found constitutional limits to state defamation laws, *Gertz* involved expression on a matter of undoubted public concern. * * *

"We have never considered whether the *Gertz* balance obtains when the defamatory statements involve no issue of public concern. To make this determination, we must employ the approach approved in *Gertz* and balance the State's interest in compensating private individuals for injury to their reputation against the First Amendment interest in protecting this type of expression. This state interest is identical to the one weighed in *Gertz.* * * *

"The First Amendment interest, on the other hand, is less important than the one weighed in *Gertz.* We have long recognized that not all speech is of equal First Amendment importance.[5] It is speech on 'matters

---

5. This Court on many occasions has recognized that certain kinds of speech are less central to the interests of the First Amendment than others. Obscene speech and "fighting words" long have been accorded no protection. *Roth; Chaplinsky.* In the area of protected speech, the most prominent example of reduced protection for certain kinds of speech concerns commercial speech. Such speech, we have noted, occupies a "subordinate position in the scale of First Amendment values." *Ohralik.* * * *

Other areas of the law provide further examples. In *Ohralik* we noted that there are "[n]umerous examples [of] communications that are regulated without offending the First Amendment, such as the exchange of information about securities, * * * corporate proxy statements, [the] exchange of price and production information among competitors, [and] employ-

of public concern' that is 'at the heart of the First Amendment's protection.' [In] contrast, speech on matters of purely private concern is of less First Amendment concern. As a number of state courts, including the court below, have recognized, the role of the Constitution in regulating state libel law is far more limited when the concerns that activated *New York Times* and *Gertz* are absent.[6] In such a case, '[t]here is no threat to the free and robust debate of public issues; there is no potential interference with a meaningful dialogue of ideas concerning self-government; and there is no threat of liability causing a reaction of self-censorship by the press. The facts of the present case are wholly without the First Amendment concerns with which the Supreme Court of the United States has been struggling.' *Harley-Davidson Motorsports, Inc. v. Markley,* 279 Or. 361, 366, 568 P.2d 1359, 1363 (1977).

"While such speech is not totally unprotected by the First Amendment, see *Connick v. Myers* [Ch. 7, III infra], its protections are less stringent. [In] light of the reduced constitutional value of speech involving no matters of public concern, we hold that the state interest adequately supports awards of presumed and punitive damages—even absent a showing of 'actual malice.'[7]

"The only remaining issue is whether petitioner's credit report involved a matter of public concern. In a related context, we have held that '[w]hether [speech] addresses a matter of public concern must be determined by [the expression's] content, form, and context [as] revealed by the whole record.' *Connick.* These factors indicate that petitioner's credit report concerns no public issue.[8] It was speech solely in the individual

---

ers' threats of retaliation for the labor activities of employees." Yet similar regulation of political speech is subject to the most rigorous scrutiny. Likewise, while the power of the State to license lawyers, psychiatrists, and public school teachers—all of whom speak for a living—is unquestioned, this Court has held that a law requiring licensing of union organizers is unconstitutional under the First Amendment. *Thomas v. Collins,* [Ch. 4, I, A infra]; see also *Rosenbloom v. Metromedia* (opinion of Brennan, J.) ("the determinant whether the First Amendment applies to state libel actions is whether the utterance involved concerns an issue of public or general concern").

6. As one commentator has remarked with respect to "the case of a commercial supplier of credit information that defames a person applying for credit"—the case before us today—"If the First Amendment requirements outlined in *Gertz* apply, there is something clearly wrong with the First Amendment or with *Gertz.*" Steven Shiffrin, *The First Amendment and Economic Regulation: Away From a General Theory of the First Amendment,* 78 Nw.L.Rev. 1212, 1268 (1983).

7. The dissent, purporting to apply the same balancing test that we do today, concludes that even speech on purely private matters is entitled to the protections of *Gertz.* * * *

The dissent's "balance" [would] lead to the protection of all libels—no matter how attenuated their constitutional interest. If the dissent were the law, a woman of impeccable character who was branded a "whore" by a jealous neighbor would have no effective recourse unless she could prove "actual malice" by clear and convincing evidence. This is not malice in the ordinary sense, but in the more demanding sense of *New York Times.* The dissent would, in effect, constitutionalize the entire common law of libel.

8. The dissent suggests that our holding today leaves all credit reporting subject to reduced First Amendment protection. This is incorrect. The protection to be accorded a particular credit report depends on whether the report's "content, form, and context" indicate that it concerns a public matter. We also do not hold, as the dissent suggests we do, that the report is subject to reduced constitutional protection because it constitutes economic or commercial speech. We

interest of the speaker and its specific business audience. Cf. *Central Hudson.* This particular interest warrants no special protection when—as in this case—the speech is wholly false and clearly damaging to the victim's business reputation. Moreover, since the credit report was made available to only five subscribers, who, under the terms of the subscription agreement, could not disseminate it further, it cannot be said that the report involves any 'strong interest in the free flow of commercial information.' *Virginia Pharmacy.* There is simply no credible argument that this type of credit reporting requires special protection to ensure that 'debate on public issues [will] be uninhibited, robust, and wide-open.' *New York Times.*

"In addition, the speech here, like advertising, is hardy and unlikely to be deterred by incidental state regulation. See *Virginia Pharmacy.* It is solely motivated by the desire for profit, which, we have noted, is a force less likely to be deterred than others. Arguably, the reporting here was also more objectively verifiable than speech deserving of greater protection. In any case, the market provides a powerful incentive to a credit reporting agency to be accurate, since false credit reporting is of no use to creditors. Thus, any incremental 'chilling' effect of libel suits would be of decreased significance.

"We conclude that permitting recovery of presumed and punitive damages in defamation cases absent a showing of 'actual malice' does not violate the First Amendment when the defamatory statements do not involve matters of public concern."

Although expressing the view that *Gertz* should be overruled and that the *New York Times* malice definition should be reconsidered, BURGER, C.J., concurring, stated that: "The single question before the Court today is whether *Gertz* applies to this case. The plurality opinion holds that *Gertz* does not apply because, unlike the challenged expression in *Gertz,* the alleged defamatory expression in this case does not relate to a matter of public concern. I agree that *Gertz* is limited to circumstances in which the alleged defamatory expression concerns a matter of general public importance, and that the expression in question here relates to a matter of essentially private concern. I therefore agree with the plurality opinion to the extent that it holds that *Gertz* is inapplicable in this case for the two reasons indicated. No more is needed to dispose of the present case."

WHITE, J., who had dissented in *Gertz,* was prepared to overrule that case or to limit it, but he disagreed with Powell, J.'s, suggestion that the plurality's resolution of the case was faithful to *Gertz:* "It is interesting that Justice Powell declines to follow the *Gertz* approach in this case. I had thought that the decision in *Gertz* was intended to reach cases that involve any false statements of fact injurious to reputation, whether the statement is made privately or publicly and whether or not it implicates a matter of public importance. Justice Powell, however, distinguishes *Gertz*

discuss such speech, along with advertising, only to show how many of the same concerns that argue in favor of reduced constitutional protection in those areas apply here as well.

as a case that involved a matter of public concern, an element absent here. Wisely, in my view, Justice Powell does not rest his application of a different rule here on a distinction drawn between media and non-media defendants. On that issue, I agree with Justice Brennan that the First Amendment gives no more protection to the press in defamation suits than it does to others exercising their freedom of speech. None of our cases affords such a distinction; to the contrary, the Court has rejected it at every turn. It should be rejected again, particularly in this context, since it makes no sense to give the most protection to those publishers who reach the most readers and therefore pollute the channels of communication with the most misinformation and do the most damage to private reputation. If *Gertz* is to be distinguished from this case, on the ground that it applies only where the allegedly false publication deals with a matter of general or public importance, then where the false publication does not deal with such a matter, the common-law rules would apply whether the defendant is a member of the media or other public disseminator or a non-media individual publishing privately. Although Justice Powell speaks only of the inapplicability of the *Gertz* rule with respect to presumed and punitive damages, it must be that the *Gertz* requirement of some kind of fault on the part of the defendant is also inapplicable in cases such as this. * * *

"The question before us is whether *Gertz* is to be applied in this case. For either of two reasons, I believe that it should not. First, I am unreconciled to the *Gertz* holding and believe that it should be overruled. Second, as Justice Powell indicates, the defamatory publication in this case does not deal with a matter of public importance."

BRENNAN, J., joined by Marshall, Blackmun and Stevens, JJ., dissented: "This case involves a difficult question of the proper application of *Gertz* to credit reporting—a type of speech at some remove from that which first gave rise to explicit First Amendment restrictions on state defamation law—and has produced a diversity of considered opinions, none of which speaks for the Court. Justice Powell's plurality opinion affirming the judgment below would not apply the *Gertz* limitations on presumed and punitive damages [because] the speech involved a subject of purely private concern and was circulated to an extremely limited audience. * * * Justice White also would affirm; he would not apply *Gertz* to this case on the ground that the subject matter of the publication does not deal with a matter of general or public importance. The Chief Justice apparently agrees with Justice White. The four who join this opinion would reverse the judgment of the Vermont Supreme Court. We believe that, although protection of the type of expression at issue is admittedly not the 'central meaning of the First Amendment,' *Gertz* makes clear that the First Amendment nonetheless requires restraints on presumed and punitive damage awards for this expression. * * *

"[Respondent urged that *Gertz* be restricted] to cases in which the defendant is a 'media' entity. Such a distinction is irreconcilable with the fundamental First Amendment principle that '[t]he inherent worth [of] speech in terms of its capacity for informing the public does not depend upon the identity of its source, whether corporation, association, union, or individual.' *First National Bank v. Bellotti* [Ch. 10 infra]. First Amendment difficulties lurk in the definitional questions such an approach would generate. And the distinction would likely be born an anachronism.[7] Perhaps most importantly, the argument that *Gertz* should be limited to the media misapprehends our cases. We protect the press to ensure the vitality of First Amendment guarantees. This solicitude implies no endorsement of the principle that speakers other than the press deserve lesser First Amendment protection. * * *

"The free speech guarantee gives each citizen an equal right to self-expression and to participation in self-government. [Accordingly,] at least six Members of this Court (the four who join this opinion and Justice White and The Chief Justice) agree today that, in the context of defamation law, the rights of the institutional media are no greater and no less than those enjoyed by other individuals or organizations engaged in the same activities.[10] * * *

"Purporting to 'employ the approach approved in *Gertz*,' Justice Powell balances the state interest in protecting private reputation against the First Amendment interest in protecting expression on matters not of public concern.[11]

"The five Members of the Court voting to affirm the damage award in this case have provided almost no guidance as to what constitutes a protected 'matter of public concern.' Justice White offers nothing at all, but his opinion does indicate that the distinction turns on solely the subject matter of the expression and not on the extent or conditions of dissemination of that expression. Justice Powell adumbrates a rationale that would appear to focus primarily on subject matter.[12] The opinion

---

7. Owing to transformations in the technological and economic structure of the communications industry, there has been an increasing convergence of what might be labeled "media" and "nonmedia."

10. Justice Powell's opinion does not expressly reject the media/nonmedia distinction, but does expressly decline to apply that distinction to resolve this case.

11. One searches *Gertz* in vain for a single word to support the proposition that limits on presumed and punitive damages obtained only when speech involved matters of public concern. *Gertz* could not have been grounded in such a premise. Distrust of placing in the courts the power to decide what speech was of public concern was precisely the rationale *Gertz* offered for rejecting the *Rosenbloom* plurality approach. * * *

12. Justice Powell also appears to rely in part on the fact that communication was limited and confidential. Given that his analysis also relies on the subject matter of the credit report, it is difficult to decipher exactly what role the nature and extent of dissemination plays in Justice Powell's analysis. But because the subject matter of the expression at issue is properly understood as a matter of public concern, it may well be that this element of confidentiality is crucial to the outcome as far as Justice Powell's opinion is concerned. In other words, it may be that Justice Powell thinks this particular expression could not contribute to public welfare because the public generally does not receive it. This factor does not suffice to save the analysis. See n. 18 infra.

[In fn. 18, Brennan, J., indicated that, "Dun & Bradstreet doubtless provides thousands of credit reports to thousands of subscribers who receive the information pursuant to the same strictures imposed on the recipients in this case. As a systemic matter, therefore, today's decision diminishes the free flow of information because Dun & Bradstreet will generally be made more reticent in providing information to all its subscribers."]

relies on the fact that the speech at issue was 'solely in the individual interest of the speaker and its *business* audience.' Analogizing explicitly to advertising, the opinion also states that credit reporting is 'hardy' and 'solely motivated by the desire for profit.' These two strains of analysis suggest that Justice Powell is excluding the subject matter of credit reports from 'matters of public concern' because the speech is predominantly in the realm of matters of economic concern."

Brennan, J., pointed to precedents (particularly labor cases) protecting speech on economic matters and argued that, "the breadth of this protection evinces recognition that freedom of expression is not only essential to check tyranny and foster self-government but also intrinsic to individual liberty and dignity and instrumental in society's search for truth."

Moreover, he emphasized the importance of credit reporting: "The credit reporting of Dun & Bradstreet falls within any reasonable definition of 'public concern' consistent with our precedents. Justice Powell's reliance on the fact that Dun & Bradstreet publishes credit reports 'for profit' is wholly unwarranted. Time and again we have made clear that speech loses none of its constitutional protection 'even though it is carried in a form that is "sold" for profit.' *Virginia Pharmacy.* More importantly, an announcement of the bankruptcy of a local company is information of potentially great concern to residents of the community where the company is [located]. And knowledge about solvency and the effect and prevalence of bankruptcy certainly would inform citizen opinions about questions of economic regulation. It is difficult to suggest that a bankruptcy is not a subject matter of public concern when federal law requires invocation of judicial mechanisms to effectuate it and makes the fact of the bankruptcy a matter of public record. * * *

"Even if the subject matter of credit reporting were properly considered—in the terms of Justice White and Justice Powell—as purely a matter of private discourse, this speech would fall well within the range of valuable expression for which the First Amendment demands protection. Much expression that does not directly involve public issues receives significant protection. Our cases do permit some diminution in the degree of protection afforded one category of speech about economic or commercial matters. 'Commercial speech'—defined as advertisements that 'do no more than propose a commercial transaction'—may be more closely regulated than other types of speech. [Credit] reporting is not 'commercial speech' as this Court has defined the term.

"[In] *every* case in which we have permitted more extensive state regulation on the basis of a commercial speech rationale—the speech being regulated was pure advertising—an offer to buy or sell goods and services or encouraging such buying and selling. Credit reports are not commercial advertisements for a good or service or a proposal to buy or sell such a product. We have been extremely chary about extending the 'commercial speech' doctrine beyond this narrowly circumscribed category of advertising because often vitally important speech will be uttered to advance economic interests and because the profit motive making such speech hardy dissipates rapidly when the speech is not advertising."[a]

Finally, Brennan, J., argued that even if credit reports were characterized as commercial speech, "unrestrained" presumed and punitive damages would violate the commercial speech requirement that "the regulatory means chosen be narrowly tailored so as to avoid any unnecessary chilling of protected expression. [Accordingly,] Greenmoss Builders should be permitted to recover for any actual damage it can show resulted from Dun & Bradstreet's negligently false credit report, but should be required to show actual malice to receive presumed or punitive damages."

NOTES AND QUESTIONS

1. Which of the following are "private" according to the opinions of Powell, J., Burger, C.J., and White, J.? (a) a report in the *Wall Street Journal* that Greenmoss has gone bankrupt; (b) a confidential report by Dun & Bradstreet to a bank that a famous politician has poor credit. Would it be different if the subject of the report were an actor? (c) a statement in the campus newspaper or by one student to another that a law professor is an alcoholic. Would it make a difference if the law professor was being considered for a Supreme Court appointment?

Consider the relationship between the public/private focus of the *Greenmoss* decision and the "public controversy" aspect of the public figure definition. If the speech does not relate to a "public" controversy, can it be "public" within the terms of *Greenmoss*? See Rodney Smolla, *Law of Defamation* 3–15 (1986). Reconsider *Time, Inc. v. Firestone,* Ch. 1, II, C supra.[b]

Finally, does it matter why the D & B subscribers received the information about Greenmoss? Suppose, for investment or insurance purposes, the subscribers had asked for reports on all aspects of the construction industry in Vermont? Compare *Lowe v. SEC,* Ch. 4, III infra.

2. Should the focus of the decision have been commercial speech instead of private speech? Would an expansion of the commercial speech definition

---

a. Brennan, J., cited *Consolidated Edison Co. v. Public Service Comm'n,* 447 U.S. 530 (1980), which invalidated a regulation that prohibited a utility company from inserting its views on "controversial issues of public policy" into its monthly electrical bill mailings. The mailing that prompted the regulation advocated nuclear power.

b. For discussion of the treatment of *Greenmoss* in the lower courts, see Ruth Walden & Derigan Silver, *Deciphering Dun and Bradstreet,* 14 Comm.L. & Pol'y 1 (2009). For discussion of the different meanings of public and private speech, see Nat Stern, *Private Concerns of Private Plaintiffs: Revisiting a Problematic Defamation Category,* 65 Mo. L.Rev. 597 (2000); Schauer, *"Private" Speech and the "Private" Forum: Givhan v. Western Line School District,* 1979 Sup.Ct.Rev. 217. Compare Michael Perry, *Freedom of Expression: An Essay on Theory and Doctrine,* 78 Nw.U.L.Rev. 1137 (1983) (denying any meaningful distinction between personal and political decisions). See generally sources cited in Ch. I, 2, E; Symposium, *The Public/Private Distinction,* 130 U.Pa.L.Rev. 1289 (1982); Risa Lieberwitz, *Freedom of Speech in Public Sector Employment: The Deconstitutionalization of the Public Sector Workplace,* 19 U.C.Davis L.Rev. 597 (1986); Toni Massaro, *Significant Silences: Freedom of Speech in the Public Sector Workplace,* 61 S.Cal.L.Rev. 1, 68–76 (1987). Comment, *A Conflict in the Public Interest,* 31 Santa Clara L.Rev. 997 (1991). For commentary on the question of whether Gertz should extend to non-media defendants see e.g. sources cited in note 1 after *Gertz,* Ch. 1, II, C supra.

have been preferable to the promotion of ad hoc decisionmaking about the nature of "private" speech? Consider Shiffrin, *The First Amendment and Economic Regulation: Away From A General Theory of the First Amendment,* 78 Nw.U.L.Rev. 1212, 1269 n. 327 (1983): "[D]rawing lines based on underlying First Amendment values is a far cry from sending out the judiciary on a general ad hoc expedition to separate matters of general public interest from matters that are not. A commitment to segregate certain commercial speech from *Gertz* protection is not a commitment to general ad hoc determinations."

3. According to Powell, J., in fn. 5, are the *Ohralik* examples, i.e., exchange of information about securities, corporate proxy statements and the like, examples of protected speech subject to regulation? In what sense, are those examples of communication protected? What is the significance of Powell, J.'s suggestion that they are something other than commercial speech?[c] Where do those examples fit into Brennan, J.'s view of the First Amendment?

4. Should (does?) the public/private distinction of Greenmoss apply to newspapers and broadcasters? C. Edwin Baker, *Autonomy and Informational Privacy, or Gossip: The Central Meaning of the First Amendment,* 21 Social Phil. & Pol'y 215, 247 (2004): "The business of credit reporting is in many respects more like professions that are regulated than like the press. Just as an accountant sells tax advice, a credit reporting agency sells specific, individualized financial information to clients who seek the information to guide their commercial transactions. These features distinguish credit reporting from both individuals' noncommercial speech and media communications."

IV. CONCEIVING AND RECONCEIVING THE STRUCTURE OF FIRST AMENDMENT DOCTRINE: HATE SPEECH REVISITED—AGAIN

R.A.V. v. ST. PAUL

505 U.S. 377, 112 S.Ct. 2538, 120 L.Ed.2d 305 (1992).

JUSTICE SCALIA delivered the opinion of the Court.

In the predawn hours of June 21, 1990, petitioner and several other teenagers allegedly assembled a crudely-made cross by taping together broken chair legs. They then allegedly burned the cross inside the fenced yard of a black family that lived across the street from the house where petitioner was staying. Although this conduct could have been punished under any of a number of laws, one of the two provisions under which respondent city of St. Paul chose to charge petitioner (then a juvenile) was the St. Paul Bias–Motivated Crime Ordinance, which provides: "Whoever places on public or private property a symbol, object, appellation, characterization or graffiti, including, but not limited to, a burning cross or Nazi swastika, which one knows or has reasonable grounds to know arouses

---

c. Consider *Board of Trustees v. Fox,* Ch. 3, II supra (dictum stating that attorneys or tutors dispensing advice for a fee is not commercial speech and strongly suggesting that regulations prohibiting such speech in college dormitories may be unconstitutional).

anger, alarm or resentment in others on the basis of race, color, creed, religion or gender commits disorderly conduct and shall be guilty of a misdemeanor." * * *

I. [W]e accept the Minnesota Supreme Court's authoritative statement that the ordinance reaches only those expressions that constitute "fighting words" within the meaning of Chaplinsky. [W]e nonetheless conclude that the ordinance is facially unconstitutional in that it prohibits otherwise permitted speech solely on the basis of the subjects the speech addresses.

[From] 1791 to the present, our society, like other free but civilized societies, has permitted restrictions upon the content of speech in a few limited areas, which are "of such slight social value as a step to truth that any benefit that may be derived from them is clearly outweighed by the social interest in order and morality." *Chaplinsky.* * * *

We have sometimes said that these categories of expression are "not within the area of constitutionally protected speech," *Roth; Beauharnais; Chaplinsky;* or that the "protection of the First Amendment does not extend" to them, *Bose Corp. v. Consumers Union of United States, Inc.* [Ch. 1, II, B supra]; *Sable Communications of Cal., Inc. v. FCC* [Ch. 8, II infra]. Such statements must be taken in context, however, and are no more literally true than is the occasionally repeated shorthand characterizing obscenity "as not being speech at all," Cass Sunstein, *Pornography and the First Amendment*, 1986 Duke L.J. 589, 615, n. 146. What they mean is that these areas of speech can, consistently with the First Amendment, be regulated *because of their constitutionally proscribable content* (obscenity, defamation, etc.)—not that they are categories of speech entirely invisible to the Constitution, so that they may be made the vehicles for content discrimination unrelated to their distinctively proscribable content. Thus, the government may proscribe libel; but it may not make the further content discrimination of proscribing *only* libel critical of the government. * * *

Our cases surely do not establish the proposition that the First Amendment imposes no obstacle whatsoever to regulation of particular instances of such proscribable expression, so that the government "may regulate [them] freely," (White, J., concurring in judgment). That would mean that a city council could enact an ordinance prohibiting only those legally obscene works that contain criticism of the city government or, indeed, that do not include endorsement of the city government. Such a simplistic, all-or-nothing-at-all approach to First Amendment protection is at odds with common sense and with our jurisprudence as well.[1] It is not

---

1. Justice White concedes that a city council cannot prohibit only those legally obscene works that contain criticism of the city government, but asserts that to be the consequence, not of the First Amendment, but of the Equal Protection Clause. Such content-based discrimination would not, he asserts, "be rationally related to a legitimate government interest." But of course the only *reason* that government interest is not a "legitimate" one is that it violates the First Amendment. This Court itself has occasionally fused the First Amendment into the Equal Protection Clause in this fashion, but at least with the acknowledgment (which Justice White cannot afford to make) that the First Amendment underlies its analysis. * * *

true that "fighting words" have at most a "de minimis" expressive content or that their content is *in all respects* "worthless and undeserving of constitutional protection"; sometimes they are quite expressive indeed. We have not said that they constitute "*no* part of the expression of ideas," but only that they constitute "no *essential* part of any exposition of ideas." *Chaplinsky.*

The proposition that a particular instance of speech can be proscribable on the basis of one feature (e.g., obscenity) but not on the basis of another (e.g., opposition to the city government) is commonplace, and has found application in many contexts. We have long held, for example, that nonverbal expressive activity can be banned because of the action it entails, but not because of the ideas it expresses—so that burning a flag in violation of an ordinance against outdoor fires could be punishable, whereas burning a flag in violation of an ordinance against dishonoring the flag is not. See *Johnson.* See also *Barnes* (Scalia, J., concurring in judgment) (Souter, J., concurring in judgment); *O'Brien.* Similarly, we have upheld reasonable "time, place, or manner" restrictions, but only if they are "justified without reference to the content of the regulated speech." *Ward;* see also *Clark* (noting that the *O'Brien* test differs little from the standard applied to time, place, or manner restrictions). And just as the power to proscribe particular speech on the basis of a noncontent element (e.g., noise) does not entail the power to proscribe the same speech on the basis of a content element; so also, the power to proscribe it on the basis of *one* content element (e.g., obscenity) does not entail the power to proscribe it on the basis of *other* content elements.

In other words, the exclusion of "fighting words" from the scope of the First Amendment simply means that, for purposes of that Amendment, the unprotected features of the words are, despite their verbal character, essentially a "non-speech" element of communication. Fighting words are thus analogous to a noisy sound truck: Each [is,] a "mode of speech,"; both can be used to convey an idea; but neither has, in and of itself, a claim upon the First Amendment. As with the sound truck, however, so also with fighting words: The government may not regulate use based on hostility—or favoritism—towards the underlying message expressed.

The concurrences describe us as setting forth a new First Amendment principle that prohibition of constitutionally proscribable speech cannot be "underinclusiv[e]" (White, J., concurring in judgment)—a First Amendment "absolutism" whereby "within a particular 'proscribable' category of expression, [a] government must either proscribe *all* speech or no speech at all" (Stevens, J., concurring in judgment). That easy target is of the concurrences' own invention. In our view, the First Amendment imposes not an "underinclusiveness" limitation but a "content discrimination" limitation upon a State's prohibition of proscribable speech. There is no problem whatever, for example, with a State's prohibiting obscenity (and other forms of proscribable expression) only in certain media or markets, for although that prohibition would be "underinclusive," it would not discriminate on the basis of content. See, e.g., *Sable Communications* (upholding 47 U.S.C. § 223(b)(1) (1988), which prohibits obscene *telephone* communications).

Even the prohibition against content discrimination that we assert the First Amendment requires is not absolute. It applies differently in the context of proscribable speech than in the area of fully protected speech. The rationale of the general prohibition, after all, is that content discrimination "rais[es] the specter that the Government may effectively drive certain ideas or viewpoints from the marketplace," *Simon & Schuster*, [Ch. 1, V, A infra]. But content discrimination among various instances of a class of proscribable speech often does not pose this threat.

When the basis for the content discrimination consists entirely of the very reason the entire class of speech at issue is proscribable, no significant danger of idea or viewpoint discrimination exists. Such a reason, having been adjudged neutral enough to support exclusion of the entire class of speech from First Amendment protection, is also neutral enough to form the basis of distinction within the class. To illustrate: A State might choose to prohibit only that obscenity which is the most patently offensive *in its prurience*—i.e., that which involves the most lascivious displays of sexual activity. But it may not prohibit, for example, only that obscenity which includes offensive *political* messages. And the Federal Government can criminalize only those threats of violence that are directed against the President, see 18 U.S.C. § 871—since the reasons why threats of violence are outside the First Amendment (protecting individuals from the fear of violence, from the disruption that fear engenders, and from the possibility that the threatened violence will occur) have special force when applied to the person of the President. See *Watts* [Ch. 1, I, D supra] (upholding the facial validity of § 871 because of the "overwhelmin[g] interest in protecting the safety of [the] Chief Executive and in allowing him to perform his duties without interference from threats of physical violence"). But the Federal Government may not criminalize only those threats against the President that mention his policy on aid to inner cities. And to take a final example (one mentioned by Justice Stevens), a State may choose to regulate price advertising in one industry but not in others, because the risk of fraud (one of the characteristics of commercial speech that justifies depriving it of full First Amendment protection) is in its view greater there. Cf. *Morales v. Trans World Airlines, Inc.*, 504 U.S. 374 (1992) (state regulation of airline advertising); *Ohralik* (state regulation of lawyer advertising). But a State may not prohibit only that commercial advertising that depicts men in a demeaning fashion.

Another valid basis for according differential treatment to even a content-defined subclass of proscribable speech is that the subclass happens to be associated with particular "secondary effects" of the speech, so that the regulation is "*justified* without reference to the content of [the] speech," *Renton*. A State could, for example, permit all obscene live performances except those involving minors. Moreover, since words can in some circumstances violate laws directed not against speech but against conduct (a law against treason, for example, is violated by telling the enemy the nation's defense secrets), a particular content-based subcategory of a proscribable class of speech can be swept up incidentally within the reach of a statute directed at conduct rather than speech. Thus, for example, sexually derogatory "fighting words," among other words, may produce a violation of Title VII's general prohibition against sexual discrimination in employment practices. Where the government does not target conduct on the basis of its expressive content, acts are not shielded from regulation merely because they express a discriminatory idea or philosophy.

These bases for distinction refute the proposition that the selectivity of the restriction is "even arguably 'conditioned upon the sovereign's agreement with what a speaker may intend to say.' '" There may be other such bases as well. Indeed, to validate such selectivity (where totally proscribable speech is at issue) it may not even be necessary to identify any particular "neutral" basis, so long as the nature of the content discrimination is such that there is no realistic possibility that official suppression of ideas is afoot. (We cannot think of any First Amendment interest that would stand in the way of a State's prohibiting only those obscene motion pictures with blue-eyed actresses.) Save for that limitation, the regulation of "fighting words," like the regulation of noisy speech, may address some offensive instances and leave other, equally offensive, instances alone. See *Posadas*.[2]

II. [Although] the phrase in the ordinance, "arouses anger, alarm or resentment in others," has been limited by the Minnesota Supreme Court's construction to reach only those symbols or displays that amount to "fighting words," the remaining, unmodified terms make clear that the ordinance applies only to "fighting words" that insult, or provoke violence, "on the basis of race, color, creed, religion or gender." Displays containing abusive invective, no matter how vicious or severe, are permissible unless they are addressed to one of the specified disfavored topics. Those who wish to use "fighting words" in connection with other ideas— to express hostility, for example, on the basis of political affiliation, union membership, or homosexuality—are not covered. The First Amendment does not permit St. Paul to impose special prohibitions on those speakers who express views on disfavored subjects.

In its practical operation, moreover, the ordinance goes even beyond mere content discrimination, to actual viewpoint discrimination.[a] Displays containing some words—odious racial epithets, for example—would be

---

2. Justice Stevens cites a string of opinions as supporting his assertion that "selective regulation of speech based on content" is not presumptively invalid. [A]ll that their contents establish is what we readily concede: that presumptive invalidity does not mean invariable invalidity, leaving room for such exceptions as reasonable and viewpoint-neutral content-based discrimination in nonpublic forums, or with respect to certain speech by government employees.

a. Consider Alan E. Brownstein, *Alternative Maps for Navigating the First Amendment Maze*, 16 Const. Comm. 101, 105 (1999): "Even an ostensibly innocuous subject matter regulation that prohibits speech about dogs, for example, may directly restrict at least one of the viewpoints that might be expressed in a debate about what constitutes the best household pet."

prohibited to proponents of all views. But "fighting words" that do not themselves invoke race, color, creed, religion, or gender—aspersions upon a person's mother, for example—would seemingly be usable ad libitum in the placards of those arguing *in favor* of racial, color, etc. tolerance and equality, but could not be used by that speaker's opponents. One could hold up a sign saying, for example, that all "anti-Catholic bigots" are misbegotten; but not that all "papists" are, for that would insult and provoke violence "on the basis of religion." St. Paul has no such authority to license one side of a debate to fight freestyle, while requiring the other to follow Marquis of Queensbury Rules.

What we have here, it must be emphasized, is not a prohibition of fighting words that are directed at certain persons or groups (which would be *facially* valid if it met the requirements of the Equal Protection Clause); but rather, a prohibition of fighting words that contain (as the Minnesota Supreme Court repeatedly emphasized) messages of "bias-motivated" hatred and in particular, as applied to this case, messages "based on virulent notions of racial supremacy." One must wholeheartedly agree with the Minnesota Supreme Court that "[i]t is the responsibility, even the obligation, of diverse communities to confront such notions in whatever form they appear," but the manner of that confrontation cannot consist of selective limitations upon speech. St. Paul's brief asserts that a general "fighting words" law would not meet the city's needs because only a content-specific measure can communicate to minority groups that the "group hatred" aspect of such speech "is not condoned by the majority." The point of the First Amendment is that majority preferences must be expressed in some fashion other than silencing speech on the basis of its content. * * *

[T]he reason why fighting words are categorically excluded from the protection of the First Amendment is not that their content communicates any particular idea, but that their content embodies a particularly intolerable (and socially unnecessary) *mode* of expressing *whatever* idea the speaker wishes to convey. St. Paul has not singled out an especially offensive mode of expression—it has not, for example, selected for prohibition only those fighting words that communicate ideas in a threatening (as opposed to a merely obnoxious) manner. Rather, it has proscribed fighting words of whatever manner that communicate messages of racial, gender, or religious intolerance. Selectivity of this sort creates the possibility that the city is seeking to handicap the expression of particular ideas.

* * * St. Paul argues that the ordinance [is] aimed only at the "secondary effects" of the speech, see *Renton*. According to St. Paul, the ordinance is intended, "not to impact on [sic] the right of free expression of the accused," but rather to "protect against the victimization of a person or persons who are particularly vulnerable because of their membership in a group that historically has been discriminated against." Even assuming that an ordinance that completely proscribes, rather than merely regulates, a specified category of speech can ever be considered to be directed only to the secondary effects of such speech, it is clear that the St.

Paul ordinance is not directed to secondary effects within the meaning of *Renton*. As we said in *Boos* "[l]isteners' reactions to speech are not the type of 'secondary effects' we referred to in *Renton*." * * * *[7]

Finally, St. Paul [asserts] that the ordinance helps to ensure the basic human rights of members of groups that have historically been subjected to discrimination, including the right of such group members to live in peace where they wish. We do not doubt that these interests are compelling, and that the ordinance can be said to promote them. But the "danger of censorship" presented by a facially content-based statute requires that that weapon be employed only where it is *"necessary* to serve the asserted [compelling] interest". The existence of adequate content-neutral alternatives thus "undercut[s] significantly" any defense of such a statute, casting considerable doubt on the government's protestations that "the asserted justification is in fact an accurate description of the purpose and effect of the law." [An] ordinance not limited to the favored topics, for example, would have precisely the same beneficial effect. In fact the only interest distinctively served by the content limitation is that of displaying the city council's special hostility towards the particular biases thus singled out. That is precisely what the First Amendment forbids. The politicians of St. Paul are entitled to express that hostility—but not through the means of imposing unique limitations upon speakers who (however benightedly) disagree. * * *

Let there be no mistake about our belief that burning a cross in someone's front yard is reprehensible. But St. Paul has sufficient means at its disposal to prevent such behavior without adding the First Amendment to the fire. * * *

JUSTICE WHITE, with whom JUSTICE BLACKMUN and JUSTICE O'CONNOR join, and with whom JUSTICE STEVENS joins except as to Part I(A), concurring in the judgment. * * *

I.A. [T]he majority holds that the First Amendment protects those narrow categories of expression long held to be undeserving of First Amendment protection—at least to the extent that lawmakers may not regulate some fighting words more strictly than others because of their content. [Should] the government want to criminalize certain fighting words, the Court now requires it to criminalize all fighting words.

To borrow a phrase, "Such a simplistic, all-or-nothing-at-all approach to First Amendment protection is at odds with common sense and with our jurisprudence as well." It is inconsistent to hold that the government may proscribe an entire category of speech because the content of that speech is evil, but that the government may not treat a subset of that

---

7. St. Paul has not argued in this case that the ordinance merely regulates that subclass of fighting words which is most likely to provoke a violent response. But even if one assumes (as appears unlikely) that the categories selected may be so described, that would not justify selective regulation under a "secondary effects" theory. The only reason why such expressive conduct would be especially correlated with violence is that it conveys a particularly odious message; because the "chain of causation" thus *necessarily* "run[s]" through the persuasive effect of the expressive component" of the conduct, it is clear that the St. Paul ordinance regulates on the basis of the "primary" effect of the speech—i.e., its persuasive (or repellent) force.

category differently without violating the First Amendment; the content of the subset is by definition worthless and undeserving of constitutional protection.

The majority's observation that fighting words are "quite expressive indeed," is no answer. Fighting words are not a means of exchanging views, rallying supporters, or registering a protest; they are directed against individuals to provoke violence or to inflict injury. Therefore, a ban on all fighting words or on a subset of the fighting words category would restrict only the social evil of hate speech, without creating the danger of driving viewpoints from the marketplace.

Therefore, the Court's insistence on inventing its brand of First Amendment underinclusiveness puzzles me.[3] [T]he Court's new "under-breadth" creation [invites] the continuation of expressive conduct that in this case is evil and worthless in First Amendment terms until the city of St. Paul cures the underbreadth by adding to its ordinance a catch-all phrase such as "and all other fighting words that may constitutionally be subject to this ordinance."

Any contribution of this holding to First Amendment jurisprudence is surely a negative one, since it necessarily signals that expressions of violence, such as the message of intimidation and racial hatred conveyed by burning a cross on someone's lawn, are of sufficient value to outweigh the social interest in order and morality that has traditionally placed such fighting words outside the First Amendment.[4] Indeed, by characterizing fighting words as a form of "debate" the majority legitimates hate speech as a form of public discussion. * * *

B.   [Although] the First Amendment does not apply to categories of unprotected speech, such as fighting words, the Equal Protection Clause requires that the regulation of unprotected speech be rationally related to a legitimate government interest. A defamation statute that drew distinctions on the basis of political affiliation or "an ordinance prohibiting only those legally obscene works that contain criticism of the city government" would unquestionably fail rational basis review.[9]

Turning to the St. Paul ordinance and assuming arguendo, as the majority does, that the ordinance is not constitutionally overbroad there is

---

3. The assortment of exceptions the Court attaches to its rule belies the majority's claim that its new theory is truly concerned with content discrimination. See Part I(C), infra (discussing the exceptions).

4. This does not suggest, of course, that cross burning is always unprotected. Burning a cross at a political rally would almost certainly be protected expression. Cf. *Brandenburg.* But in such a context, the cross burning could not be characterized as a "direct personal insult or an invitation to exchange fisticuffs," *Texas v. Johnson,* to which the fighting words doctrine.

9. The majority is mistaken in stating that a ban on obscene works critical of government would fail equal protection review only because the ban would violate the First Amendment. While decisions such as *Mosley* recognize that First Amendment principles may be relevant to an equal protection claim challenging distinctions that impact on protected expression, there is no basis for linking First and Fourteenth Amendment analysis in a case involving unprotected expression. Certainly, one need not resort to First Amendment principles to conclude that the sort of improbable legislation the majority hypothesizes is based on senseless distinctions.

no question that it would pass equal protection review. The ordinance [reflects] the City's judgment that harms based on race, color, creed, religion, or gender are more pressing public concerns than the harms caused by other fighting words. In light of our Nation's long and painful experience with discrimination, this determination is plainly reasonable. Indeed, as the majority concedes, the interest is compelling.

C. The Court has patched up its argument with an apparently nonexhaustive list of ad hoc exceptions, in what can be viewed either as an attempt to confine the effects of its decision to the facts of this case, or as an effort to anticipate some of the questions that will arise from its radical revision of First Amendment law. * * *

To save the statute [making it illegal to threaten the life of the President], the majority has engrafted the following exception onto its newly announced First Amendment rule: Content-based distinctions may be drawn within an unprotected category of speech if the basis for the distinctions is "the very reason the entire class of speech at issue is proscribable." * * *

The exception swallows the majority's rule. Certainly, it should apply to the St. Paul ordinance, since "the reasons why [fighting words] are outside the First Amendment [have] special force when applied to [groups that have historically been subjected to discrimination]."

To avoid the result of its own analysis, the Court suggests that fighting words are simply a mode of communication, rather than a content-based category, and that the St. Paul ordinance has not singled out a particularly objectionable mode of communication. Again, the majority confuses the issue. A prohibition on fighting words is not a time, place, or manner restriction; it is a ban on a class of speech that conveys an overriding message of personal injury and imminent violence, a message that is at its ugliest when directed against groups that have long been the targets of discrimination. Accordingly, the ordinance falls within the first exception to the majority's theory.

As its second exception, the Court posits that certain content-based regulations will survive under the new regime if the regulated subclass "happens to be associated with particular 'secondary effects' of the speech" which the majority treats as encompassing instances in which "words [can] violate laws directed not against speech but against conduct."[11] Again, there is a simple explanation for the Court's eagerness to craft an exception to its new First Amendment rule: Under the general rule the Court applies in this case, Title VII hostile work environment claims would suddenly be unconstitutional.

---

11. The consequences of the majority's conflation of the rarely-used secondary effects standard and the *O'Brien* test for conduct incorporating "speech" and "nonspeech" elements, see generally *O'Brien*, present another question that I fear will haunt us and the lower courts in the aftermath of the majority's opinion.

Title VII * * * regulations covering hostile workplace claims forbid "sexual harassment," which includes "[u]nwelcome sexual advances, requests for sexual favors, and other verbal or physical conduct of a sexual nature" which creates "an intimidating, hostile, or offensive working environment." The regulation does not prohibit workplace harassment generally; it focuses on what the majority would characterize as the "disfavored topi[c]" of sexual harassment. In this way, Title VII is similar to the St. Paul ordinance that the majority condemns because it "impose[s] special prohibitions on those speakers who express views on disfavored subjects." * * *

Hence, the majority's second exception, which the Court indicates would insulate a Title VII hostile work environment claim from an underinclusiveness challenge because "sexually derogatory 'fighting words' [may] produce a violation of Title VII's general prohibition against sexual discrimination in employment practices." But application of this exception to a hostile work environment claim does not hold up under close examination.

First, the hostile work environment regulation is not keyed to the presence or absence of an economic quid pro quo, but to the impact of the speech on the victimized worker. Consequently, the regulation would no more fall within a secondary effects exception than does the St. Paul ordinance. Second, the majority's focus on the statute's general prohibition on discrimination glosses over the language of the specific regulation governing hostile working environment, which reaches beyond any "incidental" effect on speech. If the relationship between the broader statute and specific regulation is sufficient to bring the Title VII regulation within O'Brien, then all St. Paul need do to bring its ordinance within this exception is to add some prefatory language concerning discrimination generally.

As the third exception to the Court's theory for deciding this case, the majority concocts a catchall exclusion to protect against unforeseen problems. [It] would apply in cases in which "there is no realistic possibility that official suppression of ideas is afoot." As I have demonstrated, this case does not concern the official suppression of ideas. The majority discards this notion out-of-hand. * * *

II.   * * * I would decide the case on overbreadth grounds. * * *

In construing the St. Paul ordinance, [I understand the Minnesota Supreme Court] to have ruled that St. Paul may constitutionally prohibit expression that "by its very utterance" causes "anger, alarm or resentment."

Our fighting words cases have made clear, however, that [t]he mere fact that expressive activity causes hurt feelings, offense, or resentment does not render the expression unprotected. See Eichman; Texas v. Johnson; Falwell. * * *[13] The ordinance is therefore fatally overbroad and invalid on its face.

---

13. Although the First Amendment protects offensive speech, it does not require us to be subjected to such expression at all times, in all settings. We have held that such expression may

JUSTICE BLACKMUN, concurring in the judgment.

[B]y deciding that a State cannot regulate speech that causes great harm unless it also regulates speech that does not (setting law and logic on their heads), the Court seems to abandon the categorical approach, and inevitably to relax the level of scrutiny applicable to content-based laws. [The] simple reality is that the Court will never provide child pornography or cigarette advertising the level of protection customarily granted political speech. If we are forbidden from categorizing, as the Court has done here, we shall reduce protection across the board. * * *

[There] is the possibility that this case will not significantly alter First Amendment jurisprudence, but, instead, will be regarded as an aberration—a case where the Court manipulated doctrine to strike down an ordinance whose premise it opposed, namely, that racial threats and verbal assaults are of greater harm than other fighting words. I fear that the Court has been distracted from its proper mission by the temptation to decide the issue over "politically correct speech" and "cultural diversity," neither of which is presented here. If this is the meaning of today's opinion, it is perhaps even more regrettable.

I see no First Amendment values that are compromised by a law that prohibits hoodlums from driving minorities out of their homes by burning crosses on their lawns, but I see great harm in preventing the people of Saint Paul from specifically punishing the race-based fighting words that so prejudice their community. * * *

JUSTICE STEVENS, with whom JUSTICE WHITE and JUSTICE BLACKMUN join as to Part I, concurring in the judgment. * * *

I.   [Our] First Amendment decisions have created a rough hierarchy in the constitutional protection of speech. Core political speech occupies the highest, most protected position; commercial speech and nonobscene, sexually explicit speech are regarded as a sort of second-class expression; obscenity and fighting words receive the least protection of all. Assuming that the Court is correct that this last class of speech is not wholly "unprotected," it certainly does not follow that fighting words and obscenity receive the *same* sort of protection afforded core political speech. Yet in ruling that proscribable speech cannot be regulated based on subject matter, the Court does just that. Perversely, this gives fighting words *greater* protection than is afforded commercial speech. If Congress can prohibit false advertising directed at airline passengers without also prohibiting false advertising directed at bus passengers and if a city can prohibit political advertisements in its buses while allowing other advertisements, it is ironic to hold that a city cannot regulate fighting words based on "race, color, creed, religion or gender" while leaving unregulated fighting words based on "union membership or homosexuality." * * * Perhaps because the Court recognizes these perversities, it quickly offers

be proscribed when it intrudes upon a "captive audience." And expression may be limited when it merges into conduct. *O'Brien.* However, because of the manner in which the Minnesota Supreme Court construed the St. Paul ordinance, those issues are not before us in this case.

some ad hoc limitations on its newly extended prohibition on content-based regulations.[b]

[T]he Court recognizes that a State may regulate advertising in one industry but not another because "the risk of fraud (one of the characteristics that justifies depriving [commercial speech] of full First Amendment protection)" in the regulated industry is "greater" than in other industries. "[O]ne of the characteristics that justifies" the constitutional status of fighting words is that such words "by their very utterance inflict injury or tend to incite an immediate breach of the peace." *Chaplinsky.* Certainly a legislature that may determine that the risk of fraud is greater in the legal trade than in the medical trade may determine that the risk of injury or breach of peace created by race-based threats is greater than that created by other threats.

Similarly, it is impossible to reconcile the Court's analysis of the St. Paul ordinance with its recognition that "a prohibition of fighting words that are directed at certain persons or groups [would] be facially valid." A selective proscription of unprotected expression designed to protect "certain persons or groups" (for example, a law proscribing threats directed at the elderly) would be constitutional if it were based on a legitimate determination that the harm created by the regulated expression differs from that created by the unregulated expression (that is, if the elderly are more severely injured by threats than are the nonelderly). Such selective protection is no different from a law prohibiting minors (and only minors) from obtaining obscene publications. St. Paul has determined—reasonably in my judgment—that fighting-word injuries "based on race, color, creed, religion or gender" are qualitatively different and more severe than fighting-word injuries based on other characteristics. Whether the selective proscription of proscribable speech is defined by the protected target ("certain persons or groups") or the basis of the harm (injuries "based on race, color, creed, religion or gender") makes no constitutional difference: what matters is whether the legislature's selection is based on a legitimate, neutral, and reasonable distinction. * * *

III.   [Unlike] the Court, I do not believe that all content-based regulations are equally infirm and presumptively invalid; unlike Justice White, I do not believe that fighting words are wholly unprotected by the First Amendment. To the contrary, I believe our decisions establish a more complex and subtle analysis, one that considers the content and

---

b. In an earlier passage and footnote of his opinion, Stevens, J., argued: "[W]hile the Court rejects the 'all-or-nothing-at-all' nature of the categorical approach, it promptly embraces an absolutism of its own: within a particular 'proscribable' category of expression, the Court holds, a government must either proscribe all speech or no speech at all. The Court disputes this characterization because it has crafted two exceptions, one for 'certain media or markets' and the other for content discrimination based upon 'the very reason that the entire class of speech at issue is proscribable.' These exceptions are, at best, ill-defined. The Court does not tell us whether, with respect to the former, fighting words such as cross-burning could be proscribed only in certain neighborhoods where the threat of violence is particularly severe, or whether, with respect to the second category, fighting words that create a particular risk of harm (such as a race riot) would be proscribable. The hypothetical and illusory category of these two exceptions persuades me that either my description of the Court's analysis is accurate or that the Court does not in fact mean much of what it says in its opinion."

context of the regulated speech, and the nature and scope of the restriction on speech. * * * Whatever the allure of absolute doctrines, it is just too simple to declare expression "protected" or "unprotected" or to proclaim a regulation "content-based" or "content-neutral."

In applying this analysis to the St. Paul ordinance, I assume arguendo—as the Court does—that the ordinance regulates *only* fighting words and therefore is *not* overbroad. Looking to the content and character of the regulated activity, two things are clear. First, by hypothesis the ordinance bars only low-value speech, namely, fighting words. * * * Second, the ordinance regulates "expressive conduct [rather] than [the] written or spoken word."

Looking to the context of the regulated activity, it is again significant that the statute (by hypothesis) regulates *only* fighting words. Whether words are fighting words is determined in part by their context. Fighting words are not words that merely cause offense; fighting words must be directed at individuals so as to "by their very utterance inflict injury." By hypothesis, then, the St. Paul ordinance restricts speech in confrontational and potentially violent situations. The case at hand is illustrative. The cross-burning in this case—directed as it was to a single African–American family trapped in their home—was nothing more than a crude form of physical intimidation. That this cross-burning sends a message of racial hostility does not automatically endow it with complete constitutional protection.

Significantly, the St. Paul ordinance regulates speech not on the basis of its subject matter or the viewpoint expressed, but rather on the basis of the *harm* the speech causes. * * * Contrary to the Court's suggestion, the ordinance regulates only a subcategory of expression that causes *injuries based on* "race, color, creed, religion or gender," not a subcategory that involves *discussions* that concern those characteristics.[9] * * *

Finally, it is noteworthy that the St. Paul ordinance is, as construed by the Court today, quite narrow. The St. Paul ordinance does not ban all "hate speech," nor does it ban, say, all cross-burnings or all swastika displays. Rather it only bans a subcategory of the already narrow category of fighting words. Such a limited ordinance leaves open and protected a vast range of expression on the subjects of racial, religious, and gender equality. As construed by the Court today, the ordinance certainly does not " 'raise the specter that the Government may effectively drive certain

---

9. The Court contends that this distinction is "wordplay," reasoning that "[w]hat makes [the harms caused by race-based threats] distinct from [the harms] produced by other fighting words [is] the fact that [the former are] caused by a *distinctive idea*." In this way, the Court concludes that regulating speech based on the injury it causes is no different from regulating speech based on its subject matter. This analysis fundamentally miscomprehends the role of "race, color, creed, religion [and] gender" in contemporary American society. One need look no further than the recent social unrest in the Nation's cities to see that race-based threats may cause more harm to society and to individuals than other threats. Just as the statute prohibiting threats against the President is justifiable because of the place of the President in our social and political order, so a statute prohibiting race-based threats is justifiable because of the place of race in our social and political order. * * * [S]uch a place and is so incendiary an issue, until the Nation matures beyond that condition, laws such as St. Paul's ordinance will remain reasonable and justifiable.

ideas or viewpoints from the marketplace.' " Petitioner is free to burn a cross to announce a rally or to express his views about racial supremacy, he may do so on private property or public land, at day or at night, so long as the burning is not so threatening and so directed at an individual as to "by its very [execution] inflict injury." Such a limited proscription scarcely offends the First Amendment. * * *c

NOTES AND QUESTIONS

1. **The harm of insults based on race, gender, and religion.** Consider Steven J. Heyman, *Spheres of Autonomy: Reforming the Content Neutrality Doctrine in First Amendment Jurisprudence*, 10 Wm. & Mary Bill Rts. J. 647, 695 (2002): "How should we answer the critical question in *R.A.V.*? Do insults based on race, gender, and religion cause greater injury than insults in general? [First,] unlike insults that express merely personal dislike, group-based insults often deny the very humanity of those against whom they are directed. In this way, they inflict a deeper injury on their targets. Second, in an important sense, group-based insults are directed not only against specific individuals, but also against the group in general. For this reason, they may inflict injury on a greater number of people, and may tend to provoke violence on a broader scale. By exacerbating tensions between groups, such insults also tend to cause greater harm to the community as a whole. And all of these injuries are heightened when the insults are directed against members of groups that have historically been subjected to discrimination and oppression."

2. **The harm of cross burning.** Is cross burning not a particularly virulent form of fighting words? Consider Michel Rosenfeld, *Hate Speech in Constitutional Jurisprudence: A Comparative Analysis*, 24 Cardozo L. Rev. 1523, 1540 (2003): [T]hough both the proposed march in *Skokie* and the cross burning in *R.A.V.* were meant to incite hatred on the basis of religion and race respectively, their effects were quite different. *Skokie* mainly produced contempt for the marchers and a reminder that there was little danger of an embrace of Nazism in the United States. *R.A.V.*, on the other hand, played on pervasive, and to a significant degree justified, fears concerning race relations in America. Undoubtedly, cross burning itself is rejected as repugnant by the vast majority of Americans. The underlying racism associated with it, and the message that blacks should remain in their own segregated neighborhoods, however, unfortunately still have adherents among a non-negligible portion of whites in America." Consider also Consider Steven Shiffrin, *Racist Speech, Outsider Jurisprudence, and the Meaning of America*, 80 Corn.L.Rev. 43, 59, 57 (1994): "If the argument is that a particular subject matter implicates the very risks the category was designed to cover, but in a more severe way, what

---

c. For background on *R.A.V.*, see Edward Cleary, *Beyond the Burning Cross* (1994). For additional commentary, see Symposium, *Hate Speech After R.A.V.: More Conflict Between Free Speech and Equality*, 18 Wm. Mitchell L.Rev. 889 (1992); Akhil Amar, *The Case of the Missing Amendments*, 106 Harv.L.Rev. 124 (1992); Joshua Cohen, *Freedom of Expression*, 22 Phil. & Pub.Aff. 207 (1993); Elena Kagan, *The Changing Faces of First Amendment Neutrality*, 1992 Sup.Ct.Rev. 29; Elena Kagan, *Regulation of Hate Speech and Pornography After R.A.V.*, 60 U.Chi.L.Rev. 873 (1993); Charles Lawrence, *Crossburning and the Sound of Silence*, 37 Vill.L.Rev. 787 (1992); Shiffrin, supra.

difference does it make that the category of speech involved is not the most offensive *mode* of speech? The question is whether it causes the most serious form of injury. Since when is the mere possibility of idea discrimination in regulating less than fully protected speech of such enormous constitutional import? [Scalia, J.'s] description of the case law breathes new life into the expression about ostriches hiding their heads in the sand. When the government outlaws threats against the President, advertisements for casino gambling or alcoholic beverages, or the burning of draft cards, or when it engages in a campaign of zoning adult theaters out of neighborhoods, no one but a person wearing a black robe with a strong will to believe or befuddle could possibly suppose that 'there is no realistic possibility that official suppression of ideas is afoot.' Point-of-view discrimination permeates these categories. If point-of-view discrimination were as major an evil as the Court often supposes, one would think that a demanding test would have been applied in some of these cases. But many of the justices presumably share the governmental view that advertisements for casino gambling or alcoholic beverages, the burning of draft cards, and the kind of films shown in adult theaters are not worth much. They either do not look for point-of-view discrimination or devise tests that command them not to look. Perhaps they cannot see the ways in which they themselves discriminate."

3. (a) At the capital sentencing phase of a murder case, the prosecution sought to introduce evidence that the defendant was a member of the Aryan Brotherhood which was stipulated to be a "white racist gang." DAWSON v. DELAWARE, 503 U.S. 159 (1992), per REHNQUIST, C.J., held that its admission violated the First Amendment: "Even if the Delaware group to which Dawson allegedly belongs is racist, those beliefs, so far as we can determine, had no relevance to the sentencing proceeding in this case. For example, the Aryan Brotherhood evidence was not tied in any way to the murder of Dawson's [white] victim. [Moreover], we conclude that Dawson's First Amendment rights were violated by the admission of the Aryan Brotherhood evidence in this case, because the evidence proved nothing more than Dawson's abstract beliefs. [Delaware] might have avoided this problem if it had presented evidence showing more than mere abstract beliefs on Dawson's part, but on the present record one is left with the feeling that the Aryan Brotherhood evidence was employed simply because the jury would find these beliefs morally reprehensible."

THOMAS, J., dissented: "Dawson introduced mitigating character evidence that he had acted kindly toward his family. The stipulation tended to undercut this showing by suggesting that Dawson's kindness did not extend to members of other racial groups. Although we do not sit in judgment of the morality of particular creeds, we cannot bend traditional concepts of relevance to exempt the antisocial."

(b) WISCONSIN v. MITCHELL, 508 U.S. 476 (1993), per REHNQUIST, C.J., found no First Amendment violation when Wisconsin permitted a sentence for aggravated battery to be enhanced on the ground that the white victim had been selected because of his race. The Court observed that, unlike *R.A.V.*, the Wisconsin statute was aimed at conduct, not speech, that a chilling effect on speech was unlikely, that the focus on motive was no different from that employed in anti-discrimination statutes, and that bias-inspired conduct is more likely "to provoke retaliatory crimes, inflict distinct emotional harms on their victims, and incite community unrest." Consistent with *R.A.V.*?[d] After *Mitchell*, could the state "enact a general regulation against the use of fighting words, and then have a sentence enhancement based on racial motivation"? See Daniel A. Farber, *The First Amendment* 115 (1998): "There seems to be a reasonable argument for distinguishing *R.A.V.* even when the enhancement is applied to a speech-based regulation."[e]

4. Consider Shiffrin, supra, at 65: "[Scalia, J., maintains] that the rationale of the prohibition against content discrimination is the 'specter that the government may effectively drive certain ideas or viewpoints from the marketplace.' That concern, however, is difficult to take seriously in the context of *R.A.V.* St. Paul prohibited only a small class of 'fighting words,' words which make a slight contribution to truth—just a particular socially unacceptable *mode* of presentation in Justice Scalia's view. It is hard to see how that raises the 'specter that the Government may effectively drive certain ideas or viewpoints from the marketplace.' Even more telling is Justice Scalia's 'content-neutral' alternative to the St. Paul ordinance: a 'pure' fighting words statute, which, he maintains, could serve the valid government interests in protecting basic human rights of members of groups historically subject to discrimination. But this content-neutral alternative would drive the very same ideas and viewpoints (along with others) from the marketplace." Is there a better rationale?

5. Consider Elena Kagan, *Private Speech, Public Purpose: The Role of Governmental Motive in First Amendment Doctrine*, 63 U.Chi.L.Rev. 413 (1996): "[H]alf hidden beneath a swirl of doctrinal formulations, the crux of the dispute between the majority and the concurring opinions concerned the proper understanding of St. Paul's motive in enacting its hate-speech law. The majority understood this motive as purely censorial—a simple desire to blot out ideas of which the government or a majority of its citizens disapproved. The concurring Justices saw something different: an effort by the government, divorced from mere hostility toward ideas, to counter a severe and objectively ascertainable harm caused by (one form of) an idea's expression."

6. In distinguishing Title VII law, Scalia, J., states that if government does not target discriminatory conduct on the basis of its expressive content, government may regulate, apparently without First Amendment scrutiny, even if the conduct expresses a discriminatory idea or philosophy. Is this consistent with *O'Brien*? The opinions in *Barnes* other than Scalia, J.'s? Suppose St. Paul outlawed all conduct that tended to create a racially or sexually hostile environment. Consider Richard Fallon, *Sexual Harassment, Content Neutrality, and the First Amendment Dog That Didn't Bark*, 1994 Sup.Ct.Rev. 1, 16: "A statute of this kind, which would restrict the press,

---

d. See Frederick Lawrence, *Punishing Hate: Bias Crimes Under American Law* (1999); James B. Jacobs & Kimberly Potter, *Hate Crimes, Criminal Law and Identity Politics* (1998); Alon Herel & Gideon Parchomovsky, *On Hate and Equality,* 109 Yale L.J 507 (1999); Alan E. Brownstein, *Rules of Engagement for Cultural Wars,* 29 U.C. Davis L.Rev. 553 (1996); Susan Gellman, *Sticks and Stones Can Put You in Jail, But Can Words Increase Your Sentence?,* 39 U.C.L.A.L.Rev. 333 (1991); See generally Laurence Tribe, *The Mystery of Motive, Private and Public: Some Notes Inspired by the Problems of Hate Crime and Animal Sacrifice,* 1993 Sup.Ct.Rev. 1.

e. California's anti-paparazzi legislation provides stiffer penalties for trespass if the purpose is to photograph or videotape someone without their permission. Constitutional?

political orators, and private citizens engaged in conversation in their homes, would surely offend the First Amendment. Certainly Justice Scalia [does] not believe otherwise." Could St. Paul outlaw racial harassment under Scalia, J.'s rationale and apply it to the facts of *R.A.V.* without First Amendment scrutiny?

Are many applications of sexual harassment law problematic under the First Amendment?**f**

7. After *R.A.V.*, what is (should be) the constitutional status of statutes imposing "penalties for filing false complaints against police officers, bans on defamatory statements about political candidates, prohibitions on falsely imputing unchastity to women, and civil liability for defamation of agricultural products." See Nat Stern, *The Doubtful Validity of Victim-Specific Libel Laws*, 52 Vill. L.Rev. 533 (2007).

————

In 1952, Virginia declared it a felony publicly to burn a cross with the intent of intimidating any person or group of persons. In 1968, Virginia added a provision that any such burning shall be prima facie evidence of an intent to intimidate. Barry Black led a Ku Klux Klan rally in which a cross was burned after a series of speeches marked by racial hostility, including one speaker saying that he "would love to take a .30/.30 and just random[ly] shoot the blacks." Forty to fifty cars passed the site during the rally, and eight to ten houses were located in its vicinity. The trial court used a Virginia Model Instruction that "the burning of a cross by itself is sufficient evidence from which you may infer the required intent."

Richard Elliot and Jonathan O'Mara attempted to burn a cross at the residence of an African–American. O'Mara pled guilty of attempted burning, reserving the right to challenge the statute; Elliot was convicted in a trial in which the jury was instructed that the Commonwealth had to show the intent to burn the cross and the intent to intimidate. The trial court did not instruct on the meaning of the prima facie provision of the statute, nor did it give the Model Instruction.

---

f. For a variety of views, see Kent Greenawalt, *Fighting Words* 77–96 (1995); J.M. Balkin, *Free Speech and Hostile Environments*, 99 Colum. L.Rev. 2295 (1999); Kingsley Browne, *Title VII as Censorship: Hostile-Environment Harassment and the First Amendment*, 52 Ohio St.L.J. 481 (1991); Cynthia L. Estlund, *Freedom of Expression in the Workplace and the Problem of Discriminatory Harassment*, 75 Texas L.Rev. 687 (1997); Cynthia L. Estlund, *The Architecture of the First Amendment and the Case of Workplace Harassment*, 72 Notre Dame L.Rev. 1361 (1997); Fallon, supra; Jules B. Gerard, *The First Amendment in a Hostile Environment: A Primer on Free Speech and Sexual Harassment*, 68 Notre D.L.Rev. 579 (1995); Linda S. Greene, *Sexual Harassment Law and the First Amendment*, 71 Chi.-Kent L.Rev. 729 (1995); Susanne Sangree, *Title VII Prohibitions Against Hostile Environment Sexual Harassment and the First Amendment: No Collision in Sight*, 47 Rutgers L.Rev. 461 (1995); Marcy Strauss, *Sexist Speech in the Workplace*, 25 Harv.C.R.–C.L.L.Rev. 1 (1990); Nadine Strossen, *Regulating Workplace Sexual Harassment and Upholding the First Amendment—Avoiding a Collision*, 37 Vill. L.Rev. 757 (1992); Eugene Volokh, *Freedom of Speech and Workplace Harassment*, 39 U.C.L.A.L.Rev. 1791 (1992); Eugene Volokh, *How Harassment Law Restricts Free Speech*, 47 Rutgers L.Rev. 563 (1995); Eugene Volokh, *What Speech Does "Hostile Work Environment" Harassment Law Restrict?*, 85 Geo. L.J. 627, 647 (1997). See also *Davis v. Monroe County Board of Educ.*, 526 U.S. 629 (1999) (Kennedy, J., dissenting).

The Virginia Supreme Court declared the statute unconstitutional in light of *R.A.V.* and overturned the convictions of the three defendants. VIRGINIA v. BLACK, 538 U.S. 343 (2003), per O'CONNOR, J., upheld the cross burning with intent to intimidate provision, struck down the prima facie evidence provision as interpreted by the jury instruction in the Black case, and, thereby, affirmed the dismissal of Black's prosecution while vacating and remanding for further proceedings with respect to Elliot and O'Mara: "[T]he First Amendment [permits] a State to ban a 'true threat.' [*Watts.*, Ch. 1, I, D, fn. d supra.] Intimidation in the constitutionally proscribable sense of the word is a type of true threat. [The] First Amendment permits Virginia to outlaw cross burnings done with the intent to intimidate because burning a cross is a particularly virulent form of intimidation. Instead of prohibiting all intimidating messages, Virginia may choose to regulate this subset of intimidating messages in light of cross burning's long and pernicious history as a signal of impending violence. Thus, just as a State may regulate only that obscenity which is the most obscene due to its prurient content, so too may a State choose to prohibit only those forms of intimidation that are most likely to inspire fear of bodily harm. A ban on cross burning carried out with the intent to intimidate is fully consistent with our holding in *R.A.V.* and is proscribable under the First Amendment."

In a section of the opinion joined by Rehnquist, C.J., Stevens and Breyer, JJ., O'Connor, J., addressed the prima facie evidence provision: "The Supreme Court of Virginia has not ruled on the meaning of the prima facie evidence provision. It has, however, stated that 'the act of burning a cross alone, with no evidence of intent to intimidate, will nonetheless suffice for arrest and prosecution and will insulate the Commonwealth from a motion to strike the evidence at the end of its case-in-chief.' The jury in the case of Richard Elliott did not receive any instruction on the prima facie evidence provision, and the provision was not an issue in the case of Jonathan O'Mara because he pleaded guilty. The court in Barry Black's case, however, instructed the jury that the provision means: 'The burning of a cross, by itself, is sufficient evidence from which you may infer the required intent.'

"The prima facie evidence provision, as interpreted by the jury instruction, renders the statute unconstitutional. Because this jury instruction is the Model Jury Instruction, and because the Supreme Court of Virginia had the opportunity to expressly disavow the jury instruction, the jury instruction's construction of the prima facie provision 'is a ruling on a question of state law that is as binding on us as though the precise words had been written into' the statute. [As] construed by the jury instruction, the prima facie provision strips away the very reason why a State may ban cross burning with the intent to intimidate. The prima facie evidence provision permits a jury to convict in every cross-burning case in which defendants exercise their constitutional right not to put on a defense. And even where a defendant like Black presents a defense, the prima facie evidence provision makes it more likely that the jury will find an intent to intimidate regardless of the particular facts of the case. The provision permits the Commonwealth to arrest, prosecute, and convict a person based solely on the fact of cross burning itself.

"The act of burning a cross may mean that a person is engaging in constitutionally proscribable intimidation. But that same act may mean only that the person is engaged in core political speech. The prima facie evidence provision in this statute blurs the line between these two meanings of a burning cross. As interpreted by the jury instruction, the provision chills constitutionally protected political speech because of the possibility that a State will prosecute—and potentially convict—somebody engaging only in lawful political speech at the core of what the First Amendment is designed to protect. * * *

"For these reasons, the prima facie evidence provision, as interpreted through the jury instruction and as applied in Barry Black's case, is unconstitutional on its face. We recognize that the Supreme Court of Virginia has not authoritatively interpreted the meaning of the prima facie evidence provision. Unlike Justice Scalia, we refuse to speculate on whether *any* interpretation of the prima facie evidence provision would satisfy the First Amendment. Rather, all we hold is that because of the interpretation of the prima facie evidence provision given by the jury instruction, the provision makes the statute facially invalid at this point. We also recognize the theoretical possibility that the court, on remand, could interpret the provision in a manner different from that so far set forth in order to avoid the constitutional objections we have described. We leave open that possibility. We also leave open the possibility that the provision is severable, and if so, whether Elliott and O'Mara could be retried * * *.

"With respect to Barry Black, we agree with the Supreme Court of Virginia that his conviction cannot stand, and we affirm the judgment of the Supreme Court of Virginia. With respect to Elliott and O'Mara, we vacate the judgment of the Supreme Court of Virginia, and remand the case for further proceedings."

SCALIA, J., joined by Thomas, J., concurring and dissenting, agreed that the cross burning/intimidation portion of the statute was constitutional, but he denied that the prima facie evidence aspect of the statute was unconstitutional on its face. In a portion of his opinion not joined by Thomas, J., Scalia J., nonetheless concurred with the plurality's view that that the jury instruction was invalid: "I believe the prima-facie-evidence provision in Virginia's cross-burning statute is constitutionally unproblematic. Nevertheless, because the Virginia Supreme Court has not yet offered an authoritative construction of [that provision], I concur in the Court's decision to vacate and remand the judgment with respect to respondents Elliott and O'Mara. I also agree that respondent Black's conviction cannot stand. As noted above, the jury in Black's case was instructed that '[t]he burning of a cross, *by itself,* is sufficient evidence from which you may infer the required intent.' Where this instruction has been given, it is impossible to determine whether the jury has rendered its verdict (as it must) in light of the entire body of facts before it—*including* evidence that might rebut the presumption that the cross burning was done with an intent to intimidate—or, instead, has chosen to ignore such rebuttal evidence and focused exclusively on the fact that the defendant burned a cross. Still, I cannot go along with the Court's decision to affirm the judgment with respect to Black. In that judgment, the Virginia Supreme Court, having erroneously concluded that § 18.2–423 is over-broad, not only vacated Black's conviction, but dismissed the indictment against him as well. Because I believe the constitutional defect in Black's conviction is rooted in a jury instruction and not in the statute itself, I would not dismiss the indictment and would permit the Commonwealth to retry Black if it wishes to do so. It is an interesting question whether the plurality's willingness to let the Virginia Supreme Court resolve the plurality's make-believe facial invalidation of the statute extends as well to the facial invalidation insofar as it supports dismissal of the indictment against Black. Logically, there is no reason why it would not."

SOUTER, J., joined by Kennedy and Ginsburg, JJ., concurring in part and dissenting in part, argued that both the cross burning/intimidation section and the prima facie evidence section were unconstitutional: "I agree with the majority that the Virginia statute makes a content-based distinction within the category of punishable intimidating or threatening expression, the very type of distinction we considered in *R.A.V.* I disagree that any exception should save Virginia's law from unconstitutionality under the holding in *R.A.V.* or any acceptable variation of it. [Because] of the burning cross's extraordinary force as a method of intimidation, the *R.A.V.* exception most likely to cover the statute is the first of the three mentioned there, which the *R.A.V.* opinion called an exception for content discrimination on a basis that 'consists entirely of the very reason the entire class of speech at issue is proscribable.' This is the exception the majority speaks of here as covering statutes prohibiting 'particularly virulent' proscribable expression. [RAV] explained that when the subcate-gory is confined to the most obviously proscribable instances, 'no signifi-cant danger of idea or viewpoint discrimination exists,' and the explana-tion was rounded out with some illustrative examples. None of them, however, resembles the case before us.

"[One example] of permissible distinction is for a prohibition of obscenity unusually offensive 'in its prurience,' with citation to a case in which the Seventh Circuit discussed the difference between obscene de-pictions of actual people and simulations. As that court noted, distinguish-ing obscene publications on this basis does not suggest discrimination on the basis of the message conveyed. *Kucharek v. Hanaway,* 902 F.2d 513, 517–518 (7th Cir. 1990). The opposite is true, however, when a general prohibition of intimidation is rejected in favor of a distinct proscription of intimidation by cross burning. The cross may have been selected because of its special power to threaten, but it may also have been singled out because of disapproval of its message of white supremacy, either because a legislature thought white supremacy was a pernicious doctrine or because it found that dramatic, public espousal of it was a civic embarrassment. Thus, there is no kinship between the cross-burning statute and the core prurience example. * * *

"The majority's approach could be taken as recognizing an exception to *R.A.V.* when circumstances show that the statute's ostensibly valid reason for punishing particularly serious proscribable expression probably is not a ruse for message suppression, even though the statute may have a greater (but not exclusive) impact on adherents of one ideology than on others. * * *

"My concern here, in any event, is not with the merit of a pragmatic doctrinal move. For whether or not the Court should conceive of exceptions to *R.A.V.*'s general rule in a more practical way, no content-based statute should survive even under a pragmatic recasting of *R.A.V.* without a high probability that no 'official suppression of ideas is afoot,' I believe the prima facie evidence provision stands in the way of any finding of such a high probability here. * * *

"As I see the likely significance of the evidence provision, its primary effect is to skew jury deliberations toward conviction in cases where the evidence of intent to intimidate is relatively weak and arguably consistent with a solely ideological reason for burning. To understand how the provision may work, recall that the symbolic act of burning a cross, without more, is consistent with both intent to intimidate and intent to make an ideological statement free of any aim to threaten. One can tell the intimidating instance from the wholly ideological one only by reference to some further circumstance. In the real world, of course, and in real-world prosecutions, there will always be further circumstances, and the factfinder will always learn something more than the isolated fact of cross burning. Sometimes those circumstances will show an intent to intimidate, but sometimes they will be at least equivocal, as in cases where a white supremacist group burns a cross at an initiation ceremony or political rally visible to the public. In such a case, if the factfinder Black's case is aware of the prima facie evidence provision, as the jury was in respondent, the provision will have the practical effect of tilting the jury's thinking in favor of the prosecution. [The] provision will thus tend to draw nonthreatening ideological expression within the ambit of the prohibition of intimidating expression. * * *

"To the extent the prima facie evidence provision skews prosecutions, then, it skews the statute toward suppressing ideas. Thus, the appropriate way to consider the statute's prima facie evidence term, in my view, is not as if it were an overbroad statutory definition amenable to severance or a narrowing construction. The question here is not the permissible scope of an arguably overbroad statute, but the claim of a clearly content-based statute to an exception from the general prohibition of content-based proscriptions, an exception that is not warranted if the statute's terms show that suppression of ideas may be afoot. Accordingly, the way to look at the prima facie evidence provision is to consider it for any indication of what is afoot. And if we look at the provision for this purpose, it has a very obvious significance as a mechanism for bringing within the statute's prohibition some expression that is doubtfully threatening though certainly distasteful.

"It is difficult to conceive of an intimidation case that could be easier to prove than one with cross burning, assuming any circumstances suggesting intimidation are present. The provision, apparently so unnecessary to legitimate prosecution of intimidation, is therefore quite enough to raise the question whether Virginia's content-based statute seeks more than mere protection against a virulent form of intimidation. It consequently bars any conclusion that an exception to the general rule of *R.A.V.* is warranted on the ground 'that there is no realistic [or little realistic] possibility that official suppression of ideas is afoot.'

"I conclude that the statute under which all three of the respondents were prosecuted violates the First Amendment, since the statute's content-based distinction was invalid at the time of the charged activities, regardless of whether the prima facie evidence provision was given any effect in any respondent's individual case. In my view, severance of the prima facie evidence provision now could not eliminate the unconstitutionality of the whole statute at the time of the respondents' conduct. I would therefore affirm the judgment of the Supreme Court of Virginia vacating the respondents' convictions and dismissing the indictments. Accordingly, I concur in the Court's judgment as to respondent Black and dissent as to respondents Elliott and O'Mara."

THOMAS, J., dissenting, maintained that the statute was constitutional: "Although I agree with the majority's conclusion that it is constitutionally permissible to 'ban ... cross burning carried out with intent to intimidate,' I believe that the majority errs in imputing an expressive component to the activity in question. In my view, whatever expressive value cross burning has, the legislature simply wrote it out by banning only intimidating conduct undertaken by a particular means. A conclusion that the statute prohibiting cross burning with intent to intimidate sweeps beyond a prohibition on certain conduct into the zone of expression overlooks not only the words of the statute but also reality.

" 'The world's oldest, most persistent terrorist organization is not European or even Middle Eastern in origin. Fifty years before the Irish Republican Army was organized, a century before Al Fatah declared its holy war on Israel, the Ku Klux Klan was actively harassing, torturing and murdering in the United States. Today [its] members remain fanatically committed to a course of violent opposition to social progress and racial equality in the United States.' M. Newton & J. Newton, *The Ku Klux Klan: An Encyclopedia* vii (1991). * * *

"As the Solicitor General points out, the association between acts of intimidating cross burning and violence is well documented in recent American history. [Virginia's] experience has been no exception. [In]

February 1952, in light of [a] series of cross burnings and attendant reports that the Klan, 'long considered dead in Virginia, is being revitalized in Richmond,' Governor Battle announced that 'Virginia might well consider passing legislation to restrict the activities of the Ku Klux Klan.' [As] newspapers reported at the time, the bill was 'to ban the burning of crosses and other similar evidences of *terrorism.*' * * *

"Strengthening [my] conclusion, that the legislature sought to criminalize terrorizing *conduct* is the fact that at the time the statute was enacted, racial segregation was not only the prevailing practice, but also the law in Virginia. And, just two years after the enactment of this statute, Virginia's General Assembly embarked on a campaign of 'massive resistance' in response to *Brown v. Board of Education.* It strains credulity to suggest that a state legislature that adopted a litany of segregationist laws self-contradictorily intended to squelch the segregationist message. Even for segregationists, violent and terroristic conduct, the Siamese twin of cross burning, was intolerable. The ban on cross burning with intent to intimidate demonstrates that even segregationists understood the difference between intimidating and terroristic conduct and racist expression. It is simply beyond belief that, in passing the statute now under review, the Virginia legislature was concerned with anything but penalizing conduct it must have viewed as particularly vicious.

"Accordingly, this statute prohibits only conduct, not expression. And, just as one cannot burn down someone's house to make a political point and then seek refuge in the First Amendment, those who hate cannot terrorize and intimidate to make their point. In light of my conclusion that the statute here addresses only conduct, there is no need to analyze it under any of our First Amendment tests.

"[Even] assuming that the statute implicates the First Amendment, in my view, the fact that the statute permits a jury to draw an inference of intent to intimidate from the cross burning itself presents no constitutional problems. [The] inference is rebuttable and, as the jury instructions given in this case demonstrate, Virginia law still requires the jury to find the existence of each element, including intent to intimidate, beyond a reasonable doubt."

NOTES AND QUESTIONS

1. *R.A.V.* struck the ordinance down on its face, but did not rely on the overbreadth doctrine. The Court interpreted the ordinance to apply only to fighting words; it, therefore, could not have been overbroad. The concurring justices in *R.A.V.* interpreted the ordinance to sweep beyond fighting words, and maintained that the ordinance should have been invalidated on overbreadth grounds. Does O'Connor, J., rely on overbreadth analysis in *Black?* If so, how would the analysis relate to *Brockett v. Spokane Arcades?* Recall that *Brockett* referred to the "normal rule that partial, rather than facial invalidation" of statutes is to be preferred and observed that: "[A]n individual whose own speech or expressive conduct may validly be prohibited or sanctioned is

permitted to challenge a statute on its face because it also threatens others not before the court—those who desire to engage in legally protected expression but who may refrain from doing so rather than risk prosecution or undertake to have the law declared partially invalid. If the overbreadth is 'substantial,' the law may not be enforced against anyone, including the party before the court, until it is narrowed to reach only unprotected activity, whether by legislative action or by judicial construction or partial invalidation.

"It is otherwise where the parties challenging the statute are those who desire to engage in protected speech that the overbroad statute purports to punish, or who seek to publish both protected and unprotected material. There is then no want of a proper party to challenge the statute, no concern that an attack on the statute will be unduly delayed or protected speech discouraged. The statute may forthwith be declared invalid to the extent that it reaches too far, but otherwise left intact."[a] How does Black's activity fit into this scheme? In any event, is the Virginia statute substantially overbroad?

2.   Consider Erwin Chemerinsky, *Striking a Balance on Hate Speech*, 39 July Trial 78, 79 (2003): "The Court, with only Thomas dissenting, affirmed the Virginia Supreme Court's conclusion that Black's conviction, for burning a cross on a relatively isolated farm as part of a rally, violated the First Amendment. The cross was burned not to intimidate a person or group, but as part of a Klan rally to express that organization's views. [T]he Court struck a balance likely to be important in future cases involving hate speech. 'True threats' are not protected by the First Amendment, and hate speech, such as cross-burning, may be banned when it constitutes a true threat. But the burden is on the government to prove that an action is a true threat under the circumstances." But cf. Jeannine Bell, *O Say, Can You See: Free Expression by the Light of Fiery Crosses*, 39 Harv. C.R.-C.L. L. Rev. 335, 345, 367 (2004): "For minorities and enemies of the Klan there were few, if any, innocent cross burnings. The association between the burning cross and violent intimidation of racial, ethnic and religious minorities—or anyone else who might be an enemy of the Klan—was strengthened as cross burnings continued to be accompanied by acts of violence. [A] cross burning by the Klan at one of its gatherings, especially a gathering staged in a way that others will see it, is intended to serve two goals at the same time: promoting group solidarity and causing intimidation."[b]

---

a.   After the Court has declared that the statute is invalid to the extent it reaches too far, the remaining portion of the statute will be examined to determine whether that portion is severable. That is, it could well be the intent of the legislature that the statute stands or falls as a single package. To invalidate a part, then, could be to invalidate the whole. Alternatively, the legislature may have intended to salvage whatever it might. The question of severability is regarded as one of legislative intent, but, at least with respect to federal legislation, courts will presume that severability was intended. See, e.g., *Regan v. Time, Inc.*, 468 U.S. 641 (1984). The question of whether a provision of a state statute is severable is one of state law.

b.   For discussion of the violence and discrimination associated with hate speech, see Alexander Tsesis, *Dignity and Speech: The Regulation of Hate Speech in a Democracy*, 44 Wake For. L. Rev. 497 (2009); On the importance of context regarding threats, see Kenneth Karst, *Threats and Meanings: How the Facts Govern First Amendment Doctrine*, 58 Stan.L.Rev. 1337 (2006).

CHAPTER 4

PRIOR RESTRAINTS

■ ■ ■

Prior restraint is a technical term in First Amendment law. A criminal statute prohibiting all advocacy of violent action would *restrain* speech and would have been enacted *prior* to any restrained communication. The statute would be overbroad, but it would not be a prior restraint. A prior restraint refers only to closely related, distinctive methods of regulating expression that are said to have in common their own peculiar set of evils and problems, in addition to those that accompany most any governmental interference with free expression. "The issue is not whether the government may impose a particular restriction of substance in an area of public expression, such as forbidding obscenity in newspapers, but whether it may do so by a particular method, such as advance screening of newspaper copy. In other words, restrictions which could be validly imposed when enforced by subsequent punishment are, nevertheless, forbidden if attempted by prior restraint." Thomas Emerson, *The Doctrine of Prior Restraint,* 20 Law and Contemp.Prob. 648 (1955).

The classic prior restraints were the English licensing laws which required a license in advance to print any material or to import or to sell any book.[a] One of the questions raised in this chapter concerns the types of government conduct beyond the classic licensing laws that should be characterized as prior restraints. Another concerns the question of when government licensing of speech, press, or assembly should be countenanced. Perhaps, most important, the Section explores the circumstances in which otherwise protected speech may be restrained on an ad hoc basis.

I. FOUNDATION CASES

A. LICENSING

LOVELL v. GRIFFIN, 303 U.S. 444 (1938), per HUGHES, C.J., invalidated an ordinance prohibiting the distribution of handbooks, advertising or literature within the city of Griffin, Georgia without obtaining written permission of the City Manager: "[T]he ordinance is invalid on its face.

---

a. For a persuasive chronicling of the abuses in a modern licensing system, see generally Lucas Powe, *American Broadcasting and the First Amendment* (1987).

284

Whatever the motive which induced its adoption, its character is such that it strikes at the very foundation of the freedom of the press by subjecting it to license and censorship. The struggle for the freedom of the press was primarily directed against the power of the licensor. It was against that power that John Milton directed his assault by his 'Appeal for the Liberty of Unlicensed Printing.' And the liberty of the press became initially a right to publish *without* a license what formerly could be published only *with* one.' While this freedom from previous restraint upon publication cannot be regarded as exhausting the guaranty of liberty, the prevention of that restraint was a leading purpose in the adoption of the constitutional provision. Legislation of the type of the ordinance in question would restore the system of license and censorship in its baldest form.

"The liberty of the press is not confined to newspapers and periodicals. It necessarily embraces pamphlets and leaflets. These indeed have been historic weapons in the defense of liberty, as the pamphlets of Thomas Paine and others in our own history abundantly attest. The press in its historic connotation comprehends every sort of publication which affords a vehicle of information and opinion. * * *

"The ordinance cannot be saved because it relates to distribution and not to publication. 'Liberty of circulating is as essential to that freedom as liberty of publishing; indeed, without the circulation, the publication would be of little value.' *Ex parte Jackson*, 96 U.S. (6 Otto) 727, 733 (1877).

"[As] the ordinance is void on its face, it was not necessary for appellant to seek a permit under it. She was entitled to contest its validity in answer to the charge against her."[a]

NOTES AND QUESTIONS

1. ***First Amendment procedure.*** Notice that Lovell would get the benefit of the prior restraint doctrine even if the material she distributed was obscene or otherwise unprotected. In that respect, the prior restraint doctrine is similar to the doctrines of overbreadth and vagueness. For particular concerns that underlie the prior restraint doctrine, consider Thomas Emerson, *The System of Freedom of Expression* 506 (1970): "A system of prior restraint is in many ways more inhibiting than a system of subsequent punishment: It is likely to bring under government scrutiny a far wider range of expression; it shuts off communication before it takes place; suppression by a stroke of the pen is more likely to be applied than suppression through a criminal process; the procedures do not require attention to the safeguards of the criminal process; the system allows less opportunity for public appraisal and criticism; the dynamics of the system drive toward excesses, as the history of all censorship shows."[b]

---

a. Cardozo, J., took no part.

b. But see Richard Posner, *Free Speech in an Economic Perspective*, 20 Suff.L.Rev. 1, 13 (1986): "The conventional arguments for why censorship is worse than criminal punishment are

2. ***Scope and character of the doctrine.*** What is the vice of the licensing scheme in *Lovell*? Is the concern that like vague statutes it affords undue discretion and potential for abuse? Is the real concern the uncontrolled power of the licensor to deny licenses? Suppose licenses were automatically issued to anyone who applied?

To what extent should the prior restraint doctrine apply to non-press activities? To a licensing ordinance that otherwise forbids soliciting membership in organizations that exact fees of their members? See *Staub v. Baxley,* 355 U.S. 313 (1958) (yes). To a licensing ordinance that otherwise prohibits attempts to secure contributions for charitable or religious causes? See *Cantwell v. Connecticut,* 310 U.S. 296 (1940) (yes).

Should the prior restraint doctrine apply to all aspects of newspaper circulation? See *Lakewood v. Plain Dealer Publishing Co.,* 486 U.S. 750 (1988) (invalidating ordinance granting Mayor power to grant or deny annual permits to place newsracks on public property).[c]

Suppose, in the above cases, that the authority of the licensor were confined by narrow, objective, and definite standards or that licenses were automatically issued to anyone who applied. *Hynes v. Mayor,* 425 U.S. 610 (1976), per Burger, C.J., stated in dictum that a municipality could regulate house to house soliciting by requiring advance notice to the police department in order to protect its citizens from crime and undue annoyance: "A narrowly drawn ordinance, that does not vest in municipal officials the undefined power to determine what messages residents will hear, may serve these important interests without running afoul of the First Amendment." But cf. *Thomas v. Collins,* 323 U.S. 516 (1945) (registration requirement for paid union organizers invalid prior restraint); *Talley v. California,* 362 U.S. 60 (1960) (ban on anonymous handbills "void on its face," noting that the "obnoxious press licensing law of England, which was also enforced on the Colonies was due in part to the knowledge that exposure of the names of printers, writers and distributors would lessen the circulation of literature critical of the government").

WATCHTOWER BIBLE & TRACT SOCIETY v. STRATTON, 536 U.S. 150 (2002), per STEVENS, J., struck down a village ordinance requiring door to door advocates or distributors of literature to register with the mayor: "It is offensive—not only to the values protected by the First Amendment, but to the very notion of a free society—that in the context of everyday public discourse a citizen must first inform the government of her desire to speak to her neighbors and then obtain a permit to do so. Even if the issuance of permits by the mayor's office is a ministerial task that is performed promptly and at no cost to the applicant, a law requiring

---

little better than plausible (though I think there is at least one good argument)" [observing that speech ordinarily does not produce sufficient damage to justify sifting through massive materials].

c. White, J., joined by Stevens and O'Connor, JJ., dissenting, contended that *Lovell* should apply only if the newspaper had a constitutional right to place newsracks on public sidewalks. Otherwise, the newspaper should be required to show that a denial was based on improper reasons. .

a permit to engage in such speech constitutes a dramatic departure from our national heritage and constitutional tradition."

Stevens, J., argued that required licensing impinged on the speaker's interest in anonymity. In addition, "requiring a permit as a prior condition on the exercise of the right to speak imposes an objective burden on some speech of citizens holding religious or patriotic views. As our World War II-era cases dramatically demonstrate, there are a significant number of persons whose religious scruples will prevent them from applying for such a license. There are no doubt other patriotic citizens, who have such firm convictions about their constitutional right to engage in uninhibited debate in the context of door-to-door advocacy, that they would prefer silence to speech licensed by a petty official.

"[Moreover,] there is a significant amount of spontaneous speech that is effectively banned by the ordinance. A person who made a decision on a holiday or a weekend to take an active part in a political campaign could not begin to pass out handbills until after he or she obtained the required permit. Even a spontaneous decision to go across the street and urge a neighbor to vote against the mayor could not lawfully be implemented without first obtaining the mayor's permission. * * *

"Also central to our conclusion that the ordinance does not pass First Amendment scrutiny is that it is not tailored to the Village's stated interests. Even if the interest in preventing fraud could adequately support the ordinance insofar as it applies to commercial transactions and the solicitation of funds, that interest provides no support for its application to petitioners, to political campaigns, or to enlisting support for unpopular causes. The Village, however, argues that the ordinance is nonetheless valid because it serves the two additional interests of protecting the privacy of the resident and the prevention of crime.

"With respect to the former, it seems clear that § 107 of the ordinance, which provides for the posting of 'No Solicitation' signs and which is not challenged in this case, coupled with the resident's unquestioned right to refuse to engage in conversation with unwelcome visitors, provides ample protection for the unwilling listener. [The] annoyance caused by an uninvited knock on the front door is the same whether or not the visitor is armed with a permit.

"With respect to the latter, it seems unlikely that the absence of a permit would preclude criminals from knocking on doors and engaging in conversations not covered by the ordinance. They might, for example, ask for directions or permission to use the telephone, or pose as surveyers or census takers. Or they might register under a false name with impunity because the ordinance contains no provision for verifying an applicant's identity or organizational credentials. Moreover, the Village did not assert an interest in crime prevention below, and there is an absence of any evidence of a special crime problem related to door-to-door solicitation in the record before us.

"The rhetoric used in the World War II-era opinions that repeatedly saved petitioners' coreligionists from petty prosecutions reflected the Court's evaluation of the First Amendment freedoms that are implicated in this case. The value judgment that then motivated a united democratic people fighting to defend those very freedoms from totalitarian attack is unchanged. It motivates our decision today."

BREYER, J., joined by Souter and Ginsburg, JJ., concurred: "While joining the Court's opinion, I write separately to note that the dissent's 'crime prevention' justification for this ordinance is not a strong one. For one thing, there is no indication that the legislative body that passed the ordinance considered this justification. In the intermediate scrutiny context, the Court ordinarily does not supply reasons the legislative body has not given. That does not mean, as the Chief Justice suggests, that only a government with a 'battery of constitutional lawyers,' could satisfy this burden. It does mean that we expect a government to give its real reasons for passing an ordinance.

"Because Stratton did not rely on the crime prevention justification, because Stratton has not now 'present[ed] more than anecdote and supposition,' and because the relationship between the interest and the ordinance is doubtful, I am unwilling to assume that these conjectured benefits outweigh the cost of abridging the speech covered by the ordinance."

SCALIA, J., joined by Thomas, J., concurring in the judgment, agreed with some of the Court's opinion, but did not "agree, for example, that one of the causes of the invalidity of Stratton's ordinance is that some people have a religious objection to applying for a permit, and others (posited by the Court) 'have such firm convictions about their constitutional right to engage in uninhibited debate in the context of door-to-door advocacy, that they would prefer silence to speech licensed by a petty official.'

"If a licensing requirement is otherwise lawful, it is in my view not invalidated by the fact that some people will choose, for religious reasons, to forgo speech rather than observe it. That would convert an invalid free-exercise claim into a valid free-speech claim—and a more destructive one at that. Whereas the free-exercise claim, if acknowledged, would merely exempt Jehovah's Witnesses from the licensing requirement, the free-speech claim exempts everybody, thanks to Jehovah's Witnesses.

"As for the Court's fairy-tale category of 'patriotic citizens,' who would rather be silenced than licensed in a manner that the Constitution (but for their 'patriotic' objection) would permit: If our free-speech jurisprudence is to be determined by the predicted behavior of such crackpots, we are in a sorry state indeed."

REHNQUIST, C.J., dissented: "The town had little reason to suspect that the negligible burden of having to obtain a permit runs afoul of the

First Amendment . For over 60 years, we have categorically stated that a permit requirement for door-to-door canvassers, which gives no discretion to the issuing authority, is constitutional. The District Court and Court of Appeals, relying on our cases, upheld the ordinance. The Court today, however, abruptly changes course and invalidates the ordinance. [With] respect to the interest in protecting privacy, the Court concludes that '[t]he annoyance caused by an uninvited knock on the front door is the same whether or not the visitor is armed with a permit.' True, but that misses the key point: the permit requirement results in fewer uninvited knocks. Those who have complied with the permit requirement are less likely to visit residences with no trespassing signs, as it is much easier for the authorities to track them down.

"The Court also fails to grasp how the permit requirement serves Stratton's interest in preventing crime. We have approved of permit requirements for those engaging in protected First Amendment activity because of a common-sense recognition that their existence both deters and helps detect wrongdoing. And while some people, intent on committing burglaries or violent crimes, are not likely to be deterred by the prospect of a misdemeanor for violating the permit ordinance, the ordinance's effectiveness does not depend on criminals registering. The ordinance prevents and detects serious crime by making it a crime not to register."

Rehnquist, C.J., referred to a double murder that had taken place in Hanover, New Jersey: "The murderers did not achieve their objective until they visited their fifth home over a period of seven months. If Hanover had a permit requirement, the teens may have been stopped before they achieved their objective. One of the residents they visited may have informed the police that there were two canvassers who lacked a permit. Such neighborly vigilance, though perhaps foreign to those residing in modern day cities, is not uncommon in small towns. Or the police on their own may have discovered that two canvassers were violating the ordinance. Apprehension for violating the permit requirement may well have frustrated the teenagers' objectives; it certainly would have assisted in solving the murders had the teenagers gone ahead with their plan.

"Of course, the Stratton ordinance does not guarantee that no canvasser will ever commit a burglary or violent crime. The Court seems to think this dooms the ordinance, erecting an insurmountable hurdle that a law must provide a fool-proof method of preventing crime. In order to survive intermediate scrutiny, however, a law need not solve the crime problem, it need only further the interest in preventing crime. Some deterrence of serious criminal activity is more than enough to survive intermediate scrutiny."

B. INJUNCTIONS

NEAR v. MINNESOTA

283 U.S. 697, 51 S.Ct. 625, 75 L.Ed. 1357 (1931).

CHIEF JUSTICE HUGHES delivered the opinion of the Court.

[The *Saturday Press* published articles charging that through graft and incompetence named public officials failed to expose and punish gangsters responsible for gambling, bootlegging, and racketeering in Minneapolis. It demanded a special grand jury and special prosecutor to deal with the situation and to investigate an alleged attempt to assassinate one of its publishers. Under a statute that authorized abatement of a "malicious, scandalous and defamatory newspaper" the state secured, and its supreme court affirmed, a court order that "abated" the Press and perpetually enjoined the defendants from publishing or circulating "any publication whatsoever which is a malicious, scandalous or defamatory newspaper." The order did not restrain the defendants from operating a newspaper "in harmony with the general welfare."]

The object of the statute is not punishment, in the ordinary sense, but suppression of the offending newspaper. [In] the case of public officers, it is the reiteration of charges of official misconduct, and the fact that the newspaper [is] principally devoted to that purpose, that exposes it to suppression. [T]he operation and effect of the statute [is] that public authorities may bring the owner or publisher of a newspaper or periodical before a judge upon a charge of conducting a business of publishing scandalous and defamatory matter—in particular that the matter consists of charges against public officers of official dereliction—and, unless the owner or publisher is able and disposed to bring competent evidence to satisfy the judge that the charges are true and are published with good motives and for justifiable ends, his newspaper or periodical is suppressed and further publication is made punishable as a contempt. This is of the essence of censorship.

The question is whether a statute authorizing such proceedings [is] consistent with the conception of the liberty of the press as historically conceived and guaranteed. [I]t has been generally, if not universally, considered that it is the chief purpose of the guaranty to prevent previous restraints upon publication. The struggle in England, directed against the legislative power of the licenser, resulted in renunciation of the censorship of the press. The liberty deemed to be established was thus described by Blackstone: "The liberty of the press is indeed essential to the nature of a free state; but this consists in laying no *previous* restraints upon publications, and not in freedom from censure for criminal matter when published. Every freeman has an undoubted right to lay what sentiments he pleases before the public; to forbid this, is to destroy the freedom of the press; but if he publishes what is improper, mischievous or illegal, he must take the consequence of his own temerity." [The] criticism upon Blackstone's statement has not been because immunity from previous restraint upon publication has not been regarded as deserving of special emphasis, but chiefly because that immunity cannot be deemed to exhaust the conception of the liberty guaranteed by State and Federal Constitutions.

[T]he protection even as to previous restraint is not absolutely unlimited. But the limitation has been recognized only in exceptional cases. [N]o one would question but that a government might prevent actual obstruction to its recruiting service or the publication of the sailing dates of transports or the number and location of troops. On similar grounds, the primary requirements of decency may be enforced against obscene publications. The security of the community life may be protected against incitements to acts of violence and the overthrow by force of orderly [government].[a] * * *

The fact that for approximately one hundred and fifty years there has been almost an entire absence of attempts to impose previous restraints upon publications relating to the malfeasance of public officers is significant of the deep-seated conviction that such restraints would violate constitutional right. Public officers, whose character and conduct remain open to debate and free discussion in the press, find their remedies for false accusations in actions under libel laws providing for redress and punishment, and not in proceedings to restrain the publication of newspapers and periodicals. [The] fact that the liberty of the press may be abused by miscreant purveyors of scandal does not make any the less necessary the immunity of the press from previous restraint in dealing with official misconduct. Subsequent punishment for such abuses as may exist is the appropriate remedy, consistent with constitutional [privilege].

The statute in question cannot be justified by reason of the fact that the publisher is permitted to show, before injunction issues, that the matter published is true and is published with good motives and for justifiable ends. If such a statute, authorizing suppression and injunction on such a basis, is constitutionally valid, it would be equally permissible for the Legislature to provide that at any time the publisher of any newspaper could be brought before a court, or even an administrative officer (as the constitutional protection may not be regarded as resting on mere procedural details), and required to produce proof of the truth of his publication, or of what he intended to publish and of his motives, or stand enjoined. If this can be done, the Legislature may provide machinery for determining in the complete exercise of its discretion what are justifiable ends and restrain publication accordingly. And it would be but a step to a complete system of censorship.

---

a. For critical commentary on the concessions in *Near,* see Hans Linde, *Courts and Censorship,* 66 Minn.L.Rev. 171 (1981); Jeffery Smith, *Prior Restraint: Original Intentions and Modern Interpretations*, 28 Wm. & M.Rev. 439, 462 (1987). For criticism of the overuse of preliminary injunctions in a variety of intellectual property contexts, see Mark A. Lemley & Eugene Volokh, *Freedom of Speech and Injunctions in Intellectual Property Cases,* 48 Duke L.J. 147 (1998). For the contention that some of the "exceptions" to the prior restraint doctrine are not properly classified as prior restraints, see Michael I. Meyerson, *The Neglected History of the Prior Restraint Doctrine: Rediscovering the Link Between the First Amendment and the Separation of Powers*, 34 Ind. L. Rev. 295 (2001).

[For] these reasons we hold the statute, so far as it authorized the proceedings in this action, [to] be an infringement of the liberty of the press guaranteed by the Fourteenth Amendment. * * *

JUSTICE BUTLER (dissenting).

[T]he *previous restraints* referred to by [Blackstone] subjected the press to the arbitrary will of an administrative officer. [The] Minnesota statute does not operate as a *previous* restraint on publication within the proper meaning of that phrase. It does not authorize administrative control in advance such as was formerly exercised by the licensers and censors, but prescribes a remedy to be enforced by a suit in equity. In this case [t]he business and publications unquestionably constitute an abuse of the right of free press. [A]s stated by the state Supreme Court [they] threaten morals, peace, and good order. [The] restraint authorized is only in respect of continuing to do what has been duly adjudged to constitute a nuisance. [It] is fanciful to suggest similarity between the granting or enforcement of the decree authorized by this statute to prevent *further* publication of malicious, scandalous, and defamatory articles and the *previous restraint* upon the press by licensers as referred to by Blackstone and described in the history of the times to which he alludes. * * *

It is well known, as found by the state supreme court, that existing libel laws are inadequate effectively to suppress evils resulting from the kind of business and publications that are shown in this case. The doctrine [of this decision] exposes the peace and good order of every community and the business and private affairs of every individual to the constant and protracted false and malicious assaults of any insolvent publisher who may have purpose and sufficient capacity to contrive and put into effect a scheme or program for oppression, blackmail or extortion. * * *

JUSTICE VAN DEVANTER, JUSTICE MCREYNOLDS, and JUSTICE SUTHERLAND concur in this opinion.[b]

NOTES AND QUESTIONS

1. ***Near and seditious libel: a misuse of prior restraint?*** *Near* was decided three decades before *New York Times v. Sullivan*. Should the Court have looked to the substance of the regulation rather than its form? Consider John Jeffries, *Rethinking Prior Restraint*, 92 Yale L.J. 409, 416–17 (1983): "In truth, *Near* involved nothing more or less than a repackaged version of the law of seditious libel, and this the majority rightly refused to countenance. Hence, there was pressure, so typical of this doctrine, to cram the law into the disfavored category of prior restraint, even though it in fact functioned very differently from a scheme of official licensing. Here there was no license and no censor, no ex parte determination of what was prohibited, and no suppression of publication based on speculation about what somebody might say. Here the decision to suppress was made by a judge (not a bureaucrat), after

---

b. For background, see Fred Friendly, *Minnesota Rag* (1981); Paul Murphy, *Near v. Minnesota in the Context of Historical Developments*, 66 Minn.L.Rev. 95, 133–60 (1981).

adversarial (not ex parte) proceedings, to determine the legal character of what had been (and not what might be) published. The only aspect of prior restraint was the incidental fact that the defendants were commanded not to repeat that which they were proved to have done.

"[I]f *Near* reached the right result, does it really matter that it gave the wrong reason? The answer [is that] *Near* has become a prominent feature of the First Amendment landscape—a landmark, as the case is so often called, from which we chart our course to future decisions. [T]he Court has yet to explain (at least in terms that I understand) what it is about an injunction that justifies this independent rule of constitutional disfavor."

Should a court be able to enjoin the continued distribution of material it has finally adjudicated to be unprotected defamation under existing law? Suppose it enjoins the publication of any material that does not comply with the mandates of *New York Times* and *Gertz*?

2. ***The collateral bar rule.*** Does the collateral bar rule shed light on the relationship between prior restraints and injunctions? That rule insists "that a court order must be obeyed until it is set aside, and that persons subject to the order who disobey it may not defend against the ensuing charge of criminal contempt on the ground that the order was erroneous or even unconstitutional." Stephen Barnett, *The Puzzle of Prior Restraint,* 29 Stan. L.Rev. 539, 552 (1977). Is this rule defensible to protect the integrity of the judiciary and important state interests that could be thwarted by the speech restrained? Richard Favata, *Filling the Void in First Amendment Jurisprudence: Is There a Solution for Replacing the Impotent System of Prior Restraints?,* 72 Fordham L.Rev. 169, 193 (2003).

WALKER v. BIRMINGHAM, 388 U.S. 307 (1967) upheld the rule against a First Amendment challenge in affirming the contempt conviction of defendants for violating an ex parte injunction issued by an Alabama court enjoining them from engaging in street parades without a municipal permit issued pursuant to the city's parade ordinance. The Court, per STEWART, J., (Warren, C.J., Brennan, Douglas, and Fortas, JJ., dissenting) held that because the petitioners neither moved to dissolve the injunction nor sought to comply with the city's parade ordinance, their claim that the injunction and ordinance were unconstitutional[c] did not need to be considered: "This Court cannot hold that the petitioners were constitutionally free to ignore all the procedures of the law and carry their battle to the streets. [R]espect for judicial process is a small price to pay for the civilizing hand of law, which alone can give abiding meaning to constitutional freedom." Although *Walker* suggested that its holding might be different if the court issuing the injunction lacked jurisdiction or if the injunction were "transparently invalid or had only a frivolous pretense to validity," it held that Alabama's invocation of the collateral bar rule was not itself unconstitutional.

Cf. *Poulos v. New Hampshire,* 345 U.S. 395 (1953) (claim of arbitrary refusal to issue license for open air meeting need not be entertained when a licensing statute is considered to be valid on its face in circumstance where

---

c. Indeed, the ordinance in question was declared unconstitutional two years later. *Shuttlesworth v. Birmingham,* 394 U.S. 147 (1969) (ordinance conferring unbridled discretion to prohibit any parade or demonstration is unconstitutional prior restraint).

speaker fails to seek direct judicial relief and proceeds without a license).[d] Does *Poulos* pose considerable danger to First Amendment interests because the low visibility of the administrative decision permits easy abridgement of free expression? See Henry Monaghan, *First Amendment "Due Process,"* 83 Harv.L.Rev. 518, 543 (1970). Do *Lovell, Walker,* and *Poulos* fit easily together? Consider Vincent Blasi, *Prior Restraints on Demonstrations,* 68 Mich.L.Rev. 1482, 1555 (1970): "A refuses to apply for a permit; he undertakes a march that could have been prohibited in the first place; he is prosecuted for parading without a permit under a statute that is defective for overbreadth. B applies for a permit; he is rudely rebuffed by a city official in clear violation of the state permit statute (which is not invalid on its face); he marches anyway in a manner that would be protected by the First Amendment, he is prosecuted for parading without a permit. C applies for a permit; he is rudely rebuffed; he notifies city officials that he will march anyway; the officials obtain an injunction against the march; the injunction is overbroad and is also based on a state statute that is overbroad; C marches in a manner ordinarily within his constitutional rights; he is prosecuted for contempt. Under the law as it now stands, A wins, but B and C lose!"

3. ***Time, place, and manner regulations.*** Should injunctions that impose time, place, or manner regulations in response to proven wrongdoing be subjected to more stringent examination than that ordinarily applied to general regulations imposed by legislative or executive action? See *Madsen v. Women's Health Center,* 512 U.S. 753 (1994).

4. ***The commentators, injunctions, and prior restraint.*** Should the link between prior restraint doctrine and injunctions depend upon the collateral bar rule? Does the analogy between licensing systems and injunctions hold only in that event? See Owen Fiss, *The Civil Rights Injunction* 30, 69–74 (1978); Barnett, note 2 supra, at 553–54. Should the prior restraint doctrine be wholly inapplicable to injunctions so long as "expedited appellate review allows an immediate opportunity to test the validity of an injunction against speech and only so long as that opportunity is genuinely effective to allow timely publication should the injunction ultimately be adjudged invalid"? Jeffries, note 1 supra, at 433.[e] Indeed should the whole concept of prior restraint be abandoned? Consider id. at 433–34: "In the context of administrative preclearance, talking of prior restraint is unhelpful, though not inapt. A more informative frame of reference would be overbreadth, the doctrine that explicitly identifies why preclearance is specially objectionable. In the context of injunctions, however, the traditional doctrine of prior restraint is not merely unhelpful, but positively misleading. It focuses on a constitutionally inconsequential consideration of form and diverts attention away from the critical substantive issues of First Amendment coverage. The result is a two-pronged danger. On the one hand, vindication of First Amendment freedoms

---

d. For consideration of when licensing statutes for assemblies are valid, see *Cox v. New Hampshire,* Ch. 6, I, A infra.

e. For the argument that regulation by injunction is generally more speech protective than regulation via subsequent punishment, see William Mayton, *Toward A Theory of First Amendment Process: Injunctions of Speech, Subsequent Punishment, and the Costs of the Prior Restraint Doctrine,* 67 Corn.L.Rev. 245 (1982). For the contention that this should count in favor of subsequent punishment in many contexts, see Martin Redish, *The Proper Role of the Prior Restraint Doctrine in First Amendment Theory,* 70 Va.L.Rev. 53, 92–93 (1984).

in the name of prior restraint may exaggerate the legitimate reach of official competence to suppress by subsequent punishment. On the other hand, insistence on special disfavor for prior restraints outside the realm of substantive protection under the First Amendment may deny to the government an appropriate choice of means to vindicate legitimate interests. In my view, neither risk is justified by any compelling reason to continue prior restraint as a doctrinally independent category of contemporary First Amendment analysis."**f**

For a nuanced argument that the prior restraint doctrine should apply to injunctions even in those jurisdictions that reject the applicability of the collateral bar rule to First Amendment arguments, see Vincent Blasi, *Toward a Theory of Prior Restraint: The Central Linkage,* 66 Minn.L.Rev. 11 (1981). Except in particular contexts, Professor Blasi does not claim that the chilling effect of injunctions on speech is more severe than those associated with criminal laws and civil liability rules. He does argue that unlike criminal laws and civil liability rules, regulation of speech by licensing and injunctions requires abstract and unduly speculative adjudication, stimulates overuse by regulatory agents, can to some extent distort the way in which audiences perceive the message at issue, and unreasonably implies that the activity of disseminating controversial communications is "a threat to, rather than an integral feature of, the social order." Id. at 85. He argues that many of these factors are aggravated if the collateral bar rule applies and that other undesirable features are added. For example, speakers are forced to reveal planned details about their communication. He concludes that the "concept of prior restraint is coherent at the core." Id. at 93.**g** Michael I. Meyerson, *Rewriting Near v. Minnesota: Creating a Complete Definition of Prior Restraint,* 52 Mercer L. Rev. 1087, 1139 (2001)(prior restraints more susceptible to discriminatory treatment).

II. PRIOR RESTRAINTS, OBSCENITY, AND COMMERCIAL SPEECH

KINGSLEY BOOKS, INC. v. BROWN, 354 U.S. 436 (1957), per Frankfurter, J., upheld a state court decree, issued pursuant to a New York statute, enjoining the publisher from further distribution of 14 booklets the state court found obscene. On appeal to the Supreme Court the publisher challenged only the prior restraint, not the obscenity finding: "The phrase 'prior restraint' is not a self-wielding sword. Nor can it serve as a talismatic test. The duty of closer analysis and critical judgment in applying the thought behind the phrase has thus been authoritatively put by one who brings weighty learning to his support of constitutionally protected liberties: 'What is needed,' writes Professor Paul A. Freund, 'is a pragmatic assessment of its operation in the particular circumstances. The

---

f. See also Marin Scordato, *Distinction Without a Difference,* 68 N.C.L.Rev. 1 (1989) (generally agreeing with Jeffries but arguing that a small part of prior restraint doctrine should be salvaged).

g. See also Daniel A. Farber, *The First Amendment* 48–49 (1998). For detailed criticism of Blasi's position, all in defense of a different core, see Redish, fn. e supra, at 59–75.

generalization that prior restraint is particularly obnoxious in civil liberties cases must yield to more particularistic analysis.' *The Supreme Court and Civil Liberties,* 4 Vand.L.Rev. 533, 539.

"Wherein does § 22–a differ in its effective operation from the type of statute upheld in *Alberts v. California,* [354 U.S. 476 (1957)]. One would be bold to assert that the in terrorem effect of [criminal] statutes less restrains booksellers in the period before the law strikes than does § 22–a. Instead of requiring the bookseller to dread that the offer for sale of a book may, without prior warning, subject him to a criminal prosecution with the hazard of imprisonment, the civil procedure assures him that such consequences cannot follow unless he ignores a court order specifically directed to him for a prompt and carefully circumscribed determination of the issue of obscenity. Until then, he may keep the book for sale and sell it on his own judgment rather than steer 'nervously among the treacherous shoals.'[a]

"Criminal enforcement and the proceeding under § 22–a interfere with a book's solicitation of the public precisely at the same stage. In each situation the law moves after publication; the book need not in either case have yet passed into the hands of the public. [H]ere as a matter of fact copies of the booklets whose distribution was enjoined had been on sale for several weeks when process was served. In each case the bookseller is put on notice by the complaint that sale of the publication charged with obscenity in the period before trial may subject him to penal consequences. In the one case he may suffer fine and imprisonment for violation of the criminal statute, in the other, for disobedience of the temporary injunction. The bookseller may of course stand his ground and confidently believe that in any judicial proceeding the book could not be condemned as obscene, but both modes of procedure provide an effective deterrent against distribution prior to adjudication of the book's content— the threat of subsequent penalization.[2]"

The Court pointed out that in both criminal misdemeanor prosecutions and injunction proceedings a jury could be called as a matter of discretion, but that defendant did not request a jury trial and did not attack the statute for its failure to require a jury.

"Nor are the consequences of a judicial condemnation for obscenity under § 22–a more restrictive of freedom of expression than the result of conviction for a misdemeanor. In *Alberts,* the defendant was fined $500, sentenced to sixty days in prison, and put on probation for two years on condition that he not violate the obscenity statute. Not only was he completely separated from society for two months but he was also serious-

---

a. In fact, § 22–a did not require a civil adjudication before criminal prosecution, as intimated by the opinion. The feasibility of such a requirement is considered in William Lockhart, *Escape from the Chill of Uncertainty,* 9 Ga.L.Rev. 533, 569–86 (1975).

2. This comparison of remedies takes note of the fact that we do not have before us a case where, although the issue of obscenity is ultimately decided in favor of the bookseller, the State nevertheless attempts to punish him for disobedience of the interim injunction. For all we know, New York may impliedly condition the temporary injunction so as not to subject the bookseller to a charge of contempt if he prevails on the issue of obscenity.

ly restrained from trafficking in all obscene publications for a considerable time. Appellants, on the other hand, were enjoined from displaying for sale or distributing only the particular booklets theretofore published and adjudged to be obscene. Thus, the restraint upon appellants as merchants in obscenity was narrower than that imposed on *Alberts.*

"Section 22–a's provision for the seizure and destruction of the instruments of ascertained wrongdoing expresses resort to a legal remedy sanctioned by the long history of Anglo–American law. See Oliver Holmes, *The Common Law,* 24–26.

"[It] only remains to say that the difference between *Near* and this case is glaring in fact. The two cases are no less glaringly different when judged by the appropriate criteria of constitutional law. Minnesota empowered its courts to enjoin the dissemination of future issues of a publication because its past issues had been found offensive. In the language of Mr. Chief Justice Hughes, 'This is of the essence of censorship.' As such, it was enough to condemn the statute wholly apart from the fact that the proceeding in *Near* involved not obscenity but matters deemed to be derogatory to a public officer. Unlike *Near,* § 22–a is concerned solely with obscenity and, as authoritatively construed, it studiously withholds restraint upon matters not already published and not yet found to be offensive."[b]

TIMES FILM CORP. v. CHICAGO

365 U.S. 43, 81 S.Ct. 391, 5 L.Ed.2d 403 (1961).

JUSTICE CLARK delivered the opinion of the Court.

Petitioner challenges on constitutional grounds the validity on its face of that portion of § 155–4[1] of the Municipal Code of the City of Chicago which requires submission of all motion pictures for examination prior to their public exhibition. Petitioner is a New York corporation owning the exclusive right to publicly exhibit in Chicago the film known as "Don Juan." It applied for a permit, as Chicago's ordinance required, and tendered the license fee but refused to submit the film for examination. The appropriate city official refused to issue the permit and his order was made final on appeal to the Mayor. The sole ground for denial was petitioner's refusal to submit the film for examination as required. Petitioner then brought this suit seeking injunctive relief ordering the issuance of the permit without submission of the [film]. Its sole ground is that the provision of the ordinance requiring submission of the film consti-

---

b. Warren, C.J., dissented, objecting that the New York law "places the book on trial" without any consideration of its "manner of use." Black and Douglas, JJ., dissented, objecting to a state-wide decree depriving the publisher of separate trials in different communities, and to substituting "punishment by contempt for punishment by jury trial." Brennan, J., dissenting, contended that a jury trial is required to apply properly the *Roth* standard for obscenity.

1. The portion of the section here under attack is as follows: "Such permit shall be granted only after the motion picture film for which said permit is requested has been produced at the office of the commissioner of police for examination or [censorship]."

tutes, on its face, a prior restraint.[2] [Admittedly,] the challenged section of the ordinance imposes a previous restraint, and the broad justiciable issue is therefore present as to whether the ambit of constitutional protection includes complete and absolute freedom to exhibit, at least once, any and every kind of motion picture. It is that question alone which we decide.

[T]here is not a word in the record as to the nature and content of "Don Juan." We are left entirely in the dark in this regard, as were the city officials and the other reviewing courts. Petitioner claims that the nature of the film is irrelevant, and that even if this film contains the basest type of pornography, or incitement to riot, or forceful overthrow of orderly government, it may nonetheless be shown without prior submission for examination. The challenge here is to the censor's basic authority; it does not go to any statutory standards employed by the censor or procedural requirements as to the submission of the film. * * *

Petitioner would have us hold that the public exhibition of motion pictures must be allowed under any circumstances. The State's sole remedy, it says, is the invocation of criminal process under the Illinois pornography statute and then only after a transgression. But this position [is] founded upon the claim of absolute privilege against prior restraint under the First Amendment—a claim without sanction in our cases. To illustrate its fallacy, we need only point to one of the "exceptional cases" which Chief Justice Hughes enumerated in *Near,* namely, "the primary requirements of decency [that] may be enforced against obscene publications." Moreover, we later held specifically "that obscenity is not within the area of constitutionally protected speech or press." *Roth.* Chicago emphasizes here its duty to protect its people against the dangers of obscenity in the public exhibition of motion pictures. [It] is not for this Court to limit the State in its selection of the remedy it deems most effective to cope with such a problem, absent, of course, a showing of unreasonable strictures on individual liberty resulting from its application in particular circumstances. * * *

As to what may be decided when a concrete case involving a specific standard provided by this ordinance is presented, we intimate no opinion. [At] this time we say no more than this—that we are dealing only with motion pictures and, even as to them, only in the context of the broadside attack presented on this record.

Affirmed.

---

2. That portion of § 155–4 of the Code providing standards is as follows: "If a picture or series of pictures, for the showing or exhibition of which an application for a permit is made, is immoral or obscene, or portrays, depravity, criminality, or lack of virtue of a class of citizens of any race, color, creed, or religion and exposes them to contempt, derision, or obloquy, or tends to produce a breach of the peace or riots, or purports to represent any hanging, lynching, or burning of a human being, it shall be the duty of the commissioner of police to refuse such permit; otherwise it shall be his duty to grant such permit.

"In case the commissioner of police shall refuse to grant a permit as hereinbefore provided, the applicant for the same may appeal to the mayor. Such appeal shall be presented in the same manner as the original application to the commissioner of police. The action of the mayor on any application for a permit shall be final." * * *

CHIEF JUSTICE WARREN, with whom JUSTICE BLACK, JUSTICE DOUGLAS and JUSTICE BRENNAN join, dissenting. * * *

I hesitate to disagree with the Court's formulation of the issue before us, but, with all deference, I must insist that the question presented in this case is *not* whether a motion picture exhibitor has a constitutionally protected, "complete and absolute freedom to exhibit, at least once, any and every kind of motion picture." [The] question here presented is whether the City of Chicago—or, for that matter, any city, any State or the Federal Government—may require all motion picture exhibitors to submit all films to a police chief, mayor or other administrative official, for licensing and censorship prior to public exhibition within the jurisdiction. * * *

The booklets enjoined from distribution in *Kingsley* were concededly obscene. There is no indication that this is true of the moving picture here. This was treated as a particularly crucial distinction. Thus, the Court has suggested that, in times of national emergency, the Government might impose a prior restraint upon "the publication of the sailing dates of transports or the number and location of troops." *Near*. But, surely this is not to suggest that the Government might require that all newspapers be submitted to a censor in order to assist it in preventing such information from reaching print. Yet in this case the Court gives its blessing to the censorship of all motion pictures in order to prevent the exhibition of those it feels to be constitutionally unprotected.

[E]ven if the impact of the motion picture is greater than that of some other media, that fact constitutes no basis for the argument that motion pictures should be subject to greater suppression. This is the traditional argument made in the censor's behalf; this is the argument advanced against newspapers at the time of the invention of the printing press. The argument was ultimately rejected in England, and has consistently been held to be contrary to our Constitution.[a] No compelling reason has been predicated for accepting the contention now. * * *[b]

NOTES AND QUESTIONS

1.   Should the producers of *Bambi* be forced to submit their film to show it in a particular city? Should they be forced to pay a license fee? Suppose hundreds of cities adopted the Chicago system? If films must be submitted before exhibition, can a city constitutionally require that books be submitted before distribution? What are the "peculiar problems" associated with films?

2.   ***Procedural safeguards.*** FREEDMAN v. MARYLAND, 380 U.S. 51 (1965), per BRENNAN, J., set out procedural safeguards designed to reduce the dangers associated with prior restraints of films. It required that the proce-

---

a. For the contention that the argument has in fact received a warm reception in the twentieth century, see Donald Lively, *Fear and the Media: A First Amendment Horror Show,* 69 Minn.L.Rev. 1071 (1985).

b. Douglas, J., joined by Warren, C.J., and Black, J., dissenting, elaborated on the evils connected with systems of censorship.

dure must "assure a prompt final judicial decision, to minimize the deterrent effect of an interim and possibly erroneous denial of a license," that the censor must promptly institute the proceedings, that the burden of proof to show that the speech in question is unprotected must rest on the censor, and that the proceedings be adversarial. The *Freedman* standards have been applied in other contexts. *Blount v. Rizzi,* 400 U.S. 410 (1971) (postal stop orders of obscene materials); *United States v. Thirty–Seven Photographs,* 402 U.S. 363 (1971) (customs seizure of obscene materials); *Southeastern Promotions Ltd. v. Conrad,* 420 U.S. 546 (1975) (denial of permit to use municipal theater for the musical, Hair); *Carroll v. President and Commissioners,* 393 U.S. 175 (1968) (10 day restraining order against particular rallies or meetings invalid because *ex parte*); *City of Littleton v. Z.J. Gifts D–4,* 541 U.S. 774 (2004) (adult business licensing ordinances including the assurance of speedy court decisions); But see *Thomas v. Chicago Park Dist.,* 534 U.S. 316 (2002)(*Freedman* does not apply to content neutral licensing requirement granting authorities for assemblies involving more than fifty persons in public park even when ordinance as a matter of course grants authorities fourteen days to decide whether permit should be issued). Cf. *FW/PBS v. Dallas,* 493 U.S. 215 (1990) (suggesting that partial application of *Freedman* standards (dispensing with burden of going to court and burden of proof, but retaining assurance of timely decision making by licensor and prompt judicial review) to ordinance licensing sexually oriented businesses ostensibly without regard to content of films or books would be appropriate). For the contention that the *Freedman* standards have been undermined in the context of parade licensing schemes, see Nick Suplina, *Crowd Control: The Troubling Mix of First Amendment Law, Political Demonstrations, and Terrorism,* 73 Geo. Wash. L. Rev. 395, 398 (2005). On the general reception of *Freedman, see* Kathryn F. Whittington, *The Prior Restraints Doctrine and the Freedman Protections: Navigating a Gigantic Labyrinth,* 52 FLA. L. REV. 809 (2000). For thorough discussion of the procedural issues, see Henry Monaghan, *First Amendment "Due Process,"* 83 Harv.L.Rev. 518 (1970).

3. ***Informal prior restraints.*** BANTAM BOOKS, INC. v. SULLIVAN, 372 U.S. 58 (1963), per BRENNAN, J., (Harlan, J. dissenting) held unconstitutional the activities of a government commission that would identify "objectionable" books (some admittedly not obscene), notify the distributor in writing, inform the distributor of the Commission's duty to recommend obscenity prosecutions to the Attorney General and that the Commission's list of objectionable books was distributed to local police departments. The Commission thanked distributors in advance for their "cooperation," and a police officer usually visited the distributor to learn what action had been taken. In characterizing these practices as a system of prior administrative restraints, rather than mere legal advice, the Court observed that it did not mean to foreclose private consultation between law enforcement officers and distributors so long as such consultations were "genuinely undertaken with the purpose of aiding the distributor to comply" with the laws and avoid prosecution. What if the Commission circulated its list to distributors, police and prosecutors without mentioning prosecution? What if the prosecutor circulates a list of sixty books he or she regards as obscene and subject to prosecution?

4. ***Comparing obscenity and commercial speech.*** To combat decep-tion, could commercial advertising be constitutionally subjected to a *Times Film* regime? Would such a scheme be permissible for advertising via some media, but not others? Reconsider fn. 24 in *Virginia Pharmacy,* Ch. 3, II supra. Should the prohibition on prior restraints be inapplicable to injunctions against commercial advertising? Should *Freedman* standards be required? Should injunctions be permitted against a newspaper that carries unprotected advertising in addition to the advertiser? PITTSBURGH PRESS CO. v. PITTSBURGH COMM'N ON HUMAN RELATIONS, 413 U.S. 376 (1973), per POWELL, J., upheld an order forbidding Pittsburgh Press to carry sex-designated "help wanted" ads, except for exempt jobs: "As described by Blackstone, the protection against prior restraint at common law barred only a system of administrative censorship. [While] the Court boldly stepped beyond this narrow doctrine in *Near* [it] has never held that all injunctions are impermissible. See *Lorain Journal Co. v. United States,* 342 U.S. 143 (1951).[c] The special vice of a prior restraint is that communication will be suppressed, either directly or by inducing excessive caution in the speaker, before an adequate determination that it is unprotected by the First Amend-ment.

"The present order does not endanger arguably protected speech. Because the order is based on a continuing course of repetitive conduct, this is not a case in which the Court is asked to speculate as to the effect of publication. Moreover, the order is clear and sweeps no more broadly than necessary. And because no interim relief was granted, the order will not have gone into effect until it was finally determined that the actions of Pittsburgh Press were unprotected."

STEWART, J., joined by Douglas, J., dissented: Putting to one side "the question of governmental power to prevent publication of information that would clearly imperil the military defense of our Nation," "no government agency can tell a newspaper in advance what it can print and what it cannot."[d]

III. LICENSING "PROFESSIONALS": A DICHOTOMY BETWEEN SPEECH AND PRESS?

LOWE v. SEC, 472 U.S. 181 (1985): The Investment Advisors Act of 1940 provides for injunctions and criminal penalties against anyone using the mails in conjunction with the advisory business who is not registered with the SEC or otherwise exempt from registration. The SEC sought an injunction against Lowe and his affiliated businesses primarily alleging that Lowe's registration with the SEC had been properly revoked because

---

c. *Lorain* upheld a Sherman Act injunction restraining a newspaper from seeking to monopo-lize commerce by refusing to carry advertising from merchants who advertised through a competing radio station.

d. Blackmun, J., dissented "for substantially the reasons stated by" Stewart, J. Burger, C.J., dissenting, argued that the majority had mischaracterized the character and interim effect of the Commission's order.

of various fraudulent activities,[a] and that by publishing investment news-letters, Lowe was using the mails as an investment advisor. The SEC did not claim that any information in the newsletters had been false or materially misleading or that Lowe had yet profited from the advice tendered. The SEC did contend that Lowe's prior criminal conduct showed his "total lack of fitness" to remain in an occupation with "numerous opportunities for dishonesty and self-dealing." Lowe denied that his newsletters were covered by the act and argued that, in any event, they were protected against registration and restraint under the First Amendment.

The Court, per STEVENS, J., denied that Lowe's publication of financial newsletters made him an investment advisor under the act. The Court's interpretation was strongly influenced by First Amendment consider-ations. The doctrine against prior restraints and the notion that freedom of the press includes everything from distributing leaflets to mass circula-tion of magazines was said to support a "broad reading" of the exclusion "that encompasses any newspaper, business publication, or financial pub-lication provided that two conditions are met. The publication must be 'bona fide,' and it must be 'of regular and general circulation.' Neither of these conditions is defined, but the two qualifications precisely differenti-ate 'hit and run tipsters' and 'touts' from genuine publishers. Presumably a 'bona fide' publication would be genuine in the sense that it would contain disinterested commentary and analysis as opposed to promotional material disseminated by a 'tout.' Moreover, publications with a 'general and regular' circulation would not include 'people who send out bulletins from time to time on the advisability of buying and selling stocks' or 'hit and run tipsters.' Because the content of petitioners' newsletters was completely disinterested, and because they were offered[b] to the general public on a regular schedule, they are described by the plain language of the [exclusion].

"The dangers of fraud, deception, or overreaching that motivated the enactment of the statute are present in personalized communications but are not replicated in publications that are advertised and sold in an open market.[57] To the extent that the chart service contains factual information about past transactions and market trends, and the newsletters contain commentary on general market conditions, there can be no doubt about the protected character of the communications,[58] a matter that concerned

---

a. For example, during the period that he was giving personal investment advice, Lowe had been convicted of misappropriating funds of a client, tampering with evidence to cover up fraud of a client, and stealing from a bank.

b. Lowe's newsletters in fact did not appear according to schedule. White, J., concurring, remarked: "As is evident from the Court's conclusion that petitioner's publications meet the regularity requirement, the Court's construction of the requirement adopts the view of our major law reviews on the issue of regular publication: good intentions are enough."

57. Cf. *Ohralik*. It is significant that the Commission has not established that petitioners have had authority over the funds of subscribers; that petitioners have been delegated decisionmaking authority to handle subscribers' portfolios or accounts; or that there have been individualized, investment-related interactions between petitioners and subscribers.

58. Moreover, because we have squarely held that the expression of opinion about a commer-cial product such as a loudspeaker is protected by the First Amendment, *Bose Corp.*, Ch. 1, II, B

Congress when the exclusion was drafted. The content of the publications and the audience to which they are directed in this case reveal the specific limits of the exclusion. As long as the communications between petitioners and their subscribers remain entirely impersonal and do not develop into the kind of fiduciary, person-to-person relationships that were discussed at length in the legislative history of the Act and that are characteristic of investment adviser-client relationships, we believe the publications are, at least presumptively, within the exclusion."[c]

WHITE, J., joined by Burger, C.J., and Rehnquist, J., concurring, argued that the Court's statutory interpretation was "improvident" and "based on a thinly disguised conviction" that the Act was unconstitutional as applied to prohibit publication by unregistered advisors. "[While] purporting not to decide the question, the Court bases its statutory holding in large measure on the assumption that Congress already knew the answer to it when the statute was enacted. The Court thus attributes to the 76th Congress a clairvoyance the Solicitor General and the Second Circuit apparently lack—that is, the ability to predict our constitutional holdings 45 years in advance of our declining to reach them." Finding it necessary to reach the constitutional question, White, J., argued that an injunction against Lowe's publications would violate the First Amendment: "The power of government to regulate the professions is not lost whenever the practice of a profession entails speech. The underlying principle was expressed by the Court in *Giboney v. Empire Storage & Ice Co.*, 336 U.S. 490 (1949): 'it has never been deemed an abridgment of freedom of speech or press to make a course of conduct illegal merely because the conduct was in part initiated, evidenced, or carried out by means of language, either spoken, written, or printed.'

"Perhaps the most obvious example of a 'speaking profession' that is subject to governmental licensing is the legal profession. Although a lawyer's work is almost entirely devoted to the sort of communicative acts that, viewed in isolation, fall within the First Amendment's protection, we have never doubted that '[a] State can require high standards of qualification, such as good moral character or proficiency in its law, before it admits an applicant to the [bar].' [To] protect investors, the Government insists, it may require that investment advisers, like lawyers, evince the qualities of truth-speaking, honor, discretion, and fiduciary responsibility.

"But the principle that the government may restrict entry into professions and vocations through licensing schemes has never been extended to encompass the licensing of speech per se or of the press. At some point, a measure is no longer a regulation of a profession but a regulation of speech or of the press; beyond that point, the statute must survive the level of scrutiny demanded by the First Amendment." [It] is for us, then, to find some principle by which to answer the question

---

supra, it is difficult to see why the expression of an opinion about a marketable security should not also be protected.

c. Powell, J., took no part.

whether the Investment Advisers Act as applied to petitioner operates as a regulation of speech or of professional conduct.

"This is a problem Justice Jackson wrestled with in his concurring opinion in *Thomas v. Collins*. His words are instructive: '[A] rough distinction always exists, I think, which is more shortly illustrated than explained. A state may forbid one without its license to practice law as a vocation, but I think it could not stop an unlicensed person from making a speech about the rights of man or the rights of labor, or any other kind of right, including recommending that his hearers organize to support his views. Likewise, the state may prohibit the pursuit of medicine as an occupation without its license, but I do not think it could make it a crime publicly or privately to speak urging persons to follow or reject any school of medical thought. So the state to an extent not necessary now to determine may regulate one who makes a business or a livelihood of soliciting funds or memberships for unions. But I do not think it can prohibit one, even if he is a salaried labor leader, from making an address to a public meeting of workmen, telling them their rights as he sees them and urging them to unite in general or to join a specific union.'

"Justice Jackson concluded that the distinguishing factor was whether the speech in any particular case was 'associat[ed] [with] some other factor which the state may regulate so as to bring the whole within its official control.' If 'in a particular case the association or characterization is a proven and valid one,' he concluded, the regulation may stand.

"These ideas help to locate the point where regulation of a profession leaves off and prohibitions on speech begin. One who takes the affairs of a client personally in hand and purports to exercise judgment on behalf of the client in the light of the client's individual needs and circumstances is properly viewed as engaging in the practice of a profession. Just as offer and acceptance are communications incidental to the regulable transaction called a contract, the professional's speech is incidental to the conduct of the profession. [Where] the personal nexus between professional and client does not exist, and a speaker does not purport to be exercising judgment on behalf of any particular individual with whose circumstances he is directly acquainted, government regulation ceases to function as legitimate regulation of professional practice with only incidental impact on speech; it becomes regulation of speaking or publishing as such, subject to the First Amendment's [command].

"[E]ven where mere 'commercial speech' is concerned, the First Amendment permits restraints on speech only when they are narrowly tailored to advance a legitimate governmental interest. The interest here is certainly legitimate: the Government wants to prevent investors from falling into the hands of scoundrels and swindlers. The means chosen, however, is extreme. [Our] commercial speech cases have consistently rejected the proposition that such drastic prohibitions on speech may be justified by a mere possibility that the prohibited speech will be fraudulent. See *Zauderer; Bates.* * * *

"I emphasize the narrowness of the constitutional basis on which I would decide this case. [I] would by no means foreclose the application of, for example, the Act's antifraud or reporting provisions to investment advisers (registered or unregistered) who offer their advice through publications. Nor do I intend to suggest that it is unconstitutional to invoke the Act's provisions for injunctive relief and criminal penalties against unregistered persons who, for compensation, offer personal investment advice to individual clients. I would hold only that the Act may not constitutionally be applied to prevent persons who are unregistered (including persons whose registration has been denied or revoked) from offering impersonal investment advice through publications such as the newsletters published by petitioner."

NOTES AND QUESTIONS

1. **Professions.** Is White, J.'s speech/profession dichotomy persuasive? Should the existence of a "profession" justify prior restraints? If so, are there free speech limits on the conditions that can be employed for admitting lawyers? Can a candidate who has persistently been engaged in racist speech be excluded on that ground? See W. Bradley Wendel, *Free Speech for Lawyers*, 28 Hast. Con. L.Q. 305, 314 (2001).

2. **Free Legal Advice.** Consider C. Edwin Baker, *First Amendment Limits on Copyright*, 55 Vand. L. Rev. 902 (2002): "Although doctrinally less clear, a nonlawyer or nondoctor should have a free speech right to give away her amateur legal or medical advice or views, at least if her manner of doing so would not cause the recipient to confuse her for a licensed lawyer or doctor, but no free speech right to charge for individualized provision of these views."

3. **Content Control of Legal Advice.** Consider Eugene Volokh, *Speech As Conduct: Generally Applicable Laws, Illegal Courses of Conduct, "Situation–Altering Utterances," and the Uncharted Zones*, 90 Cornell L. Rev. 1277, 1344 (2005): "[I]t's far from clear that the government should be completely free to regulate professionals' speech to their clients. For instance, I doubt that the government may simply ban doctors from informing patients that marijuana is the best solution to their problems. Perhaps doctors could be prevented from writing recommendations that, by operation of state law, free patients from state liability for marijuana possession, though even that is not clear. But I'm fairly certain that doctors at least have the constitutional right to inform their patients of the medical benefits of marijuana, and to urge the patients to lobby their legislators to enact a medical marijuana exception."

4. **Press privilege?** Does White, J., suggest an element of special privilege for the press? Consider Steven Shiffrin, *The First Amendment and Economic Regulation: Away From a General Theory of the First Amendment*, 78 Nw.U.L.Rev. 1212, 1276 (1983): "The doctrine of prior restraint may have been designed to put the press on an equal footing. People could speak or write without a license and that ought not to change merely because they used a printing press. Yet we now license a good deal of speech (for example, of lawyers), and those licenses are clearly prior restraints. So we have turned the law upside down. To speak you sometimes need a license; to use the press

you almost never do. A doctrine designed to create equality for the press has evolved into one that gives it a special place."

5. *Licensing limits?* If lawyers, psychiatrists, and investment advisors can be licensed, what about fortune tellers? Union organizers? Journalists?

———

RILEY v. NATIONAL FEDERATION OF THE BLIND, 487 U.S. 781 (1988), per BRENNAN, J., invalidated a scheme for licensing professional fundraisers who were soliciting on behalf of charitable organizations: "[North Carolina's] provision requires professional fundraisers to await a determination regarding their license application before engaging in solicitation, while volunteer fundraisers, or those employed by the charity, may solicit immediately upon submitting an application. [It] is well settled that a speaker's rights are not lost merely because compensation is received; a speaker is no less a speaker because he or she is paid to speak. [Generally,] speakers need not obtain a license to speak. However, that rule is not absolute. For example, states may impose valid time, place, or manner restrictions. North Carolina seeks to come within the exception by alleging a heightened interest in regulating those who solicit money. Even assuming that the State's interest does justify requiring fundraisers to obtain a license before soliciting, such a regulation must provide that the licensor 'will, within a specified brief period, either issue a license or go to court.' *Freedman.* [The] statute on its face does not purport to require when a determination must be made, nor is there an administrative regulation or interpretation doing so."

REHNQUIST, C.J., joined by O'Connor, J., dissented: "It simply is not true that [fundraisers] are prevented from engaging in any protected speech on their own behalf by the State's licensing requirements; the requirements only restrict their ability to engage in the profession of 'solicitation' without a license. We do not view bar admission requirements as invalid because they restrict a prospective lawyer's 'right' to be hired as an advocate by a client. So in this case we should not subject to strict scrutiny the State's attempt to license a business—professional fundraising—some of whose members might reasonably be thought to pose a risk of fraudulent activity."[d]

IV. PRIOR RESTRAINTS AND NATIONAL SECURITY

NEW YORK TIMES CO. v. UNITED STATES [THE PENTAGON PAPERS CASE]
403 U.S. 713, 91 S.Ct. 2140, 29 L.Ed.2d 822 (1971).

PER CURIAM.

We granted certiorari in these cases in which the United States seeks to enjoin the *New York Times* and the *Washington Post* from publishing

---

d. Stevens, J., also dissented from the Court's treatment of the licensing issue. Under what circumstances should restrictions on charitable solicitation be permitted? See John D. Inazu, *Making Sense of Schaumberg: Seeking Coherence in First Amendment Charitable Solicitation Law,* 92 Marq. L.Rev. 551 (2009). Should begging be treated differently?

the contents of a classified study entitled "History of U.S. Decision–Making Process on Viet Nam Policy."[a]

"Any system of prior restraints of expression comes to this Court bearing a heavy presumption against its constitutional validity." *Bantam Books;* see also *Near.* The Government "thus carries a heavy burden of showing justification for the enforcement of such a restraint." [The district court in the *Times* case and both lower federal courts] in the *Post* case held that the Government had not met that burden. We agree. [T]he stays entered [by this Court five days previously] are vacated. * * *

JUSTICE BLACK, with whom JUSTICE DOUGLAS joins, concurring.

I adhere to the view that the Government's case against the *Post* should have been dismissed and that the injunction against the *Times* should have been vacated without oral argument when the cases were first presented to this Court. I believe that every moment's continuance of the injunctions against these newspapers amounts to a flagrant, indefensible, and continuing violation of the First Amendment. Furthermore, after oral arguments, I agree [with] the reasons stated by my Brothers Douglas and Brennan. In my view it is unfortunate that some of my Brethren are apparently willing to hold that the publication of news may sometimes be enjoined. Such a holding would make a shambles of the First Amendment.

[F]or the first time in the 182 years since the founding of the Republic, the federal courts are asked to hold that the First Amendment does not mean what it says, but rather means that the Government can halt the publication of current news of vital importance to the people of this country. * * *

The Government does not even attempt to rely on any act of Congress. Instead it makes the bold and dangerously far-reaching contention that the courts should take it upon themselves to "make" a law abridging freedom of the press in the name of equity, presidential power and national security, even when the representatives of the people in Congress have adhered to the command of the First Amendment and refused to make such a law. To find that the President has "inherent power" to halt the publication of news by resort to the courts would wipe out the First Amendment and destroy the fundamental liberty and security of the very people the Government hopes to make "secure." [The] word "security" is a broad, vague generality whose contours should not be invoked to abrogate the fundamental law embodied in the First Amendment. * * *

JUSTICE DOUGLAS, with whom JUSTICE BLACK joins, concurring.

---

a. On June 12–14, 1971 the *New York Times* and on June 18 the *Washington Post* published portions of this "top secret" Pentagon study. Government actions seeking temporary restraining orders and injunctions progressed through two district courts and two courts of appeals between June 15–23. After a June 26 argument, ten Supreme Court opinions were issued on June 30, 1971. For discussion, see Randall Bezanson, *How Free Can the Press Be?,* 7–57 (2003).

While I join the opinion of the Court I believe it necessary to express my views more fully.

[The First Amendment leaves] no room for governmental[b] restraint on the press. There is, moreover, no statute barring the publication by the press of the material which the *Times* and *Post* seek to use. [These] disclosures may have a serious impact. But that is no basis for sanctioning a previous restraint on the press * * *.

The dominant purpose of the First Amendment was to prohibit the widespread practice of governmental suppression of embarrassing information. [A] debate of large proportions goes on in the Nation over our posture in Vietnam. That debate antedated the disclosure of the contents of the present documents. The latter are highly relevant to the debate in progress.

Secrecy in government is fundamentally anti-democratic, perpetuating bureaucratic errors. Open debate and discussion of public issues are vital to our national health. [The] stays in these cases that have been in effect for more than a week constitute a flouting of the principles of the First Amendment as interpreted in *Near*.

JUSTICE BRENNAN, concurring.

I write separately [to] emphasize what should be apparent: that our judgment in the present cases may not be taken to indicate the propriety, in the future, of issuing temporary stays and restraining orders to block the publication of material sought to be suppressed by the Government. So far as I can determine, never before has the United States sought to enjoin a newspaper from publishing information in its possession. * * *

The entire thrust of the Government's claim throughout these cases has been that publication of the material sought to be enjoined "could," or "might," or "may" prejudice the national interest in various ways. But the First Amendment tolerates absolutely no prior judicial restraints of the press predicated upon surmise or conjecture that untoward consequences may result.* Our cases, it is true, have indicated that there is a single, extremely narrow class of cases in which the First Amendment's ban on prior judicial restraint may be overridden. Our cases have thus far indicated that such cases may arise only when the Nation "is at war," [*Schenck*]. Even if the present world situation were assumed to be tantamount to a time of war, or if the power of presently available armaments would justify even in peacetime the suppression of information that would set in motion a nuclear holocaust, in neither of these actions has the Government presented or even alleged that publication of items

---

b. But see Mark Denbeaux, *The First Word of the First Amendment,* 80 Nw.U.L.Rev. 1156 (1986).

* *Freedman* and similar cases regarding temporary restraints of allegedly obscene materials are not in point. For those cases rest upon the proposition that "obscenity is not protected by the freedoms of speech and press." *Roth.* Here there is no question but that the material sought to be suppressed is within the protection of the First Amendment; the only question is whether, notwithstanding that fact, its publication may be enjoined for a time because of the presence of an overwhelming national interest. * * *

from or based upon the material at issue would cause the happening of an event of that nature. [Thus,] only governmental allegation and proof that publication must inevitably, directly and immediately cause the occurrence of an event kindred to imperiling the safety of a transport already at sea can support even the issuance of an interim restraining order. In no event may mere conclusions be sufficient: for if the Executive Branch seeks judicial aid in preventing publication, it must inevitably submit the basis upon which that aid is sought to scrutiny by the judiciary. And therefore, every restraint issued in this case, whatever its form, has violated the First Amendment—and not less so because that restraint was justified as necessary to afford the courts an opportunity to examine the claim more thoroughly. Unless and until the Government has clearly made out its case, the First Amendment commands that no injunction may issue.

Justice Stewart, with whom Justice White joins, concurring.

[I]n the cases before us we are asked neither to construe specific regulations nor to apply specific laws. [We] are asked, quite simply, to prevent the publication by two newspapers of material that the Executive Branch insists should not, in the national interest, be published. I am convinced that the Executive is correct with respect to some of the documents involved. But I cannot say that disclosure of any of them will surely result in direct, immediate, and irreparable damage to our Nation or its people. That being so, there can under the First Amendment be but one judicial resolution of the issues before us. I join the judgments * * *.

Justice White, with whom Justice Stewart joins, concurring.

I concur in today's judgments, but only because of the concededly extraordinary protection against prior restraints enjoyed by the press under our constitutional system. I do not say that in no circumstances would the First Amendment permit an injunction against publishing information about government plans or operations. Nor, after examining the materials the Government characterizes as the most sensitive and destructive, can I deny that revelation of these documents will do substantial damage to public interests. Indeed, I am confident that their disclosure will have that result. But I nevertheless agree that the United States has not satisfied the very heavy burden which it must meet to warrant an injunction against publication in these cases, at least in the absence of express and appropriately limited congressional authorization for prior restraints in circumstances such as these.

The Government's position is simply stated: The responsibility of the Executive for the conduct of the foreign affairs and for the security of the Nation is so basic that the President is entitled to an injunction against publication of a newspaper story whenever he can convince a court that the information to be revealed threatens "grave and irreparable" injury to the public interest; and the injunction should issue whether or not the material to be published is classified, whether or not publication would be lawful under relevant criminal statutes enacted by Congress and regardless of the circumstances by which the newspaper came into possession of the information.

At least in the absence of legislation by Congress, based on its own investigations and findings, I am quite unable to agree that the inherent powers of the Executive and the courts reach so far as to authorize remedies having such sweeping potential for inhibiting publications by the press. [To] sustain the Government in these cases would start the courts down a long and hazardous road that I am not willing to travel at least without congressional guidance and direction.

* * * Prior restraints require an unusually heavy justification under the First Amendment; but failure by the Government to justify prior restraints does not measure its constitutional entitlement to a conviction for criminal publication. That the Government mistakenly chose to proceed by injunction does not mean that it could not successfully proceed in another way.

* * * Congress has addressed itself to the problems of protecting the security of the country and the national defense from unauthorized disclosure of potentially damaging information. It has not, however, authorized the injunctive remedy against threatened publication. It has apparently been satisfied to rely on criminal sanctions and their deterrent effect on the responsible as well as the irresponsible press. * * *

JUSTICE HARLAN, with whom THE CHIEF JUSTICE and JUSTICE BLACKMUN join, dissenting. * * *

With all respect, I consider that the Court has been almost irresponsibly feverish in dealing with these cases. Both [the] Second Circuit and [the] District of Columbia Circuit rendered judgment on June 23. [This] Court's order setting a hearing before us on June 26 at 11 a.m., a course which I joined only to avoid the possibility of even more peremptory action by the Court, was issued less than 24 hours before. The record in the *Post* case was filed with the Clerk shortly before 1 p.m. on June 25; the record in the *Times* case did not arrive until 7 or 8 o'clock that same night. The briefs of the parties were received less than two hours before argument on June 26.

This frenzied train of events took place in the name of the presumption against prior restraints created by the First Amendment. Due regard for the extraordinarily important and difficult questions involved in these litigations should have led the Court to shun such a precipitate timetable. In order to decide the merits of these cases properly, some or all of the following questions should have been faced: * * *

2. Whether the First Amendment permits the federal courts to enjoin publication of stories which would present a serious threat to national security. See *Near* (dictum). * * *

4. Whether the unauthorized disclosure of any of these particular documents would seriously impair the national security.

5. What weight should be given to the opinion of high officers in the Executive Branch of the Government with respect to [question 4]. * * *

7. Whether the threatened harm to the national security or the Government's possessory interest in the documents justifies the issuance of an injunction against publication in light of—

a. The strong First Amendment policy against prior restraints on publication; b. The doctrine against enjoining conduct in violation of criminal statutes; and c. The extent to which the materials at issue have apparently already been otherwise disseminated.

These are difficult questions of fact, of law, and of judgment; the potential consequences of erroneous decision are enormous. The time which has been available to us, to the lower courts, and to the parties has been wholly inadequate for giving these cases the kind of consideration they deserve. It is a reflection on the stability of the judicial process that these great issues—as important as any that have arisen during my time on the Court—should have been decided under the pressures engendered by the torrent of publicity that has attended these litigations from their inception.

Forced as I am to reach the merits of these cases, I dissent from the opinion and judgments of the Court. Within the severe limitations imposed by the time constraints under which I have been required to operate, I can only state my reasons in telescoped form, even though in different circumstances I would have felt constrained to deal with the cases in the fuller sweep indicated above.

[It] is plain to me that the scope of the judicial function in passing upon the activities of the Executive Branch of the Government in the field of foreign affairs is very narrowly restricted. This view is, I think, dictated by the concept of separation of powers upon which our constitutional system [rests.] I agree that, in performance of its duty to protect the values of the First Amendment against political pressures, the judiciary must review the initial Executive determination to the point of satisfying itself that the subject matter of the dispute does lie within the proper compass of the President's foreign relations power. Constitutional considerations forbid "a complete abandonment of judicial control." Moreover, the judiciary may properly insist that the determination that disclosure of the subject matter would irreparably impair the national security be made by the head of the Executive Department concerned—here the Secretary of State or the Secretary of Defense—after actual personal consideration by that officer.[c] This safeguard is required in the analogous area of executive claims of privilege for secrets of state.

---

c. Consider Stanley Godofsky & Howard Rogatnick, *Prior Restraints: The Pentagon Papers Case Revisited,* 18 Cum.L.Rev. 527, 536–37 (1988): "Ironically, Justice Harlan's view of the Constitution might, ultimately, have presented more problems for the Government than those of most of the other Justices. Realistically, how often can the Secretary of State or Secretary of Defense devote 'actual personal consideration' to the question of whether material about to be published should be suppressed? And of what does 'actual personal consideration' consist? Must the Secretary himself read the documents? Is it sufficient 'consideration' by a Cabinet officer to

But in my judgment the judiciary may not properly go beyond these two inquiries and redetermine for itself the probable impact of disclosure on the national security. "[T]he very nature of executive decisions as to foreign policy is political, not judicial. Such decisions are wholly confided by our Constitution to the political departments of the government, Executive and Legislative. They are delicate, complex, and involve large elements of prophecy. They are and should be undertaken only by those directly responsible to the people whose welfare they advance or imperil. They are decisions of a kind for which the judiciary has neither aptitude, facilities nor responsibility and which has long been held to belong in the domain of political power not subject to judicial intrusion or inquiry." *Chicago & S. Air Lines v. Waterman S.S. Corp.* (Jackson, J.), 333 U.S. 103 (1948).

Even if there is some room for the judiciary to override the executive determination, it is plain that the scope of review must be exceedingly narrow. I can see no indication in the opinions of either the District Court or the Court of Appeals in the *Post* litigation that the conclusions of the Executive were given even the deference owing to an administrative agency, much less that owing to a co-equal branch of the Government operating within the field of its constitutional prerogative. * * *

Pending further hearings in each case conducted under the appropriate ground rules, I would continue the restraints on publication. I cannot believe that the doctrine prohibiting prior restraints reaches to the point of preventing courts from maintaining the status quo long enough to act responsibly in matters of such national importance as those involved here.

JUSTICE BLACKMUN, dissenting.

[The First Amendment] is only one part of an entire Constitution. Article II of the great document vests in the Executive Branch primary power over the conduct of foreign affairs and places in that branch the responsibility for the Nation's safety. Each provision of the Constitution is important, and I cannot subscribe to a doctrine of unlimited absolutism for the First Amendment at the cost of downgrading other provisions. First Amendment absolutism has never commanded a majority of this Court. What is needed here is a weighing, upon properly developed standards, of the broad right of the press to print and of the very narrow right of the Government to prevent. Such standards are not yet developed. The parties here are in disagreement as to what those standards should be. But even the newspapers concede that there are situations where restraint is in order and is constitutional. Mr. Justice Holmes gave us a suggestion when he said in *Schenck,* "It is a question of proximity and degree. When a nation is at war many things that might be said in time of peace are such a hindrance to its effort that their utterance will not be

---

act on the advice of his subordinates? If so, is not the 'actual personal consideration' test substantially meaningless? Could a Cabinet officer be required to testify as to the basis for his decision in order to test his 'bona fides'?"

endured so long as men fight and that no Court could regard them as protected by any constitutional right."

I therefore would remand these cases to be developed expeditiously, of course, but on a schedule permitting the orderly presentation of evidence from both sides [and] with the preparation of briefs, oral argument and court opinions of a quality better than has been seen to this point. [T]hese cases and the issues involved and the courts, including this one, deserve better than has been produced thus far. * * *d

NOTES AND QUESTIONS

1. *What did the case decide?* Do you agree that "the case [did] not make any law at all, good or bad"? That on the question "whether injunctions against the press are permissible, it is clear that [the case] can supply no precedent?" See Peter Junger, *Down Memory Lane: The Case of the Pentagon Papers,* 23 Case W.Res.L.Rev. 3, 4–5 (1971). Or do you find in several concurring opinions a discernible standard that must be satisfied before a majority of the Court would permit an injunction against the press on national security grounds? Cf. 85 Harv.L.Rev. 199, 205–06 (1971). Do you find guidance as to the outcome if Congress were to authorize an injunction in narrow terms to protect national security? Cf. id. at 204–05. Might it fairly be said that this is a separation of powers decision, like the *Steel Seizure* case, as well as a First Amendment decision? See Junger, supra, at 19.

2. *"De facto" prior restraint.* One difficulty with viewing the prior restraint doctrine as "simply creat[ing] a 'presumption' against the validity of the restraint" (Emerson's characterization of the current approach) rather than as "a prohibition on all restraints subject to certain categorical exceptions," observes Thomas Emerson, *First Amendment Doctrine and the Burger Court,* 68 Calif.L.Rev. 422, 457–58 (1980), is that "the requirement of ad hoc scrutiny of prior restraints is itself likely to result in a 'de facto' prior restraint." Pointing to Brennan, J.'s comment in *Pentagon Papers* that "every restraint issued in this case [has] violated the First Amendment—and not less so because that restraint was justified as necessary to afford the courts an opportunity to examine the claim more thoroughly," Emerson notes that "[t]his is exactly what happened when the government sought to enjoin *The Progressive* magazine from publishing an article on the manufacture of the hydrogen bomb. The Supreme Court refused to order an expedited appeal from the [federal district court] injunction against publication [and, although the case was ultimately dismissed by the Seventh Circuit,] *The Progressive* remained under effective prior restraint for nearly seven months."

---

d. Marshall, J., concurring, did not deal with First Amendment issues but only with separation of powers—the government's attempt to secure through the Court injunctive relief that Congress had refused to authorize.

Burger, C.J., dissenting, complained that because of "unseemly haste," "we do not know the facts of this case. [W]e literally do not know what we are acting on." He expressed no views on the merits, apart from his joinder in Harlan, J.'s opinion, and a statement that he would have continued the temporary restraints in effect while returning the cases to the lower courts for more thorough exploration of the facts and issues.

Compare *Near* and *Pentagon Papers* with UNITED STATES v. PRO-GRESSIVE, INC., 467 F.Supp. 990 (W.D.Wis.) (preliminary injunction issued Mar. 28, 1979), request for writ of mandamus den. sub nom. *Morland v. Sprecher,* 443 U.S. 709 (1979), case dismissed, 610 F.2d 819 (7th Cir.1979).[e] *The Progressive* planned to publish an article. "The H–Bomb Secret—How We Got It, Why We're Telling It," maintaining that the article would contribute to informed opinion about nuclear weapons and demonstrate the inadequacies of a system of secrecy and classification. Although the government conceded that at least some of the information contained in the article was "in the public domain" or had been "declassified," it argued that "national security" permitted it to censor information originating in the public domain "if when drawn together, synthesized and collated, such information acquires the character of presenting immediate, direct and irreparable harm to the inter-ests of the United States." The Secretary of State stated that publication would increase thermonuclear proliferation and that this would "irreparably impair the national security of the United States." The Secretary of Defense maintained that dissemination of the Morland article would lead to a substan-tial increase in the risk of thermonuclear proliferation and to use or threats that would "adversely affect the national security of the United States."

Although recognizing that this constituted "the first instance of prior restraint against a publication in this fashion in the [nation's history]," the district court enjoined defendants, pending final resolution of the litigation, from publishing or otherwise disclosing any information designated by the government as "restricted data" within the meaning of The Atomic Energy Act of 1954: "What is involved here is information dealing with the most destructive weapon in the history of mankind, information of sufficient destructive potential to nullify the right to free speech and to endanger the right to life itself. [Faced] with a stark choice between upholding the right to continued life and the right to freedom of the press, most jurists would have no difficulty in opting for the chance to continue to breathe and function as they work to achieve perfect freedom of expression.

"[A] mistake in ruling against *The Progressive* will seriously infringe cherished First Amendment rights. [A] mistake in ruling against the United States could pave the way for thermonuclear annihilation for us all. In that event, our right to life is extinguished and the right to publish becomes moot.

"[W]ar by foot soldiers has been replaced in large part by machines and bombs. No longer need there be any advance warning or any preparation time before a nuclear war could be commenced. [In light of these factors] publica-tion of the technical information on the hydrogen bomb contained in the article is analogous to publication of troop movements or locations in time of

---

e. The government's action against *The Progressive* was abandoned after information similar to that it sought to enjoin was published elsewhere. For discussion of the case, see David Rudenstine, *Transcript of Weapons of Mass Destruction, National Security, and a Free Press: Seminal Issues as Viewed Through the Lens of the Progressive Case,* 26 Cardozo L. Rev. 1337 (2005); Ray E. Kidder, *Weapons of Mass Destruction, National Security, and a Free Press,* 26 Cardozo L. Rev. 1389 (2005). Under what circumstances should the government be able to prosecute a nongovernmental actor for disseminating national security information? See general-ly Mary-Rose Papandrea, *Lapdogs, Watchdogs, and Scapegoats: The Press and National Security Information,* 83 Ind. L.J. 233 (2008).

war and falls within the extremely narrow exception to the rule against prior restraint [recognized in *Near*].[f]

"The government has met its burden under § 2274 of The Atomic Energy Act [, which authorizes injunctive relief against one who would communicate or disclose restricted data 'with reason to believe such data will be utilized to. injure the United States or to secure an advantage to any foreign nation.']. [I]t has also met the test enunciated by two Justices in *Pentagon Papers,* namely grave, direct, immediate and irreparable harm to the United States."

The court distinguished *Pentagon Papers*: "[T]he study involved [there] contained historical data relating to events some three to twenty years previously. Secondly, the Supreme Court agreed with the lower court that no cogent reasons were advanced by the government as to why the article affected national security except that publication might cause some embarrassment to the United States. A final and most vital difference between these two cases is the fact that a specific statute is involved here [§ 2274 of The Atomic Energy Act]."

3. ***CIA secrecy agreement.*** The Central Intelligence Agency requires employees to sign a "secrecy agreement" as a condition of employment, an agreement committing the employee not to reveal classified information nor to publish any information obtained during the course of employment without prior approval of the Agency. In SNEPP v. UNITED STATES, 444 U.S. 507 (1980), Snepp had published a book called *Decent Interval* about certain CIA activities in South Vietnam based on his experiences as an agency employee without seeking prepublication review. At least for purposes of the litigation, the government conceded that Snepp's book divulged no confidential information. The Court, per curiam (Stevens, J., joined by Brennan and Marshall, JJ., dissenting) held that Snepp's failure to submit the book was a breach of trust and the government was entitled to a constructive trust on the proceeds of the book: "[E]ven in the absence of an express agreement, the CIA could have acted to protect substantial government interests by imposing reasonable restrictions on employee activities that in other contexts might be protected by the First Amendment. The Government has a compelling interest in protecting both the secrecy of information important to our national security and the appearance of confidentiality so essential to the effective operation of our foreign intelligence service."[g] When employees or past employees do submit publications for clearance, should *Freedman* standards apply? Can former CIA employees be required to submit all public speeches relating to their former employment for clearance? Are extemporaneous remarks permit-

---

f. One of the reasons the court gave for finding that the objected-to technical portions of the article fell within the *Near* exception was that it was "unconvinced that suppression of [these portions] would in any plausible fashion impede the defendants in their laudable crusade to stimulate public knowledge of nuclear armament and bring about enlightened debate on national policy questions." Should this have been a factor in the decision to issue the preliminary injunction?

g. Compare *Haig v. Agee,* 453 U.S. 280 (1981), stating that "repeated disclosures of intelligence operations and names of intelligence personnel" for the "purpose of obstructing intelligence operations and the recruiting of intelligence personnel" are "clearly not protected by the Constitution." What if the publisher of the information merely has "reason to believe that such activities would impair or impede the foreign intelligence activities of the United States"? See 50 U.S.C. § 421.

ted? To what extent can secrecy agreements be required of public employees outside the national security area?[h]

---

h. For discussion of *Snepp*, see Mary Cheh, *Judicial Supervision of Executive Secrecy*, 69 Corn.L.Rev. 690 (1984); Frank Easterbrook, *Insider Trading, Secret Agents, Evidentiary Privileges, and the Production of Information*, 1981 Sup.Ct.Rev. 309, 339–53; Stanley Godofsky & Howard Rogatnick, *Prior Restraints: The Pentagon Papers Case Revisited*, fn. c supra, at 543–54 (1988); Judith Koffler & Bennett Gershman, *The New Seditious Libel*, 69 Corn.L.Rev. 816 (1984); Jonathan Medow, *The First Amendment and the Secrecy State: Snepp v. United States*, 130 U.Pa.L.Rev. 775 (1982). For a thorough exploration of the occasions in which secrecy has been preferred over public knowledge, see Benjamin DuVal, *The Occasions of Secrecy*, 47 U.Pitt.L.Rev. 579 (1986).

CHAPTER 5

JUSTICE AND NEWSGATHERING

■ ■ ■

This section explores three problems connected with the fair administration of justice or with newsgathering or with both. The first problem involves pre-trial publicity. The government seeks to deter or punish speech by the press that it fears will threaten the fair administration of justice, but speech of that character falls into no recognized category of unprotected speech. Thus, the courts must consider whether absolute protection is called for, or, alternatively, whether new categories or ad hoc determinations are appropriate, and whether prior restraints are permissible. Alternatively, if the press cannot be prevented from speaking about trials, can prosecutors, defense attorneys, litigants and potential witnesses be prevented from speaking to the press?

In the second problem the government seeks to fairly administer the justice system by forcing reporters to reveal their confidential sources. The press maintains that any such authorized compulsion would have a chilling effect on its ability to gather the news.

In the final problem, government seeks not to punish speech, but to administer justice in private. It refuses to let the public or press witness its handling of prisoners, or its conduct of trial or pre-trial proceedings. The question is whether the First Amendment can serve as a sword allowing the press or citizen-critics to gather information. Assuming it can, what are its limits within the justice system? Does any right of access reach beyond the justice system? Does the First Amendment require that the press be granted access not afforded the public? Does the First Amendment permit differential access? If so, what are the limits on how government defines the press?

I. PUBLICITY ABOUT TRIALS

In a number of cases, defendants have asserted that their rights to a fair trial have been abridged by newspaper publicity. SHEPPARD v. MAXWELL, 384 U.S. 333 (1966), is probably the most notorious "trial by newspaper" case. The Court, per CLARK, J., (Black, J. dissenting) agreed with the "finding" of the Ohio Supreme Court that the atmosphere of defendant's murder trial was that of a " 'Roman holiday' for the news media." The courtroom was jammed with reporters. And in the corridors outside the courtroom, "a host of photographers and television personnel" photographed witnesses, counsel and jurors as they entered and left the courtroom. Throughout the trial, there was a deluge of publicity, much of which contained information never presented at trial, yet the jurors were not sequestered until the trial was over and they had begun their deliberations.

The Court placed the primary blame on the trial judge. He could "easily" have prevented "the carnival atmosphere of the trial" since "the courtroom and courthouse premises" were subject to his control. For example, he should have provided privacy for the jury, insulated witnesses from the media, instead of allowing them to be interviewed at will, and "made some effort to control the release of leads, information, and gossip to the press by police officers, witnesses, and the counsel for both sides." No one "coming under the jurisdiction of the court should be permitted to frustrate its function."

The Court recognized that "there is nothing that proscribes the press from reporting events that transpire in the courtroom. But where there is a reasonable likelihood that prejudicial news prior to trial will prevent a fair trial, the judge should continue the case until the threat abates, or transfer it to another county not so permeated with publicity. In addition, sequestration of the jury was something the judge should have raised sua sponte with counsel. If publicity during the proceedings threatens the fairness of the trial, a new trial should be ordered. But we must remember that reversals are but palliatives; the cure lies in those remedial measures that will prevent the prejudice at its inception."

The Court, however, reiterated its extreme reluctance "to place any direct limitations on the freedom traditionally exercised by the news media for '[w]hat transpires in the courtroom is public property.' "The press "does not simply publish information about trials but guards against the miscarriage of justice by subjecting the police, prosecutors, and judicial processes to extensive public scrutiny and criticism."

———

In anticipation of the trial of Simants for a mass murder which had attracted widespread news coverage, the county court prohibited everyone in attendance from, inter alia, releasing or authorizing for publication "any testimony given or evidence adduced." Simants' preliminary hearing (open to the public) was held the same day, subject to the restrictive order. Simants was bound over for trial. Respondent Nebraska state trial judge then entered an order which, as modified by the state supreme court, restrained the press and broadcasting media from reporting any confessions or incriminating statements made by Simants to law enforcement officers or third parties, except members of the press, and from reporting other facts "strongly implicative" of the defendant. The order expired when the jury was impaneled.

In NEBRASKA PRESS ASS'N v. STUART, 427 U.S. 539 (1976), the Court granted review while Simants' conviction was pending on appeal in the state supreme court. The Court, per BURGER, C.J., struck down the state court order: "To the extent that the order prohibited the reporting of evidence adduced at the open preliminary hearing, it plainly violated settled principles: 'There is nothing that proscribes the press from reporting events that transpire in the courtroom.' *Sheppard*."[a] To the extent that the order prohibited publication "based on information gained from other sources, [the] heavy burden imposed as a condition to securing a prior restraint was not met." The portion of the order regarding "implicative" information was also "too vague and too broad" to survive scrutiny of restraints on First Amendment rights.

"[P]retrial publicity—even pervasive, adverse publicity—does not inevitably lead to an unfair trial. The capacity of the jury eventually impaneled to decide the case fairly is influenced by the tone and extent of the publicity, which is in part, and often in large part, shaped by what attorneys, police and other officials do to precipitate news coverage. [T]he measures a judge takes or fails to take to mitigate the effects of pretrial publicity—the measures described in *Sheppard*—may well determine whether the defendant receives a trial consistent [with] due process.

"[The] Court has interpreted [First Amendment] guarantees to afford special protection against orders that prohibit the publication or broadcast of particular information or commentary—orders that impose [a] 'prior' restraint on speech. None of our decided cases on prior restraint involved restrictive orders entered to protect a defendant's right to a fair and impartial jury, but [they] have a common thread relevant to this case. * * *

"The thread running through [*Near* and *Pentagon Papers*], is that prior restraints on speech and publication are the most serious and the least tolerable infringement on First Amendment rights. A criminal penalty or a judgment in a defamation case is subject to the whole panoply of protections afforded by deferring the impact of the judgment until all avenues of appellate review have been exhausted. [But] a prior restraint [has] an immediate and irreversible sanction. If it can be said that a threat of criminal or civil sanctions after publication 'chills' speech, prior restraint 'freezes' it at least for the time.

"[I]f the authors of [the first and sixth amendments], fully aware of the potential conflicts between them, were unwilling or unable to resolve the issue by assigning to one priority over the other, it is not for us to rewrite the Constitution by undertaking what they declined. [Yet] it is nonetheless clear that the barriers to prior restraint remain high unless

---

a. The Court added, however, that the county court "could not know that closure of the preliminary hearing was an alternative open to it until the Nebraska Supreme Court so construed state law."

we are to abandon what the Court has said for nearly a quarter of our national existence and implied throughout all of [it.]

"We turn now to the record in this case to determine whether, as Learned Hand put it, 'the gravity of the 'evil,' discounted by its improbability, justifies such invasion of free speech as is necessary to avoid the danger,' *Dennis* [2d Cir.], aff'd. To do so, we must examine the evidence before the trial judge when the order was entered to determine (a) the nature and extent of pretrial news coverage; (b) whether other measures would be likely to mitigate the effects of unrestrained pretrial publicity; (c) how effectively a restraining order would operate to prevent the threatened danger. The precise terms of the restraining order are also important. We must then consider whether the record supports the entry of a prior restraint on publication, one of the most extraordinary remedies known to our jurisprudence."

As to (a), although the trial judge was justified in concluding there would be extensive pretrial publicity concerning this case, he "found only 'a clear and present danger that pretrial publicity *could* impinge upon the defendant's right to a fair trial.' [Emphasis added by the Court]. His conclusion as to the impact of such publicity on prospective jurors was of necessity speculative, dealing as he was with factors unknown and unknowable."

As to (b), "there is no finding that alternative means [e.g., change of venue, postponement of trial to allow public attention to subside, searching questions of prospective jurors] would not have protected Simants' rights, and the Nebraska Supreme Court did no more than imply that such measures might not be adequate. Moreover, the record is lacking in evidence to support such a finding."

As to (c), in view of such practical problems as the limited territorial jurisdiction of the trial court issuing the order, the difficulties of predicting what information "will in fact undermine the impartiality of jurors," the problem of drafting an order that will "effectively keep prejudicial information from prospective jurors," and that the events "took place in a community of only 850 people"—throughout which, "it is reasonable to assume," rumors that "could well be more damaging than reasonably accurate news accounts" would "travel swiftly by word of mouth"—"it is far from clear that prior restraint on publication would have protected Simants' rights."

"[It] is significant that when this Court has reversed a state conviction because of prejudicial publicity, it has carefully noted that some course of action short of prior restraint would have made a critical difference. However difficult it may be, we need not rule out the possibility of showing the kind of threat to fair trial rights that would possess the requisite degree of certainty to justify restraint. [We] reaffirm that the guarantees of freedom of expression are not an absolute prohibition under all circumstances, but the barriers to prior restraint remain high and the presumption against its use continues intact. We hold that, with respect to the order entered in this case [the] heavy burden imposed as a condition to securing a prior restraint was not [met]."

BRENNAN, J., joined by Stewart and Marshall, JJ., concurring, would hold that "resort to prior restraints on the freedom of the press is a constitutionally impermissible method for enforcing [the right to a fair trial by a jury]; judges have at their disposal a broad spectrum of devices for ensuring that fundamental fairness is accorded the accused without necessitating so drastic an incursion on the equally fundamental and salutary constitutional mandate that discussion of public affairs in a free society cannot depend on the preliminary grace of judicial censors": " * * * Settled case law concerning the impropriety and constitutional invalidity of prior restraints on the press compels the conclusion that there can be no prohibition on the publication by the press of any information pertaining to pending judicial proceedings or the operation of the criminal justice system, no matter how shabby the means by which the information is obtained.[15] This does not imply, however, any subordination of Sixth Amendment rights, for an accused's right to a fair trial may be adequately assured through methods that do not infringe First Amendment values.

"[The narrow national security exception mentioned in *Near* and *Pentagon Papers*] does not mean [that] prior restraints can be justified on an ad hoc balancing approach that concludes that the 'presumption' must be overcome in light of some perceived 'justification.' Rather, this language refers to the fact that, as a matter of procedural safeguards and burden of proof, prior restraints even within a recognized exception to the rule against prior restraints will be extremely difficult to justify; but as an initial matter, the purpose for which a prior restraint is sought to be imposed 'must fit within one of the narrowly defined exceptions to the prohibition against prior restraints.' Indeed, two Justices in [*Pentagon Papers*] apparently controverted the existence of even a limited 'military security' exception to the rule against prior restraints on the publication of otherwise protected material. (Black, J., concurring); (Douglas, J., concurring). And a majority of the other Justices who expressed their views on the merits made it clear that they would take cognizance only of a 'single, extremely narrow class of cases in which the First Amendment's ban on prior judicial restraint may be overridden.' (Brennan, J., concurring). * * *

"The only exception that has thus far been recognized even in dictum to the blanket prohibition against prior restraints against publication of material which would otherwise be constitutionally shielded was the 'military security' situation addressed in [*Pentagon Papers*]. But unlike the virtually certain, direct, and immediate harm required for such a restraint [the] harm to a fair trial that might otherwise eventuate from

---

15. Of course, even if the press cannot be enjoined from reporting certain information, that does not necessarily immunize it from civil liability for libel or invasion of privacy or from criminal liability for transgressions of general criminal laws during the course of obtaining that information.

publications which are suppressed pursuant to orders such as that under review must inherently remain speculative.''

Although they joined the Court's opinion, White and Powell, JJ., also filed brief concurrences. WHITE, J., expressed ''grave doubts'' that these types of restrictive orders ''would ever be justifiable.'' POWELL, J., ''emphasize[d] the unique burden'' resting upon one who ''undertakes to show the necessity for prior restraint on pretrial publicity.'' In his judgment, a prior restraint ''requires a showing that (i) there is a clear threat to the fairness of trial, (ii) such a threat is posed by the actual publicity to be restrained, and (iii) no less restrictive alternatives are available. Notwithstanding such a showing, a restraint may not issue unless it also is shown that previous publicity or publicity from unrestrained sources will not render the restraint inefficacious. [A]ny restraint must comply with the standards of specificity always required in the First Amendment context.''

STEVENS, J., concurred in the judgment. He agreed with Brennan, J., that the ''judiciary is capable of protecting the defendant's right to a fair trial without enjoining the press from publishing information in the public domain, and that it may not do so.'' But he reserved judgment, until further argument, on ''[w]hether the same absolute protection would apply no matter how shabby or illegal the means by which the information is obtained, no matter how serious an intrusion on privacy might be involved, no matter how demonstrably false the information might be, no matter how prejudicial it might be to the interests of innocent persons, and no matter how perverse the motivation for publishing it.'' He indicated that ''if ever required to face the issue squarely'' he ''may well accept [Brennan, J.'s] ultimate conclusion.''**b**

NOTES AND QUESTIONS

1. *Why the prior restraint reliance?* Does ''the reasoning used by all of the justices premised solely on the traditional aversion to prior restraints, insufficiently'' protect the press? Robert Sack, *Principle and Nebraska Press Association v. Stuart*, 29 Stan.L.Rev. 411, 411 (1977). Would the *Nebraska Press* order have been ''equally objectionable'' if ''framed as a statutory sanction punishing publication after it had occurred''?**c** Is it objectionable at all? Gavin Phillipson, *Trial By Media: The Betrayal of the First Amendment's Purpose*, 71 Law & Contemp. Probs. 15, 21 (2008): ''The spectacle of the persistent refusal of U.S. courts to protect individuals from the prejudicial effect of media coverage of their arrest and trials by restraining the media looks from the outside the United States like the very opposite of American respect for the individual and reverence for individual liberty. Rather, it appears that the rights and freedoms of individuals are being sacrificed to the commercial interests of the mass media and the idle curiosity of the majori-

---

b. For background on *Nebraska Press*, see Fred Friendly & Martha Elliot, *The Constitution: That Delicate Balance* 148–58 (1984).

c. Id. at 415. See also Stephen Barnett, *The Puzzle of Prior Restraint*, 29 Stan.L.Rev. 539, 542–44, 560 (1977). But see Note, *Punishing the Press: Using contempt of Court to Secure the Right to a Free Trial*, 76 B.U.L. Rev. 537 (1996).

ty." See also Kathryn Webb Bradley, *The Court of Public Opinion*, 71 Law & Contemp. Probs. 15, 18 (2008): "[T]he uses the media makes of its freedom can often directly undermine the values underlying the right to free speech itself—human dignity, the state's duty to secure equal rights for the basic rights of all, and the foundations of a democratic society, among which must be the rule of law, a vital aspect of which is the right to a fair trial."

2. ***Why the Dennis citation?*** Consider Benno Schmidt, *Nebraska Press Association: An Expansion of Freedom and Contraction of Theory*, 29 Stan. L.Rev. 431, 459–60 (1977): Burger, C.J.'s reliance on *Dennis* "is remarkable, almost unbelievable, because that test is both an exceedingly odd means of determining the validity of a prior restraint and a controversial and recently neglected technique of First Amendment adjudication. [If] the [*Dennis*] test is the right one for prior restraints, what tests should govern a subsequent punishment case resting on legislation?" See also Barnett, note c supra, at 542–44. Burger, C.J.'s citation to *Dennis* should be read in conjunction with dictum in his majority opinion in *Landmark Communications, Inc. v. Virginia,* note 6 infra. There he questioned reliance upon the clear and present danger standard but observed: "Properly applied, the test requires a court to make its own inquiry into the imminence and magnitude of the danger said to flow from the particular utterance and then to balance the character of the evil, as well as its likelihood, against the need for free and unfettered expression. The possibility that other measures will serve the State's interests should also be weighed."

3. ***Application to non-press defendants.*** Should *Nebraska Press* standards apply to court orders preventing prosecutors, witnesses, potential witnesses, jurors,[d] defendants, or defense attorneys from talking to the press about the case? Would limits on law enforcement personnel alone drastically limit the threat to fair trial? Joanne Armstrong Brandwood, *You Say "Fair Trial" and I Say "Free Press": British and American Approaches to Protecting Defendants' Rights in High Profile Trials,* 75 N.Y.U. L. Rev. 1412, 1448 (2000).

Should different standards apply to different categories of those potentially subject to court orders—e.g., do defense attorneys deserve as much protection as the press? See *Gentile v. State Bar,* 501 U.S. 1030 (1991) (less stringent standard ("substantial likelihood of material prejudice") applies to defense attorneys not clear and present danger).[e]

4. ***Obstructing justice.*** A series of cases have held that the First Amendment greatly restricts contempt sanctions against persons whose comments on pending cases were alleged to have created a danger of obstruction of the judicial process. "Such repression can be justified, if at all, only by a

---

d. Marcy Strauss, *Juror Journalism,* 12 Yale L. & Pol'y Rev. 389 (1994); Comment, *Checkbook Journalism, Free Speech, and Fair Trials,* 143 U.Pa.L.Rev. 1739 (1995).

e. For relevant commentary, see W. Bradley Wendel, *Free Speech for Lawyers,* 28 Hastings Const. L.Q. 305, 314 (2001); Erwin Chemerinsky, *Silence is Not Golden,* 47 Emory L.Rev. 859 (1998); David A. Strauss, *Why It's Not Free Speech versus Fair Trial,* 1998 U.Chi.Legal F. 109; Lloyd Weinreb, *Speaking Out Outside the Courtroom,* 47 Emory L.J. 889 (1998); Monroe Freedman & Janet Starwood, *Prior Restraints on Freedom of Expression by Defendants and Defense Attorneys: Ratio Decidendi v. Obiter Dictum,* 29 Stan.L.Rev. 607 (1977); Comment, *First Amendment Protection of Criminal Defense Attorneys' Extrajudicial [Statements],* 8 Whittier L.Rev. 1021 (1987).

clear and present danger of the obstruction of justice." *New York Times*. In *Bridges v. California,* 314 U.S. 252 (1941), union leader Bridges had caused publication or acquiesced in publication of a telegram threatening a strike if an "outrageous" California state decision involving Bridges' dock workers were enforced. The Court reversed Bridges' contempt citation. Consider Tribe 1st ed., at 624: "If Bridges' threat to cripple the economy of the entire West Coast did not present danger enough, the lesson of the case must be that almost nothing said outside the courtroom is punishable as contempt."[f]

Would it make a difference if a petit jury were impaneled? Suppose Bridges published an open letter to petit jurors? What if copies were sent by Bridges to each juror? Cf. *Wood v. Georgia,* 370 U.S. 375 (1962) (open letter to press and grand jury—contempt citation reversed). But cf. *Cox v. Louisiana,* 379 U.S. 559 (1965) (statute forbidding parades near courthouse with intent to interfere with administration of justice upheld): ("[W]e deal not with the contempt power [but] a statute narrowly drawn to punish" not a pure form of speech but expression mixed with conduct "that infringes a substantial state interest in protecting the judicial process.").

5. *Confidentiality and privacy.* A series of cases has rebuffed state efforts to protect confidentiality or privacy by prohibiting publication. *Cox Broadcasting Corp. v. Cohn,* Ch. 1, II, F supra (state could not impose liability for public dissemination of the name of rape victim derived from public court documents); *Oklahoma Pub. Co. v. District Court,* 430 U.S. 308 (1977) (pretrial order enjoining press from publishing name or picture of 11-year-old boy accused of murder invalid when reporters had been lawfully present at a prior public hearing and had photographed him en route from the courthouse); *Landmark Communications, Inc. v. Virginia,* 435 U.S. 829 (1978) (statute making it a crime to publish information about particular confidential proceedings invalid as applied to non-participant in the proceedings, at least when the information had been lawfully acquired); *Smith v. Daily Mail Pub. Co.,* 443 U.S. 97 (1979) (statute making it a crime for newspapers (but not broadcasters) to publish the name of any youth charged as a juvenile offender invalid as applied to information lawfully acquired from private sources). But cf. *Seattle Times Co. v. Rhinehart,* 467 U.S. 20 (1984) (order enjoining newspaper from disseminating information acquired as a litigant in pretrial discovery valid so long as order is entered on a showing of good cause and does not restrict the dissemination of the information if gained from other sources).

II. NEWSGATHERING

A. PROTECTION OF CONFIDENTIAL SOURCES

BRANZBURG v. HAYES
408 U.S. 665, 92 S.Ct. 2646, 33 L.Ed.2d 626 (1972).

JUSTICE WHITE delivered the opinion of the Court.

---

f. Compare Carol Rieger, *Lawyers' Criticism of Judges: Is Freedom of Speech A Figure of Speech?,* 2 Const.Comm. 69 (1985).

[Branzburg, a Kentucky reporter, wrote articles describing his observations of local hashish-making and other drug violations. He refused to testify before a grand jury regarding his information. The state courts rejected his claim of a First Amendment privilege.

[Pappas, a Massachusetts TV newsman-photographer, was allowed to enter and remain inside a Black Panther headquarters on condition he disclose nothing. When an anticipated police raid did not occur, he wrote no story. Summoned before a local grand jury, he refused to answer any questions about what had occurred inside the Panther headquarters or to identify those he had observed. The state courts denied his claim of a First Amendment privilege.

[Caldwell, a N.Y. Times reporter covering the Black Panthers, was summoned to appear before a federal grand jury investigating Panther activities. A federal court issued a protective order providing that although he had to divulge information given him "for publication," he could withhold "confidential" information "developed or maintained by him as a professional journalist." Maintaining that absent a specific need for his testimony he should be excused from attending the grand jury altogether, Caldwell disregarded the order and was held in contempt. The Ninth Circuit reversed, holding that absent "compelling reasons" Caldwell could refuse even to attend the grand jury, because of the potential impact of such an appearance on the flow of news to the public.]

[Petitioners' First Amendment claims] may be simply put: that to gather news it is often necessary to agree either not to identify [sources] or to publish only part of the facts revealed, or both; that if the reporter is nevertheless forced to reveal these confidences to a grand jury, the source so identified and other confidential sources of other reporters will be measurably deterred from furnishing publishable information, all to the detriment of the free flow of information protected by the First Amendment. Although petitioners do not claim an absolute privilege [they] assert that the reporter should not be forced either to appear or to testify before a grand jury or at trial until and unless sufficient grounds are shown for believing that the reporter possesses information relevant to a crime the grand jury is investigating, that the information the reporter has is unavailable from other sources, and that the need for the information is sufficiently compelling to override the claimed invasion of First Amendment interests occasioned by the disclosure. [The] heart of the claim is that the burden on news gathering resulting from compelling reporters to disclose confidential information outweighs any public interest in obtaining the information.

[We agree] that news gathering [qualifies] for First Amendment protection; without some protection for seeking out the news, freedom of the press could be eviscerated. But this case involves no intrusions upon speech [and no] command that the press publish what it prefers to withhold. [N]o penalty, civil or criminal, related to the content of published material is at issue here. The use of confidential sources by the press is not forbidden or restricted; reporters remain free to seek news from any source by means within the law. No attempt is made to require the press to publish its sources of information or indiscriminately to disclose them on request.

The sole issue before us is the obligation of reporters to respond to grand jury subpoenas as other citizens do and to answer questions relevant to an investigation into the commission of crime.

[T]he First Amendment does not guarantee the press a constitutional right of special access to information not available to the public generally. [Although] news gathering may be hampered, the press is regularly excluded from grand jury proceedings, our own conferences, the meetings of other official bodies gathered in executive session, and the meetings of private organizations. Newsmen have no constitutional right of access to the scenes of crime or disaster when the general public is excluded, and they may be prohibited from attending or publishing information about trials if such restrictions are necessary to assure a defendant a fair trial before an impartial tribunal. [It] is thus not surprising that the great weight of authority is that newsmen are not exempt from the normal duty of appearing before a grand jury and answering questions relevant to a criminal investigation.

[Because] its task is to inquire into the existence of possible criminal conduct and to return only well-founded indictments, [the grand jury's] investigative powers are necessarily broad. [T]he long standing principle that "the public has a right to every man's evidence," except for those persons protected by a constitutional, common law, or statutory privilege, is particularly applicable to grand jury proceedings.

A [number] of States have provided newsmen a statutory privilege of varying breadth, [but] none has been provided by federal statute. [We decline to create one] by interpreting the First Amendment to grant newsmen a testimonial privilege that other citizens do not enjoy. [On] the records now before us, we perceive no basis for holding that the public interest in law enforcement and in ensuring effective grand jury proceedings is insufficient to override the consequential, but uncertain, burden on news gathering which is said to result from insisting that reporters, like other citizens, respond to relevant questions put to them in the course of a valid grand jury investigation or criminal trial.

This conclusion [does not] threaten the vast bulk of confidential relationships between reporters and their sources. Grand juries address themselves to the issues of whether crimes have been committed and who committed them. Only where news sources themselves are implicated in crime or possess information relevant to the grand jury's task need they or the reporter be concerned about grand jury subpoenas. Nothing before us indicates that a large number or percentage of *all* confidential news sources fall into either category and would in any way be deterred by [our holding]. * * *[33]

Accepting the fact, however, that an undetermined number of informants not themselves implicated in crime will nevertheless, for whatever reason, refuse to talk to newsmen if they fear identification by a reporter in an official investigation, we cannot accept the argument that the public interest in possible future news about crime from undisclosed, unverified sources must take precedence over the public interest in pursuing and prosecuting those crimes reported to the press by informants and in thus deterring the commission of such crimes in the future. * * *

[The] privilege claimed here is conditional, not absolute; given the suggested preliminary showings and compelling need, the reporter would be required to testify. [If] newsmen's confidential sources are as sensitive as they are claimed to be, the prospect of being unmasked whenever a judge determines the situation justifies it is hardly a satisfactory solution to the problem. For them, it would appear that only an absolute privilege would suffice.

We are unwilling to embark the judiciary on a long and difficult journey to such an uncertain destination. The administration of a constitutional newsman's privilege would present practical and conceptual difficulties of a high order. Sooner or later, it would be necessary to define those categories of newsmen who qualified for the privilege, a questionable procedure in light of the traditional doctrine that liberty of the press is the right of the lonely pamphleteer who uses carbon paper or a mimeograph just as much as of the large metropolitan publisher who utilizes the latest photocomposition methods. [The] informative function asserted by representatives of the organized press in the present cases is also performed by lecturers, political pollsters, novelists, academic researchers, and dramatists. Almost any author may quite accurately assert that he is contributing to the flow of information to the public, that he relies on confidential sources of information, and that these sources will be silenced if he is forced to make disclosures before a grand jury.

In each instance where a reporter is subpoenaed to testify, the courts would also be embroiled in preliminary factual and legal determinations with respect to whether the proper predicate had been laid for the reporters' appearance. [I]n the end, by considering whether enforcement of a particular law served a "compelling" governmental interest, the courts would be inextricably involved in distinguishing between the value of enforcing different criminal laws. By requiring testimony from a reporter in investigations involving some crimes but not in others, they would be making a value judgment which a legislature had declined to [make.]

---

33. In his *Press Subpoenas: An Empirical and Legal Analysis* 6–12 (1971), Prof. Blasi found that slightly more than half of the 975 reporters questioned said that they relied on regular confidential sources for at least 10% of their stories. Of this group of reporters, only 8% were able to say with some certainty that their professional functioning had been adversely affected by the threat of subpoena; another 11% were not certain whether or not they had been adversely affected. [See also Vincent Blasi, *The Newsman's Privilege: An Empirical Study,* 70 Mich.L.Rev. 229 (1971).]

At the federal level, Congress has freedom to determine whether a statutory newsman's privilege is necessary and desirable and to fashion standards and rules as narrow or broad as deemed necessary [and], equally important, to re-fashion those rules as experience from time to time may dictate. There is also merit in leaving state legislatures free, within First Amendment limits, to fashion their own standards in light of the conditions and problems with respect to the relations between law enforcement officials and press in their own [areas]. * * *

[G]rand jury investigations if instituted or conducted other than in good faith, would pose wholly different issues for resolution under the First Amendment. Official harassment of the press undertaken not for purposes of law enforcement but to disrupt a reporter's relationship with his news sources would have no justification. Grand juries are subject to judicial control and subpoenas to motions to quash. We do not expect courts will forget that grand juries must operate within the limits of the First Amendment as well as the Fifth.

We turn, therefore, to the disposition of the cases before us. [*Caldwell*] must be reversed. If there is no First Amendment privilege to refuse to answer the relevant and material questions asked during a good-faith grand jury investigation, then it is a fortiori true that there is no privilege to refuse to appear before such a grand jury until the Government demonstrates some "compelling need" for a newsman's testimony. [*Branzburg*] must be affirmed. [P]etitioner refused to answer questions that directly related to criminal conduct which he had observed and written about. [If] what petitioner wrote was true, he had direct information to provide the grand jury concerning the commission of serious crimes. [In *Pappas*, we] affirm [and] hold that petitioner must appear before the grand jury to answer the questions put to him, subject, of course, to the supervision of the presiding judge as to "the propriety, purposes, and scope of the grand jury inquiry and the pertinence of the probable testimony."

JUSTICE POWELL, concurring in the opinion of the Court.

I add this brief statement to emphasize what seems to me to be the limited nature of the Court's holding. The Court does not hold that newsmen, subpoenaed to testify before a grand jury, are without constitutional rights with respect to the gathering of news or in safeguarding their sources. [As] indicated in the concluding portion of the opinion, the Court states that no harassment of newsmen will be tolerated. If a newsman believes that the grand jury investigation is not being conducted in good faith he is not without remedy. Indeed, if the newsman is called upon to give information bearing only a remote and tenuous relationship to the subject of the investigation, or if he has some other reason to believe that his testimony implicates confidential source relationships without a legitimate need of law enforcement, he will have access to the Court on a motion to quash and an appropriate protective order may be entered. The asserted claim to privilege should be judged on its facts by the striking of a proper balance between freedom of the press and the obligation of all citizens to give relevant testimony with respect to criminal conduct. The balance of these vital constitutional and societal interests on a case-by-case basis accords with the tried and traditional way of adjudicating such questions.*

In short, the courts will be available to newsmen under circumstances where legitimate First Amendment interests require protection.

JUSTICE DOUGLAS, dissenting.

[T]here is no "compelling need" that can be shown [by the Government] which qualifies the reporter's immunity from appearing or testifying before a grand jury, unless the reporter himself is implicated in a crime. His immunity in my view is therefore quite complete, for absent his involvement in a crime, the First Amendment protects him against an appearance before a grand jury and if he is involved in a crime, the Fifth Amendment stands as a barrier. Since in my view there is no area of inquiry not protected by a privilege, the reporter need not appear for the futile purpose of invoking one to each [question.]

Two principles which follow from [Alexander Meiklejohn's] understanding of the First Amendment are at stake here. One is that the people, the ultimate governors, must have absolute freedom of and therefore privacy of their individual opinions and beliefs regardless of how suspect or strange they may appear to others. Ancillary to that principle is the conclusion that an individual must also have absolute privacy over whatever information he may generate in the course of testing his opinions and beliefs. In this regard, Caldwell's status as a reporter is less relevant than is his status as a student who affirmatively pursued empirical research to enlarge his own intellectual viewpoint. The second principle is that effective self-government cannot succeed unless the people are immersed in a steady, robust, unimpeded, and uncensored flow of opinion and reporting which are continuously subjected to critique, rebuttal, and re-examination. In this respect, Caldwell's status as a newsgatherer and an integral part of that process becomes critical. * * *

Sooner or later any test which provides less than blanket protection to beliefs and associations will be twisted and relaxed so as to provide virtually no protection at [all]. Perceptions of the worth of state objectives

---

* It is to be remembered that Caldwell asserts a constitutional privilege not even to appear before the grand jury unless a court decides that the government has made a showing that meets the three preconditions specified in [Stewart, J.'s dissent]. To be sure, this would require a "balancing" of interests by the Court, but under circumstances and constraints significantly different from the balancing that will be appropriate under the Court's decision. The newsman witness, like all other witnesses, will have to appear; he will not be in a position to litigate at the threshold the State's very authority to subpoena him. Moreover, absent the constitutional preconditions that [the dissent] would impose as heavy burdens of proof to be carried by the State, the court—when called upon to protect a newsman from improper or prejudicial questioning—would be free to balance the competing interests on their merits in the particular case. The new constitutional rule endorsed by [the dissent] would, as a practical matter, defeat such a fair balancing and the essential societal interest in the detection and prosecution of crime would be heavily subordinated.

will change with the composition of the Court and with the intensity of the politics of the [times.]

JUSTICE STEWART, with whom JUSTICE BRENNAN and JUSTICE MARSHALL join, dissenting.

The Court's crabbed view of the First Amendment reflects a disturbing insensitivity to the critical role of an independent press in our society. [While] Mr. Justice Powell's enigmatic concurring opinion gives some hope of a more flexible view in the future, the Court in these cases holds that a newsman has no First Amendment right to protect his sources when called before a grand jury. The Court thus invites state and federal authorities to undermine the historic independence of the press by attempting to annex the journalistic profession as an investigative arm of government. Not only will this decision impair performance of the press' constitutionally protected functions, but it will, I am convinced, in the long run, harm rather than help the administration of justice.

[As] private and public aggregations of power burgeon in size and the pressures for conformity necessarily mount, there is obviously a continuing need for an independent press to disseminate a robust variety of information and opinion through reportage, investigation and criticism, if we are to preserve our constitutional tradition of maximizing freedom of choice by encouraging diversity of expression. * * *

A corollary of the right to publish must be the right to gather news. [This right] implies, in turn, a right to a confidential relationship between a reporter and his source. This proposition follows as a matter of simple logic once three factual predicates are recognized: (1) newsmen require informants to gather news; (2) confidentiality—the promise or understanding that names or certain aspects of communications will be kept off-the-record—is essential to the creation and maintenance of a news-gathering relationship with informants; and (3) the existence of an unbridled subpoena power—the absence of a constitutional right protecting, in *any* way, a confidential relationship from compulsory process—will either deter sources from divulging information or deter reporters from gathering and publishing information. * * *

After today's decision, the potential informant can never be sure that his identity or off-the-record communications will not subsequently be revealed through the compelled testimony of a newsman. A public spirited person inside government, who is not implicated in any crime, will now be fearful of revealing corruption or other governmental wrong-doing, because he will now know he can subsequently be identified by use of compulsory process. The potential source must, therefore, choose between risking exposure by giving information or avoiding the risk by remaining silent.

The reporter must speculate about whether contact with a controversial source or publication of controversial material will lead to a subpoena. In the event of a subpoena, under today's decision, the newsman will know that he must choose between being punished for contempt if he refuses to testify, or violating his profession's ethics[10] and impairing his resourcefulness as a reporter if he discloses confidential information. * * *

The impairment of the flow of news cannot, of course, be proven with scientific precision, as the Court seems to demand. [But] we have never before demanded that First Amendment rights rest on elaborate empirical studies demonstrating beyond any conceivable doubt that deterrent effects exist; we have never before required proof of the exact number of people potentially affected by governmental action, who would actually be dissuaded from engaging in First Amendment activity. * * *

We cannot await an unequivocal—and therefore unattainable—imprimatur from empirical studies. We can and must accept the evidence developed in the record, and elsewhere, that overwhelmingly supports the premise that deterrence will occur with regularity in important types of newsgathering relationships. Thus, we cannot escape the conclusion that when neither the reporter nor his source can rely on the shield of confidentiality against unrestrained use of the grand jury's subpoena power, valuable information will not be published and the public dialogue will inevitably be impoverished.

[W]hen a reporter is asked to appear before a grand jury and reveal confidences, I would hold that the government must (1) show that there is probable cause to believe that the newsman has information which is clearly relevant to a specific probable violation of law; (2) demonstrate that the information sought cannot be obtained by alternative means less destructive of First Amendment rights; and (3) demonstrate a compelling and overriding interest in the information. * * *

Both the "probable cause" and "alternative means" requirements [would] serve the vital function of mediating between the public interest in the administration of justice and the constitutional protection of the full flow of information. These requirements would avoid a direct conflict between these competing concerns, and they would generally provide adequate protection for newsmen. No doubt the courts would be required to make some delicate judgments in working out this accommodation. But that, after all, is the function of courts of law. Better such judgments, however difficult, than the simplistic and stultifying absolutism adopted by the Court in denying any force to the First Amendment in these cases.[36] * * *

[In Stewart, J.'s view, the Ninth Circuit correctly ruled that in the circumstances of the case, Caldwell need not divulge confidential informa-

---

10. The American Newspaper Guild has adopted the following rule as part of the newsman's code of ethics: "Newspaper men shall refuse to reveal confidences or disclose sources of confidential information in court or before other judicial or investigative bodies."

36. The disclaimers in Mr. Justice Powell's concurring opinion leave room for the hope that in some future case the Court may take a less absolute position in this area. [For the claim that a legislative solution is better than waiting, see William E. Lee, *The Priestly Class: Reflections on a Journalist's Privilege*, 23 Card. Arts & Ent. L.J. 635 (2006). For defense of a qualified privilege extended to everyone who disseminates information to the public, see Mary-Rose Papandrea, *Citizen Journalism and the Reporter's Privilege*, 91 Minn. L.Rev. 515, 584–90 (2007)].

tion and, moreover, that in this case Caldwell had established that "his very appearance [before] the grand jury would jeopardize his relationship with his sources, leading to a severance of the news gathering relationship and impairment of the flow of news to the public." But because "only in very rare circumstances would a confidential relationship between a reporter and his source be so sensitive [as to preclude] his mere appearance before the grand jury," Stewart, J., would confine "*this* aspect of the *Caldwell* judgment [to] its own facts." Thus, he would affirm in *Caldwell* and remand the other cases for further proceedings not inconsistent with his views.]

NOTES AND QUESTIONS

1. ***Role of the press.*** Consider Vincent Blasi, *The Checking Value in First Amendment Theory,* 1977 Am.B.Found.Res.J. 521, 593: The White, J., opinion "characterized the press as a private-interest group rather than an institution with a central function to perform in the constitutional system of checks and balances [and] labeled the source relationships that the reporters sought to maintain 'a private system of informers operated by the press to report on criminal conduct' [cautioning] that this system would be 'unaccountable to the public' were a reporter's privilege to be recognized." In contrast to White, J.'s perspective, consider the remarks of Stewart, J., in a much-discussed address, *"Or of the Press,"* 26 Hast.L.J. 631, 634 (1975): "In setting up the three branches of the Federal Government, the Founders deliberately created an internally competitive[a] system. [The] primary purpose[b] of [the Free Press Clause] was a similar one: to create a fourth institution outside the Government as an additional check on the three official branches."[c] Proceeding from variations of this fourth estate view of the press, most commentators endorse a reporter's privilege. See, e.g., C. Edwin Baker, *Press Rights and Government Power to Structure the Press,* 34 U.Miami L.Rev. 819, 858 (1980) (absolute protection). But see Randall Bezanson, *The New Free Press Guarantee,* 63 Va.L.Rev. 731, 759–62 (1977) (press clause prevents special governmental assistance for press). Claims for an independent press-clause, however, need not interpret the press clause along fourth estate lines, see Rodney Smolla, *Smolla and Nimmer on Freedom of Speech* 2–104—2–129 (1984).[d]

---

a. For commentary on how the "cozy connections" between press and government demonstrate that the relationship is often more cooperative than adversarial, see Aviam Soifer, *Freedom of the Press in the United States* in Press Law in Modern Democracies 79, 108–110 (Lahav, ed., 1985).

b. For spirited debate about the historical evidence, compare David Anderson, *The Origins of the Press Clause,* 30 UCLA L.Rev. 455 (1983) with Leonard Levy, *On the Origins of the Free Press Clause,* 32 UCLA L.Rev. 177 (1984). See generally Leonard Levy, *Emergence of a Free Press* (1985).

For background on Stewart, J.'s dissent and the role it has played in the lower courts, see Stephen Bates, *Garland v. Torre and the Birth of Reporter's Privilege,* 15 Comm. L.&Pol'y 91 (2010). For the contention that media litigants have largely avoided arguing in favor of Stewart, J.'s position, see Erik Ugland, *Newsgathering, Autonomy, and the Special Rights Apocrypha,* 11 U. Pa. J. Const.L.375 (2009).

c. For Brennan, J.'s views, see *Address,* 32 Rutg.L.Rev. 173 (1979).

d. For criticism of the notion of an independent press clause, see David Lange, *The Speech and Press Clauses,* 23 UCLA L.Rev. 77 (1975); Anthony Lewis, *A Preferred Position for*

2. *Evaluating Powell, J.'s concurrence.* Did five justices—or only four—hold that grand juries may pursue their goals by any means short of bad faith? May one conclude that the information sought bears "only a remote and tenuous relationship to the subject of investigation" on grounds falling short of demonstrating "bad faith"? Does Powell, J.'s suggested test—the privilege claim "should be judged on its facts by [balancing the] vital constitutional and societal interests on a case-by-case basis"—resemble Stewart, J.'s dissenting approach more than White, J.'s? Extrajudicially, Stewart, J., has referred to *Branzburg* as a case which rejected claims for a journalist's privilege "by a vote of 5–4, or, considering Mr. Justice Powell's concurring opinion, perhaps by a vote of 4½–4½." Potter Stewart, *"Or of the Press,"* 26 Hast.L.J. 631, 635 (1975). The majority of courts applying *Branzburg* have concluded that Powell, J.'s opinion read together with the dissents affords the basis for a qualified privilege. See Jennifer Elrod, *Protecting Journalists From Compelled Disclosure: A Proposal For a Federal Statute,* 7 N.Y.U. J. Legis. & Pub. Pol'y 115, 124 (2004). Among the issues litigated are whether the privilege should be confined to journalists (or extended e.g. to academics) and the related question of how to define journalists and whether the privilege belongs to the source, the reporter, or both. See James Goodale, Joseph Moodhe & Rodney Ott, *Reporter's Privilege Cases,* 421 PLI/PAT 63 (1995). In any event, the privilege would give way if access to the source were necessary to investigate serious criminal misconduct.

The Court's most recent expression unanimously refuses, at least in the absence of bad faith, to extend a qualified First Amendment privilege to "confidential" tenure files and, in dictum, confines *Branzburg* to the recognition that the " 'bad faith' exercise of grand jury powers might raise First Amendment concerns." *University of Pennsylvania v. EEOC,* 493 U.S. 182 (1990) (gender discrimination claim).

3. *Other contexts.* Does *Branzburg's* emphasis on the grand jury's special role in the American criminal justice system warrant different treatment of the journalist's privilege when a prosecutor seeks disclosure? See Donna Murasky, *The Journalist's Privilege: Branzburg and Its Aftermath,* 52 Tex.L.Rev. 829, 885 (1974). Are the interests of civil litigants in compelling disclosure of a journalist's confidences significantly weaker than those of criminal litigants? Should there be an absolute journalist's privilege in civil discovery proceedings? See id. at 898–903. What if the journalist is a party to the litigation? Should journalists have greater protection for non-confidential

Journalism?, 7 Hof.L.Rev. 595 (1979); William Van Alstyne, *The First Amendment and the Free Press: A Comment on Some New Trends and Some Old Theories,* 9 Hof.L.Rev. 1 (1980); William Van Alstyne, *The Hazards to the Press of Claiming a "Preferred Position",* 28 Hast.L.J. 761 (1977). But see Floyd Abrams, *The Press is Different: Reflections on Justice Stewart and the Autonomous Press,* 7 Hof.L.Rev. 563 (1979). For an effort to transcend the issues involved, see generally Robert Sack, *Reflections on the Wrong Question: Special Constitutional Privilege for the Institutional Press,* 7 Hof.L.Rev. 629 (1979). Finally, for commentary on the "tension between journalism as the political, sometimes partisan fourth estate and journalism as a profession" purporting to operate as a "neutral and objective medium," see Pnina Lahav, *An Outline for a General Theory of Press Law in Democracy* in Press Law in Modern Democracies 339, 352–54 (Lahav ed. 1985). See also Lee Bollinger, *The Press and the Public Interest: An Essay on the Relationship Between Social Behavior and the Language of First Amendment Theory,* 82 Mich. L.Rev. 1447, 1457 (1984) (commenting generally on the pitfalls connected with justifying a free press by arguing that it serves the public interest: "More than most groups (compare lawyers, for example) the press is in conflict over its relationship to the world on which it regularly reports.").

information than other potential witnesses? See *Gonzales v. National Broadcasting Co.*, 155 F.3d 618 (2d Cir.1998).

4. ***Beyond confidentiality.*** Should the press receive a measure of protection from government attempts to secure information gathered on a non-confidential basis? Consider Jaynie Randall, *Freeing Newsgathering From the Reporter's Privilege*, 114 Yale L.J. 1827, 1827 (2005): "A number of recent high-profile cases have forced courts to reexamine whether reporters must respond to subpoenas seeking disclosure of confidential sources or whether they are protected from doing so by the doctrine of reporter's privilege. While these confidential-source cases have garnered the most public attention, the vast majority of subpoenas issued to reporters seek to compel disclosure of nonconfidential information. [P]reserving the checking value of the press demands protections mirroring those for attorney work products. Disclosure of the interim steps in newsgathering may result in self-censorship. * * * To the extent that resource materials, drafts, and outtakes reveal the editorial choices made by the press, they should be protected."

5. ***Defining the press.*** Consider David McGowan, *Approximately Speech*, 89 Minn. L. Rev. 1416, 1434 (2005): "[T]he transaction cost savings that distinguish firms from bloggers are not directly relevant to free speech interests, so they do not justify differential treatment. In terms of function, bloggers have shown they can nail down stories of national importance as quickly and accurately as traditional media firms. In some cases, they do better."

6. ***Reverse Branzburg.*** Suppose a reporter reveals a confidential source who sues for redress. Any First Amendment protection? See *Cohen v. Cowles Media Co.*, note 2 after *Arcara*, Ch. 2 supra.[e]

7. ***State "shield laws" and a criminal defendant's right to compulsory process.*** Most states and the District of Columbia have enacted "shield" laws.[f] Some protect only journalists' sources; some (including New Jersey) protect undisclosed information obtained in the course of a journalist's professional activities as well as sources.

IN RE FARBER, 78 N.J. 259, 394 A.2d 330 (1978), cert. denied, 439 U.S. 997 (1978): New York Times investigative reporter Myron Farber

---

e. For commentary on *Cohen*, see Anthony L. Fargo, *Testing the Boundaries of the First Amendment Press Clause*, 32 Harv. J.L. & Pub. Pol'y 1093 (2009); Dan Cohen, *Anonymous Source: At War Against the Media, A True Story* (2005); Kyu Ho Youm, *"Burning the Source": Cohen v. Cowles Media*, 23–SPG Comm. Law. 19 (2005); Alan E. Garfield, *The Mischief of Cohen v. Cowles Media*, 35 Georgia L.Rev. 1087 (2001); Jerome A. Barron, *Cohen v. Cowles Media and Its Significance for First Amendment Law and Journalism*, 3 Wm. & Mary Bill Rts. J. 419 (1994); Eric B. Easton, *Two Wrongs Mock a Right: Overcoming the Cohen Maledicta that Bar First Amendment Protection for Newsgathering*, 58 Ohio St. L.J. 1135 (1997); Lili Levi, *Dangerous Liasons: Seduction and Betrayal in Confidential Press–Source Relations*, 43 Rutgers L.Rev. 609 (1991).

f. Consider Gerald F. Uelmen, *Leaks, Gags and Shields: Taking Responsibility*, 37 Santa Clara L.Rev. 943, 945 (1997): "Current 'shield laws' encourage the leaking of information by protecting the leaker from any consequences for his breach of confidentiality, and place no responsibility on reporters for lack of restraint in promising confidentiality to their sources. Somehow the irony has escaped us, that we encourage irresponsible breaches of confidentiality by guaranteeing to violators that we will protect the confidentiality of their breach! Those who have no respect for confidentiality that protects others are rewarded by our guarantee of absolute confidentiality for their treachery."

wrote a series of articles claiming that an unidentified "Doctor X" had caused the death of several patients by poisoning. This led to the indictment and eventual prosecution of Dr. Jascalevich for murder. (He was ultimately acquitted.) In response to the defendant's request, the trial court demanded the disclosure of Farber's sources and the production of his interview notes and other information for his in camera inspection. Relying on the First Amendment and the state shield law, Farber refused to comply with the subpoenas. After White, J., and then Marshall, J., had denied stays, each deeming it unlikely that four justices would grant certiorari at this stage of the case, Farber was jailed for civil contempt and the *Times* heavily fined.

The state supreme court (5–2) upheld civil and criminal convictions of the *Times* and Farber. Under the circumstances, it ruled, the First Amendment did not protect Farber against disclosure. Nor did the New Jersey shield law, for Farber's statutory rights had to yield to Dr. Jascalevich's sixth amendment right "to have compulsory process for obtaining witnesses in his favor."[g]

———

ZURCHER v. STANFORD DAILY, 436 U.S. 547 (1978), again declined to afford the press special protection—dividing very much as in *Branzburg*.[a] A student newspaper that had published articles and photographs of a clash between demonstrators and police brought this federal action, claiming that a search of its offices for film and pictures showing events at the scene of the police-demonstrators clash (the newspaper was not involved in the unlawful acts) had violated its first and fourth amendment rights. A 5–3 majority, per WHITE, J., held that the fourth amendment does not prevent the government from issuing a search warrant (based on reasonable cause to believe that the "things" to be searched for are located on the property) simply because the owner or possessor of the place to be searched is not reasonably suspected of criminal involvement. The Court also rejected the argument that "whatever may be true of third-party searches generally, where the third party is a newspaper, there are additional [First Amendment factors justifying] a nearly per se rule forbidding the search warrant and permitting only the subpoena duces tecum. The general submission is that searches of newspaper offices for evidence of crime reasonably believed to be on the premises

———

g. For analysis of the case, see Note, 32 Rutg.L.Rev. 545 (1979). The case is also discussed at length by *New York Times* columnist Anthony Lewis, *A Preferred Position for Journalism?*, 7 Hof.L.Rev. 595, 610–18 (1979).

a. In both cases, White, J., joined by Burger, C.J., Blackmun, Powell and Rehnquist, JJ., delivered the opinion of the Court and in both cases the "fifth vote"—Powell, J.,—also wrote a separate opinion which seemed to meet the concerns of the dissent part way. In both cases Stewart, J., dissented, maintaining that the Court's holding would seriously impair "newsgathering." Stevens, J., who had replaced Douglas, J., also dissented in Zurcher, as had Douglas in *Branzburg*. Brennan, J., who had joined Stewart, J.'s dissent in *Branzburg*, did not participate in *Zurcher*.

will seriously threaten the ability of the press to gather, analyze, and disseminate news.

"[Although] [a]ware of the long struggle between Crown and press and desiring to curb unjustified official intrusions, [the Framers] did not forbid warrants where the press was involved, did not require special showing that subpoenas would be impractical, and did not insist that the owner of the place to be searched, if connected with the press, must be shown to be implicated in the offense being investigated. Further, the prior cases do no more than insist that the courts apply the warrant requirements with particular exactitude when First Amendment interests would be endangered by the search. [N]o more than this is required where the warrant requested is for the seizure of criminal evidence reasonably believed to be on the premises occupied by a newspaper. Properly administered, the preconditions for a warrant—probable cause, specificity [as to] place [and] things to be seized and overall reasonableness—should afford [the press] sufficient protection * * *.

"[R]espondents and amici have pointed to only a very few instances [since] 1971 involving [newspaper office searches]. This reality hardly suggests abuse, and if abuse occurs, there will be time enough to deal with it. Furthermore, the press [is] not easily intimidated—nor should it be."

POWELL, J., concurring, rejected Stewart, J.'s dissenting view that the press is entitled to "a special procedure, not available to others," when the government requires evidence in its possession, but added: "This is not to say [that a warrant] sufficient to support the search of an apartment or an automobile would be reasonable in supporting the search of a newspaper office. [While] there is no justification for the establishment of a separate Fourth Amendment procedure for the press, a magistrate asked to issue a warrant for the search of press offices can and should take cognizance of the independent values protected by the First Amendment—such as those highlighted by [Stewart, J., dissenting]—when he weighs such factors."[b]

STEWART, joined by Marshall, J., dissented: "A search warrant allows police officers to ransack the files of a newspaper, reading each and every document until they have found the one named in the warrant, while a subpoena would permit the newspaper itself to produce only the specific documents requested. A search, unlike a subpoena, will therefore lead to the needless exposure of confidential information completely unrelated to the purpose of the investigation. The knowledge that police officers can make an unannounced raid on a newsroom is thus bound to have a deterrent effect on the availability of confidential news sources. [The result] will be a diminishing flow of potentially important information to the public.

---

b. Powell, J., noted that his *Branzburg* concurrence may "properly be read as supporting the view expressed in the text above, and in the Court's [*Zurcher*] opinion," that under the warrant requirement "the magistrate should consider the values of a free press as well as the societal interest in enforcing the criminal laws."

"[Here, unlike *Branzburg,* the newspaper does] not claim that any of the evidence sought was privileged[, but] only that a subpoena would have served equally well to produce that evidence. Thus, we are not concerned with the principle, central to *Branzburg,* that ' "the public [has] a right to everyman's evidence," ' but only with whether any significant social interest would be impaired if the police were generally required to obtain evidence from the press by means of a subpoena rather than a search. * * *

"Perhaps as a matter of abstract policy a newspaper office should receive no more protection from unannounced police searches than, say, the office of a doctor or the office of a bank. But we are here to uphold a Constitution. And our Constitution does not explicitly protect the practice of medicine or the business of banking from all abridgement by government. It does explicitly protect the freedom of the press."[c]

NOTES AND QUESTIONS

The distinctions between search and subpoena are underscored in Tribe 2d ed., at 973: "When a subpoena is served on a newspaper, it has the opportunity to assert constitutional and statutory rights [such as 'shield laws,' enacted in many states, protecting reporters from divulging information given them in confidence] to keep certain materials confidential. Such protection is circumvented when officials can proceed *ex parte,* by search warrant. And the risk of abuse may be greatest exactly when the press plays its most vital and creative role in our political system, the role of watchdog on official corruption and abuse. Officials who find themselves the targets [of] media investigations may well be tempted to conduct searches to find out precisely what various journalists have discovered, and to retaliate against reporters who have unearthed and reported official wrongdoing."

B. ACCESS TO TRIALS AND OTHER GOVERNMENTALLY CONTROLLED INFORMATION AND INSTITUTIONS

By 1978, no Supreme Court holding contradicted Burger, C.J.'s contention for the plurality in *Houchins v. KQED,* 438 U.S. 1 (1978) that, "neither the First Amendment nor the Fourteenth Amendment mandates a right of access to government information or sources of information within the government's control." Or as Stewart, J., put it in an often-quoted statement, "The Constitution itself is neither a Freedom of Information Act nor an Official Secrets Act." *"Or of the Press,"* 26 Hast.L.J. 631, 636 (1975). *Richmond Newspapers,* infra, constitutes the Court's first break with its past denials of First Amendment rights to information within governmental control.

RICHMOND NEWSPAPERS, INC. v. VIRGINIA
448 U.S. 555, 100 S.Ct. 2814, 65 L.Ed.2d 973 (1980).

[At the commencement of his fourth trial on a murder charge (his first conviction having been reversed and two subsequent retrials having

---
c. Stevens, J., dissented on the general fourth amendment issue.

ended in mistrials), defendant moved, without objection by the prosecutor or two reporters present, that the trial be closed to the public—defense counsel stating that he did not "want any information being shuffled back and forth when we have a recess as [to] who testified to what." The trial judge granted the motion, stating that "the statute gives me that power specifically." He presumably referred to Virginia Code § 19.2–266, providing that in all criminal trials "the court may, in its discretion, exclude [any] persons whose presence would impair the conduct of a fair trial, provided that the [defendant's right] to a public trial shall not be violated." Later the same day the trial court granted appellants' request for a hearing on a motion to vacate the closure order. At the closed hearing, appellants observed that prior to the entry of its closure order the court had failed to make any evidentiary findings or to consider any other, less drastic measures to ensure a fair trial. Defendant stated that he "didn't want information to leak out," be published by the media, perhaps inaccurately, and then be seen by the jurors. Noting inter alia that "having people in the Courtroom is distracting to the jury" and that if "the rights of the defendant are infringed in any way [and if his closure motion] doesn't completely override all rights of everyone else, then I'm inclined to go along with" the defendant, the court denied the motion to vacate the closure order. Defendant was subsequently found not guilty.]

CHIEF JUSTICE BURGER announced the judgment of the Court and delivered an opinion in which JUSTICE WHITE and JUSTICE STEVENS joined.

[T]he precise issue presented here has not previously been before this Court for decision. [*Gannett Co. v. DePasquale,* 443 U.S. 368 (1979)] was not required to decide whether a right of access to *trials,* as distinguished from hearings on *pre*trial motions, was constitutionally guaranteed. The Court held that the Sixth Amendment's guarantee to the accused of a public trial gave neither the public nor the press an enforceable right of access to a *pre*trial suppression hearing. One concurring opinion specifically emphasized that "a hearing on a motion before trial to suppress evidence is not a *trial.*" (Burger, C.J., concurring). Moreover, the Court did not decide whether the First and Fourteenth Amendments guarantee a right of the public to attend trials; nor did the dissenting opinion reach this issue. [H]ere for the first time the Court is asked to decide whether a criminal trial itself may be closed to the public upon the unopposed request of a defendant, without any demonstration that closure is required to protect the defendant's superior right to a fair trial, or that some other overriding consideration requires closure.

[T]he historical evidence demonstrates conclusively that at the time when our organic laws were adopted, criminal trials both here and in England had long been presumptively open[, thus giving] assurance that the proceedings were conducted fairly to all concerned, [and] discouraging] perjury, the misconduct of participants, and decisions based on secret bias or partiality. [Moreover, the] early history of open trials in part reflects the widespread acknowledgment [that] public trials had significant therapeutic value. [When] a shocking crime occurs, a community reaction of outrage and public protest often follows. Thereafter the open processes of justice serve an important prophylactic purpose, providing an outlet for community concern, hostility, and emotion.

[The] crucial prophylactic aspects of the administration of justice cannot function in the dark; no community catharsis can occur if justice is "done in a corner [or] in any covert manner." [To] work effectively, it is important that society's criminal process "satisfy the appearance of justice," and the appearance of justice can best be provided by allowing people to observe it.

[From] this unbroken, uncontradicted history, supported by reasons as valid today as in centuries past, we are bound to conclude that a presumption of openness inheres in the very nature of a criminal trial under our system of criminal justice. [Nevertheless,] the State presses its contention that neither the Constitution nor the Bill of Rights contains any provision which by its terms guarantees to the public the right to attend criminal trials. Standing alone, this is correct, but there remains the question whether, absent an explicit provision, the Constitution affords protection against exclusion of the public from criminal trials.

[The] expressly guaranteed [First Amendment] freedoms share a common core purpose of assuring freedom of communication on matters relating to the functioning of government. Plainly it would be difficult to single out any aspect of government of higher concern and importance to the people than the manner in which criminal trials are conducted * * *.

The Bill of Rights was enacted against the backdrop of the long history of trials being presumptively open. [In] guaranteeing freedoms such as those of speech and press, the First Amendment can be read as protecting the right of everyone to attend trials so as to give meaning to those explicit guarantees. * * * Free speech carries with it some freedom to listen. "In a variety of contexts this Court has referred to a First Amendment right to 'receive information and ideas.'" *Kleindienst v. Mandel*, 408 U.S. 753 (1972).[a] What this means in the context of trials is that the First Amendment guarantees of speech and press, standing alone, prohibit government from summarily closing courtroom doors which had long been open to the public at the time that amendment was adopted.

[It] is not crucial whether we describe this right to attend criminal trials to hear, see, and communicate observations concerning them as a "right of access," cf. *Gannett* (Powell, J., concurring); *Saxbe v. Washington*

---

a. *Mandel* held that the Executive had plenary power to exclude a Belgium journalist from the country, at least so long as it operated on the basis of a facially legitimate and bona fide reason for exclusion. Although the Court decided ultimately not to balance the government's particular justification against the First Amendment interest, it recognized that those who sought personal communication with the excluded alien did have a First Amendment interest at stake. The Court apparently assumed that the excluded speaker had no rights at stake, and none were asserted on his behalf.

Post Co., 417 U.S. 843 (1974); *Pell v. Procunier,* 417 U.S. 817 (1974),[11] or a "right to gather information," for we have recognized that "without some protection for seeking out the news, freedom of the press could be eviscerated." *Branzburg v. Hayes.* The explicit, guaranteed rights to speak and to publish concerning what takes place at a trial would lose much meaning if access to observe the trial could, as it was here, be foreclosed arbitrarily.

The right of access to places traditionally open to the public, as criminal trials have long been, may be seen as assured by the amalgam of the First Amendment guarantees of speech and press; and their affinity to the right of assembly is not without relevance. From the outset, the right of assembly was regarded not only as an independent right but also as a catalyst to augment the free exercise of the other First Amendment rights with which it was deliberately linked by the draftsmen. [Subject] to the traditional time, place, and manner restrictions, streets, sidewalks, and parks are places traditionally open, where First Amendment rights may be exercised [see generally Ch. 6 infra]; a trial courtroom also is a public place where the people generally—and representatives of the media—have a right to be present, and where their presence historically has been thought to enhance the integrity and quality of what takes place.

* * * Notwithstanding the appropriate caution against reading into the Constitution rights not explicitly defined, the Court has acknowledged that certain unarticulated rights are implicit in enumerated guarantees [referring, inter alia, to the rights of association and of privacy and the right to travel. [T]hese important but unarticulated rights [have] been found to share constitutional protection in common with explicit guarantees. The concerns expressed by Madison and others have thus been [resolved].[b]

We hold that the right to attend criminal trials[17] is implicit in the guarantees of the First Amendment; without the freedom to attend such trials, which people have exercised for centuries, important aspects of freedom of speech and "of the press could be eviscerated." *Branzburg.*

[In the present case,] the trial court made no findings to support closure; no inquiry was made as to whether alternative solutions would have met the need to ensure fairness; there was no recognition of any right under the Constitution for the public or press to attend the trial. In contrast to the pretrial proceeding dealt with in *Gannett,* there exist in the

---

11. *Procunier* and *Saxbe* are distinguishable in the sense that they were concerned with penal institutions which, by definition, are not "open" or public places. [See] also *Greer v. Spock* (military bases) [Ch. 6, II infra].

b. The Chief Justice noted "the perceived need" of the Constitution's draftsmen "for some sort of constitutional 'saving clause' [which] would serve to foreclose application to the Bill of Rights of the maxim that the affirmation of particular rights implies a negation of those not expressly defined. Madison's efforts, culminating in the Ninth Amendment, served to allay the fears of those who were concerned that expressing certain guarantees could be read as excluding others."

17. Whether the public has a right to attend [civil trials is] not raised by this case, but we note that historically both civil and criminal trials have been presumptively open.

context of the trial itself various tested alternatives to satisfy the constitutional demands of fairness. [For example, there was nothing] to indicate that sequestration of the jurors would not have guarded against their being subjected to any improper information.[c] [Absent] an overriding interest articulated in findings, the trial of a criminal case must be open to the public. * * *

Reversed.[d]

JUSTICE BRENNAN, with whom JUSTICE MARSHALL joins, concurring in the judgment.

[Gannett] held that the Sixth Amendment right to a public trial was personal to the accused, conferring no right of access to pretrial proceedings that is separately enforceable by the public or the press. [This case] raises the question whether the First Amendment, of its own force and as applied to the States through the Fourteenth Amendment, secures the public an independent right of access to trial proceedings. Because I believe that [it does secure] such a public right of access, I agree [that], without more, agreement of the trial judge and the parties cannot constitutionally close a trial to the public.[1]

While freedom of expression is made inviolate by the First Amendment, and with only rare and stringent exceptions, may not be suppressed, the First Amendment has not been viewed by the Court in all settings as providing an equally categorical assurance of the correlative freedom of access to information.[2] Yet the Court has not ruled out a public access component to the First Amendment in every circumstance. Read with care and in context, our decisions must therefore be understood as holding only that any privilege of access to governmental information is subject to a degree of restraint dictated by the nature of the information and countervailing interests in security or confidentiality. [Cases such as Houchins, Saxbe and Pell] neither comprehensively nor absolutely deny that public access to information may at times be implied by the First Amendment and the principles which animate it.

---

c. Once the jurors are selected, when, if ever, will their sequestration *not* be a satisfactory alternative to closure?

d. Powell, J., took no part. In *Gannett,* he took the position that a First Amendment right of access applied to courtroom proceedings, albeit subject to overriding when justice so demanded or when confidentiality was necessary.

1. Of course, the Sixth Amendment remains the source of the *accused's* own right to insist upon public judicial proceedings. *Gannett.*

That the Sixth Amendment explicitly establishes a public trial right does not impliedly foreclose the derivation of such a right from other provisions of the Constitution. The Constitution was not framed as a work of carpentry, in which all joints must fit snugly without overlapping. * * *

2. A conceptually separate, yet related, question is whether the media should enjoy greater access rights than the general public. But no such contention is at stake here. Since the media's right of access is at least equal to that of the general public, this case is resolved by a decision that the state statute unconstitutionally restricts public access to trials. As a practical matter, however, the institutional press is the likely, and fitting, chief beneficiary of a right of access because it serves as the "agent" of interested citizens, and funnels information about trials to a large number of individuals.

The Court's approach in right of access cases simply reflects the special nature of a claim of First Amendment right to gather information. Customarily, First Amendment guarantees are interposed to protect communication between speaker and listener. When so employed against prior restraints, free speech protections are almost insurmountable. See generally Brennan, *Address,* 32 Rutg.L.Rev. 173, 176 (1979). But the First Amendment embodies more than a commitment to free expression and communicative interchange for their own sakes; it has a *structural* role to play in securing and fostering our republican system of self-government. Implicit in this structural role is not only "the principle that debate on public issues should be uninhibited, robust, and wide-open," but the antecedent assumption that valuable public debate—as well as other civic behavior—must be informed. The structural model links the First Amendment to that process of communication necessary for a democracy to survive, and thus entails solicitude not only for communication itself, but for the indispensable conditions of meaningful communication.

[A]n assertion of the prerogative to gather information must [be] assayed by considering the information sought and the opposing interests invaded. This judicial task is as much a matter of sensitivity to practical necessities as it is of abstract reasoning. But at least two helpful principles may be sketched. First, the case for a right of access has special force when drawn from an enduring and vital tradition of public entree to particular proceedings or information. Such a tradition commands respect in part because the Constitution carries the gloss of history. More importantly, a tradition of accessibility implies the favorable judgment of experience. Second, the value of access must be measured in specifics. Analysis is not advanced by rhetorical statements that all information bears upon public issues; what is crucial in individual cases is whether access to a particular government process is important in terms of that very process.

[This Court has] persistently defended the public character of the trial process. *In re Oliver,* 333 U.S. 257 (1948), established that [fourteenth amendment due process] forbids closed criminal trials [and] acknowledged that open trials are indispensable to First Amendment political and religious freedoms.

By the same token, a special solicitude for the public character of judicial proceedings is evident in the Court's rulings upholding the right to report about the administration of justice. While these decisions are impelled by the classic protections afforded by the First Amendment to pure communication, they are also bottomed upon a keen appreciation of the structural interest served in opening the judicial system to public inspection. So, in upholding a privilege for reporting truthful information about judicial misconduct proceedings, *Landmark* emphasized that public scrutiny of the operation of a judicial disciplinary body implicates a major purpose of the First Amendment—"discussion of governmental affairs." Again, *Nebraska Press* noted that the traditional guarantee against prior restraint "should have particular force as applied to reporting of criminal proceedings." And *Cox Broadcasting* instructed that "[w]ith respect to judicial proceedings in particular, the function of the press serves to guarantee the fairness of trials and to bring to bear the beneficial effects of public scrutiny upon the administration of justice."

[Open] trials play a fundamental role in furthering the efforts of our judicial system to assure the criminal defendant a fair and accurate adjudication of guilt or innocence. But, as a feature of our governing system of justice, the trial process serves other, broadly political, interests, and public access advances these objectives as well. To that extent, trial access possesses specific structural significance.

[For] a civilization founded upon principles of ordered liberty to survive and flourish, its members must share the conviction that they are governed equitably. That necessity * * * mandates a system of justice that demonstrates the fairness of the law to our citizens. One major function of the trial is to make that demonstration.

Secrecy is profoundly inimical to this demonstrative [purpose]. Public access is essential, therefore, if trial adjudication is to achieve the objective of maintaining public confidence in the administration of justice. But the trial [also] plays a pivotal role in the entire judicial process, and, by extension, in our form of government. Under our system, judges are not mere umpires, but, in their own sphere, lawmakers—a coordinate branch of *government.* [Thus], so far as the trial is the mechanism for judicial factfinding, as well as the initial forum for legal decisionmaking, it is a genuine governmental proceeding.

[More] importantly, public access to trials acts as an important check, akin in purpose to the other checks and balances that infuse our system of government. "The knowledge that every criminal trial is subject to contemporaneous review in the forum of public opinion is an effective restraint on possible abuse of judicial power," *Oliver*—an abuse that, in many cases, would have ramifications beyond the impact upon the parties before the court. * * *

Popular attendance at trials, in sum, substantially furthers the particular public purposes of that critical judicial proceeding. In that sense, public access is an indispensable element of the trial process itself. Trial access, therefore, assumes structural importance in our "government of laws."

As previously noted, resolution of First Amendment public access claims in individual cases must be strongly influenced by the weight of historical practice and by an assessment of the specific structural value of public access in the circumstances. With regard to the case at hand, our ingrained tradition of public trials and the importance of public access to the broader purposes of the trial process, tip the balance strongly toward the rule that trials be open.[23] What countervailing interests might be

---

23. The presumption of public trials is, of course, not at all incompatible with reasonable restrictions imposed upon courtroom behavior in the interests of decorum. Thus, when engaging in interchanges at the bench, the trial judge is not required to allow public or press intrusion

sufficiently compelling to reverse this presumption of openness need not concern us now,[24] for the statute at stake here authorizes trial closures at the unfettered discretion of the judge and parties.[25] [Thus it] violates the First and Fourteenth Amendments * * *.

JUSTICE STEWART, concurring in the judgment.

Whatever the ultimate answer [may] be with respect to pretrial suppression hearings in criminal cases, the First and Fourteenth Amendments clearly give the press and the public a right of access to trials themselves, civil as well as criminal. * * *

In conspicuous contrast to a military base, *Greer*; a jail, *Adderley v. Florida,* 385 U.S. 39 (1966); or a prison, *Pell,* a trial courtroom is a public place. Even more than city streets, sidewalks, and parks as areas of traditional First Amendment activity, a trial courtroom is a place where representatives of the press and of the public are not only free to be, but where their presence serves to assure the integrity of what goes on.

But this does not mean that the First Amendment right of members of the public and representatives of the press to attend civil and criminal trials is absolute. Just as a legislature may impose reasonable time, place and manner restrictions upon the exercise of First Amendment freedoms, so may a trial judge impose reasonable limitations upon the unrestricted occupation of a courtroom by representatives of the press and members of the public. Moreover, [there] may be occasions when not all who wish to attend a trial may do so.[3] And while there exist many alternative ways to satisfy the constitutional demands of a fair trial, those demands may also sometimes justify limitations upon the unrestricted presence of spectators in the courtroom.[5]

Since in the present case the trial judge appears to have given no recognition to the right [of] the press and [the] public to be present at [the] murder trial over which he was presiding, the judgment under review must be [reversed.]

JUSTICE WHITE, concurring.

This case would have been unnecessary had *Gannett* construed the Sixth Amendment to forbid excluding the public from criminal proceed-

---

upon the huddle. Nor does this opinion intimate that judges are restricted in their ability to conduct conferences in chambers, inasmuch as such conferences are distinct from trial proceedings.

24. For example, national security concerns about confidentiality may sometimes warrant closures during sensitive portions of trial proceedings, such as testimony about state secrets.

25. Significantly, closing a trial lacks even the justification for barring the door to pretrial hearings: the necessity of preventing dissemination of suppressible prejudicial evidence to the public before the jury pool has become, in a practical sense, finite and subject to sequestration.

3. In such situations, representatives of the press must be assured access, *Houchins* (concurring opinion).

5. This is not to say that only constitutional considerations can justify such restrictions. The preservation of trade secrets, for example, might justify the exclusion of the public from at least some segments of a civil trial. And the sensibilities of a youthful prosecution witness, for example, might justify similar exclusion in a criminal trial for rape, so long as the defendant's Sixth Amendment right to a public trial were not impaired.

ings except in narrowly defined circumstances. But the Court there rejected the submission of four of us to this effect, thus requiring that the First Amendment issue involved here be addressed. On this issue, I concur in the opinion of the Chief Justice.

JUSTICE BLACKMUN, concurring in the judgment.

My opinion and vote in partial dissent [in] *Gannett* compels my vote to reverse the judgment. [It] is gratifying [to] see the Court now looking to and relying upon legal history in determining the fundamental public character of the criminal trial. * * *

The Court's ultimate ruling in *Gannett,* with such clarification as is provided by the opinions in this case today, apparently is now to the effect that there is no *Sixth* Amendment right on the part of the public—or the press—to an open hearing on a motion to suppress. I, of course, continue to believe that *Gannett* was in error, both in its interpretation of the Sixth Amendment generally, and in its application to the suppression hearing, for I remain convinced that the right to a public trial is to be found where the Constitution explicitly placed it—in the Sixth Amendment.

[But] with the Sixth Amendment set to one side in this case, I am driven to conclude, as a secondary position, that the First Amendment must provide some measure of protection for public access to the trial. The opinion in partial dissent in *Gannett* explained that the public has an intense need and a deserved right to know about the administration of justice in general; about the prosecution of local crimes in particular; about the conduct of the judge, the prosecutor, defense counsel, police officers, other public servants, and all the actors in the judicial arena; and about the trial itself. It is clear and obvious to me, on the approach the Court has chosen to take, that, by closing this criminal trial, the trial judge abridged these First Amendment interests of the public. * * *

JUSTICE STEVENS, concurring.

This is a watershed case. Until today the Court has accorded virtually absolute protection to the dissemination of information or ideas, but never before has it squarely held that the acquisition of newsworthy matter is entitled to any constitutional protection whatsoever. An additional word of emphasis is therefore appropriate.

Twice before, the Court has implied that any governmental restriction on access to information, no matter how severe and no matter how unjustified, would be constitutionally acceptable so long as it did not single out the press for special disabilities not applicable to the public at large. In a dissent joined by [Brennan and Marshall, JJ.] in *Saxbe,* Justice Powell unequivocally rejected [that conclusion.] And in *Houchins,* I explained at length why [Brennan, Powell, JJ.] and I were convinced that "[a]n official prison policy of concealing * * * knowledge from the public by arbitrarily cutting off the flow of information at its source abridges [First Amendment freedoms]." Since [Marshall and Blackmun, JJ.] were unable to participate in that case, a majority of the Court neither accepted nor rejected that conclusion or the contrary conclusion expressed in the prevailing opinions. Today, however, for the first time, the Court unequivocally holds that an arbitrary interference with access to important information is an abridgment of the freedoms of speech and of the press protected by the First Amendment.

It is somewhat ironic that the Court should find more reason to recognize a right of access today than it did in *Houchins*. For *Houchins* involved the plight of a segment of society least able to protect itself, an attack on a longstanding policy of concealment, and an absence of any legitimate justification for abridging public access to information about how government operates. In this case we are protecting the interests of the most powerful voices in the community, we are concerned with an almost unique exception to an established tradition of openness in the conduct of criminal trials, and it is likely that the closure order was motivated by the judge's desire to protect the individual defendant from the burden of a fourth criminal trial.[2]

In any event, for the reasons stated [in] my *Houchins* opinion, as well as those stated by the Chief Justice today, I agree that the First Amendment protects the public and the press from abridgment of their rights of access to information about the operation of their government, including the Judicial Branch; given the total absence of any record justification for the closure order entered in this case, that order violated the First Amendment * * *.

JUSTICE REHNQUIST, dissenting.

[I] do not believe that [anything in the Constitution] require[s] that a State's reasons for denying public access to a trial, where both [the prosecution and defense] have consented to [a court-approved closure order], are subject to any additional constitutional review at our hands.

[The] issue here is not whether the "right" to freedom of the press * * * overrides the defendant's "right" to a fair trial, [but] whether any provision in the Constitution may fairly be read to prohibit what the [trial court] did in this case. Being unable to find any such prohibition in the First, Sixth, Ninth, or any other Amendments [or] in the Constitution itself, I dissent.

NOTES AND QUESTIONS

1. ***Whose right?*** Consider David A. Anderson, *Freedom of the Press*, 80 Tex. L. Rev. 429, 431–32, 450 (2002): "The Court acknowledges that courtroom access for the general public may be restricted in order to provide 'preferential seating for media representatives.' The press probably enjoys no

---

2. Neither that likely motivation nor facts showing the risk that a fifth trial would have been necessary without closure of the fourth are disclosed in this record, however. The absence of any articulated reason for the closure order is a sufficient basis for distinguishing this case from *Gannett*. The decision today is in no way inconsistent with the perfectly unambiguous holding in *Gannett* that the rights guaranteed by the Sixth Amendment are rights that may be asserted by the accused rather than members of the general public. * * *

greater freedom than the public to disclose prejudicial information about pending trials, but those members of the public most likely to publish such information (such as attorneys and defendants) may be restricted in ways that the press may not be. * * * [But] the Court's determination to avoid recognizing rights under the Press Clause is especially evident in the courtroom access cases. The Court granted the First Amendment right of access that the media demanded, but granted it to the public rather than to the press. Of course, as any nonpress citizen who tries to attend a highly publicized trial will quickly discover, it is the press that gains access under these decisions. But the Court adheres to the fiction, in obvious resistance to Justice Stevens's suggestion that the controlling principle is a First Amendment right to gather news.

2. *Beyond the justice system.* May (should) "public access to information about how government operates" (to use Stevens, J.'s phrase) be denied, as the Chief Justice suggests, simply on the ground that the place at issue has not been *traditionally* open to the public (recall how the Chief Justice distinguishes penal institutions from criminal trials) or should the government also have to advance, as Stevens, J., suggests, "legitimate justification" for "abridging" public access? Is it relevant that the constitutional convention was closed to the press, that the delegates were forbidden from talking with reporters, and that only the House debates about the Bill of Rights were open to the public? Amy Jordan, *The Right of Access: Is There a Better Fit Than the First Amendment?*, 57 VAND. L. REV. 1349, 1358–59 (2004). Compare the controversy over whether "the right to a public forum" should turn on whether the place at issue has *historically* been dedicated to the exercise of First Amendment rights or on whether the manner of expression is *basically incompatible* with the normal activity of the place at a particular time. See generally the materials on the Public Forum: New Forums, Ch. 6, II infra. See also Note, *The First Amendment Right to Gather State–Held Information*, 89 Yale L.J. 923, 933–39 (1979). Consider, too, Vincent Blasi, *The Checking Value in First Amendment Theory*, 1977 Am.B.Found.Res.J. 521, 609–10: "[U]nder the checking value, the interest of the press (and ultimately the public) in learning certain information relevant to the abuse of official power would sometimes take precedence over perfectly legitimate and substantial government interests such as efficiency and confidentiality. Thus, the First Amendment may require that journalists have access as a general matter to some records, such as certain financial documents, which anyone investigating common abuses of the public trust would routinely want to inspect, even though the granting of such access would undoubtedly entail some costs and risks. Also, the balance might be tilted even more in the direction of access if a journalist could demonstrate that there are reasonable grounds to believe that certain records contain evidence of misconduct by public officials."

But cf. Yale Kamisar, *Right of Access to Information Generated or Controlled by the Government: Richmond Newspapers Examined and Gannett Revisited* in Jesse Choper, Yale Kamisar & Laurence Tribe, The Supreme Court: Trends and Developments, 1979–80 145, 166 (1981): "[T]hese law review commentaries go quite far. But *someday* the views they advance may be the law of the land. In the meantime, however, many more battles will have to be fought. *Someday* we may look back on *Richmond Newspapers* as the '*Powell v. Alabama*' of the right of access to government-controlled information—but it was a long, hard road from *Powell* to *Gideon*."[e]

3. **Within the justice system.** How far does (should) *Richmond Newspapers* extend within the justice system? To criminal pre-trial proceedings?[f] How is a trial defined? Should it extend to conferences in chambers or at the bench? To grand jury hearings? To civil trials? To depositions? To records of any or all of the above? Should it apply outside judicial proceedings? Should wardens be permitted to completely preclude access by the public and press to prisons? To executions? What if the prisoner wants to close the execution? For wide-ranging discussion of these and related questions, see Choper, Kamisar, and Tribe, note 2 supra, at 145–206 (Professor Tribe was winning counsel in *Richmond Newspapers*). See also G. Michael Fenner & James Koley, *Access to Judicial Proceedings: To Richmond Newspapers and Beyond,* 16 Harv.Civ. Rts—Civ.Lib.L.Rev. 415 (1981).

4. **Closing trials.** After *Richmond Newspapers,* what showing should suffice to justify closure of a criminal trial? See *Globe Newspaper Co. v. Superior Court,* 457 U.S. 596 (1982) (routine exclusion of press and public during testimony of minor victim of sex offense unconstitutional); *Press-Enterprise Co. v. Superior Court,* 464 U.S. 501 (1984) (extending *Richmond Newspapers* to voir dire examination of jurors). To overcome either the First Amendment or the sixth amendment right to a public trial, the Court has required that the party seeking to close the proceedings "must advance an overriding interest that is likely to be prejudiced, the closure must be no broader than necessary to protect that interest, the trial court must consider reasonable alternatives to closing the proceeding, and it must make findings adequate to support the closure." *Waller v. Georgia,* 467 U.S. 39 (1984).

5. **Special access rights for the press.** Is a press section in public trials required when the seating capacity would be exhausted by the public? Is a press section permitted? What limits attach to government determinations of who shall get press passes? See, e.g., *Sherrill v. Knight,* 569 F.2d 124 (D.C.Cir.1977) (denial of White House press pass infringes upon First Amendment guarantees in the absence of adequate process); *Borreca v. Fasi,* 369 F.Supp. 906 (D.Haw.1974) (preliminary injunction against denial of access of a reporter to Mayor's press conferences justified when basis for exclusion is allegedly "inaccurate" and "irresponsible" reporting); *Los Angeles Free Press, Inc. v. Los Angeles,* 9 Cal.App.3d 448, 88 Cal.Rptr. 605 (1970) (exclusion of weekly newspaper from scenes of disaster and police press conferences upheld when newspaper did not report police and fire events "with some regularity"). Cf. *Los Angeles Police Dep't v. United Reporting Pub. Corp.,* 528 U.S. 32

---

e. For endorsements of generous access, see Franklyn Haiman, *Speech and Law in a Free Society* 108–14, 368–97 (1981); Mark Yudof, *When Government Speaks* 246–55 (1983); Thomas Emerson, *Legal Foundations of the Right to Know,* 1976 Wash.U.L.Q. 1, 14–17; Anthony Lewis, *A Public Right to Know about Public Institutions: The First Amendment as Sword,* 1980 Sup.Ct.Rev. 1; Mary-Rose Papandrea, *Under Attack: The Public's Right to Know and the War on Terror,* 25 B.C. Third World L. Rev. 35 (2005). But see Lillian Bevier, *An Informed Public, an Informing Press: The Search for a Constitutional Principle,* 68 Calif.L.Rev. 482 (1980).

f. See *Press–Enterprise Co. v. Superior Court,* 478 U.S. 1 (1986) ("California preliminary hearings are sufficiently like a trial" to implicate *Richmond Newspapers'* "qualified First Amendment right of access"), in addition, see *El Vocero de Puerto Rico v. Puerto Rico,* 508 U.S. 147 (1993) (reaching same conclusion as to Puerto Rican preliminary hearings).

(1999) (law mandating release of arrest records for a scholarly, journalistic, political, or governmental purpose, but not to sell a product or service, may not be challenged on its face; remanded for as applied attack).

When access is required, may the press be prevented from taking notes? Is the right to bring tape recorders into public trials protected under *Richmond Newspapers?* What about "unobtrusive" television cameras? Cf. *Chandler v. Florida,* 449 U.S. 560 (1981) (subject to certain safeguards a state may *permit* electronic media and still photography coverage of public criminal proceedings over the objection of the accused).

CHAPTER 6

GOVERNMENT PROPERTY AND THE PUBLIC FORUM[a]

■ ■ ■

The case law treating the question of when persons can speak on public property has come to be known as public forum doctrine. But "[t]he public forum saga began, and very nearly ended," Geoffrey Stone, *Fora Americana: Speech in Public Places,* 1974 Sup.Ct.Rev. 233, 236, with an effort by Holmes, J., then on the Supreme Judicial Court of Massachusetts, "to solve a difficult First Amendment problem by simplistic resort to a common-law concept," Vincent Blasi, *Prior Restraints on Demonstrations,* 68 Mich.L.Rev. 1482, 1484 (1970). For holding religious meetings on the Boston Common, a preacher was convicted under an ordinance prohibiting "any public address" upon publicly-owned property without a permit from the mayor. In upholding the permit ordinance Holmes, J., observed: "For the legislature absolutely or conditionally to forbid public speaking in a highway or public park is no more an infringement of rights of a member of the public than for the owner of a private house to forbid it in the house." *Massachusetts v. Davis,* 162 Mass. 510, 511, 39 N.E. 113, 113 (1895). On appeal, a unanimous Supreme Court adopted the Holmes position, 167 U.S. 43 (1897): "[T]he right to absolutely exclude all right to use [public property], necessarily includes the authority to determine under what circumstances such use may be availed of, as the greater power contains the lesser."

This view survived until HAGUE v. CIO, 307 U.S. 496 (1939), which rejected Jersey City's claim that its ordinance requiring a permit for an open air meeting was justified by the "plenary power" rationale of *Davis.* In rejecting the implications of the *Davis* dictum, ROBERTS, J., in a plurality opinion, uttered a famous "counter dictum," which has played a central role in the evolution of public forum theory: "Wherever the title of streets and parks may rest, they have immemorially been held in trust for the use of the public and, time out of mind, have been used for purposes of

---

a. For treatment of the related question whether, and if so under what circumstances, there is a First Amendment right of access to privately-owned facilities, such as shopping centers, see *Marsh v. Alabama,* 326 U.S. 501 (1946); *Hudgens v. NLRB,* 424 U.S. 507 (1976); *PruneYard Shopping Center v. Robins,* Ch. 9, I infra. Margaret Farrand Saxton, *Protecting the Marketplace of Ideas: Access For Solicitors in Common Interest Communities,* 51 UCLA L. Rev. 1437 (2004).

assembly, communicating thoughts between citizens, and discussing public questions. Such use of the streets and public places has, from ancient times, been a part of the privileges, immunities, rights, and liberties of citizens. [This privilege of a citizen] is not absolute, but relative, and must be exercised in subordination to the general comfort and convenience, and in consonance with peace and good order; but it must not, in the guise of regulation, be abridged or denied." Eight months later, the *Hague* dictum was given impressive content by Roberts, J., for the Court, in *Schneider* infra.

I. FOUNDATION CASES

A. MANDATORY ACCESS

SCHNEIDER v. IRVINGTON, 308 U.S. 147 (1939), per ROBERTS, J., invalidated several ordinances prohibiting leafleting on public streets or other public places: "Municipal authorities, as trustees for the public, have the duty to keep their communities' streets open and available for movement of people and property, the primary purpose to which the streets are dedicated. So long as legislation to this end does not abridge the constitutional liberty of one rightfully upon the street to impart information through speech or the distribution of literature, it may lawfully regulate the conduct of those using the streets. For example, a person could not exercise this liberty by taking his stand in the middle of a crowded street, contrary to traffic regulations, and maintain his position to the stoppage of all traffic; a group of distributors could not insist upon a constitutional right to form a cordon across the street and to allow no pedestrian to pass who did not accept a tendered leaflet; nor does the guarantee of freedom of speech or of the press deprive a municipality of power to enact regulations against throwing literature broadcast in the streets. Prohibition of such conduct would not abridge the constitutional liberty since such activity bears no necessary relationship to the freedom to speak, write, print or distribute information or opinion. * * *

"In *Lovell* [Ch. 4, I, A supra] this court held void an ordinance which forbade the distribution by hand or otherwise of literature of any kind without written permission from the city manager. [Similarly] in *Hague v. C.I.O.*, an ordinance was held void on its face because it provided for previous administrative censorship of the exercise of the right of speech and assembly in appropriate public places." The [ordinances] under review do not purport to license distribution but all of them absolutely prohibit it in the streets and, one of them, in other public places as well.

"The motive of the legislation under attack in Numbers 13, 18 and 29 is held by the courts below to be the prevention of littering of the streets and, although the alleged offenders were not charged with themselves scattering paper in the streets, their convictions were sustained upon the theory that distribution by them encouraged or resulted in such littering. We are of opinion that the purpose to keep the streets clean and of good appearance is insufficient to justify an ordinance which prohibits a person rightfully on a public street from handing literature to one willing to receive it. Any burden imposed upon the city authorities in cleaning and caring for the streets as an indirect consequence of such distribution results from the constitutional protection of the freedom of speech and press. This constitutional protection does not deprive a city of all power to prevent street littering. There are obvious methods of preventing littering. Amongst these is the punishment of those who actually throw papers on the streets.

"It is suggested that [the] ordinances are valid because their operation is limited to streets and alleys and leaves persons free to distribute printed matter in other public places. But, as we have said, the streets are natural and proper places for the dissemination of information and opinion; and one is not to have the exercise of his liberty of expression in appropriate places abridged on the plea that it may be exercised in some other place."

McReynolds, J., "is of opinion that the judgment in each case should be affirmed."

Notes and Questions

1. **Leaflets and the streets as public forum.** Consider Harry Kalven, *The Concept of the Public Forum: Cox v. Louisiana,* 1965 S.Ct.Rev. 1, 18 & 21: "Leaflet distribution in public places in a city is a method of communication that carries as an inextricable and expected consequence substantial littering of the streets, which the city has an obligation to keep clean. It is also a method of communication of some annoyance to a majority of people so addressed; that its impact on its audience is very high is doubtful. Yet the constitutional balance in *Schneider* was struck emphatically in favor of keeping the public forum open for this mode of communication. [The] operative theory of the Court, at least for the leaflet situation, is that, although it is a method of communication that interferes with the public use of the streets, the right to the streets as a public forum is such that leaflet distribution cannot be prohibited and can be regulated only for weighty reasons."

2. **Litter prevention as a substantial interest.** Does the interest in distributing leaflets always outweigh the interest in preventing littering? Suppose helicopters regularly dropped tons of leaflets on the town of Irvington?

3. **Beyond leaflets.** COX v. NEW HAMPSHIRE, 312 U.S. 569 (1941), per Hughes, C.J., upheld convictions of sixty-eight Jehovah's Witnesses for parading without a permit. They had marched in four or five groups (with perhaps twenty others) along the sidewalk in single file carrying signs and handing out leaflets: "[T]he state court considered and defined the duty of the licensing authority and the rights of the appellants to a license for their parade, with regard only to consideration of time, place and manner so as to conserve the public convenience." The licensing procedure was said to "afford opportunity for proper policing" and " 'to prevent confusion by overlapping parades, [to] secure convenient use of the streets by other travelers, and to minimize the risk of disorder.' " A municipality "undoubtedly" has "authority

to control the use of its public streets for parades or processions." But see C. Edwin Baker, *Unreasoned Reasonableness: Mandatory Parade Permits and Time, Place, and Manner Regulations,* 78 Nw.U.L.Rev. 937, 992 (1984): Approximately 26,000 people walked on the same sidewalks during the same hour the defendants in *Cox* "marched." "This single difference in what [the defendants] did—'marching in formation,' which they did for expressive purposes and which presumably is an 'assembly' that the First Amendment protects—turned out to have crucial significance. This sole difference, engaging in First Amendment protected conduct, made them guilty of a criminal offense. [Surely] something is wrong with this result."

4. ***Charging for use of public forum.*** *Cox* said there was nothing "contrary to the Constitution" in the exaction of a fee " 'incident to the administration of the [licensing] Act and to the maintenance of public order in the matter licensed.' "But see *Forsyth County v. The Nationalist Movement,* 505 U.S. 123 (1992)(speech cannot be financially burdened for expenses associated with hostile audience in a licensing context).

5. ***Reasonable time, place, and manner regulations.*** (a) As *Cox* reveals, a right of access to a public forum does not guarantee immunity from reasonable time, place, and manner regulations. In HEFFRON v. INTERNATIONAL SOC. FOR KRISHNA CONSCIOUSNESS, 452 U.S. 640 (1981), for example, the Court, per White, J., upheld a state fair rule prohibiting the distribution of printed material or the solicitation of funds except from a duly licensed booth on the fairgrounds. The Court noted that consideration of a forum's special attributes is relevant to the determination of reasonableness, and the test of reasonableness is whether the restrictions "are justified without reference to the content of the regulated speech, that they serve a significant governmental interest, and that in doing so they leave open ample alternative channels for communication of the information."[a]

WARD v. ROCK AGAINST RACISM, 491 U.S. 781 (1989), per Kennedy, J., observes that "[E]ven in a public forum the government may impose reasonable restrictions on the time, place, or manner of protected speech, provided the restrictions 'are justified without reference to the content of the regulated speech, that they are narrowly tailored to serve a significant governmental interest, and that they leave open ample alternative channels for communication of the information.' " The case reasserts that the *O'Brien* test is little different from the time, place, and manner test, and then states: "[A] regulation of the time, place, or manner of protected speech must be narrowly tailored to serve the government's legitimate content-neutral interests but [it] need not be the least-restrictive or least-intrusive means of doing so. Rather, the requirement of narrow tailoring is satisfied 'so long as [the] regulation promotes a substantial government interest that would be achieved less effectively absent the regulation.' To be sure, this standard does not mean that a time, place, or manner regulation may burden substantially more speech than is necessary to further the government's legitimate interests.

---

a. Brennan, J., joined by Marshall and Stevens, JJ., dissented in part as did Blackmun, J., in a separate opinion. Their dispute was not with the Court's test, but its application.

Government may not regulate expression in such a manner that a substantial portion of the burden on speech does not serve to advance its goals.[7]"

MARSHALL, J., dissenting, joined by Brennan and Stevens, JJ., complains of the Court's "serious distortion of the narrowly tailoring requirement" and states that the Court's rejection of the less restrictive alternative test relies on "language in a few opinions [taken] out of context." Should the time, place, and manner test be different from the *O'Brien* test? Is there any difference between those tests and the approach employed in *Schneider*?

(b) Should public universities be able to designate "free speech zones" where protest can take place (but not elsewhere) while permitting other speech elsewhere? Can it limit all public speech to such designated zones? What standards should govern? Should the standards differ if the zone is off campus? For a public library? For a place where candidates for office appear? See Joseph D. Herrold, *Capturing the Dialogue: Free Speech Zones and the "Caging" of First Amendment Rights*, 54 Drake L.Rev. 949 (2006).

B.   EQUAL ACCESS

CHICAGO POLICE DEPT. v. MOSLEY, 408 U.S. 92 (1972), invalidated an ordinance banning all picketing within 150 feet of a school building while the school is in session and one half-hour before and afterwards, except "the peaceful picketing of any school involved in a labor dispute." The suit was brought by a federal postal employee who, for seven months prior to enactment of the ordinance, had frequently picketed a high school in Chicago. "During school hours and usually by himself, Mosley would walk the public sidewalk adjoining the school, carrying a sign that read: 'Jones High School practices black discrimination. Jones High School has a black quota.' His lonely crusade was always peaceful, orderly, and [quiet]." The Court, per MARSHALL, J., viewed the ordinance as drawing "an impermissible distinction between labor picketing and other peaceful picketing": "The central problem with Chicago's ordinance is that it describes permissible picketing in terms of its subject matter. Peaceful picketing on the subject of a school's labor-management dispute is permitted, but all other peaceful picketing is prohibited. The operative distinction is the message on a picket sign. But, above all else, the First Amendment means that government has no power to restrict expression because of its message, its ideas, its subject matter, or its content.

"[U]nder the Equal Protection Clause, not to mention the First Amendment itself,[a] government may not grant the use of a forum to people whose views it finds acceptable, but deny use to those wishing to express less favored or more controversial views. And it may not select

---

7. A ban on handbilling, of course, would suppress a great quantity of speech that does not cause the evils that it seeks to eliminate, whether they be fraud, crime, litter, traffic congestion, or noise. For that reason, a complete ban on handbilling would be substantially broader than necessary to achieve the interests justifying it.

a. *Consolidated Edison Co. v. Public Service Comm'n,* abandoned equal protection and cited *Mosley* as a First Amendment case: "The First Amendment's hostility to content-based regulation extends not only to restrictions on particular viewpoints, but also to prohibition of public discussion of an entire topic." But see, e.g., *Minnesota State Board v. Knight,* 465 U.S. 271 (1984) (stating that *Mosley* is an equal protection case).

which issues are worth discussing or debating in public facilities. There is an 'equality of status in the field of ideas,' and government must afford all points of view an equal opportunity to be heard. Once a forum is opened up to assembly or speaking by some groups, government may not prohibit others from assembling or speaking on the basis of what they intend to say. Selective exclusions from a public forum may not be based on content alone, and may not be justified by reference to content alone.

"[Not] all picketing must always be allowed. We have continually recognized that reasonable 'time, place and manner' regulations of picketing may be necessary to further significant governmental interests. Similarly, under an equal protection analysis, there may be sufficient regulatory interests justifying selective exclusions or distinctions among picketers. [But] [b]ecause picketing plainly involves expressive conduct within the protection of the First Amendment, discriminations among picketers must be tailored to serve a substantial governmental interest. In this case, the ordinance itself describes impermissible picketing not in terms of time, place and manner, but in terms of subject matter. The regulation 'thus slip[s] from the neutrality of time, place and circumstance into a concern about content.' This is never permitted.[b] * * *

"Although preventing school disruption is a city's legitimate concern, Chicago itself has determined that peaceful labor picketing during school hours is not an undue interference with school. Therefore, under the Equal Protection clause, Chicago may not maintain that other picketing disrupts the school unless that picketing is clearly more disruptive than the picketing Chicago already permits. If peaceful labor picketing is permitted, there is no justification for prohibiting all nonlabor picketing, both peaceful and nonpeaceful. 'Peaceful' labor picketing, however the term 'peaceful' is defined, is obviously no less disruptive than 'peaceful' nonlabor picketing. But Chicago's ordinance permits the former and prohibits the latter.

"[We also] reject the city's argument that, although it permits peaceful labor picketing, it may prohibit all nonlabor picketing because, as a class, nonlabor picketing is more prone to produce violence than labor picketing. Predictions about imminent disruption from picketing involve judgments appropriately made on an individualized basis, not by means of broad classifications, especially those based on subject matter. Freedom of expression, and its intersection with the guarantee of equal protection, would rest on a soft foundation indeed if government could distinguish among picketers on such a wholesale and categorical basis. '[I]n our system, undifferentiated fear or apprehension of disturbance is not enough to overcome the right to freedom of expression.' *Tinker.* Some labor picketing is peaceful, some disorderly; the same is true for picketing on

---

b. Consider Daniel A. Farber, *The First Amendment* 23 (1998): "[T]he Court never really explained the basis for its rule. On the face of things, it is not clear that distinctions based on subject matter should always be considered particularly troublesome. For instance, there seems to be nothing suspicious about the decisions of the drafters of the National Labor Relations Act and the Taft–Hartley Act to regulate labor picketing but not antiwar picketing."

other themes. No labor picketing could be more peaceful or less prone to violence than Mosley's solitary vigil. In seeking to restrict nonlabor picketing which is clearly more disruptive than peaceful labor picketing, Chicago may not prohibit all nonlabor picketing at the school forum."[c]

NOTES AND QUESTIONS

1. Consider Kenneth Karst, *Equality as a Central Principle in the First Amendment,* 43 U.Chi.L.Rev. 20, 28 (1975): "*Mosley* is a landmark First Amendment decision. It makes two principal points: (1) the essence of the First Amendment is its denial to government of the power to determine which messages shall be heard and which suppressed * * *. (2) Any 'time, place and manner' restriction that selectively excludes speakers from a public forum must survive careful judicial scrutiny to ensure that the exclusion is the minimum necessary to further a significant government interest. Taken together, these statements declare a principle of major importance. The Court has explicitly adopted the principle of equal liberty of expression. [The] principle requires courts to start from the assumption that all speakers and all points of view are entitled to a hearing, and permits deviation from this basic assumption only upon a showing of substantial necessity."[d]

2. What if the *Mosley* ordinance had not excepted labor picketing, but had banned *all* picketing within 150 feet of a school during school hours? Consider Karst 37–38: "The burden of this restriction would fall most heavily on those who have something to communicate to the school [population]. Student picketers presenting a grievance against a principal, or striking custodians with a message growing out of a labor dispute, would be affected more seriously by this ostensibly content-neutral ordinance than would, say the proponents of a candidate for Governor [who could just as effectively carry their message elsewhere]. This differential impact amounts to de facto content discrimination, presumptively invalid under the First Amendment equality principle. "[The city faces] an apparent dilemma. [If it] bars all picketing within a certain area, it will effectively discriminate against those groups that can communicate to their audience only by picketing within that area. But if the city adjusts its ordinance to this differential impact, as by providing a student-picketing or labor-picketing exemption, [it runs] afoul of *Mosley* itself. The city can avoid the dilemma by amending the ordinance to ban not all picketing but only noisy picketing."[e]

3. Does equality fully explain the special concern with content regulation? Consider Geoffrey Stone, *Content Regulation and the First Amendment,*

---

c. Burger, C.J., joined the Court's opinion, but also concurred. Blackmun and Rehnquist, JJ., concurred in the result.

d. For reflections on developments since Karst's article, see Geoffrey R. Stone, *Kenneth Karst's Equality as a Central Principle in the First Amendment,* 75 U.Chi.L.Rev. 37 (2008). For commentary on the relationship between equality and freedom of speech borrowing and adapting the theory of Jurgen Habermas, see Lawrence B. Solum, *Freedom of Communicative Action,* 83 Nw.U.L.Rev. 54 (1989).

e. As Professor Karst notes, such an ordinance was upheld in *Grayned v. Rockford,* 408 U.S. 104 (1972), the companion case to *Mosley.* For additional reflection on the relationship between equality and the First Amendment, see Patrick M. Garry, *An Equal Protection View of the First Amendment,* 28 Quinn. L.Rev. 787 (2010).

25 Wm. & Mary L.Rev. 189, 207 (1983): "The problem, quite simply, is that restrictions on expression are rife with 'inequalities,' many of which have nothing whatever to do with content. The ordinance at issue in *Mosley,* for example, restricted picketing near schools, but left unrestricted picketing near hospitals, libraries, courthouses, and private homes. The ordinance at issue in *Erznoznik* restricted drive-in theaters that are visible from a public street, but did not restrict billboards. [Whatever] the effect of these content-neutral inequalities on First Amendment analysis, they are not scrutinized in the same way as content-based inequalities. Not all inequalities, in other words, are equal. And although the concern with equality may support the content-based/content-neutral distinction, it does not in itself have much explanatory power."

Is the concern with content discrimination explainable because of concerns about communicative impact, distortion of public debate, or government motivation? See generally Stone, supra. See also sources cited in notes 1 & 2 after *O'Brien,* Ch. 2 supra and Ronald Cass, *First Amendment Access to Government Facilities,* 65 Va.L.Rev. 1287, 1323–25 (1979); Paul Stephan, *The First Amendment and Content Discrimination,* 68 Va.L.Rev. 203 (1982); Geoffrey Stone, *Restrictions of Speech Because of its Content: The Peculiar Case of Subject–Matter Restrictions,* 46 U.Chi.L.Rev. 81 (1978).

4. An Illinois statute prohibited picketing residences or dwellings— except when the dwelling is "used as a place of business," or is "a place of employment involved in a labor dispute or the place of holding a meeting [on] premises commonly used to discuss subjects of general public interest," or when a "person is picketing his own [dwelling]." Can a conviction for picketing the Mayor of Chicago's home be upheld? Is *Mosley* distinguishable? See *Carey v. Brown,* 447 U.S. 455 (1980).

II. NEW FORUMS

Are First Amendment rights on government property confined to streets and parks? "[W]hat about other publicly owned property, ranging from the grounds surrounding a public building, to the inside of a welfare office, publicly run bus, or library, to a legislative gallery?" Stone, *Fora Americana,* supra, at 245.

INTERNATIONAL SOCIETY FOR KRISHNA CONSCIOUSNESS, INC. v. LEE

505 U.S. 672, 112 S.Ct. 2701, 120 L.Ed.2d 541 (1992).

CHIEF JUSTICE REHNQUIST delivered the opinion of the Court.

* * * Petitioner International Society for Krishna Consciousness, Inc. (ISKCON) is a not-for-profit religious corporation whose members perform a ritual known as sankirtan. The ritual consists of " 'going into public places, disseminating religious literature and soliciting funds to support the religion.' " The primary purpose of this ritual is raising funds for the movement.

Respondent [was] the police superintendent of the Port Authority of New York and New Jersey and was charged with enforcing the regulation at issue. The Port Authority owns and operates three major airports in the greater New York City area [which] collectively form one of the world's busiest metropolitan airport complexes. By decade's end they are expected to serve at least 110 million passengers annually. * * *

The Port Authority has adopted a regulation forbidding within the terminals the repetitive solicitation of money or distribution of literature [but permitting] solicitation and distribution on the sidewalks outside the terminal buildings. The regulation effectively prohibits petitioner from performing sankirtan in the terminals. * * *

It is uncontested that the solicitation at issue in this case is a form of speech protected under the First Amendment.[3] But it is also well settled that the government need not permit all forms of speech on property that it owns and controls. *United States Postal Service v. Council of Greenburgh Civic Assns.,* 453 U.S. 114, 129 (1981);[a] *Greer v. Spock,* 424 U.S. 828 (1976).[b] Where the government is acting as a proprietor, managing its internal operations, rather than acting as lawmaker with the power to regulate or license, its action will not be subjected to the heightened review to which its actions as a lawmaker may be subject. Thus, we have upheld a ban on political advertisements in city-operated transit vehicles, *Lehman v. City of Shaker Heights,* 418 U.S. 298 (1974), even though the city permitted other types of advertising on those vehicles. Similarly, we have permitted a school district to limit access to an internal mail system used to communicate with teachers employed by the district. *Perry Education Assn. v. Perry Local Educators' Ass'n,* 460 U.S. 37 (1983).[c]

These cases reflect, either implicitly or explicitly, a "forum-based" approach for assessing restrictions that the government seeks to place on the use of its property. *Cornelius v. NAACP Legal Defense and Educational Fund, Inc.,* 473 U.S. 788, 800 (1985).[d] Under this approach, regulation

---

3. We deal here only with [ISKCON's] claim raising the permissibility of solicitation. Respondent's cross-petition concerning the leafletting ban is disposed of in the companion case, *Lee v. International Society for Krishna Consciousness, Inc.,* infra.

a. *Greenburgh* held that the post office could prevent individuals from placing unstamped material in residential mail boxes.

b. *Greer* held that the military could bar a presidential candidate from speaking on a military base even though members of the public were free to visit the base, the President had spoken on the base, and other speakers (e.g., entertainers and anti-drug speakers) had spoken by invitation on the base.

c. *Perry* held it permissible to deny access to the mailboxes for a competing union despite permitting access for the duly elected union and access for various community groups such as the cub scouts, the YMCA, and other civic and church organizations. *Mosley* and *Carey* were distinguished: "[The] key to those decisions [was] the presence of a public forum." Compare *Lamb's Chapel v. Center Moriches Union Free School Dist.,* 508 U.S. 384 (1993) (school could not exclude religious groups from access to school property for after school meetings so long as it held the property generally open for meetings by social, civic, and recreation groups). *Good News Club v. Milford Central School,* 533 U.S. 98 (2001)(viewpoint discrimination to refuse access to elementary school classrooms after school for group engaging in religious instruction and prayer to discuss morals and character while permitting access to groups who would discuss the development of character and morals in other ways).

d. *Cornelius* upheld an executive order that included organizations providing direct health and welfare services to individuals or their families in a charity drive in the federal workplace while excluding legal defense and political advocacy organizations.

of speech on government property that has traditionally been available for public expression is subject to the highest scrutiny. Such regulations survive only if they are narrowly drawn to achieve a compelling state interest. *Perry.* The second category of public property is the designated public forum, whether of a limited or unlimited character—property that the state has opened for expressive activity by part or all of the public. Id.[e] Regulation of such property is subject to the same limitations as that governing a traditional public forum. Finally, there is all remaining public property. Limitations on expressive activity conducted on this last category of property must survive only a much more limited review. The challenged regulation need only be reasonable, as long as the regulation is not an effort to suppress the speaker's activity due to disagreement with the speaker's view.[f]

[Our] precedents foreclose the conclusion that airport terminals are public fora. Reflecting the general growth of the air travel industry, airport terminals have only recently achieved their contemporary size and character. [Moreover,] even within the rather short history of air transport, it is only "[i]n recent years [that] it has become a common practice for various religious and non-profit organizations to use commercial airports as a forum for the distribution of literature, the solicitation of funds, the proselytizing of new members, and other similar activities." 45 Fed.Reg. 35314 (1980). Thus, the tradition of airport activity does not demonstrate that airports have historically been made available for speech activity. Nor can we say that these particular terminals, or airport terminals generally, have been intentionally opened by their operators to such activity; the frequent and continuing litigation evidencing the operators' objections belies any such claim. * * *

A 4–3 majority, per O'Connor, J., determined that "government does not create a public forum by inaction or by permitting limited discourse, but only by intentionally opening a non-traditional forum for public discourse." Observing that the Court will look to the policy and practice of the government, the nature of the property and its compatibility with expressive activity in discerning intent, O'Connor, J., insisted that "we will not find that a public forum has been created in the face of clear evidence of a contrary intent, nor will we infer that the Government intended to create a public forum when the nature of the property is inconsistent with expressive activity."

Blackmun, J., dissented: "If the Government does not create a limited public forum unless it intends to provide an 'open forum' for expressive activity, and if the exclusion of some speakers is evidence that the Government did not intend to create such a forum, no speaker challenging denial of access will ever be able to prove that the forum is a limited public forum. The very fact that the Government denied access to the speaker indicates that the Government did not intend to provide an open forum for expressive activity, and [that] fact alone would demonstrate that the forum is not a limited public forum."

e. In interpreting this approach, *Perry* also stated in footnote 7 that: "a public forum may be created for a limited purpose such as use by certain groups, e.g., *Widmar v. Vincent* [Ch. 11, III] (student groups), or for discussion of certain subjects, e.g., *Madison Joint School District v. Wisconsin Employ. Relat. Comm'n*, 429 U.S. 167 (1976) (school board business)". Can a school board preclude public discussion of one of the subjects on its agenda while permitting discussion of the other subjects? For relevant commentary, see Note, *Strict Scrutiny in the Middle Forum,* 122 Harv. L.Rev. 2140 (2009).

f. Could the President not use point of view discrimination in determining who can get access to speak in the Oval Office? See Alan Brownstein, *The Nonforum as a First Amendment Category,* 42 U.C. Davis L.Rev. 717 (2009).

Petitioner attempts to circumvent the history and practice governing airport activity by pointing our attention to the variety of speech activity that it claims historically occurred at various "transportation nodes" such as rail stations, bus stations, wharves, and Ellis Island. Even if we were inclined to accept petitioner's historical account[,] we think that such evidence is of little import for two reasons. First, much of the evidence is irrelevant to *public* fora analysis, because sites such as bus and rail terminals traditionally have had *private* ownership. The development of privately owned parks that ban speech activity would not change the public fora status of publicly held parks. But the reverse is also true. The practices of privately held transportation centers do not bear on the government's regulatory authority over a publicly owned airport.

Second, the relevant unit for our inquiry is an airport, not "transportation nodes" generally. When new methods of transportation develop, new methods for accommodating that transportation are also likely to be needed. And with each new step, it therefore will be a new inquiry whether the transportation necessities are compatible with various kinds of expressive activity. [The] "security magnet," for example, is an airport commonplace that lacks a counterpart in bus terminals and train stations. And public access to air terminals is also not infrequently restricted—just last year the Federal Aviation Administration required airports for a 4–month period to limit access to areas normally publicly accessible. To blithely equate airports with other transportation centers, therefore, would be a mistake. [T]he record demonstrates that Port Authority management considers the purpose of the terminals to be the facilitation of passenger air travel, not the promotion of expression. Even if we look beyond the intent of the Port Authority to the manner in which the terminals have been operated, the terminals have never been dedicated (except under the threat of court order) to expression in the form sought to be exercised [here]. Thus, we think that neither by tradition nor purpose can the terminals be described as satisfying the standards we have previously set out for identifying a public forum.

The restrictions here challenged, therefore, need only satisfy a requirement of reasonableness. * * *

We have on many prior occasions noted the disruptive effect that solicitation may have on business. "Solicitation requires action by those who would respond: The individual solicited must decide whether or not to contribute (which itself might involve reading the solicitor's literature or hearing his pitch), and then, having decided to do so, reach for a wallet, search it for money, write a check, or produce a credit card." *United States v. Kokinda*, 497 U.S. 720 (1990). Passengers who wish to avoid the solicitor may have to alter their path, slowing both themselves and those around them. The result is that the normal flow of traffic is impeded. This is especially so in an airport, where "air travelers, who are often weighted down by cumbersome baggage [may] be hurrying to catch a plane or to arrange ground transportation." Delays may be particularly costly in this setting, as a flight missed by only a few minutes can result in hours worth of subsequent inconvenience.

In addition, face to face solicitation presents risks of duress that are an appropriate target of regulation. The skillful, and unprincipled, solicitor can target the most vulnerable, including those accompanying children or those suffering physical impairment and who cannot easily avoid the solicitation. The unsavory solicitor can also commit fraud through concealment of his affiliation or through deliberate efforts to shortchange those who agree to purchase. Compounding this problem is the fact that, in an airport, the targets of such activity frequently are on tight schedules. This in turn makes such visitors unlikely to stop and formally complain to airport authorities. As a result, the airport faces considerable difficulty in achieving its legitimate interest in monitoring solicitation activity to assure that travelers are not interfered with unduly.

[T]he sidewalk areas outside the terminals [are] frequented by an overwhelming percentage of airport users. [W]e think it would be odd to conclude that the Port Authority's terminal regulation is unreasonable despite the Port Authority having otherwise assured access to an area universally traveled. * * *

Moreover, "[if] petitioner is given access, so too must other groups. "Obviously, there would be a much larger threat to the State's interest in crowd control if all other religious, nonreligious, and noncommercial organizations could likewise move freely." As a result, we conclude that the solicitation ban is reasonable. * * *

JUSTICE O'CONNOR, concurring in 91–155 [on the solicitation issue] and concurring in the judgment in 91–339 [on the distribution of literature issue]. * * *

I concur in the Court's opinion in No. 91–155 and agree that publicly owned airports are not public fora.

[This], however, does not mean that the government can restrict speech in whatever way it likes. * * *

"The reasonableness of the Government's restriction [on speech in a nonpublic forum] must be assessed in light of the purpose of the forum and all the surrounding circumstances." *Cornelius.* " '[C]onsideration of a forum's special attributes is relevant to the constitutionality of a regulation since the significance of the governmental interest must be assessed in light of the characteristic nature and function of the particular forum involved.' " *Kokinda.* In this case, the "special attributes" and "surrounding circumstances" of the airports operated by the Port Authority are determinative. Not only has the Port Authority chosen *not* to limit access to the airports under its control, it has created a huge complex open to travelers and nontravelers alike. The airports house restaurants, cafeterias, snack bars, coffee shops, cocktail lounges, post offices, banks, telegraph offices, clothing shops, drug stores, food stores, nurseries, barber shops, currency exchanges, art exhibits, commercial advertising displays, bookstores, newsstands, dental offices and private clubs. The International Arrivals Building at JFK Airport even has two branches of BloomingFirst Amendment's.

We have said that a restriction on speech in a nonpublic forum is "reasonable" when it is "consistent with the [government's] legitimate interest in 'preserv[ing] the property [for] the use to which it is lawfully dedicated.' " *Perry.* [The] reasonableness inquiry, therefore, is not whether the restrictions on speech are "consistent [with] preserving the property" for air travel, but whether they are reasonably related to maintaining the multipurpose environment that the Port Authority has deliberately created.

Applying that standard, I agree with the Court in No. 91–155 that the ban on solicitation is reasonable. * * *

In my view, however, the regulation banning leafletting [cannot] be upheld as reasonable on this record. I therefore concur in the judgment in No. 91–339 striking down that prohibition. [W]e have expressly noted that leafletting does not entail the same kinds of problems presented by face-to-face solicitation. Specifically, "[o]ne need not ponder the contents of a leaflet or pamphlet in order mechanically to take it out of someone's [hand]. 'The distribution of literature does not require that the recipient stop in order to receive the message the speaker wishes to convey; instead the recipient is free to read the message at a later time.' " With the possible exception of avoiding litter, it is difficult to point to any problems intrinsic to the act of leafletting that would make it naturally incompatible with a large, multipurpose forum such as those at issue here. * * *

Of course, it is still open for the Port Authority to promulgate regulations of the time, place, and manner of leafletting which are "content-neutral, narrowly tailored to serve a significant government interest, and leave open ample alternative channels of communication." For example, during the many years that this litigation has been in progress, the Port Authority has not banned sankirtan completely from JFK International Airport, but has restricted it to a relatively uncongested part of the airport terminals, the same part that houses the airport chapel. In my view, that regulation meets the standards we have applied * * *.

JUSTICE KENNEDY, with whom JUSTICE BLACKMUN, JUSTICE STEVENS, and JUSTICE SOUTER join as to Part I, concurring in the judgment.

I.   [The Court] leaves the government with almost unlimited authority to restrict speech on its property by doing nothing more than articulating a non-speech-related purpose for the area, and it leaves almost no scope for the development of new public forums absent the rare approval of the government. The Court's error [in] analysis is a classification of the property that turns on the government's own definition or decision, unconstrained by an independent duty to respect the speech its citizens can voice there. The Court acknowledges as much, by reintroducing today into our First Amendment law a strict doctrinal line between the proprietary and regulatory functions of government which I thought had been abandoned long ago. *Schneider; Grayned v. Rockford,* 408 U.S. 104 (1972).[f]

[Public] places are of necessity the locus for discussion of public issues, as well as protest against arbitrary government action. At the heart of our jurisprudence lies the principle that in a free nation citizens must have the right to gather and speak with other persons in public places. The recognition that certain government-owned property is a public forum provides open notice to citizens that their freedoms may be exercised there without fear of a censorial government, adding tangible reinforcement to the idea that we are a free people. * * *

The Court's analysis rests on an inaccurate view of history. The notion that traditional public forums are property which have public discourse as their principal purpose is a most doubtful fiction. The types of property that we have recognized as the quintessential public forums are streets, parks, and sidewalks. It would seem apparent that the principal purpose of streets and sidewalks, like airports, is to facilitate transportation, not public discourse. [Similarly,] the purpose for the creation of public parks may be as much for beauty and open space as for discourse. Thus under the Court's analysis, even the quintessential public forums would appear to lack the necessary elements of what the Court defines as a public forum. * * *

One of the places left in our mobile society that is suitable for discourse is a metropolitan airport [because] in these days an airport is one of the few government-owned spaces where many persons have extensive contact with other members of the public. Given that private spaces of similar character are not subject to the dictates of the First Amendment, it is critical that we preserve these areas for protected speech. [If] the objective, physical characteristics of the property at issue and the actual public access and uses which have been permitted by the government indicate that expressive activity would be appropriate and compatible with those uses, the property is a public forum. [The] possibility of some theoretical inconsistency between expressive activities and the property's uses should not bar a finding of a public forum, if those inconsistencies can be avoided through simple and permitted regulations.

The second category of the Court's jurisprudence, the so-called designated forum, provides little, if any, additional protection for speech. [I] do not quarrel with the fact that speech must often be restricted on property of this kind to retain the purpose for which it has been designated. And I recognize that when property has been designated for a particular expressive use, the government may choose to eliminate that designation. But this increases the need to protect speech in other places, where discourse may occur free of such restrictions. In some sense the government always retains authority to close a public forum, by selling the property, changing

---

f.　*Grayned* stated that: "The crucial question is whether the manner of expression is basically incompatible with the normal activity of a particular place at a particular time." Applying that test, the Court held constitutional an ordinance forbidding the making of noise which disturbs or tends to disturb the peace or good order of a school session.

its physical character, or changing its principal use. Otherwise the State would be prohibited from closing a park, or eliminating a street or sidewalk, which no one has understood the public forum doctrine to require. The difference is that when property is a protected public forum the State may not by fiat assert broad control over speech or expressive activities; it must alter the objective physical character or uses of the property, and bear the attendant costs, to change the property's forum status.

Under this analysis, it is evident that the public spaces of the Port Authority's airports are public forums. First, the District Court made detailed findings [that] show that the public spaces in the airports are broad, public thoroughfares full of people and lined with stores and other commercial activities. An airport corridor is of course not a street, but that is not the proper inquiry. The question is one of physical similarities, sufficient to suggest that the airport corridor should be a public forum for the same reasons that streets and sidewalks have been treated as public forums by the people who use them.

Second, the airport areas involved here are open to the public without restriction. Plaintiffs do not seek access to the secured areas of the airports, nor do I suggest that these areas would be public forums. And while most people who come to the Port Authority's airports do so for a reason related to air travel, [this] does not distinguish an airport from streets or sidewalks, which most people use for travel. * * *

Third, and perhaps most important, it is apparent from the record, and from the recent history of airports, that when adequate time, place, and manner regulations are in place, expressive activity is quite compatible with the uses of major airports. The Port Authority [argues] that the problem of congestion in its airports' corridors makes expressive activity inconsistent with the airports' primary purpose, which is to facilitate air travel. The First Amendment is often inconvenient. But that is besides the point. Inconvenience does not absolve the government of its obligation to tolerate speech. * * *

[A] grant of plenary power allows the government to tilt the dialogue heard by the public, to exclude many, more marginal voices. [We] have long recognized that the right to distribute flyers and literature lies at the heart of the liberties guaranteed by the Speech and Press Clauses of the First Amendment. The Port Authority's rule, which prohibits almost all such activity, is among the most restrictive possible of those liberties. The regulation is in fact so broad and restrictive of speech, Justice O'Connor finds it void even under the standards applicable to government regulations in nonpublic forums. I have no difficulty deciding the regulation cannot survive the far more stringent rules applicable to regulations in public forums. The regulation is not drawn in narrow terms and it does not leave open ample alternative channels for communication. * * *

II. It is my view, however, that the Port Authority's ban on the "solicitation and receipt of funds" [may] be upheld as either a reasonable time, place, and manner restriction, or as a regulation directed at the nonspeech element of expressive conduct. The two standards have considerable overlap in a case like this one. * * *

I am in full agreement with the statement of the Court that solicitation is a form of protected speech. If the Port Authority's solicitation regulation prohibited all speech which requested the contribution of funds, I would conclude that it was a direct, content-based restriction of speech in clear violation of the First Amendment. The Authority's regulation does not prohibit all solicitation, however; it prohibits the "solicitation and receipt of funds." [It] reaches only personal solicitations for immediate payment of money. [The] regulation does not cover, for example, the distribution of preaddressed envelopes along with a plea to contribute money to the distributor or his organization. As I understand the restriction it is directed only at the physical exchange of money, which is an element of conduct interwoven with otherwise expressive solicitation.

[T]he government interest in regulating the sales of literature[, however,] is not as powerful as in the case of solicitation. The danger of a fraud arising from such sales is much more limited than from pure solicitation, because in the case of a sale the nature of the exchange tends to be clearer to both parties. Also, the Port Authority's sale regulation is not as narrowly drawn as the solicitation rule, since it does not specify the receipt of money as a critical element of a violation. And perhaps most important, the flat ban on sales of literature leaves open fewer alternative channels of communication than the Port Authority's more limited prohibition on the solicitation and receipt of funds. Given the practicalities and ad hoc nature of much expressive activity in the public forum, sales of literature must be completed in one transaction to be workable. Attempting to collect money at another time or place is a far less plausible option in the context of a sale than when soliciting donations, because the literature sought to be sold will under normal circumstances be distributed within the forum. * * *

Against all of this must be balanced the great need, recognized by our precedents, to give the sale of literature full First Amendment protection. We have long recognized that to prohibit distribution of literature for the mere reason that it is sold would leave organizations seeking to spread their message without funds to operate. "It should be remembered that the pamphlets of Thomas Paine were not distributed free of charge." *Murdock v. Pennsylvania,* 319 U.S. 105 (1943). The effect of a rule of law distinguishing between sales and distribution would be to close the marketplace of ideas to less affluent organizations and speakers, leaving speech as the preserve of those who are able to fund themselves. One of the primary purposes of the public forum is to provide persons who lack access to more sophisticated media the opportunity to speak. [And] while the same arguments might be made regarding solicitation of funds, the answer is that the Port Authority has not prohibited all solicitation, but only a narrow class of conduct associated with a particular manner of solicitation. * * *g

JUSTICE SOUTER, with whom JUSTICE BLACKMUN and JUSTICE STEVENS join, concurring in the judgment in No. 91–339 [on the distribution of literature issue] and dissenting in No. 91–155 [on the solicitation issue].

[R]espondent comes closest to justifying the [total ban on solicitation of money for immediate payment] as one furthering the government's interest in preventing coercion and fraud.[1] [While] a solicitor can be insistent, a pedestrian on the street or airport concourse can simply walk [away]. Since there is here no evidence of any type of coercive conduct, over and above the merely importunate character of the open and public solicitation, that might justify a ban, the regulation cannot be sustained to avoid coercion.

As for fraud, our cases do not provide government with plenary authority to ban solicitation just because it could be [fraudulent.] The evidence of fraudulent conduct here is virtually nonexistent. It consists of one affidavit describing eight complaints, none of them substantiated, "involving some form of fraud, deception, or larceny" over an entire 11–year period between 1975 and 1986, during which the regulation at issue here was, by agreement, not enforced. [B]y the Port Authority's own calculation, there has not been a single claim of fraud or misrepresentation since 1981. * * *

Even assuming a governmental interest adequate to justify some regulation, the present ban would fall when subjected to the requirement of narrow tailoring. Thus, in Schaumburg v. Citizens for a Better Environment, 444 U.S. 620 (1980), we said: "The Village's legitimate interest in preventing fraud can be better served by measures less intrusive than a direct prohibition on solicitation. Fraudulent misrepresentations can be prohibited and the penal laws used to punish such conduct directly."

[Finally,] I do not think the Port Authority's solicitation ban leaves open the "ample" channels of communication required of a valid content-neutral time, place and manner restriction. A distribution of preaddressed envelopes is unlikely to be much of an alternative. The practical reality of the regulation, which this Court can never ignore, is that it shuts off a

---

g. For commentary on Kennedy, J.'s perspective, see Steven G. Gey, *Reopening the Public Forum—From Sidewalks to Cyberspace*, 58 Ohio St. L.J. 1535 (1998); Comment, *"Objective" Approaches to the Public Forum Doctrine*, 90 Nw. U.L.Rev. 1185 (1996).

1. Respondent also attempts to justify its regulation on the alternative basis of "interference with air travelers," referring in particular to problems of "annoyance," and "congestion." The First Amendment inevitably requires people to put up with annoyance and uninvited persuasion. Indeed, in such cases we need to scrutinize restrictions on speech with special care. In their degree of congestion, most of the public spaces of these airports are probably more comparable to public streets than to the fairground as we described it in *Heffron*. Consequently, the congestion argument, which was held there to justify a regulation confining solicitation to a fixed location, should have less force here. Be that as it may, the conclusion of a majority of the Court today that the Constitution forbids the ban on the sale [Ed. Does the majority of the Court conclude that the Constitution forbids the ban on the *sale* of literature?] as well as the distribution, of leaflets puts to rest respondent's argument that congestion justifies a total ban on solicitation. While there may, of course, be congested locations where solicitation could severely compromise the efficient flow of pedestrians, the proper response would be to tailor the restrictions to those choke points.

uniquely powerful avenue of communication for organizations like the International Society for Krishna Consciousness, and may, in effect, completely prohibit unpopular and poorly funded groups from receiving funds in response to protected solicitation. * * *

LEE v. INTERNATIONAL SOCIETY FOR KRISHNA CONSCIOUSNESS, INC.

505 U.S. 830, 112 S.Ct. 2709, 120 L.Ed.2d 669 (1992).

PER CURIAM.

For the reasons expressed in the opinions of Justice O'Connor, Justice Kennedy, and Justice Souter in *ISKCON v. Lee,* the judgment of the Court of Appeals holding that the ban on distribution of literature in the Port Authority airport terminals is invalid under the First Amendment is affirmed.

CHIEF JUSTICE REHNQUIST, with whom JUSTICE WHITE, JUSTICE SCALIA and JUSTICE THOMAS join, dissenting.

Leafletting [must] be evaluated against a backdrop of the substantial congestion problem facing the Port Authority and with an eye to the cumulative impact that will result if all groups are permitted terminal access. Viewed in this light, I conclude that the distribution ban, no less than the solicitation ban, is reasonable.

[The] weary, harried, or hurried traveler may have no less desire and need to avoid the delays generated by having literature foisted upon him than he does to avoid delays from a financial solicitation. And while a busy passenger perhaps may succeed in fending off a leafletter with minimal disruption to himself by agreeing simply to take the proffered material, this does not completely ameliorate the dangers of congestion flowing from such leafletting. Others may choose not simply to accept the material but also to stop and engage the leafletter in debate, obstructing those who follow. Moreover, those who accept material may often simply drop it on the floor once out of the leafletter's range, creating an eyesore, a safety hazard, and additional cleanup work for airport staff. See *Los Angeles City Council v. Taxpayers for Vincent,* 466 U.S. 789 (1984) (aesthetic interests may provide basis for restricting speech).

[Under] the regime that is today sustained, the Port Authority is obliged to permit leafletting. But monitoring leafletting activity in order to ensure that it is *only* leafletting that occurs, and not also soliciting, may prove little less burdensome than the monitoring that would be required if solicitation were permitted. At a minimum, therefore, I think it remains open whether at some future date the Port Authority may be able to reimpose a complete ban, having developed evidence that enforcement of a differential ban is overly burdensome. * * *

NOTES AND QUESTIONS

1. **Dissent.** Do the public forum line of cases underestimate the importance of affording opportunities for dissent? Cass R. Sunstein, *Why Societies Need Dissent* 102–06 (2003); Steven H. Shiffrin, *Dissent, Injustice, and the Meanings of America* 111 (1999).

2. **The First Amendment and geography.** Consider Daniel Farber & John Nowak, *The Misleading Nature of Public Forum Analysis: Content and Context in First Amendment Adjudication,* 70 Va.L.Rev., 1219, 1234–35 (1984): "Classification of public places as various types of forums has only confused judicial opinions by diverting attention from the real First Amendment issues involved in the cases. Like the fourth amendment, the First Amendment protects people, not places. Constitutional protection should depend not on labeling the speaker's physical location but on the First Amendment values and governmental interests involved in the case. Of course, governmental interests are often tied to the nature of the place. [To] this extent, the public forum doctrine is a useful heuristic [device]. But when the heuristic device becomes the exclusive method of analysis, only confusion and mistakes can result." Compare Robert Post, *Between Governance and Management: The History and Theory of the Public Forum,* 34 U.C.L.A.L.Rev. 1713, 1777 (1987): "*Grayned's* 'incompatibility' test takes into account only the specific harm incident to a plaintiff's proposed speech; it does not recognize the generic damage to managerial authority flowing from the very process of independent judicial review of institutional decisionmaking. [The Court's] present focus 'on the character of the property at issue' is a theoretical dead end, because there is no satisfactory theory connecting the classification of government property with the exercise of First Amendment rights. But there is great potential for a rich and principled jurisprudence if the Court were to focus instead on the relationship between judicial review and the functioning of institutional authority."

3. Would the Arlington National Cemetery be open to solicitation and the distribution of literature under Kennedy, J.'s approach? Consider Comment, *"Objective" Approaches to the Public Forum Doctrine,* 90 Nw. U.L.Rev. 1185, 1240 (1996): "The only differences between the Cemetery and the typical park might be concrete tombstones instead of bird baths and the increased likelihood of solemn expressions on the faces of Cemetery visitors."

4. **Footnote 7 forums.** What is the relationship between the Court's second category of property in *Perry* and its fn. 7 (see fn. e. supra)? Is the discretion to create forums limited? Is it necessary to show that restrictions on such forums are necessary to achieve a compelling state interest? If a restriction (to certain speakers or subjects) is challenged, can the restrictions be used to show that that the property is not a public forum of the second category? Is this inadmissible circularity? See Laurence Tribe, *Equality as a First Amendment Theme: The "Government-as-Private Actor" Exception* in Jesse Choper, Yale Kamisar & Laurence Tribe, The Supreme Court: Trends and Developments 1982–1983, at 221, 226 (1984); Post, supra at 1752–56. In any event, does fn. 7 create a fourth category of property without setting guiding standards? Matthew D. McGill, *Unleashing the Limited Public Forum:*

A Modest Revision to a Dysfunctional Doctrine, 52 Stan. L. Rev. 929, 931 (2000): "Briefly stated, within a limited public forum it is impossible for one to differentiate between a presumptively invalid content-based restriction on speech and a legitimate adjustment of the content parameters that define the forum." Are content limitations acceptable so long as they are not viewpoint based? See Mary Jean Dolan, *The Special Public Purpose Forum and Endorsement Relationships: New Extensions of Government Speech*, 31 Hastings Const. L.Q. 71, 72 (2004). What if there is a serious risk that a private group's message may be attributed to the government? May the government exclude the speech from the forum? See Dolan, id.; Helen Norton, *Not for Attribution: Government's Interest in Protecting the Integrity of Its Own Expression*, 37 U.C. Davis L. Rev. 1317 (2004). Could government exclude the Klan from an Adopt-a-Highway-program? From a city website listing restaurants exclude Hooters because it did not want to be associated with a business that demeaned women? See Dolan, supra, at 133.

LEHMAN v. SHAKER HEIGHTS, 418 U.S. 298 (1974), held that a public transit system could sell commercial advertising space for cards on its vehicles while refusing to sell space for "political" or "public issue" advertising. BLACKMUN, J., joined by Burger, C.J., and White and Rehnquist, JJ., ruled that the card space is not a public forum and found the city's decision reasonable because it minimized "chances of abuse, the appearance of favoritism, and the risk of imposing upon a captive audience." DOUGLAS, J., concurring, maintained that political messages and commercial messages were both offensive and intrusive to captive audiences, noted that the commercial advertising policy was not before the Court, and voted to deny a right to spread a political message to a captive audience. BRENNAN, J., joined by Stewart, Marshall, and Powell, JJ., dissenting, observed that the "city's solicitous regard for 'captive riders' [has] a hollow ring in the present case where [it] has opened its rapid transit system as a forum for communication."

Is *Lehman* a fn. 7 forum?

5. **The relationship between the public forum tests and other tests.** In *Vincent*, a political candidate had placed signs on publicly owned utility poles, and the Court assessed the constitutionality of an ordinance that prohibited the placing of signs on public property. What test applies? A public forum test? A time, place, and manner test? The *O'Brien* test?[h]

6. In order to prevent voter intimidation and election fraud, Tennessee prohibits the soliciting of votes and the display or distribution of campaign materials within 100 feet of the entrance to a polling place. Is the campaign-

---

h. For additional commentary on public forum issues, see Curtis Berger, *Pruneyard Revisited: Political Activity on Private Lands*, 66 N.Y.U.L.Rev. 650 (1991); G. Sidney Buchanan, *The Case of the Vanishing Public Forum*, 1991 U.Ill.L.Rev. 949 (1991); David Day, *The End of the Public Forum Doctrine*, 78 Iowa L.Rev. 143 (1992); Steven G. Gey, *Reopening the Public Forum—From Public Sidewalks to Cyberspace*, 58 Ohio St.L.J. 1535 (1998); David Goldstone, *The Public Forum Doctrine in the Age of the Information Superhighway (Where Are the Public Forums on the Information Superhighway?)*, 46 Hastings L.J. 335 (1995); Ronald Krotoszynski, Jr., *Celebrating Selma: The Importance of Context in Public Forum Analysis*, 104 Yale L.J. 1411 (1995); Edward Naughton, *Is Cyberspace A Public Forum? Computer Bulletin Boards, Free Speech, and State Action*, 81 Geo.L.J. 409 (1992); Note, 46 Okla.L.Rev. 155 (1993). For commentary on speaker-based restrictions, see Geoffrey Stone, *Content Regulation and the First Amendment*, 25 Wm. & Mary L.Rev. 189, 244–51 (1983).

free zone, a public forum? Is the permitting of charitable or religious speech (including solicitation) or commercial speech while banning election speech (but not exit polling) impermissible content discrimination?

BURSON v. FREEMAN, 504 U.S. 191 (1992), upheld the statute. BLACKMUN, J., joined by Rehnquist, C.J., and White and Kennedy, JJ., argued that the 100 foot zone was a public forum, that the regulation was based on the content of the speech, that the state was required to show that its statute was necessary to achieve a compelling state interest and narrowly drawn to achieve that end, and determined that this was the "rare case" in which strict scrutiny against content regulation could be satisfied: "There is [ample evidence] that political candidates have used campaign workers to commit voter intimidation or electoral fraud. In contrast, there is simply no evidence that political candidates have used other forms of solicitation or exit polling to commit such electoral abuses. [The] First Amendment does not require states to regulate for problems that do not exist. * * *

"Here, the State, as recognized administrator of elections, has asserted that the exercise of free speech rights conflicts with another fundamental right, the right to cast a ballot in an election free from the taint of intimidation and fraud. A long history, a substantial consensus, and simple common sense shows that some restricted zone around polling places is necessary to protect that fundamental right. Given the conflict between those two rights, we hold that requiring solicitors to stand 100 feet[i] from the entrances to polling places does not constitute an unconstitutional compromise."[j]

SCALIA, J., agreed with Blackmun, J., that the regulation was justified, but maintained that the area around a polling place is not a public forum: "If the category of 'traditional public forum' is to be a tool of analysis rather than a conclusory label, it must remain faithful to its name and derive its content from *tradition.* Because restrictions on speech around polling places are as venerable a part of the American tradition as the secret ballot, [Tennessee's statute] does not restrict speech in a traditional public forum. [I] believe that the [statute] though content-based, is constitutional because it is a reasonable, viewpoint-neutral regulation of a non-public forum."

STEVENS, J., joined by O'Connor and Souter, JJ., did not address the question of whether the area around a polling place was a public forum, but agreed with Blackmun, J., that the regulation could not be upheld without showing that it was necessary to serve a compelling state interest by means narrowly tailored to that end. He contended that the existence of the secret ballot was a sufficient safeguard against intimidation[k] and that the fear of fraud from last minute campaigning could not be reconciled with *Mills v.*

---

i. Blackmun, J., argued that the question of whether the state should be required to set a smaller zone, perhaps 25 feet, would put the state to an unreasonable burden of proof, and that the difference between such zones was not of constitutional moment.

j. Kennedy, J., concurring, reaffirmed the views he had put forward in *Simon and Schuster,* but noted that the First Amendment must appropriately give way in some cases where other constitutional rights are at stake. Thomas, J., took no part.

k. Stevens, J., argued that the record showed no evidence of intimidation or abuse, nor did it offer a basis for denying election advocacy, while permitting other forms of political advocacy, e.g., environmental advocacy. He maintained that the plurality had shifted the strict scrutiny standard from the state to the candidate who wished to speak.

Alabama, 384 U.S. 214 (1966)(prohibition on election day editorials unconstitutional). In addition, Stevens, J., argued that the prohibition disproportionately affects candidates with "fewer resources, candidates from lesser visibility offices, and 'grassroots' candidates" who specially profit from "last-minute campaigning near the polling place. [The] hubbub of campaign workers outside a polling place may be a nuisance, but it is also the sound of a vibrant democracy."

III. PRIVACY AND THE PUBLIC FORUM

HILL v. COLORADO

530 U.S. 703, 120 S.Ct. 2480, 147 L.Ed.2d 597 (2000).

JUSTICE STEVENS delivered the opinion of the Court.

[A Colorado statute makes it unlawful, within 100 feet of the entrance to any health care facility, for any person to "knowingly approach" within eight feet of another person, without that person's consent, "for the purpose of passing a leaflet or handbill to, displaying a sign to, or engaging in oral protest, education, or counseling with such other person * * *." The statute] does not require a standing speaker to move away from anyone passing by. Nor does it place any restriction on the content of any message that anyone may wish to communicate to anyone else, either inside or outside the regulated areas. It does, however, make it more difficult to give unwanted advice, particularly in the form of a handbill or leaflet, to persons entering or leaving medical facilities.

[P]etitioners emphasize three propositions. First, they accurately explain that the areas protected by the statute encompass all the public ways within 100 feet of every entrance to every health care facility everywhere in the State of Colorado [even] though the legislative history makes it clear that its enactment was primarily motivated by activities in the vicinity of abortion clinics. Second, they correctly state that their leafletting, sign displays, and oral communications are protected by the First Amendment. The fact that the messages conveyed by those communications may be offensive to their recipients does not deprive them of constitutional protection. Third, the public sidewalks, streets, and ways affected by the statute are 'quintessential' public forums for free speech. * * *

On the other hand, it is a traditional exercise of the States' "police powers to protect the health and safety of their citizens." That interest may justify a special focus on unimpeded access to health care facilities and the avoidance of potential trauma to patients associated with confrontational protests. See *Madsen* [Ch. 5, I, B supra. Moreover,] rules that provide specific guidance to enforcement authorities serve the interest in even-handed application of the law. * * *

It is also important when conducting this interest analysis to recognize the significant difference between state restrictions on a speaker's right to address a willing audience and those that protect listeners from unwanted communication. This statute deals only with the latter. [The] right to avoid unwelcome speech has special force in the privacy of the home, *Rowan v. Post Office Dept.*, 397 U.S. 728 (1970), and its immediate surroundings, *Frisby v. Schultz*, 487 U.S. 474 (1988)[a] but can also be protected in confrontational settings. * * *

The dissenters argue that we depart from precedent by recognizing a "right to avoid unpopular speech in a public forum," We, of course, are not addressing whether there is such a "right." Rather, we are merely noting that our cases have repeatedly recognized the interests of unwilling listeners in situations where "the degree of captivity makes it impractical for the unwilling viewer or auditor to avoid exposure." * * *[25]

Theoretically, of course, cases may arise in which it is necessary to review the content of the statements made by a person approaching within eight feet of an unwilling listener to determine whether the approach is covered by the statute. But that review need be no more extensive than a determination of whether a general prohibition of "picketing" or "demonstrating" applies to innocuous speech. The regulation of such expressive activities, by definition, does not cover social, random, or other everyday communications. See Webster's Third New International Dictionary 600, 1710 (1993) (defining "demonstrate" as "to make a public display of sentiment for or against a person or cause" and "picket" as an effort "to persuade or otherwise influence"). Nevertheless, we have never suggested that the kind of cursory examination that might be required to exclude casual conversation from the coverage of a regulation of picketing would be problematic. * * *

The Colorado statute's regulation [places] no restrictions on—and clearly does not prohibit—either a particular viewpoint or any subject matter that may be discussed by a speaker. Rather, it simply establishes a minor place restriction on an extremely broad category of communications with unwilling listeners. Instead of drawing distinctions based on the subject that the approaching speaker may wish to address, the statute applies equally to used car salesmen, animal rights activists, fundraisers, environmentalists, and missionaries.

---

a. Anti-abortion demonstrators picketed on a number of occasions outside a doctor's home. In response, the Town Board passed an ordinance prohibiting picketing taking place solely in front of, and directed at, a residence. *Frisby*, per O'Connor, J., upheld the ordinance: "The state's interest in protecting the well-being, tranquility, and privacy of the home is certainly of the highest order in a free and civilized society." Brennan, J., joined by Marshall, J., dissenting, would have permitted the town to regulate the number of residential picketers, the hours, and the noise level of the pickets. Stevens, J., dissenting, would have limited the ban to conduct that "unreasonably interferes with the privacy of the home and does not serve a reasonable communicative purpose." He worried that a sign such as "GET WELL CHARLIE—OUR TEAM NEEDS YOU," would fall within the sweep of the ordinance.

25. Furthermore, whether there is a "right" to avoid unwelcome expression is not before us in this case. The purpose of the Colorado statute is not to protect a potential listener from hearing a particular message. It is to protect those who seek medical treatment from the potential physical and emotional harm suffered when an unwelcome individual delivers a message (whatever its content) by physically approaching an individual at close range, i.e., within eight feet. In offering protection from that harm, while maintaining free access to health clinics, the State pursues interests constitutionally distinct from the freedom from unpopular speech to which Justice Kennedy refers.

Here, the statute's restriction seeks to protect those who enter a health care facility from the harassment, the nuisance, the persistent importuning, the following, the dogging, and the implied threat of physical touching that can accompany an unwelcome approach within eight feet of a patient by a person wishing to argue vociferously face-to-face and perhaps thrust an undesired handbill upon her. The statutory phrases, "oral protest, education, or counseling," distinguish speech activities likely to have those consequences from speech activities (such as Justice Scalia's "happy speech" that are most unlikely to have those consequences. The statute does not distinguish among speech instances that are similarly likely to raise the legitimate concerns to which it responds. Hence, the statute cannot be struck down for failure to maintain "content neutrality," or for "underbreadth."

Also flawed is Justice Kennedy's theory that a statute restricting speech becomes unconstitutionally content based because of its application "to the specific locations where that discourse occurs." A statute prohibiting solicitation in airports that was motivated by the aggressive approaches of Hari–Krishnas does not become content based solely because its application is confined to airports. [A] statute making it a misdemeanor to sit at a lunch counter for an hour without ordering any food would also not be 'content based' even if it were enacted by a racist legislature that hated civil rights protesters (although it might raise separate questions about the State's legitimate interest at issue).

Similarly, the contention that a statute is 'viewpoint based' simply because its enactment was motivated by the conduct of the partisans on one side of a debate is without support. The antipicketing ordinance upheld in *Frisby*, a decision in which both of today's dissenters joined, was obviously enacted in response to the activities of antiabortion protesters * * *. We nonetheless summarily concluded that the statute was content neutral.

[The statute is a reasonable place regulation.] The 8–foot separation between the speaker and the audience should not have any adverse impact on the readers' ability to read signs displayed by demonstrators. In fact, the separation might actually aid the pedestrians' ability to see the signs by preventing others from surrounding them and impeding their view. Furthermore, the statute places no limitations on the number, size, text, or images of the placards. And, as with all of the restrictions, the 8–foot zone does not affect demonstrators with signs who remain in place.

With respect to oral statements, the distance certainly can make it more difficult for a speaker to be heard, particularly if the level of background noise is high and other speakers are competing for the pedestrian's attention. Notably, the statute places no limitation on the number of speakers or the noise level, including the use of amplification equipment, although we have upheld such restrictions in past [cases]. Finally, here there is a "knowing" requirement that protects speakers "who thought they were keeping pace with the targeted individual" at the proscribed distance from inadvertently violating the statute.

It is also not clear that the statute's restrictions will necessarily impede, rather than assist, the speakers' efforts to communicate their messages. The statute might encourage the most aggressive and vociferous protesters to moderate their confrontational and harassing conduct, and thereby make it easier for thoughtful and law-abiding sidewalk counselors like petitioners to make themselves heard. But whether or not the 8–foot interval is the best possible accommodation of the competing interests at stake, we must accord a measure of deference to the judgment of the Colorado Legislature. * * *

The burden on the ability to distribute handbills is more serious because it seems possible that an 8–foot interval could hinder the ability of a leafletter to deliver handbills to some unwilling recipients. The statute does not, however, prevent a leafletter from simply standing near the path of oncoming pedestrians and proffering his or her material, which the pedestrians can easily accept.

[The statute] will sometimes inhibit a demonstrator whose approach in fact would have proved harmless. But the statute's prophylactic aspect is justified by the great difficulty of protecting, say, a pregnant woman from physical harassment with legal rules that focus exclusively on the individual impact of each instance of behavior. [Such] individualized characterization of each individual movement is often difficult to make accurately. [A] bright-line prophylactic rule may be the best way to provide protection, and, at the same time, by offering clear guidance and avoiding subjectivity, to protect speech itself. * * *

[There] are two parts to petitioners' "overbreadth" argument. On the one hand, they argue that the statute is too broad because it protects too many people in too many places, rather than just the patients at the facilities where confrontational speech had occurred. Similarly, it burdens all speakers, rather than just persons with a history of bad conduct. On the other hand, petitioners also contend that the statute is overbroad because it "bans virtually the universe of protected expression, including displays of signs, distribution of literature, and mere verbal statements."

[T]hat the coverage of a statute is broader than the specific concern that led to its enactment is of no constitutional significance. What is important is that all persons entering or leaving health care facilities share the interests served by the statute. It is precisely because the Colorado Legislature made a general policy choice that the statute is assessed under the constitutional standard set forth in *Ward*, rather than a more strict standard. In this case, it is not disputed that the regulation affects protected speech activity, the question is thus whether it is a "reasonable restrictio[n] on the time, place, or manner of protected speech." * * *

The second part of the argument is based on a misreading of the statute [, which] does not "ban" any messages, [nor] any signs, literature, or oral statements. It merely regulates the places where communications may occur. [Petitioners] have not persuaded us that the impact of the statute on the conduct of other speakers will differ from its impact on their own sidewalk counseling. Like petitioners' own activities, the conduct of other protesters and counselors at all health care facilities are encompassed within the statute's "legitimate sweep." Therefore, the statute is not overly broad.

Petitioners also claim that [the statute] is unconstitutionally vague. [This] concern is ameliorated by the fact that [it] contains a scienter requirement. The statute only applies to a person who "knowingly" approaches within eight feet of another, without that person's consent, for the purpose of engaging in oral protest, education, or counseling. The likelihood that anyone would not understand any of those common words seems quite remote.* * *

JUSTICE SOUTER, with whom JUSTICE O'CONNOR, JUSTICE GINSBURG, and JUSTICE BREYER, join concurring. * * *

It is important to recognize that the validity of punishing some expressive conduct, and the permissibility of a time, place, or manner restriction, does not depend on showing that the particular behavior or mode of delivery has no association with a particular subject or opinion. Draft card burners disapprove of the draft, see *O'Brien*, and abortion protesters believe abortion is morally wrong, *Madsen*.[b] There is always a correlation with subject and viewpoint when the law regulates conduct that has become the signature of one side of a controversy. But that does not mean that every regulation of such distinctive behavior is content based as First Amendment doctrine employs that term. The correct rule, rather, is captured in the formulation that a restriction is content based only if it is imposed because of the content of the speech. * * *

No one disputes the substantiality of the government's interest in protecting people already tense or distressed in anticipation of medical attention (whether an abortion or some other procedure) from the unwanted intrusion of close personal importunity by strangers. The issues dividing the Court, then, go to the content neutrality of the regulation, its fit with the interest to be served by it, and the availability of other means of expressing the desired message (however offensive it may be even without physically close communication).

---

b. *Madsen*, per Rehnquist, C.J., struck down an injunction creating a 300–foot buffer zone around the homes of those who worked in abortion clinics: "The 300–foot zone around the residence is much larger than the zone approved in *Frisby*. [It] would ban '[g]eneral marching through residential neighborhoods, or even walking a route in front of an entire block of houses.' The record before us does not contain sufficient justification for this broad a ban on picketing; it appears that a limitation on the time, duration of picketing, and number of pickets outside a smaller zone could have accomplished the desired result." In separate opinions Stevens, J., Souter, J., and Scalia, J., joined by Kennedy and Thomas, JJ., joined in the judgment of the Court on this issue. For commentary, see Christina Wells, *Of Communists and Anti–Abortion Protestors: The Consequences of Falling into the Theoretical Abyss*, 33 Ga. L. Rev. 1 (1998); Alan E. Brownstein, *Rules of Engagement for Cultural Wars: Regulating Conduct, Unprotected Speech, and Protected Expression in Anti–Abortion Protests Section II*, 29 U.C.Davis L.Rev. 1163 (1996).

Each of these issues is addressed principally by the fact that [the statute does] not declare any view as unfit for expression within the 100–foot zone or beyond it. [A]ll it forbids is approaching another person closer than eight feet (absent permission) to deliver the message. * * *

This is not to say that enforcement of the approach restriction will have no effect on speech; of course it will make some difference. The effect of speech is a product of ideas and circumstances, and time, place, and manner are circumstances. The question is simply whether the ostensible reason for regulating the circumstances is really something about the ideas. Here, the evidence indicates that the ostensible reason is the true reason.* * *

JUSTICE SCALIA, with whom JUSTICE THOMAS joins, dissenting.

[What] is before us [is] a speech regulation directed against the opponents of abortion, and it therefore enjoys the benefit of the "ad hoc nullification machine" that the Court has set in motion to push aside whatever doctrines of constitutional law stand in the way of that highly favored practice. [T]he regulation as it applies to oral communications is obviously and undeniably content-based. A speaker wishing to approach another for the purpose of communicating any message except one of protest, education, or counseling may do so without first securing the other's consent. Whether a speaker must obtain permission before approaching within eight [feet] depends entirely on *what he intends to say* when he gets there. I have no doubt that this regulation would be deemed content-based *in an instant* if the case before us involved antiwar protesters, or union members seeking to 'educate' the public about the reasons for their strike. * * *

The Court asserts that this statute is not content-based for purposes of our First Amendment analysis because it neither (1) discriminates among viewpoints nor (2) places restrictions on "any subject matter that may be discussed by a speaker." But we have never held that the universe of content-based regulations is limited to those two categories, and such a holding would be absurd. Imagine, for instance, special place-and-manner restrictions on all speech except that which "conveys a sense of contentment or happiness." This "happy speech" limitation would not be "viewpoint-based"—citizens would be able to express their joy in equal measure at either the rise or fall of the NASDAQ, at either the success or the failure of the Republican Party—and would not discriminate on the basis of subject matter, since gratification could be expressed about anything at all. Or consider a law restricting the writing or recitation of poetry—neither viewpoint-based nor limited to any particular subject matter. Surely this Court would consider such regulations to be "content-based" and deserving of the most exacting scrutiny.

[The] Court's confident assurance that the statute poses no special threat to First Amendment freedoms because it applies alike to "used car salesmen, animal rights activists, fundraisers, environmentalists, and missionaries," is a wonderful replication (except for its lack of sarcasm) of

Anatole France's observation that "[t]he law, in its majestic equality, forbids the rich as well as the poor to sleep under bridges." [We] know what the Colorado legislators, by their careful selection of content ('protest, education, and counseling'), were taking aim at, for they set it forth in the statute itself: the 'right to protest or counsel against certain medical procedures' on the sidewalks and streets surrounding health care facilities.

The Court is unpersuasive in its attempt to equate the present restriction with content-neutral regulation of demonstrations and picketing—as one may immediately suspect from the opinion's wildly expansive definitions of demonstrations as "public display[s] of sentiment for or against a person or cause," and of picketing as an effort "to persuade or otherwise influence." (On these terms, Nathan Hale was a demonstrator and Patrick Henry a picket.) When the government regulates "picketing," or "demonstrating," it restricts a particular manner of expression that is, as the author of today's opinion has several times explained, "a mixture of conduct and communication." [Today], Justice Stevens gives us an opinion restricting not only handbilling but even one-on-one conversation of a particular content.

[The] Court makes too much of the statement in *Ward* that "[t]he principal inquiry in determining content neutrality ... is whether the government has adopted a regulation of speech because of disagreement with the message it conveys." That is indeed "the *principal* inquiry"—but it is not the *only* inquiry. Even a law that has as its purpose something unrelated to the suppression of particular content cannot irrationally single out that content for its prohibition. An ordinance directed at the suppression of noise (and therefore "justified without reference to the content of regulated speech") cannot be applied only to sound trucks delivering messages of "protest." * * *[2]

[The statute is invalid even if it were content neutral.] Just three Terms ago, in upholding an injunction against antiabortion activities, the Court refused to rely on any supposed "right of the people approaching and entering the facilities to be left alone." *Schenck v. Pro–Choice Network*, 519 U.S. 357 (1997)[c] Finding itself in something of a jam (the State

---

2. The Court's contention that the statute is content-neutral because it is not a "regulation of speech" but a "regulation of the places where some speech may occur," is simply baffling. First, because the proposition that a restriction upon the places where speech may occur is not a restriction upon speech is both absurd and contradicted by innumerable cases. And second, because the fact that a restriction is framed as a "regulation of the places where some speech may occur" has nothing whatever to do with whether the restriction is content-neutral—which is why *Boos* held to be content-based the ban on displaying, within 500 feet of foreign embassies, banners designed to "bring into public odium any foreign government."

c. *Schenck*, per Rehnquist, C.J., maintained that an injunction ordering abortion protesters to cease and desist from "counseling" women entering abortion clinics, who indicate they do not wish to be counseled, could not be sustained in order to protect privacy: "As [a] general matter, we have indicated that in public debate our own citizens must tolerate insulting, and often outrageous, speech in order to provide adequate breathing space to the freedoms protected by the First Amendment." This portion of the injunction was sustained on other grounds. Demonstrators had previously engaged in physical intimidation against women and their escorts. The lower court ordered demonstrators to stay 15 feet away from doorways, driveways, and driveway

here has passed a regulation that is obviously not narrowly tailored to advance any other interest) the Court today neatly re-packages the repudiated "right" as an "interest" the State may decide to protect and then places it onto the scales opposite the right to free speech in a traditional public forum.

[T]he "right to be let alone" [is] not an interest that may be legitimately weighed against the speakers' First Amendment rights (which the Court demotes to the status of First Amendment 'interests'). We have consistently held that "the Constitution does not permit the government to decide which types of otherwise protected speech are sufficiently offensive to require protection *for the unwilling listener or viewer.*" *Erznoznik.* [We] have upheld limitations on a speaker's exercise of his right to speak on the public streets *when that speech intrudes into the privacy of the home. Frisby.* [But] 'Outside the home, the burden is generally on the observer or listener to avert his eyes or plug his ears against the verbal assaults, lurid advertisements, tawdry books and magazines, and other 'offensive' intrusions which increasingly attend urban life.' L. Tribe, *American Constitutional Law* § 12–19, p. 948 (2d ed. 1988).

[The] Court displays a willful ignorance of the type and nature of communication affected by the statute's restrictions. It seriously asserts, for example, that the 8–foot zone allows a speaker to communicate at a "normal conversational distance," [but] I have never walked along the public sidewalk—and have not seen others do so—"conversing" at an 8–foot remove. The suggestion is absurd. So is the suggestion that the opponents of abortion can take comfort in the fact that the statute "places no limitation on the number of speakers or the noise level, including the use of amplification equipment." That is good enough, I suppose, for "protesting"; but the Court must know that [t]he availability of a powerful amplification system will be of little help to the woman who hopes to forge, in the last moments before another of her sex is to have an abortion, a bond of concern and intimacy that might enable her to persuade the woman to change her mind and heart. * * *

The Court [reasons] that a leafletter may, without violating the statute, stand "near the path" of oncoming pedestrians and make his "proffe[r] which the pedestrians can easily accept." [But] leafletting will be rendered utterly ineffectual by a requirement that the leafletter obtain from each subject permission to approach, or else man a stationary post (one that does not obstruct access to the facility, lest he violate subsection (2) of statute) and wait for passersby voluntarily to approach an outstretched hand. [A] leafletter, whether he is working on behalf of Operation Rescue, Local 109, or Bubba's Bar–B–Que, stakes out the best piece of real estate he can, and then walks a few steps toward individuals passing in his vicinity, extending his arm and making it *as easy as possible* for the

---

entrances except for two sidewalk counselors in order to accommodate free speech rights. The Court observed that the counselors, if ordered to desist, and other demonstrators could present their messages outside the 15–foot buffer zone and that their consignment to that area was a result of their own previous intimidation.

passerby, whose natural inclination is generally not to seek out such distributions, to simply accept the offering. * * *

"The fact," the Court says, "that the coverage of a statute is broader than the specific concern that led to its enactment is of no constitutional significance." That is true enough ordinarily, but it is not true with respect to restraints upon speech, which is what the doctrine of overbreadth is all [about.] I know of no precedent for the proposition that time, place, and manner restrictions are not subject to the doctrine of overbreadth. * * *

[T]he public forum involved here—the public spaces outside of health care facilities—has become, by necessity and by virtue of this Court's decisions, a forum of last resort for those who oppose abortion. [Those] whose concern is for the physical safety and security of clinic patients, workers, and doctors should take no comfort from today's decision. Individuals or groups intent on bullying or frightening women out of an abortion, or doctors out of performing that procedure, will not be deterred by Colorado's statute; bullhorns and screaming from eight feet away will serve their purposes well. But those who would accomplish their moral and religious objectives by peaceful and civil means, by trying to persuade individual women of the rightness of their cause, will be deterred; and that is not a good thing in a democracy. * * *

JUSTICE KENNEDY, dissenting.

[For] the first time, the Court approves a law which bars a private citizen from passing a message, in a peaceful manner and on a profound moral issue, to a fellow citizen on a public sidewalk. [The] prohibitions against "picketing" and/or "leafleting" upheld in *Frisby*, *Grace*, and *Mosley*, the Court says are no different from the restrictions on "protest, education, or counseling" imposed by the Colorado statute. [But no] examination of the content of a speaker's message is required to determine whether an individual is picketing, or distributing a leaflet, or impeding free access to a building. Under the Colorado enactment, however, [w]hen a citizen approaches another on the sidewalk in a disfavored-speech zone, an officer of the State must listen to what the speaker says. If, in the officer's judgment, the speaker's words stray too far toward "protest, education, or counseling"—the boundaries of which are far from clear—the officer may decide the speech has moved from the permissible to the criminal. The First Amendment does not give the government such power.

The statute is content based for an additional reason: [We] would close our eyes to reality were we to deny that 'oral protest, education, or counseling' outside the entrances to medical facilities concern a narrow range of topics—indeed, one topic in particular. [If], just a few decades ago, a State with a history of enforcing racial discrimination had enacted a statute like this one, regulating "oral protest, education, or counseling" within 100 feet of the entrance to any lunch counter, our predecessors would not have hesitated to hold it was content based or viewpoint based.

[To] say that one citizen can approach another to ask the time or the weather forecast or the directions to Main Street but not to initiate discussion on one of the most basic moral and political issues in all of contemporary discourse, a question touching profound ideas in philosophy and theology, is an astonishing view of the First Amendment. * * *

[The] statute's vagueness [in] the terms "protest," "counseling," "education," and "consent" [becomes] as well one source of its overbreadth. The only sure way to avoid violating the law is to refrain from picketing, leafleting, or oral advocacy altogether. Scienter cannot save so vague a statute as this. [T]he State and the Court attempt to sidestep the enactment's obvious content-based restriction by praising the statute's breadth, by telling us all topics of conversation, not just discourse on abortion, are banned within the statutory proscription. [Our] precedents do not permit content censoring to be cured by taking even more protected speech within a statute's reach. [The] happenstance of a dental office being located in a building brings the restricted-speech zone into play. If the same building also houses an organization dedicated, say, to environmental issues, a protest against the group's policies would be barred. Yet if, on the next block there were a public interest enterprise in a building with no health care facility, the speech would be unrestricted. The statute is a classic example of a proscription not narrowly tailored and resulting in restrictions of far more speech than necessary to achieve the legislature's object. * * *

The majority insists the statute aims to protect distraught women who are embarrassed, vexed, or harassed as they attempt to enter abortion clinics. If these are punishable acts, they should be prohibited in those [terms.] Citizens desiring to impart messages to women considering abortions likely do not have resources to use the mainstream media for their message, much less resources to locate women contemplating the option of abortion. [Nowhere] is the speech more important than at the time and place where the act is about to occur. As the named plaintiff, Leila Jeanne Hill, explained, "In my many years of sidewalk counseling I have seen a number of [these] women change their minds about aborting their unborn children as a result of my sidewalk counseling, and God's grace." * * *

The Court now strikes at the heart of the reasoned, careful balance I had believed was the basis for the joint opinion in *Casey*. The vital principle of the opinion was that in defined instances the woman's decision whether to abort her child was in its essence a moral one, a choice the State could not dictate. Foreclosed from using the machinery of government to ban abortions in early term, those who oppose it are remitted to debate the issue in its moral dimensions. In a cruel way, the Court today turns its back on that balance.* * *

NOTES AND QUESTIONS

1. ***Overbreadth?*** Consider Alan K. Chen, *Statutory Speech Bubbles, First Amendment Overbreadth, and Improper Legislative Purpose*, 38 HARV.

C.R.-C.L. L. REV. 31, 67 (2003): "[T]he Court rejected the plaintiffs' over-breadth claim because it believed that the bubble law's comprehensiveness (treating all speech equally) suggested that the state's purposes were legitimate. But this was simply another way of stating that the law was viewpoint and content neutral. Overbreadth law's precision requirement, however, requires that laws discriminate by ensuring that lawmakers address the state's legitimate interests and no (or little) more, without sweeping in protected speech." Does the state's privacy interest address the overbreadth claim?

2. **Privacy?** Consider Robert D. Nauman, *The Captive Audience Doctrine and Floating Buffer Zones: An Analysis of Hill v. Colorado*, 30 Cap. U. L. Rev. 769, 808–09 (2002): "Nowhere in the Court's discussion are there facts showing how the petitioners invaded the privacy rights of pedestrians, let alone how they did this in an 'intolerable manner.' Rather, the Court, after finding the substantial privacy interest, placed it 'in the scales with the right of others to communicate.' This suggests that the *Cohen* standard has been rejected in favor of a balancing approach, in which the unwilling listener will no longer be presumed to have the opportunity to avoid the unwanted speech in public. This gives much greater recognition to the interests of unwilling listeners in public fora than was present previously. It also runs the concurrent risk of establishing a 'heckler's veto,' in which the audience possesses the power to prohibit speech that it does not wish to hear simply by being present."

3. *Is manner distinguishable from content?* Consider Heidi Kitrosser, *From Marshall McLuhan to Anthropomorphic Cows: Communicative Manner and the First Amendment*, 96 Nw. U. L. Rev. 1339, 1340 (2002): "Although the Court's statements in *Hill* echo assumptions evinced in other cases, to the effect that content is synonymous with viewpoint and subject matter, these statements contradict broader definitions provided by the Court in other cases to the effect that content-based regulations target the 'communicative impact' of expression. Because the manner in which speech is delivered can have significant communicative impact upon listeners and viewers, the Court, applying the 'communicative impact' approach to defining content, has occasionally found restrictions on 'manner of speech' to be content-based, including restrictions on speech delivered in an indecent or offensive manner. Communicative manner includes expressive choices ranging from word choice (e.g., the use of profane language), to choice of visual displays to convey a message (e.g., the burning of a flag or the use of nudity), to place-and-manner choices affecting the communicative impact of a message (e.g., the decision to engage in face-to-face communication, or to picket in front of a particular location of symbolic or emotional significance)."

4. *Discriminatory impact.* Consider Kathleen M. Sullivan, *Sex, Money, and Groups: Free Speech and Association Decisions in the October 1999 Term*, 28 Pepp. L. Rev. 723, 737 (2001): "The law in Hill arguably has a viewpoint-discriminatory effect: requiring listeners affirmatively to consent to speech will inevitably have the effect of discriminating in favor of popular or widely accepted messages and against those that are unorthodox or unpopular."

5. *Severe slippery slope?* Consider Jamin B. Raskin, *Disfavored Speech About Favored Rights: Hill v. Colorado, The Vanishing Public Forum and the Need for an Objective Speech Discrimination Test*, 51 Am. U. L. Rev. 179, 226–27 (2001): "Thus, if a state is vexed by protests outside lunch counters that refuse to serve racial minorities, it can enact a regulation limiting unconsented approaches for speech purposes by any person (not just opponents of segregation) within 100 feet of the entrance of food service establishments. [Similarly,] if a state is opposed to gay rights activists leafleting on Sundays near the churches of conservative religious congregations that oppose homosexuality, it can enact a criminal law banning unconsented approaches by any person within 100 feet of the entrance of all houses of worship. [A] legislature in a right-to-work state perturbed by union picketing outside paper mills can pass a law that prohibits unconsented approaches by any person within 100 feet of the entrance of all industrial facilities for the stated purpose of ensuring the free flow of commerce, securing the right to contract, and protecting employees from stresses that diminish worker safety and productivity."

6. *Legislative dilemma.* Consider Alan K. Chen, *Statutory Speech Bubbles, First Amendment Overbreadth, and Improper Legislative Purpose*, 38 Harv. C.R.-C.L. L. Rev. 31, 89 (2003): "Such laws may be inextricably caught between the doctrine of substantial overbreadth and the doctrine of content neutrality. If such laws are to be truly viewpoint-and content-neutral, they must apply to a broad range of expression that is clearly protected by the First Amendment, but is unrelated to the government's interest. On the other hand, if such laws are read more narrowly to encompass only the state's primary interest in protecting women's access to abortion clinics, they may be invalidated because they are discriminatory."

CHAPTER 7

GOVERNMENT SUPPORT OF SPEECH

■ ■ ■

Public forum doctrine recognizes that government is obligated to permit some of its property to be used for communicative purposes without content discrimination, but public forum doctrine also allows other government property to be restricted to some speakers or for talk about selected subjects. In short, in some circumstances government can provide resources for some speech while denying support for other speech. Indeed, government is a significant actor in the marketplace of ideas. Sometimes the government speaks as government; sometimes it subsidizes speech without purporting to claim that the resulting message is its own. It supports speech in many ways: official government messages; statements of public officials at publicly subsidized press conferences; artistic, scientific, or political subsidies; even the classroom communications of public school teachers.

If content distinctions are suspect when government acts as censor, they are the norm when government speaks or otherwise subsidizes speech. Government makes editorial judgments; it decides that some content is appropriate for the occasion and other content is not. The public museum curator makes content decisions in selecting exhibits; the librarian in selecting books; the public board in selecting recipients for research grants; the public official in composing press releases.

The line between support for speech and censorship of speech is not always bright, however. In any event, the Constitution limits the choices government may make in supporting speech. For example, government support of religious speech is limited under the establishment clause. See Ch. 8. This section explores the extent to which the speech clause or constitutional conceptions of equality should limit government discretion in supporting speech.

I. SUBSIDIES OF SPEECH

Pleasant Grove, Utah permitted private groups to place a number of permanent monuments in its Pioneer Park including a Ten Commandments monument provided by the Fraternal Order of Eagles. Summum, a religious organization, requested permission to erect a monument containing Seven Aphorisms which it believes were presented by God to Moses. The city refused and Summum challenged the refusal on the ground that the city was engaging in unacceptable content discrimination in a public forum.

PLEASANT GROVE CITY v. SUMMUM, 555 U.S. 460 (2009), per ALITO, J., upheld the city's action: "[A]lthough a park is a traditional public forum for speeches and other transitory expressive acts, the display of a permanent monument in a public park is not a form of expression to which forum analysis applies. Instead, the placement of a permanent monument in a public park is best viewed as a form of government speech and is therefore not subject to scrutiny under the Free Speech Clause. [If] government entities must maintain viewpoint neutrality in their selection of donated monuments, they must either 'brace themselves for an influx of clutter' or face the pressure to remove longstanding and cherished monuments. Every jurisdiction that has accepted a donated war memorial may be asked to provide equal treatment for a donated monument questioning the cause for which the veterans fought. New York City, having accepted a donated statue of one heroic dog (Balto, the sled dog who brought medicine to Nome, Alaska, during a diphtheria epidemic) may be pressed to accept monuments for other dogs who are claimed to be equally worthy of commemoration. The obvious truth of the matter is that if public parks were considered to be traditional public forums for the purpose of erecting privately donated monuments, most parks would have little choice but to refuse all such donations." Earlier in the opinion, the Court recited limits on government speech: "This does not mean that there are no restraints on government speech. For example, government speech must comport with the Establishment Clause. The involvement of public officials in advocacy may be limited by law, regulation, or practice. And of course, a government entity is ultimately 'accountable to the electorate and the political process for its advocacy.' 'If the citizenry objects, newly elected officials later could espouse some different or contrary position.' "[a]

RUST v. SULLIVAN

500 U.S. 173, 111 S.Ct. 1759, 114 L.Ed.2d 233 (1991).

CHIEF JUSTICE REHNQUIST delivered the opinion of the Court.

---

a. The Court recognized that there might be situations where it is difficult to tell whether government is speaking or providing a forum for private speech. Stevens, J., joined by Ginsburg, J., concurring, doubted that it made a difference whether the city's acceptance of the Ten Commandment's monument was deemed to be government speech or implicit endorsement of the donor's message. Scalia, J., joined by Thomas J., concurring, expressed the view that the city's action did not violate the Establishment Clause (although the issue was not presented). Breyer, J., concurring, expressed the view that the phrase, "government speech" needed to be applied not as a label, but with an eye toward the category's purpose. He did not think the government action disproportionately burdened Summum's speech. Souter, J., concurring, applied a reasonable observer test to determine that the Ten Commandment's monument was government speech. He thought it premature to be deciding Establishment Clause issues.

These cases concern a facial challenge to Department of Health and Human Services (HHS) regulations which limit the ability of Title X fund recipients to engage in abortion-related activities. * * *

A.   In 1970, Congress enacted Title X of the Public Health Service Act (Act), 84 Stat. 1506, as amended, 42 U.S.C. §§ 300–300a–41, which provides federal funding for family-planning services. The Act authorizes the Secretary to "make grants to and enter into contracts with public or nonprofit private entities to assist in the establishment and operation of voluntary family planning projects which shall offer a broad range of acceptable and effective family planning methods and services." 42 U.S.C. § 300(a). Grants and contracts under Title X must "be made in accordance with such regulations as the Secretary may promulgate." 42 U.S.C. § 300a–4. Section 1008 of the Act, however, provides that "[n]one of the funds appropriated under this subchapter shall be used in programs where abortion is a method of family planning." 42 U.S.C. § 300a–6. * * *

In 1988, the Secretary promulgated new regulations designed to provide " 'clear and operational guidance' to grantees about how to preserve the distinction between Title X programs and abortion as a method of family planning." 53 Fed.Reg. 2923–2924 (1988). * * *

The regulations attach three principal conditions on the grant of federal funds for Title X projects. First, the regulations specify that a "Title X project may not provide counseling concerning the use of abortion as a method of family planning or provide referral for abortion as a method of family planning." 42 CFR § 59.8(a)(1) (1989). Because Title X is limited to preconceptional services, the program does not furnish services related to childbirth. Only in the context of a referral out of the Title X program is a pregnant woman given transitional information. § 59.8(a)(2). Title X projects must refer every pregnant client "for appropriate prenatal and/or social services by furnishing a list of available providers that promote the welfare of the mother and the unborn child." Id. The list may not be used indirectly to encourage or promote abortion, "such as by weighing the list of referrals in favor of health care providers which perform abortions, by including on the list of referral providers health care providers whose principal business is the provision of abortions, by excluding available providers who do not provide abortions, or by 'steering' clients to providers who offer abortion as a method of family planning." § 59.8(a)(3). The Title X project is expressly prohibited from referring a pregnant woman to an abortion provider, even upon specific request. One permissible response to such an inquiry is that "the project does not consider abortion an appropriate method of family planning and therefore does not counsel or refer for abortion." § 59.8(b)(5).

Second, the regulations broadly prohibit a Title X project from engaging in activities that "encourage, promote or advocate abortion as a method of family planning." § 59.10(a). Forbidden activities include lobbying for legislation that would increase the availability of abortion as a method of family planning, developing or disseminating materials advocating abortion as a method of family planning, providing speakers to promote abortion as a method of family planning, using legal action to make abortion available in any way as a method of family planning, and paying dues to any group that advocates abortion as a method of family planning as a substantial part of its activities. Id.

Third, the regulations require that Title X projects be organized so that they are "physically and financially separate" from prohibited abortion activities. § 59.9. To be deemed physically and financially separate, "a Title X project must have an objective integrity and independence from prohibited activities. Mere bookkeeping separation of Title X funds from other monies is not sufficient." Id. The regulations provide a list of nonexclusive factors for the Secretary to consider in conducting a case-by-case determination of objective integrity and independence, such as the existence of separate accounting records and separate personnel, and the degree of physical separation of the project from facilities for prohibited activities. Id.

[Petitioners] are Title X grantees and doctors who supervise Title X funds suing on behalf of themselves and their patients. Respondent is the Secretary of the Department of Health and Human Services. [Petitioners] contend that the regulations violate the First Amendment by impermissibly discriminating based on viewpoint because they prohibit "all discussion about abortion as a lawful option—including counseling, referral, and the provision of neutral and accurate information about ending a pregnancy—while compelling the clinic or counselor to provide information that promotes continuing a pregnancy to term." They assert that the regulations violate the "free speech rights of private health care organizations that receive Title X funds, of their staff, and of their patients" by impermissibly imposing "viewpoint-discriminatory conditions on government subsidies" and thus "penaliz[e] speech funded with non-Title X monies." Because "Title X continues to fund speech ancillary to pregnancy testing in a manner that is not even-handed with respect to views and information about abortion, it invidiously discriminates on the basis of viewpoint." Relying on *Regan v. Taxation with Representation of Washington,* 461 U.S. 540 (1983)[a] and *Arkansas Writers' Project, Inc. v. Ragland,* 481 U.S. 221 (1987),[b] petitioners also assert that while the Government may place certain conditions on the receipt of federal subsidies, it may not

---

a. *Regan* upheld tax code provisions that permitted contributions to veteran's organizations to be deductible even if they engaged in substantial lobbying while denying deductions for contributions to other religious, charitable, scientific, or educational organizations if they engaged in substantial lobbying.

b. *Arkansas Writers' Project* held it unconstitutional to impose a sales tax on general interest magazines while exempting newspapers, religious, professional, trade, and sports journals. Discriminatory taxation against the press or segments of it has generally been invalidated. *Minneapolis Star & Tribune v. Minnesota Comm. of Rev.,* 460 U.S. 575 (1983) (some press treated more favorably and press treated differently from other enterprises); *Grosjean v. American Press Co.,* 297 U.S. 233 (1936) (same). But see *Leathers v. Medlock,* 499 U.S. 439 (1991) (upholding general sales tax extension to cable that was not applicable to the print media on the grounds that it did not suppress ideas and that the tax did not target a small group of speakers).

"discriminate invidiously in its subsidies in such a way as to 'ai[m] at the suppression of dangerous ideas.' " *Regan.*

There is no question but that the statutory prohibition contained in § 1008 is constitutional. [The] Government can, without violating the Constitution, selectively fund a program to encourage certain activities it believes to be in the public interest, without at the same time funding an alternate program which seeks to deal with the problem in another way.[c] In so doing, the Government has not discriminated on the basis of viewpoint; it has merely chosen to fund one activity to the exclusion of the other. "[A] legislature's decision not to subsidize the exercise of a fundamental right does not infringe the right." *Regan.* * * *

The challenged regulations implement the statutory prohibition by prohibiting counseling, referral, and the provision of information regarding abortion as a method of family planning. They are designed to ensure that the limits of the federal program are observed. The Title X program is designed not for prenatal care, but to encourage family planning. A doctor who wished to offer prenatal care to a project patient who became pregnant could properly be prohibited from doing so because such service is outside the scope of the federally funded program. The regulations prohibiting abortion counseling and referral are of the same ilk; "no funds appropriated for the project may be used in programs where abortion is a method of family planning," and a doctor employed by the project may be prohibited in the course of his project duties from counseling abortion or referring for abortion. This is not a case of the Government "suppressing a dangerous idea," but of a prohibition on a project grantee or its employees from engaging in activities outside of its scope.

To hold that the Government unconstitutionally discriminates on the basis of viewpoint when it chooses to fund a program dedicated to advance certain permissible goals, because the program in advancing those goals necessarily discourages alternate goals, would render numerous government programs constitutionally suspect. When Congress established a National Endowment for Democracy to encourage other countries to adopt democratic principles, 22 U.S.C. § 4411(b), it was not constitutionally required to fund a program to encourage competing lines of political philosophy such as Communism and Fascism. Petitioners' assertions ultimately boil down to the position that if the government chooses to subsidize one protected right, it must subsidize analogous counterpart rights. But the Court has soundly rejected that proposition. Within far broader limits than petitioners are willing to concede, when the government appropriates public funds to establish a program it is entitled to define the limits of that program.

We believe that petitioners' reliance upon our decision in *Arkansas Writers' Project* is misplaced. That case involved a state sales tax which

---

c. The Court cited *Maher v. Roe,* 432 U.S. 464 (1977) (constitutional for government to subsidize childbirth without subsidizing abortions) and *Harris v. McRae,* 448 U.S. 297 (1980) (accord).

discriminated between magazines on the basis of their content. Relying on this fact, and on the fact that the tax "targets a small group within the press," contrary to our decision in *Minneapolis Star,* the Court held the tax invalid. But we have here not the case of a general law singling out a disfavored group on the basis of speech content, but a case of the Government refusing to fund activities, including speech, which are specifically excluded from the scope of the project funded.

Petitioners rely heavily on their claim that the regulations would not, in the circumstance of a medical emergency, permit a Title X project to refer a woman whose pregnancy places her life in imminent peril to a provider of abortions or abortion-related services. This case, of course, involves only a facial challenge to the regulations, and we do not have before us any application by the Secretary to a specific fact situation. On their face, we do not read the regulations to bar abortion referral or counseling in such circumstances. * * *

Petitioners also contend that the restrictions on the subsidization of abortion-related speech contained in the regulations are impermissible because they condition the receipt of a benefit, in this case Title X funding, on the relinquishment of a constitutional right, the right to engage in abortion advocacy and counseling.

[H]ere the government is not denying a benefit to anyone, but is instead simply insisting that public funds be spent for the purposes for which they were authorized. The Secretary's regulations do not force the Title X grantee to give up abortion-related speech; they merely require that the grantee keep such activities separate and distinct from Title X activities. Title X expressly distinguishes between a Title X *grantee* and a Title X *project.* The grantee, which normally is a health care organization, may receive funds from a variety of sources for a variety of purposes. The grantee receives Title X funds, however, for the specific and limited purpose of establishing and operating a Title X project. 42 U.S.C. § 300(a). The regulations govern the scope of the Title X *project's* activities, and leave the grantee unfettered in its other activities. The Title X *grantee* can continue to perform abortions, provide abortion-related services, and engage in abortion advocacy; it simply is required to conduct those activities through programs that are separate and independent from the project that receives Title X funds.

In contrast, our "unconstitutional conditions" cases involve situations in which the government has placed a condition on the *recipient* of the subsidy rather than on a particular program or service, thus effectively prohibiting the recipient from engaging in the protected conduct outside the scope of the federally funded program. [By] requiring that the Title X grantee engage in abortion-related activity separately from activity receiving federal funding, Congress has, consistent with our teachings in *League of Women Voters,* [Ch. 8, II infra], and *Regan,* not denied it the right to engage in abortion-related activities. Congress has merely refused to fund such activities out of the public fisc, and the Secretary has simply required a certain degree of separation from the Title X project in order to ensure the integrity of the federally funded program.

The same principles apply to petitioners' claim that the regulations abridge the free speech rights of the grantee's staff. Individuals who are voluntarily employed for a Title X project must perform their duties in accordance with the regulation's restrictions on abortion counseling and referral. The employees remain free, however, to pursue abortion-related activities when they are not acting under the auspices of the Title X project. The regulations, which govern solely the scope of the Title X project's activities, do not in any way restrict the activities of those persons acting as private individuals. The employees' freedom of expression is limited during the time that they actually work for the project; but this limitation is a consequence of their decision to accept employment in a project, the scope of which is permissibly restricted by the funding authority.

This is not to suggest that funding by the Government, even when coupled with the freedom of the fund recipients to speak outside the scope of the Government-funded project, is invariably sufficient to justify government control over the content of expression. For example, this Court has recognized that the existence of a Government "subsidy," in the form of Government-owned property, does not justify the restriction of speech in areas that have "been traditionally open to the public for expressive activity," or have been "expressly dedicated to speech activity." Similarly, we have recognized that the university is a traditional sphere of free expression so fundamental to the functioning of our society that the Government's ability to control speech within that sphere by means of conditions attached to the expenditure of Government funds is restricted by the vagueness and overbreadth doctrines of the First Amendment, *Keyishian v. Board of Regents*. It could be argued by analogy that traditional relationships such as that between doctor and patient should enjoy protection under the First Amendment from government regulation, even when subsidized by the Government. We need not resolve that question here, however, because the Title X program regulations do not significantly impinge upon the doctor-patient relationship. Nothing in them requires a doctor to represent as his own any opinion that he does not in fact hold. Nor is the doctor-patient relationship established by the Title X program sufficiently all-encompassing so as to justify an expectation on the part of the patient of comprehensive medical advice. The program does not provide post-conception medical care, and therefore a doctor's silence with regard to abortion cannot reasonably be thought to mislead a client into thinking that the doctor does not consider abortion an appropriate option for her. The doctor is always free to make clear that advice regarding abortion is simply beyond the scope of the program. In these circumstances, the general rule that the Government may choose not to subsidize speech applies with full force. * * *

JUSTICE BLACKMUN, with whom JUSTICE MARSHALL joins, with whom JUSTICE STEVENS joins as to Parts II[d] and III,[e] and with whom JUSTICE O'CONNOR joins as to Part I,[f] dissenting. * * *

II. A. Until today, the Court never has upheld viewpoint-based suppression of speech simply because that suppression was a condition upon the acceptance of public funds. Whatever may be the Government's power to condition the receipt of its largess upon the relinquishment of constitutional rights, it surely does not extend to a condition that suppresses the recipient's cherished freedom of speech based solely upon the content or viewpoint of that speech. * * *

It cannot seriously be disputed that the counseling and referral provisions at issue in the present cases constitute content-based regulation of speech. Title X grantees may provide counseling and referral regarding any of a wide range of family planning and other topics, save abortion.

The Regulations are also clearly viewpoint-based. While suppressing speech favorable to abortion with one hand, the Secretary compels anti-abortion speech with the other. For example, the Department of Health and Human Services' own description of the Regulations makes plain that "Title X projects are *required* to facilitate access to prenatal care and social services, including adoption services, that might be needed by the pregnant client to promote her well-being and that of her child, while making it abundantly clear that the project is not permitted to promote abortion by facilitating access to abortion through the referral process." 53 Fed.Reg. 2927 (1988) (emphasis added).

Moreover, the Regulations command that a project refer for prenatal care each woman diagnosed as pregnant, irrespective of the woman's expressed desire to continue or terminate her pregnancy. 42 CFR § 59.8(a)(2) (1990). If a client asks directly about abortion, a Title X physician or counselor is required to say, in essence, that the project does not consider abortion to be an appropriate method of family planning. § 59.8(b)(4). Both requirements are antithetical to the First Amendment. See *Wooley v. Maynard.*

The Regulations pertaining to "advocacy" are even more explicitly viewpoint-based. These provide: "A Title X project may not *encourage, promote or advocate* abortion as a method of family planning." § 59.10 (emphasis added). They explain: "This requirement prohibits actions to *assist* women to obtain abortions or *increase* the availability or accessibility of abortion for family planning purposes." § 59.10(a) (emphasis added). The Regulations do not, however, proscribe or even regulate anti-abortion advocacy. These are clearly restrictions aimed at the suppression of "dangerous ideas."

---

d. Part II discussed freedom of speech and portions of it are set out below.

e. Part III argued that the regulations violated the fifth amendment due process clause.

f. Part I contended that the regulations were not authorized by the statute. O'Connor, and Stevens, JJ., each filed separate dissents advancing the same contention.

Remarkably, the majority concludes that "the Government has not discriminated on the basis of viewpoint; it has merely chosen to fund one activity to the exclusion of another." But the majority's claim that the Regulations merely limit a Title X project's speech to preventive or preconceptional services rings hollow in light of the broad range of nonpreventive services that the Regulations authorize Title X projects to provide.[2] By refusing to fund those family-planning projects that advocate abortion *because* they advocate abortion, the Government plainly has targeted a particular viewpoint. The majority's reliance on the fact that the Regulations pertain solely to funding decisions simply begs the question. Clearly, there are some bases upon which government may not rest its decision to fund or not to fund. For example, the Members of the majority surely would agree that government may not base its decision to support an activity upon considerations of race. As demonstrated above, our cases make clear that ideological viewpoint is a similarly repugnant ground upon which to base funding decisions.

The majority's reliance upon *Regan* in this connection is [misplaced]. That case stands for the proposition that government has no obligation to subsidize a private party's efforts to petition the legislature regarding its views. Thus, if the challenged Regulations were confined to non-ideological limitations upon the use of Title X funds for lobbying activities, there would exist no violation of the First Amendment. The advocacy Regulations at issue here, however, are not limited to lobbying but extend to all speech having the effect of encouraging, promoting, or advocating abortion as a method of family planning. § 59.10(a). Thus, in addition to their impermissible focus upon the viewpoint of regulated speech, the provisions intrude upon a wide range of communicative conduct, including the very words spoken to a woman by her physician. By manipulating the content of the doctor/patient dialogue, the Regulations upheld today force each of the petitioners "to be an instrument for fostering public adherence to an ideological point of view [he or she] finds unacceptable." *Wooley v. Maynard.* This type of intrusive, ideologically based regulation of speech goes far beyond the narrow lobbying limitations approved in *Regan*, and cannot be justified simply because it is a condition upon the receipt of a governmental benefit.[3]

---

2. In addition to requiring referral for prenatal care and adoption services, the Regulations permit general health services such as physical examinations, screening for breast cancer, treatment of gynecological problems, and treatment for sexually transmitted diseases. 53 Fed.Reg. 2927 (1988). None of the latter are strictly preventive, preconceptional services.

3. The majority attempts to obscure the breadth of its decision through its curious contention that "the Title X program regulations do not significantly impinge upon the doctor-patient relationship." That the doctor-patient relationship is substantially burdened by a rule prohibiting the dissemination by the physician of pertinent medical information is beyond serious dispute. This burden is undiminished by the fact that the relationship at issue here is not an "all-encompassing" one. A woman seeking the services of a Title X clinic has every reason to expect, as do we all, that her physician will not withhold relevant information regarding the very purpose of her visit. To suggest otherwise is to engage in uninformed fantasy. Further, to hold that the doctor-patient relationship is somehow incomplete where a patient lacks the resources to seek comprehensive healthcare from a single provider is to ignore the situation of a vast number of Americans. As Justice Marshall has noted in a different context: "It is perfectly proper for judges to disagree about what the Constitution requires. But it is disgraceful for an interpretation of the

B. The Court concludes that the challenged Regulations do not violate the First Amendment rights of Title X staff members because any limitation of the employees' freedom of expression is simply a consequence of their decision to accept employment at a federally funded project. Ante, at 22. But it has never been sufficient to justify an otherwise unconstitutional condition upon public employment that the employee may escape the condition by relinquishing his or her job.

The majority attempts to circumvent this principle by emphasizing that Title X physicians and counselors "remain free [to] pursue abortion-related activities when they are not acting under the auspices of the Title X project." "The regulations," the majority explains, "do not in any way restrict the activities of those persons acting as private individuals." Under the majority's reasoning, the First Amendment could be read to tolerate *any* governmental restriction upon an employee's speech so long as that restriction is limited to the funded workplace. This is a dangerous proposition, and one the Court has rightly rejected in the past.

In *Abood,* it was no answer to the petitioners' claim of compelled speech as a condition upon public employment that their speech outside the workplace remained unregulated by the State.[g] Nor was the public employee's First Amendment claim in *Rankin v. McPherson,* 483 U.S. 378 (1987), derogated because the communication that her employer sought to punish occurred during business hours.[h] At the least, such conditions require courts to balance the speaker's interest in the message against those of government in preventing its dissemination.

In the cases at bar, the speaker's interest in the communication is both clear and vital. In addressing the family-planning needs of their clients, the physicians and counselors who staff Title X projects seek to provide them with the full range of information and options regarding their health and reproductive freedom. Indeed, the legitimate expectations of the patient and the ethical responsibilities of the medical profession demand no less. "The patient's right of self-decision can be effectively exercised only if the patient possesses enough information to enable an intelligent choice. * * * The physician has an ethical obligation to help the patient make choices from among the therapeutic alternatives consistent with good medical practice." Current Opinions, the Council on Ethical and Judicial Affairs of the American Medical Association ¶ 8.08 (1989). * * *

The Government's articulated interest in distorting the doctor/patient dialogue—ensuring that federal funds are not spent for a purpose outside the scope of the program—falls far short of that necessary to justify the suppression of truthful information and professional medical opinion

---

Constitution to be premised upon unfounded assumptions about how people live." *United States v. Kras,* 409 U.S. 434 (1973) (dissenting opinion).

g. *Abood v. Detroit Board of Education,* Ch. 9, II infra (compelled funding of ideological activities of union violates freedom of speech).

h. *Rankin* (expressed hope that assassination attempt of president be successful is protected speech when uttered in private to fellow employee during working hours).

regarding constitutionally protected conduct.[4] Moreover, the offending Regulation is not narrowly tailored to serve this interest. For example, the governmental interest at stake could be served by imposing rigorous bookkeeping standards to ensure financial separation or adopting content-neutral rules for the balanced dissemination of family-planning and health information. By failing to balance or even to consider the free speech interests claimed by Title X physicians against the Government's asserted interest in suppressing the speech, the Court falters in its duty to implement the protection that the First Amendment clearly provides for this important message.

C.   Finally, it is of no small significance that the speech the Secretary would suppress is truthful information regarding constitutionally protected conduct of vital importance to the listener. One can imagine no legitimate governmental interest that might be served by suppressing such information. * * *

NOTES AND QUESTIONS

1.   *Free speech?* Is the problem in *Rust* one of free speech or of the right to secure an abortion? Consider Abner S. Greene, *Government of the Good,* 53 Vand. L.Rev. 1, 5 (2000): "Should it be improper as a matter of political theory, or unconstitutional, for government to condition the funding of health clinics on their advocating condom use by teens?"

2.   *Political Speech.* Are there First Amendment limits on the extent to which government can subsidize political speech. Suppose government itself enters the political fray. Should a city government be able to buy media time to speak on behalf of candidates? To influence the outcome of initiative campaigns?[i] What about refusals to subsidize political speech? See *Ysura v. Pacatello Education Ass'n,* 129 S.Ct. 1093 (2009) (constitutional for state to permit payroll deductions for union dues while barring deductions for political purposes).

3.   *Managerial domains.* Consider Robert C. Post, *Subsidized Speech,* 106 Yale L.J. 151, 164 (1996): "Public discourse must be distinguished from ['managerial'] domains. [Within] managerial domains, the state organizes its resources so as to achieve specified ends. The constitutional value of managerial domains is that of instrumental rationality, a value that conceptualizes

---

4. It is to be noted that the Secretary has made no claim that the Regulations at issue reflect any concern for the health or welfare of Title X clients.

i. For relevant commentary, see Mark Yudof, *When Government Speaks: Politics, Law, and Government Expression in America* (1983); David Cole, *Beyond Unconstitutional Conditions: Charting Spheres of Neutrality in Government–Funded Speech,* 67 N.Y.U.L.Rev. 675 (1992). Richard Delgado, *The Language of the Arms Race,* 64 B.U.L.Rev. 961 (1984); Thomas Emerson, *The Affirmative Side of the First Amendment,* 15 Ga.L.Rev. 795 (1981); Robert Kamenshine, *The First Amendment's Implied Political Establishment Clause,* 67 Calif.L.Rev. 1104 (1979); Steven Shiffrin, *Government Speech,* 27 UCLA L.Rev. 565 (1980); Martin H. Redish & Daryl I. Kessler, *Government Subsidies and Free Expression,* 80 Minn.L.Rev. 543 (1996); Frederick Schauer, *Book Review,* 35 Stan.L.Rev. 373 (1983); Mark Yudof, *When Governments Speak: Toward A Theory of Government Expression and the First Amendment,* 57 Tex.L.Rev. 863 (1979); Edward Ziegler, *Government Speech and the Constitution: The Limits of Official Partisanship,* 21 B.C.L.Rev. 578 (1980); Note, *The Constitutionality of Municipal Advocacy in Statewide Referendum Campaigns,* 93 Harv.L.Rev. 535 (1980).

persons as means to an end rather than as autonomous agents. [T]herefore, ends may be imposed upon persons.

"Managerial domains are necessary so that a democratic state can actually achieve objectives that have been democratically agreed upon. [Thus] the state can regulate speech within public educational institutions so as to achieve the purposes of education; it can regulate speech within the judicial system so as to attain the ends of justice; it can regulate speech within the military so as to preserve the national defense; it can regulate the speech of government employees so as to promote 'the efficiency of the public services [the government] performs through its employees'; and so forth.

"As a result of this instrumental orientation, viewpoint discrimination occurs frequently within managerial domains. To give but a few obvious examples: the president may fire cabinet officials who publicly challenge rather than support Administration policies; the military may discipline officers who publicly attack rather than uphold the principle of civilian control over the armed forces; public defenders who prosecute instead of defend their clients may be sanctioned; prison guards who encourage instead of condemn drug use may be chastised. Viewpoint discrimination occurs within managerial domains whenever the attainment of legitimate managerial objectives requires it.

"[Clearly], First Amendment doctrine within managerial domains differs fundamentally from First Amendment doctrine within public discourse."[j]

Is the *Rust* situation an appropriate instance to invoke the managerial domain perspective? Or does it matter that the speakers whose speech is limited are not bureaucrats, but professionals who "must always qualify their loyalty and commitment to the vertical hierarchy of an organization by their horizontal commitment to general professional norms and standards." See id. at 172.

And consider Susan H. Williams, *Truth, Autonomy, and Speech: Feminist Theory and the First Amendment* 192–93 (New York University Press 2004): "[Post] is clearly right that certain government institutions must be seen as engaged in an activity distinct from governance; such institutions are intended to serve a particular purpose and speech within them often can be regulated in the interest of that purpose. [But] those holding power in such institutions must make themselves vulnerable to claims of injustice by other members and even by outsiders affected by the institution. Such institutions, in other words, are never only in the domain of management; they are always subject to claims of justice and not just to claims of instrumental rationality." Williams observes that this is particularly important because "It is in the nature of power hierarchies to overestimate the need for their own control

---

j. For similar First Amendment perspectives, see C. Edwin Baker, *Campaign Expenditures and Free Speech*, 33 Harv. C.R.-C.L.Rev. 1 (1998) (referring to bounded contexts); Daniel Halberstam, *Commercial Speech, Professional Speech, and the Constitutional Status of Social Institutions*, 147 U.Pa.L.Rev. 771 (1991) (referring to bounded speech institutions). For sympathetic criticism, see Mark Tushnet, *The Possibilities of Comparative Constitutional Law*, 108 Yale L.J. 1225 (1999). On the other hand, are there circumstances in which the problem of government supported speech should be regarded as outside the managerial domain and inside the realm of distributive justice where individuals are not treated as a means to an end? See Stephen J. Heyman, *State-Supported Speech*, 1999 Wis. L.Rev. 1119, 1139–40.

and underestimate the harms done to those subject to that control. For that reason, deference toward the people holding power in such institutions is generally less appropriate as the institutions are more hierarchical."

4. ***Deception.*** Consider Dorothy E. Roberts, *Rust v. Sullivan and the Control of Knowledge,* 61 Geo.Wash.L.Rev. 587, 594–95 (1993): "[P]regnancy may accelerate the progression of certain serious medical conditions, such as heart disease, hypertension, diabetes, sickle cell anemia, cancer and AIDS. For example, a woman with diabetic retinopathy who becomes pregnant may go blind. The regulations prohibited doctors from advising women suffering from these conditions that abortion may reduce the long-term risks to their health. Moreover, the recommendation of prenatal care may give the false impression that pregnancy does not jeopardize these women's health." See also Gia B. Lee, *Persuasion, Transparency, and Government Speech,* 56 Hast. L.J. 983, 1050 (2005): "While the *Rust* majority noted that, '[n]othing in [the regulations] requires a doctor to represent as his own any opinion that he does not hold,' and that '[t]he doctor is always free to make clear that advice regarding abortion is simply beyond the scope of the program,' it was also true that nothing in the regulations required the doctors to disclose the government's role in restricting the scope of their counseling."

5. ***Domination.*** Note, *Unconstitutional Conditions as "Nonsubsidies": When is Deference Inappropriate?* 80 Geo.L.J. 131, 135 (1991): "*Rust* was wrongly decided because the government's domination of the entire family planning dialogue for many of those who seek such information has made private alternatives unavailable. Poor women have a right to this information because the Constitution respects the interests of those who want to receive a particular message, not just the interests of those who speak. In the limited context of the exchange between the family planning counselor and the poor pregnant woman who wants information concerning a range of options, government has gone far toward creating a monopoly. By contrast, a broad portion of government's speech-related subsidies, such as those for the Kennedy Center, do not involve 'crowding out' of private alternatives and thus do not raise analogous First Amendment concerns."

6. ***Rust distinguished.*** The University of Virginia subsidized the printing costs of a wide variety of student organizations, but refused to fund religious activities (those that "primarily promote or manifest a particular belief in or about a deity or an ultimate reality"). ROSENBERGER v. UNIVERSITY OF VIRGINIA, 515 U.S. 819 (1995), per KENNEDY, J., also set forth Part 2, Ch. 11, II infra held that the refusal to fund religious speech violated the free speech clause: "[In *Rust*] the government did not create a program to encourage private speech but instead used private speakers to transmit specific information pertaining to its own program. We recognized that when the government appropriates public funds to promote a particular policy of its own it is entitled to say what it wishes.

"It does not follow [that] viewpoint-based restrictions are proper when the University does not itself speak or subsidize transmittal of a message it favors but instead expends funds to encourage a diversity of views from private speakers."[k]

---

k. O'Connor, J., and Thomas, J., filed concurring opinions. *Rust* was also distinguished in *Legal Services Corp. v. Velazquez,* 531 U.S. 533 (2001). The Court struck down a restriction

SOUTER, J., joined by Stevens, Ginsburg and Breyer, JJ., dissented: "If the Guidelines were written or applied so as to limit only such Christian advocacy and no other evangelical efforts that might compete with it, the discrimination would be based on viewpoint. But that is not what the regulation authorizes; it applies to Muslim and Jewish and Buddhist advocacy as well as to Christian. And since it limits funding to activities promoting or manifesting a particular belief not only 'in' but 'about' a deity or ultimate reality, it applies to agnostics and atheists as well as it does to deists and theists. The Guidelines [thus] do not skew debate by funding one position but not its competitors. [T]hey simply deny funding for hortatory speech that 'primarily promotes or manifests' any view on the merits of religion; they deny funding for the entire subject matter of religious apologetics."[1]

Consider Randall P. Bezanson and William G. Buss, *The Many Faces of Government Speech*, 86 Iowa L. Rev. 1377, 1407 (2001): "*Rosenberger* has now become the standard bearer for one of two poles in the Court's government speech jurisprudence. At one pole, the Court says, when the government makes a decision to create a forum for individual speech, the government is stuck with it. The government may not pick and choose among speakers because it prefers some messages over others. At the opposite pole, represented by *Rust v. Sullivan*, [the] Court says that the government may favor one message over another because the favored message is the government's own message, and because the government has not created any forum for the expression of individual views. Between these poles is sometimes a third one; the government may create a forum for the expression of individual views, but a forum that is not open to everyone. * * *m

"In deciding between the poles, the Court purports to hold the government to its own decision. The Court determines either that the government was speaking its own message or that it opened an avenue for individual speech opportunities and, if the latter, whether it was opening the door wide or opening only a limited forum. It seems clear that in deciding what the government has undertaken to do, the Court will be influenced by its own broad view of First Amendment tradeoffs."

7. **Funding Arts and Sciences**. The government has long funded scientific projects on the basis of their perceived merit. Could Congress constitutionally prohibit the funding of "indecent" art? Would this be an example of content discrimination or viewpoint discrimination? Does it matter? The extent to which the government may make such judgments and the role that political actors may play in the process was debated in *National Endowment for the Arts v. Finley*, 524 U.S. 569 (1998) but not resolved. Consider Abner S. Greene, *Government Speech on Unsettled Issues*, 69 Ford.

---

preventing the The Legal Services Corporation from distributing federal funds to challenge the constitutionality or the statutory validity of existing welfare laws. It concluded that the speech of lawyers on behalf of indigent clients was not government speech. Scalia, J., joined by Rehnquist, C.J., and O'Connor and Thomas, JJ., dissented.

l. For commentary on whether the Virginia practice constitutes viewpoint discrimination, see Kent Greenawalt, *Viewpoints From Olympus*, 96 Colum. L.Rev. 697 (1996).

m. Can government constitutionally permit pro choice specialty license plates while refusing to issue pro life specialty life license plates? See Amy Riley Lucas, *Speciality License Plates*, 55 UCLA L.Rev. 1971 (2008); Steven G. Gey, *Why Should the First Amendment Protect Government Speech When the Government Has Nothing to Say*, 95 Iowa L.Rev. 1259, 1303–07 (2010).

L. Rev. 1667, 1681 (2001): "[V]iewpoint discrimination is a term that we should leave for government regulation of a particular viewpoint. We should not use it to describe government speech favoring a given viewpoint. Such speech, absent monopoly, coercion, or [similar] concerns, should be considered a healthy part of the market and of democratic debate and as no intrusion on the liberty or autonomy of citizens to express contrary viewpoints." Consider also Steven J. Heyman, *State-Supported Speech*, 1999 Wis. L.Rev. 1119, 1139–40: "Suppose [a] state legislature becomes concerned about violence in popular culture and the impact it may have on young people. Instead of attempting to regulate violent entertainment, the legislature decides to create a program to support art and culture, with the proviso that no funds should be awarded to works that glorify violence. There can be little doubt that this would constitute viewpoint discrimination. Yet it seems highly implausible to suggest that if the government chooses to support non-violent art, it must support violent art as well. Instead, the proviso should be upheld on the same ground that Souter offers in defending criteria of artistic merit—that it serves a 'perfectly legitimate' governmental goal." [n]

8.   If government consistently with the First Amendment can impose a point of view on bureaucrats or on doctors when they are subsidized with government funds (*Rust*), is it nonetheless barred from telling academics the point of view they can advance in the classroom? If so, should artists on panels be considered more like bureaucrats and doctors or more like academics. How does one decide which actors favor some speech over other speech? See Frederick Schauer, *The Ontology of Censorship*, in *Censorship and Silencing* 147 (Post ed. 1998). Is there a problem with giving special protection for some institutions or professionals and not others? See generally Frederick Schauer, Principles, Institutions, and the first Amendment, 112 Harv. L. Rev. 84 (1998). [o]

II.   GOVERNMENT AS EDUCATOR AND EDITOR

Many problems involved with government speech have arisen in the school setting. Government can compel children to attend schools, but it may not compel children to attend public schools. *Pierce v. Society of Sisters*, 268 U.S. 510 (1925), infra, held that compulsory public education violated parental substantive due process rights though government may require that basic educational requirements be met even in private schools. In public schools there are limits to which the institution may be an exclusive enclave for government messages. *Tinker v. Des Moines School Dist.*, 393 U.S. 503 (1969), infra, upheld the rights of school children to wear black armbands in a classroom protest of the Vietnam War. Moreover, there are constitutional limits on the government's power

---

n.   For additional commentary, see Steven H. Shiffrin, *Dissent, Injustice and the Meanings of America* ch. 1 (1999); Owen J. Fiss, *State Activism and State Censorship*, 100 Yale L.J. 2087, 2101 (1991); Amy Sabrin, *Thinking About Contents; Can It Play An Appropriate Role in Government Funding of the Arts?* 102 Yale L/J/ 1209 (1993).

o.   Are the issues involved in supporting some speech over other speech different in the sciences than the arts? See David Wasserman, *Public Funding for Science and Art*, in *Censorship and Silencing* 169 (Post ed. 1998).

to shield students from ideas by removing books from a school library. *Board of Educ. v. Pico*, 457 U.S. 853 (1982).[a] On the other hand, school authorities have been granted broad editorial control over the school curriculum including school-sponsored publications, theatrical productions, and other expressive activities.

———

Oregon's Compulsory Education Act of 1922 required all students to attend public schools through the eighth grade.[a] Two operators of private schools, the Society of the Sisters of the Holy Names of Jesus and Mary and the Hill Military Academy, secured an injunction against the act's enforcement. PIERCE v. SOCIETY OF SISTERS, 268 U.S. 510 (1925), per McReynolds, J., held that the law violated the substantive due process rights of the parents and the schools: "The manifest purpose is to compel general attendance at public schools by normal children, between 8 and 16, who have not completed the eighth grade. [No] question is raised concerning the power of the state reasonably to regulate all schools, to inspect, supervise and examine them, their teachers and pupils; to require that all children of proper age attend some school, that teachers shall be of good moral character and patriotic disposition, that certain studies plainly essential to good citizenship must be taught, and that nothing be taught which is manifestly inimical to the public welfare.

"The inevitable practical result of enforcing the act under consideration would be destruction of appellees' primary schools, and perhaps all other private primary schools for normal children within the state of Oregon. Appellees are engaged in a kind of undertaking not inherently harmful, but long regarded as useful and meritorious. Certainly there is nothing in the present records to indicate that they have failed to

---

a. But see *United States v. American Library Associations*, Inc., 539 U.S. 194 (2003) (constitutional to condition federal funding on the adoption of "a policy of Internet safety for minors that includes the operations of a technology protection measure [that] protects against access" by all persons to "visual depictions" that constitute "obscenity" or "child pornography," and that protects against access by minors to "visual depictions" that are "harmful to minors.").

a. The statute provided exemptions for children with disabilities, or who had completed the eighth grade, or who lived considerable distances from a public school, or who held a special permit from the county superintendent. The Court did not believe these exemptions were especially important. For a thorough historical and perceptive analytical treatment, see Barbara Bennett Woodhouse, *"Who Owns the Child?"*: Meyer *and* Pierce *and the Child as Property*, 33 Wm. & Mary L. Rev. 995 (1992). In the end, despite cogent criticism, Woodhouse believes that *Pierce* reached the right result. Barbara Bennett Woodhouse, *Child Abuse, the Constitution, and the Legacy of* Pierce v. Society of Sisters, 78 U. Det. Mercy L. Rev. 479, 484 (2001). Others take the criticism further. See, e.g., Meira Levinson, *The Demands of Liberal Education* 158, 161–63 (1999) (arguing for education within common schools and requiring heavy regulation of private schools to reach liberal public school ideals, including the prohibition of religious private schools); Abner S. Greene, *Civil Society and Multiple Repositories of Power*, 75 Chi.-Kent. L. Rev. 477, 489–92 (2000); Abner S. Greene, *Why Vouchers Are Unconstitutional and Why They Are Not*, 13 Notre Dame J.L. Ethics & Pub. Pol'y 397 (1999). For defenses, see, e.g., Martha Minow, *Before and After* Pierce, 78 U. Det. Mercy L. Rev. 407, 415 (2001); William G. Ross, Pierce *After Seventy–Five Years: Reasons to Celebrate*, 78 U. Det. Mercy L. Rev. 443 (2001). For the argument that *Pierce* is rightly decided for young children, but more problematic for older children, see Steven H. Shiffrin, *The First Amendment and the Socialization of Children,* 11 Cornell J.L. & Pub. Pol'y 503 (2005).

discharge their obligations to patrons, students, or the state. And there are no peculiar circumstances or present emergencies which demand extraordinary measures relative to primary education.

"Under the doctrine of *Meyer v. Nebraska*, 262 U.S. 390 (1923), we think it entirely plain that the Act of 1922 unreasonably interferes with the liberty of parents and guardians to direct the upbringing and education of children under their control. [The] fundamental theory of liberty upon which all governments in this Union repose excludes any general power of the state to standardize its children by forcing them to accept instruction from public teachers only. The child is not the mere creature of the state; those who nurture him and direct his destiny have the right, coupled with the high duty, to recognize and prepare him for additional obligations.

"Appellees are corporations, and therefore, it is said, they cannot claim for themselves the liberty which the Fourteenth Amendment guarantees. [But] they have business and property for which they claim protection. These are threatened with destruction through the unwarranted compulsion which appellants are exercising over present and prospective patrons of their schools. * * * Generally, it is entirely true, as urged by counsel, that no person in any business has such an interest in possible customers as to enable him to restrain exercise of proper power of the state upon the ground that he will be deprived of patronage. But the injunctions here sought are not against the exercise of any proper power. Appellees asked protection against arbitrary, unreasonable, and unlawful interference with their patrons and the consequent destruction of their business and property. Their interest is clear and immediate * * * ."

NOTES AND QUESTIONS

1.   Apart from due process, did the Oregon law violate the free speech rights of the affected parents? The schools? The children?

2.   Can a law like that in *Pierce* be defended on the ground that private schools siphon off the wealthy and the academically talented from the public schools while undermining a strong base of political support for generous financing of the schools?[b] On the ground that democratic education depends on schools that are integrated in terms of race, class, and religion?

3.   If parents have a right to send their children to private schools, do they also have a right to have their children excused from instruction they find objectionable? If so, what limits, if any, accompany that right?[c] Do captive audiences of government speech have a First Amendment right not to be propagandized? Do children educated in public schools particularly have such a right? See Stephen Gottlieb, *In The Name of Patriotism: The Constitu-*

---

b.   Is the empirical assumption correct? See Amy Gutmann, *Democratic Education* 117 (1987).

c.   See generally Nomi M. Stolzenberg, *"He Drew a Circle that Shut Me Out": Assimilation, Indoctrination, and the Paradox of a Liberal Education*, 106 Harv. L. Rev. 581 (1993). On parents' free speech rights, see generally, Stephen G. Giles, *On Educating Children: A Parentalist Manifesto*, 63 U.Chi.L.Rev. 937 (1996).

tionality of "Bending" History in Public Secondary Schools, 62 N.Y.U.L.Rev. 497 (1987). If ad hoc methods of separating education from propaganda are unreliable, are any institutional structures or processes required? Should this be a constitutional right without a remedy?[d]

4.   Is public education itself objectionable? Consider John Stuart Mill, *On Liberty* 98 (D. Spitz ed. 1975): "A general State education is a mere contrivance for moulding people to be exactly like one another. An education established and controlled by the State should only exist, if it exists at all, as one of many competing experiments carried on for the purpose of example and stimulus, to keep the others up to a certain standard of excellence." Is point of view discrimination in public schools unacceptable? Can public schools teach that tobacco consumption is unwise? That racial discrimination is wrong? For a skeptical view, see Martin H. Redish and Kevin Finnerty, *What Did You Learn in School Today? Free Speech, Values Inculcation, and the Democratic–Educational Paradox,* 88 Cornell L. Rev. 62, 71 (2002).

5.   Consider Mark G. Yudof, *When Government Speaks: Politics, Law, and Government Expression in America* 229–230 (1983): "*Pierce* may be construed (whatever the original motivations of the justices) as telling governments that they are free to establish their own public schools and to make education compulsory for certain age groups, but not free to eliminate competing, private-sector educational institutions that may serve to create heterogeneity and to counter the state's dominance over the education of the young. * * * *Pierce* represents a reasonable, if imperfect, accommodation of conflicting pressures. The state may promulgate its messages in the public school, while parents are free to choose private schools with different orientations. The state must tolerate private education, but need not fund it. The state may make some demands of private schools to satisfy compulsory schooling laws, but those demands may not be so excessive as to turn private schools into public schools managed and funded by the public sector. The integrity of the communications and socialization processes in private schools and families remains intact, while the state's interest in producing informed, educated, and productive citizens is not sacrificed."

But consider Abner S. Greene, *Why Vouchers are Constitutional and Why They are Not,* 13 Notre Dame J. of L.Ethics & Pub. Policy 397, 407 (1999): "[T]he *Pierce* assumption—although, in one view, assuring multiple repositories of power by counteracting the state's school monopoly—in fact assures that children will get their basic education not from multiple sources, but rather from their parents or their parent's agents alone. [Overruling] *Pierce* would free up funds used for private schooling and would direct parental energies at improving the public schools. Different public schools would, of course, focus on different values, and parents would still therefore have significant input into the curriculum of their local public schools. But we would remove some children from the monopoly of their parents and substitute a plural system of education."

---

d.   Consider also captive audiences of prisoners, soldiers, or workers in public institutions. Do "informed consent" provisions concerning abortion raise First Amendment captive audience issues? Cf. *Public Utilities Comm'n v. Pollak,* 343 U.S. 451 (1952)(city transit company's playing of radio programs does not violate Constitution).

6. A Nebraska law outlawed the teaching of languages other than English[e] in any school to students who had yet to pass the eighth grade. The Nebraska Supreme Court upheld the conviction of an instructor who taught reading in the German language in a private elementary school during recess. The Nebraska Supreme Court thought the law had a defensible purpose: "The Legislature had seen the baneful effects of permitting foreigners, who had taken residence in this country, to rear and educate their children in the language of their native land. The result of that condition was found to be inimical to our own safety. To allow the children of foreigners, who had emigrated here, to be taught from early childhood the language of the country of their parents was to rear them with that language as their mother tongue. It was to educate them so that they must always think in that language, and, as a consequence, naturally inculcate in them the ideas and sentiments foreign to the best interests of this country. The statute, therefore, was intended not only to require that the education of all children be conducted in the English language, but that, until they had grown into that language and until it had become a part of them, they should not in the schools be taught any other language. [The] hours which a child is able to devote to study in the confinement of school are limited. It must have ample time for exercise or play. Its daily capacity for learning is comparatively small."

MEYER v. NEBRASKA, supra, per MCREYNOLDS, J., held that the statute violated due process: "While this court has not attempted to define with exactness the liberty [guaranteed under the fourteenth amendment], the term has received much consideration and some of the included things have been definitely stated. Without doubt, it denotes not merely freedom from bodily restraint but also the right of the individual to contract, to engage in any of the common occupations of life, to acquire useful knowledge, to marry, establish a home and bring up children, to worship God according to the dictates of his own conscience, and generally to enjoy those privileges long recognized at common law as essential to the orderly pursuit of happiness by free men. [Corresponding] to the right of control, it is the natural duty of the parent to give his children education suitable to their station in life; and nearly all the states, including Nebraska, enforce this obligation by compulsory laws. Practically, education of the young is only possible in schools conducted by especially qualified persons who devote themselves thereto. The calling always has been regarded as useful and honorable, essential, indeed, to the public welfare. Mere knowledge of the German language cannot reasonably be regarded as harmful. Heretofore it has been commonly looked upon as helpful and desirable. Plaintiff in error taught this language in school as part of his occupation. His right thus to teach and the right of parents to engage him so to instruct their children, we think, are within the liberty of the amendment. * * *

"It is said the purpose of the legislation was to promote civic development by inhibiting training and education of the immature in foreign tongues and ideals before they could learn English and acquire American ideals, and 'that the English language should be and become the mother tongue of all children reared in this state.' It is also affirmed that the foreign born population is

---

e.   The teaching of Latin, Greek, and Hebrew was permitted.

very large, that certain communities commonly use foreign words, follow foreign leaders, move in a foreign atmosphere, and that the children are thereby hindered from becoming citizens of the most useful type and the public safety is imperiled. * * *

"For the welfare of his Ideal Commonwealth, Plato suggested a law which should provide: 'That the wives of our guardians are to be common, and their children are to be common, and no parent is to know his own child, nor any child his parent. [The] proper officers will take the offspring of the good parents to the pen or fold, and there they will deposit them with certain nurses who dwell in a separate quarter; but the offspring of the inferior, or of the better when they chance to be deformed, will be put away in some mysterious, unknown place, as they should be.' In order to submerge the individual and develop ideal citizens, Sparta assembled the males at seven into barracks and intrusted their subsequent education and training to official guardians. Although such measures have been deliberately approved by men of great genius their ideas touching the relation between individual and state were wholly different from those upon which our institutions rest; and it hardly will be affirmed that any Legislature could impose such restrictions upon the people of a state without doing violence to both letter and spirit of the Constitution.

"The desire of the Legislature to foster a homogeneous people with American ideals prepared readily to understand current discussions of civic matters is easy to appreciate. Unfortunate experiences during the late war and aversion toward every character of truculent adversaries were certainly enough to quicken that aspiration. But the means adopted, we think, exceed the limitations upon the power of the state and conflict with rights assured to plaintiff in error.[f] The interference is plain enough and no adequate reason therefor in time of peace and domestic tranquility has been shown.

"As the statute undertakes to interfere only with teaching which involves a modern language, leaving complete freedom as to other matters, there seems no adequate foundation for the suggestion that the purpose was to protect the child's health by limiting his mental activities. It is well known that proficiency in a foreign language seldom comes to one not instructed at an early age, and experience shows that this is not injurious to the health, morals or understanding of the ordinary child."[g]

---

f. Are statutes mandating English as the only language of government constitutional? See Drucilla Cornell & William W. Bratton, *Deadweight Costs and Intrinsic Wrongs of Nativism,* 84 Corn.L.Rev. 595 (1999).

g. Holmes and Sutherland, JJ., dissented, arguing, that the Court should defer to the state's interest. In addition, to studying *Pierce* and *Meyer* in connection with due process, the student may wish to reconsider them in the course of studying freedom of religion. In that connection, consider the argument that the law in *Pierce* was substantially motivated by anti-Catholic sentiment, that the law in *Meyer* was substantially motivated by anti-German sentiment and that the purpose of teaching German in *Meyer* was to help children participate in Lutheran services which were taught in German. For rich discussion of the other purposes present in *Pierce* and *Meyer,* see Barbara B. Woodhouse, *"Who Owns the Child?": Meyer and Pierce and the Child as Property,* 33 Wm. & Mary L. Rev. 995 (1992). See generally William J. Ross, *Nativism, Education, and the Constitution, 1917–1927* (1994).

TINKER v. DES MOINES SCHOOL DISTRICT
393 U.S. 503, 89 S.Ct. 733, 21 L.Ed.2d 731 (1969).

JUSTICE FORTAS delivered the opinion of the Court.

[Petitioners, two high school students and one junior high student,[a] wore black armbands to school to publicize their objections to the Vietnam conflict and their advocacy of a truce. They refused to remove the armbands when asked to do so. In accordance with a ban on armbands which the city's school principals had adopted two days before in anticipation of such a protest, petitioners were sent home and suspended from school until they would return without the armbands. They sought a federal injunction restraining school officials from disciplining them, but the lower federal courts upheld the constitutionality of the school authorities' action on the ground that it was reasonable in order to prevent a disturbance which might result from the wearing of the armbands.]

[T]he wearing of armbands in the circumstances of this case was entirely divorced from actually or potentially disruptive conduct by those participating in it. It was closely akin to "pure speech" which, we have repeatedly held, is entitled to comprehensive protection under the First Amendment. * * *

First Amendment rights, applied in light of the special characteristics of the school environment, are available to teachers and students. It can hardly be argued that either students or teachers shed their constitutional rights to freedom of speech or expression at the schoolhouse gate. This has been the unmistakable holding of this Court for almost 50 years. In *Meyer*, this Court [held that fourteenth amendment due process] prevents States from forbidding the teaching of a foreign language to young students. Statutes to this effect, the Court held, unconstitutionally interfere with the liberty of teacher, student, and parent. * * *

The problem presented by the present case does not relate to regulation of the length of skirts or the type of clothing, to hair style or deportment. [It] does not concern aggressive, disruptive action or even group demonstrations. Our problem involves direct, primary First Amendment rights akin to "pure speech."

The school officials banned and sought to punish petitioners for a silent, passive, expression of opinion, unaccompanied by any disorder or disturbance on the part of petitioners. There is here no evidence whatever of petitioners' interference, actual or nascent, with the school's work or of collision with the rights of other students to be secure and to be let alone. Accordingly, this case does not concern speech or action that intrudes upon the work of the school or the rights of other students.

Only a few of the 18,000 students in the school system wore the black armbands. Only five students were suspended for wearing them. There is no indication that the work of the school or any class was disrupted. Outside the classrooms, a few students made hostile remarks to the children wearing armbands, but there were no threats or acts of violence on school premises.

---

a. See Mary Beth Tinker, *Reflections on Tinker,* 58 Am. U.L.Rev. 1119 (2009).

[I]n our system, undifferentiated fear or apprehension of disturbance [the District Court's basis for sustaining the school authorities' action] is not enough to overcome the right to freedom of expression. Any departure from absolute regimentation may cause trouble. Any variation from the majority's opinion may inspire fear. Any words spoken, in class, in the lunchroom or on the campus, that deviates from the views of another person, may start an argument or cause a disturbance. But our Constitution says we must take this risk [and] our history says that it is this sort of hazardous freedom—this kind of openness—that is the basis of our national strength and of the independence and vigor of Americans who grow up and live in this relatively permissive, often disputatious society.

In order for the State in the person of school officials to justify prohibition of a particular expression of opinion, it must be able to show that its action was caused by something more than a mere desire to avoid the discomfort and unpleasantness that always accompany an unpopular viewpoint. Certainly where there is no finding and no showing that the exercise of the forbidden right would "materially and substantially interfere with the requirements of appropriate discipline in the operation of the school," the prohibition cannot be sustained.

In the present case, the District Court made no such finding, and our independent examination of the record fails to yield evidence that the school authorities had reason to anticipate that the wearing of the armbands would substantially interfere with the work of the school or impinge upon the rights of other students.[b] Even an official memorandum prepared after the suspension that listed the reasons for the ban on wearing the armbands made no reference to the anticipation of such disruption.[3]

On the contrary, the action of the school authorities appears to have been based upon an urgent wish to avoid the controversy which might result from the expression, even by the silent symbol of armbands, of opposition to this Nation's part in the conflagration in Vietnam. * * *

It is also relevant that the school authorities did not purport to prohibit the wearing of all symbols of political or controversial signifi-

---

b. Would a racist t-shirt interfere with the rights of others? A t-shirt condemning homosexuality? See *Harper v. Poway Unified School Dist.,* 445 F.3d 1166 (9th Cir. 2006). For discussion, see Bonnie A. Kellman, 85 Notre Dame L.Rev. 367 (2009); Jay Alan Sekulow & Erik M. Zimmerman, *Tinker at Forty,* 58 Am. U.L. Rev. 1243, 1275–84 (2009); Francisco M. Negron, *A Foot in the Door?, The Unwitting Move toward a "New" Student Wlefar Standar in Student Speech after Morse v. Frederick,* 58 Am. U.L. Rev. 1221 (2009).

3. The only suggestions of fear of disorder in the report are these: "A former student of one of our high schools was killed in Viet Nam. Some of his friends are still in school and it was felt that if any kind of a demonstration existed, it might evolve into something which would be difficult to control.

"Students at one of the high schools were heard to say they would wear arm bands of other colors if the black bands prevailed."

Moreover, the testimony of school authorities at trial indicates that it was not fear of disruption that motivated the regulation prohibiting the armbands; the regulation was directed against "the principle of the demonstration" itself. School authorities simply felt that "the schools are no place for demonstrations," and if the students "didn't like the way our elected officials were handling things, it should be handled with the ballot box and not in the halls of our public schools."

cance. The record shows that students in some of the schools wore buttons relating to national political campaigns, and some even wore the Iron Cross, traditionally a symbol of Nazism. The order prohibiting the wearing of armbands did not extend to these. Instead, a particular symbol—black armbands worn to exhibit opposition to this Nation's involvement in Vietnam—was singled out for prohibition. Clearly, the prohibition of expression of one particular opinion, at least without evidence that it is necessary to avoid material and substantial interference with school work or discipline, is not constitutionally permissible.

In our system, state-operated schools may not be enclaves of totalitarianism. School officials do not possess absolute authority over their students. Students in school as well as out of school are "persons" under our Constitution. They are possessed of fundamental rights which the State must respect, just as they themselves must respect their obligations to the State. In our system, students may not be regarded as closed-circuit recipients of only that which the State chooses to communicate. They may not be confined to the expression of those sentiments that are officially approved. In the absence of a specific showing of constitutionally valid reasons to regulate their speech, students are entitled to freedom of expression of their views.

[The principle of prior cases underscoring the importance of diversity and exchange of ideas in the schools,] is not confined to the supervised and ordained discussion which takes place in the classroom. The principal use to which the schools are dedicated is to accommodate students during prescribed hours for the purpose of certain types of activities. Among those activities is personal intercommunication among the students. This is not only an inevitable part of the process of attending school. It is also an important part of the educational process.

A student's rights therefore, do not embrace merely the classroom hours. When he is in the cafeteria, or on the playing field, or on the campus during the authorized hours, he may express his opinions, even on controversial subjects like the conflict in Vietnam, if he does so "[without] materially and substantially interfering [with] appropriate discipline in the operation of the school" and without colliding with the rights of others. *Burnside.* But conduct by the student, in class or out of it, which for any reason—whether it stems from time, place, or type of behavior—materially disrupts classwork or involves substantial disorder or invasion of the rights of others is, of course, not immunized by the [First Amendment].

We properly read [the First Amendment] to permit reasonable regulation of speech-connected activities in carefully restricted circumstances. But we do not confine the permissible exercise of First Amendment rights to a telephone booth or the four corners of a pamphlet, or to supervised and ordained discussion in a school classroom.[c] * * *

---

[c] See also Akhil Reed Amar, *A Tale of Three Wars: Tinker in Constitutional Context,* 48 Drake L.Rev. 507 (2000); Erwin Chemerinsky, *Students Do Leave Their First Amendment Rights*

Reversed and remanded.

JUSTICE STEWART, concurring.[d]

Although I agree with much of what is said in the Court's opinion, and with its judgment in this case, I cannot share the Court's uncritical assumption that, school discipline aside, the First Amendment rights of children are co-extensive with those of adults. Indeed, I had thought the Court decided otherwise just last Term in *Ginsberg v. New York* [Ch. 1, III, B supra.] I continue to hold the view I expressed in that case: "[A] State may permissibly determine that, at least in some precisely delineated areas, a child—like someone in a captive audience—is not possessed of that full capacity for individual choice which is the presupposition of First Amendment guarantees." (concurring opinion). * * *

JUSTICE BLACK, dissenting. * * *

Assuming that the Court is correct in holding that the conduct of wearing armbands for the purpose of conveying political ideas is protected by the First Amendment [, the] crucial remaining questions are whether students and teachers may use the schools at their whim as a platform for the exercise of free speech—"symbolic" or "pure"—and whether the Courts will allocate to themselves the function of deciding how the pupils' school day will be spent. * * *

While the record does not show that any of these armband students shouted, used profane language, or were violent in any manner, detailed testimony by some of them shows their armbands caused comments, warnings by other students, the poking of fun at them, and a warning by an older football player that other, nonprotesting students had better let them alone. There is also evidence that the professor of mathematics had his lesson period practically "wrecked" chiefly by disputes with Beth Tinker, who wore her armband for her "demonstration." Even a casual reading of the record shows that this armband did divert students' minds from their regular lessons, and that talk, comments, etc., made John Tinker "self-conscious" in attending school with his armband. While the absence of obscene or boisterous and loud disorder perhaps justifies the Court's statement that the few armband students did not actually "disrupt" the classwork, I think the record overwhelmingly shows that the armbands did exactly what the elected school officials and principals foresaw it would, that is, took the students' minds off their classwork and diverted them to thoughts about the highly emotional subject of the Vietnam war.

[E]ven if the record were silent as to protests against the Vietnam war distracting students from their assigned class work, members of this Court, like all other citizens, know, without being told, that the disputes

at the Schoolhouse Door: What's Left of Tinker?, *48 Drake L.Rev. 527 (2000); Nadine Strossen,* Keeping the Constitution Inside the Schoolhouse Gate, *48 Drake L.Rev. 445 (2000); Mark Yudof,* When Governments Speak: Toward a Theory of Government Expression and the First Amendment, *57 Tex.L.Rev. 863, 884–85 (1979).*

d. White, J., also briefly concurred.

over the wisdom of the Vietnam war have disrupted and divided this country as few other issues ever have. Of course students, like other people, cannot concentrate on lesser issues when black armbands are being ostentatiously displayed in their presence to call attention to the wounded and dead of the war, some of the wounded and the dead being their friends and neighbors. It was, of course, to distract the attention of other students that some students insisted up to the very point of their own suspension from school that they were determined to sit in school with their symbolic armbands. * * *

JUSTICE HARLAN, dissenting.

I certainly agree that state public school authorities in the discharge of their responsibilities are not wholly exempt from the requirements of the Fourteenth Amendment respecting the freedoms of expression and association. At the same time I am reluctant to believe that there is any disagreement between the majority and myself on the proposition that school officials should be accorded the widest authority in maintaining discipline and good order in their institutions. To translate that proposition into a workable constitutional rule, I would, in cases like this, cast upon those complaining the burden of showing that a particular school measure was motivated by other than legitimate school concerns—for example, a desire to prohibit the expression of an unpopular point of view, while permitting expression of the dominant opinion.

Finding nothing in this record which impugns the good faith of respondents in promulgating the arm band regulation, I would affirm the judgment below.

NOTES AND QUESTIONS

1. Should the government's interest in education trump the school child's interest in speaking in the classroom? Are the two interests compatible in this case? May students be prohibited from voicing their opinions of the Vietnam War in the middle of a math class? If so, why can't they be prevented from expressing their views on the same issue in the same class by means of "symbolic speech"? Cf. Sheldon Nahmod, *Beyond Tinker: The High School as an Educational Public Forum,* 5 Harv.Civ.Rts. & Civ.Lib.L.Rev. 278 (1970).

2. Could school authorities adopt a regulation forbidding *teachers* to wear black armbands in the classroom? Or prohibiting teachers from wearing *all* symbols of political or controversial significance in the classroom or anywhere on school property? Are students a "captive" group? Do the views of a teacher occupying a position of authority carry much more influence with a student than would those of students inter sese? Consider *James v. Board of Educ.,* 461 F.2d 566 (2d Cir.1972), holding that school officials violated a high school teacher's constitutional rights by discharging him because he had worn a black armband in class in symbolic protest of the Vietnam War. But the court stressed that "the armband did not disrupt classroom activities [nor] have any influence on any students and did not engender protest from any student, teacher or parent." What if it had? By implication, did the court

confirm the potency of the "heckler's veto"? See Note, 39 Brook.L.Rev. 918 (1973). Same result if appellant had been a 3rd grade teacher rather than an 11th grade teacher? See Steven Shiffrin, *Government Speech*, 27 U.C.L.A.L.Rev. 565, 647–53 (1980).

3. **Viewpoint-discriminatory restrictions on student speech.** Can a school district prohibit the expression of racist views or anti-gay views on the ground that they threaten substantial disruption and interfere with the promotion of multicultural views with respect to race and sexual orientation? See John E. Taylor, *Tinker and Viewpoint Discrimination*, 77 UMKC L.Rev. 569 (2009); Kristi L. Bowman, *Public School Student's Religious Speech and Viewpoint Discrimination*, 110 W.Va. L. Rev. 187 (2007).

4. MORSE v. FREDERICK, 551 U.S. 393 (2007), per ROBERTS, C.J., upheld the suspension of a high school student for refusing to take down a banner at a school sponsored event that read "BONG HiTS 4 JESUS": "The concern is not that Frederick's speech is offensive, but that it was reasonably viewed as promoting illegal drug use."

ALITO, J., joined by Kennedy, J., concurring, joined the Court's opinion on the understanding that it "goes no further than to hold that a public school may restrict speech that a reasonable observer would interpret as advocating illegal drug use" and provides no support for restricting comments on political or social issues including "the wisdom of the war on drugs or legalizing marijuana for medicinal use."[e]

THOMAS, J., concurring, would overrule *Tinker*: "In light of the history of American public education, it cannot be seriously suggested that the First Amendment 'freedom of speech' encompasses a student's right to speak in public schools. Early public schools gave total control to teachers, who expected obedience and respect from students."[f]

STEVENS, J., joined by Souter and Ginsburg, JJ., dissenting, thought it was not reasonable to conclude that the message on the banner advocated drug use or that it would persuade students to use drugs.

5. **Guidance to lower courts**. The lower courts are struggling with cases involving apprehension of or threats of student violence. In addition, many cases involve student criticism of teachers and administrators. Does *Morse* provide guidance? Consider Frederick Schauer, *Abandoning the Guidance Function: Morse v. Frederick*, 2007 Sup. Ct. Rev. 205, 209–10: "Faced with an opportunity to say something helpful to and for those in the trenches, the Court not only selected a highly unrepresentative case for its first foray into the area in nineteen years, but it also decided the case on narrow grounds, and in doing so focused on those dimensions of the case least likely to be found in the conflicts that bedevil school administrators and lower courts on an almost daily basis."

---

e. Breyer, J., concurring in part and dissenting in part would not have reached the First Amendment issue except to maintain that it was close enough that the high school principal could not be held liable for monetary damages. For commentary on *Morse*, see Stephen M. Feldman, *Free Expression and Education: Between Two Democracies*, 16 Wm. & Mary Bill Rts.J. 999 (2008); Negron, fn. b supra.

f. For criticism of Thomas, J.'s methodology, see Vikram D. Amar, *Morse, School Speech, and Originalism*, 42 U.C. Davis L.Rev. 637 (2009).

6. Consider Jamin B. Raskin, *No Enclaves of Totalitarianism,* 58 Am. U.L. Rev. 1193, 1196 (2009): *Tinker* has been eroded "by the sharp undertow of sympathy for authoritarian structure on the Burger, Rehnquist, and Roberts Courts. The conservative court has carved out major exceptions to *Tinker* in the interests of social conformity, sexual prudishness, protection of sexual adults' feelings, and promotion of ideological unity for drug prohibition." Consider also Chemerinsky, fn. a supra, at 529: "[I]n the three decades since *Tinker*, the courts have made it clear that students leave most of their constitutional rights at the schoolhouse gate. The judiciary's unquestioning acceptance of the need for deference to school authority leaves relatively little room for protecting student's constitutional rights. The decisions over the past thirty years are far closer to Justice Black's dissent in *Tinker* than they are to Justice Fortas's majority opinion."**g**

HAZELWOOD SCHOOL DISTRICT v. KUHLMEIER

484 U.S. 260, 108 S.Ct. 562, 98 L.Ed.2d 592 (1988).

JUSTICE WHITE delivered the opinion of the Court. * * *

Petitioners are the Hazelwood School District in St. Louis County, Missouri; various school officials; Robert Eugene Reynolds, the principal of Hazelwood East High School, and Howard Emerson, a teacher in the school district. Respondents are three former Hazelwood East students who were staff members of Spectrum, the school newspaper. * * *

The practice at Hazelwood East during the spring 1983 semester was for the journalism teacher to submit page proofs of each Spectrum issue to Principal Reynolds for his review prior to publication. On May 10, Emerson delivered the proofs of the May 13 edition to Reynolds, who objected to two of the articles scheduled to appear in that edition. One of the stories described three Hazelwood East students' experiences with pregnancy; the other discussed the impact of divorce on students at the school.

Reynolds was concerned that, although the pregnancy story used false names "to keep the identity of these girls a secret," the pregnant students still might be identifiable from the text. He also believed that the article's references to sexual activity and birth control were inappropriate for some of the younger students at the school. In addition, Reynolds was concerned that a student identified by name in the divorce story had complained [about] her father * * *. Reynolds believed that the student's parents should have been given an opportunity to respond to these remarks or to

---

g. For a review of the cases together with opposition to the extension of *Tinker* to off campus speech, see Mary-Rose Papandreu, *Student Speech Rights in the Digital Age,* 60 Fla. L.Rev. 1027 (2008). For an argument that the appropriate test should depend whether the speaker acts in the role of a student or in the role of a citizen, Benjamin F. Heidlage, *A Relational Approach to School's Regulation of Youth Online Speech,* 84 N.Y.U.L.Rev. 572 (2009). See also Clay Calvert, *Tinker Turns 40,* 58 Am. U.L. Rev. 1167 (2009); Fiona Ruthven, *Is the True Threat the Student or the School Board? Punishing Threatening Student Expression,* 88 Iowa L. Rev. 931 (2003); Robert D. Richards and Clay Calvert, *Columbine Fallout: The Long–Term Effects on Free Expression Take Hold in Public Schools,* 83 B.U. L. Rev. 1089 (2003); Lisa M. Pisciotta, *Beyond Sticks & Stones: A First Amendment Framework for Educators Who Seek to Punish Student Threats,* 30 Seton Hall L. Rev. 635 (2000).

consent to their publication. He was unaware that Emerson had deleted the student's name from the final version of the article.

Reynolds believed that there was no time to make the necessary changes in the stories before the scheduled press run and that the newspaper would not appear before the end of the school year if printing were delayed to any significant extent. He concluded that his only options under the circumstances were to publish a four-page newspaper instead of the planned six-page newspaper, eliminating the two pages on which the offending stories appeared, or to publish no newspaper at all. Accordingly, he directed Emerson to withhold from publication the two pages containing the stories on pregnancy and divorce.[1] He informed his superiors of the decision, and they concurred. * * *

[T]he First Amendment rights of students in the public schools "are not automatically coextensive with the rights of adults in other settings," *Bethel School District No. 403 v. Fraser,* 478 U.S. 675 (1986), and must be "applied in light of the special characteristics of the school environment." *Tinker.* A school need not tolerate student speech that is inconsistent with its "basic educational mission," *Fraser,* even though the government could not censor similar speech outside the school. Accordingly, we held in *Fraser* that a student could be disciplined for having delivered a speech that was "sexually explicit" but not legally obscene at an official school [assembly]. We thus recognized that "[t]he determination of what manner of speech in the classroom or in school assembly is inappropriate properly rests with the school board," rather than with the federal courts. * * *

We deal first with the question whether Spectrum may appropriately be characterized as a forum for public expression. [T]he evidence relied upon by the Court of Appeals fails to demonstrate the "clear intent to create a public forum," *Cornelius,* that existed in cases in which we found public forums to have been created. School [officials] "reserve[d] the forum for its intended purpos[e]," *Perry,* as a supervised learning experience for journalism students. Accordingly, school officials were entitled to regulate the contents of Spectrum in any reasonable manner. * * *

The question whether the First Amendment requires a school to tolerate particular student speech—the question that we addressed in *Tinker*—is different from the question whether the First Amendment requires a school affirmatively to promote particular student speech. The former question addresses educators' ability to silence a student's personal expression that happens to occur on the school premises. The latter question concerns educators' authority over school-sponsored publications, theatrical productions, and other expressive activities that students, parents, and members of the public might reasonably perceive to bear the imprimatur of the school. These activities may fairly be characterized as part of the school curriculum, whether or not they occur in a traditional

---

1. The two pages deleted from the newspaper also contained articles on teenage marriage, runaways, and juvenile delinquents, as well as a general article on teenage pregnancy. Reynolds testified that he had no objection to these articles and that they were deleted only because they appeared on the same pages as the two objectionable articles.

classroom setting, so long as they are supervised by faculty members and designed to impart particular knowledge or skills to student participants and audiences.

[A] school may in its capacity as publisher of a school newspaper or producer of a school play "disassociate itself," *Fraser,* not only from speech that would "substantially interfere with [its] work [or] impinge upon the rights of other students," *Tinker,* but also from speech that is, for example, ungrammatical, poorly written, inadequately researched, biased or prejudiced, vulgar or profane, or unsuitable for immature audiences.[4] A school must be able to set high standards for the student speech that is disseminated under its auspices—standards that may be higher than those demanded by some newspaper publishers or theatrical producers in the "real" world—and may refuse to disseminate student speech that does not meet those standards. [Otherwise,] the schools would be unduly constrained from fulfilling their role as "a principal instrument in awakening the child to cultural values, in preparing him for later professional training, and in helping him to adjust normally to his environment." *Brown v. Board of Education.*

Accordingly, we conclude that the standard articulated in *Tinker* for determining when a school may punish student expression need not also be the standard for determining when a school may refuse to lend its name and resources to the dissemination of student expression. Instead, we hold that educators do not offend the First Amendment by exercising editorial control over the style and content of student speech in school-sponsored expressive activities so long as their actions are reasonably related to legitimate pedagogical concerns.[7] * * *a

JUSTICE BRENNAN, with whom JUSTICE MARSHALL and JUSTICE BLACKMUN join, dissenting.

[Under] *Tinker,* school officials may censor only such student speech as would "materially disrup[t]" a legitimate curricular function. Manifestly, student speech is more likely to disrupt a curricular function when it

---

4. [The] decision in *Fraser* rested on the "vulgar," "lewd," and "plainly offensive" character of a speech delivered at an official school assembly rather than on any propensity of the speech to "materially disrupt[ ] classwork or involve[ ] substantial disorder or invasion of the rights of others." Indeed, the *Fraser* Court cited as "especially relevant" a portion of Justice Black's dissenting opinion in *Tinker* "disclaim[ing] any purpose [to] hold that the Federal Constitution compels the teachers, parents and elected school officials to surrender control of the American public school system to public school students." Of course, Justice Black's observations are equally relevant to the instant case.

7. A number of lower federal courts have similarly recognized that educators' decisions with regard to the content of school sponsored newspapers, dramatic productions, and other expressive activities are entitled to substantial deference. We need not now decide whether the same degree of deference is appropriate with respect to school-sponsored expressive activities at the college and university level.

a. White, J., concluded that Principal Reynolds acted reasonably in requiring deletion of the pages from the newspaper. In addition to concerns about privacy and failure to contact persons discussed in the stories, it was "not unreasonable for the principal to have concluded that [frank talk about sexual histories, albeit not graphic, with comments about use or nonuse of birth control] was inappropriate in a school-sponsored publication distributed to 14–year-old freshmen and presumably taken home to be read by students' even younger brothers and sisters."

arises in the context of a curricular activity—one that "is designed to teach" something—than when it arises in the context of a noncurricular activity. Thus, under *Tinker,* the school may constitutionally punish the budding political orator if he disrupts calculus class but not if he holds his tongue for the cafeteria. That is not because some more stringent standard applies in the curricular context. (After all, this Court applied the same standard whether the Tinkers wore their armbands to the "classroom" or the "cafeteria.") It is because student speech in the noncurricular context is less likely to disrupt materially any legitimate pedagogical purpose.

I fully agree with the Court that the First Amendment should afford an educator the prerogative not to sponsor the publication of a newspaper article that is "ungrammatical, poorly written, inadequately researched, biased or prejudiced," or that falls short of the "high standards [for] student speech that is disseminated under [the school's] auspices." But we need not abandon *Tinker* to reach that conclusion; we need only apply it. The enumerated criteria reflect the skills that the curricular newspaper "is designed to teach." The educator may, under *Tinker,* constitutionally "censor" poor grammar, writing, or research because to reward such expression would "materially disrup[t]" the newspaper's curricular purpose. * * *

The Court relies on bits of testimony to portray the principal's conduct as a pedagogical lesson to Journalism II students who "had not sufficiently mastered those portions of [the] curriculum that pertained to the treatment of controversial issues and personal attacks, the need to protect the privacy of individuals [and] 'the legal, moral, and ethical restrictions imposed upon journalists * * *.' "

But the principal never consulted the students before censoring their work. [T]hey learned of the deletions when the paper was released. [Further,] he explained the deletions only in the broadest of generalities. In one meeting called at the behest of seven protesting Spectrum staff members (presumably a fraction of the full class), he characterized the articles as " 'too sensitive' for 'our immature audience of readers,' " and in a later meeting he deemed them simply "inappropriate, personal, sensitive and unsuitable for the newspaper." The Court's supposition that the principal intended (or the protesters understood) those generalities as a lesson on the nuances of journalistic responsibility is utterly incredible. If he did, a fact that neither the District Court nor the Court of Appeals found, the lesson was lost on all but the psychic Spectrum staffer.

The Court's second excuse for deviating from precedent is the school's interest in shielding an impressionable high school audience from material whose substance is "unsuitable for immature audiences." [*Tinker*] teaches us that the state educator's undeniable, and undeniably vital, mandate to inculcate moral and political values is not a general warrant to act as "thought police" stifling discussion of all but state-approved topics and advocacy of all but the official position. [The] mere fact of school sponsorship does not, as the Court suggests, license such thought control in the high school, whether through school suppression of disfavored viewpoints or through official assessment of topic sensitivity. [Moreover, the] State's prerogative to dissolve the student newspaper entirely (or to limit its subject matter) no more entitles it to dictate which viewpoints students may express on its pages, than the State's prerogative to close down the schoolhouse entitles it to prohibit the nondisruptive expression of antiwar sentiment within its gates.

Official censorship of student speech on the ground that it addresses "potentially sensitive topics" is, for related reasons, equally impermissible. I would not begrudge an educator the authority to limit the substantive scope of a school-sponsored publication to a certain, objectively definable topic, such as literary criticism, school sports, or an overview of the school year. Unlike those determinate limitations, "potential topic sensitivity" is a vaporous nonstandard [that] invites manipulation to achieve ends that cannot permissibly be achieved through blatant viewpoint discrimination and chills student speech to which school officials might not object. * * *b

NOTES AND QUESTIONS

1. Consider Bruce Hafen, *Hazelwood School District and the Role of First Amendment Institutions,* 1988 Duke L.J. 685, 701, 704–05: "[T]he question whether authoritarian or anti-authoritarian approaches will best develop the minds and expressive powers of children is more a matter of educational philosophy and practice than of constitutional law. For that reason alone, First Amendment theories applied by courts largely on the basis of anti-authoritarian assumptions are at best a clumsy and limited means of ensuring optimal educational development, whether the goal is an understanding of democratic values or a mastery of basic intellectual skills. Thus, one of *Hazelwood's* major contributions is its reaffirmation of schools' institutional role—and their accountability to the public for fulfilling it responsibly—in nurturing the underlying values of the First Amendment. * * *

"The First Amendment must [protect] not only individual writers, but newspapers; not only religious persons, but churches; not only individual students and teachers, but schools. These 'intellectual and moral associations' form a crucial part of the constitutional structure, for they help teach the peculiar and sometimes paradoxical blend of liberty and duty that sustains both individual freedom and the entire culture from one generation to the next."

2. Consider Martha Minow & Elizabeth Spellman, *Passion For Justice,* 10 Cardozo L.Rev. 37, 68–69 (1988): "The majority does not acknowledge the power it is exercising in the act of deferring to the 'reasonable' judgments of the [principal:] the power to signal to school officials all around the country, that it is all right to err on the side of eliminating student speech, it is all

---

b. Brennan, J. further argued that the material deleted was not conceivably tortious and that less restrictive alternatives, such as more precise deletions, were readily available.

right to indulge your paternalistic attitudes toward the students; you do not need to guard against your own discomfort with what students want to discuss, for the 'rights' really lie within your own judgment about what they need. [The] dissent is acutely sensitive to the impact of censorship on students, but less attentive to the impact of judicial review on the school officials. Although equal attention to competing sides may make a decision more difficult, refraining from seeing the power of competing arguments itself may lead to tragic blindness."

3. ***Extending Hazelwood.*** Consider Karyl Roberts Martin, *Demoted to High School: Are College Students' Free Speech Rights the Same as Those of High School Students?*, 45 B.C. L. Rev. 173, 183–184 (2003): "Since [*Hazelwood*], lower courts have consistently applied the 'legitimate pedagogical concerns' test to allow elementary and secondary schools to restrict students' and teachers' expression in a variety of 'school-sponsored' contexts. The circuit courts have disagreed, however, on the extent to which schools can regulate speech based on the particular viewpoint expressed."[c] See *Boring v. Buncombe County Board of Education*, 136 F.3d 364 (4th Cir.1998)(drama teacher selects play involving a dysfunctional divorced single parent family including a lesbian daughter and an unmarried pregnant daughter); *Ward v. Hickey*, 996 F.2d 448 (1st Cir. 1993) (teacher discusses abortion of Down's Syndrome fetus in ninth grade biology class). Should *Hazelwood* have any application at the college level?[d]

Is the "legitimate pedagogical concerns" test one for which judges have no expertise? When government manages and directs speech as its primary activity in a particular sphere, should the First Amendment be inapplicable? If making content decisions in supervising a newspaper or grading student efforts is a regular part of a teacher's job is the potential for judicial intervention an unnecessarily "stifling burden"? See Alan Brownstein, *The NonForum as a First Amendment Category*, 42 UC Davis L.Rev. 717, 790 (2009).

III. GOVERNMENT AS EMPLOYER

Ceballos, a supervising district attorney, wrote a disposition memorandum in which he recommended dismissal of a case on the ground that the affidavit in support of a search warrant contained false representations. As a result of the memorandum, which he characterized as protected speech, Ceballos maintained he was unconstitutionally transferred to a

---

c. See Jessica B. Lyons, *Defining Freedom of the College Press After Hosty v. Carter,* 59 Vand. L.Rev. 1771 (2006); Gail Sorenson & Andrew S. LaManque, *The Application of Hazelwood v. Kuhlmeier in College Litigation,* 22 J. of College & Univ. Law 971 (1996). For a range of views on academic freedom, consider Ronald Dworkin, *Freedom's Law* ch. 11 (1996); Amy Gutmann, *Democratic Education* (rev. ed. 1999); William G. Buss, *Academic Freedom and Freedom of Speech: Communicating the Curriculum,* 2 J. of Gender, Race & Justice 213 (1999); J. Peter Byrne, *Academic Freedom: A "Special Concern of the First Amendment,"* 99 Yale L.J. 251 (1989); Merle H. Weiner, *Dirty Words in the Classroom: Teaching the Limits of the First Amendment,* 66 Tenn.L.Rev. 597 (1999); William W. Van Alstyne, *Academic Freedom and the First Amendment in the Supreme Court of the United States: An Unhurried Historical Review,* 53 Law & Contemp. Probs. 79 (1990).

d. Walter E. Kuhn, *First Amendment Protection of Teacher Instructional Speech,* 55 Duke L.J. 995 (2006).

less desirable work location and denied a promotion in retaliation. GAR-CETTI v. CEBALLOS, 547 U.S. 410 (2006), per KENNEDY, J., held that the memorandum was pursuant to his official duties as a supervising district attorney and, therefore, not protected by the First Amendment: *"Pickering v. Bd. Of Educ.*, 391 U.S. 563 (1968)[a] and the cases decided in its wake identify two inquiries to guide interpretation of the constitutional protections accorded to public employee speech. The first requires determining whether the employee spoke as a citizen on a matter of public concern. If the answer is no, the employee has no First Amendment cause of action based on his or her employer's reaction to the speech. If the answer is yes, then the possibility of a First Amendment claim arises. The question becomes whether the relevant government entity had an adequate justification for treating the employee differently from any other member of the general public. This consideration reflects the importance of the relationship between the speaker's expressions and employment. A government entity has broader discretion to restrict speech when it acts in its role as employer, but the restrictions it imposes must be directed at speech that has some potential to affect the entity's operations. * * *

"When a citizen enters government service, the citizen by necessity must accept certain limitations on his or her freedom. Government employers, like private employers, need a significant degree of control over their employees 'words and actions; without it, there would be little chance for the efficient provision of public services. Public employees, moreover, often occupy trusted positions in society. When they speak out, they can express views that contravene governmental policies or impair the proper performance of governmental functions.

"At the same time, the Court has recognized that a citizen who works for the government is nonetheless a citizen. The First Amendment limits the ability of a public employer to leverage the employment relationship to restrict, incidentally or intentionally, the liberties employees enjoy in their capacities as private citizens.[b] So long as employees are speaking as citizens about matters of public concern, they must face only those speech restrictions that are necessary for their employers to operate efficiently and effectively. * * *

"The controlling factor in Ceballos' case is that his expressions were made pursuant to his duties as a calendar deputy. That consideration—the fact that Ceballos spoke as a prosecutor fulfilling a responsibility to advise his supervisor about how best to proceed with a pending case—

---

a. *Pickering* held that the First Amendment protected a teacher who published a letter in a newspaper criticizing the Board of Education. *Givhan v. Western Line Cons. School Dist.*, 439 U.S. 410 (1979), held that a private communication of an employee with an employer concerning racially discriminatory policies was similarly protected.

b. *Elrod v. Burns*, 427 U.S. 347 (1976), held that nonpolicymaking and nonconfidential employees could not be dismissed simply because they were not affiliated with a particular political party, and *Rutan v. Republican Party of Illinois*, 497 U.S. 62 (1990), extended *Elrod* to hiring decisions. But *United Public Workers v. Mitchell*, 330 U.S. 75 (1947), and *U.S. Civil Service Comm'n v. Letter Carriers*, 413 U.S. 548 (1973), upheld Hatch Act restrictions on participation by government employees in political campaigns.

distinguishes Ceballos' case from those in which the First Amendment provides protection against discipline. We hold that when public employees make statements pursuant to their official duties, the employees are not speaking as citizens for First Amendment purposes, and the Constitution does not insulate their communications from employer discipline. * * *

"This result is consistent with our precedents' attention to the potential societal value of employee speech. Refusing to recognize First Amendment claims based on government employees' work product does not prevent them from participating in public debate. The employees retain the prospect of constitutional protection for their contributions to the civic discourse. This prospect of protection, however, does not invest them with a right to perform their jobs however they see fit. * * *

"Ceballos' proposed contrary rule [would] commit state and federal courts to a new, permanent, and intrusive role, mandating judicial oversight of communications between and among government employees and their superiors in the course of official business. This displacement of managerial discretion by judicial supervision finds no support in our precedents. When an employee speaks as a citizen addressing a matter of public concern, the First Amendment requires a delicate balancing of the competing interests surrounding the speech and its consequences. When, however, the employee is simply performing his or her job duties, there is no warrant for a similar degree of scrutiny. To hold otherwise would be to demand permanent judicial intervention in the conduct of governmental operations to a degree inconsistent with sound principles of federalism and the separation of powers.

"The Court of Appeals based its holding in part on what it perceived as a doctrinal anomaly. The court suggested it would be inconsistent to compel public employers to tolerate certain employee speech made publicly but not speech made pursuant to an employee's assigned duties. This objection misconceives the theoretical underpinnings of our decisions. Employees who make public statements outside the course of performing their official duties retain some possibility of First Amendment protection because that is the kind of activity engaged in by citizens who do not work for the government. The same goes for writing a letter to a local newspaper, see *Pickering*, or discussing politics with a co-worker, see *Rankin v. McPherson*, 483 U.S. 378 (1987).[c] When a public employee speaks pursuant to employment responsibilities, however, there is no relevant analogue to speech by citizens who are not government employees.

"The Court of Appeals' concern also is unfounded as a practical matter. The perceived anomaly, it should be noted, is limited in scope: It relates only to the expressions an employee makes pursuant to his or her

---

c. *Rankin* held that a secretary in a law enforcement agency was protected in saying at work in private to a co-worker that next time she hoped an assassination attempt on President Reagan would be successful.

official responsibilities, not to statements or complaints (such as those at issue in cases like *Pickering* and *Connick v. Myers*, 461 U.S 138 (1983)[d] that are made outside the duties of employment. If, moreover, a government employer is troubled by the perceived anomaly, it has the means at hand to avoid it. A public employer that wishes to encourage its employees to voice concerns privately retains the option of instituting internal policies and procedures that are receptive to employee criticism. Giving employees an internal forum for their speech will discourage them from concluding that the safest avenue of expression is to state their views in public. * * *

"Two final points warrant mentioning. First, as indicated above, the parties in this case do not dispute that Ceballos wrote his disposition memo pursuant to his employment duties. We thus have no occasion to articulate a comprehensive framework for defining the scope of an employee's duties in cases where there is room for serious debate. We reject, however, the suggestion that employers can restrict employees' rights by creating excessively broad job descriptions. The proper inquiry is a practical one. Formal job descriptions often bear little resemblance to the duties an employee actually is expected to perform, and the listing of a given task in an employee's written job description is neither necessary nor sufficient to demonstrate that conducting the task is within the scope of the employee's professional duties for First Amendment purposes.

"Second, Justice Souter suggests today's decision may have important ramifications for academic freedom, at least as a constitutional value. There is some argument that expression related to academic scholarship or classroom instruction implicates additional constitutional interests that are not fully accounted for by this Court's customary employee-speech jurisprudence. We need not, and for that reason do not, decide whether the analysis we conduct today would apply in the same manner to a case involving speech related to scholarship or teaching."[e]

SOUTER, J., joined by Stevens and Ginsburg, JJ., dissented: "In *Givhan*, we followed *Pickering* when a teacher was fired for complaining to a superior about the racial composition of the school's administrative, cafeteria, and library [staffs]. The difference between a case like *Givhan* and this one is that the subject of Cembalos' speech fell within the scope of his job responsibilities, whereas choosing personnel was not what the

---

d. *Connick* upheld the dismissal of an Assistant D.A. for distributing a questionnaire to other assistants calling into question office transfer policy, the need for a grievance committee, office morale, the level of confidence in various supervisors, and whether employees felt pressure to participate in political campaigns.

e. The case was remanded because Ceballos had made other statements that were arguably outside the scope of his official duties that may have given rise to retaliation. In another case with implications for discussion of government operations, an acquittee in a federal fraud prosecution brought an action against criminal investigators for inducing prosecution in retaliation for political speech concerning the postal department. Despite a showing of animus by the investigators and a statement by the prosecutor that he was not galvanized to prosecute by the merits of the case, *Hartman v. Moore*, 547 U.S. 250 (2006), required that the plaintiff also show a lack of probable cause as an element of the offence. For a case showing that prisoners have more limited rights than government employees, see *Beard v. Banks*, 126 S.Ct. 2572 (2006). Does the diversity of standards in special contexts have implications for First Amendment theory?

teacher was hired to do. The effect of the majority's constitutional line between these two cases, then, is that a *Givhan* schoolteacher is protected when complaining to the principal about hiring policy, but a school personnel officer would not be if he protested that the principal disapproved of hiring minority job applicants. This is an odd place to draw a distinction, and while necessary judicial line-drawing sometimes looks arbitrary, any distinction obliges a court to justify its choice. Here, there is no adequate justification for the majority's line categorically denying *Pickering* protection to any speech uttered 'pursuant [to] official duties.'

"As all agree, the qualified speech protection embodied in *Pickering* balancing resolves the tension between individual and public interests in the speech, on the one hand, and the government's interest in operating efficiently without distraction or embarrassment by talkative or headline-grabbing employees. The need for a balance hardly disappears when an employee speaks on matters his job requires him to address; rather, it seems obvious that the individual and public value of such speech is no less, and may well be greater, when the employee speaks pursuant to his duties in addressing a subject he knows intimately for the very reason that it falls within his duties. * * *

"Nothing [accountable] on the individual and public side of the *Pickering* balance changes when an employee speaks 'pursuant' to public duties.[f] On the side of the government employer, however, something is different, and to this extent, I agree with the majority of the Court. The majority is rightly concerned that the employee who speaks out on matters subject to comment in doing his own work has the greater leverage to create office uproars and fracture the government's authority to set policy to be carried out coherently through the ranks. [Up] to a point, then, the majority makes good points: government needs civility in the workplace, consistency in policy, and honesty and competence in public service.

"But why do the majority's concerns, which we all share, require categorical exclusion of First Amendment protection against any official retaliation for things said on the job? Is it not possible to respect the unchallenged individual and public interests in the speech through a *Pickering* balance without drawing the strange line I mentioned before? This is, to be sure, a matter of judgment, but the judgment has to account for the undoubted value of speech to those, and by those, whose specific public job responsibilities bring them face to face with wrongdoing and incompetence in government, who refuse to avert their eyes and shut their mouths. And it has to account for the need actually to disrupt government if its officials are corrupt or dangerously incompetent. It is thus no adequate justification for the suppression of potentially valuable informa-

---

f. Later in his opinion, Souter, J., observed: "This ostensible domain beyond the pale of the First Amendment is spacious enough to include even the teaching of a public university professor, and I have to hope that today's majority does not mean to imperil First Amendment protection of academic freedom in public colleges and universities, whose teachers necessarily speak and write 'pursuant to official duties.'"

tion simply to recognize that the government has a huge interest in managing its employees and preventing the occasionally irresponsible one from turning his job into a bully pulpit. Even there, the lesson of *Pickering* (and the object of most constitutional adjudication) is still to the point: when constitutionally significant interests clash, resist the demand for winner-take-all; try to make adjustments that serve all of the values at stake.

"[T]he basic *Pickering* balancing scheme is perfectly feasible here. First, the extent of the government's legitimate authority over subjects of speech required by a public job can be recognized in advance by setting in effect a minimum heft for comments with any claim to outweigh it. Thus, the risks to the government are great enough for us to hold from the outset that an employee commenting on subjects in the course of duties should not prevail on balance unless he speaks on a matter of unusual importance and satisfies high standards of responsibility in the way he does it. The examples I have already given indicate the eligible subject matter, and it is fair to say that only comment on official dishonesty, deliberately unconstitutional action, other serious wrongdoing, or threats to health and safety can weigh out in an employee's favor. If promulgation of this standard should fail to discourage meritless actions [before] they get filed, the standard itself would sift them out at the summary-judgment stage."

BREYER, J., dissented: "The majority [holds] that 'when public employees make statements pursuant to their official duties, the employees are not speaking as citizens for First Amendment purposes, and the Constitution does not insulate their communications from employer discipline.' In a word, the majority says, 'never.' That word, in my view, is too absolute.

"Like the majority, I understand the need to 'affor[d] government employers sufficient discretion to manage their operations.' And I agree that the Constitution does not seek to 'displac[e] managerial discretion by judicial supervision.' Nonetheless, there may well be circumstances with special demand for constitutional protection of the speech at issue, where governmental justifications may be limited, and where administrable standards seem readily available—to the point where the majority's fears of department management by lawsuit are misplaced. [This] is such a case. * * *

"First, the speech at issue is professional speech—the speech of a lawyer. Such speech is subject to independent regulation by canons of the profession. Those canons provide an obligation to speak in certain instances. And where that is so, the government's own interest in forbidding that speech is diminished. The objective specificity and public availability of the profession's canons also help to diminish the risk that the courts will improperly interfere with the government's necessary authority to manage its work.

"Second, the Constitution itself here imposes speech obligations upon the government's professional employee. A prosecutor has a constitutional obligation to learn of, to preserve, and to communicate with the defense about exculpatory and impeachment evidence in the government's possession. So, for example, might a prison doctor have a similar constitutionally related professional obligation to communicate with superiors about seriously unsafe or unsanitary conditions in the cellblock. There may well be other examples.

"Where professional and special constitutional obligations are both present, the need to protect the employee's speech is augmented, the need for broad government authority to control that speech is likely diminished, and administrable standards are quite likely available. Hence, I would find that the Constitution mandates special protection of employee speech in such circumstances. Thus I would apply the *Pickering* balancing test here.

"While I agree with much of Justice Souter's analysis, I believe that the constitutional standard he enunciates fails to give sufficient weight to the serious managerial and administrative concerns that the majority describes. The standard would instruct courts to apply *Pickering* balancing in all cases, but says that the government should prevail unless the employee (1) 'speaks on a matter of unusual importance,' and (2) 'satisfies high standards of responsibility in the way he does it.' Justice Souter adds that 'only comment on official dishonesty, deliberately unconstitutional action, other serious wrongdoing, or threats to health and safety can weigh out in an employee's favor.'

"There are, however, far too many issues of public concern, even if defined as 'matters of unusual importance,' for the screen to screen out very much. Government administration typically involves matters of public concern. Why else would government be involved? And 'public issues,' indeed, matters of 'unusual importance,' are often daily bread-and-butter concerns for the police, the intelligence agencies, the military, and many whose jobs involve protecting the public's health, safety, and the environment. This aspect of Justice Souter's 'adjustment' of 'the basic *Pickering* balancing scheme' is similar to the Court's present insistence that speech be of 'legitimate news interest', when the employee speaks only as a private citizen. It gives no extra weight to the government's augmented need to direct speech that is an ordinary part of the employee's job-related duties.

"Moreover, the speech of vast numbers of public employees deals with wrongdoing, health, safety, and honesty: for example, police officers, firefighters, environmental protection agents, building inspectors, hospital workers, bank regulators, and so on. Indeed, this categorization could encompass speech by an employee performing almost any public function, except perhaps setting electricity rates. Nor do these categories bear any obvious relation to the constitutional importance of protecting the job-related speech at issue.

"The underlying problem with this breadth of coverage is that the standard (despite predictions that the government is likely to *prevail* in the balance unless the speech concerns 'official dishonesty, deliberately unconstitutional action, other serious wrongdoing, or threats to health and safety,') does not avoid the judicial need to *undertake the balance* in the first place. * * *

"I conclude that the First Amendment sometimes does authorize judicial actions based upon a government employee's speech that both (1) involves a matter of public concern and also (2) takes place in the course of ordinary job-related duties. But it does so only in the presence of augmented need for constitutional protection and diminished risk of undue judicial interference with governmental management of the public's affairs."[g]

NOTES AND QUESTIONS

1. **Speech within government institutions.** The doctrine affords diminished free speech protection within government institutions such as schools and workplaces. Does this shortchange the "First Amendment aims of facilitating the search for truth, promoting self-government, and checking governmental misconduct" and of "autonomy and self-fulfillment." See Gina B. Lee, *First Amendment Enforcement in Government Institutions and Programs*, 56 UCLA L.Rev. 1691, 1713–14, 1715–16 (2009). Is it consistent with *Tinker*? Consider Jamin B. Raskin, *No Enclaves of Totalitarianism*, 58 Am. U.L. Rev. 1193, 1211 (2009): "The basic meaning of *Tinker* [was] that a student at a school is still a citizen clothed with constitutional rights that she does not surrender simply because she is in a learning relationship with teachers paid by the government. Yet, Justice Kennedy essentially finds that a public employee does shed his First Amendment rights entering the gates of the government workplace."

2. **Political accountability.** Is government control over the speech of employees needed if government is to be politically accountable? See Lawrence Rosenthal, *The Emerging First Amendment of Managerial Prerogative*, 77 Ford. L.Rev. 33 (2008).

3. **Sexual harassment.** Does *Garcetti* remove any limits on government's attempts to limit what it regards as sexually harassing speech? Consider Rosenthal, id. at 79: "*Garcetti* ultimately rests on a notion that management has a right to control how public employees perform their jobs; and surely that includes how they treat each other. Just as a public employer can 'prohibit its employees from being rude to its customers,' it can insist that they not be rude to each other."

4. **Dissent.** Does *Garcetti* provide inadequate protection for dissent in the public workplace? Would balancing of the relevant values be preferable to a per se rules? See Julie A Wenell, *Garcetti v. Ceballos: Stifling the First Amendment in the Public Workplace*, 16 Wm. & Mary Bill Rights J. 621

---

g. Stevens, J., also dissented.

(2007); Sheldon H. Nahmod, *Public Employee Speech, Categorical Balancing, and § 1983*, 42 U. Rich. L. Rev. 561 (2008).

5. **Academic freedom.** Should *Garcetti* be extended to teaching in elementary and secondary classrooms or would a balancing test be preferable? See Neal H. Hutchens, *Silence at the Schoolhouse Gate*, 97 Ky. L.Rev. 37 (2008). Should *Garcetti* be extended to teaching in college classrooms? To academic research and publication? Does public forum doctrine assist in answering these questions? See Darryn Cathryn Beckstrom, *Reconciling the Public Employee Speech Doctrine and Academic Speech After Garcetti v. Ceballos*, 94 Minn. L.Rev. 1202 (2010). Should universities be regarded as First Amendment institutions? See Paul Horwitz, *Universities as First Amendment* Institutions, 54 UCLA L.Rev. 1497 (2007).

Consider Alexander Wohl, *Oiling the Schoolhouse Gate*, 58 Am. U.L.Rev. 1285, 1307 (2009): "Though *Garcetti* may indeed leave some room for the speech of college instructors, the likelihood that any protections will fall to K-12 teachers is extremely small." Does the existence of tenure mitigate this damage?

6. **Off the job speech.** (a) A long line of cases has established that employees may not be dismissed because of their affiliation with a political party. *Elrod v.* Burns, 427 U.S. 347 (1976). If employees engage in off the job speech, their protection depends upon the principles developed in *Pickering*. Will *Garcetti* provide excessive incentive for employees to go public with criticisms of their employer? Consider Consider Patrick Morvan, *A Comparison of the Freedom of Speech of Workers in French and American Law*, 84 Ind. L.J. 1015, 1020–21 (2009). By encouraging employees to inform the public instead of their supervisors of wrongdoing, does the decision encourage twenty-two million public employees "to break the chain of command and adopt an attitude otherwise more subversive and detrimental to their employer's interests?" But see Helen Norton, *Constraining Public Employee Speech*, 59 Duke L.J. 67–68 (2009): "[C]ourts too readily permit government to punish public employees for their speech away from work, deferring to government claims that even off-duty expression sufficiently reflects upon the government to justify government's control of that speech as well."

(b) May government employees constitutionally be dismissed if they publicly identify as gay? Should different rules regarding this be applied to the military? To teachers? See Fadi Hanna, *Gay Self-Identification and the Right to Political Legibility*, 2006 Wis. L.Rev. 75 (2006).

CHAPTER 8

THE ELECTRONIC MEDIA

■ ■ ■

The mass media are not invariably the most effective means of communication. For example, the right to place messages on utility poles concerning a lost dog may be more important than access to a radio or a television station. In some circumstances, picketing outside a school or placing leaflets in teachers' mailboxes may be the most effective communications medium. "Moreover, the rise of the internet and various computer applications has contributed to newspaper closings, declines in audiences for broadcasters, and layoffs in the print and broadcast media. [Nonetheless,] newspaper readership in the U.S. reaches about 100 million people daily. Network newscasts alone reach 20 to 30 million people every day." Lee C. Bollinger, *Uninhibited, Robust, and Wide-Open* 85–86 (2010). This section considers first, cases in which government seeks to force newspapers and broadcasters to grant access and cases in which the First Amendment is claimed to demand access. Second, this section considers cases involving content regulation of the electronic media, particularly those where government seeks otherwise to regulate content in broadcasting, cable, and on the internet particularly with respect to sexually oriented material.

I. ACCESS TO THE MASS MEDIA

MIAMI HERALD PUB. CO. v. TORNILLO, 418 U.S. 241 (1974), per BURGER, C.J., unanimously struck down a Florida "right of reply" statute, which required any newspaper that "assails" the personal character or official record of a candidate in any election to print, on demand, free of cost, any reply the candidate may make to the charges, in as conspicuous a place and the same kind of type, provided the reply takes up no more space than the charges. The opinion carefully explained the aim of the statute to "ensure that a wide variety of views reach the public" even though "chains of newspapers, national newspapers, national wire and news services, and one-newspaper towns, are the dominant features of a press that has become noncompetitive and enormously powerful and influential in its capacity to manipulate popular opinion and change the course of events," placing "in a few hands the power to inform the

423

American people and shape public opinion."[a] Nonetheless, the Court concluded that to require the printing of a reply violated the First Amendment: "Compelling editors or publishers to publish that which ' "reason" tells them should not be published' is what is at issue in this case. The Florida statute operates as a command in the same sense as a statute or regulation forbidding appellant from publishing specified matter. [The] Florida statute exacts a penalty on the basis of the content of a newspaper. The first phase of the penalty resulting from the compelled printing of a reply is exacted in terms of the cost in printing and composing time and materials and in taking up space that could be devoted to other material the newspaper may have preferred to print. It is correct, as appellee contends, that a newspaper is not subject to the finite technological limitations of time that confront a broadcaster but it is not correct to say that, as an economic reality, a newspaper can proceed to infinite expansion of its column space to accommodate the replies that a government agency determines or a statute commands the readers should have available.

"Faced with the penalties that would accrue to any newspaper that published news or commentary arguably within the reach of the right of access statute, editors might well conclude that the safe course is to avoid controversy and that, under the operation of the Florida statute, political and electoral coverage would be blunted or reduced. Government enforced right of access inescapably 'dampens the vigor and limits the variety of public debate,' *New York Times.*

"Even if a newspaper would face no additional costs to comply with a compulsory access law and would not be forced to forego publication of news or opinion by the inclusion of a reply, the Florida statute fails to clear the barriers of the First Amendment because of its intrusion into the function of editors. A newspaper is more than a passive receptacle or conduit for news, comment, and advertising. The choice of material to go into a newspaper, and the decisions made as to limitations on the size of the paper, and content, and treatment of public issues and public officials—whether fair or unfair—constitutes the exercise of editorial control and judgment. It has yet to be demonstrated how governmental regulation of this crucial process can be exercised consistent with First Amendment guarantees of a free press as they have evolved to this time."[b]

---

a. The opinion developed these views at greater length, citing "generally" Jerome Barron, *Access to the Press—A New First Amendment Right,* 80 Harv.L.Rev. 1641 (1967); David Lange, *The Role of the Access Doctrine in the Regulation of the Mass Media: A Critical Review and Assessment,* 52 N.C.L.Rev. 1, 8–9 (1973). For historical background and a spirited criticism of the statute, see Lucas Powe, *Tornillo,* 1987 Sup.Ct.Rev. 345. For background and criticism of the opinion, see Randall Bezanson, *How Free Can the Press Be?,* 58–82 (2003).

b. Brennan, J., joined by Rehnquist, J., joined the Court's opinion in a short statement to express the understanding that it "implies no view upon the constitutionality of 'retraction' statutes affording plaintiffs able to prove defamatory falsehoods a statutory action to require publication of a retraction."

The Federal Communications Commission for many years imposed on radio and television broadcasters the "fairness doctrine"—requiring that stations (1) devote a reasonable percentage of broadcast time to discussion of public issues and (2) assure fair coverage for each side.[a] At issue in RED LION BROADCASTING CO. v. FCC, 395 U.S. 367 (1969), were the application of the fairness doctrine to a particular broadcast[b] and two specific access regulations promulgated under the doctrine: (1) the "political editorial" rule, requiring that when a broadcaster, in an editorial, "endorses or opposes" a political candidate, it must notify the candidate opposed, or the rivals of the candidate supported, and afford them a "reasonable opportunity" to respond; (2) the "personal attack" rule, requiring that "when, during the presentation of views on a controversial issue of public importance, an attack is made on the honesty, character [or] integrity [of] an identified person or group," the person or group attacked must be given notice, a transcript of the attack, and an opportunity to respond.[c] "[I]n view of [the] scarcity of broadcast frequencies, the Government's role in allocating those frequencies, and the legitimate claims of those unable without government assistance to gain access to those frequencies for expression of their views," a 7–0 majority, per WHITE, J., upheld both access regulations:[d]

"[The broadcasters] contention is that the First Amendment protects their desire to use their allotted frequencies continuously to broadcast whatever they choose, and to exclude whomever they choose from ever using that frequency. No man may be prevented from saying or publishing what he thinks, or from refusing in his speech or other utterances to give

White, J., concurred. After agreeing that "prior compulsion by government in matters going to the very nerve center of a newspaper—the decision as to what copy will or will not be included in any given edition—collides with the First Amendment," he returned to his attack on *Gertz*, decided the same day: "Reaffirming the rule that the press cannot be forced to print an answer to a personal attack made by it [throws] into stark relief the consequences of the new balance forged by the Court in the companion case also announced today. *Gertz* goes far toward eviscerating the effectiveness of the ordinary libel action, which has long been the only potent response available to the private citizen libeled by the press. [To] me it is a near absurdity to so deprecate individual dignity, as the Court does in *Gertz,* and to leave the people at the complete mercy of the press, at least in this stage of our history when the press, as the majority in this case so well documents, is steadily becoming more powerful and much less likely to be deterred by threats of libel suits."

a. For helpful background on the origins, justification and administration of the fairness doctrine, see Roscoe Barrow, *The Fairness Doctrine: A Double Standard for Electronic and Print Media,* 26 Hast.L.J. 659 (1975); Benno Schmidt, *Freedom of the Press vs. Public Access* 157–98 (1976).

b. *Red Lion* grew out of a series of radio broadcasts by fundamentalist preacher Billy James Hargis, who had attacked Fred J. Cook, author of an article attacking Hargis and "hate clubs of the air." When Cook heard about the broadcast, he demanded that the station give him an opportunity to reply. Cook refused to pay for his "reply time" and the FCC ordered the station to give Cook the opportunity to reply whether or not he would pay for it. The Supreme Court upheld the order of free reply time. See Schmidt, fn. a supra, at 161–63.

c. Excepted were "personal attacks [by] legally qualified candidates [on] other such candidates" and "bona fide newscasts, bona fide news interviews, and on-the-spot coverage of a bona fide news event."

d. Surprisingly, none of the justices joining White, J.'s opinion felt the need to make additional remarks, but Douglas, J., who did not participate in *Red Lion,* expressed his disagreement with it in the *CBS* case, infra.

equal weight to the views of his opponents. This right, they say, applies equally to broadcasters.

"Although broadcasting is clearly a medium affected by a First Amendment interest, differences in the characteristics of new media justify differences in the First Amendment standards applied to [them]. Just as the Government may limit the use of sound-amplifying equipment potentially so noisy that it drowns out civilized private speech, so may the Government limit the use of broadcast equipment. The right of free speech of a broadcaster, the user of a sound truck, or any other individual does not embrace a right to snuff out the free speech of [others].

"Where there are substantially more individuals who want to broadcast than there are frequencies to allocate, it is idle to posit an unabridgeable First Amendment right to broadcast comparable to the right of every individual to speak, write, or publish. [It] would be strange if the First Amendment, aimed at protecting and furthering communications, prevented the Government from making radio communication possible by requiring licenses to broadcast and by limiting the number of licenses so as not to overcrowd the spectrum. * * *

"By the same token, as far as the First Amendment is concerned those who are licensed stand no better than those to whom licenses are refused. A license permits broadcasting, but the licensee has no constitutional right [to] monopolize a radio frequency to the exclusion of his fellow citizens. There is nothing in the First Amendment which prevents the Government from requiring a licensee to share his frequency with others and to conduct himself as a proxy or fiduciary with obligations to present those views and voices which are representative of his community and which would otherwise, by necessity, be barred from the airwaves.

"[The] people as a whole retain their interest in free speech by radio and their collective right to have the medium function consistently with the ends and purposes of the First Amendment. It is the right of the viewers and listeners, not the right of the broadcasters, which is paramount. [It] is the purpose of the First Amendment to preserve an uninhibited marketplace of ideas in which truth will ultimately prevail, rather than to countenance monopolization of that market, whether it be by the Government itself or a private licensee. [It] is the right of the public to receive suitable access to social, political, esthetic, moral, and other ideas and experiences which is crucial [here.]

"In terms of constitutional principle, and as enforced sharing of a scarce resource, the personal attack and political editorial rules are indistinguishable from the equal-time provision of § 315 [of the Communications Act], a specific enactment of Congress requiring [that stations allot equal time to qualified candidates for public office] and to which the fairness doctrine and these constituent regulations are important complements. [Nor] can we say that it is inconsistent with the First Amendment goal of producing an informed public capable of conducting its own affairs to require a broadcaster to permit answers to personal attacks occurring in the course of discussing controversial issues, or to require that the political opponents of those endorsed by the station be given a chance to communicate with the public. Otherwise, station owners and a few networks would have unfettered power to make time available only to the highest bidders, to communicate only their own views on public issues, people and candidates, and to permit on the air only those with whom they agreed. There is no sanctuary in the First Amendment for unlimited private censorship operating in a medium not open to all.

"[It is contended] that if political editorials or personal attacks will trigger an obligation in broadcasters to afford the opportunity for expression to speakers who need not pay for time and whose views are unpalatable to the licensees, then broadcasters will be irresistibly forced to self-censorship and their coverage of controversial public issues will be eliminated or at least rendered wholly ineffective. Such a result would indeed be a serious matter, [but] that possibility is at best speculative. [If these doctrines turn out to have this effect], there will be time enough to reconsider the constitutional implications. The fairness doctrine in the past has had no such overall effect. That this will occur now seems unlikely, however, since if present licensees should suddenly prove timorous, the Commission is not powerless to insist that they give adequate and fair attention to public issues. It does not violate the First Amendment to treat licensees given the privilege of using scarce radio frequencies as proxies for the entire community, obligated to give suitable time and attention to matters of great public concern. To condition the granting or renewal of licenses on a willingness to present representative community views on controversial issues is consistent with the ends and purposes of those constitutional provisions forbidding the abridgment of freedom of speech and freedom of the press."[e]

NOTES AND QUESTIONS

1. *Tension between Miami Herald and Red Lion.* Consider Lee Bollinger, *Freedom of the Press and Public Access: Toward a Theory of Partial Regulation of the Mass Media,* 75 Mich.L.Rev. 1, 4–6, 10–12 (1976): "What seems so remarkable about the unanimous *Miami Herald* opinion is the complete absence of any reference to the Court's unanimous decision five years earlier in *Red Lion*[, upholding] the so-called personal attack rule, [which] is almost identical in substance to the Florida statute declared

---

e. The Court noted that it "need not deal with the argument that even if there is no longer a technological scarcity of frequencies limiting the number of broadcasters, there nevertheless is an economic scarcity in the sense that the Commission could or does limit entry to the broadcasting market on economic grounds and license no more stations than the market will support. Hence, it is said, the fairness doctrine or its equivalent is essential to satisfy the claims of those excluded and of the public generally. A related argument, which we also put side, is that quite apart from scarcity of frequencies, technological or economic, Congress does not abridge freedom of speech or press by legislation directly or indirectly multiplying the voices and views presented to the public through time sharing, fairness doctrines, or other devices which limit or dissipate the power of those who sit astride the channels of communication with the general public." For background and discussion of *Red Lion,* see Fred Friendly, *The Good Guys, The Bad Guys and the First Amendment* (1975).

unconstitutional in *Miami Herald*. That omission, however, is no more surprising than the absence of any discussion in *Red Lion* of the cases in which the Court expressed great concern about the risks attending government regulation of the print media.

"[The] scarcity rationale [articulated in *Red Lion* does not] explain why what appears to be a similar phenomenon of natural monopolization within the newspaper industry does not constitute an equally appropriate occasion for access regulation. A difference in the cause of concentration—the exhaustion of a physical element necessary for communication in broadcasting as contrasted with the economic constraints on the number of possible competitors in the print media—would seem far less relevant from a First Amendment standpoint than the fact of concentration itself. [Instead] of exploring the relevance for the print media of the new principle developed in broadcasting, the Court merely reiterated the opposing, more traditional, principle that the government cannot tell editors what to publish. It thus created a paradox, leaving the new principle unscathed while preserving tradition."

2. ***Absence of balancing in Miami Herald.*** Did *Miami Herald* present a confrontation between the rights of speech and press? "Nowhere does [*Miami Herald*] explicitly acknowledge [such a confrontation], but implicit recognition of the speech interest," observes Melville Nimmer, *Is Freedom of the Press a Redundancy? What Does it Add to Freedom of Speech?*, 26 Hast.L.J. 639, 645, 657 (1975), "may be found in the Court's reference to the access advocates' argument that, given the present semimonopolistic posture of the press, speech can be effective and therefore free only if enhanced by devices such as a right of reply statute. The Court in accepting the press clause argument in effect necessarily found it to be superior to any competing speech clause claims. [But] the issue cannot be resolved merely by noting, as did [*Miami Herald*], that a right of reply statute 'constitutes the [state] exercise of editorial control and judgment.' This is but one half of the equation. [*Miami Herald*] ignored the strong conflicting claims of 'speech.' Perhaps on balance the press should still prevail, but those who doubt the efficacy of such a result are hardly persuaded by an approach that apparently fails to recognize that any balancing of speech and press rights is required."[f] Consider Gregory P. Magarian, *The Jurisprudence of Colliding First Amendment Interests,* 83 Notre Dame L.Rev. 185, 237 (2007): "Single minded emphasis on autonomy tends to favor the expressive haves over the have nots [and] tends to yield a bias toward established viewpoints."

3. ***Scope of Miami Herald.*** Consider Schmidt, fn. a supra, at 233–35: "From the perspective of First Amendment law generally, *Miami Herald* would be a stark and unexplained deviation if one were to read the decision as creating absolute prohibitions on access obligations.[g] [The] fact the Court

---

f. Does *Miami Herald* demonstrate, as Professor Nimmer believes, at 644–46, that free speech and press can be distinct, even conflicting interests? Anthony Lewis, *A Preferred Position for Journalism?*, 7 Hof.L.Rev. 595, 603 (1979), thinks not: "[T]he vice of the [Florida right of reply] law lay in the compulsion to publish; and I think the result would be no different if the case involved a compulsion to speak. If a state statute required any candidate who spoke falsely about another to make a corrective speech, would it survive challenge under the First Amendment?"

g. "Even in the area of 'the central freedom of the First Amendment,' which is criticism of the governmental acts of public officials," recalls Professor Schmidt, fn. a supra, at 232, "there is no absolute protection for expression."

offers no discussion as to why First Amendment rules respecting access should be absolute, while all other rules emanating from that Amendment are relative, suggests that the principle of *Miami Herald* probably is destined for uncharted qualifications and exceptions." But see Lucas Powe, *Tornillo,* 1987 Sup.Ct.Rev. 345, 391, 390: "Quite frankly I do not believe that a twenty page Supreme Court opinion meeting all the standards of craft (all considerations are ventilated fully and the opinion be of publishable quality for a good legal journal) can as effectively protect the right of press autonomy as the blunt rejection in *Miami Herald.* Chief Justice Burger's failure to engage, so annoying to Schmidt and other commentators, is in fact a great strength of the opinion."

Would a statute requiring nondiscriminatory access to the classified ads section of a newspaper pass muster under *Miami Herald?* A requirement that legal notices be published?

4. ***Absolute editorial autonomy—some of the time.*** Is it ironic that *Gertz* was decided the same day as *Miami Herald?* Which poses a greater threat to editorial autonomy—a negligence standard in defamation cases or the guaranteed access contemplated by the Florida statute? Whose autonomy is important—the editors or the owners? May government protect editors from ad hoc intervention by corporate owners? See generally C. Edwin Baker, *Human Liberty and Freedom of Speech* 225–71 (1989).

5. ***The threat to editorial autonomy in Red Lion.*** Consider Schmidt, fn. c supra, at 166: *Red Lion* "left broadcaster autonomy almost entirely at the mercy of the FCC." See also William Van Alstyne, *The Möbius Strip of the First Amendment: Perspectives on Red Lion,* 29 S.C.L.Rev. 539, 571 (1978): "Indeed, if one continues to be troubled by *Red Lion,* I think it is not because one takes lightly the difficulty of forum allocation in a society of scarce resources. Rather, it is because one believes that the technique of the fairness doctrine in particular may represent a very trivial egalitarian gain and a major First Amendment loss; that a twist has been given to the equal protection idea by a device the principal effect of which is merely to level down the most vivid and versatile forum we have, to flatten it out and to render it a mere commercial mirror of each community. What may have been lost is a willingness to risk the partisanship of licensees as catalysts and as active advocates with a freedom to exhort, a freedom that dares to exclaim 'Fuck the draft,' and not be made to yield by government at once to add, 'but on the other hand there is also the view, held by many.' "

6. ***The best of both worlds.*** "[T]he critical difference between what the Court was asked to do in *Red Lion* and what it was asked to do in *Miami Herald,*" maintains Professor Bollinger note 1 supra, at 27, 32–33, 36–37, "involved choosing between a partial regulatory system and a universal one. Viewed from that perspective, the Court reached the correct result in both cases": "[T]here are good First Amendment reasons for being both receptive to and wary of access regulation. This dual nature of access legislation suggests the need to limit carefully the intrusiveness of the regulation in order safely to enjoy its remedial benefits. Thus, a proper judicial response is one that will permit the legislature to provide the public with access *somewhere* within the mass media, but not throughout the press. The Court should

not, and need not, be forced into an all-or-nothing position on this matter; there is nothing in the First Amendment that forbids having the best of both worlds."[h]

For a powerful critique of the regulated world, see Lucas Powe, *American Broadcasting and the First Amendment* (1987). For a powerful critique of the unregulated world, see C. Edwin Baker, *The First Amendment in Modern Garb,* 58 Ohio St.L.J. 311 (1997).

––––––

"Like many equal protection issues," observes Karst, Ch. 6, I, B supra, at 45, "the media-access problem should be approached from two separate constitutional directions. First, what does the Constitution *compel* government to do in the way of equalizing? Second, what does the Constitution *permit* government to do in equalizing by statute?" *Red Lion* and *Miami Herald* presented the second question; the first is raised by COLUMBIA BROADCASTING SYSTEM, INC. v. DEMOCRATIC NAT'L COMMITTEE, 412 U.S. 94 (1973) (*CBS*): The FCC rejected the claims of Business Executives' Move for Vietnam Peace (BEM) and the Democratic National Committee (DNC) that "responsible" individuals and groups are entitled to purchase advertising time to comment on public issues, even though the broadcaster has complied with the fairness doctrine. The District of Columbia Circuit held that "a flat ban on paid public issue announcements" violates the First Amendment "at least when other sorts of paid announcements are accepted," and remanded to the FCC to develop "reasonable procedures and regulations determining which and how many 'editorial advertisements' will be put on the air." The Supreme Court, per BURGER, C.J., reversed, holding that neither the "public interest" standard of the Communications Act (which draws heavily from the First Amendment) nor the First Amendment itself—assuming that refusal to accept such advertising constituted "governmental action" for First Amendment purposes[a]—requires broadcasters to accept paid editorial announcements. As pointed out in Vincent Blasi, *The Checking Value in First Amendment Theory,* 1977 Am.B.Found.Res.J. 521, 613–14 although Burger, C.J. "built to some extent" on *Red Lion,* his opinion "evinced a most important change of emphasis. For whereas White, J., based his argument in *Red Lion* on the premise that broadcasters are mere 'proxies' or 'fiduciaries' for the general public, the Chief Justice's opinion [in *CBS*] invoked a concept of 'journalistic independence' or 'journalistic discretion,'

---

h. Does the existence of the threat of regulation or the Court's rhetoric about the press have a substantial impact on press decisions? Compare Lee C. Bollinger, *Images of a Free Press* (1991) with Lili Levi, *Challenging the Autonomous Press,* 78 Cornell L.Rev. 665 (1993).

a. Burger, C.J., joined by Stewart and Rehnquist, JJ., concluded that a broadcast licensee's refusal to accept an advertisement was not "governmental action" for First Amendment purposes. Although White, Blackmun and Powell, JJ., concurred in parts of the Court's opinion, they did not decide this question for, *assuming* governmental action, they found that the challenged ban did not violate the First Amendment. Douglas, J., who concurred in the result, assumed *no* governmental action. Dissenting, Brennan, J., joined by Marshall, J., found that the challenged ban did constitute "governmental action."

the essence of which is that broadcasters do indeed have special First Amendment interests which have to be considered in the constitutional calculus."

Burger, C.J. continued: "[From various provisions of the Communications Act of 1934] it seems clear that Congress intended to permit private broadcasting to develop with the widest journalistic freedom consistent with its public obligations. Only when the interests of the public are found to outweigh the private journalistic interests of the broadcasters will government power be asserted within the framework of the Act. License renewal proceedings, in which the listening public can be heard, are a principal means of such regulation.

"[W]ith the advent of radio a half century ago, Congress was faced with a fundamental choice between total Government ownership and control of the new medium—the choice of most other countries—or some other alternative. Long before the impact and potential of the medium was realized, Congress opted for a system of private broadcasters licensed and regulated by Government. The legislative history suggests that this choice was influenced not only by traditional attitudes toward private enterprise, but by a desire to maintain for licensees, so far as consistent with necessary regulation, a traditional journalistic [role.]

"The regulatory scheme evolved slowly, but very early the licensee's role developed in terms of a 'public trustee' charged with the duty of fairly and impartially informing the public audience. In this structure the Commission acts in essence as an 'overseer,' but the initial and primary responsibility for fairness, balance, and objectivity rests with the licensee. This role of the Government as an overseer and ultimate arbiter and guardian of the public interest and the role of the licensee as a journalistic 'free agent' call for a delicate balancing of competing interests. The maintenance of this balance for more than 40 years has called on both the regulators and the licensees to walk a 'tightrope' to preserve the First Amendment values written into the Radio Act and its successor, the Communications Act.

"The tensions inherent in such a regulatory structure emerge more clearly when we compare a private newspaper with a broadcast licensee. The power of a privately owned newspaper to advance its own political, social, and economic views is bounded by only two factors: first, the acceptance of a sufficient number of readers—and hence advertisers—to assure financial success; and, second, the journalistic integrity of its editors and publishers. A broadcast licensee has a large measure of journalistic freedom but not as large as that exercised by a newspaper. A licensee must balance what it might prefer to do as a private entrepreneur with what it is required to do as a 'public trustee.' To perform its statutory duties, the Commission must oversee without censoring. This suggests something of the difficulty and delicacy of administering the Communications Act—a function calling for flexibility and the capacity to adjust and readjust the regulatory mechanism to meet changing problems and needs.

"The licensee policy challenged in this case is intimately related to the journalistic role of a licensee for which it has been given initial and primary responsibility by Congress. The licensee's policy against accepting editorial advertising cannot be examined as an abstract proposition, but must be viewed in the context of its journalistic role. It does not help to press on us the idea that editorial ads are 'like' commercial ads, for the licensee's policy against editorial spot ads is expressly based on a journalistic judgment that 10– to 60–second spot announcements are ill-suited to intelligible and intelligent treatment of public issues; the broadcaster has chosen to provide a balanced treatment of controversial questions in a more comprehensive form. Obviously, the licensee's evaluation is based on its own journalistic judgment of priorities and newsworthiness.

"Moreover, the Commission has not fostered the licensee policy challenged here; it has simply declined to command particular action because it fell within the area of journalistic discretion. [The] Commission's reasoning, consistent with nearly 40 years of precedent, is that so long as a licensee meets its 'public trustee' obligation to provide balanced coverage of issues and events, it has broad discretion to decide how that obligation will be met. We do not reach the question whether the First Amendment or the Act can be read to preclude the Commission from determining that in some situations the public interest requires licensees to re-examine their policies with respect to editorial advertisements.[b] The Commission has not yet made such a determination; it has, for the present at least, found the policy to be within the sphere of journalistic discretion which Congress has left with the licensee.

"[I]t must constantly be kept in mind that the interest of the public is our foremost concern. With broadcasting, where the available means of communication are limited in both space and time, [Meiklejohn's admonition] that '[w]hat is essential is not that everyone shall speak, but that everything worth saying shall be said' is peculiarly appropriate.

"[Congress] has time and again rejected various legislative attempts that would have mandated a variety of forms of individual access. [It] has chosen to leave such questions with the Commission, to which it has given the flexibility to experiment with new ideas as changing conditions require. In this case, the Commission has decided that on balance the undesirable effects of the right of access urged by respondents would outweigh the asserted [benefits.]

---

b. *Columbia Broadcasting System, Inc. v. FCC,* 453 U.S. 367 (1981), upheld FCC administration of a statutory provision guaranteeing "reasonable" access to the airwaves for federal election candidates. The Court, per Burger, C.J., observed that "the Court has never approved a *general* right of access to the media. *Miami Herald*; *CBS v. DNC.* Nor do we do so today." But it found that the limited right of access "properly balances the First Amendment rights of federal candidates, the public, and broadcasters." White, J., joined by Rehnquist and Stevens, JJ., dissented on statutory grounds. For criticism, see Daniel Polsby, *Candidate Access to the Air: The Uncertain Future of Broadcaster Discretion,* 1981 Sup.Ct.Rev. 223.

"The Commission was justified in concluding that the public interest in providing access to the marketplace of 'ideas and experiences' would scarcely be served by a system so heavily weighted in favor of the financially affluent, or those with access to wealth. Even under a first-come-first-served system [the] views of the affluent could well prevail over those of others, since they would have it within their power to purchase time more frequently. Moreover, there is the substantial danger [that] the time allotted for editorial advertising could be monopolized by those of one political persuasion.

"These problems would not necessarily be solved by applying the Fairness Doctrine, including the *Cullman* doctrine [requiring broadcasters to provide free time for the presentation of opposing views if a paid sponsor is unavailable], to editorial advertising. If broadcasters were required to provide time, free when necessary, for the discussion of the various shades of opinion on the issue discussed in the advertisement, the affluent could still determine in large part the issues to be discussed. Thus, the very premise of the Court of Appeals' holding—that a right of access is necessary to allow individuals and groups the opportunity for self-initiated speech—would have little meaning to those who could not afford to purchase time in the first instance.

"If the Fairness Doctrine were applied to editorial advertising, there is also the substantial danger that the effective operation of that doctrine would be jeopardized. To minimize financial hardship and to comply fully with its public responsibilities a broadcaster might well be forced to make regular programming time available to those holding a view different from that expressed in an editorial advertisement. [The] result would be a further erosion of the journalistic discretion of broadcasters in the coverage of public issues, and a transfer of control over the treatment of public issues from the licensees who are accountable for broadcast performance to private individuals who are not. The public interest would no longer be 'paramount' but rather subordinate to private whim especially since, under the Court of Appeals' decision, a broadcaster would be largely precluded from rejecting editorial advertisements that dealt with matters trivial or insignificant or already fairly covered by the broadcaster. If the Fairness Doctrine and the *Cullman* doctrine were suspended to alleviate these problems, as respondents suggest might be appropriate, the question arises whether we would have abandoned more than we have gained. Under such a regime the congressional objective of balanced coverage of public issues would be seriously threatened.

"Nor can we accept the Court of Appeals' view that every potential speaker is ''he best judge' of what the listening public ought to hear or indeed the best judge of the merits of his or her views. All journalistic tradition and experience is to the contrary. For better or worse, editing is what editors are for; and editing is selection and choice of material. That editors—newspaper or broadcast—can and do abuse this power is beyond doubt, but that is not reason to deny the discretion Congress provided. Calculated risks of abuse are taken in order to preserve higher values. The presence of these risks is nothing new; the authors of the Bill of Rights accepted the reality that these risks were evils for which there was no acceptable remedy other than a spirit of moderation and a sense of responsibility—and civility—on the part of those who exercise the guaranteed freedoms of expression.

"It was reasonable for Congress to conclude that the public interest in being informed requires periodic accountability on the part of those who are entrusted with the use of broadcast frequencies, scarce as they are. In the delicate balancing historically followed in the regulation of broadcasting Congress and the Commission could appropriately conclude that the allocation of journalistic priorities should be concentrated in the licensee rather than diffused among many. This policy gives the public some assurance that the broadcaster will be answerable if he fails to meet their legitimate needs. No such accountability attaches to the private individual, whose only qualifications for using the broadcast facility may be abundant funds and a point of view. To agree that debate on public issues should be 'robust, and wide-open' does not mean that we should exchange 'public trustee' broadcasting, with all its limitations, for a system of self-appointed editorial commentators.

"[T]he risk of an enlargement of Government control over the content of broadcast discussion of public issues [is] inherent in the Court of Appeals' remand requiring regulations and procedures to sort out requests to be heard—a process involving the very editing that licensees now perform as to regular programming. [Under] a constitutionally commanded and government supervised right-of-access system urged by respondents and mandated by the Court of Appeals, the Commission would be required to oversee far more of the day-to-day operations of broadcasters' conduct, deciding such questions as whether a particular individual or group has had sufficient opportunity to present its viewpoint and whether a particular viewpoint has already been sufficiently aired. Regimenting broadcasters is too radical a therapy for the ailment respondents complain of. * * *

"The Commission is also entitled to take into account the reality that in a very real sense listeners and viewers constitute a 'captive audience.' [It] is no answer to say that because we tolerate pervasive commercial advertisement [we] can also live with its political counterparts.

"The rationale for the Court of Appeals' decision imposing a constitutional right of access on the broadcast media was that the licensee impermissibly discriminates by accepting commercial advertisements while refusing editorial advertisements. The court relied on [lower court cases] holding that state-supported school newspapers and public transit companies were forbidden by the First Amendment from excluding controversial editorial advertisements in favor of commercial advertisements.[c] The court also attempted to analogize this case to some of our decisions holding that States may not constitutionally ban certain protected speech

---

c. But see *Lehman v. Shaker Heights*, Ch. 6, II supra.

while at the same time permitting other speech in public areas [citing e.g., *Grayned* and *Mosley,* Ch. 6 supra].

"These decisions provide little guidance, however, in resolving the question whether the First Amendment required the Commission to mandate a private right of access to the broadcast media. In none of those cases did the forum sought for expression have an affirmative and independent statutory obligation to provide full and fair coverage of public issues, such as Congress has imposed on all broadcast licensees. In short, there is no 'discrimination' against controversial speech present in this case. The question here is not whether there is to be discussion of controversial issues of public importance on the broadcast media, but rather who shall determine what issues are to be discussed by whom, and when."

DOUGLAS, J., concurred in the result, but "for quite different reasons." Because the Court did not decide whether a broadcast licensee is "a federal agency within the context of this case," he assumed that it was not. He "fail[ed] to see," then "how constitutionally we can treat TV and the radio differently than we treat newspapers": "I did not participate in [*Red Lion* and] would not support it. The Fairness Doctrine has no place in our First Amendment regime. It puts the head of the camel inside the tent and enables administration after administration to toy with TV or radio in order to serve its sordid or its benevolent ends. [The uniqueness of radio and TV] is due to engineering and technical problems. But the press in a realistic sense is likewise not available to all. [T]he daily newspapers now established are unique in the sense that it would be virtually impossible for a competitor to enter the field due to the financial exigencies of this era. The result is that in practical terms the newspapers and magazines, like the TV and radio, are available only to a select few. [That] may argue for a redefinition of the responsibilities of the press in First Amendment terms. But I do not think it gives us carte blanche to design systems of supervision and control nor empower [the government to] make 'some' laws 'abridging' freedom of the press. * * *

"Licenses are, of course, restricted in time and while, in my view, Congress has the power to make each license limited to a fixed term and nonreviewable, there is no power to deny renewals for editorial or ideological reasons [for] the First Amendment gives no preference to one school of thought over the others.

"The Court in today's decision by endorsing the Fairness Doctrine sanctions a federal saddle on broadcast licensees that is agreeable to the traditions of nations that never have known freedom of press and that is tolerable in countries that do not have a written constitution containing prohibitions as absolute as those in the First Amendment."[d]

BRENNAN, J., joined by Marshall, J., dissented, viewing "the *absolute* ban on the sale of air time for the discussion of controversial issues" as

---

d. Noting that his views "closely approach those expressed by Mr. Justice Douglas," Stewart, J., also concurred.

"governmental action"[e] violating the First Amendment: "As a practical matter, the Court's reliance on the Fairness Doctrine as an 'adequate' alternative to editorial advertising seriously overestimates the ability—or willingness—of broadcasters to expose the public to the 'widest possible dissemination of information from diverse and antagonistic sources.' [Indeed,] in light of the strong interest of broadcasters in maximizing their audience, and therefore their profits, it seems almost naive to expect the majority of broadcasters to produce the variety and controversiality of material necessary to reflect a full spectrum of viewpoints. Stated simply, angry customers are not good customers and, in the commercial world of mass communications, it is simply 'bad business' to espouse—or even to allow others to espouse—the heterodox or the controversial. As a result, even under the Fairness Doctrine, broadcasters generally tend to permit only established—or at least moderated—views to enter the broadcast world's 'marketplace of ideas.'[24]

"Moreover, the Court's reliance on the Fairness Doctrine as the *sole* means of informing the public seriously misconceives and underestimates the public's interest in receiving ideas and information directly from the advocates of those ideas without the interposition of journalistic middlemen. Under the Fairness Doctrine, broadcasters decide what issues are 'important,' how 'fully' to cover them, and what format, time and style of coverage are 'appropriate.' The retention of such *absolute* control in the hands of a few government licensees is inimical to the First Amendment, for vigorous, free debate can be attained only when members of the public have at least *some* opportunity to take the initiative and editorial control into their own hands.

"[S]tanding alone, [the Fairness Doctrine] simply cannot eliminate the need for a further, complementary airing of controversial views through the limited availability of editorial advertising. Indeed, the availability of at least *some* opportunity for editorial advertising is imperative if we are ever to attain the 'free and general discussion of public matters [that] seems absolutely essential to prepare the people for an intelligent exercise of their rights as citizens.'

"Moreover, a proper balancing of the competing First Amendment interests at stake in this controversy must consider, not only the interests of broadcasters and of the listening and viewing public, but also the independent First Amendment interest of groups and individuals in effective self-expression. [I]n a time of apparently growing anonymity of the individual in our society, it is imperative that we take special care to preserve the vital First Amendment interest in assuring 'self-fulfillment [of expression] for each individual.' For our citizens may now find greater than ever the need to express their own views directly to the public, rather than through a governmentally appointed surrogate, if they are to feel

---

e.   See fn. a supra.

24.   [Citing many secondary sources to support this statement.]

that they can achieve at least some measure of control over their own destinies.

"[F]reedom of speech does not exist in the abstract. [It] can flourish only if it is allowed to operate in an effective forum—whether it be a public park, a schoolroom, a town meeting hall, a soapbox, or a radio and television frequency. For in the absence of an effective means of communication, the right to speak would ring hollow indeed. And, in recognition of these principles, we have consistently held that the First Amendment embodies not only the abstract right to be free from censorship, but also the right of an individual to utilize an appropriate and effective medium for the expression of his views.

"[W]ith the assistance of the Federal Government, the broadcast industry has become what is potentially the most efficient and effective 'marketplace of ideas' ever devised. [Thus], although 'full and free discussion' of ideas may have been a reality in the heyday of political pamphleteering, modern technological developments in the field of communications have made the soapbox orator and the leafleteer virtually obsolete. And, in light of the current dominance of the electronic media as the most effective means of reaching the public, any policy that *absolutely* denies citizens access to the airwaves necessarily renders even the concept of 'full and free discussion' practically meaningless.

"[T]he challenged ban can be upheld only if it is determined that such editorial advertising would unjustifiably impair the broadcaster's assertedly overriding interest in exercising *absolute* control over 'his' frequency. Such an analysis, however, hardly reflects the delicate balancing of interests that this sensitive question demands. Indeed, this 'absolutist' approach wholly disregards the competing First Amendment rights of all 'nonbroadcaster' citizens, ignores the teachings of our recent decision in *Red Lion,* and is not supported by the historical purposes underlying broadcast regulation in this Nation. [T]here is simply no overriding First Amendment interest of broadcasters that can justify the *absolute* exclusion of virtually all of our citizens from the most effective 'marketplace of ideas' ever devised.

"[T]his case deals *only* with the allocation of *advertising* time—airtime that broadcasters regularly relinquish to others without the retention of significant editorial control. Thus, we are concerned here not with the speech of broadcasters themselves but, rather, with their 'right' to decide which *other* individuals will be given an opportunity to speak in a forum that has already been opened to the public.

"Viewed in this context, the *absolute* ban on editorial advertising seems particularly offensive because, although broadcasters refuse to sell any airtime whatever to groups or individuals wishing to speak out on controversial issues of public importance, they make such airtime readily available to those 'commercial' advertisers who seek to peddle their goods and services to the public. [Yet an] individual seeking to discuss war, peace, pollution, or the suffering of the poor is denied this right to speak.

Instead, he is compelled to rely on the beneficence of a corporate 'trustee' appointed by the Government to argue his case for him.

"It has been long recognized, however, that although access to public forums may be subjected to reasonable 'time, place, and manner' regulations, '[s]elective exclusions from a public forum, may not be based on *content* alone.' *Mosley* (emphasis added). Here, of course, the differential treatment accorded 'commercial' and 'controversial' speech clearly violates that principle. Moreover, and not without some irony, the favored treatment given 'commercial' speech under the existing scheme clearly reverses traditional First Amendment priorities. For it has generally been understood that 'commercial' speech enjoys *less* First Amendment protection than speech directed at the discussion of controversial issues of public importance."

NOTES AND QUESTIONS

1. *Confronting scarcity.* Consider Tribe 2d ed., at 1005: "*CBS* took a step away from *Red Lion* by its treatment of broadcasters as part of the 'press' with an important editorial function to perform rather than as analogous to the postal or telephone systems, but *CBS* was firmly in the *Red Lion* tradition when it refused to consider the possibility that either the technologically scarce radio and television channels, or the finite time available on such channels, might be allocated much as economically scarce newspaper opportunities are allocated: by a combination of market mechanisms and chance rather than by government design coupled with broadcaster autonomy."

Suppose the government sold the airwaves to the highest bidder and allowed subsequent exchange according to property and contract law. Consider Note, *Reconciling Red Lion and Tornillo: A Consistent Theory of Media Regulation,* 28 Stan.L.Rev. 563, 583 (1976): "This regulatory strategy would remove the government from direct determination of the particular individuals who are allowed to broadcast, leaving this decision to market forces, and would avoid the need for specific behavioral commands and sanctions now necessary to secure compliance by broadcasters with the various obligations imposed by the public interest standard. [Under] strict scrutiny, then, the existence of this clearly identifiable less restrictive alternative indicates that the Communications Act is unconstitutional."

But see Van Alstyne, at 563: "Congress may indeed be free to 'sell off' the airwaves, and it may be wholly feasible to allocate most currently established broadcast signals by competitive bidding that, when done, may well produce private licensees operating truly without subsidy. But only a singularly insensitive observer would believe that this choice is not implicitly also a highly speech-restrictive choice by Congress. It is fully as speech-restrictive as though, in the case of land, government were to withdraw from *all* ownership and all subsidized maintenance of all land, including parks, auditoriums, and streets and to remain in the field exclusively as a policeman to enforce the proprietary decisions of all private landowners."**f**

---

f. For detailed, but traditional, criticism of the scarcity argument, see Matthew Spitzer, *Controlling the Content of Print and Broadcast,* 58 S.Cal.L.Rev. 1349 (1985). But see *Metro*

Should it be constitutional for the government to exercise "ownership" over the entire broadcast spectrum?[g]

2. ***The "fairness" doctrine criticized.*** The Court's assumption that the fairness doctrine works tolerably well has been roasted by the commentators. See, e.g., Ford Rowan, *Broadcast Fairness: Doctrine, Practice, Prospects* (1984); Steven Simmons, *The Fairness Doctrine and the Media* (1978); Johnson & Dystel, *A Day in the Life: The Federal Communications Commission*, 82 Yale L.J. 1575 (1973). Consider Thomas Krattenmaker & Lucas Powe, *The Fairness Doctrine Today: A Constitutional Curiosity and an Impossible Dream*, 1985 Duke L.J. 151, 175: "If the doctrine is to be taken seriously then suspected violations lurk everywhere and the FCC should undertake continuous oversight of the industry. If the FCC will not—or cannot—do that, then the doctrine must be toothless except for the randomly-selected few who are surprised to feel its bite after the fact." For a vigorous defense of the fairness doctrine, see Charles Ferris & James Kirkland, *Fairness—The Broadcaster's Hippocratic Oath*, 34 Cath.U.L.Rev. 605 (1985).

3. ***The fairness doctrine repealed.*** The FCC concluded a 15 month administrative proceeding with an official denunciation of the fairness doctrine, pointing in particular to the marked increase in the information services marketplace since *Red Lion* and the effects of the doctrine in application. FCC, [*General*] *Fairness Doctrine Obligations of Broadcast Licensees*, 102 F.C.C.2d 143 (1985). *Syracuse Peace Council*, 2 FCC Rcd 5043 (1987) held that "under the constitutional standard established by *Red Lion* and its progeny, the fairness doctrine contravenes the First Amendment and its enforcement is no longer in the public interest."[h]

4. ***The worst of both worlds.*** Evaluate the following hypothetical commentary: "*CBS v. DNC* allows government to grant virtually exclusive control over American's most valuable communication medium to corporations who regard it as their mission to 'deliver' audiences to advertisers. The system gives us the worst of both worlds: the world of profit-seeking—without a free market; the world of regulation—without planning." Consider Richard Moon, *The Constitutional Protection of Freedom of Expression* 81 (2000): "The domination of public discourse by advertising also means that the unnatural images or absurd associations of a particular ad seem unexceptional. Because the principal channels of public discourse are controlled by commercial

---

Broadcasting v. FCC, 497 U.S. 547 (1990)(reaffirming the government's power to regulate the "limited number" of broadcast licensees in the context of upholding minority ownership policies designed to effectuate more diverse programming and to safeguard the "rights of the viewing and listening audiences"). For criticism of the scarcity argument in light of new technology, see Lawrence Lessig, *Code* 182–85 (1999).

g. See Glen O. Robinson, *The Electronic First Amendment: An Essay for the New Age*, 47 Duke L.J. 899, 911–13 (1998); Matthew Spitzer, *The Constitutionality of Licensing Broadcasters*, 64 N.Y.U.L.Rev. 990 (1989); Steven Shiffrin, *Government Speech*, 27 UCLA L.Rev. 565, 587 n. 122, 644–45 (1980).

h. *Syracuse Peace Council v. FCC*, 867 F.2d 654 (D.C.Cir.1989), affirmed the FCC's determination that the fairness doctrine no longer serves the public interest without reaching constitutional issues. On June 20, 1987, President had vetoed congressional legislation designed to preserve the fairness doctrine on the ground that the legislation was unconstitutional. *Radio-Television News Directors Assoc. v. FCC*, 229 F.3d 269 (D.C.Cir.2000), ordered the FCC to vacate the personal attack rules with the understanding that the rules might be reinstituted if the Commission conducted a new rule-making proceeding to determine whether the public interest, consistent with the First Amendment, required them.

interests and carry only ads and advertising-funded programming, the underlying message of advertising, that self-realization is achieved through consumption, is an almost unchallengeable cultural assumption." For the contention that advertising control undermines the quality, quantity, and diversity of programming, see Christopher S. Yoo, *Architectural Censorship and the FCC*, 78 S. Cal. L. Rev. 669 (2005).

5. *Candidate debates on public television.* A third party candidate was excluded from a debate sponsored by a public television station on the ground that he had little popular support. He claimed a right of access. ARKANSAS EDUCATIONAL TELEVISION COMM'N v. FORBES, 523 U.S. 666 (1998), concluded that a candidate debate sponsored by a state-owned public television broadcaster was a nonpublic forum subject to constitutional restraints (because the views expressed were those of the candidates, not the broadcaster and because of the importance of such debates to the political process), but that the broadcaster's decision to exclude a candidate was reasonable: "We conclude that, unlike most other public television programs, the candidate debate was subject to constitutional constraints applicable to nonpublic fora under our forum precedents. Even so, the broadcaster's decision to exclude the candidate was a reasonable, viewpoint-neutral exercise of journalistic discretion."

Consider Frederick Schauer, *Principles, Institutions, and the First Amendment*, 112 Harv. L. Rev. 84 (1998): "Beyond designated public forums, [it] is hard to see the point of forum analysis in government enterprise cases. In the typical case, the complaint is not about access, but about discriminatory treatment. And at the heart of this issue is the seemingly banal but quite important point that content-based discriminatory treatment is appropriate in some contexts, but not in others. Yet once we recognize this idea, the point of combining the determination of which contexts permit content discrimination and which do not with public forum analysis is elusive. If access is mandatory, then the focus on content discrimination is redundant. But if access is not mandatory, then the existence (or not) of a public forum is superfluous. What is not superfluous is the question whether this is one of the government enterprises which may control for content or viewpoint, and as to this question public forum doctrine offers no assistance.[i] [That] forum analysis plays no role at all in *Finley*, and that the conclusory distinction between a nonpublic forum and a non-forum does all of the work in *Forbes*, serves only to underscore the point."

Should the exclusion of Forbes have been invalidated on the ground that the exclusion skews public debate? Should the state's purpose matter? Consider Jamin B. Raskin, *Disfavored Speech About Favored Rights: Hill v. Colorado, The Vanishing Public Forum and the Need For an Objective Speech Discrimination Test*, 51 Am. U. L. Rev. 179, 210 (2001): "[T]he Court found that the exclusion of the Independent candidate from a televised, government-run election debate was not viewpoint discriminatory because it was not based on officially expressed animosity towards his views. But the whole purpose and function of excluding an Independent is to block off a political viewpoint

---

i. But see Anthony E. Varona, *Out of Thin Air: Using First Amendment Public Forum Analysis to Redeem American Public Broadcasting Regulation*, 39 U. Mich. J.L. Reform 149 (2006).

based on its perceived unpopularity." See also Owen Fiss, *The Censorship of Television*, 93 Nw.U.L.Rev. 1215, 1233 (1999). Consider the test proposed in Tim Cramm, *The Designated Nonpublic Forum: Remedying the Forbes Mistake*, 67 Alb. L. Rev. 89, 149 (2003): "Where the public has a separate and independent interest in the forum being accessible to the broadest possible class of potential speakers, and that interest is at least as strong as the governmental interest in regulating the forum by excluding speakers, the forum is a designated nonpublic forum. Conversely, where the public's interest is less than the government's interest, the forum is a nonpublic forum akin to those discussed in *Cornelius* and *Perry*."

Suppose Congress required state owned broadcast stations to admit all official candidates to televised debates. Constitutional?

Did the public broadcast station have First Amendment rights? Consider Randall P. Bezanson and William G. Buss, *The Many Faces of Government Speech*, 86 Iowa L. Rev. 1377, 1441–1442 (2001): "*Forbes* may be the first decision in which the government's role as a speaker with a claim to First Amendment freedom has been expressly acknowledged other than by dicta. [V]irtually every regulatory act of government could be transformed into an act of government expression, and then sheltered from attack under the shield of the First Amendment. For example, one might argue that government's decisions about candidate access to the ballot are, in reality, editorial judgments protected under the First Amendment, for they result in specific content being included or excluded from a printed ballot, a communicative artifact of the government's making. Is it clear that deciding which names will appear on a ballot is any different, for analytical purposes, from deciding which candidates will appear on the program of a government-sponsored debate?"

6. Do access proposals miss the central problem? Is television at the heart of an "amusement-centered culture" that substitutes images and sound bites for serious public discourse while encouraging a privatized nonengaged citizenry? Consider Ronald Collins & David Skover, *The First Amendment in an Age of Paratroopers*, 68 Tex.L.Rev. 1087, 1088–89 (1990): "With entertainment as the paradigm for most public discourse, traditional First Amendment values—which stress civic restraint and serious dialogue—are overshadowed. Given these core values and the anticensorial direction of First Amendment theory, is there anything that could (or should) be done to thwart, rather than to feed, an amusement-centered culture?

"In attempting to answer this question, we confront a paradox: by saving itself, the First Amendment destroys itself. On the one hand, to preserve its anticensorial ideals, the First Amendment must protect both the old and new media cultures. Accordingly, it must constrain most governmental controls over expression, including those over the commercial use of electronic media. On the other hand, if the First Amendment's protections do not differentiate between the old and new media cultures, the modern obsession with self-amusement will trivialize public discourse and undermine the traditional aim of the First Amendment."[j]

---

j. For discussion of the Collins–Skover paradox by Max Lerner, David M. O'Brien, Martin Redish, Edward Rubin, Herbert Schiller, and Mark Tushnet, see Colloquy: *The First Amendment and the Paratroopers Paradox*, 68 Texas L.Rev. 1087 (1990).

7. Consider Henry Geller, *The Transformation of Television News: Articles and Comments: Fairness and the Public Trustee Concept: Time to Move On,* 47 Fed.Com.L.J. 79, 83–84 (1994): "It makes no sense to try to impose effective, behavioral regulation [when] conventional television faces such fierce and increasing competition, and viewership is declining rather than growing. It would be much sounder to truly deregulate broadcasting by eliminating the public trustee requirement and in its place substituting a reasonable spectrum fee imposed on existing stations (and an auction for all new frequency assignments), with the sums so obtained dedicated to public telecommunications. [For] the first time, we would have a structure that works to accomplish explicit policy goals. The commercial system would continue to do what it already does—deliver a great variety of entertainment and news-type programs. The noncommercial system would have the funds to accomplish its goals—to supply needed public service such as educational programming for children, cultural fare, minority presentations, and in-depth informational programs."

8. **Cable television.** Can government require cable operators to grant an access channel for the public, for the government, and for educational institutions? Which is the better analogy: *Red Lion* or *Miami Herald?* Need government lease space or otherwise afford access to utility poles under its control (and grant rights of way) to all competing cable companies? Is the appropriate analogy to *Schneider? Perry? Vincent? Red Lion? Miami Herald?*

LOS ANGELES v. PREFERRED COMMUNICATIONS, INC., 476 U.S. 488 (1986), per REHNQUIST, J., upheld the refusal to dismiss a complaint brought by a cable company demanding access to a city's utility poles and asserting a right to be free of government-mandated channels: "Cable television partakes of some of the aspects of speech and the communication of ideas as do the traditional enterprises of newspapers and [book publishers]. Respondent's proposed activities would seem to implicate First Amendment interests as do the activities of wireless broadcasters, which were found to fall within the ambit of the First Amendment in [*Red Lion*]. Of course, ['Even] protected speech is not equally permissible in all places and at all times.' *Cornelius.* Moreover, where speech and conduct are joined in a single course of action, the First Amendment values must be balanced against competing societal interests. See, e.g., *Los Angeles City Council v. Taxpayers for Vincent; O'Brien.*" The Court postponed fuller discussion of any cable rights until a factual record had been developed.[k]

---

k. For cogent discussion, see Daniel Brenner, *Cable Television and the Freedom of Expression,* 1988 Duke L.J. 329. See also Powe, supra, at 216–47; David Saylor, *Municipal Ripoff: The Unconstitutionality of Cable Television Franchise Fees and Access Support Payments,* 35 Cath. U.L.Rev. 671 (1986); Ithiel de Sola Pool, *Technologies of Freedom* 151–88 (1983); Monroe Price, *Taming Red Lion: The First Amendment and Structural Approaches to Media Regulation,* 31 Fed.Comm.L.J. 215 (1979); Comment, *Access to Cable Television: A Critique of the Affirmative Duty Theory of the First Amendment,* 70 Calif.L.Rev. 1393 (1982). For discussion of other technologies, see Special Issue, *Videotex,* 36 Fed.Comm.L.J. 119 (1984). Monroe Price, *Free Expression and Digital Dreams: The Open and Closed Terrain of Speech,* 22 Critical Inquiry 64 (1995).

The Cable Television and Consumer Protection and Competition Act of 1992 required cable television systems to devote a portion of their channels to local broadcasters including commercial stations and public broadcast stations.[a] Congress was concerned about the monopolistic character of cable operations in most localities and the economic incentives for cable operators to favor their own programming. It also pointed to the importance of maintaining local broadcasting. TURNER BROADCASTING SYSTEM, INC. v. FCC, 512 U.S. 622 (1994), per KENNEDY, J., joined by Rehnquist, C.J., and Blackmun and Souter, JJ., upheld the requirement so long as the Government could demonstrate on remand that in the absence of legislation, a large number of broadcast stations would not be carried or would be adversely repositioned, that such stations would be at serious risk of financial difficulty, that the cable operators' programming selections (as opposed to using unused channel capacity) would not be excessively affected, and that no less restrictive alternative means existed. The plurality, joined by Stevens, J., argued that the antitrust interests of government were content neutral, but concluded that "some measure of heightened First Amendment scrutiny" was appropriate because the act was not a generally applicable law but directed at cable operators: "The scope and operation of the challenged provisions make clear [that] Congress designed the must-carry provisions not to promote speech of a particular content, but to prevent cable operators from exploiting their economic power to the detriment of broadcasters, and thereby to ensure that all Americans, especially those unable to subscribe to cable, have access to free television programming—whatever its content."[b]

O'CONNOR, J., joined by Scalia, Thomas and Ginsburg, JJ., concurring and dissenting in part, would have held the requirements unconstitutional without a remand. They argued that strict scrutiny was appropriate because the preference for broadcasters over cable programmers on many channels was based on content (referring to findings about local public affairs programming and public television).[c] Although the interest in public affairs programming was said to be weighty, O'Connor, J., observed that public affairs cable-programming could be displaced: "In the rare circumstances where the government may draw content-based distinctions to serve its goals, the restrictions must serve the goals a good deal more precisely than this." O'Connor, J., also argued that the requirements should fail content neutral scrutiny as well because the act disadvantaged

---

a. It also required that they be placed in the same numerical position as when broadcast over the air.

b. Blackmun, J., concurring, emphasized the importance of deferring to Congress during the new proceedings. Stevens, J., concurring, reluctantly joined the order to remand; he would have preferred to affirm the must-carry legislation without further proceedings. Ginsburg, J., concurred in parts of the Court's opinion (including the section arguing for intermediate First Amendment scrutiny regarding the antitrust interest), filed a separate concurring opinion, and joined O'Connor, J's opinion.

c. Kennedy, J., argued that such findings showed "nothing more than the recognition that the services provided by broadcast television have some intrinsic value and, thus, are worth preserving against the threats posed by cable."

cable operators with no anti-competitive motives and favored broadcasters who could financially survive even if dropped from a cable system.[d]

NOTES AND QUESTIONS

1. ***Permissible content regulation.*** Has the United States "consistently and properly engaged in content-motivated structuring of the communications realm" in ways that have usually "benefited the nation"? See C. Edwin Baker, *Turner Broadcasting: Content–Based Regulation of Persons and Presses*, 1994 Sup.Ct.Rev. 57, 94. See also Marvin Ammori, *Beyond Content Neutrality*, 61 Fed. Comm. L.J. 273 (2009). Does the dissent's emphasis on content discrimination shortchange the government's interest in assuring a robust communications system? Would such an emphasis lead to the conclusion that commercial broadcasters deserved no preference but public broadcasters did? Consider Donald Hawthorne & Monroe Price, *Rewiring the First Amendment: Meaning, Content and Public Broadcasting*, 12 Cardozo Arts & Ent.L.J. 499, 504 (1994): "If the absence of a meaningful content basis for preferring commercial broadcasters should impair their entitlement to 'must-carry' treatment, precisely the converse is true for noncommercial broadcasters. These entities have been mandated to carry on government's historic responsibility to educate the citizenry and more recent undertaking to subsidize the arts."[e]

Given the steep decline in international news coverage and the need for more international news in an increasingly interdependent globalized setting, could government require that broadcasters set a particular amount of time for international and global issues? Lee C. Bollinger, *Uninhibited, Robust, and Wide-Open* 129 (2010). Cable operators?

2. ***Compelled speech?*** Consider C. Edwin Baker, *First Amendment Limits on Copyright*, 55 Vand. L. Rev. 938 (2002): "[T]he Court's apparent contradictory holdings in *Barnette*, Ch. 9, I supra, and *Turner I* got it right in both cases. Compulsion (or prohibition) is impermissible as to the individual's freedom of speech (*Barnette*) but sometimes permissible as a means to improve the overall communications environment in relation to a free press (*Turner I*). Since the cases involved no censorship, the Court could approve compelled speech in the press context that would improperly impinge on individual liberty in the speech context."

3. **The digital revolution.** Consider Neil Weinstock Netanel, *New Media in Old Bottles?*, 76 Geo. Wash. L.Rev. 952, 954 (2008): "The bulk of scholarly and activist attention among those who sympathize with Barron's [fn. a in *Miami Herald*] egalitarian vision of the First Amendment has moved from how to regulate mass media to promote expressive diversity to how to

---

d. Thomas, J., did not join this section of the opinion.

e. For additional commentary, see Cass R. Sunstein, *One Case at a Time* 172–82 (1999); Glen O. Robinson, *The Electronic First Amendment: An Essay for the New Age*, 47 Duke L.J. 899, 933–39 (1998); Jerome Barron, *Reading Turner through a Tornillo Lens*, 13 Comm. Lawyer (1995); Monroe Price & Donald Hawthorne, *Saving Public Television*, Hast.Comm./Ent.L.J. 65 (1994); Cass Sunstein, *The First Amendment in Cyberspace*, 104 Yale L.J. 1757 (1995); Mark Tushnet, *Weak Form Judicial Review and "Core" Civil Liberties*, 41 Harv. C.R.-C.L. L.Rev. 1 (2006); R. George Wright, *Content-Based and Content-Neutral Regulation of Speech: The Limitations of a Common Distinction*, 60 U. Miami L.Rev. 333, 354–55 (2006).

assure that individual speakers and new media have access to the conduits of digital communication." Consider Jack M. Balkin, *Digital Speech and Democratic Culture: A Theory of Freedom of Expression for the Information Society*, 79 N.Y.U. L. REV. 20 (2004): "The digital revolution has undermined one of the traditional justifications for structural regulation of the mass media— scarcity of bandwidth. Cable can accommodate hundreds of channels, as can satellite broadcasting. The number of speakers on the Internet seems limitless. Broadcast media now compete with cable, satellite, and the Internet for viewer attention. In theory, at least, digital technologies offer everyone the potential to become broadcasters." See also Yoo, note 4 after *CBS*; Michael J. Burstein, *Towards a New Standard for First Amendment Review of Structural Media Regulation*, 79 N.Y.U. L. Rev. 1030, 1035–1036 (2004). And consider Randall P. Bezanson and William G. Buss, *The Many Faces of Government Speech*, 86 Iowa L. Rev. 1377, 1447 (2001): "With the scarcity rationale no longer available, and with the shelter of *FCC v. Pacifica Foundation* unavailing because the scope of government editorial discretion extended beyond the obscene and beyond material considered indecent for children, the Court rested its decision explicitly on the cable medium and its influence. 'Cable television systems, including access channels, "have established a uniquely pervasive presence in the lives of all Americans." ' [T]he logic of the Court's attitude toward cable strongly suggests the conclusion that pervasiveness and intrusiveness mask concerns about the power of the medium in shaping personal and cultural values, the persuasiveness of its multi-sensory and real-time character, and the added dimensions of force and immediacy that unrestricted access to multi-sensory stimuli provides."

4. After remand, TURNER BROADCASTING SYSTEM, INC. v. FCC, 520 U.S. 180 (1997), per KENNEDY, J., joined by Rehnquist, C.J., Stevens, and Souter, JJ., upheld the must-carry provisions. Applying the *O'Brien* test, he emphasized the importance of deferring to Congress so long as it had "drawn reasonable inferences based upon substantial evidence." He found that the legislation was narrowly tailored to preserve the benefits of local broadcast television, to promote widespread dissemination of information from a multiplicity of sources, and to promote fair competition.

BREYER, J., concurring, joined Kennedy, J.'s opinion except for his discussion and conclusion regarding the fair competition rationale:[f] "Whether or not the statute does or does not sensibly compensate for some significant market defect, it undoubtedly seeks to provide over-the-air viewers who *lack* cable with a rich mix of over-the-air programming by guaranteeing the over-the-air stations that provide such programming with the extra dollars that an additional cable audience will generate. I believe that this purpose-to assure the over-the-air public 'access to a multiplicity of information sources,' provides sufficient basis for rejecting appellants' First Amendment claim.

"I do not deny that the compulsory carriage that creates the 'guarantee' extracts a serious First Amendment price. It interferes with the protected interests of the cable operators to choose their own programming; it prevents displaced cable program providers from obtaining an audience; and it will sometimes prevent some cable viewers from watching what, in its absence,

---

f. Stevens, J., also filed a concurring opinion.

would have been their preferred set of programs. This 'price' amounts to a 'suppression of speech.' ''

Breyer, J., observed that a cable system, physically dependent upon the availability of space along city streets, at present (perhaps less in the future) typically faces little competition, that it therefore constitutes a kind of bottleneck that controls the range of viewer choice (whether or not it uses any consequent economic power for economically predatory purposes), and that *some* degree-at least a limited degree of governmental intervention and control through regulation can prove appropriate when justified under *O'Brien* (at least when not 'content based'). Cf. *Red Lion.* Breyer, J., concluded that the statute survived '' 'intermediate scrutiny,' whether or not the statute [was] properly tailored to Congress' purely economic objectives.''

O'CONNOR, J., joined by Scalia, Thomas, and Ginsburg, JJ., dissenting, argued again that strict scrutiny should apply, agreed that deference was owed to Congress "in its predictive judgments and its evaluation of complex economic questions," but maintained that even under intermediate scrutiny, the Court had an independent duty to examine with care the Congressional interests, the findings, and the fit between the goals and consequences. She criticized the Court for being too deferential even on the assumption that the legislation was content neutral. On her analysis, the record did not support either the conclusion that cable posed a significant threat to local broadcast markets or that the act was narrowly tailored to deal with anti-competitive conduct.[g]

Consider Owen M. Fiss, *The Censorship of Television,* in *Eternally Vigilant: Free Speech in the Modern Era* 275 (Lee C. Bollinger & Geoffrey R. Stone eds., 2002): "Breyer's entire approach represents a revitalization of *Red Lion,* and his discussion of the economic power of cable operators allows the principle of that case to transcend the specific technological context in which it was born.''

II.   THE ELECTRONIC MEDIA AND CONTENT REGULATION

FCC v. PACIFICA FOUNDATION
438 U.S. 726, 98 S.Ct. 3026, 57 L.Ed.2d 1073 (1978).

JUSTICE STEVENS delivered the opinion of the Court (Parts I, II, III, and IV–C) and an opinion in which CHIEF JUSTICE BURGER and JUSTICE REHNQUIST joined (Parts IV–A and IV–B).

[In an early afternoon weekday broadcast which was devoted that day to contemporary attitudes toward the use of language, respondent's New York radio station aired a 12–minute selection called "Filthy Words,"

---

g. Would *Turner* justify the application of "must carry" rules to segments of the Internet? See also Cass Sunstein, *republic.com* (2001); Andrew Chin, *Making the World Wide Web Safe for Democracy: A Medium–Specific First Amendment Analysis,* 19 Hast. Comm/Ent L.J. 309 (1997).

from a comedy album by a satiric humorist, George Carlin. The monologue, which had evoked frequent laughter from a live theater audience, began by referring to Carlin's thought about the seven words you can't say on the public airwaves, "the ones you definitely wouldn't say ever." He then listed the words ("shit," "piss," "fuck," "motherfucker," "cocksucker," "cunt," and "tits"), "the ones that will curve your spine, grow hair on your hands and (laughter) maybe, even bring us, God help us, peace without honor (laughter) um, and a bourbon (laughter)," and repeated them over and over in a variety of colloquialisms. Immediately prior to the monologue, listeners were advised that it included sensitive language which some might regard as offensive. Those who might be offended were advised to change the station and return in fifteen minutes.

[The FCC received a complaint from a man stating that while driving in his car with his young son he had heard the broadcast of the Carlin monologue. The FCC issued an order to be "associated with the station's license file, and in the event that subsequent complaints are received, the Commission will then decide whether it should utilize any of the available sanctions it has been granted by Congress."][a]

The Commission characterized the language used in the Carlin monologue as "patently offensive," though not necessarily obscene, and expressed the opinion that it should be regulated by principles analogous to those found in the law of nuisance where the "law generally speaks to *channeling* behavior more than actually prohibiting [it]."[5]

Applying these considerations to the language used in the monologue as broadcast by respondent, the Commission concluded that certain words depicted sexual and excretory activities in a patently offensive manner, noted that they "were broadcast at a time when children were undoubtedly in the audience (i.e., in the early afternoon)," and that the prerecorded language, with these offensive words "repeated over and over," was "deliberately broadcast." In summary, the Commission stated: "We therefore hold that the language as broadcast was indecent [under 18 U.S.C. 1464]."

IV. Pacifica [argues] that the Commission's construction of the statutory language broadly encompasses so much constitutionally protected speech that reversal is required even if Pacifica's broadcast of the "Filthy Words" monologue is not itself protected by the First Amendment.
* * *

A. The first argument fails because our review is limited to the question whether the Commission has the authority to proscribe this particular broadcast. As the Commission itself emphasized, its order was "issued in a specific factual context." That approach is appropriate for

---

a. The FCC's action is placed in the context of other similar actions in Lucas Powe, *American Broadcasting and the First Amendment* 162–90 (1987). See Christine A. Corcos, *George Carlin, Constitutional Law Scholar*, 39 Stet. L.Rev. 899 (2008).

5. Thus, the Commission suggested, if an offensive broadcast had literary, artistic, political or scientific value, and were preceded by warnings, it might not be indecent in the late evening, but would be so during the day, when children are in the audience.

courts as well as the Commission when regulation of indecency is at stake, for indecency is largely a function of context—it cannot be adequately judged in the abstract. * * *

It is true that the Commission's order may lead some broadcasters to censor themselves. At most, however, the Commission's definition of indecency will deter only the broadcasting of patently offensive references to excretory and sexual organs and activities.[18] While some of these references may be protected, they surely lie at the periphery of First Amendment concern. * * * Invalidating any rule on the basis of its hypothetical application to situations not before the Court is "strong medicine" to be applied "sparingly and only as a last resort." *Broadrick* [Ch. 1, VI supra]. We decline to administer that medicine to preserve the vigor of patently offensive sexual and excretory speech.

B. [The] words of the Carlin monologue are unquestionably "speech" within the meaning of the First Amendment. [The] question in this case is whether a broadcast of patently offensive words dealing with sex and excretion may be regulated because of its content.[20] Obscene materials have been denied the protection of the First Amendment because their content is so offensive to contemporary moral standards. *Roth.* But the fact that society may find speech offensive is not a sufficient reason for suppressing it. Indeed, if it is the speaker's opinion that gives offense, that consequence is a reason for according it constitutional protection. For it is a central tenet of the First Amendment that the government must remain neutral in the marketplace of ideas. If there were any reason to believe that the Commission's characterization of the Carlin monologue as offensive could be traced to its political content—or even to the fact that it satirized contemporary attitudes about four letter words[22]—First Amendment protection might be required. But that is simply not this case. These words offend for the same reasons that obscenity offends. Their place in the hierarchy of First Amendment values was aptly sketched by Justice Murphy when he said, "such utterances are no essential part of any exposition of ideas, and are of such slight social value as a step to truth that any benefit that may be derived from them is clearly outweighed by the social interest in order and morality." *Chaplinsky.*

---

18. A requirement that indecent language be avoided will have its primary effect on the form, rather than the content, of serious communication. There are few, if any, thoughts that cannot be expressed by the use of less offensive language. [*FCC v. Fox Television Stations, Inc.*, 129 S.Ct. 1800 (2009), per Scalia, J., observed that "any chilled references to excretory and sexual material surely lie at the periphery of First Amendment concern.' "].

20. Although neither Justice Powell nor Justice Brennan directly confronts this question, both have answered it affirmatively, the latter explicitly, at fn. 3, infra, and the former implicitly by concurring in a judgment that could not otherwise stand.

22. The monologue does present a point of view; it attempts to show that the words it uses are "harmless" and that our attitudes toward them are "essentially silly." The Commission objects, not to this point of view, but to the way in which it is expressed. The belief that these words are harmless does not necessarily confer a First Amendment privilege to use them while proselytizing just as the conviction that obscenity is harmless does not license one to communicate that conviction by the indiscriminate distribution of an obscene leaflet.

Although these words ordinarily lack literary, political, or scientific value, they are not entirely outside the protection of the First Amendment. Some uses of even the most offensive words are unquestionably protected. Indeed, we may assume, arguendo, that this monologue would be protected in other contexts. [It] is a characteristic of speech such as this that both its capacity to offend and its "social value," to use Justice Murphy's term, vary with the circumstances. Words that are commonplace in one setting are shocking in another. To paraphrase Justice Harlan, one occasion's lyric is another's vulgarity. Cf. *Cohen v. California*.[25]

In this case it is undisputed that the content of Pacifica's broadcast was "vulgar," "offensive," and "shocking." Because content of that character is not entitled to absolute constitutional protection under all circumstances, we must consider its context in order to determine whether the Commission's action was constitutionally permissible.

C.   We have long recognized that each medium of expression presents special First Amendment problems. And of all forms of communication, it is broadcasting that has received the most limited First Amendment [protection.]

The reasons for these distinctions are complex, but two have relevance to the present case. First, the broadcast media have established a uniquely pervasive presence in the lives of all Americans. Patently offensive, indecent material presented over the airwaves confronts the citizen, not only in public, but also in the privacy of the home, where the individual's right to be let alone plainly outweighs the First Amendment rights of an intruder. *Rowan v. Post Office Dept.*, 397 U.S. 728 (1970). Because the broadcast audience is constantly tuning in and out, prior warnings cannot completely protect the listener or viewer from unexpected program content. To say that one may avoid further offense by turning off the radio when he hears indecent language is like saying that the remedy for an assault is to run away after the first blow.[27] * * *

Second, broadcasting is uniquely accessible to children, even those too young to read. Although Cohen's written message might have been incomprehensible to a first grader, Pacifica's broadcast could have enlarged a child's vocabulary in an instant. Other forms of offensive expression may be withheld from the young without restricting the expression at its source. Bookstores and motion picture theaters, for example, may be

---

25.   The importance of context is illustrated by the *Cohen* case. [So] far as the evidence showed no one in the courthouse was offended by [Cohen's jacket.]

In holding that criminal sanctions could not be imposed on Cohen for his political statement in a public place, the Court rejected the argument that his speech would offend unwilling viewers; it noted that "there was no evidence that persons powerless to avoid [his] conduct did in fact object to it." In contrast, in this case the Commission was responding to a listener's strenuous complaint, and Pacifica does not question its determination that this afternoon broadcast was likely to offend listeners. It should be noted that the Commission imposed a far more moderate penalty on Pacifica than the state court imposed on Cohen. Even the strongest civil penalty at the Commission's command does not include criminal prosecution.

27.   Outside the home, the balance between the offensive speaker and the unwilling audience may sometimes tip in favor of the speaker, requiring the offended listener to turn away. See *Erznoznik*. * * *

prohibited from making indecent material available to children. We held in *Ginsberg* [Ch. 1, III, B supra] that the government's interest in the "well being of its youth" and in supporting "parents' claim to authority in their own household" justified the regulation of otherwise protected expression.[28] * * *

It is appropriate, in conclusion, to emphasize the narrowness of our holding. This case does not involve a two-way radio conversation between a cab driver and a dispatcher, or a telecast of an Elizabethan comedy. We have not decided that an occasional expletive in either setting would justify any sanction or, indeed, that this broadcast would justify a criminal prosecution. The Commission's decision rested entirely on a nuisance rationale under which context is all-important.

[R]eversed.

JUSTICE POWELL, with whom JUSTICE BLACKMUN joins, concurring.

[T]he language employed is, to most people, vulgar and offensive. It was chosen specifically for this quality, and it was repeated over and over as a sort of verbal shock treatment. [In] essence, the Commission sought to "channel" the monologue to hours when the fewest unsupervised children would be exposed to it. In my view, this consideration provides strong support for the Commission's holding.

[The] Commission properly held that the speech from which society may attempt to shield its children is not limited to that which appeals to the youthful prurient interest. The language involved in this case is as potentially degrading and harmful to children as representations of many erotic acts.

In most instances, the dissemination of this kind of speech to children may be limited without also limiting willing adults' access to it. Sellers of printed and recorded matter and exhibitors of motion pictures and live performances may be required to shut their doors to children, but such a requirement has no effect on adults' access. See *Ginsberg*. The difficulty is that [d]uring most of the broadcast hours, both adults and unsupervised children are likely to be in the broadcast audience, and the broadcaster cannot reach willing adults without also reaching children. This, as the Court emphasizes, is one of the distinctions between the broadcast and other media to which we often have adverted as justifying a different treatment of the broadcast media for First Amendment purposes. In my view, the Commission was entitled to give substantial weight to this difference in reaching its decision in this case.

---

28. The Commission's action does not by any means reduce adults to hearing only what is fit for children. Cf. *Butler v. Michigan* [Ch. 1, III, B supra]. Adults who feel the need may purchase tapes and records or go to theatres and nightclubs to hear these words. In fact, the Commission has not unequivocally closed even broadcasting to speech of this sort; whether broadcast audiences in the late evening contain so few children that playing this monologue would be permissible is an issue neither the Commission nor this Court has decided. [Would the rationale based on supporting parental authority rule out banning Carlin's monologue in the early evening? See Baker, *The Evening Hours During Pacifica Standard Time,* 3 Vill. Sports & Ent. L.J. 45 (1996)].

[Another difference] is that broadcasting—unlike most other forms of communication—comes directly into the home, the one place where people ordinarily have the right not to be assaulted by uninvited and offensive sights and sounds. *Erznoznik; Cohen; Rowan.* * * * "That we are often 'captives' outside the sanctuary of the home and subject to objectionable speech and other sound does not mean we must be captives everywhere." *Rowan.* The Commission also was entitled to give this factor appropriate weight in the circumstances of the instant case. This is not to say, however, that the Commission has an unrestricted license to decide what speech, protected in other media, may be banned from the airwaves in order to protect unwilling adults from momentary exposure to it in their homes.[2] * * *

[M]y views are generally in accord with what is said in Part IV(C) of opinion. I therefore join that portion of his opinion. I do not join Part IV(B), however, because I do not subscribe to the theory that the Justices of this Court are free generally to decide on the basis of its content which speech protected by the First Amendment is most "valuable" and hence deserving of the most protection, and which is less "valuable" and hence deserving of less protection.[3] In my view, the result in this case does not turn on whether Carlin's monologue, viewed as a whole, or the words that comprise it, have more or less "value" than a candidate's campaign speech. This is a judgment for each person to make, not one for the judges to impose upon him.[4]

The result turns instead on the unique characteristics of the broadcast media, combined with society's right to protect its children from speech generally agreed to be inappropriate for their years, and with the interest of unwilling adults in not being assaulted by such offensive speech in their homes. Moreover, I doubt whether today's decision will prevent any adult who wishes to receive Carlin's message in Carlin's own words from doing so, and from making for himself a value judgment as to the merit of the message and words. These are the grounds upon which I join the judgment of the Court as to Part IV.

JUSTICE BRENNAN, with whom JUSTICE MARSHALL joins, dissenting.

---

2. It is true that the radio listener quickly may tune out speech that is offensive to him. In addition, broadcasters may preface potentially offensive programs with warnings. But such warnings do not help the unsuspecting listener who tunes in at the middle of a program. In this respect, too, broadcasting appears to differ from books and records, which may carry warnings on their faces, and from motion pictures and live performances, which may carry warnings on their marquees.

3. The Court has, however, created a limited exception to this rule in order to bring commercial speech within the protection of the First Amendment. See *Ohralik* [Ch. 3, II supra].

4. For much the same reason, I also do not join Part IV(A). I had not thought that the application vel non of overbreadth analysis should depend on the Court's judgment as to the value of the protected speech that might be deterred. Except in the context of commercial speech, see *Bates* [Ch. 3, II supra], it has not in the past. See, e.g., *Lewis v. New Orleans; Gooding.*

As Justice Stevens points out, however, the Commission's order was limited to the facts of this case; "it did not purport to engage in formal rulemaking or in the promulgation of any regulations." In addition, since the Commission may be expected to proceed cautiously, as it has in the past, I do not foresee an undue "chilling" effect on broadcasters' exercise of their rights. I agree, therefore, that respondent's overbreadth challenge is meritless.

[T]he Court refuses to embrace the notion, completely antithetical to basic First Amendment values, that the degree of protection the First Amendment affords protected speech varies with the social value ascribed to that speech by five Members of this Court. See opinion of Justice Powell. Moreover, [all] Members of the Court agree that [the monologue] does not fall within one of the categories of speech, such as "fighting words," or obscenity, that is totally without First Amendment protection. [Yet] a majority of the Court[1] nevertheless finds that, on the facts of this case, the FCC is not constitutionally barred from imposing sanctions on Pacifica for its airing of the Carlin monologue. * * *

[A]n individual's actions in switching on and listening to communications transmitted over the public airways and directed to the public at-large do not implicate fundamental privacy interests, even when engaged in within the home. Instead, because the radio is undeniably a public medium, these actions are more properly viewed as a decision to take part, if only as a listener, in an ongoing public discourse. Although an individual's decision to allow public radio communications into his home undoubtedly does not abrogate all of his privacy interests, the residual privacy interests he retains vis-à-vis the communication he voluntarily admits into his home are surely no greater than those of the people present in the corridor of the Los Angeles courthouse in *[Cohen]*.

Even if an individual who voluntarily opens his home to radio communications retains privacy interests of sufficient moment to justify a ban on protected speech if those interests are "invaded in an essentially intolerable manner," *Cohen,* the very fact that those interests are threatened only by a radio broadcast precludes any intolerable invasion of privacy; for unlike other intrusive modes of communication, such as sound trucks, "[t]he radio can be turned off"—and with a minimum of effort. [Whatever] the minimal discomfort suffered by a listener who inadvertently tunes into a program he finds offensive during the brief interval before he can simply extend his arm and switch stations or flick the "off" button, it is surely worth the candle to preserve the broadcaster's right to send, and the right of those interested to receive, a message entitled to full First Amendment protection. * * *

The Court's balance, of necessity, fails to accord proper weight to the interests of listeners who wish to hear broadcasts the FCC deems offensive. It permits majoritarian tastes completely to preclude a protected message from entering the homes of a receptive, unoffended minority. No decision of this Court supports such a result. Where the individuals comprising the offended majority may freely choose to reject the material being offered, we have never found their privacy interests of such moment to warrant the suppression of speech on privacy grounds. [In] *Rowan,* the Court upheld a statute, permitting householders to require that mail advertisers stop sending them lewd or offensive materials and remove

---

1. Where I refer without differentiation to the actions of "the Court," my reference is to this majority, which consists of my Brothers Powell and Stevens and those Members of the Court joining their separate opinions.

their names from mailing lists. Unlike the situation here, householders who wished to receive the sender's communications were not prevented from doing so. Equally important, the determination of offensiveness vel non under the statute involved in *Rowan* was completely within the hands of the individual householder; no governmental evaluation of the worth of the mail's content stood between the mailer and the householder. In contrast, the visage of the censor is all too discernable here. * * *

Because the Carlin monologue is obviously not an erotic appeal to the prurient interests of children, the Court, for the first time, allows the government to prevent minors from gaining access to materials that are not obscene, and are therefore protected, as to them.[2] It thus ignores our recent admonition that "[s]peech that is neither obscene as to youths nor subject to some other legitimate proscription cannot be suppressed solely to protect the young from ideas or images that a legislative body thinks unsuitable for them." *Erznoznik*.[3] The Court's refusal to follow its own pronouncements is especially lamentable since it has the anomalous subsidiary effect, at least in the radio context at issue here, of making completely unavailable to adults material which may not constitutionally be kept even from children. * * * *Yoder* and *Pierce,* hold that parents, *not* the government, have the right to make certain decisions regarding the upbringing of their children. As surprising as it may be to individual Members of this Court, some parents may actually find Mr. Carlin's unabashed attitude towards the seven "dirty words" healthy, and deem it desirable to expose their children to the manner in which Mr. Carlin defuses the taboo surrounding the words. Such parents may constitute a minority of the American public, but the absence of great numbers willing to exercise the right to raise their children in this fashion does not alter the right's nature or its existence. Only the Court's regrettable decision does that.

As demonstrated above, neither of the factors relied on by both [Powell and Stevens, JJ.]—the intrusive nature of radio and the presence of children in the listening audience—can, when taken on its own terms, support the FCC's disapproval of the Carlin monologue. [N]either of the opinions comprising the Court serve to clarify the extent to which the FCC may assert the privacy and children-in-the-audience rationales as justification for expunging from the airways protected communications the Com-

---

2. Even if the monologue appealed to the prurient interest of minors, it would not be obscene as to them unless, as to them, "the work, taken as a whole, lacks serious literary, artistic, political, or scientific value." *Miller.*

3. It may be that a narrowly drawn regulation prohibiting the use of offensive language on broadcasts directed specifically at younger children constitutes one of the "other legitimate proscription[s]" alluded to in *Erznoznik.* This is so both because of the difficulties inherent in adapting the *Miller* formulation to communications received by young children, and because such children are "not possessed of that full capacity for individual choice which is the presupposition of the First Amendment guarantees." *Ginsberg.* (Stewart, J., concurring). I doubt, as my Brother Stevens suggests, that such a limited regulation amounts to a regulation of speech based on its content, since, by hypothesis, the only persons at whom the regulated communication is directed are incapable of evaluating its content. To the extent that such a regulation is viewed as a regulation based on content, it marks the outermost limits to which content regulation is permissible.

mission finds offensive. Taken to their logical extreme, these rationales would support the cleansing of public radio of any "four-letter words" whatsoever, regardless of their context. The rationales could justify the banning from radio of a myriad of literary works, novels, poems, and plays by the likes of Shakespeare, Joyce, Hemingway, Ben Jonson, Henry Fielding, Robert Burns, and Chaucer; they could support the suppression of a good deal of political speech, such as the Nixon tapes; and they could even provide the basis for imposing sanctions for the broadcast of certain portions of the Bible.

In order to dispel the spectre of the possibility of so unpalatable a degree of censorship, and to defuse Pacifica's overbreadth challenge, the FCC insists that it desires only the authority to reprimand a broadcaster on facts analogous to those present in this case. [Powell and Stevens, JJ.] take the FCC at its word, and consequently do no more than permit the Commission to censor the afternoon broadcast of the "sort of verbal shock treatment" involved [here]. I would place the responsibility and the right to weed worthless and offensive communications from the public airways where it belongs and where, until today, it resided: in a public free to choose those communications worthy of its attention from a marketplace unsullied by the censor's hand. * * *

My Brother Stevens [finds] solace in his conviction that "[t]here are few, if any, thoughts that cannot be expressed by the use of less offensive language." The idea that the content of a message and its potential impact on any who might receive it can be divorced from the words that are the vehicle for its expression is transparently fallacious. A given word may have a unique capacity to capsule an idea, evoke an emotion, or conjure up an image. Indeed, for those of us who place an appropriately high value on our cherished First Amendment rights, the word "censor" is such a word. Justice Harlan, speaking for the Court, recognized the truism that a speaker's choice of words cannot surgically be separated from the ideas he desires to express when he warned that "we cannot indulge the facile assumption that one can forbid particular words without also running a substantial risk of suppressing ideas in the process."

[Stevens, J.] also finds relevant to his First Amendment analysis the fact that "[a]dults who feel the need may purchase tapes and records or go to theatres and nightclubs to hear [the tabooed] words." [Powell, J.,] agrees. [The] opinions of my Brethren display both a sad insensitivity to the fact that these alternatives involve the expenditure of money, time, and effort that many of those wishing to hear Mr. Carlin's message may not be able to afford, and a naive innocence of the reality that in many cases, the medium may well be the message.

The Court apparently believes that the FCC's actions here can be analogized to the zoning ordinances upheld in *American Mini Theatres.* For two reasons, it is wrong. First, the zoning ordinances found to pass constitutional muster [had] valid goals other than the channeling of protected speech. No such goals are present here. Second, [the] ordinances did not restrict the access of distributors or exhibitors to the market or impair the viewing public's access to the regulated material. Again, this is not the situation here.

[T]here runs throughout the opinions of my Brothers Powell and Stevens [a] depressing inability to appreciate that in our land of cultural pluralism, there are many who think, act, and talk differently from the Members of this Court, and who do not share their fragile sensibilities. It is only an acute ethnocentric myopia that enables the Court [to blink at] persons who do not share the Court's view as to which words or expressions are acceptable and who, for a variety of reasons, including a conscious desire to flout majoritarian conventions, express themselves using words that may be regarded as offensive by those from different socio-economic backgrounds.[8] In this context, the Court's decision may be seen for what, in the broader perspective, it really is: another of the dominant culture's inevitable efforts to force those groups who do not share its mores to conform to its way of thinking, acting, and speaking. * * *b

NOTES AND QUESTIONS

1. Consider Steven H. Shiffrin, *The First Amendment, Democracy, and Romance* 80 (1990): "Most people with any First Amendment bones in their bodies are troubled by [*Pacifica*]. But the nub of the First Amendment insult has little to do with self-government or with the marketplace of ideas. The concern does not flow from a worry that voters will be deprived of valuable information. Concern that the truth about vulgar language might not emerge in the marketplace of ideas may be well placed, but is not a sufficient concern to explain the widespread outrage against the decision. Again, the decision is an affront to a notion of content neutrality, but there are many of those. The *Pacifica* case produces heat precisely because Carlin's speech is considered by many to be precisely what the First Amendment is *supposed* to protect. Carlin is attacking conventions; assaulting the prescribed orthodoxy; mocking the stuffed shirts; Carlin *is* the prototypical dissenter.

"It matters not at all whether the target of his invective is society at large or a public official. The outrage is that the stuffed shirts are in a position to silence Carlin, or at least in a position to keep him from 'offending' the mass audience."[c]

2. **Market failure and communitarian vision.** Does the market encourage programming that is inherently harmful to children? Does it lead

---

8. Under the approach taken by my Brother Powell, the availability of broadcasts *about* groups whose members comprise such audiences might also be affected. Both news broadcasts about activities involving these groups and public affairs broadcasts about their concerns are apt to contain interviews, statements, or remarks by group leaders and members which may contain offensive language to an extent my Brother Powell finds unacceptable.

b. Stewart, J., joined by Brennan, White, and Marshall, JJ., dissenting maintained that the Commission lacked statutory authority to issue its order and did not reach the constitutional question.

c. For a compelling account of the censorship battles surrounding the colorful comic and critic Lenny Bruce, see Ronald K.L. Collins & David M. Skover, *The Trials of Lenny Bruce: The Fall and Rise of an American Icon* (2003).

broadcasters to pursue adult-driven ratings pushing the "boundaries of the existing indecency rules?" Does a communitarian vision of the public airwaves help to salvage the weaknesses of the scarcity argument for broadcast regulation? See generally Joshua B. Gordon, *Pacifica is Long Dead. Long Live Pacifica,* 79 S.Cal. L.Rev. 1451, 1494–97 (2006).

3. ***Cohen distinguished?*** Consider R. George Wright, *An Emotion–Based Approach to Freedom of Speech,* 34 Loy. U. Chi. L.J. 429, 445 (2003): "*Cohen* emphasized that even slight changes in wording may change the emotive, if not the cognitive, message conveyed, and that there might be no fully adequate substitute available, in some contexts, for particular words. *Pacifica Foundation,* however, concluded that in an indecent radio broadcast case, requiring more decorous language tended chiefly to affect the form, as opposed to the content of the message, and that few indecently expressed thoughts were not expressible in more decorous language."

4. ***Implications for broadcasting.*** Consider Thomas Krattenmaker & Lucas Powe, *Televised Violence: First Amendment Principles and Social Science Theory,* 64 Va.L.Rev. 1123, 1228 (1978): *Pacifica* "marks the first time any theory other than scarcity has received the official imprimatur of the Court. [S]carcity could not have authorized the result in *Pacifica* because regardless of whether one thinks the incredible abundance of radio stations in the United States (and especially in New York City) is insufficient, scarcity supports adding voices not banning them." What is the significance of the Court's comment that "the broadcast media have established a uniquely pervasive presence in the lives of all Americans"? Consider Daniel Brenner, *Censoring the Airwaves: The Supreme Court's Pacifica Decision* in Free But Regulated: Conflicting Traditions in Media Law 175, 177 & 79 (1982): "[N]ewspapers, drive-in movies, direct mail advertisements and imprinted T-shirts are media that have also 'established a uniquely pervasive presence' in our lives, in and out of [home]. Offhand comments about broadcasting enjoying 'the most limited' First Amendment protection—What of comic books? Playing cards? Chinese cookie fortunes?—are not simply harmless baffle; they constitute Delphic pronouncements made at a watershed period in the development of electronic media." See also Powe, supra fn. a, at 210–11.

Is the Court suggesting that the broadcast media are uniquely powerful? If so, should that factor cut for or against government regulation?[d] Does *Pacifica* support regulation of sex and violence on television, of "offensive" commercials, of advertising directed toward children? See generally Matthew Spitzer, *Seven Dirty Words and Six Other Stories* (1986) (criticizing *Pacifica's* distinctions between print and broadcast).

5. FCC v. LEAGUE OF WOMEN VOTERS, 468 U.S. 364 (1984), per BRENNAN, J., invalidated a federal law prohibiting editorializing on public broadcast stations: "As our cases attest, [broadcast restrictions] have been upheld only when we were satisfied that the restriction is narrowly tailored to

---

d. See Powe, supra, at 211–15; Lucas Powe, *"Or of the [Broadcast] Press,"* 55 Tex.L.Rev. 39, 58–62 (1976). On the various justifications for broadcast regulation, see J.M. Balkin, *Media Filters, the V–Chip, and the Foundations of Broadcast Regulation,* 45 Duke L.J. 1131 (1996).

further a substantial governmental interest, such as ensuring adequate and balanced coverage of public issues.[13]"

6. ***Public/Private.*** David Cole, *Playing by Pornography's Rules: The Regulation of Sexual Expression,* 143 U.Pa.L.Rev. 111, 140 (1994); "The Court's sexual expression decisions can be organized along a similar public/private axis. The Court's zoning decisions allow communities to demand that when sexually explicit speech appears in public, it must be relegated to dark and distant parts of town. The Court's affirmance of the FCC's 'indecency' regulation permits the zoning of sexual speech to less 'public' times of day. And while private possession of obscenity cannot be regulated, the state is free to regulate obscenity in a public place even if it is enjoyed only by consenting adults, and even where it is only being transported through public channels for private home use. What is immune from regulation in private becomes suppressible in public, even if the very same speakers, listeners, and speech are involved."

7. ***Anti-abortion advertising.*** Is graphic anti-abortion advertising indecent? Should it be channeled to the late evening hours? From the perspective of Stevens, J.? Powell, J.? See Lili Levi, *The FCC, Indecency, and Anti-Abortion Political Advertising,* 3 Vill.Spts. & Ent.L.J. 85 (1996).

8. **Other Media. (a)** *Telephonic "indecency" compared.* SABLE COMMUNICATIONS v. FCC, 492 U.S. 115 (1989), per White, J., invalidated a congressional ban on "indecent" interstate commercial telephone messages, i.e., "dial-a-porn."[e] The Court thought *Pacifica* was "readily distinguishable from this case, most obviously because it did not involve a total ban on broadcasting indecent material. [Second,] there is no 'captive audience' problem here; callers will generally not be unwilling listeners. [Third,] the congressional record contains no legislative findings that would justify us in concluding that there is no constitutionally acceptable less restrictive means, short of a total ban, to achieve the Government's interest in protecting minors."

(b) *Internet "indecency" compared.* Two provisions of the Communications Decency Act ("CDA") sought to protect minors from indecent or patently offensive material on the Internet. 47 U.S.C. § 223(a) prohibited the knowing transmission of indecent messages to any recipient under 18 years of

---

13. [*Pacifica*] is consistent with the approach taken in our other broadcast cases. There, the Court focused on certain physical characteristics of broadcasting—specifically, that the medium's uniquely pervasive presence renders impossible any prior warning for those listeners who may be offended by indecent language, and, second, that the case with which children may gain access to the medium, especially during daytime hours, creates a substantial risk that they may be exposed to such offensive expression without parental supervision. The governmental interest in reduction of those risks through Commission regulation of the timing and character of such "indecent broadcasting" was thought sufficiently substantial to outweigh the broadcaster's First Amendment interest in controlling the presentation of its programming. In this case, by contrast, we are faced not with indecent expression, but rather with expression that is at the core of First Amendment protections, and no claim is made by the Government that the expression of editorial opinion by noncommercial stations will create a substantial "nuisance" of the kind addressed in *Pacifica.*

e. The Court upheld a ban on "obscene" interstate commercial telephonic messages. Scalia, J., concurring, noted: "[W]hile we hold the Constitution prevents Congress from banning indecent speech in this fashion, we do not hold that the Constitution requires public utilities to carry it." Brennan, J., joined by Marshall and Stevens, JJ., concurred on the indecency issue and dissented on the obscenity issue.

age. 47 U.S.C. § 223(d) prohibited the knowing sending or displaying of patently offensive messages in a manner that is available to a person under 18 years of age. Patently offensive was defined as any "image or other communication that in context, depicts or describes, in terms patently offensive as measured by contemporary community standards, sexual or excretory activities or organs."

RENO v. AMERICAN CIVIL LIBERTIES UNION, 521 U.S. 844 (1997), invalidated both provisions: "The breadth of the CDA's coverage is wholly unprecedented. Unlike the regulations upheld in *Ginsberg* and *Pacifica*, the scope of the CDA is not limited to commercial speech or commercial entities. [The] general, undefined terms 'indecent' and 'patently offensive' cover large amounts of nonpornographic material with serious educational or other value. Moreover, the 'community standards' criterion as applied to the Internet means that any communication available to a nation-wide audience will be judged by the standards of the community most likely to be offended by the message.[f] The regulated subject matter includes any of the seven 'dirty words' used in the *Pacifica* monologue, the use of which the Government's expert acknowledged could constitute a felony. It may also extend to discussions about prison rape or safe sexual practices, artistic images that include nude subjects, and arguably the card catalogue of the Carnegie Library."[g] Compare *Ashcroft v. American Civil Liberties Union* (II), 542 U.S. 656 (2004), which struck down the Child Online Protection Act prohibiting the placement of material obscene for children on the web unless proof of age for access was required. The Court concluded that Congress could encourage the use of software that would block pornography as a less restrictive alternative. Scalia, J., dissenting, argued that strict scrutiny was inappropriate and Breyer, J., argued that encouragement of filtering software had been tried and found wanting.[h]

(c) Consider Robert Corn-Revere, *Can Indecency Broadcast Regulations Be Extended to Cable Television and Satellite Radio?*, 30 S. Ill.U.L.J. 243

---

f. Nonetheless, *Ashcroft v. American Civil Liberties Union*, 535 U.S. 564 (2002), held that the Child Online Protection Act's requirement in defining obscenity that prurient interest to children and patent offensiveness for children be determined by reference to "community standards" did not by itself render the statute substantially overbroad.

g. Consider Marjorie Heins, *Indecency: The Ongoing American Debate Over Sex, Children, Free Speech, and Dirty Words* (1997): "It remains to be seen whether *Reno v. ACLU* will prove an idiosyncratically broad response to a broadly drafted law, or whether its recognition of the positive value of some speech about some speech, even for minors, will mark the beginning of a long-overdue process of actually examining the presumption that sexual explicitness or crude language is intrinsically harmful to the young." The Court suggested that regulations of speech on the internet should be subject to stricter scrutiny than broadcast regulations, prompting Stuart Minor Benjamin, *Proactive Legislation and the First Amendment*, 99 Mich. L. Rev. 281, 320 (2000) to observe: [T]he Supreme Court stated, as one of its reasons for subjecting Internet regulation to stricter scrutiny than broadcast regulation, that broadcast has a history of government regulation and has been regulated since its inception, whereas the Internet has no comparable history of regulation. This creates a somewhat perverse incentive for legislatures— regulate a medium in its infancy or lose your chance to regulate at all."

h. The Court used strict scrutiny because content discrimination was present. Given that the speech is non-political and that no viewpoint discrimination was present, would it be better advised to employ middle level scrutiny? Should it assess the degree of burden as a part of its determination as to which level of scrutiny to employ? See generally Patrick M. Garry, *A New First Amendment Model for Evaluating Content-Based Regulation of Internet Pornography*, 2007 B.Y.U.L. Rev. 1595 (2007).

(2006): "[I]ndecency regulations restrict what may be transmitted on over-the-air broadcasting but have been struck down for other media, including print, film, the mails, cable television, and the internet. As a result of this technology-specific approach, one click on the TV remote can mean the difference between full constitutional protection for a program and heavy fines."

———

Cable operators are required under federal law to reserve channels for commercial lease ("leased access channels"). For some years federal law prevented cable operators from employing any editorial control over the content of leased access. The Cable Television Consumer Protection and Competition of 1992, however, permitted cable operators to prohibit the broadcast of material that the cable operator "reasonably believes describes or depicts sexual or excretory activities or organs in a patently offensive manner" on leased access channels (47 U.S.C. § 10(a)).

DENVER AREA EDUCATIONAL TELECOMMUNICATIONS CONSORTIUM, INC. v. FCC, 518 U.S. 727 (1996), upheld the constitutionality of § 10(a).[a] BREYER, J., joined by Stevens, O'Connor, and Souter, JJ., argued that the statute was sufficiently tailored to address a significant problem: "Justices Kennedy and Thomas would have us decide this case simply by transferring and applying literally categorical standards this Court has developed in other contexts. For Justice Kennedy, leased access channels are like a common carrier, cablecast is a protected medium, strict scrutiny applies, § 10(a) fails this test, and, therefore, § 10(a) is invalid. For Justice Thomas, the case is simple because the cable operator who owns the system over which access channels are broadcast, like a bookstore owner with respect to what it displays on the shelves, has a predominant First Amendment interest. Both categorical approaches suffer from the same flaws: they import law developed in very different contexts into a new and changing environment, and they lack the flexibility necessary to allow government to respond to very serious practical problems without sacrificing the free exchange of ideas the First Amendment is designed to protect. * * *

"Over the years, this Court has restated and refined [basic] First Amendment principles, adopting them more particularly to the balance of competing interests and the special circumstances of each field of application. [This] tradition teaches that the First Amendment embodies an overarching commitment to protect speech from Government regulation

---

a. O'Connor, J's concurring opinion is omitted. The Court also struck down (1) a provision permitting a cable operator to prohibit indecent speech on public access channels, distinguishing leased access channels in part because the presence of other supervisory mechanisms for public access channels made the provision seem less needed; (2) a provision requiring that a cable operator scramble or otherwise block any indecent speech permitted on leased access channels allowing for unscrambling on written request; and (3) a similar provision blocking provision for channels primarily dedicated to sexual programming. With respect to the blocking requirements, the Court was troubled by the inconsistent treatment between channels and the breadth of the restrictions.

through close judicial scrutiny, thereby enforcing the Constitution's constraints, but without imposing judicial formulae so rigid that they become a straightjacket that disables Government from responding to serious problems. This Court, in different contexts, has consistently held that the Government may directly regulate speech to address extraordinary problems, where its regulations are appropriately tailored to resolve those problems without imposing an unnecessarily great restriction on speech. Justices Kennedy and Thomas would have us further declare which, among the many applications of the general approach that this Court has developed over the years, we are applying here. But no definitive choice among competing analogies (broadcast, common carrier, bookstore) allows us to declare a rigid single standard, good for now and for all future media and purposes. That is not to say that we reject all the more specific formulations of the standard—they appropriately cover the vast majority of cases involving Government regulation of speech. Rather, aware as we are of the changes taking place in the law, the technology, and the industrial structure, related to telecommunications, we believe it unwise and unnecessary definitively to pick one analogy or one specific set of words now.

"[W]e can decide this case more narrowly, by closely scrutinizing § 10(a) to assure that it properly addresses an extremely important problem, without imposing, in light of the relevant interests, an unnecessarily great restriction on speech. The importance of the interest at stake here—protecting children from exposure to patently offensive depictions of sex; the accommodation of the interests of programmers in maintaining access channels and of cable operators in editing the contents of their channels; the similarity of the problem and its solution to those at issue in *Pacifica*, and the flexibility inherent in an approach that permits private cable operators to make editorial decisions, lead us to conclude that § 10(a) is a sufficiently tailored response to an extraordinarily important problem. * * *

"[W]e part company with Justice Kennedy on two issues. First, Justice Kennedy's focus on categorical analysis forces him to disregard the cable system operators' interests. We, on the other hand, recognize that in the context of cable broadcast that involves an access requirement (here, its partial removal), and unlike in most cases where we have explicitly required 'narrow tailoring,' the expressive interests of cable operators do play a legitimate role. Cf. *Turner*. While we cannot agree with Justice Thomas that everything turns on the rights of the cable owner, we also cannot agree with Justice Kennedy that we must ignore the expressive interests of cable operators altogether. Second, Justice Kennedy's application of a very strict 'narrow tailoring' test depends upon an analogy with a category ('the public forum cases'), which has been distilled over time from the similarities of many cases. Rather than seeking an analogy to a category of cases, however, we have looked to the cases themselves. And, [we find] that *Pacifica* provides the closest analogy. * * *

"The Court's distinction in *Turner*, [between] cable and broadcast television, relied on the inapplicability of the spectrum scarcity problem to cable. While that distinction was relevant in *Turner* to the justification for structural regulations at issue there (the 'must carry' rules), it has little to do with a case that involves the effects of television viewing on children. Those effects are the result of how parents and children view television programming, and how pervasive and intrusive that programming is. In that respect, cable and broadcast television differ little, if at all.

"[I]f one wishes to view the permissive provisions before us through a 'public forum' lens, one should view those provisions as limiting the otherwise totally open nature of the forum that leased access channels provide for communication of other than patently offensive sexual material—taking account of the fact that the limitation was imposed in light of experience gained from maintaining a totally open 'forum.' One must still ask whether the First Amendment forbids the limitation. But unless a label alone were to make a critical First Amendment difference (and we think here it does not), the features of this case that we have already discussed—the government's interest in protecting children, the 'permissive' aspect of the statute, and the nature of the medium—sufficiently justify the 'limitation' on the availability of this forum."

STEVENS, J., concurring, agreed with Breyer, J., that it was unwise to characterize leased channels as public fora: "When the Federal Government opens cable channels that would otherwise be left entirely in private hands, it deserves more deference than a rigid application of the public forum doctrine would allow. At this early stage in the regulation of this developing industry, Congress should not be put to an all or nothing-at-all choice in deciding whether to open certain cable channels to programmers who would otherwise lack the resources to participate in the marketplace of ideas."

SOUTER, J., concurred: "All of the relevant characteristics of cable are presently in a state of technological and regulatory flux. Recent and far-reaching legislation not only affects the technical feasibility of parental control over children's access to undesirable material but portends fundamental changes in the competitive structure of the industry and, therefore, the ability of individual entities to act as bottlenecks to the free flow of information. As cable and telephone companies begin their competition for control over the single wire that will carry both their services, we can hardly settle rules for review of regulation on the assumption that cable will remain a separable and useful category of First Amendment scrutiny. And as broadcast, cable, and the cyber-technology of the Internet and the World Wide Web approach the day of using a common receiver, we can hardly assume that standards for judging the regulation of one of them will not have immense, but now unknown and unknowable, effects on the others. * * *

"The upshot of appreciating the fluidity of the subject that Congress must regulate is simply to accept the fact that not every nuance of our old standards will necessarily do for the new technology, and that a proper choice among existing doctrinal categories is not obvious. Rather than definitively settling the issue now, Justice Breyer wisely reasons by direct analogy rather than by rule, concluding that the speech and the restriction at issue in this case may usefully be measured against the ones at issue in *Pacifica*. If that means it will take some time before reaching a final method of review for cases like this one, there may be consolation in recalling that 16 years passed, from *Roth* to *Miller*, before the modern obscenity rule jelled; that it took over 40 years, from *Hague v. CIO* to *Perry*, for the public forum category to settle out; and that a round half-century passed before the clear and present danger of *Schenck* evolved into the modern incitement rule of *Brandenburg*.

"I cannot guess how much time will go by until the technologies of communication before us today have matured and their relationships become known. But until a category of indecency can be defined both with reference to the new technology and with a prospect of durability, the job of the courts will be just what Justice Breyer does today: recognizing established First Amendment interests through a close analysis that constrains the Congress, without wholly incapacitating it in all matters of the significance apparent here, maintaining the high value of open communication, measuring the costs of regulation by exact attention to fact, and compiling a pedigree of experience with the changing subject. These are familiar judicial responsibilities in times when we know too little to risk the finality of precision, and attention to them will probably take us through the communications revolution. Maybe the judicial obligation to shoulder these responsibilities can itself be captured by a much older rule, familiar to every doctor of medicine: 'First, do no harm.' "

KENNEDY, J., joined by Ginsburg, J., concurring in part and dissenting in part, faulted the plurality opinion for upholding § 10(a): "The plurality opinion, insofar as it upholds § 10(a) [is] adrift. The opinion treats concepts such as public forum, broadcaster, and common carrier as mere labels rather than as categories with settled legal significance; it applies no standard, and by this omission loses sight of existing First Amendment doctrine. When confronted with a threat to free speech in the context of an emerging technology, we ought to have the discipline to analyze the case by reference to existing elaborations of constant First Amendment principles. This is the essence of the case-by-case approach to ensuring protection of speech under the First Amendment, even in novel settings. * * *

"The plurality begins its flight from standards with a number of assertions nobody disputes. I agree, of course, that it would be unwise 'to declare a rigid single standard, good for now and for all future media and purposes.' I do think it necessary, however, to decide what standard applies to discrimination against indecent programming on cable access channels in the present state of the industry. We owe at least that much to public and leased access programmers whose speech is put at risk nationwide by these laws. * * *

"The plurality claims its resistance to standards is in keeping with our case law, where we have shown a willingness to be flexible in confronting novel First Amendment problems. [W]e have developed specialized or more or less stringent standards when certain contexts demanded them; we did not avoid the use of standards altogether. Indeed, the creation of standards and adherence to them, even when it means affording protection to speech unpopular or distasteful, is the central achievement of our First Amendment jurisprudence. Standards are the means by which we state in advance how to test a law's validity, rather than letting the height of the bar be determined by the apparent exigencies of the day. They also provide notice and fair warning to those who must predict how the courts will respond to attempts to suppress their speech. Yet formulations like strict scrutiny, used in a number of constitutional settings to ensure that the inequities of the moment are subordinated to commitments made for the long run mean little if they can be watered down whenever they seem too strong. They mean still less if they can be ignored altogether when considering a case not on all fours with what we have seen before.

"The plurality seems distracted by the many changes in technology and competition in the cable industry. The laws challenged here, however, do not retool the structure of the cable industry. [The] straightforward issue here is whether the Government can deprive certain speakers, on the basis of the content of their speech, of protections afforded all others. There is no reason to discard our existing First Amendment jurisprudence in answering this question.

"While it protests against standards, the plurality does seem to favor one formulation of the question in this case: namely, whether the Act 'properly addresses an extremely important problem, without imposing, in light of the relevant interests, an unnecessarily great restriction on speech.' [This] description of the question accomplishes little, save to clutter our First Amendment case law by adding an untested rule with an uncertain relationship to the others we use to evaluate laws restricting speech. * * *

"Justice Souter recommends to the Court the precept 'First, do no harm.' The question, though, is whether the harm is in sustaining the law or striking it down. If the plurality is concerned about technology's direction, it ought to begin by allowing speech, not suppressing it. We have before us an urgent claim for relief against content-based discrimination, not a dry run.

"The constitutionality under *Turner Broadcasting* of requiring a cable operator to set aside leased access channels is not before us. For purposes of this case, we should treat the cable operator's rights in these channels as extinguished, and address the issue these petitioners present: namely, whether the Government can discriminate on the basis of content in affording protection to certain programmers. I cannot agree with Justice Thomas that the cable operator's rights inform this analysis.

"Laws requiring cable operators to provide leased access are the practical equivalent of making them common carriers, analogous in this respect to telephone companies: They are obliged to provide a conduit for the speech of others. [Laws] removing common-carriage protection from a single form of speech based on its content should be reviewed under the same standard as content-based restrictions on speech in a public forum. Making a cable operator a common carrier does not create a public forum in the sense of taking property from private control and dedicating it to public use; rather, regulations of a common carrier dictate the manner in which private control is exercised. A common-carriage mandate, nonetheless, serves the same function as a public forum. It ensures open, nondiscriminatory access to the means of communication.

"*Pacifica* did not purport, however, to apply a special standard for indecent broadcasting. Emphasizing the narrowness of its holding, the Court in *Pacifica* conducted a context-specific analysis of the FCC's restriction on indecent programming during daytime hours. It relied on the general rule that 'broadcasting [has] received the most limited First Amendment protection.' We already have rejected the application of this lower broadcast standard of review to infringements on the liberties of cable operators, even though they control an important communications medium. *Turner.* * * *

"[Indecency] often is inseparable from the ideas and viewpoints conveyed, or separable only with loss of truth or expressive power. Under our traditional First Amendment jurisprudence, factors perhaps justifying some restriction on indecent cable programming may all be taken into account without derogating this category of protected speech as marginal.

"Congress does have, however, a compelling interest in protecting children from indecent speech. So long as society gives proper respect to parental choices, it may, under an appropriate standard, intervene to spare children exposure to material not suitable for minors. This interest is substantial enough to justify some regulation of indecent speech even under, I will assume, the [strict scrutiny standard].

"[Section 10(a) nonetheless is] not narrowly tailored to protect children from indecent programs on access channels. First, to the extent some operators may allow indecent programming, children in localities those operators serve will be left unprotected. Partial service of a compelling interest is not narrow tailoring. Put another way, the interest in protecting children from indecency only at the caprice of the cable operator is not compelling. Perhaps Congress drafted the law this way to avoid the clear constitutional difficulties of banning indecent speech * * *, but the First Amendment does not permit this sort of ill fit between a law restricting speech and the interest it is said to serve.

"Second, to the extent cable operators prohibit indecent programming on access channels, not only children but adults will be deprived of it."

THOMAS, J., joined by Rehnquist, C.J., and Scalia, J., concurring in part and dissenting in part, argued that § 10(a) validly protected the constitutional rights of cable operators: "It is one thing to compel an operator to carry leased [access] speech, in apparent violation of *Tornillo*, but it is another thing altogether to say that the First Amendment forbids Congress to give back part of the operators' editorial discretion, which all recognize as fundamentally protected, in favor of a broader access right. It is no answer to say that leased [is] content neutral and that [§ 10(a) is] not, for that does not change the fundamental fact, which petitioners never address, that it is the operators' journalistic freedom that is infringed, whether the challenged restrictions be content neutral or content based.

"Because the access provisions are part of a scheme that restricts the free speech rights of cable operators, and expands the speaking opportunities of access programmers, who have no underlying constitutional right to speak through the cable medium, I do not believe that access programmers can challenge the scheme, or a particular part of it, as an abridgment of their 'freedom of speech.' Outside the public forum doctrine, government intervention that grants access programmers an opportunity to speak that they would not otherwise enjoy—and which does not directly limit programmers' underlying speech rights—cannot be an abridgement of the same programmers' First Amendment rights, even if the new speaking opportunity is content-based.

"The permissive nature of [§] 10(a) is important in this regard. If Congress had forbidden cable operators to carry indecent programming on leased * * * channels, that law would have burdened the programmer's right, recognized in *Turner* to compete for space on an operator's system. The Court would undoubtedly strictly scrutinize such a law."

NOTES AND QUESTIONS

1. Consider Yochai Benkler, *Free as the Air to Common Use: First Amendment Constraints on Enclosure of the Public Domain*, 74 N.Y.U. L. Rev. 354 (1999): "Beneath the veneer of an indecency case, *Denver Area* was a case about access rights. [A] majority of the justices acknowledged that access rights to the cable medium served the First Amendment by permitting many and diverse sources to reach viewers over this concentrated medium. These justices treated decisions by cable operators not to carry programming as 'censorial,' and acknowledged that the availability of access to the medium was a question of constitutional moment. Only the partial dissent by Justice Thomas thought that government intervention by requiring access rights was the relevant constitutional concern." Compare Jerome A. Barron, *The Electronic Media and the Flight From First Amendment Doctrine: Justice Breyer's New Balancing Approach*, 31 U. Mich. J.L. Ref. 817, 868, 870 (1998): "[Breyer, J.'s balancing approach provided] specific consideration to the access for expression dimension of the cable regulations under review in *Denver Area*. Access rights must be weighed against the free speech rights of the cable operator. For Justice Thomas, no First Amendment rights conflicted in *Denver Area* because the only rights asserted that merit First Amendment status were those of the cable operator. [Thomas, J.,] noted that the rationale

behind the plurality was not 'intuitively obvious' as to why programmers and viewers have any First Amendment rights. In reality, however, it is not intuitively obvious that cable operators enjoy the whole panoply of First Amendment rights either. [T]o say that mandatory public access and leased access channels violate *Tornillo* would be an extravagant statement. If the rights of the communications entity's owners were intended to trump all other claims to First Amendment protection for all media, *Tornillo* would have been the ideal occasion to make that statement. The *Tornillo* Court instead directed itself to the print media alone and did not so much as cite *Red Lion*, the most obvious contrary electronic media precedent then extant."

2. Consider Jonathan Weinberg, *Cable TV, Indecency and the Court*, 21 Colum.-VLA J.L. & Arts 95, 128 (1997): "[*Pacifica's*] reasoning and jurisprudential approach are back. This is disturbing. The history of First Amendment decision making in this century suggests that rules are more effective than ad hoc analysis in protecting speech from the fears and repression of the moment. Justice Breyer, in the *Denver Area* plurality opinion, attributed his contextual approach to 'the changes taking place in the law, the technology, and the industrial structure,' which, he said, made any attempt to enunciate abstract doctrine premature. The deeper message of the plurality opinion, though, is that no matter how technology evolves, *Pacifica's* contextual approach—not the law of rules—will continue to guide content-based regulation of media that feel like television." But cf. Suzanna Sherry, *Hard Cases Make Good Judges*, 99 Nw. U. L. Rev. 3, 27 (2004): "Echoing Justice Scalia's distaste for anything other than the brightest of lines, Kennedy suggests that the plurality's approach "end[s] up being a legalistic cover for an ad hoc balancing of interests." Yet Justice Kennedy was perfectly content to apply highly manipulable intermediate scrutiny to the regulation of commercial speech, voted to uphold the zoning ordinance in *Alameda Books* in an opinion that carefully recognized that characterizing the ordinance as 'content neutral' was 'imprecise,' and has shown a refreshing sensitivity to fact-specific context in other areas of the law. Why not here?"

3. § 505 of the Telecommunications Act of 1996 requires that cable television operators who provide channels "primarily dedicated to sexually-oriented programming" either "fully scramble or otherwise fully block" the channels so that non-subscribers to the programming would not be able to hear or see it. The art of scrambling has not been perfected, however. "Signal bleed" occurs on many channels, allowing some of the visual and audio aspects of the programming to be heard or seen. In the case of signal bleed, the act requires that the programming be blocked except during hours when children are unlikely to be viewing. The F.C.C.'s regulations provide that those hours are between 10 p.m. and 6 a.m ("the safe harbor provision"). § 504 of the same act required operators to block other programming upon a subscriber's request. A cable television programmer challenged § 505.

United States v. Playboy Entertainment Group, 529 U.S. 803 (2000), applied strict scrutiny to the restriction and struck it down because the cable systems had the capacity to block unwanted channels. The dissenters argued that this alternative was impractical.[b]

---

b. For commentary, see Ashutosh Bhagwat, *What if I Want My Kids to Watch Pornograph?: Protecting Children From "Indecent" Speech*, 11 Wm. & Mary Bill Rts. J. 671, 674, 695 (2003).

CHAPTER 9

THE RIGHT NOT TO SPEAK, THE RIGHT TO ASSOCIATE, AND THE RIGHT NOT TO ASSOCIATE

■ ■ ■

NAACP v. Alabama ex rel. Patterson, 357 U.S. 449 (1958), per Harlan, J., held that the Constitution barred Alabama from compelling production of NAACP membership lists. The opinion used the phrase freedom of association repeatedly, "elevat[ing] freedom of association to an independent right, possessing an equal status with the other rights specifically enumerated in the First Amendment." Thomas Emerson, *Freedom of Association and Freedom of Expression,* 74 Yale L.J. 1, 2 (1964).[a]

From the materials on advocacy of illegal action (Ch. 1, I supra) onward, it has been evident that individuals have rights to join with others for expressive purposes. This section explores other aspects of the freedom to associate and its corollary, the freedom not to associate. First, we explore cases which the Court bases on a right not to speak, but might better be understood as establishing a right not to be associated with particular ideas. Second, instead of persons resisting forced membership in a group, we confront groups resisting members. Finally, we explore aspects of free association in the employment context.

I. THE RIGHT NOT TO BE ASSOCIATED WITH PARTICULAR IDEAS

WEST VIRGINIA STATE BD. OF EDUC. v. BARNETTE, 319 U.S. 624 (1943), per JACKSON, J., upheld the right of public school students to refuse to salute the flag:[a] "To sustain the compulsory flag salute we are required to say that a Bill of Rights which guards the individual's right to

---

a. For discussion of the evolution of the right of association, see John Inazu, *The Strange Origins of the Constitutional Rights of Association,* 77 Tenn. L.Rev. 485 (2010).

a. The Court observed that it was constitutional to otherwise involve students in the recitation of the pledge (which at that time did not include "Under God") during a school day. When a teacher leads a class in the pledge of allegiance, is psychological coercion involved even in the absence of a legal requirement? Should psychological coercion be sufficient to trigger a free speech violation? See Abner Greene, *The Pledge of Allegiance Problem,* 64 Ford.L.Rev. 451 (1995).

speak his own mind, left it open to public authorities to compel him to utter what is not in his mind. * * * Struggles to coerce uniformity of sentiment in support of some end thought essential to their time and country have been waged by many good as well as by evil men. [Ultimate] futility of such attempts to compel coherence is the lesson of every such effort from the Roman drive to stamp out Christianity as a disturber of its pagan unity, the Inquisition, as a means to religious and dynastic unity, the Siberian exiles as a means to Russian unity, down to the fast failing efforts of our present totalitarian enemies. Those who begin coercive elimination of dissent soon find themselves exterminating dissenters. Compulsory unification of opinion achieves only the unanimity of the graveyard. * * *

"If there is any fixed star in our constitutional constellation, it is that no official, high or petty, can prescribe what shall be orthodox in politics, nationalism, religion, or other matters of opinion or force citizens to confess by word or act their faith therein. If there are any circumstances which permit an exception, they do not now occur to us. We think the action of the local authorities in compelling the flag salute and pledge transcends constitutional limitations on their power and invades the sphere of intellect and spirit which it is the purpose of the First Amendment to our Constitution to reserve from all official control."[b]

NOTES AND QUESTIONS

1. Is it a sufficient answer to *Barnette* that the audience need not be misled into believing that the speaker believes what he is forced to say?

2. **Mind control.** Consider Seana Valentine Shiffrin, *What Is Really Wrong With Compelled Association?*, 99 Nw. U. L. Rev. 839, 854 (2005): "One may worry that compulsory, frequent repetition of the Pledge will have an influence on what and how one thinks, independent of one's direct deliberations on its subject matter. Routine recitation may make its message familiar. Through regularity, it may become a comfort and an internal source of authority for consultation. At a later point, one might instinctively, without further thought and without awareness of the origin of the thought, characterize the polity as a republic, or as a place where there is freedom and justice, or perhaps more plausibly, be more likely assent to another's assertion to that effect."

3. **Sincerity.** Consider Seana Valentine Shiffrin, *What Is Really Wrong With Compelled Association?*, 99 Nw. U. L. Rev. 839, 860–861, 863 (2005): "[C]ompelled speech requirements of the sort at issue in *Barnette* conflict with recognition of and respect for the value of sincerity, a virtue that is integrally related to the well-functioning of a robust First Amendment culture. [In] the case of the Pledge, students are compelled to pledge to something that they may not believe is worth pledging to, or that they may

---

b. Black and Douglas, JJ., concurred, abandoning their position taken in a recent flag salute case *Minersville School Dist. v. Gobitis*, 310 U.S. 586 (1940), which the Court reconsidered in *Barnette*; Roberts and Reed, JJ., citing their position in *Gobitis*, and Frankfurter, J., taking a position on the judicial role similar to that which he had expressed in *Dennis*, dissented.

believe is unworthy of or an inappropriate object for such commitment. [The rote recitation and sincerity arguments] appeal not to the comprehension by the compelled speaker's audience but rather to the conditions of respect for the character, the autonomous cognitive life, and the mental contents of the compelled party."

4. **Dignity.** Consider Laurence H. Tribe, *Disentangling Symmetries: Speech, Association, Parenthood*, 28 Pepp. L. Rev. 641, 645 (2001): "The right that all of these cases affirm is better understood as a right not to be used or commandeered to do the state's ideological bidding by having to mouth, convey, embody, or sponsor a message, especially the state's message, with one's voice or body or resources, on one's personal possessions, through the composition of the associations one joins or forms, or in their selection of teachers, exemplars, and leaders." See also Vincent Blasi & Seana V. Shiffrin, *The Story of West Virginia State Board of Education v. Barnette*, in Constitutional Law Stories 432 (Michael C. Dorf ed. 2004); James P. Madigan, *Questioning the Coercive Effect of Self–Identifying Speech*, 87 Iowa L. Rev. 75, 113 (2001); Greene, supra note a.

———

New Hampshire required that noncommercial vehicles bear license plates embossed with the state motto, "Live Free or Die." "Refus[ing] to be coerced by the State into advertising a slogan which I find morally, ethically, religiously and politically abhorrent," appellee, a Jehovah's Witness, covered up the motto on his license plate, a misdemeanor under state law. After being convicted several times of violating the misdemeanor statute, appellee sought federal injunctive and declaratory relief. WOOLEY v. MAYNARD, 430 U.S. 705 (1977), per BURGER, C.J., held that requiring appellee to display the motto on his license plates violated his First Amendment right to "refrain from speaking": "[T]he freedom of thought protected by the First Amendment [includes] both the right to speak freely and the right to refrain from speaking at all. See *Barnette*. The right to speak and the right to refrain from speaking are complementary components of the broader concept of 'individual freedom of mind.' This is illustrated [by] *Miami Herald* [infra], where we held unconstitutional a Florida statute placing an affirmative duty upon newspapers to publish the replies of political candidates whom they had criticized.

" * * * Compelling the affirmative act of a flag salute [the situation in *Barnette*] involved a more serious infringement upon personal liberties than the passive act of carrying the state motto on a license plate, but the difference is essentially one of degree. Here, as in *Barnette,* we are faced with a state measure which forces an individual as part of his daily life— indeed constantly while his automobile is in public view—to be an instrument for fostering public adherence to an ideological point of view he finds unacceptable. In doing so, the State 'invades the sphere of intellect and spirit which it is the purpose of the First Amendment [to] reserve from all official control.' *Barnette*.

"New Hampshire's statute in effect requires that appellees use their private property as a 'mobile billboard' for the State's ideological message—or suffer a penalty, as Maynard already has. [The] fact that most individuals agree with the thrust of [the] motto is not the test; most Americans also find the flag salute acceptable. The First Amendment protects the right of individuals to hold a point of view different from the majority and to refuse to foster, in the way New Hampshire commands, an idea they find morally objectionable."

The Court next considered whether "the State's countervailing interest" was "sufficiently compelling" to justify appellees to display the motto on their license plates. The two interests claimed by the state were (1) facilitating the identification of state license plates from those of similar colors of other states and (2) promoting "appreciation of history, state pride, [and] individualism." As to (1), the record revealed that these state license plates were readily distinguishable from others without reference to the state motto and, in any event, the state's purpose could be achieved by "less drastic means," i.e., by alternative methods less restrictive of First Amendment freedoms. As to (2), where the State's interest is to communicate an "official view" as to history and state pride or to disseminate any other "ideology," "such interest cannot outweigh an individual's First Amendment right to avoid becoming the courier for such message."

REHNQUIST, J., joined by Blackmun, J., dissented, not only agreeing with what he called "the Court's implicit recognition that there is no protected 'symbolic speech' in this case," but maintaining that "that conclusion goes far to undermine the Court's ultimate holding that there is an element of protected expression here. The State has not forced appellees to 'say' anything; and it has not forced them to communicate ideas with nonverbal actions reasonably likened to 'speech,' such as wearing a lapel button promoting a political candidate or waving a flag as a symbolic gesture. The State has simply required that *all* noncommercial automobiles bear license tags with the state motto. [Appellees] have not been forced to affirm or reject that motto; they are simply required by the State [to] carry a state auto license tag for identification and registration purposes. [The] issue, unconfronted by the Court, is whether appellees, in displaying, as they are required to do, state license tags, the format of which is known to all as having been prescribed by the State, would be considered to be advocating political or ideological views.

"[H]aving recognized the rather obvious differences between [*Barnette* and this case], the Court does not explain why the same result should obtain. The Court suggests that the test is whether the individual is forced 'to be an instrument for fostering public adherence to an ideological point of view he finds unacceptable,' [but] these are merely conclusory words. [For] example, were New Hampshire to erect a multitude of billboards, each proclaiming 'Live Free or Die,' and tax all citizens for the cost of erection and maintenance, clearly the message would be 'fostered' by the individual citizen-taxpayers and just as clearly those individuals would be 'instruments' in that communication. Certainly, however, that case would not fall within the ambit of *Barnette*. In that case, as in this case, there is no *affirmation* of belief. For First Amendment principles to be implicated, the State must place the citizen in the position of either appearing to, or actually, 'asserting as true' the message. This was the focus of *Barnette*, and clearly distinguishes this case from that one.''[c]

NOTES AND QUESTIONS

1. ***Speech?*** Consider Randall P. Bezanson, *Speaking Through Others' Voices: Authorship, Originality, and Free Speech*, 38 Wake Forest L. Rev. 983, 1102 (2003): "Maynard's act was an exercise of his liberty, but the question is whether it is an exercise of his liberty to speak, which is a liberty to communicate his ideas or beliefs or information to [others]. Maynard's private conceit that he was speaking when driving with the license plate was divorced from the communicative interaction with others that the First Amendment speech guarantee presumes. Since there was no evidence that anyone understood the carrying of the motto on a car to be an act of speech, much less an act of Maynard's speech, Maynard was simply speaking into the air. He was exercising his own conscience, but he was not, without more, speaking, a status that at least requires communication to others.''

2. ***Coercive inculcation of values.*** Consider Larry Alexander, *Compelled Speech*, 23 Const. Comm. 147, 152 (2006): "*Wooley* seems particularly difficult to explain as a case of coercive inculation of beliefs/values. Whether or not the motto was visible or taped over, it would be largely invisible to the vehicle's driver and passengers. Other vehicles' license plates would be much more effective for that purpose than the plates of Maynard's own vehicle, in which case the demand should have been to eliminate the motto from all license plates.''

3. ***Double irony.*** Consider Laurence H. Tribe, *Disentangling Symmetries: Speech, Association, Parenthood*, 28 Pepp. L. Rev. 641, 643–644 (2001): "Apparently suffering from an 'irony deficiency,' the 'Granite State' of New Hampshire had threatened to imprison those of its citizens who refused to adorn their cars with that 'Live Free or Die' motto. But, there is actually a double irony here: By holding that individuals have a right to refuse this state slogan on their plates while letting the state keep distributing plates bearing the slogan, the Court was forcing those who are most offended by the slogan to come out of the closet. No longer able to just blend in as law abiding citizens whose views nobody could guess from their license plates, now those keeping the "Live Free or Die" slogan would be marked as having no objection to the sentiment it expressed, while those replacing it would be marked as having affirmatively rejected the slogan.''

4. ***Use of private property as a forum for the speech of others***. (a) Appellees sought to enjoin a shopping center from denying them access to the center's central courtyard in order to solicit signatures from passersby for petitions opposing a U.N. resolution. The California Supreme Court held they

---

c. White, J., joined by Blackmun and Rehnquist, JJ., dissented on procedural grounds.

were entitled to conduct their activity at the center, construing the state constitution to protect "speech and petitioning, reasonably exercised, in shopping centers, even [when] privately owned." The shopping center appealed, arguing that its First Amendment rights had been violated. PRUNEYARD SHOPPING CENTER v. ROBINS, 447 U.S. 74 (1980), per REHNQUIST, J., disagreed with the shopping center: "[In *Wooley,*] the government itself prescribed the message, required it to be displayed openly on appellee's personal property that was used 'as part of his daily life,' and refused to permit him [to] cover up the motto even though the Court found that the display of the motto served no important state interest. Here, by contrast, [the center] is not limited to the personal use of appellants, [but is] a business establishment that is open to the public to come and go as they please. The views expressed by members of the public in passing out pamphlets or seeking signatures for a petition thus will not likely be identified with those of the owner. Second, no specific message is dictated by the State to be displayed on appellants' property. There consequently is no danger of government discrimination for or against a particular message. Finally, [it appears] appellants can expressly disavow any connection with the message by simply posting signs in the area where the speakers or handbillers stand."

Unlike *Barnette,* appellants "are not [being] compelled to affirm their belief in any governmentally prescribed position or view, and they are free to publicly dissociate themselves from the views of the speakers or handbillers. [*Miami Herald*] rests on the principle that the State cannot tell a newspaper what it must print. [There was also a danger that the statute requiring a newspaper to publish a political candidate's reply to previously published criticism would deter] editors from publishing controversial political [statements]. Thus, the statute was found to be an 'intrusion into the function of editors.' These concerns obviously are not present here."[d]

POWELL, J., joined by White, J., concurring in the judgment, maintained that "state action that transforms privately owned property into a forum for the expression of the public's views could raise serious First Amendment questions": "I do not believe that the result in *Wooley* would have changed had [the state] directed its citizens to place the slogan 'Live Free or Die' in their shop windows rather than on their automobiles. [*Wooley*] protects a person who refuses to allow use of his property as a market place for the ideas of others. [One] who has merely invited the public onto his property for commercial purposes cannot fairly be said to have relinquished his right 'to decline to be an instrument for fostering public adherence to an ideological point of view he finds unacceptable.' *Wooley.*

"[E]ven when [as here] no particular message is mandated by the State, First Amendment interests are affected by state action that forces a property owner to admit third-party speakers. [A] right of access [may be] no less intrusive than speech compelled by the State itself. [A] law requiring that a

---

d. Could *PruneYard* be extended to parts of the Internet? To America Online? To Netscape? Are parts of the Internet already public fora. For various views, see Laurence H. Tribe, *The Constitution in Cyberspace,* The Humanist, Sept.–Oct. 1991, at 15; Edward V. Di Lello, *Functional Equivalency and Its Application to Freedom of Speech on Computer Bulletin Boards,* 26 Colum. J.L. & Soc. Probs. 199 (1993); Note, *Sidewalks in Cyberspace: Making Space for Public Forums in the Electronic Environment,* 12 Harv. J.L. & Tech. 149 (1998); Note, *Is Cyberspace a Public Forum? Computer Bulletin Boards, Free Speech, and State Action,* 81 Geo.L.J. 409 (1992).

newspaper permit others to use its columns imposes an unacceptable burden upon the newspaper's First Amendment right to select material for publication. *Miami Herald.*

"[If] a state law mandated public access to the bulletin board of a freestanding store [or] small shopping center [or allowed soliciting or pamphleteering in the entrance area of a store,] customers might well conclude that the messages reflect the view of the proprietor. [He] either could permit his customers to receive a mistaken impression [or] disavow the messages. Should he take the first course, he effectively has been compelled to affirm someone else's belief. Should he choose the second, he has been forced to speak when he would prefer to remain silent. In short, he has lost control over his freedom to speak or not to speak on certain issues. The mere fact that he is free to dissociate himself from the views expressed on his property cannot restore his 'right to refrain from speaking at all.' *Wooley.*

"A property owner may also be faced with speakers who wish to use his premises as a platform for views that he finds morally repugnant[, for example, a] minority-owned business confronted with leafleteers from the American Nazi Party or the Ku Klux Klan, [or] a church-operated enterprise asked to host demonstrations in favor of abortion. [The] pressure to respond is particularly apparent [in the above cases, but] an owner who strongly objects to some of the causes to which the state-imposed right of access would extend may oppose ideological activities 'of *any* sort' that are not related to the purposes for which he has invited the public onto his property. See *Abood.* To require the owner to specify the particular ideas he finds objectionable enough to compel a response would force him to relinquish his 'freedom to maintain his own beliefs without public disclosure.' *Abood.* * * *

"[On this record] I cannot say that customers of this vast center [occupying several city blocks and containing more than 65 shops] would be likely to assume that appellees' limited speech activity expressed the views of [the center]. [Moreover, appellants] have not alleged that they object to [appellees' views, nor asserted] that some groups who reasonably might be expected to speak at [the center] will express views that are so objectionable as to require a response even when listeners will not mistake their source. [Thus,] I join the judgment of the Court, [but] I do not interpret our decision today as a blanket approval for state efforts to transform privately owned commercial property into public forums."

(b) *Pacific Gas & Electric Co. v. Public Utilities Comm'n*, 475 U.S. 1 (1986), per Powell, J., joined by Burger, C.J., and Brennan and O'Connor, JJ., (together with Marshall, J., concurring), struck down a commission requirement that a private utility company include in its billing envelope materials supplied by a public interest group that were critical of some of the company's positions.[e] Was the result required by *Miami Herald*? Consistent with *PruneYard*?[f]

---

e. Burger, C.J., filed a concurring opinion; Rehnquist, J., joined by White and Stevens, JJ., dissented; Stevens, J., filed a separate dissent; Blackmun, J., took no part.

f. Consider Alan Hirsch, *"The Corporate Conscience" and Other First Amendment Follies in Pacific Gas & Electric*, 41 San Diego L. Rev. 483, 495–496 (2004): "The Court's treatment of *Tornillo* and *Prune Yard*, taken together, suggests the bankruptcy of its opinion. The utility

(c) The Solomon Amendment provides that if any part of an institution of higher education denies military recruiters access equal to that afforded to other recruiters, the entire institution would be deprived of federal funds. A consortium of law schools filed suit, alleging that this violated the First Amendment. RUMSFELD v. FORUM FOR ACADEMIC AND INSTITUTIONAL RIGHTS, INC., 547 U.S. 47 (2006), per ROBERTS, C.J., held that it did not: "The Solomon Amendment neither limits what law schools may say nor requires them to say anything. Law schools remain free under the statute to express whatever views they may have on the military's congressionally mandated employment policy, all the while retaining eligibility for federal funds. See Tr. Of Oral Arg. 25 (Solicitor General acknowledging that law schools "could put signs on the bulletin board next to the door, they could engage in speech, they could help organize student protests"). As a general matter, the Solomon Amendment regulates conduct, not speech. It affects what law schools must *do*—afford equal access to military recruiters—not what they may or may not *say*. * * *

"Compelling a law school that sends scheduling e-mails for other recruiters to send one for a military recruiter is simply not the same as forcing a student to pledge allegiance, or forcing a Jehovah's Witness to display the motto 'Live Free or Die,' and it trivializes the freedom protected in *Barnette* and *Wooley* to suggest that it is."[g]

5. ***Paraders' rights***. Boston authorized the South Boston Allied War Veterans Council to conduct the St. Patrick's Day–Evacuation parade (commemorating the evacuation of British troops from the city in 1776). The Veterans Council refused to let the Irish–American Gay, Lesbian and Bisexual Group of Boston march in the parade, but the Massachusetts courts ruled that the Council's refusal violated a public accommodations law in that the parade was an "open recreational event." HURLEY v. IRISH–AMERICAN GAY, LESBIAN AND BISEXUAL GROUP OF BOSTON, 515 U.S. 557 (1995), per SOUTER, J., held that "[t]his use of the State's power violates the fundamental rule of protection under the First Amendment, that a speaker has the autonomy to choose the content of his own message. * * *

"[The Council's] claim to the benefit of this principle of autonomy to control one's own speech is as sound as the South Boston parade is expressive. Rather like a composer, the Council selects the expressive units of the parade from potential participants, and though the score may not produce a particularized message, each contingent's expression in the Council's eyes comports with what merits celebration on that day. Even if this view gives the Council credit for a more considered judgment than it actively made, the Council clearly decided to exclude a message it did not like from the communication it chose to make, and that is enough to invoke its right as a private speaker to shape its expression by speaking on one subject while remaining silent on another. * * *

---

company bears a far greater resemblance to a shopping center owner than to a newspaper, but the Court distinguished it from the latter and likened it to the former."

g. For criticism of FAIR, see Paul Horwitz, *Three Faces of* Deference, 83 Notre Dame L.Rev. 1061 (2008); Chai R. Feldblum, *Moral Conflict and Liberty: Gay Rights and Religion,* 72 Brook. L.Rev. 61 (2006). See generally Paul Horwitz, *Universities as First Amendment* Institutions, 54 UCLA L.Rev. 1497 (2007).

"Unlike the programming offered on various channels by a cable network, the parade does not consist of individual, unrelated segments that happen to be transmitted together for individual selection by members of the audience. Although each parade unit generally identifies itself, each is understood to contribute something to a common theme, and accordingly there is no customary practice whereby private sponsors disavow any 'identity of viewpoint' between themselves and the selected participants. Practice follows practicability here, for such disclaimers would be quite curious in a moving parade. [*PruneYard* found] that the proprietors were running 'a business establishment that is open to the public to come and go as they please,' that the solicitations would 'not likely be identified with those of the owner,' and that the proprietors could 'expressly disavow any connection with the message by simply posting signs in the area where the speakers or handbillers stand.' "[h]

6. ***Economic pressure to engage in political activity.*** NAACP v. CLAIBORNE HARDWARE CO., 458 U.S. 886 (1982): The NAACP had organized a consumer boycott whose principal objective was, according to the lower court, "to force the white merchants [to] bring pressure upon [the government] to grant defendants' demands or, in the alternative, to suffer economic ruin." Mississippi characterized the boycott as a tortious and malicious interference with the plaintiffs' businesses. The Court, per Stevens, J., held for the NAACP: Although labor boycotts organized for economic ends had long been subject to prohibition, "speech to protest racial discrimination" was "essential political speech lying at the core of the First Amendment" and was therefore distinguishable. Is the boycott protected association? Are there association rights on the other side? Does the state have a legitimate interest in protecting merchants from being forced to support political change they would otherwise oppose? Cf. *NLRB v. Retail Store Employees Union,* 447 U.S. 607 (1980) (ban on labor picketing encouraging consumer boycott of neutral employer upheld). Are the white merchants neutral?[i] For commentary, compare Michael Harper, *The Consumer's Emerging Right to Boycott: NAACP v. Claiborne Hardware and Its Implications for American Labor Law,* 93 Yale L.J. 409 (1984) with Maimon Schwarzschild & Larry Alexander, *Consumer Boycotts and Freedom of Association: Comment on a Recently Proposed Theory,* 22 San Diego L.Rev. 555 (1985).

7. ***Orthodoxy and commercial advertising.*** ZAUDERER v. OFFICE OF DISCIPLINARY COUNSEL, 471 U.S. 626 (1985), per White, J., upheld an Ohio requirement that an attorney advertising availability on a contingency basis must disclose in the ad whether the clients would have to pay costs if their lawsuits should prove unsuccessful: "[T]he interests at stake in this case are not of the same order as those discussed in *Wooley, Miami Herald,* and *Barnette.* Ohio has not attempted to 'prescribe what shall be orthodox in politics, nationalism, religion, or other matters of opinion or force citizens to

---

h. For incisive pre-*Hurley* commentary, see Larry W. Yackle, *Parading Ourselves: Freedom of Speech at the Feast of St. Patrick,* 73 B.U.L.Rev. 791 (1993). Is *Hurley* consistent with the particularized message requirement of *Spence?* If not, how is expressive conduct defined? For commentary, see Angelica M. Sinopole, *"No Saggy Pants,"* 113 Penn. St.L.Rev. 328 (2008).

i. Stevens, J., also argued in *Claiborne* that the boycott was protected as a right to petition the government. Are the white merchants the government?

confess by word or act their faith therein.' The State has attempted only to prescribe what shall be orthodox in commercial advertising [regarding] purely factual and uncontroversial[j] information about the terms under which his services will be available. Because the extension of First Amendment protection to commercial speech is justified principally by the value to consumers of the information such speech provides, *Virginia Pharmacy*, appellant's constitutionally protected interest in *not* providing any particular factual information in his advertising is minimal. [We] recognize that unjustified or unduly burdensome disclosure requirements might offend the First Amendment by chilling protected commercial speech. But we hold that an advertiser's rights are adequately protected as long as disclosure requirements are reasonably related to the State's interest in preventing deception of consumers."

The Court stated that the First Amendment interests "implicated by disclosure requirements are substantially weaker than those at stake when speech is actually suppressed." Accordingly it rejected any requirement that the advertisement in question be shown to be deceptive absent the disclosure or that the state meet a "least restrictive means" analysis.

BRENNAN, J., joined by Marshall, J., dissenting on this issue, conceded that the distinction between disclosure and suppression "supports some differences in analysis," but thought the Court had exaggerated the importance of the distinction: "[A]n affirmative publication requirement 'operates as a command in the same sense as a statute or regulation forbidding [someone] to publish specified matter,' and that [a] compulsion to publish that which 'reason tells [one] should not be published' therefore raises substantial First Amendment concerns. *Miami Herald*." Accordingly, he would have required a demonstration that the advertising was inherently likely to deceive or record evidence that the advertising was in fact deceptive, or a showing that another substantial interest was directly [advanced]. Applying this standard, Brennan, J., agreed with the Court that a state may require an advertising attorney to include a costs disclaimer, but concluded that the state had provided Zauderer with inadequate notice of what he was required to include in the advertisement.

---

j. What if the requested disclosures are controverted? Do cigarette companies have First Amendment grounds to resist forced disclosures?

Do doctors have a First Amendment right to resist state mandated disclosures to patients regarding abortion? Consider joint opinion of O'Connor, Kennedy, and Souter, JJ., in *Planned Parenthood v. Casey*, 505 U.S. 833 (1992): "[This] is, for constitutional purposes, no different from a requirement that a doctor give certain specific information about any medical procedure. [To] be sure, the physician's First Amendment rights not to speak are implicated, see *Wooley*, but only as part of the practice of medicine, subject to reasonable licensing and regulation by the State." See Robert Post, *Informed Consent to Abortion*, 2007 U.Ill.L.Rev. 939. Is there a First Amendment right against compelled listening in some circumstances? Should it apply in the abortion context? See Caroline M. Corbin, *The First Amendment Right Against Compelled Listening*, 89 B.U. L. Rev. 939 (2009).

Can professional fundraisers be required to disclose their professional status before soliciting funds? The percent of charitable contributions that have been turned over to charity in the past 12 months? See *Riley v. National Federation of the Blind*, Ch. 4, III supra (the former can be required, not the latter). But cf. *Illinois ex rel. Madigan v. Telemarketing Associates, Inc.*, 538 U.S. 600 (2003)(fraud action cognizable when solicitor represents that a significant amount will go to charity when only 15 cents per dollar would be distributed for such purpose). On compelled commercial speech, see generally Note, *Can the Budweiser Frogs Be Forced to Sing A New Tune?*, 84 Va. L.Rev. 1195 (1998).

Milavetz, Gallop & Milavetz, P.A., et al., v. United States, 130 S.Ct. 1324 (2010), reaffirmed *Zauderer*, holding that "an advertiser's rights are adequately protected as long as disclosure requirements are reasonably related to the State's interest in preventing deception of consumers."

8. ***Compelled monetary subsidies.*** A series of cases have invalidated government forced monetary contributions for support of speech opposed by the contributors. *Abood v. Detroit Bd. of Educ.*, 431 U.S. 209 (1977)(members of public employee bargaining unit who are not members of a union can be compelled to pay service fees to union, but rebates must be provided if they object to the union's support of political candidates or political views unrelated to the union's duties as exclusive bargaining representative); *Davenport v. Washington Education Ass'n*, 551 U.S. 177 (2007) (public-sector unions may be required to receive affirmative authorization from a nonmember before spending that person's compelled fees for election purposes, though nonmembers fees need not be commingled with members' fees); *Keller v. State Bar of California*, 496 U.S. 1 (1990) (compulsory bar dues could only be used if "reasonably incurred for the purpose of regulating the legal profession or improving the quality of the legal service available to the people of the State" not to endorse or advance a gun control or nuclear weapons freeze initiative); *United States v. United Foods, Inc.*, 533 U.S. 405 (2001) (objecting mushroom handlers can not be compelled to fund generic advertisements supporting mushroom sales).[k] Nonetheless, taxpayers routinely fund speech activities to which they are opposed without First Amendment rights being violated.

This paradox was addressed in a case involving beef subsidies. Pursuant to the Beef Promotion and Research Act, the Secretary of Agriculture established a beef promotion and research board funded by government compelled contributions from the sales and importation of cattle. More than 1 billion dollars have been collected, much of it used to promote the sale of beef employing the slogan, "Beef: It's What's for Dinner." Many of the promotional messages state that they are funded by America's beef producers. Plaintiffs brought suit maintaining that compelled financial support of generic advertisements for beef impeded their efforts to promote the superiority of American beef, grain-fed beef, or certified Angus or Hereford beef, and violated the First Amendment.

JOHANNS v. LIVESTOCK MARKETING ASSOCIATION, 544 U.S. 550 (2005), per SCALIA, J., concluded that compelled support of private speech raised First Amendment issues, that such compelled support of government speech did not raise First Amendment issues, and that the beef promotional messages were government speech: "We have sustained First Amendment challenges to allegedly compelled expression in two categories of cases: true

---

k. Despite ideological objections, compulsory exactions might be justified by the strength of the government interest. See *Abood* (forced support of union collective bargaining activities permissible despite ideological objection); *Board of Regents v. Southworth*, 529 U.S. 217 (2000)(no refund appropriate of mandatory student fee so long as allocation of funding is viewpoint neutral because the interest in stimulating diverse ideas on campus outweighs the interests of objecting students). Is the First Amendment objection mistaken because "the mere act of paying a mandatory assessment does not identify the payer with the message her payments help fund"? Gregory Klass, *The Very Idea of a First Amendment Right Against Compelled Subsidization*, 38 U.C. Davis L. Rev. 1087, 1116–1117 (2005). Can *United Foods* be reconciled with *Zauderer*? For doubts, see Robert Post, *Transparent and Efficient Markets*, 40 Val.U.L.Rev. 555 (2006).

'compelled speech' cases, in which an individual is obliged personally to express a message he disagrees with, imposed by the government; and 'compelled subsidy' cases, in which an individual is required by the government to subsidize a message he disagrees with, expressed by a private entity. We have not heretofore considered the First Amendment consequences of government-compelled subsidy of the government's own speech.

"Our compelled-subsidy cases have consistently respected the principle that '[c]ompelled support of a private association is fundamentally different from compelled support of government.' ['The] government, as a general rule, may support valid programs and policies by taxes or other exactions binding on protesting parties. Within this broader principle it seems inevitable that funds raised by the government will be spent for speech and other expression to advocate and defend its own policies.' We have generally assumed, though not yet squarely held, that compelled funding of government speech does not alone raise First Amendment concerns. * * *

"Respondents [assert] that the challenged promotional campaigns differ dispositively from the type of government speech that, our cases suggest, is not susceptible to First Amendment challenge. They point to the role of the Beef Board and its Operating Committee in designing the promotional campaigns, and to the use of a mandatory assessment on beef producers to fund the advertising. * * *

'The Secretary of Agriculture does not write ad copy himself. Rather, the Beef Board's promotional campaigns are designed by the Beef Board's Operating Committee. [Nonetheless, the] message set out in the beef promotions is from beginning to end the message established by the Federal Government.[5]

"Congress has directed the implementation of a 'coordinated program' of promotion, 'including paid advertising, to advance the image and desirability of beef and beef products.' * * * Congress and the Secretary have set out the overarching message and some of its elements, and they have left the development of the remaining details to an entity whose members are answerable to the Secretary (and in some cases appointed by him as well).

"Moreover, the record demonstrates that the Secretary exercises final approval authority over every word used in every promotional campaign. All proposed promotional messages are reviewed by Department officials both for substance and for wording, and some proposals are rejected or rewritten by the Department. * * *

"The compelled-*subsidy* analysis is altogether unaffected by whether the funds for the promotions are raised by general taxes or through a targeted assessment. Citizens may challenge compelled support of private speech, but have no First Amendment right not to fund government speech. And that is no less true when the funding is achieved through targeted assessments devoted exclusively to the program to which the assessed citizens object.

---

5. The principal dissent suggests that if this is so, then the Government has adopted at best a mixed message, because it also promulgates dietary guidelines that, if followed, would discourage excessive consumption of beef. Even if we agreed that the protection of the government-speech doctrine must be forfeited whenever there is inconsistency in the message, we would nonetheless accord the protection here. The beef promotions are perfectly compatible with the guidelines' message of moderate consumption—the ads do not insist that beef is also What's for Breakfast, Lunch, and Midnight Snack.

"[R]espondents' contend that crediting the advertising to 'America's Beef Producers' impermissibly uses not only their money but also their seeming endorsement to promote a message with which they do not agree. Communications cannot be 'government speech,' they argue, if they are attributed to someone other than the government; and the person to whom they are attributed, when he is, by compulsory funding, made the unwilling instrument of communication, may raise a First Amendment objection.

"We need not determine the validity of this argument—which relates to compelled *speech* rather than compelled *subsidy*—with regard to respondents' facial challenge. Since neither the Beef Act nor the Beef Order requires attribution, neither can be the cause of any possible First Amendment harm. The District Court's order enjoining the enforcement of the Act and the Order thus cannot be sustained on this theory.

"[This theory might form] the basis for an as-applied challenge—if it were established, that is, that individual beef advertisements were attributed to respondents. [Whether] the *individual* respondents who are beef producers would be associated with speech labeled as coming from 'America's Beef Producers' is a question on which the trial record is altogether silent. We have only the funding tagline itself, a trademarked term that, standing alone, is not sufficiently specific to convince a reasonable factfinder that any particular beef producer, or all beef producers, would be tarred with the content of each trademarked ad."[1]

BREYER, J., concurred: "The beef checkoff program in these cases is virtually identical to the mushroom checkoff program in which the Court struck down on First Amendment grounds. The 'government speech' theory the Court adopts today was not before us in *United Foods* [where I dissented] based on my view that the challenged assessments involved a form of economic regulation, not speech. * * *

"I remain of the view that the assessments in these cases are best described as a form of economic regulation. However, I recognize that a majority of the Court does not share that view. Now that we have had an opportunity to consider the 'government speech' theory, I accept it as a solution to the problem presented by these cases."

GINSBURG, J., concurred in the judgment: "I resist ranking the promotional messages funded under the Beef Promotion and Research Act of 1985 as government speech, given the message the Government conveys in its own name [discouraging the consumption of trans fatty acids found in cattle and sheep]. I remain persuaded, however, that the assessments in these cases qualify as permissible economic regulation."

SOUTER, J., joined by Stevens and Kennedy, JJ., dissented: "I take the view that if government relies on the government-speech doctrine to compel specific groups to fund speech with targeted taxes, it must make itself politically accountable by indicating that the content actually is a government message, not just the statement of one self-interested group the government is currently willing to invest with power. Sometimes, as in these very cases,

---

1. Thomas, J. concurred. Kennedy, J., dissented. For discussion of the food cases, see Kathleen Sullivan & Robert C. Post, *It's What's For Lunch: Nectarines, Mushrooms, and Beef - The First Amendment and Compelled Commercial Speech*, 41 Loy. L.A. L.Rev. 359 (2007).

government can make an effective disclosure only by explicitly labeling the speech as its own.

"[T]he requirement of effective public accountability means the ranchers ought to prevail, it being clear that the Beef Act does not establish an advertising scheme subject to effective democratic checks. The reason for this is simple: the ads are not required to show any sign of being speech by the Government, and experience under the Act demonstrates how effectively the Government has masked its role in producing the ads. Most obviously, many of them include the tag line, '[f]unded by America's Beef Producers,' which all but ensures that no one reading them will suspect that the message comes from the National Government. But the tag line just underscores the point that would be true without it, that readers would most naturally think that ads urging people to have beef for dinner were placed and paid for by the beef producers who stand to profit when beef is on the table. No one hearing a commercial for Pepsi or Levi's thinks Uncle Sam is the man talking behind the curtain. Why would a person reading a beef ad think Uncle Sam was trying to make him eat more steak? Given the circumstances, it is hard to see why anyone would suspect the Government was behind the message unless the message came out and said so."

Consider Note, 119 Harv. L. Rev. 169, 277 (2005): "The ranchers argued that the attribution of many of the advertisements to 'America's Beef Producers' wrongly associated them with the government's message. The Court sidestepped this argument by noting that the respondents had brought a facial challenge to the statute and that while the program as applied might appear to attribute the speech to the plaintiffs—contrary to *Wooley*—the text of the statute did not mandate this result." On the problem of concealing the government's involvement in a private message, see Brian P. Morrisey, *Speech and Taxes*, 81 Notre Dame L.Rev. 2059 (2006); Abner S. Greene, *Government of the Good*, 53 Vand. L.Rev. 1 (2000); Gia B. Lee, *Persuasion, Transparency, and Government Speech*, 56 Hast. L.J. 983, 1010 (2005).

Leaving aside the government speech question, is the claim of the ranchers unappealing because it is little more than "economic interest dressed up as constitutional principle"? Suppose the objectors instead were small organic farmers opposing undifferentiated product descriptions on moral and political grounds relating to the environment, consumer health, or humane treatment of animals? See Seana V. Shiffrin, *Compelled Association, Morality, and Market Dynamics*, 41 Loy. U.L. Law. Rev. 317, 322 (2007).

9. *A right not to speak?* *Wooley* and succeeding cases establish a right not to be associated with ideas to which one is ideologically opposed. Yet individuals are forced to speak in a wide variety of situations. Does it violate the First Amendment to ·compel witnesses to speak in court or legislative proceedings? Should such compulsion have limits? Consider *Barenblatt v. United States,* 360 U.S. 109 (1959)(witness can be compelled before Congress to testify about his political connections with the Communist Party if he does not invoke the fifth amendment). Other cases are more sympathetic to those who choose to remain silent.

(a) *Anonymous political speech.* McINTYRE v. OHIO ELECTIONS COMM'N, 514 U.S. 334 (1995), per STEVENS, J., held that Ohio's prohibition against the distribution of anonymous campaign literature was unconstitutional: "Under our Constitution, anonymous pamphleteering is not a pernicious, fraudulent practice, but an honorable tradition of advocacy and of dissent. [The] State may and does punish fraud directly. But it cannot seek to punish fraud indirectly by indiscriminately outlawing a category of speech, based on its content, with no necessary relationship to the danger sought to be prevented."[m]

THOMAS, J., concurred, but argued that instead of asking whether " 'an honorable tradition' of free speech has existed throughout American history, [we] should seek the original understanding when we interpret the Speech and Press clauses, just as we do when we read the Religion Clauses of the First Amendment." According to Thomas, J., the original understanding approach also protected anonymous speech.

SCALIA, joined by Rehnquist, C.J., dissenting, asserted that it was the "Court's (and society's) traditional view that the Constitution bears its original meaning and is unchanging." Applying that approach, he concluded that anonymous political speech is not protected under the First Amendment.

(b) *Compelled election disclosures.* BROWN v. SOCIALIST WORKERS, 459 U.S. 87 (1982), per MARSHALL, J., held that an Ohio statute requiring every political party to report the names and addresses of campaign contributors and recipients of campaign disbursements could not be applied to the Socialist Workers Party. Citing *Buckley v. Valeo,* Ch. 10 infra, the Court held that the " 'evidence offered [by a minor party] need show only a reasonable probability that the compelled disclosure [of] names will subject them to threats, harassment, or reprisals from either Government officials or private parties.' " Consider Geoffrey Stone & William Marshall, *Brown v. Socialist Workers: Inequality As A Command of the First Amendment,* 1983 Sup.Ct.Rev. 583, 592: "[I]n *Brown* the Court expressly exempted particular political parties from an otherwise content-neutral regulation for reasons directly related to the content of their expression. [The] constitutionally compelled exemption substitutes a content-based law for one that is content neutral. It stands the presumption in favor of 'content neutrality' on its head." Is the decision, nonetheless, consistent with First Amendment values? See Stone & Marshall, supra.

---

m. Ginsburg, J., concurred. Consider Randall P. Bezanson, *Speech Stories: How Free Can Speech Be?* 50 (1998): "The Court's decision appears to have rested on the fact that McIntyre's leaflet was an expression of *opinion,* not just of fact, and that its quality as opinion subordinated any claims about authorship that might be based on its factual content, thus avoiding any need to discuss its factual elements." What if the leaflet did not contain opinion?

See also Buckley v. American Constitutional Law Foundation, 525 U.S. 182 (1999), per Ginsburg, J., which held unconstitutional a Colorado statute requiring that circulators of initiatives wear identification badges bearing their names and that sponsors of the initiative report the names and addresses of all paid circulators. By contrast, the Court was satisfied that the requirement of the filing of an affidavit containing the name and address of the circulator of petitions was consistent with the First Amendment. Compare *John Doe No. 1 v. Reed,* 130 S.Ct. 2811 (2010), holding that a state, in order to protect the integrity of the elections process could constitutionally make the names of those who sign referendum petitions a matter of public record, but the Court stated that a state could not do so in cases where there was a "reasonable probability" of harassment, threats, or reprisals. For broad-ranging commentary on the relationship between privacy and disclosure, see Kreimer, *Sunlight, Secrets, and Scarlet Letter: The Tension Between Privacy and Disclosure in Constitutional Law,* 140 U.Pa.L.Rev. 1, 70 (1991).

(c) *Compelled disclosure of desire to receive communist mail.* LA-MONT v. POSTMASTER GENERAL, 381 U.S. 301 (1965), per Douglas, J., invalidated a federal statute permitting delivery of "communist political propaganda" only if the addressee specifically requested in writing that it be delivered: "We rest on the narrow ground that the addressee in order to receive his mail must request in writing that it be delivered. [The] addressee carries an affirmative obligation which we do not think the government may impose on him. This requirement is almost certain to have a deterrent effect, especially as respects those who have sensitive positions. [Public] officials, like school teachers who have no tenure, might think they would invite disaster if they read what the Federal Government says contains the seeds of treason. Apart from them, any addressee is likely to feel some inhibition in sending for literature which federal officials have condemned as 'communist political propaganda.' "[n]

II. INTIMATE ASSOCIATION AND EXPRESSIVE ASSOCIATION

ROBERTS v. UNITED STATES JAYCEES, 468 U.S. 609 (1984): Appellee U.S. Jaycees, a nonprofit national membership corporation whose objective is to pursue educational and charitable purposes that promote the growth and development of young men's civic organizations, limits regular membership to young men between the ages of 18 and 35. Associate membership is available to women and older men. An associate member may not vote or hold local or national office. Two local chapters in Minnesota violated appellee's bylaws by admitting women as regular members. When they learned that revocation of their charters was to be considered, members of both chapters filed discrimination charges with the Minnesota Department of Human Rights, alleging that the exclusion of women from full membership violated the Minnesota Human Rights Act (Act), which makes it an "unfair discriminatory practice" to deny anyone "the full and equal enjoyment of goods, services, facilities, privileges, advantages, and accommodations of a place of public accommodation" because, inter alia, of sex.

Before a hearing on the state charge took place, appellee brought federal suit, alleging that requiring it to accept women as regular members would violate the male members' constitutional "freedom of association." A state hearing officer decided against appellee and the federal district court certified to the Minnesota Supreme Court the question whether appellee is "a place of public accommodation" within the meaning of the Act. With the record of the administrative hearing before it, the state Supreme Court answered that question in the affirmative. The U.S. Court of Appeals held that application of the Act to appellee's membership policies would violate its freedom of association.[a]

---

n. Compare *Meese v. Keene*, 481 U.S. 465 (1987)(government may label and require registration of films involving "political propaganda," so long as it permits distribution).

a. When the state supreme court held that appellee was "a place of public accommodation" within the meaning of the Act, it suggested that, unlike appellee, the Kiwanis Club might be

In rejecting appellee's claims,[b] the Court, per BRENNAN, J., pointed out that the Constitution protects " 'freedom of association' in two distinct senses," what might be called "freedom of intimate association" and "freedom of expressive association": "In one line of decisions, the Court has concluded that choices to enter into and maintain certain intimate human relationships must be secured against undue intrusion by the State because of the role of such relationships in safeguarding the individual freedom that is central to our constitutional scheme. In this respect, freedom of association receives protection as a fundamental element of personal liberty. In another set of decisions, the Court has recognized a right to associate for the purpose of engaging in those activities protected by the First Amendment—speech, assembly, petition for the redress of grievances, [and] religion. The Constitution guarantees freedom of association of this kind as an indispensable means of preserving other individual liberties."

The freedom of intimate association was deemed important because, "certain kinds of personal bonds have played a critical role in the culture and traditions of the Nation by cultivating and transmitting shared ideals and beliefs; they thereby foster diversity and act as critical buffers between the individual and the power of the State. Moreover, the constitutional shelter afforded such relationships reflects the realization that individuals draw much of their emotional enrichment from close ties with others. Protecting these relationships from unwarranted state interference therefore safeguards the ability independently to define one's identity that is central to any concept of liberty.

"The personal affiliations that exemplify these considerations [are] distinguished by such attributes as relative smallness, a high degree of selectivity in decisions to begin and maintain the affiliation, and seclusion from others in critical aspects of the relationship. [A]n association lacking these qualities—such as a large business enterprise—seems remote from the concerns giving rise to this constitutional protection. * * *

"Between these poles, of course, lies a broad range of human relationships that may make greater or lesser claims to constitutional protection from particular incursions by the State. [We] need not mark the potentially significant points on this terrain with any precision. We note only that factors that may be relevant include size, purpose, policies, selectivity, congeniality, and other characteristics that in a particular case may be pertinent. In this case, however, several features of the Jaycees clearly place the organization outside of the category of relationships worthy of this kind of constitutional protection.

---

sufficiently "private" to be outside the scope of the Act. Appellee then amended its complaint to allege that the state court's interpretation of the Act rendered it unconstitutionally vague. The Eighth Circuit so held, but the Supreme Court reversed.

b. There was no dissent. Rehnquist, J., concurred in the judgment. O'Connor, J., joined part of the Court's opinion and concurred in the judgment. See infra. Burger, C.J., and Blackmun, J., took no part.

"[T]he local chapters of the Jaycees are large and basically unselective groups. [Apart] from age and sex, neither the national organization nor the local chapters employs any criteria for judging applicants for membership, and new members are routinely recruited and admitted with no inquiry into their backgrounds. In fact, a local officer testified that he could recall no instance in which an applicant had been denied membership on any basis other than age or sex. [Furthermore], numerous non-members of both genders regularly participate in a substantial portion of activities central to the decision of many members to associate with one another, including many of the organization's various community programs, awards ceremonies, and recruitment meetings.

"[We] turn therefore to consider the extent to which application of the Minnesota statute to compel the Jaycees to accept women infringes the group's freedom of expressive association. * * *

"Government actions that may unconstitutionally infringe upon [freedom of expressive association] can take a number of forms. Among other things, government may seek to impose penalties or withhold benefits from individuals because of their membership in a disfavored group; it may attempt to require disclosure of the fact of membership in a group seeking anonymity; and it may try to interfere with the internal organization or affairs of the group. [There] can be no clearer example of an intrusion into the internal structure or affairs of an association than a regulation that forces the group to accept members it does not desire. Such a regulation may impair the ability of the original members to express only those views that brought them together. Freedom of association therefore plainly presupposes a freedom not to associate. See *Abood*.

"The right to associate for expressive purposes is not, however, absolute. Infringements on that right may be justified by regulations adopted to serve compelling state interests, unrelated to the suppression of ideas, that cannot be achieved through means significantly less restrictive of associational freedoms.

"[I]n upholding Title II of the Civil Rights Act of 1964, which forbids race discrimination in public accommodations, we emphasized that its 'fundamental object [was] to vindicate "the deprivation of personal dignity that surely accompanies denials of equal access to public establishments." ' *Heart of Atlanta Motel,* 379 U.S. 241 (1964). That stigmatizing injury, and the denial of equal opportunities that accompanies it, is surely felt as strongly by persons suffering discrimination on the basis of their sex as by those treated differently because of their race.

"Nor is the state interest in assuring equal access limited to the provision of purely tangible goods and services. A State enjoys broad authority to create rights of public access on behalf of its citizens. *PruneYard.* Like many States and municipalities, Minnesota has adopted a functional definition of public accommodations that reaches various forms of public, quasi-commercial conduct. This expansive definition reflects a recognition of the changing nature of the American economy and of the importance, both to the individual and to society, of removing the barriers to economic advancement and political and social integration that have historically plagued certain disadvantaged groups, including women. * * *

"In applying the Act to the Jaycees, the State has advanced those interests through the least restrictive means of achieving its ends. Indeed, the Jaycees have failed to demonstrate that the Act imposes any serious burdens on the male members' freedom of expressive association. See *Hishon v. King & Spalding,* 467 U.S. 69 (1984) (law firm 'has not shown how its ability to fulfill [protected] function[s] would be inhibited by a requirement that it consider [a woman lawyer] for partnership on her merits'). To be sure, a 'not insubstantial part' of the Jaycees' activities constitutes protected expression on political, economic, cultural, and social affairs. [There] is, however, no basis in the record for concluding that admission of women as full voting members will impede the organization's ability to engage in these protected activities or to disseminate its preferred views. The Act requires no change in the Jaycees' creed of promoting the interests of young men, and it imposes no restrictions on the organization's ability to exclude individuals with ideologies or philosophies different from those of its existing members. Moreover, the Jaycees already invite women to share the group's views and philosophy and to participate in much of [its] activities. Accordingly, any claim that admission of women as full voting members will impair a symbolic message conveyed by the very fact that women are not permitted to vote is attenuated at best.

"[In] claiming that women might have a different attitude about such issues as the federal budget, school prayer, voting rights, and foreign relations, or that the organization's public positions would have a different effect if the group were not 'a purely young men's association,' the Jaycees rely solely on unsupported generalizations about the relative interests and perspectives of men and women. Although such generalizations may or may not have a statistical basis in fact with respect to particular positions adopted by the Jaycees, we have repeatedly condemned legal decisionmaking that relies uncritically on such assumptions. In the absence of a showing far more substantial than that attempted by the Jaycees, we decline to indulge in the sexual stereotyping [of appellees].

"In any event, even if enforcement of the Act causes some incidental abridgement of the Jaycees' protected speech, that effect is no greater than is necessary to accomplish the State's legitimate purposes. [A]cts of invidious discrimination in the distribution of publicly available goods, services, and other advantages cause unique evils that government has a compelling interest to prevent—wholly apart from the point of view such conduct may transmit. Accordingly, like violence or other types of potentially expressive activities that produce special harms distinct from their communicative impact, such practices are entitled to no constitutional protection."[c]

---

c. For cases following or extending *Roberts,* see *Board of Directors of Rotary International v. Rotary Club of Duarte,* 481 U.S. 537 (1987); *New York State Club Ass'n v. New York,* 487 U.S. 1

O'CONNOR, J., concurring, joined the Court's opinion except for its analysis of freedom of expressive association: "[T]he Court has adopted a test that unadvisedly casts doubt on the power of States to pursue the profoundly important goal of ensuring nondiscriminatory access to commercial opportunities" yet "accords insufficient protection to expressive associations and places inappropriate burdens on groups claiming the protection of the First Amendment":

"[The] Court declares that the Jaycees' right of association depends on the organization's making a 'substantial' showing that the admission of unwelcome members 'will change the message communicated by the group's speech.' [S]uch a requirement, especially in the context of the balancing-of-interests test articulated by the Court, raises the possibility that certain commercial associations, by engaging occasionally in certain kinds of expressive activities, might improperly gain protection for discrimination. The Court's focus raises other problems as well. [W]ould the Court's analysis of this case be different if, for example, the Jaycees membership had a steady history of opposing public issues thought (by the Court) to be favored by women? It might seem easy to conclude, in the latter case, that the admission of women to the Jaycees' ranks would affect the content of the organization's message, but I do not believe that should change the outcome of this case. Whether an association is or is not constitutionally protected in the selection of its membership should not depend on what the association says or why its members say it.

"The Court's readiness to inquire into the connection between membership and message reveals a more fundamental flaw in its analysis. The Court pursues this inquiry as part of its mechanical application of a 'compelling interest' test, [and] entirely neglects to establish at the threshold that the Jaycees is an association whose activities or purposes should engage the strong protections that the First Amendment extends to expressive associations.

"On the one hand, an association engaged exclusively in protected expression enjoys First Amendment protection of both the content of its message and the choice of its members. * * * Protection of the association's right to define its membership derives from the recognition that the formation of an expressive association is the creation of a voice, and the selection of members is the definition of that voice. [A] ban on specific group voices on public affairs violates the most basic guarantee of the First Amendment—that citizens, not the government, control the content of public discussion.

"On the other hand, there is only minimal constitutional protection of the freedom of *commercial* association. There are, of course, some constitutional protections of commercial speech—speech intended and used to

---

(1988) (upholding city ordinance against facial challenge that prohibits discrimination based on race, creed, or sex by institutions (except benevolent orders or religious corporations) with more than 400 members that provide regular meal service and receive payment from nonmembers for the furtherance of trade or business); *Dallas v. Stanglin*, 490 U.S. 19 (1989) (upholding ordinance restricting admission to certain dance halls to persons between the ages of 14 and 18).

promote a commercial transaction with the speaker. But the State is free to impose any rational regulation on the commercial transaction itself. The Constitution does not guarantee a right to choose employees, customers, suppliers, or those with whom one engages in simple commercial transactions, without restraint from the State.

"[A]n association should be characterized as commercial, and therefore subject to rationally related state regulation of its membership and other associational activities, when, and only when, the association's activities are not predominantly of the type protected by the First Amendment. It is only when the association is predominantly engaged in protected expression that state regulation of its membership will necessarily affect, change, dilute, or silence one collective voice that would otherwise be heard. An association must choose its market. Once it enters the marketplace of commerce in any substantial degree it loses the complete control over its membership that it would otherwise enjoy if it confined its affairs to the marketplace of ideas.

"[N]otwithstanding its protected expressive activities, [appellee] is, first and foremost, an organization that, at both the national and local levels, promotes and practices the art of solicitation and management. The organization claims that the training it offers its members gives them an advantage in business, and business firms do indeed sometimes pay the dues of individual memberships for their employees. Jaycees members hone their solicitation and management skills, under the direction and supervision of the organization, primarily through their active recruitment of new members. [The] 'not insubstantial' volume of protected Jaycees activity found by the Court of Appeals is simply not enough to preclude state regulation of the Jaycees' commercial activities. The State of Minnesota has a legitimate interest in ensuring nondiscriminatory access to the commercial opportunity presented by membership in the Jaycees."

NOTES AND QUESTIONS

1. *Freedom of intimate association*. The reference to the freedom of intimate association is the first in the Court's history, but the notion that the concept should serve as an organizing principle is found in Kenneth Karst, *Freedom of Intimate Association*, 89 Yale L.J. 624 (1980). To what extent should freedom of intimate association itself be regarded as a First Amendment right? Compare Karst with C. Edwin Baker, *Scope of the First Amendment Freedom of Speech*, 25 UCLA L.Rev. 964 (1978) and Reena Raggi, *An Independent Right to Freedom of Association*, 12 Harv.Civ.Rts.-Civ.Lib.L.Rev. 1 (1977).

2. *Freedom of expressive association.* Should freedom of association be confined to groups that are intimate or have a message to propound? Consider Shiffrin, note 1 after *Barnette*, Ch. 9, I, supra, at 865: "An association may have no message at all and nonetheless serve important First Amendment values. To wit, an important function of private associations is

that they provide sites in which the thoughts and ideas of members are formed and in which the content of their expressions is generated and germinated (although not necessarily in harmony with other members), not merely concentrated and exported. That is, associations are important from a freedom of speech perspective because of what happens inside of them, not solely or even necessarily by virtue of their relationships to the outside world or even by virtue of any internal shared beliefs.'' Is Brennan, J.'s conception of association's value too narrowly conceived? See also George Kateb, *The Value of Association* in *Freedom of Association* 35, 49(Amy Gutmann ed. 1998).[d]

3. ***Commercial associations.*** Is O'Connor, J.'s distinction of commercial associations defensible? Consider Shiffrin, supra, at 877: ''Regulation to promote inclusive membership practices is justified when applied to associations whose primary purpose is participation in the commercial milieu because of the central importance of fair access to material resources and mechanisms of power. Second, because such associations operate within a highly competitive marketplace and have a fairly focused singular purpose whose pursuit is largely guided by this competitive context and aim of profitable operation, these associations do not function in a context that is likely to be conducive to the free, sincere, uninhibited, and undirected social interaction and consideration of ideas and ways of life.''[e] To what extent should government be able to limit the discriminatory policies of groups that are commercial and expressive? What about private schools? Should they be able to discriminate in the selection of teachers but not with respect to construction workers or secretaries? See Dale Carpenter, *Expressive Association and Anti–Discrimination Law After Dale: A Tripartite Approach*, 85 Minn. L. Rev. 1515 (2001). Should hate speech codes on private college campuses be protected against government prohibition on associational grounds? See David E. Bernstein, *The Right of Expressive Association and Private Universities' Racial Preferences and Speech Codes*, 9 Wm. & Mary Bill Rts. J. 619 (2001).

What about newspapers? Should a similar analysis apply to them? Should the freedom of association concept apply to the press, or should the press clause apply? Christopher R. Edgar, *The Right to Freedom of Expressive Association and the Press*, 55 Stan. L. Rev. 191 (2002). Does the concept of freedom of association support or engulf the academic freedom enjoyed by universities? See Paul Horwitz, *Grutter's First Amendment*, 46 B.C. L. Rev. 461, 546 (2005).

––––––––

James Dale's position as an assistant scoutmaster of a New Jersey troop of the Boy Scouts of America was revoked. The Scouts learned that he was gay and the co-President of the Rutgers University Lesbian/Gay Alliance. Dale had been publicly quoted on the importance in his own life

---

d. On the value of discriminatory associations, see generally Nancy L. Rosenblum, *Membership and Morals* (1998).

e. See generally Michael Burns, *The Exclusion of Women From Influential Men's Clubs: The Inner Sanctum and the Myth of Full Equality,* 18 Harv.Civ.Rts.-Civ.Lib.L.Rev. 321 (1983).

on the need for gay role models. Dale sued, and the New Jersey Supreme Court ultimately held that New Jersey's anti-discrimination public accommodation law required that the Scouts readmit him.

BOY SCOUTS OF AMERICA v. DALE, 530 U.S. 640 (2000), per REHNQUIST, C.J., held that the New Jersey law violated the expressive association rights of the Boy Scouts: "The First Amendment's protection of expressive association is not reserved for advocacy groups. But to come within its ambit, a group must engage in some form of expression, whether it be public or private."

Rehnquist, C.J., cited portions of the Scout Oath requiring Scouts to be "morally straight" and to be "Clean": "The Boy Scouts [says] that it 'teach[es] that homosexual conduct is not morally straight' * * *. We need not inquire further to determine the nature of the Boy Scouts' expression with respect to homosexuality. But because the record before us contains written evidence of the Boy Scouts' viewpoint, we look to it as instructive, if only on the question of the sincerity of the professed beliefs. * * *

"We must [also] give deference to an association's view of what would impair its expression. [That] is not to say that an expressive association can erect a shield against antidiscrimination laws simply by asserting that mere acceptance of a member from a particular group would impair its message. But here Dale, by his own admission, is one of a group of gay Scouts who have 'become leaders in their community and are open and honest about their sexual orientation.' [His] presence in the Boy Scouts would, at the very least, force the organization to send a message, both to the youth members and the world, that the Boy Scouts accepts homosexual conduct as a legitimate form of behavior.[a] * * *

"We recognized in cases such as *Roberts* and *Duarte* that States have a compelling interest in eliminating discrimination against women in public accommodations. But in each of these cases we went on to conclude that the enforcement of these statutes would not materially interfere with the ideas that the organization sought to express. * * * New Jersey's public accommodations law directly and immediately affects associational rights, in this case associational rights that enjoy First Amendment protection. Thus, *O'Brien*['s] intermediate standard of review [is] inapplicable."

---

a. Stevens, J., dissenting, responded: "Dale's inclusion in the Boy Scouts [sends] no cognizable message to the Scouts or to the world. Unlike GLIB, Dale did not carry a banner or a sign; he did not distribute any fact sheet; and he expressed no intent to send any message. If there is any kind of message being sent, then, it is by the mere act of joining the Boy Scouts. [S]ome acts are so imbued with symbolic meaning that they qualify as 'speech' under the First Amendment. At the same time, however, '[w]e cannot accept the view that an apparently limitless variety of conduct can be labeled 'speech' whenever the person engaging in the conduct intends thereby to express an idea.' *O'Brien*. [Indeed], if merely joining a group did constitute symbolic speech; and such speech were attributable to the group being joined; and that group has the right to exclude that speech (and hence, the right to exclude that person from joining), then the right of free speech effectively becomes a limitless right to exclude for every organization, whether or not it engages in any expressive activities. That cannot be, and never has been, the law."

STEVENS, J., joined by Souter, Ginsburg, and Breyer, JJ., dissenting, contended that: "at a minimum, a group seeking to prevail over an antidiscrimination law must adhere to a clear and unequivocal view" and that the Scouts had not done so. Nor did precedent favor the Scouts claim: "Several principles are made perfectly clear by *Jaycees* and *Rotary Club*. First, to prevail on a claim of expressive association in the face of a State's antidiscrimination law, it is not enough simply to engage in *some kind* of expressive activity. Both the Jaycees and the Rotary Club engaged in expressive activity protected by the First Amendment, yet that fact was not dispositive. Second, it is not enough to adopt an openly avowed exclusionary membership policy. Both the Jaycees and the Rotary Club did that as well. Third, it is not sufficient merely to articulate *some* connection between the group's expressive activities and its exclusionary policy." Stevens, J., argued that it was necessary to show a serious burden on the association's expression: "The evidence before this Court makes it exceptionally clear that BSA has, at most, simply adopted an exclusionary membership policy and has no shared goal of disapproving of homosexuality [or] collective effort to foster a belief about homosexuality at all—let alone one that is significantly burdened by admitting homosexuals." Stevens argued that the majority's deferential posture toward the allegations of the Scouts reflected "an astounding view of the law. I am unaware of any previous instance in which our analysis of the scope of a constitutional right was determined by looking at what a litigant asserts in his or her brief and inquiring no further."

NOTES AND QUESTIONS

1. **What speech?** Consider Randall P. Bezanson, *Speaking Through Others' Voices: Authorship, Originality, and Free Speech*, 38 Wake Forest L. Rev. 983, 990 (2003): "*Dale* represents an instance of speakerless speech since the speaker (the Scouts) never physically articulated a message. Yet the *Dale* case involved an identifiable message that was likely understood by an audience. To complicate matters further, the speaker in *Dale* (the Scouts) had no intention to communicate the message, or indeed to communicate any message whatever, by the act of employing or firing Dale." Are the Scouts entitled to exclude Dale because his coming out in a context other than scouting imputes a message to it? If so, what is Dale's message? See James P. Madigan, *Questioning the Coercive Effect of Self–Identifying Speech*, 87 Iowa L. Rev. 75 (2001); Nancy J. Knauer, *"Simply So Different": The Uniquely Expressive Character of the Openly Gay Individual After Boy Scouts of America v. Dale*, 89 Ky. L.J. 997 (2001). Consider Laurence H. Tribe, *Disentangling Symmetries: Speech, Association, Parenthood*, 28 Pepp. L. Rev. 641, 647 (2001): "[T]he right not to have government force on you an unwanted associate cannot be overcome by the fact that it might be as clear as day to the whole world that the unwanted associate is not your idea, and that your agreement to let him or her into your group reflects nothing more than your obedience to the law. Thus, the fact that the Chief Justice overplayed his hand when he said that forcing the Boy Scouts to accept an openly gay scout

leader would compel them to send a pro-gay signal to the world at large should not lead anyone to conclude that the majority's result in that case was necessarily wrong."

2. *Standard of review.* Does the Court apply a more demanding standard of review to the application of the statute than it did in *O'Brien*? Adam M. Samaha, *Litigant Sensitivity in First Amendment Law*, 98 Nw. U. L. Rev. 1291, 1342 (2004). Is this a particular problem for Justice Scalia? See Stephen Clark, *Judicially Straight? Boy Scouts v. Dale and the Missing Scalia Dissent*, 76 S. Cal. L. Rev. 521 (2003).

Consider Laurence H. Tribe, *Disentangling Symmetries: Speech, Association, Parenthood*, 28 Pepp. L. Rev. 641, 651–652 (2001): "The state's objection to the exclusion of openly gay men by groups like the Boy Scouts cannot be simply that such groups must be acting on ignorant stereotypes, using sexual orientation as a statistical proxy or as shorthand for something else that really matters to them—the sort of objection conventionally made to the use of race, and sometimes to the use of gender, as proxies for something else. That kind of objection would not carry the day against the Boy Scouts, who are, for better or for worse, using heterosexual status as a defining component of their ideal. As a result, it becomes difficult to regard the application of the anti-discrimination laws in this setting as a 'neutral' instance of mere error-correction. Rather, it becomes a direct clash of competing images of 'the good life.' And, in such a clash, the teaching of the First Amendment has long been that the state loses."

What accounts for the Court's deferential review of the Scout's ideology? Is it to be explained by hostility to civil rights for gays? See Neal Troum, *Expressive Association and the Right to Exclude: Reading Between the Lines in Boy Scouts of America v. Dale*, 35 Creighton L. Rev. 641, 686–687 (2002); Darren L. Hutchinson, *"Closet Case": Boy Scouts of America v. Dale and the Reinforcement of Gay, Lesbian, Bisexual, and Transgender Invisibility*, 76 Tul. L. Rev. 81, 99 (2001). Would a contrary result mean that the Scouts could be required to be sexually integrated? For discussion, see Evelyn Brody, *Entrance, Voice, and Exit: The Constitutional Bounds of the Right of Association*, 35 U.C. Davis L. Rev. 821, 901 n.116 (2002).

3. *Children.* Does it matter that unlike *Roberts* the Scouts are children? See Seana Valentine Shiffrin, *What Is Really Wrong With Compelled Association?*, 99 Nw. U. L. Rev. 839 (2005) (contending that it makes it more difficult to defend the result).

4. *The joy of ambiguity.* Consider Andrew Koppelman, *Should Noncommercial Associations Have an Absolute Right to Discriminate?*, 67–FALL Law & Contemp. Probs. 27, 57–58 (2004): "In the end, we have a choice of pathologies. We can either live with the little pathologies created by the message-based rule, or with the big pathologies that would be created by either of the large and clear rules—absolute protection for discrimination, or no freedom of association at all—between which it uneasily perches. Ambiguity has its virtues. There is this much to be said for the Court's confused opinion in *Dale*: it has thickened the fog where clarity would be deadly." Does O'Connor, J.'s approach in *Roberts* avoid the "big" pathologies?

5. ***Restrictions on freedom of association and limited public forums.*** (a) CHRISTIAN LEGAL SOCIETY v. MARTINEZ, 130 S.Ct. 2971 (2010), per GINSBURG, J., held that Hastings Law School could condition official recognition of a student group—and the resulting eligibility for financial resources and access to certain facilities—on its agreement to open its membership and eligibility for access to leadership positions to all students ("all-comers" policy).[a] The Christian Legal Society restricted membership to Christians and denied access to those who "engage in unrepentant homosexual conduct." Ginsburg, J., concluded that the policy, denying the Society access to a limited public forum, was viewpoint neutral; indeed it drew no distinction between groups based on their message or perspective; it regulated conduct, not speech.

She also maintained that the policy was "reasonable." It ensured that students were afforded leadership, educational, and social opportunities, that Hastings students are not forced through student fees to fund a group that would reject them as members, helped Hastings enforce its anti-discrimination policy (and state anti-discrimination laws) without the necessity of determining the basis for membership restrictions, and by bringing together people of diverse backgrounds encouraged toleration, cooperation, and learning. Any claim that hostile students would take over an organization was contrary to the experience of the school and unduly speculative.

The reasonableness of the policy was also indicated by its measured character. The school offered the Society access to school facilities to conduct meetings and the use of chalkboards and some bulletin boards, and it could take advantage of electronic media and social networking sites. "It is beyond dissenter's license * * * constantly to maintain that nonrecognition of a group is equivalent to prohibiting its members from speaking."

Nor did the policy impinge on the Society's freedom of association right to choose its members. Although the Society had a right to be selective in its membership, it had no right for the state to subsidize its selectivity. Finally, the Court rejected claims that the policy had been applied in a discriminatory way and that it was a pretext to single out the Christian Legal Society for special treatment. Ginsburg, J., maintained that such claims were not before the Court because the parties stipulated that Hastings current policy was an all-comers policy and that it applied equally to religious and political groups. The Court remanded to permit the lower court to explore claims of pretext if they were still open to the plaintiffs.

STEVENS, J., concurring, argued that Hastings' exclusion of the Society from its limited public forum would have been justified even under a policy that only excluded groups discriminating on the basis of race, gender, religion, and sexual orientation: Hastings "excludes students who will not sign its Statement of Faith or who engage in 'unrepentant homosexual conduct.' [Other] groups may exclude or mistreat Jews, blacks and women—or those who do not share their contempt for Jews, blacks and women. A free society

---

a. The Hastings brief observed that recognized student organizations can require students to pay dues, maintain good attendance, refrain from gross misconduct, or to pass a skill-based test, such as the writing competitions administered by the law journals. The dissent stated that this admission transformed the all-comers policy into a some-comers policy.

may tolerate such groups. It need not subsidize them, give them its official imprimatur, or grant them equal access to law school facilities."[b]

ALITO, J., joined by Roberts, C.J., Scalia and Thomas, JJ., dissented, mostly disagreeing with the majority's reading of the record. Alito, J., argued that the Hastings policy shifted over the years, that it had been applied in a discriminatory way (including the denial of access to facilities), that it was ultimately pretextual, and that such issues were rightly before the Court, and that the decision was a "serious setback for freedom of expression in this country."

As to the all-comers policy, even applied in a non-discriminatory way, he argued that it was unreasonable in large part because it impinged on freedom of association by denying access to needed facilities, and that subsidies were a minor part of the case. Respecting freedom of association also promoted leadership, educational, and social opportunities. He denied that the difficulty of enforcing a nondiscrimination policy was greater than other policies it sought to enforce and denied that California law called into question that right of religious groups to discriminate on the basis of religion. He maintained that furthering toleration, cooperation, and learning skills was consistent with pluralism. Alito, J., also denied that the all-comers policy was viewpoint neutral in that it opened the door for hostile groups to take over organizations and because of his view of discriminatory purpose and treatment.

(b) If Hastings had a policy prohibiting discrimination on the basis of race, gender, sexual orientation, and religion instead of an all-comers policy, would it be constitutional? See generally Eugene Volokh, *Freedom of Expressive Association and Government Subsidies,* 58 Stan. L.Rev. 1919 (2006)(subject to limited exceptions, government need not subsidize such discrimination).

(c) Conservative justices have tended to deny equality claims in subsidy cases and liberal justices have tended to support them except in *Rosenberger* and in *Hastings.* Why the departure in those cases? For discussion, see Kathleen M. Sullivan, *Two Concepts of Freedom of Speech,* 124 Harv. L.Rev. 143, 165–66 (2010).

––––––––

In the *Rumsfeld* case, note 4(c) supra, the law schools, citing *Dale,* argued that the Solomon Amendment violated law schools' freedom of expressive association. The Court disagreed: "To comply with the statute, law schools must allow military recruiters on campus and assist them in whatever way the school chooses to assist other employers. Law schools therefore 'associate' with military recruiters in the sense that they

---

b. Kennedy, J., concurring, argued that Hastings could reasonably believe that the process of learning how to create arguments in a "convincing, rational, and respectful manner and to express doubt and disagreement in a professional way" is best enhanced when dialogue is "vibrant" which cannot occur if "students wall themselves off from opposing points of view."

interact with them.   But recruiters are not part of the law school.
Recruiters are, by definition, outsiders who come onto campus for the
limited purpose of trying to hire students—not to become members of the
school's expressive association.   This distinction is critical.   Unlike the
public accommodations law in *Dale,* the Solomon Amendment does not
force a law school 'to accept members it does not desire.' "

CHAPTER 10

WEALTH AND THE POLITICAL PROCESS: CONCERNS FOR EQUALITY

■ ■ ■

The idea of equality has loomed large throughout this chapter. Some feel it should be a central concern of the First Amendment. See Laurence Tribe, *Constitutional Choices* 188–220 (1985); Kenneth Karst, *Equality as a Central Principle in the First Amendment*, 43 U.Chi.L.Rev. 20 (1975). Equality has been championed by those who seek access to government property and to media facilities. It has been invoked in support of content regulation and against it. This section considers government efforts to prevent the domination of the political process by wealthy individuals and business corporations. In the end, it would be appropriate to reconsider the arguments for and against a marketplace conception of the First Amendment, to ask whether the Court's interpretations overall (e.g., taking the public forum materials, the media materials, and the election materials together) have adequately considered the interest in equality, and to inquire generally about the relationship between liberty and equality in the constitutional scheme.

BUCKLEY v. VALEO
424 U.S. 1, 96 S.Ct. 612, 46 L.Ed.2d 659 (1976).

PER CURIAM.

[In this portion of a lengthy opinion dealing with the validity of the Federal Election Campaign Act of 1971, as amended in 1974, the Court considers those parts of the Act limiting *contributions* to a candidate for federal office (all sustained), and those parts limiting *expenditures* in support of such candidacy (all held invalid).]

A. *General Principles.* The Act's contribution and expenditure limitations operate in an area of the most fundamental First Amendment activities. Discussion of public issues and debate on the qualifications of candidates are integral to the operation of the system of government established by our Constitution.

[Appellees] contend that what the Act regulates is conduct, and that its effect on speech and association is incidental at most. Appellants

respond that contributions and expenditures are at the very core of
political speech, and that the Act's limitations thus constitute restraints
on First Amendment liberty that are both gross and [direct.]

Contributions are not considered conduct

We cannot share the view [that] the present Act's contribution and
expenditure limitations are comparable to the restrictions on conduct
upheld in *O'Brien* [Ch. 2 supra]. The expenditure of money simply cannot
be equated with such conduct as destruction of a draft card. Some forms of
communication made possible by the giving and spending of money
involve speech alone, some involve conduct primarily, and some involve a
combination of the two. Yet this Court has never suggested that the
dependence of a communication on the expenditure of money operates
itself to introduce a non-speech element or to reduce the exacting scrutiny
required by the First Amendment. * * *

Regulation fails O'Brien standard — government has an interest in regulating speech

Even if the categorization of the expenditure of money as conduct
were accepted, the limitations challenged here would not meet the *O'Brien*
test because the governmental interests advanced in support of the Act
involve "suppressing communication." The interests served by the Act
include restricting the voices of people and interest groups who have
money to spend and reducing the overall scope of federal election campaigns. [Unlike] *O'Brien*, where [the] interest in the preservation of draft
cards was wholly unrelated to their use as a means of communication, it is
beyond dispute that the interest in regulating the alleged "conduct" of
giving or spending money "arises in some measure because the communication allegedly integral to the conduct is itself thought to be harmful."

Nor can the Act's contribution and expenditure limitations be sustained, as some of the parties suggest, by reference to the constitutional
principles reflected in such decisions as *Adderley* 385 U.S. 39 (1966) and
Kovacs v. Cooper, 336 U.S. 77 (1949). [The] critical difference between this
case and those time, place and manner cases is that the present Act's
contribution and expenditure limitations impose direct quantity restrictions on political communication and association by persons, groups,
candidates and political parties in addition to any reasonable time, place,
and manner regulations otherwise imposed.

A restriction on the amount of money a person or group can spend on
political communication during a campaign necessarily reduces the quantity of expression by restricting the number of issues discussed, the depth of
their exploration, and the size of the audience reached. This is because
virtually every means of communicating ideas in today's mass society
requires the expenditure of [money].

The expenditure limitations contained in the Act represent substantial rather than merely theoretical restraints on the quantity and diversity
of political speech. The $1,000 ceiling on spending "relative to a clearly
identified candidate," 18 U.S.C. § 608(e)(1), would appear to exclude all
citizens and groups except candidates, political parties and the institution-

al press from any significant use of the most effective modes of communication.[20] * * *

By contrast with a limitation upon expenditures for political expression, a limitation [on] the amount of money a person may give to a candidate or campaign organization [involves] little direct restraint on his political communication, for it permits the symbolic expression of support evidenced by a contribution but does not in any way infringe the contributor's freedom to discuss candidates and issues. While contributions may result in political expression if spent by a candidate or an association to present views to the voters, the transformation of contributions into political debate involves speech by someone other than the contributor.

[There] is no indication [that] the contribution limitations imposed by the Act would have any dramatic adverse effect on the funding of campaigns and political associations.[23] The overall effect of the Act's contribution ceilings is merely to require candidates and political committees to raise funds from a greater number of persons and to compel people who would otherwise contribute amounts greater than the statutory limits to expend such funds on direct political expression, rather than to reduce the total amount of money potentially available to promote political expression. * * *

In sum, although the Act's contribution and expenditure limitations both implicate fundamental First Amendment interests, its expenditure ceilings impose significantly more severe restrictions on protected freedoms of political expression and association than do its limitations on financial contributions.

B. *Contribution Limitations.* [Section] 608(b) provides, with certain limited exceptions, that "no person shall make contributions to any candidate with respect to any election for Federal office which, in the aggregate, exceeds $1,000."[a]* * *

Appellants contend that the $1,000 contribution ceiling unjustifiably burdens First Amendment freedoms, employs overbroad dollar limits, and discriminates against candidates opposing incumbent officeholders and against minor-party candidates in violation of the Fifth Amendment.

---

20. The record indicates that, as of January 1, 1975, one full-page advertisement in a daily edition of a certain metropolitan newspaper costs $6,971.04—almost seven times the annual limit on expenditures "relative to" a particular candidate imposed on the vast majority of individual citizens and associations by § 608(e)(1).

23. Statistical findings agreed to by the parties reveal that approximately 5.1% of the $73,483,613 raised by the 1161 candidates for Congress in 1974 was obtained in amounts in excess of $1,000. In 1974, two major-party senatorial candidates, Ramsey Clark and Senator Charles Mathias, Jr., operated large-scale campaigns on contributions raised under a voluntarily imposed $100 contribution limitation.

a. As defined, "person" includes "an individual, partnership, committee, association, corporation or any other organization or group." The limitation applies to: (1) anything of value, such as gifts, loans, advances, and promises to give, (2) contributions made direct to the candidate or to an intermediary, or a committee authorized by the candidate, (3) the aggregate amounts contributed to the candidate for each election, treating primaries, run-off elections and general elections separately and all Presidential primaries within a single calendar year as one election.

[In] view of the fundamental nature of the right to associate, governmental "action which may have the effect of curtailing the freedom to associate is subject to the closest scrutiny." Yet, it is clear that "[n]either the right to associate nor the right to participate in political activities is absolute." *Letter Carriers*, Ch. 7, III. Even a " 'significant interference' with protected rights of political association" may be sustained if the State demonstrates a sufficiently important interest and employs means closely drawn to avoid unnecessary abridgment of associational freedoms. * * *

It is unnecessary to look beyond the Act's primary purpose—to limit the actuality and appearance of corruption resulting from large individual financial contributions—in order to find a constitutionally sufficient justification for the $1,000 contribution limitation. [The] increasing importance of the communications media and sophisticated mass mailing and polling operations to effective campaigning make the raising of large sums of money an ever more essential ingredient of an effective candidacy. To the extent that large contributions are given to secure political quid pro quos from current and potential office holders, the integrity of our system of representative democracy is undermined. Although the scope of such pernicious practices can never be reliably ascertained, the deeply disturbing examples surfacing after the 1972 election demonstrate that the problem is not an illusory one.

Of almost equal concern as the danger of actual quid pro quo arrangements is the impact of the appearance of corruption stemming from public awareness of the opportunities for abuse inherent in a regime of large individual financial contributions. In *Letter Carriers,* the Court found that the danger to "fair and effective government" posed by partisan political conduct on the part of federal employees charged with administering the law was a sufficiently important concern to justify broad restrictions on the employees' right of partisan political association. Here, as there, Congress could legitimately conclude that the avoidance of the appearance of improper influence "is also critical [if] confidence in the system of representative Government is not to be eroded to a disastrous extent."[29]

Appellants contend that the contribution limitations must be invalidated because bribery laws and narrowly-drawn disclosure requirements constitute a less restrictive means of dealing with "proven and suspected quid pro quo arrangements." But laws [against] bribes deal with only the most blatant and specific attempts of those with money to influence governmental action. [And] Congress was surely entitled to conclude that disclosure was only a partial measure, and that contribution ceilings were a necessary legislative concomitant to deal with the reality or appearance of corruption inherent in a system permitting unlimited financial contri-

---

29. Although the Court in *Letter Carriers* found that this interest was constitutionally sufficient to justify legislation prohibiting federal employees from engaging in certain partisan political activities, it was careful to emphasize that the limitations did not restrict an employee's right to express his views on political issues and candidates.

butions, even when the identities of the contributors and the amounts of their contributions are fully disclosed.

→ no broader than necessary

The Act's $1,000 contribution limitation focuses precisely on the problem of large campaign contributions—the narrow aspect of political association where the actuality and potential for corruption have been identified—while leaving persons free to engage in independent political expression, to associate actively through volunteering their services. [The] Act's contribution limitations [do] not undermine to any material degree the potential for robust and effective discussion of candidates and campaign [issues].

We find that, under the rigorous standard of review established by our prior decisions, the weighty interests served by restricting the size of financial contributions to political candidates are sufficient to justify the limited effect upon First Amendment freedoms caused by the $1,000 contribution ceiling.[b]

C. *Expenditure Limitations.* [1.] Section 608(e)(1) provides that "[n]o person may make any expenditure [relative] to a clearly identified candidate during a calendar year which, when added to all other expenditures made by such person during the year advocating the election or defeat of such candidate, exceeds $1,000." [Its] plain effect [is] to prohibit all individuals, who are neither candidates nor owners of institutional press facilities, and all groups, except political parties and campaign organizations, from voicing their views "relative to a clearly identified candidate" through means that entail aggregate expenditures of more than $1,000 during a calendar year. The provision, for example, would make it a federal criminal offense for a person or association to place a single one-quarter page advertisement "relative to a clearly identified candidate" in a major metropolitan newspaper.

[Although] "expenditure," "clearly identified," and "candidate" are defined in the Act, there is no definition clarifying what expenditures are "relative to" a candidate. [But the "when" clause in § 608(e)(1)] clearly permits, if indeed it does not require, the phrase "relative to" a candidate to be read to mean "advocating the election or defeat of" a candidate.

---

b. The Court rejected the challenges that the $1,000 limit was overbroad because (1) most large contributors do not seek improper influence over a candidate, and (2) much more than $1,000 would still not be enough to influence improperly a candidate or office holder. With respect to (1), "Congress was justified in concluding that the interest in safeguarding against the appearance of impropriety requires that the opportunity for abuse inherent in the process of raising large monetary contributions be eliminated." With respect to (2), "As the Court of Appeals observed, '[a] court has no scalpel to probe, whether, say, a $2,000 ceiling might not serve as well as $1,000.' Such distinctions in degree become significant only when they can be said to amount to differences in kind."

The Court also rejected as without support in the record the claims that the contribution limitations worked invidious discrimination between incumbents and challengers to whom the same limitations applied.

The Court then upheld (1) exclusion from the $1,000 limit of the value of unpaid volunteer services and of certain expenses paid by the volunteer up to a maximum of $500; (2) the higher limit of $5,000 for contributions to a candidate by established, registered political committees with at least 50 contributing supporters and fielding at least five candidates for federal office; and (3) the $25,000 limit on total contributions to all candidates by one person in one calendar year.

But while such a construction of § 608(e)(1) refocuses the vagueness question, [it hardly] eliminates the problem of unconstitutional vagueness altogether. For the distinction between discussion of issues and candidates and advocacy of election or defeat of candidates may often dissolve in practical application. Candidates, especially incumbents, are intimately tied to public issues involving legislative proposals and governmental actions. Not only do candidates campaign on the basis of their positions on various public issues, but campaigns themselves generate issues of public interest.

[Constitutionally deficient uncertainty which "compels the speaker to hedge and trim"] can be avoided only by reading § 608(e)(1) as limited to communications that include explicit words of advocacy of election or defeat of a candidate, much as the definition of "clearly identified" in § 608(e)(2) requires that an explicit and unambiguous reference to the candidate appear as part of the communication. This is the reading of the provision suggested by the non-governmental appellees in arguing that "[f]unds spent to propagate one's views on issues without expressly calling for a candidate's election or defeat are thus not covered." We agree that in order to preserve the provision against invalidation on vagueness grounds, § 608(e)(1) must be construed to apply only to expenditures for communications that in express terms advocate the election or defeat of a clearly identified candidate for federal office.[c]

We turn then to the basic First Amendment question—whether § 608(e)(1), even as thus narrowly and explicitly construed, impermissibly burdens the constitutional right of free expression. * * *

We find that the governmental interest in preventing corruption and the appearance of corruption is inadequate to justify § 608(e)(1)'s ceiling on independent expenditures. First, assuming arguendo that large independent expenditures pose the same dangers of actual or apparent quid pro quo arrangements as do large contributions, § 608(e)(1) does not provide an answer that sufficiently relates to the elimination of those dangers. Unlike the contribution limitations' total ban on the giving of large amounts of money to candidates, § 608(e)(1) prevents only some large expenditures. So long as persons and groups eschew expenditures that in express terms advocate the election or defeat of a clearly identified candidate, they are free to spend as much as they want to promote the candidate and his views. The exacting interpretation of the statutory language necessary to avoid unconstitutional vagueness thus undermines the limitation's effectiveness as a loophole-closing provision by facilitating circumvention by those seeking to exert improper influence upon a candidate or office-holder. It would naively underestimate the ingenuity and resourcefulness of persons and groups desiring to buy influence to believe

---

c. On the issues raised by this interpretation, see Richard Briffault, *Issue Advocacy: Redrawing the Elections/Politics Line,* 77 Texas L.Rev. 1751 (1999); Allison R. Hayward, *When Does an Advertisement about Issues Become an "Issues" Ad,* 49 Cath. U.L.Rev. 63 (1999); Glenn J. Moramarco, *Beyond "Magic Words": Using Self–Disclosure to Regulate Electioneering,* 49 Cath. U.L.Rev. 107 (1999).

that they would have much difficulty devising expenditures that skirted the restriction on express advocacy of election or defeat but nevertheless benefitted the candidate's campaign. * * *

Second, [the] independent advocacy restricted by the provision does not presently appear to pose dangers of real or apparent corruption comparable to those identified with large campaign contributions. The parties defending § 608(e)(1) contend that it is necessary to prevent would-be contributors from avoiding the contribution limitations by the simple expedient of paying directly for media advertisements or for other portions of the candidate's campaign activities. [Section] 608(b)'s contribution ceilings rather than § 608(e)(1)'s independent expenditure limitation prevent attempts to circumvent the Act through prearranged or coordinated expenditures amounting to disguised contributions.[53] By contrast, § 608(e)(1) limits expenditures for express advocacy of candidates made totally independently of the candidate and his campaign. [The] absence of prearrangement and coordination of an expenditure with the candidate or his agent not only undermines the value of the expenditure to the candidate, but also alleviates the danger that expenditures will be given as a quid pro quo for improper commitments from the candidate. Rather than preventing circumvention of the contribution limitations, § 608(e)(1) severely restricts all independent advocacy despite its substantially diminished potential for abuse.

While the independent expenditure ceiling thus fails to serve any substantial governmental interest in stemming the reality or appearance of corruption in the electoral process, it heavily burdens core First Amendment expression. [Advocacy] of the election or defeat of candidates for federal office is no less entitled to protection under the First Amendment than the discussion of political policy generally or advocacy of the passage or defeat of legislation.

It is argued, however, that the ancillary governmental interest in equalizing the relative ability of individuals and groups to influence the outcome of elections serves to justify the limitation on express advocacy of the election or defeat of candidates imposed by § 608(e)(1)'s expenditure ceiling. But the concept that government may restrict the speech of some elements of our society in order to enhance the relative voice of others[d] is

---

53. Section 608(e)(1) does not apply to expenditures "on behalf of a candidate within the meaning of" § 608(2)(B). That section provides that expenditures "authorized or requested by the candidate, an authorized committee of the candidate, or an agent of the candidate" are to be treated as expenditures of the candidate and contributions by the person or group making the expenditure. [In] view of [the] legislative history and the purposes of the Act, we find that the "authorized or requested" standard of the Act operates to treat all expenditures placed in cooperation with or with the consent of a candidate, his agents, or an authorized committee of the candidate as contributions subject to the limitations set forth in § 608(b). [Eds. Subsequent cases have held that group expenditures on behalf of a candidate that are not coordinated with the candidate may not constitutionally be restricted. FEC v. National Conservative Political Action Comm., 470 U.S. 480 (1985)].

d. For sustained defense of this aspect of *Buckley*, see Martin H. Redish & Kirk J. Kaludis, *The Right of Expressive Access in First Amendment Theory: Redistributive Values and the Democratic Dilemma*, 93 Nw.U.L.Rev. 1083 (1999). For reaffirmation, see *Davis v. Federal Election Commission*, 554 U.S. 724 (2008). On the other hand, the lower court characterized the

wholly foreign to the First Amendment, which was designed "to secure 'the widest possible dissemination of information from diverse and antagonistic sources,' " and " 'to assure unfettered interchange of ideas for the bringing about of political and social changes desired by the people.' " *New York Times Co. v. Sullivan.* The First Amendment's protection against governmental abridgement of free expression cannot properly be made to depend on a person's financial ability to engage in public discussion.[55]

* * * *Mills v. Alabama,* 384 U.S. 214 (1966), held that legislative restrictions on advocacy of the election or defeat of political candidates are wholly at odds with the guarantees of the First Amendment. [Yet] the prohibition on election day editorials invalidated in *Mills* is clearly a lesser intrusion on constitutional freedom than a $1,000 limitation on the amount of money any person or association can spend *during an entire election year* in advocating the election or defeat of a candidate for public office.

For the reasons stated, we conclude that § 608(e)(1)'s independent expenditure limitation is unconstitutional under the First Amendment. * * *e

2. [The] Act also sets limits on expenditures by a candidate "from his personal funds, or the personal funds of his immediate family, in connection with his campaigns during any calendar year." § 608(a)(1).[f]

The ceiling on personal expenditures by candidates on their own behalf [imposes] a substantial restraint on the ability of persons to engage in protected First Amendment expression. The candidate, no less than any other person, has a First Amendment right to engage in the discussion of public issues and vigorously and tirelessly to advocate his own election and the election of other candidates. Indeed, it is of particular importance that candidates have the unfettered opportunity to make their views known so that the electorate may intelligently evaluate the candidates' personal qualities and their positions on vital public issues before choosing among them on election day. [Section] 608(a)'s ceiling on personal expenditures

---

issue somewhat differently: Can "the wealthy few [claim] a constitutional guarantee to a stronger political voice than the unwealthy many because they are able to give and spend more money, and because the amounts they give and spend cannot be limited"? 519 F.2d 821, 841 (D.C.Cir.1975).

55. Neither the voting rights cases nor the Court's decision upholding the FCC's fairness doctrine lends support to appellees' position that the First Amendment permits Congress to abridge the rights of some persons to engage in political expression in order to enhance the relative voice of other segments of our [society].

e. The Court invalidated restrictions on the amount of personal funds candidates could spend on their own behalf and on the amount of overall campaign expenditures by federal candidates. The anti-corruption rationale did not apply in the former instance and was already served by the act's contribution and disclosure provisions. On the other hand, the Court also stated that, "[A]cceptance of federal funding entails voluntary acceptance of an expenditure ceiling."

f. $50,000 for Presidential or Vice Presidential candidates; $35,000 for Senate candidates; $25,000 for most candidates for the House of Representatives. *Davis v. FEC,* fn. d supra, held that Congress could not increase the contribution limits for a candidate whose opponent had achieved a specified spending advantage by virtue of his or her personal funds. The Court maintained that the anti-corruption rationale did not apply and that equalizing electoral opportunities is not a sufficient interest to override First Amendment rights, but it indicated that Congress could raise contribution limits for *both* candidates.

by a candidate in furtherance of his own candidacy thus clearly and directly interferes with constitutionally protected freedoms.

The primary governmental interest served by the Act—the prevention of actual and apparent corruption of the political process—does not support the limitation on the candidate's expenditure of his own personal funds. [Indeed], the use of personal funds reduces the candidate's dependence on outside contributions and thereby counteracts the coercive pressures and attendant risks of abuse to which the Act's contribution limitations are directed.

- EQUALIZATION NOT ENOUGH TO PRUTE MANY EXPENDITURE CEILING

The ancillary interest in equalizing the relative financial resources of candidates competing for elective office, therefore, provides the sole relevant rationale for Section 608(a)'s expenditure ceiling. That interest is clearly not sufficient to justify the provision's infringement of fundamental First Amendment rights. First, the limitation may fail to promote financial equality among candidates. [Indeed], a candidate's personal wealth may impede his [fundraising efforts]. Second, and more fundamentally, the First Amendment simply cannot tolerate § 608(a)'s restriction upon the freedom of a candidate to speak without legislative limit on behalf of his own candidacy. We therefore hold that § 608(a)'s restrictions on a candidate's personal expenditures is unconstitutional.

3.   [Section] 608(c) of the Act places limitations on overall campaign expenditures by candidates [seeking] election to federal office. [For Presidential candidates the ceiling is $10,000,000 in seeking nomination and $20,000,000 in the general election campaign; for House of Representatives candidates it is $70,000 for each campaign—primary and general; for candidates for Senator the ceiling depends on the size of the voting age population.]

No governmental interest that has been suggested is sufficient to justify [these restrictions] on the quantity of political expression. [The] interest in alleviating the corrupting influence of large contributions is served by the Act's contribution limitations and disclosure provisions rather than by § 608(c)'s campaign expenditure ceilings. [There] is no indication that the substantial criminal penalties for violating the contribution ceilings combined with the political repercussion of such violations will be insufficient to police the contribution provisions. Extensive reporting, auditing, and disclosure requirements applicable to both contributions and expenditures by political campaigns are designed to facilitate the detection of illegal contributions. * * *

The interest in equalizing the financial resources of candidates competing for federal office is no more convincing a justification for restricting the scope of federal election campaigns. Given the limitation on the size of outside contributions, the financial resources available to a candidate's campaign, like the number of volunteers recruited, will normally vary with the size and intensity of the candidate's support. There is nothing invidious, improper, or unhealthy in permitting such funds to be spent to carry the candidate's message to the electorate. Moreover, the equalization of permissible campaign expenditures might serve not to equalize the opportunities of all candidates but to handicap a candidate who lacked substantial name recognition or exposure of his views before the start of the campaign.

The campaign expenditure ceilings appear to be designed primarily to serve the governmental interests in reducing the allegedly skyrocketing costs of political campaigns. [But the] First Amendment denies government the power to determine that spending to promote one's political views is wasteful, excessive, or unwise. In the free society ordained by our Constitution it is not the government but the people individually as citizens and candidates and collectively as associations and political committees who must retain control over the quantity and range of debate on public issues in a political campaign.[65]

For these reasons we hold that § 608(c) is constitutionally invalid.

* * *

CHIEF JUSTICE BURGER, concurring in part and dissenting in part.

[I] agree fully with that part of the Court's opinion that holds unconstitutional the limitations the Act puts on campaign expenditures. [Yet] when it approves similarly stringent limitations on contributions, the Court ignores the reasons it finds so persuasive in the context of expenditures. For me contributions and expenditures are two sides of the same First Amendment coin.

[Limiting] contributions, as a practical matter, will limit expenditures and will put an effective ceiling on the amount of political activity and debate that the Government will permit to take place.[5]

The Court attempts to separate the two communicative aspects of political contributions—the "moral" support that the gift itself conveys, which the Court suggests is the same whether the gift is of $10 or $10,000,[6] and the fact that money translates into communication. The Court dismisses the effect of the limitations on the second aspect of

---

65. [Congress] may engage in public financing of election campaigns and may condition acceptance of public funds on an agreement by the candidate to abide by specified expenditure limitations. Just as a candidate may voluntarily limit the size of the contributions he chooses to accept he may decide to forgo private fundraising and accept public funding. [On the merits and demerits of public financing, compare Richard Briffault, *Public Funding and Democratic Elections,* 148 U.Pa.L.Rev. 563 (1999) with Bradley A. Smith, *Some Problems with Taxpayer-funded Political Campaigns,* id. at 591].

5. The Court notes that 94.9% of the funds raised by congressional candidates in 1974 came in contributions of less than $1,000, n. 27, and suggests that the effect of the contribution limitations will be minimal. This logic ignores the disproportionate influence large contributions may have when they are made early in a campaign; "seed money" can be essential, and the inability to obtain it may effectively end some candidacies before they begin. Appellants have excerpted from the record data on nine campaigns to which large, initial contributions were critical. Campaigns such as these will be much harder, and perhaps impossible, to mount under the Act.

6. Whatever the effect of the limitation, it is clearly arbitrary—Congress has imposed the same ceiling on contributions to a New York or California senatorial campaign that it has put on House races in Alaska or Wyoming. Both the strength of support conveyed by the gift of $1,000 *and* the gift's potential for corruptly influencing the recipient will vary enormously from place to place. * * *

contributions: "[T]he transformation of contributions into political debate involves speech by someone other than the contributor." On this premise—that contribution limitations restrict only the speech of "someone other than the contributor"—rests the Court's justification for treating contributions differently from expenditures. The premise is demonstrably flawed; the contribution limitations will, in specific instances, limit exactly the same political activity that the expenditure ceilings limit, and at least one of the "expenditure" limitations the Court finds objectionable operates precisely like the "contribution" limitations.[8]

The Court's attempt to distinguish the communication inherent in political *contributions* from the speech aspects of political *expenditures* simply will not wash. We do little but engage in word games unless we recognize that people—candidates and contributors—spend money on political activity because they wish to communicate ideas, and their constitutional interest in doing so is precisely the same whether they or someone else utter the words.

[T]he restrictions are hardly incidental in their effect upon particular campaigns. Judges are ill-equipped to gauge the precise impact of legislation, but a law that impinges upon First Amendment rights requires us to make the attempt. It is not simply speculation to think that the limitations on contributions will foreclose some candidacies.[9] The limitations will also alter the nature of some electoral contests drastically.[10]

[In] striking down the limitations on campaign expenditures, the Court relies in part on its conclusion that other means—namely, disclosure and contribution ceilings—will adequately serve the statute's aim. It is not clear why the same analysis is not also appropriate in weighing the need for contribution ceilings in addition to disclosure requirements. Congress may well be entitled to conclude that disclosure was a "partial measure," but I had not thought until today that Congress could enact its conclusions in the First Amendment area into laws immune from the most searching review by this Court. * * *[g]

JUSTICE WHITE, concurring in part and dissenting in part. * * *

---

8. The Court treats the Act's provisions limiting a candidate's spending from his *personal resources* as *expenditure* limits, as indeed the Act characterizes them, and holds them unconstitutional. As Mr. Justice Marshall points out, infra, by the Court's logic these provisions could as easily be treated as limits on *contributions,* since they limit what the candidate can give to his own campaign.

9. Candidates who must raise large initial contributions in order to appeal for more funds to a broader audience will be handicapped. See n. 5, supra. It is not enough to say that the contribution ceilings "merely require candidates [to] raise funds from a greater number of persons," where the limitations will effectively prevent candidates without substantial personal resources from doing just that.

10. Under the Court's holding, candidates with personal fortunes will be free to contribute to their own campaigns as much as they like, since the Court chooses to view the Act's provisions in this regard as unconstitutional "expenditure" limitations rather than "contribution" limitations. See n. 8, supra.

g. Blackmun, J., also dissented separately from that part of the Court's opinion upholding the Act's restrictions on campaign contributions, unpersuaded that "a principled constitutional distinction" could be made between the contribution and expenditure limitations involved.

I [agree] with the Court's judgment upholding the limitations on contributions. I dissent [from] the Court's view that the expenditure limitations [violate] the First Amendment. [This] case depends on whether the nonspeech interests of the Federal Government in regulating the use of money in political campaigns are sufficiently urgent to justify the incidental effects that the limitations visit upon the First Amendment interests of candidates and their supporters.

[The Court] accepts the congressional judgment that the evils of unlimited contributions are sufficiently threatening to warrant restriction regardless of the impact of the limits on the contributor's opportunity for effective speech and in turn on the total volume of the candidate's political communications by reason of his inability to accept large sums from those willing to give.

The congressional judgment, which I would also accept, was that other steps must be taken to counter the corrosive effects of money in federal election campaigns. One of these steps is § 608(e), which [limits] what a contributor may independently spend in support or denigration of one running for federal office. Congress was plainly of the view that these expenditures also have corruptive potential; but the Court strikes down the provision, strangely enough claiming more insight as to what may improperly influence candidates than is possessed by the majority of Congress that passed this Bill and the President who signed it. Those supporting the Bill undeniably included many seasoned professionals who have been deeply involved in elective processes and who have viewed them at close range over many years.

It would make little sense to me, and apparently made none to Congress, to limit the amounts an individual may give to a candidate or spend with his approval but fail to limit the amounts that could be spent on his behalf. Yet the Court permits the former while striking down the latter limitation. [I] would take the word of those who know—that limiting independent expenditures is essential to prevent transparent and widespread evasion of the contribution limits. * * *

The Court also rejects Congress' judgment manifested in § 608(c) that the federal interest in limiting total campaign expenditures by individual candidates justifies the incidental effect on their opportunity for effective political speech. I disagree both with the Court's assessment of the impact on speech and with its narrow view of the values the limitations will serve.

[M]oney is not always equivalent to or used for speech, even in the context of political campaigns. [There are] many expensive campaign activities that are not themselves communicative or remotely related to speech. Furthermore, campaigns differ among themselves. Some seem to spend much less money than others and yet communicate as much or more than those supported by enormous bureaucracies with unlimited financing. The record before us no more supports the conclusion that the communicative efforts of congressional and Presidential candidates will be crippled by the expenditure limitations than it supports the contrary. The judgment of Congress was that reasonably effective campaigns could be conducted within the limits established by the Act and that the communicative efforts of these campaigns would not seriously suffer. In this posture of the case, there is no sound basis for invalidating the expenditure limitations, so long as the purposes they serve are legitimate and sufficiently substantial, which in my view they are.

[E]xpenditure ceilings reinforce the contribution limits and help eradicate the hazard of corruption. [Without] limits on total expenditures, campaign costs will inevitably and endlessly escalate. Pressure to raise funds will constantly build and with it the temptation to resort in "emergencies" to those sources of large sums, who, history shows, are sufficiently confident of not being caught to risk flouting contribution [limits.]

The ceiling on candidate expenditures represents the considered judgment of Congress that elections are to be decided among candidates none of whom has overpowering advantage by reason of a huge campaign war chest. At least so long as the ceiling placed upon the candidates is not plainly too low, elections are not to turn on the difference in the amounts of money that candidates have to spend. This seems an acceptable purpose and the means chosen a common sense way to achieve [it.]

I also disagree with the Court's judgment that § 608(a), which limits the amount of money that a candidate or his family may spend on his campaign, violates the Constitution. Although it is true that this provision does not promote any interest in preventing the corruption of candidates, the provision does, nevertheless, serve salutary purposes related to the integrity of federal campaigns. By limiting the importance of personal wealth, § 608(a) helps to assure that only individuals with a modicum of support from others will be viable candidates. This in turn would tend to discourage any notion that the outcome of elections is primarily a function of money. Similarly, § 608(a) tends to equalize access to the political arena, encouraging the less wealthy, unable to bankroll their own campaigns, to run for political office.[h]

NOTES AND QUESTIONS

1. **Equality and democracy.** Is it "foreign" to the First Amendment to curb the spending of the wealthy in an effort to preserve the integrity of

---

h. Marshall, J., dissented from that part of the Court's opinion invalidating the limitation on the amount a candidate or his family may spend on his campaign. He considered "the interest in promoting the reality and appearance of equal access to the political arena" sufficient to justify the limitation: "[T]he wealthy candidate's immediate access to a substantial personal fortune may give him an initial advantage that his less wealthy opponent can never overcome. [With the option of large contributions removed by § 608(b)], the less wealthy candidate is without the means to match the large initial expenditures of money of which the wealthy candidate is capable. In short, the limitations on contributions put a premium on a candidate's personal wealth. [Section 608(a) then] emerges not simply as a device to reduce the natural advantage of the wealthy candidate, but as a provision providing some symmetry to a regulatory scheme that otherwise enhances the natural advantage of the wealthy."

For background on the *Buckley* case, see Fred Friendly & Martha Elliot, *The Constitution: That Delicate Balance* 91–107 (1984).

the elections process? Does copyright law curb the speech of some in order to enhance the speech of others? Rebecca Tushnet, *Copyright as a Model for Free Speech Law: What Copyright Has in Common with Anti–Pornography Laws, Campaign Finance Reform, and Telecommunications Regulation,* 42 B.C. L. Rev. 1, 38 (2000). In any event, would it have been "foreign" to First Amendment doctrine to engage in some type of balancing? Does the Court's expenditure ruling denigrate the interests in equality and democracy?[i] See Stephen Breyer, *Our Democratic Constitution,* 77 N.Y.U. L. Rev. 245, 253 (2002).

2. ***The nature of democracy.*** Lori Ringhand, *Defining Democracy: The Supreme Court's Campaign Finance Dilemma,* 56 Hast. L.J. 77, 85 (2004–2005): "In *Buckley*, the Court found that prohibiting the appearance or actuality of quid pro quo-type corruption was a sufficiently compelling governmental interest to justify restrictions on political speech. Equalizing the ability of groups or individuals to participate in the public debate by limiting campaign expenditures, however, was not. By accepting the government's corruption rationale while denying the government's equalization rationale, *Buckley* implicitly endorsed a pluralist-inspired view of democracy. To the Court, protecting a pluralistic political process by regulating things like quid pro quo bribery, which potentially interfere with an elected official's duty to vote in accordance with pluralist preferences, is constitutionally acceptable. But regulating overall political expenditures in order to promote the civic republican ideals of political equality and public deliberation is constitutionally unacceptable."

3. ***Advancing equality values?*** To what extent are campaign finance laws likely to advance equality values?[j] Aren't they most likely to benefit incumbents? See Richard Epstein, *Modern Republicanism—Or the Flight From Substance,* 97 Yale L.J. 1633, 1643–45 (1988); Jon Macey, *The Missing Element in the Republican Revival,* 97 Yale L.J. 1673, 1680–81 (1988). Do incumbents possess ordinarily insuperable advantages apart from the campaign finance system? Would campaign finance legislation free incumbents from the need to rely on interest group funding and improve the quality of representation? Vincent Blasi, *Free Speech and the Widening Gyre of Fund–Raising,* 94 Colum.L.Rev. 1281 (1994). Is increased legislative autonomy desirable?[k]

---

i. See, e.g., Laurence Tribe, *Constitutional Choices* 193–94 (1985); Owen Fiss, *Money and Politics,* 97 Colum. L.Rev. 2470 (1997; Burt Neuborne, *Toward a Democracy–Centered Reading of the First Amendment,* 93 Nw.U.L.Rev. 1055 (1999); Marlene Nicholson, *Buckley v. Valeo: The Constitutionality of the Federal Election Campaign Act Amendments of 1974,* 1977 Wis.L.Rev. 323, 336; J. Skelly Wright, *Money and the Pollution of Politics: Is the First Amendment an Obstacle to Political Equality?,* 82 Colum.L.Rev. 609 (1982).

j. Consider Paul Brest, *Further Beyond the Republican Revival,* 97 Yale L.J. 1623, 1627 (1988): " 'Those who are better off participate more, and by participating more they exercise more influence on government officials.' Unequal resources produce unequal influence in determining which issues get on the political [agenda]. Campaign finance regulations barely begin to remedy the systematic ways in which inequalities of wealth distort the political process." But see Edward B. Foley, *Equal–Dollars–Per Voter: A Constitutional Principle of Campaign Finance,* 94 Colum.L.Rev. 1204 (1994); Jamin Raskin & John Bonifaz, *Equal Protection and the Wealth Primary,* 11 Yale L. & Pol'y Rev. 273 (1993). For a variety of views, see *Symposium on Campaign Finance Reform,* 94 Colum.L.Rev. 1125 (1994).

k. Compare Cass Sunstein, *Beyond the Republican Revival,* 97 Yale L.J. 1539 (1988) with Michael Fitts, *Look Before You Leap,* 97 Yale L.J. 1651 (1988); Michael Fitts, *The Vices of Virtue,* 136 U.Pa.L.Rev. 1567 (1988).

4. ***Mitigating corruption.*** Will campaign finance laws mitigate public perception of corruption? Or is the cynicism of the American people too deep to allow that? Kelli Lammie, *Perceptions of Corruption and Campaign Finance: When Public Opinion Determines Constitutional Law*, 153 U. Pa. L. Rev. 119, 120 (2004). Would such laws affect actual corruption? Consider Jamin B. Raskin, *The Campaign–Finance Crucible: Is Laissez Fair?*, 101 Mich. L. Rev. 1532, 1536 (2003): "[I]f corruption simply means compromising the moral purity or 'true beliefs' of the politician, then the claim that money corrupts legislatures seems highly doubtful. The kinds of politicians that receive huge sums from agri-business interests are the kinds of politicians that would robotically serve these interests anyway. Corporate power does not have to buy politicians in American elections; it spawns them. [W]e need a definition [of corruption] that does not focus on the impressionable soul of the politician but rather on keeping the channels of popular democracy safe from capture by predatory elite factions, which are always made up of both politicians and the broader interests they serve."

5. ***Bet-hedging.*** Should contributors who give to both opposing candidates be protected under the First Amendment? See Jason Cohen, *The Same Side of Two Coins: The Peculiar Phenomenon of Bet-Hedging in Campaign Finance*, 26 N. Ill. U.L. Rev. 271 (2006).

6. **Varying scrutiny.** (a) Did *Buckley* apply less exacting scrutiny to impairment of associational freedoms by contribution limits than to impairment of free expression by expenditure limits? Cf. 90 Harv.L.Rev. 178–79 (1976). "Granted that freedom of association is merely ancillary to speech, a means of amplifying and effectuating communication but logically secondary to speech," is this also "true of expenditures of money in aid of speech"? See Daniel Polsby, *Buckley v. Valeo: The Special Nature of Political Speech*, 1976 Sup.Ct.Rev. 1, 22. Can a lesser scrutiny be justified for contributions? Or were the differing results based on the Court's perceiving a greater threat to First Amendment interests in expenditure limits and less risk of corruption and undue influence in unlimited independent expenditures? Cf. Nicholson, note 1 supra, at 340–45. For a defense of strict scrutiny across the board, see Lillian BeVier, *Money and Politics: A Perspective on the First Amendment and Campaign Finance Reform*, 73 Calif.L.Rev. 1045 (1985). For the argument that strict scrutiny is inappropriate in institutionally bounded contexts and that elections are such contexts, see C. Edwin Baker, *Campaign Expenditures and Free Speech*, 33 Harv. C.R.-C.L.Rev. 1 (1998).[1]

(b) ***The O'Brien analogy.*** May the Court's rejection of the less-exacting *O'Brien* standard on the ground that the expenditure of money did not introduce a non-speech element fairly be criticized for asking the wrong

---

1. For similar views, see Richard Briffault, *Issue Advocacy: Redrawing the Elections/Politics Line*, 77 Texas L.Rev. 1751 (1999); Frederick Schauer & Richard H. Pildes, *Electoral Exceptionalism and the First Amendment*, 77 Texas L. Rev. 1803 (1999); and Burt Neuborne, *The Supreme Court and Free Speech: Love and A Question*, 42 St. Louis U.L.J. 789, 800 (1998): "If we can conceive of an election campaign as a great deliberative assembly of the people, why shouldn't we allow ourselves to establish a content-neutral, meta-Roberts' Rules of Order to help assure that our elections are preceded by debate calculated to permit our democratic institutions to perform at an acceptable level, an electoral debate where political discourse is not completely dominated by the wealthy?" But see Kathleen M. Sullivan, *Against Campaign Finance Reform*, 1998 Utah L.Rev. 311, 318–20 (1998); Robert Post, *Commentary: Regulating Election Speech Under the First Amendment*, 77 Texas L.Rev 1837 (1999).

question: whether *"pure speech* can be regulated where there is some incidental effect on *money,"* rather than whether "the use of *money* can be regulated, by analogy to such conduct as draft-card burning, where there is an undoubted incidental effect on *speech"*? See J. Skelly Wright, *Politics and the Constitution: Is Money Speech?,* 85 Yale L.J. 1001, 1007 (1976). But compare J.M. Balkin, *Some Realism About Pluralism: Legal Realist Approaches to the First Amendment,* 1990 Duke L.J. 375, 414: "I suspect that the slogan 'money is not speech' is attractive because it appeals to a certain humanistic vision—that there is something quite different between the situation of a lone individual expressing her views and the purchase of hired mouths using hired expressions created by hired minds to saturate the airwaves with ideological drivel. Yet in one sense, this humanistic vision really turns upon a set of unstated egalitarian assumptions about economic and social power. Certainly we would have no objection to a person with a speech impediment hiring someone to do her talking for her; that is because we think that, under these circumstances, it is fair for such a person to boost her communicative powers. Modern political campaigns seem a far cry from this example because of the massive amounts of economic power expended to get the message across. I think we should isolate the egalitarian assumptions implicit in the 'money is not speech' position and put them to their best use—the justification of campaign finance reforms on the ground that gross inequalities of economic power destroy the integrity of the political process. [G]overnment is responsible for inequalities in access to the means of communication because it has created the system of property rights that makes such inequalities possible. Therefore, it is not only wrong but also incoherent for opponents of campaign finance reform to contend that the government should not regulate access to the political process. Government already regulates access to the political process—the First Amendment simply demands that it do so fairly."

7. *Judicial elections.* Are judicial elections different? Should strict scrutiny be applied to contribution limits in judicial elections? Is *Republican Party v. White,* 536 U.S. 765 (2002) (applying strict scrutiny and invalidating a canon of judicial conduct that prohibited candidates for judicial election in that State from announcing their views on disputed legal and political issues) relevant to this? Should a state be permitted to prohibit a candidate from promising to decide cases in a particular way?[m]

8. **Vitality of Buckley.** Vermont's 1997 campaign finance statute limited the amount that state candidates could spend on their campaigns and that individuals, organizations, and parties could contribute to those campaigns. RANDALL v. SORRELL, 548 U.S. 230 (2006), struck down both the expenditure limitations and the contribution limitations with a diversity of views concerning the authority of *Buckley.* BREYER, J., announced the judgment of the Court in an opinion joined by Roberts, C.J., and, in part, by Alito, J. He determined that the expenditure provision was unconstitutional on the

---

m. For discussion of *White,* see e.g., Richard Briffault, *Judicial Campaign Codes After Republican Party of Minnesota v. White,* 153 U. Pa. L. Rev. 181 (2004); Matthew J. Medina, *The Constitutionality of the 2003 Revisions to Canon 3(E) of the Model Code of Judicial Conduct,* 104 Colum. L. Rev. 1072 (2004); Ronald D. Rotunda, *Judicial Elections, Campaign Financing, and Free Speech,* 2 Election L.J. 79, 89–90 (2003); Erwin Chemerinsky, *Judicial Elections and the First Amendment,* 38–Nov Trial 78, 81 (2002); Robert M. O'Neil, *The Canons in the Courts: Recent First Amendment Rulings,* 35 Ind. L. Rev. 701, 715 (2002).

strength of *Buckley.* On the basis of stare decisis, he declined what he perceived to be an invitation to overrule *Buckley's* ruling on candidate expenditure limits,[a] and he rejected the view that *Buckley* could be distinguished on the ground that it failed to consider the argument that such limitations are justified because they help to prevent candidates from spending too much time raising money. With respect to the contribution limits, Breyer, J., maintained that they were too restrictive, noting, for example, that the limit on contributions for governor (adjusted for inflation) was slightly more than one-twentieth of the limit on contributions to federal office before the Court in *Buckley.* He also determined that Vermont's per election contribution limit was the lowest in the nation. Breyer, J., concluded that such limits would impair the ability of some candidates running against incumbent officeholder to mount an effective challenge.

Thomas, J., joined by Scalia, J., concurred in the judgment, demanding strict scrutiny in examining both expenditure and contributions limitations,[b] and arguing that the plurality's attempt to distinguish permissible from impermissible contribution limits could not be administered in a principled way: "[T]he plurality's determination that this statute clearly lies on the *impermissible* side of the constitutional line gives no assistance in drawing this line, and it is clear that no such line can be drawn rationally. There is simply no way to calculate just how much money a person would need to receive before he would be corrupt or perceived to be corrupt (and such a calculation would undoubtedly vary by person). Likewise, there is no meaningful way of discerning just how many resources must be lost before speech is 'disproportionately burden[ed].'"

Stevens, J., dissenting, would depart from *Buckley's* strict scrutiny of candidate expenditure limits. He would uphold such limits "so long as the purposes they serve are legitimate and sufficiently substantial:" "The interest in freeing candidates from the fundraising straitjacket [is] compelling. Without expenditure limits, fundraising devours the time and attention of political leaders, leaving them too busy to handle their public responsibilities effectively. That fact was well recognized by backers of the legislation reviewed in *Buckley,* by the Court of Appeals judges who voted to uphold the expenditure limitations in that statute, and by Justice White—who not incidentally had personal experience as an active participant in a Presidential campaign. The validity of their judgment has surely been confirmed by the mountains of evidence that has been accumulated in recent years concerning the time that elected officials spend raising money for future campaigns and the adverse effect of fundraising on the performance of their official duties."

Souter, J., joined by Ginsburg, J., and, on the contributions issue, by Stevens, J., dissented, arguing that the question whether to relax *Buckley's* standard on expenditure requirements was not properly before the Court. He voted to affirm the Court of Appeals decision to remand on the expenditures issue to determine if the record met the requirements of *Buckley,* and to

---

a. Alito, J., concurring in part and in the judgment, argued that the question whether to overrule *Buckley's* standard for contributions and expenditures was not properly presented to the Court and should not have been reached.

b. Kennedy, J., who has also maintained that *Buckley's* standard regarding contributions is too relaxed, concurred in the judgment.

uphold the contribution limits: "I believe the Court of Appeals correctly rejected the challenge to the contribution limits. Low though they are, one cannot say that 'the contribution limitation[s are] so radical in effect as to render political association ineffective, drive the sound of a candidate's voice below the level of notice, and render contributions pointless.' *Nixon* v. *Shrink Missouri Government PAC*, 528 U.S. 377 (2000). The limits set by Vermont are not remarkable departures either from those previously upheld by this Court or from those lately adopted by other States. The plurality concedes that on a per-citizen measurement Vermont's limit for statewide elections 'is slightly more generous,' than the one set by the Missouri statute approved by this Court in *Shrink*."[c]

CITIZENS UNITED v. FEC

___ U.S. ___, 130 S.Ct. 876, 175 L.Ed.2d 753 (2010).

JUSTICE KENNEDY delivered the opinion of the Court.

[In January 2008, Citizens United, a nonprofit corporation that accepts a small portion of its funds from for-profit companies, released a film entitled *Hillary: The Movie*. The film was a documentary arguing that Senator Hilary Clinton was an unsuitable candidate for President. Citizens United had released its film in theaters and on DVD, but it also wished to make the film available through video-on-demand on cable and to promote the film with ads on broadcast and cable television.]

Federal law prohibits corporations and unions from using their general treasury funds to make independent expenditures for speech defined as an "electioneering communication" or for speech expressly advocating the election or defeat of a candidate. Federal Election Campaign Act of 1971, 2 U.S.C. § 441b. Limits on electioneering communications were upheld in *McConnell v. Federal Election Comm'n*, (2003). The holding of *McConnell* rested to a large extent on an earlier case, *Austin v. Michigan Chamber of Commerce*, 494 U.S. 652 (1990). *Austin* had held that political speech may be banned based on the speaker's corporate identity.

In this case we are asked to reconsider *Austin* and, in effect, *McConnell*. * * * We [hold] that stare decisis does not compel the continued acceptance of *Austin*. The Government may regulate corporate political speech through disclaimer and disclosure requirements, but it may not suppress that speech altogether.

Before the Bipartisan Campaign Reform Act of 2002 (BCRA), federal law prohibited-and still does prohibit—corporations and unions from using general treasury funds to make direct contributions to candidates or independent expenditures that expressly advocate the election or defeat of a candidate, through any form of media, in connection with certain qualified federal elections. BCRA § 203 amended § 441b to prohibit any

---

c. In response, Breyer, J., argued: "[T]his does not necessarily mean that Vermont's limits are less objectionable than the limit upheld in *Shrink*. A campaign for state auditor is likely to be less costly than a campaign for governor; campaign costs do not automatically increase or decrease in precise proportion to the size of an electoral district."

"electioneering communication" as [well,] defined as "any broadcast, cable, or satellite communication" that "refers to a clearly identified candidate for a Federal office" and is made [well] within 30 days of a primary or 60 days of a general [election.]ᵃ Corporations and unions [may] establish, however, a "separate segregated fund" (known as a political action committee, or PAC) for these purposes. The moneys received by the segregated fund are limited to donations from stockholders and employees of the corporation or, in the case of unions, members of the union. * * *

[T]he following acts would all be felonies under § 441b: The Sierra Club runs an ad, within the crucial phase of 60 days before the general election, that exhorts the public to disapprove of a Congressman who favors logging in national forests; the National Rifle Association publishes a book urging the public to vote for the challenger because the incumbent U.S. Senator supports a handgun ban; and the American Civil Liberties Union creates a Web site telling the public to vote for a Presidential candidate in light of that candidate's defense of free speech. These prohibitions are classic examples of censorship.

[A] PAC is a separate association from the corporation. So the PAC exemption from § 441b's expenditure ban does not allow corporations to speak. Even if a PAC could somehow allow a corporation to speak—and it does not—the option to form PACs does not alleviate the First Amendment problems with § 441b. PACs are burdensome alternatives; they are expensive to administer and subject to extensive regulations. For example, every PAC must appoint a treasurer, forward donations to the treasurer promptly, keep detailed records of the identities of the persons making donations, preserve receipts for three years, and file an organization statement and report changes to this information within 10 days. * * *

By taking the right to speak from some and giving it to others, the Government deprives the disadvantaged person or class of the right to use speech to strive to establish worth, standing, and respect for the speaker's voice. The Government may not by these means deprive the public of the right and privilege to determine for itself what speech and speakers are worthy of consideration. The First Amendment protects speech and speaker, and the ideas that flow from each.

The Court has upheld a narrow class of speech restrictions that operate to the disadvantage of certain persons, but these rulings were based on an interest in allowing governmental entities to perform their functions. See, e.g., *Bethel School Dist. No. v. Fraser,* 478 U.S. 675, 683 (1986) (protecting the "function of public school education"); *Jones v. North Carolina Prisoners' Labor Union, Inc.,* 433 U.S. 119, 129 (furthering "the legitimate penological objectives of the corrections system");

---

a. The law exempted any news story, commentary, or editorial distributed through the facilities of any broadcasting station, newspaper, magazine, or other periodical publication, unless such facilities are owned or controlled by any political party, political committee, or candidate.

Parker v. Levy, 417 U.S. 733, 759 (1974) (ensuring "the capacity of the Government to discharge its [military] responsibilities"); *Civil Service Comm'n v. Letter Carriers,* 413 U.S. 548, 557 (1973) ("[F]ederal service should depend upon meritorious performance rather than political service"). The corporate independent expenditures at issue in this case, however, would not interfere with governmental functions, so these cases are inapposite. These precedents stand only for the proposition that there are certain governmental functions that cannot operate without some restrictions on particular kinds of speech. By contrast, it is inherent in the nature of the political process that voters must be free to obtain information from diverse sources in order to determine how to cast their votes. At least before *Austin,* the Court had not allowed the exclusion of a class of speakers from the general public dialogue.

[Laws] that burden political speech are "subject to strict scrutiny," which requires the Government to prove that the restriction "furthers a compelling interest and is narrowly tailored to achieve that interest." *Austin* identified a new governmental interest in limiting political speech: an antidistortion interest. *Austin* found a compelling governmental interest in preventing "the corrosive and distorting effects of immense aggregations of wealth that are accumulated with the help of the corporate form and that have little or no correlation to the public's support for the corporation's political ideas." [As] for *Austin's* antidistortion rationale, the Government does little to defend it. * * *

If the First Amendment has any force, it prohibits Congress from fining or jailing citizens, or associations of citizens, for simply engaging in political speech. If the antidistortion rationale were to be accepted, however, it would permit Government to ban political speech simply because the speaker is an association that has taken on the corporate form. The Government contends that *Austin* permits it to ban corporate expenditures for almost all forms of communication stemming from a corporation. If *Austin* were correct, the Government could prohibit a corporation from expressing political views in media beyond those presented here, such as by printing books. The Government responds "that the FEC has never applied this statute to a book," and if it did, "there would be quite [a] good as-applied challenge." This troubling assertion of brooding governmental power cannot be reconciled with the confidence and stability in civic discourse that the First Amendment must secure. * * *

Austin sought to defend the antidistortion rationale as a means to prevent corporations from obtaining "an unfair advantage in the political marketplace" by using "resources amassed in the economic marketplace." But *Buckley* rejected the premise that the Government has an interest "in equalizing the relative ability of individuals and groups to influence the outcome of elections." *Buckley* was specific in stating that "the skyrocketing cost of political campaigns" could not sustain the governmental prohibition. The First Amendment's protections do not depend on the speaker's "financial ability to engage in public discussion."

[*Austin*] undertook to distinguish wealthy individuals from corporations on the ground that "[s]tate law grants corporations special advantages—such as limited liability, perpetual life, and favorable treatment of the accumulation and distribution of assets." This does not suffice, however, to allow laws prohibiting speech. "It is rudimentary that the State cannot exact as the price of those special advantages the forfeiture of First Amendment rights."

It is irrelevant for purposes of the First Amendment that corporate funds may "have little or no correlation to the public's support for the corporation's political ideas." All speakers, including individuals and the media, use money amassed from the economic marketplace to fund their speech. The First Amendment protects the resulting speech, even if it was enabled by economic transactions with persons or entities who disagree with the speaker's ideas.

Austin's antidistortion rationale would produce the dangerous, and unacceptable, consequence that Congress could ban political speech of media corporations [now] exempt from § 441b's ban on corporate expenditures. Yet media corporations accumulate wealth with the help of the corporate form, the largest media corporations have "immense aggregations of wealth," and the views expressed by media corporations often "have little or no correlation to the public's support" for those views. Thus, under the Government's reasoning, wealthy media corporations could have their voices diminished to put them on par with other media entities. There is no precedent for permitting this [nor any] precedent supporting laws that attempt to distinguish between corporations which are deemed to be exempt as media corporations and those which are not. "We have consistently rejected the proposition that the institutional press has any constitutional privilege beyond that of other speakers." * * *

[T]he Government falls back on the argument that corporate political speech can be banned in order to prevent corruption or its appearance. In *Buckley,* the Court found this interest "sufficiently important" to allow limits on contributions but did not extend that reasoning to expenditure limits. * * *

With regard to large direct contributions, *Buckley* reasoned that they could be given "to secure a political quid pro quo," and that "the scope of such pernicious practices can never be reliably ascertained." The practices *Buckley* noted would be covered by bribery laws if a quid pro quo arrangement were proved. The Court, in consequence, has noted that restrictions on direct contributions are preventative, because few if any contributions to candidates will involve quid pro quo arrangements. The *Buckley* Court, nevertheless, sustained limits on direct contributions in order to ensure against the reality or appearance of corruption. That case did not extend this rationale to independent expenditures, and the Court does not do so here. * * *

When *Buckley* identified a sufficiently important governmental interest in preventing corruption or the appearance of corruption, that interest was limited to quid pro quo corruption. The fact that speakers may have influence over or access to elected officials does not mean that these officials are corrupt: "[It] is in the nature of an elected representative to favor certain policies, and, by necessary corollary, to favor the voters and contributors who support those policies. It is well understood that a substantial and legitimate reason, if not the only reason, to cast a vote for, or to make a contribution to, one candidate over another is that the candidate will respond by producing those political outcomes the supporter favors. Democracy is premised on responsiveness." Reliance on a "generic favoritism or influence theory ... is at odds with standard First Amendment analyses because it is unbounded and susceptible to no limiting principle."

The appearance of influence or access, furthermore, will not cause the electorate to lose faith in our democracy. By definition, an independent expenditure is political speech presented to the electorate that is not coordinated with a candidate. The fact that a corporation, or any other speaker, is willing to spend money to try to persuade voters presupposes that the people have the ultimate influence over elected officials. This is inconsistent with any suggestion that the electorate will refuse "to take part in democratic governance" because of additional political speech made by a corporation or any other speaker.

The *McConnell* record was "over 100,000 pages" long, yet it "does not have any direct examples of votes being exchanged for ... expenditures," This confirms *Buckley*'s reasoning that independent expenditures do not lead to, or create the appearance of, quid pro quo corruption. In fact, there is only scant evidence that independent expenditures even ingratiate. Ingratiation and access, in any event, are not corruption. The BCRA record establishes that certain donations to political parties, called "soft money," were made to gain access to elected officials. This case, however, is about independent expenditures, not soft money. [If] elected officials succumb to improper influences from independent expenditures; if they surrender their best judgment; and if they put expediency before principle, then surely there is cause for concern. We must give weight to attempts by Congress to seek to dispel either the appearance or the reality of these influences. The remedies enacted by law, however, must comply with the First Amendment; and, it is our law and our tradition that more speech, not less, is the governing rule.

The Government contends further that corporate independent expenditures can be limited because of its interest in protecting dissenting shareholders from being compelled to fund corporate political speech. This asserted interest, like *Austin*'s antidistortion rationale, would allow the Government to ban the political speech even of media corporations. Assume, for example, that a shareholder of a corporation that owns a newspaper disagrees with the political views the newspaper expresses. Under the Government's view, that potential disagreement could give the Government the authority to restrict the media corporation's political speech. The First Amendment does not allow that power. There is, furthermore, little evidence of abuse that cannot be corrected by shareholders "through the procedures of corporate democracy."

Those reasons are sufficient to reject this shareholder-protection interest; and, moreover, the statute is both underinclusive and overinclusive. As to the first, if Congress had been seeking to protect dissenting shareholders, it would not have banned corporate speech in only certain media within 30 or 60 days before an election. A dissenting shareholder's interests would be implicated by speech in any media at any time. As to the second, the statute is overinclusive because it covers all corporations, including nonprofit corporations and for-profit corporations with only single shareholders. As to other corporations, the remedy is not to restrict speech but to consider and explore other regulatory mechanisms. The regulatory mechanism here, based on speech, contravenes the First Amendment.

[441b] is not limited to corporations or associations that were created in foreign countries or funded predominately by foreign shareholders. Section 441b therefore would be overbroad even if we assumed, arguendo, that the Government has a compelling interest in limiting foreign influence over our political process.

Austin is overruled, [thus] "effectively invalidat[ing] not only BCRA Section 203, but also 441b's prohibition on the use of corporate treasury funds for express advocacy." Section 441b's restrictions on corporate independent expenditures are therefore invalid and cannot be applied to *Hillary*.

Given our conclusion we are further required to overrule the part of *McConnell* that upheld BCRA § 203's extension of § 441b's restrictions on corporate independent expenditures. * * *b

JUSTICE STEVENS, with whom JUSTICE GINSBURG, JUSTICE BREYER, and JUSTICE SOTOMAYOR join, concurring in part c and dissenting in part.

Pervading the Court's analysis is the ominous image of a "categorical ba[n]" on corporate speech. [But our] cases have repeatedly pointed out that, "[c]ontrary to the [majority's] critical assumptions," the statutes upheld in *Austin* and *McConnell* do "not impose an *absolute* ban on all forms of corporate political spending." For starters, both statutes provide exemptions for PACs, separate segregated funds established by a corporation for political purposes. "The ability to form and administer separate segregated funds," we observed in *McConnell,* "has provided corporations and unions with a constitutionally sufficient opportunity to engage in express advocacy. That has been this Court's unanimous view."

---

b. Thomas, J., joined the opinion of Kennedy, J., except for a section upholding disclosure requirements. Roberts, C.J., joined by Alito, J., concurring argued that the principle of stare decisis did not apply. Scalia, J., joined by Alito, J., and Thomas, J., in part, concurring, argued that the Stevens, J., dissent did not properly assess the original understanding of the First Amendment.

c. Stevens, J., joined by Ginsburg, Breyer, and Sotomayor, JJ., joined that part of the Court's opinion upholding disclosure requirements.

A significant and growing number of corporations avail themselves of this option; during the most recent election cycle, corporate and union PACs raised nearly a billion dollars. Administering a PAC entails some administrative burden, but so does complying with the disclaimer, disclosure, and reporting requirements that the Court today upholds, and no one has suggested that the burden is severe for a sophisticated for-profit corporation. To the extent the majority is worried about this issue, it is important to keep in mind that we have no record to show how substantial the burden really is, just the majority's own unsupported factfinding.

The laws upheld in *Austin* and *McConnell* leave open many additional avenues for corporations' political speech. Consider the statutory provision we are ostensibly evaluating in this case, BCRA § 203. It has no application to genuine issue advertising—a category of corporate speech Congress found to be far more substantial than election-related advertising or to Internet, telephone, and print advocacy. [It] also allows corporations to spend unlimited sums on political communications with their executives and shareholders, to fund additional PAC activity through trade associations, to distribute voting guides and voting records, to underwrite voter registration and voter turnout activities, to host fundraising events for candidates within certain limits, and to publicly endorse candidates through a press release and press conference. * * *

In many ways, then, § 203 functions as a source restriction or a time, place, and manner restriction. It applies in a viewpoint-neutral fashion to a narrow subset of advocacy messages about clearly identified candidates for federal office, made during discrete time periods through discrete channels. In the case at hand, all Citizens United needed to do to broadcast *Hillary* right before the primary was to abjure business contributions or use the funds in its PAC, which by its own account is "one of the most active conservative PACs in America."

[Laws] such as § 203 target a class of communications that is especially likely to corrupt the political process, that is at least one degree removed from the views of individual citizens, and that may not even reflect the views of those who pay for it. Such laws burden political speech, and that is always a serious matter, demanding careful scrutiny. But the majority's incessant talk of a "ban" aims at a straw man. * * *

The second pillar of the Court's opinion is its assertion that "the Government cannot restrict political speech based on the speaker's ... identity." [Yet] in a variety of contexts, we have held that speech can be regulated differentially on account of the speaker's identity, when identity is understood in categorical or institutional terms. The Government routinely places special restrictions on the speech rights of students, prisoners, members of the Armed Forces, foreigners, and its own employees. When such restrictions are justified by a legitimate governmental interest, they do not necessarily raise constitutional problems. [T]he Court, of course, is right that the First Amendment closely guards political speech. But in [the election] context, too, the authority of legislatures to enact viewpoint-neutral regulations based on content and identity is well settled. We have, for example, allowed state-run broadcasters to exclude independent candidates from televised debates. We have upheld statutes that prohibit the distribution or display of campaign materials near a polling place. Although we have not reviewed them directly, we have never cast doubt on laws that place special restrictions on campaign spending by foreign nationals. And we have consistently approved laws that bar Government employees, but not others, from contributing to or participating in political [activities].

* * * Undergirding the majority's approach to the merits is the claim that the only "sufficiently important governmental interest in preventing corruption or the appearance of corruption" is one that is "limited to quid pro quo corruption." [On] numerous occasions we have recognized Congress' legitimate interest in preventing the money that is spent on elections from exerting an "undue influence on an officeholder's judgment" and from creating "the appearance of such influence," beyond the sphere of quid pro quo relationships. Corruption can take many forms. Bribery may be the paradigm case. But the difference between selling a vote and selling access is a matter of degree, not kind. And selling access is not qualitatively different from giving special preference to those who spent money on one's behalf. Corruption operates along a spectrum, and the majority's apparent belief that quid pro quo arrangements can be neatly demarcated from other improper influences does not accord with the theory or reality of politics. It certainly does not accord with the record Congress developed in passing BCRA, a record that stands as a remarkable testament to the energy and ingenuity with which corporations, unions, lobbyists, and politicians may go about scratching each other's backs-and which amply supported Congress' determination to target a limited set of especially destructive practices.

Stevens, J., then quoted the district court: "The factual findings of the Court illustrate that corporations and labor unions routinely notify Members of Congress as soon as they air electioneering communications relevant to the Members' elections. The record also indicates that Members express appreciation to organizations for the airing of these election-related advertisements. Indeed, Members of Congress are particularly grateful when negative issue advertisements are run by these organizations, leaving the candidates free to run positive advertisements and be seen as 'above the fray.' Political consultants testify that campaigns are quite aware of who is running advertisements on the candidate's behalf, when they are being run, and where they are being run. Likewise, a prominent lobbyist testifies that these organizations use issue advocacy as a means to influence various Members of Congress. [Finally], a large majority of Americans (80%) are of the view that corporations and other organizations that engage in electioneering communications, which benefit specific elected officials, receive special consideration from those officials when matters arise that affect these corporations and organizations."

[When] private interests are seen to exert outsized control over officeholders solely on account of the money spent on (or withheld from) their campaigns, the result can depart so thoroughly "from what is pure or correct" in the conduct of Government that it amounts to a "subversion [of] the electoral process." [Starting] today, corporations with large war chests to deploy on electioneering may find democratically elected bodies becoming much more attuned to their interests. * * *

The fact that corporations are different from human beings might seem to need no elaboration, except that the majority opinion almost completely elides it. *Austin* set forth some of the basic differences. Unlike natural persons, corporations have "limited liability" for their owners and managers, "perpetual life," separation of ownership and control, "and favorable treatment of the accumulation and distribution of assets [that] enhance their ability to attract capital and to deploy their resources in ways that maximize the return on their shareholders' investments." [It] might also be added that corporations have no consciences, no beliefs, no feelings, no thoughts, no desires. Corporations help structure and facilitate the activities of human beings, to be sure, and their "personhood" often serves as a useful legal fiction. But they are not themselves members of "We the People" by whom and for whom our Constitution was established. * * *

It is an interesting question "who" is even speaking when a business corporation places an advertisement that endorses or attacks a particular candidate. Presumably it is not the customers or employees, who typically have no say in such matters. It cannot realistically be said to be the shareholders, who tend to be far removed from the day-to-day decisions of the firm and whose political preferences may be opaque to management. Perhaps the officers or directors of the corporation have the best claim to be the ones speaking, except their fiduciary duties generally prohibit them from using corporate funds for personal ends. * * *

In critiquing *Austin's* antidistortion rationale and campaign finance regulation more generally, our colleagues place tremendous weight on the example of media corporations. Yet it is not at all clear that *Austin* would permit § 203 to be applied to them. The press plays a unique role not only in the text, history, and structure of the First Amendment but also in facilitating public discourse * * *. Our colleagues have raised some interesting and difficult questions about Congress' authority to regulate electioneering by the press, and about how to define what constitutes the press. *But that is not the case before us.* Section 203 does not apply to media corporations, and even if it did, Citizens United is not a media corporation. * * *

Interwoven with *Austin's* concern to protect the integrity of the electoral process is a concern to protect the rights of shareholders from a kind of coerced speech: electioneering expenditures that do not "reflec[t] [their] support." When corporations use general treasury funds to praise or attack a particular candidate for office, it is the shareholders, as the residual claimants, who are effectively footing the bill. Those shareholders who disagree with the corporation's electoral message may find their financial investments being used to undermine their political convictions.

The PAC mechanism, by contrast, helps assure that those who pay for an electioneering communication actually support its content and that managers do not use general treasuries to advance personal agendas. [The] shareholder protection rationale has been criticized as underinclusive, in that corporations also spend money on lobbying and charitable contributions in ways that any particular shareholder might disapprove. But those expenditures do not implicate the selection of public officials, an area in which "the interests of unwilling ... corporate shareholders [in not being] forced to subsidize that speech" "are at their zenith." And in any event, the question is whether shareholder protection provides a basis for regulating expenditures in the weeks before an election, not whether additional types of corporate communications might similarly be conditioned on voluntariness.

Recognizing the limits of the shareholder protection rationale, the *Austin* Court did not hold it out as an adequate and independent ground for sustaining the statute in question. Rather, the Court applied it to reinforce the antidistortion rationale, in two main ways. First, the problem of dissenting shareholders shows that even if electioneering expenditures can advance the political views of some members of a corporation, they will often compromise the views of others. Second, it provides an additional reason, beyond the distinctive legal attributes of the corporate form, for doubting that these "expenditures reflect actual public support for the political ideas espoused." * * *

While American democracy is imperfect, few outside the majority of this Court would have thought its flaws included a dearth of corporate money in politics.

NOTES AND QUESTIONS

1. ***Court's opinion.*** Should the Court have reached the question regarding the First Amendment rights of business corporations? (a) *Documentary films.* Should the Court have ruled that the Act applied to advertising, but not to documentary films? Was there a history of corruption or its appearance arising from documentary films? If the Act did apply to documentary films, might it be argued that the difference between advertising and films is of constitutional dimension? (b) *Video on demand.* Might it be argued that the Act did not apply to video on demand because viewers decide to see such videos in ways they do not do with ads? (c) *Advocacy corporations.* The Court had already held that non-profit corporations not involved in business and formed for the purpose of advocacy were as free as individuals to engage in campaign spending so long as they had no shareholders with claims on its assets and earnings and did not receive contributions from business corporations or unions. *FEC v. Massachusetts Citizens for Life,* 479 U.S. 238 (1986). Should the Court have ruled that Citizens United should be

treated like MCFL because the amount of business funds it received was small enough that it could not be considered as a surrogate for business corporations?

2. *First Amendment values.* The Court had previously granted First Amendment protection to corporations in a variety of contexts. It routinely granted protection to press corporations, and, as discussed in note 1, it granted protection to advocacy corporations. But it also granted protection to business corporations in the context of commercial speech cases (see, e.g., *Central Hudson*; *Linmark Associates*). And it afforded protection for the political speech of business corporations in the context of opposing a referendum proposal. *First National Bank of Boston v. Bellotti*, 435 U.S. 765 (1978). But, as the opinion makes clear, prior to *Citizens United,* protection was not granted in candidate elections. Leaving press corporations and advocacy corporations aside, did it ever make sense to afford protection to non-media business corporations in commercial [d] or political contexts? What precisely are the values furthered by protection for business corporations? Is it fair to say that the speech of business corporations is dictated by their competitive needs in the market? If so, is there a liberty interest? If so, is the speech of business corporations the speech of the kind of association the First Amendment should protect? Is speech that is not necessarily connected to the genuine views of those who finance it likely to make a contribution to the marketplace of ideas? Should it be dominant in that marketplace? Should the lack of citizenship of corporations disqualify it from participation in the elections process (other than through PACs)?

3. *Corruption interest and contributions.* Does the reasoning of the Court apply to corporate contributions as well as corporate independent expenditures? See Kathleen M. Sullivan, *Two Concepts of Freedom of Speech,* 124 Harv. L.Rev. 143, 167–68 (2010). Although corporations may use their treasuries to solicit funds donated to a segregated independent political fund, they are not permitted to make direct contributions from their treasuries in federal election campaigns. Constitutional? Consider also Floyd Abrams, *Speaking Freely* 268 (2005): "If the purpose of McCain-Feingold was truly to prevent corruption, real or apparent, why were PACs permitted? Such a statute, the NRA argued, 'makes no more sense than a bribery statute requiring corporations to pay for their bribes using funds from PACs.'"

4. *Contracting Corporations.* Could Congress prohibit those who contract with government to give contributions or make political expenditures after *Citizens United?* See Samuel Issacharoff, *On Political Corruption,* 124 Harv. L. Rev. 118, 138–42 (2010).

5. *Media corporations.* Do most of the concerns of the last note also apply to media corporations? Can media corporations be easily distinguished from business corporations? Consider David A. Anderson, *Freedom of the Press,* 80 Tex. L. Rev. 429, 455 (2002): "As recently as 1990, the Supreme Court assured us that 'media corporations differ significantly from other

---

d. Does the refusal to create a hierarchy among speakers in *Citizens United* suggest that the Court will refuse to create hierarchies of speech and abandon the lower place of commercial speech in the free speech hierarchy? See Darrel C. Menthe, *The Market Place Metaphor and Commercial Speech Doctrine,* 38 Hast. Con. L.Q. 131 (2010).

corporations in that their resources are devoted to the collection of information and its dissemination to the public.' The Court held that this 'valid distinction' constituted a compelling reason for the state to exempt media corporations from campaign finance laws that restricted other corporations' ability to influence politics. This argument may or may not have been persuasive in 1990, but it is extremely dubious today. NBC is owned by General Electric, ABC by Walt Disney Co., and CBS by Viacom, Inc.; each of these conglomerate parents owns many other businesses, media and nonmedia. Today's major media owners seem indistinguishable in most respects from other conglomerates. They devote their resources to a vast array of activities, only a fraction of which involve the gathering and dissemination of information to the public, and it is difficult to believe that they are any less eager to influence politics than their nonmedia counterparts. Through their media subsidiaries they are allowed to influence political campaigns in ways that are forbidden to other corporations, and the resulting difficulty of justifying this disparate treatment has become a significant obstacle to regulation of campaign finance.''

6. *Soft money.* *Citizens United* reopens a loophole that the Bipartisan Campaign Reform Act [BRCA] sought to close. But the same Act sought to close another loophole as well. As interpreted, the Federal Election Campaign Act of 1971 ("FECA") distinguishes between hard and soft money. Hard money is contributed money that falls under the specified contribution limits and complies with certain source limitations. Soft money encompasses contributions not subject to those restrictions which are for the most part ostensibly designed to encourage party-building activities benefitting the political parties in general, but not specific candidates. Under FECA, as interpreted, however, wealthy donors were able to use soft money directly or indirectly in ways that benefited federal candidates.

BRCA sought to close the soft money loophole. It forbids national party committees from soliciting, receiving, or directing the use of soft-money; prohibits state and local party committees from using soft money (although it permits their use of hard money and some additional funding) for activities affecting federal elections, including voter registration activity during the 120 days before a federal election, and get-out-the-vote drives conducted in connection with an election in which a federal candidate appears on the ballot; forbids the use of soft money by state and local party committees or state and local candidates and officeholders for any public communication that supports or attacks a federal candidate, whether or not the communication specifically asks for a vote for or against a particular candidate.

McCONNELL v. FEC, per STEVENS and O'CONNOR, JJ., joined by Souter, Ginsburg and Breyer, JJ. (the "Joint Opinion"), upheld the soft money provisions of the Act against a facial constitutional challenge: "Of the two major parties' total spending, soft money accounted for 5% ($21.6 million) in 1984, 11% ($45 million) in 1988, 16% ($80 million) in 1992, 30% ($272 million) in 1996, and 42% ($498 million) in 2000. The national parties transferred large amounts of their soft money to the state parties, which were allowed to use a larger percentage of soft money to finance mixed-purpose activities under FEC rules. In the year 2000, for example, the national parties diverted $280 million—more than half of their soft money—to state parties.

"Many contributions of soft money were dramatically larger than the contributions of hard money permitted by FECA. For example, in 1996 the top five corporate soft-money donors gave, in total, more than $9 million in nonfederal funds to the two national party committees. In the most recent election cycle the political parties raised almost $300 million—60% of their total soft-money fundraising—from just 800 donors, each of which contributed a minimum of $120,000. Moreover, the largest corporate donors often made substantial contributions to both parties. Such practices corroborate evidence indicating that many corporate contributions were motivated by a desire for access to candidates and a fear of being placed at a disadvantage in the legislative process relative to other contributors, rather than by ideological support for the candidates and parties."

Despite the fact that many of the soft money restrictions regulated spending, the Joint Opinion concluded that the less than strict scrutiny applied to the contribution limits in *Buckley* and *Nixon v. Shrink Missouri Government PAC,* 528 U.S. 377 (2000), was appropriately applied to the soft money restrictions: "The relevant inquiry is whether the mechanism adopted to implement the contribution limit, or to prevent circumvention of that limit, burdens speech in a way that a direct restriction on the contribution itself would not. That is not the case here." Applying the *Buckley* contribution limits standard, it concluded that the soft money restrictions were "closely drawn to match the important governmental interests of preventing corruption and the appearance of corruption"[a]

The dissents employed themes about incumbent protection, the failure to show quid pro quo corruption, lack of precision, and deep invasion of treasured First Amendment rights.[b]

Do the limitations approved by *McConnell* taken together with the denial in *Elrod* v. Burns, 427 U.S. 347 (1976), of the parties ability to use patronage as a system of reward cripple the power of parties in the political system?[c]

---

a. The Joint Opinion argued that the application of soft money restrictions to minor parties was permissible because the corruption and appearance of corruption interests were not a function of the number of legislators elected and that an as-applied challenge could be brought if the act prevented the massing of sufficient resources for effective advocacy. The Court had previously held that limitations on independent expenditures of the major parties were unconstitutional, *Colorado Republican Fed. Campaign Comm. v. FEC,* 518 U.S. 604 (1996), but prohibitions of expenditures coordinated with a candidate were constitutional. *FEC v. Colorado Republican Fed. Campaign Comm.,* 533 U.S. 431 (2001).

b. Scalia, J., dissented. Thomas, J., joined in part by Scalia, J., dissented. Kennedy, joined Rehnquist, C.J., and in part by Scalia and Thomas, JJ., dissented. Rehnquist, C.J., joined by Scalia and Kennedy, JJ., dissented.

c. The Court has generally upheld the association rights of the major parties. *California Democratic Party v. Jones,* 530 U.S. 567 (2000), invalidated California's "blanket primary" which required parties to permit citizens to vote in the primary of any party for any office regardless of their party membership. *Eu v. San Francisco County Democratic Central Comm.,* 489 U.S. 214 (1989) struck down California election provisions prohibiting political parties from endorsing candidates in party primaries. *Tashjian v. Republican Party of Conn.,* 479 U.S. 208 (1986) denounced Connecticut's closed-primary statute requiring voters in a party primary to be registered party members. At the same time, the Court has decided a number of cases that favor the interests of a two party system or the candidates of the two parties. *Timmons v. Twin Cities Area New Party,* 520 U.S. 351 (1997) upheld Minnesota legislation prohibiting political candidates

To the extent that the campaign finance restrictions enhance the power of advocacy groups at the expense of parties. Is this a good thing?[d] Is this aspect of *McConnell* likely to survive *Citizens United.*

7. ***Impact on campaigns.*** It is not clear that *United Citizens* will have a substantial impact on election campaigns. The Court had already narrowed the limitation on electioneering ads in ways that provided substantial leeway for business corporations. Wisconsin Right to Life, Inc., a non profit advocacy corporation, ran three broadcast ads from its treasury funds, which included contributions of $50,000 from business corporations, for the ads. Wisconsin Right to Life had previously campaigned against Senator Feingold, and one of its concerns was his support of filibustering of judicial nominees. The ads spoke out against filibustering and asked citizens to contact Senators Feingold and McCain without referring to Feingold's position on the issue (though his position was well known in Wisconsin). The ads appeared to violate BCRA § 203.

FEC v. WISCONSIN RIGHT TO LIFE, INC., 551 U.S. 449 (2007), per ROBERTS, C.J., joined only by Alito, J., concluded that § 203 was constitutional only as applied to ads that are "susceptible of no reasonable interpretation other than as an appeal to vote for or against a specific candidate." Because of the importance of political speech, any doubt on the matter was to be resolved in favor of the ads. Neither the intent nor the effect of the ads counted in the determination. Roberts, C.J., found Wisconsin Right to Life's ads to be protected under the First Amendment.[e]

SOUTER, J., joined by Stevens, Ginsburg, and Breyer, JJ., dissenting, found it hard to imagine that the majority would ever find an ad unprotected unless it contained words of express advocacy.

8. ***First Amendment overview.*** Having examined the doctrine overall, how free is free speech? For general discussion, see Daniel Farber, *The Categorical Approach to Protecting Speech in American Constitutional Law,* 84

---

from appearing on the ballot as candidates for more than one party. *Storer v. Brown,* 415 U.S. 724 (1974) approved a California statute denying ballot positions to independent candidates who had recently been registered with a political party. *Burdick v. Takushi,* 504 U.S. 428 (1992) validated Hawaii's ban on write-in voting. On the other hand, burdens on minor parties have occasionally been struck down particularly when they have been regarded as severe. For example, *Anderson v. Celebrezze,* 460 U.S. 780 (1983) held that unreasonably early filing deadlines for independent candidates violated the association rights of their supporters. *Williams v. Rhodes,* 393 U.S. 23 (1968) invalidated unduly stringent ballot access requirements on equal protection grounds.

But *Crawford v. Marion County Elecs. Bd.,* 553 U.S. 181 (2008), upheld Indiana's government issued photo identification voting requirement against an equal protection challenge.

In other developments, *New York State Bd. of Elec. v. Torres,* 552 U.S. 196 (2008), upheld New York's party convention scheme for nominating judges against a First Amendment claim that democratic primaries would give aspiring party nominees a more realistic chance than a convention process responsive to the wishes of party leaders. And *Washington State Grange v. Washington Republican Party,* 552 U.S. 442 (2008), upheld a blanket party scheme, that narrowed the candidate field to two regardless of party affiliation, against a claim that the system infringed upon the associational rights of political parties.

d. For discussion, see Nathaniel Persily, *Soft Parties and Strong Money,* 3 Election L.J. 315, 318 (2004).

e. Alito, J., concurring, observed that the Court would presumably be asked to reconsider its holding that § 203 is facially constitutional. Scalia, J., joined by Kennedy and Thomas, JJ., concurring in the judgment, would have overruled *McConnell's* upholding of § 203.

Ind. L.J. 917 (2009); Rodney A. Smolla, *Words "Which By Their Very Utterance Inflict Injury": The Evolving Treatment of Inherently Dangerous Speech in Free Speech Law and Theory,* 36 Pepp. L.Rev. 317 (2009).

Part 2

Freedom of Religion

■ ■ ■

CHAPTER 11

ESTABLISHMENT CLAUSE

■ ■ ■

I. INTRODUCTION

Many authorities view the Establishment Clause as seeking to assure some form of separation of church and state in a nation that has become characterized by religious pluralism. Prior to 1947, only two decisions concerning the Establishment Clause produced any significant consideration by the Court. *Bradfield v. Roberts*, 175 U.S. 291 (1899) upheld federal appropriations to a hospital in the District of Columbia, operated by the Catholic Church, for ward construction and care of indigent patients. *Quick Bear v. Leupp*, 210 U.S. 50 (1908) upheld federal disbursement of funds, held in trust for the Sioux Indians, to Catholic schools designated by the Sioux for payment of tuition costs.

In the Court's first modern decision, *Everson v. Board of Educ.* (1947), Part II infra, Rutledge, J., observed that "no provision of the Constitution is more closely tied to or given content by its generating history than the religious clause of the First Amendment." Black, J., writing for the majority, recounted that the Religion Clauses "reflected in the minds of early Americans a vivid mental picture of conditions and practices which they fervently wished to stamp out in order to preserve liberty for themselves and for their posterity." Black, J., detailed the history of religious persecution in Europe "before and contemporaneous with the colonization of America" and the "repetition of many of the old world practices" in the colonies. For example, in Massachusetts, Quakers, Baptists, and other religious minorities suffered harshly and were taxed for the established Congregational Church. In 1776, the Maryland "Declaration of Rights" stated that "only persons professing the Christian religion" were entitled to religious freedom, and not until 1826 were Jews permitted to hold public office. The South Carolina Constitution of 1778 stated that "the Christian Protestant religion shall be deemed [the] established religion of this state." Black, J., explained that "abhorrence" of these practices "reached its dramatic climax in Virginia in 1785–86" when "Madison wrote his great Memorial and Remonstrance" against renewal of "Virginia's tax levy for support of the established church" and the Virginia Assembly "enacted the famous 'Virginia Bill for Religious

Liberty' originally written by Thomas Jefferson. [T]he provisions of the First Amendment, in the drafting and adoption of which Madison and Jefferson played such leading roles, had the same objective and were intended to provide the same protection against governmental intrusion on religious liberty as the Virginia statute."

Still, the specific historical record suggests that rather than disclosing a coherent "intent of the Framers," those who influenced the framing of the First Amendment were animated by several distinct and sometimes conflicting goals. Thus, Jefferson believed that the integrity of government could be preserved only by erecting "a wall of separation" between church and state. A sharp division of authority was essential, in his view, to insulate the democratic process from ecclesiastical depradations and excursions. Madison shared this view, but also perceived church-state separation as benefiting religious institutions. Even more strongly, Roger Williams, one of the earliest colonial proponents of religious freedom, posited an evangelical theory of separation, believing it vital to protect the sanctity of the church's "garden" from the "wilderness" of the state.[a] Finally, there is evidence that one purpose of the Establishment Clause was to protect the existing state-established churches from the newly ordained national government.[b] (Indeed, although disestablishment was then well under way, the epoch of state-sponsored churches did not close until 1833 when Massachusetts separated church and state.)

The varied ideologies that prompted the founders do, however, disclose a dominant theme: constitutional status for the integrity of individual conscience.[c] Moreover, as revealed in Virginia's Bill for Religious Liberty, a practice seen by many as anathema to religious freedom was forcing the people to support religion through compulsory taxation, although there was a division of opinion as to whether non-preferential aid to religion violated liberty of conscience.[d]

---

a. For the view that "the Constitution was written on the assumption [that] government is a threat to human liberty [and] not the other way around [i.e.,] the First Amendment constrains Congress, not churches," see Douglas Laycock, *Continuity and Change in the Threat to Religious Liberty: The Reformation Era and the Late Twentieth Century*, 80 Minn.L.Rev. 1047 (1996).

b. In *Elk Grove Unified School Dist. v. Newdow*, Part IV infra, Thomas, J., stated that "text and history * * * strongly suggest" that the Establishment Clause is only "a federalism provision." For the broader view that both "religion clauses amounted to a decision by the national government not to address substantive questions concerning the proper relationship between religion and government," but rather "did no more and no less than confirm the constitutional allocation of jurisdiction over religion to the states," see Steven D. Smith, *Foreordained Failure: The Quest for a Constitutional Principle of Religious Freedom* (1995). Compare Kurt T. Lash, *The Second Adoption of the Establishment Clause: The Rise of the Nonestablishment Principle*, 27 Ariz.St.L.J. 1085 (1995) (this understanding had changed by the time of the Fourteenth Amendment). For a different perspective, see Richard C. Schragger, *The Role of the Local in the Doctrine and Discourse of Religious Liberty*, 117 Harv.L.Rev. 1810, 1815, 1852, 1892 (2004) ("Decentralization should be incorporated as a substantive Religion Clause value" because the exercise of national and state power is "the chief threat to religious liberty," and "the dispersal of political authority over religious burdens and benefits enhances local public authority, enabling it to serve as a counterweight to private religious power.").

c. See Noah Feldman, *The Intellectual Origins of the Establishment Clause*, 77 N.Y.U.L.Rev. 346 (2002).

d. The view that it did not do so was endorsed by Rehnquist, J., in *Wallace v. Jaffree*, Part III, and Thomas, J., found "much to commend" this position in *Rosenberger v. University of Virginia*, Part II infra.

A final matter involving the history of the Establishment Clause concerns *Everson*'s unanimous ruling that it was "made applicable to the states" by the Fourteenth Amendment.[e]

II. AID TO RELIGION

EVERSON v. BOARD OF EDUC., 330 U.S. 1 (1947), involved one of the major areas of controversy under the Establishment Clause: public financial assistance to church-related institutions (mainly parochial schools). A New Jersey township reimbursed parents for the cost of

---

e. *Application of the Establishment Clause to the states.* Is nonestablishment as "implicit in the concept of ordered liberty" as the freedoms of speech, press, religious exercise, and assembly? See *Palko v. Connecticut,* 302 U.S. 319 (1937). Is it "fundamental to the American scheme"? See *Duncan v. Louisiana,* 391 U.S. 145 (1968).

Brennan, J., stated: "It has been suggested [that] absorption of the [Establishment Clause] is conceptually impossible because the Framers meant [it] also to foreclose any attempt by Congress to disestablish the existing official state churches. [But] the last of the formal state establishments was dissolved more than three decades before the Fourteenth Amendment was ratified, and thus the problem of protecting official state churches from federal encroachments could hardly have been any concern of those who framed the post-Civil War Amendments. [T]he Fourteenth Amendment created a panoply of new federal rights for the protection of citizens of the various States. And among those rights was freedom from such state governmental involvement in the affairs of religion as the Establishment Clause had originally foreclosed on the part of Congress.

"It has also been suggested that the 'liberty' guaranteed by the Fourteenth Amendment logically cannot absorb the Establishment Clause because that clause is not one of the provisions of the Bill of Rights which in terms protects a 'freedom' of the individual. The fallacy in this contention, I think, is that it underestimates the role of the Establishment Clause as a coguarantor, with the Free Exercise Clause, of religious liberty. * * *

"Finally, it has been contended that absorption of the Establishment Clause is precluded by the absence of any intention on the part of the Framers of the Fourteenth Amendment to circumscribe the residual powers of the States to aid religious activities and institutions in ways which fell short of formal establishments. That argument relies in part upon the express terms of the abortive Blaine Amendment—proposed several years after the adoption of the Fourteenth Amendment—which would have added to the First Amendment a provision that '[n]o state shall make any law respecting an establishment of religion.' Such a restriction would have been superfluous, it is said, if the Fourteenth Amendment had already made the Establishment Clause binding upon the States.

"The argument proves too much, for the Fourteenth Amendment's protection of the free exercise of religion can hardly be questioned; yet the Blaine Amendment would also have added an explicit protection against state laws abridging that liberty." *School Dist. v. Schempp,* Part III infra (concurring opinion).

Consider Mark D. Howe, *The Constitutional Question,* in Religion and the Free Society 49, 55 (1958): "The Court did not seem to be aware [that] some legislative enactments respecting an establishment of religion affect most remotely, if at all, the personal rights of religious liberty. [So, the Court might allow] the states to take such action in aid of religion as does not appreciably affect the religious or other constitutional rights of individuals."

Compare Jesse H. Choper, *The Establishment Clause and Aid to Parochial Schools,* 56 Calif.L.Rev. 260, 274–75 (1968): "[A] central design of the establishment clause was that it [prevent] government generally from coercing religious belief and specifically from compulsorily taxing individuals for strictly religious purposes. If nonsecular federal action involves either of these consequences, [it] has seemingly violated the fourteenth amendment by 'significantly' affecting personal liberty. However, if federal action involves neither consequence, then [the] establishment clause itself—as a matter of constitutional construction—has probably not been breached." See also Noah Feldman, *The Framers' Church-State Problem—and Ours,* in The Constitution 2020, p. 221 (Jack Balkin & Reva Siegel, eds. 2009) ("no coercion and no money").

Several opinions of Thomas, J., see Part IV infra, support the non-incorporation position. For discussion of recent scholarship on the issue, see Steven D. Smith, *The Jurisdictional Establishment Clause: A Reappraisal,* 81 Notre D. L. Rev. 1843 (2006).

sending their children "on regular buses operated by the public transportation system," to and from schools, including nonprofit private and parochial schools. The Court, per BLACK, J., rejected a municipal taxpayer's contention that payment for Catholic parochial school students violated the Establishment Clause:

"The 'establishment of religion' clause of the First Amendment means at least this: Neither a state nor the Federal Government can set up a church. Neither can pass laws which aid one religion, aid all religions, or prefer one religion over another. Neither can force nor influence a person to go to or to remain away from church against his will or force him to profess a belief or disbelief in any religion. No person can be punished for entertaining or professing religious beliefs or disbeliefs, for church attendance or non-attendance. No tax in any amount, large or small can be levied to support any religious activities or institutions, whatever they may be called, or whatever form they may adopt to teach or practice religion. Neither a state nor the Federal Government can, openly or secretly, participate in the affairs of any religious organizations or groups and vice versa. In the words of Jefferson, the clause against establishment of religion by law was intended to erect 'a wall of separation between Church and State.'

"We must [not invalidate the New Jersey statute] if it is within the state's constitutional power even though it approaches the verge of that power. New Jersey [cannot] contribute tax-raised funds to the support of an institution which teaches the tenets and faith of any church. On the other hand, other language of the amendment commands that New Jersey cannot hamper its citizens in the free exercise of their own religion. Consequently, it cannot exclude individual Catholics, Lutherans, Mohammedans, Baptists, Jews, Methodists, Non-believers, Presbyterians, or the members of any other faith, *because of their faith, or lack of it,* from receiving the benefits of public welfare legislation. While we do not mean to intimate that a state could not provide transportation only to children attending public schools, we must be careful, in protecting the citizens of New Jersey against state-established churches, to be sure that we do not inadvertently prohibit New Jersey from extending its general State law benefits to all its citizens without regard to their religious belief."

Noting that "the New Jersey legislature has decided that a public purpose will be served" by having children "ride in public buses to and from schools rather than run the risk of traffic and other hazards incident to walking or 'hitchhiking,'" the Court conceded "that children are helped to get to church schools. There is even a possibility that some of the children might not be sent to the church schools if the parents were compelled to pay their children's bus fares out of their own pockets when transportation to a public school would have been paid for by the State. [But] state-paid policemen, detailed to protect children going to and from church schools from the very real hazards of traffic, would serve much the same [purpose]. Similarly, parents might be reluctant to permit their children to attend schools which the state had cut off from such general government services as ordinary police and fire protection, connections for sewage disposal, public highways and sidewalks. Of course, cutting off church schools from these services, so separate and so indisputably marked off from the religious function, would make it far more difficult for the schools to operate. But such is obviously not the purpose of the First Amendment. That Amendment requires the state to be a neutral in its relations with groups of religious believers and non-believers; it does not require the state to be their adversary. * * *

"This Court had said that parents may, in the discharge of their duty under state compulsory education laws, send their children to a religious rather than a public school if the school meets the secular educational requirements which the state has power to impose. See *Pierce v. Society of Sisters,* [Ch. 12, I]. It appears that these parochial schools meet New Jersey's requirements. The State contributes no money to the schools. [Its] legislation, as applied, does no more than provide a general program to help parents get their children, regardless of their religion, safely and expeditiously to and from accredited schools.

"The First Amendment has erected a wall between church and state. That wall must be kept high and impregnable. We could not approve the slightest breach. New Jersey has not breached it here."

RUTLEDGE, J., joined by Frankfurter, Jackson and Burton, JJ., filed the principal dissent, arguing that the statute aided children "in a substantial way to get the very thing which they are sent to the particular school to secure, namely, religious training and [teaching.] Commingling the religious with the secular teaching does not divest the whole of its religious permeation and emphasis or make them of minor part, if proportion were material. Indeed, on any other view, the constitutional prohibition always could be brought to naught by adding a modicum of the secular. [Transportation] cost is as much a part of the total expense, except at times in amount, as the cost of textbooks, of school lunches, of athletic equipment, of writing and other [materials]. Payment of transportation is [no] less essential to education, whether religious or secular, than payment for tuitions, for teachers' salaries, for buildings, equipment and necessary materials. [Now], as in Madison's time, not the amount but the principle of assessment is wrong.

" * * * Public money devoted to payment of religious costs, educational or other, brings the quest for more. It brings too the struggle of sect against sect for the larger share or for any. Here one by numbers alone will benefit most, there another. That is precisely the history of societies which have had an established religion and dissident groups. It is the very thing Jefferson and Madison experienced and sought to guard [against]. The end of such strife cannot be other than to destroy the cherished liberty. The dominating group will achieve the dominant benefit; or all will embroil the state in their dissensions. [Nor] is the case comparable to one of furnishing fire or police protection, or access to public highways. These things are matters of common right, part of the general need for safety. Certainly the fire department must not stand idly by while the church burns."

The Court did not again confront the subject of aid to parochial schools for more than two decades.[a] During the intervening years, however, the Court continued to develop its Establishment Clause rationale in cases involving other issues, emphasizing the "purpose and primary effect" of the challenged government action (see Part III infra).

WALZ v. TAX COM'N, 397 U.S. 664 (1970), per BURGER, C.J., upheld state tax exemption for "real or personal property used exclusively for religious, educational or charitable purposes": "The legislative purpose of a property tax exemption is neither the advancement nor the inhibition of religion; it is neither sponsorship nor hostility. New York, in common with the other states, has determined that certain entities that exist in a harmonious relationship to the community at large, and that foster its 'moral or mental improvement,' should not be inhibited in their activities by property taxation or the hazard of loss of those properties for nonpayment of taxes. It [has] granted exemption to all houses of religious worship within a broad class of property owned by nonprofit, quasi-public corporations which include hospitals, libraries, playgrounds, scientific, professional, historical and patriotic groups. * * *

"We find it unnecessary to justify the tax exemption on the social welfare services or 'good works' that some churches perform for parishioners and others—family counselling, aid to the elderly and the infirm, and to children. [To] give emphasis to so variable an aspect of the work of religious bodies would introduce an element of governmental evaluation and standards as to the worth of particular social welfare programs, thus producing a kind of continuing day-to-day relationship which the policy of neutrality seeks to minimize. * * * We must also be sure that the end result—the effect—is not an excessive government entanglement with religion. The test is inescapably one of degree. * * * Elimination of exemption would tend to expand the involvement of government by giving rise to tax valuation of church property, tax liens, tax foreclosures, and the direct confrontations and conflicts that follow in the train of those legal processes.

"Granting tax exemptions to churches necessarily operates to afford an indirect economic benefit and also gives rise to some, but yet a lesser, involvement than taxing them. * * * Obviously a direct money subsidy would be a relationship pregnant with involvement and, as with most governmental grant programs, could encompass sustained and detailed administrative relationships for enforcement of statutory or administrative standards, but that is not this case. * * *

----

a. See *Board of Educ. v. Allen* (1968), discussed by Souter, J., in *Zelman*, infra.

"It is obviously correct that no one acquires a vested or protected right in violation of the Constitution by long use * * *. Yet an unbroken practice of according the exemption to churches [is] not something to be lightly cast aside."

BRENNAN, J., concurred: "Tax exemptions and general subsidies [both] provide economic assistance, [but a] subsidy involves the direct transfer of public monies to the subsidized enterprise and uses resources exacted from taxpayers as a whole. An exemption, on the other hand, involves no such transfer.[b] It assists the exempted enterprise only passively." Harlan, J., also concurred.

DOUGLAS, J., dissented: "If history be our guide, then tax exemption of church property in this country is indeed highly suspect, as it arose in the early days when the church was an agency of the state. [The] financial support rendered here is to the church, the place of worship. A tax exemption is a subsidy."

NOTES AND QUESTIONS

1. **Size of government.** Consider William W. Van Alstyne, *Constitutional Separation of Church and State: The Quest for a Coherent Position*, 57 Am.Pol.Sci.Rev. 865, 881 (1963): "To finance expanding government services, [taxes] may gradually divert an increasing fraction of total personal income, necessarily leaving proportionately less money in the private sector to each person to spend according to his individual choice, in support of religion or other undertakings. To the extent that the tax revenues thus collected may not be spent by government to support religious enterprises, but must be used exclusively for secular purposes, the net effect, arguably, is to reduce the relative supply of funds available to religion." Does this warrant tax exemption for "religion"? Does it "warrant the judicial junking of the establishment clause"? Id. Is it "equally arguable that government fiscal activity, far from reducing disposable personal income, actually increases it"? Id. See also Alan Schwarz, *The Nonestablishment Principle: A Reply to Professor Giannella*, 81 Harv.L.Rev. 1465, 1469–70 (1968).

2. **"Neutrality" and "endorsement."** TEXAS MONTHLY, INC. v. BULLOCK, 489 U.S. 1 (1989), held violative of the Establishment Clause a Texas sales tax exemption for books and "periodicals that are published or distributed by a religious faith and that consist wholly of writings promulgating the teaching of the faith." BRENNAN, J., joined by Marshall and Stevens, JJ., referred to several important themes in the Court's developing Establishment Clause rationale:[c] "[*Walz*] emphasized that the benefits derived by religious organizations flowed to a large number of nonreligious groups as [well]. However, when government directs a subsidy exclusively to religious

---

b. What of the fact that exemption for churches augments the tax bills of others? For the view that there is a constitutional distinction between tax exemptions ("a standing arrangement open to a wide array of organizations") and annual appropriations, see Edward A. Zelinsky, *Are Tax "Benefits" Constitutionally Equivalent to Direct Expenditures*, 112 Harv.L.Rev. 379 (1998).

c. "Neutrality" and "endorsement" are discussed further in the materials in this Part. A third theme—"coercion"—is considered more fully in Part IV infra.

organizations [that] either burdens nonbeneficiaries markedly or cannot reasonably be seen as removing a significant state-imposed deterrent to the free exercise of religion, as Texas has done, it 'provide[s] unjustifiable awards of assistance to religious organizations' and cannot but 'conve[y] a message of endorsement' to slighted members of the community. This is particularly true where, as here, the subsidy is targeted at writings that *promulgate* the teachings of religious faiths. It is difficult to view Texas' narrow exemption as anything but state sponsorship of religious belief [which] lacks a secular objective.''

BLACKMUN, J., joined by O'Connor, J., concurred: ''[A] tax exemption *limited* to the sale of religious literature * * * offends our most basic understanding of what the establishment clause is all about.'' White, J., concurred on freedom of press grounds. Scalia, J., joined by Rehnquist, C.J., and Kennedy, J., dissented from Brennan, J.'s distinction of *Walz*.

———

In 1971, LEMON v. KURTZMAN, 403 U.S. 602, per BURGER C.J., which invalidated state salary supplements to teachers of secular subjects in nonpublic schools, articulated a three-part test for judging Establishment Clause issues. This test is most frequently invoked by the lower courts and—as the materials that follow indicate—has not been overruled: ''First, the statute must have a secular legislative purpose; second, its principal or primary effect must be one that neither advances nor inhibits religion;''[d] finally, the statute must not foster ''an excessive government entanglement with religion.'' During the next fifteen years, the Court, using the *Lemon* test, invalidated a large number of aid programs for elementary and secondary schools, even though it found that virtually all had a ''secular'' purpose.[e] The *Lemon* Court began with a critical premise: the mission of church related elementary and secondary schools is to teach religion, and all subjects are, or carry the potential of being, permeated with religion. Thus, states would have to engage in a ''comprehensive, discriminating, and continuing state surveillance'' to prevent misuse of

d. Compare Douglas Laycock, *Towards a General Theory of the Religion Clauses: The Case of Church Labor Relations and the Right to Church Autonomy*, 81 Colum.L.Rev. 1373, 1381, 1384 (1981): ''The 'inhibits' language is at odds with the constitutional text and with the Court's own statements of the origins and purposes of [the] clause. Government support for religion is an element of every establishment claim, just as a burden or restriction on religion is an element of every free exercise claim. Regulation that burdens religion, enacted because of the government's general interest in regulation, is simply not establishment.''

e. ''This reflects, at least in part, our reluctance to attribute unconstitutional motives to the states, particularly when a plausible secular purpose for the state's program may be discerned from the face of the statute.'' *Mueller v. Allen*, discussed infra. *Mueller* added: ''A state's decision to defray the cost of educational expenses incurred by parents—regardless of the type of schools their children attend—evidences a purpose that is both secular and understandable. An educated populace is essential to the political and economic health of any community, and a state's efforts to assist parents in meeting the rising cost of educational expenses plainly serves this secular purpose of ensuring that the state's citizenry is well-educated. Similarly, [states] could conclude that there is a strong public interest in assuring the continued financial health of private schools, both sectarian and non-sectarian. By educating a substantial number of students such schools relieve public schools of a correspondingly great burden—to the benefit of all taxpayers. In addition, private schools may serve as a benchmark for public schools.''

tax funds for religious purposes, which would be impermissibly entangling, and "pregnant with dangers of excessive government direction of church schools and hence of churches."[f] Furthermore, state assistance risked another sort of entanglement: "divisive political potential" along religious lines.[g]

Zelman v. Simmons–Harris, infra, is the most recent case on the subject. It is preceded by *Mitchell v. Helms* because of its strong emphasis of the "neutrality" theme. Both review the important decisions since *Lemon.*

MITCHELL v. HELMS, 530 U.S. 793 (2000), involved a federal program that lends "secular, neutral and nonideological" educational materials (mainly for libraries and computers)—which may not "supplant funds from non-Federal sources"—to elementary and secondary schools, both public and private. THOMAS, J., joined by Rehnquist, C.J., and Scalia and Kennedy, JJ., upheld the program, overruling *Meek v. Pittenger*, 421 U.S. 349 (1975) and *Wolman v. Walter*, 433 U.S. 229 (1977), "in which we held unconstitutional programs that provided many of the same sorts of materials and equipment," and noting that *Agostini v. Felton*, 521 U.S. 203 (1997), "in which we approved a program [that] provided public employees to teach remedial classes at private schools, including religious schools, [had] overruled *Aguilar v. Felton*, 473 U.S. 402 (1985), and partially overruled *School Dist. of Grand Rapids v. Ball*, 473 U.S. 373 (1985), both of which had involved such a program": "[W]e have consistently turned to the principle of neutrality. [I]f the government, seeking to further some legitimate secular purpose, offers aid on the same terms, without regard to religion, to all who adequately further that purpose,

---

f. White, J., dissenting in *Lemon,* accused the Court of "creat[ing] an insoluble paradox for the State and the parochial schools. The State cannot finance secular instruction if it permits religion to be taught in the same classroom; but if it exacts a promise that religion not be so taught—a promise the school and its teachers are quite willing and on this record able to give—and enforces it, it is then entangled in the 'no entanglement' aspect of the Court's Establishment Clause jurisprudence."

g. *Lemon* reasoned: "In a community [where] pupils are served by church-related schools, it can be assumed that state assistance will entail considerable political activity [by partisans and opponents]. Candidates will be forced to declare and voters to choose. It would be unrealistic to ignore the fact that many people confronted with issues of this kind will find their votes aligned with their faith.

"Ordinarily political debate and division, however vigorous or even partisan, are normal and healthy manifestations of our democratic system of government, but political division along religious lines was one of the principal evils against which the First Amendment was intended to protect. Paul A. Freund, *Public Aid to Parochial Schools*, 82 Harv.L.Rev. 1680, 1692 (1969)."

Compare Alan Schwarz, *No Imposition of Religion: The Establishment Clause Value*, 77 Yale L.J. 692, 711 (1968): "If avoidance of strife were an independent [Establishment Clause] value, no legislation could be adopted on any subject which aroused strong and divided [religious] feelings." See Choper, fn. e, Ch. 11, I supra, at 273: "Nor would a denial of aid to parochial schools largely diminish the extent of religious political activity. In fact, it 'might lead to greater political ruptures caused by the alienation of segments of the religious community.' Those who send their children to parochial schools might intensify opposition to increased governmental aid to public education." For the view that the historical evidence contradicts the significance of political division along religious lines, see Peter M. Schotten, *The Establishment Clause and Excessive Governmental-Religious Entanglement*, 15 Wake For.L.Rev. 207 (1979). For the view that the doctrine is "misguided and quixotic," see Richard W. Garnett, *Religion, Division, and the First Amendment,* 94 Geo. L. J. 1667 (2006).

then it is fair to say that any aid going to a religious recipient only has the effect of furthering that secular purpose.[a]

"[T]here was a period [when] whether a school that receives aid [was] pervasively sectarian [mattered, particularly if it] was a primary or secondary school. But that period [is] thankfully long past. [The] religious nature of a recipient should not matter to the constitutional analysis, so long as the recipient adequately furthers the government's secular purpose. [T]he inquiry into the recipient's religious views required by a focus on whether a school is pervasively sectarian is not only unnecessary but also offensive. It is well established [that] courts should refrain from trolling through a person's or institution's religious beliefs * * *.

"Finally, hostility to aid to pervasively sectarian schools has a shameful pedigree * * *. Opposition to aid to 'sectarian' schools acquired prominence in the 1870's with Congress's consideration (and near passage) of the Blaine Amendment, which would have amended the Constitution to bar any aid to sectarian institutions. Consideration of the amendment arose at a time of pervasive hostility to the Catholic Church and to Catholics in general, and it was an open secret that 'sectarian' was code for 'Catholic.' [When the Court coined the term 'pervasively sectarian,' it] could be applied almost exclusively to Catholic parochial schools [and] even today's dissent exemplifies chiefly by reference to such schools."

O'CONNOR, J., joined by Breyer, J., concurred only in the result: "[W]e have never held that a government-aid program passes constitutional muster solely because of the neutral criteria it employs as a basis for distributing aid." Rather, under *Agostini*, "we [ask] whether the program results in governmental indoctrination or defines its recipients by reference to religion," and plaintiffs in this case have failed to "prove that the aid in question actually is, or has been, used for religious purposes."[a]

SOUTER, J., joined by Stevens and Ginsburg, JJ., dissented: "[I]f we looked no further than evenhandedness, and failed to ask what activities the aid might support, or in fact did support, religious schools could be blessed with government funding as massive as expenditures made for the benefit of their public school counterparts, and religious missions would thrive on public money. This is [why] neutrality has never been recognized as dispositive and has always been teamed with attention to other

---

a. See also Carl H. Esbeck, *When Accommodations for Religion Violate the Establishment Clause: Regularizing the Supreme Court's Analysis*, 110 W. Va. L. Rev. 359, 382–83 (2007) (excluding religious organizations from aid programs for educational and social services "puts pressure on individuals, as well as the faith-based organizations they have created, to adapt their religious choices to the government's favored behaviors").

a. The plurality reasoned that "whether governmental aid to religious schools results in governmental indoctrination is ultimately a question whether any religious indoctrination that occurs in those schools could reasonably be attributed to governmental action. We have also indicated that the answer to the question of indoctrination will resolve the question whether a program of educational aid 'subsidizes' religion, as our religion cases use that term. In distinguishing between indoctrination that is attributable to the State and indoctrination that is not, we have consistently turned to the principle of neutrality."

facts bearing on the substantive prohibition of support for a school's religious objective.* * *[19]"

ZELMAN v. SIMMONS–HARRIS

536 U.S. 639, 122 S.Ct. 2460, 153 L.Ed.2d 604 (2002).

CHIEF JUSTICE REHNQUIST delivered the opinion of the Court.

* * * Cleveland's public schools have been among the worst performing public schools in the Nation. In 1995, a Federal District Court declared a "crisis of magnitude" and placed the entire Cleveland school district under state control. Shortly thereafter, the state auditor found that Cleveland's public schools [had] failed to meet any of the 18 state standards for minimal acceptable performance. Only 1 in 10 ninth graders could pass a basic proficiency examination, and students at all levels performed at a dismal rate compared with students in other Ohio public schools. More than two-thirds of high school students either dropped or failed out before graduation. [Of] those students who did graduate, few could read, write, or compute at levels comparable to their counterparts in other cities.

It is against this backdrop that Ohio enacted, among other initiatives, its Pilot Project Scholarship Program [which] provides financial assistance to families in any Ohio school district that is or has been "under federal court order requiring supervision and operational management of the district by the state superintendent." Cleveland is the only Ohio school district to fall within that category.

[First,] the program provides tuition aid for students [to] attend a participating public or private school of their parent's choosing. Second, the program provides tutorial aid for students who choose to remain enrolled in public school.

[Any] private school, whether religious or nonreligious, may participate in the tuition aid portion of [the] program [so] long as the school is located within the boundaries of a covered district and meets statewide educational standards. Participating private schools must agree not to discriminate on the basis of race, religion, or ethnic background, or to "advocate or foster unlawful behavior or teach hatred of any person or group on the basis of race, ethnicity, national origin, or religion." Any public school located in a school district adjacent to the covered district may also participate [and is] eligible to receive a $2,250 tuition grant for each program student accepted in addition to the full amount of per-pupil state funding attributable to each additional student.

---

19. Adopting the plurality's rule would permit practically any government aid to religion so long as it could be supplied on terms ostensibly comparable to the terms under which aid was provided to nonreligious recipients. As a principle of constitutional sufficiency, the manipulability of this rule is breathtaking. A legislature would merely need to state a secular objective in order to legalize massive aid to all religions, one religion, or even one sect, to which its largess could be directed through the easy exercise of crafting facially neutral terms under which to offer aid favoring that religious group. Short of formally replacing the Establishment Clause, a more dependable key to the public fisc or a cleaner break with prior law would be difficult to imagine.

Tuition aid is distributed to parents according to financial need. Families with incomes below 200% of the poverty line are given priority [and] receive 90% of private school tuition up to $2,250. For these lowest-income families, participating private schools may not charge a parental co-payment greater than $250. For all other families, the program pays 75% of tuition costs, up to $1,875, with no co-payment cap. [If] parents choose a private school, checks are made payable to the parents who then endorse the checks over to the chosen school.

[In] the 1999–2000 school year, 56 private schools participated in the program, 46 (or 82%) of which had a religious affiliation. None of the public schools in districts adjacent to Cleveland have elected to participate. More than 3,700 students participated in the scholarship program, most of whom (96%) enrolled in religiously affiliated schools. Sixty percent of these students were from families at or below the poverty line. * * *

The program is part of a broader undertaking by the State to enhance the educational options of Cleveland's schoolchildren in response to the 1995 takeover. That undertaking includes programs governing community and magnet schools. Community schools are funded under state law but are run by their own school boards, not by local school districts. These schools enjoy academic independence to hire their own teachers and to determine their own curriculum. They can have no religious affiliation and are required to accept students by lottery. During the 1999–2000 school year, there were 10 start-up community schools in the Cleveland City School District with more than 1,900 students enrolled. For each child enrolled in a community school, the school receives state funding of $4,518, twice the funding a participating program school may receive.

Magnet schools are public schools operated by a local school board that emphasize a particular subject area, teaching method, or service to students. For each student enrolled in a magnet school, the school district receives $7,746, including state funding of $4,167, the same amount received per student enrolled at a traditional public school. As of 1999, parents in Cleveland were able to choose from among 23 magnet schools, which together enrolled more than 13,000 students in kindergarten through eighth grade. These schools provide specialized teaching methods, such as Montessori, or a particularized curriculum focus, such as foreign language, computers, or the arts.

[There] is no dispute that the program challenged here was enacted for the valid secular purpose of providing educational assistance to poor children in a demonstrably failing public school system. Thus, the question presented is whether the Ohio program nonetheless has the forbidden "effect" of advancing or inhibiting religion.

To answer that question, our decisions have drawn a consistent distinction between government programs that provide aid directly to religious schools, *Mitchell*; *Rosenberger v. University of Virginia*, 515 U.S.

819, 842 (1995),[t] and programs of true private choice, in which government aid reaches religious schools only as a result of the genuine and independent choices of private individuals. While our jurisprudence with respect to the constitutionality of direct aid programs has "changed significantly" over the past two decades, our jurisprudence with respect to true private choice programs has remained consistent and unbroken. Three times we have confronted Establishment Clause challenges to neutral government programs that provide aid directly to a broad class of individuals, who, in turn, direct the aid to religious schools or institutions of their own choosing. Three times we have rejected such challenges.

In *Mueller v. Allen,* 463 U.S. 388 (1983), we rejected an Establishment Clause challenge to a Minnesota program authorizing tax deductions for various educational expenses, including private school tuition costs, even though the great majority of the program's beneficiaries (96%) were parents of children in religious schools. [In] *Witters v. Washington Dept. of Servs. for Blind,* 474 U.S. 481 (1986), we used identical reasoning to reject an Establishment Clause challenge to a vocational scholarship program that provided tuition aid to a student studying at a religious institution to become a pastor. [Finally,] in *Zobrest v. Catalina Foothills School Dist.,* 509 U.S. 1 (1993), we applied *Mueller* and *Witters* to reject an Establishment Clause challenge to a federal program that permitted sign-language interpreters to assist deaf children enrolled in religious schools. * * *

Mueller, Witters, and *Zobrest* thus make clear that where a government aid program is neutral with respect to religion, and provides assistance directly to a broad class of citizens who, in turn, direct government aid to religious schools wholly as a result of their own genuine and independent private choice, the program is not readily subject to challenge under the Establishment Clause. [The] incidental advancement of a religious mission, or the perceived endorsement of a religious message, is

---

t. The *Rosenberger* majority, Ch. 7, Sec. 1, I, which consisted of the *Mitchell* plurality and O'Connor, J., held that the Establishment Clause permits a public university to fund a student newspaper that proselytized a Christian perspective as part of a program that generally funded student publications. Although recognizing "special Establishment Clause dangers" in direct aid to religious entities, the plurality noted that its decision "cannot be read as addressing an expenditure from a general tax fund." Rather, the money came from a "special student activities fund from which any group of students with [recognized] status can draw for purposes consistent with the University's educational mission." As in *Lamb's Chapel v. Center Moriches Union Free School Dist.,* 508 U.S. 384 (1993), holding that a school district did not violate the Establishment Clause in permitting a church's after-hours use of school facilities to show a religiously oriented film series on family values when the school district also permitted presentation of views on the subject by nonreligious groups, "a public university may maintain its own computer facility and give student groups access to that facility, including the use of the printers, on a religion neutral, say first-come-first-served, basis." This is no different than "a school paying a third-party contractor to operate the facility on its behalf. The latter occurs here." Since the University made payments for publication costs directly to the printing companies, "we do not confront a case where, even under a neutral program that includes nonsectarian recipients, the government is making direct money payments to an institution or group that is engaged in religious activity."

The dissenters, who were the same as in *Zelman,* distinguished cases like *Lamb's Chapel* as based "on the recognition that all speakers are entitled to use the street corner (even though the State paves the roads and provides police protection to everyone on the street) and on the analogy between the public street corner and open classroom space. [T]he cases cannot be lifted to a higher plane of generalization without admitting that new economic benefits are being extended directly to religion in clear violation of the principle barring direct aid."

reasonably attributable to the individual recipient, not to the government, whose role ends with the disbursement of benefits [citing the opinions of the plurality and O'Connor, J., in *Mitchell*].ᵘ [It] is precisely for these reasons that we have never found a program of true private choice to offend the Establishment Clause.

We believe that the program challenged here is a program of true private choice. [It] is neutral in all respects toward religion. It is part of a general and multifaceted undertaking by the State of Ohio to provide educational opportunities to the children of a failed school district. It confers educational assistance directly to a broad class of individuals defined without reference to religion. [The] program permits the participation of *all* schools within the district, religious or nonreligious. Adjacent public schools also may participate and have a financial incentive to do so. [The] only preference stated anywhere in the program is a preference for low-income families* * *.

There are no "financial incentive[s]" that "ske[w]" the program toward religious schools. *Witters*. Such incentives "[are] not present [where] the aid is allocated on the basis of neutral, secular criteria that neither favor nor disfavor religion, and is made available to both religious and secular beneficiaries on a nondiscriminatory basis." *Agostini*. The program here in fact creates financial *dis*incentives for religious schools, with private schools receiving only half the government assistance given to community schools and one-third the assistance given to magnet schools. Adjacent public schools, should any choose to accept program students, are also eligible to receive two to three times the state funding of a private religious [school]. Parents that choose to participate in the scholarship program and then to enroll their children in a private school (religious or nonreligious) must copay a portion of the school's tuition. Families that choose a community school, magnet school, or traditional public school pay nothing. Although such features of the program are not necessary to its constitutionality, they clearly dispel the claim that the program "creates * * * financial incentive[s] for parents to choose a sectarian school." *Zobrest*.[22]

---

u. O'Connor, J. reasoned: "In terms of public perception, a government program of direct aid to religious schools based on the number of students attending each school differs meaningfully from the government distributing aid directly to individual students who, in turn, decide to use the aid at the same religious schools. In the former example, if the religious school uses the aid to inculcate religion [, the] reasonable observer would naturally perceive the aid program as *government* support for the advancement of religion. That the amount of aid received by the school is based on the school's enrollment does not separate the government from the endorsement of the religious message. [In] contrast, when government aid supports a school's religious mission only because of independent decisions made by numerous individuals to guide their secular aid to that [school,] endorsement of the religious message is reasonably attributed to the individuals who select the path of the aid."

The "endorsement" theme—highly influential in the present Court's reasoning—is considered in further detail in Part III, and particularly Part IV infra.

22. Justice Souter suggests the program is not "neutral" because program students cannot spend scholarship vouchers at traditional public schools. This objection is mistaken: Public schools in Cleveland already receive $7,097 in public funding per pupil—$4,167 of which is attributable to the State. Program students who receive tutoring aid and remain enrolled in

[Any] objective observer familiar with the full history and context of the Ohio program would reasonably view it as one aspect of a broader undertaking to assist poor children in failed schools, not as an endorsement of religious schooling in general.

There also is no evidence that the program fails to provide genuine opportunities for Cleveland parents to select secular educational options for their school-age children. Cleveland schoolchildren [may] remain in public school as before, remain in public school with publicly funded tutoring aid, obtain a scholarship and choose a religious school, obtain a scholarship and choose a nonreligious private school, enroll in a community school, or enroll in a magnet school. That 46 of the 56 private schools now participating in the program are religious schools does not condemn it as [t]he Establishment Clause question is whether Ohio is coercing parents into sending their children to religious schools, and that question must be answered by evaluating *all* options * * *.

Justice Souter speculates that because more private religious schools currently participate in the program, the program itself must somehow discourage the participation of private nonreligious schools.[23] But Cleveland's preponderance of religiously affiliated private schools certainly did not arise as a result of the program; it is a phenomenon common to many American cities. Indeed, by all accounts the program has captured a remarkable cross-section of private schools, religious and nonreligious. It is true that 82% of Cleveland's participating private schools are religious schools, but it is also true that 81% of private schools in Ohio are religious schools. To attribute constitutional significance to this figure, moreover, would lead to the absurd result that a neutral school-choice program might [be] constitutional in some States, such as Maine or Utah, where less than 45% of private schools are religious schools, but not in other States, such as Nebraska or Kansas, where over 90% of private schools are religious schools.

---

traditional public schools therefore direct almost twice as much state funding to their chosen school as do program students who receive a scholarship and attend a private school.* * *

23. Justice Souter appears to base this claim on the unfounded assumption that capping the amount of tuition charged to low-income students (at $2,500) favors participation by religious schools. [But] the record [shows] that nonreligious private schools operating in Cleveland also seek and receive substantial third-party contributions. Indeed, the actual operation of the program refutes Justice Souter's [argument]: Ten secular private schools operated within the Cleveland City School District when the program was adopted. All 10 chose to participate in the program and have continued to participate to this day. And while no religious schools have been created in response to the program, several *nonreligious* schools have been created in spite of the fact that a principal barrier to entry of new private schools is the uncertainty caused by protracted litigation which has plagued the program since its inception. See also 234 F.3d 945, 970 (CA6 2000) ("There is not a scintilla of evidence in this case that any school, public or private, has been discouraged from participating in the school voucher program because it cannot 'afford' to do so") (Ryan, J., concurring in part and dissenting in part). Similarly mistaken is Justice Souter's reliance on the low enrollment of scholarship students in nonreligious schools during the 1999–2000 school year. These figures ignore the fact that the number of program students enrolled in nonreligious schools has widely varied from year to year, underscoring why the constitutionality of a neutral choice program does not turn on annual tallies of private decisions made in any given year by thousands of individual aid recipients.

Respondents and Justice Souter claim [that] we should attach constitutional significance to the fact that 96% of scholarship recipients have enrolled in religious schools. They claim that this alone proves parents lack genuine choice, even if no parent has ever said so. We need not consider this argument in detail, since it was flatly rejected in *Mueller*, where we found it irrelevant that 96% of parents taking deductions for tuition expenses paid tuition at religious schools. [The] constitutionality of a neutral educational aid program simply does not turn on whether and why, in a particular area, at a particular time, most private schools are run by religious organizations, or most recipients choose to use the aid at a religious school. As we said in *Mueller*, "[s]uch an approach would scarcely provide the certainty that this field stands in need of, nor can we perceive principled standards by which such statistical evidence might be evaluated."

This point is aptly illustrated here. The 96% figure upon which respondents and Justice Souter rely discounts entirely (1) the more than 1,900 Cleveland children enrolled in alternative community schools, (2) the more than 13,000 children enrolled in alternative magnet schools, and (3) the more than 1,400 children enrolled in traditional public schools with tutorial assistance. Including some or all of these children in the denominator of children enrolled in nontraditional schools during the 1999–2000 school year drops the percentage enrolled in religious schools from 96% to under 20%. The 96% figure also represents but a snapshot of one particular school year. In the 1997–1998 school year, by contrast, only 78% of scholarship recipients attended religious schools. The difference was attributable to two private nonreligious schools that had accepted 15% of all scholarship students electing instead to register as community schools, in light of larger per-pupil funding for community schools and the uncertain future of the scholarship program generated by this litigation.[24] Many of the students enrolled in these schools as scholarship students remained enrolled as community school students, thus demonstrating the arbitrariness of counting one type of school but not the other to assess primary effect.[25] * * *

Respondents finally claim that we should look to *Committee for Public Ed. & Religious Liberty v. Nyquist*, 413 U.S. 756 (1973) [involving a state

---

24. The fluctuations seen in the Cleveland program are hardly atypical. Experience in Milwaukee, which since 1991 has operated an educational choice program similar to the Ohio program, demonstrates that the mix of participating schools fluctuates significantly from year to year based on a number of factors, one of which is the uncertainty caused by persistent litigation. Since the Wisconsin Supreme Court declared the Milwaukee program constitutional in 1998, several nonreligious private schools have entered the Milwaukee market, and now represent 32% of all participating schools. [There] are currently 34 nonreligious private schools participating in the Milwaukee program, a nearly a five-fold increase from the 7 nonreligious schools that participated when the program began in 1990. * * *

25. Justice Souter and Justice Stevens claim that community schools and magnet schools are separate and distinct from program schools, simply because the program itself does not include community and magnet school options. But none of the dissenting opinions explain how there is any perceptible difference between scholarship schools, community schools, or magnet schools from the perspective of Cleveland parents looking to choose the best educational option for their school-age children.* * *

partial tuition tax credit to parents who sent their children to nonpublic schools; for parents too poor to be liable for income taxes and therefore unable to benefit from a tax credit, the state gave an outright grant of up to fifty percent of tuition] to decide these cases. We disagree for two reasons. First, the program in *Nyquist* was quite different from the program challenged [here.] Although the program was enacted for ostensibly secular purposes, we found that its "function" was "unmistakably to provide desired financial support for nonpublic, sectarian institutions." Its genesis, we said, was that private religious schools faced "increasingly grave fiscal problems." [It] provided tax benefits "unrelated to the amount of money actually expended by any parent on tuition," ensuring a windfall to parents of children in religious schools. It similarly provided tuition reimbursements designed explicitly to "offe[r] an incentive to parents to send their children to sectarian schools." Indeed, the program flatly prohibited the participation of any public school, or parent of any public school enrollee. Ohio's program shares none of these features.

Second, [we] expressly reserved judgment with respect to "a case involving some form of public assistance (e.g., scholarships) made available generally without regard to the sectarian-nonsectarian, or public-nonpublic nature of the institution benefited." That, of course, is the very question now before us, and it has since been answered [in *Mueller*, *Witters*, and *Zobrest*].[26]

The judgment of the Court of Appeals is reversed.

Jᴜsᴛɪᴄᴇ O'Cᴏɴɴᴏʀ, concurring. * * *

These cases are different from prior indirect aid cases in part because a significant portion of the funds appropriated for the voucher program reach religious schools without restrictions on the use of these funds.[c] The share of public resources that reach religious schools is not, however, as significant as respondents suggest. [Even if] all voucher students came from low-income families and that each voucher student used up the entire $2,250 voucher, at most $8.2 million of public funds flowed to religious schools under the voucher program in 1999–2000. Although just over one-half as many students attended community schools as religious private schools on the state fisc, the State spent over $1 million more [on] students in community schools than on students in religious private schools because per-pupil aid to community schools is more than double the per-pupil aid to private schools under the voucher program. Moreover, the amount spent on religious private schools is minor compared to the

---

26. Justice Breyer would raise the invisible specters of "divisiveness" and "religious strife" to find the program unconstitutional [but] the program has ignited no "divisiveness" or "strife" other than this litigation. * * * We quite rightly have rejected the claim that some speculative potential for divisiveness bears on the constitutionality of educational aid programs. *Mitchell*.

[The plurality in *Mitchell* argued that the Court had "recast *Lemon's* entanglement inquiry as simply one criterion relevant to determining a statute's effect."]

c. If at least *some* voucher funds might be used to support "religious indoctrination," would the program fail O'Connor, J.'s burden of proof standard in *Mitchell*. If so, what of *Witters* (and the GI Bill)?

$114.8 million the State spent on students in the Cleveland magnet schools.

Although $8.2 million is no small sum, it pales in comparison to the amount of funds that federal, state, and local governments already provide religious institutions. Religious organizations may qualify for exemptions from the federal corporate income tax, the corporate income tax in many States, and property taxes in all 50 States, and clergy qualify for a federal tax break on income used for housing expenses. In addition, the Federal Government provides [a] tax deduction for charitable contributions to qualified religious groups. Finally, the Federal Government and certain state governments provide tax credits for educational expenses, many of which are spent on education at religious schools.

[The] state property tax exemptions for religious institutions alone amount to very large sums annually. For example, available data suggest [that] Wisconsin's exemption lowers revenues by approximately $122 million. [As] for the Federal Government, the tax deduction for charitable contributions reduces federal tax revenues by nearly $25 billion annually, and it is reported that over 60 percent of household charitable contributions go to religious charities. [Federal] dollars also reach religiously affiliated organizations through public health programs such as Medicare and Medicaid, through educational programs such as the Pell Grant program and the G. I. Bill of Rights, and through child care programs such as the Child Care and Development Block Grant Program. [A] significant portion of the funds appropriated for these programs reach religiously affiliated institutions, typically without restrictions on its subsequent use.[d]

JUSTICE SOUTER, with whom JUSTICE STEVENS, JUSTICE GINSBURG, and JUSTICE BREYER join, dissenting.

[In] the city of Cleveland the overwhelming proportion of large appropriations for voucher money must be spent on religious schools if it is to be spent at all, and will be spent in amounts that cover almost all of tuition. The money will thus pay for eligible students' instruction not only in secular subjects but in religion as well, in schools that can fairly be characterized as founded to teach religious doctrine and to imbue teaching in all subjects with a religious dimension.[2] * * *

---

d. The concurring opinion of Thomas, J.—questioning whether the Establishment Clause should be applied to the states (see his opinion in *Van Orden v. Perry*, Sec. IV infra), and rejecting use of the Fourteenth Amendment "to oppose neutral programs of school choice through the incorporation of the Establishment Clause"—is omitted.

2. See, e.g., App. (Saint Jerome School Parent and Student Handbook 1999–2000, p. 1) ("FAITH must dominate the entire educational process so that the child can make decisions according to Catholic values and choose to lead a Christian life"); id., (Westside Baptist Christian School Parent–Student Handbook, p. 7) ("Christ is the basis of all learning. All subjects will be taught from the Biblical perspective that all truth is God's truth").

[Compare Eugene Volokh, *Equal Treatment Is Not Establishment*, 13 Not.D.J.L.Eth. & Pub.Pol. 341, 346 (1999): "The religious schools do teach a religious value system—just as secular schools teach a secular value system. There's [no] reason why the government is obligated to discriminate against one or the other system, and thus against the parents who choose to teach their children one or the other system. Just as we wouldn't tolerate discrimination against atheistic schools, or

The majority's statements of Establishment Clause doctrine cannot be appreciated without some historical perspective on the Court's announced limitations on government aid to religious education, and its repeated repudiation of limits previously set. My object here [is] to set out the broad doctrinal stages covered in the modern era, and to show that doctrinal bankruptcy has been reached today.

Viewed with the necessary generality, the cases can be categorized in three groups. In the period from 1947 to 1968, the basic principle of no aid to religion through school benefits was unquestioned. Thereafter for some 15 years, the Court termed its efforts as attempts to draw a line against aid that would be divertible to support the religious, as distinct from the secular, activity of an institutional beneficiary. Then, starting in 1983, concern with divertibility was gradually lost in favor of approving aid in amounts unlikely to afford substantial benefits to religious schools, when offered evenhandedly without regard to a recipient's religious character, and when channeled to a religious institution only by the genuinely free choice of some private individual. Now, the three stages are succeeded by a fourth, in which the substantial character of government aid is held to have no constitutional significance, and the espoused criteria of neutrality in offering aid, and private choice in directing it, are shown to be nothing but examples of verbal formalism.

[Souter, J., began with *Everson* and continued with *Board of Educ. v. Allen*, 392 U.S. 236 (1968), upholding a program for lending state approved secular textbooks to all schoolchildren, including those attending church-related schools.] The Court relied [on] the theory that the in-kind aid could only be used for secular educational purposes, and found it relevant that "no funds or books are furnished [directly] to parochial schools, and the financial benefit is to parents and children, not to schools.⁴" * * *

Allen recognized the reality that "religious schools pursue two goals, religious instruction and secular education;" if state aid could be restricted to serve the second, it might be permissible under the Establishment Clause. But in the retrenchment that followed, the Court saw that the two educational functions were so intertwined in religious primary and secondary schools that aid to secular education could not readily be segregated, and the intrusive monitoring required to enforce the line itself raised Establishment Clause concerns about the entanglement of church and state. See *Lemon*. To avoid the entanglement, the Court's focus in the post-*Allen* cases was on the principle of divertibility. [The] greater the risk of diversion to religion (and the monitoring necessary to avoid it), the less

---

discrimination against secular schools, so we shouldn't assume that the Constitution requires discrimination against religious schools."]

4. The Court noted that "the record contains no evidence that any of the private schools . . . previously provided textbooks for their students," and "[t]here is some evidence that at least some of the schools did not." This was a significant distinction: if the parochial schools provided secular textbooks to their students, then the State's provision of the same in their stead might have freed up church resources for allocation to other uses, including, potentially, religious indoctrination.

legitimate the aid scheme was under the no-aid principle. On the one hand, the Court tried to be practical, and when the aid recipients were not so "pervasively sectarian" that their secular and religious functions were inextricably intertwined, the Court generally upheld aid earmarked for secular use. See, e.g., *Roemer v. Board of Public Works*, 426 U.S. 736 (1976); *Hunt v. McNair*, 413 U.S. 734 (1973); *Tilton v. Richardson,* 403 U.S. 672 (1971).[e] But otherwise the principle of nondivertibility was enforced strictly, with its violation being presumed in most cases, even when state aid seemed secular on its face. Compare, e.g., *Levitt v. Committee for Public Ed. & Religious Liberty*, 413 U.S. 472 (1973) (striking down state program reimbursing private schools' administrative costs for teacher-prepared tests in compulsory secular subjects), with *Wolman* (upholding similar program using standardized tests [and] permitting state aid for diagnostic speech, hearing, and psychological testing).

The fact that the Court's suspicion of divertibility reflected a concern with the substance of the no-aid principle is apparent in its rejection of stratagems invented to dodge it. [The] *Nyquist* Court dismissed warranties of a "statistical guarantee," that the scheme provided at most 15% of the total cost of an education at a religious school which could presumably be matched to a secular 15% of a child's education at the school. And it rejected the idea that the path of state aid to religious schools might be dispositive: "far from providing a per se immunity from examination of the substance of the State's program, the fact that aid is disbursed to parents rather than to the schools is only one among many factors to be considered." The point was that "the effect of the aid is unmistakably to provide desired financial support for nonpublic, sectarian institutions." [The Court's object] had always been a realistic assessment of facts aimed at respecting the principle of no aid. In *Mueller*, however, that object began to fade, for *Mueller* started down the road from realism to formalism.

[If] regular, public schools (which can get no voucher payments) "participate" in a voucher scheme with schools that can, and public expenditure is still predominantly on public schools, then the majority's reasoning would find neutrality in a scheme of vouchers available for private tuition in districts with no secular private schools at all. "Neutrality" as the majority employs the term is, literally, verbal and nothing more. * * *

---

e. These cases all involved higher education. *Tilton* and *Roemer* upheld direct government grants to church-related colleges and universities as part of general programs for construction of buildings and other activities not involving sectarian activities. *Tilton* noted: "The 'affirmative, if not dominant, policy' of the instruction in pre-college church-schools is 'to assure future adherents to a particular faith by having control of their total education at an early age.' There is substance to the contention that college students are less impressionable and less susceptible to religious indoctrination. [Further], by their very nature, college and postgraduate courses tend to limit the opportunities for sectarian influence by virtue of their own internal disciplines. Many church-related colleges and universities are characterized by a high degree of academic freedom and seek to evoke free and critical responses from their students." For detailed criticism of the Court's distinction of higher education from elementary and secondary schools, see Mark Strasser, *Death by a Thousand Cuts: The Illusory Safeguards Against Funding Pervasively Sectarian Institutions of Higher Learning,* 56 Buff. L. Rev. 353 (2008).

The majority addresses the issue of choice the same way it addresses neutrality, by asking whether recipients or potential recipients of voucher aid have a choice of public schools among secular alternatives to religious schools. [But this] ignores the whole point of the choice test: it is a criterion for deciding whether indirect aid to a religious school is legitimate because it passes through private hands that can spend or use the aid in a secular school. [The] majority now has transformed this question about private choice in channeling aid into a question about selecting from examples of state spending (on education) including direct spending on magnet and community public schools that goes through no private hands and could never reach a religious school under any circumstance. [And] because it is unlikely that any participating private religious school will enroll more pupils than the generally available public system, it will be easy to generate numbers suggesting that aid to religion is not the significant intent or effect of the voucher scheme.* * *

If, contrary to the majority, we ask the right question about genuine choice to use the vouchers, the answer shows that something is influencing choices in a way that aims the money in a religious direction: * * * 96.6% of all voucher recipients go to religious schools, only 3.4% to nonreligious [ones.] One answer to these statistics, for example, which would be consistent with the genuine choice claimed to be operating, might be that 96.6% of families choosing to avail themselves of vouchers choose to educate their children in schools of their own religion. This would not, in my view, render the scheme constitutional, but it would speak to the majority's choice criterion. Evidence shows, however, that almost two out of three families using vouchers to send their children to religious schools did not embrace the religion of those schools. The families made it clear they had not chosen the schools because they wished their children to be proselytized in a religion not their own, or in any religion, but because of educational opportunity.

Even so, [that] some 2,270 students chose to apply their vouchers to schools of other religions might be consistent with true choice if the students "chose" their religious schools over a wide array of private nonreligious options, or if it could be shown [that] Ohio's program had no effect on educational choices and thus no impermissible effect of advancing religious education. But both possibilities are contrary to fact. First, even if all existing nonreligious private schools in Cleveland were willing to accept large numbers of voucher students, only a few more than the 129 currently enrolled in such schools would be able to attend, as the total enrollment at all nonreligious private schools in Cleveland for kindergarten through eighth grade is only 510 children, and there is no indication that these schools have many open seats.[13] Second, the $2,500 cap that the program places on tuition for participating low-income pupils has the

---

13. Justice O'Connor points out that "there is no record evidence that any voucher-eligible student was turned away from a nonreligious private school in the voucher program." But there is equally no evidence to support her assertion that "many parents with vouchers selected nonreligious private schools over religious alternatives," and in fact the evidence is to the contrary, as only 129 students used vouchers at private nonreligious schools.

effect of curtailing the participation of nonreligious schools: "nonreligious schools with higher tuition (about $4,000) stated that they could afford to accommodate just a few voucher students."[14] By comparison, the average tuition at participating Catholic schools in Cleveland in 1999–2000 was $1,592, almost $1,000 below the cap.

Of course, the obvious fix would be to increase the value of vouchers so that existing nonreligious private and non-Catholic religious schools would be able to enroll more voucher students, and to provide incentives for educators to create new such schools given that few presently exist. [But] it is simply unrealistic to presume that parents of elementary and middle schoolchildren in Cleveland will have a range of secular and religious choices even arguably comparable to the statewide program for vocational and higher education in *Witters*. And to get to that hypothetical point would require that such massive financial support be made available to religion as to disserve every objective of the Establishment Clause even more than the present scheme does.

[And] contrary to the majority's assertion, public schools in adjacent districts hardly have a financial incentive to participate in the Ohio voucher program, and none has.[17] [It] is entirely irrelevant that the State did not deliberately design the network of private schools for the sake of channeling money into religious institutions. The criterion is one of genuinely free choice on the part of the private individuals who choose, and a Hobson's choice is not a choice, whatever the reason for being Hobsonian. * * *

The scale of the aid to religious schools approved today is unprecedented, both in the number of dollars and in the proportion of systemic school expenditure supported. Each measure has received attention in previous cases. [In] paying for practically the full amount of tuition for thousands of qualifying students, the scholarships purchase everything that tuition purchases, be it instruction in math or indoctrination in faith. [T]he majority makes no pretense that substantial amounts of tax money are not systematically underwriting religious practice and indoctrination.

It is virtually superfluous to point out that every objective underlying the prohibition of religious establishment is betrayed by this scheme, but something has to be said about the enormity of the violation. [The first objective is] respect for freedom of conscience. Jefferson described it as the

---

14. Of the 10 nonreligious private schools that "participate" in the Cleveland voucher program, 3 currently enroll no voucher students. And of the remaining seven schools, one enrolls over half of the 129 students [while] only two others enroll more than 8 voucher students. Such schools can charge full tuition to students whose families do not qualify as "low income," but unless the number of vouchers are drastically increased, it is unlikely that these students will constitute a large fraction of voucher recipients, as the program gives preference in the allocation of vouchers to low-income children.

17. As the Court points out, an out-of-district public school that participates will receive a $2,250 voucher for each Cleveland student on top of its normal state funding. The basic state funding, though, is a drop in the bucket as compared to the cost of educating that student, as much of the cost (at least in relatively affluent areas with presumptively better academic standards) is paid by local income and property taxes. * * *

idea that no one "shall be compelled [to] support any religious worship, place, or ministry whatsoever."

As for the second objective, to save religion from its own corruption, [t]he risk is already being realized. In Ohio, for example, a condition of receiving government money under the program is that [the] school may not give admission preferences to children who are members of the patron faith. [In addition], a participating religious school may well be forbidden to choose a member of its own clergy to serve as teacher or principal over a layperson of a different religion claiming equal qualification for the job. Indeed, a separate condition that "[t]he school [not] teach hatred of any person or group on the basis [of] religion," could be understood (or subsequently broadened) to prohibit religions from teaching traditionally legitimate articles of faith as to the error, sinfulness, or ignorance of [others].

For perspective on this foot-in-the-door of religious regulation, it is well to remember that the money has barely begun to flow. [T]here is no question that religious schools in Ohio are on the way to becoming bigger businesses with budgets enhanced to fit their new stream of tax-raised income. See, e.g., People for the American Way Foundation, A Painful Price 5, 9, 11 (Feb. 14, 2002) (of 91 schools participating in the Milwaukee program, 75 received voucher payments in excess of tuition, 61 of those were religious and averaged $185,000 worth of overpayment per school, justified in part to "raise low salaries"). [A] move in the Ohio State Senate [would] raise the current maximum value of a school voucher from $2,250 to the base amount of current state spending on each public school student ($4,814 for the 2001 fiscal year). Ohio, in fact, is merely replicating the experience in Wisconsin, where a similar increase in the value of educational vouchers in Milwaukee has induced the creation of some 23 new private schools, some of which, we may safely surmise, are religious. New schools have presumably pegged their financial prospects to the government from the start, and the odds are that increases in government aid will bring the threshold voucher amount closer to the tuition at even more expensive religious schools. * * *[f]

Justice Breyer, with whom Justice Stevens and Justice Souter join, dissenting.

[T]he Court's 20th century Establishment Clause cases—both those limiting the practice of religion in public schools and those limiting the public funding of private religious education—focused directly upon social conflict, potentially created when government becomes involved in religious education. [The] Court appreciated the religious diversity of contemporary American society. [It] understood the Establishment Clause to prohibit (among other things) [favoring some religions at the expense of others]. Yet *how* did the Clause achieve that objective? Did it simply

---

f. For brief discussion of dangers to religious liberty from "creeping regulation" and "responsiveness to financial incentives," see Kent Greenawalt, 2 *Religion and the Constitution* 418–19 (2008).

require the government to give each religion an equal chance to introduce religion into the primary schools? [T]he Court concluded that the Establishment Clause required "separation," in part because an "equal opportunity" approach was not workable. With respect to religious activities in the public schools, [i]n many places there were too many religions, too diverse a set of religious practices, too many whose spiritual beliefs denied the virtue of formal religious training. * * *

With respect to government aid to private education, did not history show that efforts to obtain equivalent funding for the private education of children whose parents did not hold popular religious beliefs only exacerbated religious strife? * * * America boasts more than 55 different religious groups and subgroups with a significant number of members. [V]oucher programs finance the religious education of the young. And, if widely adopted, they may well provide billions of dollars that will do so. Why will different religions not become concerned about, and seek to influence, the criteria used to channel this money to religious schools? Why will they not want to examine the implementation of the programs that provide this money—to determine, for example, whether implementation has biased a program toward or against particular sects, or whether recipient religious schools are adequately fulfilling a program's criteria? If so, just how is the State to resolve the resulting controversies without provoking legitimate fears of the kinds of religious favoritism that, in so religiously diverse a Nation, threaten social dissension? * * *

I concede that the Establishment Clause currently permits States to channel various forms of assistance to religious schools, for example, transportation costs for students, computers, and secular texts. [V]oucher programs differ, however, in both *kind* and *degree* from aid programs upheld in the past. They differ in kind because they direct financing to a core function of the church: the teaching of religious truths to young [children]. History suggests, not that such private school teaching of religion is undesirable, but that *government funding* of this kind of religious endeavor is far more contentious than providing funding for secular textbooks, computers, vocational training, or even funding for adults who wish to obtain a college education at a religious university. [H]istory also shows that government involvement in religious primary education is far more divisive than state property tax exemptions for religious institutions or tax deductions for charitable contributions, both of which come far closer to exemplifying the neutrality that distinguishes, for example, fire protection on the one hand from direct monetary assistance on the other. * * *

I do not believe that the "parental choice" aspect of the voucher program sufficiently offsets the concerns I have mentioned. Parental choice cannot help the taxpayer who does not want to finance the religious education of children. It will not always help the parent who may see little real choice between inadequate nonsectarian public education and adequate education at a school whose religious teachings are contrary to his own. It will not satisfy religious minorities unable to participate because they are too few in number to support the creation of their own private schools. It will not satisfy groups whose religious beliefs preclude them from participating in a government-sponsored program, and who may well feel ignored as government funds primarily support the education of children in the doctrines of the dominant religions. And it does little to ameliorate the entanglement problems or the related problems of social division * * *.[g]

NOTES AND QUESTIONS

1. **"Endorsement" and "private choice."** The *Mitchell* plurality explained the "voucher" in *Witter* as "no different from a government issuing a paycheck to one of its employees knowing that the employee would direct the funds to a religious institution." Compare Ira C. Lupu, *The Increasingly Anachronistic Case Against School Vouchers*, 13 Not.D.J.L.Eth. & Pub.Pol. 375, 379–80 (1999): "When the state pays its employees a wage, they can spend the money for any lawful purpose, including for the advancement of religion. In such circumstances, the state cannot be held responsible for any religious benefit arising from the unfettered spending choices of its employees. By contrast, when the state constrains the benefit in certain ways—for example, a state income tax deduction for all charitable contributions—the probability and forseeability of a boost to religion are markedly increased. Contemporary voucher programs tend to constrain yet further, limiting parents to the mix of participating schools, in which sectarian institutions will be heavily represented, at least in the short run." Does this argument survive *Zelman*? Does *Zelman* place any limits on a "neutral" voucher plan? On a program of public funding charter schools that includes religious groups whose school "accommodates religious observance without promoting it, and grounds its teaching in [religious] values and culture without indoctrinating religion"? See Benjamin S. Hillman, Note, *Is There a Place for Religious Charter Schools?*, 118 Yale L. J. 554 (2008).

2. **"Charitable Choice."** After *Zelman*, what result if a state provides vouchers for an important social service that may be used in privately operated programs. What difference does it make if (a) the program is a legal requirement (education), (b) it is an economic necessity (childcare for a single parent who must work in order to obtain welfare), (c) its purpose is to instill personal attitudes and values (drug abuse treatment), (d) there are a large (or small) number of nonreligious providers, (e) government policies affect the mix of religious/nonreligious providers (because of voucher amount), (f) a provider's religious component may be separated from its delivery of the service (schools), (g) recipients can opt out of any religious component (prayer at meals), (h) religious providers have visible symbols of their faith on the premises (summer camp)? See generally Ira C. Lupu & Robert Tuttle, *Sites of Redemption: A Wide–Angle Look at Government Vouchers and Sectarian Service Providers*, 18 J.L. & Pol. 539 (2002). See also David Cole, *Faith and*

---

g. Stevens, J.'s brief separate dissent—stating that "whenever we remove a brick from the wall that was designed to separate religion and government, we increase the risk of religious strife and weaken the foundation of our democracy"—is omitted.

Funding: Toward an Expressivist Model of the Establishment Clause, 75 So.Cal.L.Rev. 559 (2002).

If a voucher program results in the fact that, although there are many elementary schools in the community, the only "good" one is church-related, what constitutional issues arise and how may they be remedied?

3. ***Other approaches.*** Commentators have proposed various "tests" to measure the validity of public aid to church-related schools. In evaluating those that follow, what results would they produce in the decided cases?

(a) Choper, fn. e, Sec. 1 supra, at 265–66: "[G]overnmental financial aid may be extended directly or indirectly to support parochial schools [so] long as such aid does not exceed the value of the secular educational service rendered by the school."[a] Would such aid have "a secular legislative purpose and a primary effect that neither advances nor inhibits religion"? Compare Harold D. Hammett, *The Homogenized Wall*, 53 A.B.A.J. 929, 932–33 (1967): "If the net effect of the financial aid is to increase proportionally the influence of both the church and the state, so that their influence relative to each other remains at the same original ratio, the 'primary' effect on religion has been neutral." Contrast Stephen D. Sugarman, *New Perspectives on "Aid" to Private School Users*, in Nonpublic School Aid 64, 66 (West ed. 1976): "Even if the [effect] principle were limited to cases in which there was (or the legislature knew there would be) a *large* beneficial impact on religion, it would intolerably inhibit secular government action. For example, perhaps building roads and running public transportation on Sunday may be shown to have large beneficial impacts on religion. [For] me the concerns underlying the Establishment Clause could be satisfied with an affirmative answer to this hypothetical question: Would the legislature have acted as it did were there no interdependency with religion involved? If so, then I think it would be fair to say that there is no subsidy of religion, that the religious benefits are constitutionally permitted side effects."[b]

(b) Ira C. Lupu, *To Control Faction and Protect Liberty: A General Theory of the Religion Clauses*, 7 J.Contemp.Leg.Issues 357, 373 (1996): "The worry expressed so widely [about] coercive taxation to support religious teaching is a holdover relic from the Virginia story of coercive assessments earmarked for the support of Christian ministers and teachers. Such an exaction, taking from all to support a few on religious grounds and for religious ends, of course violates the Establishment Clause. [When] the state, however, makes funds available in a religion-neutral way for secular ends ["such as educational attainment, health care, or social services"], those objections quickly become attenuated. Such programs should survive, unless the challenger can persuasively demonstrate that the program (despite facially neutral criteria) is in essence a cover for sectarian discrimination."

---

a. For further analysis, see Michael W. McConnell & Richard Posner, *An Economic Approach to Issues of Religious Freedom*, 56 U.Chi.L.Rev. 1 (1989); Note, *The Supreme Court, Effect Inquiry, and Aid to Parochial Education*, 37 Stan.L.Rev. 219 (1984).

b. Problems under the Free Exercise Clause raised by the exclusion of parochial schools from public aid programs are considered in note 2(c), p. 629 infra.

III. RELIGION AND PUBLIC SCHOOLS

WALLACE v. JAFFREE

472 U.S. 38, 105 S.Ct. 2479, 86 L.Ed.2d 29 (1985).

JUSTICE STEVENS delivered the opinion of the Court.

[In 1978, Alabama enacted § 16–1–20 authorizing a one-minute period of silence in all public schools "for meditation"; in 1981, it enacted § 16–1–20.1 authorizing a period of silence "for meditation or voluntary prayer." Appellees] have not questioned the holding that § 16–1–20 is valid. Thus, the narrow question for decision [concerns § 16–1–20.1].

[T]he Court has unambiguously concluded that the individual freedom of conscience protected by the First Amendment embraces the right to select any religious faith or none at all. This conclusion derives [from] recognition of the fact that the political interest in forestalling intolerance extends beyond intolerance among Christian sects—or even intolerance among "religions"—to encompass intolerance of the disbeliever and the uncertain. * * *

[Under *Lemon*,] even though a statute that is motivated in part by a religious purpose may satisfy the first criterion, the First Amendment requires that a statute must be invalidated if it is entirely motivated by a purpose to advance religion. In applying the purpose test, it is appropriate to ask "whether government's actual purpose is to endorse or disapprove of religion."[42] In this case, the answer to that question is dispositive. * * *

The sponsor of the bill that became § 16–1–20.1, Senator Donald Holmes, inserted into the legislative record—apparently without dissent—a statement indicating that the legislation was an "effort to return voluntary prayer" to the public schools. Later Senator Holmes confirmed this purpose before the District Court. In response to the question whether he had any purpose for the legislation other than returning voluntary prayer to public schools, he stated: "No, I did not have no other purpose in mind."[44] The State did not present evidence of *any* secular purpose. * * *

The legislative intent to return prayer to the public schools is, of course, quite different from merely protecting every student's right to engage in voluntary prayer during an appropriate moment of silence during the schoolday. The 1978 statute already protected that right,

---

42. *Lynch v. Donnelly,* [Sec. IV infra] (O'Connor, J., concurring) ("The purpose prong of the *Lemon* test asks whether government's actual purpose is to endorse or disapprove of religion. The effect prong asks whether, irrespective of government's actual purpose, the practice under review in fact conveys a message of endorsement or disapproval. An affirmative answer to either question should render the challenged practice invalid").

44. [The] evidence presented to the District Court elaborated on the express admission of the Governor of Alabama (then Fob James) that the enactment of § 16–1–20.1 was intended to "clarify [the State's] intent to have prayer as part of the daily classroom activity," and that the "expressed legislative purpose in enacting Section 16–1–20.1 (1981) was to 'return voluntary prayer to public schools.' "

containing nothing that prevented any student from engaging in voluntary prayer during a silent minute of meditation. [The] legislature enacted § 16–1–20.1, despite the existence of § 16–1–20 for the sole purpose of expressing the State's endorsement of prayer activities for one minute at the beginning of each schoolday. The addition of "or voluntary prayer" indicates that the State intended to characterize prayer as a favored practice. Such an endorsement is not consistent with the established principle that the government must pursue a course of complete neutrality toward religion.

The importance of that principle does not permit us to treat this as an inconsequential case involving nothing more than a few words of symbolic speech on behalf of the political majority.[51] For whenever the State itself speaks on a religious subject, one of the questions [is] "whether the government intends to convey a message of endorsement or disapproval of religion." * * *

JUSTICE O'CONNOR concurring in the judgment.

* * * Although a distinct jurisprudence has enveloped each of [the Religion] Clauses, their common purpose is to secure religious liberty. On these principles the Court has been and remains unanimous. [O]ur goal should be "to frame a principle for constitutional adjudication that is not only grounded in the history and language of the first amendment, but one that is also capable of consistent application to the relevant problems." Jesse H. Choper, *Religion in the Public Schools: A Proposed Constitutional Standard,* 47 Minn.L.Rev. 329, 332–333 (1963). Last Term, I proposed a refinement of the *Lemon* test with this goal in mind. *Lynch v. Donnelly* (concurring opinion).

The *Lynch* concurrence suggested that the religious liberty protected by the Establishment Clause is infringed when the government makes adherence to religion relevant to a person's standing in the political community. Direct government action endorsing religion or a particular religious practice is invalid under this approach because it "sends a message to nonadherents that they are outsiders, not full members of the political community, and an accompanying message to adherents that they are insiders, favored members of the political community." [In] this country, church and state must necessarily operate within the same community. Because of this coexistence, it is inevitable that the secular interests of government and the religious interests of various sects and

---

51. As this Court stated in *Engel v. Vitale,* [infra]: "The Establishment Clause, unlike the Free Exercise Clause, does not depend upon any showing of direct governmental compulsion and is violated by the enactment of laws which establish an official religion whether those laws operate directly to coerce nonobserving individuals or not." Moreover, this Court has noted that "[w]hen the power, prestige and financial support of government is placed behind a particular religious belief, the indirect coercive pressure upon religious minorities to conform to the prevailing officially approved religion is plain." Id. This comment has special force in the public-school context where attendance is mandatory. Justice Frankfurter acknowledged this reality in *McCollum v. Board of Education,* [note 1(a) infra] (concurring opinion): "That a child is offered an alternative may reduce the constraint; it does not eliminate the operation of influence by the school in matters sacred to conscience and outside the school's domain. The law of imitation operates, and non-conformity is not an outstanding characteristic of children." * * *

their adherents will frequently intersect, conflict, and combine. A statute that ostensibly promotes a secular interest often has an incidental or even a primary effect of helping or hindering a sectarian belief. Chaos would ensue if every such statute were invalid under the Establishment Clause. For example, the State could not criminalize murder for fear that it would thereby promote the Biblical command against killing.[a] The task for the Court is to sort out those statutes and government practices whose purpose and effect go against the grain of religious liberty protected by the First Amendment.

The endorsement test does not preclude government from acknowledging religion or from taking religion into account in making law and policy. It does preclude government from conveying or attempting to convey a message that religion or a particular religious belief is favored or preferred. Such an endorsement infringes the religious liberty of the nonadherent * * *.

Twenty-five states permit or require public school teachers to have students observe [a] moment of silence at the beginning of the schoolday during which students may meditate, pray, or reflect on the activities of the day. * * * Relying on this Court's decisions disapproving vocal prayer and Bible reading in the public schools, see *School Dist. v. Schempp,* 374 U.S. 203 (1963); *Engel v. Vitale,* 370 U.S. 421 (1962), the courts that have struck down the moment of silence statutes generally conclude that their purpose and effect are to encourage prayer in public schools.

The *Engel* and *Schempp* decisions are not dispositive. [In] *Engel,* a New York statute required teachers to lead their classes in a vocal prayer.[b] The Court concluded that "it is no part of the business of government to compose official prayers for any group of the American people to recite as part of a religious program carried on by the government." In *Schempp,* the Court addressed Pennsylvania and Maryland statutes that authorized morning Bible readings in public schools.[c] The

---

a. On this analysis, *McGowan v. Maryland,* 366 U.S. 420 (1961), per Warren, C.J., upheld Maryland's Sunday Closing Laws. Although "the original laws which dealt with Sunday labor were motivated by religious forces," the Court showed that secular emphases in language and interpretation have come about, that recent "legislation was supported by labor groups and trade associations," and that "secular justifications have been advanced for making Sunday a day of rest, a day when people may recover from the labors of the week just passed and may physically and mentally prepare for the week's work to come. [It] would seem unrealistic for enforcement purposes and perhaps detrimental to the general welfare to require a State to choose a common day of rest other than that which most persons would select of their own accord."

Douglas, J., dissented: "No matter how much is written, no matter what is said," Sunday is a Christian holiday. "There is an 'establishment' of religion [if] any practice of any religious group has the sanction of law behind it."

b. The prayer, composed by the N.Y. Board of Regents, provided: "Almighty God, we acknowledge our dependence upon Thee, and we beg Thy blessings upon us, our parents, our teachers and our country."

c. The reading of the Bible, without comment, was followed by recitation of the Lord's Prayer. In Pennsylvania, various students read passages they selected from any version of the Bible. Plaintiff father testified that "specific religious doctrines purveyed by a literal reading of the Bible" were contrary to the family's Unitarian religious beliefs; one expert testified that "portions of the New Testament were offensive to Jewish tradition" and, if "read without explanation, they could [be] psychologically harmful to the child and had caused a divisive force within the social

Court reviewed the purpose and effect of the statutes, concluded that they required religious exercises, and therefore found them to violate the Establishment Clause. Under all of these statutes, a student who did not share the religious beliefs expressed in the course of the exercise was left with the choice of participating, thereby compromising the nonadherent's beliefs, or withdrawing, thereby calling attention to his or her nonconformity. The decisions acknowledged the coercion implicit under the statutory schemes, see *Engel*,[d] but they expressly turned only on the fact that the government was sponsoring a manifestly religious exercise.[e]

A state-sponsored moment of silence in the public schools is different from state-sponsored vocal prayer or Bible reading. First, a moment of silence [unlike] prayer or Bible reading, need not be associated with a religious exercise. Second, [d]uring a moment of silence, a student who objects to prayer is left to his or her own thoughts, and is not compelled to listen to the prayers or thoughts of others. [It] is difficult to discern a serious threat to religious liberty from a room of silent, thoughtful schoolchildren.

By mandating a moment of silence, a State does not necessarily endorse any activity that might occur during the period. Even if a statute specifies that a student may choose to pray silently during a quiet moment, the State has not thereby encouraged prayer over other specified alternatives. Nonetheless, it is also possible that a moment of silence statute, either as drafted or as actually implemented, could effectively favor the child who prays over the child who does not. For example, the message of endorsement would seem inescapable if the teacher exhorts children to use the designated time to pray. Similarly, the fact of the statute or its legislative history may clearly establish that it seeks to encourage or promote voluntary prayer over other alternatives, rather than merely provide a quiet moment that may be dedicated to prayer by those so inclined. The crucial question is whether the State has conveyed or attempted to convey the message that children should use the moment of silence for prayer.[2] This question cannot be answered in the abstract,

---

media of the school''; a defense expert testified "that the Bible [was] non-sectarian within the Christian faiths."

d. See fn. 51 in the Court's opinion, supra.

e. *Engel* distinguished "the fact that school children and others are officially encouraged to express love for our country by reciting historical documents such as the Declaration of Independence which contain references to the Deity or by singing officially espoused anthems which include the composer's professions of faith in a Supreme Being, or with the fact that there are many manifestations in our public life of belief in God. Such patriotic or ceremonial occasions bear no true resemblance to the unquestioned religious exercise that the State of New York has sponsored in this instance."

2. Appellants argue that *Zorach v. Clauson*, [note 1(b) infra], suggests there is no constitutional infirmity in a State's encouraging a child to pray during a moment of silence. [There] the Court stated that "[w]hen the state encourages religious instruction—*[by] adjusting the schedule of public events to sectarian needs*, it follows the best of our traditions." When the State provides a moment of silence during which prayer may occur at the election of the student, it can be said to be adjusting the schedule of public events to sectarian needs. But when the State also encourages the student to pray during a moment of silence, it converts an otherwise inoffensive moment of silence into an effort by the majority to use the machinery of the State to encourage the minority to participate in a religious exercise.

but instead requires courts to examine the history, language, and administration of a particular statute to determine whether it operates as an endorsement of religion.

[T]he inquiry into the purpose of the legislature in enacting a moment of silence law should be deferential and limited. In determining whether the government intends a moment of silence statute to convey a message of endorsement or disapproval of religion, a court has no license to psychoanalyze the legislators. If a legislature expresses a plausible secular purpose for a moment of silence statute in either the text or the legislative history, or if the statute disclaims an intent to encourage prayer over alternatives during a moment of silence, then courts should generally defer to that stated intent. It is particularly troublesome to denigrate an expressed secular purpose due to postenactment testimony by particular legislators or by interested persons who witnessed the drafting of the statute.[f] Even if the text and official history of a statute express no secular purpose, the statute should be held to have an improper purpose only if it is beyond purview that endorsement of religion or a religious belief "was and is the law's reason for existence." *Epperson v. Arkansas,* [note 3(b) infra]. Since there is arguably a secular pedagogical value to a moment of silence in public schools, courts should find an improper purpose behind such a statute only if the statute on its face, in its official legislative history, or in its interpretation by a responsible administrative agency suggests it has the primary purpose of endorsing prayer.

[It is] possible that a legislature will enunciate a sham secular purpose for a statute. I have little doubt that our courts are capable of distinguishing a sham secular purpose from a sincere one, or that the *Lemon* inquiry into the effect of an enactment would help decide those close cases where the validity of an expressed secular purpose is in doubt. [T]he *Lynch* concurrence suggested that the effect of a moment of silence law is not entirely a question of [fact]. The relevant issue is whether an objective observer, acquainted with the text, legislative history, and implementation of the statute, would perceive it as a state endorsement of prayer in public schools. A moment of silence law that is clearly drafted and implemented so as to permit prayer, meditation, and reflection within the prescribed period, without endorsing one alternative over the others, should pass this test.

[M]oment of silence laws in many States should pass Establishment Clause scrutiny because they do not favor the child who chooses to pray during a moment of silence over the child who chooses to meditate or reflect. §16–1–20.1 does not stand on the same footing. However deferentially one examines its text and legislative history, however objectively one views the message attempted to be conveyed to the public, the conclusion is unavoidable that the purpose of the statute is to endorse prayer in public schools.* * *

CHIEF JUSTICE BURGER dissenting.

---

f. For further discussion of this point, see Burger, C.J.'s opinion infra.

* * * Today's decision recalls the observations of Justice Goldberg: "[U]ntutored devotion to the concept of neutrality can lead to invocation or approval of results which partake not simply of that noninterference and noninvolvement with the religious which the Constitution commands, but of a brooding and pervasive dedication to the secular and a passive, or even active, hostility to the religious. Such results are not only not compelled by the Constitution, but, it seems to me, are prohibited by it." *Schempp* (concurring opinion). * * *

Curiously, the opinions do not mention that *all* of the sponsor's statements relied upon—including the statement "inserted" into the Senate Journal—were made *after* the legislature had passed the statute; [there] is not a shred of evidence that the legislature as a whole shared the sponsor's motive or that a majority in either house was even aware of the sponsor's view of the bill when it was [passed.]

Even if an individual legislator's after-the-fact statements could rationally be considered relevant, all of the opinions fail to mention that the sponsor also testified that one of his purposes in drafting [the] moment-of-silence bill was to clear up a widespread misunderstanding that a schoolchild is legally *prohibited* from engaging in silent, individual prayer once he steps inside a public school building. That testimony is at least as important as the statements the Court relies upon, and surely that testimony manifests a permissible purpose. * * *

The several preceding opinions conclude that the principal difference between § 16–1–20.1 and its predecessor statute proves that the sole purpose behind the inclusion of the phrase "or voluntary prayer" in § 16–1–20.1 was to endorse and promote prayer. This reasoning is simply a subtle way of focusing exclusively on the religious component of the statute rather than examining the statute as a whole. Such logic—if it can be called that—would lead the Court to hold, for example, that a state may enact a statute that provides reimbursement for bus transportation to the parents of all schoolchildren, but may not *add* parents of parochial school students to an existing program providing reimbursement for parents of public school students.

* * * Without pressuring those who do not wish to pray, the statute simply creates an opportunity to think, to plan, or to pray if one wishes— as Congress does by providing chaplains and chapels. [If] the government may not accommodate religious needs when it does so in a wholly neutral and noncoercive manner, the "benevolent neutrality" that we have long considered the correct constitutional standard will quickly translate into the "callous indifference" that the Court has consistently held the Establishment Clause does not require. * * *

JUSTICE REHNQUIST, dissenting.

[There] is simply no historical foundation for the proposition that the Framers intended to build the "wall of separation" that was constitutionalized in *Everson*.[g] [And the "purpose and effect" tests] are in no way based on either the language or intent of the drafters. [If] the purpose prong is intended to void those aids to sectarian institutions accompanied by a stated legislative purpose to aid religion, the prong will condemn nothing so long as the legislature utters a secular purpose and says nothing about aiding religion. [I]f the purpose prong is aimed to void all statutes enacted with the intent to aid sectarian institutions, whether stated or not, then most statutes providing any aid, such as textbooks or bus rides for sectarian school children, will fail because one of the purposes behind every statute, whether stated or not, is to aid the target of its largesse. * * *

If a constitutional theory has no basis in the history of the amendment it seeks to interpret, is difficult to apply and yields unprincipled results, I see little use in it. [It] would come as much of a shock to those who drafted the Bill of Rights as it will to a large number of thoughtful Americans today to learn that the Constitution [prohibits] the Alabama Legislature from "endorsing" prayer. George Washington himself, at the request of the very Congress which passed the Bill of Rights, proclaimed a day of "public thanksgiving and prayer, to be observed by acknowledging with grateful hearts the many and signal favors of Almighty God." History must judge whether it was the Father of his Country in 1789, [the] Court today, which has strayed from the meaning of the Establishment Clause. * * *

NOTES AND QUESTIONS

1. ***Released time.*** (a) McCOLLUM v. BOARD OF EDUC., 333 U.S. 203 (1948), per BLACK, J., held that a public school released time program violated the Establishment Clause. Privately employed religious teachers held weekly classes, on public school premises, in their respective religions, for students whose parents signed request cards, while non-attending students pursued secular studies in other parts of the building: "[N]ot only are the state's tax-supported public school buildings used for the dissemination of religious doctrines. The State also affords sectarian groups an invaluable aid in that it helps to provide pupils for their religious classes through use of the state's compulsory public school machinery."[a]

(b) ZORACH v. CLAUSON, 343 U.S. 306 (1952), per DOUGLAS, J., upheld a released time program when the religious classes were held in church buildings: "[This] involves neither religious instruction in public school class-rooms nor the expenditure of public funds. All costs, including the application blanks, are paid by the religious organizations. The case is therefore unlike *McCollum.*

"[The] nullification of this law would have wide and profound effects. A Catholic student applies to his teacher for permission to leave the school

---

g. See also Philip Hamburger, *Separation and Interpretation*, 18 J.L. & Pol. 7, 37 (2002) ("after two centuries, it now is time for an express rejection of this non-constitutional phrase that has distorted and diminished the Constitution's religious liberty").

a. Frankfurter and Jackson, JJ., each filed concurrences. Reed, J., dissented.

during hours on a Holy Day of Obligation to attend a mass. A Jewish student asks his teacher for permission to be excused for Yom Kippur. A Protestant wants the afternoon off for a family baptismal ceremony. In each case the teacher requires parental consent in writing [and] to make sure the student is not a truant, goes further and requires a report from the priest, the rabbi, or the minister. The teacher in other words cooperates in a religious program to the extent of making it possible for her students to participate in it. Whether she does it occasionally for a few students, regularly for one, or pursuant to a systematized program designed to further the religious needs of all the students does not alter the character of the act.

"We are a religious people whose institutions presuppose a Supreme Being. We guarantee the freedom to worship as one chooses. [When] the state encourages religious instruction or cooperates [by] adjusting the schedule of public events to sectarian needs, [it] respects the religious nature of our people and accommodates the public service to their spiritual needs. To hold that it may not would [be] preferring those who believe in no religion over those who do believe. [The] problem, like many problems in constitutional law, is one of degree."

JACKSON, J., dissented: "If public education were taking so much of the pupils' time as to [encroach] upon their religious opportunity, simply shortening everyone's school day would facilitate voluntary and optional attendance at Church classes. But that suggestion is rejected upon the ground that if they are made free many students will not go to the Church. [Here,] schooling is more or less suspended during the 'released time' so the nonreligious attendants will not forge ahead of the churchgoing absentees. But it serves as a temporary jail for a pupil who will not go to Church. It takes more subtlety of mind than I possess to deny that this is governmental constraint in support of religion."[b]

(c) *Cost*. Brennan, J., has distinguished the cases "not [because] of the difference in public expenditures involved. True, the *McCollum* program involved the regular use of school facilities, classrooms, heat and light and time from the regular school day—even though the actual incremental cost may have been negligible. [But the] deeper difference was that the *McCollum* program placed the religious instructor in the public school classroom in precisely the position of authority held by the regular teachers of secular subjects, while the *Zorach* program did not. [This] brought government and religion into that proximity which the Establishment Clause forbids." *Schempp* (concurring opinion).

(d) *Coercion. Zorach* found "no evidence [that] the system involves the use of coercion to get public school students into religious classrooms. [If] it were established that any one or more teachers were using their office to persuade or force students to take the religious instruction, a wholly different case would be presented.[7]" Would the *Zorach* plan be inherently coercive, and

---

b. Black and Frankfurter, JJ., also filed separate dissents.

For a description of the interaction of the justices in fashioning the *Everson, McCollum* and *Zorach* opinions, see Note, *The "Released Time" Cases Revisited: A Study of Group Decisionmaking by the Supreme Court*, 83 Yale L.J. 1202 (1974).

7. [The] only allegation in the complaint that bears on the issue is that the operation of the program "has resulted and inevitably results in the exercise of pressure and coercion upon

therefore unconstitutional, if it were shown that most children found religious instruction more appealing than remaining in the public schools? Even if the alternative for those remaining was secular instruction with academic credit? If so, would it be permissible to excuse children from classes to enable them to attend special religious services of their faith? Would the First Amendment forbid attendance at parochial schools, as an alternative to public schools, on the ground that this was simply one hundred per cent released time?

Under this analysis, would a program of "dismissed time" as described by Jackson, J., in *Zorach* (all children released early permitting those who so wish to attend religious schools) be unconstitutional? Would "dismissed time" be nonetheless invalid if it could be shown that the *purpose* for the early school closing was to facilitate religious education? Or is this merely an accommodation "adjusting the schedule of public events to sectarian needs"?

What of the argument that the *Zorach* program is inherently coercive, and therefore unconstitutional, because, as Frankfurter, J., contended in *McCollum*, "the law of imitation operates" placing "an obvious pressure upon children to attend" religious classes? Under this analysis, what result for excusing students to attend a religious service? For parochial schools? For "dismissed time"? What of Jackson, J.'s assertion in *McCollum* that "it may be doubted whether the Constitution [protects] one from the embarrassment that always attends nonconformity, whether in religion, politics, behavior or dress"?

(e) *Use of public property.* Is the use of public school classrooms for religious education during *non*school hours distinguishable from *McCollum?* Consider Tribe 2d ed., at 1175: "Religious instructors will no longer stand in 'the position of authority held by the regular teachers,' because the activities lie outside the mandatory school day. Although coercion is conceivable, it is not inherent, as it probably is with official school prayer; students who do not want to take part in the religious activities may take part in other activities or leave the campus. [Thus,] the state neither lends power to religion, nor borrows legitimacy from religion. Permitting a religious group to use school facilities during non-school hours, accordingly, conveys no message of endorsement."

2. *School prayer and the relevance of coercion.* (a) Should *Engel* and *Schempp* (and *McCollum*) have been explicitly based on "the coercion implicit under the statutory schemes"? Consider Stewart, J., dissenting in *Schempp:* "[T]he duty laid upon government in connection with religious exercises in the public schools is that of refraining from so structuring the school environment as to put any kind of pressure on a child to participate in those exercises; it is not that of providing an atmosphere in which children are kept scrupulously insulated from any awareness that some of their fellows may want to open the school day with prayer, or of the fact that there exist in our pluralistic society differences of religious belief. [A] law which provided for religious exercises during the school day and which contained no excusal provision would obviously be unconstitutionally coercive. [E]ven under a law containing an excusal provision, if the exercises were held during the school

---

parents and children to secure attendance by the children for religious instruction." But this charge does not even implicate the school authorities. * * *

day, and no equally desirable alternative were provided by the school authorities, the likelihood that children might be under at least some psychological compulsion to participate would be great. [Here,] the record shows no more than a subjective prophecy by a parent of what he thought would happen if a request were made to be excused from participation* * *. I think we must not assume that school boards so lack the qualities of inventiveness and good will as to make impossible the achievement of that goal."

What evidence of coercion does Stewart, J. require? That the objectors first ask to be excused from participation and then show that social pressures were brought to bear on them? Would this force an objector to surrender his rights in order to vindicate them? Or would Stewart, J., accept the testimony of social scientists that the program was coercive? Could this be judicially noticed? Or would he require a showing that these particular objectors were coerced? Were likely to be coerced? If so, is this a desirable approach?

(b) **Establishment vs. free exercise.** If the decisions *should* turn on the element of coercion, would it have been preferable to base them on "the narrower ground of freedom of religion or of conscience, explaining why the considerations advanced in support of the prayer were outweighed by the rights of the objectors, and why under the circumstances the feature of voluntary participation did not sufficiently protect the interests of objectors"? Paul Kauper, *Prayer, Public Schools and the Supreme Court,* 61 Mich.L.Rev. 1031, 1065–66 (1963). Would this analysis permit prayer in an elementary school where every child was willing to participate? In *any* high school? Consider Louis Pollak, *Public Prayers in Public Schools,* 77 Harv.L.Rev. 62, 70 (1963): "[T]o have pitched the decision [on the Free Exercise Clause] would presumably have meant that the prayer programs were constitutionally unobjectionable unless and until challenged, [and] school boards would have been under no discernible legal obligation [to] suspend ongoing prayer programs on their own initiative. [Indeed,] the hypothetical schoolchild plaintiff, whose free exercise rights would thus be enforced, would have to be a child with the gumption not only to disassociate himself from the prayer program but to prefer litigation to the relatively expeditious exit procedure contemplated by the excusal proviso."

3. **Secular purpose.** Several decisions, in addition to *Jaffree,* have invalidated public school practices because their "purpose" has been found to be "religious":

(a) STONE v. GRAHAM, 449 U.S. 39 (1980), per curiam, held that a Kentucky statute—requiring "the posting of a copy of the Ten Commandments, purchased with private contributions, on the wall of each public classroom in the State," with the notation at the bottom that "The secular application of the Ten Commandments is clearly seen in its adoption as the fundamental legal code of Western Civilization and the Common Law of the United States"—had "no secular legislative purpose": "The Ten Commandments is undeniably a sacred text in the Jewish and Christian faiths, and no legislative recitation of a supposed secular purpose can blind us to that [fact]. Posting of religious texts on the wall serves [no] educational function. If [they] are to have any effect at all, it will be to induce the school children to read, meditate upon, perhaps to venerate and obey, the Commandments.

However desirable this might be as a matter of private devotion, it is not a permissible state objective under the Establishment Clause."[a]

(b) EPPERSON v. ARKANSAS, 393 U.S. 97 (1968), per FORTAS, J., held that an "anti-evolution" statute, forbidding public school teachers "to teach the theory or doctrine that mankind ascended or descended from a lower order of animals," violated both religion clauses: "Arkansas' law selects from the body of knowledge a particular segment which it proscribes for the sole reason that it is deemed to conflict with a particular religious doctrine." Citing newspaper advertisements and letters supporting adoption of the statute in 1928, the Court found it "clear that fundamentalist sectarian conviction was and is the law's reason for existence.* * * Arkansas did not seek to excise from the curricula of its schools and universities all discussion of the origin of man."

BLACK, J., concurring on the ground of "vagueness," found the First Amendment questions "troublesome": "Since there is no indication that the literal Biblical doctrine of the origin of man is included in the curriculum of Arkansas schools, does not the removal of the subject of evolution leave the State in a neutral position. [A] state law prohibiting all teaching of human development or biology is constitutionally quite different from a law that compels a teacher to teach as true only one theory of a given doctrine. It would be difficult to make a First Amendment case out of a state law eliminating the subject of higher mathematics, or astronomy, or biology from its curriculum. [T]here is no reason I can imagine why a State is without power to withdraw from its curriculum any subject deemed too emotional and controversial for its public schools."[b]

(c) EDWARDS v. AGUILLARD, 482 U.S. 578 (1987), per BRENNAN, J., held that a Louisiana statute, barring "teaching of the theory of evolution in public schools unless accompanied by instruction in 'creation science,'" had "no clear secular purpose": "True, the Act's stated purpose is to protect academic freedom. [While] the Court is normally deferential to a State's articulation of a secular purpose, it is required that the statement of such purpose be sincere and not a sham. See *Jaffree; Stone; Schempp.* [It] is clear from the legislative history [that] requiring schools to teach creation science with evolution does not advance academic freedom. The Act does not grant teachers a flexibility that they did not already possess to supplement the present science curriculum with the presentation of theories, besides evolution, about the origin of life. [While] requiring that curriculum guides be developed for creation science, the Act says nothing of comparable guides for evolution. [The] Act forbids school boards to discriminate against anyone who 'chooses to be a creation-scientist' or to teach 'creationism,' but fails to protect those who choose to teach evolution or any other non-creation science theory, or who refuse to teach creation science.

---

a. Rehnquist, J., dissented from "the Court's summary rejection of a secular purpose articulated by the legislature and confirmed by the state court." Stewart, J., also dissented. Burger, C.J., and Blackmun, J., dissented from not giving the case plenary consideration. For recent decisions on posting the Ten Commandments in public places other than schools, see Part IV infra.

b. Harlan, J., concurred in the Court's "establishment of religion" rationale. Stewart, J., concurred on the ground of vagueness.

"If the Louisiana legislature's purpose was solely to maximize the comprehensiveness and effectiveness of science instruction, it would have encouraged the teaching of all scientific theories about the origins of humankind. But [the] legislative history documents that the Act's primary purpose was to change the science curriculum of public schools in order to provide persuasive advantage to a particular religious doctrine that rejects the factual basis of evolution in its entirety [and that] embodies the religious belief that a supernatural creator was responsible for the creation of humankind. [T]eaching a variety of scientific theories about the origins of humankind to school children might be validly done with the clear secular intent of enhancing the effectiveness of science instruction. But because the primary purpose of the Creationism Act is to endorse a particular religious doctrine, the Act furthers religion in violation of the Establishment Clause."[a]

SCALIA, J., joined by Rehnquist, C.J., dissented: "Even if I agreed with the questionable premise that legislation can be invalidated under the Establishment Clause on the basis of its motivation alone, without regard to its effects, I would still find no justification for today's decision. [The] Legislature explicitly set forth its secular purpose ('protecting academic freedom') [which] meant: *students'* freedom from *indoctrination*. The legislature wanted to ensure that students would be free to decide for themselves how life began, based upon a fair and balanced presentation of the scientific evidence. [The] legislature did not care *whether* the topic of origins was taught; it simply wished to ensure that *when* the topic was taught, [it] be 'taught as a theory, rather than as proven scientific fact' and that scientific evidence inconsistent with the theory of evolution (viz., 'creation science') be taught as well. [The law] treats the teaching of creation the same way. It does *not* mandate instruction in creation science; *forbids* teachers to present creation science 'as proven scientific fact'; and *bans* the teaching of creation science unless the theory [is] 'discredit[ed] at every turn' with the teaching of evolution. It surpasses understanding how the Court can see in this a purpose 'to restructure the science curriculum to conform with a particular religious viewpoint,' 'to provide a persuasive advantage to a particular religious doctrine,' 'to promote the theory of creation science which embodies a particular religious tenet,' and 'to endorse a particular religious doctrine.'

"[The] Louisiana legislators had been told repeatedly that creation scientists were scorned by most educators and scientists, who themselves had an almost religious faith in evolution. It is hardly surprising, then, that in seeking to achieve a balanced, 'nonindoctrinating' curriculum, the legislators protected from discrimination only those teachers whom they thought were *suffering* from discrimination. [In] light of the unavailability of works on creation science suitable for classroom use (a fact appellees concede) and the existence of ample materials on evolution, it was entirely reasonable for the Legislature to conclude that science teachers attempting to implement the Act would need a curriculum guide on creation science, but not on evolution.
* * *

---

a. Powell, J., joined by O'Connor, J., joined the Court's opinion but wrote separately "to emphasize that nothing in the Court's opinion diminishes the traditionally broad discretion accorded state and local school officials in the selection of the public school curriculum." White, J., concurred only in the judgment.

"It is undoubtedly true that what prompted the Legislature to direct its attention to the misrepresentation of evolution in the schools (rather than the inaccurate presentation of other topics) was its awareness of the tension between evolution and the religious beliefs of many children. But [a] valid secular purpose is not rendered impermissible simply because its pursuit is prompted by concern for religious sensitivities.[b] [I] am astonished by the Court's unprecedented readiness to [disbelieve] the secular purpose set forth in the Act [and to conclude] that it is a sham. [I] can only attribute [this] to an intellectual predisposition [and] an instinctive reaction that any governmentally imposed requirements bearing upon the teaching of evolution must be a manifestation of Christian fundamentalist repression. In this case, however, it seems to me the Court's position is the repressive one. [Perhaps] what the Louisiana Legislature has done is unconstitutional because there *is* no [scientific] evidence, and the scheme they have established will amount to no more than a presentation of the Book of Genesis. But we cannot say that on the evidence before us in this summary judgment context, which includes ample uncontradicted testimony that 'creation science' is a body of scientific knowledge rather than revealed belief.[c] *Infinitely less* can we say (or should we say) that the scientific evidence for evolution is so conclusive that no one could be gullible enough to believe that there is any real scientific evidence to the contrary, so that the legislation's stated purpose must be a lie. Yet that illiberal judgment, that *Scopes*-in-reverse, is ultimately the basis on which the Court's facile rejection of the Louisiana Legislature's purpose must rest. * * *

"[W]hile it is possible to discern the objective 'purpose' of a statute (i.e., the public good at which its provisions appear to be directed),[d] or even the formal motivation for a statute where that is explicitly set forth (as it was, to no avail, here), discerning the subjective motivation of those enacting the statute [is] almost always an impossible task. The number of possible motivations [is] not binary, or indeed even finite. In the present case, for example, a particular legislator need not have voted for the Act either because he wanted to foster religion or because he wanted to improve education. He may have

---

b. See also Scalia, J., joined by Rehnquist, C.J., and Thomas, J., dissenting from denial of certiorari in *Tangipahoa Parish Board of Educ. v. Freiler*, 530 U.S. 1251 (2000), which invalidated, as "not sufficiently neutral," a policy that when "the scientific theory of evolution" is taught, a statement of "disclaimer from endorsement of such theory" shall be made "to inform students of the scientific concept and not intended to influence or dissuade the Biblical version of Creation," and urging students "to exercise critical thinking and gather all information possible and closely examine each alternative."

For further discussion, compare Jay D. Wexler, *Darwin, Design, and Disestablishment: Teaching the Evolution Controversy in Public Schools*, 56 Vand.L.Rev. 751 (2003) with David K. DeWolf, Stephen C. Meyer, and Mark Edward DeForest, *Teaching the Origins Controversy: Science, or Religion, or Speech*, 39 Utah. L. Rev. 29 (2000).

c. "The only evidence in the record [defining] 'creation science' is found in five affidavits filed by appellants. In those affidavits, two scientists, a philosopher, a theologian, and an educator, all of whom claim extensive knowledge of creation science, swear that it is essentially a collection of scientific data supporting the theory that the physical universe and life within it appeared suddenly and have not changed substantially since appearing."

d. See generally Andrew Koppelman, *Secular Purpose*, 88 Va.L.Rev. 87 (2002). Compare Suzanna Dokupil, *"Thou Shalt Not Bear False Witness": "Sham" Secular Purposes in Ten Commandments Displays*, 28 Harv.J.L. & Pub.Pol. 609 (2005) ("secular purpose analysis rarely changes ultimate conclusion"; "focusing solely on observer's perception of overall effect would improve clarity"). Contrast Josh Blackman, *This Lemon Comes as a Lemon: The Lemon Test and the Pursuit of a Statute's Secular Purpose,* 20 Geo. Mason Civ. Rts. L. J. 351 (2010).

thought the bill would provide jobs for his district, or may have wanted to make amends with a faction of his party he had alienated on another vote, or he may have been a close friend of the bill's sponsor, or he may have been repaying a favor he owed the Majority Leader, or he may have hoped the Governor would appreciate his vote and make a fundraising appearance for him, or he may have been pressured to vote for a bill he disliked by a wealthy contributor or by a flood of constituent mail, or he may have been seeking favorable publicity, or he may have been reluctant to hurt the feelings of a loyal staff member who worked on the bill, or he may have been settling an old score with a legislator who opposed the bill, or he may have been mad at his wife who opposed the bill, or he may have been intoxicated and utterly *un*motivated when the vote was called, or he may have accidentally voted 'yes' instead of 'no,' or, of course, he may have had (and very likely did have) a combination of some of the above and many other motivations. To look for *the sole purpose* of even a single legislator is probably to look for something that does not exist."

(d) Is it meaningful to distinguish between *secular* vs. *religious* purposes? Consider Phillip E. Johnson, *Concepts and Compromise in First Amendment Religious Doctrine*, 72 Calif.L.Rev. 817, 827 (1984): "Governments usually act out of secular motives, even when they are directly aiding a particular religious sect. An atheistic ruler might well create an established church because he thinks it a useful way of raising money, or of ensuring that the clergy do not preach seditious doctrines. In democratic societies, elected officials have an excellent secular reason to accommodate (or at least to avoid offending) groups and individuals who are religious, as well as groups and individuals who are not. They wish to be re-elected, and they do not want important groups to feel that the community does not honor their values." Do any (all) of these "purposes" implicate Madison's concern with "employing religion as an engine of civil policy"?

(e) If the "purpose" of government action is found to be "religious," *should* that alone be enough to invalidate it under the Establishment Clause? If so, what result in *Zorach*? For a public school "dismissed time" program implemented to facilitate religious education?[e] Consider Tribe 2d ed., at 1211: "The secular purpose requirement [might] be used to strike down laws whose effects are utterly secular. A legislature might, for example, vote to increase welfare benefits because individual legislators feel religiously compelled to do so. [A] visible religious purpose may independently convey a message of endorsement or exclusion, but such a message, standing alone, should rarely if ever suffice to transform a secular action into an establishment clause violation. A religious message may be conveyed by the legislative debates concerning a bill, but the same result is possible from debates that lead to no legislation; it can hardly be said that the debates themselves establish a religion." Compare Arnold H. Loewy, *Morals Legislation and the Establishment Clause*, 55 Ala.L.Rev. 159, 161, 175 (2003): "[If] the legislature simply

---

e. For use of this test to invalidate the "religiously motivated" Utah firing squad, see Martin R. Gardner, *Illicit Legislative Motivation as a Sufficient Condition for Unconstitutionality Under the Establishment Clause*, 1979 Wash.U.L.Q. 435. For discussion of whether laws whose historical or current basis is a "function of religious morality" violate the Establishment Clause, see Scott C. Idleman, *Religious Premises, Legislative Judgments, and the Establishment Clause*, 12 Corn. J.L. & Pub.Pol. 1 (2002).

condemns the activity because it is immoral"—i.e., "forces all citizens to act in accordance with the religious dictates of some [under] pain of criminal penalty"—"the law should be held to violate the Establishment Clause. [But] if the legislation is predicated [on] morality that serves a secular function, the law should be sustained." Why should the former type law be confined to *criminal* penalties and not to other disadvantages, e.g., government benefits?

See also Jesse H. Choper, *The Religion Clauses of the First Amendment: Reconciling the Conflict,* 41 U.Pitt.L.Rev. 673, 686–87 (1980): "[I]t is only when religious purpose is coupled with threatened impairment of religious freedom that government action should be held to violate the Establishment Clause. [Conceding] that the [*Epperson*] statute had a solely religious purpose, [there] was no evidence that religious beliefs were either coerced, compromised or influenced. That is, it was not shown, nor do I believe that it could be persuasively argued, that the anti-evolution law either (1) induced children of fundamentalist religions to accept the biblical theory of creation, or (2) conditioned other children for conversion to fundamentalism. [Thus, it] should have survived the Establishment Clause challenge." Similarly, "I would find that the creation science law had a religious purpose [to] placate those religious fundamentalists whose beliefs rejected the Darwinian theory of evolution. But [so] long as the theory of creation science is taught in an objective rather than a proselytizing fashion, it does not seem to me to pose a danger to religious liberty [and] should not be held to violate the Establishment Clause." Jesse H. Choper, *Church, State and the Supreme Court: Current Controversy,* 29 Ariz.L.Rev. 551, 557 (1987).

4. ***Purpose, primary effect, and "neutrality."*** (a) BOARD OF EDUC. v. MERGENS, 496 U.S. 226 (1990), interpreted the Equal Access Act, passed by Congress, to apply to public secondary schools that (a) receive federal financial assistance, and (b) give official recognition to noncurriculum related student groups (e.g., chess club and scuba diving club in contrast to Latin club and math club) in such ways as allowing them to meet on school premises during noninstructional time. The Act prohibited these schools from discriminating against student groups "on the basis of the religious, political, philosophical, or other content of the speech at [their] meetings." O'CONNOR, J., joined by Rehnquist, C.J., and White and Blackmun, JJ., held that the Establishment Clause did not forbid Westside High School from including within its thirty recognized student groups a Christian club "to read and discuss the Bible, to have fellowship and to pray together": "In *Widmar v. Vincent,* 454 U.S. 263 (1981), we applied the three-part *Lemon* test to hold that an 'equal access' policy, at the university level, does not violate the Establishment Clause. We concluded that 'an open-forum policy, including nondiscrimination against religious speech, would have a secular purpose,' and would in fact *avoid* entanglement with religion. See id. ("[T]he University would risk greater 'entanglement' by attempting to enforce its exclusion of 'religious worship' and 'religious speech' "). We also found that although incidental benefits accrued to religious groups who used university facilities, this result did not amount to an establishment of religion. First, we stated that a university's forum does not 'confer any imprimatur of state approval on religious sects or practices.' Indeed, the message is one of neutrality rather than endorsement; if a State refused to let religious groups use facilities open

to others, then it would demonstrate not neutrality but hostility toward religion. Second, we noted that '[t]he [University's] provision of benefits to [a] broad spectrum of groups'—both nonreligious and religious speakers—was 'an important index of secular effect.'

"We think the logic of *Widmar* applies [here.] Congress' avowed purpose—to prevent discrimination against religious and other types of speech—is undeniably secular. Even if some legislators were motivated by a conviction that religious speech in particular was valuable and worthy of protection, that alone would not invalidate the Act, because what is relevant is the legislative *purpose* of the statute, not the possibly religious *motives* of the legislators who enacted [it].

"Petitioners' principal contention is that the Act has the primary effect of advancing religion. Specifically, [that] because the student religious meetings are held under school aegis, and because the state's compulsory attendance laws bring the students together (and thereby provide a ready-made audience for student evangelists), an objective observer in the position of a secondary school student will perceive official school support for such religious meetings.

"We disagree. First, [there] is a crucial difference between *government* speech endorsing religion, which the Establishment Clause forbids, and *private* speech endorsing religion, which the Free Speech and Free Exercise Clauses protect. We think that secondary school students are mature enough and are likely to understand that a school does not endorse or support student speech that it merely permits on a nondiscriminatory basis. * * *

"Second, we note that the Act expressly limits participation by school officials at meetings of student religious groups, and that any such meetings must be held during 'noninstructional time.' The Act therefore avoids the problems of 'the students' emulation of teachers as role models' and 'mandatory attendance requirements,' *Aguillard;* see also *McCollum.* To be sure, the possibility of *student* peer pressure remains, but there is little if any risk of official state endorsement or coercion where no formal classroom activities are involved and no school officials actively participate."

KENNEDY, J., joined by Scalia, J., concurred, emphasizing his disagreement with the plurality's "endorsement test" developed further in *Allegheny County v. ACLU,* Sec. IV infra: "I should think it inevitable that a public high school 'endorses' a religious club, in a common-sense use of the term, if the club happens to be one of many activities that the school permits students to choose [in] an extracurricular setting. But no constitutional violation occurs if the school's action is based upon a recognition of the fact that membership in a religious club is one of many permissible ways for a student to further his or her own personal enrichment. The inquiry with respect to coercion must be whether the government imposes pressure upon a student to participate in a religious activity. This inquiry, of course, must be undertaken with sensitivity to the special circumstances that exist in a secondary school where the line between voluntary and coerced participation may be difficult to draw. No such coercion, however, has been shown to exist as a necessary result of this statute, either on its face [or] on the facts of this case."[f]

---

f. Marshall, J., joined by Brennan, J., concurred "to emphasize the steps Westside must take to avoid appearing to endorse the Christian Club's goals."

STEVENS, J., dissented: "[If] a school continues to allow students to participate in such familiar and innocuous activities as a school chess or scuba diving club, it must also allow religious groups to make use of school facilities. [This] comes perilously close to an outright command to allow organized prayer [on] school premises."[g]

(b) GOOD NEWS CLUB v. MILFORD CENTRAL SCHOOL, 533 U.S. 98 (2001), per THOMAS, J., used similar analysis to find no Establishment Clause violation for a public school's permitting a Christian organization to use schoolrooms for weekly after school meetings, which involved religious instruction and worship, when the school allowed such use by other groups for "the moral and character development of children": "Milford attempts to distinguish *Lamb's Chapel* and *Widmar* by emphasizing that Milford's policy involves elementary school children. [This] is unpersuasive.

"First, we have held that 'a significant factor in upholding governmental programs [is] their *neutrality* towards religion.' [Second,] to the extent we consider whether the community would feel coercive pressure to engage in the Club's activities, [b]ecause the children cannot attend without their parents' permission, they cannot be coerced into engaging in the Good News Club's religious activities. [Third, here], where the school facilities are being used for a nonschool function and there is no government sponsorship of the Club's activities, *Lee v. Weisman*, [Part IV infra, involving prayer at graduation exercises,] is inapposite. [Fourth,] even if we were to consider the possible misperceptions by schoolchildren [, the] facts of this case simply do not support Milford's conclusion. [The] meetings were held in a combined high school resource room and middle school special education room, not in an elementary school classroom. The instructors are not schoolteachers. And the children in the group are not all the same age as in the normal classroom setting; their ages range from 6 to 12. In sum, these circumstances simply do not support the theory that small children would perceive endorsement here."

SCALIA, J., concurred to underline his view, expressed in *Lamb's Chapel*, fn. a in *Zelman*, Part II supra, that "perceptions of endorsement [do] not count [when] giving [a private religious group] nondiscriminatory access to school facilities." In contrast, BREYER, J., concurred to emphasize his view that "government's 'neutrality' [is] only one of the considerations relevant to deciding whether a public school's policy violates the Establishment Clause. See, e.g., *Mitchell* (O'Connor, J., concurring). [A] child's perception that the school has endorsed a particular religion or religion in general may also prove critically important. [Today's opinion holds only] that the school was not entitled to summary judgment [and] both parties, if they so desire, should have a fair opportunity to fill the evidentiary gap."[h]

---

g. May elementary or secondary schools permit their facilities to be used for instruction by religious groups if they also permit instruction by outside teachers of art, music, crafts, dance, etc. (cf. *McCollum*)? May they post the Ten Commandments if they also post the symbols of other civic or charitable groups (cf. *Stone*)? See Douglas Laycock, *Equal Access and Moments of Silence: The Equal Status of Religious Speech by Private Speakers*, 81 Nw.U.L.Rev. 1, 33–35 (1986).

The most recent decisions on Religion and Public Schools are considered in Part IV infra.

h. Souter, J., dissented on this ground, because of "the majority's refusal to remand," adding that "there is a good case that Good News's exercises blur the line between public classroom

5. ***Military chaplains.*** In rejecting the argument that prayer exercises in public schools furthered "the majority's right to free exercise of religion," *Schempp* did "not pass upon a situation such as military service, where the Government regulates the temporal and geographic environment of individuals to a point that, unless it permits voluntary religious services to be conducted with the use of government facilities, military personnel would be unable to engage in the practice of their faiths." Might it be that, while free exercise considerations may justify government provision for opportunity to worship, the Establishment Clause nonetheless bars a government subsidized ministry? "Could the governmental interest be satisfied merely by allowing free time for the serviceman to seek non-military worship or by merely giving the religious orders the right to come into the military environment, at their own expense, to provide the opportunity for worship?" M. Albert Figinski, *Military Chaplains—A Constitutionally Permissible Accommodation Between Church and State*, 24 Md.L.Rev. 377, 409 (1964). Or might it be "that the Government need not necessarily provide chapels and chaplains to those of its armed personnel who are *not* cut off from civilian church facilities"? Klaus J. Herrmann, *Some Considerations on the Constitutionality of the United States Military Chaplaincy*, 14 Am.U.L.Rev. 24, 34 (1964). For the view that "the military chaplaincy system should represent the 'poster child' of an Establishment Clause violation," see Steven K. Green, *Reconciling the Irreconcilable: Military Chaplains and the First Amendment*, 110 W. Va. L. Rev. 167, 170 (2007). For fuller consideration of the "conflict" between the Religion Clauses, see Ch. 14 infra.

6. ***Public school secularism.*** *Schempp* emphasized that "it might well be said that one's education is not complete without a study of comparative religion or the history of religion and its relationship to the advancement of civilization. It certainly may be said that the Bible is worthy of study for its literary and historic qualities. Nothing we have said here indicates that such study of the Bible or of religion, when presented objectively as part of a secular program of education, may not be [effected]." Compare Stewart, J., dissenting in *Schempp*: "[A] compulsory state educational system so structures a child's life that if religious exercises are held to be an impermissible activity in schools, [this] is seen, not as the realization of state neutrality, but rather as the establishment of a religion of secularism, or at the least, as government support of the beliefs of those who think that religious exercises should be conducted only in private." Contrast Kent Greenawalt, *Teaching About Religion in the Public Schools*, 18 J.L. & Pol. 329, 337–38 (2002): "[W]hatever tenet one might ascribe to secular humanism, [it] is generally consistent with many (liberal) religious tenets. [The] crucial educational and constitutional question is not whether the schools explicitly teach a religion of secular humanism, but whether they convey messages that [are] antithetical to *many* religious believers and go to the core of their religious faith." May public schools inculcate "fundamental civic and democratic" values? Consider William H. Clune, *The Constitution and Vouchers for Religious Schools: The Demise of Separatism and the Rise of Non-discrimination as Measures of State*

---

instruction and private religious indoctrination, leaving a reasonable elementary school pupil unable to appreciate that the former instruction is the business of the school while the latter evangelism is not." Stevens, J., dissented on free speech grounds.

Neutrality, Working Paper No. 31 of the Earl Warren Legal Institute, Law School, University of California–Berkeley (1999): "The idea of brainwashing in religious schools only makes sense if it is contrasted with a supposed condition of free choice in secular public education. [But principles] of secularism and secular humanism, that the child should be able to choose among ultimate values on the basis of individual rational choice (as that faculty gradually matures) now seems just as much a value position and a value choice by parents and society as the opposite view that certain values have absolute priority and should be strongly socialized into the child's value system. Indeed the idea that individuals should choose values according to 'rational' criteria operates conceptually as the ultimate value position of secular humanism, just as the idea that individuals should choose values on the basis of religious criteria operates as the ultimate value in religious education."[i] If government requires that public employees be of "good moral character," is this a "religious test" for public office?

IV. OFFICIAL ACKNOWLEDGMENT OF RELIGION

ALLEGHENY COUNTY v. ACLU

492 U.S. 573, 109 S.Ct. 3086, 106 L.Ed.2d 472 (1989).

JUSTICE BLACKMUN announced the judgment of the Court and delivered the opinion of the Court with respect to Parts III–A, IV, and V, an opinion with respect to Parts I and II, in which JUSTICE O'CONNOR and JUSTICE STEVENS join, an opinion with respect to Part III–B, in which JUSTICE STEVENS joins, and an opinion with respect to Part VI.

This litigation concerns the constitutionality of two recurring holiday displays located on public property in downtown Pittsburgh. The first is a crèche placed on the Grand Staircase of the Allegheny County Courthouse. The second is a Chanukah menorah placed just outside the City–County Building, next to a Christmas tree and a sign saluting liberty. * * *

I.A. [The] crèche [is] a visual representation of the scene in the manger in Bethlehem shortly after the birth of Jesus, as described in the Gospels of Luke and Matthew. The crèche includes [an] angel bearing a banner that proclaims "Gloria in Excelsis Deo!" A plaque stated it had been donated by the Holy Name Society.

[III.A.] Although "the myriad, subtle ways in which Establishment Clause values can be eroded," are not susceptible to a single verbal formulation, this Court has attempted to encapsulate the essential precepts. [Thus,] in *Everson,* the Court gave this often-repeated summary [stating the second ¶ on p. 531 supra]. In *Lemon,* the Court sought to refine these principles by focusing on three "tests." [In] recent years, we have paid particularly close attention to whether the challenged governmental practice either has the purpose or effect of "endorsing" religion. [See] *Lynch* (O'Connor, J., concurring).

---

i. For a discerning discussion of how teachers might (must) deal with these matters in various courses, see Greenawalt, supra.

B. [In *Lynch*,] we considered whether the city of Pawtucket, R.I., had violated the Establishment Clause by including a crèche in its annual Christmas display, located in a private park within the downtown shopping district.[a] By a 5–4 decision[,] the Court [held] that the inclusion of the crèche did not have the impermissible effect of advancing or promoting religion. [First,] the opinion states that the inclusion of the crèche in the display was "no more an advancement or endorsement of religion" than other "endorsements" this Court has approved in the past—but the opinion offers no discernible measure for distinguishing between permissible and impermissible endorsements. Second, the opinion observes that any benefit the government's display of the crèche gave to religion was no more than "indirect, remote, and incidental"—without saying how or why. * * * Justice O'Connor['s] concurrence [provides] a sound analytical framework for evaluating governmental use of religious symbols.

First and foremost, the concurrence [recognizes] any endorsement of religion as "invalid," because it "sends a message to nonadherents that they are outsiders, not full members of the political community, and an accompanying message to adherents that they are insiders, favored members of the political community."

Second, [it] articulates a method for determining whether the government's use of an object with religious meaning has the effect of endorsing religion[:] the question is "what viewers may fairly understand to be the purpose of the display." That inquiry, of necessity, turns upon the context in which the contested object appears: "a typical museum setting, though not neutralizing the religious content of a religious painting, negates any message of endorsement of that content." * * *

The concurrence applied this mode of analysis to the Pawtucket crèche, seen in the context of that city's holiday celebration as a whole. In addition to the crèche the city's display contained: a Santa Claus House with a live Santa distributing candy, reindeer pulling Santa's sleigh; a live 40–foot Christmas tree strung with lights; statues of carolers in old-fashioned dress; candy-striped poles; a "talking" wishing well; a large banner proclaiming "SEASONS GREETINGS"; a miniature "village" with several houses and a church, and various "cut-out" figures, including those of a clown, a dancing elephant, a robot, and a teddy bear. The concurrence concluded that both because the crèche is "a traditional symbol" of Christmas, a holiday with strong secular elements, and because the crèche was "displayed along with purely secular symbols," the crèche's setting "changes what viewers may fairly understand to be the purpose of the display" and "negates any message of endorsement" of "the Christian beliefs represented by the crèche."

The four *Lynch* dissenters agreed with [O'Connor, J.'s approach but] concluded that the other elements of the Pawtucket display did not negate

a. "[Ten years ago], when [the] crèche was acquired, it cost the City $1365; it now is valued at $200. The erection and dismantling of the crèche costs the City about $20 per year; nominal expenses are incurred in lighting the crèche. No money has been expended on its maintenance for the past 10 years."

the endorsement of Christian faith caused by the presence of the crèche. [Thus,] despite divergence at the bottom line, the five Justices in concurrence and dissent in *Lynch* agreed upon the relevant constitutional principles [which] are sound, and have been adopted by the Court in subsequent cases. [*Grand Rapids.*][b]

IV. We turn first to the county's crèche display. [U]nlike *Lynch*, nothing in the context of the display detracts from the crèche's religious message. [T]he crèche sits on the Grand Staircase, the "main" and "most beautiful part" of the building that is the seat of county government. No viewer could reasonably think that it occupies this location without the support and approval of the government [which] has chosen to celebrate Christmas in a way that has the effect of endorsing a patently Christian message: Glory to God for the birth of Jesus Christ. * * *

V. Justice Kennedy and the three Justices who join him would [uphold] display of the crèche. [The] reasons for deciding otherwise are so far-reaching in their implications that they require a response in some depth:

A. In *Marsh v. Chambers*, 463 U.S. 783 (1983) [upholding the practice of legislative prayer], the Court relied specifically on the fact that Congress authorized legislative prayer at the same time that it produced the Bill of Rights.[c] Justice Kennedy, however, argues that *Marsh* legitimates all "practices with no greater potential for an establishment of religion" than those "accepted traditions dating back to the Founding." Otherwise, the Justice asserts, such practices as our national motto ("In God We Trust") and our Pledge of Allegiance (with the phrase "under God," added in 1954) are in danger of invalidity.

Our previous opinions have considered in dicta the motto and the pledge, characterizing them as consistent with the proposition that government may not communicate an endorsement of religious belief. We need not return to the subject of "ceremonial deism,"[d] because there is an

---

b. For the view that the endorsement theory changed the Establishment Clause, which had been "designed and understood to protect religious liberty," into "a guarantor of equality," and that "equality is being used not to justify the separation of church and state, but to subvert it," see Noah Feldman, *From Liberty to Equality: The Transformation of the Establishment Clause*, 90 Calif.L.Rev. 673, 697, 729 (2002).

c. *Marsh* also pointed, inter alia, to the practice in the colonies (including Virginia after adopting its Declaration of Rights which has been "considered the precursor of both the Free Exercise and Establishment Clauses"), to the opening invocations in federal courts (including the Supreme Court), and in the Continental Congress and First Congress: "[T]he practice of opening sessions with prayer has continued without interruption ever since that early session of Congress. It has also been followed consistently in most of the states." Brennan, Marshall and Stevens, JJ., dissented.

Is it relevant that, subsequently, "Madison acknowledged that he had been quite mistaken in approving—as a member of the House, in 1789—bills for the payment of congressional chaplains"? William W. Van Alstyne, *Trends in the Supreme Court: Mr. Jefferson's Crumbling Wall*, 1984 Duke L.J. 770, 776. See also Christopher C. Lund, *The Congressional Chaplaincies*, 17 Wm. & Mary Bill Rts. J. 1171, 1173–74 (2009): "[T]he history [is] more checkered than *Marsh* seemed to believe. [C]haplaincies have sometimes been the locus of significant religious and political conflict."

d. Brennan, J., joined by Marshall, Blackmun and Stevens, JJ., dissenting in *Lynch* "suggest[ed] that such practices as the designation of 'In God We Trust' as our national motto, or the obvious distinction between crèche displays and references to God in the motto and the pledge. However history may affect the constitutionality of nonsectarian references to religion by the government,[52] history cannot legitimate practices that demonstrate the government's allegiance to a particular sect or creed. [The] history of this Nation, it is perhaps sad to say, contains numerous examples of official acts that endorsed Christianity specifically [but] this heritage of official discrimination against non-Christians has no place in the jurisprudence of the Establishment Clause. * * *

C. Although Justice Kennedy repeatedly accuses the Court of harboring a "latent hostility" or "callous indifference" toward religion, nothing could be further from the truth. [The] government does not discriminate against any citizen on the basis of the citizen's religious faith if the government is secular in its functions and operations. On the contrary, the Constitution mandates that the government remain secular, rather than affiliating itself with religious beliefs or institutions, precisely in order to avoid discriminating among citizens on the basis of their religious faiths. A secular state, it must be remembered, is not the same as an atheistic or antireligious state. A secular state establishes neither atheism nor religion as its official creed. * * *[59]

VI. The display of the Chanukah menorah in front of the City–County Building may well present a closer [issue. The] question for Establishment Clause purposes is whether the combined display of the tree, the sign, and the menorah has the effect of endorsing both Christian and Jewish faiths, or rather simply recognizes that both Christmas and Chanukah are part of the same winter-holiday season, which has attained

---

references to God contained in the Pledge of Allegiance can best be understood [as] a form of 'ceremonial deism,' protected from Establishment Clause scrutiny chiefly because they have lost through rote repetition any significant religious content."

For the view that "secularizing religious practices conveniently preserves the inclusion of symbols and practices that many Americans understand as fundamental to American identity, [but] it also threatens the purity and integrity of both government and religion. In addition, such strained legal justification jeopardizes the historically neutral relationship between religion and the state," see Alexandra D. Furth, *Secular Idolatry and Sacred Traditions: A Critique of the Supreme Court's Secularization Analysis*. 146 U.Pa.L.Rev. 579 (1998). See also Steven B. Epstein, *Rethinking the Constitutionality of Ceremonial Deism*, 96 Colum.L.Rev. 2083 (1996) (extensive review concluding that most forms "violate a core purpose of the Establishment Clause").

52. It is worth noting that just because *Marsh* sustained the validity of legislative prayer, it does not necessarily follow that practices like proclaiming a National Day of Prayer are constitutional. Legislative prayer does not urge citizens to engage in religious practices, and on that basis could well be distinguishable from an exhortation from government to the people that they engage in religious conduct. But, as this practice is not before us, we express no judgment about its constitutionality.

59. In his attempt to legitimate the display of the crèche on the Grand Staircase, Justice Kennedy repeatedly characterizes it as an "accommodation" of religion. But an accommodation of religion, in order to be permitted under the Establishment Clause, must lift "an identifiable burden *on the exercise of religion.*" *Corporation of Presiding Bishop v. Amos*, [Ch. 14 infra]. Prohibiting the display of a crèche at this location [does] not impose a burden on the practice of Christianity (except to the extent some Christian sect seeks to be an officially approved religion), and therefore permitting the display is not an "accommodation" of religion in the conventional sense.

["Accommodation" of religion and the relationship between the Establishment and Free Exercise Clauses is considered in Ch. 14 infra.]

a secular status in our society. Of the two interpretations of this particular display, the latter seems far more plausible* * *.[64]

The Christmas tree, unlike the menorah, is not itself a religious symbol. [The] widely accepted view of the Christmas tree as the preeminent secular symbol of the Christmas holiday season serves to emphasize the secular component of the message communicated by other elements of an accompanying holiday display, including the Chanukah menorah.[66] The tree, moreover, is clearly the predominant element in the city's display. The 45–foot tree occupies the central position [in] the City–County Building; the 18–foot menorah is positioned to one side. Given this configuration, it is much more sensible to interpret the meaning of the menorah in light of the tree, rather than vice versa. * * *

Although the city has used a symbol with religious meaning as its representation of Chanukah, this is not a case in which the city has reasonable alternatives that are less religious in nature. [Where] the government's secular message can be conveyed by two symbols, only one of which carries religious meaning, an observer reasonably might infer from the fact that the government has chosen to use the religious symbol that the government means to promote religious faith. See *Schempp* (Brennan, J., concurring) (Establishment Clause forbids use of religious means to serve secular ends when secular means suffice). But where, as here, no such choice has been made, this inference of endorsement is not present.[68]

The Mayor's sign further diminishes the possibility that the tree and the menorah will be interpreted as a dual endorsement of Christianity and Judaism. The sign states that during the holiday season the city salutes liberty. Moreover, the sign draws upon the theme of light, common to both Chanukah and Christmas as winter festivals, and links that theme with this Nation's legacy of freedom, which allows an American to celebrate the holiday season in whatever way he wishes, religiously or otherwise. [While] an adjudication of the display's effect must take into account the perspective of one who is neither Christian nor Jewish, as well as of those who adhere to either of these religions, the constitutionality of its effect

---

64. [The] conclusion that Pittsburgh's combined Christmas–Chanukah display cannot be interpreted as endorsing Judaism alone does not mean, however, that it is implausible, as a general matter, for a city like Pittsburgh to endorse a minority faith. The display of a menorah alone might well have that effect.

66. Although the Christmas tree represents the secular celebration of Christmas, its very association with Christmas (a holiday with religious dimensions) makes it conceivable that the tree might be seen as representing Christian religion when displayed next to an object associated with Jewish religion. For this reason, I agree with Justice Brennan and Justice Stevens that one must ask whether the tree and the menorah together endorse the *religious* beliefs of Christians and Jews. For the reasons stated in the text, however, I conclude the city's overall display does not have this impermissible effect.

68. In *Lynch*, in contrast, there was no need for Pawtucket to include a crèche in order to convey a secular message about Christmas. (Blackmun, J., dissenting). [In] displaying the menorah next to the tree, the city has demonstrated no preference for the *religious* celebration of the holiday season. This conclusion, however, would be untenable had the city substituted a crèche for its Christmas tree or if the city had failed to substitute for the menorah [a] more secular, representation of Chanukah.

must also be judged according to the standard of a "reasonable observer." When measured against this standard, the menorah need not be excluded from this particular display.

The conclusion [here] does not foreclose the possibility that the display of the menorah might violate either the "purpose" or "entanglement" prong of the *Lemon* analysis. These issues [may] be considered [on] remand. * * *

JUSTICE KENNEDY, with whom THE CHIEF JUSTICE, JUSTICE WHITE, and JUSTICE SCALIA join, concurring in the judgment in part and dissenting in part. * * *

I.   In keeping with the usual fashion of recent years, the majority applies the *Lemon* [test]. Persuasive criticism of *Lemon* has emerged. See *Aguillard* (Scalia, J., dissenting); *Aguilar v. Felton* (O'Connor, J., dissenting); *Jaffree* (Rehnquist, J., dissenting); *Roemer* (White, J., concurring in judgment). Our cases often question its utility in providing concrete answers to Establishment Clause questions, calling it but a "helpful signpos[t]" or "guidelin[e]", to assist our deliberations rather than a comprehensive test. *Mueller;* see *Lynch* ("we have repeatedly emphasized our unwillingness to be confined to any single test or criterion in this sensitive area").[e] Substantial revision of our Establishment Clause doctrine may be in order;[f] but it is unnecessary to undertake that task today, for even the *Lemon* test, when applied with proper sensitivity to our traditions and our caselaw, supports the conclusion that both the crèche and the menorah are permissible displays in the context of the holiday season. * * *

Rather than requiring government to avoid any action that acknowledges or aids religion, the Establishment Clause permits government some latitude in recognizing and accommodating the central role religion plays in our society. *Lynch; Walz.* Any approach less sensitive to our heritage would border on latent hostility toward religion, as it would require

---

e.   In *Marsh*, Brennan, J., joined by Marshall, J. dissenting, noted that "the Court makes no pretense of subjecting Nebraska's practice of legislative prayer to any of the formal 'tests' that have traditionally structured our inquiry under the Establishment Clause": "[I]f any group of law students were asked to apply the principles of *Lemon* to the question of legislative prayer, they would nearly unanimously find the practice to be unconstitutional. [W]e are faced here with the regularized practice of conducting official prayers, on behalf of the entire legislature, as part of the order of business constituting the formal opening of every single session of the legislative term."

f.   Four years later, concurring in *Lamb's Chapel*, Scalia, J., joined by Thomas, J., noted that six "of the currently sitting Justices" have disagreed with *Lemon*—Rehnquist, C.J., and White, O'Connor, and Kennedy, JJ., in addition to themselves: "For my part, I agree with the long list of constitutional scholars who have criticized *Lemon* and bemoaned the strange Establishment Clause geometry of crooked lines and wavering shapes its intermittent use has produced. See, e.g., Jesse H. Choper, *The Establishment Clause and Aid to Parochial Schools—An Update,* 75 Cal.L.Rev. 5 (1987); William P. Marshall, *"We Know It When We See It": The Supreme Court and Establishment,* 59 S.Cal.L.Rev. 495 (1986); Michael W. McConnell, *Accommodation of Religion,* 1985 S.Ct.Rev. 1; Philip B. Kurland, *The Religion Clauses and the Burger Court,* 34 Cath. U.L.Rev. 1 (1984); Robert Cord, *Separation of Church and State* (1982); Jesse H. Choper, *The Religion Clauses of the First Amendment: Reconciling the Conflict,* 41 U.Pitt.L.Rev. 673 (1980). I will decline to apply *Lemon*—whether it validates or invalidates the government action in question—and therefore cannot join the opinion of the Court today."

government in all its multifaceted roles to acknowledge only the secular. [A] categorical approach would install federal courts as jealous guardians of an absolute "wall of separation," sending a clear message of disapproval. In this century, as the modern administrative state expands to touch the lives of its citizens in such diverse ways and redirects their financial choices through programs of its own, it is difficult to maintain the fiction that requiring government to avoid all assistance to religion can in fairness be viewed as serving the goal of neutrality. * * *

The ability of the organized community to recognize and accommodate religion in a society with a pervasive public sector requires diligent observance of the border between accommodation and establishment. Our cases disclose two limiting principles: government may not coerce anyone to support or participate in any religion or its exercise; and it may not, in the guise of avoiding hostility or callous indifference, give direct benefits to religion in such a degree that it in fact "establishes a [state] religion or religious faith, or tends to do so." *Lynch.* These two principles, while distinct, are not unrelated, for it would be difficult indeed to establish a religion without some measure of more or less subtle coercion, be it in the form of taxation to supply the substantial benefits that would sustain a state-established faith, direct compulsion to observance, or governmental exhortation to religiosity that amounts in fact to proselytizing.

[The] freedom to worship as one pleases without government interference or oppression is the great object of both the Establishment and the Free Exercise Clauses. Barring all attempts to aid religion through government coercion goes far toward attainment of this object. [S]ome of our recent cases reject the view that coercion is the sole touchstone of an Establishment Clause violation. See *Engel* (dictum) [see fn. 53 in *Jaffree*]; *Schempp; Nyquist.* That may be true if by "coercion" is meant *direct* coercion in the classic sense of an establishment of religion that the Framers knew. But coercion need not be a direct tax in aid of religion or a test oath. Symbolic recognition or accommodation of religious faith may violate the Clause in an extreme case.[1] I doubt not, for example, that the Clause forbids a city to permit the permanent erection of a large Latin cross on the roof of city hall. This is not because government speech about religion is per se suspect, as the majority would have it, but because such an obtrusive year-round religious display would place the government's weight behind an obvious effort to proselytize on behalf of a particular religion. Speech may coerce in some circumstances, but this does not justify a ban on all government recognition of religion. As Chief Justice Burger wrote for the Court in *Walz:* "[W]e will not tolerate either governmentally established religion or governmental interference with religion. Short of those expressly proscribed governmental acts there is

---

1. [The] prayer invalidated in *Engel* was unquestionably coercive in an indirect manner, as the *Engel* Court itself recognized * * *.

[*Marsh* noted that "here, the individual claiming injury by the practice is an adult, presumably not readily susceptible to 'religious indoctrination,' see *Tilton,* or peer pressure, compare *Schempp* (Brennan, J., concurring)."]

room for play in the joints productive of a benevolent neutrality which will permit religious exercise to exist without sponsorship and without interference." * * * Absent coercion, the risk of infringement of religious liberty by passive or symbolic accommodation is minimal. [In] determining whether there exists an establishment, or a tendency toward one, we refer to the other types of church-state contacts that have existed unchallenged throughout our history, or that have been found permissible in our caselaw [discussing *Lynch* and *Marsh*].

II. These principles are not difficult to apply to the facts of the case before us. [If] government is to participate in its citizens' celebration of a holiday that contains both a secular and a religious component, enforced recognition of only the secular aspect would signify the callous indifference toward religious faith that our cases and traditions do not require; [the] government would be refusing to acknowledge [the] historical reality, that many of its citizens celebrate its religious aspects as well. [The] Religion Clauses do not require government to acknowledge these holidays or their religious component; but our strong tradition of government accommodation and acknowledgment permits government to do so.

There is no suggestion here that the government's power to coerce has been used to further the interests of Christianity or Judaism in any way. No one was compelled to observe or participate in any religious ceremony or activity. Neither the city nor the county contributed significant amounts of tax money to serve the cause of one religious faith. The crèche and the menorah are purely passive symbols of religious holidays. Passersby who disagree with the message conveyed by these displays are free to ignore them, or even to turn their backs, just as they are free to do when they disagree with any other form of government speech.

[Crucial to the decision in *Lynch* was] the simple fact that, when displayed by government during the Christmas season, a crèche presents no realistic danger of moving government down the forbidden road toward an establishment of religion. Whether the crèche be surrounded by poinsettias, talking wishing wells, or carolers, the conclusion remains the same, for the relevant context is not the items in the display itself but the season as a whole. * * *

[III.] Even if *Lynch* did not control, I would not commit this Court to [the] notion that cases arising under the Establishment Clause should be decided by an inquiry into whether a " 'reasonable observer' " may " 'fairly understand' " government action to " 'sen[d] a message to nonadherents that they are outsiders, not full members of the political community.' " [This is a] most unwelcome, addition to our tangled Establishment Clause jurisprudence. * * *

[A.] *Marsh* stands for the proposition, not that specific practices common in 1791 are an exception to the otherwise broad sweep of the Establishment Clause, but rather that the meaning of the Clause is to be determined by reference to historical practices and understandings.[7] Whatever test we choose to apply must permit not only legitimate practices two centuries old but also any other practices with no greater potential for an establishment of religion. [Few] can withstand scrutiny under a faithful application [the endorsement test].

Some examples suffice to make plain my concerns. Since the Founding of our Republic, American Presidents have issued Thanksgiving Proclamations establishing a national day of celebration and prayer. The first such proclamation was issued by President Washington at the request of the First Congress [and] the forthrightly religious nature of these proclamations has not waned with the years. President Franklin D. Roosevelt went so far as to "suggest a nationwide reading of the Holy Scriptures during the period from Thanksgiving Day to Christmas" so that "we may bear more earnest witness to our gratitude to Almighty God." It requires little imagination to conclude that these proclamations would cause non-adherents to feel excluded.* * *.[9]

The Executive has not been the only Branch of our Government to recognize the central role of religion in our society. [T]his Court opens its sessions with the request that "God save the United States and this honorable Court." [The] Legislature has gone much further, not only employing legislative chaplains, but also setting aside a special prayer room in the Capitol for use by Members of the House and Senate. The room is decorated with a large stained glass panel that depicts President Washington kneeling in prayer; around him is etched the first verse of the 16th Psalm: "Preserve me, O God, for in Thee do I put my trust." * * * Congress has directed the President to "set aside and proclaim a suitable day each year [as] a National Day of Prayer, on which the people of the United States may turn to God in prayer and meditation at churches, in groups, and as individuals." [Also] by statute, the Pledge of Allegiance to the Flag describes the United States as "one Nation under God." To be sure, no one is obligated to recite this phrase, see *West Virginia State Bd. of Educ. v. Barnette,* [Ch. 12, I infra] but it borders on sophistry to suggest that the " 'reasonable' " atheist would not feel less than a " 'full membe[r] of the political community' " every time his fellow Americans recited, as part of their expression of patriotism and love for country, a phrase he believed to be false. Likewise, our national motto, "In God we trust," which is prominently engraved in the wall above the Speaker's dias in the Chamber of the House of Representatives and is reproduced on every coin minted and every dollar printed by the Federal Government, must have the same effect.

---

7. [T]he relevant historical practices are those conducted by governmental units which were subject to the constraints of the Establishment Clause. Acts of "official discrimination against non-Christians" perpetrated in the eighteenth and nineteenth centuries by States and municipalities are of course irrelevant to this inquiry, but the practices of past Congresses and Presidents are highly informative.

9. Similarly, our presidential inaugurations have traditionally opened with a request for divine blessing. * * *

If the intent of the Establishment Clause is to protect individuals from mere feelings of exclusion, then legislative prayer cannot escape invalidation. It has been argued that "[these] government acknowledgments of religion serve, in the only ways reasonably possible in our culture, the legitimate secular purposes of solemnizing public occasions, expressing confidence in the future, and encouraging the recognition of what is worthy of appreciation in society." *Lynch* (O'Connor, J., concurring). I fail to see why prayer is the only way to convey these messages; appeals to patriotism, moments of silence, and any number of other approaches would be as effective, were the only purposes at issue the ones described by the *Lynch* concurrence. [No] doubt prayer is "worthy of appreciation," but that is most assuredly not because it is secular. Even accepting the secular-solemnization explanation at face value, moreover, it seems incredible to suggest that the average observer of legislative prayer who either believes in no religion or whose faith rejects the concept of God would not receive the clear message that his faith is out of step with the political norm.[10]

[B.]   If there be such a person as the "reasonable observer," I am quite certain that he or she will take away a salient message from our holding in this case: [the] First Amendment creates classes of religions based on the relative numbers of their adherents. Those religions enjoying the largest following must be consigned to the status of least-favored faiths so as to avoid any possible risk of offending members of minority religions. * * *

[IV.]   The case before us is admittedly a troubling one. It must be conceded that, however neutral the purpose of the city and county, the eager proselytizer may seek to use these symbols for his own ends. The urge to use them to teach or to taunt is always present. It is also true that some devout adherents of Judaism or Christianity may be as offended by the holiday display as are nonbelievers, if not more so. To place these religious symbols in a common hallway or sidewalk, where they may be ignored or even insulted, must be distasteful to many who cherish their meaning. For these reasons, I might have voted against installation [were] I a local legislative official. But [the] principles of the Establishment Clause and our Nation's historic traditions of diversity and pluralism allow communities to make reasonable judgments respecting the accommodation or acknowledgment of holidays with both cultural and religious aspects. No constitutional violation occurs when they do so by displaying a symbol of the holiday's religious origins. * * *

---

10. If the majority's test were to be applied logically, it would lead to the elimination of all nonsecular Christmas caroling in public buildings or, presumably, anywhere on public property. It is difficult to argue that lyrics like "Good Christian men, rejoice," "Joy to the world! the Savior reigns," "This, this is Christ the King," "Christ, by highest heav'n adored," and "Come and behold Him, Born the King of angels," have acquired such a secular nature that nonadherents would not feel "left out" by a government-sponsored or approved program that included these carols. [Like] Thanksgiving Proclamations, the reference to God in the Pledge of Allegiance, and invocations to God in sessions of Congress and of this Court, they constitute practices that the Court will not proscribe, but that the Court's reasoning today does not explain.

JUSTICE O'CONNOR with whom JUSTICE BRENNAN and JUSTICE STEVENS join as to Part II, concurring in part and concurring in the judgment. * * *

II. In his separate opinion, Justice Kennedy asserts that the endorsement test "is flawed in its fundamentals and unworkable in practice." * * *

An Establishment Clause standard that prohibits only "coercive" practices or overt efforts at government proselytization, but fails to take account of the numerous more subtle ways that government can show favoritism to particular beliefs or convey a message of disapproval to others, would [not] adequately protect the religious liberty or respect the religious diversity of the members of our pluralistic political community. Thus, this Court has never relied on coercion alone as the touchstone of Establishment Clause analysis. To require a showing of coercion, even indirect coercion, as an essential element of an Establishment Clause violation would make the Free Exercise Clause a redundancy. [Moreover,] as even Justice Kennedy recognizes, any Establishment Clause test limited to "*direct* coercion" clearly would fail to account for forms of "[s]ymbolic recognition or accommodation of religious faith" that may violate the Establishment Clause.

[To] be sure, the endorsement test depends on a sensitivity to the unique circumstances and context of a particular challenged practice and, like any test that is sensitive to context, it may not always yield results with unanimous agreement at the margins. But that is true of many standards in constitutional law, and even the modified coercion test offered by Justice Kennedy involves judgment and hard choices at the margin. He admits as much by acknowledging that the permanent display of a Latin cross at city hall would violate the Establishment Clause, as would the display of symbols of Christian holidays alone. Would the display of a Latin cross for six months have such an unconstitutional effect, or the display of the symbols of most Christian holidays and one Jewish holiday? Would the Christmas-time display of a crèche inside a courtroom be "coercive" if subpoenaed witnesses had no opportunity to "turn their backs" and walk away? Would displaying a crèche in front of a public school violate the Establishment Clause under Justice Kennedy's test? * * *

Justice Kennedy submits that the endorsement test [would] invalidate many traditional practices. [But] historical acceptance of a practice does not in itself validate that practice under the Establishment Clause if the practice violates the values protected by that Clause, just as historical acceptance of racial or gender based discrimination does not immunize such practices from scrutiny under the 14th Amendment.[g] [On] the

---

g. In contending that "specific historical practice should [not] override [the] clear constitutional imperative," Brennan, J., joined by Marshall, J., dissenting in *Marsh*, noted that "the sort of historical argument made by the Court should be advanced with some hesitation in light of certain other skeletons in the congressional closet. See, e.g., An Act for the Punishment of certain Crimes against the United States (1790) (enacted by the First Congress and requiring that

contrary, the "history and ubiquity" of a practice is relevant because it provides part of the context in which a reasonable observer evaluates whether a challenged governmental practice conveys a message of endorsement of religion. [Thus,] the celebration of Thanksgiving as a public holiday, despite its religious origins, is now generally understood as a celebration of patriotic values rather than particular religious beliefs.[h]
* * *

III.   For reasons which differ somewhat from those set forth in Part VI of Justice Blackmun's opinion, I also conclude [that] Pittsburgh's combined holiday display [does] not have the effect of conveying an endorsement of religion. [But] Justice Blackmun's new rule that an inference of endorsement arises every time government uses a symbol with religious meaning if a "more secular alternative" is available, is too blunt an instrument for Establishment Clause analysis, which depends on sensitivity to the context and circumstances presented by each [case.]

JUSTICE BRENNAN, with whom JUSTICE MARSHALL and JUSTICE STEVENS join, concurring in part and dissenting in part.

* * * I continue to believe that the display of an object that "retains a specifically Christian [or other] religious meaning," is incompatible with the separation of church and state demanded by our Constitution. I therefore agree with the Court that Allegheny County's display of a crèche at the county courthouse signals an endorsement of the Christian faith in violation of the Establishment Clause, and join Parts III–A, IV, and V of the Court's opinion. I cannot agree, however, [with] the decision as to the menorah [which] rests on three premises: the Christmas tree is a secular symbol; Chanukah is a holiday with secular dimensions, symbolized by the menorah; and the government may promote pluralism by sponsoring or condoning displays having strong religious associations on its property. None of these is sound.

[I.]   Even though the tree alone may be deemed predominantly secular, it can hardly be so characterized when placed next to such a forthrightly religious symbol. Consider a poster featuring a star of David, a statue of Buddha, a Christmas tree, a mosque, and a drawing of Krishna. [W]hen found in such company, the tree serves as an unabashedly religious symbol. * * *

---

persons convicted of certain theft offenses 'be publicly whipped, not exceeding thirty-nine stripes'); Act of July 23, 1866 (reaffirming the racial segregation of the public schools in the District of Columbia; enacted exactly one week after Congress proposed Fourteenth Amendment to the States).''

   Brennan, J., concurring in *Schempp,* further observed that "today the Nation is far more heterogeneous religiously, including as it does substantial minorities not only of Catholics and Jews but as well of those who worship according to no version of the Bible and those who worship no God at all. In the face of such profound changes, practices which may have been objectionable to no one in the time of Jefferson and Madison may today be highly offensive to many persons, the deeply devout and the non-believers alike. [Thus], our use of the history of their time must limit itself to broad purposes, not specific practices.''

   h.   Brennan, J.'s dissent in *Lynch* expressed a similar view.

[II.] The menorah is indisputably a religious symbol, used ritually in a celebration that has deep religious significance. That [is] all that need be said. Whatever secular practices the holiday of Chanukah has taken on in its contemporary observance are beside the [point.] Pittsburgh's secularization of an inherently religious symbol [recalls] the effort in *Lynch* to render the crèche a secular symbol. As I said then: "To suggest [that] such a symbol is merely 'traditional' and therefore no different from Santa's house or reindeer is not only offensive to those for whom the crèche has profound significance, but insulting to those who insist for religious or personal reasons that the story of Christ is in no sense a part of 'history' nor an unavoidable element of our national 'heritage.' " * * *

III. Justice Blackmun, in his acceptance of the city's message of "diversity," and, even more so, Justice O'Connor, in her approval of the "message of pluralism and freedom to choose one's own beliefs," appear to believe that, where seasonal displays are concerned, more is better. * * * I know of no principle under the Establishment Clause, however, that permits us to conclude that governmental promotion of religion is acceptable so long as one religion is not favored. We have, on the contrary, interpreted that Clause to require neutrality, not just among religions, but between religion and nonreligion. [The] uncritical acceptance of a message of religious pluralism also ignores the extent to which even that message may offend. Many religious faiths are hostile to each other, and indeed, refuse even to participate in ecumenical services designed to demonstrate the very pluralism Justices Blackmun and O'Connor extol. * * *

JUSTICE STEVENS, with whom JUSTICE BRENNAN and JUSTICE MARSHALL join, concurring in part and dissenting in part. * * *

In my opinion the Establishment Clause should be construed to create a strong presumption against the display of religious symbols on public property. There is always a risk that such symbols will offend nonmembers of the faith being advertised as well as adherents who consider the particular advertisement disrespectful. [Even] though "[p]assersby who disagree with the message conveyed by these displays are free to ignore them, or even turn their backs," displays of this kind inevitably have a greater tendency to emphasize sincere and deeply felt differences among individuals than to achieve an ecumenical goal. The Establishment Clause does not allow public bodies to foment such disagreement.

Application of a strong presumption [will not] "require a relentless extirpation of all contact between government and religion," (Kennedy, J., concurring and dissenting), for it will prohibit a display only when its message, evaluated in the context in which it is presented, is nonsecular. For example, a carving of Moses holding the Ten Commandments, if that is the only adornment on a courtroom wall, conveys an equivocal message, perhaps of respect for Judaism, for religion in general, or for law. The addition of carvings depicting Confucius and Mohammed may honor religion, or particular religions, to an extent that the First Amendment does not tolerate any more than it does "the permanent erection of a large

Latin cross on the roof of city hall." Placement of secular figures such as
Caesar Augustus, William Blackstone, Napoleon Bonaparte, and John
Marshall alongside these three religious leaders, however, signals respect
not for great proselytizers but for great lawgivers. It would be absurd to
exclude such a fitting message from a courtroom,[13] as it would to exclude
religious paintings by Italian Renaissance masters from a public museum.[i]
Far from "border[ing] on latent hostility toward religion," this careful
consideration of context gives due regard to religious and nonreligious
members of our society. * * *

NOTES AND QUESTIONS

1. **Secular purpose.** (a) *Lynch* found that "Pawtucket has *a* secular
purpose for its display": "The City [has] principally taken note of a significant
historical religious event long celebrated in the Western World. [Were] the
test that the government must have 'exclusively secular' objectives, much of
the conduct and legislation this Court has approved in the past would have
been invalidated."

Brennan, J.'s dissent in *Lynch,* reasoned: "When government decides to
recognize Christmas day as a public holiday, it does no more than accommodate the calendar of public activities to the plain fact that many Americans
will expect on that day to spend time visiting with their families, attending
religious services, and perhaps enjoying some respite from preholiday activities. [If] public officials go further and participate in the *secular* celebration of
Christmas—by, for example, decorating public places with such secular images
as wreaths, garlands or Santa Claus figures—they move closer to the limits of
their constitutional power but nevertheless remain within the boundaries set
by the Establishment Clause. But when those officials participate in or appear
to endorse the distinctively religious elements of this otherwise secular event,
they encroach upon First Amendment freedoms. [The] Court seems to assume
that forbidding Pawtucket from displaying a crèche would be tantamount to
forbidding a state college from including the Bible or Milton's *Paradise Lost*
in a course on English literature. But in those cases the religiously-inspired
materials are being considered solely as literature. [In] this case, by contrast,
the crèche plays no comparable secular role. [It] would be another matter if
the crèche were displayed in a museum setting, in the company of other
religiously-inspired artifacts, as an example, among many, of the symbolic
representation of religious myths. In that setting, we would have objective
guarantees that the crèche could not suggest that a particular faith had been
singled out for public favor and recognition."

Does the dissent's approach require that government have "exclusively
secular" objectives? If so, is this inconsistent with the Court's subsequent
opinion in *Jaffree* (joined by all the *Lynch* dissenters) that "a statute that is

---

13. All these leaders, of course, appear in friezes on the walls of our courtroom.

i. As an example of government "reference to our religious heritage," *Lynch* noted that "the
National Gallery in Washington, maintained with Government support [has] long exhibited
masterpieces with religious messages, notably the Last Supper, and paintings depicting the Birth
of Christ, the Crucifixion, and the Resurrection, among many others with explicit Christian
themes and messages."

motivated in part by a religious purpose may satisfy the first [*Lemon*] criterion."

(b) Two cases in 2005 involving the Ten Commandments further considered the issue of secular purpose. *McCreary*, below, was the first since *Allegheny County* to invalidate a public acknowledgment of religion outside the context of the public schools.

McCREARY COUNTY v. ACLU, 545 U.S. 844 (2005), per SOUTER, J. held that posting copies of the Ten Commandments in two Kentucky county courthouses violated the Establishment Clause because of a "predominantly religious purpose": "When government acts with the ostensible and predominant purpose of advancing religion, it violates that central Establishment Clause value of official religious neutrality, [even though] given its generality as a principle, an appeal to neutrality alone cannot possibly lay every issue to rest, or tell us what issues on the margins are substantial enough for constitutional significance * * *.

"Examination of purpose is a staple of statutory interpretation [and] governmental purpose is a key element of a good deal of constitutional doctrine, e.g., *Washington v. Davis*, 426 U.S. 229 (1976) (discriminatory purpose required for Equal Protection violation); *Hunt v. Washington State Apple Advertising Comm'n*, 432 U.S. 333 (1979) (discriminatory purpose relevant to dormant Commerce Clause claim); *Church of Lukumi Babalu Aye, Inc. v. Hialeah*, [Ch. 12, I infra] (discriminatory purpose raises level of scrutiny required by free exercise claim). [S]crutinizing purpose does make practical sense, [where] an understanding of official objective emerges from readily discoverable fact, without any judicial psychoanalysis of a drafter's heart of hearts [, and when "openly available data supported a commonsense conclusion that a religious objective permeated the government's action."] The eyes that look to purpose belong to an 'objective observer,' one who takes account of the traditional external signs that show up in the 'text, legislative history, and implementation of the statute,' or comparable official act. *Santa Fe Ind. School Dist.* [note 3 infra].[a] [A]lthough a legislature's stated reasons will generally get deference, the secular purpose required has to be genuine, not a sham, and not merely secondary to a religious objective.[13]"

The Court's detailed examination of the record showed that the counties first posted only the Ten Commandments. When suit was filed, the counties adopted "resolutions reciting that the Ten Commandments are 'the precedent legal code upon which the civil and criminal codes [of] Kentucky are founded,' and stating several grounds for taking that position," most of which were related to religion. The displays were expanded to include "eight other documents in smaller frames, each either

---

a. For the view favoring "a search for actual purpose" because the "form and function" of the "reasonable observer" are "unprecedently malleable and thus dangerously uncertain," see Kristi L. Bowman, *Seeing Government Purpose Through the Objective Observer's Eyes: The Evolution-Intelligent Design Debates*, 29 Harv. J. L. & Pub. Policy 419 (2006).

13. The dissent nonetheless maintains that the purpose test is satisfied so long as any secular purpose for the government action is apparent. [While] heightened deference to legislatures is appropriate for the review of economic legislation, an approach that credits any valid purpose, no matter how trivial, has not been the way the Court has approached government action that implicates establishment.

having a religious theme or excerpted to highlight a religious element," including the Preamble to the Constitution, the Mayflower Compact, and Presidential Proclamations. After a preliminary injunction was issued, the counties installed another display, "the third within a year," entitled "The Foundations of American Law and Government Display," made up "of nine framed documents of equal size" including the Bill of Rights and a picture of Lady Justice, all [with] statements about their historical and legal significance.

"[T]he Commandments 'are undeniably a sacred text in the Jewish and Christian faiths' [*Stone v. Graham*]. This is not to deny that the Commandments have had influence on civil or secular law; [but where] the text is set out, the insistence of the religious message is hard to avoid in the absence of a context plausibly suggesting a message going beyond an excuse to promote the religious point of view.[b] [W]e do not decide that the Counties' past actions forever taint any effort on their part to deal with the subject matter. [But] a conclusion that centuries-old purposes may no longer be operative says nothing about the relevance of recent evidence of purpose.[c] [Nor] do we have occasion here to hold that a sacred text can never be integrated constitutionally into a governmental display on the subject of law, or American history. * * *

"The dissent, however, puts forward a limitation on the application of the neutrality principle [to] show that the Framers understood the ban on establishment of religion as sufficiently narrow to allow the government to espouse submission to the divine will [and] that government may espouse a tenet of traditional monotheism. [This] apparently means that government should be free to approve the core beliefs of a favored religion over the tenets of others, a view that should trouble anyone who prizes religious liberty. [But] there is also evidence supporting the proposition that the Framers intended the Establishment Clause to require governmental neutrality in matters of religion, including neutrality in statements acknowledging religion."

SCALIA, joined by Rehnquist, C.J., and Thomas, J., and by Kennedy, J., in final two ¶s infra, dissented: "[B]oth historical fact [pointing to actions beginning with President Washington and the First Congress to Congress's unanimous action in 2002 approving "under God" in the Pledge of Allegiance] and current practice ["federal, state and local governments across the Nation" have displayed the Ten Commandments] [contradict] the demonstrably false principle that the government cannot favor religion over irreligion. [T]he principle that the government cannot favor one religion over another [is valid] where public aid or assistance to religion

---

b. As for *Marsh* and *Lynch*, "créches placed with holiday symbols and prayers by legislators do not insistently call for religious action on the part of citizens; the history of posting the Commandments expressed a purpose to urge citizens to act in prescribed ways as a personal response to divine authority."

c. Does the Court's analysis "penalize government actors for good-faith efforts to conform their actions to the Establishment Clause while litigation is in progress"? See Edith B. Clement, *Public displays of Affection ... For God: Religious Monuments After McCreary and Van Orden*, 32 Harv. J. L. & Pub. Pol'y 231, 251 (2009).

[or] where the free exercise of religion is at issue, but it necessarily applies in a more limited sense to public acknowledgment of the Creator. [Nothing] stands behind the Court's assertion that governmental affirmation of the society's belief in God is unconstitutional except the Court's own say-so, citing as support only the unsubstantiated say-so of earlier Courts going back no farther than the mid–20th [century.] Publicly honoring the Ten Commandments cannot be reasonably understood as a government endorsement of a particular religious viewpoint. [We must] recognize that in the context of public acknowledgments of God there are legitimate *competing* interests: On the one hand, the interest of that minority in not feeling 'excluded'; but on the other, the interest of the overwhelming majority of religious believers in being able to give God thanks and supplication *as a people,* and with respect to our national endeavors.[d]

"[T]he legitimacy of a government action with a wholly secular effect [cannot] turn on the *misperception* of an imaginary observer that the government officials behind the action had the intent to advance religion. [The] constitutional problem, the Court says, is with the Counties' *purpose* in erecting the Foundations Displays, not the displays themselves. The Court [adds]: 'One consequence of taking account of the purpose underlying past actions is that the same government action may be constitutional if taken in the first instance and unconstitutional if it has a sectarian heritage.' This inconsistency may be explicable in theory, but I suspect that the 'objective observer' with whom the Court is so concerned will recognize its absurdity in [practice.] Displays erected in silence (and under the direction of good legal advice) are permissible, while those hung after discussion and debate are deemed unconstitutional. Reduction of the Establishment Clause to such minutiae trivializes the Clause's protection against religious establishment; indeed, it may inflame religious passions by making the passing comments of every government official the subject of endless litigation.

"In any event, the Court's conclusion that the Counties exhibited the Foundations Displays with the purpose of promoting religion is doubtful. [If,] as discussed above, the Commandments have a proper place in our civic history, even placing them by themselves can be civically motivated—especially when they are placed [in] a courthouse. [What] Justice Kennedy said of the crèche in *Allegheny County* is equally true of the Counties' original Ten Commandments displays [quoting p. 579 (Part II)]. [They] are assuredly a religious symbol, but they are not so closely associated with a single religious belief that their display can reasonably be understood as preferring one religious sect over another. The Ten Commandments are recognized by Judaism, Christianity, and Islam alike as divinely given. [The] Court may well be correct in identifying the third displays as the fruit of a desire to display the Ten Commandments, but neither our

---

d. For strong criticism of Scalia, J.'s opinion, see Thomas B. Colby, *A Constitutional Hierarchy of Religions? Justice Scalia, the Ten Commandments, and the Future of the Establishment Clause,* 100 Nw. U. L. Rev. 1097 (2006).

cases nor our history support its assertion that such a desire renders the fruit poisonous.''[e]

VAN ORDEN v. PERRY, 545 U.S. 677 (2005), upheld the display of a monument, donated by the Eagles, inscribed with the Ten Commandments on the Texas State Capitol grounds "between the Capitol and the Supreme Court building. [The] 22 acres contain 17 monuments and 21 historical markers commemorating the 'people, ideals, and events that compose Texan identity.'[1] [A]n eagle grasping the American flag, an eye inside of a pyramid, and two small tablets with what appears to be an ancient script are carved above the text of the Ten Commandments. Below the text are two Stars of David and the superimposed Greek letters Chi and Rho, which represent Christ. The bottom of the monument bears the inscription 'PRESENTED TO THE PEOPLE AND YOUTH OF TEXAS BY THE FRATERNAL ORDER OF EAGLES OF TEXAS 1961.' '' Rehnquist, C.J., joined by Scalia, Kennedy, and Thomas, JJ. wrote the plurality opinion: "Our institutions presuppose a Supreme Being, yet these institutions must not press religious observances upon their citizens. Reconciling [these] requires that we neither abdicate our responsibility to maintain a division between church and state nor evince a hostility to religion by disabling the government from in some ways recognizing our religious heritage. * * *

"Whatever may be the fate of the *Lemon* test in the larger scheme of Establishment Clause jurisprudence, we think it not useful in dealing with the sort of passive monument that Texas has erected on its Capitol grounds. Instead, our analysis is driven both by the nature of the monument and by our Nation's history. As we explained in *Lynch,* 'There is an unbroken history of official acknowledgment by all three branches of government of the role of religion in American life from at least 1789.' * * * Recognition of the role of God in our Nation's heritage has also been reflected in our decisions. We have acknowledged, for example, that 'religion has been closely identified with our history and government,' *Schempp,* and that '[t]he history of man is inseparable from the history of religion,' *Engel.* This recognition has led us to hold that the Establishment Clause permits a state legislature to open its daily

---

e. For development of the thesis that "government is not forbidden to act on religious beliefs or to make religious expressions [but] should avoid acting on religion in ways that are unnecessarily or gratuitously narrow or exclusionary," see Steven D. Smith, *Nonestablishment "Under God"? The Nonsectarian Principle,* 50 Vill.L.Rev. 1 (2005). Contrast Frederick M. Gedicks & Roger Hendrix, *Uncivil Religion: Judeo-Christianity and the Ten Commandments,* 110 W. Va. L. Rev. 275, 278, 299 (2007): "Judeo-Christianity excludes too many Americans for it to function as a unifying civil religion" for two reasons: (1) "dramatic increases in unbelievers, practitioners of non-Western religions, and adherents to postmodern spirituality now leave large numbers of Americans outside the boundaries of Judeo-Christianity" and (2) "the sectarianization of Judeo-Christianity by conservative Christians makes it difficult even for some monotheistic believers to see their beliefs reflected in its symbols and practices."

1. The monuments are: Heroes of the Alamo, Hood's Brigade, Confederate Soldiers, Volunteer Fireman, Terry's Texas Rangers, Texas Cowboy, Spanish–American War, Texas National Guard, Ten Commandments, Tribute to Texas School Children, Texas Pioneer Woman, The Boy Scouts' Statue of Liberty Replica, Pearl Harbor Veterans, Korean War Veterans, Soldiers of World War I, Disabled Veterans, and Texas Peace Officers.

sessions with a prayer by a chaplain paid by the State. *Marsh.*[8] Such a practice, we thought, was 'deeply embedded in the history and tradition of this country.' [In] this case we are faced with a display of the Ten Commandments on government property outside the Texas State Capitol. [Such] acknowledgments [are] common throughout America [and] can be seen throughout a visitor's tour of our Nation's Capital. * * *

"Of course, the Ten Commandments are religious. [According] to Judeo–Christian belief, the Ten Commandments were given to Moses by God on Mt. Sinai. But Moses was a lawgiver as well as a religious leader. And the Ten Commandments have an undeniable historical meaning, as the foregoing examples demonstrate. Simply having religious content or promoting a message consistent with a religious doctrine does not run afoul of the Establishment Clause. There are, of course, limits to the display of religious messages or symbols. [*Stone*] stands as an example of the fact that we have 'been particularly vigilant in monitoring compliance with the Establishment Clause in elementary and secondary schools.' [The] placement of the Ten Commandments monument on the Texas State Capitol grounds is a far more passive use of those texts than was the case in *Stone,* where the text confronted elementary school students every day."

SCALIA, J. also concurred briefly: "I would prefer to reach the same result by adopting an Establishment Clause jurisprudence that is in accord with our Nation's past and present practices, and that can be consistently applied. [See] *McCreary* (Scalia, J., dissenting)."

THOMAS, J., also concurred: Attempting "to balance out its willingness to consider almost any acknowledgment of religion an establishment, in other cases Members of this Court have concluded that the term or symbol at issue has no religious meaning by virtue of its ubiquity or rote ceremonial invocation. [Even] when this Court's precedents recognize the religious meaning of symbols or words, that recognition fails to respect fully religious belief or disbelief. [R]ather than trying to suggest meaninglessness where there is meaning, the Chief Justice rightly recognizes that the monument has 'religious significance.' " Preferably, however, the Court should "return to the views of the Framers" and hold that the Establishment Clause does not apply to the states, or even if it does, the Court should "adopt coercion as the touchstone for our Establishment Clause inquiry."

BREYER, J. concurred only in the judgment: "[T]he Establishment Clause does not compel the government to purge from the public sphere all that in any way partakes of the religious. Such absolutism is not only inconsistent with our national traditions, but would also tend to promote the kind of social conflict the Establishment Clause seeks to avoid. Thus, [the] Court has found no single mechanical formula that can accurately draw the constitutional line in every case. [T]ests designed to measure 'neutrality' alone are insufficient, both because it is sometimes difficult to determine when a legal rule is 'neutral,' and because 'untutored devotion to the concept of neutrality can lead to invocation or approval of results which partake not simply of that noninterference and noninvolvement with the religious which the Constitu-

---

8. Indeed, [i]n *Marsh,* the prayers were often explicitly Christian, but the chaplain removed all references to Christ the year after the suit was filed.

tion commands, but of a brooding and pervasive devotion to the secular and a passive, or even active, hostility to the religious.' * * *

"If the relation between government and religion is one of separation, but not of mutual hostility and suspicion, one will inevitably find difficult borderline cases. And in such cases, I see no test-related substitute for the exercise of legal judgment. That judgment is not a personal judgment. Rather, as in all constitutional cases, it must reflect and remain faithful to the underlying purposes of the Clauses, and it must take account of context and consequences measured in light of those purposes. While the Court's prior tests provide useful guideposts—and might well lead to the same result the Court reaches today—no exact formula can dictate a resolution to such fact-intensive cases. [In] certain contexts, a display of the tablets of the Ten Commandments can convey not simply a religious message but also a secular moral message (about proper standards of social conduct). And in certain contexts, a display of the tablets can also convey a historical message (about a historic relation between those standards and the law)—a fact that helps to explain the display of those tablets in dozens of courthouses throughout the Nation, including the Supreme Court of the United States.

"Here [t]he group that donated the monument, the Fraternal Order of Eagles, a private civic (and primarily secular) organization, while interested in the religious aspect of the Ten Commandments, sought to highlight the Commandments' role in shaping civic morality as part of that organization's efforts to combat juvenile delinquency. [The] monument sits in a large park containing 17 monuments and 21 historical markers, all designed to illustrate the 'ideals' of those who settled in Texas and of those who have lived there since that time. The setting does not readily lend itself to meditation or any other religious activity. [T]he context suggests that the State intended the display's moral message—an illustrative message reflecting the historical 'ideals' of Texans—to predominate. [The] 40 years [that] passed in which the presence of this monument, legally speaking, went unchallenged suggest [that] the public visiting the capitol grounds has considered the religious aspect of the tablets' message as part of what is a broader moral and historical message reflective of a cultural heritage. [This] case also differs from *McCreary County*, where the short (and stormy) history of the courthouse Commandments' displays demonstrates the substantially religious objectives of those who mounted them, and the effect of this readily apparent objective upon those who view them. [This] display has stood apparently uncontested for nearly two generations. That experience helps us understand that as a practical matter of *degree* this display is unlikely to prove divisive. And this matter of degree is, I believe, critical in a borderline case such as this one.

"At the same time, to reach a contrary conclusion [would], I fear, lead the law to exhibit a hostility toward religion [that] might well encourage disputes concerning the removal of longstanding depictions of the Ten Commandments from public buildings across the Nation. And it could thereby create the very kind of religiously based divisiveness that the Establishment Clause seeks to avoid."[a]

---

a. For the view that legislative prayers (upheld in *Marsh)* present a more "divisive political issue" than other public acknowledgements of religion (such as Ten Commandments) where

STEVENS, J., joined by Ginsburg, J., dissented: "Viewed on its face, Texas' display has no purported connection to God's role in the formation of Texas or the founding of our Nation; nor does it provide the reasonable observer with any basis to guess that it was erected to honor any individual or organization. The message transmitted by Texas' chosen display is quite plain: This State endorses the divine code of the 'Judeo–Christian' God. [In] my judgment, at the very least, the Establishment Clause has created a strong presumption against the display of religious symbols on public property. [We] have repeatedly reaffirmed that neither a State nor the Federal Government 'can constitutionally pass laws or impose requirements which aid all religions as against non-believers, and neither can aid those religions based on a belief in the existence of God as against those religions founded on different beliefs.' I do not discount the importance of avoiding an overly strict interpretation of [this principle]. This Court has often recognized 'an unbroken history of official acknowledgment [of] the role of religion in American life.' [This] case, however, is not about historic preservation or the mere recognition of religion. [This] Nation's resolute commitment to neutrality with respect to religion is flatly inconsistent with the plurality's wholehearted validation of an official state endorsement of the message that there is one, and only one, God.

"When the Ten Commandments monument was donated to the State of Texas in 1961, it was not for the purpose of commemorating a noteworthy event in Texas history. [B]y disseminating the 'law of God'—directing fidelity to God and proscribing murder, theft, and adultery—the Eagles hope that this divine guidance will help wayward youths conform their behavior and improve their lives. In my judgment, the significant secular by-products that are intended consequences of religious instruction—indeed, of the establishment of most religions—are not the type of 'secular' purposes that justify government promulgation of sacred religious messages. [The] State may admonish its citizens not to lie, cheat or steal, to honor their parents and to respect their neighbors' property; and it may do so by printed words, in television commercials, or on granite monuments in front of its public buildings. Moreover, the State may provide its schoolchildren and adult citizens with educational materials that explain the important role that our forebears' faith in God played. [The] message at issue in this case, however, is fundamentally different from either a bland admonition to observe generally accepted rules of behavior or a general history lesson. [It] cannot be analogized to an appendage to a common article of commerce ('In God we Trust') or an incidental part of a familiar recital ('God save the United States and this honorable Court'). [Attempts] to secularize what is unquestionably a sacred text defy credibility and disserve people of faith.

"Even if [the] message of the monument, despite the inscribed text, fairly could be said to represent the belief system of all Judeo–Christians,[c] it would still run afoul of the Establishment Clause by prescribing a compelled code of

---

"government has virtually no discretion over the religious content," see Christopher C. Lund, *Legislative Prayer and the Secret Costs of Religious Endorsements,* 94 Minn. L. Rev. 972, 1047–48 (2010).

c. "There are many distinctive versions of the Decalogue, ascribed to by different religions and even different denominations within a particular faith; to a pious and learned observer, these differences may be of enormous religious significance. See Lubet, *The Ten Commandments in Alabama,* 15 Constitutional Commentary 471, 474–476 (1998)."

conduct from one God, namely a Judeo–Christian God, that is rejected by prominent polytheistic sects, such as Hinduism, as well as nontheistic religions, such as Buddhism. * * * Critical examination of the Decalogue's prominent display at the seat of Texas government, rather than generic citation to the role of religion in American life, unmistakably reveals on which side of the 'slippery slope,' (Breyer, J., concurring in judgment), this display must fall. * * *

"The speeches and rhetoric characteristic of the founding era [do] not answer the question before us. [W]hen public officials deliver public speeches, we recognize that their words are not exclusively a transmission from *the* government because those oratories have embedded within them the inherently personal views of the speaker as an individual member of the polity. The permanent placement of a textual religious display on state property is different in kind; it amalgamates otherwise discordant individual views into a collective statement of government approval. [T]here is another critical nuance lost in the plurality's portrayal of history. Simply put, many of the Founders who are often cited as authoritative expositors of the Constitution's original meaning understood the Establishment Clause to stand for a *narrower* proposition than the plurality [is] willing to accept. Namely, many of the Framers understood the word 'religion' in the Establishment Clause to encompass only the various sects of Christianity. [Scalia, J.'s] inclusion of Judaism and Islam [in his *McCreary* dissent] is a laudable act of religious tolerance, but it is one that is unmoored from the Constitution's history and text, and moreover one that is patently arbitrary in its inclusion of some, but exclusion of other (e.g., Buddhism), widely practiced non-Christian religions. * * *

"A reading of the First Amendment dependent on [the] purported original meanings [would] eviscerate the heart of the Establishment Clause. [It] would permit States to construct walls of their own choosing—Baptists inside, Mormons out; Jewish Orthodox inside, Jewish Reform out. [As] we have said in the context of statutory interpretation, legislation 'often [goes] beyond the principal evil [at which the statute was aimed] to cover reasonably comparable evils, and it is ultimately the provisions of our laws rather than the principal concerns of our legislators by which we are governed.' In similar fashion, we have construed the Equal Protection Clause [to] prohibit segregated schools, even though those who drafted [the Fourteenth] Amendment evidently thought that separate was not unequal. We have held that the same Amendment prohibits discrimination against individuals on account of their gender, despite the fact that the contemporaries of the Amendment 'doubt[ed] very much whether any action of a State not directed by way of discrimination against the negroes as a class, or on account of their race, will ever be held to come within the purview of this provision,' And we have construed 'evolving standards of decency' to make impermissible practices that were not considered 'cruel and unusual' at the founding. * * *

"The principle that guides my analysis is neutrality.[35] [As] religious pluralism has expanded, so has our acceptance of what constitutes valid belief

---

35. Justice Thomas contends that the Establishment Clause [reaches] only the governmental coercion of individual belief or disbelief. In my view, [that] cannot be the full extent of the

systems. The evil of discriminating today against atheists, "polytheists[,] and believers in unconcerned deities," *McCreary County,* (Scalia, J., dissenting), is in my view a direct descendent of the evil of discriminating among Christian sects. The Establishment Clause thus forbids it and, in turn, forbids Texas from displaying the Ten Commandments monument the plurality so casually affirms."

SOUTER, J., joined by Stevens and Ginsburg, JJ., also dissented:[d] "A governmental display of an obviously religious text cannot be squared with neutrality, except in a setting that plausibly indicates that the statement is not placed in view with a predominant purpose on the part of government either to adopt the religious message or to urge its acceptance by others.[1]

"[A] pedestrian happening upon the monument at issue here needs no training in religious doctrine to realize that the statement of the Commandments, quoting God himself, proclaims that the will of the divine being is the source of obligation to obey the rules, including the facially secular ones. [To] ensure that the religious nature of the monument is clear to even the most casual passerby, the word 'Lord' appears in all capital letters (as does the word 'am'), so that the most eye-catching segment of the quotation is the declaration 'I AM the LORD thy God.' [It] would therefore be difficult to miss the point that the government of Texas is telling everyone who sees the monument to live up to a moral code because God requires it, with both code and conception of God being rightly understood as the inheritances specifically of Jews and Christians. [It] stands in contrast to any number of perfectly constitutional depictions of [the Commandments], the frieze of our own Courtroom providing a good example, where the figure of Moses stands among history's great lawgivers. [N]o one looking at the lines of figures in marble relief is likely to see a religious purpose behind the assemblage or take away a religious message from it. [T]he viewers may just as naturally see the tablets of the Commandments (showing the later ones, forbidding things like killing and theft, but without the divine preface) as background from which the concept of law emerged. [But] 17 monuments with no common appearance, history, or esthetic role scattered over 22 acres is not a museum, and anyone strolling around the lawn would surely take each memorial on its own terms without any dawning sense that some purpose held the miscellany together more coherently than fortuity and the edge of the grass.[6]

---

provision's reach. [Thomas, J.'s] "coercion view," [would] not prohibit explicit state endorsements of religious orthodoxies of particular sects, actions that lie at the heart of what the Clause was meant to regulate. The government could, for example, take out television advertisements lauding Catholicism as the only pure religion. [T]hose programs would not be coercive because the viewer could simply turn off the television or ignore the ad.

Further, [e]nshrining coercion as the Establishment Clause touchstone fails to eliminate the difficult judgment calls regarding "the form that coercion must take." * * *

d. O'Connor, J., dissented, "for essentially the reasons given by Justice Souter."

1. [In this] case, the religious purpose was evident on the part of the donating organization. [I]t was not just the terms of the moral code, but the proclamation that the terms of the code were enjoined by God, that the Eagles put forward in the monuments they donated.

6. [A]lthough the nativity scene in *Allegheny County* was donated by the Holy Name Society, we concluded that "[n]o viewer could reasonably think that [the scene] occupies [its] location [at the seat of county government] without the support and approval of the government."

"To be sure, Kentucky's compulsory-education law [in *Stone*] meant that the schoolchildren were forced to see the display every day, whereas many see the monument by choice, and those who customarily walk the Capitol grounds can presumably avoid it if they choose. But in my judgment [this] distinction should make no difference. The monument in this case sits on the grounds of the Texas State Capitol[,] the civic home of every one of the State's citizens. If neutrality in religion means something, any citizen should be able to visit that civic home without having to confront religious expressions clearly meant to convey an official religious position that may be at odds with his own religion, or with rejection of religion.

"Finally, though this too is a point on which judgment will vary, I do not see a persuasive argument for constitutionality in the plurality's observation that Van Orden's lawsuit comes '[f]orty years after the monument's erection.' [We] have approved framing-era practices because they must originally have been understood as constitutionally permissible, e.g., *Marsh*, and we have recognized that Sunday laws have grown recognizably secular over time, *McGowan*. There is also an analogous argument, not yet evaluated, that ritualistic religious expression can become so numbing over time that its initial Establishment Clause violation becomes at some point too diminished for notice. [But] other explanations may do better in accounting for the late resort to the courts. Suing a State over religion puts nothing in a plaintiff's pocket and can take a great deal out, and even with volunteer litigators to supply time and energy, the risk of social ostracism can be powerfully deterrent."[e]

2. ***Differing interpretations of the "coercion" test.*** (a) LEE v. WEISMAN, 505 U.S. 577 (1992), per KENNEDY, J., held violative of the Establishment Clause the practice of public school officials inviting members of the clergy to offer invocation and benediction prayers at graduation ceremonies: "[The] school district's supervision and control of a high school graduation ceremony places public pressure, as well as peer pressure, on attending students to stand as a group or, at least, maintain respectful silence during the Invocation and Benediction. This pressure, though subtle and indirect, can be as real as any overt compulsion. * * *

"Finding no violation [would] place objectors in the dilemma of participating, with all that implies, or protesting. * * * Research in psychology supports the common assumption that adolescents are often susceptible to pressure from their peers towards conformity, and that the influence is strongest in matters of social convention.[a] [That] the intrusion was in the course of promulgating religion that sought to be civic or nonsectarian rather than pertaining to one sect does not lessen the offense or isolation to the

---

e. See also Alan Brownstein, *A Decent Respect for Religious Liberty and Religious Equality: Justice O'Connor's Interpretation of the Religion Clause of the First Amendment*, 32 McG.L.Rev. 837, 854–55 (2001): "Often minority groups tolerate what they cannot change because they realize it is futile to express opposition or are intimidated from doing so. Majorities, on the other hand, will all too often choose to misinterpret resigned acceptance to unequal treatment as an indication that no real harm is being done and that the system is operating fairly."

a. For criticism of the psychological evidence relied on by the Court, see Donald N. Bersoff & David J. Glass, *The Not–So Weisman: The Supreme Court's Continuing Misuse of Social Science Research*, 2 U.Chi.L.S.Roundtable 279 (1995).

objectors. At best it narrows their number, at worst increases their sense of isolation and affront.

"[I]n our society and in our culture high school graduation is one of life's most significant occasions. * * * Attendance may not be required by official decree, yet it is apparent that a student is not free to absent herself from the graduation exercise in any real sense of the term 'voluntary,' for absence would require forfeiture of these intangible benefits which have motivated the student through youth and all her high school years.[b] [To] say that a student must remain apart from the ceremony at the opening invocation and closing benediction is to risk compelling conformity in an environment analogous to the classroom setting, where we have said the risk of compulsion is especially high. See *Engel* and *Schempp*. [The] atmosphere at the opening of a session of a state legislature [as in *Marsh*] where adults are free to enter and leave with little comment and for any number of reasons cannot compare with the constraining potential of the one school event most important for the student to attend. * * * People may take offense at all manner of religious as well as nonreligious messages, but offense alone does not in every case show a violation. We know too that sometimes to endure social isolation or even anger may be the price of conscience or nonconformity. But, by any reading of our cases, the conformity required of the student in this case was too high an exaction to withstand the test of the Establishment Clause."

BLACKMUN, J., joined by Stevens and O'Connor, JJ., who joined the Court's opinion, concurred: "[I]t is not enough that the government restrain from compelling religious practices: it must not engage in them either. [To] that end, our cases have prohibited government endorsement of religion, its sponsorship, and active involvement in religion, whether or not citizens were coerced to conform."

SOUTER, J., (who also joined the Court's opinion), joined by Stevens and O'Connor, JJ., concurred: "The Framers adopted the Religion Clauses in response to a long tradition of coercive state support for religion, particularly in the form of tax assessments, but their special antipathy to religious coercion did not exhaust their hostility to the features and incidents of establishment. Indeed, Jefferson and Madison opposed any political appropriation of religion, [and] saw that [an] official endorsement of religion can impair religious liberty. [O]ne can call any act of endorsement a form of coercion, but only if one is willing to dilute the meaning of 'coercion' until there is no meaning left. * * *

---

b. Consider Steven G. Gey, *Religious Coercion and the Establishment Clause*, 1994 U.Ill. L.Rev. 463, 503: "But a citizen of Allegheny County may also be compelled to transact business in the county courthouse, which would inevitably require that person to pass by the prominent display of the birth of the Christian savior. If the Allegheny County citizen is not coerced by being required to respectfully pass by the religious display, why is [the] student coerced by respectfully remaining silent during a one-minute prayer? Conversely, if 'the act of standing or remaining silent' during a graduation prayer is 'an expression of participation' in the prayer, why is walking by an overtly Christian display in respectful silence not also 'an expression of participation' in the display?"

To what extent does *Lee* apply to similar practices at public universities? See *Bunting v. Mellen*, 541 U.S. 1019 (2004) (opinions respecting denial of certiorari).

For an intensive dissection of the "coercion" approach, see Mark Strasser, *The Coercion Test: On Prayer, Offense, and Doctrinal Inculcation*, 53 St. Louis U. L. J. 417 (2009).

"Religious students cannot complain that omitting prayers from their graduation ceremony would, in any realistic sense, 'burden' their spiritual callings. To be sure, many of them invest this rite of passage with spiritual significance, but they may express their religious feelings about it before and after the ceremony. They may even organize a privately sponsored baccalaureate if they desire the company of likeminded students. Because they accordingly have no need for the machinery of the State to affirm their beliefs, the government's sponsorship of prayer at the graduation ceremony is most reasonably understood as an official endorsement of religion and, in this instance, of theistic religion."

SCALIA, J., joined by Rehnquist, C.J., and White and Thomas, JJ., dissented: "Three terms ago, I joined an opinion recognizing that 'the meaning of the [Establishment] Clause is to be determined by reference to historical practices and understandings.' * * * *Allegheny County* (Kennedy, J., concurring in judgment in part and dissenting in part). These views of course prevent me from joining today's opinion, which is conspicuously bereft of any reference to history [and] lays waste a tradition that is as old as public-school graduation ceremonies themselves, and that is a component of an even more longstanding American tradition of nonsectarian prayer to God at public celebrations generally.

"[Since] the Court does not dispute that students exposed to prayer at graduation ceremonies retain (despite 'subtle coercive pressures,') the free will to sit, there is absolutely no basis for the Court's decision. It is fanciful enough to say that 'a reasonable dissenter,' standing head erect in a class of bowed heads, 'could believe that the group exercise signified her own participation or approval of it.' It is beyond the absurd to say that she could entertain such a belief while pointedly declining to rise. But let us assume the very worst, that the nonparticipating graduate is 'subtly coerced' * * * to stand! Even that half of the disjunctive does not remotely establish a 'participation' (or an 'appearance of participation') in a religious exercise. * * *

"The deeper flaw in the Court's opinion does not lie in its wrong answer to the question whether there was state-induced 'peer-pressure' coercion; it lies, rather, in the Court's making violation of the Establishment Clause hinge on such a precious question. The coercion that was a hallmark of historical establishments of religion was coercion of religious orthodoxy and of financial support by force of *law and threat of penalty*. [I] concede that our constitutional tradition [has] ruled out of order government-sponsored endorsement of religion—even when no legal coercion is present, and indeed even when no ersatz, 'peer-pressure' psycho-coercion is present—where the endorsement is sectarian, in the sense of specifying details upon which men and women who believe in a benevolent, omnipotent Creator and Ruler of the world, are known to differ (for example, the divinity of Christ). But there is simply no support for the proposition that the officially sponsored nondenominational invocation and benediction read by Rabbi Gutterman—with no one legally coerced to recite them—violated the Constitution of the United States.[c] To

---

c. Compare Gey, supra, at 507: "If dissenting audience members at a state-sponsored public event may walk away from the affair without subjecting themselves to legal penalties, it should not matter whether a prayer given at that function incorporates the tenets of a particular sect, or comments unfavorably on the tenets of another sect. It should not matter even if the government

the contrary, they are so characteristically American they could have come from the pen of George Washington or Abraham Lincoln himself.

"The Court relies on our 'school prayer' cases, *Engel* and *Schempp*. But whatever the merit of those cases, they do not support, much less compel, the Court's psycho-journey. In the first place, *Engel* and *Schempp* do not constitute an exception to the rule, distilled from historical practice, that public ceremonies may include prayer; rather, they simply do not fall within the scope of the rule (for the obvious reason that school instruction is not a public ceremony). Second, we have made clear our understanding that school prayer occurs within a framework in which legal coercion to attend school (i.e., coercion under threat of penalty) provides the ultimate backdrop. * * * Voluntary prayer at graduation—a one-time ceremony at which parents, friends and relatives are present—can hardly be thought to raise the same concerns."

(b) ELK GROVE UNIFIED SCHOOL DIST. v. NEWDOW, 542 U.S. 1 (2004), reversed the Ninth Circuit's decision that daily classroom recitation by the teacher of the Pledge of Allegiance, with the words "Under God" added in 1954 by Congress, violates the Establishment Clause. The Court held that the father of the schoolgirl had no standing. Three justices reached the merits and would reverse. REHNQUIST, C.J., joined by O'Connor, J., noted that the sponsor of the 1954 amendment "said its purpose was to contrast this country's belief in God with the Soviet Union's embrace of atheism. We do not know what other Members of Congress thought about the purpose of the amendment. Following the decision of the Court of Appeals in this case, Congress passed legislation that made extensive findings about the historic role of religion in the political development of the Nation and reaffirmed the text of the Pledge. To the millions of people who regularly recite the Pledge, and who have no access to, or concern with, such legislation or legislative history, 'under God' might mean several different [things]. Examples of patriotic invocations of God and official acknowledgments of religion's role in our Nation's history abound. * * *

"I do not believe that the phrase 'under God' in the Pledge converts its recital into a 'religious exercise' of the sort described in *Lee*. [It is] in no sense a prayer, nor an endorsement of any religion. [It] is a patriotic exercise, not a religious one; participants promise fidelity to our flag and our Nation, not to any particular God, faith, or church."

O'CONNOR, J., added: "For centuries, we have marked important occasions or pronouncements with references to God and invocations of divine assistance. [These] can serve to solemnize an occasion instead of to invoke divine provenance. The reasonable observer [,] fully aware of our national history and the origins of such practices, would not perceive these [as] signifying a government endorsement of any specific religion, or even of religion over non-religion.[a]

---

sponsors a prayer overtly hostile to one or more faiths, so long as the dissenters are allowed to ignore the government's advice and practice their own beliefs freely."

a. Compare Steven H. Shiffrin, *The Pluralistic Foundations of the Religion Clauses*, 90 Corn.L.Rev. 9, 67 (2004): "[C]hildren of atheists, agnostics, and Buddhists to name a few, are quite unlikely to be aware of this history. [If] their views match their parents, they are

"There are no de minimis violations of the Constitution—no constitutional harms so slight that the courts are obliged to ignore them. Given the values that the Establishment Clause was meant to serve, however, I believe that government can, in a discrete category of cases, acknowledge or refer to the divine without offending the Constitution. This category of 'ceremonial deism' most clearly encompasses such things as the national motto ("In God We Trust"), religious references in traditional patriotic songs such as the Star–Spangled Banner, and the words with which the Marshal of this Court opens each of its sessions. See *Allegheny County* (opinion of O'Connor, J.). * * *

"This case requires us to determine whether the appearance of the phrase 'under God' in the Pledge of Allegiance constitutes an instance of such ceremonial deism. Although it is a close question, I conclude that it [does.]**b** "The Pledge complies with [the] requirement [that "no religious acknowledgment could claim to be an instance of ceremonial deism if it explicitly favored one particular religious belief system over another"]. It does not refer to a nation 'under Jesus' or 'under Vishnu,' but instead acknowledges religion in a general way: a simple reference to a generic 'God.' Of course, some religions—Buddhism, for instance—are not based upon a belief in a separate Supreme Being. But one would be hard pressed to imagine a brief solemnizing reference to religion that would adequately encompass every religious belief expressed by any citizen of this Nation."**c**

THOMAS, J., also concurred: "Adherence to *Lee* would require us to strike down the Pledge policy, which, in most respects, poses more serious difficulties. [I] believe, however, that *Lee* was wrongly decided. [The] kind of coercion implicated by the Religion Clauses is that accomplished *by force of law and threat of penalty. Lee* (Scalia, J., dissenting). Peer pressure, unpleasant as it may be, is not coercion."

3. ***Prayer at other school activities—issues of government purpose and involvement***. SANTA FE IND. SCHOOL DIST. v. DOE, 530 U.S. 290 (2000), per STEVENS, J., relied on *Lee* to hold "invalid on its face" the school district's policy authorizing a student election (1) to determine whether to have a student "deliver a brief invocation and/or message [at] varsity football games to solemnize the event, to promote good sportsmanship and student safety, and to establish the appropriate environment for the competition," and (2) to select "a student volunteer who is [to] decide what statement or invocation to deliver, consistent with the goals and purposes of this policy. Any message and/or invocation delivered by a student must be nonsectarian and nonproselytizing." The Court found "the evolution of the current policy [to be] most striking," pointing to the earlier practice of having an elected "Student Chaplain [deliver] a prayer over the public address system before each varsity football game," and to the title—"Prayer at Football Games"—of

---

overwhelmingly likely to think that they are 'outsiders, not full members of the political community.' "

b. For the view that "the Court's precedents provide abundant support" for the Ninth Circuit's decision, see Steven G. Gey, *"Under God," The Pledge of Allegiance, and Other Constitutional Trivia*, 81 N.C.L.Rev. 1865 (2003).

c. For the view that "under God" emphasizes "that the state is limited by human dignity and rights of transcendent status [, and therefore this is] a powerful reason that the Establishment Clause must permit the state to recognize this religious rationale," see Thomas C. Berg, *The Pledge of Allegiance and the Limited State*, Tex.Rev.L. & Pol. 41 (2003).

the most recent preceding policy, which was similar to the school's policy for prayer at graduations. The Court also emphasized the parties' stipulation that "students voted to determine whether a student would deliver prayer at varsity football games," all of which led the Court "to infer that the specific purpose of the policy was to preserve a popular 'state-sponsored religious practice.' "[a]

"[T]he District first argues that [the] messages are private student speech, not public speech. [But] these invocations are authorized by a government policy and take place on government property at government-sponsored school-related events. [Unlike] the type of forum discussed in [*Rosenberger* and similar cases, here,] the school allows only one student, the same student for the entire season, to give the invocation. [T]he majoritarian process implemented by the District guarantees, by definition, that minority candidates will never prevail and that their views will be effectively silenced. [This] encourages divisiveness along religious lines in a public school setting, a result at odds with the Establishment Clause. [And] the members of the listening audience must perceive the pregame message as a public expression of the views of the majority of the student body delivered with the approval of the school administration."

As for "coercion," "we may assume [that] the informal pressure to attend an athletic event is not as strong as a senior's desire to attend her own graduation ceremony. [But] to assert that [many] high school students do not feel immense social pressure, or have a truly genuine desire, to be involved in the extracurricular event that is American high school football is 'formalistic in the extreme.' "

Rehnquist, C.J., joined by Scalia and Thomas, JJ., dissented: "[The] policy should not be invalidated on its face. [I]t is possible that the students might vote not to have a pregame speaker, in which case there would be no threat of a constitutional violation. It is also possible that the election would not focus on prayer, but on public speaking ability or social popularity. And if student campaigning did begin to focus on prayer, the school might decide to implement reasonable campaign restrictions.[b]

"[A]ny speech that may occur as a result of the election process here would be private, not government, speech. [Unlike *Lee*, the] elected student, not the government, would choose what to say. [A] newly elected prom king or queen, could use opportunities for public speaking to say prayers. Under the Court's view, the mere grant of power to the students to vote for such offices,

---

a. "[Further], the policy, by its terms, invites and encourages religious messages. The policy itself states that the purpose of the message is 'to solemnize the event.' A religious message is the most obvious method of solemnizing an event. Moreover, the requirements that the message 'promote good citizenship' and 'establish the appropriate environment for competition' further narrow the types of message deemed appropriate, suggesting that a solemn, yet nonreligious, message, such as commentary on United States foreign policy, would be prohibited. Indeed, the only type of message that is expressly endorsed in the text is an 'invocation'—a term that primarily describes an appeal for divine assistance. In fact, as used in the past at Santa Fe High School, an 'invocation' has always entailed a focused religious message."

b. The Court responded: "Under the *Lemon* standard, a court must invalidate a statute if it lacks 'a secular legislative purpose.' [E]ven if no Santa Fe High School student were ever to offer a religious message, [the] attempt by the District to encourage prayer is also at issue. Government efforts to endorse religion cannot evade constitutional reproach based solely on the remote possibility that those attempts may fail."

in light of the fear that those elected might publicly pray, violates the Establishment Clause.[c]

"[T]he Court dismisses the [policy's "plausible secular purpose"] of solemnization.[d] [But] it is easy to think of solemn messages that are not religious in nature, for example urging that a game be fought fairly. And sporting events often begin with a solemn rendition of our national anthem, with its concluding verse 'And this be our motto: "In God is our trust."' Under the Court's logic, a public school that sponsors the singing of the national anthem before football games violates the Establishment Clause."

   4. ***Differing interpretations of the "endorsement" test.*** (a) CAPITOL SQUARE REVIEW & ADVISORY BOARD v. PINETTE, 515 U.S. 753 (1995), per Scalia, J., relying on *Widmar* and *Lamb's Chapel*, held that petitioner's permitting the Ku Klux Klan to place a Latin cross in Capitol Square—"A 10–acre, state-owned plaza surrounding the Statehouse in Columbus, Ohio"—when it had also permitted such other unattended displays as "a State-sponsored lighted tree during the Christmas season, a privately-sponsored menorah during Chanukah, a display showing the progress of a United Way fundraising campaign, and booths and exhibits during an arts festival," did not violate the Establishment Clause: "The State did not sponsor respondents' expression, the expression was made on government property that had been opened to the public for speech, and permission was requested through the same application process [for] other private groups."

   The seven-justice majority divided, however, on the scope of the "endorsement" test. Scalia, J., joined by Rehnquist, C.J., and Kennedy and Thomas, JJ., rejected petitioners' claim based on "the forum's proximity to the seat of government, which, they contend, may produce the perception that the cross bears the State's approval": "[W]e have consistently held that it is no violation for government to enact neutral policies that happen to benefit religion. Where we have tested for endorsement of religion, the subject of the test was either expression by the government itself, *Lynch*, or else government action alleged to discriminate in favor of private religious expression or activity, *Allegheny County*. The test petitioners propose, which would attribute to a neutrally behaving government private religious expression, has no

---

   c. The Court responded: "If instead of a choice between an invocation and no pregame message, the first election determined whether a political speech should be made, and the second election determined whether the speaker should be a Democrat or a Republican, it would be rather clear that the public address system was being used to deliver a partisan message reflecting the viewpoint of the majority rather than a random statement by a private individual.

   "The fact that the District's policy provides for the election of the speaker only after the majority has voted on her message identifies an obvious distinction between this case and the typical election of a 'student body president, or even a newly elected prom king or queen.'"

   After *Lee,* what result if the class valedictorian begins her speech with a prayer? If students are selected to give "brief inspirational messages" that are broadcast each day over the school's public address system and some messages contain religious content? For comprehensive treatment, see Kathleen A. Brady, *The Push to Private Religious Expression: Are We Missing Something?*, 70 Ford.L.Rev. 1147, 1172 (2002) ("Where student-initiated speech takes place at a school-sponsored event in a captive audience situation, the context changes the purely private character of the speech, but it does not convert the speech into government expression.").

   d. The Court responded: "When a governmental entity professes a secular purpose for an arguably religious policy, the government's characterization is, of course, entitled to some deference. But it is nonetheless the duty of the courts to 'distinguis[h] a sham secular purpose from a sincere one.' (O'Connor, J., concurring in judgment)."

antecedent in our jurisprudence. [O]ne can conceive of a case in which a governmental entity manipulates its administration of a public forum close to the seat of government (or within a government building) in such a manner that only certain religious groups take advantage of it, creating an impression of endorsement that is in fact accurate. But those situations, which involve governmental favoritism, do not exist here. * * *

"The contrary view, most strongly espoused by Justice Stevens [infra], but endorsed by Justice Souter and Justice O'Connor [and Breyer, J.] as well, [infra], exiles private religious speech to a realm of less-protected expression. [It] is no answer to say that the Establishment Clause tempers religious speech. By its terms that Clause applies only to the words and acts of government. It [has] never been read by this Court to serve as an impediment to purely private religious speech connected to the State only through its occurrence in a public forum."[a]

O'CONNOR, J., joined by Souter and Breyer, JJ., concurred in part: "Where the government's operation of a public forum has the effect of endorsing religion, even if the governmental actor neither intends nor actively encourages that result, the Establishment Clause is violated [because] the State's own actions (operating the forum in a particular manner and permitting the religious expression to take place therein), and their relationship to the private speech at issue, actually convey a message of endorsement."[b]

STEVENS, J., dissented: "[W]hile this unattended, freestanding wooden cross was unquestionably a religious symbol, [some] might have perceived it as a message of love, others as a message of hate, still others as a message of exclusion—a Statehouse sign calling powerfully to mind their outsider status. [It] is especially important to take account of the perspective of a reasonable observer who may not share the particular religious belief it expresses. A paramount purpose of the Establishment Clause is to protect such a person from being made to feel like an outsider in matters of faith, and a stranger in the political community. If a reasonable person could perceive a government endorsement of religion from a private display, then the State may not allow its property to be used as a forum for that display. No less stringent rule can adequately protect non-adherents from a well-grounded perception that their sovereign supports a faith to which they do not subscribe.[c,5]

---

a. Thomas, J., filed a brief concurrence, emphasizing "a cross erected by the Ku Klux Klan [is] a political act, not a Christian one."

b. Souter, J., joined by O'Connor and Breyer, JJ., concurred "in large part because of the possibility of affixing a sign to the cross adequately disclaiming any government sponsorship or endorsement of it.

"[As] long as the governmental entity does not 'manipulat[e]' the forum in such a way as to exclude all other speech, the plurality's opinion would seem to [invite] government encouragement [of religion], even when the result will be the domination of the forum by religious displays and religious speakers. [Something] of the sort, in fact, may have happened here. Immediately after the District Court issued the injunction ordering petitioners to grant the Klan's permit, a local church council [invited] all local churches to erect crosses, and the Board granted 'blanket permission' for 'all churches friendly to or affiliated with' the council to do so. The end result was that a part of the square was strewn with crosses, and while the effect in this case may have provided more embarrassment than suspicion of endorsement, the opportunity for the latter is clear."

c. O'Connor, J., responded: "Under such an approach, a religious display is necessarily precluded so long as some passersby would perceive a governmental endorsement thereof. [But

"[The] very fact that a sign is installed on public property implies official recognition and reinforcement of its message. That implication is especially strong when the sign stands in front of the seat of the government itself. The 'reasonable observer' of any symbol placed unattended in front of any capitol in the world will normally assume that the sovereign [has] sponsored and facilitated its message. [Even] if the disclaimer at the foot of the cross (which stated that the cross was placed there by a private organization) were legible, that inference would remain, because a property owner's decision to allow a third party to place a sign on her property conveys the same message of endorsement as if she had erected it herself. [This] clear image of endorsement was lacking in *Widmar* and *Lamb's Chapel*, in which the issue was access to government facilities. Moreover, there was no question in those cases of an unattended display; private speakers, who could be distinguished from the state, were present. * * *

"The battle over the Klan cross underscores the power of such symbolism. The menorah prompted the Klan to seek permission to erect an antisemitic symbol, [which] not only prompted vandalism but also motivated other sects to seek permission to place their own symbols in the Square. These facts illustrate the potential for insidious entanglement that flows from state-endorsed proselytizing."

GINSBURG, J., also dissented, reserving the question of whether an unequivocal disclaimer, "legible from a distance," "that Ohio did not endorse the display's message" would suffice: "Near the stationary cross were the government's flags and the government's statues. No human speaker was present to disassociate the religious symbol from the State. No other private display was in sight. No plainly visible sign informed the public that the cross belonged to the Klan and that Ohio's government did not endorse the display's message."

(b) SALAZAR v. BUONO, 130 S.Ct. 1803 (2010): In 1934, members of the Veterans of Foreign Wars placed a Latin cross on federal land to honor American soldiers who died in World War I. Easter services have been regularly held there over the years. After a federal court held this violative of the Establishment Clause, Congress prohibited spending governmental funds

---

the] reasonable observer in the endorsement inquiry must be deemed aware of the history and context of the community and forum in which the religious display appears. [An] informed member of the community will know how the public space in question has been used in the past—and it is that fact, not that the space may meet the legal definition of a public forum, which is relevant to the endorsement inquiry. [The] reasonable observer would recognize the distinction between speech the government supports and speech that it merely allows in a place that traditionally has been open to a range of private speakers accompanied, if necessary, by an appropriate disclaimer."

5. [O'Connor, J.'s] 'reasonable person' comes off as a well-schooled jurist, a being finer than the tort-law model. With respect, I think this enhanced tort-law standard is singularly out of place in the Establishment Clause context. It strips of constitutional protection every reasonable person whose knowledge happens to fall below some 'ideal' standard. * * * Justice O'Connor's argument that 'there is always someone' who will feel excluded by any particular governmental action, ignores the requirement that such an apprehension be objectively reasonable. A person who views an exotic cow at the zoo as a symbol of the Government's approval of the Hindu religion cannot survive this test.

[*Query*: Should the Court "develop a national standard, rather than leaving final assessments about endorsement to local juries and courts, who are better able to reflect perceptions about displays in different communities"? 2 Greenawalt 89.]

to remove the cross and directed the Secretary of the Interior to transfer the cross and land to VFW in exchange for privately owned land elsewhere in the Preserve. The statute provided that the property would revert to the Government if not maintained "as a memorial commemorating United States participation in World War I and honoring the American veterans of that war." A splintered 5–4 majority reversed on grounds of (1) rules pertaining to the law of injunctions or (2) standing. Four justices reached the constitutional issue but their discussion was somewhat influenced by their view of injunction doctrine.

ALITO, J., who was part of the majority, would uphold the statute: "Assuming that it is appropriate to apply the so-called 'endorsement test,' [the "reasonable observer"] would be familiar with the origin and history of the monument and would also know both that the land on which the monument is located is privately owned and that the new owner is under no obligation preserve the monument's present design. [A] well-informed observer would appreciate that the transfer represents an effort by Congress to address a unique situation and to find a solution that best accommodates conflicting concerns [to] commemorate our Nation's war dead and to avoid the disturbing symbolism that would have been created by the destruction of the monument."[a]

STEVENS, J., joined by Ginsburg and Sotomayor, JJ., dissented: "[I]t is undisputed that the Latin cross is the preeminent symbol of Christianity. It is exclusively a Christian symbol, and not a symbol of any other religion. * * * I certainly agree that the Nation should memorialize the service of those who fought and died in World War I, but it cannot lawfully do so by continued endorsement of a starkly sectarian message.

"[T]he transfer [statute] would not end government endorsement of the cross for two independently sufficient reasons. First, after the transfer it would continue to appear to any reasonable observer that the Government has endorsed the cross, notwithstanding that the name has changed on the title to a small patch of underlying land. This is particularly true because the Government has designated the cross as a national memorial, and that endorsement continues regardless of whether the cross sits on public or private land. Second, the transfer continues the existing government endorsement of the cross because the purpose of the transfer is to preserve its display. Congress' intent to preserve the display of the cross maintains the Government's endorsement of the cross."

(c) **_Reasonable observer._** Consider William P. Marshall, _"We Know It When We See It," The Supreme Court and Establishment,_ 59 So.Cal.L.Rev. 495, 537 (1986): "Is the objective observer (or average person) a religious person, an agnostic, a separationist, a person sharing the predominate religious sensibility of the community, or one holding a minority view? Is there any 'correct' perception?" Compare Note, _Religion and the State,_ 100 Harv. L.Rev. 1606, 1648 (1987): "[If the test] is governed by the perspective of the

---

a. Alito, J.'s analysis generally conforms to the discussion in the plurality opinion by Kennedy, J., joined by Roberts, C.J., and Alito, J., which based its conclusion on the law of injunctions. Breyer, J., also relied on the law of injunctions, but dissented. Scalia, J., joined by Thomas, J., concurred in the judgment on the ground that respondent had no standing.

majority, it will be inadequately sensitive. [If] the establishment clause is to prohibit government from sending the message to religious minorities or nonadherents that the state favors certain beliefs and that as nonadherents they are not fully members of the political community, its application must turn on the message received *by the minority or nonadherent.*" Concurring in *Van Orden*, THOMAS, J., argued: "['Reasonable observer'] analysis is not fully satisfying to either nonadherents or adherents. For the nonadherent, who may well be more sensitive than the hypothetical 'reasonable observer,' or who may not know all the facts, this test fails to capture completely the honest and deeply felt offense he takes from the government conduct. For the adherent, this analysis takes no account of the message sent by removal of the sign or display, which may well appear to him to be an act hostile to his religious faith."

(d) *Ambiguities.* (i) Consider Steven D. Smith, *Symbols, Perceptions, and Doctrinal Illusions: Establishment Neutrality and the "No Endorsement" Test,* 86 Mich.L.Rev. 266, 283, 301–03, 310–12 (1987): "[E]vidence of the test's indeterminate character appears in [Arnold H. Loewy, *Rethinking Government Neutrality Towards Religion Under the Establishment Clause: The Untapped Potential of Justice O'Connor's Insight,* 64 N.C.L.Rev. 1049 (1986), who] concludes that Pawtucket's sponsorship of a nativity scene violated the establishment clause, that Alabama's 'moment of silence' law probably did *not* violate the clause, and that ceremonial invocations of deity, such as those occurring in the Pledge of Allegiance or the opening of a Supreme Court session, *do* violate the 'no endorsement' test. In each instance, Justice O'Connor would disagree. [From] the Continental Congress[139] through the framing of the Bill of Rights[140] and on down to the present day, government and government officials—including Presidents [not] to mention the Supreme Court itself[141]—have frequently expressed approval of religion and religious ideas. Such history [at] least demonstrates that many Americans, including some of our early eminent statesmen, have *believed* such approval was proper. That fact alone is sufficient to show that the 'no endorsement' principle is controversial, not easily self-evident. [If] public institutions employ religious symbols, persons who do not adhere to the predominant religion may feel like 'outsiders.'[d] But if religious symbols are banned from such contexts, some religious people will feel that their most central values and concerns [have] been excluded from a public culture devoted purely to secular concerns. [We] might conclude, however, that any alienation felt by [the latter] groups, although perfectly sincere, should be disregarded because their dissatisfaction actually results [from] the very meaning of the establishment clause." Contrast Jesse H. Choper, *Securing*

---

139. [The] Continental Congress "sprinkled its proceedings liberally with the mention of God, Jesus Christ, the Christian religion, and many other religious references."

140. Shortly after approving the Bill of Rights, [including] the Establishment Clause, the first Congress resolved to observe a day of thanksgiving and prayer in appreciation of "the many signal favors of Almighty God."

141. See, e.g., *Zorach* ("We are a religious people whose institutions presuppose a Supreme Being."); *Church of the Holy Trinity v. United States,* 143 U.S. 457, 471 (1892) (asserting that "this is a Christian nation").

d. For support of O'Connor, J.'s approach in this setting, see Steven G. Gey, *When Is Religious Speech Not "Free Speech"?* 2000 U.Ill.L.Rev. 379.

Religious Liberty: Principles for Judicial interpretation of the Religion Clauses 28–29 (1995): "[T]his would grant [a] self-interested veto for the minority. [Although] justices of the Supreme Court 'cannot become someone else,' they should, with their own solicitude for the values of religious liberty, either assume the view of a reasonable member of the political community who is faithful to the Constitution's protection of individual rights or ask whether a *reasonable minority observer*, who would be 'acquainted with the text, legislative history, and implementation of the [challenged state action],' *should feel* less than a full member of the political community.[112]" For critical appraisal of the "inherent difficulties" of the endorsement test, see Mark Strasser, *The Protection and Alienation of Religious Minorities: On the Evolution of the Endorsement Test*, 2008 Mich. St. L. Rev. 667: The test "is invoked to rationalize a result that has been reached some other way."

(ii) Do government accommodations for religion (such as exempting the sacramental use of wine during Prohibition) violate the endorsement test? Consider Mark Tushnet, *"Of Church and State and the Supreme Court": Kurland Revisited*, 1989 Sup.Ct.Rev. 373, 395 n. 73: "They use religion as a basis for government classification, and they do [so] precisely in order to confer a benefit on some religions that does not flow either to nonbelievers or to all religions." Compare Michael W. McConnell, *Religious Freedom at a Crossroads*, 59 U.Chi.L.Rev. 115, 150 (1992): "Any action the government takes on issues of this sort inevitably sends out messages, and it is not surprising that reasonable observers from different legal and religious perspectives respond to these messages in different ways. These examples raise some of the most important and most often litigated issues under the Establishment Clause, and the concept of endorsement does not help to resolve them." Contrast Jesse H. Choper, *The Endorsement Test: Its Status and Desirability*, 18 J.L. & Pol. 499, 524, 529 (2002): "[A]ttempts by government to accommodate *either minority or mainstream* religions are often (indeed, usually) benign, genuine, and sometimes even important to the larger society. These efforts should be upheld even though they may fairly be seen as endorsing or approving religion and even though they may cause reasonable people to feel offended or alienated. It is surely regrettable when state policies that address issues of faith produce a sense of subordination or resentment in a segment of the populace. But this alone should not suffice for a judicial holding of unconstitutionality. [That] makes a decision to protect the distressed sensibilities of the religious minority (or nonbelievers) and to ignore those of the religious majority. [In] the absence of any tangible threat to religious liberty, it is not at all apparent that the minorities' feelings ought to prevail. Indeed, where equal perceptions of subordination exist, a strong case can be made to favor majority preference."

5. ***Proposal to reconcile Establishment Clause problems.*** Consider Michael W. McConnell, *State Action and the Supreme Court's Emerging Consensus on the Line Between Establishment and Private Religious Expression*, 28 Pepp.L.Rev. 681 (2001): The Establishment Clause "is a limitation on

---

112. Although this process is basically normative rather than empirical, the Court's judgment should obviously be influenced by the perception (if fairly discernible) of 'average' members of minority religious faiths and should be more strongly affected if their response is very widely shared.

the power of government. It is not a limitation on the activities of private citizens." The "decisive question" is: "Was the religious activity that took place properly attributable to the government or to private parties?" If "religious activity"—even when undertaken by private parties—"is instigated, encouraged, or—in the strongest case—coerced by the government, the government's acts are unconstitutional. But if religious activity is the product of private judgment, it is permissible—even welcome—within the public sphere. [Thus], to the extent that religious teaching is to be a part of the education of young Americans, this must be the product of decisions made by individual families and religious societies and not of government direction." In respect to individual choice of schools, "the Establishment Clause does not limit the right of private institutions to engage in religious teaching, even with the benefit of neutrally available public resources."

CHAPTER 12

FREE EXERCISE CLAUSE AND RELATED PROBLEMS

■ ■ ■

I. CONFLICT WITH STATE REGULATION

The most common problem respecting free exercise of religion has involved a generally applicable government regulation, whose purpose is nonreligious, that either makes illegal (or otherwise burdens) conduct that is dictated by some religious belief, or requires (or otherwise encourages) conduct that is forbidden by some religious belief. REYNOLDS v. UNITED STATES, 98 U.S. 145 (1878), the first major decision on the Free Exercise Clause, upheld a federal law making polygamy illegal as applied to a Mormon whose religious duty was to practice polygamy: "Congress was deprived of all legislative power over mere opinion, but was left free to reach actions which were in violation of social duties or subversive of good order." CANTWELL v. CONNECTICUT, 310 U.S. 296 (1940), reemphasized this distinction between religious opinion or belief, on the one hand, and action taken because of religion, on the other, although the Court this time spoke more solicitously about the latter: "Freedom of conscience and freedom to adhere to such religious organization or form of worship as the individual may choose cannot be restricted by law. [Free exercise] embraces two concepts,—freedom to believe and freedom to act. The first is absolute but, in the nature of things, the second cannot be. [The] freedom to act must have appropriate definition to preserve the enforcement of that protection [although] the power to regulate must be so exercised as not, in attaining a permissible end, unduly to infringe the protected freedom."

Beginning with *Cantwell*—which first held that the Fourteenth Amendment made the free exercise guarantee applicable to the states—a number of cases invalidated application of state laws to conduct undertaken pursuant to religious beliefs. Like *Cantwell*, these decisions, a number of which are set forth in Part 1,[a] rested in whole or in part on the freedom of expression protections of the First and Fourteenth Amendments. Simi-

---

a. E.g., *Schneider v. Irvington*, Ch. 6, I, A; *Lovell v. Griffin*, Ch. 4, I, A (involving distribution of religious literature). See also *Marsh v. Alabama*, Ch. 6, 3.

larly, WEST VIRGINIA STATE BD. OF EDUC. v. BARNETTE, 319 U.S. 624 (1943),[b] held that compelling a flag salute by public school children whose religious scruples forbade it violated the First Amendment: "[The] freedoms of speech and of press, of assembly, and of worship [are] susceptible of restriction only to prevent grave and immediate danger to interests which the state may lawfully protect. [The] freedom asserted by these appellees does not bring them into collision with rights asserted by any other individual. It is such conflicts which most frequently require intervention of the State to determine where the rights of one end and those of another begin. [T]he compulsory flag salute and pledge requires *affirmation of a belief* and an *attitude of mind*. [If] there is any fixed star in our constitutional constellation, it is that no official, high or petty, can prescribe what shall be orthodox in politics, nationalism or other matters of opinion or force citizens to confess by word or act their faith therein."

It was not until 1963, in *Sherbert v. Verner* (discussed in *Hobbie* below), that the Court held conduct protected by the Free Exercise Clause alone.

HOBBIE v. UNEMPLOYMENT APPEALS COMM'N

480 U.S. 136, 107 S.Ct. 1046, 94 L.Ed.2d 190 (1987).

JUSTICE BRENNAN delivered the opinion of the Court.

Appellant's employer discharged her when she refused to work certain scheduled hours because of sincerely-held religious convictions adopted after beginning employment. [Under] our precedents, the [Florida] Appeals Commission's disqualification of appellant from receipt of [unemployment compensation] benefits violates the Free Exercise [Clause]. *Sherbert v. Verner*, 374 U.S. 398 (1963); *Thomas v. Review Board*, 450 U.S. 707 (1981). In *Sherbert* we considered South Carolina's denial of unemployment compensation benefits to a Sabbatarian who, like Hobbie, refused to work on Saturdays. The Court held that the State's disqualification of Sherbert "force[d] her to choose between following the precepts of her religion and forfeiting benefits, on the one hand, and abandoning one of the precepts of her religion in order to accept work, on the other hand. Governmental imposition of such a choice puts the same kind of burden upon the free exercise of religion as would a fine imposed against [her] for her Saturday worship." * * *

In *Thomas,* [a] Jehovah's Witness, held religious beliefs that forbade his participation in the production of armaments. He was forced to leave his job when the employer closed his department and transferred him to a division that fabricated turrets for tanks. Indiana then denied Thomas unemployment compensation benefits. * * *

We see no meaningful distinction among the situations [and] again affirm, as stated in *Thomas:* "Where the state conditions receipt of an important benefit upon conduct proscribed by a religious faith, *or where it*

---

b. Overruling *Minersville School Dist. v. Gobitis,* 310 U.S. 586 (1940).

denies such a benefit because of conduct mandated by religious belief, thereby putting substantial pressure on an adherent to modify his behavior and to violate his beliefs, a burden upon religion exists. While the compulsion may be indirect, the infringement upon free exercise is nonetheless substantial" (emphasis added).

Both *Sherbert* and *Thomas* held that such infringements must be subjected to strict scrutiny and could be justified only by proof by the State of a compelling interest. The Appeals Commission does not seriously contend that its denial of benefits can withstand strict scrutiny;[a] rather it urges that we hold that its justification should be determined under the less rigorous standard articulated in Chief Justice Burger's opinion in *Bowen v. Roy:* "the Government meets its burden when it demonstrates that a challenged requirement for governmental benefits, neutral and uniform in its application, is a reasonable means of promoting a legitimate public interest."[b] 476 U.S. 693, 707–08 (1986). Five Justices expressly rejected this argument in *Roy.* [As] Justice O'Connor pointed out in *Roy,* "[s]uch a test has no basis in precedent and relegates a serious First Amendment value to the barest level of minimal scrutiny that the Equal Protection Clause already provides." See also *Wisconsin v. Yoder,* 406 U.S. 205, 215 (1972)[c] ("[O]nly those interests of the highest order and those not otherwise served can overbalance legitimate claims to the free exercise of religion"). * * *

The Appeals Commission also attempts to distinguish this case by arguing that [in] *Sherbert* and *Thomas,* the employees held their respec-

---

a. In *Sherbert,* the state "suggest[ed] no more than a possibility that the filing of fraudulent claims by unscrupulous claimants feigning religious objections to Saturday work [might] dilute the unemployment compensation fund [but] there is no proof whatever to warrant such fears of malingering or deceit [and] it is highly doubtful whether such evidence would be sufficient to warrant a substantial infringement of religious liberties. For [it] would plainly be incumbent upon the [state] to demonstrate that no alternative forms of regulation would combat such abuses without infringing First Amendment rights."

b. Burger, C.J., joined by Powell and Rehnquist, JJ., prefaced this statement in *Roy*: "[G]overnment regulation that indirectly and incidentally calls for a choice between securing a governmental benefit and adherence to religious beliefs is wholly different from [action] that criminalizes religiously inspired activity or inescapably compels conduct that some find objectionable for religious reasons. Although the denial of governmental benefits over religious objection can raise serious Free Exercise problems, these two very different forms of government action are not governed by the same constitutional standard. * * * Absent proof of an intent to discriminate against particular religious beliefs or against religion in general, the Government meets its burden [etc.]"

c. *Yoder* invalidated a law compelling school attendance to age 16 as applied to Amish parents who refused on religious grounds to send their children to high school, noting no "showing that upon leaving the Amish community Amish children, with their practical agricultural training and habits of industry and self-reliance, would become burdens on society because of educational shortcomings. [The] independence and successful social functioning of the Amish community for a period approaching almost three centuries [is] strong evidence that there is at best a speculative gain, [in] meeting the duties of citizenship from an additional one or two years of compulsory formal education."

Only Douglas, J., dissented: If parents "are allowed a religious exemption, the inevitable effect is to impose the parents' notions of religious duty upon their children. Where the child is mature enough to express potentially conflicting desires, it would be an invasion of the child's rights to permit such an imposition without canvassing his views." On the question of "whether children should be afforded rights of religious exercise independent of their parents," see Emily Buss, *What Does Frieda Yoder Believe?,* 2 U.Pa.J.Con.L. 53 (1999).

tive religious beliefs at the time of hire; subsequent changes in the conditions of employment made *by the employer* caused the conflict between work and belief. In this case, Hobbie's beliefs changed during the course of her employment. [This] asks us to single out the religious convert for different, less favorable treatment. * * * We decline to do so. * * *

Finally, we reject the Appeals Commission's argument that the awarding of benefits to Hobbie would violate the Establishment Clause. This Court has long recognized that the government may (and sometimes must) accommodate religious practices and that it may do so without violating the Establishment Clause.[10] See e.g., *Yoder* (judicial exemption of Amish children from compulsory attendance at high school); *Walz* (tax exemption for churches). * * *

Reversed.[d]

CHIEF JUSTICE REHNQUIST, dissenting.

I adhere to the views I stated in dissent in *Thomas* [where Rehnquist, J., stated: "As to the proper interpretation of the Free Exercise Clause, I would accept the decision of *Braunfeld v. Brown,* 366 U.S. 599 (1961), and the dissent in *Sherbert.* In *Braunfeld,* we held that Sunday closing laws do not violate the First Amendment rights of Sabbatarians. Chief Justice Warren explained that the statute did not make unlawful any religious practices of appellants; it simply made the practice of their religious beliefs more expensive. We concluded that '[t]o strike down, without the most critical scrutiny, legislation which imposes only an indirect burden on the exercise of religion, i.e., legislation which does not make unlawful the religious practice itself, would radically restrict the operating latitude of the legislature.'[e] Likewise in this case, it cannot be said that the State discriminated against Thomas on the basis of his religious beliefs or that he was denied benefits *because* he was a Jehovah's Witness.[11] Where, as here, a State has enacted a general statute, the purpose and effect of which is to advance the State's secular goals, the Free Exercise Clause

---

10. In the unemployment benefits context, the majorities *and* those dissenting have concluded that, were a state voluntarily to provide benefits to individuals in Hobbie's situation, [it] would not violate the Establishment Clause. See *Thomas* (Rehnquist, J., dissenting); *Sherbert* (Harlan, J., dissenting). [The conflict between the Establishment and Free Exercise Clauses is considered in Ch. 14 infra.]

d. The opinions of Powell and Stevens, JJ., concurring in the judgment, are omitted.

e. *Braunfeld* continued: "Statutes which tax income and limit the amount which may be deducted for religious contributions impose an indirect economic burden on the observance of the religion of the citizen whose religion requires him to donate a greater amount to his church; statutes which require the courts to be closed on Saturday and Sunday impose a similar indirect burden on the observance of the religion of the trial lawyer whose religion requires him to rest on a weekday. The list of legislation of this nature is nearly limitless."

Query: If a statute makes a religious practice unlawful but maximum penalty is a fine, is this a "direct" or "indirect" burden?

1. [T]he Indiana Supreme Court *has* construed the State's unemployment statute to make every personal subjective reason for leaving a job a basis for disqualification. [Because] Thomas left his job for a personal reason, the State of Indiana should not be prohibited from disqualifying him from receiving benefits.

does not in my view require the State to conform that statute to the dictates of religious conscience of any group."]

NOTES AND QUESTIONS

1. *Scope of decisions.* After *Sherbert, Thomas* and *Hobbie,* may a state deny unemployment benefits (a) to a member of a pacifist religion who agreed to produce tanks as a condition of employment and who was fired for subsequently refusing to do so because of religious beliefs, see *Employment Division v. Smith,* 485 U.S. 660 (1988); (b) to a Sabbatarian who is dismissed from a post office job for refusal to work on Saturday because to grant an exemption would require paying overtime to another employee?[a] May (c) a state deny worker's compensation to the widow of an employee who, after being injured at work, died because of his refusal on religious grounds to accept a blood transfusion?

2. *Rejections of free exercise claims.* (a) *Taxation.* (i) JIMMY SWAGGART MINISTRIES v. BOARD OF EQUAL., 493 U.S. 378 (1990), per O'CONNOR, J., unanimously held that the Free Exercise Clause does not prohibit imposing a sales and use tax on sale of religious materials by a religious organization. The Court distinguished *Murdock v. Pennsylvania,* 319 U.S. 105 (1943) and *Follett v. McCormick,* 321 U.S. 573 (1944), which had invalidated license taxes for sellers as applied to Jehovah's Witnesses who went from house to house selling religious pamphlets, because of the "particular nature of the challenged taxes—flat license taxes that operated as a prior restraint on the exercise of religious liberty": "[T]o the extent that imposition of a generally applicable tax merely decreases the amount of money appellant has to spend on its religious activities, any such burden is not constitutionally significant. [B]ecause appellant's religious beliefs do not forbid payment of the sales and use tax, appellant's reliance on *Sherbert* and its progeny is misplaced. [Although] it is of course possible to imagine that a more onerous tax, even if generally applicable, might effectively choke off an adherent's religious practices, cf. *Murdock* (the burden of a flat tax could render itinerant evangelism 'crushed and closed out by the sheer weight of the toll or tribute which is exacted town by town'), we face no such situation in this case."

(ii) UNITED STATES v. LEE, 455 U.S. 252 (1982), per BURGER, C.J., held that the Free Exercise Clause does not require an exemption for members of the Old Order Amish from payment of social security taxes even though "both payment and receipt of social security benefits is forbidden by the Amish faith": "The state may justify a limitation on religious liberty by showing that it is essential to accomplish an overriding governmental interest [and] mandatory participation is indispensable to the fiscal vitality of the social security system. [To] maintain an organized society that guarantees religious freedom to a great variety of faiths requires that some religious practices yield to the common good. [The] tax system could not function if denominations were

---

a. See also *TWA v. Hardison,* 432 U.S. 63 (1977), interpreting the Civil Rights Act ban on religious discrimination in employment as permitting dismissal of a Sabbatarian if accommodating his work schedule would require "more than a de minimis cost" by the employer. Brennan and Marshall, JJ., dissented.

allowed to challenge the tax system because tax payments were spent in a manner that violates their religious belief."

STEVENS, J., concurred in the judgment: "As a matter of fiscal policy, an enlarged exemption probably would benefit the social security system because the nonpayment of these taxes by the Amish would be more than offset by the elimination of their right to collect benefits.[b] * * * Nonetheless, I agree with the Court's conclusion that the difficulties associated with processing other claims to tax exemption on religious grounds justify a rejection of this claim.[2]"

(b) *Conscription.* (i) GILLETTE v. UNITED STATES, 401 U.S. 437 (1971), per MARSHALL, J., held that the Free Exercise Clause does not forbid Congress from "conscripting persons who oppose a particular war on grounds of conscience and religion. * * *[23]": "The conscription laws [are] not designed to interfere with any religious ritual or practice, and do not work a penalty against any theological position. The incidental burdens felt by [petitioners] are strictly justified by substantial governmental interests that relate directly to the very impacts questioned. And more broadly [is] the Government's interest in procuring the manpower necessary for military purposes * * *."

DOUGLAS, J., dissented: "[M]y choice is the dicta of Chief Justice Hughes who, dissenting in *Macintosh*, spoke for Holmes, Brandeis, and Stone: '[Among] the most eminent statesmen here and abroad have been those who condemned the action of their country in entering into wars they thought to be unjustified. [If] the mere holding of religious or conscientious scruples against all wars should not disqualify a citizen from holding office in this country, or an applicant otherwise qualified from being admitted to citizenship, there would seem to be no reason why a reservation of religious or conscientious objection to participation in wars believed to be unjust should constitute such a disqualification.' "[d]

---

b. Stevens, J., found the distinction between this case and *Yoder* "unconvincing because precisely the same religious interest is implicated in both cases and Wisconsin's interest in requiring its children to attend school until they reach the age of 16 is surely not inferior to the federal interest in collecting these social security taxes."

2. [T]he principal reason for adopting a strong presumption against such claims is not a matter of administrative convenience. It is the overriding interest in keeping the government— whether it be the legislature or the courts—out of the business of evaluating the relative merits of differing religious claims. The risk that governmental approval of some and disapproval of others will be perceived as favoring one religion over another is an important risk the Establishment Clause was designed to preclude.

23. We are not faced with the question whether the Free Exercise Clause itself would require exemption of any class other than objectors to particular wars. * * * We note that the Court has previously suggested that relief for conscientious objectors is not mandated by the Constitution. See *Hamilton v. Regents*, 293 U.S. 245 (1934); *United States v. Macintosh*, 283 U.S. at 623–24 (1931).

d. Did *Gillette* discard the "alternative means" approach found in *Sherbert*? Consider Tribe 2d ed., at 1266: "In light of the relative ease with which the conscientious-objector exemption has been administered throughout our history without placing a noticeable burden on the country's military manpower needs, a court might well require a concrete showing of threat to such needs in order to justify abolition of the exemption. The use of conscientious objectors—even selective conscientious objectors—in paramedical or other non-military roles could meet both the personnel argument and the morale argument well enough to constitute a required alternative under *Sherbert*."

(ii) In JOHNSON v. ROBISON, 415 U.S. 361 (1974), a federal statute granted educational benefits for veterans who served on active duty but disqualified conscientious objectors who performed alternate civilian service. The Court, per BRENNAN, J., found a "rational basis" for the classification and thus no violation of equal protection, because the "disruption caused by military service is quantitatively greater [and] qualitatively different." Further, the statute "involves only an incidental burden upon appellee's free exercise of religion—if, indeed, any burden exists at [all.]¹⁹ Government's substantial interest in raising and supporting armies is of 'a kind and weight' clearly sufficient to sustain the challenged legislation, for the burden upon appellee's free exercise [is] not nearly of the same order or magnitude as" in *Gillette*. Douglas, J., dissented.

(c) *Tax exemption*. BOB JONES UNIV. v. UNITED STATES, 461 U.S. 574 (1983), per BURGER, C.J., held that IRS denial of tax exempt status to private schools that practice racial discrimination on the basis of sincerely held religious beliefs does not violate the Free Exercise Clause: "[T]he Government has a fundamental, overriding interest in eradicating racial discrimination in education [which] substantially outweighs whatever burden denial of tax benefits places on petitioners' exercise of their religious beliefs. The interests asserted by petitioners cannot be accommodated with that compelling governmental interest, see *Lee;* and no 'less restrictive means' are available to achieve the governmental interest."ᵉ Rehnquist, J., agreeing with the Court's free exercise analysis, dissented on the ground that Congress had not authorized the IRS denial of tax exemption.ᶠ

(d) *Internal government affairs*. LYNG v. NORTHWEST INDIAN CEMETERY PROTECTIVE ASS'N, 485 U.S. 439 (1988), per O'CONNOR, J., held the federal government's building a road [in] a national forest did not violate the free exercise rights of American Indian tribes even though this would "virtually destroy the Indians' ability to practice their religion" because it would irreparably damage "sacred areas which are an integral and necessary part of [their] belief systems": "In *Bowen v. Roy,* we considered a challenge to a federal statute that required the States to use Social Security numbers in administering certain welfare programs. Two applicants [contended] that their religious beliefs prevented them from acceding to the use of a Social Security number [that had been assigned to] their two-year-old daughter because the use of a numerical identifier would ' "rob the spirit" of [their]

---

19. * * * Congress has bestowed relative benefits upon conscientious objectors by permitting them to perform their alternate service obligation as civilians. Thus, [to] grant educational benefits to military servicemen might arguably be viewed as an attempt to equalize the burdens of military service and civilian alternate service, rather than an effort [to] place a relative burden upon a conscientious objector's free exercise of religion. [See also Kent Greenawalt, 1 *Religion and the Constitution* 53 (2006): "The government can grant everyone an option between a term of military service and *a longer term* of civilian service, or an option between a certainty of civilian service and a chance of military service.]

e. Contra, Douglas Laycock, *Tax Exemptions for Racially Discriminatory Religious Schools,* 60 Tex.L.Rev. 259 (1982); Mayer G. Freed & Daniel D. Polsby, *Race, Religion, and Public Policy: Bob Jones University v. United States,* 1983 Sup.Ct.Rev. 1, 20–30.

f. Four justices also rejected the claim that Nebraska's denial of a driver's license to a person whose sincerely held religious beliefs—pursuant to the Second Commandment prohibition of "graven images"—forbade her to be photographed, violated the Free Exercise Clause. *Quaring v. Peterson,* 728 F.2d 1121 (8th Cir.1984) (free exercise violation), affirmed by an equally divided Court, 472 U.S. 478 (1985).

daughter and prevent her from attaining greater spiritual power.' [The] Court rejected [this]: 'The Free Exercise Clause simply cannot be understood to require the Government to conduct its own internal affairs in ways that comport with the religious beliefs of particular citizens. Just as the Government may not insist that [the Roys] engage in any set form of religious observance, so [they] may not demand that the Government join in their chosen religious practices by refraining from using a number to identify their daughter. [The] Free Exercise Clause affords an individual protection from certain forms of governmental compulsion; it does not afford an individual a right to dictate the conduct of the Government's internal procedures.'

"The building of a road [on] publicly owned land cannot meaningfully be distinguished from the use of a Social Security number in *Roy*. In both cases, the challenged government action would interfere significantly with private persons' ability to pursue spiritual fulfillment according to their own religious beliefs. In neither case, however, would the affected individuals be coerced by the Government's action into violating their religious beliefs; nor would either governmental action penalize religious activity by denying any person an equal share of [benefits]. [G]overnment simply could not operate if it were required to satisfy every citizen's religious needs and desires. A broad range of government activities—from social welfare programs to foreign aid to conservation projects—will always be considered essential to the spiritual well-being of some citizens, often on the basis of sincerely held religious beliefs. Others will find the very same activities deeply offensive, and perhaps incompatible with their own search for spiritual fulfillment and with the tenets of their religion. The First Amendment must apply to all citizens alike, and it can give to none of them a veto over public programs that do not prohibit the free exercise of religion.

"[The] dissent now offers to distinguish [*Roy*] by saying that the Government was acting there 'in a purely internal manner,' whereas land-use decisions 'are likely to have substantial external effects.' [But robbing] the spirit of a child, and preventing her from attaining greater spiritual power, is both a 'substantial external effect' and one that is remarkably similar to the injury claimed [today]."[g]

Brennan, J., joined by Marshall and Blackmun, JJ., dissented: "[T]oday's ruling sacrifices a religion at least as old as the Nation itself, along with the spiritual well-being of its approximately 5,000 adherents, so that the Forest Service can build a six-mile segment of road that two lower courts found had only the most marginal and speculative utility, both to the Government itself and to the private lumber interests that might conceivably use it." Kennedy, J., did not participate.

EMPLOYMENT DIVISION v. SMITH
494 U.S. 872, 110 S.Ct. 1595, 108 L.Ed.2d 876 (1990).

Justice Scalia delivered the opinion of the Court. * * *

---

g. *Nature of remedy.* Is there a difference between the remedy needed to satisfy the free exercise claim in *Roy* and that in *Lyng?* If so, what about the required remedy in the other instances in which the Court has sustained the free exercise claim?

Respondents [were] fired from their jobs with a private drug rehabilitation organization because they ingested peyote for sacramental purposes at a ceremony of the Native American Church, of which both are members. When respondents applied to petitioner [for] unemployment compensation, they were determined to be ineligible for benefits because they had been discharged for work-related "misconduct." [We believe] that "if a State has prohibited through its criminal laws certain kinds of religiously motivated conduct without violating the First Amendment, it certainly follows that it may impose the lesser burden of denying unemployment compensation benefits to persons who engage in that conduct."

[The] free exercise of religion means, first and foremost, the right to believe and profess whatever religious doctrine one desires. Thus, the First Amendment obviously excludes all "governmental regulation of religious *beliefs* as such." The government may not compel affirmation of religious belief, see *Torcaso v. Watkins,* [Part II infra], punish the expression of religious doctrines it believes to be false, *United States v. Ballard,* [Part II infra], impose special disabilities on the basis of religious views or religious status, see *McDaniel v. Paty,* 435 U.S. 618 (1978) [state rule disqualifying clergy from being legislators]; cf. *Larson v. Valente,* [Ch. 13 infra] or lend its power to one or the other side in controversies over religious authority or dogma, see *Presbyterian Church v. Hull Church,* [Ch. 13 infra].

But the "exercise of religion" often involves not only belief and profession but the performance of (or abstention from) physical acts: assembling with others for a worship service, participating in sacramental use of bread and wine, proselytizing, abstaining from certain foods or certain modes of transportation. It would be true, we think (though no case of ours has involved the point), that a state would be "prohibiting the free exercise [of religion]" if it sought to ban such acts or abstentions only when they are engaged in for religious reasons, or only because of the religious belief that they display. It would doubtless be unconstitutional, for example, to ban the casting of "statues that are to be used for worship purposes," or to prohibit bowing down before a golden calf.

Respondents [seek] to carry the meaning of "prohibiting the free exercise [of religion]" one large step further. They contend that their religious motivation for using peyote places them beyond the reach of a criminal law that is not specifically directed at their religious practice, and that is concededly constitutional as applied to those who use the drug for other reasons. [As] a textual matter, we do not think the words must be given that meaning. It is no more necessary to regard the collection of a general tax, for example, as "prohibiting the free exercise [of religion]" by those citizens who believe support of organized government to be sinful, than it is to regard the same tax as "abridging the freedom [of] the press" of those publishing companies that must pay the tax as a condition of staying in business. It is a permissible reading of the text [to] say that if prohibiting the exercise of religion (or burdening the activity of printing) is not the object of the tax but merely the incidental effect of a generally applicable and otherwise valid provision, the First Amendment has not been offended. Compare *Citizen Publishing Co. v. United States*, 394 U.S. 131 (1969) (upholding application of antitrust laws to press), with *Grosjean v. American Press Co.*, [fn. b, p. 386 supra] (striking down license tax applied only to newspapers with weekly circulation above a specified level); see generally *Minneapolis Star & Tribune Co. v. Minnesota Commissioner of Revenue* [p. 386 supra].

Our decisions reveal that the latter reading is the correct one. We have never held that an individual's religious beliefs excuse him from compliance with an otherwise valid law prohibiting conduct that the State is free to regulate. [In] *Prince v. Massachusetts*, 321 U.S. 158 (1944), we held that a mother could be prosecuted under the child labor laws for using her children to dispense literature in the streets, her religious motivation notwithstanding. [The opinion also discusses *Braunfeld, Gillette*, and *Lee*.]

The only decisions in which we have held that the First Amendment bars application of a neutral, generally applicable law to religiously motivated action have involved [the] Free Exercise Clause in conjunction with other constitutional protections, such as freedom of speech and of the press, see *Cantwell* (invalidating a licensing system for religious and charitable solicitations under which the administrator had discretion to deny a license to any cause he deemed nonreligious); *Murdock*; *Follett*, or the right of parents, acknowledged in *Pierce v. Society of Sisters* [Sec. 2 supra] to direct the education of their children, see *Yoder*.[1] Some of our cases prohibiting compelled expression, decided exclusively upon free speech grounds, have also involved freedom of religion, cf. *Wooley v. Maynard* [Ch. 9, I] (invalidating compelled display of a license plate slogan that offended individual religious beliefs); *Barnette*. And it is easy to envision a case in which a challenge on freedom of association grounds would likewise be reinforced by Free Exercise Clause concerns. Cf. *Roberts v. United States Jaycees* [Ch. 9, II] ("An individual's freedom to speak, to worship, and to petition the government for the redress of grievances could not be vigorously protected from interference by the State [if] a correlative freedom to engage in group effort toward those ends were not also guaranteed."). * * *

---

1. [*Yoder*] said that "[*Pierce*] stands as a charter of the rights of parents to direct the religious upbringing of their children. And, when the interests of parenthood are combined with a free exercise claim of the nature revealed by this record, more than merely a 'reasonable relation to some purpose within the competency of the State' is required to sustain the validity of the State's requirement under the First Amendment."

[Compare Mark V. Tushnet, *Questioning the Value of Accommodating Religion*, in Law & Religion 245, 246 (Stephen M. Feldman ed. 2000): "In virtually every case a careful litigant can identify another constitutional claim that rides along with the free exercise one: most obviously, free speech claims, but occasionally substantive due process claims as well." For a review of post-*Smith* decisions in the lower courts, concluding that "hybrid rights claims have overwhelmingly failed to succeed," see Steven H. Aden & Lee J. Strang, *When a "Rule" Doesn't Rule: The Failure of the Oregon Employment Division v. Smith "Hybrid Rights Exception,"* 108 Penn St.L.Rev. 573 (2003). See further, Note, *The Best of a Bad Lot: Compromise and Hybrid Religious Exemptions*, 123 Harv. L. Rev. 1494 (2010).]

Respondents argue that [the] claim for a religious exemption must be evaluated under the balancing test set forth in *Sherbert*[:] governmental actions that substantially burden a religious practice must be justified by a compelling governmental interest. [We] have never invalidated any governmental action on the basis of the *Sherbert* test except the denial of unemployment compensation. Although we have sometimes purported to apply the *Sherbert* test in contexts other than that, we have always found the test satisfied, see *Lee, Gillette*. In recent years we have abstained from applying the *Sherbert* test (outside the unemployment compensation field) at all [discussing *Roy* and *Lyng*]. In *Goldman v. Weinberger,* 475 U.S. 503 (1986), we rejected application of the *Sherbert* test to military dress regulations that forbade the wearing of yarmulkes. In *O'Lone v. Shabazz,* 482 U.S. 342 (1987), we sustained, without mentioning the *Sherbert* test, a prison's refusal to excuse inmates from work requirements to attend worship services.[a]

[The] *Sherbert* test [was] developed in a context that lent itself to individualized governmental assessment of the reasons for the relevant conduct. [O]ur decisions in the unemployment cases stand for the proposition that where the State has in place a system of individual exemptions, it may not refuse to extend that system to cases of "religious hardship" without compelling reason.[b]

Whether or not the decisions are that limited, they at least have nothing to do with an across-the-board criminal prohibition on a particular form of conduct. [T]he sounder approach, and the approach in accord with the vast majority of our precedents, is to hold the test inapplicable to such challenges. [To] make an individual's obligation to obey such a law contingent upon the law's coincidence with his religious beliefs, except where the State's interest is "compelling"—permitting him, by virtue of

a. For a careful review of the cases, both in the Supreme Court and in the U.S. courts of appeals for ten years preceding *Smith*, concluding that "despite the apparent protection afforded claimants by the language of the compelling interest test, courts overwhelmingly sided with the government when applying that test," see James E. Ryan, *Smith and the Religious Freedom Restoration Act: An Iconoclastic Assessment,* 78 Va.L.Rev. 1407 (1992). See also Jesse H. Choper, *The Rise and Decline of the Constitutional Protection of Religious Liberty,* 70 Neb.L.Rev. 651, 659–70 (1991).

b. For the view that the system of discretionary hearings involved in the unemployment cases presents "a fertile ground for the undervaluation of minority religious interests" and is therefore "vulnerable to a distinct constitutional objection," see Christopher L. Eisgruber & Lawrence G. Sager, *The Vulnerability of Conscience: The Constitutional Basis for Protecting Religious Conduct,* 61 U.Chi.L.Rev. 1245 (1994). For an empirical study reaching an opposite conclusion, see Prabha S. Bhandari, *The Failure of Equal Regard to Explain the Sherbert Quartet,* 72 N.Y.U.L.Rev. 97 (1997). See also Ira C. Lupu, *The Case Against Legislative Codification of Religious Liberty,* 21 Card.L.Rev. 565, 573 (1999): "Long prior to *Smith*, our civil liberties tradition had recognized the dangers of permitting local officials to exercise licensing authority over expressive activity without the benefit of determinate criteria. The absence of such criteria invites discriminatory treatment of groups disfavored by local decision makers. Identical concerns [favor] aggressive implementation of [the] anti-discrimination principle of free exercise with the individual assessment principle which *Smith* purports to preserve."

For review of lower court decisions that have attempted to "evade" *Smith* through the "individual exemptions" analysis and the "hybrid rights exemption," see Carol M. Kaplan, *The Devil is in the Details: Neutral, Generally Applicable Laws and Exceptions from Smith,* 75 N.Y.U.L.Rev. 1045 (2000).

his beliefs, "to become a law unto himself," *Reynolds*—contradicts both constitutional tradition and common sense.[2]

The "compelling government interest" requirement seems benign, because it is familiar from other fields. But using it as the standard that must be met before the government may accord different treatment on the basis of race, or before the government may regulate the content of speech, is not remotely comparable to using it for the purpose asserted here. What it produces in those other fields—equality of treatment, and an unrestricted flow of contending speech—are constitutional norms; what it would produce here—a private right to ignore generally applicable laws—is a constitutional anomaly.[3]

Nor is it possible to limit the impact of respondents' proposal by requiring a "compelling state interest" only when the conduct prohibited is "central" to the individual's religion. It is no more appropriate for judges to determine the "centrality" of religious beliefs [than] it would be for them to determine the "importance" of ideas before applying the "compelling interest" test in the free speech field. What principle of law or logic can be brought to bear to contradict a believer's assertion that a particular act is "central" to his personal faith? [I]n many different contexts, we have warned that courts must not presume to determine the place of a particular belief in a religion or the plausibility of a religious claim. See, e.g., *Thomas* [Part II infra]; *Jones v. Wolf,* [Ch. 13]; *Ballard*.[4]

If the "compelling interest" test is to be applied at all, then, it must be applied across the board, to all actions thought to be religiously commanded. Moreover, if "compelling interest" really means what it says (and watering it down here would subvert its rigor in the other fields

---

2. Justice O'Connor seeks to distinguish *Lyng* and *Roy* on the ground that those cases involved the government's conduct of "its own internal affairs." [But] it is hard to see any reason in principle or practicality why the government should have to tailor its health and safety laws to conform to the diversity of religious belief, but should not have to tailor its management of public lands, *Lyng,* or its administration of welfare programs, *Roy.*

3. [Just] as we subject to the most exacting scrutiny laws that make classifications based on race or on the content of speech, so too we strictly scrutinize governmental classifications based on religion, see *McDaniel;* see also *Torcaso.* But we have held that race-neutral laws that have the *effect* of disproportionately disadvantaging a particular racial group do not thereby become subject to compelling-interest analysis under the Equal Protection Clause, see *Washington v. Davis,* 426 U.S. 229 (176) (police employment examination); and we have held that generally applicable laws unconcerned with regulating speech that have the *effect* of interfering with speech do not thereby become subject to compelling-interest analysis under the First Amendment, see *Citizen Publishing Co. v. United States* (antitrust laws). Our conclusion [today] is the only approach compatible with these precedents.

4. [In] any case, dispensing with a "centrality" inquiry is utterly unworkable. It would require, for example, the same degree of "compelling state interest" to impede the practice of throwing rice at church weddings as to impede the practice of getting married in church. There is no way out of the difficulty that, if general laws are to be subjected to a "religious practice" exception, *both* the importance of the law at issue *and* the centrality of the practice at issue must reasonably be considered. * * *

[For the conclusion that "the Court has never required that the claimant establish either centrality or compulsion to receive protection under the First Amendment," see Steven C. Seeger, *Restoring Rights to Rites: The Religious Motivation Test and the Religious Freedom Restoration Act,* 95 Mich.L.Rev. 1472 (1997).]

where it is applied), many laws will not meet the test. Any society adopting such a system would be courting anarchy, but that danger increases in direct proportion to the society's diversity of religious [beliefs].[c] Precisely because "we are a cosmopolitan nation made up of people of almost every conceivable religious preference," and precisely because we value and protect that religious divergence, we cannot afford the luxury of deeming *presumptively invalid,* as applied to the religious objector, every regulation of conduct that does not protect an interest of the highest order. The rule respondents favor would open the prospect of constitutionally required religious exemptions from civic obligations of almost every conceivable kind—ranging from compulsory military service, see, e.g., *Gillette,* to the payment of taxes, see, e.g., *Lee,* to health and safety regulation such as manslaughter and child neglect laws, compulsory vaccination laws, drug laws, and traffic laws, to social welfare legislation such as minimum wage laws, see *Tony and Susan Alamo Foundation v. Secretary of Labor,* 471 U.S. 290 (1985), child labor laws, see *Prince;* animal cruelty laws, see, e.g., *Church of the Lukumi Babalu Aye Inc. v. Hialeah,* [note 1 infra], environmental protection laws, and laws providing for equality of opportunity for the races, see e.g., *Bob Jones University.* The First Amendment's protection of religious liberty does not require this.[5]

[A] number of States have made an exception to their drug laws for sacramental peyote use. But to say that a nondiscriminatory religious-practice exemption is permitted, or even that it is desirable, is not to say that it is constitutionally required, and that the appropriate occasions for its creation can be discerned by the courts.[d] It may fairly be said that

---

c. Contra, Gary Simson, *Endangering Religious Liberty*, 84 Calif.L.Rev. 441, 461 (1996): "[I]t is far from clear that the government's ability to govern effectively would be seriously undermined as a result. After all, since the legislative process generally makes allowance for the needs of adherents of mainstream religions, court-ordered exemptions typically would be limited in scope to affected members of relatively small groups."

5. Justice O'Connor contends that the "parade of horribles" in the text only "demonstrates [that] courts have been quite capable of strik[ing] sensible balances between religious liberty and competing state interests." But the cases we cite have struck "sensible balances" only because they have all applied the general laws, despite the claims for religious exemption. In any event, Justice O'Connor mistakes the purpose of our parade: it is not to suggest that courts would necessarily permit harmful exemptions from these laws (though they might), but to suggest that courts would constantly be in the business of determining whether the "severe impact" of various laws on religious practice (to use Justice Blackmun's terminology) or the "constitutiona[l] significan[ce]" of the "burden on the particular plaintiffs" (to use Justice O'Connor's terminology) suffices to permit us to confer an exemption. It [is] horrible to contemplate that federal judges will regularly balance against the importance of general laws the significance of religious practice.

[Compare Douglas Laycock & Oliver S. Thomas, *Interpreting the Religious Freedom Restoration Act,* 73 Tex. L. Rev. 209, 221 (1994): "Whatever the theoretical values of republican deliberation, the reality of the legislative process is totally unsuited to principled decisions about whether one faction's desire to suppress an annoying religious practice is really the least restrictive means of serving a compelling government interest."]

d. Does a "religious-practice exemption" violate the Religion Clauses principle of "neutrality"? Consider Phillip Kurland, *Religion and the Law* 112 (1962): "The [Free Exercise and Establishment] clauses should be read as stating a single precept: that government cannot utilize religion as a standard for action or inaction because these clauses, read together as they should be, prohibit classification in terms of religion either to confer a benefit or to impose a burden." For thoughtful comment, see Paul Kauper, *Book Review,* 41 Texas L.Rev. 467 (1963); Leo Pfeffer,

leaving accommodation to the political process will place at a relative disadvantage those religious practices that are not widely engaged in;[e] but that unavoidable consequence of democratic government must be preferred to a system in which each conscience is a law unto itself or in which judges weigh the social importance of all laws against the centrality of all religious beliefs. * * *[f]

JUSTICE O'CONNOR, with whom JUSTICE BRENNAN, JUSTICE MARSHALL, and JUSTICE BLACKMUN join as to [Part II], concurring in the judgment. * * *

II. [A] law that prohibits certain conduct—conduct that happens to be an act of worship for someone—manifestly does prohibit that person's free exercise of his religion [regardless] of whether the law prohibits the conduct only when engaged in for religious reasons, only by members of that religion, or by all persons.

[If] the First Amendment is to have any vitality, it ought not be construed to cover only the extreme and hypothetical situation in which a State directly targets a religious practice. [Yoder] expressly rejected the interpretation the Court now adopts: "[T]o agree that religiously grounded conduct must often be subject to the broad police power of the State is not to deny that there are areas of conduct protected by the Free Exercise Clause [and] thus beyond the power of the State to control, *even under regulations of general applicability*. [A] regulation neutral on its face may, in its application, nonetheless offend the constitutional requirement for government neutrality if it unduly burdens the free exercise of religion."

The Court endeavors to escape from our decisions in *Cantwell* and *Yoder* by labeling them "hybrid" decisions but there is no denying that both cases expressly relied on the Free Exercise Clause. [I]n each of the other cases cited by the Court to support its categorical rule, we rejected the particular constitutional claims before us only after carefully weighing the competing interests. [That] we rejected the free exercise claims in those cases hardly calls into question the applicability of First Amendment doctrine.

[W]e have never distinguished between cases in which a State conditions receipt of a benefit on conduct prohibited by religious beliefs and cases in which a State affirmatively prohibits such conduct. The *Sherbert* compelling interest test applies in both kinds of cases. [A] neutral criminal law prohibiting conduct that a State may legitimately regulate is, if

---

Religion–Blind Government, 15 Stan.L.Rev. 389 (1963); John Mansfield, *Book Review*, 52 Calif.L.Rev. 212 (1964). For consideration of "the extent to which equality, as a constitutional value, constrains our understanding of religious guarantees," see Laura S. Underkuffler–Freund, *Yoder and the Question of Equality*, 25 Cap.U.L.Rev. 789 (1996).

e. Since *Smith*, "more than half the states appear to have adopted some version of the *Sherbert-Yoder* test." Douglas Laycock, *Comment: Theology Scholarships, the Pledge of Allegiance, and Religious Liberty: Avoiding the Extremes but Missing the Liberty*, 118 Harv.L.Rev. 155, 212 (2004).

f. For a comprehensive and sensitive discussion of the role of judges in reviewing the nature of the burden on religious exercise and the strength of the state interest in not granting an exemption, see 1 Greenawalt ch. 13.

anything, *more* burdensome than a neutral civil statute placing legitimate conditions on the award of a state benefit.

[Even] if, as an empirical matter, a government's criminal laws might usually serve a compelling interest in health, safety, or public order, the First Amendment at least requires a case-by-case determination of the question, sensitive to the facts of each particular claim. Given the range of conduct that a State might legitimately make criminal, we cannot assume, merely because a law carries criminal sanctions and is generally applicable, that the First Amendment *never* requires the State to grant a limited exemption for religiously motivated conduct.

Moreover, we have not "rejected" or "declined to apply" the compelling interest test in our recent cases. See, e.g., *Hobbie*. The cases cited by the Court signal no retreat from our consistent adherence to the compelling interest test. In both *Roy* and *Lyng*, for example, we expressly distinguished *Sherbert* on the ground that the First Amendment does not "require the Government *itself* to behave in ways that the individual believes will further his or her spiritual development. * * * " This distinction makes sense because "the Free Exercise Clause is written in terms of what the government cannot do to the individual, not in terms of what the individual can exact from the government." *Sherbert* (Douglas, J., concerning).[g] Because [this case] plainly falls into the former category, I would apply those established precedents to the facts of this case.

Similarly, the other cases cited by the Court for the proposition that we have rejected application of the *Sherbert* test outside the unemployment compensation field are distinguishable because they arose in the narrow, specialized contexts in which we have not traditionally required the government to justify a burden on religious conduct by articulating a compelling interest. See *Goldman v. Weinberger* ("Our review of military regulations challenged on First Amendment grounds is far more deferential than constitutional review of similar laws or regulations designed for civilian society"); *O'Lone v. Shabazz* ("[P]rison regulations alleged to infringe constitutional rights are judged under a 'reasonableness' test less restrictive than that ordinarily applied to alleged infringements of fundamental constitutional rights"). That we did not apply the compelling interest test in these cases says nothing about whether the test should continue to apply in paradigm free exercise cases such as the one presented here.

[As] the language of the Clause itself makes clear, an individual's free exercise of religion is a preferred constitutional activity. A law that makes criminal such an activity therefore [triggers] heightened judicial scrutiny. [Our] free speech cases similarly recognize that neutral regulations that

---

g. For the view that *Lyng's* approach, which "seems to involve neither social science nor theology," attracts the Court because it functions to "reduce the number of claims that must be afforded the searching inquiry demanded by the free exercise clause" and to permit the Court to avoid resolving the difficult issues of "cognizability of the asserted burden, the sincerity of the claimant, and religiosity of the claim," see Ira C. Lupu, *Where Rights Begin: The Problem of Burdens on The Free Exercise of Religion,* 102 Harv.L.Rev. 933 (1989).

affect free speech values are subject to a balancing, rather than categorical, approach. See, e.g., *United States v. O'Brien,* [Ch. 2]; *Renton v. Playtime Theatres, Inc.,* [Ch. 3, I]; cf. *Anderson v. Celebrezze,* 460 U.S. 780 (1983) (generally applicable laws may impinge on free association concerns). * * *

Finally, the Court today suggests that the disfavoring of minority religions is an "unavoidable consequence" under our system of government and that accommodation of such religions must be left to the political process. In my view, however, the First Amendment was enacted precisely to protect the rights of those whose religious practices are not shared by the majority and may be viewed with hostility. The history of our free exercise doctrine amply demonstrates the harsh impact majoritarian rule has had on unpopular or emerging religious groups such as the Jehovah's Witnesses and the Amish.[h] [The] compelling interest test reflects the First Amendment's mandate of preserving religious liberty to the fullest extent possible in a pluralistic society. For the Court to deem this command a "luxury," is to denigrate "[t]he very purpose of a Bill of Rights."

III. The Court's holding today [is] unnecessary to this case. I would reach the same result applying our established free exercise jurisprudence.

There is no dispute that Oregon's criminal prohibition of peyote places a severe burden on the ability of respondents to freely exercise their religion. Peyote is a sacrament of the Native American Church and is regarded as vital to respondents' ability to practice their religion. * * *

There is also no dispute that Oregon has a significant interest in enforcing laws that control the possession and use of controlled substances by its citizens. [Indeed,] under federal law (incorporated by Oregon law in relevant part), peyote is specifically regulated as a Schedule I controlled substance, which means that Congress has found that it has a high potential for abuse, that there is no currently accepted medical use, and that there is a lack of accepted safety for use of the drug under medical supervision. In light of our recent decisions holding that the governmental interests in the collection of income tax, *Hernandez v. Comm'n,* [Ch. 13

---

h. See also Douglas Laycock, *Formal, Substantive, and Disaggregated Neutrality Toward Religion,* 39 De Paul L.Rev. 993, 1016 (1990): "Of course, inadvertence can interact with hostility, or with an insensitivity that borders on hostility. Consider what might happen when Frances Quaring [fn. f in *Bob Jones*] writes her legislator [who] may find it so impossible to empathize with her belief that he never seriously considers whether an exemption would be workable. Even if he empathizes, the legislative calendar is crowded, and the original statute having been enacted, all the burdens of legislative inertia now work against an exemption."

Compare Eisengruber & Sager, supra, at 1304: "[After *Lyng,*] the political process responded to interests the judiciary had not protected, and the Bureau of Land Management relocated the road. [After *Lee,*] Congress accommodated churches that had religious objections to participating in the social security system. [After *Goldman,*] Congress granted relief. And [after *Smith,*] Oregon legislated an exemption to its law," and Congress protected religious use of peyote in all states. But contrast Dhananjai Shivakumar, *Neutrality and the Religion Clauses,* 33 Harv. Civ. Rts.—Civ. Lib. L. Rev. 505, 512 n. 28 (1998): "[R]ejection of meaningful judicial review will deprive free exercise claimants of one historically effective way of eliciting attention and public support[:] litigation. Many well-known examples of political accommodation were preceded by lengthy, well-publicized free exercise litigation."

infra], a comprehensive social security system, see *Lee,* and military conscription, see *Gillette,* are compelling, respondents do not seriously dispute that Oregon has a compelling interest in prohibiting the possession of peyote. [Although] the question is close, I would conclude that uniform application of Oregon's criminal prohibition is "essential to accomplish," *Lee,* its overriding interest in preventing the physical harm caused by the use of a Schedule I controlled substance. [Because] the health effects caused by the use of controlled substances exist regardless of the motivation of the user, [use] for religious purposes, violates the very purpose of the laws that prohibit them. Moreover, in view of the societal interest in preventing trafficking[,] uniform application of the criminal prohibition at issue is essential to the effectiveness of Oregon's stated interest in preventing any possession of peyote. * * *

Respondents contend that any incompatibility is belied by the fact that the Federal Government and several States provide exemptions for the religious use of peyote. But other governments may surely choose to grant an exemption without Oregon, with its specific asserted interest in uniform application of its drug laws, being *required* to do so by the First Amendment. Respondents also note that the sacramental use of peyote is central to the tenets of the Native American Church, but I agree with the Court [that] "[i]t is not within the judicial ken to question the centrality of particular beliefs or practices to a faith." [This] does not mean [that] courts may not make factual findings as to whether a claimant holds a sincerely held religious belief that conflicts with [the] challenged law. The distinction between questions of centrality and questions of sincerity and burden is admittedly fine, but it is one that is an established part of our free exercise doctrine * * *.[i]

JUSTICE BLACKMUN, with whom JUSTICE BRENNAN and JUSTICE MARSHALL join, dissenting.

This Court over the years painstakingly has developed a consistent and exacting standard to test the constitutionality of a state statute that burdens the free exercise of religion. Such a statute may stand only if the law in general, and the State's refusal to allow a religious exemption in particular, are justified by a compelling interest that cannot be served by less restrictive means.

[I]t is important to articulate in precise terms the state interest involved. It is not the State's broad interest in fighting the critical "war

---

i. In *Boerne v. Flores,* fn. i infra, O'Connor, J., joined by Breyer, J., argued that "the historical evidence [bears] out the conclusion that, at the time the Bill of Rights was ratified, it was accepted that government should, when possible, accommodate religious practice." Scalia, J., joined by Stevens, J., disagreed: "The historical evidence put forward by the dissent does nothing to undermine the conclusion we reached in *Smith.*" For an extensive review, see Michael W. McConnell, *Freedom From Persecution or Protection of the Rights of Conscience?: A Critique of Justice Scalia's Historical Arguments,* 39 Wm. & M. L. Rev. 819 (1998). For support at the time of the Fourteenth Amendment for O'Connor, J.'s position, see Kurt T. Lash, *The Second Adoption of the Free Exercise Clause: Religious Exemptions Under the Fourteenth Amendment,* 88 Nw.U.L.Rev. 1106, 1149–55 (1994). For the view that the original understanding of the Free Exercise Clause was an "unqualified" right to be free from "penalty" or "discrimination" on the basis of religion, see Phillip Hamburger, *More Is Less,* 90 Va.L.Rev. 835 (2004).

on drugs" that must be weighed against respondents' claim, but the State's narrow interest in refusing to make an exception for the religious, ceremonial use of peyote. [The] State cannot plausibly assert that unbending application of a criminal prohibition is essential to fulfill any compelling interest, if it does not, in fact, attempt to enforce that prohibition. * * * Oregon has never sought to prosecute respondents, and does not claim that it has made significant enforcement efforts against other religious users of peyote. The State's asserted interest thus amounts only to the symbolic preservation of an unenforced prohibition. * * *

Similarly, this Court's prior decisions have not allowed a government to rely on mere speculation about potential harms, but have demanded evidentiary support for a refusal to allow a religious exception. [In] this case, the State [offers] no evidence that the religious use of peyote has ever harmed anyone. The factual findings of other courts cast doubt on the State's assumption that religious use of peyote is harmful. See *State v. Whittingham,* 19 Ariz.App. 27, 30, 504 P.2d 950, 953 (1973) ("the State failed to prove that the quantities of peyote used in the sacraments of the Native American Church are sufficiently harmful to the health and welfare of the participants * * * "); *People v. Woody,* 61 Cal.2d 716, 722–723, 40 Cal.Rptr. 69, 74, 394 P.2d 813, 818 (1964) ("as the Attorney General [admits,] the opinion of scientists and other experts is 'that peyote [works] no permanent deleterious injury to the Indian' ").

The fact that peyote is classified as a Schedule I controlled substance does not, by itself, show that any and all uses of peyote, in any circumstance, are inherently harmful and dangerous. The Federal Government [does] not find peyote so dangerous as to preclude an exemption for religious use.[5] Moreover, other Schedule I drugs have lawful uses. See *Olsen v. Drug Enforcement Administration,* 878 F.2d 1458 (D.C.Cir.1989) (medical and research uses of marijuana).

The carefully circumscribed ritual context in which respondents used peyote is far removed from the irresponsible and unrestricted recreational use of unlawful drugs.[6] * * * *[7] [J]ust as in *Yoder,* the values and interests of those seeking a religious exemption in this case are congruent, to a great degree, with those the State seeks to promote through its drug laws. See *Yoder* (since the Amish accept formal schooling up to 8th grade, and then provide "ideal" vocational education, State's interest in enforcing its law against the Amish is "less substantial than [for] children generally"). Not only does the Church's doctrine forbid nonreligious use of peyote; it also generally advocates self-reliance, familial responsibility, and absti-

---

5. [Moreover,] 23 States, including many that have significant Native American populations, have statutory or judicially crafted exemptions in their drug laws for religious [use].

6. In this respect, respondents' use of peyote seems closely analogous to the sacramental use of wine by the Roman Catholic Church. During Prohibition, the Federal Government exempted such use of wine from its general [ban]. However compelling the Government's then general interest in prohibiting the use of alcohol may have been, it could not plausibly have asserted an interest sufficiently compelling to outweigh Catholics' right to take communion.

7. The use of peyote is, to some degree, self-limiting. [It] is extremely bitter, and eating it is an unpleasant experience, which would tend to discourage casual or recreational use.

nence from alcohol. There is considerable evidence that the spiritual and social support provided by the Church has been effective in combatting the tragic effects of alcoholism on the Native American population. * * *

The State also seeks to support its refusal to make an exception [by] invoking its interest in abolishing drug trafficking. There is, however, practically no illegal traffic in peyote. Also, the availability of peyote for religious use, even if Oregon were to allow an exemption from its criminal laws, would still be strictly controlled by federal regulations, see 21 U.S.C. §§ 821–823 (registration requirements for distribution of controlled substances); and by the State of Texas, the only State in which peyote grows in significant quantities. Peyote simply is not a popular drug; its distribution for use in religious rituals has nothing to do with the vast and violent traffic in illegal narcotics that plagues this country.

Finally, the State argues that, [if] it grants an exemption for religious peyote use, a flood of other claims to religious exemptions will follow. It would then be placed in a dilemma, it says, between allowing a patchwork of exemptions that would hinder its law enforcement efforts, and risking a violation of the Establishment Clause by arbitrarily limiting its religious exemptions. [But almost] half the States, and the Federal Government, have maintained an exemption for religious peyote use for many years, and apparently have not found themselves overwhelmed by claims to other religious exemptions.[8] [The] unusual circumstances that make the religious use of peyote compatible with the State's interests in health and safety and in preventing drug trafficking would not apply to other religious claims. Some religions, for example, might not restrict drug use to a limited ceremonial context, as does the Native American Church. See, e.g., *Olsen* ("the Ethiopian Zion Coptic Church [teaches] that marijuana is properly smoked 'continually all day' "). Some religious claims involve drugs such as marijuana and heroin, in which there is significant illegal traffic, [so] that it would be difficult to grant a religious exemption without seriously compromising law enforcement efforts.[9] [Though] the State must treat all religions equally, and not favor one over another, this obligation is fulfilled by the uniform application of the "compelling interest" *test* to all free exercise claims, not by reaching uniform *results* as to all claims. * * *

Respondents believe, and their sincerity has *never* been at issue, that the peyote plant embodies their deity, and eating it is an act of worship and communion. Without peyote, they could not enact the essential ritual of their religion. [This] potentially devastating impact must be viewed in light of the federal policy—reached in reaction to many years of religious

---

8. [V]arious sects have raised free exercise claims regarding drug use. In no reported case, except those involving claims of religious peyote use, has the claimant prevailed.

9. Thus, this case is distinguishable from *Lee,* in which the Court concluded that there was "no principled way" to distinguish other exemption claims, and the "tax system could not function if denominations were allowed to challenge the tax system because tax payments were spent in a manner that violates their religious belief."

persecution and intolerance—of protecting the religious freedom of Native Americans. See American Indian Religious Freedom Act. * * *j

Notes and Questions

1. **_Significance of other constitutional provisions._** What result under the _Smith_ rule if a state law barring religious discrimination in employment is applied to churches' selection of their clergy? If a church is sued for "negligent supervision of employees" because its clergy have been found guilty of sexual abuse? Of what relevance is the freedom of expressive association (_Boy Scouts of America v. Dale_, Ch. 9, II)? See Mark Tushnet, _The Redundant Free Exercise Clause?_, 33 Loy.U.Chi.L.J. 71 (2001); Kathleen A. Brady, _Religious Organizations and Free Exercise: The Surprising Lessons of Smith_, 2004 B.Y.U.L.Rev. 1633, 1636, 1676 ("_Smith_ supports a broad right of church autonomy" because of its emphasis that "religious _beliefs_ as such" are absolutely protected and the fact that religious groups "play an important role in the formation of religious beliefs"); Ira C. Lupu & Robert W. Tuttle, _Sexual Misconduct and Ecclesiastical Immunity_, 2004 B.Y.U.L.Rev. 1789, 1815 (_Smith's_ recognition of "ecclesiastical immunities," which are rooted in the Establishment Clause, forbids the state to "adjudicate or regulate the ways in which communities of faith are organized"). See further _Jones v. Wolf_, Ch. 13 infra. Compare Paul Horwitz, _Churches as First Amendment Institutions: Of Sovereignty and Spheres_, 44 Harv. Civ. Rts.—Civ. Libs. L. Rev. 79, 120 (2009) (under "sphere sovereignty" approach, "churches are entitled to a substantial degree of decision-making autonomy with respect to membership and employment matters, regardless of the nature of the employee or the grounds of discrimination") with Ira C. Lupu & Robert W. Tuttle, _Courts, Clergy, and Congregations: Disputes Between Religious Institutions and Their Leaders_, 7 Geo. J. L. & Pub. Pol'y, 119, 163 (2009) (permitting "adjudication between clergy and their employers" when "limited to secular and temporal concerns"). Contrast Laura S. Underkuffler, _Thoughts on Smith and Religious–Group Autonomy_, 2004 B.Y.U.L.Rev. 1773, 1787 ("there is no convincing basis for distinguishing individual religious exemptions, struck down in _Smith_, from aggressive forms of religious-group autonomy" which "pose far more dangers of individual oppression, governmental interference, and undermining of societal norms than autonomously acting individuals"). For the view that free exercise claims should be treated "no differently than free expression claims," see Marshall, _Solving the Free Exercise Dilemma: Free Exercise as Expression_, 67 Minn.L.Rev. 545 (1983). For a general discussion of the comparative advantages of the Free Speech and Free Exercise Clauses in protecting religious liberty, see Alan Brownstein, _Protecting Religious Liberty:_

---

j. In 1993, Congress passed the Religious Freedom Restoration Act which effectively reinstated the _Sherbert-Yoder_ test for generally applicable laws that burden religious practices. RFRA was held unconstitutional in _Boerne v. Flores_, 521 U.S. 507 (1997).

For the view that the "core meaning of the Establishment Clause" prevents congressional efforts to "tell states what relation their laws must have to the fostering of one or all religions," which "means that Congress may not try to dictate church-state relations even to vindicate religious toleration or free exercise," see Jed Rubenfeld, _Antidisestablishmentarianism: Why RFRA Really Was Unconstitutional_, 95 Mich.L.Rev. 2347 (1997).

The False Messiahs of Free Speech Doctrine and Formal Neutrality, 18 J.L. & Pol. 119–85 (2002).

2. ***Discrimination.*** (a) CHURCH OF THE LUKUMI BABALU AYE, INC. v. HIALEAH, 508 U.S. 520 (1993), per KENNEDY, J., held that city ordinances barring ritual animal sacrifice violated the Free Exercise Clause: "[I]f the object of a law is to infringe upon or restrict practices because of their religious motivation, the law is not neutral, see *Smith;* and it is invalid unless it is justified by a compelling interest and is narrowly tailored to advance that interest. [The] ordinances had as their object the suppression of [the Santeria] religion. The [record] discloses animosity to Santeria adherents and their religious practices; the ordinances by their own terms target this religious exercise; the texts of the ordinances were gerrymandered with care to proscribe religious killings of animals but to exclude almost all secular killings; and the ordinances suppress much more religious conduct than is necessary in order to achieve the legitimate ends asserted in their defense. [A] law that targets religious conduct for distinctive treatment or advances legitimate governmental interests only against conduct with a religious motivation will survive strict scrutiny only in rare cases. [T]hese ordinances cannot withstand this scrutiny."

SOUTER, J., concurred specially "for I have doubts whether the *Smith* rule merits adherence": Because "*Smith* refrained from overruling prior free-exercise cases that [are] fundamentally at odds with the rule *Smith* declared, [in] a case presenting the issue, the Court should re-examine the rule *Smith* declared."

BLACKMUN, J., joined by O'Connor, J., concurred only in the judgment: "I continue to believe that *Smith* was wrongly decided, because it ignored the value of religious freedom as an affirmative individual liberty and treated the Free Exercise Clause as no more than an antidiscrimination principle." Moreover, "when a law discriminates against religion as such, as do the ordinances in this case, it automatically will fail strict scrutiny [because] a law that targets religious practice for disfavored treatment both burdens the free exercise of religion and, by definition, is not precisely tailored to a compelling governmental interest.

"[This] case does not [decide] whether the Free Exercise Clause would require a religious exemption from a law that sincerely pursued the goal of protecting animals from cruel treatment. [That] is not a concern to be treated lightly."

(b) ***Scope.*** Does the *Smith-Lukumi* rule bar only those laws whose "object is suppression" of a religious practice? For the view that "empirical data show conclusively" a "persistent judicial bias and religious insensitivity" in applying strict scrutiny under *Sherbert,* and that a rule requiring the government to "bear the burden of establishing the actual reason for the law" would "provide a powerful tool for rooting out more subtle forms of discrimination against unpopular minority religions," see Ronald J. Krotoszynski, Jr., *If Judges Were Angels: Religious Equality, Free Exercise, and the (Under-appreciated) Merits of Smith,* 102 Nw. U. L. Rev. 1189, 1196–99 (2008). After *Lukumi,* what result in *Smith* if Oregon had permitted the medicinal use of peyote (or marijuana) in designated circumstances to relieve pain? Would the law barring other uses of peyote (including sacramental use) be "generally applicable"? Or would it "target religious conduct"? Of what relevance is *Smith's* reaffirmation of *Sherbert's* "individualized governmental assessment" context? Consider Richard F. Duncan, *Free Exercise Is Dead, Long Live Free Exercise: Smith, Lukumi and the General Applicability Requirement,* 3 U.Pa. J.Con.L. 850, 862 (2001): "[W]henever you are dealing with burdensome regulations administered by [government,] there will often be some process for requesting an exemption, waiver, or variance. Even if the regulation [is] generally applicable on its face, if a state agency grants ad hoc exemptions [in] even a few cases involving secular claims, it may not refuse to grant similar exemptions [for] 'religious hardship' without satisfying strict scrutiny." See also Frederick M. Gedicks, *The Normalized Free Exercise Clause: Three Abnormalities,* 75 Ind. L.J. 77, 117–120 (2000): "[T]he free exercise of religion is a fundamental right, the protection of which is specified by the constitutional text [but] the Court is not treating free exercise rights like privacy, speech, travel, and other fundamental [rights.] Fundamental rights/equal protection analysis makes clear that any law or government action that excuses—by administrative exemption, legislative exemption, or otherwise—one or more secular activities but not *comparable* religious practices creates a classification that impermissibly burdens the fundamental right of free exercise of religion, and thus should normally be subject to strict scrutiny."

If a state bars ingestion of all alcoholic beverages but exempts sacramental use, may it bar ingestion of all hallucinogenic substances without exempting sacramental use? See Michael J. Perry, *Freedom of Religion in the United States: Fin de Siècle Sketches,* 75 Ind.L.J. 295, 305 (2000). If "a school committed to the Montessori philosophy of education, or to a pacifist or multiculturalist approach, is legally free to require that its staff adhere to that ideology," may a religious school be forbidden to discriminate in employment on the basis of religion? Suppose it receives vouchers as part of a general program? See Thomas C. Berg, *Vouchers and Religious Schools: The New Constitutional Questions,* 72 U.Cinc.L.Rev. 151, 216 (2003).

What result if Hialeah's ordinance barred "all other exhibitionistic killings, like those that are sometimes performed by entertainers or as part of college fraternity or other initiation ceremonies." See Lino A. Graglia, *Church of the Lukumi Babalu Aye: Of Animal Sacrifice and Religious Persecution,* 85 Geo. L. J. 1, 36 (1996). What result under the *Smith-Lukumi* rule if a state prohibits *all* polygamous marriages after a religious group that engages in the practice becomes active in the state? See Garrett Epps, *What We Talk About When We Talk About Free Exercise,* 30 Ariz.St.L.J. 563 (1998).

(c) ***Aid to religious schools.*** Is the Court's statement, that denial of financial benefits to religious schools does not infringe the free exercise rights of attending children,[a] consistent with *Smith* and *Lukumi*? Could a student bus transportation program include all nonprofit private schools except religious schools? See *Luetkemeyer v. Kaufmann,* 419 U.S. 888 (1974). Would affording aid to *all* schools (public and nonpublic) *except* those that are

---

a. See the dictum in *Sloan v. Lemon,* 413 U.S. 825 (1973): "[V]alid aid to nonpublic, nonsectarian schools would provide no lever for aid to their sectarian counterparts."

church-related "target religious conduct" (*Lukumi*)? Consider Jesse H. Choper, *Federal Constitutional Issues*, in *School Choice and Social Controversy* 235, 249 (Sugarman & Kemerer eds. 1999): "First, such a program would plainly discriminate on its face against 'some or all religious beliefs,' violating the basic protections of the Free Exercise Clause, unless justified after strict scrutiny. Second, since all schools teach values, the state could be fairly seen as discriminating against religious viewpoints, much as the University of Virginia had done in *Rosenberger*, and would also be subject to strict scrutiny under the Free Speech Clause [see Ch.7, I]. *Lukumi* and *Rosenberger* would appear to compel the inclusion of religious schools in any voucher program or other plan of aid to education that included nonreligious private schools."

Indeed, might it be argued that *Sherbert* would require aid for parochial schools even though public support was given only to public schools? If some religions impose a duty on parents to send children to religious schools, may these parents argue that, since they must pay public school taxes, the state's failure to support parochial as well as public schools imposes a serious financial burden on their exercise of religion? That "conditioning the availability of benefits upon their willingness to violate a cardinal principle of their religious faith effectively penalizes the free exercise of their constitutional liberties" (*Sherbert*); that there is no "compelling state interest to justify the substantial infringement of their First Amendment rights"? May these parents further argue that their position is stronger than *Sherbert*, *Thomas* and *Hobbie* because the purpose of granting an exemption in that case was *solely* to aid religion whereas there is a wholly nonreligious purpose in giving aid to all nonpublic schools—improving the quality of the secular education? What result after *Smith*? See Choper, supra, at 246–48.

(d) LOCKE v. DAVEY, 540 U.S. 712 (2004), per REHNQUIST, C.J., held that the exclusion (as required by the state constitution) from Washington's postsecondary education Promise Scholarship Program to assist academically gifted students, of pursuit of a devotional theology degree (i.e., one "designed to induce religious faith"), did not violate the Free Exercise Clause: "[W]e have long said that 'there is room for play in the points' between [the religion clauses]. *Walz*. In other words, there are some state actions permitted by the Establishment Clause but not required by the Free Exercise Clause. [And] there is no doubt that the State could, consistent with the Federal Constitution, permit Promise Scholars to pursue a degree in devotional theology, see *Witters* * * *.

"[Respondent] contends that [under] *Lukumi*, the program is presumptively unconstitutional because it is not facially neutral with respect to religion. [But here], the State's disfavor of religion (if it can be called that) is of a far milder kind [than in *Lukumi*]. It imposes neither criminal nor civil sanctions on any type of religious service or rite. It does not deny to ministers the right to participate in the political affairs of the community. See *McDaniel*. And it does not require students to choose between their religious beliefs and receiving a government benefit.[4] See *Hobbie*; *Sherbert*. The State has merely chosen not to fund a distinct category of instruction.[a]

---

4. Promise Scholars may still use their scholarship to pursue a secular degree at a different institution from where they are studying devotional theology.

"[M]ajoring in devotional theology is akin to a religious calling as well as an academic pursuit. [T]he interest that [the Washington constitution] seeks to further is scarcely novel. In fact, we can think of few areas in which a State's antiestablishment interests come more into play. Since the founding of our country, there have been popular uprisings against procuring taxpayer funds to support church leaders, which was one of the hallmarks of an 'established' religion. * * *

Most States that sought to avoid such an establishment around the time of the founding placed in their constitutions formal prohibitions against using tax funds to support the ministry. [T]hat early state constitutions saw no problem in explicitly excluding *only* the ministry from receiving state dollars reinforces the conclusion that religious instruction is of a different ilk.

"Far from evincing the hostility toward religion which was manifest in *Lukumi,* we believe that the entirety of the Promise Scholarship Program goes a long way toward including religion in its benefits.[8] The program permits students to attend pervasively religious schools, so long as they are accredited [and] students are still eligible to take devotional theology courses."

SCALIA, J., joined by Thomas, J., dissented, finding *Lukumi* "irreconcilable with today's decision": "When the State makes a public benefit generally available, that benefit becomes part of the baseline against which burdens on religion are measured; and when the State withholds that benefit from some individuals solely on the basis of religion, it violates the Free Exercise Clause no less than if it had imposed a special tax.

"[No] field of study but religion is singled out for disfavor. [The history relied on by the Court] involved not the inclusion of religious ministers in public benefits programs like the one at issue here, but laws that singled them out for financial aid. [No] one would seriously contend, for example, that the Framers would have barred ministers from using public roads on their way to church.[1]

"[T]he State already has all the play in the joints it needs. There are any number of ways it could respect both its unusually sensitive concern for the conscience of its taxpayers *and* the Federal Free Exercise Clause. It could make the scholarships redeemable only at public universities (where it sets the curriculum), or only for select courses of study. Either option would

---

a. For the view that *Davey's* "goal was to extend the *Lukumi* rules from regulation to funding. That effort failed; *Lukumi* does not apply to funding. But neither was *Lukumi* rolled back as applied to regulation," see Laycock, fn. e in *Smith,* at 216 (criticizing *Locke*). For a rationale that permits government to "single out many religious actors and entities for exclusion from its support programs," see Nelson Tebbe, *Excluding Religion,* 156 U. Pa. L. Rev. 1263 (2008).

8. Washington has also been solicitous in ensuring that its constitution is not hostile towards religion, and at least in some respects, its constitution provides greater protection of religious liberties than the Free Exercise Clause (rejecting standard in *Smith*) * * *.

1. No State [with] a constitutional provision [that] prohibited the use of tax funds to support the ministry [has,] so far as I know, ever prohibited the hiring of public employees who use their salary to conduct ministries, or excluded ministers from generally available disability or unemployment benefits. * * *

replace a program that facially discriminates against religion with one that just happens not to subsidize it.

"[T]he interest to which the Court defers is not fear of a conceivable Establishment Clause violation, budget constraints, avoidance of endorsement, or substantive neutrality—none of these. It is a pure philosophical preference: the State's opinion that it would violate taxpayers' freedom of conscience *not* to discriminate against candidates for the ministry. This sort of protection of 'freedom of conscience' has no logical limit and can justify the singling out of religion for exclusion from public programs in virtually any context.[b] The Court never says whether it deems this interest compelling (the opinion is devoid of any mention of standard of review) but, self-evidently, it is not.[2]

"The Court makes no serious attempt to defend the program's neutrality, and instead identifies two features thought to render its discrimination less offensive. The first is the lightness of Davey's burden. The Court offers no authority for approving facial discrimination against religion simply because its material consequences are not severe. I might understand such a test if we were still in the business of reviewing facially neutral laws that merely happen to burden some individual's religious exercise, but we are not. See *Smith*. Discrimination *on the face of a statute* is something else. The indignity of being singled out for special burdens on the basis of one's religious calling is so profound that the concrete harm produced can never be dismissed as insubstantial. The Court has not required proof of 'substantial' concrete harm with other forms of discrimination, see, e.g., *Brown v. Board of Education,* and it should not do so here. * * *

"The other reason the Court thinks this particular facial discrimination less offensive is that the scholarship program was not motivated by animus toward religion. [If] a State deprives a citizen of trial by jury or passes an ex post facto law, we do not pause to investigate whether it was actually trying to accomplish the evil the Constitution prohibits. It is sufficient that the citizen's rights have been infringed. [We] do sometimes look to legislative intent to smoke out more subtle instances of discrimination, but we do so as a *supplement* to the core guarantee of facially equal treatment, not as a replacement for it.

"[This] case is about discrimination against a religious minority. Most citizens of this country identify themselves as professing some religious belief, but [t]hose the statutory exclusion actually affects—those whose belief in their religion is so strong that they dedicate their study and their lives to its ministry—are a far narrower set. One need not delve too far into modern popular culture to perceive a trendy disdain for deep religious conviction."

    (e) Does *Locke* permit a state to exclude religious elementary and secondary schools (or colleges and universities)—at least those that are "pervasively

---

    b. The Court responded that "the only interest at issue here is the State's interest in not funding the religious training of clergy."

    2. [If] religious discrimination required only a rational basis, the Free Exercise Clause would impose no constraints other than those the Constitution already imposes on all government action. The question is not whether theology majors are different, but whether the differences are substantial enough to justify a discriminatory financial penalty that the State inflicts on no other major. Plainly they are not. * * *

religious"—from a generally available program of state aid to education? See fn. b in *Locke*. May a state choose not to fund religious aspects of the education provided by recipient schools? See Laycock, fn. e in *Smith*, at 184–200; Ira C. Lupu & Robert W. Tuttle, *The Faith-Based Initiative and the Constitution*, 55 De Paul L. Rev. 1, 46–50 (2005).

3. ***Action vs. inaction.*** Of what significance is it that all the decisions sustaining free exercise claims against government regulations of conduct (*Sherbert—Thomas—Hobbie, Yoder* and *Bowen v. Roy*) involved *inaction*, i.e., religious refusal to engage in conduct required by government rather than religiously dictated action forbidden by the state? In the case of *action* due to religious beliefs, should a distinction be drawn between action that is requested by the people affected and action that is imposed on others? Should the conviction of a religious Spiritualist for fortune telling be sustained despite the fact that fortunes were told only upon request? If not, how do you distinguish the polygamy cases?[a]

II. UNUSUAL RELIGIOUS BELIEFS AND PRACTICES

1. ***Validity and sincerity.*** In UNITED STATES v. BALLARD, 322 U.S. 78 (1944), defendant was indicted for mail fraud. He had solicited funds for the "I Am" movement, asserting, inter alia, that he had been selected as a divine messenger, had the divine power of healing incurable diseases, and had talked with Jesus and would transmit these conversations to mankind. The Court, per DOUGLAS, J., held that the First Amendment barred submitting to the jury the question of whether these religious beliefs were true: "Men may believe what they cannot [prove.] Religious experiences which are as real as life to some may be incomprehensible to others. [The] miracles of the New Testament, the Divinity of Christ, life after death, the power of prayer are deep in the religious convictions of many. If one could be sent to jail because a jury in a hostile environment found those teachings false, little indeed would be left of religious freedom."

(a) *Ballard* permits the prosecution to prove that, irrespective of whether the incidents described by defendant happened, he did not honestly believe that they had. If so, may the prosecution introduce evidence that the incidents did not in fact happen and that therefore defendant could not honestly believe that they did? Should this line of proof be permitted in the prosecution of an official of the Catholic church for soliciting funds to construct a shrine commemorating the Miracle of Fatima in 1930?

(b) Is it relevant that in *Ballard* the alleged divine revelation was made to defendant himself? Would it be material if the experiences had

---

a. For several recent approaches that evaluate a wide range of factors in considering religious exemptions from generally applicable laws, see Eugene Volokh, *A Common–Law Model for Religious Exemptions*, 46 UCLA L.Rev. 1465 (1999); Eugene Volokh, *Intermediate Questions of Religious Exemptions—A Research Agenda with Test Suites*, 21 Card.L.Rev. 595 (1999); Jesse H. Choper, *Securing Religious Liberty* ch. 3 (1995).

allegedly occurred at a definite time and place? Many Biblical happenings are so identified. Could the prosecution introduce evidence that Ballard was not physically present at the alleged place at the alleged time? If Protestant, Catholic or Jewish clergy were prosecuted and there was overwhelming scientific evidence disputing the Biblical doctrine, what would the jury be likely to find as to the honesty of the beliefs? Should the First Amendment permit people to obtain money in the name of religion by knowingly making false statements? See Ronald J. Krotoszynski, Jr., The Apostle, *Mr. Justice Jackson, and the "Pathological Perpsective" of the Free Exercise Clause,* 65 Wash. & Lee L. Rev. 1071, 1084 ("inquiries into subjective good faith are virtually certain to devolve into questions about the cultural acceptability—indeed plausibility—of a particular sect"). Compare Tribe 2d ed., at 1243–47.

(c) Should the prosecution be able to prove that defendant had stated on many occasions that he believed none of his representations but that by saying that he did he was amassing great wealth? Suppose it can be shown that a priest or rabbi is *somewhat* skeptical as to the truth of certain Biblical occurrences? See John T. Noonan, Jr., *How Sincere Do You Have to Be to Be Religious,* 1988 U.Ill.L.Rev. 713. After *Smith,* could Ballard be convicted on the ground that fraudulent procurement of money is a generally applicable regulation of conduct which may be constitutionally prohibited even if done in the name of religion?

2. ***What is "religion"?*** May the Court determine that asserted religious beliefs and practices do not constitute a valid religion? Consider Jonathan Weiss, *Privilege, Posture and Protection—"Religion" in the Law,* 73 Yale L.J. 593, 604 (1964): "[A]ny definition of religion would seem to violate religious freedom in that it would dictate to religions, present and future, what they must [be]. Furthermore, an attempt to define religion, even for purposes of increasing freedom for religions, would run afoul of the 'establishment' clause as excluding some religions, or even as establishing a notion respecting religion."

Is it relevant that the beliefs of a group do not include the existence of God? TORCASO v. WATKINS, per BLACK, J., 367 U.S. 488 (1961), invalidated a Maryland provision requiring a declaration of belief in God as a test for public office, stated: "Neither [a state nor the federal government can] impose requirements which aid all religions as against nonbelievers, and neither can aid those religions based on a belief in the existence of God as against those religions founded on different beliefs." The Court noted that "among religions [that] do not teach what would generally be considered a belief in the existence of God are Buddhism, Taoism, Ethical Culture, Secular Humanism and others."

Are atheism and agnosticism "religions"? Contrast Douglas Laycock, *Religious Liberty as Liberty,* 7 J. Contemp. Leg. Issues 313 (1996) ("for constitutional purposes, any answer to religious questions is religion") and 1 Greenawalt at 149–150 ("atheists have free exercise rights [that do] not necessarily parallel rights of traditional believers"). Consider Paul G.

Kauper, *Religion and the Constitution* 31 (1964): "What makes secular humanism a religion? Is it because it is an ideology or system of belief that attempts to furnish a rationale of life? [If so], must not democracy, fascism, and communism also qualify as religions? [S]ome find in these systems an adequate explanation of the meaning and purpose of life and the source of values that command faith and devotion."

May a single person establish his or her own religion? Consider Milton Konvitz, *Religious Liberty and Conscience* 84 (1968): "[Many religions] had their origin in a 'private and personal' religious experience. Mohammed did not take over an on-going, established religion; the history of Islam records the names of his first three converts. John Wesley is given credit as the founder of Methodism. Mrs. Mary Baker Eddy was the founder of the Christian Science church. Menno Simons organized a division of Anabaptists that in due course became the sect known as the Mennonites. Jacob Ammon broke away from the Mennonites and founded the sect known as the Amish."

How important is it that the group has regular weekly services? Designated leaders who conduct these services? Ceremonies for naming, marrying and burying members? Does the First Amendment extend only to those groups that conform to the "conventional" concept of religion? Consider Harvey Cox (Harvard Divinity School), N.Y. Times 25 (Feb. 16, 1977): "[C]ourts [often] turn to some vague 'man-in-the-street' idea of what 'religion' should be. [But] a man-in-the-street approach would surely have ruled out early Christianity, which seemed both subversive and atheistic to the religious Romans of the day. The truth is that one man's 'bizarre cult' is another's true path to salvation, and the Bill of Rights was designed to safeguard minorities from the man-on-the-street's uncertain capacity for tolerance." To what extent should a group's "brainwashing," mental coercion techniques affect its constitutional status as a "religion"? Compare Richard Delgado, *Religious Totalism: Gentle and Ungentle Persuasion Under the First Amendment*, 51 So.Cal.L.Rev. 1 (1977) with 1 Greenawalt 310–15.

Suppose that a group has certain characteristics of "traditional" religions, such as a holy book, ministers, houses of worship, prescribed prayers, a strict moral code, a belief in the hereafter and an appeal to faith, but also has announced social and economic tenets? (Methodism developed originally out of social concerns.) Consider Note, *Toward a Constitutional Definition of Religion*, 91 Harv.L.Rev. 1056, 1069 (1978): "[A] spokesman for the new 'liberation theology' within Catholicism argues that true religion is to be found in ['the] creation of a new social consciousness and as a social appropriation not only of the means of production, but also of the political processes.' The church, he says, seeks 'the abolition of the exploitation of man by man.' The views [of] significant Christian theologians coalesce around one important theme: the Christian church will find itself only by discarding what until now has been perceived to be religious and by immersing itself in the secular world." Does the First Amendment encompass any political, philosophical, moral or social doctrine that some group sincerely espouses as its religion?

UNITED STATES v. SEEGER, 380 U.S. 163 (1965), interpreted § 6(j) of the Universal Military Training and Service Act, which exempted from combat any person "who, by reason of religious training and belief, is conscientiously opposed to participation in war in any form. Religious training and belief in this [means] an individual's belief in a relation to a Supreme Being involving duties superior to those arising from any human relation, but does not include essentially political, sociological or philosophical views or a merely personal moral code."[a] The Court, per CLARK, J., avoided constitutional questions and upheld claims for exemption of three conscientious objectors. One declared "that he preferred to leave the question as to his belief in a Supreme Being open, [and] that his was a 'belief in and devotion to goodness and virtue for their own sakes, and a religious faith in a purely ethical creed.'" Another said "that he felt it a violation of his moral code to take human life and that he considered this belief superior to his obligation to the state. As to whether his conviction was religious, he [quoted] Reverend John Haynes Holmes' definition of religion as 'the consciousness of some power manifest in nature which helps man in the ordering of his life in harmony with its demands * * *; it is man thinking his highest, feeling his deepest, and living his best.' The source of his conviction he attributed to reading and meditation 'in our democratic American culture, with its values derived from the western religious and philosophical tradition.' As to his belief in a Supreme Being, Peter stated that he supposed 'you could call that a belief in the Supreme Being or God. These just do not happen to be the words I use.'"

The Court "concluded that Congress, in using the expression 'Supreme Being' [was] merely clarifying the meaning of religious training and belief so as to embrace all religions and to exclude essentially political, sociological, or philosophical views [and that] the test of belief 'in a relation to a Supreme Being' is whether a given belief that is sincere and meaningful occupies a place in the life of its possessor parallel to that filled by the orthodox belief in God of one who clearly qualifies for the exemption. [No] party claims to be an atheist * * *. We do not deal with [that. The] use by Congress of the words 'merely personal' seems to us to restrict the exception to a moral code which [is] in no way related to a Supreme Being. [Congress did] not distinguish between externally and internally derived beliefs. Such a determination [would] prove impossible as a practical matter."

In WELSH v. UNITED STATES, 398 U.S. 333 (1970), petitioner, in his application for exemption, "struck the word 'religious' entirely and later characterized his beliefs as having been formed 'by reading in the

---

a. The statute was subsequently amended to omit the "belief in a Supreme Being" element. For the view that "religion" under the First Amendment "involves some conception of God," see Michael S. Paulsen, *God is Great, Garvey is Good: Making Sense of Religious Freedom*, 72 Not.D.L.Rev. 1597, 1623 (1997): "Text and historical evidence of original meaning should settle the matter. If this seems illiberal today, that is unfortunate, but irrelevant to the task of textual interpretation of the constitutional provision the framers wrote."

fields of history and sociology.'" BLACK, J., joined by Douglas, Brennan and Marshall, JJ., held that, under *Seeger,* "if an individual deeply and sincerely holds beliefs which are purely ethical or moral in source and content but that nevertheless impose upon him a duty of conscience to refrain from participating in any war at any time, those beliefs certainly occupy in the life of that individual 'a place parallel to that filled [by] God' in traditionally religious persons." "Although [Welsh] originally character-ized his beliefs as nonreligious, he later upon reflection wrote a long and thoughtful letter to his Appeal Board in which he declared that his beliefs were 'certainly religious in the ethical sense of that word.' [§ 6(j)'s] exclusion of those persons with 'essentially political, sociological, or philo-sophical views or a merely personal moral code' should [not] be read to exclude those who hold strong beliefs about our domestic and foreign affairs or even those whose conscientious objection to participation in all wars is founded to a substantial extent [on] public policy. The two groups of registrants which obviously do fall within these exclusions from the exemption are those whose beliefs are not deeply held and those whose objection to war does not rest at all upon moral, ethical, or religious principle but instead rests solely upon considerations of policy, pragma-tism, or expediency."[b]

3. ***What is "religious belief"?*** (a) Of what significance is it that the practice is an "age-old form" of religious conduct (*Murdock*)? A "cardinal principle" of the asserted religious faith (*Sherbert*)? Consider Laycock, fn. d in *Lemon,* Ch. 11, Sec. II, at 1390–91: "Many activities that obviously are exercises of religion are not required by conscience or doctrine. Singing in the church choir and saying the Roman Catholic rosary are [two] examples. Any activity engaged in by a church as a body is an exercise of religion. [Indeed,] many would say that an emphasis on rules and obligations misconceives the essential nature of some religions." Compare Donald Giannella, *Religious Liberty Nonestablishment and Doc-trinal Development,* 80 Harv.L.Rev. 1381, 1427–28 (1967): "Personal alien-ation from one's Maker, frustration of one's ultimate mission in life, and violation of the religious person's integrity are all at stake when the right to worship is threatened. Although the seeker of new psychological worlds [through use of hallucinogens] may feel equally frustrated when deprived of his gropings for a higher reality, there is not the same sense [of] loss of the Be-all and End-all of life. [A] different problem presents itself when an individual who does not believe in a supernatural or personal God asserts conscientious objection to certain conduct because of its injurious effects on his fellow man. [T]his ethical belief may be held with such a degree of

---

b. In separate opinions, Harlan, J., and White, J., (joined by Burger, C.J., and Stewart, J.) dissented on the issue of statutory construction. For their views on the constitutional issue, see Ch. 14.

See generally Note, *The Sacred and the Profane: A First Amendment Definition of Religion,* 61 Tex.L.Rev. 139 (1982). For criticism of "sincerity," see Comment, *The Legal Relationship of Conscience to Religion: Refusals to Bear Arms,* 38 U.Chi.L.Rev. 583 (1971).

intensity that its violation occasions the same interior revulsion and anguish as does violation of the law of God to the pious." Under this approach, on what evidence should these factual questions be determined?

For the view that "belief [in] 'extratemporal consequences'—whether the effects of actions taken pursuant or contrary to the dictates of a person's beliefs extend in some meaningful way beyond his lifetime—is a sensible and desirable criterion (albeit plainly far short of ideal) for determining when the free exercise clause should trigger judicial consideration of whether an exemption from general government regulations of conduct is constitutionally required," see Jesse H. Choper, *Defining "Religion" in the First Amendment,* 1982 U.Ill.L.Rev. 579, 599, 603–04:[c] "It may be persuasively argued that *all* beliefs that invoke a transcendent reality—and especially those that provide their adherents with glimpses of meaning and truth that make them so important and so uncompromisable—should be encompassed by the special constitutional protection granted 'religion' by the free exercise clause. [In] many ways, however, transcendental explanations of worldly realities are essentially no different [than] conventional exegeses for temporal outcomes that are based on such 'rational' disciplines as economics, political science, sociology, or psychology, or even such 'hard' sciences [as] physics. When justifying competing government policies on such varied matters as social welfare, the economy, and military and foreign affairs, there is at bedrock only a gossamer line between 'rational' and 'supernatural' causation—the former really being little more capable of 'scientific proof' than the latter."[d] Compare Kent Greenawalt, *Religion as a Concept in Constitutional Law,* 72 Calif.L.Rev. 753, 763, 815 (1984): "No specification of essential conditions will capture all and only the beliefs, practices, and organizations that are regarded as religious in modern culture and should be treated as such under the Constitution. [Rather, determining] whether questionable beliefs, practices, and organizations are religious by seeing how closely they resemble what is undeniably religious is a method that has been implicitly used by courts in difficult borderline cases [and] is consonant with Supreme Court decisions."[e]

(b) *Judicial role.* In THOMAS v. REVIEW BD., Part I supra, petitioner testified that, although his religious convictions forbade him to

---

c. For criticism of this view, see Stanley Ingber, *Religion or Ideology: A Needed Clarification of the Religion Clauses,* 41 Stan.L.Rev. 233, 274–77 (1989); Note, *Religion and Morality Legislation: A Reexamination of Establishment Clause Analysis,* 59 N.Y.U.L.Rev. 301, 346–52 (1984); Note, *Defining "Religion" in the First Amendment: A Functional Approach,* 74 Corn.L.Rev. 532 (1989).

d. For the view that religion should be defined as dealing with "quintessentially religious questions," "addressing the profound questions of human existence," "such as God's existence or the proper definition of life and death," see Tom Stacy, *Death, Privacy, and the Free Exercise of Religion,* 77 Corn.L.Rev. 490 (1992).

e. Accord, George C. Freeman, III, *The Misguided Search for the Constitutional Definition of "Religion,"* 71 Geo.L.J. 1519 (1983). See also Eduardo Peñalver, *The Concept of Religion,* 107 Yale L.J. 791 (1997) (supporting "analogical" approach that "takes into account the evolutionary nature of language" and "tries to minimize [western] judicial bias"). For the view that "the original meaning of religion is a monotheistic belief system, such as Christianity, that holds true to a future state of rewards and punishments and thus imposes duties on believers in this world," see Lee J. Strang, *The Meaning of "Religion" in the First Amendment,* 40 Duq.L.Rev. 181, 238 (2002).

manufacture weapons, "he could, in good conscience, engage indirectly in the production, [for] example, as an employee of a raw material supplier." The state court, viewing petitioner's positions as inconsistent, ruled that he had made a "personal philosophical choice rather than a religious choice." The Court, per BURGER, C.J. reversed: "[D]etermination of what is a 'religious' belief or practice is more often than not a difficult and delicate task, [but] resolution of that question is not to turn upon a judicial perception of the particular belief or practice in question; religious beliefs need not be acceptable, logical, consistent, or comprehensible to others in order to merit First Amendment protection. [Thomas] drew a line and it is not for us to say that the line he drew was an unreasonable one. Courts should not undertake to dissect religious beliefs because the believer admits that he is 'struggling' with his position or because his beliefs are not articulated with the clarity and precision that a more sophisticated person might employ.

"The Indiana court also appears to have given significant weight to the fact that another Jehovah's Witness had no scruples about working on tank turrets; for that other Witness, at least, such work was 'scripturally' acceptable. Intra-faith differences of that kind are not uncommon [and] the judicial process is singularly ill equipped to resolve such differences in relation to the Religion Clauses. [The] narrow function of a reviewing court in this context is to determine whether there was an appropriate finding that petitioner terminated his work because of an honest conviction that such work was forbidden by his religion."

4. ***Variable definition.*** May "religion" be defined differently for purposes of the Establishment Clause than the Free Exercise Clause? Consider Marc S. Galanter, *Religious Freedom in the United States: A Turning Point?* 1966 Wis.L.Rev. 217, 266–67: "[For purposes of the Establishment Clause, the] effect and purpose of government action are not to be assessed by the religious sensibilities of the person who is complaining of the alleged establishment. It must be essentially religious in some widely shared public understanding. [But, for the Free Exercise Clause, the] claimants' view of religion controls the characterization of their objection as a religious one." Does this analysis solve the dilemma of Leonard F. Manning, *The Douglas Concept of God in Government*, 39 Wash.L.Rev. 47, 66 (1964): "If religion need not be predicated on a belief in God or even in a god and if it may not be tested by the common consensus of what reasonable men would reasonably call religion, [might] not a group of gymnasts proclaiming on their trampolines that physical culture is their religion be engaged in a religious exercise? And if Congress, in a particular Olympic year, appropriated funds to subsidize their calisthenics would this not [be] an establishment of religion?" See generally Note, *Transcendental Meditation and the Meaning of Religion Under the Establishment Clause*, 62 Minn.L.Rev. 887 (1978); 1 Greenawalt at 141–42.

CHAPTER 13

PREFERENCE AMONG RELIGIONS

■ ■ ■

In BOARD OF EDUC. OF KIRYAS JOEL v. GRUMET, 512 U.S. 687 (1994), a New York statute constituted the Village of Kiryas Joel—"a religious enclave of Satmar Hasidim, practitioners of a strict form of Judaism"—as a separate school district. Most of the children attend pervasively religious private schools. The newly created district "currently runs only a special education program for handicapped [Satmar] children" who reside both inside and outside the village. The statute was passed "to enable the village's handicapped children to receive a secular, public-school education" because when they previously attended public schools in the larger school district outside the village, they suffered "panic, fear and trauma [in] leaving their own community and being with people whose ways were so different." The Court, per SOUTER, J., invoked "a principle at the heart of the Establishment Clause, that government should not prefer one religion to another. [Because] Kiryas Joel did not receive its new governmental authority simply as one of many communities eligible for equal treatment under a general law, we have no assurance that the next similarly situated group seeking a school district of its own will receive one; [and] a legislature's failure to enact a special law is itself unreviewable.[a] [Here] the benefit flows only to a single sect,[b] [and] therefore

---

a. Kennedy, J., disagreed: if another religious community were denied legislative help, it "could sue the State of New York, contending that New York's discriminatory treatment of the two religious communities violated the Establishment Clause. [T]he court would have only to determine whether the community does indeed bear the same burden on its religious practice as [did] Kiryas Joel. See *Olsen v. Drug Enforcement Admin.*, [p. 625 supra] (R.B. Ginsburg, J.) (rejecting claim that the members of the Ethiopian Zion Coptic Church were entitled to an exemption from the marijuana laws on the same terms as the peyote exemption for the Native American Church). While a finding of discrimination would then raise a difficult question of relief, compare *Olsen* ('Faced with the choice between invalidation and extension of any controlled-substances religious exemption, which would the political branches choose? It would take a court bolder than this one to predict [that] extension, not invalidation, would be the probable choice'), with *Califano v. Westcott*, 443 U.S. 76 (1979) (curing gender discrimination in the AFDC program by extending benefits to children of unemployed mothers instead of denying benefits to children of unemployed fathers), the discrimination itself would not be beyond judicial remedy."

b. Compare Thomas C. Berg, *Slouching Towards Secularism*, 44 Emory L.J. 433, 468–69 (1995): "[T]he legislature specifically accommodated the Satmars [because] their plight was unique: no other group of children was being denied effective special education because they were traumatized by the atmosphere of the mainstream public schools. [Even] if the children of other groups had been harmed by the public school ethos, few if any such groups live together

crosses the line from permissible accommodation to impermissible establishment."[c]

KENNEDY, J., concurred in the judgment: "Whether or not the purpose is accommodation and whether or not the government provides similar gerrymanders to people of all religious faiths, the Establishment Clause forbids the government to use religion [as] a criterion to draw political or electoral lines."[d]

SCALIA, J., joined by Rehnquist, C.J., and Thomas, J., dissented: "[A]ll the residents of the Kiryas Joel Village School District are Satmars. But all its residents also wear unusual dress, have unusual civic customs, and have not much to do with people who are culturally different from them. [I]t was not theology but dress, language, and cultural alienation that posed the educational problem for the children [and caused the Legislature to] provide a public education for these students, in the same way it addressed, by a similar law, the unique needs of children institutionalized in a hospital. [T]he creation of a special, one-culture school district for the benefit of [children whose] parents were nonreligious commune dwellers, or American Indians, or gypsies [would] pose no problem. The neutrality demanded by the Religion Clauses requires the same indulgence towards cultural characteristics that are accompanied by religious belief."[e]

NOTES AND QUESTIONS

1. **Delegation of government power.** In *Kiryas Joel,* SOUTER, J., joined by Blackmun, Stevens and Ginsburg, JJ., found an additional ground for invalidating the statute: "delegating the State's discretionary authority over public schools to a group defined by its character as a religious community, in a legal and historical context that gives no assurance that governmental power has been or will be exercised neutrally." They relied on LARKIN v. GRENDEL'S DEN, INC., 459 U.S. 116 (1982), per BURGER, C.J., which held that a Massachusetts law (§ 16C), giving churches and schools the power "to veto applications for liquor licenses within a five hundred foot radius of the church or school, violates the Establishment Clause": "§ 16C is not simply a legislative exercise of zoning power [because it delegates] discretionary governmental powers [to] religious bodies.

---

communally so as to permit the solution of a geographically based school district such as that drawn for the Satmars." But see Ira C. Lupu, *The Lingering Death of Separationism,* 62 Geo.Wash.L.Rev. 230, 269 (1994): "Is it imaginable that New York State would create a new public school district at the behest of an insular group of Branch Davidians or members of the Unification Church, whose children [may] suffer panic, fear, and trauma at encountering those outside their own community?"

c.　Within ten days of *Kiryas Joel,* the New York legislature passed a new law allowing "any municipality situated wholly within a single school district" to form its own district if it meets designated criteria regarding population, enrollment and property wealth. Constitutional when used by the Village of Kiryas Joel?

d.　For similarities and differences between the use of religion and race in drawing political districts, see Abner S. Greene, *Kiryas Joel and Two Mistakes About Equality,* 96 Colum.L.Rev. 1, 27–57 (1996).

e.　Is this persuasive when there is total congruence between a religion and distinctive cultural needs *and* the cultural distinctiveness is defined by the religion?

"[The] valid secular objectives [of protecting] spiritual, cultural, and educational centers from the 'hurly-burly' associated with liquor outlets [can] be readily accomplished by [an] absolute legislative ban on liquor outlets within reasonable prescribed distances from churches, schools, hospitals and like institutions, or by ensuring a hearing for the views of affected institutions at licensing proceedings. [But the] churches' power under the statute is standardless [and] may therefore be used [for] explicitly religious goals, for example, favoring liquor licenses for members of that congregation or adherents of that faith. [And] the mere appearance of a joint exercise of legislative authority by Church and State provides a significant symbolic benefit to religion in the minds of some by reason of the power conferred. It does not strain our prior holdings to say that the statute can be seen as having a 'primary' and 'principal' effect of advancing religion. [Finally, § 16C] enmeshes churches in the processes of government and creates the danger of 'political fragmentation and divisiveness along religious lines.' "

REHNQUIST, J., dissented in *Grendel's Den:* A "flat ban [on] the grant of an alcoholic beverages license to any establishment located within 500 feet of a church or a [school], which the majority concedes is valid, is more protective of churches and more restrictive of liquor sales than the present § 16C. * * * Nothing in the Court's opinion persuades me why the more rigid prohibition would be constitutional, but the more flexible not. [It] does not sponsor or subsidize any religious group or activity. It does not encourage, much less compel, anyone to participate in religious activities or to support religious institutions. [If] a church were to seek to advance the interests of its members [by favoring them for licenses], there would be an occasion to determine whether it had violated any right of an unsuccessful applicant for a liquor license. But our ability to discern a risk of such abuse does not render § 16C violative of the Establishment Clause."

Scalia, J., joined by Rehnquist, C.J., and Thomas, J., dissenting in *Kiryas Joel*, argued that *Grendel's Den* had ruled that "a state may not delegate its civil authority *to a church*," and did not involve delegation to "groups of people sharing a common religious and cultural heritage": "If the conferral of governmental power upon a religious institution *as such* (rather than upon American citizens who belong to the religious institution) is not the test of *Grendel's Den* invalidity, there is no reason why giving power to a body that is overwhelmingly dominated by the members of one sect would not suffice to invoke the Establishment Clause. That might have made the entire States of Utah and New Mexico unconstitutional at the time of their admission to the Union."

2. ***"Excessive government entanglement" in ecclesiastical disputes.*** (a) In JONES v. WOLF, 443 U.S. 595 (1979), a majority of the Vineville Presbyterian Church voted to separate from the Presbyterian Church in the United States (PCUS). A commission of PCUS, acting pursuant to the PCUS constitution (called the Book of Church Order), declared the Vineville minority to be "the true congregation." The minority sued [for] the local church property. The state court applied "the 'neutral principles of law' method for resolving church property disputes. The court examined the deeds to the properties, the state statutes dealing with implied trusts, and the Book of Church Order, to determine whether there was any basis for a trust in

favor of the general church. Finding [none], the court awarded the property on the basis of legal title, which was in the local church."

The Court, per BLACKMUN, J., stated the established principle that "the First Amendment prohibits civil courts from resolving church property disputes on the basis of religious doctrine and practice. *Presbyterian Church v. Hull Church*, 393 U.S. 440 (1969). As a corollary [, the] Amendment requires that civil courts defer to the resolution of issues of religious doctrine or polity by the highest court of a hierarchical church organization. *Serbian Eastern Orthodox Diocese v. Milivojevich*, 426 U.S. 696 (1976).[a] Subject to these limitations, [however,] 'a State may adopt *any* of various approaches for settling church property [disputes].' *Maryland & Virginia Eldership v. Sharpsburg Church*, 396 U.S. 367 (1970) (Brennan, J., concurring).

"[W]e think the 'neutral principles of law' approach is consistent with the foregoing constitutional principles. [It] relies extensively on objective, well-established concepts of trust and property law familiar to lawyers and judges. It thereby promises to free civil courts completely from entanglement in questions of religious doctrine, polity, and practice. Furthermore, the neutral principles analysis [affords] flexibility [to] reflect the intentions of the parties. Through appropriate reversionary clauses and trust provisions, religious societies can specify what is to happen to church property in the event of a particular contingency. [The] neutral principles method [does require] a civil court to examine certain religious documents, such as a church constitution, for language of trust in favor of the general church. [A] civil court must take special care to scrutinize the document in purely secular terms, and not to rely on religious precepts in determining whether the document indicates that the parties have intended to create a trust. [If] the interpretation of the instruments of ownership would require the civil court to resolve a religious controversy, then the court must defer to the resolution of the doctrinal issue by the authoritative ecclesiastical body. *Serbian.*"

POWELL, J., joined by Burger, C.J., and Stewart and White, JJ., dissented, finding that the neutral principles "approach inevitably will increase the involvement of civil courts in church controversies": "Until today, [the] first question presented in a case involving an intrachurch dispute over church property was where within the religious association the rules of polity, accepted by its members before the schism, had placed ultimate authority over the use of the church property. The courts, in answering this question have recognized two broad categories of church government. One is congregational, in which authority over questions of church doctrine, practice, and administration rests entirely in the local congregation or some body within [it]. *Watson v. Jones*, 80 U.S. (13 Wall.) 679 (1871). The second is hierarchical

---

a. *Serbian*, per Brennan, J., reversed a state court decision that the Mother Church's removal of respondent as bishop of the American–Canadian diocese was "procedurally and substantively defective under the internal regulations of the Mother Church and were therefore arbitrary and invalid": "[W]hether or not there is room for 'marginal civil court review' under the narrow rubrics of 'fraud' or 'collusion' when church tribunals act in bad faith for secular purposes, no 'arbitrariness' exception—in the sense of an inquiry whether the decisions of the highest ecclesiastical tribunal of a hierarchical church complied with church laws and regulations—is consistent with the constitutional mandate. [I]t is the essence of religious faith that ecclesiastical decisions are reached and are to be accepted as matters of faith whether or not rational or measurable by objective criteria." Rehnquist and Stevens, JJ., dissented.

[and] this Court has held that the civil courts must give effect to the duly made decisions of the highest body within the hierarchy that has considered the dispute." See generally 1 Greenawalt ch. 16.

(b) *Scope of the decision.* After *Jones,* what results for the following: (i) A donor who made a bequest "to the First Methodist Church" seeks return of the money because subsequently a majority of the church's members decided to affiliate with another denomination. Suppose the bequest had been "to the First Methodist Church so long as it does not substantially deviate from existing doctrine"? (ii) A statute makes it a crime for sellers to falsely represent food to be "kosher." See Kent Greenawalt, *Religious Law and Civil Law: Using Secular Law to Assure Observance of Practices with Religious Significance,* 71 So.Cal.L.Rev. 781 (1998). (iii) An adult sues a member of the clergy for "malpractice" based on consensual sexual acts with plaintiff. See Scott C. Idleman, *Tort Liability, Religious Entities, and the Decline of Constitutional Protection,* 75 Ind. L.J., 219 (2000).

———

LARSON v. VALENTE, 456 U.S. 228 (1982), involved a challenge by the Unification Church ("Moonies") to "a Minnesota statute, imposing certain registration and reporting requirements upon only those religious organizations that solicit more than fifty per cent of their funds from nonmembers." The Court, per BRENNAN, J., noting that "the clearest command of the establishment clause is that one religious denomination cannot be officially preferred over another, [*Everson*]," and that the "constitutional prohibition of denominational preferences is inextricably connected with the continuing vitality of the Free Exercise Clause," held that the statute violated the Establishment Clause because it did not survive "strict scrutiny."[a] Assuming that the state's "valid secular purpose [in] protecting its citizens from abusive practices in the solicitation of funds for charity" is "compelling," the state "failed to demonstrate that the fifty per cent rule [is] 'closely fitted'" to furthering that interest. Moreover, the statute failed the third *Lemon* "test": "The fifty per cent [rule] effects the *selective* legislative imposition of burdens and advantages upon particular denominations. The 'risk of politicizing religion' that inheres in such legislation is obvious, and indeed is confirmed by the

———

a. The Court reasoned that this "is not simply a facially neutral statute, the provisions of which happen to have a 'disparate impact' upon different religious organizations. On the contrary [it] makes explicit and deliberate distinctions between different religious organizations [and] effectively distinguishes between 'well-established churches' that have 'achieved strong but not total financial support from their members,' on the one hand, and 'churches which are new [or,] which, as a matter of policy, may favor public solicitation over general reliance on financial support from members,' on the other hand."

The Court found *Gillette v. United States,* Ch. 12, I, "readily distinguishable": "[W]e rejected an Establishment Clause attack upon § 6(j) of the Military Selective Service Act of 1967, which afforded 'conscientious objector' status to any person who, 'by reason of religious training and belief,' was 'conscientiously opposed to participation in war in any form. [§ 6(j)] 'focused on individual conscientious belief, not on sectarian affiliation.' Under § 6(j), conscientious objector status was available on an equal basis to both the Quaker and the Roman Catholic, despite the distinction drawn by the latter's church between 'just' and 'unjust' wars. [In] contrast, the statute challenged in the case before us focuses precisely and solely upon religious organizations."

provision's legislative history [which] demonstrates that the provision was drafted with the explicit intention of including particular religious denominations and excluding others."

WHITE, J., joined by Rehnquist, J., dissented,[b] disagreeing with the Court's view "that the rule [is] an explicit and deliberate preference for some religious beliefs over others": "The rule [names] no churches or denominations. [Some] religions will qualify and some will not, but this depends on the source of their contributions, not on their brand of religion. [The Court's assertion] that the limitation might burden the less well-organized denominations [is contrary to the state's claim] that both categories include not only well-established, but also not so well-established organizations." Further, "I cannot join the Court's easy rejection of the state's submission [of] a valid secular [purpose]."[c]

NOTES AND QUESTIONS

1. **_The Gillette rationale._** (a) Should a "neutral, secular basis" justify government preference—de jure or de facto—among religions? Consider Kent Greenawalt, _All or Nothing at All: The Defeat of Selective Conscientious Objection,_ 1971 Sup.Ct.Rev. 31, 71: "If a sociological survey indicated that Protestants generally work harder than Catholics, the government might simplify its hiring problems by interviewing only Protestants. If the doctors of Catholic hospitals were determined to be on the average more qualified than those at Lutheran hospitals, aid might be limited to the Catholic hospitals." How significant was the Court's observation that the _Gillette_ law "attempts to accommodate free exercise values"?

(b) Was the Draft Act of 1917, which exempted only conscientious objectors affiliated with some "well-recognized religious sect" whose principles forbade participation in war, valid under _Gillette_ and _Larson?_ See Jeremy Patrick-Justice, _Strict Scrutiny for Denominational Preferences: Larson in Retrospect,_ 8 N. Y. City L. Rev. 53, 96–101 (2005). Consider 48 Minn.L.Rev. 776–77 (1964): "Since pacifism often arises from religious beliefs, a workable method for ascertaining sincerity may have to be couched in terms of those beliefs. Such a test should be permissible, even though it may theoretically 'prefer' some sincere conscientious objectors over others, if it reasonably advances the [statute's] purpose by aiding local draft boards in administering the act. [S]ince membership in an organized pacifist sect may be better evidence of sincerity than the mere assertion of pacificist beliefs, a requirement to that effect should be permissible." May (should) an exemption for peyote be limited to religious groups like the Native American Church that consider its use essential? (The federal exemption is limited to that church.) See Greenawalt, 1 _Religion and the_ Constitution at 71–74. See also id. at 98–100.

---

b.   Rehnquist, J., joined by Burger, C.J. and White and O'Connor, JJ., also dissented on the ground that the church had no standing.

c.   _Gillette_ held that there was no religious "gerrymander" if there was "a neutral, secular basis for the lines government has drawn."

For a comprehensive analysis concluding that "the Court's accommodation decisions represent a surprisingly coherent model [that] religious accommodations must satisfy four" norms, see Ira C. Lupu & Robert W. Tuttle, *Instruments of Accommodation: The Military Chaplaincy and the Constitution,* 110 W. Va. L. Rev. 89, 93–94 (2007): (1) "a reasonable effort to relieve a government-imposed burden on religious practice"; (2) beneficiaries must "participate voluntarily"; (3) the accommodation must be "available on a denominationally-neutral basis"; and (4) must not "impose significant burdens on third parties."

2. ***The Larson rationale.*** (a) Consider Jesse H. Choper, *The Free Exercise Clause: A Structural Overview and An Appraisal of Recent Developments,* 27 Wm. & M.L.Rev. 943, 958–61 (1986): "*Larson* should be seen as a free exercise clause decision parading in an establishment clause disguise. [The] major thrust of the Court's opinion [used] classic free exercise clause analysis[:] strict scrutiny. [Even if] the Minnesota statute did not specifically give preference to some religions over others, it did expressly deal with the subject of religion, and it resulted in favoring some and disfavoring others. In my view, it should have [been] subject to the same level of scrutiny—as a general, neutral law that says nothing about religion but that happens to have an adverse impact on some faiths, [as] in *Yoder.* The problem is that when the [pre-*Smith*] Court has invoked the establishment clause, it has applied a much more lenient test to laws that expressly deal with religion and subject some faiths to discriminatory treatment than it has applied under the free exercise clause to general, neutral laws that come into conflict with religious beliefs. [In] reality, I believe that the Selective Service Act survived strict scrutiny in *Gillette* [because of the] powerful government interest in raising an army and the difficulties in administering a draft exemption based on 'just war' beliefs. [In] sum, the doctrine in *Gillette,* that a valid secular basis for de facto religious discrimination is enough to sustain it under the establishment clause, plainly supports Justice White's dissent in *Larson.* The *Gillette* doctrine, however, effectively has been abandoned, and rightly so."

(b) HERNANDEZ v. COMMISSIONER, 490 U.S. 680 (1989), per MARSHALL, J., found no violation of the Establishment Clause in not permitting federal taxpayers to deduct as "charitable contributions" payments to the Church of Scientology for "auditing" and "training" sessions. A central tenet of the Church requires "fixed donations" for these sessions to study the faith's tenets and to increase spiritual awareness. The proceeds are the Church's primary source of income. *Larson* was distinguished on the ground that IRS disallowance for payments made "with some expectation of a quid pro quo in terms of goods or services [makes] no 'explicit and deliberate distinctions between different religious organizations.' [It] may be that a consequence of the quid pro quo orientation of the 'contribution or gift' requirement is to impose a disparate burden on those charitable and religious groups that rely on sales of commodities or services as a means of fundraising, relative to those groups that raise funds primarily by soliciting unilateral donations. But a statute primarily having a secular effect does not violate the Establishment Clause merely because it 'happens to coincide or harmonize with the tenets of some or all religions.' *McGowan.*"

Because of the absence of "a proper factual record," the Court did not consider the contention of O'CONNOR, J., joined by Scalia, J., dissenting, that "at least some of the fixed payments which the IRS has treated as charitable deductions [are as much a 'quid pro quo exchange'] as the payments [here]": "In exchange for their payment of pew rents, Christians receive particular seats during worship services. Similarly, in some synagogues attendance at the worship services for Jewish High Holy Days is often predicated upon the purchase of a general admission ticket or a reserved seat ticket. Religious honors such as publicly reading from Scripture are purchased or auctioned periodically in some synagogues of Jews from Morocco and Syria. Mormons must tithe ten percent of their income as a necessary but not sufficient condition to obtaining a 'temple recommend,' i.e., the right to be admitted into the temple. A Mass stipend—a fixed payment given to a Catholic priest, in consideration of which he is obliged to apply the fruits of the Mass for the intention of the donor—has similar overtones of exchange. [Thus, the case] involves the differential application of a standard based on constitutionally impermissible differences drawn by the Government among religions." Brennan and Kennedy, JJ., did not participate.

3. **Preference for "religious" objectors.** Is Congress' limitation of draft exemption to "religious" conscientious objectors valid? Consider John H. Mansfield, *Conscientious Objection—1964 Term,* 1965 Relig. & Pub.Or. 3, 76: "[Compared to a] non-religious conscientious objector [t]he religious objector's opposition rests on somewhat more fundamental grounds [and] makes reference to realities that can more easily be described as spiritual. But the non-religious conscientious objector's opposition does rest on basic propositions about the nature of reality and the significance of human existence; this is what distinguishes it from objection that is not even conscientious." Does the "religious" exemption result in more or less government "entanglement" with religion than an exemption for *all* conscientious objectors?

CHAPTER 14

CONFLICT BETWEEN THE CLAUSES

■ ■ ■

The decision in *Employment Division v. Smith* appeared to have relieved some of the tension that had existed between the doctrines that the Court had developed under the Establishment and Free Exercise Clauses. But substantial questions remained, e.g., do (a) the decisions in *Sherbert (Thomas, Hobbie), Yoder* and *Roy,* and (b) statutes granting religious exemptions from laws of general applicability violate the Establishment Clause because they impermissibly aid religion?

CORPORATION OF THE PRESIDING BISHOP OF THE CHURCH OF JESUS CHRIST OF LATTER–DAY SAINTS v. AMOS

483 U.S. 327, 107 S.Ct. 2862, 97 L.Ed.2d 273 (1987).

JUSTICE WHITE delivered the opinion of the Court.

Section 702 of the Civil Rights Act of 1964 exempts religious organizations from Title VII's prohibition against discrimination in employment on the basis of religion. [The] Deseret Gymnasium (Gymnasium) in Salt Lake City, Utah, is a nonprofit facility, open to the public, run by [an] unincorporated religious association sometimes called the Mormon or LDS Church. Appellee Mayson worked at the Gymnasium for some 16 years as an assistant building engineer and then building engineer. He was discharged in 1981 because he failed to qualify for a temple recommend, that is, a certificate that he is a member of the Church and eligible to attend its temples. Mayson [contended that] § 702 violates the Establishment Clause. * * *

"This Court has long recognized that the government may (and sometimes must) accommodate religious practices [without] violating the Establishment Clause." It is well established, too, that "[t]he limits of permissible state accommodation to religion are by no means co-extensive with the noninterference mandated by the Free Exercise Clause." *Walz.*[a]

---

a. Consider Michael W. McConnell, *Accommodation of Religion,* 1985 Sup.Ct.Rev. 1, 34: "[S]ome government employees may view attendance at religious services on a holy day a sacred duty; they could make out a plausible free exercise case if the government refused them leave. Others may view attendance at services as no more than a spiritually wholesome activity; their

[At] some point, accommodation may devolve into "an unlawful fostering of religion," but this is not such a [case].

Lemon requires [a] "secular legislative purpose." This does not mean that the law's purpose must be unrelated to religion. [Rather,] *Lemon's* "purpose" requirement aims at preventing the relevant governmental decisionmaker—in this case, Congress—from abandoning neutrality and acting with the intent of promoting a particular point of view in religious matters.

Under the *Lemon* analysis, it is a permissible legislative purpose to alleviate significant governmental interference with the ability of religious organizations to define and carry out their religious missions.[b] Appellees argue that there is no such purpose here because § 702 provided adequate protection for religious employers prior to the 1972 amendment, when it exempted only the religious activities of such employers from the statutory ban on religious discrimination. We may assume for the sake of argument that the pre–1972 exemption was adequate in the sense that the Free Exercise Clause required no more. Nonetheless, it is a significant burden on a religious organization to require it, on pain of substantial liability, to predict which of its activities a secular court will consider religious. The line is hardly a bright one, and an organization might understandably be concerned that a judge would not understand its religious tenets [and] affect the way an organization carried out what it understood to be its religious mission. * * *

The second requirement under *Lemon* is that the law in question have "a principal or primary effect [that] neither advances nor inhibits religion." Undoubtedly, religious organizations are better able now to advance their purposes than they were prior to the 1972 amendment to § 702. But religious groups have been better able to advance their purposes on account of many laws that have passed constitutional muster: for example, the property tax exemption at issue in *Walz,* or the loans of school books to school children, including parochial school students, upheld in *Allen.* A law is not unconstitutional simply because it *allows* churches to advance religion, which is their very purpose. For a law to have forbidden "effects" under *Lemon,* it must be fair to say that the *government itself* has advanced religion through its own activities and influence. [Moreover,] we find no persuasive evidence in the record before us that the Church's ability to propagate its religious doctrine through the

---

free exercise claim would be much weaker. It is not unreasonable for the government to disregard these distinctions—to implement a general policy permitting leave for employees on the holy days of their faith. * * * Religious liberty is not enhanced by a rule confining government accommodations to the minimum compelled under the Constitution."

b. See also Wilbur Katz, *Note on the Constitutionality of Shared Time,* 1964 Relig. & Pub.Or. 85, 88: "It is no violation of neutrality for the government to express its concern for religious freedom by measures which merely neutralize what would otherwise be restrictive effects of government action. Provision for voluntary worship in the armed forces is constitutional, not because government policy may properly favor religion, but because the government is not required to exercise its military powers in a manner restrictive of religious freedom. Affirmative government action to maintain religious freedom in these instances serves the secular purpose of promoting a constitutional right, the free exercise of religion."

Gymnasium is any greater now than it was prior to the passage of the Civil Rights Act in 1964. In such circumstances, we do not see how any advancement of religion achieved by the Gymnasium can be fairly attributed to the Government, as opposed to the Church.[15]

We find unpersuasive [that] § 702 singles out religious entities for a benefit. [The Court] has never indicated that statutes that give special consideration to religious groups are per se invalid. That would run contrary to [our] cases that there is ample room for accommodation of religion under the Establishment Clause. Where, as here, government acts with the proper purpose of lifting a regulation that burdens the exercise of religion, we see no reason to require that the exemption come packaged with benefits to secular [entities.] *Larson* indicates that laws discriminating *among* religions are subject to strict scrutiny, and that laws "affording a uniform benefit to *all* religions" should be analyzed under *Lemon*. In a case such as this, where a statute is neutral on its face and motivated by a permissible purpose of limiting governmental interference with the exercise of religion, we see no justification for applying strict scrutiny to a statute that passes the *Lemon* [test.] § 702 is rationally related to the legitimate purpose of alleviating significant governmental interference with the ability of religious organizations to define and carry out their religious missions. * * *

JUSTICE BRENNAN, with whom JUSTICE MARSHALL joins, concurring in the judgment.

[Any] exemption from Title VII's proscription on religious discrimination [says] that a person may be put to the choice of either conforming to certain religious tenets or losing a job opportunity. [The] potential for coercion created by such a provision is in serious tension with our commitment to individual freedom of conscience in matters of religious belief.

At the same time, religious organizations have an interest in autonomy in ordering their internal affairs * * *. Determining that certain activities are in furtherance of an organization's religious mission, and that only those committed to that mission should conduct them, is thus a means by which a religious community defines itself. Solicitude for a church's ability to do so reflects the idea that furtherance of the autonomy of religious organizations often furthers individual religious freedom as well.[a] * * *

This rationale suggests that, ideally, religious organizations should be able to discriminate on the basis of religion *only* with respect to religious activities [because] the infringement on religious liberty that results from

---

15. Undoubtedly, Mayson's freedom of choice in religious matters was impinged upon, but it was the Church [and] not the Government, who put him to the choice of changing his religious practices or losing his job. * * *

a. For the view that the Establishment Clause requires an exemption from a neutral, generally applicable law that "interferes with the relationship between clergy and church" or "intrudes on religious organizations' sphere of autonomy," see Carl H. Esbeck, *The Establishment Clause as a Structural Restraint on Governmental Power*, 84 Ia.L.Rev. 1 (1998).

conditioning performance of *secular* activity upon religious belief cannot be defended as necessary for the community's self-definition. Furthermore, the authorization of discrimination in such circumstances is not an accommodation that simply enables a church to gain members by the normal means of prescribing the terms of membership for those who seek to participate in furthering the mission of the community. Rather, it puts at the disposal of religion the added advantages of economic leverage in the secular realm. * * *

What makes the application of a religious-secular distinction difficult is that the character of an activity is not self-evident [and] requires a searching case-by-case analysis. This results in considerable ongoing government entanglement in religious affairs [and] raises concern that a religious organization may be chilled in its Free Exercise activity. * * *

The risk [is] most likely to arise with respect to *nonprofit* activities. The fact that an operation is not organized as a profit-making commercial enterprise makes colorable a claim that it is not purely secular in orientation. * * *

Sensitivity to individual religious freedom dictates that religious discrimination be permitted only with respect to employment in religious activities.[b] Concern for the autonomy of religious organizations demands that we avoid the entanglement and the chill on religious expression that a case-by-case determination would produce. We cannot escape the fact that these aims are in tension. Because of the nature of nonprofit activities, I believe that a categorical exemption for such enterprises appropriately balances these competing concerns. * * *

JUSTICE O'CONNOR, concurring in the judgment.[c] * * *

In *Jaffree,* I noted [that, "on] the one hand, a rigid application of the *Lemon* test would invalidate legislation exempting religious observers from generally applicable government obligations. By definition, such legislation has a religious purpose and effect in promoting the free exercise of religion.[d] On the other hand, judicial deference to all legislation that purports to facilitate the free exercise of religion would completely vitiate the Establishment Clause. Any statute pertaining to religion can be viewed as an 'accommodation' of free exercise rights."[e]

---

b. If the employee engaging in "religious activities" is paid with public funds, does this "result in religious indoctrination" (Ch. 11, II) and thus violate the Establishment Clause? Does this mean that the *most* protected activities may *not* be funded, but the least protected may? See Steven K. Green, *Religious Discrimination, Public Funding, and Constitutional Values*, 30 Hast.Con.L.Q. 1 (2002).

c. Blackmun, J., concurred in the judgment, "essentially for the reasons set forth in Justice O'Connor's opinion."

d. In her *Jaffree* concurrence, O'Connor, J., added: "Indeed, the statute at issue in *Lemon* [can] be viewed as an accommodation of the religious beliefs of parents who choose to send their children to religious schools."

e. In *Jaffree,* O'Connor, J. added: "It [is] difficult to square any notion of 'complete neutrality' [see fn. e in *Smith*] with the mandate of the Free Exercise Clause that government must sometimes exempt a religious observer from an otherwise generally applicable obligation. [The] solution [lies] in identifying workable limits to the Government's license to promote the

In my view, the opinion for the Court leans toward the second of the two unacceptable options described [above.] Almost any government benefit to religion could be recharacterized as simply "allowing" a religion to better advance itself, unless perhaps it involved actual proselytization by government agents. In nearly every case of a government benefit to religion, the religious mission would not be advanced if the religion did not take advantage of the benefit; even a direct financial subsidy to a religious organization would not advance religion if for some reason the organization failed to make any use of the funds. * * *

The necessary first step in evaluating an Establishment Clause challenge to a government action lifting from religious organizations a generally applicable regulatory burden is to recognize that such government action *does* have the effect of advancing religion. The necessary second step is to separate those benefits to religion that constitutionally accommodate the free exercise of religion from those that provide unjustifiable awards of assistance to religious organizations. As I have suggested in earlier opinions, the inquiry framed by the *Lemon* test should be "whether government's purpose is to endorse religion and whether the statute actually conveys a message of endorsement." [T]he relevant issue is how it would be perceived by an objective observer, acquainted with the text, legislative history, and implementation of the statute.[f] [This] case involves a government decision to lift from a nonprofit activity of a religious organization the burden of demonstrating that the particular nonprofit activity is religious as well as the burden of refraining from discriminating

---

free exercise of religion. [O]ne can plausibly assert that government pursues free exercise clause values when it lifts a government-imposed burden on the free exercise of religion. [T]hen the standard Establishment Clause test should be modified accordingly. [T]he Court should simply acknowledge that the religious purpose of such a statute is legitimated by the Free Exercise Clause."

See also Abner S. Greene, *The Political Balance of the Religion Clauses*, 102 Yale L.J. 1611, 1644 (1993): "[I]f we construe the Establishment Clause to prohibit legislation enacted for the express purpose of advancing religious values, then the predicate for universal obedience to law has been removed. A religious conscientious objector may legitimately claim that because she was thwarted from offering her values for majority acceptance as law, she should have at least a prima facie right of exemption from law that conflicts with her religion. The Free Exercise Clause works as a counterweight to the Establishment Clause; it gives back what the Establishment Clause takes away." Compare Suzanna Sherry, *Lee v. Weisman: Paradox Redux*, 1992 Sup.Ct.Rev. 123, 145: "This formulation can also be reversed: protecting the values of the Establishment Clause should constitute a compelling government interest sufficient to justify the impact of neutral laws on religious exercise. Whichever clause serves as the compelling interest trumps the other. Which formulation one prefers depends solely on whether one places a higher priority on the values of the Establishment Clause or on those of the Free Exercise Clause."

f. In *Jaffree*, O'Connor, J., added: "[C]ourts should assume that the 'objective observer,' is acquainted with the Free Exercise Clause and the values it promotes. Thus individual perceptions, or resentment that a religious observer is exempted from a particular government requirement, would be entitled to little weight if the Free Exercise Clause strongly supported the exemption."

Compare William P. Marshall, *The Religious Freedom Restoration Act: Establishment, Equal Protection and Free Speech Concerns*, 56 Mont.L.Rev. 227, 236 (1995): "Prior to *Smith*, one could argue that the Constitution demanded some accommodation from general laws of neutral applicability for free exercise interests. Legislative exemptions from neutral laws, which provided this accommodation, could therefore be defended as in accord with this constitutional mandate. The denial of the free exercise right in *Smith*, however, suggests that exempting religion from neutral laws is no longer based upon a constitutional requirement. Accordingly, after *Smith*, the strength of the state interest supporting the legislative exemption is necessarily diminished."

on the basis of religion. Because there is a probability that a nonprofit activity of a religious organization will itself be involved in the organization's religious mission, in my view the objective observer should perceive the government action as an accommodation of the exercise of religion rather than as a government endorsement of religion.

[U]nder the holding of the Court, [the] constitutionality of the § 702 exemption as applied to for-profit activities of religious organizations remains open.

NOTES AND QUESTIONS

1. ***Draft exemption***. Did the statute in *Gillette*, exempting only "religious" conscientious objectors, impermissibly prefer religion over nonreligion? In WELSH v. UNITED STATES, Ch. 12, II, WHITE, J., joined by Burger, C.J., and Stewart, J., found it valid: "First, § 6(j) may represent a purely practical judgment that religious objectors, however admirable, would be of no more use in combat than many others unqualified for military service. [On] this basis, the exemption has neither the primary purpose nor the effect of furthering religion. [Second], Congress may have [believed that] to deny the exemption would violate the Free Exercise Clause or at least raise grave problems in this respect. [It] cannot be ignored that the First Amendment itself contains a religious classification [and the Free Exercise Clause] protects conduct as well as religious belief and speech. [It] was not suggested [in *Braunfeld*] that the Sunday closing laws in 21 States exempting Sabbatarians and others violated the Establishment Clause because no provision was made for others who claimed nonreligious reasons for not working on some particular day of the week. Nor was it intimated in *Zorach* that the no-establishment holding might be infirm because only those pursuing religious studies for designated periods were released from the public school routine; neither was it hinted that a public school's refusal to institute a released time program would violate the Free Exercise Clause. The Court in *Sherbert* construed the Free Exercise Clause to require special treatment for Sabbatarians under the State's unemployment compensation law. But the State could deal specially with Sabbatarians whether the Free Exercise Clause required it or not * * *."

HARLAN, J., disagreed, believing that "having chosen to exempt, [Congress] cannot draw the line between theistic or nontheistic religious beliefs on the one hand and secular beliefs on the other. [I]t must encompass the class of individuals it purports to exclude, those whose beliefs emanate from a purely moral, ethical, or philosophical source.[9] The common denominator must be the intensity of moral [conviction]. *Everson, McGowan* and *Allen*, all sus-

---

9. * * * I suggested [in *Sherbert*] that a State could constitutionally create exceptions to its program to accommodate religious scruples. [But] any such exception in order to satisfy the Establishment Clause [would] have to be sufficiently broad so as to be religiously neutral. This would require creating an exception for anyone who, as a matter of conscience, could not comply with the statute. * * *

[See also Lisa S. Bressman, *Accommodation and Equal Liberty*, 42 Wm. & M. L.Rev. 1007 (2001) (legislatures may "respond to religious requests for accommodation [if they] extend any such accommodation to similarly situated nonreligious claimants"). *Query*: If a religious accommodation is granted for peyote, must a medical accommodation also be granted? See id.]

tained legislation on the premise that it was neutral [notwithstanding] that it may have assisted religious groups by giving them the same benefits accorded to nonreligious groups.[12] To the extent that *Zorach* and *Sherbert* stand for the proposition that the Government may (*Zorach*), or must (*Sherbert*), shape its secular programs to accommodate the beliefs and tenets of religious groups, I think these cases unsound.[13]"

2. *Unemployment compensation.* (a) Did the Court's decisions in *Sherbert, Thomas* and *Hobbie* impermissibly prefer religion? In THOMAS v. REVIEW BD., Ch. 12, II, Rehnquist, J., dissented, finding the result "inconsistent with many of our prior Establishment Clause cases"[2]: "If Indiana were to legislate [an] unemployment compensation law which permitted benefits to be granted to those persons who quit their jobs for religious reasons—the statute would 'plainly' violate the Establishment Clause as interpreted in such cases as [*Lemon*]. First, [the] proviso would clearly serve only a religious purpose. It would grant financial benefits for the sole purpose of accommodating religious beliefs. Second, [the] primary effect of the proviso would be to 'advance' religion by facilitating the exercise of religious belief. Third, [it] would surely 'entangle' the State in religion. [By] granting financial benefits to persons solely on the basis of their religious beliefs, the State must necessarily inquire whether the claimant's belief is 'religious' and whether it is sincerely [held.] I believe that Justice Stewart, dissenting in *Schempp,* accurately stated the reach of the Establishment Clause [as] limited to 'government support of proselytizing activities of religious sects by throwing the weight of secular authorities behind the dissemination of religious tenets.' See *McCollum* (Reed, J., dissenting) (impermissible aid is only 'purposeful assistance directly to the church itself or to some religious [group] performing ecclesiastical functions'). Conversely, governmental assistance which does not have the effect of 'inducing' religious belief, but instead merely 'accommodates' or implements an independent religious choice does not impermissibly involve the government in religious choices and therefore does not violate the Establishment [Clause]. I would think that in this case, as in *Sherbert,* had

---

12. [I] fail to see how [§ 6(j)] has "any substantial legislative purpose" apart from honoring the conscience of individuals who oppose war on only religious grounds. * * *

13. [At] the very least the Constitution requires that the State not excuse students early for the purpose of receiving religious instruction when it does not offer to nonreligious students the opportunity to use school hours for spiritual or ethical instruction of a nonreligious nature. Moreover, whether a released-time program cast in terms of improving "conscience" to the exclusion of artistic or cultural pursuits, would be "neutral" and consistent with the requirement of "voluntarism," is by no means an easy question. * * *

2. To the extent *Sherbert* was correctly decided, it might be argued that cases such as *McCollum, Engel, Schempp, Lemon,* and *Nyquist* were wrongly decided. The "aid" rendered to religion in these latter cases may not be significantly different, in kind or degree, than the "aid" afforded Mrs. Sherbert or Thomas. For example, if the State in *Sherbert* could not deny compensation to one refusing work for religious reasons, it might be argued that a State may not deny reimbursement to students who choose for religious reasons to attend parochial schools. The argument would be that although a State need not allocate any funds to education, once it has done so, it may not require any person to sacrifice his religious beliefs in order to obtain an equal education. There can be little doubt that to the extent secular education provides answers to important moral questions without reference to religion or teaches that there are no answers, a person in one sense sacrifices his religious belief by attending secular schools. And even if such "aid" were not constitutionally compelled by the Free Exercise Clause, Justice Harlan may well be right in *Sherbert* when he finds sufficient flexibility in the Establishment Clause to permit the States to voluntarily choose to grant such benefits to individuals.

the state voluntarily chosen to pay unemployment compensation benefits to persons who left their jobs for religious reasons, such aid would be constitutionally permissible because it redounds directly to the benefit of the individual."

(b) *Accommodation/inducement/imposition/coercion.* Consider Alan Schwarz, *No Imposition of Religion: The Establishment Clause Value,* 77 Yale L.J. 692, 693, 723, 728 (1968): "[T]he establishment clause [should] be read to prohibit only aid which has as its motive or substantial effect the imposition of religious belief or [practice]. Exemption of Mrs. Sherbert [represents] a judgment that the exercise of Seventh-day Adventism is more worthy than bowling on Saturdays, but the exemption has no significant effect [on] whether someone becomes a Seventh-day Adventist. Similarly, the Sabbatarian exemption from Sunday closing laws does not induce one to become a Jew; draft exemption to conscientious objectors does not normally induce one to become a Quaker; closing the public schools on all religious holidays or on every Wednesday at 2 P.M. does not induce the adoption of religion; and compulsory Sunday closing, while implementing an independent desire to attend church services, has no substantial effect upon the creation of such desire. The availability of preferential aid to religious exercise may, to be sure, induce false claims of religious belief, but the establishment clause is not concerned with false claims of belief, only with induced belief." Does this distinguish *McCollum, Engel* and *Schempp* from *Sherbert?* Do you agree with all of the *factual* assumptions made? Under this analysis, what result in *Epperson?* What of a small governmental payment to all persons who would lose salary because they have to be absent from their jobs in order to attend religious services? Would the state's failure to provide Sherbert with unemployment compensation be the same as its not having on-premises released time and school prayer in that all of these actions simply "make the practice of religious beliefs more expensive"?

Compare Jesse H. Choper, *The Religion Clauses of the First Amendment: Reconciling the Conflict,* 41 U.Pitt.L.Rev. 673, 691, 697–700 (1980): "My proposal for resolving the conflict between the two Religion Clauses seeks to implement their historically and contemporarily acknowledged common goal: to safeguard religious liberty. [I]t is only when an accommodation would jeopardize religious liberty—when it would coerce, compromise, or influence religious choice—that it would fail. [For example, in *Yoder,* unless] it could be shown that relieving the Amish [would] tend to coerce, compromise, or influence religious choice—and it is extremely doubtful that it could—the exemption was permissible under the Establishment Clause. In contrast, in *Sherbert,* [the] exemption results in impairment of religious liberty because compulsorily raised tax funds must be used to subsidize Mrs. Sherbert's exercise of religion.[a] [In the draft exemption cases], draftees seeking exemption had to formulate a statement of personal doctrine that would pass

---

a. See also Jesse H. Choper, *The Free Exercise Clause,* 27 Wm. & M.L.Rev. 943, 951 n. 25 (1986): "Under Justice Rehnquist's [and Professor Schwarz's] rationale, if a municipally-owned bus company wanted to waive the fare to take people to churches, it could do so. According to Justice Rehnquist, the waiver would not 'induce' religion, but would simply 'accommodate' a religious choice that already had been made. That may be true, but the waiver also would result in what the religion clauses protect against—the use of tax funds for exclusively religious purposes."

muster. This endeavor would involve deep and careful thought, and perhaps reading in philosophy and religion. Some undoubtedly would be persuaded by what they read. Moreover, the theory of 'cognitive dissonance'—which posits that to avoid madness we tend to become what we hold ourselves to be and what others believe us to be—also suggests that some initially fraudulent claims of belief in a personal religion would develop into true belief. Thus, a draft exemption for religious objectors threatens values of religious freedom by encouraging the adoption of religious beliefs by those who seek to qualify for the benefit.''

(c) *Breadth of exemption.* In TEXAS MONTHLY, INC. v. BULLOCK, Ch. 11, II, SCALIA, J., joined by Rehnquist, C.J., and Kennedy, J., charged that according to Brennan, J.'s plurality opinion, "no law is constitutional whose 'benefits [are] confined to religious organizations,' except, of course, those laws that are unconstitutional *unless* they contain benefits confined to religious organizations. [But] 'the limits of permissible state accommodation to religion are by no means co-extensive with the noninterference mandated by the Free Exercise Clause.' Breadth of coverage is essential to constitutionality whenever a law's benefiting of religious activity [is] defended [as] merely the incidental consequence of seeking to benefit *all* activity that achieves a particular secular goal. But that is a different rationale—more commonly invoked than accommodation of religion [but] not preclusive of it. Where accommodation of religion is the justification, by definition religion is being singled out." Finally, "the proper lesson to be drawn from" the fact that the Free Exercise Clause may not require the Texas sales tax exemption and "that *Murdock* and *Follett* are narrowly distinguishable" is that "if the exemption comes so close to being a constitutionally required accommodation, there is no doubt that it is at least a permissible one.''[b]

BRENNAN, J., joined by Marshall and Stevens, JJ., responded: "[W]e in no way suggest that *all* benefits conferred exclusively upon religious groups or upon individuals on account of their religious beliefs are forbidden by the Establishment Clause unless they are mandated by the Free Exercise Clause. Our decisions in *Zorach* and *Amos* offer two examples. Similarly, if the Air Force provided a sufficiently broad exemption from its dress requirements for servicemen whose religious faiths commanded them to wear certain headgear, [see] *Goldman v. Weinberger,* that exemption presumably would not be invalid under the Establishment Clause even though this Court has not found it to be required by the Free Exercise Clause.

"All of these cases, however, involve legislative exemptions that did not or would not impose substantial burdens on nonbeneficiaries while allowing others to act according to their religious [beliefs]. New York City's decision to release students from public schools so that they might obtain religious instruction elsewhere, which we upheld in *Zorach,* was found not to coerce students who wished to remain behind to alter their religious beliefs, nor did it impose monetary costs on their parents or other taxpayers who opposed or were indifferent to the religious instruction given to students who were

---

b. Why didn't Texas' exemption violate the Establishment Clause test articulated by Kennedy, J. (joined by Rehnquist, C.J., and White and Scalia, JJ.) in *Allegheny County v. ACLU,* Ch 11, IV, because it gave "direct benefits to religion" and involved "subtle coercion [in] the form of taxation"?

released. The hypothetical Air Force uniform exemption also would not place a monetary burden on those required to conform to the dress code or subject them to any appreciable privation. And the application of Title VII's exemption for religious organizations that we approved in *Amos* though it had some adverse effect on those holding or seeking employment with those organizations (if not on taxpayers generally), prevented potentially serious encroachments on protected religious freedoms.

"Texas' tax exemption, by contrast, does not remove a demonstrated and possible grave imposition on religious activity sheltered by the Free Exercise Clause. Moreover, it burdens nonbeneficiaries by increasing their tax bills by whatever amount is needed to offset the benefit bestowed on subscribers to religious publications."

3. *Sabbath observance.* THORNTON v. CALDOR, INC., 472 U.S. 703 (1985), per BURGER, C.J., held that a Connecticut law—"that those who observe a Sabbath any day of the week as a matter of religious conviction must be relieved of the duty to work on that day, no matter what burden or inconvenience this imposes on the employer or fellow workers"—"has a primary effect that impermissibly advances a particular religious practice" and thus violates the Establishment Clause: "The statute arms Sabbath observers with an absolute and unqualified right not to work on whatever day they designate as their Sabbath [and thus] goes beyond having an incidental or remote effect of advancing religion."[c]

O'CONNOR, J., joined by Marshall, J., concurred, distinguishing "the religious accommodation provisions of Title VII of the Civil Rights Act [which] require private employers to reasonably accommodate the religious practices of employees unless to do so would cause undue hardship to the employer's business": "Since Title VII calls for reasonable rather than absolute accommodation and extends [to] all religious beliefs and practices rather than protecting only the Sabbath observance, I believe an objective observer would perceive it as an anti-discrimination law rather than an endorsement of religion or a particular religious practice."

Was the purpose or effect of the *Caldor* statute any different than that of the *Amos* statute or the Court's decisions in *Sherbert, Thomas, Hobbie, Roy* and *Yoder*? *Amos* distinguished *Caldor* on the ground that in *Amos*, "appellee was not legally obligated to take the steps necessary to qualify for a temple recommend, and his discharge was not required by statute." Should it make a difference that, unlike the other cases, the *Caldor* statute sought to alleviate burdens on religion posed by private parties rather than the state?

---

c. Rehnquist, J., dissented without opinion.

Consider Richard A. Epstein, *Religious Liberty in the Welfare State*, 31 Wm. & M.L.Rev. 375, 406 (1990): "[It would plainly be unconstitutional] if the state offered to pay a small sum [to] the employer to defray the additional costs it had to bear to keep the religious worker on its payroll. [If] a public subsidy of religious workers is not acceptable under the establishment clause, then a public mandate of a private subsidy is unacceptable as well."

For the view that since "securing individual constitutional rights often (or almost always) imposes impediments to the smooth functioning of our system, if accommodations for religion impose only imprecise social/economic costs, then these prices of religious tolerance are permitted to be paid," see Jesse H. Choper, *Securing Religious Liberty* 123–26 (1995).

Does the *Caldor* statute "promote" and "endorse" a particular "religion" or "religious belief" or "religious practice" any more than the Court's decisions in *Sherbert, Thomas, Hobbie, Yoder* and *Roy,* or than the statutory exemptions from the draft or Sunday Closing laws? *Hobbie* distinguished *Caldor* as follows: "Florida's provision of unemployment benefits to religious observers does not single out a particular class of such persons for favorable treatment and thereby have the effect of implicitly endorsing a particular religious belief. Rather, the provision of unemployment benefits generally available within the State to religious observers who must leave their employment due to an irreconcilable conflict between the demands of work and conscience neutrally accommodates religious beliefs and practices, without endorsement."

In *Kiryas Joel,* Ch. 13, SCALIA, J., joined by Rehnquist, C.J., and Thomas, J., disagreed with the Court's conclusion that New York had impermissibly preferred one religion: "[M]ost efforts at accommodation seek to solve a problem that applies [to] only one or a few religions. Not every religion uses wine in its sacraments, but that does not make an exemption from Prohibition for sacramental wine-use impermissible, nor does it require the State granting such an exemption to explain [how] it will treat every other claim for dispensation from its controlled-substances laws. Likewise, not every religion uses peyote in its services, but we have suggested that legislation which exempts the sacramental use of peyote from generally applicable drug laws is not only permissible, but desirable, see *Smith,* without any suggestion that some 'up front' legislative guarantee of equal treatment for sacramental substances used by other sects must be provided." Kennedy, J., expressed a similar view: "It is normal for legislatures to respond to problems as they [arise.] Most accommodations cover particular religious practices."

Is a *general* rule for free exercise exemptions—as under *Sherbert-Yoder,* or the Religious Freedom Restoration Act (fn. a after *Smith*)—preferable to a specific exemption for religion (as the statutes in *Texas Monthly* and *Caldor*)? Consider Thomas C. Berg, *The New Attacks on Religious Freedom Legislation, and Why They are Wrong,* 21 Card.L.Rev. 415, 435–36 (1999): "Requiring the same standard for all religious freedom claims, in the less political forum of the courts, serves the goal of religious equality by minimizing the chance that only politically powerful groups will get accommodations, while individuals or very small groups without a lobbyist will escape the legislature's attention altogether.[89]" What result if a state grants an exemption from compulsory education for religions with beliefs like the Amish but not for farmers who badly need their children for farming, or an exemption for sacramental, but not medical, use of peyote? See William K. Kelley, *The Primacy of Political Actors in Accommodation of Religion,* 22 U. of Haw. L. Rev. 403 (2000).

    4. ***Unanimous approval.*** CUTTER v. WILKINSON, 544 U.S. 709 (2005), per GINSBURG, J., relying on *Amos* and language in *Smith,* held that the Religious Land Use and Institutionalized Persons Act of 2000—"No government shall impose a substantial burden on the religious exercise of a

---

89. See Ira C. Lupu, *Reconstructing the Establishment Clause: The Case Against Discretionary Accommodation of Religion,* 140 U.Pa.L.Rev. 555 (1991) (claiming that statute-by-statute legislative accommodations are unconstitutional because they reflect the varying political power of different religious groups).

person residing [in] an institution," unless the burden furthers "a compelling governmental interest," and does so by "the least restrictive means"—does not violate the Establishment Clause:

RLUIPA "does not, on its face, exceed the limits of permissible government accommodation [because] it alleviates exceptional government-created burdens on private religious exercise. [Further], the Act [does] not founder on shoals the Court's prior decisions have identified: Properly applying RLUIPA, courts must take adequate account of the burdens a requested accommodation may impose on nonbeneficiaries, see *Caldor*, and they must be satisfied that the Act's prescriptions [are] administered neutrally among different faiths, see *Kiryas Joel*.[8] [It] covers state-run institutions—mental hospitals, prisons, and the like—in which the government exerts a degree of control unparalleled in civilian society and severely disabling to private religious exercise.[9] * * *[10] * * *

"[RLUIPA's sponsors] anticipated that courts would apply the Act's standard with 'due deference to the experience and expertise of prison and jail administrators in establishing necessary regulations and procedures to maintain good order, security and discipline, consistent with consideration of costs and limited resources.' "

5. ***School prayer.*** In *Jaffree*, O'CONNOR, J., applied her "solution"[d] to Alabama's moment of silence law: "No law prevents a student who is so inclined from praying silently in public schools. [Of] course, the State might argue that § 16–1–20.1 protects not silent prayer, but rather group silent prayer under State sponsorship. Phrased in these terms, the burden lifted by the statute is not one imposed by the State of Alabama, but by the Establishment Clause as interpreted in *Engel* and *Schempp*. In my view, it is beyond the authority of the State of Alabama to remove burdens imposed by the Constitution itself."

6. ***Reconciling the conflict.*** Assuming the validity of the distinction between *McCollum*, *Engel*, *Schempp* and *Jaffree* on one hand, and programs such as that in *Amos* and draft exemption etc. on the other, are *all* exemptions undesirable because they often result not merely in protection of free exercise (or neutrality or accommodation) but in relieving persons with certain religious beliefs of significant burdens from which many others

---

8. Directed at obstructions institutional arrangements place on religious observances, RLUIPA does not require a State to pay for an inmate's devotional accessories.

9. See, e.g., *Charles v. Verhagen*, 348 F.3d 601 (C.A.7 2003) (prison's regulation prohibited Muslim prisoner from possessing ritual cleansing oil); *Young v. Lane*, 922 F.2d 370, 375–376 (C.A.7 1991) (prison's regulation restricted wearing of yarmulkes); *Hunafa v. Murphy*, 907 F.2d 46, 47–48 (C.A.7 1990) (noting instances in which Jewish and Muslim prisoners were served pork, with no substitute available).

10. Respondents argue [that RLUIPA] advances religion by encouraging prisoners to "get religion." [While] some accommodations of religious observance, notably the opportunity to assemble in worship services, might attract joiners seeking a break in their closely guarded day, we doubt that all accommodations would be perceived as "benefits." For example, congressional hearings on RLUIPA revealed that one state corrections system served as its kosher diet "a fruit, a vegetable, a granola bar, and a liquid nutritional supplement—each and every meal." The argument, in any event, founders on the fact that Ohio already facilitates religious services for mainstream faiths. The State provides chaplains, allows inmates to possess religious items, and permits assembly for worship.

d. See fn. e in *Amos*.

strongly desire to be exempted? That, in this sense, there is "preference" for minority religions and "discrimination" against the other persons because of their religion or lack of it?[e]

Might religious exemptions be seen as "restorative or equalizing" (Galanter, note 4, Ch. 12, II)? Consider James D. Gordon III, *The New Free Exercise Clause*, 26 Cap.U. L.Rev. 65, 91–92 (1997): "In a democracy, laws inevitably will reflect the majority's values, and [consequently] majority religions generally have a kind of inherent exemption from the force of law. In addition, politically powerful minority religions often are able to obtain express exemptions from legislation. [The] accommodation principle provides powerless minority religions with some measure of the same protection that other religions already enjoy in the democratic process." What about exemptions (accommodations) for majority (mainstream) religions? Consider Greene, fn.d in *Kiryas Joel*, at 74: "When a majority pushes for governmentally organized prayer in public schools or for the placement of its favored religious symbols in the halls of government, it is wrong to call such actions 'accommodation.' [But] when the effect of the majority's actions is to make life easier for a minority, there is no concern about an 'Establishment' of religion. It also seems wrong to say that accommodation of minority religions constitutes a symbolic endorsement of those religions; rather, accommodation in this context suggests that the majority is coming to the aid of a burdened minority, not that the majority agrees with the minority on any matter of religious truth." Compare Ira C. Lupu, *Uncovering the Village of Kiryas Joel*, 96 Colum.L.Rev. 104, 117–18 (1996): "If Jews are a relatively small minority in New York State but a sizable minority or a majority in some New York City area suburbs, may the state close public schools on Yom Kippur while the suburb is forbidden from doing likewise? May Pennsylvania accommodate Mormon traditions, while Utah may not?"

---

e. Should the Court "either suggest or require that an alternative burden be imposed on individuals who would otherwise qualify for religious exemptions"? Choper, fn. c supra, at 92. See generally Alan Brownstein, *Taking "Free Exercise Rights Seriously,* 57 Case W. Res. L. Rev. 55, 70–81 (2006).

INDEX

References are to Pages

†